ALSO BY WOODY HOLTON

Abigail Adams

Black Americans in the Revolutionary Era:
A Brief History with Documents

Unruly Americans and the Origins of the Constitution

Forced Founders: Indians, Debtors, Slaves, and the
Making of the American Revolution in Virginia

LIBERTY
Is SWEET

———— ◆ ————

*The Hidden History
of the American Revolution*

WOODY HOLTON

SIMON & SCHUSTER

New York   London   Toronto   Sydney   New Delhi

Simon & Schuster
1230 Avenue of the Americas
New York, NY 10020

First Simon & Schuster hardcover edition October 2021

SIMON & SCHUSTER and colophon are registered trademarks of Simon & Schuster, Inc.

For information about special discounts for bulk purchases, please contact Simon &
Schuster Special Sales at 1-866-506-1949 or business@simonandschuster.com.

The Simon & Schuster Speakers Bureau can bring authors to your live event.
For more information or to book an event, contact the Simon & Schuster Speakers Bureau
at 1-866-248-3049 or visit our website at www.simonspeakers.com.

Interior design by Carly Loman

Manufactured in the United States of America

10 9 8 7 6 5 4 3 2 1

Library of Congress Cataloging-in-Publication Data

Names: Holton, Woody, author.
Title: Liberty is sweet : the hidden history of the American Revolution / Woody Holton.
Other titles: Hidden history of the American Revolution
Description: First Simon & Schuster hardcover edition. | New York : Simon & Schuster,
    2021. | Includes bibliographical references and index.
Identifiers: LCCN 2020049257 | ISBN 9781476750378 (hardcover) | ISBN 9781476750385
    (trade paperback) | ISBN 9781476750392 (ebook)
Subjects: LCSH: United States—History--Revolution, 1775–1783—Indians. | United
    States—History—Revolution, 1775–1783—Participation, African American. | United
    States—History—Revolution, 1775–1783—Women. | Minorities—United States—
    History—18th century.
Classification: LCC E209 .H655 2021 | DDC 973.308—dc23

ISBN 978-1-4767-5037-8
ISBN 978-1-4767-5039-2 (ebook)

for Henry

CONTENTS

PART THREE:
ROADS OPENED, ROADS CLOSED

LIBERTY
Is SWEET

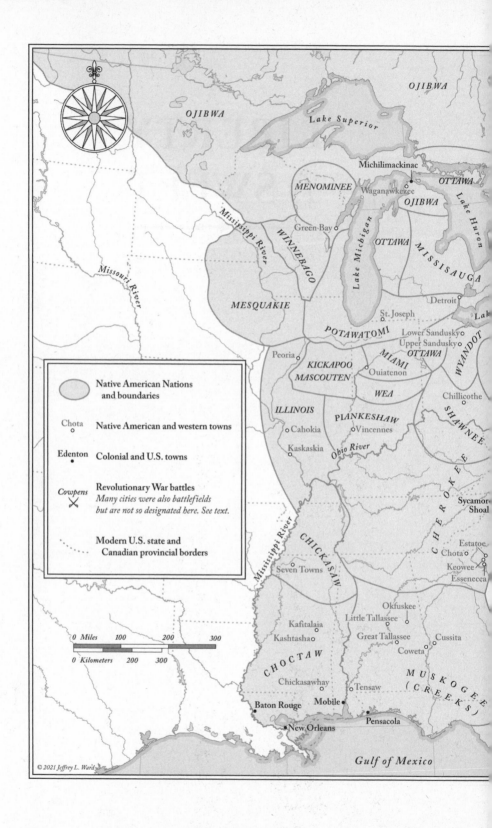

OJIBWA

Lake Superior

OJIBWA

Michilimackinac

Waganakwezee

MENOMINEE

OTTAWA

OJIBWA

Green Bay

Mississippi River

Lake Michigan

Lake Huron

OTTAWA

MISSISAUGA

WINNEBAGO

Missouri River

Detroit

Lak

St. Joseph

MESQUAKIE

POTAWATOMI

Lower Sandusky

Peoria

Upper Sandusky

WYANDOT

MIAMI

OTTAWA

KICKAPOO

Ouiatenon

Chillicothe

MASCOUTEN

WEA

Native American Nations
and boundaries

ILLINOIS

SHAWNEE

PIANKESHAW

Chota   Native American and western towns

Cahokia

Vincennes

Kaskaskia

Ohio River

Edenton   Colonial and U.S. towns

Cowpens   Revolutionary War battles
Many cities were also battlefields
but are not so designated here. See text.

CHEROKEE

Sycamore
Shoal

Modern U.S. state and
Canadian provincial borders

Mississippi River

CHICKASAW

Estatoe

Chota

Seven Towns

Keowee

Essenecca

0 Miles   100   200   300

Okfuskee

Little Tallassee

0 Kilometers   200   300

Kafitalaia

Great Tallassee

Cussita

Kashtasha

Coweta

CHOCTAW

MUSKOGEE

Chickasawhay

Tensaw

(CREEKS)

Baton Rouge

Mobile

New Orleans

Pensacola

Gulf of Mexico

© 2021 Jeffrey L. Ward

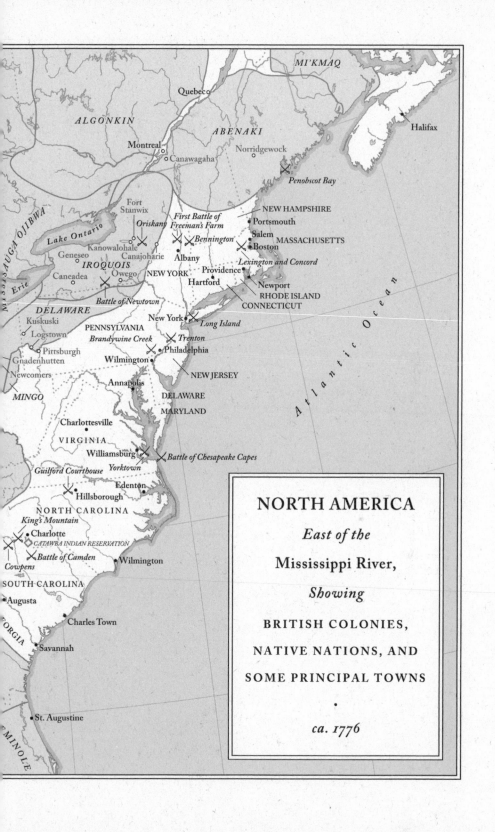

MI'KMAQ

Quebec

ALGONKIN

ABENAKI

Montreal
Canawagaha

Norridgewock

Halifax

Penobscot Bay

MISSISAUGA/OJIBWA

Fort
Stanwix

Lake Ontario

Oriskany

First Battle of
Freeman's Farm

NEW HAMPSHIRE

Portsmouth

Salem
Boston

MASSACHUSETTS

Kanowalohale

Geneseo

Canajoharie

Bennington

Albany

IROQUOIS

Caneadea

Owego

NEW YORK

Lexington and Concord

Providence

Hartford

Newport

RHODE ISLAND

CONNECTICUT

Erie

Battle of Newtown

DELAWARE

Kuskuski

Logstown

Pittsburgh

PENNSYLVANIA

New York

Long Island

Brandywine Creek

Trenton

Philadelphia

Gnadenhutten

Newcomers

Wilmington

NEW JERSEY

MINGO

Annapolis

DELAWARE

MARYLAND

Charlottesville

VIRGINIA

Williamsburg

Yorktown

Battle of Chesapeake Capes

Guilford Courthouse

Edenton

Hillsborough

NORTH CAROLINA

King's Mountain

Charlotte

CATAWBA INDIAN RESERVATION

Battle of Camden

Cowpens

Wilmington

SOUTH CAROLINA

Augusta

Charles Town

GEORGIA

Savannah

St. Augustine

SEMINOLE

Atlantic Ocean

NORTH AMERICA

East of the

Mississippi River,

Showing

BRITISH COLONIES,

NATIVE NATIONS, AND

SOME PRINCIPAL TOWNS

•

ca. 1776

WORDS AND BOUNDARIES

Jeff Ward's two-page map at the start of this book differs from many depictions of eastern North America in the eighteenth century in showing the boundaries between native nations as well as European colonies. But it is worth remembering that, as with Europeans and settlers, Native American neighbors often disagreed about where exactly the lines ran. And even agreed-upon boundaries disguised considerable intermingling, as will be seen throughout the book.

Liberty Is Sweet identifies *indigenous* people by their nation—be it Cherokee, Shawnee, or what have you—whenever the sources provide it, but they do not always do so. Moreover, during the revolutionary era, disparate native nations often coalesced, or tried to. In those cases, should they be referred to as *Indians*, *Native Americans*, or what? To call people who lived eight thousand miles from South Asia *Indians*, as the ever-hopeful Columbus did, is of course absurd, but *Native American* seems no better, since they reached these shores about thirty thousand years before Amerigo Vespucci. And for my generation, at least, even *natives* reeks of "the natives are restless." *Indigenous* (the term preferred in most of Latin America) people come up hundreds of times in this story, so simply for variety's sake, I follow their modern-day descendants in alternating among all these terms. Sometimes, when I have made my subject clear, I employ the Canadian term *First Nations*, which is dead-on accurate but little known outside that country. I refer to the Native Americans who lived principally in what is now Alabama and Georgia not as Creeks, as their British contemporaries did and most historians do, but as Muskogees, the term they appear to have preferred, though even that masks the fact that they were, as Bernard Romans called them, a "confederacy of remnants": the sole survivors of more than a dozen native nations annihilated by European disease and slave traders.[1]

In addition to referring to "African Americans" and "Blacks," I occasionally talk about *enslaved people*, a term more and more historians are using to emphasize that *slaves* was *what* they were, not *who* they were.

Finally, I faithfully preserve my sources' creative spelling and grammar, along with their often random capitalization.

An Invisible Enemy

July 1755

O N JULY 2, 1775, WHEN GEORGE WASHINGTON RODE INTO CAM-
bridge, Massachusetts, to take command of the Continental Army,
he expected to be attacked at any moment by the British soldiers camped
across the Charles River in Boston and commanded by Gen. Thomas
Gage.[1] Washington knew Gage. They had also fought twenty years earlier and five hundred miles to the southwest, near modern-day Pittsburgh, Pennsylvania, only that time on the same side.

In the Battle of the Monongahela, on July 9, 1755, the twenty-three-
year-old Washington had served as an aide to the commander-in-chief
of British forces in North America, Edward Braddock. Six other future
Continental Army generals also served under Braddock, as did at least
one colonist who would battle the redcoats at Lexington and Concord.[2]
Gage led the advance troops. Daniel Boone drove a wagon and managed
its woeful team. Benjamin Franklin did not accompany the army out to
the Monongahela River but did more than anyone to get it there.

As the redcoats waded north across the river, fewer than three hundred French marines and provincials, accompanied by more than six
hundred Native American warriors, marched down a hill toward them.
Like their British counterparts, many of the French and native survivors
of this battle would fight again in the American War of Independence.[3]

The Battle of the Monongahela was the first major engagement of the
world's first global war. Today most Americans call it the French and
Indian War, though in truth it drew in numerous additional belligerents
as far away as India. In most of Europe, it is known as the Seven Years'
War, though it actually dragged on for more than a decade. Canadians
derive their term for it, the War of the Conquest, from one of its most
dramatic outcomes: France ceded Québec and the eastern half of the

vast Mississippi Valley to Britain. Actually, though, Native Americans retained control over most of that region for the rest of the century.

Exultant as they were at the outcome of the war, the British believed it had exposed fatal flaws in their relationship with their own North American colonists, and Parliament soon rolled out a package of imperial reforms. These British initiatives seemed tyrannical to the provincials, who contested every one of them. In a sense, the American Revolution, like the Seven Years' War, began on the banks of the Monongahela on July 9, 1755. So we would do well to start there, too.

It was fitting that Braddock fought the French and their Algonquian allies in Indian country. In July 1755—as in July 1776, when thirteen British colonies seceded from Britain, and in July 1861, when eleven rebel states defeated the rest in their first major encounter—the key to the controversy was Native American land. Today West Virginia is known as the Mountain State, and western Pennsylvania is just as hilly, but over the millennia, many of the region's streams, including the Ohio, carved out exceptionally fertile floodplains.[4] In the Seven Years' War, as the empires of France and Great Britain fought in and over the Upper Ohio Valley, they also had to contend with much older claimants: the Shawnees, Delawares, and Six Nations of the Iroquois (Senecas, Cayugas, Onondagas, Oneidas, Mohawks, and Tuscaroras).

In 1753, France had attempted to strengthen its grip on the region by constructing a fort where the Monongahela and Allegheny Rivers converge to become the Ohio: modern-day Pittsburgh. The French post was known as Fort Duquesne, and Braddock's task was to destroy it and scatter, capture, or kill its garrison.

Having served in the army for forty-five of his sixty years—somehow without ever seeing combat—Braddock had acquired a reputation as a crack administrator. In March 1755, he landed his troops at Alexandria, Virginia (just across and down the Potomac River from modern-day Washington, D.C.), where he was greeted by many of the colonists who would accompany him on his westward trek. One was an unabashed anglophile named George Washington. He had been to the forks of the Ohio before.[5]

Two years earlier, Washington had inveigled from Virginia lieutenant governor Robert Dinwiddie the hapless task of informing Jacques Legardeur de Saint-Pierre, the commander of French forces in the trans-Appalachian region, that he and his soldiers were squatting on Virginia property and would have to leave. During the latter stage of his journey

Washington was accompanied by several Haudenosaunee (Iroquois). In a message to one of them, the Half King (viceroy) Tanaghrisson, he laid claim to the name the Iroquois had bestowed upon his great-grandfather, John Washington: Connotaucarious—"devourer of villages."[6] In his journal of the expedition, Washington referred to another of his Iroquois escorts, a young Seneca, as simply "the Hunter." His real name was Guyasuta (often spelled Kiasutha or Kiashuta), and his and Washington's paths would cross again.[7]

Washington's party reached Fort Le Boeuf, the French headquarters on the Buffalo River in what is now northwestern Pennsylvania, on December 11, 1753. Legardeur and his officers balanced their contempt for Governor Dinwiddie's outrageous demand with amused goodwill toward his earnest messenger. They loaded Washington down with ample food and drink for the trip home. The following year, the Virginian returned to the region, heading a party of provincial soldiers and Iroquois warriors and hoping to beat a French force to the forks of the Ohio. The French won the race, built Fort Duquesne, and sent a party to gather intelligence on Lt. Col. Washington. On May 28, 1754, he and forty Virginia provincials, goaded on by the anti-French Iroquois leader Tanaghrisson, surprised and easily defeated the reconnoiterers, who were not expecting a war. But five weeks later, on July 4, Washington and his troops had to surrender their outpost, Fort Necessity, to the French and their native allies, exchanging an abject confession of culpability for the privilege of going home.[8]

The following year, the news that Braddock was planning to attack Fort Duquesne by way of Virginia placed Washington in a quandary. He had long desired a commission in the British army, and serving in the expedition would gain him valuable experience, contacts, and possibly renown. But an army regulation required provincial officers to take orders from regular officers of like rank, a humiliation he could not abide. When Braddock learned of Washington's dilemma—and that the young Virginian knew the Upper Ohio Valley as well as any white man living—he offered him an unpaid place in his official "Family" (personal staff), and Washington eagerly accepted.[9]

On April 12, 1755, the first of Braddock's soldiers set out from Alexandria on their westward journey through backcountry Virginia, Maryland, and Pennsylvania. The commander-in-chief expected to find two hundred carts and 2,500 horses waiting for him in Frederick, Maryland, fifty miles to the northeast. Only one-tenth that number appeared, and one colonist reported that Braddock in his fury seemed "more intent on an Expedition against us than against the French." Pennsylvania's effort to supply the general had fallen victim to its internal divisions: the assembly would levy the necessary taxes only if the colony's largest landholders, the proprietary Penn family, would pay their share. But the Penns' handpicked governor vowed to veto any tax on their land. Nonetheless determined to combat the general's "violent Prejudices" against Pennsylvania, and also to assist a second British army advancing up the Mohawk River, legislative leaders printed up £15,000 worth of paper currency to supply the troops.[10]

Meanwhile Braddock commissioned Benjamin Franklin of Philadelphia to find him 150 wagons. In an advertisement that appeared in German as well as English, Franklin offered farmers silver and gold coin for the use of their wagons and teams. Describing Braddock's deputy quartermaster general, John St. Clair, as a "Hussar"—one of the brutal light horsemen many Pennsylvanians thought they had left behind in the German states—Franklin assured them that whatever he was unable to buy, St. Clair would seize.[11] Franklin did *not* appeal to his fellow colonists' British patriotism, an omission that was all the more surprising in light of the deep affection for the mother country that he shared with George Washington. Indeed, while Franklin loved his adoptive hometown of Philadelphia, it would take a sudden and last-minute "Americanization" to land him on the colonial side of the imperial divide just in time to help write the Declaration of Independence.[12]

Franklin had the farmers bring their wagons and horses to the junction of Wills Creek and the Upper Potomac River, the staging area for Braddock's ascent of the Allegheny Mountains. Years earlier, a group of wealthy Virginians and Marylanders calling themselves the Ohio Company had received a preliminary grant of up to 500,000 acres at the forks of the Ohio. The company also purchased animal pelts from Native American trappers and stored them at Wills Creek. Recently fortified, the Ohio Company's storehouse was being called Fort Cumberland—modern-day Cumberland, Maryland. On May 10, when the general arrived, 150 wagons were waiting for him.[13]

At Fort Cumberland, Braddock welcomed a delegation representing the three nations that lived and hunted in the Upper Ohio Valley—the Shawnees, the Delawares, and a southern offshoot of the Iroquois called the Mingos. The Upper Ohio nations were inclined to help him, since they were worried about the growing French presence on their land.

And their aid might prove decisive: between them, the Shawnees and Delawares boasted more than one thousand warriors. Moreover, their presence in Braddock's army would discourage their many allies in the region from contesting its passage. But first the Delaware sachem Shingas sat down with the British commander to ascertain "what he intended to do with the Land if he Coud drive the French and their Indians away."[14]

How you think Braddock replied to that question depends on which witnesses you believe. Shingas later shared his version with Charles Stuart, a white man his nation had captured and adopted. In his memoirs, Stuart claimed that Braddock announced "that the English Shoud Inhabit & Inherit the Land." When Shingas "askd Genl Braddock whether the Indians that were Freinds to the English might not be Permitted to Live and Trade Among the English and have Hunting Ground sufficient To Support themselves and Familys," Braddock's reply was categorical: "No Savage Shoud Inherit the Land."[15]

Stuart noted that in keeping with native diplomatic protocol, Braddock's visitors made no reply until the following day, when "Shingas and the other Chiefs answered That if they might not have Liberty To Live on the Land they woud not Fight for it," whereupon all of the Delawares and Shawnees and most of the Mingos left Fort Cumberland.[16]

Shingas's version of his conversation with Braddock was contradicted by several British and colonial witnesses, who claimed that the general had treated him courteously. Indeed it would have been unwise and out of character for Braddock to deliberately alienate the very warriors he was trying to enlist. Perhaps the best explanation for the contradiction between the native and white accounts is that Shingas gleaned the general's real intentions from his own long history with British colonists and from the two thousand soldiers milling about Fort Cumberland.[17]

One thing is certain: Braddock enlisted a grand total of eight Native Americans—all members of the roughly six-thousand-person Iroquois confederacy. Led by Scarouady, the Iroquois Half King in the Ohio Valley, they would serve as guides. Scarouady helped Braddock in order to maintain Iroquois sovereignty over the Upper Ohio in the face of Shawnee, Delaware, and French counterclaims.[18]

Even without many actual natives in his camp, Braddock still had the option of preparing his redcoats to fight Indian-style, as recommended by many of his American officers. That would not be necessary, he said. "These Savages may indeed be a formidable Enemy to your raw American Militia," he reportedly told Benjamin Franklin, "but upon the King's regular and disciplin'd Troops, Sir, it is impossible they should make any Impression."[19]

By June 10, when Braddock set out from Fort Cumberland, he knew that French authorities in Québec had sent Fort Duquesne's three-hundred-man garrison massive reinforcements: about nine hundred French and First Nations fighters. However, a report apparently originating from Native Americans living or traveling on the Buffalo River (a branch of the Allegheny known today as French Creek) indicated that a drought had left that stream too little water to float the craft transporting the French troops' food and other supplies. That raised the possibility that Braddock could beat the enemy reinforcements to Fort Duquesne, capture it, and claim the tremendous advantage of fighting from behind its walls. With that prospect in mind, Washington, who had navigated the Buffalo two winters earlier, urged Braddock to hasten ahead with a "small but chosn Band."[20]

Braddock had worn the uniform for twice as long as Washington had lived, but he respected the young American's forest lore and heeded his advice. Neither man knew they had already lost the race: by June 18, when Braddock divided his army, the French soldiers had made it down the Buffalo River to the Allegheny. Indeed, such was the greater efficiency of water travel in this motorless age that despite the drought, the enemy reinforcements covered the six hundred miles from Montréal to Fort Duquesne three and a half weeks faster than the British could complete their 250-mile march from Alexandria.[21]

As the 1,300 men in Braddock's flying column approached Fort Duquesne along an Indian path, native war parties began picking off stragglers, and anxiety spread through the ranks.[22] Yet as the men gazed into their nightly campfires, some were already thinking about the years ahead. One of Franklin's Pennsylvania teamsters, John Findley, held forth on the amazing fertility of "Kanta-ke," three hundred miles down the Ohio River. Once the French were gone, he said, men with the gumption to settle there could make "a great speck"—enormous profits as land speculators. The idea captivated at least one of Findley's fellow teamsters, the twenty-one-year-old Daniel Boone.[23]

NOT ALL OF THOSE who marched with Braddock were men. In a letter to his brother Jack, Washington said "most of the Women" traveling with the army stayed back with the baggage and Col. Thomas Dunbar's 48th Regiment—but that fifty others were adjudged valuable enough to march ahead with the flying column. Washington had to hang back with severe dysentery, but he improved enough to join the advance troops on the evening of July 8, as they made camp about a mile east of the Monongahela River and only twelve miles from Fort Duquesne.[24]

In its lower reaches, the Monongahela flows mostly northwestward. The redcoats were on the right bank, as was Fort Duquesne. But to avoid a defile—a narrow path between the river and the base of a cliff, a virtual tunnel that practically invited ambush—they would have to wade the Monongahela, march two miles downriver, and then, eight miles from the fort, recross to the twelve-foot-high north bank. Surely if the French meant to attack, it would be during the recrossing. Before the men ventured back out into the river, Braddock moved them from column formation into a line of battle. As they clambered safely up the north bank, they "hugg'd themselves with joy," convinced that there would be no ambush that day. Braddock ordered his soldiers back into their columns and moved them out under an "excessive hot sun."[25]

Braddock's conviction that the Monongahela River crossing was the best place for the French to ambush him was shared by the commander of Fort Duquesne. The previous day, Capt. Claude-Pierre Pécaudy, sieur de Contrecoeur, had ordered up an attack by a force of Canadian militiamen, French infantry, and native warriors: mostly Ottawas, Ojibwas, Mississaugas, and other Great Lakes nations but also a handful of Ohio Valley warriors, including Guyasuta, the Mingo who had hunted game for Washington less than two years earlier. Contrecoeur's decision to deploy his First Nations allies at the river's edge rather than in the final defense of Fort Duquesne reflected his realization that Eastern Woodlands Indians almost never contested the possession of forts, as either attackers or defenders.[26] As it was, some of the natives in his 1,600-man force hesitated to strike Braddock's army, which numbered nearly 1,400, and their objections delayed the sortie's departure nearly two hours, preventing it from reaching the Monongahela until after Braddock's troops had recrossed it.[27]

When the two armies collided just north of the river, both were surprised. Both opened fire, and the third British volley killed Daniel Liénard de Beaujeu, the French commander. Unfazed, his native allies spread out in a horseshoe pattern, occupying a hill on the British right. In short order, fifteen of the eighteen officers in the British vanguard became casualties, and the survivors fell back. Meanwhile Braddock rushed the main body forward, and the two British units became entangled. In the chaos, the few remaining officers lost contact with their men.[28]

The area where the British and French met was less forested than the rough country through which Braddock and his men had just marched—and probably not by accident, for Native Americans periodically burned forests to reduce cover, attracting more deer. But the vegetation was thicker than in the European fields where the British officers had learned to fight, if they had learned at all, and they struggled to convert their columns into firing lines.[29] When a few men—rarely more than a platoon—managed to line up, their training did them a disservice. They had been drilled and drilled in platoon firing: the moment one man pulls his trigger, the rest must follow. But with the enemy dispersed among the trees, the first man to shoot tended to be the only one who had actually spotted a target. Many British survivors of the battle reported that "they did not see One of the Enemy the whole day," and one attributed the growing panic to "the Novelty of an invisible enemy."[30]

As native warriors scalped wounded captives, assailants' screams mingled with those of their victims, terrifying the remaining redcoats. George Washington, who had experience in forest warfare, would later voice contempt for the redcoats, who, as he put it, "broke, and run as Sheep pursued by dogs." Frightened sheep do not always take flight. Sometimes they bunch up, and just so with the British, one officer reporting that "the men were sometimes 20 or 30 deep, and he thought himself securest, who was in the Center."[31]

All the while, Braddock rode furiously among them, constantly exposing himself to enemy fire as he tried to gather platoons into companies. Four or five horses were successively shot from under him. His secretary and two of his aides-de-camp were wounded, leaving him only Washington, still miserable from lingering dysentery and so beset with hemorrhoids that he had had to tie cushions over his saddle. When he was not carrying the general's messages, Washington remained at his side. Lead balls pierced his jacket and hat, but he somehow escaped injury.

Washington and several of Braddock's American officers repeated their earlier suggestion about fighting the Indians in their own way. The rear guard, apparently acting on the orders of Capt. Adam Stephen, who had been with Washington at Fort Necessity, adopted this tactic and fared better than the rest. But Braddock refused, and when he found men taking cover behind trees, he used threats and the flat edge of his sword to force them back into line.[32]

Braddock was probably wise not to change tactics under fire, for numerous men sent into the forest would surely have run away. When scores of soldiers took to the woods in defiance of Braddock's orders, many were mistaken for enemies. "The greatest part of the men who were behind trees, were either kill'd or wounded by our own People," wrote one survivor. As many as two-thirds of the redcoats who fell that day were victims of friendly fire.[33]

Surprisingly, the natives also had a technological advantage over the redcoats. Most of their firelocks were rifles, not muskets, as indicated by the sound they made when fired—"Pop[p]ing shots, with little explosion, only a kind of Whiszing noise"—and by the smaller-than-normal lead balls that surgeons later extracted from the few wounded who made it off the battlefield; rifles fired smaller rounds. Rifles were seldom used on traditional European battlefields, since they did not carry bayonets and took three times longer to load. But in the forest, where trees and underbrush prevented bayonet charges, where the fighter could take cover while reloading, and where the target was not a platoon but one individual at a time, the advantage passed to the rifled barrel, which sent the ball spinning toward its target, greatly improving accuracy, range, and stopping power.[34]

Many of Franklin's teamsters cut horses from their traces and rode off, but most of the troops and some of the teamsters (including Daniel Boone, per his own later claim) held firm for three hours, until they ran out of ammunition and a musket ball threw Braddock himself from his horse. Then the men began to break and run. One wounded officer begged the soldiers racing past to stop and help him, but none would. Finally, he reported, "an *American Virginian*" came along and said, "Yes, Countryman . . . I will put you out of your Misery, these Dogs shall not burn you." The man "levelled his Piece at my Head, I cried out and dodged him behind the Tree, the Piece went off and missed me."[35] The Virginian ran on, and the wounded officer got help from someone else.

The soldiers scrambled down the steep northern bank of the Monongahela and waded out into the stream. The Indians "shot many in the Water," but pursued the rest no farther, preferring to harvest scalps, plunder, and captives back at the battlefield. An officer described the road to Dunbar's camp as "full of Dead and people dieing who with fatigue or Wounds Could move on no further; but lay down to die." The first survivor straggled in at 5 a.m. on July 10. About one-third of Braddock's officers were dead, with another third wounded. Enlisted men suffered in the same proportion. Altogether, of a force of fewer than 1,500, approximately 450 were killed and roughly the same number were wounded. At least 70 of the injured men eventually died, pushing the fatalities over 500. On the other side, only about 28 French infantrymen and 11 natives were killed.[36]

Among the British casualties were the majority of the fifty or so women who had marched with the flying column. Many died on the battlefield, a few escaped, and others were taken captive, along with some of the men. Bringing home captives was a principal goal of native warfare and won a warrior greater renown and more spiritual power than bringing in a scalp, owing to the greater danger and difficulty. Many male captives would be ritually tortured to death, but some of the men and most of the women would be adopted as replacements for deceased kin.[37]

Braddock lingered for four days, finally succumbing as the retreating army camped near the ruins of Fort Necessity, where Washington had suffered his own humiliating defeat the previous year. Washington made sure the general was buried under the road so that (as one veteran put it) "all the Wagons might March Over him and the Army [as well] to hinder any Suspision of the French Indiens," lest they "take him up and Scalp him." At Braddock's death, the command of the expedition fell to Col. Dunbar. Spooked by the survivors' accounts, he opted not to renew the attack and would not even accede to local officials' pleas that the army at least remain at Fort Cumberland in order to help protect frontier settlers. Instead he announced plans to march to Philadelphia; Washington and others scoffed at his going into *Winter* Quarter's" in August.[38]

During Braddock's westward crawl across the Allegheny Mountains in June, native war parties had taken scalps and captives as far east as Fort Cumberland, but after July 9, the raids multiplied all along the frontier. Among the attackers was Shingas, the Delaware leader who had offered to fight for the British in return for quiet possession of his land.[39]

White colonists also faced another danger. Less than a week after Braddock's defeat, King George County, Virginia, slaves "apear'd in a Body" at the home of Charles Carter, and Carter's father, who commanded the county militia, sent a posse after them. Virginia governor Robert Dinwiddie recommended making "an Example of one or two" of the slaves—by which he meant trying them for their lives. A week later, Dinwiddie informed the earl of Halifax that Virginia slaves had been "very audacious on the Defeat on the Ohio"; he agonized over how many of each county's militiamen to send against native raiders and how many to leave behind to guard the slaves. Dinwiddie reported that "These poor Creatures imagine the Fr[ench] will give them their

Freedom," and this was a real possibility. The king of Spain, who often joined his French cousins in intermittent warfare against Britain, had offered freedom to any British slave who could make it to Spanish Florida, and in 1739 this invitation had prompted a slave revolt near Charles Town (which would not be shortened to Charleston until 1783), South Carolina. It was the largest ever seen in colonial British North America. Like many white Virginians, Dinwiddie owed his fortune to slaves but also feared them. "We have too many here," he wrote.[40]

Others shared the governor's fears. In the wake of Braddock's defeat, Samuel Davies, a Presbyterian minister in Hanover County, Virginia, warned his flock of "the danger of insurrection and massacre from some of our own gloomy domestics."[41]

NO ONE COULD HAVE anticipated that one survivor of the Battle of the Monongahela, George Washington, would one day command an American army of insurrection or that his unofficial wagon master, Benjamin Franklin, would polish the rebels' declaration of independence before sailing off to seek a French alliance. After all, both men had helped Braddock in hopes of *deepening* their connections to the mother country, and after the general's death and defeat, both redoubled these efforts. Franklin joined the campaign to take Pennsylvania away from the Penn family and turn it into a royal colony.[42] Washington, who had enlisted with Braddock partly in hopes of procuring an army commission, continued that pursuit after 1755. Had he been commissioned, he might still have fought in the American War of Independence, just on the other side. Although Washington's hopes for immediate professional preferment died with Braddock, he had made valuable contacts, especially with Thomas Gage.

Why did Americans like Washington and Franklin later turn against their beloved British empire? The roots of the American Revolution ran even farther back than the Seven Years' War. At the conclusion of their previous clash with France and Spain (the War of Jenkins' Ear, 1739–1748), the British resolved to exert greater control over their North American possessions. In 1751, Parliament prohibited New England from printing paper money that was legal tender, meaning that creditors were required to accept it. (Even today, American currency is "legal tender for all debts.") Royal officials hoped to extend the currency ban to the provinces south of New England—and also crack down on colonial smuggling and rein in the real estate speculators who engrossed vast quantities of native land. But then the disaster on the Monongahela brought British politicians heart and soul into the crusade against the French and Indians.[43] Victory would depend, above all, on whether the colonists also fully committed, so while the war raged on, Britain had to wink at their transgressions.

Viewed from London, though, the North Americans' actions during the Seven Years' War only strengthened the case for root-and-branch reform. Textbooks err in stating that the reason Parliament tried to tax the colonists in the 1760s was to reduce the debt it had incurred fighting the French. But the war did pave the way for the Revolution in another way: by teaching British officials that they needed to overhaul the empire.

Many of the lessons Britain thought it learned during the Seven Years' War had to do with groups that Braddock had not noticed until too late and that even today remain invisible in most accounts of the origins of American Revolution. For example, in the wake of the disaster on the Monongahela, Britain came to believe that it could never defeat France and Spain in North America without Native American allies. To win the natives over, imperial officials promised to keep their colonists off their land.[44]

Britain somewhat succeeded at placating the Native Americans—but at the same time infuriated a significant portion of its own colonists: those who had hoped to make or improve their fortunes selling Native American land. Many of these men had fought at the Monongahela and learned their own lessons there: not that the First Nations had to be appeased but that their land possessed immense potential value—all the more so now that army engineers had built a road to it. Here was the most important way in which the Battle of the Monongahela set the stage for the American Revolution: British officials and American colonists came out of it with conflicting ideas about Indians.

Later events of the Seven Years' War taught British officials additional lessons that colonists wished they had not learned. In 1760, when black Jamaicans carried out Britain's largest slave revolt yet—suppressed only at great cost to the British army and navy—they gave London still another reason to shorten the American colonists' leash. Near the close of the interimperial struggle, France deeded Louisiana, which included New Orleans and all of the land along rivers flowing into the Mississippi from the west, to Spain. The combined Spanish and Native American threats contributed to the British cabinet's fateful December 1762 decision to leave twenty battalions—ten thousand troops—in America after the peace treaty. British taxpayers were already straining to pay the interest on the British government's debt, which had nearly doubled during the war, so imperial officials decided to push the cost of the peacekeeping troops onto the Americans they protected. That meant taxing them.[45]

Like the British government, many of the mother country's most powerful interest groups learned important lessons from the Seven Years' War. The paper money that the Pennsylvania legislature spent provisioning Braddock's soldiers held its value, but much of the colonial currency issued later in the prolonged conflict depreciated, often dramatically. In equal measure, hyperinflation benefited debtors but cheated creditors, including British merchants, who went to war against the colonists' paper money.[46]

The Seven Years' War also awakened other interest groups. Even as British and French soldiers shot and stabbed each other, merchants based in Philadelphia, Newport, Boston, and other colonial ports illegally traded with the French sugar islands in the Caribbean. The most vocal opposition to this smuggling came from the British Caribbean slaveholders who competed with the French (and the Spanish and Dutch) for the privilege of supplying North America with sugarcane, especially in the form of molasses, the principal ingredient in rum.[47]

In the four arenas of taxes, territory, treasury notes (paper money), and trade—conveniently summarized as the four Ts—the colonists had long violated official British policy. Then the Seven Years' War freed them to stray even further from imperial orthodoxy. If Britain came down too hard on the colonists' smuggling, tried to tax them, or burned the crude cabins they built beyond the Anglo-Indian boundary, it would jeopardize their support for the war. Thomas Hutchinson, who was both lieutenant governor of Massachusetts and chief justice of the colony's superior court, became so unpopular, especially for his aggressive pursuit of smugglers, that the legislature voted to cut his salary. But there was nothing he could do—at least not yet. "We wish for a good peace with foreign enemies," Hutchinson wrote a friend in 1762. "It would enable us to make a better defence against our domestick foes."[48]

Hutchinson was not alone. British politicians as well as hapless colonial officials spent the final years of the Seven Years' War drawing up plans, pigeonholing them, and anxiously awaiting the end of the war.

PART ONE

THE KING'S GRIEVANCES

CHAPTER 1

Awing and Protecting the Indians

1763

UPPER OHIO VALLEY WARRIORS TOOK THE BATTLE OF THE Monongahela as a signal to attack colonists everywhere west of the Appalachian Mountains, killing many, capturing still more, and chasing survivors back east into Pennsylvania, Maryland, and Virginia. The raids continued until October 1758, when British officials signed the Treaty of Easton, committing colonists to never again breaching the Appalachians.[1] The treaty not only stopped the Upper Ohioans' attacks but persuaded them to back out of their alliance with France just as a second British army marched west toward Fort Duquesne. Unable to defend themselves without native help, the French evacuated, burning the fort to the ground on their way out. Redcoats occupied the smoking ruins on November 24 and immediately set to work on a new fort that they named for William Pitt, the cabinet secretary who had secured virtually unlimited parliamentary funding for the war.

British colonists immediately violated the Treaty of Easton. Some set up just outside Fort Pitt and christened their settlement Pittsburgh. In July 1760, members of the land-speculating Ohio Company, who now included George Washington, offered Henry Bouquet, the British commander at Fort Pitt, a share of its stock if he would allow them to sell land west of the Appalachians. Indignantly refusing (his own real estate ventures lay east of the mountains), Bouquet awarded only one "Lot of Ground on the Bank of the Monongahela" River. It went to Samuel Lightfoot of Chester County, Pennsylvania, "so as to take in his sons Grave who dyed there" with Gen. Braddock.[2]

Undaunted, the Ohio Company found other ways to advance its claim.

ESTIMATED POPULATION OF THE CARIBBEAN AND NORTH AMERICA EAST OF THE MISSISSIPPI, C. 1776

	TOTAL	AFRICAN AMERICAN[1]	NATIVE AMERICAN	WHITE	DATE	SOURCES CONSULTED
New England Colonies						
Connecticut	199,200	6,400	1,400	191,400	1774	CT, CB, PH
Massachusetts[2]	290,900	5,000	2,000	283,900	1776	HS, CJ, RW
New Hampshire	81,400	700[3]		80,700	1775	HS
Rhode Island	59,700	3,700	1,500	54,500	1774	RI, CJ, RW
Middle Colonies						
Delaware	35,500				1770	CJ
New Jersey	130,000		9,700	119,000	1775	HS, CJ, RW
New York	163,400	19,900		143,500	1771	HS, RW, CJ
Pennsylvania[4]	302,000	7,200		294,800	1775	CB, Bo, GN
Southern Colonies						
East Florida	5,500	2,500		3,000	1774	Sm, PW, CJ
West Florida	5,000	1,200		3,800	c. 1775	Sm, PW, CJ
Georgia[5]	33,000	15,000		18,000	1775	PW, CB
Maryland	223,000	90,000		133,000	1775	CB, RW
New Orleans[6]	3,500				1779	PL, KH
North Carolina	209,600	52,300	500	156,800	1775	PW
South Carolina	179,400	107,300	500	71,600	1775	PW, CB
Virginia	466,100	186,400	200	279,500	1775	PW
Canada						
Newfoundland	12,400				1775	RW
Nova Scotia	11,000				1775	RW, WBK
Quebec	76,500		1,500	75,000	c. 1762	HT, RW
Caribbean and Bermuda						
Antigua (Br.)	40,400	37,800		2,600	1774	Ba, Sh, CL
Bahamas (Br.)[7]	4,300	2,300		2,000	1773	RW
Barbados (Br.)	87,600	69,100		18,500	1773	CG
Bermuda (Br.)[8]	11,100	5,000		6,100	1774	RW
Cuba (Sp.)	171,600	75,200		96,400	1774	CG
Dominica (Br.)	22,600	18,800		3,800	1774	RW

	TOTAL	AFRICAN AMERICAN[1]	NATIVE AMERICAN	WHITE	DATE	SOURCES CONSULTED
Caribbean and Bermuda *(cont.)*						
Grenada (Br.)	36,400	35,100		1,300	1777	EW, TM
Guadeloupe (Fr.)	114,000				1767	CL
Jamaica (Br.)	216,000	197,300		18,700	1775	CG, RW
Martinique (Fr.)	85,800	74,200		11,600	1776	CG
Montserrat (Br.)[9]	10,600	9,500		1,100	c. 1780	CL, RW
Nevis (Br.)	9,500	8,400		1,100	1756	RW
Puerto Rico (Sp.)	71,300	42,000		29,300	1775	CG, CB, RL
Saint-Domingue (Fr.)	330,500	310,300		20,200	1784	CG
St. Christopher (Br.)	25,400	23,500		1,900	1774	VH, RW
St. Eustatius (Du.)	3,200	1,600		1,600	1779	VE
St. Vincent (Br.)	9,200	7,300		1,900	1764	RW, JS
Tobago (Br.)	9,000	8,600		400	1775	RW
Virgin Islands (Br.)	7,300	6,100		1,200	1756	RW
First Nations (Native American)						
Abenaki[10]	3,000		3,000		1750	DG
Cherokee	10,700	200	8,500	2,000	1775	PW, JM
Chickasaw, Choctaw	16,400		16,300	100	1775	PW, JM
Delaware, Munsee	3,500		3,500		1768	HT, JM
Fox (Mesquakie)	1,500		1,500		1768	HT, JK
Illinois	2,200		2,200		1768	HT, JM
Iroquois (6 Nations)	6,000				1778	JM
Kickapoo, Mascouten	2,000		2,000		1768	HT, JM
Mi'kmaq	3,000		3,000		c. 1775	PB
Muskogee (Creek)	14,000		14,000		1775	PW, JM
Ojibwa (Ojibwe), Mississauga	15,000		10,200		1768	HT
Ottawa (Odawa)	5,000		5,000		1768	HT, JM
Piankeshaw, Miami, Wea	4,000		4,000		1768	HT, JM
Potawatomi	3,000		3,000		1768	HT, JM
Sauk	2,000		2,000		1769	HT, JK
Shawnee	1,800		1,800		1768	HT, JM
Wyandot (Huron)	1,000		1,000		1768	HT, JM

Prepared by Riley K. Sutherland, University of South Carolina

Key to Sources (see bibliography for detailed source citations)

Ba - Ballester	GN - Nash	RI - Rhode Island Census
Bo - Bouton	HS - *Historical Statistics*	RL - Logan
CB - US Census Bureau	HT - Tanner	RW - Wells
CG - Cohen and Greene	JK - Kay	Sh - Sheridan
CJ - Coulson and Joyce	JM - Muller	Sm - Smith
CL - Carey and Lea	JS - Spinelli	TM - Murphy
CT - Connecticut Census	PB - Block	VE - Enthoven
DG - Ghere	PL -Lachane	VH - Hubbard
EW - Williams	PH - Hinks	WBK - Kerr
	PW - Wood	WC - Calderhead

Notes

Blank cells indicate that no data is available. All estimates are rounded to the nearest hundred.

1. Numerous mixed-race individuals lived in both native and colonial societies, but sources rarely estimate their numbers.

2. African American, Native American, and white populations of Massachusetts, New Jersey, Maryland, Nevis, and the Virgin Islands were estimated by applying Robert Wells's proportions to estimates of the colonies' total populations.

3. For New Hampshire, Maryland, the Bahamas, and St. Eustatius, the sources estimate the number of enslaved people, not the slightly larger number of African Americans.

4. Estimates of Pennsylvania's African American and white populations in 1775 were derived using Bouton's figures for their proportions of the 1780 population.

5. Wood combines his headcounts for the Creeks/Muskogees (14,000) and Georgia. Here these figures have been disaggregated.

6. The sole portion of the Spanish North American empire that lay east of the Mississippi River was New Orleans. The headcount given here is an average of New Orleans's 1769 and 1788 populations.

7. This Bahamas estimate includes 150 inhabitants of Turks Island. Since the source provides a racial breakdown for the Bahamas but not Turks, it is assumed to be the same for both.

8. The sources for Bermuda, Dominica, and Tobago do not supply headcounts for African Americans and whites but do estimate each group's proportion of the population. In each case, these proportions have been applied to the total populations.

9. Estimates of white and African American populations in Nevis and the Virgin Islands were reached by applying the proportion of each race in all of the Leeward Islands. Although sources do not provide individual racial proportions for either location, Wells estimates that their racial proportions varied from that of all Leeward Islands by less than two percent. Additionally, population statistics for the Virgin Islands were estimated by averaging Wells's estimate of the islands' 1756 population and Carey and Lea's estimate from 1805.

10. The number of Abenaki warriors (640) in 1750 was multiplied by five, as suggested by David Ghere, to estimate the total Abenaki population.

The scramble for Ohio Valley land was fueled by a combination of greed and mass depopulation. For 250 years, European disease and violence had ravaged native communities, leaving the so-called New World much less populous than the Old. Just as nature abhors even a relative

vacuum, America's lower population density made land there compara-
tively cheap, drawing a continuous stream of immigrants from Europe.
As soon as they could, many of the new arrivals bought slaves, seeing no
other way to wealth in this land where free workers were scarce enough
to demand a decent wage. By the eighteenth century, forced immigrants
from Africa outnumbered voluntary arrivals from Europe.[3]

But the movement of peoples across the Atlantic, forced and free,
was only the second largest contributor to the demographic boom that
saw the Black and white populations of the future United States double every generation, from about 300,000 in 1706, the year of Benjamin Franklin's birth, to four million at his death in 1790.[4] Even more
significant was natural increase: excess of births over deaths. In North
America, cheap land enabled young couples to marry and start having
children—not always in that order—sooner than in Europe. And a more
dispersed population inhibited the spread of disease, allowing mothers
to live longer and deliver more children than their cousins in densely
populated Europe.

The same diffusionary process that drew immigrants across the Atlantic propelled thousands of settlers westward, always preceded, at least
on paper, by real estate speculators, who counted on the surge of new
arrivals to push the price of Native American land ever higher.

On September 8, 1760, Britain captured Montréal, prompting the
French to surrender all of New France (Canada) and setting off a land
rush. At the beginning of the Seven Years' War, Virginia had recruited
soldiers for its provincial regiment by promising each a share of 200,000
acres of Ohio Valley land. The bounty was for enlisted men, but in 1762,
George Washington led their officers in appealing to the provincial council for the lion's share of the plunder. Land fever struck Connecticut,
too. That colony's 1663 charter claimed every acre all the way out to the
Pacific Ocean, encroaching not only on numerous native nations but on
the northern third of Pennsylvania. Before the war, Connecticut residents had formed the Susquehannah Company to exploit the disputed
territory, and in 1762, they dispatched settlers to the Susquehanna Valley
(home of today's Wilkes-Barre and Scranton, Pennsylvania).[5]

Native Americans learned that the removal of the French had fundamentally transformed their relationship to the British government as
well. After Braddock's defeat, London had tried to strip away France's
native allies by redressing their grievances. But many officers serving in
America viewed every victory over the French as reducing the need to

placate Native Americans. For example, in July 1759, less than three weeks after Britain captured Fort Niagara, an officer rejoiced that "We can now talk to our new Allies"—the natives—"in a proper Stile, as their Services are not Necessary." Jeffery Amherst, the army's commander-in-chief for North America, believed the conclusion of the war in February 1763 had disclosed both the need to stop buying the First Nations' favor—the war had been Britain's costliest up to that time, nearly doubling its debt, from £73 million to £137 million—and an opportunity to do so: reducing Indian gifts.[6] Guyasuta, the Seneca who had accompanied George Washington in 1753, had since become a sachem, and he could see what was afoot. In a May 1765 conference with Indian agent George Croghan, a fellow veteran of the Battle of the Monongahela (albeit on the other side), Guyasuta fondly recalled that just a few years earlier, Britain had generously supplied its native allies with European manufactures. But that "was only when the war was doubtful," he said. "As soon as you conquered the French, you did not care how you treated us, as you then did not think us worth your notice."[7]

Amherst's austerity had both practical and symbolic consequences. Most Native Americans living east of the Mississippi (and even some farther west) relied more heavily upon European manufactured goods—from cloth to rum to guns—than many backcountry whites. Having already lost French aid, many native nations suffered terribly when Amherst also cut them off. They were also insulted, since they valued the exchange of gifts as the core of any alliance.[8] Guyasuta twice helped recruit far-flung native nations for conspiracies against the British and

James A. West, *Point of View*, featuring George
Washington and Guyasuta

later explained his motives to Croghan. When you Englishmen stopped supplying us with arms and ammunition, he said, you "gave all the nations in this country a suspicion that you had designs against them."[9]

The French evacuation also freed the British from having to placate another group of North Americans, their own colonists. Now they could finally begin reforming the empire. The Declaration of Independence would be framed as an indictment of King George III, who ascended to the throne on October 25, 1760, at the age of twenty-two. But the truth was that no monarch had ruled Great Britain since the "Glorious Revolution" of 1688. The policies promulgated in the king's name were actually the work of his cabinet: the fewer than ten men who held the highest posts in government. Granted, George had the power of appointment, but he had to choose cabinet secretaries who could command parliamentary majorities. So long as they did so, they could cling to power even in the face of royal disapproval. George III more closely resembled Elizabeth II (1926–)—a figurehead—than the all-but-omnipotent Elizabeth I (1533–1603). Already in 1763, every speech he gave to Parliament was a ventriloquist act, dictated to him by his ministers.[10]

The real head of the British government, increasingly referred to as the prime minister, was the first lord of the treasury—a post that modern British PMs still hold. When France and Spain sued for peace in 1762, the first lord was the Earl of Bute, the "royal favourite." In December, the Bute ministry adopted a new policy that, although virtually unknown today, ended up playing a pivotal role in provoking the American Revolution. In 1749, at the conclusion of its previous contest against France and Spain—the War of the Austrian Succession—Britain had left about two thousand troops behind in North America. But Bute and his team opted for a much larger peacetime colonial establishment: ten thousand soldiers.[11] Many British Americans believed the ministry intended this army "as a rod and check over us." But that was not true, at least not at first. A fourth of the men went to the Caribbean. The rest would police newly conquered regions like Canada, Florida—and the trans-Appalachian west. London also augmented the peacetime establishment in other corners of its empire; Ireland got six thousand additional soldiers.[12]

Thomas Gage, who had commanded Gen. Braddock's advance at the Battle of the Monongahela, identified the expanded American garrison's primary mission: "keeping the Indians in awe and Subjection." But Britain also hoped to prevent its own land pirates and often larcenous fur traders from abusing Native Americans. In the aftermath of the Battle of the Monongahela, imperial officials had been stunned to see nearly every native nation side with France—and then proceed, as Gage noted, to "over run our Frontiers." Britain incurred enormous costs in transporting troops—and, even worse, their equipment—hundreds of miles overland in pursuit of warriors who knew how to avoid or ambush them. Indeed, Indian wars were widely considered "the most ruinous and expensive that can be waged." Thus the cabinet resolved never again to fight France or Spain in America without drawing at least some native towns into its own column. That meant "awing as well as protecting the Indian nations." A ten-thousand-man peacetime garrison would itself come at a high cost—but not to Britain, for Bute and his ministers planned to tax the Americans to pay for it.[13]

The Seven Years' War officially ended with the Treaty of Paris, signed on February 10, 1763, at the Hôtel de Grinberghen, just across the Seine from the Louvre. In it, France gave Britain all of its North American possessions except two tiny fishing islands, St. Pierre and Miquelon, off the coast of Newfoundland. On April 9, Prime Minister Bute, having achieved his principal aim, resigned, sticking George III with a new first lord of the treasury whom he intensely disliked. The fifty-year-old George Grenville was, as one admirer noted, "a man born to public business." A decade earlier, he had become the first treasurer of the Royal Navy to force the admirals to pay their sailors on time. Allegedly Grenville once "stole a turnpike bill out of somebody's pocket at a concert and read it in a corner in despite of all the efforts of the finest singers to attract his attention."[14]

Two of Grenville's highest priorities were slowing the British empire's descent into debt and halting American smuggling. More than half of the government's revenue went to interest on its bonds. But if anyone could impose fiscal discipline, it was Grenville, as he had already shown in his private life. By living simply, he managed to survive on the interest on his inheritance, investing every shilling of his government salary and accumulating £154,674 by the time of his death in 1770.[15]

One way to reduce the deficit was to crack down on smugglers, who not only cheated the government but enriched themselves at the expense of honest traders and damaged the mercantilist system that had made Great Britain great. In America, the key to halting illegal trade was a simple fact known to everyone at the time but hardly anyone today: Britain did not have thirteen colonies in the New World but

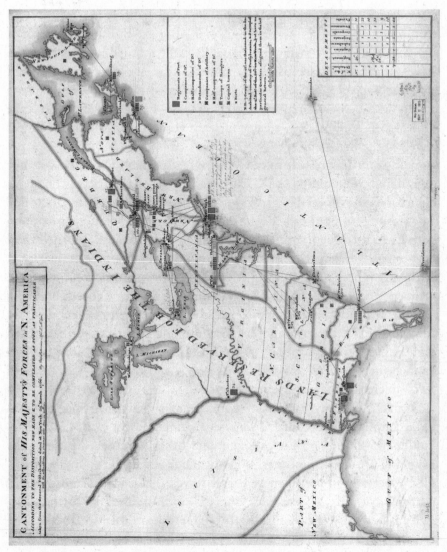

Daniel Paterson, *Cantonment of His Majesty's Forces in North America* (1767)

twenty-six. In addition to the provinces that later declared independence and three others in Canada, there were Bermuda and the Bahamas out in the Atlantic, along with the two Floridas: the southern peninsula was called East Florida, and West Florida ran from the modern state's panhandle westward to just short of New Orleans, which France ceded to Spain in 1762. And Britain also had six colonies in the Caribbean.[16]

As importers, the residents of the future United States played a crucial role in Britain's industrial revolution, taking a fifth of its exports and employing about a million artisans and laborers. But in their exports, North Americans were far less valuable to the mother country than the slaves in the sugar islands. The mainland's largest crop, tobacco, sold for an average of £750,000 a year. But the British West Indies' sugarcane and its derivatives—molasses, sugar, and rum—fetched an annual average of nearly £4 million. Say what you want about tobacco, "the brightest jewels in the British crown" were in the Caribbean.[17]

The islands were just as crucial to North America (which was not considered as including the Caribbean in those days). Slaves on sugar plantations were forced to grow most of their own food during their one day's respite from the cane fields, but that provided too little nutrition to keep them working, especially when El Niño hurricanes flattened their plantain groves. Sugar planters purchased about half of the grain grown in the breadbasket colonies of New York, New Jersey, Pennsylvania, Delaware, and increasingly Maryland and Virginia.[18] Indeed, by 1770, George Washington grew no tobacco at Mount Vernon, having fully converted his fields and laborers to wheat and corn. Yankee fishermen sent the best of the catch to southern Europe, where the Catholic Church banned meat on Fridays and saints' days, and the rest—the "refuse" fish—to enslaved sugarcane workers in the Caribbean.[19]

Many today may have trouble imagining the Nutmeg State as cowpoke country, but colonial Connecticut annually sent Caribbean slaveholders thousands of horses, oxen, and other livestock. Much of the mainland's lumber and other forest products also went to the West Indies, especially in the form of barrel staves. The sugar islands bought nearly two-thirds of what New England sold, and British North Americans as a whole exported more to the Caribbean than to Britain. The return cargoes included not only molasses but coveted gold and silver. If, like Atlantis, the sugar islands had disappeared beneath the waves, much of North America would have sunk right along with them. Daniel Defoe, who knew something about islands, put it well: "*no* Islands, *no* Continent."[20]

Fewer than 5 percent of New England and middle colonies residents were enslaved. But given that two-thirds of North American grain, forest products, and livestock ended up on Caribbean sugar plantations, the colonies between New Hampshire and Pennsylvania were as dependent on the work of African Americans as Virginia and South Carolina. In the vitally important economic sphere they, too, were slave societies.[21]

Since 1733, Parliament had used prohibitive taxes to force North American merchants to buy their sugar, rum, and—most of all—molasses from British West Indian provinces such as Barbados and Jamaica rather than such foreign sugar islands as Spanish Cuba and Puerto Rico, Dutch Surinam and Berbice on the northern coast of South America, and, most crucially, French Saint-Domingue (the future Haiti). The stark reality, however, was that most North American vessels arriving in the Caribbean illegally filled their holds at foreign islands, for economically unassailable reasons.

The British West Indies could not consume nearly as much food, livestock, or forest products as British North America produced, and they were even less capable of satisfying its appetite for molasses. Jamaican and Barbadian planters forced their slaves not only to grow sugarcane and mill it into table sugar and molasses but also to distill most of the molasses into rum, leaving little for export to the more than one hundred rum distilleries in North America. Mainlanders always had the option of importing Barbadian and Jamaican rum, but they knew that the real profits lay in turning a sweetener into an intoxicant. And not just for domestic use, for New England rum was a major export. Taking it away would throw North America into permanent trade deficit.[22]

All this time, slaves in Saint-Domingue cranked out more molasses than all of the British islands combined, and their owners offered it to North Americans for a song, since Louis XV would not let them send either molasses or rum home to France to compete with brandy. Yet French islanders did refine vast quantities of sugar, with molasses as a by-product. The all but inevitable result was that less than one-sixteenth of the molasses entering British North American ports like Newport, Rhode Island, and Boston came in from Anglophone islands—which is to say, legally.[23]

British North America's importation of foreign molasses continued even as Britain battled France and Spain in the so-called Great War for Empire; in fact it quintupled. On August 23, 1760, Secretary Pitt commanded mainland governors and customs agents to stop colonists from succoring Britain's enemies. Officials briefly stepped up enforcement but hesitated to push the Americans too hard at a time when all hands were needed for the fight against the French.[24]

But then the Treaty of Paris gave the British government a freer hand. Early in April 1763, while serving as Bute's first lord of the admiralty, George Grenville helped draft the Hovering Act, which made Royal

Navy battleships the maritime equivalent of the ten thousand troops the ministry left in America at the end of the war. Benjamin Franklin spoke for countless North Americans when he denounced Parliament for converting "the brave honest Officers of your Navy into pimping Tide-waiters and Colony Officers of the Customs." And years later, John Adams would write, "I know not why we should blush to confess that molasses was an essential ingredient in American independence."[25]

THE EIGHTEENTH-CENTURY BRITISH POLITICAL system was surprisingly apolitical. Opposition MPs jockeyed for power less by offering alternatives to the governing faction's program than by assembling often diverse coalitions to magnify its missteps in hopes of eroding its majority, taking its place, and tasting the "loaves and fishes": lucrative government jobs, pensions, and contracts. But George Grenville's accession as first lord of the treasury marked the beginning of something like genuine party politics, for he and his team staked out clear policy differences with one of the nation's most popular figures, his brother-in-law William Pitt.[26]

Pitt had joined the cabinet in 1757, at the low point of the struggle against the French. Immediately becoming its dominant force, he had turned the tide of war, primarily by showering borrowed funds on the army, the navy—and the provincial legislatures.[27] Then in 1761, he resigned, leaving his colleagues with the tab. In March 1763, when the Bute administration proposed to tax cider and perry (fermented pear juice) in order to trim Pitt's debt, he had no compunction about leading the populist opposition. But he did have to answer a pointed query from Grenville: "*Where* is your money,—*where* are your means" of eliminating the deficit? In reply, Pitt merely hummed a popular ballad: "Oh *where*,—Oh *Gentle Shepherd*! tell me *where*." Laughter filled the room, and opposition politicians and newspaper wags took to calling Grenville the Gentle Shepherd.[28]

Grenville and Pitt both sought to squeeze more money out of Britain's overseas possessions, differing only in whether the windfall should go to merchants or the government. One of their sharpest disputes centered on the East India Company (EIC), whose global reach was even wider than its name implied. Foreigners owned about a third of the firm's stock, and EIC ships sailed not just to India but all the way to Canton (Guangdong). The company traded on more or less equal terms with the powerful Cantonese mercantile houses that sold it tea, primarily in return for Spanish American silver.[29] But in India, the EIC went in more for straight plunder. Bengal's healthy combination of cottage industry (especially spinning and weaving) and farming produced great wealth. By the mid-1760s, the company extracted more than half of it, primarily through taxation, and sent it home in the form of calico (printed and painted cotton cloth) that was then reexported all over the Atlantic. That arrangement made sense to Grenville, but parliamentary spokesmen for the British merchant class wanted to abolish the EIC's monopoly, throwing India open to private adventurers. Commercial competition, they said, would lower the prices of goods traveling in either direction between Britain and India, vastly increasing the trade.[30]

In America as in India, Pitt wished to foster commerce, while Grenville sought to maximize tax revenue, primarily in order to make good on Lord Bute's pledge to make the Americans pay for their protection. The new first lord was also determined to rescue the primary victims of American smuggling, the British sugar planters. That meant coming down hard, not only on the smugglers but on their enablers in the customs service. Numerous British-born revenue officers, addicted to the comforts of home, remained there, farming out their duties to subordinates, who accepted smugglers' bribes in return for underreporting their importation of foreign molasses. So on July 25, 1763, the Grenville administration told the absentee colonial officeholders to occupy their posts—in person, immediately—or forfeit them. It also sent additional warships to America to hunt for smugglers.[31]

The crucial fact about the emerging conflict between colonies and crown—so often missed by the mythmakers—was that British officials, not American colonists, were the ones demanding change.

CHAPTER 2

—•◦•—

The First American Revolution

1763

Michigan's upper and lower peninsulas are separated by the straits that drain Lake Michigan into Lake Huron, but since 1957 the two Michigans have been linked by a five-mile-long bridge. A few hundred feet west of the bridge's southern terminus, just off the beach, stands the restored Fort Michilimackinac, site in June 1763 of an extraordinary incident that began with a game of baggataway, also known as lacrosse.

Every year, British subjects all over the world celebrated the king's birthday with toasts and fireworks. On June 4, 1768, Boston's artillery company took the occasion of George III's thirtieth birthday to introduce two cannon it had just received from England. Five years earlier, the revelers converging on Fort Michilimackinac included a group of Ojibwas (Chippewas). Though George had ascended to the throne only two and a half years earlier, his Ojibwa children (as, per custom, they called themselves in diplomatic talks) had no trouble remembering the date. In fact they reached Michilimackinac early and offered to open the festivities with an exhibition game of baggataway, to be played just outside the fort's walls against a team of Sacs.[1]

These Ojibwa families hunted farther west but summered near the fort, and their relations with the British had been fairly amicable since September 1761, when the French Lt. Charles-Michel Mouet de Langlade handed the keys to Fort Michilimackinac to British Capt. George Etherington. Langlade stayed on as a fur trader, and he was still there three years later, as was Capt. Etherington.

In the midst of the June 2 baggataway match, an Ojibwa lobbed the ball over the stockade fence, and he and his teammates pursued it, right through the open gate. All morning Ojibwa women had been milling about inside the fort, as they often did, since it doubled as a trading post and women figured prominently in the fur trade. But as soon as the baggataway players entered Fort Michilimackinac, the women drew tomahawks, knives, and other weapons from under their blankets and handed them to their brothers and husbands, who set upon the garrison. The warriors' victory was as complete as the soldiers' surprise. Sixteen redcoats and one trader were killed on the spot; the rest, including Etherington, were captured.[2]

Many more soldiers would have died that day had Charles Langlade not pled their case. With an Ottawa mother and French father, he had spent most of the previous decade battling the British, for instance at the massacre of the Fort William Henry garrison in 1757, the incident immortalized in James Fenimore Cooper's *Last of the Mohicans.* But having reconciled himself to the new order, he helped persuade a party of Ottawas to transport Etherington and the other survivors of the 1763 attack more than five hundred miles down the Great Lakes and St. Lawrence River to Montreal.[3]

The Ojibwas had taken Fort Michilimackinac at the instigation of the natives who lived along the *etroit,* or strait, that drains Lake St. Clair into Lake Erie. They had planned an assault of their own, on Fort Detroit, named for the strait. But Maj. Henry Gladwin, a veteran of Braddock's expedition and the fort's commander, "was luckily informed the night before" the planned attack, possibly by his Native American lover. Having lost the element of surprise, the Ottawas elected not to storm the fort; like other Eastern Woodlands Indians, they almost never initiated battles where they appeared likely to lose large numbers. Instead they laid a siege.[4]

Like the Ojibwas at Michilimackinac, the Detroit River natives had acted in response to diplomatic communiqués: wampum (beaded) belts from the Upper Ohio Valley nations and the westernmost members of the Iroquois league, the Senecas, who lived around modern-day Rochester, New York. The Seneca headmen had tried to pull the other Iroquois nations into the conspiracy, and "the Women of the Senecas" had likewise "spoke with a Belt to the Women of the other [Iroquois] Nations." When these invitations were declined, the Senecas joined the plot on their own.[5]

Why had the Senecas, Shawnees, Mingos, and Delawares rebelled? Because to colonial settlers as well as real estate speculators, news of the Anglo-French peace treaty had sounded like a starter's pistol. The

Virginia-based Ohio Company's 500,000-acre land grant had lapsed during the war, but in 1763 the partners sent an agent to London to try to revive it.[6] One Ohio Company member, George Washington, who had gotten his start as a surveyor, also helped found another real estate firm, the Mississippi Company. On June 3, 1763, the day after Ojibwa warriors captured distant Fort Michilimackinac, Washington and his partners composed an audacious request for 2.5 million acres all the way out at the confluence of the Ohio and Mississippi Rivers.[7] The thirty-one-year-old Virginian saw in the trans-Appalachian west not only untold riches but the prospect of escape.

In 1759, Washington had married Martha Dandridge Custis, the wealthiest widow in Virginia. It began as something less than a love match, at least on Washington's side, as evidenced by the love letters he continued sending a close friend's wife throughout his and Custis's engagement.[8] Under English common law, the marriage entitled Washington to the profits on his wife's real estate—and absolute ownership of all her other property. He invested heavily in "Lands and Negroes," along with the carriage, English suits, and other accoutrements appropriate to his new station. By 1763, those purchases, combined with bad weather and lower-than-expected tobacco prices, had left him £2,000 in debt to a British supplier.[9] He could have cleared his accounts by selling some of his wife's land—so long as she consented—but his natural reluctance to do so was exacerbated by the stark reality that the American colonies' chronic shortage of circulating cash all but guaranteed that big-ticket items like real estate would not fetch a fraction of what had been paid for them.

While eastern gentlemen like Washington dreamed of recouping their fortunes by obtaining title to the First Nations' land, other colonists simply moved out onto it—that is, until the spring and summer of 1763, when native war parties struck as far east as Carlisle, Pennsylvania, about halfway between Pittsburgh and Philadelphia. Their goal, as white settlers understood, was "to prevent our settling any farther than we have, viz., much about the main Blue Ridge of mountains."[10] The rebels were also fueld by spiritual passion. Around 1760, a Delaware had a life-changing religious vision and took the name Neolin ("The Enlightened"). In many ways, he resembled a Christian evangelist. Turning to prophecy after an instant conversion, he aroused audiences by delivering highly charged sermons, "almost constantly crying," as he urged his followers to address the Master of Life by way of his son. And while most Native

Americans expected to be punished only for violating prescribed rituals, Neolin arraigned his flock for "Sins & Vices," especially their embrace of such European depravities as drunkenness and firearms. Natives, he said, must retrain themselves in making and using their own weapons, tools, and clothing. Neolin circulated a schematic drawing summarizing his "new Plan of Religion." It depicted the Indians at the bottom, heaven at the top—and Europeans and their ways blocking the path between.[11]

The prophet's diagram traveled as far east as Iroquoia and as far west as present-day Minnesota. On April 17, 1763, it served as the principal theme of a council speech given in a native village ten miles from Fort Detroit. The speaker was Pontiac, the principal conspirator against that post. Pontiac belonged to the same Ottawa nation that had saved most of the Fort Michilimackinac garrison; that some Ottawas helped Capt. Etherington even as Pontiac and his neighbors plotted against Maj. Gladwin should dispel forever the myth of natives belonging to homogenous tribes.[12]

Great Lakes Indians modified Neolin's message to suit their needs. Having enjoyed more than a century of good relations with the French fur traders and officers who armed and otherwise supplied them, they did not seek to dismantle forts like Detroit and Michilimackinac but to persuade the French army to re-occupy them. Leading insurgents spread a rumor that France already planned to return. Their evident purpose was to recruit enough additional Native Americans to persuade Louis XV that by reviving his native alliances, he could reconquer the American west. Thus the rebels' false claims of French backing would belatedly turn true.[13]

The insurgents' hopes for a French restoration were not as naive as they might seem. Étienne-François, duc de Choiseul, the foreign minister, really did expect France to return to North America as soon as it rebuilt its military,

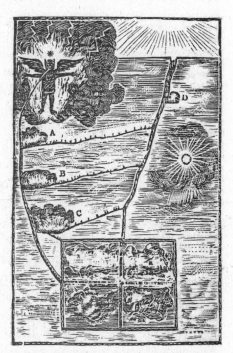

Neolin, diagram illustrating his call to Native Americans to depart from the European (left) path (copy by unknown artist)

and it did return in 1778.[14] According to British Indian agent William Johnson, few Native Americans wanted either European power to "swallow up the other." Hoping instead "to preserve a kind of equilibrium between us," they would always "throw their weight into the lightest scale." These people, Johnson observed, were "not bad politicians."[15]

In one of the most successful Native American revolts in history, the insurgents captured nine British posts. Fort Pitt in western Pennsylvania was not among them, however. On June 24, the Swiss-born Simeon Ecuyer, who commanded the 250-man garrison, invited his besiegers to a parley. Afterward, per diplomatic custom, he sent them away with presents, including blankets — taken, as it turned out, from the fort's smallpox ward, for Ecuyer knew of his enemies' acute susceptibility to the virus. Astonishingly but revealingly, Gen. Amherst in New York City was just then sending Ecuyer a message proposing this exact strategy.[16]

British colonists and soldiers found one aspect of the native revolt especially disturbing. "The Indians are saving & Carressing all the Negroes they take," Virginia militia lieutenant William Fleming reported in July 1763, adding that should this policy lead to a slave "Insurrection it may be attended with the most serious Consequences." Less than two weeks later, a clergyman in the same province observed with alarm that "for the first time," Native Americans attacking British settlements had chosen to capture many African Americans rather than kill them or leave them behind. A settler in Albany, New York, learned from some of his slaves that the native rebels had somehow gotten them word that they "would be in no Danger" when the natives attacked.[17]

The siege of Fort Detroit that had begun in May dragged on until late October, when rebel leaders received a message from Pierre-Joseph Neyon de Villiers, the commander of France's not yet evacuated Fort de Chartres out on the Mississippi River, confirming that Louis XV had no plans to return North America, whereupon they lifted the siege. They had failed to drive the British off, but they had inflicted many more casualties than they suffered, killing or capturing four or five hundred British soldiers and more than two thousand civilians. The uprising also led to significant changes in imperial policy. Amherst was recalled to London and replaced by Gen. Thomas Gage, who reverted to the earlier policy of plying the First Nations with gifts. More than two thousand Native Americans, many of whom had participated in attacks against British settlements just weeks earlier, attended a congress at Fort Niagara in July 1764, taking home about £38,000 worth of merchandise.[18]

Most significant of all, the native revolt induced imperial officials to fast-track a momentous policy reversal. On October 7, the Privy Council prohibited British settlement and speculation west of the Appalachian Mountains. By turning the land on "the Western Waters"—rivers that ultimately flow into the Mississippi River and the Gulf of Mexico—into a vast new Indian reservation, London hoped not only to pacify the Native Americans but to stem the tide of migration from the British isles to North America.[19] (See map, "NATIVE AND BRITISH ATTACKS AGAINST SPANISH, U.S., AND PRO-U.S. NATIVE SETTLEMENTS," page 409.)

The Privy Council underscored that it was only banning trans-Appalachian land grants "for the present," but real estate speculators were furious. "I shall call upon you some Time next Week and condole with you in your late Misfortune," Virginian David Robinson wrote fellow land speculator William Thompson when he heard about the decree. Robinson lambasted the government for trading the natives land—their own land—for peace. "'Tis a great Mercy that Roanok [River] has not in like Manner been given as a Compliment [to] our good Friends and faithfull Allies, the Shanee Indians," he wrote. Anglican minister Jonathan Boucher reported that a friend had planned to settle west of the Appalachian Mountains, "But This is put a Stop to by a very impolitic, as well as unjust Proclama'n, forbidding any of the King's Subjects to settle Lands so far back." When Virginia lieutenant governor Francis Fauquier learned about the Proclamation Line, he warned of residents seeking compensation from Parliament or "retaliating upon the Indians for the Injuries they do" in procuring the Proclamation of 1763.[20]

SEVEN MILES SOUTHWEST OF Lancaster, Pennsylvania, the Conestogas—actually the intermarried remnants of other native nations—had lived in peace with their white neighbors ever since signing a treaty with William Penn back in 1701. They dressed like Europeans, socialized with them, worshipped the same God, and eked out a living renting them land and selling them baskets and brooms. None of the Conestogas showed any support for the Indian uprising. Yet on the morning of December 14, in the midst of a snowstorm, more than fifty white vigilantes known as the Paxton Boys rode to Conestoga Manor and killed everyone they found: four men—including one who had known William Penn—and two women. Three Conestoga families that had been out peddling their wares made for the safest place they could think of, the Lancaster work-house. But on December 27, whites broke into the building and killed them all, including two three-year-olds, whom they scalped.[21]

About 140 other native Christians sought refuge in Philadelphia, and in early February, some five hundred Paxton Boys set off after them. Benjamin Franklin, declaring whites who killed innocent Indians the real savages, led a delegation that met them at the edge of town and cajoled and threatened them into turning around. But the killers' neighbors protected them from prosecution.[22]

The native uprising of 1763–1764 thus indirectly fueled a long-standing conflict between eastern and western Pennsylvanians, but its greatest impact was on relations between the colonies and the crown. Already British leaders had stationed a peacetime army garrison in North America and cracked down on molasses smugglers. And now they had gone after the time-honored and profitable business of taking and selling the Native Americans' land.

CHAPTER 3

Confederacy of Smugglers

1763–1764

AFTER SOME FUMBLING ABOUT, MASSACHUSETTS GOVERNOR FRANcis Bernard finally found an apt comparison for New Englanders' dismay at the British government's ever-tightening clampdown on molasses smuggling: it "caused a greater alarm . . . than the taking of *Fort William Henry* did in 1757." Cornered, the smugglers improvised. When customs agents or Royal Navy crews seized vessels carrying contraband, colonists sometimes took them back.[1] More commonly, they went after the enforcers. Providence, Rhode Island, merchant Nicholas Brown reported that by June 1764 only one revenuer, "that pussy William Mumford," still insisted on reporting the full amount of foreign molasses unloaded on his watch. Brown made sure Mumford knew he was not "out of the reach of wanting the favors of this Town," and the captain of a sugar ship stated that Mumford "must be taught better by some means or other."[2]

Such methods brought only temporary and partial relief. But the Molasses Act of 1733, the parliamentary statute placing a prohibitive duty on the importation of foreign molasses, was set to expire in 1764, and North American merchants pledged their "united strength" against its renewal. In December 1763, the Society for Encouraging Trade and Commerce, a Boston trade association, began circulating a "State of the Trade" demonstrating North America's urgent need for foreign molasses. The campaign quickly spread to Providence, Newport, New York, and Philadelphia, becoming America's "first known instance of intercolonial mercantile cooperation."[3]

Instead of renewing the Molasses Act, Parliament strengthened it. The American Duties (Sugar) Act, which passed the House of Commons on April 5, 1764, actually cut the prohibitive sixpence per gallon on foreign molasses in half, but it also ratcheted up enforcement. Grenville and his cabinet hoped the new law would fill the pockets of the British sugar planters while extracting an annual £60,000 to £80,000 from their foreign competitors, all for "defending, protecting, and securing" the British American colonies.[4]

Thus molasses smugglers, like land speculators, entered 1763 anticipating a much brighter future, only to see the British government heed voices other than theirs. Everyone in the sugar trade—from rum distillers to the fishermen who sold half their catch to the Caribbean—mobilized against the American Duties Act and the "overgrown West Indians" they credited with getting it through Parliament. "Should the welfare of millions," Pennsylvania attorney John Dickinson asked, "be sacrificed to the magnificence of a few?"[5]

Colonists' fury at the "rich, proud, and overbearing Planters of the West-Indies" appears to have had a surprising side effect. Up to this time, opposition to slavery had largely been confined to the Society of Friends (Quakers)—and to the slaves themselves. But in the 1760s, antislavery sentiment began to spill over into other groups—at least north of the Mason-Dixon line, which runs along the southern border of Pennsylvania. No Americans were more deeply implicated in what they euphemistically termed the African trade than those who lived in highly commercial Rhode Island. Yet that colony's governor, Stephen Hopkins, explicitly linked his constituents' grievances against the sugar barons with those of enslaved cane cutters. The planters, he claimed, were so "used to an arbitrary and cruel Government over Slaves" that they reflexively viewed "Two Millions of free and loyal British Subjects, Inhabitants of the Northern [i.e., mainland] Colonies, in the same Light"—in other words, as prey.[6]

Most Americans referred to the new legislation as the Sugar Act, but it actually covered a host of commodities, invariably, as they saw it, enriching both the government and some rival interest group at their expense. For example, Parliament favored British textile manufacturers with new taxes on foreign cloth transshipped through the mother country to the colonies. The price of Indian calico was expected to rise by 12 to 16 percent.[7]

The new law also benefited British merchants. To take one example, Parliament had previously permitted wine ships to travel from Madeira, the Azores, and other "wine islands" in the eastern Atlantic directly to America. Indeed, the North Atlantic's clockwise trade winds actually made it faster and cheaper to ship wine from Madeira to London by way of North America—despite the two Atlantic crossings, which quadrupled the distance traveled to six thousand miles. But the American Duties Act sought to send wine in the opposite direction, making Britain rather than America the entrepôt. Toward that end, every tun (252 gallons) of island wine carried directly to America would pay the enormous duty of 140 shillings (sterling), even if it was subsequently reexported to Britain (where it would pay another import tax). By contrast, wine traveling counterclockwise, against the wind, from Madeira or the Azores through Britain to North America, would only pay 80 shillings.[8]

Colonial merchants had freely acknowledged that their reasons for opposing the Molasses Act of 1733 were economic. But the American Duties Act was different, for with it, Parliament claimed the right not only to regulate their trade but to tax it. And that meant the colonists could take a principled stand against having to pay taxes to a body in which they were not represented. No one made that case more forcefully than Boston attorney James Otis.

During the 1760s, while most Americans merely reacted to Parliament's efforts to alter the imperial relationship, James Otis proposed changes of his own—most spectacularly in 1761. Normally customs officers who wanted to search for contraband on land could only get help from sheriffs and constables by naming their informers, exposing them to retribution. But decades earlier, Parliament had ordered colonial courts to issue "general writs of assistance," which carried no such requirement. The writs had to be renewed when the monarch died, as George II did in October 1760. The following February, sixty-three Boston merchants came to the Massachusetts superior court, whose members also served as the colony's executive council, with the extraordinary request that they not renew the writs. They were represented by James Otis.[9]

The hearing took place in the council chambers on the second floor of the Town House, which still stands, albeit with a subway station in its basement. The judges wore "new, fresh, rich robes of scarlet English broadcloth" and "immense judicial wigs," as one spectator, John Adams, recalled in 1817. Attorney Adams had plenty of time to attend the trial, since, having opened his practice just two years previously, he had not yet built up much of a clientele.[10]

Otis's argument was simple: since general writs of assistance allowed government officials onto innocent subjects' property, the parliamentary statutes authorizing them were unconstitutional. Otis thus became the first American to openly question the omnipotence of Parliament. "Then

and there," John Adams declared, "the child Independence was born."
Chief Justice Thomas Hutchinson, who was also Massachusetts's lieutenant governor, had already angered many colonists with his successful
opposition to paper money. Ruling against Otis and issuing the writs
made him the most hated man in the province.[11]

The verdict also intensified the feud between Hutchinson and Otis.[12]
Years earlier, the governor of Massachusetts had promised Otis's father
the next vacant seat on the colony's superior court, but when the position
finally opened up, a new governor, Francis Bernard, gave it to Hutchinson instead, and the younger Otis never forgave Governor Bernard—or
Hutchinson.

In July 1764, Otis published *The Rights of the British Colonies Asserted and Proved*, arguing that the American Duties Act set a dangerous
precedent. "If a shilling in the pound may be taken from me against my
will," he asked, "why may not twenty shillings[?]" (In other words, the
whole pound.) But Otis's position was complex. Even though the American Duties Act was unconstitutional, he declared, Americans owed it
their "most perfect and ready obedience." Like most British freemen,
Otis revered the sovereignty that Parliament had asserted ever since its
victory over the king in 1688. Judges could nullify parliamentary statutes, he believed, but for anyone else to do so would be "an end of all
government."[13]

In his pamphlet, Otis denounced the British sugar planters for "making their own posterity, white as well as black, worse slaves" than those
who cut their cane. And having brought up the Caribbean's African
laborers, Otis did not shrink from asserting that they, too, possessed
natural rights. "The Colonists are by the law of nature free born, as
indeed all men are, white or black," he declared. Did the sugar planters
really believe they could justify enslaving Africans by saying they had
dark skin and "short curl'd hair like wool, instead of christian hair . . .?"
Slaveholders who made such claims had hearts "as hard as the nether
millstone"; they lacked "sensibility" to the joy as well as suffering of
others.[14]

After the journeymen printers had set the type for *The Rights of the
British Colonies*, Otis apparently had second thoughts about laying into
the British Caribbean planters. So he added a postscript: "I have been
credibly informed that the British Sugar colonists are humane towards
their slaves, in comparison with the others. Therefore in page 29, let it
be read, foreign Sugar-Islanders."[15]

In another pamphlet published the following year, Otis denied that

Members of Parliament could virtually represent Americans, of whom they knew no more than "the savages in *Calafornia*." But he moderated his criticism of British taxes after Bernard made his father probate judge for Barnstable County and chief justice of the county's court of common pleas. "Jemmy railed at upper folks when Jemmy's DAD was out," a newspaper critic noted. "But Jemmy's DAD now has a place so Jemmy's turned about."[16]

North America's "Confederacy of Smugglers" (as one London merchant called them) simultaneously protested and evaded the American Duties Act. During the summer of 1764, the naval schooner *St. John* angered residents of Newport, Rhode Island, by seizing not only molasses but men (to replace sailors lost to sickness and desertion). When three of the *St. John*'s crew stole pigs and chickens from a local farmer, their captain would not allow the local sheriff aboard to apprehend them. That led two members of the colony's executive council to have a shore battery fire nearly a dozen shots at the *St. John* (none hit it). On April 6, 1765, John Robinson, the customs collector for Narragansett Bay, discovered that the captain of the sloop *Polly*, just arrived from the Dutch colony of Surinam, had paid the tax on only half of the molasses in his hold. Robinson seized the ship, but two nights later, men with blackened faces clambered aboard and carried off the *Polly*'s sails, rigging, and cargo. Then the owner had Robinson thrown in jail. George Grenville expected the molasses duty to bring in at least £60,000 annually, but in 1765, its first full year, it raised only £4,000.[17]

LOOKING BACK FROM THE twenty-first century, it often seems that before the modern welfare state, the government mostly stayed out of people's lives. Eighteenth-century Americans knew better. The government took Native Americans' land, put down slave revolts, and even interfered in the lives of whites: by taxing them, sending them to war, and regulating their business affairs—especially relations between debtors and creditors. Then as now, most debt arose when people bought merchandise on credit. A few Americans posted positive balances on the books of their English or Scottish trading partners, but credit nearly always flowed from the Old World to the New, and by 1774, the colonists collectively owed British merchants about £6 million.[18]

In the enduring struggle between colonial debtors and British creditors, provincial legislators naturally favored their constituents, and Members of Parliament occasionally intervened on behalf of theirs. In the mother country, creditors who won lawsuits against their debtors could only seize their personal property, not their land. But in 1732, metropolitan merchants persuaded Parliament to pass the Colonial Debtors Act, allowing them to take delinquent Americans' land and slaves as well. Typically in this era, when a storekeeper in the mother country sued a delinquent customer, he or she had to document the debt by carrying the store ledger to court. But the Colonial Debtors Act allowed British merchants collecting American debts to skip this step—and with it, a trip across the ocean. Defenders of the law pointed out that it encouraged Britons to extend credit to Americans, but colonists such as Richard Henry Lee, a Virginia assemblyman who owed large sums in Britain, denounced this "too speedy a change in property" from American debtors to British creditors. In 1766, he proposed to repeal Virginia's law complying with the Colonial Debtors Act, a move far too radical for his colleagues in the House of Burgesses.[19]

One of the most consequential ways in which governments mediated between debtors and creditors was also the least visible: by regulating the money supply. Runaway inflation allows borrowers and credit purchasers to cancel their debts with worthless paper, while reducing the quantity of circulating cash can have the opposite effect of magnifying debts. Today few Americans realize that the nation's official money supply is determined by the Federal Open Market Committee (whose membership is appointed partly by the president and partly by private bankers), but in the eighteenth century every colonist knew that this power lay with the provincial assemblies—unless Parliament intervened.[20]

British merchant-creditors declared war on colonial paper money, and in 1744, a House of Commons committee voted to ban it. But Britain was in the midst of the War of Austrian Succession and could not risk alienating the colonists. After making peace with France and Spain, however, Parliament adopted the Currency Act of 1751, prohibiting New England assemblymen—widely seen as the worst offenders—from making their paper money legal tender.[21] When Rhode Island governor Stephen Hopkins heard about the new statute, he allegedly demanded of several dinner companions, "What have the King and Parliament to do with making a Law or Laws to govern us by, any more than the Mohawks have?"[22]

After Parliament approved the Currency Act, the British empire's Board of Trade started vetoing colonial currency even outside New England. But the outbreak of the Seven Years' War once again checked the home government's inclination to offend its indispensable colonial allies.

And even paper money's bitterest enemies conceded that the American legislatures could not field troops against the French without some means of paying them.[23]

The volume of paper that issued forth from colonial presses appalled British merchants. In the midst of the war, they renewed their anti-currency campaign, specifically targeting Virginia, where the House of Burgesses began printing money in May 1755 to support Braddock's march to Fort Duquesne, eventually churning out £440,000. In February 1759, the Board of Trade, speaking through Governor Fauquier, ordered assemblymen to allow the British business community to refuse Virginia debtors' paper money. Colonists knew that having to convert their currency into sterling— British bills of exchange (similar to modern bank checks) or gold or silver coin—would have the effect of driving up their debts. So the House of Burgesses took the extraordinary step of defying the Board of Trade.[24]

The moment the Seven Years' War ended, metropolitan merchant-creditors stepped up their assault on colonial currency. "To what purpose do we protect the Colonies and expend such sums in their defence if we are ultimately to be undone by them?" one asked. Finally Fauquier called the House of Burgesses into special session and again ordered them to take away their money's status as legal tender for British debts. It was May 1763, the low point of the postwar recession, and one representative, George Washington, predicted that the battle over the money supply would "set the whole Country in Flames." And sure enough, the Virginians once again disregarded the imperial government's unambiguous order.[25]

Governor Fauquier punished the assemblymen's defiance by sending them all home—and Parliament's reaction was even harsher. One MP, Anthony Bacon, traded both to Virginia and to North Carolina, which had also allowed its debtors to foist paper money on their British creditors. On April 4, 1764, he proposed to extend the ban on colonial currency to the provinces south of New England.[26] Like its predecessor of 1751, the Currency Act of 1764 entered the statute books at the conclusion of an imperial war, when the colonists' military service was no longer required.

Parliament's ban on fiat currency infuriated Americans, especially in the middle colonies, which had had great success with paper. The Pennsylvania, New York, and South Carolina assemblies all instructed their London agents (lobbyists) to urge the government to reconsider.[27] Since Parliament's interest in the colonial money supply was aroused by the flood of provincial paper that funded the epic struggle against France and its native allies, the Currency Act was one more link between the Seven Years' War and the American Revolution.

Parliament's newfound attentiveness to the American economy prompted many settlers to reflect on ancient grievances. Mercantilist theory made colonies captive markets for the mother country's manufactures, but from the beginnings of English settlement in North America, provincials had tried to reduce their dependence on the mother country's merchandise, especially its textiles. Spinning and, increasingly, weaving enabled colonial women to turn idle hours to account. But North Americans imported more cloth than they made—in the south, *much* more—and everyone knew why: colonial America's low population density permitted free workers to demand such high wages that its manufacturing never took off.[28]

There were exceptions to this bleak picture. Old-growth forests fostered shipbuilding. And land travel was so expensive—primarily owing to the high cost of feeding teams (twenty pounds per animal per day, William Tecumseh Sherman would later estimate) as well as teamsters—that families living far back from navigable water had no choice but to produce much of what they consumed. (Before canals and railroads, it cost no more to move cargo three thousand miles across the Atlantic than to cart it thirty miles overland.) Yet like modern Americans, most of their colonial forebears acknowledged that "We can import Manufactures cheaper than we can make them."[29]

But if Americans were all but obligated to wear British dress, dressing *up* was another matter, and they occasionally declared war on fashionable attire. The most passionate jeremiads came from New England, where Puritans had always abhorred extravagance, and many of these focused on funerals. Bereaved family members were expected to send their guests home with special scarves and gloves—and sometimes even rings. At his uncle's funeral in 1738, Peter Faneuil distributed four thousand pairs of gloves.[30]

The American Duties Act breathed new life into the frugality crusade and gave it a political cast. What better way to underscore the colonists' most powerful argument against Grenville's smuggling crackdown—that it would prevent them from purchasing British merchandise—than by actually canceling orders? In August 1764, more than fifty "principal Merchants in Boston" agreed to "curtail many Superfluities in Dress." When friends and loved ones died, they would no longer wear elaborate mourning suits, just black crepe hatbands and armbands. In theory, these people could have curbed their spending on their own, as George Grenville did, but acting in unison allowed them to attribute their frugality to "a sincere concern for the publick" rather than individual distress or a "parcemonous spirit." When Ellis Callender died a month into the retrenchment compact, his father strictly complied with it as he planned the funeral, inspiring prominent citizens who had never met Ellis to attend out of "Esteem for a Family who have shown Virtue enough to break a Custom too long established."[31]

Many of the appeals to frugality targeted women. A *Pennsylvania Journal* essayist wanted "the fair Ladies" to know "how much more amiable they will appear in decent plain dresses made in their own country, than in the gaudy, butterfly, vain, fanstastick, and expensive dresses brought from Europe." So close was the association between women and luxury, at least in men's minds, that some of the anonymous exhortations to abstinence at least claimed to come from female pens. "We don't set our trinkets and baubles in competition with the prosperity of North-America," "Sophia Thrifty" told readers of the *New-York Mercury*.[32]

Brief summaries of the origins of the American Revolution often begin with Parliament approving the Stamp Act in February 1765. But free colonists believed that by that time, Parliament had already subverted their vital interests to those of British sugar planters hoping to corner the molasses market, Native Americans trying to defend their land, and British merchants bent on bleeding them dry, especially by shrinking their money supply.

The Great Financier (1765), satirizing George Grenville

CHAPTER 4

Hungry Caterpillars

1765

I N THE SUMMER OF 1764, THOMAS GAGE, WHO SUCCEEDED JEFFERY Amherst as commander-in-chief of British forces in North America, sent two armies to burn the native rebels' crops and kill anyone who stood in their way. The first, led by Col. John Bradstreet, sailed up the St. Lawrence River and Lakes Ontario and Erie, and the second marched northwest from Fort Pitt under Col. Henry Bouquet. Neither ended up killing a soul.[1]

At Presque Isle (Erie, Pennsylvania), Bradstreet negotiated peace with a diverse array of Native Americans led by Guyasuta, the ubiquitous Seneca who had accompanied George Washington into the wilderness in 1753. Bouquet marched to the forks of the Muskingum River in modern-day Ohio, but the Shawnees, Delawares, and Mingos—again including Guyasuta—staved off attacks on their villages by suing for peace and agreeing to return their scores of Black and white captives.[2]

One great obstacle remained. The prisoners had been adopted by native families, and many had no desire to return to their previous homes. John M'Cullough had been about eight years old back in July 1756, when a war party abducted him from western Pennsylvania. A Delaware family took him in to replace a dead kinsman, dunked him (nearly drowning him, he said) in the Allegheny River by way of purification, and told him he was "then an Indian." Nearly seven years later, when his birth father tracked him down, he "wept bitterly" at being kidnapped yet again. M'Cullough's father tied him atop a horse and headed for Pittsburgh, but that night the boy slipped his cords and escaped back to the Delawares. But when Bouquet's army marched into Delaware country in the autumn of 1764, M'Cullough was once again given up, along with two hundred other captives. Adoptees who had been snatched up

Benjamin West, *Indians Delivering Up the
English Captives to Col. Bouquet* (1766)

as children could be expected to refuse repatriation to homes they did
not remember. But many who refused were adult women. "No wonder
why they are so loath to come," an Iroquois representative told his British counterparts as he returned Seven Years' War prisoners, "when you
make Servants of them."[3]

From the British imperial standpoint, the most useful military expedition dispatched in the wake of the Native Americans' revolt may
have been the one led by Indian agent George Croghan. Accompanied
by several Shawnees and Delawares, Croghan's party floated down the
Ohio in the spring of 1765 to negotiate peace with the native nations of
the Illinois country. On June 8, Croghan's two bateaux (rowboats with
flat, narrow bottoms, usually about twelve feet long) were assaulted,
for unknown reasons, by about eighty warriors from the Wabash River
towns in present-day Illinois and Indiana. Two of Croghan's servants
and three Shawnees were killed, and he himself took a blow to the head,
crediting his deliverance to his thick skull. The attack turned two prominent participants in the 1763 uprising, the Shawnees and the Wabash
River nations, into bitter enemies. By blundering into an effective de-

ployment of the British empire's ancient strategy of divide and conquer, Croghan had inflicted more damage on the natives' anti-British coalition than Bradstreet and Bouquet with all their marching.[4]

IN THE WINTER OF 1764–1765, as molasses smugglers and First Nations rebels eluded imperial punishment, a third kind of revolt was breaking out in the home of an impoverished Newport, Rhode Island, school-teacher named Sarah Osborn. In time it would have a bigger impact on those most involved than the red-letter political events of the 1760s, for they became convinced that Osborn could bring them to Christ. No one else they knew had ever been so powerfully transformed by the trans-atlantic religious upheaval that is known today as the Great Awakening. Although scattered across thousands of miles and dozens of years, the revivals all shared a singular focus on the necessity of being born again. Conversion was generally seen as instantaneous, but it had not gone that way for Osborn. After joining her local church in 1737, she almost immediately backslid and would experience true conversion only after experiencing sermons by the English itinerant minister George White-field and his American protégé, Gilbert Tennent.[5]

In 1753, Osborn wrote a letter to a distressed friend that a clergy ac-quaintance found so reassuring that he had it printed, placing her among the .3 percent of colonial America's published authors who were female.[6] In 1764, an African-born slave named Quaum (or Quamanee) wrote the fifty-year-old Osborn describing his own recent conversion and seeking her help joining the church. Then several Black Newport residents ap-proached her with an extraordinary request: would she assemble them once a week to lead them in prayer?

Initially Osborn agreed merely to invite a few African Americans and "white Lads" to her family's weekly devotions. But as word spread and attendance swelled, by her careful count, to 312, she wrote Stonington, Connecticut, pastor Joseph Fish confessing, "I know not what to do." Still, she affirmed, in a paraphrase of Luke 9:62, "I Have set my hand to the plow and dare not look back." Like most women of her era, Osborn had long since mastered self-deprecation, but even her effort to put her-self down betrayed a swelling sense of accomplishment. "Who would ever have thot that God by such a Mean despicable worm would have Gatherd such a Number as now stately resorts to this House every Week," she wrote.[7]

Osborn was no racial liberal. Two decades earlier, when her eleven-year-old son died (unsaved, she feared), her friends had given her an enslaved infant named Bobey. Caring for him would ease her pain, they reasoned, and then when he grew up, she could sell him. Bobey's mother shamed Osborn out of sending him to the auction block, but as he matured she did rent him out, and his wages supplied a larger and larger portion of her meager income. Meanwhile other African Americans found practical as well as spiritual benefit in Osborn's ministry: "Intent upon Learning to read etc. . . . They call[ed] it School."[8] As she read aloud from the Bible—and, increasingly, shared her own thoughts—she brushed right up against Paul's categorical command, "Let your women keep silence in the churches."[9]

But someone had to lead the men in prayer! Osborn avoided obvious solutions like having them take turns "Lest they be Lift'd up with Pride and proceed from praying to Exhorting"—preaching. Instead she led the prayers herself, reasoning that Paul had only banned women from praying in front of *adult* men—and African Americans were "no otherwise now th[a]n children tho for Stature men and women."[10] Thus did ugly racial mythology justify transgression of a gender taboo.

By 1766, Osborn's revival was also attracting other Newporters. Even many white men proved willing to follow Blacks into this female-led revival. Osborn's rebellion against the local patriarchy coincided with the American Revolution but bore few signs of its influence. She could be found, early most mornings, lying facedown in bed, her "stomach soported with bolster and Pillows," reading and writing "almost Every thing of a religious Nature" for an hour or two before breakfast.[11]

LIKE OSBORN AND MANY of her followers, residents of Mecklenburg County, North Carolina, eight hundred miles southwest of Newport, followed the battle over parliamentary enactments but worried more about local threats. In 1761, as the Seven Years' War wound down, Henry McCulloh Sr., a London merchant who had obtained title to upward of a million acres in Carolina, sent his son and namesake across the Atlantic to turn his and several associates' land titles into cash.[12]

Henry Eustace McCulloh was just the man for the job. Oversharing in a letter to his friend Edmund Fanning, the young bachelor candidly acknowledged being equally hungry for "Proc" (North Carolina's "proclamation money") and sex. "I long after the Flesh & the Proc of thy Western regions," he told Fanning in February 1766, adding that since he had "reduced F——n [fornication] almost to a regular matrimonial

System"—apparently by taking a regular sex partner—he could focus on his other passion.[13]

Farm families had already settled much of this land. McCulloh's assignment was to make them purchase it or leave, but the price he demanded was higher than most would or could pay.[14] On March 5, 1765, he led a team of surveyors onto a contested parcel not far from the infant town of Charlotte and even closer to Sugar Creek. He had the law, or at least the lawmen, on his side, but the farmers had numbers. One hundred and forty-three of them informed him that they had "joined themselves together," mutually vowing never to pay more than two and a half pence per acre. By 9 a.m. the next day, about a hundred men, some with guns, had gathered on the land, and they began to taunt McCulloh with questions like "whether he thought he would have as many Men attend him to his Grave or not?"[15]

As McCulloh's surveyors prepared their equipment, settlers knocked his compass off its staff and "contemptuously seized and broke the Surveying Chain in several pieces," forcing him to withdraw. Two months later, after a dozen men with blackened faces beat up one of his surveying teams, McCulloh grimly informed Fanning that if that "pack of ungrateful brutal Sons of Bitches" murdered him, he expected his friend to "be one of my Executors & . . . one of their Executioners."[16]

Nor was the "war of Sugar Creek" (as McCulloh called it) North Carolina's only internal conflict. When colonial-era creditors sued their debtors, the losing party—almost always the defendant—had to pay hefty fees to both sides' lawyers, to the deputy sheriff who sold off his property to discharge the debt, and to the court clerk who drew up the documents. Attorneys were only supposed to charge 15 shillings per case, but George Sims of Granville County claimed the "damned Lawyer" typically demanded twice that sum. Since very little money circulated in the backcountry, farmers often had to work off these additional debts, laboring as much as a month to pay the clerk for paperwork he had completed in "one long minute." When Sims publicly called upon the North Carolina legislature to investigate these "hungry caterpillars," the clerks sued him for libel.[17]

As SARAH OSBORN INAUGURATED her religious revival and Henry McCulloh battled western settlers, George Grenville and his cabinet stepped up their challenge to American autonomy, proposing that Parliament require colonists to purchase special paper, pre-stamped with a royal seal, for most legal documents, including wills, deeds, apprentice contracts, ship clearances, tavern licenses, and court papers. The mother country would also raise the cost of gambling by taxing dice and playing cards. Prosecutors would have the option of taking alleged violators to vice-admiralty court, where cases were decided by judges rather than juries.[18]

Many people today believe Grenville wanted to tax American colonists in order to reduce Britain's enormous war debt. But the actual purpose of both the American Duties Act and the Stamp Act was to safeguard the spoils of war. Parliament had decided to leave ten thousand redcoats in America as a western border wall—and now it was going to make the colonists pay for it. On both sides of the Atlantic, prints decrying the proposed stamp duties depicted America as an (often female) Indian warrior. No surprise there, given that Europeans were even more prone than provincials to use Native Americans as avatars for both America and liberty. But in this case the iconography was ironic, for actual First Nations warriors had played a crucial if indirect role in giving birth to the Stamp Act.[19]

Grenville announced the stamp tax a year in advance so colonists could get used to it, but he actually just aroused their hopes of smothering it in the crib. One of the most comprehensive critiques came, surprisingly enough, from the lieutenant governor of Massachusetts. Thomas Hutchinson understood that the principal purpose of the Stamp Act was to fund the British troops guarding against the Native Americans. But he insisted that colonists encountering native rebels for the first time could handle them as New Englanders had, on their own. And Americans would rather "lay waste" to the natives' cornfields themselves, financing the war "by a tax of their own raising," than submit to the Stamp Act so the imperial army could do it for them.[20]

Hutchinson anticipated some, though not all, of his fellow colonists' case against stamped paper. For example, he denied that Parliament could tax Americans but conceded its right to legislate for them. But his privately circulated essay lacked passion—which would have surprised none of his contemporaries. Tall, thin, and colorless, the lieutenant governor had risen to the pinnacle of Massachusetts society—his numerous properties around Boston included two wharves and eight homes—largely by avoiding risk. Massachusetts had exiled his great-great-grandmother, Anne Hutchinson, back in 1637 not only for her unorthodox religious activities (she had even allegedly preached to men) but because she had criticized the Puritan establishment. Thomas felt sympathy for Anne but no affinity. Noting that she had "considered herself divinely commissioned for some great purpose," he categorized her as an "enthusiast," meaning that she claimed direct communication with God. Thomas, by contrast, was determined to "not be singular" (unusual). He once asked, "Is not prudence a part of morality?"[21]

WHEN GRENVILLE FORMALLY INTRODUCED his stamps legislation on February 6, 1765, he invoked the government's financial straits and essentially characterized Americans as freeloaders. By modern estimates, they handed the tax man only about a tenth as much as residents of the mother country.[22] "The true way to relieve all is to make all contribute their proper share," he declared. British subjects living on the eastern side of the Atlantic Ocean were less wealthy than free colonists, yet they had long paid stamp duties that were 33 to 50 percent higher than what Grenville planned to charge Americans.[23]

Besides, the prime minister insisted, few forms of taxation were less oppressive than stamp duties. Much of the revenue that governments take in from tariffs and excises goes right back out to the officers who search for contraband. But the administration could implement Grenville's proposal simply by sending a single stamp distributor to each province. Since legal documents not printed on stamped paper would be null and void, colonists would actually choose to use it; such a tax "in a great degree executes itself."[24]

MP Isaac Barré, whose face bore the scars of his American service during the Seven Years' War, warned that the Stamp Act would provoke fierce opposition from Americans, whom he called "Sons of Liberty." But on a preliminary motion, the Commons endorsed Grenville's proposal by a vote of 245 to 49, so when it came up for a final vote on February 27, no one even bothered to ask for a count.[25]

The globalist movement in American history has enabled twenty-first-century scholars to see, as few of their forebears could, that Britain's post–Seven Years' War attempt at comprehensive imperial reform did not just target the American colonies. Royal officials also sought changes in Ireland and India, and other European empires enacted reform agendas of their own. In the wake of their stunning loss to Britain, both France and Spain adopted the Bourbon reforms, reducing restrictions on American trade even as they increased the colonists' taxes in order to enlarge the garrisons that guarded them in both senses. In the Spanish provinces as in North America, the home government's fiscal offensive provoked rebellion. But Britain encountered the most widespread, organized, and successful resistance, because it sought the most thoroughgoing reform.[26] Often a country coming off a major victory will feel less of a call to self-reflection than the enemies it has just defeated. And sure enough, George III at first objected to the initiative that the Stamp Act was intended to finance: Bute's decision to leave ten thousand redcoats in America. But he eventually recognized that Britain had the most changes to make for the simple reason that it had the most to lose. "As to the ten thousand in America," the king wrote, "that is become necessary from our successes."[27]

Historians have proposed countless theories about why free Americans chose to declare independence from Britain, but all this time, we seem to have been asking the wrong question. The smuggling and territorial expansion crackdowns of 1763, the American Duties Act and Currency Act of 1764, and the Stamp Act of 1765 all showed that the great dissatisfaction with the British empire of 1763 was not in the colonies but in Parliament. So the place to find the revolution's origins is not Boston or Philadelphia but London.[28]

Yet historians of North America still have a role to play in explaining where Americans acquired the self-confidence to resist Parliament's initiatives. Evangelical Christians and rationalist thinkers not only battled one another but tended to define themselves in opposition to each other. Yet both movements promoted the colonists' blessed self-assurance, with the Enlightenment teaching them that reason and science were on their side and the religious revivals saying God was. Evangelicals and religious skeptics also contributed to the dissolution of parliamentary authority in other ways, for instance by opposing Anglican church leaders' plan to appoint American bishops.[29] Finally, the late colonial proliferation of religious options—all along the spectrum, but especially at the pious and skeptical extremes—fostered resistance to parliamentary encroachment by accustoming individuals to making their own decisions. If we can choose our ministers, colonists reasoned, why not our ministers of state? This "corrosive logic of choice" (as T. H. Breen has called it) was further reinforced by a more worldly eighteenth-century trend: colonists' access to an ever-expanding array of consumer goods.[30]

For their part, most British leaders attributed colonial resistance to the victory over France. Gen. Gage recalled that at the height of the Seven Years' War, Americans had welcomed army garrisons. But now that Europe's two superpowers had made peace, "the People in general begin to be Sensible, that they are not obliged to do, what they submitted to, in Times of Danger."[31] Numerous historians echo this interpretation. But if the impetus for altering the imperial relationship came from London, that is where we ought to see the removal of the Gallic Peril having its greatest impact. And sure enough, the Seven Years' War awakened British officials to colonial disobedience in four arenas—taxation, territory, treasury bills, and trade—but only the removal of the French and the return of peace allowed them to act. On May 16, New York merchant John Watts reported that his fellow colonists "seem to wish Canada again French[;] it made the of some Consequence, which Consequence they lost when it was conquerd."[32]

The British government never subjected its colonists to anything like the brutality it routinely inflicted on Native Americans (often with British Americans' help), but provincials like John Watts and Native Americans like Seneca sachem Guyasuta described Britain's reaction to its Seven Years' War victory in remarkably similar terms.

Historians have an advantage over the Weather Channel: the events we predict have already happened. But it seems safe to say that in the absence of the Seven Years' War, Parliament would not have come down so hard on the thirteen provinces from Georgia to New Hampshire. And without a parliamentary crackdown, those colonists might have traveled the same peaceful and gradual path to independence that Canada strode a century later.[33]

George Grenville's search for military expenses to shift onto American shoulders did not cease with the Stamp Act. Every year, Parliament passed a law called the Mutiny Act, not only enforcing discipline in the army but also requiring localities hosting redcoats to house them and keep them supplied with lodging-related necessities such as bedding, firewood, and spirits. As memories of the Seven Years' War faded, Gen. Gage detected growing resistance to these requirements. For example, when, in preparing for the winter of 1764–1765, Gage asked New York City mayor John H. Cruger to send the soldiers stationed in his town a supply of firewood, Cruger refused.[34]

Informed of this defiance, Parliament in May 1765 passed a special Mutiny Act just for America. Known there as the Quartering Act, it required the colonies to house and supply the British soldiers billeted among them. Gage had sought authority, when no barracks or empty buildings were available, to quarter redcoats in private homes. Instead, Parliament, for the first time ever, prohibited army officers from imposing soldiers on unwilling homeowners—in short, the exact opposite of what most people today think the Quartering Act did.[35]

THE QUARTERING ACT, STAMP ACT, and other ministerial initiatives encountered so little opposition in Parliament that supporters dared to hope that colonists would also acquiesce. Then came the news from Virginia, Britain's oldest American province and also, with 328,000 souls in 1760, its largest.[36] The conservatives who controlled the House of Burgesses had spoken out against the Stamp Act before it was approved but opted not to revisit it afterward. Enter, on May 20, a just-elected burgess from Louisa County, Patrick Henry. Tradition dictated that new members warm the backbench and watch their tongues, but only nine days after taking office, the gentleman from Louisa demanded the floor to talk about the Stamp Act.

The newest addition to the assembly's ranks was one of its best known, primarily for his battles against the ministers of Virginia's established church, the Church of England (today's Episcopalians). The preachers received their salaries in tobacco, and twice in the 1750s short crops drove the price of the weed sky high, giving them a massive if temporary raise. But the House of Burgesses took away both windfalls, whereupon several ministers sued. After the Board of Trade took their side, jurors ruled in their favor. But in December 1763, when the jury hearing a test case deliberated on damages, Henry, representing the vestry (church board), offered the same argument about the Board of Trade's ruling that James Otis had made two years earlier about Parliament's writs of assistance: it was unconstitutional. By taking the parsons' side, Henry charged, the king had "degenerated into a Tyrant." Several spectators as well as opposing counsel cried out "Treason, Treason!" but the jury sided with Henry, awarding the plaintiff only one penny.[37]

On May 29, 1765—Henry's twenty-ninth birthday—the assembly's "Young, hot, and Giddy Members" (as Governor Fauquier called them) offered seven successively more radical resolutions against the stamp tax. It was late in the session, and only 39 of the 116 burgesses—disproportionately hotheads—remained. They scheduled a vote for the next day.[38]

Weeks earlier, three Black Virginians had been convicted of stealing £300—enough to buy their freedom—from the clerk of the colony's executive council. Before dawn on May 30, the three were taken from Virginia's public jail, just down the hill from the capitol, carted to the gallows on the edge of town, and hanged. That afternoon, Henry spoke against the Stamp Act. The House of Burgesses chamber had no gallery, but visitors could watch from the adjoining lobby, and that day they included twenty-two-year-old Thomas Jefferson, living in Williamsburg while training for the law. Decades later, he recalled the "torrents of sublime eloquence" that Henry had contributed to the "most bloody" debate.[39] Nearby was Charles Murray, a young Catholic wine merchant on a grand tour of the colonies, and he reported that Henry compared King George III to the most infamous tyrants of Roman and English history—each of whom had eventually met his match: "In former times tarquin and Jul[i]us [Caesar] [each] had their Brutus, Charles had his Cromwell, and he Did not Doubt but some good american would stand up, in favour of his Country."[40]

Leaping to his feet, Speaker John Robinson cried that Henry "had spoke traison." Henry apologized, but his first four resolutions easily passed. The fifth, claiming the Stamp Act had "a manifest Tendency to destroy British as well as American Freedom," slipped through, 20 votes to 19, whereupon Attorney General Peyton Randolph stormed out of the chamber, reportedly murmuring, "By God, I would have given 500 guineas for a single vote."[41]

The conspiratorial terms in which Henry and other colonists described parliamentary taxation have led some historians to characterize them as almost neurotically hypersensitive about seemingly trivial encroachments on their freedom.[42] Ideological or even psychological analysis may indeed be appropriate when a man who owns slaves equates the inoffensive George III with Julius Caesar and Charles I, but Henry was not alone—and not paranoid—in viewing the Stamp Act as an opening wedge. Thomas Whately, one of Grenville's secretaries and a coauthor of the legislation, recommended that the duties "begin low." Then they could be increased, and other taxes added, once "the right of Parliament to lay an internal tax upon the colonies" had been established.[43]

Figuring his work was done, Henry left Williamsburg that evening, and the next day conservatives mustered their forces and repealed his controversial fifth resolve. But newspapers in other colonies printed all five, along with two still more radical resolutions that Henry had opted to hold back, without noting that only the first four represented Virginia's official view.[44]

As Charles Murray, the wine merchant who had observed the debate alongside Jefferson, continued his journey, he thrilled audiences— including barflies and ferry passengers but also several governors—with his rendition of Henry's stirring speech. For two and half centuries, no one knew much about Murray—not even his name, since his journal was unsigned. But then in 2005, a graduate student at William and Mary (the college that, then as now, stood at the opposite end of Williamsburg's Duke of Gloucester Street from the colonial capitol) unearthed persuasive evidence that he was exactly what the most fanatic Protestant colonists imagined every Catholic among them to be: a spy for the French government.[45]

Murray's reports must have cheered hearts at Versailles, for in the wake of the Virginia assembly's action, British Americans described the Stamp Act in ever starker terms. Some wanted the mother country to remember the international context. "Let the worst Come to the worst," they told Murray, "we'l Call the french to our sucour." But if the western world's second largest empire awaited the colonists' invitation, the home government could also count on allies. The three corpses that hung from the nearby gallows as Henry spoke were a grim reminder that one in five colonial Americans owed no loyalty to the self-styled freedom fighters who claimed to own them.[46]

CHAPTER 5

———•◆•———

A Hobnail or a Horseshoe

1765–1766

O N July 11, 1765 — ABOUT HALFWAY BETWEEN THE ENACTMENT OF the Stamp Act and its November 1 implementation date — George III sacked George Grenville and most of his cabinet. Many of the king's American admirers praised him for removing the perpetrator of the Stamp Act, but his motives had actually been more personal. Grenville took excessive pride in his policy expertise, talked too much, and seemed incapable of dismounting his "hobbyhorse, the reduction of expenses." Moreover, he wanted to decide who got every job at the king's disposal, and he enforced all of these demands with constant threats to resign.[1] When, on July 10, George finally ordered Grenville to give up his seal of office — the device used by the first lord of the treasury to press his seal into the hot wax that closed up documents — he explained that he could no longer stand being told "what he was to *obey*." The master of St James Palace complaining — and, for two years, *only* complaining — about having to obey; what must the lurking ghosts of Elizabeth I and Henry VIII have thought of *that*?[2]

The dominant force in the new cabinet, though not an official member, would be the king's uncle, Prince William Augustus, the Duke of Cumberland, best known for annihilating the Jacobite uprising in the Scottish Highlands twenty years earlier.[3] The new first lord of the treasury, and thus the nominal head of the cabinet, would be the Marquess of Rockingham, who could boast experience as a lord of the bedchamber.[4]

In an effort to make the stamp duties as painless as possible, Grenville had placed the heaviest burden on the wealthiest colonists. The single largest fee, £10, was assessed on attorneys. Printers would pay an annual tax plus a small additional sum for every pamphlet, almanac, and newspaper advertisement they published. Some of the heaviest and most progressive duties were assessed on land speculators, who had previously paid the same low, flat processing fees as the recipients of smaller grants. If George Washington's Mississippi Company received the 2.5 million acres it had requested in 1763, it would have to pay £1,750 in stamp duties.[5]

The problem with targeting the well-to-do was that they were uniquely poised to put up a fight. In the summer 1765, they and other opponents of the Stamp Act decided to take down the men who would distribute the stamped paper in return for 7.5 percent of the proceeds. During the night of August 13–14, two and a half months before the tax went into effect, a never identified group of Bostonians hung an effigy of Andrew Oliver, the Massachusetts stamp distributor, from the Liberty Tree, a towering elm in the South End. Meant to evoke the suicide of Judas Iscariot, who had likewise betrayed his friends for silver, the effigy carried a sign:

What greater Joy Can New England see
Than Stamp men hanging on a tree.[6]

Toward evening, the effigy was cut down and paraded through town. The crowd was led by a twenty-seven-year-old shoemaker named Ebenezer Mackintosh.

For years, gangs representing Boston's North and South Ends had commemorated November 5, the date in 1605 when Catholics led by Guy Fawkes had allegedly plotted to blow up Parliament, by battling for control of the city's streets. It was known elsewhere as Guy Fawkes Day but in Boston as Pope's Day, a reminder that Massachusetts's established church had acquired the epithet *Puritan* not through any special commitment to sexual purity but because of its zeal to purify the Church of England of its last vestiges of Catholicism. The 1764 melee had gotten out of hand, with a boy dying under the wheels of a cart carrying a papal effigy. During the summer of 1765, Mackintosh, the leader of the South End gang, sat down with the Loyal Nine, leaders of a powerful proto-political party known as the Boston Caucus, and agreed that the two gangs should join together to force Oliver to resign. They would have help from a shadowy organization that took its name from Isaac Barré's speech against the Stamp Act: the Sons of Liberty.[7]

As night fell on August 14, Mackintosh's men broke into Oliver's house and destroyed the windows and furniture, much of the wainscoting (paneling), and "a looking glass said to be the largest in North-America." The next day, Oliver promised to resign. The crowd reassembled on August 26 and gutted three additional homes. Two belonged to officials who had distinguished themselves in the fight against foreign molasses. The third victim, Thomas Hutchinson, had privately worked to stop the Stamp Act but now publicly urged compliance.[8]

The glee with which the crowd systematically destroyed Hutchinson's house—it took them three hours just to topple the cupola— betokened something more than a political dispute. Boston during the Seven Years' War has been compared to a crucible, the ceramic vessel where compounds are heated to separate their elements, since the war and ensuing recession had similarly sifted the town. Many, especially war widows, could not afford sufficient firewood for the interminable New England winter, while a fortunate few made a killing by privateering (raiding enemy shipping), supplying the army, or simply profiting off wartime price spikes. The sheriff arrested Mackintosh for leading the assault on Hutchinson's house but then freed him after his supporters threatened to attack the customs office. Friends rescued some imprisoned rioters, and authorities had to release others when no grand jury would indict them.[9]

On August 27, the day after the second Boston riot, residents of Newport, Rhode Island, staged their own protest, hanging the local stamp distributor and two of his allies in effigy. As if to remind royal officials that they were also angry at the American Duties Act, Newporters attacked customs collector John Robinson, forcing him to take refuge on a British warship. Pennsylvanians furious at their London agent, Benjamin Franklin, for failing to prevent the Stamp Act marched to his home. He was still overseas, but just as he had stood up to the Paxton Boys the previous year, his wife, Deborah, faced down the stamp rioters, brandishing a musket at a second-story window until they moved on. On September 2, 1765, a crowd tore down the home of Maryland stamp distributor Zachariah Hood, who then disappeared, leaving the colony without stamped paper.[10]

In Connecticut, Pennsylvania, and Virginia, where the lucrative post of stamp distributor went to members of the provincial assembly's ruling party, the Stamp Act became a powerful tool in the hands of the opposition.[11] Some of Virginia's most determined tax resisters lived in the Northern Neck, the peninsula between the Potomac and Rappahannock Rivers, where the local gentry had long felt shortchanged in the distribution of political appointments and other plums. On September 24, Richard Henry Lee staged a procession in Montross, the county seat of Westmoreland County, where participants hung effigies of Grenville ("the infamous projector of AMERICAN SLAVERY") and Virginia's stamp distributor, George Mercer (who was made to say, "SLAVERY I LOVE"). Reinforcing the slavery motif, perhaps unintentionally, Lee staffed his rural replica of the earlier urban protests largely with his own slaves. It would be nearly a year before Mercer's friends revealed that Lee himself had applied for the job of Virginia stamp distributor.[12]

In South Carolina, the only North American province where African Americans outnumbered whites, a merchant's wife, standing on her balcony in Charles Town, thought she heard two slaves planning a revolt, to begin when whites dropped their guard while celebrating Christmas Eve. Her testimony put the town "in an uproar" that only intensified when, as Governor William Bull claimed, "One Hundred and Seven Negroes [who] had left their plantations soon after the Intended Insurrection had been discovered . . . joined a large number of runaways in Colleton County which increase to a formidible Body." Meanwhile a group of slaves reportedly marched through Charles Town chanting a slogan borrowed from whites' anti–Stamp Act procession two months earlier: "Liberty." The authorities responded by declaring martial law, calling up the militia, and hiring Catawba Indians to "hunt out the runaways now in the Woods and destroy their several camps."[13]

Grenville had hoped to soften the Americans' opposition to the new law by awarding the potentially highly remunerative stamp distributorships to their fellow colonists, but this strategy backfired. Tax collectors sent from Britain might have held out indefinitely, simply by taking refuge on navy ships, but Grenville's appointees owned houses and businesses within easy reach of colonial crowds, and most resigned rather than see them torched. Of the future rebel provinces, only Georgia received a nonresident distributor. Before escaping the colony, George Angus managed to get stamped paper into the hands of the customs officers, who used it to clear some sixty ships out of Savannah. But when a crowd threatened to march on the capital, Governor James Wright secured the stamps on a warship, where they were safe but useless.[14]

The Stamp Act was fully implemented in Nova Scotia, Quebec, the Floridas, and the Caribbean.[15] But in most of North America, port officials were compelled to sign unstamped ship clearances, allowing trade to proceed as usual. The vast majority of colonial justices had to hold court without stamped paper, since none could be had. But judges in several provinces took the opposite tack, insisting that they had no choice but to close their courts. Thousands of Americans were in debt to British merchants, who now had a powerful new reason to hate the Stamp Act. A Philadelphia merchant explained to his British creditors that he could only remit a fraction of what he owed, since he could "recover no outstanding Debts by a course of Law."[16]

In October, nine colonies sent delegations to New York City to discuss the stamp tax and American Duties Act. The Stamp Act Congress's "Declaration" was mild. It denounced Parliament's refusal to even read the colonists' petitions and insisted upon their right to send them.[17] Still, the chairman of the Stamp Act Congress, Timothy Ruggles, found its resolutions too radical and refused to sign or publish them, eliciting such harsh criticism from one delegate, Thomas McKean of Delaware, that the two nearly fought a duel. For the British, the gathering was most significant as disturbing evidence of the Americans' growing capacity for intercolonial cooperation.[18]

THE PROVINCIALS' MOST EFFECTIVE weapon against Grenville's aggressions was economic. Traders in all of the major North American ports instructed their British suppliers not to send them any merchandise until the Stamp Act and the American Duties Act were repealed. The idea spread quickly, with activists even handing out printed forms that merchants could use to cancel their orders.[19]

One inspiration for the boycott came from England. When a protective tariff on Italian silk cleared the Commons, only to die in the House of Lords at the hands of the Duke of Bedford, silk weavers in the Spitalfields section of London stoned Bedford's carriage, attacked his house, and surrounded the Lords as they heard an address from the king. The American boycotters hoped to pressure Parliament by provoking unemployment, and thus unrest, not only in London but in all of Britain's manufacturing towns. Rather than see Americans "loose their liberty," wrote John Adams in the homey persona of Humphry Ploughjogger, "I'de rather the Spittlefield weavers should pull down all the houses in old England, and knock the brains out of all the wicked great men there."[20]

The boycott also revived the colonists' long-standing but so far unsuccessful effort to curb their dependence on British manufactured goods, especially textiles. Years earlier, when the Seven Years' War had driven up the price of European cloth, female New Englanders had occasionally held "Spinning Entertainment[s]" to produce their own. In 1765 and 1766, as Americans protested the Stamp Act in part by boycotting British cloth, women in Rhode Island and Connecticut came to their aid by again assembling with their spinning wheels. Meanwhile leading citizens of New York, Philadelphia, and Boston sought to augment North America's wool supply by pledging not to eat lamb.[21]

A handful of colonial newspapers shut down on November 1, but most appeared on unstamped paper in defiance of the law. The same editors also published numerous pamphlets denouncing the Stamp Act. Several essayists made the intriguing argument that during the Seven Years' War, status-conscious Americans of means had lavishly entertained visiting British army officers, inadvertently giving them the false impression that all free colonists were, in John Dickinson's words, "wallowing in wealth and luxury." Carried home to the mother country, this myth fostered the mistaken British notion that Americans could effortlessly afford parliamentary taxation.[22] Maryland attorney Daniel Dulany wistfully recalled that the Lords and Commons had once adhered so firmly to the principle of no taxation without representation that they permitted Ireland's female landowners a role in setting real estate taxes. He conceded that the highly touted "virtual representation"—which held that Parliament represented all of the king's subjects, whether or not they could vote—worked well enough in the mother country, where voters had to pay the same taxes as nonvoters, who thus received some "Security . . . against Oppression." But a Member of Parliament could sign on to colonial laws such as the Stamp Act without worrying about harming his constituents, who would actually benefit from transferring some of their tax burden across the pond.[23]

AMERICANS ALSO REBUTTED ONE of the primary justifications for the Stamp Act: that they shared in all the British empire's benefits without ever picking up the tab. Historians often refer to northern provinces like Massachusetts and New York as the "commercial colonies," but southern staple growers, enslaved and free, actually imported more of what they consumed and exported more of what they produced. Thus they bore the brunt of the Navigation Acts, also known as the Acts of Trade, the century-old statutes granting the mother country a monopoly of colonial trade. Most glaringly, all of Maryland's and Virginia's tobacco had to go to Britain, though only about a fifth was consumed there, the rest being sent on to continental Europe. When English clergyman Andrew Burnaby toured Virginia in 1759, residents told him that being deprived of "an unlimited trade to every part of the world" was a great "hardship."[24] But these were only private grumblings, and only one colonist is known to have openly denounced the Acts of Trade before the imperial dispute of the mid-1760s. When he did, Richard Henry Lee's youngest brother, Arthur, was twenty-three years old and more than 3,500 miles from home.

While studying medicine at the University of Edinburgh in 1764, Lee read *The Theory of Moral Sentiments*, published five years earlier by Edinburgh professor Adam Smith (who would go on to write *The Wealth of Nations* in 1776). Advancing the notion that all healthy humans possess "fellow feeling"—the ability and even compulsion to share in the pain and pleasure of others, roughly equivalent to the as yet uncoined term *empathy*—Smith mused in passing that anyone who could claim to own another human must lack fellow feeling. Lee published a rebuttal declaring that the Virginia gentry were the ones who actually deserved the world's sympathy. With "their commerce confined" by Parliament, families like his had to submit "to the arbitrary impositions of the British merchants, who fix, like cankers, on their estates, and utterly consume them."[25]

After Parliament adopted the Stamp Act, colonial criticism of the Navigation Acts ticked upward. "Why," another Virginian, Richard Bland, demanded in a 1766 pamphlet, "is the Trade of the Colonies more circumscribed than the Trade of *Britain*?" And Richard Henry Lee complained of Virginia being "extremely fettered and confined, both in export and import."[26] But others held their tongues, figuring that the Acts of Trade, "the true cause of the British greatness," would never be relinquished—and that questioning them would only alienate the British merchants and manufacturers then leading the fight against parliamentary taxation. When Benjamin Franklin proposed that the mother country repeal the Navigation Acts in return for the colonists helping cover imperial expenses, his English friends warned him that "The Monopoly of the American Commerce could never be given up, and the Proposing it would only [give] Offence."[27]

Still, numerous Americans founded their opposition to the Stamp Act on the tribute they were already paying. Many joined George Washington in claiming Grenville and his tax collectors had showed up too late, because "the whole produce of our labour hitherto has centred in Great Britain" already.[28] Since British merchants charged their colonial customers much higher prices than they could have in a free market, Pennsylvanian John Dickinson asked, "may not the difference between these prices be called an *enormous tax* paid by them to *Great Britain*?" Other provincials echoed this assertion that the combination of the Navigation Acts and the Stamp Act amounted to double taxation, perhaps without realizing that they thereby forfeited their claim that allowing Parliament to tax them would violate sacred precedent.[29]

Most histories of the Stamp Act focus on just two combatants, Parliament and the American colonists. But as we have seen, the primary purpose of the stamp duties was to fund the troops seeking to prevent another war against the Native Americans, so they were a crucial part of the story. Likewise, free Americans' resistance to the stamps was aggravated by their resentment of the Navigation Acts, whose fiercest defenders were the British merchant princes, so no thorough account of the Stamp Act can omit them, either.

The Duke of Cumberland could not brook the thought of caving in to the rioters, but as the Stamp Act's November 1 implementation date approached, more and more observers predicted that only troops could enforce it. Even if Cumberland could convince the cabinet to go that far, how could soldiers compel merchants to place orders? The ministers agreed to consider all these matters at Cumberland's house in Grosvenor Square on the evening of October 31.[30]

But Cumberland died of a heart attack or stroke just hours before the meeting, and by late November, British merchants had begun their campaign to repeal the Stamp Act. Prime Minister Rockingham encouraged these efforts behind the scenes—not the first or last time a politician orchestrated grassroots pressure on himself.[31]

In the House of Commons, supporters of the stamp tax contended that colonists who attacked Parliament's sovereignty imperiled its 1688 victory over the king. (Agreeing, a modern historian has provocatively labeled American resistance to Parliament "royalism.") Some warned that the colonials would not stop with the repeal of the Stamp Act; eventually they might even come after the mother country's monopoly of their trade.[32]

William Pitt, who opposed the stamp tax, responded to those warnings on January 14, 1766. He had already spoken that morning and was reminded that House of Commons rules prohibited any member from addressing the same issue twice in one day, to which he artfully replied, "I do not speak twice. I only finish." Amid shouts of "Go on! Go on!"

he assured the House that he would never countenance any provincial challenge to the Navigation Acts. Should the colonists "manufacture a lock of wool, or a horse shoe" or even a "hobnail," he would fill *their Towns with Troops, & their Ports with Ships of War*."[33]

By early February, London bookies were giving three-to-one odds that Parliament would repeal the Stamp Act, but first the House of Commons wished to hear from witnesses on both sides. Most of the pro-repeal testimony came from British merchants, who blamed the tax for a drastic reduction in provincial demand for their wares that actually owed much to the recession that followed the Seven Years' War. Opponents of the Stamp Act assured MPs that Americans only objected to *internal* taxes such as stamp duties; several, including Benjamin Franklin, stated that Americans would cheerfully pay taxes on their imports.[34]

Franklin also offered another olive branch, proposing that the North American assemblies aid in imperial defense according to "the old established usage": by levying their own taxes—thus preserving the principle of no taxation without representation—and using the revenue to hire provincial troops, as they had during the Seven Years' War.[35] Such a compromise might have prevented the American War of Independence, and the failure to achieve one has long perplexed historians. Recall, though, that the Stamp Act was supposed to fund the army's colonial garrison, including the troops keeping Native Americans and western settlers apart. Experience had taught Parliament not to trust the protection of the First Nations to the colonists, so if they were going to contribute to the peacekeeping mission, it would have to be in cash, not in kind.

Franklin did not confine his criticism to the Stamp Act, for he believed it had combined with two other recent British measures—the Currency Act and the Grenville administration's assault on molasses smuggling—to deprive the North American economy of its lifeblood: circulating currency.[36]

At 1:30 a.m. on February 22, the House of Commons voted 275 to 167 to repeal the Stamp Act. As they emerged from Westminster Palace, a crowd huzzaed Pitt and booed Grenville, who grabbed the nearest heckler by the collar and had to be pulled off. On March 18, George III affixed his signature to the repeal bill—and also to the Declaratory Act, affirming Parliament's right to rule for the colonies "in all cases whatsoever."[37]

Many Americans expected this same session of Parliament to repeal the Currency Act. It did not do that, but it did temper the American

Duties (Sugar) Act of 1764. The 1766 statute was copied, nearly word for word, from a proposal by the "Meeting of the Committees of the West Indian and North American Merchants." For example, the Lords and Commons accepted the merchants' proposal to reduce the three-penny import duty on foreign molasses to a single penny. The government figured Americans would swallow their constitutional scruples and pay that small sum rather than tangle with Customs. And sure enough, over the next decade, the colonists paid molasses import taxes in excess of £15,000 a year.[38]

CHAPTER 6

Who Should Rule at Home?

1766

Oᴺᴇ ᴡɪᴛɴᴇss ᴛᴏ Cʜᴀʀʟᴇs Tᴏᴡɴ, Sᴏᴜᴛʜ Cᴀʀᴏʟɪɴᴀ's, ᴄᴇʟᴇʙʀᴀ-tion of the repeal of the Stamp Act was a Carolina native named Gustavus Vassa (also Olaudah Equiano). Born into slavery and made to work on merchant vessels, he had earned enough money trading on his own account to purchase his freedom. "I saw the town illuminated," he recalled years later, "the guns were fired, and bonfires an[d] other demonstrations of joy shewn."[1] Other ports' parties were even more lavish.

But many Americans were more ambivalent. In 1909, the historian Carl Becker put forth the arresting claim that the Founding Fathers' storied struggle for home rule was accompanied by a host of battles over "who should rule at home."[2] One of these lesser-known conflicts, pitting American farmers against mercantile firms on both sides of the Atlantic, colored some colonists' responses to the repeal of the Stamp Act.

George Mason had a question for the London merchants who wanted him to thank Parliament for backing down. "Is the Indulgence of Great Britain manifested by prohibiting her Colonys from exporting to foreign Countrys such Commoditys as she does not want, & from importing such as she does not produce or manufacture & therefore can not furnish but upon extravagant Terms?" he asked in an anonymous essay he sent to the London *Public Ledger*. Mason's neighbor George Washington thanked his London correspondents, Capel and Osgood Hanbury, for lobbying against the Stamp Act, but then added, "I coud wish it was in my power to congratulate you with success, in having the Commercial System of these Colonies put upon a more enlargd and extensive foot-ing." An anonymous newspaper writer called Parliament's gesture "*a gift to blind your eyes*, whilst they continue to clog your TRADE."[3]

Continuing tensions between farmers and merchants were also evident in an incident at Benjamin Mosby's ordinary (tavern) in Cumberland County, Virginia, on June 3, 1766. Its origins were economic, religious, political, and even ethnic.

Robert Routledge observed the king's twenty-eighth birthday a day early by draining multiple glasses of wine, for he had reasons of his own to celebrate. A prosperous storekeeper, Routledge furnished his customers with West Indian as well as European goods. But few paid him in cash or even tobacco, so he spent much of his time dunning debtors—that is, until Virginia judges protested the Stamp Act by closing their courts, robbing Routledge and other debt collectors of the indispensable threat of legal action. But Virginians had just learned that Parliament had repealed the stamp tax, meaning the courts would soon reopen.[4]

John Chiswell also spent much of June 3 in Benjamin Mosby's ordinary, but not celebrating. Neck deep in debt, he would have dreaded the resumption of lawsuits at any time, but especially now, because his largest creditor, his father-in-law, John Robinson, had just died. While serving as treasurer for Virginia's provincial government, John Robinson had lent more than £100,000 of public money to friends and kin. Now the administrators of his estate would discover the defalcation and set about recovering the money. But Chiswell did not have it.

Something led Chiswell to call Routledge a "Scotch rebel," a reference to the 1745 Jacobite rebellion, named for James Stuart, whose birth in 1688 had given his father, James II, England's Catholic king, a male heir—and Parliament compelling reason to overthrow the king. Chiswell's insult was topical, for James Stuart had died on New Year's Day 1766. The Jacobite rebellion had centered in Scotland, but "Scotch rebel" was a strange insult to level at Routledge, since he hailed from northern England—and Chiswell's own family was Scottish.[5]

Chiswell went on to call Routledge "a villain who came to Virginia to cheat and defraud men of their property." During the previous two decades, countless Scottish traders, and a few from England, had opened stores in Virginia and Maryland, over time compiling long lists of debtors. Upper-class Virginians like Chiswell additionally resented the storekeepers for supplanting them as the middlemen linking small farmers to the wider world. Chiswell called Routledge "Scotch" because that ethnic term had come to denote an economic class.[6]

The dispute escalated, and Chiswell ordered his slave to bring him his sword. The young man refused at first, producing the weapon only after

Chiswell threatened to kill him. Other patrons tried to escort Routledge to safety, but just as he reached the tavern door, Chiswell delivered a final insult, invoking Scotland's dominant religion: "Presbyterian fellow." Then he stabbed Routledge in the heart, killing him instantly.[7]

On the night before his murder trial, the defendant committed suicide. Years earlier, John Chiswell had partnered with two countrymen in a lead mine that ended up on the wrong side of the Proclamation Line of 1763. On New Year's Eve 1776, another of the partners, the deeply indebted William Byrd III, shot himself. And a nineteenth-century Virginia historian claimed that the third co-owner, Chiswell's father-in-law, John Robinson, yet another debtor, had also died at his own hands. Whether all three or only two of the owners of the lead mine killed themselves, it was clear that the Virginia gentry was experiencing a profound crisis.[8]

Economic historians see the £4 million that Virginians, Marylanders, and North Carolinians owed their British trading partners in 1774 as a healthy investment in the developing Chesapeake economy, where land values rose faster than the rate of interest. But the tobacco growers who owed the largest balances seldom viewed them in the same favorable light. After the Revolution, Thomas Jefferson stated that "The torment of mind I endure till the moment shall arrive when I shall not owe a shilling on earth is such really as to render life of little value."[9]

Elite Americans offered numerous explanations for their predicament. Many blamed their debts on supposedly extravagant wives and daughters; "old women are remarkable for golden dreams," one man declared. The historian Aubrey Land aptly described the builders of the great Chesapeake fortunes not as tobacco growers but as "merchant-planters," earning less from their crops than from side businesses such as the fur trade and the sale of British merchandise, African slaves, and Native American land. But starting around the middle of the eighteenth century, this middleman income dried up. British interlopers took over the stores, and white settlers drove the First Nations farther and farther west, greatly diminishing the flow of peltry and deerskins to the Atlantic coast. Then the Seven Years' War and the Proclamation of 1763 all but stopped real estate speculators from obtaining vast western tracts to divide up for retail sale.[10]

The colonists' most satisfying explanation for their enormous debts was that commerce was, as the wealthy Virginian tobacco grower Landon Carter described it, "a Profession that kicks Conscience out of doors like a fawning Puppy." Americans had always addressed their British correspondents as "friends," but the polite veneer was wearing thin. New Yorker John Watts believed British manufacturers considered it "no more real harm to outwit a poor American, than an American would an Indian," and George Washington characterized the goods his London correspondents sent him as "mean in quality but not in price." Another prominent Virginian claimed that overwhelming debt had turned white Virginians like him into a "species of property annexed to certain mercantile houses in London." Thomas Jefferson thus declared himself a slave.[11]

Yet most colonists attributed the British merchants' and manufacturers' fortunes less to chicanery than to their influence over Parliament, evident in legislation ranging from the first Navigation Act in 1651 to the Currency Act of 1764. Modern scholars emphasize that the Acts of Trade strengthened the British state, but they also enriched English and Scottish businessmen, and we will never understand the American perspective until we put the merchants back in mercantilism.

As colonists challenged Britain's government and its largest trading houses, they often fought each other as well. Nothing sowed division like the Great Awakening, as Sarah Osborn's friend Joseph Fish, pastor of the established Congregational (Puritan) church in Stonington, Connecticut, learned to his dismay. Initially welcoming the revivals, which filled his pews, especially with young people, Reverend Fish frequently relinquished his pulpit to the fiery James Davenport—that is, until Reverend Davenport questioned Fish's own conversion. Like many so-called New Light ministers, Davenport also had an antimaterialist streak that alarmed well-to-do colonists. At his peak in 1743, he led his followers in piling their fancy clothes (including the pants he was wearing), along with books by Old Light ministers, on a New London wharf and setting them ablaze. Within a year Davenport experienced a conversion of his own, concurring with the Old Lights in ascribing such actions to the *"false spirit"* (Satan). But when Reverend Fish denounced his flock's New Lights, they seceded and formed their own church, as did other congregations' evangelicals—and even Old Lights when they found themselves in the minority.[12]

Like Virginia, Connecticut persecuted evangelicals, but there many defended themselves by entering politics. By 1759, they had taken over the provincial legislature, inadvertently exposing themselves to a new challenge, as unconverted but ambitious men pushed onto their bandwagon.

Soon the evangelical faction became associated with the Susquehannah Company, the Connecticut land speculators claiming the northern third of Pennsylvania. The New Lights were strongest in the eastern half of the province, and their battle against western Old Lights became less and less religious and increasingly economic and sectional.[13]

By 1766, the only remaining obstacle to the Connecticut New Lights' ascendancy was the council of assistants. Every member, including the governor, was elected at large, so to replace them the insurgents held a convention to nominate a council slate. Meanwhile Governor Thomas Fitch and most of the assistants followed Thomas Hutchinson's path of privately opposing the Stamp Act before its adoption but publicly acquiescing in it afterward. In the April elections, the New Lights turned out Governor Fitch, the deputy governor, half the House of Representatives, and the entire council.[14]

NORTH CAROLINIANS ALSO BRAWLED over religion and politics. At the August 1766 session of the Orange County court, farmers came forward to say someone was stealing tax money. In North Carolina as in other colonies, sheriffs doubled as tax collectors, and Governor William Tryon claimed they had "embezzled more than one half of the public money ordered to be raised and collected by them."[15]

Probing the root causes of official corruption, the Orange County farmers found a flaw in North Carolina's system of representation. Assemblymen were elected by the counties, but western counties like Orange were so vast, and their inhabitants so dispersed, that neither of the two representatives ever got to know more than about a tenth of their constituents and thus could not discover their needs. Nor could more than a handful of freeholders find out how their representative had voted. So the Orange County farmers had come up with a way to make representation real.

The scheme appears to have been the brainchild of Hermon Husband, a farmer, miller, and religious prophet whose six-hundred-acre spread was one of the largest in Orange County. Although born into the Church of England in Maryland in 1724, he had found no satisfaction there. "It seem'd to me there was no true Worship in Spirit among them," he later said of the Anglicans, "he seemed the best Fellow who first found the Place of the Book the Minister was in, and to answer him, and to know when to rise up and sit down." After witnessing sermons by George Whitefield and Gilbert Tennent, the same evangelical ministers who had converted Sarah Osborn in Newport, Husband experienced the new birth and became a Presbyterian. Shortly after resettling in North Carolina, he moved even further toward the fringe by joining the Quakers, only to be expelled from his meeting (as Quaker congregations were called) after refusing to acquiesce in its response to the rape of a fifteen-year-old girl. Several Friends joined Husband in entering the political realm during the summer of 1766, as did Baptists and other evangelicals.[16] Nearly all of their opponents, the men who dominated county and provincial government, belonged to the established Church of England.

Husband proposed that farmers in each Orange County neighborhood assemble once a year to choose representatives who would then sit down—"at a suitable Place, where there is no Liquor"—with the county's vestrymen (who levied taxes on inhabitants of all faiths) and assemblymen. At these meetings, the officeholders would "give an Account of their Stewardship." Husband's larger goal was to combat farmers' dim view of their capacity for effective political action. Many believed the Masons (a secretive gentlemen's club) exerted such tight control over the county "that it would be vain for the Planters, or common People, to make any attempt, by an election, either to turn the present Officers out, or to chuse others, from amongst themselves." Orange County's two assemblymen and several members of the vestry agreed to attend the first accountability session, scheduled for October 10.[17]

The farmers elected their neighborhood representatives, who arrived at the meeting site, a grist mill, early in the morning to find that none of the officeholders had showed up. Toward evening a message arrived from Edmund Fanning, who occupied one of Orange County's assembly seats as well as the lucrative post of register of deeds. He would not attend a meeting in a mill, he said, and besides, the farmers' assertion of "a Right to call him to an Account" amounted to "an Insurrection."[18]

ANOTHER INTERNAL CONFLICT, IN the Hudson River Valley, went back decades but took a violent turn in 1766. In the seventeenth century, the provincial governments of New Netherland and New York had deeded vast manorial estates along the river to families such as the Livingstons and Van Rensselaers, pitting them against not only the farmers who worked the land but also the Stockbridge and Wappinger Indians, who denied having relinquished title to it and, in the eastern valley, Massachusetts and Connecticut leaders claiming jurisdiction over the disputed border region. Sometimes the manor lords' diverse opponents formed alliances. For example, when the Philipse family produced a spurious deed to 200,000 acres of Wappinger land in the Hudson Highlands fifty miles north of New York City and demanded rent, local farmers agreed to pay it—to the Wappingers, who were realistic enough about their place in the colonial order to keep their own demands moderate.[19]

Wappinger sachem Daniel Nimham and most of his warriors fought on Britain's side in the Seven Years' War, and the Philipse family took advantage of their absence to press its claim to their land. At war's end, the new landlords shortened leases, demanded rent in scarce cash instead of produce, and evicted all who objected, seizing not only their land but also their homes and other improvements—all without compensation. In March 1765, the Wappingers brought their case to the provincial council, which sided with the Philipses. The following November, settlers, denouncing the "largeness of Rents and Shortness of Leases," went on strike. They were led by an Irish immigrant and Philipse tenant, William Prendergast, whose description of colonial America clashed with those in most modern textbooks: "There was no Law for poor Men."[20]

The tenants named their group after the organization battling the Stamp Act, the Sons of Liberty, and New York governor Henry Moore drew his own link between the two rebellions: local authorities' failure to punish the anti-stamp rioters had taught inhabitants "that at this time every thing which had the appearance of resisting Government might be undertaken with impunity."[21]

Whenever a landlord evicted and replaced a family for not paying rent, a crowd of club-wielding men in turn evicted the interloper, beating him and reinstalling the original tenants. On May 25, a crowd marched to the home of a replacement tenant named Robert Hughson. He was away, so they beat his wife. When Justice Samuel Peters came out to investigate, a dozen Sons of Liberty seized him and convened an open-air trial. Even if George III himself sailed up the Hudson, Prendergast declared, "he would serve him as he had done Peters," for "Mobs had overcome Kings before." Peters won release only by vowing never to arrest his captors.[22]

The Hudson Valley farmers also took on other tormentors. Decrying conventional legal procedure, whereby county sheriffs satisfied creditors by seizing and selling their debtors' property, generally well below what they had paid for it, the Sons of Liberty invited their indebted neighbors to offer assets directly to their creditors, with the value determined by impartial appraisers. Convinced that "it could do no good to imprison persons who had nothing," the Sons also stormed jails to free debtors.[23] When officials in New York City threw two rebels in prison, several hundred others marched toward the provincial capital. On the way, they sent a message to the better-known version of the Sons of Liberty seeking their help.

They got none. John Montrésor, Gen. Gage's chief engineer and fellow survivor of Braddock's defeat, was amused to learn that the men who had nullified the Stamp Act were "of opinion no one is entitled to Riot but themselves." One of the farmers who marched toward New York City later recalled that he and his fellows had also "expected to be assisted by the poor people there," but that alliance did not materialize, either, and the tenants went home empty-handed.[24]

Tenants on Livingston Manor and Rensselaerswyck, farther up the Hudson, also rebelled in 1766. In June, two hundred marched to Robert Livingston's manor house, threatening to "level" the place and kill its owner unless he reduced their rent. Assembling forty armed men, Livingston's son forced the crowd to disperse. On June 26, tenants battled a sheriff's posse outside the home of rebel leader Robert Noble; three rebels and one man in the posse were killed. The landlords persuaded Gen. Gage to send in British troops, one of whom died fighting the rebels near Patterson, New York, less than four miles west of the Connecticut line.[25]

More than sixty tenants captured by the soldiers were put on trial, and Prendergast was charged with high treason. At the time, any Englishman convicted of this crime would be hanged but then cut down while still living so that his entrails could be cut out and burned before his eyes, after which he would be beheaded and quartered. Prevailing legal practice denied Prendergast a lawyer, but he was ably assisted in his August 6 trial by his wife. The jury found him guilty but recommended mercy. According to Montrésor (whose cynical attitude toward elite New Yorkers admittedly undermines his credibility), Prendergast then told the judges, nearly all of whom had taken the lead in nullifying the Stamp Act, that "If opposition to Government was deemed Rebellion, no member of that Court were entitled to set upon his Tryal." Sentenced to die, he was pardoned by George III.[26]

EVEN AS REDCOATS SUPPRESSED the New York rebellion, the colony's landlord-dominated legislature withheld some of their living expenses. The Quartering Act of 1765 required American provinces hosting troops to cover their lodging, including their firewood and spirits. In 1766,

Gen. Gage moved several companies from Canada down to New York City, both in order to cut costs and to handle any additional riots like those against the Stamp Act. But New York assemblymen refused to supply the garrison with alcohol, vinegar, or salt, and New Jersey followed suit. None of these amenities cost much, but the two assemblies withheld them as proof that the contributions they did make were voluntary. The New Jersey council "look'd upon the Act of Parliament for quartering Soldiers in America, to be virtually as much an Act for laying Taxes on the Inhabitants as the Stamp Act"—and just as clear a case of taxation without representation.[27]

Nor did free Americans like having a standing army kept among them during peacetime without their consent in violation of the English Bill of Rights of 1689. Most people today, especially in the United States, would consider it hopelessly utopian to muster troops only when war threatens, but that was a realistic prospect for the American colonists, since most had firearms and knew how to use them. Here was another way in which Native Americans' resistance to colonial encroachment, coupled with slaves' occasional rebellions, established a foundation for colonial resistance against Parliament. Freeholders' compulsory militia service and extensive gun ownership would both encourage them to resist Britain, eventually militarily, and also contribute to their success.[28]

Shortly after the New York assembly took its stand against the Quartering Act, 240 of the colony's merchants sent the House of Commons a petition declaring that its recent amendments to the American Duties Act still left their trade "severely clogged and restricted." Boston businessmen echoed these complaints. The Massachusetts assembly had not been fully reconciled to the imperial government, either. Ordered to compensate Thomas Hutchinson and other victims of the August 1765 riots, the representatives did so, but used the same legislation to pardon all the rioters.[29]

CHAPTER 7

———— ·•·•· ————

From Bengal to Boston

1767–1768

B Y THE WINTER OF 1767, BOTH SARAH OSBORN'S MINISTER, WIL-liam Vinal, and her best male friend, Stonington, Connecticut, pastor Joseph Fish, had concluded that her good intentions had led her astray. The letter Reverend Fish sent her that February does not survive, but the depth of his concern courses through her lengthy reply. Fish urged the fifty-three-year-old Osborn to stop hosting the initiators of the revival, the African Americans who worshipped with her every Sunday night. Osborn refused as politely as she could. "Pray my dear Sir," she wrote, "dont Look upon it as a rejecting your council; that I Have not yet dismist" them. Like many of the era's white missionaries, she contended that she had actually benefited the slaves' owners, by making their human property less "saucy."[1]

Fish was even more worried about Osborn violating gender conventions. She had permitted about twenty women to participate in the meetings initially set aside for men, and she had addressed these mixed-gender assemblies in clear violation of the apostle Paul's command. Osborn assured Fish that she never spoke at the men's meetings unless spoken to, and she had a plausible explanation for opening them to a limited number of other women. Several of her female worshippers had begun devoting their Friday evenings to a women's group associated with Newport's Baptist church, and Osborn had hit upon the idea of inviting them to her men's group, which met at the same time, "as a Means Gradualy to draw them off" from the Baptists. Making a similarly sectarian case for including African Americans in her services, she warned that one of these Black men had begun hosting religious meetings in the home of his master, who belonged to the Church of England.[2]

Fish's gravest concern was that Osborn's revival appeared to have pulled her out of the feminine sphere. She stood up to him, albeit in a manner that was anything but feminist. Portraying her role in the revival as entirely passive, she complained, "I dont know How to Let Go." Rebutting Fish's concern about her religious services drawing her away from feminine duties such as sewing, she offered that without them, she might idle away her evenings in the stereotypically female practice of receiving visitors for "some chat Less to Edification." Far from depleting her, the "Sweet refreshing Evenings" of spiritual communion were her "resting reaping times." When Fish reminded Osborn that Jethro had persuaded his son-in-law Moses to delegate authority to others, she once again replied as one who knew her place. "Moses was Head of the people and So Had it in His power to comply with Jethros advice by appointing Elders etc. to take part with Him, but I am rather as a Servant," "unworthy and unequal" of wielding authority and consequently of delegating it, she wrote.[3]

Osborn's mounting self-confidence certainly seems to have arisen from her success as a revival leader, but she herself would no doubt have attributed it to the "*Work of Grace* wrought in my soul." Behind her meek persona, she perfectly embodied the self-assurance that was evangelicalism's great gift to all who were born again.[4] Living in Newport, cockpit of opposition to the molasses tax, the Stamp Act, and other British measures, Osborn was powerfully affected by the American Revolution—but much more so by her conversion to Christ.

THE NEVER-STRONG ROCKINGHAM MINISTRY fell in July 1766. Gout and other chronic illnesses—including, specialists believe, depression—prevented William Pitt from serving as first lord of the treasury, but he accepted the obscure post of Privy Seal, along with an earldom, with the understanding that he would call the shots in a ministry nominally led by the Duke of Grafton.[5]

Giving Pitt almost sole credit for persuading Parliament to repeal the Stamp Act, colonists erected numerous statues of him and exulted when he returned to power as Lord Chatham. But his love of America had its limits, and he was furious that New Jersey and New York had defied the Quartering Act, that Massachusetts had pardoned the Stamp Act rioters, and, most of all, that the New York City merchants had sent in their "absurd," "highly improper," and "most grossly fallacious and offensive" petition for greater commercial freedom.[6]

But the Grafton ministry's primary focus was on a profound financial crisis. The landowners who had the exclusive right to vote in parliamentary elections were furious at their MPs for continuing to tax real estate income at the elevated wartime level of four shillings in the pound or 20 percent. During a January 26, 1767, debate in the House of Commons, George Grenville pointed out that every shilling of the land tax brought in about £500,000 a year: slightly more than the cost of the ten thousand redcoats stationed in America. If the government pared back its colonial expenses, especially by abandoning some of the costliest posts deep in Indian country, and if it forced the colonists to pay the soldiers who remained, as Grenville had originally proposed, it could knock the real estate tax back down to its prewar level of 15 percent.[7]

The administration's response to Grenville's provocation came from Charles Townshend, the chancellor of the exchequer, and it was a shocker: the Grafton ministry was already planning to charge the Americans for their defense. A month later, on February 27, opposition MPs leaned heavily upon Townshend's announcement in persuading their colleagues to defy the wishes of the ministry and vote, 206 to 188, to slash the real estate tax. No British administration had suffered a fiscal defeat like that in twenty-five years. It was the sort of thing that usually brought a ministry down.[8]

But Townshend's hint about future American revenue was only one reason the MPs had cut the land tax, for they had also discovered another pot of gold on the opposite side of the globe. A decade earlier, even as Britain and its American colonists suffered some of their worst defeats of the Seven Years' War, the British East India Company won a stunning victory in Bengal, an Indian province larger and more populous than France. At the Battle of Plassey on June 23, 1757, Robert Clive and the firm's private soldiers defeated the nawab (ruler) of Bengal, Siraj ud-Daulah, the man behind the much mythologized Black Hole of Calcutta. Then in 1764, Company troops also crushed Siraj ud-Daulah's successor, leading India's Mughal emperor to give the EIC the *diwani*—the sole right to collect taxes—for Bengal and two neighboring provinces. The company soon doubled its new subjects' real estate taxes and estimated that the *diwani* would bring in £2 million per year, whereupon its stock price doubled. But the British government, which had contributed £4.5 million to the East India Company's military operations, demanded a share of the plunder. The firm indignantly replied that it already supplied about a third of Britain's customs revenue, but when Members of Parliament started talking about capping stockholders' annual dividends at 10 percent, EIC officials agreed to sit down with the chancellor of the exchequer to negotiate an additional subsidy.[9]

Townshend, who had invested heavily in the East India Company, in part with funds embezzled from the Pay Office, hinted at a sweetheart deal, and the firm's stock, initially offered at £100 per share, soared to £278. But then he sold his EIC shares at a £7,000 profit and began negotiating more aggressively. In the end the Company agreed to hand the government £400,000 a year.[10]

Even after securing this windfall, Townshend decided to proceed with his earlier plan to tax merchandise arriving in American ports. During the campaign against the Stamp Act, most colonists had also objected to the previous year's American Duties (Sugar) Act. A few, however, had cast themselves as moderates by only objecting to internal taxes like stamp duties. In testimony before the House of Commons and an essay appearing in the *London Chronicle* early in April 1767, just as the chancellor of the exchequer completed his proposals, Benjamin Franklin practically begged Parliament to tax America's trade. Like most MPs, Townshend believed Parliament had just as much right to tax colonists

Benjamin West, *Shah Alam Conveying the Grant of the Diwani to Lord Clive*

internally as externally. But "since the Americans were pleased to make that distinction," he was "willing to indulge them."[11]

Townshend did not touch the colonists' single largest British import, textiles. He proposed to tax their lead, glass, paper, and "painters colours" (the dies and lead used in painting), but half of the income from the "Townshend duties" would come from a single article, tea. Even if every colonist faithfully paid them—hah!—Townshend's taxes would only bring in about £40,000 a year. And the cabinet decided not to spend this money on the army's American garrison, as Townshend had originally proposed. Instead it would pay the salaries of American governors, attorneys general, and superior court justices, freeing them from dependence on local legislators.[12] Thus both of the infamous taxes that Parliament tried to levy on the American colonists in the 1760s actually played handmaiden to other imperial objectives. The Stamp Act would pay for the ten thousand peacekeeping troops that Parliament had left in America, and the Townshend duties would stiffen the spines of officeholders charged with cracking down on smugglers.

Townshend's new American duties were part of a larger legislative package that also eliminated the 25 percent tax that the East India Company paid when it sold tea in Britain for reexport to America and Ireland. The directors were expected to pass this reduction on to their colonial customers. Even with the new colonial tax of three pence per pound—about 8 percent—Americans would pay much less for EIC tea, in fact little more than Dutch smugglers charged. Moreover, by using this new revenue to pay colonial officials' salaries, Parliament would save the provincial legislatures money. The EIC would also benefit; its American sales were expected to triple to about £1.5 million every year.[13]

Yet by paying the new duties, colonists would forfeit their only check on provincial placemen (government appointees) and at the same time establish a precedent for parliamentary taxation. In an echo of Thomas Whately's plans for the Stamp Act, Townshend repeatedly assured the House of Commons that the duties he proposed were "a beginning only."[14]

Townshend also had other ideas about how to crack down on American smuggling. Although customs agents in Massachusetts and New Hampshire had obtained the writs of assistance they had requested, the constitutional issues raised by James Otis had prevented other provinces from adopting the procedure, and Townshend now moved to extend it to all of them. He also favored establishing an American customs board on the British model; its headquarters would be in Boston—with not quite 16,000 inhabitants, the third largest of the colonial ports, behind Philadelphia and New York. Parliament enacted Townshend's entire program and also approved his proposed response to New York's violation of the Quartering Act, shutting down the provincial assembly until it sent British soldiers stationed in New York every item it owed them.[15]

The New York Suspending Act, which received the royal assent on July 2, was obviously punitive, but in a sense, so was the rest of Townshend's program. Parliament endorsed it in a fury over the seeming ingratitude with which the colonists greeted its earlier decision to repeal the Stamp Act and much of the American Duties Act.

Born in part of American resistance, the new legislation inevitably provoked more. Judges in nearly every province found excuses for not granting writs of assistance, and a quarter century later, the Fourth Amendment to the U.S. Constitution would require government officials seeking search warrants to show probable cause.[16]

Aghast at Parliament for once again trying to tax their stock-in-trade, America's newspaper editors, who were much freer than their British counterparts, churned out dozens of essays and pamphlets denouncing Townshend's entire program.[17] Most famously, Philadelphia attorney John Dickinson published a series of essays in the *Pennsylvania Chronicle* over the pseudonym "A Farmer"—farming being, then as now, more popular than the practice of law. Appropriately enough, given that the equally odious Stamp Act and Townshend duties both taxed paper, Dickinson compared them to the first and second editions of a book. Whether Parliament taxed the colonists internally or externally, it violated their rights, since there were no American MPs, Dickinson declared. His letters ran in nineteen of the twenty-three American newspapers, and the pamphlet version was reprinted as far away as Paris.[18]

ON AUGUST 31, 1767, "A.F.," an anonymous essayist, took to the pages of the *Boston Gazette* to exhort Americans to overturn the New York Suspending Act the same way they had killed the Stamp Act: by boycotting British merchandise, with the exception of "such articles as are absolutely necessary to carry on our fisheries, and provide us against the inclemency of the seasons." The Boston town meeting took up the suggestion two months later but modified it in telling ways. It did not mention either the New York Suspending Act or the Townshend duties. The real problem, as Boston saw it, was that its trade had "for several Years been on the decline," resulting in a massive trade deficit and acute shortage of circulating cash. Parliament's "heavy Impositions" on American trade were one source of the commercial crisis, but so were Massachusetts's "very burthensome Taxes" to pay off its Seven Years' War debt; here was one more link between "the late Warr" and the crown–colony conflict of the 1760s. But "the chief Cause" of Bostonians' distress was their own "excessive use of Forreign Superfluities."[19]

Boston's merchant community balked at A.F.'s proposal to boycott most British imports, so instead the town voted to escape its "embarrassed & distressed Circumstances" by boycotting the merchants. Signers of the association would stop buying two categories of goods sourced from Britain: (1) luxuries such as china, "Gold & Silver Buttons," and ready-made clothing, and (2) items that could be replaced locally, including nails, rope, and shoes. One commodity noticeably absent from either list was tea. But Bostonians vowed to continue "to adhere to the late regulations respecting Funerals," which were estimated to have already saved them £100,000. The agreement appeared in newspapers throughout the colonies under the heading "Save your MONEY, and you save your COUNTRY!"[20]

The town meeting also named a committee to look into reviving the linen manufactory that had opened amid fanfare in 1751 only to sputter out over the ensuing decade.[21]

Other New England towns drew up their own lists of merchandise to forgo. Like Boston, most allowed the continued importation of tea. But numerous newspaper essays urged women, who supposedly drank more tea than men, to give it up. In mid-December, Newport, Rhode Island, women "most judiciously rejected the poisonous Bohea"—the most common form of tea—and other women soon followed. British ceramics makers had cashed in on the repeal of the Stamp Act by hawking commemorative teapots emblazoned "No Stamp Act" and "American Liberty Restored." These sold well, but not for long, because by early 1768, few Americans had any need for them.[22]

Some women sought not just to give up British wares but to replace them, at least symbolically. Although a handful of American women had protested the Stamp Act by holding spinning bees, the movement had not spread far be-

Teapot made in England c. 1766–1770. The opposite side is inscribed with the phrase "American Liberty Restored."

fore the tax was repealed. But once Parliament enacted the Townshend duties, eighteen Providence women sought to revive them. Gathering at the home of Capt. Esek Hopkins on December 18, 1767, they drank only coffee and an herbal tea discovered by Native Americans, while spinning "upwards of 40 skeines of fine linen yarn." A newspaper account praised them for setting young men "an example of industry."[23]

No one stepped forward to emulate the Providence women, but early in March 1768, a hundred Boston merchants proposed to turn the city's limited nonconsumption pledge into full-on nonimportation. What had changed their minds? Apparently nonconsumption, limited though it was, had sapped demand for their wares. The historian Merrill Jensen argues that far from being true converts to nonimportation, Boston's business leaders "were forced into it by popular pressure." Still, by seizing the initiative, they gained an important advantage: unlike its predecessor, the March 1768 agreement came with an escape clause, suspending it until the other major ports signed on. New York readily did so, but Philadelphia's powerful Quakers and merchants refused, killing the boycott not only there but in Boston and New York.[24]

Many Philadelphians were furious at their city's traders, and a forty-year-old Quaker named Hannah Griffitts wrote a poem calling upon women to step into the breach:

If the Sons (so degenerate) the Blessing despise,
Let the Daughters of Liberty, nobly arise.

Griffitts was all too aware of the limitations on women's activism, but she reminded them of their power to *not* act, for instance by simply not consuming the items Parliament taxed. Audaciously, she called women's potential influence a "negative" (veto)—a right none of His Majesty's female subjects had ever exercised, and no monarch had since Queen Anne.

tho we've no Voice, but a negative here,
The use of the Taxables, let us forbear.

Griffitts called her poem "The Female Patriots." She did not publish it in the modern sense, by having it printed, but she did circulate it in manuscript, and in December 1769 it found its way into the *Pennsylvania Chronicle*.[25]

CHAPTER 8

Red Flag Over Boston

1768–1769

THE AMERICAN BOARD OF CUSTOMS COMMISSIONERS REACHED Boston in November 1767 and set to work investigating the yawning chasm between the theory and practice of imperial trade regulation. Discovering that port authorities had seized only six ships in two and a half years of supposedly tightened enforcement, the board called in reinforcements. Meanwhile the colonists who had forced the resignation of the stamp distributors went to work on the commissioners. William Burch's wife described a mob "surroundg her house with most hideous howlings as the Indians, when they attack."[1]

March 18, 1768, would mark the second anniversary of Stamp Act repeal. To juice up the festivities, the city's Whigs—as they were starting to call themselves—postponed Saint Patrick's Day, celebrated by many Irish Protestants even in this most anti-Catholic of cities, by one day. To Governor Bernard's great relief, March 18 "produced Terror only, and not actual Mischief." The customs commissioners nonetheless sought additional protection, and Wills Hill, Lord Hillsborough, the secretary of Britain's new American department, made the fateful decision to dispatch redcoats: initially a single regiment but later changed to two. Meanwhile the *Romney*, a fifty-cannon man-of-war, arrived to aid in customs enforcement, and the captain, John Corner, sent impressment gangs aboard merchant ships sailing into Boston Harbor. Merchant mariners aching to greet their families after months-long voyages were instead forced into indefinite service on the *Romney*.[2]

The previous November, one of Boston's wealthiest merchants, John Hancock, had held his cadet company back from the official ceremony welcoming the customs board. Early in May, Hancock's sloop *Liberty* arrived from Madeira, and the commissioners took their revenge. When

Parliament repealed much of the American Duties Act, it left in place the onerous 140 shillings per tun duty on imported wine. On the afternoon of May 9, two customs officers called tidewaiters rowed out to the *Liberty* to supervise its unloading. One of them, Thomas Kirk, later claimed that Hancock's men had confined him belowdecks on the *Liberty* while they clandestinely removed most of its cargo.[3]

By the time Kirk came forward, Hancock's workers had filled the *Liberty* with pine tar and spermaceti (whale) oil for its outbound voyage—all in advance of posting bond at the Custom House, a common practice that was technically illegal. Officials cited this infraction, not the smuggling of the Madeira or the detention of Kirk, in instructing Capt. Corner to seize the *Liberty* on June 10. A crowd of sailors and dockworkers tried but failed to recapture the sloop. In their frustration, they set upon several customs officers, pelting them with "Clubs, Stones and Brickbats." One victim, thrown down and "dragged . . . by the Hair of his Head," did not even work for Customs. His father, an agent, had chosen this day to bring his son to work.[4]

Three days after the riot, two thousand Bostonians rallied under a red flag. None of the *Liberty* rioters was ever punished, since none of their victims came forward. Why should they, when the grand jury included a leading rioter? But one victim, Benjamin Hallowell, Boston's comptroller of the customs, carried his complaints all the way to London, where they depressed the value of British government bonds and persuaded the ministry to send two additional regiments to Boston.[5]

Back in February, the Massachusetts assemblymen had protested Parliament's recent actions in a circular protest letter to the other colonies. Hillsborough ordered them to rescind it, but they stood by it, 92 to 17, whereupon Governor Bernard sent them all home and Paul Revere engraved a scene of the seventeen pro-ministry representatives marching to hell. Other governors were also instructed to dissolve their assemblies if they endorsed Massachusetts's letter—and these orders did even more for the colonists' unity than the Massachusetts circular had.[6]

The De Lanceys, one of the two rival families that contested control of the New York legislature, rode the Massachusetts circular letter out of the political wilderness. The dominant Livingstons were not required to call an election until 1775, but the De Lanceys shamed them into endorsing the circular letter, prompting Governor Henry Moore to dissolve the assembly, triggering new elections that the De Lanceys handily won.[7]

✵　　✵　　✵

IN NORTH CAROLINA, THE most vicious conflicts of 1768 were internal. The provincial assembly levied a regressive poll (head) tax to complete a £15,000 palace for Governor William Tryon, and by the end of April, farmers in at least four counties had mutually pledged to defy the tax man. Members of North Carolina's "Court Party" blamed the agitation on Hermon Husband, the man who had sought to call Orange County officeholders to account. Actually, Husband considered the new associations too "hot and rash" and feared they would turn violent. "If a devouring Vermin came to take his Hens," the onetime Quaker told an associator, "they must take four or five before he could be provoked enough to shoot it to take its Life; much more to shoot Men." By this time, Husband had expanded on his earlier proposal for yearly citizens' conventions, proposing that they nominate their own candidates for office.[8]

By the spring of 1768, the rebelling farmers had begun calling themselves Regulators. English subjects seeking to regulate officeholders' extortion had taken that name back in the 1650s, but North Carolinians apparently picked it up from an insurgency then in progress just south of their border. Yet the South Carolina Regulators were nothing like their northern namesakes; they were vigilantes.[9] The entire colonial backcountry had a reputation for lawlessness, and in the mid-1760s the leading men of western South Carolina detected spikes in all kinds of crime, from vagrancy to rape. According to these southern Regulators' chief spokesman, Church of England missionary Charles Woodmason, innocent frontiersmen were sometimes "wantonly tortured in the Indian Manner for to be made [to] confess where they secreted their Effects from Plunder."[10] Most infuriating, the outlaws stole numerous horses.

Well-to-do westerners traced the crime wave partly to lowcountry neglect. All of South Carolina's courts met in the capital, more than a hundred miles from outlying settlements. With few victims and witnesses willing to travel that far, the backcountry in effect had no judicial system, so leading westerners meted out their own rough justice, whipping errant spouses and often lynching horse thieves. In April 1768, assemblymen and Governor Charles Montague finally took notice, declaring war on the vigilantes and at the same time establishing circuit courts throughout the province and inviting prominent Regulators to command new ranger (elite woodsmen) companies tasked with suppressing backcountry crime.[11]

Not yet satisfied, hundreds of insurgents assembled in June 1768 at
the Congaree River near present-day Columbia, South Carolina, and
agreed on a "Plan of Regulation." When Capt. Joseph Holland led a militia company against them, the militiamen were captured and whipped
like so many horse thieves. One later claimed that the rebel band included
"a great number of People of different Colours ... Whites, Blacks, and
Mulattoes." The leading Regulator, Gideon Gibson, did in fact have African as well as European ancestors, but one of his fellow insurgents'
motivations for going after the livestock rustlers was that many of them
were Black.[12]

Meanwhile Hermon Husband failed in his quest to keep the North
Carolina Regulators peaceful. On April 8, 1768, Orange County sheriff
Tyree Harris seized a mare from a delinquent taxpayer, and the owner's
friends recaptured it. Then they tied up the sheriff and paraded him into
Hillsborough, capital of Orange County, and fired shots into the home
of their chief tormentor, Edmund Fanning. As soon as they freed Sheriff Harris, he assembled a posse and arrested William Butler, who had
helped rescue the mare, along with Hermon Husband.[13]

Learning of the arrests, a reported seven hundred armed men, accompanied by scores of women and children, assembled just outside
Hillsborough. Husband heard that Governor Tryon had "Represented
us as a Faction of *Quakers* and *Baptists*, who aimed to overset the
Church of England," and Husband himself called the protest "a Work
of Providence." Indeed, he wrote, "Methinks when a Reformation can be
brought about in our Constitution by a legal and constitutional Manner,
then will commence that Thousand Years Reign with Christ."[14]

"I have but one Life," Butler declared upon learning that he and Husband might be executed, "and I freely can give that up for this Cause."
Husband, however, was no readier to die than to kill, and he offered to
try to confine his criticism of court officials to election season if Fanning
would release him. Fearing that the crowd lurking on the outskirts of
Hillsborough would try to rescue both prisoners, Fanning freed them
on bond. But Husband's ordeal had only begun, for Regulators pressed
him more urgently than ever to join their ranks. "I was for my Safety
obliged to abscond from them as well as the Governor, and took [to] the
Woods for two Weeks," he wrote.[15]

Meanwhile residents of Rowan County also rescued a horse from a
tax collector, and crowds in Anson and Johnston counties shut down
local courts.[16] Tryon accused the Regulators of demanding "an abolition

of taxes and debts," but they disclaimed any desire to redistribute wealth. Like the New York land rioters, the North Carolinians compared themselves to the Sons of Liberty, insisting that "no People have a right to be taxed, but by consent of themselves or their Delegates." And far from admitting to trying to evade their just debts, the rebels accused provincial assemblymen of overtaxing them and local court officers, including lawyers, of levying exorbitant fees—all exacerbated by "the great scarcity of Money" resulting from another state action, Parliament's adoption of the Currency Act.[17]

Butler and Husband were to be tried for insurrection in Hillsborough, where Governor Tryon posted more than 1,400 troops.[18] A group of soldiers dragged Husband into a tavern, forced him to stand on a table, and (as he later reported) "made Sport of me" until their commander told them, "Hold, don't carry the joke too far." Back in prison awaiting trial, Butler, Husband, and about ten other accused Regulators were confined in a space so small that they could not all lie down at the same time. The bookish Husband was reminded of "East-India Imprisonments"—the Black Hole of Calcutta—and Europe's "Inquisitions."[19]

The jury found Husband not guilty, and he was released. Butler and two other Regulators received prison sentences and fines, but two escaped, leading Tryon to pardon all three. The court also convicted Edmund Fanning on multiple charges of extortion but fined him only one penny for each.[20]

Backcountry North Carolinians sent the provincial legislature a long list of demands. Assembly elections should be by secret ballot, but legislators' votes should be public. Neither lawyers nor country clerks should serve in the assembly. Families that homesteaded on western land, clearing forests and putting up fences and houses, should have first crack at buying it. Militia training, work on public roads, and other compulsory labor consumed as much as a month of the farmer's year and had to be curtailed. Pastors of dissenting (non-Anglican) churches should be allowed to officiate at weddings. Provincial taxes must be made less regressive—and church taxes should be abolished.[21]

MEANWHILE BOSTONIANS WITNESSED A strange coda to the *Liberty* riot. A schooner entering the harbor was seized for smuggling thirty hogsheads (giant barrels) of molasses. On July 8, in an apparent replay of the events of May 9, a crowd boarded the vessel and imprisoned the customs agents in the cabin while its cargo vanished. Boston's most prominent Whigs were embarrassed at seeing crowd violence used so blatantly to protect a smuggler, and so the next day, the contraband molasses magically reappeared.[22]

Early in September 1768, when Bostonians learned that the ministry planned to comply with the customs commissioners' request for British troops, the town meeting asked Governor Bernard to call a special session of the legislature. When he refused, Boston invited the other Massachusetts towns to an extralegal convention. Fewer than half sent delegates, but the convention operated just like the provincial House of Representatives, even asking its speaker, Thomas Cushing, to chair the proceedings. Boston had, in effect, usurped the governor's authority to convene the assembly.[23]

THREE HUNDRED MILES TO the west, in what is now upstate New York, imperial government encountered opposition of a different sort. Early in 1768, the Board of Trade decided to establish a permanent Anglo-native border, and it ordered Indian agents John Stuart and William Johnson to sit down with indigenous leaders in their districts to work out the details.[24]

Numerous land speculators coveted the region west of the Board of Trade's proposed boundary, and many had had the foresight to partner with Johnson, who had valuable connections with the powerful Six Nations of the Iroquois. Thus when the northern Indian agent convened Iroquois representatives at Fort Stanwix (present-day Rome, New York) on October 24, 1768, they made a strange demand: Britain must accept millions of acres more than it had requested. The Board of Trade's boundary would have left the western portions of North Carolina and Virginia, most of present-day West Virginia, and all of modern Kentucky in Indian country. But in the treaty negotiated at Fort Stanwix, the Iroquois sold Britain all of this land—everything east of the Ohio River. Within this giant tract, the Iroquois made particular grants to Johnson's assistant George Croghan and to a group calling itself the Suffering Traders of which Johnson was secretly a member.[25]

By giving Britain land where they did not live or hunt, the Iroquois apparently hoped to channel the tide of British encroachment away from their own territory. In addition, they walked away from Fort Stanwix with the down payment on more than £10,000 worth of trade goods— the largest amount Britain had ever paid Native Americans for land.[26]

*　　*　　*

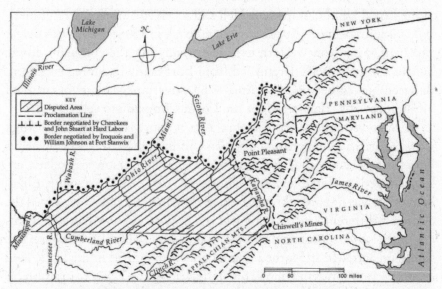

Region William Johnson obtained from the Iroquois at Fort Stanwix
in violation of his instructions, November 5, 1768

FOR FIVE YEARS, SPECULATORS seeking fortunes in rising land prices
had been held back by the Proclamation of 1763. So in every British
colony with any claim to the region ceded at Fort Stanwix, Johnson's
purchase set off a land rush. George Washington again mobilized Virginians who had led troops against the French and Indians to demand the
land bounties that their men had been promised. He also began buying
up his fellow veterans' claims. Washington instructed his brother Charles
to approach them "in a joking way, rather than in earnest at first" so as
not to alert them to the land's potential value. By 1770, Washington's
surveyor, William Crawford, a fellow survivor of Braddock's campaign,
would be warning him that his former comrades-in-arms were "a good
deel shagereend" at his engrossing "the cream of the Country" (as Washington called it).[27]

Today Dr. Thomas Walker of Albemarle County, Virginia, is best
remembered as Thomas Jefferson's physician. But he was also, as his
great-grandson put it, "as great a land-monger as General Washington"—
the first president being the gold standard against which lesser speculators were judged. Walker, who was yet another veteran of Braddock's
campaign, headed Virginia's delegation to the Fort Stanwix congress, in
which he had a deep personal interest. He was the most active member

of the Loyal Land Company, which had received a preliminary grant to 800,000 acres of trans-Appalachian land back in 1748. Braddock's defeat and British bans on western expansion had shut the company down, but the moment Walker returned from Fort Stanwix, he reactivated it. Between November 1768 and April 1769, government surveyors marked off hundreds of homesteads for the Loyal Company to sell.[28]

Jefferson sought to profit from the Fort Stanwix deal in two distinct ways. More than once while his friend John Walker was serving as his father's clerk at the Anglo-Iroquois congress, Jefferson (as he later acknowledged) "offered love to a handsome lady"—Walker's wife, Elizabeth.[29] He was indignantly rebuffed, but the Iroquois cession opened the door to a different kind of conquest. The eldest son of a deceased member of the Loyal Company, Jefferson asked Dr. Walker for his share: five thousand acres. In 1754, the imperial government had limited new land grants to one thousand acres, but Jefferson evaded that restriction by joining two new land syndicates, each promising him the thousand-acre maximum. Altogether, he now sought seven thousand acres, all west of the Proclamation Line. And Stanwix fever struck just as hard in New York and Pennsylvania.[30]

Once again, the speculators celebrated too soon. Three weeks before Johnson sat down with the Iroquois, John Stuart had met Cherokee representatives at a town the British phonetically translated as Hard Labor to negotiate the southern portion of the Anglo-native boundary. Even as the Iroquois sold Johnson the eastern half of the Ohio Valley, Stuart complied with his instructions, leaving this same vast region in Cherokee country.[31]

In April 1769, the Hard Labor agreement compelled Virginia's executive council to void the hundreds of plats that surveyors had drawn up for the Loyal Company. But the councilors' sympathies—and in many cases their investments—were with the speculators. They informed Stuart that his Cherokee boundary "would be highly injurious to this Colony, and to the Crown of Great Britain, by giving to the Indians, an extensive tract of land." In full agreement, the House of Burgesses petitioned the governor, Lord Botetourt, for permission to occupy Kentucky and the adjacent region. In a body whose members included George Washington, Patrick Henry, Thomas Jefferson, and numerous other real estate speculators, the vote in favor of the western land petition was unanimous.[32]

Imperial approval of Virginia's petition would give speculators more than six million acres for which they had already received preliminary grants and nearly double the colony's land area. But allowing Virginians onto this land would mean abrogating both the Proclamation of 1763 and the boundary that Stuart had negotiated with the Cherokees.[33]

By this time, bluegrass seed arriving from England in the guts of livestock had spread west into Kentucky, and bluegrass meadows would eventually transform Kentucky into some of the finest horse country in the world. But the Virginians' success at obtaining this rich land would hinge, to a surprising extent, upon the Native Americans who hunted there. Imperial officials carefully scrutinized the House of Burgesses' claim that "no Tribe of *Indians*, at present, sets up any Pretensions" to Kentucky or the adjacent regions.[34] Alexander McKee, whose mother was Shawnee, was a British agent charged with monitoring the Shawnees, Delawares, and Mingos. He wrote that the "Numbers of White people and Surveyors" that made their way to the Ohio River Valley in the spring of 1769 had "set all their Warriors in a rage."[35]

Like Britain's sovereignty over North America, the Iroquois's claim to the eastern Ohio Valley depended to a great extent on its not being exercised. The Shawnees acknowledged the "Six Nations as our elder Brethren and as such have listened to them while we found their advice good," headman Red Hawk told British representatives, "but their power extends no further with us." The Iroquois based their power to deed away Delaware land on the latter's having agreed, decades earlier, to play the role of "women" in indigenous diplomacy. But Delaware leaders insisted that they had become women not in the subservient English sense but in the Native American sense, as peacemakers.[36]

No native nation acting alone could do the British much damage; the First Nations' power hinged upon their ability to unite. As the year 1769 opened, native unity seemed less likely than ever. Although Upper Ohioans and Wabash River warriors had joined together in the 1763–1764 uprising, when a Wabash River war party attacked the Shawnees and Delawares accompanying George Croghan down the Ohio River in 1765, they placed themselves and their former allies in a virtual state of war. But then in the spring of 1769, as leading colonists in Virginia, Pennsylvania, and other provinces jockeyed for the land that the Iroquois had ceded at Fort Stanwix, the female peace chiefs of the Wabash River nations sent diplomatic communiqués in the form of wampum belts to their counterparts among the Upper Ohio Valley Indians (the Shawnees and Delawares), two hundred miles to the east.[37]

Most of the First Nations in the region that is now the American Midwest recognized four types of leaders. Male war chiefs led attacks against enemies, but male peace chiefs conducted village affairs during peacetime. Female war chiefs helped decide both the advisability of attacks and the fate of war captives, while female peace chiefs collaborated with male peace chiefs on civil governance.[38]

The Wabash River matrons had addressed their counterparts among the Shawnees and Delawares because they wanted to make peace, and their offer was accepted. Then, on the basis of the women's reconciliation, the Upper Ohio chiefs, male and female, set about rebuilding the anti-British confederacy of 1763–1764. The Shawnees and Delawares also decided to seek the assistance of the native nations south of the Ohio River: the seven thousand Cherokees, the thirteen thousand Muskogees, and the Chickasaws and Choctaws, who had a combined population of about fifteen thousand. These populous nations would enable the new league to mount the most resolute resistance the British had ever faced.[39]

But could the Shawnees and Delawares actually draw any southerners into their coalition? Pontiac and his cohorts had not even tried, and it was easy to see why. The southern nations often went to war with each other. For instance, between 1765 and 1771, an on-again, off-again conflict pitting the Muskogees against the Choctaws had claimed at least six hundred lives. In addition, the native nations living on the opposite banks of the Ohio River had raided each other's towns for decades.[40]

Then on May 8, 1765, Overhill Cherokees passing through western Virginia on their way north to raid the Upper Ohioans were attacked near the town of Staunton by twenty to thirty Virginians, who killed six of them. Virginia's leaders anticipated devastating revenge raids. Instead, Attakullakulla or Little Carpenter, a gifted Cherokee diplomat, asked the British for restitution in an unusual form: they must use their enormous political and economic influence to help the Cherokees make peace, both with the Upper Ohio Indians that their war party had been en route to attack and with the Iroquois. Royal officials agreed, and by the end of 1768 both disputes had been settled.[41]

After the "Charroky paice," the Shawnee promoters of an anti-British confederacy "inlarged thire plan," recruiting not only Cherokees but also other southern natives. For decades, a host of native nations had fought over Kentucky, prompting an Overhill Cherokee headman named Tsi'yu-gûnsini (Dragging Canoe) to refer to the region as "the bloody Ground."[42] But now that British colonists had set their sights on

Kentucky, the natives' overlapping claims to the region might actually seal their alliance.

The Upper Ohioans' recruitment of southern Indians began in the spring of 1769, when they persuaded six visiting Cherokees to send "a vast number of long Speeches" as well as "Two Belts, and Several Strings of Wampum" beads to their old enemies north of the Ohio River. By the end of the year, a deputation of Shawnees and Delawares had made a diplomatic tour of the southern nations, where they "complained much of encroachments upon their lands and of the Extensive cession obtained by Sir William Johnson from the Six Nations," as Johnson's southern counterpart, John Stuart, learned.[43]

The specter of a costly woodlands war against a united bloc of indigenous nations had frightened British officials first into leaving ten thousand troops in North America in 1763 and then into prohibiting colonial settlement and speculation west of the Appalachian Mountains. Now that the natives seemed to be building their broadest anti-British coalition yet, would they once again influence the British empire's approach to the American West?

CHAPTER 9

The Music of the Wheels

1769

ON AUGUST 1, 1768, BOSTON MERCHANTS REVIVED THE IDEA OF boycotting British merchandise. They noted that they had plunged deep into debt, as a result not only of parliamentary taxes and trade restrictions but also "the bad success of our Cod Fishery this season and the discouraging prospect of the Whale Fishery." In response, they agreed to stop importing the merchandise covered by the Townshend duties until they were repealed—and most other goods until December 31, 1769, no matter what Parliament did.[1] The boycotters' equal emphasis on economic and political concerns should warn us against any effort to explain the American Revolution in strictly ideological terms.

This time, the movement caught on. On March 10, 1769, Philadelphia merchants yielded to pressure from neighbors like Hannah Griffitts and joined up. By the end of March, the boycott had reached George Washington, who shared the northern merchants' conviction that it would benefit Americans economically as well as politically. He explained to George Mason, his neighbor just down the Potomac River, that while a Virginian trapped in debt could theoretically just curtail his expenses, it was actually not that easy. "For how can I, *says he*, who have lived in such & such a manner change my method? I am ashamed to do it." So to keep up appearances, he keeps on spending beyond his means until his exasperated creditors force him to sell everything he owns. But an anti-British boycott would allow this "extravagant & expensive man" to forgo his luxury while preserving his honor, since it would give him "a pretext to live within bounds."[2]

Washington soon found a chance to propagate the boycott. In January 1769, the Duke of Bedford, furious at colonial jurors for not punishing their neighbors for rioting against stamp distributors and customs agents, proposed a remedy. Back in the 1544, under Henry VIII, Parliament had decreed that English subjects accused of treason while living overseas could be brought home for trial. Bedford wanted to use this long-forgotten statute to have Boston's 1768 rioters tried in England, and early the following year the Lords and Commons endorsed the idea. On May 16, the Virginia House of Burgesses denounced Bedford's plan and other parliamentary encroachments, and the next day Governor Botetourt dissolved the assembly. The former representatives walked down Duke of Gloucester Street to Raleigh Tavern, where they unanimously endorsed nonimportation.[3]

The Virginians modified the plan they had received from the north to fit their own needs. Instead of imposing a blanket boycott and then enumerating exceptions, as northerners had, they identified several dozen items—mostly luxuries—that they would not purchase and allowed everything else in. Their one addition to the prohibited list was African slaves.[4]

Like northern merchants the previous year, traders in Charles Town, South Carolina, balked at a protest tactic that would deprive them of their livelihood. Since the business community's *"private interest* is *glaringly* against us," Christopher Gadsden reasoned in an anonymous *South-Carolina Gazette* essay, leadership would have to come from the city's mechanicks (artisans). In the previous year's assembly election, three of the six artisan-backed candidates won seats, and Charles Town's was arguably the most powerful artisan community in America. Meeting on July 3 and 4, the mechanicks announced a boycott of British merchandise, enslaved Africans, and expensive funerals—and also a pledge to patronize American manufactures. Both agreements would be enforced by a committee comprising merchants, artisans, and planters: thirteen of each.[5]

MALES IN EVERY COLONY understood that the success of the anti-British boycott would "depend greatly upon the female sex," since both genders had indulged in the century's consumer revolution. Moreover, American women had always turned imported British fabric into clothing, and for nonimportation to succeed, they would now need to produce cloth as well. Never in history had there been a time, a *Boston Evening-Post* essayist declared, when "the spinning wheel could more influence the affairs of men."[6]

Thousands of women embraced this new role. Charity Clarke, a New York City teenager, told an English cousin that she "felt Nationly"

Saxony spinning wheel

knitting stockings from homespun yarn. She imagined imperial officials finally succumbing to "a fighting army of amazones . . . armed with spinning wheels."[7] Some families that had gotten rid of their spinning wheels or never owned one now set about obtaining them. John Parker, the farmer who would command the Lexington militia on the town common on April 19, 1775, was also a woodworker. In previous years he had received orders for two or three flax wheels, but in 1767 he sold nine and in 1768, *eighteen*. Early in 1769, women revived the practice of assembling with their spinning wheels in a tavern or, more often, at the local minister's house, in which case, "after the musick of the wheels was over," the host treated the "daughters of Liberty" to dinner and a sermon on the virtue of hard work. Some of the gatherings attracted "many Spectators of both Sexes"; Rev. Ezra Stiles estimated the audience at his spinning bee at six hundred. Many of the events were described as "spinning match[es]," with the highest praise reserved for the woman—or girl; participants ranged as young as eleven—who could spin the most thread in a single day. Towns also competed against each other. Newspapers reported the totals but seldom named participants other than the male host, such being the custom when ladies, as opposed to women, made news.[8]

Just in the last six months of 1769, a single Boston newspaper reported on twenty-eight spinning matches. But these events could not begin to make up for the vast quantity of cloth that the colonies ordinarily imported from the mother country; nor were they intended to. Their real purpose was to combat middle- and upper-class women's prejudice against the spinning wheel. Already by this time, the term *spinster* had acquired its colloquial, and disparaging, alternate definition: the never-wed woman who rotated among married kin and contributed to her upkeep by working the wheel. More broadly, most women associated spinning with either poverty or backwoods isolation, and the matches were designed to enhance its respectability.[9] A report on the December 19, 1767, "spinning entertainment" in Providence, Rhode Island, emphasized that the participants belonged to "as good families as any in town." Two years earlier, during the struggle against the Stamp Act, a writer in the same city had rejoiced to see so many women consider it "no disgrace to turn the spinning wheel." (It was equally gratifying to hear that men as well as women found "no disgrace" in giving up fancy clothes.)[10]

Americans who yearned to participate in the boycott of British finery, whether as customers or spinners, were constrained by their fear of losing status, and the solution in both cases was to do it together.

Sometimes male writers' tributes to the spinners exhibited less than flattering assumptions about women in general. A Boston newspaper reported that sixteen young women in Huntington, Long Island, had "met to spend the day together, not in idle dissipation, (as is too often the case,) but with a truly laudable design of promoting industry."[11] In September 1769, a South Carolinian using the pseudonym "Frileuthras" addressed an open letter to "The Fair Sex of South-Carolina," accusing them of considering themselves too good to spin, even though "Ladies of the very first Rank among the ancient Greeks, Romans, and other polite Nations" had done so with pride. Frileuthras's lecture elicited a tart reply from an anonymous woman writer who noted that men's dissipations—from gambling on horses and gamecocks to the "intemperate Use of Spirituous Liquors"—wasted far more time and money than women's "innocent Amusements" such as visiting each other at day's end or attending the occasional fancy-dress ball. But she did not deny her adversary's claim that women disdained the spinning wheel. Until men "shew us *better* EXAMPLES of OEconomy, than many of them have hitherto done," she concluded, "we shall not think ourselves obliged to wear out our Fingers, either by *carding* or *spining*."[12]

This writer, who signed herself "Margery Distaff—Conditionally," was not alone. In the south, the association between spinning and enslavement was so strong that there is no record of female Whigs ever holding a spinning bee.[13]

Black women were another matter. White southerners exhorted their neighbors to prod their human property to step up textile production. Certainly these women had the skills; already those who worked in gentry homes like Mount Vernon and Monticello spent at least as much time sewing as they did cooking, waiting table, and cleaning. Free southern women supported the Whig cause by attending social events "apparelled in Virginia growth"—that is, in slave-made cloth. A member of the Virginia House of Burgesses, Robert Wormeley Carter, asked his father,

Landon, to let his slave Winey know how many compliments he had received on the suit she had made for him.[14]

Some slaveholders who ordered their enslaved workers to spin and weave encountered resistance. James Hill, George Washington's steward, reported that a spinner on the New Kent County estate that Martha Custis brought to their marriage insisted that mistress and slave had agreed on a quota of only three pounds of wool per week. In addition, Hill wrote, an enslaved woman named Old Nanney "wont Spin a thread & Says her Mistress left her only to Sew."[15]

CROWDS IN NEW YORK and Boston spent much of 1769 brawling with British soldiers. In New York, the controversy centered on the liberty pole that Whigs erected in March 1766 to celebrate the repeal of the Stamp Act. This sixty-eight-foot ship's mast carried special symbolism for the working people who put it up, and when redcoats stationed nearby chopped it down, Whigs rebuilt it, with blacksmiths adding iron hoops. Down it came again, then back up, a process that continued until an early 1770 incident known as the Battle of Golden Hill, in which a New Yorker was stabbed to death.[16]

Pierre Eugène du Simitière, raising of a liberty pole in New York City in 1770.
(*Courtesy of The Library Company of Philadelphia*)

New Yorkers also had to contend with internal enemies. Eighty-year-old lieutenant governor Cadwallader Colden took the place of the deceased Governor Moore and struck a deal with the De Lancey faction that ruled the provincial legislature, allowing it to issue paper money in return for its complying with the Quartering Act and paying him his full salary. New Yorkers were furious—none so much as Alexander McDougall, who had immigrated with his family from the desolate Scottish island of Islay at the age of six and then worked in his father's milk business before making his fortune during the Seven Years' War as a privateer. McDougall published a pamphlet denouncing the assembly's corrupt bargain, prompting legislative leaders to investigate him for seditious libel and imprison him twice, for a total of 162 days. Supporters compared McDougall to John Wilkes, the wildly popular English radical who had been briefly jailed on a general warrant, akin to a general writ of assistance, for criticizing George Grenville; Wilkes was repeatedly elected to the House of Commons, which would not seat him. When McDougall finally emerged from prison, he immediately took command of the New York crowd, despite a speech impediment so severe that the few times he spoke in public, he had to state each point twice.[17]

The first two army regiments requested by Boston's customs agents landed on October 1, 1768. Less than two weeks later, Whigs introduced an occasional publication, the *Journal of the Times*, chronicling the troops' alleged crimes, from gang rape to "advising several Negro Slaves in the Town to beat, abuse and cut their Masters Throats, promising them as a Reward . . . to make them free."[18] The redcoats' arrival also affected Bostonians' finances. Recognizing that enlisted men earned too little to live on, officers allowed them, when off-duty, to take odd jobs. They thus competed with local laborers, even as favored merchants received lucrative contracts to supply the army with necessities such as food and fuel. The divergent economic impacts of military occupation complicated the cheek-by-jowl intimacy of cramming an army of two thousand men and several hundred camp women (mostly soldiers' wives but in many cases also army employees) into a city of two thousand families on a narrow peninsula.[19]

The soldiers' arrival stiffened the spines of Boston merchants who opposed nonimportation. A handful, including Ame and Elizabeth Cuming, never subscribed to the association. Thomas Hutchinson's sons held out longer than most but finally surrendered and signed.

The senior Hutchinson, who became acting governor upon Francis Bernard's departure for England in August 1769, was an avid student of Massachusetts history, and he accused his countrymen of treating nonassociators just as they had earlier eccentrics, including his "Antinomian" ancestor, Anne Hutchinson. "The frenzy was not higher when they banished my pious great grandmother, when they hanged the Quakers, [or] when they afterwards hanged the poor innocent witches," he wrote.[20]

Boston printer and bookseller John Mein claimed the boycott had forced him to reduce both his own workforce and his purchases from the local paper mill. He also used Custom House records to expose Whigs who surreptitiously violated the association. John Hancock, he claimed, had imported one hundred pieces of British linen. Assaulted by a crowd and threatened with worse, Mein sought a brighter future in England.[21]

Theophilus Lillie not only refused to sign the association but accused its promoters of violating the Golden Rule. "It always seemed strange to me," he told readers of the *Boston News-Letter*, "that people who contend so much for civil and religious Liberty should be so ready to deprive others of their natural liberty." On February 22, 1770, an angry crowd or mob consisting mostly of boys gathered outside Lillie's shop in the North End. When a onetime customs informer named Ebenezer Richardson came to his neighbor's defense, the boys chased him back into his house and proceeded to pelt the building with sticks and rocks, breaking every window. When a stone struck Richardson's wife, he fired his musket into the crowd, killing ten-year-old Christopher Seider. The crowd laid hold of Richardson, beat him, and nearly lynched him before hustling him off to jail. Meanwhile town leaders organized a funeral for young Seider: six boys carried his coffin to the Old Granary burial ground, accompanied by another five hundred youngsters and at least two thousand adults.[22]

Killing of Christopher Seider

＊　　＊　　＊

DESPITE RESISTANCE FROM PEOPLE like Lillie and the Cuming sisters, the Whigs succeeded at enforcing their boycott. New England merchants imported two-thirds less British merchandise in 1769 than the previous year, and New Yorkers' purchases went from £490,673 in 1768 to just £75,930 in 1769. Yet nonimportation did not have the desired effect on the mother country's manufacturers and merchants. By 1768, only about 16 percent of Britain's exports went to North America, and supply contracts arising from the Russo-Turkish War, as well as a surge in German demand for British woolens, allowed the British to make up much of what they lost in America. Still, many British merchants suffered. Most glaringly, slave traders estimated that free colonists' pledge not to buy Africans had cost them £300,000.[23]

On May 1, 1769, British cabinet ministers asked Parliament to repeal most of the Townshend duties. Yet in what would prove to be one of the most consequential one-vote margins in American history, the cabinet voted, five to four, to keep the tax on tea. The ministry's incomplete turnabout carried some of the same ambiguity as Rockingham's decision, four years earlier, to couple the repeal of the Stamp Act with a declaration of Parliament's sovereignty over the North American colonies. But the Declaratory Act had been entirely symbolic, while tea accounted for three-quarters of the revenue arising from the Townshend duties.[24] Colonists saw partial repeal as a ploy to break nonimportation, and Bostonians tried to counter it with a new association specifically targeting tea—and also closing a crucial loophole. All tea came from the same Chinese province, Fukien (now Fujian), and the same plant, *Camellia sinensis*. No one could say whether any given quantity had passed through Britain in violation of the boycott or been "honestly smuggled" in by the Dutch. So on January 23, 1770, a group of mostly male Bostonians vowed not to drink tea of any kind "upon *any pretence whatever*." Eight days later, Boston women, acknowledging that they had been "reproached for not being so ready as could be desired, to lend our Assistance" to nonimportation, also agreed to forgo tea. They circulated this pledge door-to-door, and eventually 536 women signed it. But eighteenth-century wives' and mothers' responsibilities included health care, and Boston's female associators considered tea a medicine, so in defiance of the men's categorial ban, they made an exception for sickness, one that numerous female healers invoked.[25]

Boston women defied the Whig leadership in another way as well.

Males thought they should boycott not only Britain's merchandise but its men, refusing to intermarry or even dance with the officers and soldiers of the occupying army. But the historian Serena Zabin estimates that about forty Boston women married British officers and soldiers between 1768 and 1772.[26]

On January 26, 1770, a ministerial defeat in the perennial parliamentary quarrel over John Wilkes and the apparent suicide of a member of the cabinet prompted the Duke of Grafton to resign as first lord of the treasury. His replacement was Frederick, Lord North—a man who almost certainly would have failed at modern politics. "Nothing could be more coarse or clumsy or ungracious than his outside," Horace Walpole wrote of him, be it his "two large prominent eyes that rolled about to no purpose" or his "wide mouth, thick lips, and inflated visage." But North had served on the Treasury Board for six years, and his command of government finance approached that of George Grenville. He was witty, often at his own expense. Asked once if he knew the unattractive woman across the room, he replied, "It is my wife, and we are reckoned the ugliest couple in London." (The two had seven children over their thirty-six-year marriage.) Awkward but eloquent and indomitable, North calls to mind another Anglophone whose elevation sparked a rebellion that he prosecuted to its conclusion, despite similarly lapsing into melancholy upon every report of mass casualties, Abraham Lincoln.[27]

In March 1770, North carried out his predecessor's pledge to have Parliament repeal all of Townshend's taxes except the one on tea. Already George Evans, master of the Liverpool-based snow *Sally*, had placed his bet that North Americans would soon resume their imports. The shutdown of the African slave trade had created a severe labor shortage in Charles Town, South Carolina, so on May 2, Capt. Evans brought the *Sally*, carrying 345 West Africans, over the sandbar into Charleston Harbor and asked local Whigs to let him remain until they revoked their slave import ban. But Parliament had not yet repealed any of the Townshend duties, so after two weeks of back-and-forth, the Whigs ordered Evans out to sea, and he steered his vessel down the coast to Savannah, where merchants had never stopped importing slaves. While he and the Whig leadership argued over the Africans' fate, five of them had died.[28]

A Charles Town newspaper warned that any and all South Carolinians who rode down to Savannah to purchase slaves from Capt. Evans would be treated as "Enemies to the Liberties of America."[29]

CHAPTER 10

———•◦•———

Town Born, Turn Out!

1770–1772

A N EIGHTEENTH-CENTURY OCEANGOING VESSEL REQUIRED HUN-
dreds of yards of hempen rope, and Boston, as a major shipbuilding center, was home to several ropewalks. An off-duty British soldier,
probably Pvt. Patrick Walker of the 29th Regiment, was walking past one
of them, owned by John Gray, on Friday, March 2, 1770, when he was
hailed by a journeyman named William Green.

"Soldier, do you want work?"

"Yes, I do, faith," an excited Walker replied.

"Well, then go and clean my shithouse."[1]

Walker lunged. Green's coworkers, who shared his anxiety about
moonlighting soldiers taking their jobs, pushed Walker to the ground.
The private retreated to his barracks, only to return with thirty to forty
club-wielding compatriots, led by a tall Black drummer who shared his
last name: Thomas Walker. As the redcoats passed the home of a local
judge, he yelled down to their leader, "You black rascal, what have you
to do with white people's quarrels?"

"I suppose I may look on," he replied.[2]

The ropeworkers grabbed clubs, including the "wouldring sticks"
they used in beating braided rope tight, and found reinforcements of
their own. After a smart skirmish, the soldiers withdrew. The troops
and townsmen fought again the next day, a Saturday. Everyone expected
further violence after the Sabbath, and each side would later accuse the
other of premeditating an attack. But the next dispute actually arose over
a disputed barber's bill.[3]

On the morning of March 5, Capt.-Lt. John Goldfinch of the 14th
Regiment went to wigmaker John Piemont, on King Street, for a shave
and a haircut. Piemont had a redcoat working for him part-time, but

amid growing tensions between soldiers and civilians, he contemptuously fobbed Goldfinch off on an apprentice. The officer accepted the haircut but reciprocated the insult by walking off without paying.[4] That night, another of Piemont's apprentices, Edward Gerrish (or Garrick), spotted Goldfinch farther up King Street, near the Custom House, and shouted, "There goes the fellow who hath not paid my master for dressing his hair."[5] Goldfinch refused the bait, but Hugh White, the private standing sentry in front of the Custom House, defended him, telling the boy he was "a gentleman, and if he owes you anything he will pay it."[6]

A gentleman? Gerrish retorted that "there was none in the Regiment."[7]

White swung his musket, striking Gerrish's head and causing him to "reel and stagger, and cry much."[8] Apprentices descended on the Custom House, and people started ringing church bells, in those days a call to the bucket brigade. It was now about 9 p.m. — hours past sunset — and as the streets began to fill, the crowd around White taunted him. "Damned rascally Scoundrel Lobster Son of a Bitch," some yelled, referring to the army's policy of whipping refractory soldiers until their bloodied backs were as red as a lobster.[9]

The unnerved White banged on the door of the Custom House, but the residents, government officials and their families, dared not unbar the door. Finally the sentry yelled "Turn out *Main Guard*" — a desperate appeal to the soldiers at army headquarters just up King Street. A member of the crowd also sought reinforcements, repeatedly yelling "*Town born*, turn out."[10]

The officer of the day was the Irish-born Capt. Thomas Preston, who ran to the Main Guard to assemble a rescue team. His first thought was for White, but he also worried that the crowd would break into the Custom House and rob the king's revenue. Soon Preston and seven grenadiers — men recruited into the British army for their immense height, essential to their traditional task of hurling grenades — reached White and formed a semicircle. At least three of Preston's soldiers had participated in the ropewalk affrays of March 2 and 3, as had many of the boys and men in the crowd, which had grown to around 125 with the arrival of twenty to thirty merchant mariners, many armed with clubs.

Like the redcoats who had assaulted Gray's ropewalk three days earlier, the Jack Tars had a nonwhite leader, one who would appear neither in Paul Revere's engraving of this night's events nor in the Henry Pelham engraving that Revere plagiarized. Crispus Attucks, a six foot two dockworker, was apparently the son of an African American father and a Native American mother. Many of Attucks's followers wielded two clubs, and as they repeatedly struck them together, the ominous staccato could be heard over the church bells. Months later, one of the soldiers' defense attorneys said the crowd had also been "making the mob whistle as they call it, which . . . when made by a multitude, is a most hideous shriek, almost as terrible as an Indian yell."[11]

Boston's streets were paved with oyster shells, and soon the crowd was winging these at the soldiers, along with snowballs, chunks of ice,

Paul Revere, *Bloody [Boston] Massacre* (1770)

and large sticks, one of which struck Pvt. Hugh Montgomery, sending him toward the ground. As he regained his footing, Montgomery fired his musket, and Crispus Attucks fell dead.[12]

Some of the civilians present that night later claimed that Capt. Preston had commanded his men to fire. But Preston acknowledged only that Montgomery *thought* he had heard such an order, because a carpenter in the crowd was taunting the captain with, "Why do you not fire? God damn you, fire!"[13]

After Montgomery discharged his weapon, there followed an interval of about thirty seconds—plenty of time for Preston to order his other soldiers to hold their fire. But he gave no clear command, and they released a volley. Some witnesses would later claim that Montgomery's compatriots had taken his shot as a signal to fire; others said seeing Attucks fall enraged the townspeople, causing them to shower the soldiers with everything at hand, in turn provoking their fusillade. In an instant, two more men lay dead: Samuel Gray (no relation to John Gray, but a worker at his ropewalk) and James Caldwell. Two others were mortally wounded. One, Samuel Maverick, was an innocent bystander who was leaving the scene when a ball ricocheted off the ground and struck him in the hip. The other was a leatherworker and—surprisingly enough, given Boston's history—Roman Catholic named Patrick Carr. He lingered for ten days, stating before he died that "he did not blame the man whoever he was, that shot him," since the soldiers had fired in self-defense. Six other men were wounded.[14]

Conferring later that night, Governor Hutchinson and Lt. Col. William Dalrymple, commander of the troops in Boston, agreed to transfer his men from Boston to Castle William, on an island three miles southeast of town. The superior court agreed to postpone the shooters' trials until autumn in hopes passions would cool. John Adams took the soldiers' case, demonstrating that even redcoats could get a fair trial in Boston. His friend Josiah Quincy had previously made the same bold choice, but neither found it as unpopular as he might have anticipated. In June, Boston elected Adams to the legislature. The prosecution team was headed by Josiah Quincy's brother Samuel. As the colony's solicitor general, he, like his brother and attorney Adams, represented the side that he opposed politically.[15]

Historians of the Boston Massacre too often ignore its economic roots. The reason the army had occupied the town—and placed a guard at the Custom House—was that Bostonians had rioted against customs agents, especially on March 18 and June 10, 1768.[16] And the riots had come in response to Britain's increased enforcement of its merchants' and sugar planters' monopoly of North American trade, especially the molasses market. Even after off-duty soldiers joined Boston's labor pool, they might in a stronger economy have posed less of a threat to local workers, possibly preventing the brawl at Gray's ropewalk that lit the fuse for the King Street riot three days later. Christopher Seider, too, was as much an economic as a political martyr, since he died helping enforce a nonimportation association aimed in part at relieving Boston's distress.

Grafton and North had bet that if Parliament repealed all but one of the Townshend duties, as it finally did on April 12, it could break the colonial boycott of British merchandise. Sure enough, early in July, New York merchants informed their counterparts in the other seaports that they had sent orders to their British suppliers. Princeton students spoke for other Whigs when they ceremoniously burned the New Yorkers' letter. One protester, nineteen-year-old James Madison, thereby commenced a political career that would span sixty-six years. Angry Philadelphians considered boycotting New York, but they and other colonists could not or would not carry on the fight while their competitors went back to making money, and soon most were importing everything but tea.[17]

ON AUGUST 14, AS Bostonians commemorated the fifth anniversary of the riot that drove stamp distributor Andrew Oliver from office, George Whitefield came to town on his seventh American tour. Although his asthma had recently flared up, the great itinerant preached at least once a day for the next three weeks. Gen. Gage described pro-Parliament, Bostonians as rejoicing that Whitefield was "preaching up Subordination to Government, and Obedience to the Laws," but no one who actually heard his sermons described them that way. Whitefield was scheduled to speak in Newburyport, thirty-five miles north of Boston, on September 30, but the previous night he had an asthma attack, and by 6 a.m., he was dead.[18]

Colonists mourned Whitefield as a friend both to true religion and North America. In "the last Sermon I heard him preach," John Adams's wife, Abigail, informed an English cousin, "he told us that he had been a very great traveller, yet he had never seen so much of the real appearance of Religion in any Country, as in America."[19] Whitefield felt real sympathy for the colonists, wrote the African-born poet Phillis Wheatley, who had been brought to Boston in chains in 1761.

When his AMERICANS were burden'd sore,
When streets were crimson'd with their guiltless gore!
Unrival'd friendship in his breast now strove:
The fruit thereof was charity and love
Towards *America*.[20]

Wheatley imagined White-
field reaching out to African
Americans, encouraging them
by vouching for God's color
blindness:

Take HIM ye *Africans*, he
    longs for you;
Impartial SAVIOUR, is his
    title due:
If you chuse to walk in
    grace's road,
You shall be sons, and
    kings, and priests to
    GOD.[21]

Wheatley had published
her first verse in Rhode Island
three years earlier, apparently

Scipio Moorhead[?], *Phillis Wheatley* (1773)

through the offices of Sarah Osborn. But her "elegiac poem" on Whitefield, printed as a broadside, marked the real beginning of her public
career. It concluded with an apostrophe to Whitefield's patron, the
Countess of Huntingdon. Wheatley sent her a copy, thus initiating a
lifelong collaboration.[22]

Phillis Wheatley could scarcely have been more different from Hermon Husband, the ex-Anglican and ex-Quaker then picking fights with
the powerful in rural North Carolina. Yet for both of these once obscure
Americans, George Whitefield had loosened the lid.

Capt. Thomas Preston's trial in the Massachusetts superior court
ran from October 24 to October 30 but effectively ended the first day,
when defense attorneys managed to seat five strong supporters of the
royal government as jurors. The panel took only three hours to find

Preston innocent. The enlisted men's trial, which opened on November 27, did not go so smoothly. Several admitted to firing their weapons, and unlike Preston, they faced an unbiased jury. But they had brilliant and determined lawyers in John Adams and Josiah Quincy. Adams described Crispus Attucks, the martyred Whig leader, as a "a stout Molatto fellow, whose very looks, was enough to terrify any person" and who had led a "motley rabble" of other "negroes and molattoes," as well as "saucy boys," "Irish teagues" (a Gaelic-derived epithet roughly equivalent to *Micks*) and "out landish jack tarrs"—British seamen who were not actually British.[23]

Jurors later revealed that they wanted to convict all eight defendants of manslaughter, but the defense proved that one soldier had not fired, and no one knew which. So the only guilty verdicts were against the two men who had indisputably discharged their weapons. The prescribed punishment for manslaughter was execution, but ancient English custom allowed female as well as male defendants convicted for the first time of lesser crimes than murder to plead "benefit of clergy," falsely claiming to be priests and thereby escaping the noose. But to alert any future court that they had used up their one reprieve, each was branded with an M on his right thumb.[24]

Every year from 1771 to 1783, Boston's town fathers asked a distinguished orator to commemorate the unprovoked attack on their fellow citizens. In 1773, they invited John Adams, but he prudently declined.[25]

A month after the massacre trials, Samuel Cooper, one of Boston's leading ministers, believed he had discerned "a Pause in Politics." Most historians concur, calling the years from 1770 to 1772 the "quiet period." Now that Britain had pulled the troops out of Boston, reduced the molasses duty to a penny a gallon, and repealed the Stamp Act and all but one of the Townshend duties, most free colonists appear to have reconciled themselves to the taxation without representation and other imperial interference that remained.[26]

Another reason for improving relations between Parliament and the North American colonies was that colonial economic conditions improved. Between 1771 and 1774, provincials imported 62 percent more merchandise from Britain than during the previous four years. In the Chesapeake colonies, tobacco prices rallied, boosting the importation of African slaves as well.[27] But even as free colonists made peace with the crown, violence among Americans intensified.

* * *

By 1770, THE REGULATOR rebellions in North and South Carolina had taken different paths. Seven South Carolina insurgents won seats in the Commons House, where they obtained redress for several grievances. The North Carolina revolt might also have been settled amicably, since in July 1769 voters elected Hermon Husband and a half dozen other rebellion sympathizers to the assembly. But the new representatives' most urgent demands were ignored.[28]

North Carolina's superior court, which had repeatedly put off prosecuting officeholders accused of extortion, rode circuit. On the morning of September 24, 1770, a single justice, Richard Henderson, was about to open proceedings in Hillsborough when about 150 farmers burst into the courtroom, demanding that he immediately begin trying extortionists—and not with a jury packed in their favor. He refused, whereupon the insurgents attacked Hillsborough's merchants, county officials, and lawyers with the same weapons South Carolina Regulators had wielded against livestock rustlers: fists and whips. To these farmers, "Extortioners and Exactors of taxes [were] certainly more dangerous" than any "Gang of Horse Thieves."[29]

No one suffered worse that day, and the next, than Edmund Fanning. The rebels "struck him with their whips and clubs, kicked him, and spit and spurned at him" before gutting his home. After Justice Henderson fled Hillsborough, the crowd took over the courthouse. There they found a Black man taken from his owner for an unpaid debt, and they made him play the role of attorney in a mock trial of county officers. Before leaving town, the Regulators filled the judge's chair with excrement, ransacked several stores, and broke nearly every window in town.[30]

On January 15, 1771, the provincial assembly adopted a Riot Act. Alleged rioters, including those who had sacked Hillsborough four months earlier, could be hauled before any court in the colony. If they did not appear, they would automatically be found guilty of a felony and outlawed, making it "lawful to and for any Person to kill and destroy" them. The legislation also authorized Governor Tryon to raise an army, and he personally led 1,185 militiamen west toward Orange County.[31]

On May 16, at Great Alamance Creek near the present-day town of Burlington, the governor's soldiers clashed with an estimated two to three thousand Regulators. The insurgents' numerical advantage was canceled out by their lack of artillery or leadership. When one man was asked to take charge, he replied that "We are all free men; and every

one must command himself."
Nine government soldiers
were killed and sixty-one
were wounded, but the Regulators lost twice as many: up
to twenty dead and more than
a hundred wounded. The rest
fled. A month after the battle,
twelve captured Regulators
were found guilty of violating the Riot Act. Tryon pardoned six. Those chosen for
hanging were first allowed
to make dying speeches from
atop their barrels, but the moment James Pugh began cat-
aloguing Edmund Fanning's
crimes, the governor had his
barrel kicked away.[32]

Roadside marker commemorating
North Carolina Regulators

Tryon was unable to pun-
ish Pugh's brother-in-law, Hermon Husband, whom he considered the
chief insurgent, for he had fled the province under an assumed name,
"Tuscape Death."[33]

MEANWHILE NATIVE AMERICANS ON either side of the Ohio River diplomatic divide kept working on uniting against the colonists. The obstacles were numerous, but the coalition builders were creative. Starting in
the summer of 1769, northern and southern nations held a grand conference every year near the mouth of the Scioto River, a northern tributary
of the Ohio. The sessions took place in early August, during the Green
Corn Ceremony, a widely practiced ritual of purification, celebration,
and reconciliation that struck organizers as the perfect opportunity to
bury former animosities.[34] Just as powerful as religion in promoting
pan-Indian unity was the fiction of race. A Shawnee diplomat told participants in one conference, "Have only the same mind, all of you who
Inhabit the same Continent, and are of the same Colour."[35]

British spies, especially cultural hybrids such as Alexander McKee,
impressed their superiors with their skill at penetrating the First Nations' "secret councils . . . in the woods." But it seems likely that the na-

tive rebels actually wanted the British to know what they were up to. If the mere threat of a massive—and, for both sides, costly—Anglo-native war intimidated the British into keeping their colonists out of Kentucky and the adjacent regions, then the indigenous insurgents could accomplish their designs without subjecting their fragile coalition to a trial of strength. When the Shawnee chief Red Hawk sent Indian agent George Croghan a message regarding an upcoming meeting about his nation's territorial grievances, he pointedly added that there would be "Chiefs from the Southren Indians as well as from all the Western Nations to speak to him at that time." After receiving Red Hawk's message, Croghan observed that the Shawnees "Seem[ed] to gaskinade or T[h]reaten."[36]

The native rebels accomplished their goal, at least for the moment. British leaders turned down the Virginia House of Burgesses' petition for Kentucky and the adjacent region, and they stood by the Proclamation Line of 1763. The home government's ban on western expansion affected speculators and actual settlers differently. As an anonymous newspaper writer pointed out, "not even a second Chinese wall, unless guarded by a million of soldiers, could prevent the settlement of the lands on Ohio and its dependencies." And North American colonists further eased their way onto the Native Americans' land by refusing to pay for the troops stationed on their frontier. Once Parliament repealed the Stamp Act, its leaders reduced American expenses by evacuating all but the most vital western forts.[37] Now it was simpler than ever to glide across the home government's imaginary boundary.

Speculators were a different matter. Against them, the Proclamation of 1763, like the stamp duties that Parliament had tried to levy on legal documents, executed itself. Men like Thomas Jefferson and Patrick Henry could not profit from trans-Appalachian land because they could not obtain title to it. In filtering out speculators while allowing actual settlers to flow on west, the Proclamation actually helped the so-called squatters, since no one could make them pay for their land. (To be sure, many settlers also dabbled in speculation.)[38]

Then in the summer of 1772, the battle over the Indians' land took an unexpected turn. For nearly a decade, an assemblage of Pennsylvania speculators had campaigned for an enormous land grant in the Upper Ohio Valley. At the notorious Fort Stanwix treaty congress of 1768, the Iroquois set aside two million acres of the land they ceded for the Pennsylvania partners. Since then, the leading member of the group, Samuel

Wharton, had been in London lobbying for imperial confirmation of the grant. He offered to pick up the £10,460 tab for the Stanwix deed and distributed shares in his company to influential Londoners such as Lords Gower and Rochford (both in the cabinet), George Grenville (who unhelpfully died in 1770), and banker and Member of Parliament Thomas Walpole. The firm became known as the Walpole Associates, and its petition triggered vehement opposition, both from well-to-do Virginians with claims on the same land and from Lord Hillsborough, the American secretary, who worried that the projected settlement would drain population away not only from Britain but from Ireland, where he rented out most of his nearly 100,000 acres. (He was "terribly *afraid of dispeopling Ireland*," Benjamin Franklin claimed.) Hillsborough also warned that whites who settled in the region would place themselves outside the ambit of British merchants and soldiers and that they would provoke a "general Indian War, the expense whereof will fall on this Kingdom."[39]

Hillsborough deployed a clever stratagem against the Walpole Associates, advising Wharton and his partners to expand their request tenfold, to twenty million acres—enough to form a new inland colony, to be called Vandalia in honor of Queen Charlotte, who was said to be descended from the Vandals. He figured that tentupling the acreage would entail a tenfold increase in the purchase price as well—and that the Walpole Associates would never come up with £100,000. Hillsborough was dumbfounded when, in January 1770, the Lords of the Treasury agreed to charge the Walpole Associates only the £10,000 they had initially offered. He should not have been so surprised; both treasury secretaries were also associates.[40]

Hillsborough and the Board of Trade were able to stall the Vandalia grant for two and a half years, but finally, in August 1772, the Privy Council gave its approval. Left holding "the shitten end of the stick," Hillsborough resigned.[41] But the struggle was not over.

THE REGULATOR REBELLIONS IN the Carolinas had broken out in the late 1760s, when southern staples were selling well, and that warns us against any simple linkage between hard times and insurgency. On the other hand, the recession that began in 1772, one of the worst of the colonial era, would powerfully influence relations between the colonies and the crown. The downturn had multiple origins, including shady banking practices in England and Scotland and a credit-fueled expansion of Chesapeake tobacco production that glutted the market. But the trigger was the escape of Alexander Fordyce.

Born in Scotland, Fordyce had moved to London, speculated in stock, and amassed a fortune, most of which he invested in a bank that he founded with three associates. Like the many other private banks that cropped up all over Britain in the 1760s, Neale, James, Fordyce, and Down courted investment from Britons who had earned more money than they knew what to do with as Seven Years' War contractors. For example, Richard Oswald, who would negotiate peace with the rebel colonies in 1782, had supplied bread to British and allied troops in Germany in the late 1750s, earning upward of £100,000. In the winter of 1771–1772, Fordyce went all in on a decrease in the value of East India Company stock that did not materialize, at least not soon enough for Fordyce, who covered his losses by dipping into his bank's funds. Meanwhile, early in 1772, the Bank of England grew anxious about the depletion of its cash reserves and stopped accepting bills of exchange from most of its clients, especially Jews who traded with Amsterdam and Scots like Fordyce. Unable to meet his obligations, Fordyce evaded the sheriff by fleeing London on June 10 and taking refuge in France. His bank failed, setting off a financial panic that spread throughout the North Atlantic and soon spilled over into the world of imperial politics.[42]

A year into the recession, in June 1773, Parliament heeded Americans' demands for repeal of the Currency Act—to an extent. Henceforth colonial assemblies could print paper money and tax it back into their treasuries, but they still could not require private creditors to accept it.[43] When it came to their money supply, as to taxation, territory, and trade, the colonists were by no means satisfied.

CHAPTER 11

Cry for Liberty

1772–1773

THE SCENARIO IS ALMOST IMPOSSIBLE FOR US TO IMAGINE: MORE than sixty residents of Providence, Rhode Island, including some of its most prominent business leaders, row out to a U.S. Coast Guard cutter anchored in their river. After shooting the captain and removing the crew, they burn the vessel to the water's edge. Yet right after midnight on the night of June 9–10, 1772, at just about the exact instant that Alexander Fordyce fled London, a Providence crowd did all of these things, and more. Their target was a two-masted naval schooner, the *Gaspee*. Its skipper, William Duddingston, barely survived the bullets that struck him in the arm and groin that night.[1] What had he done to provoke Rhode Island's wrath?

In his zeal to halt illegal trade in Narragansett Bay, Duddingston had stopped and searched nearly every vessel that hoisted a sail. Moreover, per custom, his roughly twenty crewmen had requisitioned food, firewood, and other supplies from local farmers. Then on June 9, the *Gaspee* ran aground, prompting Providence merchant John Brown to assemble the party that boarded her that night.[2]

Like Americans' resistance to the American Duties Act of 1764, the attack on the *Gaspee* grew out of the British government's campaign against provincial smuggling. Duddingston's was not even the first naval vessel that colonists burned. Back in 1768, the Royal Navy officers who commandeered John Hancock's sloop *Liberty* for smuggling had added it to their fleet—that is, until Rhode Islanders set it ablaze. But in violently laying hold of the *Gaspee*, the colonists had essentially become, in British eyes, pirates. The North administration appointed a Commission of Inquiry to identify suspects and send them home to England for trial.[3]

It had been so dark on the night of June 9–10 that most of the *Gaspee's* crew could not even tell whether their assailants had been "blacked or negroes." And only one raider turned against the others: a teenaged servant named Aaron Biggs (or Briggs), of mixed African and Narragansett Indian ancestry. Claiming his involvement had been forced, Biggs fled to another navy ship and gave a deposition. Some of the most prominent men in Rhode Island insisted that he was lying in hopes of claiming the reward money and his freedom. One commissioner found "much to be suspected" in Biggs's testimony. This was New York chief justice Daniel Horsmanden, who had presided over the 1741 trial that ended in the execution by hanging or burning of thirty alleged slave plotters, along with four white accomplices.[4] For their part, Whig leaders charged that the government's plan to try the alleged *Gaspee* assailants in England would rob them of their sacred right to trial by a jury of their peers.

ABOUT THREE-QUARTERS OF COLONIAL American adults—slaves, the propertyless, and women of all ranks—were denied the vote, and the franchise was even narrower in the mother country, where fewer than 5 percent of adults could vote in House of Commons elections.[5] Yet ordinary British subjects still found ways to influence events; witness James Somerset.

Kidnapped as a child in West Africa and sold to a slave trader, Somerset survived the indescribable "middle passage" to Virginia, where he was purchased by a colonial customs agent named Charles Steuart (or Stewart). In November 1769, Steuart—then serving as paymaster general to the American Board of Customs Commissioners—took Somerset with him to London. Two years later, learning that his owner planned to move him again, this time to Jamaica—to be sold—Somerset slipped off and disappeared into the London crowd. It took Steuart's representatives nearly two months, until November 26, 1771, to track Somerset down and have him chained belowdecks on a Jamaica-bound vessel anchored in the Thames.[6]

Somerset's friends, including a white Londoner named Elizabeth Cade, enlisted the aid of Granville Sharp, an abolitionist who had been seeking just such a chance to test the legality of English slavery. Sharp's legal team persuaded Lord Mansfield, chief justice of the court of King's Bench, that slavery was so inconsistent with English common law that it could not be enforced unless explicitly sanctioned by law. But Parliament had never enacted a slave code, so Mansfield ruled on June 22, 1772, that Steuart had no right to carry Somerset out of the kingdom. The

Dido Elizabeth Belle with her cousin, Lady Elizabeth Murray (1779)

verdict did not require that every slave in England be immediately freed, but it was widely interpreted that way. Mansfield had implored the two parties to settle out of court, saving him from having to issue a decree. In ultimately choosing to meet the moment, he may have been influenced by his affection for his mixed-race grandniece. Since Dido Elizabeth Belle's mother had been an enslaved African, she, too, had been born a slave and apparently still was, technically, though she lived in splendor at Kenwood House with the childless Lord and Lady Mansfield.[7]

Newspapers, Black sailors, and other media quickly carried word of Mansfield's ruling to enslaved Americans. In short order, advertisements seeking the return of fugitive slaves started conjecturing that they had taken ship for England in order to avail themselves of *Somerset v. Steuart*. The verdict also inspired African Americans to file antislavery petitions and freedom suits. For many slaveholders, it strengthened the case against the king.[8]

Another decision made in London in the summer of 1772 proved equally decisive. On August 7, 1772, in one of his last acts as secretary of state for America, Lord Hillsborough announced that the associate justices of the Massachusetts superior court would no longer receive their salaries from the provincial legislature. Instead they would be paid out of the revenue arising from the tea tax. In response, Boston radical Samuel Adams persuaded the town meeting to establish a committee of correspondence to open communication with the other Massachusetts towns, many of which created committees of their own.[9] On March 12, 1773, the Virginia House of Burgesses cited the *Gaspee* commission's power to send American suspects to England for trial (which it ended up not exercising) in establishing its own committee of correspondence. Most of the other colonies followed suit, hastening their transformation into British North America.[10]

Benjamin Franklin also helped revive the imperial dispute. Several Massachusetts officials, including Thomas Hutchinson (who succeeded Francis Bernard in the governor's chair in 1771) and Lieutenant Governor Andrew Oliver (the onetime stamp distributor), regularly corresponded with Thomas Whately, an undersecretary of state. When Whately died on May 26, 1772, many of these letters somehow fell into the hands of Franklin, London agent for Massachusetts and several other colonies. He packed them off to Thomas Cushing, the speaker of the Massachusetts House of Representatives, with instructions to share them with only a few provincial leaders. But in June 1773, the assembly found an excuse to publish them.[11] Hutchinson and Oliver had written little to Whately that they had not also said in public. But one line of Hutchinson's stood out: Americans must reconcile themselves to an "abridgement of what are called English liberties."[12]

In the summer of 1773, as the purloined letters circulated in Massachusetts, Franklin took a brief break from imperial politics to spend a social hour with a fellow American who had just arrived in London. Still a slave but crossing the Atlantic under vastly different conditions than in 1761, Phillis Wheatley had come over, accompanied by her owners' son, to promote her health and her *Poems on Various Subjects*—the first book of poetry ever published by an African American. Dr. Franklin later observed that in his eagerness to meet the acclaimed Black poet, he had accidentally slighted her chaperon. "Before I left the House," he told a friend shortly after the visit, "I understood her Master was there and had sent her to me but did not come into the Room himself. . . . I should perhaps have enquired first for him; but I had heard nothing of him."[13]

Wheatley prudently edited her work for an English audience. For example, *Poems on Various Subjects* reprinted her elegy to George Whitefield—minus its allusion to the Boston Massacre. The author's tribute to Christopher Seider disappeared altogether.[14]

One of Wheatley's poems had originated in a challenge. In October 1772, she met Thomas Woolridge, who was visiting Boston on a fact-finding mission for Lord Dartmouth, the new American secretary. Suspecting that this young Black woman might not have actually written the poems ascribed to her, Woolridge challenged her to address some verses to Dartmouth on the spot. She did so, taking the opportunity to beseech the earl not to allow Parliament to "enslave" America—a threat she understood better than most, since "I, young in life, by seeming cruel fate / Was snatch'd from *Afric's* fancy'd happy seat."[15]

Note Wheatley's qualifications: her kidnapping had only *seemed* cruel, since back in Africa she had only been happy in *fancy* (imagination). For modern readers, that language can be disturbing—though not nearly so much as another of her 1773 poems, "On Being Brought from Africa to America":

'Twas mercy brought me from my *Pagan* land,
Taught my benighted soul to understand
That there's a God, that there's a *Saviour* too:
Once I redemption neither sought nor knew.[16]

Did Wheatley actually believe her conversion to Christianity justified her kidnapping, shipment as cargo across the Atlantic, and subsequent enslavement? The answer may lie in how she concluded the poem:

Some view our sable race with scornful eye,
[saying] "Their colour is a diabolic die."
Remember, *Christians*, *Negros*, black as *Cain*,
May be refin'd, and join th' angelic train.[17]

In eight lines, the poet had journeyed from justifying Europe's commerce in African slaves—something fewer and fewer *whites* were doing by this time—to underscoring the contradiction between the trade's two principal justifications: her own, that Africans thereby received the gift of Christianity, and the racist notion that they were incapable of true conversion (or much else). Wheatley was willing to concede the morality of chattel slavery in order to upend racial prejudice—a painful choice but also logical, if you believe, as she did, that racism was the root and slavery only its venomous stem, incapable of living without it. And she offered herself as evidence of African Americans' capacity for greatness, even though that meant constantly having to prove that her poems were actually hers. Indeed the ship captain who agreed to sell her book to a London publisher found no takers until she supplied a testimonial signed by Governor Hutchinson and seventeen other Massachusetts notables.[18]

Within a month of Wheatley's return to Boston on September 13, her owners manumitted her. Biographer Vincent Carretta notes that the *Somerset* decision prevented them from taking her home against her will, and he offers the reasonable conjecture that she had returned only on condition of being freed.[19] In March 1774, she celebrated her emancipation—without actually mentioning it—in an open letter to Samson Occom, a Mohegan Indian who had become a Presbyterian missionary. "In every human Breast, God has implanted a Principle, which we call Love of Freedom," she wrote. "It is impatient of Oppression, and pants for Deliverance." A year later the English lexicographer Samuel Johnson would wonder why "we hear the loudest yelps for liberty among the drivers of negroes?" but Wheatley had already caught that contradiction, marveling that many of the same people who set up the "Cry for Liberty" nonetheless harbored "the reverse Disposition for the Exercise of oppressive Power over others."[20]

IN THE GLOBAL ECONOMY that took shape in the seventeenth century, recessions typically inflict their worst harm on sectors that depend upon a single commodity—as shown by the fate of tea and tobacco in 1772.

In 1767, the East India Company had seemed so profitable that Parliament had laid it under an annual contribution of £400,000. But then, between June 1768 and May 1773, the firm's stock price tumbled 40 percent.[21] By 1772, the EIC owed the British government £1 million—and Parliament was not the only source of its travails. Between 1767 and 1769, it fought a costly war against Haidar (or Hyder) Ali, the de facto ruler of Mysore. Then in 1769 and 1770, a drought and famine killed more than a million Bengalis, reducing the Company's tax revenue despite its best efforts. The firm derived more than 90 percent of its trading profits from tea, but by 1773, seventeen million pounds of unsold leaf was slowly rotting in its warehouses, primarily because most British subjects on both sides of the Atlantic passed it up in favor of identical but cheaper leaf smuggled in from Holland. And the widening credit crisis further reduced consumer demand and also compelled the Bank of England to cut off the EIC's credit, pushing it to the brink of insolvency.[22]

As a multinational corporation, the East India Company was too big to fail, so the government stepped in with a bailout. Most of the Tea Act that passed Parliament on May 10, 1773, had nothing to do with America; its centerpiece was a £1.4 million loan to the EIC. But Britain also sought permanent solutions to the Company's woes, including a boost in its tea sales to America. MPs ended their long-standing requirement that India House sell its tea in London to the middlemen (including many

Americans) who shipped it across the Atlantic. From now on, the EIC could transport tea to America or "foreign parts" on its own account, assuming the risks and keeping the profits. Designated merchants in each port would, like modern-day consignment shops, move the merchandise and take a fixed commission: 6 percent.[23]

The Tea Act also promised an important side benefit. Since the collapse of nonimportation in 1770, Americans had purchased 600,000 pounds of East India Company tea, even though that meant paying the Townshend duty; John Hancock alone had imported 120,000 pounds in violation of the boycott. Yet Hancock's Massachusetts neighbors continued to obtain five-sixths of their tea from the Netherlands, and the smuggled proportion of tea sales was even higher in the middle colonies. But that would change after the EIC cut out the middleman, because then it could lower its price. In combination with Americans' grudging acceptance of the molasses duty, their increased consumption of tax-bearing British tea would solidify their acquiescence in Parliament's right to tax them. Whigs' fear that the Tea Act would "for ever after be pleaded as precedent for every imposition the parliament of Great-Britain shall think proper to saddle us with" explains why they detected "the yoke of slavery" in a law that, like Charles Townshend's program six years earlier, actually reduced the price of their tea.[24]

Private merchants, American as well as British, could still buy tea at the East India Company's semiannual auctions in London, and many did. But Americans feared that by allowing the EIC to compete with the independent traders, Parliament had effectively granted it a monopoly. Many worried that the consignment system would spread to other branches of trade, eventually leaving the northern seaports with a Chesapeake-style "factor" system, in which storekeepers employed by giant British firms replaced American merchants altogether.[25]

As with tea, so with tobacco: by the spring of 1773, the market was glutted. A long-term problem—indebted farmers' inability to hold out indefinitely for higher prices—combined with a more immediate one—four successive bumper crops—to fill the warehouses with excess inventory even as the recession sapped demand. In the fall of 1772, a pound of tobacco had sold for 2.4 pence per pound (Virginia currency), but by June 1773 its price had fallen nearly 40 percent, to 1.5 pence per pound—"too low for the Makers to live."[26] Unlike the mother country's tea barons, tobacco farmers could expect little help from Parliament. But for all its shortcomings, tobacco has one great advantage: properly stored, it can sit for years without losing much value. Thus many farmers responded to the price slump by holding their tobacco back from the market.

Tobacco growers soon discovered that they did not need to wait around for their staple to regain its former value. If large numbers of them withheld their crops, they could extract higher prices from captains with holds to fill. On June 17, 1773, James Robison, director of Virginia operations for one of the mammoth Scottish tobacco firms, reported that farmers in the lower counties of the Northern Neck "entered into an Association, lodged their tobacco in certain persons' hands, and have determined not to sell unless they can procure" 2.16 pence per pound—a third higher than the prevailing price. According to Robison, the group "tie[d] up 1,000 hogsheads" of tobacco. In Bedford County in western Virginia, a newly formed farmers' association agreed "Not to pay their Debts"—that is, not to deliver their tobacco to their creditors—"unless they can get such Prices for their Commodities as they have affixed."[27]

Although the crop-withholding associations that growers formed early in the summer of 1773 could create fleeting neighborhood shortages of tobacco, temporarily raising the local price, farmers understood that a sustained increase would require a much broader movement. But in trying to build one, they faced a seemingly insurmountable obstacle: if they did not eventually deliver their crops to their merchant-creditors, they were going to be sued.

WOMEN OF THE REVOLUTIONARY era never forgot a truth that sometimes eluded their politically minded fathers and husbands: that the vast majority of human beings—women and children, slaves and servants— were less affected by the actions of monarchs and mayors than by their *masters*, the customary term not only for slaveholders and ship captains but for all heads of households. The enduring significance of household government was evident in a document that was not published at the time and in fact never has been. Mary Fish Noyes of Stonington, Connecticut, was a graduate of Sarah Osborn's Newport, Rhode Island, boarding school. On August 3, 1773, widowed for six years and finally contemplating remarriage, Noyes completed an essay she called "Portrait of a Good Husband."[28]

English common law gave the husband nearly total control over his wife's real estate—and absolute possession of everything else she brought to the marriage. Single women had nearly the same property rights as men, but hardly any free females of the colonial and revolutionary eras dared court community disapproval by never marrying. Yet by the middle of the eighteenth century, they at least enjoyed wider discretion than their grandmothers had had in choosing their spouses. And once widowed, they suffered no stigma in choosing not to remarry. Noyes had sufficient means to wait for a partner who would respect her, but there would be no turning back if she chose wrong. Thus her "Portrait."

Many of Noyes's requirements had to do with household economy. Would Mary's second husband be a miser, or would he willingly see their "table spread with the bounties of God's providence"? Would he treat her slaves well once they became his? Above all, Noyes needed to know whether her new partner would despoil his stepchildren of their inheritances or be "a father to my fatherless children."[29]

Noyes understood that with husbands' legal supremacy came terrible emotional power. "Let the mantle of love be drawn over my imperfections," she implored whatever man she might marry, "and let them not be [commented] on before company."[30] Like the other positive qualities that Noyes enumerated, this one implied its opposite. Her determination to find a partner who would not publicly humiliate her is at once terribly sad and an indication that even in the absence of organized feminism, many or most women could not abide male arrogance. Further evidence is the frequency with which eighteenth-century females (and some males) mockingly referred to men as the "Lords of the Creation."[31] And any claim that the American Revolution raised free women's consciousness about their subjugation must reckon with the advanced views that women like Noyes had already expressed.

Lords of the Creation (c. 1865)

As of the autumn of 1773, Mary Noyes had yet to encounter a man who measured up to her "Portrait," so she elected to remain single—or, in the language of the time, "a Daughter of *Liberty*."[32]

THE EAST INDIA COMPANY moved quickly to exploit its new privileges. In their first-ever direct shipment to North America, the directors instructed dockworkers to load 600,000 pounds of tea into two thousand chests and stow them on seven ships headed to the continent's four busiest seaports: Charles Town, Philadelphia, New York, and Boston. Opponents of the Tea Act could have responded by reviving the anti-tea pledge they had taken four years earlier and never officially abandoned. But as William Gordon stated in his 1788 history of the Revolution, widespread violation of the boycott had shown that "the virtue of the people . . . was too precarious a ground on which to risk the salvation of their country."[33] So instead the Whigs demanded that the tea consignees ship the tea back and resign their commissions.

Some of the consignees chose instead to fight back. In a letter to their counterparts in New York, James & Drinker of Philadelphia recommended "obtaining from the Custom House books in Boston and Rhode Island a certified account of all Teas imported there from England which have paid the duty" levied by Parliament. "Such an account will tend much to quiet any opposition that may be made here," they wrote.[34] But this attempt at divide-and-conquer failed, and the New York and Philadelphia consignees ultimately had to send their cargoes back.

In Charles Town, the tea came ashore as contraband, seized for nonpayment of the Townshend tax, but customs agents dared not try to recoup the lost revenue by putting it up for sale. In Boston, an anonymous veteran of the Seven Years' War urged his countrymen to resist the landing of the tea the same way "the French and Indians fought General Braddock's Army." But the boycotters would have to contend with Thomas Hutchinson, who refused to follow the governors of Pennsylvania and New York in abandoning the tea consignees to their fate. Why should he, when the consignees included two of his sons and a son-in-law? Governor Hutchinson also ordered the tea ships not to return to England without landing their cargoes and paying the tax. If any did, Alexander Leslie, commandant of Castle William, had orders to fire on them. Nor did the captains have the luxury of doing nothing. If they failed to land their cargoes and pay all duties within twenty days, the tea would be impounded, as in Charles Town. That could prove ruinous not only for the captains, consignees, and Company but also for the Whigs, since sequestered tea might seep into the market disguised as Dutch leaf.[35]

The deadline for the first-arriving ship, the *Dartmouth*, was December 17. On the 16th, Whigs filled the cavernous Old South Church, and at sunset a messenger brought them word that Hutchinson still refused to allow the tea ships to leave. Samuel Adams announced that "This meeting can do no more to save the country," whereupon leather dresser Adam Colson allegedly yelled, "Boston Harbor a tea-pot this night!" A group of men appeared in the doorway dressed and painted as Native Americans—not out of any thought that they could make people believe they were actual Indians but because for them, the native warrior perfectly symbolized both bravery and freedom.[36]

In the venerable tradition of English poachers, other Whigs darkened their faces with lamp black. Also like English lawbreakers, many treated themselves to alcoholic refreshment, seeing it as not only removing their inhibitions but giving them strength.[37]

Three tea ships were moored to Griffin's Wharf. The 100 to 150 men who carried out the Boston Tea Party (the name lay fifty years in the future) came from all walks of life. Two-thirds were artisans. Skilled sailors took the lead in turning the winches that brought the 350-pound tea chests topside, where men with axes and hatchets split them open and dumped them overboard. Shoemaker George Hewes earned a leading role thanks to his "whistling talent." The only other sounds were the creaking of the decks and the splitting open of chests. The men prided themselves on damaging nothing but tea, and when they accidentally destroyed a padlock, they quickly replaced it. Two who tried to pocket some of the accursed leaves were punished.[38]

Then tragedy struck. As a chest was being hoisted onto the main deck, it struck carpenter John Crane, apparently killing him; the body was carried ashore and hidden in a nearby woodshop under a pile of shavings. The death toll could have been much higher, since several Royal Navy ships were anchored within cannon shot. "During the whole of this transaction," Adm. John Montagu later reported, "neither the Govr Magistrates, [ship] Owners or the Revenue Officers of this place ever called for my Assistance. If they had, I could easily have prevented the execution of this plan but must have endangered the Lives of many innocent People by firing upon the Town."[39] Governor Hutchinson was inflexible, not insane.

By 9 p.m., after less than three hours of work, the group had emptied 340 chests of 90,000 pounds of tea, with an estimated value of £9,659. As an added bonus, when the men who had hidden the body of John Crane went back for it, they found him very much alive.[40]

Other towns soon followed Boston's example. In April 1774, a New York crowd boarded the ship *London* and dumped the captain's eighteen half-chests of pricey Hyson tea into their harbor. Then in October, residents of Annapolis, Maryland, compelled Anthony Stewart, the owner of the brigantine *Peggy Stewart*, which had brought in two thousand pounds of tea, to set fire to his own vessel, burning it to the water's edge. Tea would also be destroyed in New York City, Greenwich, New Jersey, Charles Town, South Carolina, and elsewhere.[41]

On February 19, 2009, a stockbroker and cable news financial analyst, fed up with President Barack Obama's mortgage relief plan, declared on cable television, "We're thinking of having a Chicago Tea Party in July," and a nationwide movement was born.[42] The twenty-first-century tea party had much in common with its eighteenth-century forebear: both denounced the central government for interfering in market relations by using taxpayer funds to bail out politically powerful multinational corporations. The anti-Obama Tea Party was often ridiculed for its members' more outlandish predictions—for instance, that the president was about to imprison dissenters and confiscate their firearms. But the fact is that eighteenth-century Whigs made some outrageous claims of their own, for example that Parliament wished not just to extract revenue from them but to enslave them.[43]

But the eighteenth- and twenty-first-century tea parties differed in important ways. The Bostonians who dumped East India Company tea into their harbor were less concerned about the *amount* of money demanded of them than about not being represented in Parliament. By contrast, the twenty-first-century Tea Party organizations faced the taller challenge of combating taxation *with* representation.

THE MORNING AFTER THE destruction of the tea, John Adams took to his diary to speculate about how the British government might respond. "Will they punish Us?" he asked. "How? By quartering Troops upon Us? By annulling our Charter?—by laying on more duties? By restraining our Trade?" Parliament laid no more taxes, but Adams's other three predictions all came true. When news of the tea riot reached London, Lord Chatham, the former William Pitt, pronounced it "criminal." Even

Benjamin Franklin called it "an Act of violent Injustice on our part," and he and other Whigs urged Boston or Massachusetts to reimburse the East India Company.[44]

By this time Franklin was already hurtling toward his own climactic confrontation with British officialdom. In the summer of 1773, when Londoners learned about the publication of Hutchinson's and Oliver's letters to Thomas Whately, Whately's brother William set out to find the leaker. Eventually his suspicion fell on John Temple, a pro-American member of the American Board of Customs Commissioners who had been sacked three years earlier. Temple denied the charge, and on December 11, 1773, he wounded Whately in a Hyde Park duel. When Franklin learned that the two men planned to return to the field of honor, his conscience compelled him to come forward and take the consequences. These would prove enormous.[45]

CHAPTER 12

In the Common Cause

1774

WILLIAM FRANKLIN, THE ROYAL GOVERNOR OF NEW JERSEY, AND his father, Benjamin, had been drifting apart for years, but the elder Franklin's confession that he had leaked the Whately letters severed the tie. It also had a much broader impact, fusing in the British mind with the news that Bostonians had destroyed the East India Company's tea. For a decade, numerous Members of Parliament had pled America's cause. But now "I suppose we never had since we were a People, so few Friends in Britain," Benjamin Franklin wrote home from London. "The violent Destruction of the Tea seems to have united all Parties here against our Province"[1]

As the Massachusetts House of Representatives' agent before Parliament, Franklin had presented its petition for the removal of Governor Hutchinson and Lieutenant Governor Andrew Oliver, and the Privy Council invited him to appear before its committee on plantation affairs on January 29, 1774. The committee gathered less than a hundred paces east of Prime Minister North's official, though rarely used, residence at 10 Downing Street, in a building known as the Cockpit, since it had originally hosted cockfights. When Franklin realized that the hearing was not going to focus on Hutchinson and Oliver but on himself, he grasped at once that it was going to be more of a bear-baiting.[2]

Massachusetts Whigs had accused Hutchinson and Oliver of poisoning the London government against them, and Solicitor General Alexander Wedderburn used one of Franklin's own favorite weapons, wit, to turn that accusation right back on him. Having obtained the governor's and lieutenant governor's private correspondence by some "fraudulent or corrupt means," the inventor of the lightning rod had made himself the "prime conductor of this whole contrivance." One spectator credited Dr. Franklin with preserving his dignity throughout Wedderburn's performance: "The muscles of his face had been previously composed, so as to afford a placid tranquil expression of countenance, and he did not suffer the slightest alteration of it to appear during the continuance of the speech." But the room was with Wedderburn, and the committee concluded that Massachusetts's petition was "groundless, Vexatious and Scandalous and calculated only for the Seditious Purpose of keeping up a Spirit of Clamour and Discontent."[3]

Although often depicted as the quintessential self-made man, Franklin always acknowledged his dependence upon patrons, especially in government. He once estimated that colonial governments had paid him more to print their currency than he earned publishing newspapers (which themselves benefited from government advertising and other patronage). Appointed deputy postmaster general for North America in 1753, Franklin had made money for the imperial government as well as himself. But the day after Wedderburn's speech, he was sacked. Franklin also wrote a very public letter giving up his shares in the Walpole Associates, the real estate venture whose proposal for a fourteenth colony in the American interior had received preliminary but not final approval. The letter was fake—Franklin actually retained his holdings—and also ineffective. "The Ship Ohio [is] still aground," he reported to his associate Joseph Galloway in February 1774, and the firm never received its land grant.[4]

ON MARCH 14, LORD North asked Parliament to close Boston's harbor until it complied with all taxes and trade regulations, paid for the East India Company's tea, and reimbursed customs officers for the property they had lost to rioters. The fundamental problem, he told the House of Commons, was that many colonists considered Britain and America "two independent states"—and they and the government could no longer agree to disagree. "We must control them or submit to them," North declared. Even Isaac Barré, who had coined the term "Sons of Liberty," supported the Boston Port Act, which passed the House of Commons on the evening of March 25. The colonists who had spent the previous century perfecting the art of nullifying parliamentary legislation would not be able to ignore the Boston Port Act, because the ministry also instructed the army, which had left Boston in the wake of the Massacre, to resume it occupation.[5]

Outside Massachusetts, many Americans were less aware of tensions with Parliament than of their own struggles against each other. For ex-

ample, Virginia battled Pennsylvania for the same prize Edward Braddock had sought two decades earlier: the Upper Ohio Valley. Late in
1773, Governor Dunmore's representative, Dr. John Connolly, ironically
a native Pennsylvanian, arrived at the forks of the Ohio, gave the abandoned Fort Pitt a new name — Fort Dunmore — and provoked a border
war against his former countrymen. Arthur St. Clair, prothonotary (chief
clerk) of Westmoreland County, Pennsylvania, jailed Connolly. Released
pending trial, he ordered the arrest of several Westmoreland County
judges. As soon as they got out, they reimprisoned Connolly.[6]

Far more lethal was Connolly's confrontation with the other principal claimants to the region, the Delawares, Shawnees, and Mingos. On
April 21, 1774, he issued a bellicose circular letter that frontier whites
interpreted as a license to kill Native Americans. The worst of the ensuing attacks occurred on April 30, about fifty miles down the Ohio
River from Fort Dunmore, at the mouth of Yellow Creek. A group led
by Daniel Greathouse massacred thirteen Mingo men, women, and children. Among the dead was the wife of John Gibson, a Pittsburgh-based
Indian trader, who had met her while a captive during Pontiac's Rebellion. The couple's child was spared and sent to Gibson.[7]

John Logan (Tahgahjute or Tachnechdorus), a half-French Mingo
sachem, was the brother of Gibson's murdered wife and the husband
of another victim. Logan had long maintained good relations with the
British but now declared war, joined by a handful of Shawnee warriors
who had also lost kin at Yellow Creek. Several months later, Logan justified his revenge raids with a speech paraphrasing Matthew 25:35–40:
"I appeal to any white man to say, if ever he entered Logan's cabin
hungry, and he gave him not meat: if ever he came cold and naked, and
he clothed him not." But now, he said, "there runs not a drop of my
blood in the veins of any living creature. . . . Who is there to mourn for
Logan? — Not one."[8]

Gibson carried Logan's speech to Dunmore at the governor's palace
in Williamsburg, and it eventually made its way to Thomas Jefferson,
who, more than a decade later, printed it in his *Notes on the State of
Virginia* to refute a French naturalist's claim that animals, including humans, degenerated in the New World. Jefferson was accused of fabricating the speech. He denied that charge in the 1803 edition of his book but
went on to point out that it refuted the Frenchman's slander either way.
"Whether Logan's or mine, it would still have been American," President
Jefferson wrote.[9]

As much as Virginia land speculators like Jefferson admired Logan's "eminence in oratory," they were even more excited about his reprisal raids. For years, they had sought a "pretence" for attacking their native neighbors, and now they had one.[10]

AMERICAN COLONISTS ARE USUALLY portrayed as responding to the Boston Port Act and Parliament's other so-called Coercive Acts by sending delegates to an intercolonial congress that gathered in Philadelphia in September 1774 and stood up to Britain by boycotting its trade. But that neat sequence masks the rockiness of the actual road to what would become the Continental Association.

The Boston Port Act reached Boston on May 10, 1774, less than three weeks before the harbor was to close. Thomas Gage, commander-in-chief of British forces in North America, arrived three days later to take up an additional assignment, replacing Thomas Hutchinson as royal governor. Also on May 13, the Boston town meeting proposed that Americans revive their boycott of British merchandise. In addition, and for the first time ever, the town asked colonists to stop exporting their crops to the mother country or the British sugar islands in the Caribbean.[11]

By May 17, when Boston's messenger, Paul Revere, reached New York City, the mechanicks' party there, led by Isaac Sears and Alexander McDougall, had already devised a boycott plan so similar to Boston's as to suggest prior coordination. Like the Bostonians, McDougall and Sears wanted to cut off exports to the West Indies and all trade, in either direction, with the British Isles, but to continue importing Caribbean molasses. The city's Whigs called a series of mass meetings to gauge and drum up popular support. One of these, on May 19, elicited revealing commentary from twenty-two-year-old Gouverneur Morris, literally to the manor born, that manor being "Morrisania," his family's feudal estate in what was then Westchester County.[12]

Morris viewed the meeting from a second-floor balcony. "On my right hand," he reported to John Penn, "were ranged all the people of property, with some few poor dependants." To his left were "all the tradesmen" (artisans). Morris likened the tradesmen and day laborers to sheep and their social superiors—men like himself—to shepherds. In between these two classes stood crowd leaders like Alexander Mac-Dougall, whom Morris compared to the sheep with bells on their collars that the rest were trained to follow. At first "the belwethers jingled merrily, and roared out liberty, and property, and religion," and "the simple flock put themselves entirely under the protection of these most excellent shepherds." But then "a great metamorphosis," akin to Ovid's, had "converted the belwethers into shepherds": they no longer took orders from the gentry. Switching metaphors, Morris compared ordinary New Yorkers to snakes: "It is with them a vernal morning; they are struggling to cast off their winter's slough, they bask in the sunshine, and ere noon they will bite, depend upon it. The gentry begin to fear this."[13]

For the moment, though, New York merchants retained control of the Committee of Fifty-One, charged with responding to the Coercive Acts, and it broke the momentum of colonial resistance by postponing any boycott of British merchandise until after a continental congress — which it made no move to organize. Philadelphia merchants offered a similarly vague endorsement of a congress, advised Boston to pay for the tea, and characterized a commercial boycott as only a "last resource." A gleeful Governor Gage reported that North America's two leading ports had given the suffering Bostonians "little more than fair words."[14]

In sharp contrast, Providence, Rhode Island, actually outdid Boston, voting to cut off all trade, in both directions, with Britain, the West Indies, and even Ireland. Providence residents also offered a proposal of their own. Although theirs was one of America's premier slave-trading ports, they believed that while "engaged in the preservation of their rights and liberties," they were compelled by consistency to abolish the African slave trade. Even more astonishing, the Providence town meeting asked the provincial assembly to decree "that all negroes born in the Colony should be free at attaining to a certain age." As the historian J. Franklin Jameson would observe a century and half later, "the stream of revolution, once started, could not be confined within narrow banks, but spread abroad upon the land." Less than a week after Providence met, "A Grate Number" of enslaved people in neighboring Massachusetts asserted that "we have in common With all other men a naturel right to our freedoms" and demanded immediate emancipation.[15] This May 25, 1774, petition was the first in which Black Americans linked their freedom struggle to whites' dispute with the mother country. It would not be the last.

When Bostonians learned that New York and Philadelphia had rejected their plea for an immediate trade embargo, they were dismayed but not surprised. Even in Massachusetts, many merchants balked at shuttering their stores, just as they had in 1767. The Boston committee of correspondence proposed the same countermeasure as before: boycotting the merchants themselves. "If there are no Purchasers of British Goods," the committeemen pointed out, "there will be no Importers." The nonconsumption agreement that Boston adopted on May 30, 1774, was modest, targeting only those British wares for which townspeople could find acceptable local substitutes. But it was a start.[16]

June 2 brought shocking news: the North ministry had proposed two additional punitive statutes. The Massachusetts Government Bill would fundamentally alter the colony's eighty-three-year-old charter. Royally appointed governors had often been stymied by the provincial council, whose members were annually voted in by the House of Representatives and the previous year's council. For example, after the Boston Tea Party, councilors would not even let Hutchinson offer a reward for information on the culprits. But from now on, the British government would appoint the Massachusetts council, just as in other royal colonies. In addition, Governor Gage and his successors could hire and fire judges and county sheriffs without consulting the council. The sheriffs in turn would take over from town meetings and local constables the crucial responsibility of empaneling juries so that they could no longer be *"packt"* in favor of rioters and other malefactors. The Massachusetts Government Bill even attacked that iconic New England institution, the town meeting. In hopes of stifling the towns' frequent denunciations of Parliament, the North administration banned them from meeting other than to elect officers.[17]

Under the Administration of Justice Bill, which North introduced in the House of Commons on April 15, if a British official suppressing a riot or enforcing a customs law in Massachusetts was accused of murder or some other capital crime, the governor could determine that the only way to give him a fair trial was to send him to another colony or even England. Massachusetts Whigs interpreted this legislation as giving British soldiers and officials license to kill, and they dubbed it the Murdering Bill.[18]

These additional parliamentary assaults prompted the Boston committee of correspondence to set aside the town meeting's feeble nonconsumption pledge in favor of a thoroughgoing boycott. The committee's "Solemn League and Covenant," named for the 1643 antiroyalist alliance between Scottish Presbyterians and the English Parliament, went far beyond Boston's previous associations, for instance in baning all trade, in either direction, with the mother country and in explicitly seeking the signatures of "all adult persons of both sexes."[19]

Boston merchants accused the committee of persecuting them and exceeding its authority. They thought the town meeting should "remove Censure and annihilate the Committee of Correspondence." Boston stood by its committeemen, but only seven of the colony's other 259 towns and districts signed on to the Solemn League.[20]

BOSTON'S PROPOSAL FOUND A warmer welcome in the Chesapeake. The problem there was a collective debt to British merchants of £4 million. Farmers who wished to withhold their tobacco in order to pressure Parliament would run the same risks as those already doing so because of the price slump: not paying their debts meant damaging their credit ratings and possibly being sued.[21]

Virginians and Marylanders were nonetheless determined to adopt nonexportation, not only to punish Parliament but also for their own "pecuniary advantage." An announcement that they were going to hold an entire crop back from the market would create a sudden shortage—or at least the fear of one, which amounted to the same thing—and that in turn would raise the price.[22]

But what if British merchants sued their Chesapeake debtors? Virginia assemblyman Richard Henry Lee had a plan for that. The province's county courts could not operate unless the House of Burgesses periodically reenacted the law setting officers' fees, and the previous fee act was fortuitously about to expire. On May 10, Lee proposed to not renew it, thus closing the courts.[23]

That was too barefaced for Lee's assembly colleagues, but two weeks later they discovered a less direct route to the same destination. On May 24, Lee, Thomas Jefferson, Patrick Henry, and a half dozen other burgesses convinced their colleagues to proclaim June 1, when the Boston Port Act would go into effect, a day of "Fasting, Humiliation and Prayer." The assembly's resolution was a direct challenge to Lord Dunmore, not only in denouncing Parliament but in usurping his prerogative of proclaiming fast days. On May 26—after returning from a day of hunting with George Washington—the governor formally dissolved the assembly.[24]

Back in 1769, New York's De Lancey faction had deliberately provoked Governor Moore to dissolve the provincial assembly, and now Virginians had similarly forced Dunmore's hand. Desperate to snuff out the fee act so the colony's indebted majority could join in nonexportation but loath to leave fingerprints, the burgesses had goaded the governor into doing it for them.

Maryland found a different way to enable debtors to hang on to their crops. Agreeing on May 25 to halt exports as well as imports, Annapolis residents asked the colony's lawyers to stop trying creditors' cases until exports resumed, and other towns and counties soon echoed that request.[25] Now nonexportation could spread throughout the Chesapeake, not only pressuring Parliament to repeal the Coercive Acts but also driving up the price of tobacco.

Meanwhile Parliament fired one more arrow at Massachusetts. Whig leaders had tried to confine the British soldiers who occupied Boston between 1768 and 1772 to Castle William, three miles from town, and after the Boston Massacre, they had succeeded. So the Quartering Act of 1774 clarified that Gage, in his role as commander-in-chief, had the right to quarter the soldiers in Boston proper, and the ministry sent over four regiments—the same number as in 1768. Wave upon wave of Whig bile had erased the last traces of the countless positive interactions between Bostonians and those earlier occupiers, and the new arrivals looked like foreign invaders.[26]

All of these laws applied only to Massachusetts, and all were explicitly punitive. That same summer of 1774, Parliament also adopted two other American statutes of broader relevance. It did not intend either as punishment, but colonists saw both that way.

Colonial entrepreneurs' dreams of going into textile manufacturing had never overcome North America's high wage rates, but starting in the 1760s, aspiring industrialists also detected a threat from Parliament. In April 1769, George Washington warned his neighbor George Mason that if the mother country got away with taxing Americans, it might also seek "to restrain our manufactories" as well. During the summer of 1774, Mason's brother Thomson predicted in Clementina Rind's *Virginia Gazette* that Parliament would soon prohibit Americans from "manufacturing the smallest article for your own use"—even, he whimsically warned in only the latest reference to British America's native heritage, from "fashioning a canoe."[27] These fears were justified, because influential British writers like the agricultural reformer Arthur Young were just then warning their countrymen that America was in fact moving into large-scale manufacturing. Workers in Lynn, Massachusetts, annually turned out forty thousand pairs of women's shoes, Young claimed. Even worse, "there is a very large linen manufacture at Boston, and another in the neighbourhood of Philadelphia." Responding to these concerns, the House of Commons voted on May 26 to prohibit anyone from transporting "Tools or Utensils" used in "Cotton or Linen Manufactures" beyond Britain's shores.[28]

Lord North and his cabinet also decided to address a problem that the short-lived ministries of the 1760s had all avoided: the roughly seventy-five thousand colonists living in Quebec. Britain had promised the colony's propertied white men the privilege of electing assemblymen. But how could that possibly work? Nearly every European resident of Quebec was Catholic, and the militantly Protestant British empire had a firm policy of denying Catholics the vote. That meant a Quebec legislature would be chosen by the tiny and unpopular Protestant minority: mostly newly arrived British traders. So on May 2, the ministry proposed to entrust the province to a royally appointed governor and council. In addition, while Quebec would try accused criminals under English common law, it would settle other disputes using French-style "civil" law, which, among other eccentricities, permitted judges rather than juries to decide civil cases and married women to own and control property. Moreover, in an astonishing indulgence for a bigoted age, Catholic as well as Protestant churches would be allowed to support their priests by a tax on parishioners—a provision that critics in Parliament as well as the colonies denounced as "establishing . . . the Roman Catholic religion throughout those vast regions."[29]

The ministry also proposed to vastly extend Quebec's borders. Several east coast colonies had sea-to-sea charters, and residents believed that the 1763 peace treaty, which made the Mississippi River the border between British North America and Spanish Louisiana, confined but also confirmed their western claims. Yet the Quebec bill would give that province all the land between the Ohio and Mississippi Rivers: the eastern half of the modern Midwest. In support of the new border, Alexander Wedderburn (Franklin's nemesis from the Cockpit) begged the House of Commons not to tell seaboard colonists, "Cross the Ohio, you will find the Utopia of some great and mighty empire."[30]

The Quebec Act received the royal assent on June 22, 1774. Philadelphia attorney Joseph Reed suspected that Parliament had chosen to protect the French-descended *habitants*' religion and the First Nations' land in hopes of "bringing down the Canadians and savages upon the English Colonies," a scheme he called "odious and dreadful," "cruel and unnatural." William Lee, a Virginian living in London, was more succinct: "every tie of allegiance is broken by the Quebec act."[31]

In the minds of most free colonists, the Quebec Act merged with

Paul Revere, print protesting the Quebec Act (1774)

Parliament's anti-Massachusetts legislation as the Intolerable Acts. But Quebec's new boundary was only the latest in a series of royal restraints on the coastal colonies' westward expansion. Grenville had intended the Proclamation of 1763 to be temporary, and as Arthur Young noted, his successors at 10 Downing Street received "repeated petitions from all parts of those colonies, for leave to penetrate into the back country." But as the trans-Appalachian Indian confederacy grew, the government stood by the proclamation. Even today, Canadian attorneys and judges sometimes cite it.[32]

North and his team even made it harder for colonists to acquire land in the east. Previously a British American seeking government land only had to pay clerical fees and the cost of the survey; the land itself was free. But on February 3, 1774, the Privy Council ordered the governors to dispose of unoccupied land at auction. In June, Virginia attorney and would-be real estate peddler Edmund Pendleton condemned the ministry "for degrading Royaltie into the Pedlar hawking Lands for sale." One of the last free grants—157 acres near the intersection of today's Interstates 64 and 81, including Natural Bridge— went to Thomas Jefferson. He and other colonists boycotted the new auctions.[33]

*   *   *

IN 1774, WHITE GEORGIANS desperately needed London's help in their war against the Muskogee Indians. But starting in June, the twelve colonies north of Georgia began choosing delegates to an intercolonial congress. Gen. Gage tried to send Massachusetts assemblymen home before they could choose a delegation, but they locked his messenger out while electing Samuel Adams, his cousin John, John Hancock, and two others. Where the governor successfully prevented legislators from choosing congressmen, colonists gathered at the local level to send representatives to provincial conventions that in turn elected congressmen. Bostonians had claimed they were suffering "in the common cause," and dozens of these local and provincial gatherings used that exact phrase to characterize their plight.[34]

The most radical statement appearing in the summer of 1774 was a foiled ventriloquist's act on the part of Thomas Jefferson. Elected to Virginia's provincial convention by his Albemarle County neighbors, Jefferson contracted diarrhea on the road, had to turn back, and decided to participate indirectly by drafting an address for the convention to propose to the intercolonial congress. The convention took a pass on Jefferson's essay, but several members had Clementina Rind print it under the title *A Summary View of the Rights of British America*. This accidental pamphlet was the first Jefferson ever published—one of very few.[35]

More than two decades earlier, Rhode Island governor Stephen Hopkins had responded to the adoption of the Currency Act of 1751 with a bold rhetorical question, "What have the King and Parliament to do with making a Law or Laws to govern us by, any more than the Mohawks have?" But that was in private conversation, and no 1760s pamphlet had gone that far. Parliament founded its claim to bind the colonies "in all cases whatsoever" on the notion that sovereignty is indivisible: Parliament either had total control over the colonies or none at all. For nearly a decade, Americans had replied that Parliament had authority over them in some matters, such as regulating trade, but not in others, such as taxation. Jefferson in *Summary View* and Pennsylvania attorney James Wilson, in a pamphlet also published during the summer of 1774, took a different approach, conceding that sovereignty, being indivisible, must reside in a single body—in this case, the American assemblies. Far from wishing the colonies independent, Jefferson and Wilson believed that in relation to Parliament, they already were. Since this declaration flew in the face of long-standing experience, *Summary View* invented a new history of colonial Americans in which they had never acknowledged the authority of Parliament—an audacious move, yet very English in its reliance upon immemorial usage.[36]

The only Briton Americans had to obey was its more or less fictitious king. Jefferson reinforced his point about the sovereignty of the North American colonies by sometimes calling them *states*, which, like the French *état* and Spanish *estado*, meant *nation*.

Jefferson's constitutional concerns grew out of practical grievances. Most fundamentally, he complained that British merchants' state-sponsored monopoly of America's trade enabled them to jack up the price of their wares "to the double and treble of what they sold for before such exclusive privileges were given them, and of what better commodities of the same kind would cost us elsewhere." Jefferson's denunciation of the mother country's new policy of auctioning off (Native) American land reached even further back into English history. He noted that the only English noblemen whose land William the Conqueror seized were those who had tried to stop him at the Battle of Hastings (depicted in the Bayeux Tapestry). Since no one in Europe in 1066 even knew that America existed, William could not have intended to confiscate it, thus establishing the precedent that English kings had "no right to grant lands" there. (Of course the First Nations had resisted European conquest of their land just as stoutly as those English noblemen, so by Jefferson's logic, it belonged to the king.)[37]

ONE GRIEVANCE THAT JEFFERSON raised in *Summary View*—and also in his draft of the Declaration of Independence—dated back to before his birth in 1743: that (as he put it in the Declaration) the British had "obtruded" African captives on white Americans. *Obtrude* strikes most modern eyes as a strange word for a strange notion: that free colonists had purchased slaves only because Britain forced them to. But it contained an element of truth. Once a colony's African American births exceeded deaths, many white residents, including slaveholders, invariably started listing reasons to stop importing slaves. More workers meant more tobacco or rice, exerting downward pressure on prices. In addition, the proliferation of forced African immigrants discouraged Europeans from crossing the ocean voluntarily. And slave purchases drained away the colonies' meager stocks of gold and silver.[38]

Some free Americans opposed the transatlantic commerce in human beings out of compassion. Indeed, by the 1760s, a handful of white colonists opposed slavery itself. Few went so far as Pennsylvanian Benjamin

Lay, who destroyed his wife's tea set lest she sweeten her brew with slave-grown sugar. But in their twos and threes, Quakers and a few other whites, especially in New England, were turning against the institution that had made British America rich.[39]

Even many provincials who had no desire to give up their Black workers sought to distinguish themselves from the worst slaveholders by opposing the brutal African trade. Others took the same stand out of fear—of the growing number of slaves but especially of those born in Africa, whom they viewed as more dangerous than those who had never known freedom. Louisiana was well on its way to a Black majority when numerous African Americans joined in the Natchez Indian revolt of 1729, prompting the French government to ban bringing any more of them in. William Byrd II wanted to limit Virginia's Black population lest Black insurgents "tinge our rivers as wide as they are with blood."[40]

Byrd and other major slave owners who tried to limit forced African immigration ran into opposition from neighbors who suspected them of trying to shore up the value of their human property in the internal trade. But the most ardent defenders of continuing the flow of Africans across the Atlantic were in Britain. Occasionally the imperial government would allow a colony to shut down the trade for a limited time. For example, no one objected when South Carolina responded to the Stono Rebellion of 1739 with a prohibitive tariff.[41] But in subsequent decades, London's attitude hardened. At the end of the Seven Years' War, Virginia had the largest Black population of any North American province: an estimated 131,000 out of 328,000 souls. In 1767 and again in 1769, the House of Burgesses tried to increase its head tax on every new African arrival from 10 to 20 percent. The Privy Council not only vetoed both measures but instructed the governor to block any future attempts. And yet on April 1, 1772, the burgesses unanimously approved a petition beseeching George III to abolish the African trade. There was no other way, they said, of "averting a Calamity of a most alarming Nature": slave insurrection.[42]

The apparent author of the assembly's petition was Richard Henry Lee, who at the time was soliciting a consignment of Africans. But Virginians who opposed the trade found a more consistent champion in their new governor, Lord Dunmore, who predicted that some future invader would ally with the slaves and make "a conquest of this Country . . . in a very short time."[43] Dunmore could not have imagined that less than three years later, he himself would attempt to fulfill that dire prophecy.

In the meantime, no other royal governor joined Virginia's in assailing the slave trade. To the contrary, in eight of the thirteen colonies that later rebelled against Britain, imperial officials overturned legislative efforts to bring in fewer kidnapped Africans.[44] White colonists were sure they knew why. Jefferson complained in *Summary View* that British leaders preferred "the immediate advantages of a few African corsairs to the lasting interests of the American states." More than a decade after independence, as free Virginians debated whether to ratify the United States Constitution, George Mason would proclaim the royal government's stubborn support of the slave traders "one of the great causes of our separation from Great Britain."[45]

British merchants also transported convicted criminals to America, selling them as servants, usually for fourteen years. So early as 1751, after the Privy Council vetoed a Pennsylvania tax on imported convicts, Benjamin Franklin stated that if Britons insisted on shipping their jailbirds west across the Atlantic, Americans owed them a return cargo of rattlesnakes.[46]

"The whole art of government consists in the art of being honest," Jefferson lectured the ruler of the British empire in the final paragraph of *Summary View*. "Let not the name of George the third be a blot in the page of history." The author's audacity was one reason his pamphlet was widely reprinted on both sides of the Atlantic. Another was his fluid writing. "Let those flatter, who fear," he wrote. "It is not an American art."[47]

CHAPTER 13

·—•◦•—·

The Hindmost Horse

1774–1775

PARLIAMENT ALLOWED FIREWOOD AND FOOD INTO BOSTON, BUT Whigs feared that for the city's poor, unemployment would spell starvation. So by June 1, when the Boston Port Act took effect, Americans had begun sending them food—philanthropy that doubled as propaganda. Residents of Newport, Rhode Island, hired out-of-work Boston carpenters to build them a new meeting house. A benefit production of *Busiris, King of Egypt*—an allegorical play about tyranny—was staged in Charles Town, South Carolina, with tickets selling for rice that was then shipped north.[1]

Meanwhile Americans argued about how best to defend Boston. One South Carolinian urged freemen to reject fancy dress even if it meant being "obliged to wear the same garb your slaves hitherto have." Fashion is socially constructed, he declared: "Nothing but custom makes the curl-pated beau a more agreeable sight with his powder and pomatum, than the tawney savage with his paint and bear's grease." Five years earlier, George Washington had promoted nonimportation as giving overextended gentlemen a "pretext to live within bounds," and this anonymous South Carolinian similarly observed that traders as well as farmers were "greatly in arrears to the merchants" of Great Britain. "A stoppage of importation," he noted, "would give them all an opportunity to extricate themselves from debt."[2]

Often, though, the nonimportation debate divided a city's social classes. In New York City, Alexander McDougall chaired a mass meeting that instructed New York's representatives to support the boycott at the upcoming congress. But the merchant-dominated Committee of Fifty-One repudiated these instructions, whereupon McDougall and other militants tried to replace the committee's conservative delegates with more determined men. Voters ended up endorsing the Committee of Fifty-One's congressmen—but only after all but one endorsed the boycott.[3]

Nonimportation also alarmed the Charles Town, South Carolina, Chamber of Commerce. The colony's congressional delegation was to be popularly elected, yet the only polling place was in Charles Town, and merchants marched their clerks there en masse to vote for an anti-boycott ticket. But by "appearing in a body" (as John Drayton, an early South Carolina historian, observed), the clerks caused boycott supporters to "take the alarm." They "ran to all parts of the town, to collect people, and bring them to the poll; in consequence of which, the merchants were defeated." Only two of the five pro-business candidates won, and South Carolina empowered its representatives to go along with whatever measures their congressional colleagues favored, including a trade boycott.[4]

Numerous local meetings proposed to stop bringing in kidnapped African slaves, as several provinces had during the 1769–1770 boycott. Whigs also discussed withholding their crops, with some pointing out that the imperial government depended heavily upon its tobacco import tariff, which tripled the weed's final cost. Since the tobacco tax paid the interest on several series of government bonds, a sudden cutoff of American shipments might even provoke a British fiscal crisis.[5] But the Virginia convention insisted on delaying nonexportation for a year, admittedly eroding its political impact but allowing farmers to market their 1774 crops at the high prices they could expect from Europeans laying up for the lean years.

The summer 1774 meetings also debated whether to cut off exports to Ireland and the British West Indies, which could have a tremendous, if indirect, impact on the mother country. If the Irish farmer had no flaxseed to plant and the West Indian sugar planter had to shift his slaves and fields from sugarcane to food, neither would have crops to send their British creditors—or, for that matter, wooden barrels in which to ship them. That in turn might "oblige whole streets" of British merchants "to shut up at once, and hasten to Parliament with such tales of woe as the stubborn omnipotence of that haughty House could not refuse to hear."[6]

BEFORE 1774, MOST OF the resistance to Parliament had come from the coast, but that changed when Parliament adopted the Coercive Acts. Indeed, eastern and western Massachusetts reversed roles, with protest dying down in Boston, now home to equal numbers of adult male civilians and British soldiers, even as it lit up the countryside. Rural crowds tracked down the new royally appointed provincial councilors to force them to resign. The appointees' only hope was to escape to Boston, often with an angry mob at their heels. When Worcester County farmers arrived at the home of John Murray to demand his resignation, they discovered that he had made tracks for the capital. So they had to content themselves with stabbing his portrait—a punishment that Massachusetts Whigs also meted out to John Singleton Copley portraits of two other British officials. On August 27, between 1,500 and 3,000 Whigs caught another member of council, Timothy Paine, and forced him to read his resignation out loud, over and over, as he was paraded down Main Street to the courthouse. Three thousand angry colonists gathered on Cambridge Common, next to Harvard College, to demand that Thomas Oliver, who had replaced the deceased Andrew Oliver (no relation) as lieutenant governor, resign his position on the council. When a delegation met with Oliver and allowed him to keep his post, the crowd repudiated the concession and enforced its original demand.[7]

Virginians and Marylanders had shut down their county courts earlier in the summer so that indebted farmers could withhold their crops, and Bay Colony residents now did the same for a different reason: to prevent royally appointed judges and royally packed juries from rendering verdicts. Whereas the closing of the Chesapeake courts had been engineered by the provincial elite, in Massachusetts the initiative came from ordinary farmers. A hamlet called Great Barrington finally lived up to its aspirational name on August 16, when an enormous crowd, consisting mostly of town militia companies, prevented the Berkshire County justices from conducting court. Farmers in six other Massachusetts counties followed suit. On September 6, about six thousand people gathered in Worcester (capital of the county of the same name), formed a lane, and made the judges march down it, repeatedly reading out their resignations. Justice Timothy Paine, having run a similar Worcester gauntlet just eight days earlier while relinquishing his council seat, at least knew the drill.[8]

The four thousand residents of Plymouth County were so jubilant at having forced both their judges and their pro-Parliament militia officers to resign that they decided to roll Plymouth Rock from the water's edge up to town. (It would not budge.) Judicial proceedings even had to cease in British-occupied Boston, since no Whig would serve on a jury and no one else dared. New England towns had the right to instruct their assemblymen, and when Worcester ordered its representative to take a hard line, fifty-two prominent citizens entered their protest into the town records. Each man was later forced to cross out his signature, and the clerk smeared ink over the protest itself. Massachusetts's small Anglican minority had lent disproportionate support to Parliament and now

Blotted-out Worcester County protest from the Worcester Town Record, Aug. 22, 1774

paid the price. While John Adams was in Philadelphia for the congress, Abigail gleefully informed him that in their hometown of Braintree, the Anglican "church parson thought they were comeing after him, and run up garret they say, an other jumpt out of his window and hid among the corn whilst a third crept under his bord fence, and told his Beads."[9]

Before 1774, Concord, Massachusetts, had been too distracted by its internal squabbles to pay much attention to Parliament. But the Coercive Acts awakened Concord, along with dozens of other inland towns.[10]

For everyone who still dreamed of reconciliation, the most disturbing event of the summer began at 4:30 a.m. on September 1, when about 260 soldiers from the Boston garrison ventured out to the stone powderhouse on Quarry Hill (which still stands, in Powderhouse Square in Somerville) and carried off more than two hundred half-barrels of gunpowder. The story got better as it traveled west, insisting by the time it reached Marlborough, less than thirty miles from Boston, that Gage had ordered Royal Navy battleships to bombard the town. As many as 100,000 New Englanders grabbed their muskets and headed to Boston as women and children set to work making cartridges (paper bags containing gunpowder and lead balls) and other war matériel. The false news was eventually corrected, but the region had demonstrated its willingness to take up arms.[11]

Meanwhile in the south, war had already begun. The reprisal raids launched by the surviving kin of the Shawnee and Mingo victims of the Yellow Creek Massacre gave Virginia militiamen all the justification they needed to cross to the west bank of the Ohio River and burn the Shawnee town of Wakatomika, along with six Mingo towns. Two additional Virginia armies, one personally led by Governor Dunmore, crossed the Ohio in October. On the 19th, John Gibson, who had lost his Mingo wife to Indian haters back in May, translated as Dunmore obtained Shawnee leaders' marks on a treaty giving up their claim to the entire region east and south of the Ohio River, including Kentucky. The Mingos refused to sign, so a detachment of 250 militiamen "killed 5 & took 14 prisoners chiefly Women & Children the rest escaping under Cover of the Night."[12]

THE IDEA FOR A continental congress had originated with merchants seeking to avoid boycotting Britain, but Parliament's additional punitive legislation guaranteed that the delegates' primary task would be designing the boycott. Joseph Galloway, the conservative speaker of the Pennsylvania assembly, offered his colony's elegant statehouse (the future Independence Hall), but the delegates instead accepted the Carpenters' Company's spacious Hall, which doubled as the Library Company of Philadelphia. These were master carpenters, some quite well-to-do, but there is truth to the claim that the Revolution began in a union hall.[13]

Like Native American rebels, the congressional delegates knew they would succeed only if they overcame their differences. The colonists varied in ethnicity, class, religion, and language. John Adams not only fretted about these centrifugal tendencies but also exhibited most of them. On their way south, he and the other Massachusetts delegates learned that many New Yorkers vividly recalled the Yankees' "hanging the Quakers" on Boston Common more than a century earlier. Equally infamous was their supposed belief in "levelling"—the redistribution of wealth. Conversations with his new colleagues confirmed Adams, a rabid New England patriot, in his conviction that "Our Language is better, our Persons are handsomer, our Spirit is greater, our Laws are wiser, our Religion is superiour, [and] our Education is better." Determined, all the same, to rise above his roots, he even worshipped at a Catholic church.[14]

The Puritans' decision to place a cross rather than a crucifix at the front of their churches was emblematic of their austere faith, and the Philadelphia Catholics' altarpiece filled Adams with delicious horror. Christ was depicted "in the Agonies, and the Blood dropping and streaming from his Wounds"—and the sight was just the start of it. "Here is every Thing which can lay hold of the Eye, Ear, and Imagination. Every Thing which can charm and bewitch the simple and igno-rant," Adams wrote. "I wonder how Luther ever broke the spell." But his greatest contempt was reserved for his fellow worshippers: "The poor Wretches, fingering their Beads, chanting Latin, not a Word of which they understood, their Pater Nosters and Ave Maria's." Only one Philadelphia minister impressed Adams: a Methodist who had come over in 1755 with Gen. Braddock.[15]

The delegates labored to dispel their colleagues' prejudices. At home, Samuel Adams sometimes called the Church of England the Whore of Babylon, but on September 6, he avowed that "he was no Bigot" and proposed that Anglican minister Jacob Duché open the next session. The false rumor about the Royal Navy bombarding Boston reached Philadelphia that night, and the following morning, Duché read the Book of Common Prayer passage prescribed for that day: "Plead my cause, O LORD, with them that strive with me: fight against them that fight against me," a coincidence that most delegates considered "prov-idential."[16]

Yet the congress could not even establish its procedures (mostly copied from Parliament) without the large and small colonies brawling over how they would be represented. Patrick Henry's declaration that "I am not a Virginian, but an American" has been quoted as proof of the Americans' growing nationalism, but it was actually just the op-posite. He wanted each province to be represented in proportion to its population, favoring the larger ones, like his. But smaller colonies like Delaware and New Jersey demanded—and got—equal representation for every province. Another conflict pitted Pennsylvania and New York conservatives against a radical coalition led by Richard Henry Lee and the two Adamses.[17]

The delegates sent memorials to the British public and George III— but not Parliament, since they denied its authority—alleging numerous violations of colonial rights. Richard Henry Lee considered the Quebec Act "the worst grievance" of all; he opposed it "on territorial consider-ations," a New York representative reported, while the New Englanders did so "under pretence of religion."[18] Before 1774, most colonists had stifled their criticism of the mother country's trade monopoly for fear of alienating the British businessmen helping them hold the line against parliamentary encroachments. But now, with most of the merchants "infamously deserting their cause," colonists saw no point in placating them. Delegates to a Pennsylvania provincial congress spoke for many of their countrymen when they metaphorically described themselves "as slaves of *Great Britain*, shut up in a large work-house, constantly kept at labour in procuring such materials as she prescribes, and wearing such clothes as she sends."[19] Such expressions all but forced the congress to confront the mother country's monopoly of American trade. Richard Henry Lee called it "a Capital Violation" of colonial rights but also warned that "to strike at the Navigation Acts would unite every Man in Britain against us, because the Kingdom could not exist without them." A resolution denouncing the British merchants' commercial privileges received the support of exactly half the delegations. Under the congress's rules, that killed it.[20]

As the delegates moved from complaints to remedies, Joseph Galloway proposed to offer Parliament a grand compromise: no legislation would become law without approval from both Parliament and a new pan-American assembly. Viewing Galloway's "Plan of Union" as yet another attempt to put off the boycott of British trade, the delegates quickly cast it aside in favor of the Continental Association, the colonists' most thoroughgoing nonintercourse agreement yet. After December 1, signers would give up not only British merchandise but African slaves and tax-bearing commodities from China, the Wine Islands like Madeira, and the Caribbean. They would also "discountenance and discourage every Species of Extravagance and Dissipation, especially all Horse-racing, and all Kinds of Gaming [gambling], Cock-fighting, Exhibitions of Shows, Plays, and other expensive Diversions and Entertainments."[21]

As instructed, the Virginia delegates demanded and received the right to sell their tobacco for one more year, meaning it would continue arriving in Britain through most of 1775. We will never know whether immediate nonexportation would have forced Parliament to make concessions, preventing the imperial conflict from turning into a revolutionary war.

Another controversy around nonexportation came to a head only on October 20, after the delegates had begun signing the Continental Association. The South Carolinians suddenly announced that they wanted an exception for their two largest exports, rice and indigo, which, unlike tobacco, were selling well. Rebuffed, all but one walked out of the congress, returning only after the other delegations agreed to a compromise: South Carolina could continue shipping rice to its most important market, the mother country.[22] Since the final copy of the Association had already been drawn up, the draftsman merely added the rice exception at the end of the nonexportation article.

Like many other Americans, the delegates believed their mercantile neighbors had enforced the 1768–1770 boycott about as effectively as foxes guard henhouses, so they protected the Association in two ways: by asking Americans to pledge neither to import *nor consume* British merchandise and by entrusting enforcement not to businessmen but elected local committees, which many towns and counties had already formed. Every violator's name would be published in the local newspaper so that neighbors could "break off all Dealings with him, or her."[23]

Town government in New England was among the most democratic on earth, and even today, annual citizens' meetings rule many of the region's villages. But south of the Hudson, most freeholders had no say in their local governments, all power—not just judicial—residing in county judges, who were generally chosen by the governor. He in turn was elected by the freeholders only in Connecticut and Rhode Island. Governors were appointed by the Penn family in Pennsylvania and Delaware, the Calvert family in Maryland, and the king everywhere else. In sharp contrast, what is known as the First Continental Congress entrusted the choice of local committeemen to the freeholders.[24]

Before adjourning on October 26, the delegates proposed that if Parliament failed to redress American grievances, the colonies should send delegates back to Philadelphia the following May.[25]

ORDINARY COLONISTS DID NOT just help elect the committees charged with enforcing the Continental Association; many won seats of their own. Apparently as a result, most committees soon proved more radical than provincial assemblies and even conventions. In Caroline County, Virginia, trader Andrew Leckie disparaged the Continental Association in the most offensive way possible, by ostentatiously urging a slave to sign; the committee extracted a public apology. In February 1775, Israel Williams, one of the "River Gods" who had long dominated the prosperous Connecticut River Valley in western Massachusetts, was accused of opposing the Association. A crowd forced him and his son, another dissident, to spend a night in a smokehouse, whereupon both men signed a denunciation of the Coercive Acts.[26]

Richard Henry Lee had urged the Philadelphia congress to advise the colonies to appoint, train, and arm militias, but his fellow delegates deemed such a move too radical. Still, hardly anyone thought the four regiments occupying Boston would stand by while mobs nullified the Massachusetts Government Act. Especially in New England, a growing number of colonists took it upon themselves to prepare for war. Early in October, the British ambassador to the Netherlands learned that Rhode Islanders had sent a ship to Amsterdam for artillery and gunpowder. Later that same month, the Massachusetts provincial congress ordered twenty-two field guns, a thousand barrels of gunpowder, five thousand muskets and rifles, and other weaponry. On December 14, residents of Portsmouth, New Hampshire, overpowered the small army garrison in nearby Fort William and Mary, helping themselves to its hundred barrels of gunpowder.[27]

Gen. Gage and other British governors proved nearly as aggressive in taking munitions from the rebels. On February 26, 1775, soldiers descended upon Salem, Massachusetts, fifteen miles north of Boston, to haul away the cannon stored there. The locals thwarted them by raising a drawbridge, prompting Col. Alexander Leslie, the commander of the British force, to threaten an amphibious landing. Eventually the two sides worked out a face-saving compromise that called to mind the agree-to-disagree relationship between crown and colonies before 1763. The townspeople would lower the drawbridge, allowing Leslie and his men to enter Salem, upon which they would immediately turn around and return to Boston empty-handed.[28]

Southerners were also getting ready to defend themselves. On September 21, Whigs in Fairfax County, Virginia, formed an "independant Company of Voluntiers." Maryland, like Virginia, had a militia, but mostly just on paper. In early December, a provincial convention urged all freemen to organize themselves and begin drills.[29] Given that ordinary Americans were so much readier than their congressmen to discuss a possible military confrontation, we might well ask why historians narrating the autumn of 1774 focus on the worthies assembled in Philadelphia. [30] It is consistent with their fixation on parliamentary adoption of the Intolerable Acts to the exclusion of the troops who landed in Boston to enforce them, but it is like cheering throughout the derby for the hindmost horse.

Neither imperial officials nor the colonists wanted a war or blame for starting one. But Americans plausibly expected the army to impose the Coercive Acts by force, so they collected munitions and trained for war. Understandably misconstruing the colonists' intentions as aggressive— and also wanting to clear the way for whatever offensive maneuvers they might be ordered to undertake—Gage and other imperial officials dispatched troops to disarm them. It was all but inevitable that the two sides' defensive preparations would spark violence; the only question was when the steel would strike the flint.

As free Americans prepared for war, so did many of their slaves. In the fall of 1774, two groups of enslaved Georgians plotted insurrections. Many slave conspiracies, possibly including these two, existed only in whites' fevered imaginations. But if either or both of these was real, the leaders whom whites captured and burned alive can be considered the Revolutionary War's first martyrs. What is certain is that the racial equation fundamentally changed with the addition of British troops—and often just with enslaved Americans' anticipation of their arrival. On September 22, Abigail Adams informed John, who was attending the congress in Philadelphia, that several enslaved Massachusetts residents had sent Governor Gage a written offer to "fight for him provided he would arm them and engage to liberate them if he conquerd." No British soldiers would land in Virginia until the summer of 1775, but James Madison reported on November 26, 1774, that slaves in a neighboring county had "met together & chose a leader who was to conduct them when the English Troops should arrive." The following April, on the docks of Charles Town, South Carolina, the free Black pilot and "very good fisherman" Thomas Jeremiah used strikingly similar language as he reportedly advised slaves "to go in to His Majesty's troops when any should arrive, for they were then all to be made free."[31]

Like the Whigs, enslaved conspirators tried to stockpile arms and ammunition. Early in 1775, a white farmer in Ulster County, New York (on the Hudson River, about a third of the way from Manhattan to Albany), overheard two slaves discussing how to obtain gunpowder. Twenty Blacks were arrested. Thomas Jeremiah allegedly told his brother-in-law he "wanted more arms" and "would try to get as many as he could."[32]

The Whigs' increasing militance cost them many of their British friends. London cartoonist Philip Dawe had responded to the Boston Port Act with a mezzotint (a new form of engraving allowing for mixed tones) that was highly sympathetic to the Whigs. But less than a year later, in early 1775, he began depicting Americans differently. For example, he had male Whigs seduce fifty-one women in Edenton, North Carolina, into signing the anti-British boycott. And the women themselves were mannish gavel-wielders who deserted their children and pets.[33]

MANY FREE AMERICANS HOPED the fall 1774 House of Commons election, the first to focus on America, would bring in new MPs favoring

Philip Dawe[?], *Bostonians in Distress*
(1774)

Philip Dawe[?], *Alternative of Williamsburg*
(1775)

Philip Dawe[?], *Society of
Patriotic Ladies* (1775)

accommodation. But fewer than a third of the 558 incumbents faced serious contests, and the new Parliament, which convened on November 30, supported the ministry by the same lopsided majority as the old.[34] So did the hereditary House of Lords. On February 1, 1775, Lord Chatham proposed that Parliament promise not to tax the colonists in return for their acknowledging its right to legislate for them. The American assemblies would have to help pay the Seven Years' War debt, a demand that even George Grenville had never dared to make. Finally, Chatham wanted Parliament to repeal all of its major American legislation, including the Coercive Acts, but at the same time reaffirm its commitment to the Acts of Trade. As ever, the British merchants' bottom line was his as well.[35]

Lord Dartmouth was so eager to accommodate the rebels that he praised Chatham's plan, only to back down under pressure from his colleagues in the cabinet.[36] The House of Lords defeated it two to one, and it attracted no more support in America, where few free colonists wanted to acknowledge Parliament's authority and many were beginning to imagine life after the Navigation Acts.

On March 22, when Edmund Burke rose to offer a compromise that resembled Chatham's and suffered the same fate, everyone at least credited him with masterfully making the case. The colonists were hypersensitive, he explained. Whereas most people, including Britons, will complain only in response to "an actual grievance," Americans "augur misgovernment at a distance; and snuff the approach of tyranny in every tainted breeze." Burke traced the provincials' "mercurial" political temperament to their daily exposure to "vast multitudes of slaves." In slave country, "those who are free, are by far the most proud and jealous of [i.e., anxious about] their freedom."[37]

The day after Burke gave his most famous speech, Patrick Henry gave his. A second Virginia convention was meeting, not in Williamsburg but upriver in Richmond, and on March 23, Henry addressed the delegates in the emotional tones of an evangelical minister. He was Anglican, but in his youth he and his mother had regularly worshipped with dissenters — once, it was said, with George Whitefield. And as an attorney, he had defended Baptist ministers jailed for practicing their faith. A Virginian who admired his oratory described him as a "son of Thunder" — a biblical term normally reserved for evangelical preachers.[38]

Henry embodied the American hypersensitivity that Burke described. "There is no retreat, but in submission and slavery!" he declared, for "Our chains are forged" already. "Is life so dear, or peace so sweet, as to be purchased at the price of chains, and slavery?" he asked. "As for me, give me liberty, or give me death!"[39]

Henry was by no means the only American slaveholder to accuse Parliament of trying to reduce him to slavery, but in 1974 the historian Fawn Brodie offered additional context for his address. His wife, Sarah, had just died of what appears to have been puerperal psychosis—an extreme form of postpartum depression. Deemed a threat to herself and others, she had spent her final weeks in a strait-dress. Brodie suggested that Patrick's struggles with Sarah added color to his depiction of the colonists' ordeal:

> We have petitioned—we have remonstrated—we have supplicated. . . . Our petitions have been slighted; our remonstrances have produced additional violence and insult; our supplications have been disregarded; and we have been spurned, with contempt.[40]

Henry stated his case so effectively that later generations have overstated his impact. He and the other radical delegates were only able to persuade the Virginia convention to copy the statement issued by its Maryland counterpart a long three months earlier. Indeed, in urging every freeman to sign up for military training, the Marylanders had traveled considerably farther than the Virginians, who merely asked every county to establish a single independent military company, as many already had.[41]

Like its Maryland counterpart, the Virginia convention maintained that if Parliament had relied upon the North American militia, it could have avoided the whole dispute over its right to station ten thousand British regulars in America at colonial expense. But in glorifying militiamen, the delegates gave up the chance to seriously consider a radical proposal to field a regular army. This unsuccessful substitute motion would have embodied ten thousand regular troops—the exact number the Bute ministry had left in North America in 1763. That coincidence, and the conservative Robert Carter Nicholas's authorship of the substitute, raises the possibility that its actual purpose was to *prevent* the delegates from embodying regulars by reminding Whigs of what they had condemned in Lord Bute.[42]

Meanwhile Parliament approached the Americans with a combination of carrots and sticks. Any colony that agreed to pay its share of the imperial government's American expenses would be rewarded with an exemption from parliamentary taxation. This offer was less generous—

and less similar to Chatham's—than it seemed. By extending it to each colony individually, Britain hoped to divide them.[43]

North also proposed an ominous response to the Americans' latest boycott: "If they refused to trade with Great Britain, Great Britain would take care they should trade no where else."[44] In theory the Acts of Trade already gave the mother country a monopoly of colonial commerce, but Parliament had always made exceptions, for example allowing North Americans to export grain, forest products, and livestock to foreign provinces in the Caribbean. But in March and April, Parliament closed these loopholes with a pair of laws called the Restraining Acts, exempting only the four colonies—Georgia, North Carolina, Delaware, and New York—that it hoped to separate from the herd. This harsh new approach was partly the result of external pressure. While ports and manufacturing towns continued to petition their MPs for leniency, others demanded a harder line.[45]

In this climate, even the irrepressible Benjamin Franklin had to acknowledge that the candle had burned down on accomodation. On March 20, 1775, two days before Burke's famous speech, he took ship for Philadelphia.

IN MARCH 1775, AS white Americans inched toward separation from the mother country, a group of Cherokees carried out a rebellion of their own. At Sycamore Shoals on the Watauga River in modern-day East Tennessee, the Transylvania Company, led by Judge Richard Henderson (who had felt the North Carolina Regulators' wrath four years earlier) convinced the heads of the Cherokee nation to part with 27,000 square miles of land, including most of Kentucky and the northern portion of Tennessee. At the climax of the negotiations, Dragging Canoe, whose kinsman Little Carpenter was a principal signatory to the sale, stood up and denounced it, warning the colonists that they would find Kentucky "dark, and difficult to settle." Then he and other Cherokee critics of the Treaty of Sycamore Shoals stormed out.[46]

"THE CHILD IS ALREADY spoilt, gentle correction is of no use." Alexander Leslie, who commanded the British troops at Castle William in Boston Harbor, did not have it quite right. The mother country had not pampered her colonists or even treated them with "wise and salutary neglect," as Edmund Burke claimed of the good old days before 1763. The reason the empire had not previously tried to impose its will on the

American colonists was that it had needed their help against France. Defeating the Catholics had taken nearly a century, culminating in the Seven Years' War, which fortified Britain's conviction that North America was overdue for root-and-branch reform. The changes immediately followed the peace treaty, and when Americans resisted them, Parliament in turn responded with the Coercive and Restraining Acts. The Seven Years' War had also laid the foundation for the imperial conflict in other ways, for instance by requiring burdensome provincial taxes that aggravated American resistance to parliamentary impositions and by enriching British military contractors, giving rise to the speculative boom that culminated in the crash of 1772. In India as in America, Britain's spectacular conquests of the late 1750s and early 1760s had yielded treasure but also challenges.[47]

A half century of research by social historians of the founding era has laid bare the many ways in which the deterioration in the relationship between the colonies and the crown was influenced by other, lesser known, disputes. In a fast day sermon delivered in his hometown of Concord, Massachusetts, early in April 1775, Rev. William Emerson paraphrased Micah 7:6 and Matthew 10:36: "Verily our enemies are of our own household." Emerson, grandfather of Ralph Waldo Emerson, was referring to colonists—including his own brother-in-law—who had cooperated with Governor-General Gage, but he gestured toward a larger reality of the revolution: it was in part a conflict among Americans, including many that are often omitted from the founding narrative: natives, African Americans, and women of all races and ranks.[48]

If Native Americans had not repeatedly rebelled against the settlers and speculators who coveted their land, the Bute administration would have left many fewer than ten thousand troops in America in 1763, and Parliament might have felt no need to adopt the Stamp Act. Nor would the Privy Council have banned settlement and speculation west of the Appalachian Mountains—a prohibition that was initially intended as temporary and would have remained so if female peace chiefs out on the Wabash River had not founded a pan-Indian confederacy to battle the British or at least convincingly threaten to do so.

In other ways, too, Whigs repeatedly revealed that the natives were never far from their minds. James Otis denied that Members of Parliament could "virtually" represent Americans, who were "as perfect strangers" to the men who sat in the Lords and Commons "as the savages in *Calafornia*." Defending the Boston Massacre soldiers, John Adams pointed out that the crowd harassing them had been "making the mob whistle," which was "almost as terrible as an Indian yell." A Boston newspaper writer hoped colonists would resist the British the same way "the French and Indians fought General Braddock's Army."[49] Forced immigrants from Africa also resisted their subjugation, contributing mightily to many whites' desire to halt the transatlantic slave trade—if only the Liverpool slave merchants and their creatures in government would let them.

Free women gave more than their mite to the resistance against Parliament, both by boycotting British commodities and by symbolically replacing some of them. But they also stood up to male Whigs, for instance by marrying officers and soldiers, pushing back when caricatured as spendthrifts, and swearing off tea only after obtaining a medical exemption. Free southern women associated spinning with slavery and refused to hold bees like those in New England.[50]

The Revolution was by no means the only source of women's mounting defiance. One reason Mary Fish Noyes summoned the nerve to write "Portrait of a Good Husband" was that the English common law accorded widows like her a large measure of independence. When ministers and other males tried to shut down Sarah Osborn's ministry, her blessed self-assurance fortified her in defying them, albeit artfully rather than openly. Religious conversion also emboldened other women, including Phillis Wheatley, along with obscure males like Hermon Husband, Samson Occom, and the Black men who initiated Osborn's revival.[51]

Even as free colonists felt the influence of all these internal conflicts, they also believed the British government danced to the tune of distant and hostile economic interests. The "superior Interest of the West India Planters" pushed the imperial government to cut off their supplies of foreign molasses.[52] The mother country's merchants persuaded Parliament to ban American paper money and rebuff colonial offers to share in the cost of imperial administration in return for commercial freedom. The colonists' troubled relationship with metropolitan businessmen also fueled their desire first to boycott British merchandise and later to withhold their exports.

Free Americans' dispute with the British government was even affected by conflicts in which they were not involved. Parliament might never have adopted the Tea Act of 1773 if Haidar Ali's forces had not bedeviled the East India Company, contributing to its near bankruptcy.

Historians typically depict British reformers somewhere along the spectrum between bumbling placemen and problem solvers. But Americans knew that Parliament also responded to external pressure, whether from the "few African corsairs" who defended their sacred right to sell captive Africans or the First Nations rebels who remotely wrote the Proclamation of 1763.[53]

The conflicts that eventuated in the American Revolution were kaleidoscopically diverse, yet the participants pursued surprisingly similar strategies. For example, the indispensability of unity was apparent to everyone from members of the First Continental Congress and farmers trying to drive up the price of tobacco to Native Americans plotting against encroaching settlers. Unity even brought important psychological and sociological benefits. Indebted Virginia gentlemen like George Washington were too embarrassed to abandon extravagance on their own, but could do so collectively, as patriots. Young women who normally associated spinning with the poor or, well, spinsters gladly worked the wheel alongside fellow Whigs from "as good families as any in town."[54]

It was not just people but impersonal forces that contributed to the breakdown of imperial authority. Caribbean hurricanes, which hit food crops especially hard, all but guaranteed that French, Spanish, and Dutch sugar planters would subsist their slaves partly by trading their molasses to the North American breadbasket, no matter what London said. Britain's effort to force Wine Islands merchants to send their nectar to North America via Britain flew in the face of the Atlantic trade winds, which rarely blew counterclockwise. The famine that hit Bengal in 1769 deprived the East India Company of nearly a million taxpayers, strengthening the company's case for the Tea Act of 1773. And America's relatively sparse yet rapidly multiplying population of settlers made land speculation irresistibly lucrative, setting up a conflict between elite Americans and the British government, even as it made manufacturing unprofitable, leaving colonists anxiously dependent upon British merchandise and easily convinced to boycott it.

As late as the winter of 1775, few Americans had any desire to go to war against the imperial army. But the colonists would never reconcile themselves to the Coercive Acts, and Parliament would never repeal them. The question was how far Britain was willing to go to enforce them.

PART TWO

PUSH ON

INTRODUCTION

THE FAMILY OF MARIE-JOSEPH-PAUL-YVES-ROCH GILBERT DU Motier enjoyed prominence in its hometown of Chavaniac, three hundred miles south of Paris, but it took a series of untimely deaths to transform little Gilbert into the marquis de Lafayette. He was not yet two when, on August 1, 1759, his father died fighting the British at the Battle of Minden in Prussia. By the time he turned five, the death of his uncle had brought him immense wealth and status but also, as he matured, an acute awareness of having done nothing to earn either.[1]

And then, in 1775, he met the younger brother of the British king.

The Duke of Gloucester harbored an immense admiration for the American rebels and easily imparted it to Lafayette, who resolved to earn his eminence by joining them. Neither his guardian (who was also his father-in-law) nor his king (who was secretly arming the Americans but unready for an open rupture) would hear of the idea. So the nineteen-year-old marquis disguised himself as a courier to escape to Spain, whence he and a party of like-minded French noblemen sailed for America. On July 31, 1777, Congress gave the tall, thin, pale, redheaded aristocrat a commission as a major general in the Continental Army. It was meant to be honorary, but Lafayette could not win glory without commanding troops. So when George Washington invited him onto his personal staff, he accepted the post as an apprenticeship.[2]

The childless commander-in-chief and the fatherless marquis formed an instant bond. But Lafayette had to wait more than three years for an independent command. When he finally got one, the impetus was a devastating storm.[3]

On the last day of 1780, the American traitor and British general Benedict Arnold invaded Washington's home state of Virginia, seizing and destroying massive quantities of war matériel and high-priced tobacco. He also liberated hundreds of slaves and holed up with them in the town of Portsmouth in the southeastern corner of the state. The Virginia militia was too weak to attack Gen. Arnold, who in any event always had the option of sailing off into Chesapeake Bay. But then on January 22, 1781, a storm blew through the mid-Atlantic states, disabling two British men-of-war cruising Long Island Sound. The French expeditionary force that had landed in Newport, Rhode Island, back in August 1780 had done essentially nothing since then, but now the French admiral, Charles-René-Dominique Sochet Destouches, finally had more ships in the water than the British, and he rushed three of them south to capture Arnold and his army.[4]

On February 3, the comte de Rochambeau, who commanded the French troops stationed at Newport, wrote George Washington informing him of Destouches's plan. Four days later, before receiving Rochambeau's letter, Washington also realized that the storm offered the allies an opportunity to bag the "arch traitor." He urged the two French commanders to expand their southern expedition, sending the rest of the Newport squadron and one thousand soldiers. For his part, Washington dispatched 1,200 Continental veterans under Lafayette. Like many bold military maneuvers, this one was born of desperation. "We stood in need of something to keep us a float," Washington explained to his former aide John Laurens, since, with the plunge in the value of the Continental dollar, "we are at the end of our tether."[5]

The prospect of capturing Arnold spurred Lafayette's troops southward, but Destouches sent no additional ships, and Rochambeau kept all of his soldiers in Newport. Washington could offer Lafayette no reinforcements, since he had already depleted his own army, first by sending troops up the Hudson River to fight the Iroquois and then by allowing hundreds of mutinying soldiers to return to their families. He was furious at Destouches and Rochambeau and said so in a note to a cousin that was intercepted and published in a Loyalist (pro-British) newspaper, embarrassing all three of them.[6]

Eventually Washington persuaded Destouches to take his entire fleet to Virginia, but the British prevented it from entering the Chesapeake. Dejected, Lafayette's soldiers began the long trek back to New York, only to learn that Washington wanted them to continue southward, possibly even into the Carolinas. The marquis was distraught, for he feared that while he wandered "in the southern wilderness," Washington's and Rochambeau's armies would drive the British from New York City, ending the war. But he warmed to his assignment when he learned that Gen. William Phillips, the man he believed had killed his father at Minden, had just joined Arnold's troops in Virginia, superseding the traitor in command.[7]

Yet Lafayette's soldiers, most of whom hailed from northern states, had their own objections to an extended sojourn in the "Unwholesome Climate" of the American south just at the start of the sickly season. Expecting a quick campaign against Arnold, few had packed much clothing or other supplies, and none had brought his wife—a practical as well as emotional necessity at a time when, for example, most shirts were sewn at home. As Lafayette noted, when a soldier's linen shirt wore out, his woolen coat chafed his skin, causing "Galle"—painful swelling and sores (and the root of the modern adjective "galling").[8] With each passing mile, more men deserted and headed back north. Fearing that the army he commanded would "not Have Six Hundred Men By the time we would Arrive at our Destination," he executed a recaptured deserter but also boldly offered a pass home to any man so base as to openly quit the cause (few did).[9]

The young general also acted on the troops' complaints about their worn-out shirts and shoes. The previous summer, the women of Philadelphia had undertaken a fundraising effort—Lafayette had donated a thousand guineas in the name of his wife back in France—and then used the money to buy enough cloth to make more than two thousand shirts for the Continental troops. The women's campaign had spread into several other states, including Maryland, where Lafayette now resolved to revive it. From the Baltimore merchants, he bought £2,000 worth of supplies (primarily linen cloth) on the promise that if the French and American governments failed to pay the debt by September 1782, when he turned twenty-five and came into his inheritance, he would cover it himself. He asked the city's women to use the material to sew shirts for the solders, and they readily agreed.[10]

Late in the summer of 1781, Rochambeau's and Washington's troops joined Lafayette's in Virginia, and the combined army captured Lord Charles Cornwallis's eight thousand redcoats and Germans at Yorktown. But before Rochambeau and Washington even arrived, Lafayette's summer 1781 campaign had already encapsulated many of the complexities of the American War of Independence. It was by no means the only Revolutionary War expedition set in motion by a storm or the only southward march disrupted by northern soldiers' fears of the sickly south. Wealthy white southerners' preference for African laborers derived partly from their supposed immunity to tropical disease, and the wider distribution of the sickle cell trait among Africans really did strengthen them against malaria and yellow fever—somewhat. A third of South Carolina's forced African immigrants died during their first year in the colony.[11]

Washington was not the first Continental general to inadvertently offend America's indispensable French allies. Lafayette's prediction that the war's climactic battle would be fought in the north was inaccurate but not ill-founded, for Washington believed he could defeat the British only by annihilating them on the streets of Boston, Philadelphia, or New York. Possibly the commander-in-chief's greatest contribution to the American victory was repeatedly deciding, often at the last minute, not to act on that instinct.

Throughout the war as in 1781, Washington had sent detachments to fight Native Americans and African Americans as well as redcoats, German mercenaries, and Loyalists. Mass desertion imperiled this multi-pronged mission, and sometimes Continental soldiers rebelled in still more dramatic fashion. And when the Baltimore seamstresses redressed Lafayette's army—and thus one of its most pressing grievances—they only revived a patriotic campaign orchestrated by a much larger group of American women the previous year.

In short, the American Revolutionary War was a colonial rebellion, just as the textbooks say. But it was also much more.

CHAPTER 14

— ·◆· —

Declare Freedom

Early 1775

THE WINTER OF 1774–1775 FOUND THOMAS GAGE, GOVERNOR OF Massachusetts and commander-in-chief of British forces in North America, in an impossible position. Even pulling many of his dispersed troops into Boston gave him only about 3,500. That was roughly equivalent to the number of adult males in Boston, but Gage stressed in letters home that he no longer confronted only "a Boston Rabble but the freeholders and farmers of the country." Again and again he begged for reinforcements—ideally twenty thousand. Until they arrived, he would not attempt to enforce the Coercive Acts, and he urged Lord North to suspend them.[1]

North and the cabinet did send additional troops, though many fewer than Gage requested, and they rejected his protestations of impotence. Gage's military service went back to the annihilation of Bonnie Prince Charlie's rebels at Culloden in 1745, and he had served loyally and often boldly in America ever since commanding the advance force at the Battle of the Monongahela in 1755, but now underlings as well as superiors took to calling him "an *Old Woman.*"[2]

Gage's dispute with the ministry came to a head in a letter Lord Dartmouth wrote him on January 27, 1775. Although the American commander had explicitly denied that the rebel colonists were only a "rabble," Dartmouth insisted on that term—and also accused Gage of shirking his duty. The governor-general had warned that arresting the leaders of the Massachusetts provincial congress would provoke a war, but Dartmouth demanded that he take them anyway, adding that "it will surely be better that the conflict should be brought on upon such ground than in a riper state" of provincial military preparation.[3] In demanding this pointless provocation, Dartmouth not only brought the two sides closer to war but also foretold the outcome—of this and most imperial efforts to suppress wide-ranging citizen insurgencies.

On April 16, when Dartmouth's letter finally reached Gage, he knew he had to act—but also that any move against John Hancock and Samuel Adams would probably fail and certainly inflame the colonists. So instead his men would step up their months-long scramble for munitions, seizing or destroying the weapons, including cannon, that colonists had stashed in and around the town of Concord, seventeen miles west of Boston. Lt. Col. Francis Smith would lead seven to eight hundred elite troops: half light infantry, chosen for their fleetness of foot and for traveling light, and the rest grenadiers.[4] They would move out on Tuesday evening, April 18, ideally reaching Concord by daybreak on Wednesday, before anyone knew they were coming.

Given the multiple connections between Gen. Gage's troops and the people of Boston, his expectation of surprising the sleeping denizens of Concord seems naive. The sergeants roused their men by "putting their hands on them, and whispering gently to them," and they bayonetted a barking dog. Yet a senior British officer crossing Boston Common overheard two locals discussing the impending expedition. Even if Gage and his troops could have somehow preserved the element of surprise, the trip to Concord would still have been pointless, since Whigs, anticipating just such a move, had already dispersed most of its military stores.[5]

Gage might well have suspected that he was sending Smith on a fool's errand. But at least he could say he had tried.

Henry Wadsworth Longfellow's "Paul Revere's Ride" (1860) evokes a lone rider—almost a lone ranger—singlehandedly alarming the countryside, but the Boston silversmith was actually only one element in an extensive Whig network. At its center stood Dr. Joseph Warren, a member of the Massachusetts Committee of Safety. Knowing that Gage had ordered mounted patrols to detain all riders heading west, Warren dispatched Revere and a tanner named William Dawes on the same errand. Neither man shouted, "The British are coming," since both considered themselves British Americans—though the events of the next twenty-four hours would compel them and thousands of other colonists, especially in New England, to begin thinking of themselves as simply Americans.[6]

In case neither he nor Dawes made it out of Boston, Revere arranged for the sexton and a vestryman of the Anglican church in the town's North End to inform Whigs in Charlestown, across the river, of the redcoats' intentions by hanging two lanterns in the steeple if they were coming across the Charles River and one if they planned to take the more southerly and considerably longer land route over Boston Neck, the narrow isthmus connecting the capital to the mainland.

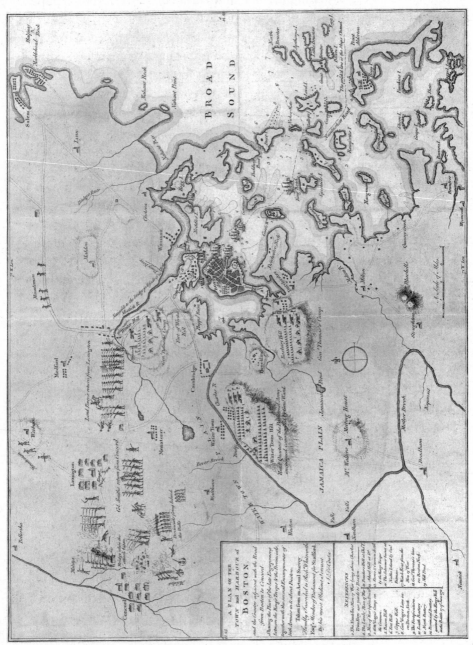

A Plan of the Town and Harbour of Boston (1775)

Dawes left ahead of Revere, somehow talking his way past the British sentries on the Neck. Meanwhile two of Revere's confederates rowed him north across the Charles, and he reached the town of Lexington, ten miles to the west, at midnight, a half hour ahead of Dawes. At each population center they passed, the two paused to convey the news, which then radiated out in every direction. Smith's troops were rowed across the Charles starting around 10 p.m. but did not start their march west until just after 2 a.m., by which time colonists as far away as New Hampshire already knew they were coming. The army marched in two divisions: about 320 light infantry, commanded by Marine Maj. John Pitcairn, followed by 350 grenadiers under Lt. Col. Smith.[7]

Dawes and Revere warned John Hancock and Samuel Adams, who were staying in Lexington, and then continued on toward Concord, accompanied by Dr. Samuel Prescott, a Concord resident who had paid a late call on his sweetheart. A British patrol accosted the messengers, and only Prescott escaped to convey the news to Concord.[8]

Meanwhile John Parker, wheelwright and captain of Lexington's militia company, mustered about 130 men on the town common (now Lexington Green). With the British infantry running hours behind Revere and Dawes, Capt. Parker permitted the militiamen to head home or to nearby Buckman's Tavern. Just before dawn, Thaddeus Bowman galloped in with the news that the British advance, consisting of about two hundred light infantry, had reached the edge of town.[9] Unable to collect more than half the troops he had had hours earlier, Parker ordered his men not to challenge the redcoats but just to stand in silent witness.

The redcoats were supposed to leave Lexington Common on their right. The militiamen lined up there were not blocking their path, but no officer worth his salt would incur the enormous risk of exposing a flank to an armed and seemingly hostile force. When the officers in the column's "front party" spotted the militiamen lined up on the Common, ahead of them on their right, they instinctively and collectively made the fateful decision to lead the column out onto the Common to confront them head-on.[10]

At the sight of two hundred light infantrymen marching toward them, several militiamen decamped, whereupon Capt. Parker dismissed the rest. That was not good enough for Maj. Pitcairn, who commanded them to leave their muskets behind. None did.[11]

Someone discharged his weapon. Every witness on both sides—with the exception of prisoners interviewed by their captors—would swear that someone on the other side had fired first. Either way, that first shot had the same effect as the one fired outside the Custom House in Boston on March 5, 1770: the British front line took it as a signal to let fly. Seven militiamen fell dead, and nine others were wounded, two mortally. A few of the provincials returned fire, but the only casualty on the government side was a private who was grazed in the thigh. (A half century later, with Concord residents boasting that they and not their Lexington neighbors had been the first to draw British blood, Lexington's surviving witnesses were "induced to try again." Several told stories of heroic resistance, especially on the part of Capt. Parker.)[12]

The Battle of Lexington would not have occurred if the officers leading the British column had known that the colonists were determined not to be the aggressors. Maj. Pitcairn and Col. Smith finally regained control of their men and led them down the road toward Concord and another battle that neither side wanted.[13]

The minute companies (so designated because they could be called up on a moment's notice) and other militiamen who gathered in Concord were, like the Lexington militia, greatly outnumbered. So as the regulars entered town around 10 a.m., they pulled back, over the North Bridge spanning the Concord River and up onto Punkatasset Hill, nearly a mile behind the town.[14]

British soldiers set about destroying the supplies they had found in the center of Concord. Seven companies marched to North Bridge, with three

Ralph Earl and Amos Doolittle, *The Battle of Lexington, April 19th. 1775*

remaining to guard the road and bridge while the rest crossed to the west bank and marched two miles upriver to search for the weaponry said to be hidden on the farm of Col. James Barrett, a sixty-five-year-old miller.[15]

Barrett commanded the Middlesex County militiamen on Punkatasset Hill, as a growing crowd of women and children looked on. Suddenly someone noticed smoke rising up through the trees. While burning war matériel, the redcoats had accidentally set fire to the blacksmith's shop and courthouse. They were now helping extinguish the blaze, but the militiamen outside town did not know that. Lt. Joseph Hosmer, leader of the town's younger generation and viewed by a pro-Parliament attorney as "the most dangerous man in Concord," demanded of Col. Barrett, in a voice loud enough for everyone around to hear, "Will you let them burn the town down?"[16]

Other militiamen made it clear to Barrett that they, too, were determined to confront the redcoats guarding North Bridge, and he grudgingly agreed to lead them. As the opposing detachments converged, the redcoats fired over the bridge, and Abner Hosmer, brother of Joseph, fell dead, along with another militiaman. The rest returned fire. At Lexington that morning, redcoats had killed colonists for the first time since the Boston Massacre five years earlier. Now at Concord, Whig militiamen killed British soldiers—three of them—for the first time ever.[17]

Ralph Earl and Amos Doolittle, *The Engagement at the North Bridge in Concord* (1775)

In the Massachusetts militia as in most modern armies, lieutenants stood near the bottom of the hierarchy of commissioned officers, out-ranking only ensigns. When Lt. Joseph Hosmer, wrongly thinking the British were burning Concord, pressured Col. Barrett to attack the red-coats guarding North Bridge, he foretold the many ways in which the American War of Independence would be influenced by people other than its titular commanders. Another similarity between April 19 and many later battles was the crucial role of misperception.

The outnumbered British survivors of the battle of North Bridge fled back into Concord, carrying some of their nine wounded with them but leaving others where they lay. A frightened young American attempted to finish off a badly wounded redcoat with an axe blow to the head, spill-ing his brains out onto the ground and giving rise to British accusations that he had been scalped. (Astonishingly, the wounded soldier appears to have survived the ordeal.) Meanwhile the four companies that had visited Col. Barrett's farm rejoined their fellows in Concord center, and Lt. Col. Smith gave the order to head back to Boston. It was about noon; the soldiers had discovered and destroyed more than two dozen cannon wheels—but only two cannon.[18]

A mile down the road, at Meriam's Corner, militiamen fired at the redcoats from behind trees and stone walls, opening up a sixteen-mile gauntlet back to Boston. Both sides received reinforcements, including, on the colonial side, several African Americans. "A Woman shot one of the Marines," claimed a British colonel who had remained in the capital, "so you see all Ages and Sexes are united." Fewer than twenty men had died at Lexington and Concord, but by 8 p.m., when the last redcoats staggered into Charlestown, where they would spend the night in rela-tive safety before being ferried across the Charles into Boston the next morning, they had suffered 272 casualties to the colonists' 94.[19]

The ratio of regulars who were wounded (180) rather than killed (65) on April 19 was about three to one—typical for eighteenth-century bat-tles. But more Americans were killed (50) than wounded (39), an ex-tremely rare outcome. Many had initially suffered non-life-threatening injuries only to be finished off, most often at bayonet's end, by exasper-ated regulars.[20] But the stark fact that the British suffered three times the colonial casualties calls into question the modern depiction of pro-vincial Davids miraculously triumphing over an imperial Goliath. The militiamen actually had the advantage not only in numbers and position but in experience. The Seven Years' War had ended twelve years earlier, before five-sixths of Col. Smith's soldiers enlisted. By contrast, many of the militiamen were middle-aged veterans who had learned hard-won lessons in forest warfare. "The rebels followed the Indian manner of fighting, concealing themselves behind hedges [and] trees and skulking in woods and houses," a British officer reported. British leaders compared the New Englanders to the Native American winners of the Battle of the Monongahela, and the militiamen did indeed understand forest warfare. At least one had marched with Braddock.[21]

Another Seven Years' War veteran, seventy-eight-year-old Samuel Whittemore, killed at least one redcoat and then took a bullet in the face and fourteen bayonet wounds but somehow survived.[22]

Long before the shooting stopped, Whig leaders sent express riders south and west with the astounding news that British soldiers had killed numerous colonists. Throughout New England, men dropped everything but their muskets and made for Massachusetts, where they established a fortified crescent around British-controlled Boston. On April 26, at least eight thousand people from Philadelphia and surrounding towns gathered outside the Pennsylvania statehouse to create a military association—not technically a militia, since none had been authorized by the colony's Quaker-dominated legislature.[23]

Neither side had wanted war, but each had expected the other to attack, so the Whigs had struggled to stockpile ammunition, and Governor-General Gage had resolved to take it from them. This standoff, itself a kind of powder keg, was set off by multiple sparks, ranging from Dartmouth's goading of Gen. Gage to an accidental or unsanctioned musket shot at Lexington and, in Concord, the militiamen's reasonable but erroneous deduction about the smoke arising from their town. To deny the war's inevitability, to say the two sides could have worked things out, is no mere hypothesis, for that was precisely how the redcoats' expedition to Salem had concluded just two months earlier.

From New Hampshire to North Carolina, the Battle of Lexington and Concord was described as having thrown colonists into a "frenzy."[24] With it, the American War of Independence officially began. But many Americans, especially in New England, viewed April 19, 1775, less as a beginning than an end: the final argument for independence.

IN THE SOUTH AS in Massachusetts, the spring 1775 scramble for munitions turned numerous colonists irrevocably against the crown, but there the struggle was heavily influenced by the 40 percent of the population that was enslaved. During the third week of April 1775, numerous whites in the James River watershed in southern Virginia came to believe their slaves were plotting a rebellion. Even more ominous, rebels in multiple localities, from the port town of Norfolk (where two men were executed for insurrection) to Prince Edward County, 130 miles upriver, seemed to be in touch with each other. They might well have been, given that most of the region's watermen were Black.[25]

Then, early on Friday morning, April 21, amid mounting African American expectations and white fears, Governor Dunmore sent sailors from HMS *Magdalen* into Virginia's principal ammunition depot, the octagonal, cone-roofed, "magazine" in the center of Williamsburg, to seize fifteen half-barrels of gunpowder. Many white Virginians believed the governor's timing was no coincidence, that he had, as one claimed, "designed, by disarming the people, to weaken the means of opposing an insurrection of the slaves . . . for a protection against whom in part the magazine was at first built."[26] When furious whites warned Dunmore to return the gunpowder or face attack, he replied with a threat of his own: if he or any other British official was assaulted, he would "declare freedom to the slaves & reduce the City of Wmsburg to ashes." As one Whig told the governor, he had forfeited "the Confidence of the People not so much for having taken the Powder as for the declaration he made of raising and freeing the Slaves."[27]

Provincial leaders labored to avoid further antagonizing Dunmore, but by April 29, more than six hundred fighters had rendezvoused at Fredericksburg, eighty-four miles northwest of Williamsburg, in order to march to the capital. Panicked Whig officials persuaded most of them to go home, but farther south in Hanover County, the independent company, led by Patrick Henry, voted on May 2 to proceed.[28] Several slaves presented themselves at the governor's palace, offering to fight alongside Dunmore in return for their freedom. He turned them away but said he would welcome them if Henry's group attacked. The crisis ended in a compromise, with the governor keeping the gunpowder but paying for it. Yet his relations with white colonists had soured forever, partly owing to the bold actions of a handful of Black Virginians.[29]

And Virginia was by no means unique. During the late spring and early summer of 1775, numerous white southerners circulated the rumor that the British government was about to free their slaves. In late May, South Carolina newspapers claimed the North ministry had shipped 78,000 muskets to African Americans, natives, and Canadians.

Even more disturbing to whites, a handful of their fellow freemen were publicly encouraging the slaves to rebel. On Maryland's Eastern Shore, a wheelwright named John Simmons stated that he "understood that the gentlemen were intending to make us all fight for their land and negroes." "Damn them," Simmons declared, "if I had a few more white people to join me I could get all the Negroes in the county to back us, and they would do more good in the night than the white people could do in the day."[30]

Simmons was tarred, feathered, and banished. In Charles Town, South Carolina, James Dealey, a Roman Catholic, received the same punishment for a similar crime: broadcasting the "good news" that the imperial government had sent weapons to anti-Whig Indians, African Americans, and Catholics.[31]

THREE WEEKS AFTER THE Battle of Lexington and Concord, rebel colonists launched their first offensive. Appropriately enough, given the centrality of native land to the imperial dispute, their first target was in the west. During the Seven Years' War, French troops had successfully defended, and then abandoned, a post they called Fort Carillon, at the mouth of the stream that drains Lake George into Lake Champlain. In 1759, the British moved into the fort and revived its Mohawk name, Ticonderoga ("between the two great waters"). After the war, the fort had fallen into disrepair, with the army maintaining only a token garrison of fifty soldiers, accompanied by twenty-four women and children, to guard Ticonderoga's hundred-odd cannon.[32]

The idea of capturing the fort and its artillery occurred at the same time to a group of Connecticut assemblymen and the Massachusetts Committee of Safety. The Connecticut group recruited about fifty soldiers in western Massachusetts but relied most heavily upon a band of fighters that had formed five years earlier in the region bordered on the east by the Connecticut River and on the west by Lake Champlain and the Hudson. This territory was claimed both by New York and New Hampshire, and many of the men who had received their land titles from New Hampshire defended them in a militia known as the Green Mountain Boys. Their leader, Ethan Allen, believed that if they could capture Fort Ticonderoga, on the New York (west) side of Lake Champlain, they would strike a triple blow, against Britain, its native allies, and the province of New York.[33]

One of the principal towns in the Hampshire Grants—soon to be rechristened Vermont—was Bennington, just ten miles north of the north-western corner of Massachusetts. As militiamen gathered there to plan their assault, the Massachusetts Committee of Safety commissioned a Connecticut native, Benedict Arnold, to lead an assault against Ticonderoga; the future traitor's commission was signed by committee chairman Benjamin Church, who had already secretly defected to the British side. Arnold galloped west to join the expedition already in progress.[34]

The Green Mountain Boys might have welcomed Arnold—except that he insisted on commanding them. Allen refused to serve under the interloper but allowed him to join in attacking Ticonderoga at 4 a.m. on May 10. Caught unawares, the garrison offered no resistance as Allen reportedly shouted to its commander, "Come out of there, you damned British rat." When asked on what authority he acted, Allen replied, "In the name of the great Jehovah, and the Continental Congress." Jehovah, maybe, but not Congress. The First Continental Congress had adjourned back in October 1774, and the second one did not convene until May 10, 1775, the very day of the Ticonderoga assault. As the delegates settled into their new assembly room, on the first floor of the Pennsylvania statehouse, they implored their fellow colonists to remain on the defensive.[35]

THE OUTBREAK OF WAR disrupted the rhythms of everyday life but did not shut them down. In March 1775, seven years after the death of her husband, Mary Fish Noyes of New Haven, Connecticut, received a marriage proposal from Gold Selleck Silliman, who had lost his own partner just seven months earlier. Before replying, she wanted to hear his reaction to the "Portrait of a Good Husband" she had penned two years earlier. At first Silliman's reply must have surprised her. He could not give her an ironclad guarantee that he would be the man her essay had described, but he added that "he had a wish to be." Apparently Noyes admired the man's honesty, for the two were married on May 24, 1775.[36]

EARLY IN 1775, BEFORE learning of the Battle of Lexington and Concord, the North ministry sent Gage three British generals—William Howe, John Burgoyne, and Henry Clinton—to serve both as advisors and as evidence of the ministry's disgust with his apparent dithering. The three crossed the Atlantic aboard the *Cerberus*, named for the three-headed watchdog of Greek mythology, and one London wit delighted in the coincidence:

Behold the *Cerberus* the Atlantic plow,
Her precious cargo, Burgoyne, Clinton, Howe.
Bow, wow, wow![37]

All three men would play decisive roles in the American War of Independence, starting with William Howe, who became Gage's second-in-command. He was tall, athletic, taciturn, and dark-complexioned—so much so that in his youth his siblings called him "the Savage." Howe's grandmother had been the illegitimate half sister of King George I, and he and his two elder brothers all became career army officers. The eldest, George Augustus, was killed in 1758 in an unsuccessful British assault on Fort Carillon. When Massachusetts placed a memorial in his honor in Westminster Abbey, it forged a lasting bond with the surviving Howe brothers. In 1759, when the British captured the city of Québec, William led the advance guard.[38]

The *Cerberus* put into Boston Harbor on May 25, and Howe soon convinced Gage, who had taken no major initiatives since the disastrous expedition to Concord, to let him try to break out of Boston. Starting at dawn on June 18, the redcoats would occupy both Dorchester Heights south of Boston and Bunker Hill on the Charlestown Peninsula, north of town. Then they would move against the main rebel camp in Cambridge.[39]

As in April, Gage's plans leaked, and the Massachusetts Committee of Safety resolved to beat his army to the top of Bunker Hill, only a few hundred yards beyond cannon range from Boston. At sunset on June 16, a fatigue (construction) crew, accompanied by two generals, headed to the summit to build a redoubt. One of the generals—either Connecticut's Israel Putnam or his unnamed colleague—convinced his fellow officers to deviate from the committee's orders, positioning the enclosure six hundred yards farther out the Charlestown Peninsula, atop seventy-five-

Contemporary drawing of the three hills of the Charlestown Peninsula,
including Bunker Hill (left), Breed's Hill (middle), and Morton's Hill (right),
as well as the village of Charlestown

foot-high Breed's Hill—just across the narrow Charles River from Boston. Vulnerable now to Whig bombardment, the British had no choice but to try to drive the Americans off.[40]

By disobeying orders and fortifying Breed's instead of Bunker Hill, a general whose name will probably never be known provoked the battle that, for the British, would become the deadliest of the seven-year war. He thereby exerted the same outsized influence as the lieutenants who had triggered the battles at Lexington and Concord.

CHAPTER 15

Pyramids of Fire

Spring – Summer 1775

As the sun rose over the Whig redoubt atop Breed's Hill on June 17, Col. William Prescott, who commanded its 1,500 to 1,700 troops, detached a party to fortify it with a breastwork. The breastwork would run the length of the redoubt's eastern wall, just in front of it, and then continue two hundred feet down the northern face of the hill. With this addition, the American fortifications resembled a lowercase d.[1]

During the night of June 16–17, Gen. Henry Clinton, who had commandeered John Hancock's elegant mansion atop Beacon Hill, had trouble sleeping, went for a stroll—and detected unusual sounds coming from the north. It sounded like digging. Dashing back to his quarters, he took up a spyglass and was just barely able to make out what a crewman on HMS *Lively* had already detected: militiamen and provincial soldiers at work on their redoubt. Generals Gage and Howe were alerted. The commander-in-chief put off deciding whether to ascend Breed's Hill until sunrise, when he confirmed his colleague's suspicion and ordered Howe (who outranked Clinton) to attack at once.[2]

At the time and ever since, Gen. Howe has been accused of blithely marching his men up Breed's Hill with no earthly idea that the mass of undisciplined provincials occupying its summit could possibly slow his progress. A recent account has one of his servants accompanying him "carrying a silver tray with a decanter of wine."[3]

Actually, Howe had no intention of assaulting the American redoubt head-on. Instead he adopted one of the most popular strategies in the European military manuals: striking the enemy's flank. The redcoats would land on Morton's (or Moulton's) Point, at the northeastern tip of the Charlestown Peninsula. From there, half would march west along the northern shore of the peninsula and then turn to the left and assault

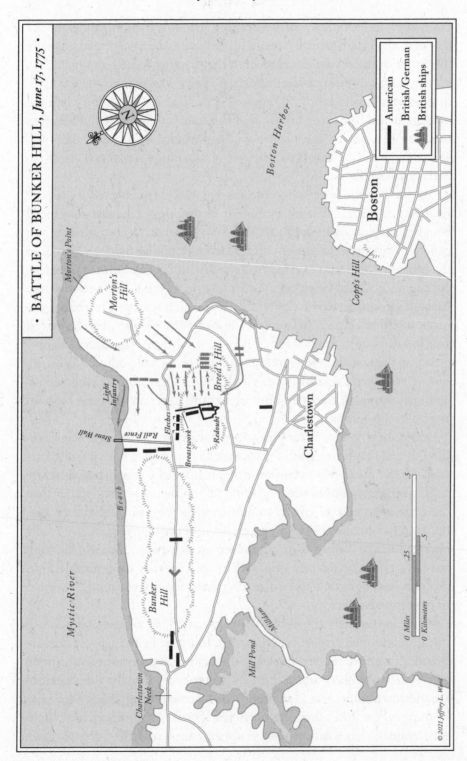

· BATTLE OF BUNKER HILL, *June 17, 1775* ·

American
British/German
British ships

Boston Harbor

Boston

Copp's Hill

Morton's Point

Morton's Hill

Breed's Hill

Light Infantry

Stone Wall

Rail Fence

Fleches

Breastwork

Redoubt

Charlestown

Beach

Mystic River

Bunker Hill

Charlestown Neck

Mill Pond

Mill

0 Miles   .25   .5

0 Kilometers   .5

© 2021 Jeffrey L. Ward

the American fort's low northern wall. Once this flanking attack broke through, the other half of Howe's soldiers would move directly against the Americans, serving as the anvil to the flanking force's hammer.[4]

Far from exhibiting overconfidence, Howe was, if anything too careful, directing his nearly 1,500 men to wait at Morton's Point while the boats returned to Boston for his 700-man reserve. That gave the colonists time to run a line all the way down the northern slope of Breed's Hill, somewhat behind the fort but capable of blocking his planned attack on their northern flank.[5]

As the Americans awaited the enemy, they were cheered by the arrival of Dr. Joseph Warren, president of the Massachusetts provincial congress, which had voted just three days earlier to commission him general. Warren occasionally suffered from crippling headaches, and on the morning of June 17, as he conferred with his Committee of Safety colleagues in Cambridge, an attack came on, forcing him to retire to a darkened room to drink chamomile tea, which was said to reduce the black bile that caused melancholia. Shortly after 3 p.m., he finally felt able to head out to Breed's Hill. There he was offered his choice of commanding the troops in the redoubt or those crouched behind a rail fence on the northern slope of Breed's Hill. But he had not yet received his commission, so he declined both invitations and served in the redoubt as a common soldier.[6]

Howe held to his earlier plan to try to turn the Americans' left flank, though this maneuver would now have to commence with a frontal assault on the northerly extension of their line. In a short speech before setting off, he implored the men to rely upon their bayonets rather than their firelocks, and he vowed to remain with them throughout the battle, as in fact he did. Howe warned that if the colonists managed to dig in atop Breed's Hill, within cannon range of Boston, the British might have "to go on board our ships, which will be very disagreeable to us all," not least because deadly diseases spread rapidly within the confines of overcrowded transports.[7]

On the southern shore of the peninsula, Whig fighters took cover in the abandoned city of Charlestown, founded in 1629, a year before Boston. From there they sniped at the British left. In response, cannon crews on Royal Navy vessels hurled two types of incendiary devices into Charlestown: superheated cannonballs and round metal cages filled with burning tallow and other combustibles. The latter so resembled butchered animals—in smell as well as appearance—that they were known as "carcasses." For good measure, Adm. Samuel Graves, Britain's naval commander in North America, sent sailors ashore with torches. Standing on Copp's Hill in Boston, just across the Charles River from Charlestown, Gen. John Burgoyne—known as "Gentleman Johnny" for his respectful attitude toward his enlisted men—marveled at the results: "a large and noble town in one great blaze—the church steeples being timber, were great pyramids of fire above the rest."[8]

At the opposite end of the battlefield, on Howe's far right, his light infantry, led by the famed Welch Fusiliers, marched west along the shore of the Mystic River. When they came within range of Col. John Stark's New Hampshire troops, taking cover behind a hastily constructed but solid stone wall, the effect was like pressing a stick of butter into a hot skillet: "the head of the column simply melted away." Just to the south, up on the bluff, the grenadiers fared no better. A series of fences repeatedly forced them to stop and re-form—all while taking scattered fire. Then when Howe's force came within thirty yards of the rebels, their entire line opened up. Working in pairs, one reloading while the other let fly, the colonists provided nearly continuous fire.[9]

Never before had a British army suffered such heavy casualties.[10] The stunned survivors turned and ran. Without the diversion of a successful flank attack, the troops on their left, who had approached the fort directly, also had to retreat.

Howe immediately organized a second attempt. Abandoning his suicidal offensive against the stone wall blocking the beach, he shifted his whole flanking force southward. The light infantry would march against the rail fence, while the grenadiers, led by Howe himself, reinforced the soldiers assaulting the American fort head-on. The troops climbing the hill were reorganized from battle lines (shoulder to shoulder) into columns, increasing casualties (since a bullet that missed the foremost soldier might still hit one behind him) but also the likelihood that some would get through. The dogged infantrymen urged each other forward with shouts of "Push on! Push on!"[11]

As before, the soldiers encountered "a continued sheet of fire for near thirty minutes." And they once again fell back.[12]

The mounting British casualties stiffened Howe's resolve to give meaning to this massive sacrifice by obtaining a victory. In their third assault, the redcoats would have a crucial advantage: in the face of heavy and continuous enemy fire, several of their gun crews had managed to position themselves a few yards west of the breastwork extending northward from the American fort. They would now be able to provide enfilade (flanking) fire—the most devastating kind—into the line of previously protected rebel soldiers. Loading their cannons with grapeshot (an array of metal objects, all in one charge), the artillerymen in several cases managed to bring down several Americans with a single shot. The survivors were forced into the redoubt, which now became the sole focus of the battle.[13]

The British had also gained another advantage of which they were not immediately aware: the Americans were almost out of gunpowder.

Soon small groups of British soldiers—marines on the left, grenadiers in the center—made it to the ditches in front of the Whig redoubt and began scaling its front wall. Rebel defenders peered over the parapet just long enough to fire at them: straight down and point-blank. Maj. John Pitcairn, who had commanded the light infantry at Lexington, had almost reached the redoubt when he took a bullet, apparently fired by another veteran of the April 19 battle, a Black man named Peter Salem, who seems to have obtained his freedom by enlisting. The major died in the arms of his son, an ensign in the marines.[14]

Finally the bravest of the redcoats clambered up into the redoubt, and the defenders ran to the back wall to get off one last shot. As the surging redcoats "tumbled over the dead to get at the living," Americans who had run out of gunpowder threw stones. Finally they fled, some scrambling over the back wall of the redoubt and others rushing the sally port, forced by clouds of dust and smoke "to feel about for the outlet." About thirty either failed to make it out or chose to stay and cover their fellows' escape; all died at the end of British bayonets.[15]

As the colonials scampered down the western slope of Breed's Hill, the redcoats did not pursue them, choosing instead to pick them off from the summit. More than half of the provincials killed or wounded on June 17 fell during the retreat. Joseph Warren made it sixty yards down the hill before taking a shot in the face and dying instantly. Despite the heavy fire, the Americans managed to bring off most of their wounded as they ceded the entire Charlestown Peninsula to the enemy and began fortifying Winter Hill and Prospect Hill on the mainland.

IN THE DAYS AFTER the battle, Whigs praised the tenacity of the men who successfully repelled two British assaults before finally withdrawing, and Joseph Warren became their first martyr. But the officers who survived the attack were so appalled at the cowardice of some of their comrades, including some officers, that they demanded courts-martial, and several were punished.[16] Some Americans, trapped in the conventional eighteenth-century mindset that awarded a battle's laurels to whichever side commanded the ground at the end of the day, pronounced Bunker Hill a defeat.

The casualties told a different story. About 450 Americans were killed or wounded, a devastating loss. But the British reported 1,054 casualties—nearly half of the men who had crossed the Charles with Gen. Howe. The officers suffered disproportionately, largely because the rebels had targeted them, though the highest-ranking British fatality, Col. James Abercrombie, commander of Howe's grenadiers, was a victim of friendly fire. As the wounded were ferried back to Boston, their comrades commandeered every available cart, carriage, and wheelbarrow to transport them to makeshift hospitals. There were so many funerals that Gen. Gage ordered the church bells silenced lest their constant tolling dispirit the troops. On both sides, numerous accounts of the Battle of Bunker Hill paraphrased the famous dispatch that gave rise to the term pyrrhic victory. "If we are victorious in one more battle with the Romans," Pyrrhus had reportedly said, "we shall be utterly ruined."[17]

In the Americans' stubborn defense of Breed's Hill, Gage, who had repeatedly warned that the Whigs were more than "the despicable rabble too many have supposed them to be," found bittersweet vindication. But even the general's expectations had fallen short. "These People Shew a Spirit and Conduct against us, they never shewed against the French," he wrote Lord Barrington, the secretary at war. Gage attributed the rebels' fanaticism to evangelical "zeal and enthusiasm," an American advantage that his officers had already detected. "It is not possible," Col. Abercrombie had written on May 21, "to conceive the phrenzy that prevails amongst the people & to what a pitch of enthusiasm their clergy have brought them."[18]

Gage's superiors did not agree that Bunker Hill justified his earlier caution, and in its wake the cabinet proceeded with its long-contemplated plan to call him home, with William Howe taking his place. Still, in an indirect way, Gage's superiors admitted that he had been right all along. His October 1774 request for twenty thousand additional soldiers had been mocked as absurdly excessive, but after Bunker Hill the government agreed to send over precisely that many reinforcements in time for the 1776 campaign.[19]

Gen. Howe would in fact command the largest expeditionary force ever sent out from Europe. Yet he feared it would never defeat the rebels, for they had stumbled upon a foolproof strategy. "The intentions of these wretches," he wrote five days after capturing Breed's Hill, "are to fortify every post in our way; wait to be attacked at every one, having their rear secure, destroying as many of us as they can before they set out to their next strong situation."[20] Modern historians routinely describe the American colonists as triumphing over Britain "against all odds." But John Burgoyne shared his soon-to-be commander's fear that the rebels would force the British army into a war of attrition that it could not possibly win. He noted that they would never "risk a general combat or a pitched battle, or even stand at all, except behind entrenchments as at Boston." And immediately upon their being "driven from one hill, you will see the enemy continually retrenched upon the next."[21]

Americans had similarly fired from cover along the road from Concord back to Boston two months earlier, but the two battles differed in one crucial particular. In taking potshots at Lt. Col. Smith's column from behind trees and walls on April 19, Massachusetts militiamen had violated Europe's prevailing rules of war, leading many observers, even on the American side, to liken them to Indians. But militiamen incurred no such disgrace in firing upon the British from the relative safety of their fortifications on June 17, since the attackers always had the option of turning back. More than two centuries after Breed's Hill, the playwright Lin-Manuel Miranda would depict the American rebels as "a ragtag volunteer army in need of a shower," and the characterization was apt, for the Americans could win the war simply by turning dirt into walls and trenches and trading them for British blood.[22]

Armies that assault forts often incur horrendous casualties, but North American geography tilted the odds even farther toward the rebels. The continent was "full of woods, swamps, stone walls, and other enclosures and hiding places," Gen. Burgoyne observed. In this terrain, the American fighter could "turn every tree and bush into a kind of temporary fortress, from whence, when he hath fired his shot with all the deliberation, coolness, and certainty which hidden safety inspires, he will skip as it were, to the next."[23]

Starting more than a decade earlier, when the Bute administration decided to leave ten thousand troops in America and compel the colonists to pay for them, the imperial government had picked this fight. But the outbreak of war left the British with only two options: go on the offensive or go home. And such were the natural disadvantages that eighteenth-century warfare imposed on every aggressor that, at least by their own reckoning, the British must be considered the underdogs.

Startlingly, even as Gen. Howe and other British commanders fretted about the Americans' natural advantage, the colonists failed to detect it. Their intention in fortifying Bunker—not Breed's—Hill had simply been to contain the British in Boston, not to provoke a high-casualty British assault. From this point forward, the great question of the Revolutionary War would be this: how long would it take the Americans to discover the foolproof strategy that their opponents had already discerned as they buried the victims of the war's first major battle?

THREE DAYS BEFORE BUNKER HILL, on June 14, Congress had voted to send the New Englanders bottling up the British in Boston reinforcements: ten companies of Pennsylvania, Maryland, and Virginia riflemen. The delegates also believed the hodgepodge of provincial units in eastern Massachusetts needed a commander-in-chief. George Washington was one of the few members of Congress with military experience, and he also looked the part. When ordering clothing from Europe, he described himself as exactly six feet tall, but his contemporaries, including the man who ordered his coffin in 1799, swore he was six foot three. Apparently Washington's bearing added three inches to his height.[24]

Since being reelected to Congress, Washington had advertised his availability for military command by attending sessions in the uni-
form he had designed for the Fairfax County independent company, a blue coat over a buff (yellowish beige) vest and breeches.[25] John Hancock, the president of Congress, had no combat experience but still wished to lead the new army—or at least to be asked. But to Hancock's chagrin, Washington's only real competition came from Artemas Ward, then in command of the troops outside Boston. When John Adams discussed the matter with members of the Virginia delegation, he was surprised to find "more than one very cool about the Appointment of Washington." But Adams and other New England delegates harbored doubts about Ward's

Charles Willson Peale, George Washington in his Virginia Regiment uniform (1772)

abilities—and also about other colonies' willingness to adopt the army if it came complete with a New England commander. On June 15, Congress unanimously selected Washington, who modestly acknowledged that his elevation was "assisted by a political motive": preserving comity among the regions.[26]

Washington was thoroughly versed in forest warfare, but his experience with European-style battles consisted of a single incident at twilight on November 12, 1758, when he had led his troops into a brief skirmish, producing several fatalities on both sides—from what turned out to be friendly fire. Yet Congress's choice was widely seen as inspired. The *Pennsylvania Packet* excerpted a sermon that Rev. Samuel Davies, a Virginia Presbyterian, had given in the wake of Braddock's defeat in 1755. Davies had honored "that heroic youth *COLONEL WASHINGTON*, whom I cannot but hope providence has hitherto preserved in so *signal* a manner for some *important service* to his country." Twenty years later, Washington assumed command with humility and even foreboding, telling fellow Virginia delegate Patrick Henry, "from the day I enter upon the command of the American armies, I date my fall, and the ruin of my reputation."[27]

Like most Americans, the man who received his commission as commander-in-chief on June 17, even as New Englanders extracted an intolerable price for Breed's Hill, failed to notice what seemed so plain to Howe and other British generals: that the strategy forced upon the the colonists in that battle could win them the war. Indeed, within weeks of his July 2 arrival at the American camp in Cambridge, Washington resolved to launch his own dramatic frontal assault on Fortress Boston. Eventually the American commander would be likened to the Roman general Fabius, who had defeated Hannibal not by striking him head-on but by avoiding battle except to seize upon golden opportunities. But in June 1775, Washington was less a Fabius than a Hotspur—Shakespeare's rebel commander who was forever spoiling for a fight.

Having selected Washington, Congress set about recruiting troops for what it called the Continental Army. To pay the soldiers and buy them weapons, uniforms—the same blue-and-buff Washington had worn to Congress—and other supplies, the delegates voted to print $2 million worth of paper money. By the end of the year, they would issue $4 million more.[28]

One of the most vexing issues confronting Congress that summer was Canada. Still hoping to persuade the Québécois to join the rebellion of their own free will, the delegates voted on June 1 "That no expedition or incursion ought to be undertaken or made, by any colony, or body of colonists, against or into Canada." But by that time, Ethan Allen had already sent Congress a proposal to invade Quebec. The British governor of the province, Guy Carleton, was sturdy as an oak, having been injured during the Seven Years' War in British assaults on Québec, Havana, and the French coast. But he had not managed to recruit many Canadians to defend the colony against the rebels. Quebec would be an easy conquest, men like Allen and Benedict Arnold claimed. On June 27, Congress ordered Gen. Philip Schuyler, its recently appointed commander in the province of New York, to lead his army north over the border.[29]

EARLY IN THE SUMMER of 1775, colonists learned that Parliament had voted to offer them an "Olive Branch": any colonial assembly that wished to save its constituents from British taxation could do so by levying sufficient taxes of its own to cover its share of imperial expenses. Thomas Jefferson drafted the Virginia House of Burgesses' response, which emphasized white Virginians' willingness to provide the requested subsidy—so long as Parliament reciprocated by allowing Virginians "a free trade with all the world." In stating that Britain's "monopoly of our trade . . . brings greater loss to us and benefit to them than the amount of our proportional contributions to the common defence," the burgesses revealed the inadequacy of studies of the origins of the American Revolution that neglect the Navigation Acts in favor of taxation. Benjamin Franklin went a step further, offering that if Parliament would repeal its restrictions on American trade, the American assemblies would show their gratitude by levying sufficient taxes to pay down the British government's entire £230 million debt.[30]

Immediately after writing Virginia's response to North's Olive Branch, Jefferson set out for Philadelphia to begin a term in Congress, arriving in time to help pen that body's reply as well. In their July 6 "Declaration . . . Setting Forth the Causes and Necessity of Their Taking Up Arms," the delegates branded North's strategy of reaching out to the provincial assemblies—rather than their representatives in Congress—"an insidious Manoeuvre calculated to divide us." They also explained why they had spent the final days of June planning the invasion of Canada that they had forsworn at the start of the month. Gen. Carleton, they claimed, "is instigating the People of that Province and the Indians to fall upon us."

The July 6 declaration also contained Congress's first accusation that Britain was trying "to excite domestic Enemies"—the slaves—against white Americans. Ominously, the delegates warned that if the imperial dispute continued, "foreign Assistance" was "undoubtedly attainable."[31] Still, two days later, they extended their own olive branch in the form of a polite but unyielding petition to George III.

MEANWHILE IN MASSACHUSETTS, AN earlier battle over the numerous islands in Boston Harbor intensified. The British garrison was desperate for food and forage and had the means to seize them, but the farmers who had planted hayseed and pastured their horses and cattle on the islands were willing to run considerable risks to ensure that they and not the British reaped the harvest. In a July 12 skirmish, a group of Whigs landed on Long Island (not to be confused with New York's Long Island, a hundred miles to the southwest) to burn haystacks and buildings. British cutters surrounded the island and let fly at the Whigs, who took to their boats. As a navy vessel bore down on one rebel whaleboat, the British captain yelled to his rebel counterpart to "yield for he was his Prisoner," to which the Whig captain replied, in the curt New England fashion, "Not yet." Straining every nerve, his oarsmen made it to shore.[32]

A hundred and sixty miles northwest of Boston Harbor, at Fort Ticonderoga, Philip Schuyler repeatedly delayed his invasion of Canada. So on August 28, while he was off in Albany conferring with Iroquois sachems, his second-in-command, Richard Montgomery, seized the initiative. The Irish-born Montgomery had served in the British army in America during the Seven Years' War and then immigrated to New York a decade later, after being denied a captain's commission. He now loaded about 1,200 troops into small craft and sailed north, first down Lake Champlain and then down the Richelieu River, its outlet, to the town of Saint-Jean. On September 6, in the woods outside Saint-Jean, Montgomery's troops were repulsed, twice, primarily by about sixty pro-British Indians. The warriors' stout defense of Saint-Jean bought the garrison time to build up its fortifications; in their absence, the Americans might have quickly captured Canada. But hardly any British soldiers or Loyalists had participated in the September 6 battle, and the disgusted warriors decamped.[33]

Montgomery did not dare proceed against Montreal, less than twenty miles to the northwest, while Saint-Jean remained in British hands. But two of the officers nominally serving under him, John Brown of New York and Green Mountain Boys leader Ethan Allen, decided to attack Montreal on their own. Allen and his troops made it across to the north bank of the St. Lawrence, but Brown's party, operating separately, did not. Isolated and outnumbered, Allen had to surrender to Ensigns Peter Johnson and Walter Butler. Johnson, just sixteen years old, was the son of the late Indian agent William Johnson and an Iroquois matron. Allen was sent to England in chains.[34]

Saint-Jean held out for more than seven weeks but finally yielded on November 2, and the Americans immediately moved on Montreal. That city's British garrison embarked for Quebec City, 150 miles down the St. Lawrence, and on November 13 the civilian leaders surrendered. Over the next few days, Montgomery's boats managed to overtake most of the fleeing garrison—but not Guy Carleton and his top officers, who used a little-known passageway through the labyrinth of islands in the St. Lawrence to evade their pursuers and reach Quebec City.[35]

On his way down the river, Carleton learned of an additional threat. Back in August, George Washington had embarked upon his first major initiative as commander-in-chief. In support of Montgomery's invasion of Canada, he would send his own expedition—1,100 volunteers led by Benedict Arnold—north along a path blazed by the Abenaki Indians: up the Kennebec River through the district of Maine (which would remain part of Massachusetts until 1820), then overland to the Chaudière River, which flows northward, emptying into the St. Lawrence less than ten miles above Quebec. Arnold would force Carleton to divide his limited forces, and he might even capture Quebec City just as Saint-Jean and Montreal fell to Montgomery.[36]

Arnold's men included ten regular infantry companies armed with muskets but also three companies comprising a total of about 250 riflemen. Seaboard colonists credited these backwoodsmen—"painted like Indians, armed with tomahawks and rifles, dressed in hunting shirts and mackasons"—with an almost aboriginal power. The expedition set out on September 11. Two days later, the men reached Newburyport, Massachusetts, where Rev. George Whitefield had died five years earlier. Some of the soldiers had Whitefield's crypt opened and took swatches of his clothing for good luck. Arnold himself had been largely untouched by the evangelical revolt that Whitefield led, and his expedition thus epitomized the Whig alliance of opposites, rationalists and evangelicals.[37]

By September 22, the expedition had reached Gardinerstown (today's

Pittston, Maine), twenty-five miles up the Kennebec, where Arnold and his troops took possession of the bateaux that would carry their food, ammunition, and gear. At Fort Western (modern Augusta), Arnold estimated that they were 180 miles and twenty days south of Quebec. He got the direct distance about right, but his assessment of how quickly he could cover it would prove far wide of the mark.

The hastily constructed bateaux leaked, and several overset, spoiling much of the expedition's food. At many of the Kennebec's numerous rapids, Arnold's bateauxmen had to pull the boats from the water and painfully carry them on their shoulders. Sometimes steep rock walls lining both riverbanks prevented the soldiers from hauling the boats out, so they had to be dragged up over the waterfalls. One portage—around an impassible stretch of the Kennebec to a tributary, the optimistically named Dead River (which actually has numerous Class IV rapids)—was twelve miles long. To get everything across, the men had to make more than half a dozen trips.[38]

Early in the nineteenth century, John Joseph Henry, a survivor of the expedition, shamefully recalled that it had been "the silly fashion of those times, for riflemen to ape the manners of savages," for instance by wearing hunting shirts and moccasins and carrying tomahawks and scalping knives. But at the time, Arnold's troops had highly valued the skills of their native guides.[39]

Before heading upriver, Arnold had warned his men to watch out for an Abenaki named Natanis, a reputed British spy who was to be captured or killed. On October 4, the advance troops came upon Natanis's empty cabin, and later that afternoon they reached a fork in the river and could not figure out which branch to take. Then a soldier found a stake in the ground with a notched top holding a neatly folded piece of birchbark. On it, Natanis or one of his kin had drawn a map indicating the proper way forward. Natanis was actually sympathetic to the Americans' cause but could not approach them until they figured out that he was not their enemy. So he was shadowing them, aiding them only indirectly. On the other hand, the Abenaki entrusted by Arnold to carry a letter to Gen. Schuyler took it straight to Gen. Carleton.[40]

Arnold had carried twice as much food as he thought he would need, but a month into the expedition, the provisions ran out, and the men began eating leather goods—moccasins, shot pouches, and breeches—along with candle wax, hair grease, and an officer's dog. The officers of the rear division, led by Lt. Col. Roger Enos, voted, without consulting Arnold, to take its three companies back downriver toward home.[41]

On October 28, the soldiers abandoned the bateaux they had dragged up the Kennebec and Dead Rivers and began their portage over the Height of Land to the Chaudière. Daniel Morgan, a Virginia rifle captain who had served as a teamster with Gen. Braddock, was alone in requiring his company to carry its boats over the mountain pass, only to lose most of them in the rapids of the aptly named Chaudière, which is French for cauldron.

At one point the troops had to wade three-quarters of a mile across a pond. Years later, John Henry recalled using his rifle butt to break through a thin layer of ice before stepping into the waist-deep mire. Like nearly every British or American military expedition of the eighteenth century, this one included women. As the soldiers slogged through the frigid pond, Henry recalled, a sergeant's wife "had got before me. My mind was humbled, yet astonished, at the exertions of this good woman. Her clothes more than waist high, she waded before me to the firm ground." Jemima Warner had also accompanied her husband, and when he became too ill to continue, she sat with him, hugging him and crying with him until he died. Then she covered his body with leaves, took up his musket, and set off down the path. Twenty miles on, she caught up with the army.[42]

Many of the soldiers had eaten nothing for a week or longer, and John Henry was contemplating suicide. Finally, on November 3, a foraging party returned with a herd of oxen, purchased from French-speaking settlers farther down the Chaudière. An ox was immediately slaughtered and placed before the ravenous soldiers. A day before his seventeenth birthday, Henry saw a man gorge himself to death. Other soldiers would die in the same way later in the war.[43]

New Englanders normally celebrated Pope's Day every November 5 by burning effigies of the Roman Catholic pontiff. Back in Cambridge, Gen. Washington prohibited his troops from indulging in this "ridiculous and childish Custom" at a time when American diplomats were desperately seeking help from Quebec as well as France.[44] Arnold's soldiers did not need to be told to skip Pope's Day, for the Catholic farmers of the Chaudière Valley had just saved them from starvation.

On November 8, Arnold finally stood on the south bank of the St. Lawrence opposite Quebec, which he had often visited in his prewar career as a ship captain. One of Washington's central objectives in sending Arnold up the Kennebec had been to force Carleton to reinforce Quebec, thus weakening his own defense of Saint-Jean and Montreal against Schuyler and Montgomery. But by the time Carleton learned of the much delayed Kennebec expedition, he had already abandoned both upriver towns. Had Washington known he would not be able to compel Carleton to divide his forces, and had he still wanted to send some of his own troops to Schuyler, they could have caught up with him at Ticonderoga, which they could have reached using the same easy roads Arnold had traveled the previous spring. Indeed a British couple had recently ridden from Boston to Lake George, which empties into Lake Champlain at Ticonderoga, in a *carriage*.[45]

A surprisingly small number of Arnold's men had drowned, died of disease, or starved or frozen to death: perhaps fewer than twenty. But every person on the expedition had suffered immeasurably, and all for naught.

During the night of November 13–14, the ragged American army crossed to the Plains of Abraham, just outside the walls of the fortified city. Here on September 13, 1759, Gen. James Wolfe's redcoats had defeated the city's French defenders under Louis-Joseph de Montcalm—with the loss of both generals—ensuring the British conquest of Canada. Death, illness, injury, and—most of all—the departure of Enos's division had cut Arnold's force nearly in half, to fewer than six hundred effectives, and Arnold knew he stood no chance of reprising Wolfe's triumph without help from Montgomery and his troops. While waiting for them, Arnold's soldiers spread out in search of food and shelter. Some made it as far up the St. Lawrence as Trois-Rivières, halfway to Montreal, where, for several hours, they unknowingly shared a house with Governor Carleton, hastening downriver to organize the defense of Quebec.[46]

Even when Montgomery's army linked up with Arnold's on December 2, the combined force could not be confident of capturing Quebec. Most of the town stood atop a tall promontory on the peninsula formed by the junction of the St. Charles and St. Lawrence Rivers. The British soldiers, Indian warriors, and Canadian militiamen guarding this natural fortress outnumbered the at most one thousand American invaders by as much as two to one. Then an outbreak of smallpox in the invaders' camp placed them at a further disadvantage. When Montgomery wrote Carleton demanding that he surrender, the governor had his letter thrown in the fire. (It did not help that Montgomery had chosen a woman to carry the message; she was jailed for several days and then drummed out of town.) Montgomery also wrote an appeal to the city's merchants and had copies attached to arrows that his Indian allies shot over the city walls, but these proved no more effective.[47]

Although outnumbered and facing a well-fortified enemy, the rebels worried that turning back without striking at Quebec would undermine Whig morale. Moreover, many of Montgomery's soldiers' enlistments would expire on December 31, and they "threatened to leave him immediately if the attempt were not made."[48] So he and Arnold decided to launch a two-pronged attack against the Lower Town, at the tip of Quebec's peninsula and the foot of its iconic cliffs. Arnold would lead a detachment that approached from the north while Montgomery and his soldiers came in from the south. Once the two divisions met, they would ascend to the Upper Town.

Gen. Carleton knew the two land approaches to the Lower Town were his weak spots, so he lined both with soldiers in homes and behind series of barricades. In hopes of gaining the element of surprise, the Americans struck during the night of December 30–31, in a severe snowstorm. But the foul weather did not diminish the British soldiers' vigilance, and early in the attack, Montgomery took a musket ball in the head and died instantly. Arnold was shot in the leg and had to be escorted to the rear.

John Trumbull, *Death of General Montgomery* (1786)

Daniel Morgan did not hold the highest rank among Arnold's remaining officers, but by acclamation, he replaced the fallen Montgomery. He displayed superhuman bravery, more than once vaulting over a British barricade despite knowing that enemy cannon and muskets were trained on the opposite wall. As Morgan's men strained to keep up with him, a gap opened between his advance troops and the rest, and British soldiers rushed into this breach, surrounding and capturing the advance, including Morgan, who defiantly surrendered his sword to a clergyman.

Like the redcoats who took Breed's Hill six months earlier, the Americans who assailed Quebec suffered nearly 50 percent casualties (in this case, mostly prisoners). Only seven British soldiers were killed.[49] Arnold, having escaped capture only because he had been wounded and sent to the rear, assumed command of the remains of the American force.

CHAPTER 16

Instigated Insurrections?

1775

MEANWHILE, FAR TO THE SOUTH, WHIG LEADERS PREPARED FOR concurrent battles against redcoats, locals who supported Parliament, Native Americans, and their own enslaved workers. On June 4, 1775—the king's birthday, as was widely noted—the South Carolina provincial congress created a military association and a 1,500-man army, justifying it by citing the North ministry's "arbitrary impositions," the Battle of Lexington and Concord—and the danger of "instigated insurrections" by the slaves. Henry Laurens, the president of the congress, announced still another reason to arm: "hostilities from the Indians." The vote in favor of the army was close and might well have gone the other way if the delegates' only concern had been the British.[1]

Loyalists in the upcountry responded to the Whigs' military association with a "Counter-Association" swearing to stand by the king—but also to oppose any uprising by Indians or slaves. In July, when eastern leaders sent delegations into the western Carolinas to counter the Loyalist threat, they were careful to include representatives of two dissenting sects then sweeping the backcountry: Baptists and Presbyterians. Two German American Whigs traveled to German-speaking settlements such as Saxe-Gotha, across the Congaree River from present-day Columbia, South Carolina.[2]

South Carolina Whigs also carried out at least one covert operation. In June 1775, when Georgia governor James Wright sent William Campbell, his Carolina counterpart, a packet of letters to be forwarded to various British officials, he chose the wrong messenger, and the whole packet went straight to the members of the Whig committee in Charles Town. They forged their own version of Wright's June 27 message to Gen. Gage. The governor had fastened his letter with hot wax, to which he had added his seal, but an ingenious Whig counterfeited the seal by making a clay impression. In the forged letter, the governor states that "there is nothing really formidable in the proceedings or designs of our neighbours of South-Carolina." The counterfeit Governor Wright also assured Gage that he did not need any additional British troops, but on this key point, the rewrite was redundant. The real Governor Wright had no desire to provoke the Whigs by receiving reinforcements, at least not until he could be assured of overwhelming superiority.[3]

Wright's caution was atypical. The other southern governors pleaded with Gage for reinforcements, but with too few troops to go around, none received more than token help.

Early in July, in the Chehaw district south of South Carolina's Edisto River, a Black preacher named George announced that George III "was about to alter the World, & set the Negroes Free." He was summarily executed. Slaves in the Tar River region of North Carolina reportedly agreed to meet up on July 8 and then head west, destroying everything in their path before rendezvousing with imperial officials and establishing "a free government of their own" beyond the mountains. Whites discovered the plot on the day it was to be set in motion.[4]

Like the participants in the Carolina conspiracies, a teenaged slave belonging to Andrew Estave, Virginia's official vintner, counted upon British help. In early July 1775, she was accused of a horrific crime: sexually molesting her owner's three-year-old daughter. She got away and "made to the palace": the governor's mansion in the center of Williamsburg. The governor had just made his own escape to the safety of a British warship, and she was captured and returned to Estave, who gave her eighty lashes and then poured embers on her back. The young woman was surprisingly successful at disseminating her side of the story, even among whites. Why else would Estave have taken to the pages of the *Virginia Gazette* to respond to her charges, even though it meant publicly exposing his young child?[5]

Back in mid-June, Charles Town officials had imprisoned the free Black harbor pilot Thomas Jeremiah, but with little evidence against him, they had not dared bring him to trial. On August 11, perhaps in reaction to the previous month's wave of slave insurrection scares, authorities finally tried and convicted Jeremiah. With an estate, including slaves, estimated at £1,000, Jeremiah was one of the wealthiest Black men in America. Governor Campbell considered the evidence against him weak, but Whigs warned that if Jeremiah was pardoned, he would be lynched before the governor's door. On August 18, as a crowd watched, Jeremiah was hanged, and then his body was burned.[6]

Other British officeholders took up Campbell's claim that South Carolina Whigs had hanged an innocent man, with the earl of Sandwich even mentioning the case on the floor of the House of Lords. To this day, historians disagree, not only about Jeremiah's involvement in the spring 1775 conspiracy but also about the actual extent of the slave rebellions reported that summer.[7] Many unrealized plots never made it into the written record. On the other hand, whites all but invited false accusations by offering to free slaves who betrayed their compatriots' plans. Indeed, in any slave insurrection, the conspirator most likely to gain freedom was the one who ratted out the rest.

Many of the leaders of the 1775 plots asserted that the whole reason for the war between colonies and crown was that George III had ordered white Americans to free their slaves. They thus embraced the same tactic Indian rebels had used in 1763: fabricating assurances of overseas support in hopes of recruiting enough foot soldiers to create a movement formidable enough to attract still more recruits—including, potentially, actual foreign allies—thus making war out of rumors of war.[8]

Like Thomas Jeremiah, Joseph Harris of Hampton, Virginia, was a pilot, but in the summer of 1775 he was still a slave. One night late in July 1775, he escaped to a Royal Navy squadron and was immediately set to work piloting a warship called the *Liberty*. On September 2, 1775, a hurricane swept through Chesapeake Bay, driving the *Liberty* ashore near Hampton, a Whig stronghold. The shipwrecked crew included not only Harris but Mathew Squire, the commander of the *Liberty*'s mother ship. For Squire, capture by the Whigs would be humiliating. For Harris, it might mean death, since in Whig eyes he was not just a runaway or an enemy but a rebel.[9]

Harris procured a canoe from a Hampton slave and rowed Squire across Hampton Roads, back to Norfolk and the safety of the British fleet. On October 27, Squire attacked Hampton with a schooner, two sloops, and two pilot boats. In the ensuing firefight, as many as nine British soldiers and sailors were killed, and the Whigs captured Harris's vessel, along with "five white men, a woman, and two slaves." But Harris and the lieutenant commanding the vessel escaped by plunging at the last instant into the Hampton River and swimming together to safety.[10] That made twice in two months that Harris had piloted his captain out of the Whigs' clutches.

The first battle of American War of Independence fought south of New England, the Battle of Hampton, might never have occurred if Joseph Harris had fit the long-dominant depiction of slaves as passive. Without Harris as a source of contention, Squire and the Hampton leadership might well have reached an accommodation.

By this time Governor Dunmore had begun forming Virginia Loyalists into two army regiments. One was staffed by whites, but the other was all Black and known as the Ethiopian Regiment. Dunmore also backed a plan by John Connolly, his onetime viceroy in Virginia's border war against Pennsylvanians and Indians in the Upper Ohio Valley, to raise an army of Native Americans, British soldiers from Kaskaskia out on the Mississippi River, and backwoods Loyalists to drive the Whigs out of Fort Pitt (as the fort at the forks of the Ohio was again being called). This mixed force would then follow Gen. Braddock's route, only in reverse, to the Potomac River port of Alexandria, Virginia, eight miles upriver from Mount Vernon, where it would link up with the governor's Black and white troops.

By this time Dunmore had made the momentous decision to draw up an emancipation proclamation that in many ways resembled the one Abraham Lincoln would sign four score and seven years later. Blacks claimed by Loyalists could not take advantage of the emancipation offer, any more than border state slaves could in the Civil War. Just as Lincoln delayed his announcement until the Union army's September 17, 1862, victory at Antietam, when he could act from a position of strength, Dunmore postponed his proclamation until November 15. Earlier that day, at Kemp's Landing, just south of Norfolk, his predominantly Black army had defeated as many as three hundred militiamen from neighboring Princess Anne County. Col. Joseph Hutchings, the commander of the militia, was captured by one of his own former slaves.[11]

Over the next six months, perhaps as many as a thousand enslaved Virginians escaped to Governor Dunmore. Among them was a mixed-race man whites called Yellow Peter. He disappeared one day in 1775 or 1776 and was later seen "in Governor Dunmore's regiment with a musquet on his back and a sword by his side," having changed his name to *Captain* Peter. Although Dunmore apparently meant to limit his emancipation offer to able-bodied men, nearly half of the Black Virginians who joined him were women and children. In a typical case, one night early in 1776, Francis Rice's slave Mary grabbed up her daughter Phillis, who was about three years old, and set out for the British lines. They made it in, survived the war, and then left America free.[12]

The proclamation also had a tremendous impact on white Virginians. Just a year earlier, Dunmore had forced the Shawnees and Mingos to give up all of their land east of the Ohio River, making him, as a fellow Scot noted, "as popular as a Scotsman can be amongst weak prejudiced people." But whites now literally demonized their governor's "Damned, infernal, Diabolical proclamation" and all "his infernal tribe." Virginia congressman Benjamin Harrison reported that "Our Devil of a Governor goes on at a Devil of a rate indeed." Dunmore had invited Black Virginians to become soldiers, not rebels or murderers, but whites acknowledged no such distinction.[13]

Rumor had long made the governor out to be a philanderer, and as early as June 1, 1775, just after Dunmore threatened to free the slaves, John Pinkney's *Virginia Gazette* had given that accusation a racial tinge, predicting that "The BLACK LADIES ... will be jollily entertained" at an upcoming dance at the governor's palace. When Dunmore issued his emancipation proclamation, the tobacco planter Landon Carter predicted that he would soon receive "some missive commission to Silence all his iniquities both male and female."[14]

Carter meant that Dunmore was about to be recalled, but no one in the British government objected to his proclamation—though no one formally endorsed it, either—and by the spring of 1776, several leading Virginia Loyalists had begun to drift toward the Whig camp. The previous spring, William Byrd III, a member of the provincial council, had offered to lead British troops suppressing the Whig rebellion. But after Dunmore announced his alliance with Black Virginians, Byrd tendered his services to the Whigs.[15]

Some Whig leaders affected to view Dunmore's proclamation as cause for celebration, since it had "united every Man" in the white population against him. "The Proclamation from L[or]d D[unmore], has had a most extensive good consequence," Archibald Cary of Chesterfield County near Richmond wrote; white "Men of all ranks resent the pointing a dagger to their Throats, thru the hands of their Slaves." Edward Rutledge of South Carolina believed Dunmore's proclamation would tend "more effectually to work an eternal separation between Great Britain and the Colonies,—than any other expedient, which could possibly have been thought of."[16]

All of these comments depicted Governor Dunmore as rousing enslaved Virginians from their slumber, but the events of the previous year told a different story. The first report of slaves planning to rise up "when

the English Troops should arrive" came in November 1774, a year before Dunmore published his emancipation proclamation.[17] In May 1775,
when the governor first threatened to free the slaves, Black Virginians
knocked on his door, only to be turned away. But they kept coming.
Some, like the young woman accused of molesting Andrew Estave's
child, did not make it, but others did, to include the pilot Joseph Harris
and the eventual victors in the Battle of Kemp's Landing. Only after all
these Black activists proved their mettle did Governor Dunmore make
their emancipation official. And no other document—not even Thomas
Paine's *Common Sense* or the Declaration of Independence—did more
than Dunmore's proclamation to convert white residents of Britain's
most populous American colony to the cause of independence

And something very similar was happening in South Carolina.

IF YOU STAND AT the far southern tip of Charleston, South Carolina—
not in the summer, but in the autumn, when the haze clears—and peer
southeastward into the harbor, you can make out, on a tiny island just
over three miles away, Fort Sumter, where the American Civil War began.
If you shift your gaze just a few degrees toward the north, you will see,
about a half mile farther out, at the mouth of Charleston Harbor, the
much larger Sullivan's Island, site of a pivotal early episode in another
battle over slavery and sovereignty, the American Revolution.

Vessels transporting kidnapped West Africans to Charleston Harbor
had to stop at Sullivan's Island on the way in for ten days of quarantine.
More than 40 percent of the captives who reached North America during
the eighteenth century came in through Sullivan's Island, leading the
historian Peter H. Wood to christen it "the Ellis Island of black Americans."[18]

For a brief period in the fall of 1775, a small number of Black South
Carolinians turned this entry point to American slavery into an exit.
On September 15, Governor William Campbell fled to a British warship riding at anchor in Charleston Harbor's Rebellion Road. That left
Sullivan's Island, which lay under the guns of Campbell's squadron, as
the one swath of South Carolina still under British control, and "nearly
five-hundred" escaped slaves reportedly found refuge there. In this latest African American overture to the British, watermen once again led
the way, often literally. Scipio Handley, a free Black fisherman whose
property included ten hogs and a fishing boat, carried messages between
Governor Campbell and certain unnamed persons in Charles Town.

Captured by the Whigs and convicted of "acting against the Congress," Handley was sentenced to death. But a friend smuggled a file into his jail cell, enabling him to jump from his window. He made it to the relative safety of Sullivan's Island. (Later Handley would travel to Barbados, but he returned in 1778 to participate in the British capture and then defense of Savannah.)[19]

The Council of Safety found out about the Black encampment on Sullivan's Island and dispatched a Whig ranger company of more than fifty men. Striking during the night of December 18–19, the rangers recaptured a handful of fugitives and killed those "that would not be taken," but nearly twenty Black South Carolinians made it to the British fleet. Aghast at the Royal Navy captains' informal alliance with the Black fugitives, the Council of Safety informed them that they would no longer be permitted to purchase food onshore "unless the fugitive slaves of the inhabitants which receive protection from them, are forthwith delivered up."[20] The council hoped the raid on Sullivan's Island would "serve to humble our negroes," and in case they did not get the message, it built a fort there. But fugitive slaves continued escaping to British ships.[21]

In Virginia, too, the tricornered struggle among Whigs, the British military, and fugitive slaves came to a head in December 1775, as the provincial convention marched one of its two regiments toward the governor's base in Norfolk, near the coast. Dunmore resolved to halt the rebel advance at the Elizabeth River. When two parties of rebels crossed the river and attacked a small British fort on the east bank, its garrison, composed primarily of African Americans, drove them back. Farther upriver, at Great Bridge, British grenadiers defended a larger fort. When Dunmore learned that Whig reinforcements would soon arrive from North Carolina as well as Williamsburg, he decided to seize the initiative. He ordered Capt. Samuel Leslie, commander of his Great Bridge garrison, to send two companies of Black soldiers across the Elizabeth to attack the rebel breastworks from behind, sowing disorder and facilitating a frontal assault across the bridge. When it turned out that these Black infantrymen had been sent on another mission, Leslie decided—"imprudently," Dunmore believed—to nonetheless proceed with his frontal assault.[22]

At dawn on December 9, two hundred British soldiers moved forward, first across the bridge and then over a long open causeway, all the while facing "a very heavy fire" from the rebels on the west bank. A Black Whig named William or Billy Flora advanced toward the onrushing grenadiers and reportedly got off eight shots before finally joining his comrades behind the breastwork. The Whigs killed about seventeen of the British attackers and wounded nearly fifty, and the rest took to their heels. William Woodford, the Whig commander at Great Bridge, called it "a second Bunker's Hill affair, in miniature; with this difference, that we kept our post."[23]

After his defeat at the Battle of Great Bridge, Dunmore abandoned Norfolk. Even as the African American survivors of the December 19 Whig raid on Sullivan's Island found refuge on Royal Navy vessels in Charleston Harbor, Dunmore's soldiers, Black and white, likewise had to take to their ships.

Another element of Dunmore's plan for restoring royal authority also collapsed at about this time. As John Connolly prepared to head out to the Ohio Valley to assemble his army of redcoats, backwoods Loyalists, and native warriors, he sent the Indian trader John Gibson (whose native wife had been killed in the Yellow Creek Massacre of April 30, 1774) a message to be forwarded to the Delaware chief White Eyes, but Gibson turned it over to Whig authorities, who began looking out for Connolly. Although Connolly had initially planned to reach Indian country via Quebec, the American invasion of that province diverted him to Maryland, where Whigs captured him. He would spend most of the rest of the war in prison, and his scheme exerted its greatest influence in further alienating white colonists against the British crown. Thomas Paine was probably correct that there were "thousands, and tens of thousands, who would think it glorious to expel from the continent, that barbarous and hellish power, which hath stirred up the Indians and Negroes to destroy us."[24]

EVEN AMONG WHITE WHIGS, tensions mounted in the fall of 1775, especially over military service. A year earlier, well-to-do Virginians had begun organizing independent military companies. Precisely because all of the early enlistees belonged to the elite, the companies' rank and file were allowed to choose their officers, and no one had the nerve to reverse that policy even when growing numbers of common farmers signed up. But then in the summer of 1775, Virginia's provincial convention voted to replace the independent companies with a more traditional military establishment centered on sixteen minuteman battalions enrolling a total of eight thousand men.

All over the province, farmers refused to serve as minutemen, and one reason was that they could no longer choose their officers. Many also balked at the exemptions granted to owners of multiple slaves—more or less the same policy that would lead many Confederate families to label the Civil War a rich man's war and a poor man's fight. George Gilmer, friend and doctor to Thomas Jefferson, was appointed to command Albemarle County's minuteman battalion but found his recruitment efforts stymied by the convention's decision "to exempt the gentlemen and to throw the whole burthen on the poor."[25]

Another reason Virginians chose not to enlist as minutemen was the enormous (albeit conventional) pay disparity between officers and men: top officers earned eleven times as much as privates.[26] But the largest disincentive was that minutemen were required to perform so many days of military service that they could not successfully manage their farms, yet they were only paid for days of actual service, which was too little to live on. In response to these complaints, a December 1775 convention eliminated the slaveholders' exemption and shifted much of the responsibility for defending white Virginians onto an augmented regular army—which also became a source of contention.

Other conflicts among white Americans arose from the commercial boycott of Britain. One reason Whigs stopped buying British merchandise on December 1, 1774, was to provoke unemployment, and thus riots, in the mother country. But the boycott ended up sparking civil disorder in America instead. By December 1775, Virginians were running out of the salt they depended upon to preserve meat. Farmers in Hanover and Henrico counties, in the Piedmont, accused local traders of hoarding salt, and armed bands broke open the alleged hoarders' stores, taking what they needed. By March 1776, Richard Henry Lee worried that the salt shortage would "produce universal riot and convulsion."[27]

Another source of civil conflict was Lee himself. As in other colonies, Virginia's Whig authorities funded the war with paper money that was widely expected to depreciate. As the owner of numerous small farms in Fauquier County in northern Virginia, Lee refused—as did many other landlords—to allow his tenants to pay him using the new currency at its face value. For their part, tenants pointed out that the closing of Virginia's ports on September 10, 1775, prevented them from obtaining anything but paper money for their crops. Soldiers were also paid in paper, and the Whig convention had commanded all Virginians to accept it. Annual rental payments were typically due on Christmas, but tenants in Fauquier and neighboring counties simply refused to pay. It was "Cruel in the Land Holders to expect their Rents when there is no market for the produce of the Land," they said. Landlords responded with a double-barreled threat to haul rent strikers before the local Whig committee and have county officials seize their belongings. But the tenants were "not at all Intimidated," and many issued threats of their own. They would overthrow the county committee, and they would "Punish the First officer" who came for their property.[28]

In upcountry South Carolina, white-on-white conflict turned fatal. Late in the summer of 1775, the Cherokees, suffering like other Americans from nonimportation, sent Whig authorities in Charles Town a desperate plea for ammunition for their fall hunt. Spotting an opportunity to buy Cherokee support, or at least neutrality, the colony's Whig congress dispatched a shipment of gunpowder and lead. On November 3, as the wagon train followed the Saluda River west, a band of Loyalists waylaid it and seized the precious cargo.[29]

Whig authorities in Charles Town sent two parties of militiamen to the upcountry to try to recapture the munitions. On November 19, Maj. Andrew Williamson's five hundred Whig militiamen reached the town of Ninety Six (named by fur traders for its distance from the Cherokee town of Keowee). As they were throwing up a fence-rail fort, more than 1,500 Loyalists surrounded them and opened fire. Over the next three days, about a dozen Whigs and fifty Loyalists were wounded—one fatally on each side. On November 22, the two sides agreed to a truce: in return for the Whigs dismantling their fort, the Loyalists allowed them safe passage out of it. Less than three weeks after Joseph Harris helped bring on Virginia's first battle of the Revolutionary War, nonwhites thus played an equally crucial role in spreading the war to South Carolina.[30]

Throughout the south, elite rebels feared the British would turn non-slaveholding whites against them. Late in the summer of 1775, when a Whig delegation from Charles Town visited upcountry farmers in a bid for their support, Loyalist Thomas Fletchall told his neighbors, "the people below wanted them to go down and assist them against the Negroes." The following spring, a British squadron sailed up Virginia's Rappahannock River, whereupon one dissident "asked the People if they were such fools to go to protect the Gentlemen's houses on the river side; he thought it would be the better if they were burnt down."[31]

FAR TO THE NORTH in Cambridge, Massachusetts, the relationship between George Washington and the common soldiers in his army was nearly as contentious. An astonishing proportion of those who met the new commander-in-chief during the summer and fall of 1775 described him by using forms of the same word—"dignity"—and yet he was unable to awe his troops into submission. A constant succession of courts-martial tried privates and even officers for cowardice, desertion, brawling, and theft.[32]

Such might be expected from an agglomeration of mostly young men that was considerably larger than nearby Boston. But Washington blamed the disorder on the structure of the New England militia, in which mid-level officers were elected by the provincial assembly or congress—and junior officers were chosen by the men they commanded. Every commander feared being severe with his troops, lest they use their collective political influence to block his advancement or even get him dismissed. Washington found New England's rank and file "exceeding dirty & nasty," and the officers, especially those from Massachusetts, "nearly of the same Kidney with the Privates." To this proud Virginian, Yankees of all ranks seemed "inattentive to every thing but their Interest."[33]

These were private comments to close associates, but somehow they leaked out. Artemas Ward, commander of the militiamen outside Boston before Congress took them into Continental service, had greeted the new commander-in-chief courteously. But in October, Ward informed John Adams that New England soldiers knew precisely "what was said of them by some that came from the Southward last summer." Indeed, the widespread recognition that Washington and other officers from outside New England "despised" the region made its males "backward in Inlisting."[34]

One group of New Englanders shocked and offended Washington simply by serving in the Continental Army. African Americans had fought at Lexington and Concord and Bunker Hill, but on October 8, Washington's council of war expelled every Black soldier from the army. But less than two months later, on December 30, Washington decided to allow free Blacks back into to the Continental ranks. He changed his mind for several reasons.

Historians like to say a *rage militaire* filled the ranks of the Continental Army in 1775, only to give way to apathy in later years, but Washington detected the decline much sooner. As the sand ran out on 1775, his army was draining away, too, and few of the soldiers whose enlistments would expire on December 31 had reupped.[35] Moreover, the veterans of Lexington, Concord, and Breed's Hill, while by no means free of racial prejudice, knew a good soldier when they saw one. On

December 5, fourteen Continental officers petitioned the Massachusetts assembly on behalf of Salem Poor, a free Black man who had behaved at Breed's Hill "like an Experienced officer, as well as an Excellent Soldier."[36] Some of these same men may have pressed their commander to reverse his decision.

Washington was also feeling a different kind of pressure. Less than a month after Lexington and Concord, Whigs like Esther Reed, the wife of Washington's secretary, were receiving reports that significant numbers of African Americans were accepting Gen. Gage's invitation to serve in the British army. Moreover, when the general's cousin Lund Washington, who managed Mount Vernon in his absence, informed him of Lord Dunmore's emancipation proclamation, he warned that it might provoke the estate's white servants as well as its Black slaves to try to run to the British. And why not? "Liberty is sweet," Lund Washington wrote.[37] The commander-in-chief fully comprehended the threat that Dunmore posed. "If . . . that Man is not crushed before Spring," he told Richard Henry Lee on December 26, "he will become the most formidable Enemy America has—his strength will Increase as a Snow ball by Rolling."[38]

Actually, Dunmore and his Ethiopian Regiment would be compelled to abandon Virginia in August 1776, forced off by an army of white Virginians—and even more so, by smallpox and other diseases. Among the dead was Joseph Harris, whose service to the Royal Navy had included piloting its ships and helping two of its captains elude Whig pursuers.[39] But Washington could not predict Dunmore's fate, and he worried that even in northern colonies with small Black populations, the pressing need for subsistence might compel Black men to enlist with the British. Given the American commander's belief that the only way to keep free Blacks out of the British army was to readmit them to his own, the Black Virginians who had initiated an informal alliance with Governor Dunmore deserved some of the credit, ironically enough, for the numerous accomplishments of the Black Continentals.

Washington's reversal may also have been driven in part by sentiment. On October 26, 1775, Phillis Wheatley sent him a poem she had written in his honor. Wheatley's timing—less than three weeks after the banishment of the Black Continentals—invites the surmise that she knew about it and wished to try the effects of flattery in getting it reversed. The master of Mount Vernon read Wheatley's poem in December, just before welcoming free Blacks back to the army. He did not get around to thanking Wheatley until February 1776, but when he did, he invited her to visit him in Cambridge.[40]

Washington changed his mind about free Blacks but not about slaves, and on January 16, Congress limited his offer still further, to free Blacks who had previously served in the army. But at least Salem Poor was able to reenlist in the Continental Army, along with Peter Salem—the former slave credited with killing John Pitcairn at Breed's Hill—and many others. In violation of Congress's directive, northern colonies soon began enlisting other free Blacks as well, and before long, they also accepted slaves. Several southern colonies and later states also welcomed freedmen—though never slaves, at least not officially. By war's end, some nine thousand African Americans had served in the Whig army and navy—roughly the same number who enlisted with the British.[41]

On September 8, 1775, barely two months after taking over the army, Washington proposed a dramatic two-pronged assault on the British garrison in Boston. One column would make an amphibious landing while another overwhelmed the British defenses on Boston Neck. Gen. Charles Lee, a fellow veteran of Braddock's expedition, supported his chief's proposal in theory, saying "the spirit of attack . . . has undoubtedly an advantage over the mere simple spirit of defence," but he worried that rank-and-file Continentals would refuse to execute it. "The fatal perswasion has taken deep root in the minds of the Americans from the highest to the lowest order," Lee told Philadelphia doctor Benjamin Rush, "that they are no match for the [British] Regulars, but when cover'd by a wall or breast work." And in an American assault on Boston, the British infantrymen and cannon crews would be the ones covered by breastworks. Thus Lee and the other generals unanimously voted down their commander's proposal.[42]

But then Washington gained a powerful ally. Congress was appalled at the staggering cost of maintaining nearly twenty thousand Continental troops in eastern Massachusetts. Operating on the hopeful assumption that if the redcoats left Boston, they would not land somewhere else, the delegates on October 2 ordered the Continental Army to attack them "as soon as a favourable Opportunity shall offer." But unlike Washington, many of his generals had participated in the slaughter of the redcoats on Breed's Hill on June 17. Since then the British had fortified Boston, ready to repay the Americans in kind. On October 18, the council of war once again voted unanimously to remain on defense. Later in the fall, the British in Boston inadvertently acquired an additional layer of protection. A smallpox epidemic struck, and Gen. Howe had all soldiers inoculated, which temporarily made them contagious. Even Washington had to admit, briefly, that this was no time to storm the city.[43]

At this early stage of the war, Washington did not think Congress had authorized him to overrule his council of war, and in his heart he knew the generals were right. Still, many Americans had come to see the as-yet-untested Continental Army as invincible, and Washington could not disabuse them—for instance, by revealing his artillerymen's dire shortage of gunpowder—without also tipping off the enemy. To the public, and even to many soldiers, the army's failure to strike Boston looked like excess caution or even cowardice.[44]

THE COLONISTS WOULD HAVE ample opportunity to test their mettle against the British regulars in the coming year, for the imperial government's attitude was hardening. On August 23, George III officially declared the Americans in rebellion, whereupon Gen. Gage and Adm. Graves launched a naval campaign to bomb them into submission. Lt. Henry Mowat would lead four vessels against the seaports north of Boston. On October 18, his cannon crews opened fire on the town of Falmouth in the district of Maine, and a landing party completed the destruction of 139 dwellings and 278 other buildings, mostly in the part of Falmouth that would later become Portland.[45]

Abigail Adams's immediate reaction to the burning of Falmouth read like a Puritan jeremiad: "We have done Evil or our Enimies would be at peace with us," she told husband John. "The Sin of Slavery as well as many others is not washed away."[46] The October 18 attack further alienated the Adamses and other free Americans against the mother country, but it could have been much worse. Mowat had given Falmouth residents ample time to evacuate; no one was killed. Moreover, Mowat had spent his wrath on Falmouth; he did not destroy even one other town.

Had Mowat tried to maximize rather than prevent civilian casualties, and if he and other British officers had repeated the process throughout North America, they might possibly have driven the rebels to despair, resignation, and submission. Wholesale violence had served Britain well against rebellious Native Americans, slaves, and people of color the world over—and against Irish Catholics closer to home. But the residents of towns like Falmouth were white Protestants, primarily of English stock. Had the North ministry carried fire and sword among them, it could not have maintained its majority in Parliament. Over the next seven years, redcoats and rebels would abuse each other with increasing brutality, but the American Revolution is nonetheless a reminder that the same racial and religious prejudices that often license atrocities against Others can also raise taboos against mistreating wayward members of one's own tribe. In North America in the 1770s, these cultural restraints favored the Whigs, for the simple reason that they began the war in possession of most of the territory in dispute.[47]

A more savage policy would also have alienated the Loyalists, whom British army commanders counted on to hold the territory they liberated from the rebels. Surely the Loyalists must vastly outnumber the rebels, imperial officials reasoned; after all, the vast majority of free colonists looked, worshipped, and spoke a lot like themselves.[48]

On November 10, Lord Dartmouth, recognizing that he was not the man to carry out the imperial crackdown, handed his post as American secretary to Lord George Germain, who assured the House of Commons that he would be "decisive, direct and firm." A decade and a half earlier at the Battle of Minden, Germain had been accused of cowardice (probably unjustly), and colonists worried that he would now seek to reclaim his manhood at their expense.[49] On December 22, Parliament adopted the American Prohibitory Act, subjecting all vessels trading to America and all American ships (even those merely engaged in coastal trade) to seizure and sale and also authorizing the impressment of American crews into the Royal Navy.

By this time Congress had already carried the war out into the Atlantic, refitting several commercial vessels to intercept the enemy's supplies. In addition, merchants in many ports began sending out their own privateers to prey on British shipping. The crew of every privateersman received a portion of its plunder, which helps explain both why many Americans were far more eager to enlist on privateersmen than in the Continental Army—and why many Whigs viewed privateering as at best a necessary evil. When the Continental soldiers crewing one privateersman seized a ship owned by a Whig merchant and were ordered to release it, they refused. In November, George Washington informed Joseph Reed that "Our Rascally privateers-men, go on at the old rate, Mutinying if they can not do as they please."[50]

At the start of the war, the Royal Navy was so destitute of sailors as well as vessels that it could not always arrange proper escorts, even for ships transporting arms, ammunition, and soldiers, and several fell victim to the privateers. Eventually Britain's wartime blockade of America's trade would all but empty its store shelves, but in both the civilian and the military sectors, privateersmen mitigated the shortages.[51]

SWASHBUCKLING ACCOUNTS OF THE American Revolution's battlefield heroics sometimes lose sight of a simple fact: like most wars, this one's most significant short-term impact was in accelerating the circulation of disease. Smallpox instilled by far the most terror, but taken together, ordinary ailments such as dysentery, yellow fever, and malaria claimed even more lives, among soldiers as well as civilians. Some British and American officers fought heroically to protect their men from such sources of infection as human waste and sick compatriots, but seldom with much success. An early example was the epidemic of dysentery—often called "bloody flux"—that broke out in the nearly ten-mile-long semicircle of Continental encampments around Boston during the summer of 1775.

Soldiers came into daily contact with civilians, and the bacteria soon spread across the lines into Boston and throughout eastern Massachusetts and into Connecticut, where it nearly killed Mary Fish Noyes Silliman, the author of "Portrait of a Good Husband." This one epidemic reportedly claimed in excess of a thousand lives: more than all of the bullets and balls British and American soldiers exchanged throughout 1775. Loyalist Benjamin Thompson claimed the Continental Army sent sick soldiers home, "spreading the infection among their relatives and friends" and causing "such a general mortality throughout New England as was never known since its first planting. . . . Some towns 'tis said have lost near one-third of their inhabitants." Factoring in the spread of disease, and recognizing that only a small percentage of the troops served long stints, it appears that the Revolutionary War killed more U.S. civilians than soldiers and roughly equal numbers of women and men.[52]

John Adams was off at Congress when the 1775 dysentery epidemic struck, but by early September the scourge had killed his brother Elihu, a soldier stationed in Cambridge, and also struck several members of his Braintree, Massachusetts, household. Every day, Abigail Adams's fifty-three-year-old mother, Elizabeth Smith, rode over from neighboring Weymouth to help out, and inevitably she, too, contracted the disease. Her death on October 1 was an incalculable blow to Abigail, who sought comfort in Isaiah, Job, and the psalms.[53]

CHAPTER 17

Freedom Hath Been Hunted

Early 1776

T HE FIRST EDITION OF *COMMON SENSE*, WHICH APPEARED ON JAN-
uary 10, 1776, was only forty-six pages long. The anonymous
author, Thomas Paine, magnanimously donated his profits to the Continental Army—a larger gift than he could have imagined, since printers
sold an unprecedented 120,000 copies over the next three months, at least
according to Paine. No other Whig production, not even the Declaration of Independence, brought as many colonists around to the position
that Paine succinctly summarized as, "'TIS TIME TO PART." "There
is abundance talked about independency," the reluctant rebel Landon
Carter of Richmond County, Virginia, stated in March 1776. "It is all
from Mr. Common sense."[1]

What made *Common Sense* different? Many have sought the answer in
Paine's crystal-clear prose. At a time when most other texts brimmed with
classical quotations (often in the original Latin and Greek), all of the ancient wisdom in *Common Sense* comes from the Bible. The prophet Mo-
hammed only comes up once, but that is more than all of ancient Greece.

Having sailed into Philadelphia in December 1774, Paine had the recent immigrant's unique vision of America's destiny:

> Every spot of the old world is overrun with oppression. Freedom
> hath been hunted round the globe. Asia, and Africa, have long ex-
> pelled her—Europe regards her like a stranger, and England hath
> given her warning to depart. O! receive the fugitive, and prepare
> in time an asylum for mankind.[2]

Paine's eloquence tends to obscure a more straightforward explanation for his outsized influence. He was one of the first authors to give

readers what many passionately desired: an explicit call for independence. Furthermore, violating that taboo gained him access to polemical ground that had been off limits to previous writers. For example, he could predict that the colonists would only need a few more months to defeat the British empire, since its fabled global reach had stretched it way too thin.[3]

Yet Paine did not stop at embracing independence. For more than a decade, Americans had criticized Britain's policies but not its form of government. Indeed, they had issued such dire warnings about corrupt parliamentary leaders upsetting the age-old balance among Commons, Lords, and king that some historians have branded them royalists.[4] But Paine argued that the English constitution, with its vaunted separation of powers, was itself fundamentally flawed, since legislative proposals that cleared the Commons could still be thwarted by the House of Lords or king. The governments of the thirteen rebel colonies were similarly mixed, and much of the popularity of *Common Sense* derived from its demand that Americans replace them with pure republics, in which popularly elected assemblies would reign supreme.

Paine opposed monarchy not just in principle but for a host of practical reasons. No king can be counted on to preach peace, since none can be conscripted and yet all have first claim to any plunder. "In the early ages of the world," Paine affirmed, "there were no kings; the consequence of which was there were no wars." The adoptive Pennsylvanian drove home his attack on kingship and aristocracy with two of his most lethal weapons: sarcasm and scripture. Modern monarchy, he reminded readers, had reached England in 1066 in the person of William the Norman ("the Conqueror"), whose parents had never married. "A French bastard landing with an armed banditti, and establishing himself king of England against the consent of the natives, is in plain terms a very paltry rascally original," he wrote. Reaching even further back, the future author of *The Age of Reason* pointed out that for generations, the Israelites had been content to be governed by judges. But then in the time of Samuel, they demanded a king. And God in his anger obliged them.[5]

PAINE'S DISCONTENT WAS WIDELY shared, but not all of the anger was directed against George III. Lund Washington, the commander-in-chief's cousin and estate manager, informed him on the last day of February 1776 that James Cleveland, George Washington's former employee, had "turn'd Politition," placing himself at the forefront of a farmers' revolt.

Most of the rioters rented land in Loudoun County in northern Virginia, and Cleveland crystallized many of their grievances against the Whig leadership in a series of radical slogans. At a time when nonexportation and the British embargo had prevented farmers from selling their crops, he argued that "The Tennants should pay no Rents." Turning to the army, he declared that "There is no inducement for a poor Man to Fight, for he has nothing to defend." He also criticized the immense income disparity between senior officers and enlisted men, contending that in a republican army, "The pay of officers and Soldiers should be the same." Most importantly, Congress's and Gen. Washington's mostly defensive posture threatened small farmers with ruin: "Let us go and Fight the Battle at once, and not be Shilly Shally, in this way, until all the Poor, people are ruined."[6]

Little did Cleveland know that his former employer, now the commander-in-chief, would have been all too happy to storm the British ramparts at Boston. Washington's sense of honor had influenced everything about him, from his pursuit of western wealth to his embrace of the anti-British boycott of 1769. It pained him to hear "Chimney Corner Hero's" constantly "censuring my inactivity." He was not the obstacle; his troops were.[7]

To be sure, the mostly youthful Continentals were at least as restless as the Loudoun rioters and Washington himself, as evidenced by occasional eruptions. More than a thousand soldiers joined in a snowball fight pitting New Englanders against southern riflemen, and just as the commander-in-chief happened by, the brawl turned violent. According to ten-year-old Israel Trask, who had accompanied his father to war, Washington

> rushed into the thickest of the melee, with an iron grip seized two tall, brawny, athletic, savage-looking riflemen by the throat, keeping them at arm's length, alternately shaking and talking to them. In this position the eye of the belligerents caught sight of the general. Its effect on them was instantaneous flight at the top of their speed in all directions.[8]

Washington admired what these rambunctious youngsters had accomplished at Breed's Hill, but he noted that they would not "allways have an Intrenchment, or a Stone Wall as a safe guard or Shield," and he feared they would not "stand exposed in a plain," much less "March boldly up to a [breast]Work." After Montgomery's death outside Quebec at the end of 1775, many of his troops reportedly had run away. Washington needed men who would storm the even more heavily fortified city of Boston, and he was not at all sure he had them.[9]

But there was one way to find out. In that cooler era, the Charles River froze nearly every winter, and with the arrival of the 1776 freeze, Washington proposed to approach Boston across the ice. Granted, a frontal assault on the British fortifications posed enormous risks. But one of Washington's generals, Nathanael Greene, echoed his claim that it might just "put a finishing stroke to the war."[10] Yet on February 16, when the commander pitched his idea to the council of war, urging haste lest the ice melt or Gage receive reinforcements, no one thought it could succeed unless the Americans first softened up the enemy with a massive cannonade for which they did not possess sufficient gunpowder. Horatio Gates was a former British army officer who had known Washington since their service together under Braddock. He argued that rather than attacking the British "in their Fortifications," the Continentals ought to "leave it to them to give us the Advantage, by attacking Ours."[11]

Washington was so eager to attack across the ice that he tried to depict the gunpowder shortage as an advantage. Boston Harbor was not frozen, so if the Continental Army could have bombarded the British, they would have simply embarked in their transports, which were already "Wooded & Watered," and sailed away. But with no Continental cannonade, the enemy would stay, fight, and lose, giving him and his army the dramatic triumph both needed.[12]

Two days after the council of war shot down his idea, Washington wrote an unusually reflective letter to John Hancock, the president of Congress. He acknowledged that the "Irksomeness of my Situation"—the insinuations that he had not stormed Boston because he was afraid—"might have inclin'd me to put more to the hazard than was consistent with prudence."[13]

Later in February the temperature moderated, foreclosing talk of an assault over the ice, but Washington was still bent on storming Boston. Perhaps believing that the best way to wean him from his fixation was with a specific alternative, his generals proposed that rather than attack Gen. Howe, the Americans should do what they had inadvertently but successfully done on Breed's Hill: tempt him to attack them.

Neither army had occupied Dorchester Heights, the chain of hills rising nearly one hundred feet above a peninsula jutting into Boston

Harbor southeast of the capital. Howe's failure to secure the Heights is often offered as evidence of his incompetence, but the reality is that he feared stretching his nine thousand troops too thin. In any event, several American generals saw Dorchester Heights as an opportunity. They informed Washington that if the Americans could drag cannon to the summit, they would be able to hit the south end of Boston, leaving Howe no choice but to drive them off, perhaps at the cost of even more casualties than on Breed's Hill.[14]

Such a maneuver would require numerous cannon, but the Continentals finally had plenty of those, owing to a secret expedition Washington had sent out the previous November. Henry Knox, the bear-sized Boston bookseller who had become his artillery commander, had led a crew of teamsters to Fort Ticonderoga, 160 miles northwest of Cambridge, to collect most of the cannon that Ethan Allen and Benedict Arnold had seized along with the fort. For Knox's teamsters—not to mention their animals—sledding nearly sixty artillery pieces back to Boston, sometimes over snow but just as often over bare soil or insufficiently frozen rivers, was a brutal ordeal. But on January 18, they delivered "a fine train of artillery" to Framingham, twenty miles west of the capital.[15]

Washington endorsed the plan to fortify Dorchester Heights but made a crucial change. Even as one detachment of Continentals installed Knox's cannon on the summit, another four thousand would assemble in Cambridge on the north bank of the Charles. If the American occupation of the Heights succeeded in "drawing out the Enemy," leaving only about half of Howe's troops in town, the Cambridge contingent would row across the river and storm the city.[16] Washington had turned the council of war's cautious and cunning strategy of forcing the British to undertake a perilous frontal attack up Dorchester Heights into a renewed opportunity to defeat them on the streets of Boston with a head-on assault of his own.

Most of the Continental generals acquiesced in this change, but William Heath dilated on the folly of assaulting even an understrength British garrison. He noted that as the Americans rowed a mile and a half across the Charles to Boston, they could expect not only cannonballs, and at close range grapeshot, from the British artillery crews on the west side of town but also enfilade fire from Boston Neck.[17]

On the night of March 4—chosen so that the next day's battle would take place on the anniversary of the Boston Massacre—a convoy of more than three hundred ox carts hauled cannon, ammunition, and other equipment up Dorchester Heights. The ground was too frozen for trenches or breastworks, so the soldiers brought their defensive works with them: baskets of rocks, wooden frames to be filled with hay and earth, and heavy barrels that would first stop British bullets and then be rolled down onto the soldiers ascending the Heights.[18]

Just as they had on June 17, 1775, the British awoke on March 5, 1776, to find Americans atop a hill commanding the town. One officer said the rebels' two redoubts had been "raised with an expedition [speed] equal to that of the Genii belonging to Aladdin's Wonderful Lamp."[19]

The Continentals did not possess sufficient gunpowder or am-munition for a sustained cannonade from Dorchester Heights—but Gen. Howe did not know that.[20] Just as the Americans had hoped, he immediately set in motion a plan to drive them off. About 2,400 red-coats embarked in transports for the short run to the eastern tip of the Dorchester peninsula, where they were to land just after sunset. Then, early on March 6, they would ascend the Heights and attack the enemy as another division stormed the northern slope.

During the afternoon of March 5, a storm struck Boston, rendering the harbor unnavigable until March 7 and giving the drenched but deter-mined Americans on Dorchester Heights two additional days to dig in. Recognizing that an uphill attack would now cost him even more casual-ties than before, Howe canceled it. Although he raged at the tempest for robbing him of this newest opportunity to break out of Boston, several historians have speculated that he actually viewed it as a providential pretext for not storming rebel fortifications on what looked suspiciously like Breed's Hill.[21]

Howe still had the option of leaving by water, and until the Americans completed their batteries atop Dorchester Heights, he could do so unmo-lested. Back in September 1775, the ministry had advised him to evacuate Boston, and he had agreed to, but he had repeatedly delayed his departure in hopes of collecting enough vessels to carry away not only his army and its supplies but the Massachusetts Loyalists and their belongings. Now Howe could no longer wait. Contrary winds delayed his sailing for ten days, but the Continentals allowed him to proceed in peace in return for not destroying Boston on his way out.[22] Finally, on March 17, nine thou-sand redcoats and more than a thousand civilians embarked.

Harvard celebrated the expulsion of the British by awarding Wash-ington an honorary degree, and John Hancock commissioned a portrait of him with Dorchester Heights as the background. But astonishingly, the general himself felt nothing but "disappointment" at the redcoats' departure. He had not wanted to chase them to their boats—indeed, he had correctly predicted that they would leave soon of their own accord—but to kill or capture them, thus bringing honor to his army and himself.[23] In a strange way, his reaction to his March 1776 triumph resembled William Howe's response to capturing Breed's Hill nine months earlier. Neither victor exhibited the expected glee, because neither was naive enough to measure success in acres acquired.

Only with time did Washington recognize that Dorchester Heights had given his army something it needed more than enemy casualties: a public relations coup. Hardly anyone knew that Howe had planned to pull his army out of Boston, so the Continentals got credit for forcing his hand. In the nineteenth century, as thousands of Irish Catholics poured into the city, their leaders would implore the Protestant Old Guard to recognize St. Patrick's Day. Finally, the town fathers relented in their own way, agreeing to honor the British exodus rather than the Irish saint. In Boston, March 17—Evacuation Day—is still an official holiday.[24] The Dorchester Heights episode foretold several themes that would persist throughout the war: the pesssism that overcame British generals the moment they gained the top spot, the instinctive and unhelpful aggressiveness of George Washington, and the powerful influence of external forces such as sudden storms.

When Washington rode into Boston on March 18, the sheer volume of war matériel that Howe's men had had to demolish on their way out of town reminded him of "Dunbars destruction of Stores after Genl Braddocks defeat." The old soldier was no less impressed with the British defensive works, which he described as "almost impregnable," with "every avenue fortified." Others agreed. Ensign Henry Sewall acknowledged being "greatly astonish'd at the strength &c. of the Works on Bunker's hill &c &c &c." Continental Gen. William Heath felt immeasurable relief that his soldiers had avoided a house-to-house fight. "Kind Heaven," he wrote, had "saved the Americans when they would have destroyed themselves." He could have added that in the months leading up to Dorchester Heights, he and the other Continental generals had, by resisting their commander's determination to storm Boston, spared the lives of hundreds of American soldiers. They had saved Washington, too.[25]

THE BRITISH FLEET HEADED northeast, to Halifax, Nova Scotia, to deliver the Massachusetts Loyalists and to await supplies, especially food, from the mother country. But everyone knew that Gen. Howe's ultimate destination was New York City. Many New Yorkers, including the mayor, were known to oppose the Revolution. The city's commercial domination of the eastern seaboard lay in the future, but with roughly 25,000 souls, it was about to dethrone Philadelphia (with just over 30,000) as the largest town north of Mexico City and Havana. Finally, it was the gateway to the Hudson River, a principal thoroughfare to North America's most important loyal colony, Quebec.[26]

Meanwhile the imperial government dispatched a six-thousand-man army under Gen. John Burgoyne to Quebec, also with New York as its ultimate destination. Both the North administration and the rebels had long believed that if Britain occupied the Hudson Valley, it would separate New England, the seat of the rebellion, from the other colonies. And if Burgoyne's troops sailed southward up Lake Champlain, then portaged over to the Hudson and united with Howe's army coming up the river, the combined force could head east into Massachusetts and crush the rebellion by the time it reached Boston.[27]

On March 18, the day after Howe's fleet set sail, Washington began sending soldiers southward, and he himself reached New York on April 13. The army also continued to take in new recruits. The combination of motives that went into each man's enlistment was evident in the Connecticut farm boy Joseph Plumb Martin, who committed to a six-month stint in late June, four months shy of his sixteenth birthday. Martin acknowledged that he was excited about the recruitment bounty and the prospect of adventure and bragging rights but added that he also felt a duty to finish what his fellow Americans had started. Paraphrasing Luke 9:62, he stated that the colonists must not "put the hand to the plough and look back." He knew he was courting danger, but he expected to be home soon: "the Americans were invincible, in my opinion."[28]

In 1776, New York City covered only the narrow southern tip of Manhattan Island, and none of its buildings was out of range of the artillery crews aboard British warships. The rebels' navy was no match for Parliament's, but they had a few cannon and an infinite supply of dirt, so from April to August they dug ditches and threw up redoubts, not only on the shores of Manhattan but on every harbor island of any size. Some batteries had earth-and-timber roofs to protect the gun crews from snipers firing down from the crow's nests of warships.[29]

Near the northern tip of Manhattan, where the Hudson narrows (and where the modern-day George Washington Bridge crosses the river), the Continentals built underwater obstructions and prepared fireships, which could be set ablaze and then allowed to drift into the British fleet. They also constructed Fort Washington on the New York side of the river and Fort Constitution (also called Fort Lee) across from it in New Jersey. Tests confirmed that the range of the two forts' cannon overlapped, potentially closing the Hudson to British warships.

Even before Howe left Massachusetts, one of his generals, Henry Clinton, received word that he was to command a British army coming over from Ireland to invade the south. Clinton, who as the son of a former governor of New York had spent most of his youth in North America, would meet the transports near the mouth of the Cape Fear River, which flows eastward through southern North Carolina on its way to the Atlantic. Clinton's troops were to conquer as much territory as possible before summer, when they would repair to New York to assist Gen. Howe.[30] Historians are not wrong in saying the American War of Independence had a northern phase (1775 to 1778) and a southern phase (1778 to 1782), but that was not British war planners' original intent. Especially in the early years of the conflict, they tried to concentrate on the south (and later the Caribbean as well) during the winter, when frost and snow cleared northern fields of forage, and the north during the summer, when rising temperatures seemed to turn the south into a Pandora's box of tropical diseases.

Clinton expected to rendezvous with two distinct groups of North Carolina Loyalists. First, Josiah Martin, who had succeeded William Tryon as governor in 1771, had made numerous overtures to the defeated and abused Regulators, even going so far as advising George III to pardon all of them except Hermon Husband.[31] Second, thousands of Scottish Highlanders had just immigrated to North Carolina, too recently to have caught the Whig infection.

Martin's prediction that throngs of Loyalists would welcome Clinton as a liberator proved only half right. The Regulators spotted roughly equal numbers of their tormentors on either side of the imperial dispute, and most tried to steer clear of it.[32] The Scottish Highlanders had their own history as rebels: many had participated in the Jacobite insurrection of 1745, and at least one, Flora MacDonald, had aided in the escape of Bonnie Prince Charlie. But with little attachment to North Carolina, most were eager to flaunt their rehabilitation by fighting for their king.

Gen. Gage had given Lt. Col. Donald MacDonald (no direct relation to Flora) the local rank of brigadier general and sent him to the heavily Scottish region around Cross Creek (modern-day Fayetteville), 110 miles up the Cape Fear River, where he enlisted six hundred Highlanders, along with about eight hundred other Loyalists, including Regulators. On February 18, he led his troops out of Cross Creek toward a planned junction with Clinton at Negro-Head Point, near the town of Wilmington. More than a thousand Whig militiamen tried to stop MacDonald's force at the Black River, a tributary of the Cape Fear. But a slave led him and his troops to an undefended crossing farther up the Black, and the Whigs had to drop back to the south bank of Moore's Creek, just seventeen miles from Wilmington.[33]

By the evening of February 26, when MacDonald's advance party reached Moore's Creek, desertion had reduced his ranks to eight hundred, nearly all Highlanders, many carrying only broadswords. Before daylight on February 27, as MacDonald prepared to cross the bridge, one of his officers heard men on the other side of the creek. Unable to determine their affiliation, he "challenged them in Ga[e]lic." When they made no reply, he knew he had met the enemy. After sunrise, the Highlanders approached the bridge. The Whigs had removed the planks and greased the stringers (side-rails), slowing the Highlanders' crossing to a crawl and making them easy marks. Thirty of their bodies were found on the battlefield, and many more were fished out of the creek. Over the next few days, Whigs would apprehend another 850 Loyalists while losing only one man of their own.[34]

Even if the Highlanders had made it to Wilmington, they would not have found Clinton (who would not arrive until March 12) or the promised British troops. Delayed both in their departure and at sea, the bulk of the Irish transports would reach Cape Fear only on May 3.[35] As he waited, Henry Clinton kept busy, for instance welcoming slaves fleeing Whig plantations and enrolling them in a noncombatant regiment he called the Black Guides and Pioneers. Among the new recruits was an African-born resident of Wilmington who had worked as a wheelwright to earn money for his owner. His name was Thomas Peters, and half his journey lay before him.

On May 31, Clinton's army set sail for Charles Town, South Carolina, the fourth largest port in the rebel colonies. The general did not have enough time or troops to storm the city, so he set the more modest objective of capturing the structure that controlled access to Charleston Harbor: the sand-and-palmetto-log fort the Whigs had built on Sullivan's Island.

On June 18, Clinton's troops landed on an island adjacent to Sullivan's and separated from it only by a narrow inlet. He had been told that the inlet could be waded at low tide, but it proved to be seven feet deep, with strong currents. So on June 28, Peter Parker, the commodore of the fleet that had brought Clinton to South Carolina, attempted to bomb Sullivan's Island into submission. Over a period of nearly ten hours, nine British warships hurled more than twelve thousand cannonballs and exploding shells toward the Whig fort, but most simply bounced off its palmetto walls. In sharp contrast, the British warships had no protection against return fire from the fort. A frigate was forced aground and had to be scuttled, and other vessels were the scenes of horrific carnage. Every single person on the quarterdeck of one vessel, the *Bristol*, was killed or wounded. In all 115 British fighters but only seven Americans were killed.[36]

Clinton had no choice but to withdraw. A year earlier, he had reached Boston just in time for the calamitous British assault on Breed's Hill, and now, on the outskirts of another of North America's largest seaports, he had presided over a disastrous offensive of his own. Breed's Hill and Sullivan's Island taught the same lesson as the Battles of Great Bridge and Moore's Creek Bridge: Americans enjoying the protection of earth and log defensive works could invariably hold out long enough to inflict crippling casualties on British assailants. And while men standing in an open field would tarnish their cherished honor by hitting the dirt in the face of enemy fire, there was nothing unmanly about taking cover in a fort.

As Clinton's army sailed off to join Gen. Howe, who had reached the entrance to New York Harbor on July 31, white South Carolinians designed a state seal featuring a palmetto tree. In 1861, once again pushed to secession to preserve everything they held dear, especially slaves like those who had built the fort on Sullivan's Island, they added the palmetto to their flag.[37]

——————

CHAPTER 18

The Mouse in the Maze

Early 1776

As white colonists agonized over whether to make their separation from the mother country official, they also had to consider, "What next?" Thomas Paine wanted them not only to cut loose from the old imperial system but also replace it with something far more democratic. Thus the appearance on January 10 of his pamphlet *Common Sense* had the ironic effect of causing some Whigs, especially among the elite, to hesitate at the threshold of independence. For others, though, the prospect of gaining a greater say in government was reason enough to sever the last lingering ties.

In the spring of 1776, numerous conservative colonists—not only the "Barons of the south," as John Adams called them, but also leading residents of mid-Atlantic and even New England provinces—gave vent to their fear that "if we become independant we shall become a commonwealth," with no monarch or House of Lords to rein in the popularly elected legislature.[1] Carter Braxton, a wealthy Virginia tobacco planter and congressman, described independence as "a delusive Bait which Men inconsiderately catch at without knowing the hook to which it is affixed." The hook was democratization, and Braxton spoke for many conservative Whigs when he claimed that the New England descendants of the Puritan radicals who had convulsed Old England in the seventeenth century favored secession from Britain precisely in order to embrace "their darling Democracy." George Washington believed many of his fellow Virginia gentlemen would already have joined him in endorsing independence were it not for their "steady Attachment heretofore to Royalty."[2]

Americans who feared republicanism warned that it would entail a wide variety of evils. Nearly a decade after encouraging Philadelphia women to pressure their men to boycott British merchandise, Hannah Griffitts still considered herself a good Whig, albeit a "moderate" one. But she pronounced the author of *Common Sense* a "Snake beneath the Grass" and anticipated numerous male thinkers, including Thomas Jefferson, in piercing the mystique of representative government. "Sixty as well as one can tyrannize," she wrote. Soon Griffitts, who had ridiculed anyone who would trade their freedom for cheap tea, was offering the contrary claim that tea drinking cured both sexes' supposedly distinguishing flaws, bringing "To Men, Politeness, & to Ladies Sense."[3]

John Adams was responding to conservatives such as Griffitts as well as radicals like Thomas Paine when, in April 1776, he published a pamphlet called *Thoughts on Government, Applicable to the Present State of the American Colonies*. Rebutting Paine's brief for republican government, Adams offered a model state constitution in which neither the governor nor the upper house of the legislature would be elected directly by the voters.[4]

The wide range of responses to *Thoughts on Government* reflected white America's deep divisions. The moment Paine got his hands on it, he hurried to Adams's lodgings in Philadelphia to voice his objections. In his diary, Adams reported telling Paine that he was "as much afraid of his Work [as] he was of mine," deeming it "so democratical, without any restraint or even an Attempt at any Equilibrium or Counterpoise, that it must produce confusion and every Evil Work." At the other extreme, Carter Braxton contended that model constitutions like Adams's were "fraught with all the tumult and riot incident to simple democracy" and might even lead to "an equal division of property." Americans like Braxton worried that such factors as the war, the closing of the courts, the flight of the royal governors, and the cessation of trade had already unleashed disorder that would spread even faster if Americans ventured down the "dark and untrodden way of Independence and Republicanism."[5]

In that fertile spring of 1776, independence advocates discovered that the stubborn fears articulated by men like Braxton could be turned to good account. They argued that the only way to prevent the colonies from lapsing into anarchy was to revive international trade and reestablish the formal institutions of government, neither of which could happen until Americans declared independence.

Much of the social conflict that beset the rebel colonies in late 1775 and early 1776 was caused by the cessation of overseas commerce. Upon learning of the Americans' boycott of British trade, Parliament ordered navy captains to prevent them from trading with other nations. The resultant cutoff of imports into North America had provoked shortages, most glaringly of salt, and nonexportation had deprived colonists of the income they needed to pay their rent and taxes and to purchase the few items they could still find on store shelves. With shortages and unemployment causing mounting social unrest, many Americans made the case that nothing short of formal separation from Britain would enable them to revive overseas trade, specifically with Britain's enemies. The most powerful navy in the western world would inevitably step up its campaign against this illicit commerce, but France coveted the rebels' business and seemed willing to fight for it—once they declared independence.

Formal separation from Britain would also increase the influx of French military aid, many writers stressed. In the spring of 1776, Vergennes, the French foreign minister, established a shell company to ship arms to the rebels in return for Chesapeake tobacco. But his government's need for plausible deniability limited the flow of this covert aid. If the Americans declared independence, France would send Continental officers the weapons they needed to comply with James Cleveland's injunction to "go and Fight the Battle at once." Moreover, many colonists opposed inviting French troops onto American soil, but all agreed that if France were to attack Britain in Europe and the Caribbean, the British would have to divert ships and soldiers from North America.[6]

Separating from Britain would check the "rising disorders" in another way as well, independence advocates argued. Royal government had ceased in most colonies by the fall of 1775, and one New Yorker insisted that "without a new legal Government, universal disorder must ensue." A Pennsylvania writer agreed that the only way for freemen "to avoid the terrible Consequences of Anarchy" was to "form such Establishments, as . . . lead to a Separation from *Great Britain*."[7] The clearest articulation of this viewpoint appeared in a series of letters that Virginia congressman Francis Lightfoot Lee sent home to his Richmond County neighbor, the crotchety Landon Carter, in April and May 1776. When a worried Carter informed Lee that "licentiousness begins to prevail in Virg[ini]a," Lee made no effort to reassure him. "The old Government being dissolved, & no new one substituted in its stead; Anarchy must be the consequence," he wrote. Six weeks later, Lee assured Carter that declaring independence would not only help the colonists defeat Britain but foster "internal peace & good order."[8]

By the fall of 1775, even many elites who were otherwise skeptical about independence began to see it as the only way to restore order. On December 1, Maryland planter Charles Carroll informed his son and namesake that the time had come to "Establish a Government," since "Nothing Essentiall to Generall safety Can be done as things are now." Soon even the conservative Virginia congressman Carter Braxton concluded that the time had come to "assume the reins of government, and no longer suffer the people to live without the benefit of law."[9]

Braxton illustrated as well as anyone the British North American ruling class's tortuous path to revolution. He and other well-to-do colonists had initially sought only to turn back the clock: to regain the privileges they had enjoyed until 1763. But their protests provoked a host of British punitive measures, culminating in the Coercive Acts. When Americans resisted these punishments, each side, expecting an attack from the other, trained for war and sought to capture the other's munitions. These defensive preparations in turn led to events such as Gage's expedition to Concord, a series of southern slave conspiracies, and Dunmore's emancipation proclamation, all of which turned even moderate freemen against the crown. Like a mouse in a maze, conservatives like Carter Braxton always chose their direction but never their destination. And the same was true of every player in the revolution drama. Over time, imperceptibly, their in-the-moment decisions led to independence.

The notion that colonial freemen had sought separation from Britain right from the start, still popular among nonspecialists, might have persisted among historians, too, if Benjamin Quarles and other early scholars of enslaved workers had not shown how the seemingly least-powerful Americans helped transform their white neighbors' resistance to imperial reform into a demand for revolution. Here was one more way in which Black history has, during my lifetime, fought its way from the back of the bus to the driver's seat, contributing mightily to our understanding not only of the lives of African Americans but incidentally of the broader American story.[10]

Even as conservatives worried that separation from Britain was going to forever transform America internally, other colonists embraced independence partly in the hope that it would. Some anonymous newspaper writers and even New England town meetings went so far as to endorse a concept that frightened other British freemen on both sides of the Atlantic: "true Democracy."[11]

Historians often diagnose the American revolutionaries with a bad case of pessimism—about human nature and consequently about the inability of human institutions to prevent evil men from clawing their way to absolute power. They often call this cast of mind "republicanism," but a *Pennsylvania Packet* writer who chose the pen name "Demophilus" (Lover of the People) worried that political pessimism was actually *preventing* Pennsylvania from becoming a republic. In his view, antirepublican writers were trying to scare their neighbors out of giving popular rule a fair trial. Another anonymous Pennsylvanian acknowledged that conflict between patricians and plebeians had torn earlier republics asunder but went on to contend that America would avoid that fate simply by "having no rank above that of freemen." In addition, Americans' wages, which far exceeded Britain's, would enable nearly all of them to afford sufficient education to detect demagogues.[12]

AMERICANS WHO RELISHED THE prospect of republican government recited a long list of specific demands. Many wanted to subject officeholders to term limits. Numerous Marylanders petitioned the provincial convention to open its proceedings to the public and publish its votes. Only in New England did colonial charters condone popular election of local officials, and residents of other regions now demanded that right.[13]

Many reformers focused on preventing either the upper house of the legislature (soon to be known in most states as the senate) or the governor from thwarting the popular will as expressed by the annually elected lower house of assembly. Some demanded direct annual election of the upper house, while others wanted to abolish it altogether. Voters in provinces other than Connecticut and Rhode Island wished to join them in electing the governor directly. Some colonists wanted to take away the governor's veto power, and a few proposed to jettison the position altogether in favor of a plural executive.[14]

The most thoroughgoing reform program appeared in an eleven-page pamphlet called *The People the Best Governors*. Its anonymous author promoted the direct election of governors, congressmen, members of executive councils, and judges at all levels. In populous states, the capital should shuttle between the two largest regions. Finally, every state should abolish property qualifications for voting and officeholding, along with the upper house of assembly and the governor's right to veto laws.[15]

The founders of all of the colonies except Pennsylvania and Rhode Island had established a firm alliance between the government and the dominant church. Now, throughout the rebel provinces, religious dissenters saw the movement for independence as their chance for liberation. In Virginia, where government officials as well as gentry-led mobs had harassed Baptists, often violently, dissenters in Prince William County, Virginia, offered the provincial convention a trade. If Virginia would grant them religious freedom, they in turn would "gladly unite with our Brethren of other denominations, and to the utmost of our ability promote the common cause of Freedom."[16]

Several issues typically associated with the later battle over the U.S. Constitution actually first arose during the run-up to independence. For example, should Americans keep their election districts small, at once enabling voters to keep a close eye on their representative and him to stay abreast of their needs? In Connecticut, where freeholders directly elected congressmen, the author of a June 10, 1776, essay favored limiting congressmen to thirty thousand constituents—the same ceiling used thirteen years later in the first Constitutional Amendment that Congress sent the states.[17] In Pennsylvania, where the extraordinarily large counties were also the assembly districts, one spring 1776 writer pled for much smaller constituencies.[18]

Americans also demanded more progressive fiscal and economic policies. The colonial era's poll (head) taxes fell heaviest on the poor, and some writers wanted to abolish them. Since eighteenth-century North America suffered from a chronic shortage of hard money (gold and silver coin), the freemen of Talbot County, on the Eastern Shore of Maryland, sought the right to pay their rent, taxes, and debts using farm produce instead. Just across the Chesapeake in Anne Arundel County, home to Annapolis, farmers sought exemption from paying interest on their debts until after the war.[19]

NOT EVEN THE MOST radical proposals appearing in American newspapers in the spring of 1776 envisaged any formal political role for women, but beneath the surface of printed discourse, the spirit of reform spread to a handful of female colonists. Abigail Adams had more than one reason to be in an upbeat mood that spring: the mercury finally rose above freezing, her new friend George Washington had driven the British out of Boston, and Congress seemed to be on the cusp of declaring independence. Anything seemed possible. On March 31, Adams wrote John, who was off in Philadelphia serving in Congress, updating him on events in Massachusetts and affirming her support for independence. Then, in as casual a tone as she could muster, she added, "By the way in the new Code of Laws which I suppose it will be necessary for you to make I desire you would Remember the Ladies, and be more generous and favourable to them than your ancestors."[20]

Adams did not ask for the right to vote or even for legislation enabling married women like herself to control property. All she wanted was a modicum of protection for abused wives—an intensely personal issue for her, since her alcoholic brother William had mistreated his wife, Catharine. Abigail knew John and his congressional colleagues would be shocked at her "List of Female Grievances," so she lightened the mood by joking that if Congress ignored women, they would "foment a Rebellion." And knowing how much John appreciated irony as well as flattery, she turned two of his own favorite slogans against him. "Remember," she wrote, "all Men would be tyrants if they could." She and other women would not "hold ourselves bound by any Laws in which we have no voice, or Representation."[21]

Not that American women needed to learn about their subjugation from their husbands' rhetoric about natural rights; recall the implicit critique of patriarchal tyranny in Mary Fish Noyes's "Portrait of a Good Husband." But the Revolution did give women an opportunity to express their grievances and a language in which to do so. No one was more alert to this threat than John Adams. "As to your extraordinary Code of Laws," he wrote in reply to his wife's "Remember the Ladies" letter, "I cannot but laugh." A month later, when John learned that a fellow Massachusetts revolutionary wanted to extend the franchise to propertyless men, he warned him not to open Pandora's box. "There will be no End of it," he wrote. "New Claims will arise. Women will demand a Vote. Lads from 12 to 21 will think their Rights not enough attended to, and every Man, who has not a Farthing, will demand an equal Voice with any other in all Acts of State."[22]

Adams's prophecy was soon fulfilled. In 1778, Hannah Lee Corbin, the sister of two signers of the Declaration of Independence and a Virginia widow whose property far exceeded her state's qualification for voting, protested her disfranchisement in a letter to her brother Richard Henry Lee, who stunned her by replying that he "would at any time give my consent" to propertied widows voting. Two years later, another Virginian, Mary Willing Byrd, who had inherited much of her husband's estate after he killed himself, likewise complained to Governor Thomas Nelson that "I have paid my taxes and have not been Personally, or Virtually represented" in the House of Burgesses.[23]

*   *   *

ALTHOUGH THE UNIVERSAL ASSOCIATION between separation from Britain and republican government divided free Americans, with some drawing back from independence and others favoring it more enthusiastically than ever, British policy had the contrary tendency of uniting them. As the one high-ranking British officer in all of North America whom the rebels still felt they could trust, Maryland governor Robert Eden had been permitted to remain in Annapolis. But in April, an American privateer operating in Chesapeake Bay captured two letters Lord Germain had sent Eden, and they revealed that the governor had secretly been working with the imperial government all along. In 1775, the North ministry had infuriated white colonists by joining forces with Native American warriors and freedom-seeking African American slaves. During the first week of May 1776, colonists received confirmation that the imperial government had also signed contracts to rent soldiers from seven German states.[24]

While the revelations about Eden and the Germans augmented colonists' ire at the mother country, a growing number of them endorsed independence for more practical reasons. Many judges had found ways to continue holding criminal trials, but others had not, so civilians accused of terrible crimes had to be jailed indefinitely, illegally tried by courts-martial, or set free. Other matters of practical necessity also pointed Americans toward a formal break. Legalizing exports to France would not only rescue individual farmers and give Whig leaders the means to buy arms and ammunition, as already noted, but also slow the depreciation of the provincial and Continental currencies.[25]

Numerous threats still loomed—and many of these also became arguments for independence. Many colonists believed Gen. Howe posed less of a danger on the battlefield than in his secondary role as peacemaker. The British cabinet had designated Howe and his brother Richard as a commission to negotiate peace with the rebel provinces. Fearful that their more moderate neighbors might heed the siren call of reconciliation, Americans who favored independence redoubled their efforts to go ahead and sever the tie.

Throughout the spring of 1776, colonists on both sides of the imperial dispute promoted the rumor that Britain was thinking about dividing the thirteen colonies with the Bourton monarchies of France and Spain in return for their help in putting down the rebellion. These fears were not entirely fanciful, for during the winter of 1775–1776, the British and Bourbons actually did contemplate an entente. Charles Inglis, an

Anglican clergyman and the author of a pamphlet denouncing *Common Sense*, tried to use the "partition" rumor to scare the revolutionaries into reconciliation with the mother country. But rebel leaders replied that if the colonies remained much longer in limbo, neither reconciling with the mother country nor formally severing ties, Britain and France would cut a deal at their expense.[26]

Even the Whigs' failures contributed to their success at bringing their neighbors around to the cause of independence. The North ministry might have made the Americans a better offer, tempting many to reconcile, if their trade boycott had accomplished its purpose of prostrating the British economy or if their invasion of Quebec had not so spectacularly failed.[27]

On May 6, three vessels carrying British reinforcements, having dodged most of the ten- and twelve-foot ice chunks in the St. Lawrence River, reached Quebec. Throughout the winter and spring of 1776, Governor Carleton had been widely criticized for not sallying forth to stamp out the remnants of the American army lurking just outside the city's gates. But on the very day the relief fleet arrived, Carleton and his troops marched out "to see what those mighty boasters were about." Abandoning its cannon and its sick, the Whig army fled up the St. Lawrence.[28]

Three weeks later, Carleton received additional reinforcements from Brunswick, one of the German states that rented soldiers to the British for use against the North Americans, and from Ireland. Within a week, his whole army had ascended to Trois-Rivières. American Gen. William Thompson's numbers had been reduced to two thousand by smallpox, and he did not realize that the enemy's ranks had swelled to some six thousand. On June 8, Thompson attacked. The redcoats and Brunswickers killed him and made casualties of about four hundred of his soldiers while only losing about a dozen of their own men.[29] The first battle of the War of Independence to involve German mercenaries had taken place in a Loyal British province where the majority of the colonists spoke French.

Other Americans farther up the St. Lawrence fared no better. On May 18, a combined force of redcoats and 160 native warriors attacked a Continental detachment stationed at the Cedars, twenty-eight miles upriver from Montreal. Over the next two days, the Anglo-Indian army obtained the surrender both of the Cedars garrison and of an additional 129 Continental soldiers who had force-marched in vain to its relief. The victorious Indians stripped many of their captives of their clothing, much of which was infected with smallpox. Returning to their homes, the warriors carried the virus as far west as Fort Michilimackinac, on the straits between Lakes Michigan and Huron.[30]

Carleton, who shared William Howe's caution, ordered Burgoyne to shadow the Continentals southward up the Richelieu River but not to bring on an engagement. On June 19, the Whigs reached Saint-Jean, where a fleet was waiting to carry them up Lake Champlain. Carleton's warships could not pass the Richelieu rapids, and he had no large vessels on Lake Champlain, so the Continentals made it safely to Fort Ticonderoga.

Reaching Saint-Jean shortly after the Whigs escaped, Carleton set about collecting a fleet to carry his army to Ticonderoga. Shipwrights built seven hundred bateaux and assembled fourteen single-cannon gunboats that had come from England in sections. British warships on the St. Lawrence were disassembled and dragged piecemeal around the Richelieu rapids and reassembled at Saint-Jean. By early September, he had four of them, but when he learned of the American fleet awaiting him on Lake Champlain—its commodore was Benedict Arnold—he decided he needed one more: the *Inflexible*, which mounted eighteen 12-pounders.[31] Transporting the *Inflexible* around the falls required nearly a month, delaying the departure of Carleton's fleet until October 4.

ON THE SOUTHERN FRONTIER as well, the enemies of the rebellion seemed to have gained the offensive. In April 1776, a pack train carrying twenty-one horse-loads of ammunition left the Gulf Coast port of Mobile in Britain's thirteen-year-old colony of West Florida and headed north. It reached Chota, a principal Cherokee town on the Little Tennessee River in present-day East Tennessee, on the 24th. Its leader was Henry Stuart, assistant to his brother John, Britain's southern Indian agent. Rebel colonists on the eastern seaboard knew that imperial officials like the Stuarts were in touch with the Cherokees, and they assumed that Britain was trying to incite the Cherokees and other Indians to attack frontier settlements. Actually the Stuarts wanted the Cherokees to hold off on raiding white settlements until British regulars arrived both to reinforce them and prevent them from killing or capturing Loyalists.[32]

On the other hand, Henry Stuart and another British Indian agent, Alexander Cameron, did agree to the Cherokee headmen's request that they send a letter of warning to whites who had settled west of the Anglo-Cherokee boundary in present-day Kentucky and Tennessee.

TOP: Thomas Whyte, Chota exterior
BOTTOM: Thomas Whyte, interior of a Chota
winter townhouse

One unnamed recipient of this message saw it as an opportunity. Recognizing that easterners would be much likelier to join the fight against the Cherokees if they seemed to be doing Britain's bidding, he or she forged a circular letter threatening to unleash the Indians on any colonist who refused "to take up arms in defence of the king's just rights"—and then signed it Henry Stuart. Published in the *Virginia Gazette* and discussed in Congress, the forged letter strengthened white southerners' conviction that if the Cherokees attacked them, it would be because British agents had put them up to it.[33]

The forged letter had something in common with Jefferson's claim, in his rough draft of the Declaration of Independence, that George III had incited enslaved Americans "to rise in arms among us." Both documents sought to vilify the British for instigating people of color to kill whites, and both had the incidental effect of falsely portraying Native and African Americans as passively quiescent until set in motion by whites.

Meanwhile in the rebel colonies, the final push for independence came not from the Continental Congress, as implied in plays and popular histories, but from other provincial congresses, along with county conventions, town meetings, grand juries, and even individual colonists who circulated petitions among their neighbors. The historian Pauline Maier discovered that more than ninety grassroots groups declared or demanded independence before Congress finally did so on July 2.[34]

Free Virginians made their wishes clear at the annual election of provincial convention delegates, held in April. In those days, freeholders had the power to instruct their representatives, and many received instructions to vote for independence. In about a third of the counties, voters replaced their anti-independence or lukewarm burgesses with "determined men." The peevish Landon Carter of Richmond County described its election, held on April 1, as "a kind of April fool," since even some of the incumbents' relatives and tenants joined in turning them out.[35]

Conservatives like Carter took alarm at the class resentment that the election unearthed. As he informed George Washington, many ordinary farmers voted to separate from Britain in the hope that "being independt of the rich men eve[r]y man would then be able to do as he pleasd." When Patrick Henry of all people voiced misgivings about declaring independence, Charles Lee, then in Williamsburg on a tour of southern defenses, informed him "the spirit of the people (except a very few in these lower parts of Virginia whose little blood has been suck'd out by musketoes) cry out for this Declaration," and that "the military in particular, men and officers are outrageous on the subject." It would be "dangerous" to disappoint them, Lee warned.[36]

On May 15, the Virginia convention instructed the colony's members of Congress to formally propose that the body declare independence and begin soliciting foreign alliances. Richard Henry Lee complied on June 7, and the delegates debated his motion for three days but then postponed action for three weeks to allow the provincial congresses and conventions to weigh in. In the meantime, they appointed a committee to draw up a document justifying independence should the delegates choose that path. As the first-named member of the committee, Thomas Jefferson chaired it and served as its penman.[37]

FREEMEN IN BRITAIN'S MOST populous North American province had overthrown the old order in an election, but the transition was much rougher in the second largest colony, Pennsylvania. The colonial assemblymen who still ran Pennsylvania had instructed the congressional delegation to oppose independence, and they would not face the voters again until autumn. Pennsylvanians who wanted to secede from Britain concluded that their only recourse was to overthrow the legislature. On May 10, 1776, Congress adopted a resolution aimed primarily at Pennsylvania. It urged colonists who deemed their provincial governments inadequate to replace them. Five days later, in a preface to the May 10 resolution, Congress did something it had never done in any of its previous addresses, resolves, and memorials. Instead of attacking Parliament and its leaders, as they always had in the past, the delegates blamed America's troubles on George III. Britain's figurehead king was the one element of the imperial government whose authority Americans had always acknowledged. By indicting him, Congress paved the way for independence.[38]

On May 20, as Congress deliberated in the Pennsylvania statehouse, a mass meeting just outside invited the colony's voters to send delegates to a special convention to write a constitution for an independent commonwealth. The gathering also demanded that Pennsylvania assemblymen rescind their anti-independence instruction, and less than three weeks later, in a last-ditch effort to prevent a constitutional convention, they did so.[39] The legislature also freed, though it did not require, Pennsylvania's members of Congress to vote for secession. But the majority were not yet ready to go that far.

In Maryland, too, much of the final impetus for independence came from ordinary freemen. On May 21, when the news that Virginia had embraced separation reached Maryland, that province's convention did not follow suit. Instead the delegates reaffirmed their earlier instruction *against* independence. But during the ensuing four weeks, two distinct sets of events forced them to reconsider. The first was an escalation in the civil disorder that had bedeviled Maryland for more than a year. In Caroline County on the Eastern Shore, "evil-disposed persons . . . prevailed on several Companies of Militia to lay down their arms." The Somerset County committee of observation reported on June 25 that the county was "unhappily convulsed, not only by external, but by internal enemies."[40]

During these same weeks, freeholders in several Maryland counties gathered to instruct their convention delegates to support independence. Many of these instructions also proposed republican reforms. The delegates spent the morning of June 28 discussing an interracial insurrection that was reportedly being planned on the Eastern Shore. That same afternoon, they withdrew their instruction against independence. Later that day, Samuel Chase, one of Maryland's earliest advocates for independence, invited his friend John Adams to behold "the glorious Effects of County Instructions."[41]

CHAPTER 19

——•◦•——

Liberty Further Extended

Summer 1776

Landon Carter was astonished when eight of his slaves absconded during the night of June 25–26, 1776—and not at all surprised exactly a month later, when one of them, "Postillion Tom," came crawling back. As Carter reported in his diary, the man "appeared most wretchedly meager and wan. He told me of their great sorrow" and announced that "He had come to ask if I would endeavor to get them pardoned, should they come in, for they knew they should be hanged for what they had done." It was a gratifying image of domestic harmony restored. But it rapidly dissolved, as Carter awakened, not as if from a dream but from an actual one. Eight of his slaves really had escaped to the British fleet during the night of June 25–26, but the whole story of their wanting to return to him, cap in hand, had unfolded entirely in his imagination. Even after recording the dream in his diary, Carter acknowledged that he was "just weak enough to fancy we shall soon hear about them."[1]

Carter was by no means the only American slaveholder who deluded himself during the summer of 1776. Henry Laurens toured his Savannah River plantations in May and then, on August 14, wrote his son John in England boasting, "My Negroes, all to a man, are strongly attached to me," not one having tried to reach the British. That very day, a neighbor reported that five of Laurens's slaves had escaped to the loyal British province of East Florida along with their overseer.[2]

White leaders in British provinces with lopsided black majorities prudently stayed out of the American Revolution, but even in those, enslaved people sometimes turned the war to their own purposes. During the summer of 1776, whites in the northwest corner of Jamaica discovered a slave insurrection plot. Some blamed fellow planters who had indiscreetly discussed the Whigs' natural rights arguments in the presence of their domestic slaves. But the ideological link between the North American and Jamaican rebellions may have been less significant than a more practical one: the royal army's 50th Regiment was stationed in Jamaica until July 3, when British officials sent it north to reinforce William Howe in New York. On July 15, a young slave was discovered removing the bullets from his owner's pistols and jamming the barrels with cotton. A search revealed that slaves had tampered with numerous other firearms as well. Needing white sailors' help against the rebels, Governor Basil Keith embargoed outgoing shipping. Eventually white Jamaicans put 135 of their slaves on trial; 62 won acquittal, but 45 were transported to other slave colonies, 11 were whipped, and 17 were executed.[3]

AT THE END OF June, another slaveholder, Thomas Jefferson, completed his draft of the Declaration of Independence. The largest section was a twenty-seven-point indictment of the British government, interspersing the reforms it had tried to impose on North Americans in the 1760s with the measures it had taken to punish them for resisting its reforms. Since 1774, radicals like Jefferson had claimed that Parliament had no more authority over, say, Pennsylvania, than that colony's assembly had over Scotland or Wales. In the Declaration of Independence, he emphasized this jurisdictional claim in a clever way, never mentioning Parliament in his list of oppressive parliamentary statutes. Instead he blamed these offenses on an alliance between George III and unnamed "others." It would have been more honest to exclude the king, by this time little more than a puppet. Silencing the ventriloquist and amplifying the dummy enabled Jefferson to refer to anti-American statutes such as the Stamp Act and Coercive Acts as "pretended acts of legislation"—mere make-believe, since only America's assemblies could legislate for Americans.[4]

Jefferson was just as strategic in his description of the colonists' specific grievances. His complaint about George III and his parliamentary collaborators "cutting off our trade with all parts of the world" was ambiguous. The phrasing resembled Jefferson's earlier denunciations of Britain's monopoly of American trade, and many Loyalists and British officials would cite it as proof that he and other colonists had aimed at the Navigation Acts all along. But the same clause could plausibly be explained away as referring only to the mother country's 1775 decision to punish the refractory colonists by closing the few remaining loopholes in its monopoly of their trade.[5]

One section of Jefferson's bill of indictment stood out: his castigation of George III for enslaving—and then freeing—African Americans. This was his final grievance, and in the eighteenth century, orators and writers knew to save the best for last. At 168 words, it was also more than three times as long as any of the others. Nowhere else in the document does Jefferson accuse George III of being a bad Christian. Only in castigating the king for enslaving his fellow "MEN" does he fall back on that ultimate expedient of the rookie writer: ALL CAPS.[6]

Jefferson's clear implication was that most free Americans not only opposed the Atlantic slave trade but wished to give up slavery itself. That was not true, but many had in fact expressed misgivings. "I abhor slavery," South Carolina rice planter and former slave merchant Henry Laurens told his son John in his August 14 letter. He had gone along with it because it was sanctioned by law and custom and because his children and grandchildren expected large inheritances (Laurens reckoned the value of his human property at about £20,000)—but most of all because the British had somehow forced him to. But amid all his excuses, Laurens experienced a moment of self-awareness, acknowledging that one reason slavery survived was "my own & the avarice of my Country Men." Laurens's candid if awkwardly phrased admission faintly echoed Patrick Henry's forthright reply, three years earlier, to the Quaker abolitionist who had challenged him to prove his commitment to freedom by freeing his slaves: "I am drawn along by the general Inconveniancy of living without them."[7]

In the northern colonies, which relied heavily upon trade with Caribbean plantations but much less upon the labor of their own slaves, many owners cleared themselves of the charge of hypocrisy by manumitting their own slaves or endorsing emancipation. But for wealthy white southerners, manumission meant a lower of standard of living, and few were ready to go that far. So they found a different solution to the hypocrisy problem, supplementing ancient prejudices with more modern justifications. Sometimes they imagined African Americans of all ages as childlike creatures who required white guidance. Just as often, they portrayed Blacks as hellish monsters in need of constant restraint. These two mutually contradictory justifications for slavery may have wrought even more damage than the original crime, which may explain why Phillis Wheatley was even willing to concede the morality of the African slave trade if that was the only way to upend racism. For slavery could be abolished with the stroke of a pen, and in 1865, with the ratification of the Thirteenth Amendment, it was. But the racial ideology that justified it proved far more durable and is with us still.

More than any of Jefferson's other grievances, his discussion of slavery is a testament to the inadequacy of any modern-day depiction of the American Revolution that only includes North American colonists and George III's government. British merchants had contributed to the Declaration of Independence not only by clinging to their government-enforced monopoly of American imports and exports but also by obtaining imperial protection from provincial legislatures seeking to curb the African slave trade. And in denouncing Britain's informal alliance with enslaved Americans, Jefferson showed that slaves, too, had played an important role in bringing their owners to the point of seceding from Britain. Jefferson charged George III with "exciting" the slaves to rebel. He would have stood on firmer ground if he had accused the slaves of inciting the British.[8]

Jefferson poured nearly as much passion into his message to ordinary Britons. By reelecting the members of Parliament who had sent soldiers, including "Scotch & foreign mercenaries," to slay Americans, the people of Great Britain had "given the last stab to agonizing affection," he wrote. Not that Americans could easily forget their "former love" for the British:

> we might have been a free & great people together; but a communication of grandeur & of freedom it seems is below their dignity. be it so, since they will have it: the road to glory & happiness is open to us too; we will climb it in a separate state, and acquiesce in the necessity which pronounces our everlasting Adieu![9]

There was something eerily personal about Jefferson's exclamation. The Virginian's mother had died just three months earlier, and the psychobiographer Fawn Brodie speculated that he may have felt abandoned. Perhaps so. But phrases such as "former love" and "agonizing affection" and maudlin musings on what "we might have been," all culminating in an "everlasting Adieu!"—were these not the snufflings of a jilted lover?[10]

Yet the most striking feature of Jefferson's Declaration of Independence remains its elegance. In his penultimate paragraph, the author had Americans vow to hold the British people "as we hold the rest of mankind, enemies in war, in peace friends." Under English law, captured traitors forfeited their lives and property, and countless Whigs had pledged to make a willing sacrifice of both. Jefferson adds a crucial third element, having members of Congress wrap up their declaration by vowing to support it with "our lives, our fortunes, & our sacred honour."[11]

WHILE JEFFERSON PREPARED HIS draft declaration for Congress, the Whig convention in his home colony went ahead and declared independence on its own and began formulating a constitution for the Commonwealth of Virginia. George Mason drew up a declaration of rights, but some of his fellow delegates identified a problem in its very first sentence, declaring that "all Men are born equally free and independent," with "certain inherent natural Rights." Their worry was that enslaved Virginians would think this clause mandated their immediate emancipation. Before approving the declaration on June 12, the convention inserted a clarification that men's rights only kicked in "when they enter into a state of society." The qualification ran counter to natural rights philosophy, which holds that the freest men of all are those who have not formed societies, but it accomplished the desired purpose of excluding Black Virginians. Many newspapers in other colonies published Mason's original, more expansive, version of the declaration, which was used much more often than the final draft as a model for other states' bills of rights.[12]

Virginia adopted its first state constitution on June 29, and just four days later New Jersey did the same. The previous month, New Jersey voters had elected a new provincial congress that sent a thoroughly pro-independence slate of delegates to Philadelphia. By publishing a constitution on July 2, the provincial congress transformed New Jersey into a state. The authors of the document enfranchised "all inhabitants of this Colony, of full age, who are worth fifty pounds," opening up the possibility of propertied women voting. Some historians contend that the delegates deliberately chose this gender-neutral language, but it was probably accidental, perhaps the result of haste. After all, it was also on July 2 that the first British soldiers landed on Staten Island, separated from Essex County, New Jersey, by nothing more than the half-mile-wide Arthur Kill.[13]

Whether by accident or design, the authors of the New Jersey constitution had provided propertied women an opening, and soon many of them pushed right through it. The adoption of the new state constitutions also advanced the cause of women's rights in another, more subtle, way. Since most ordinary freemen could already vote during the colonial era, many historians question just how much the Revolution democratized America. But American men *believed* they had embarked upon a bold experiment in republican governance, and many women seized that moment. When the ultimate New England chauvinist John Adams told his wife, Abigail, that "the Heroes, the statesmen, [and] the Philosophers" that the new nation required could only come from his region's superior colleges, Abigail replied that "If we mean to have Heroes, Statesmen and Philosophers, we should have learned women." Other reformers, male and female, also made the case that women could not possibly raise and maintain a nation of virtuous male citizens unless they themselves received more education. And sure enough, in the years after the Revolution, "female academies" opened up all over the country. But the impact of the Revolution and its republican ideology must not be exaggerated, since British women's chances of receiving more than basic instruction also leapt up during the American founding era. Besides, women's educational opportunities had already greatly expanded as a result of religious revivalists' devotion to biblical litera(l)cy.[14]

BY JULY 1, ONLY nine of the thirteen congressional delegations wished to separate from Great Britain. Congressional rules did not require a unanimous vote, but many delegates hesitated to take the fateful step while nearly a third of the colonies held out.

Then, literally overnight, the picture changed. Caesar Rodney, a Delaware delegate who supported independence, had gone home to Dover, eighty miles away. By the time he learned that the rest of his province's delegation was deadlocked, he was so dangerously ill that his doctors prohibited him from leaving his bed. He nonetheless jumped on his horse, rode all night, and reached Philadelphia the next morning, tipping Delaware into the Yes column. The South Carolina delegation switched from opposing to supporting independence. Two Pennsylvanians who were not ready to separate, Robert Morris and John Dickinson, agreed to take a walk during the vote, which was scheduled for July 2. When Charles Thomson, Congress's secretary, called the roll, the New York representatives had to report that they had been instructed to abstain. But the other twelve delegations all voted for independence.[15]

The next day, John Adams wrote Abigail advocating as well as predicting that "The Second Day of July 1776, will be the most memorable Epocha, in the History of America" and "ought to be solemnized with

Pomp and Parade, with Shews, Games, Sports, Guns, Bells, Bonfires and Illuminations from one End of this Continent to the other from this Time forward forever more."[16]

He was close. Starting with the first anniversary in 1777, the United States chose not to commemorate the second of July, when Congress voted to sever ties with Britain, but the fourth.[17] The reason was clear: most Americans learned about independence from the Declaration, which was dated July 4. Even today, in a powerful reminder of the mythology that clouds every nation's origins, Americans celebrate the press release rather than the act itself.

We do not know whether Thomas Jefferson, who hated speaking in public, personally read his Declaration to the assembled delegates or palmed that task off onto a clerk, but either way, Jefferson literally orchestrated the event. Following a system developed by music and poetry critics, he used symbols resembling quotation marks to indicate where the reader should pause for emphasis: one stroke for a short pause, two for a longer one, and three for the longest.[18]

This first oral performance of the Declaration set up three days of intense debate eventuating in major changes—primarily erasures. The delegates reduced Jefferson's 168-word discussion of the African slave trade and the Anglo-Black alliance to a seven-word euphemism: "he has excited domestic insurrections amongst us." Nor were African Americans the only group Congress blotted out. A member of the Chesapeake gentry, which had long clashed with interloping storekeepers from Scotland, Jefferson denounced George III for fighting his American colonists using "Scotch" mercenaries. Congress excised that slur, along with Jefferson's denunciation of Loyalists, which admitted too much—namely,

Jefferson, rough draft of the Declaration of Independence showing
diacritical marks (' and ") to denote pauses

that thousands of free Americans opposed independence. Jefferson's fellow delegates also toned down his melodramatic farewell to the British people; adieu to "Adieu!" Altogether they deleted about a fourth of his verbiage.[19]

Congress also made the declaration more religious. Both versions assert that all men are created equal, but Jefferson's colleagues scratched out his claim that "from that equal creation they derive rights inherent & inalienable" and insisted instead that humans' rights are "endowed by their Creator." In the final paragraph, Congress inserted an appeal "to the Supreme Judge of the world" and an affirmation of its "firm reliance on the protection of divine Providence."[20]

Congress in addition took the Declaration further in a direction that Jefferson had already moved. The Virginian had twice mentioned Parliament, by name, but no form of that word appears in the final draft—even though everyone understood that the policies animating the rebellion came from Parliament rather than from George III. Congress's studied omission of "Parliament" reflected a larger difference between the first and final versions of the Declaration. The drafting committee replaced Jefferson's term for George III, "his present majesty," with "the present king of Great Britain"—the sort of phrase a foreigner might use. By announcing free Americans' determination "to advance from that subordination in which they have hitherto remained," Jefferson had acknowledged their previous subjugation. Instead the committee stated that the colonists had chosen "to dissolve the political bands which have connected them" to Britain, implying that even before independence, the two societies had been nothing more than allies. In short, Congress out-Jeffersoned Jefferson, giving Britain and America not only distinct destinies but separate pasts.[21]

As Julian P. Boyd, founding editor of the definitive edition of Jefferson's papers, wrote in 1945, the Declaration of Independence "bore no necessary antagonism to the idea of kingship in general"—only to George III. Congress devoted the largest section of the document to enumerating the king's crimes. That made sense, because nearly everyone agreed in principle that societies have the right to overthrow governments that become oppressive, the sole question being whether Britain had met that standard. Even Congress's invocation of humans' equal entitlement to "Life, Liberty and the pursuit of Happiness" served primarily to introduce their concomitant right of revolution.[22] And that bold affirmation merely set up the delegates' insistence upon the analogous right of any society in alliance with another to break it off—in this case, for thirteen elements of the British empire to sever ties with the rest—which in turn led to the heart of the Declaration, Congress's twenty-six-count indictment of the king. In Europe as in the United States, most whites who celebrated the Declaration focused on the specific grievances and on states' right to secede and did not quote either "created equal" or "Life, Liberty, and the pursuit of Happiness."[23]

But phrases that had seemed unimportant to Congress caught the attention of Americans who hated slavery. Before the year 1776 was out, Lemuel Haynes, a free Black soldier in the Continental Army, had drafted an essay called "Liberty Further Extended." He opened by quoting the Declaration of Independence's offhand assertions "that all men are created equal" and "that they are endowed by their Creator with certain unalienable Rights." By highlighting these claims, Haynes began the process of shifting the meaning of the Declaration of Independence, from Congress's ordinance of secession to a universal declaration of human rights. This movement would be carried forward by other abolitionists—the only Americans whose initial reactions to the Declaration focused on its equality and rights clauses—joined later by women's rights advocates and eventually by freedom lovers all over the world.[24]

The same Americans who first glimpsed the modern meaning of the Declaration were also the ones who immortalized the bell that *may* have been rung to announce the first public reading of the Declaration of In-

dependence on the steps of the Pennsylvania statehouse on July 8. At the time no one gave the statehouse bell much thought. But years earlier, it had been engraved with a passage from Leviticus—"Proclaim liberty throughout the land"—and starting in 1835 Black and white abolitionists pointed out that slavery dishonored both the bell's inscription and its reputed role in heralding the Declaration. They adopted it as their symbol, and it became known as the Liberty Bell.[25]

Most other American cities and towns welcomed the Declaration as warmly as Philadelphia had. In New

Lemuel Haynes

York City, capital of the only colony whose congressmen had abstained on the question of independence, Whigs and their slaves tore down the city's equestrian statue of George III and beheaded it. The statue was made of lead covered with gold leaf, and the townswomen of Litchfield, Connecticut, melted it down into forty thousand musket balls.[26] On July 18, 1776, the entire town of Boston was under inoculation for smallpox; anyone who had never been infected and wished to remain that way was warned to stay inside or out of town. But the mass immunization did not stop Col. Thomas Crafts from reading the Declaration of Independence from the Town House balcony to a concourse of soldiers and civilians, including Abigail Adams. "As soon as he ended," she wrote, "the cry from the Belcona, was God Save our American States and then 3 cheers which rended the air, the Bells rang, the privateers fired, the forts and Batteries, the cannon were discharged, the platoons followed and every face appeard joyfull."[27]

Congress's primary objective in declaring independence was "forming foreign alliances." Later in July, it took up a "plan of treaties," especially to be used in negotiating with Louis XVI. One of the few conditions was that France not tax the molasses it shipped to the United States. As a means toward an immediate commercial and military alliance with the French, the Declaration of Independence *failed*; that would take another nineteen months—a lifetime in wartime. But Americans like Lemuel Haynes would turn the Declaration into one of the most consequential documents ever composed.[28]

Congress also named one member from each colony to a committee to frame articles of confederation.[29] As its starting point, the committee took a proposed confederation that Benjamin Franklin had drawn up the previous year. Fittingly enough, Franklin, a Pennsylvanian, wanted to get rid of the existing arrangement, which assigned each state delegation one vote, and instead distribute the delegates according to population. Franklin also wanted Congress to circulate annually among the states.

In preparing the committee's proposal for Congress, chair John Dickinson omitted these two innovations but retained others. Most strikingly, the rebel colonies would enter into "A perpetual Alliance offensive & defensive" with their Native American neighbors, guaranteeing them periodic gifts, providing agents to protect them from unscrupulous traders, and even preventing white encroachment on their land.[30] Dickinson also added progressive clauses of his own. For example, he borrowed the gender-inclusive clause of Pennsylvania's 1682 "Charter of Privileges" guaranteeing that no one would be "molested or prejudiced in his or her person or Estate for his or her religious persuasion."[31]

Dickinson's colleagues on the drafting committee eliminated his protections for Indians and male and female religious dissenters, but the Articles of Confederation that they presented to Congress on July 12 nonetheless stirred controversy, prefiguring many of the conflicts that have roiled American politics ever since. Small- and large-state delegates clashed over whether congressional representation should be equal or proportionate to population. The majority of the committee wanted to shift many of the states' powers to Congress, but that idea alarmed their southern colleagues, including Edward Rutledge of South Carolina, who accused New Englanders of seeking to remake the south in their own image. "I dread their low Cunning, and . . . levelling Principles," Rutledge told a fellow delegate. "I am resolved to vest the Congress with no more Power than what is absolutely necessary." Southern congressmen also balked at the committee's proposal to apportion federal expenses among the states according to their population, free and enslaved. Why, these delegates asked, should slaves figure in apportioning taxes when northerners' livestock did not? Because "Slaves rather weaken than strengthen the State," Benjamin Franklin replied. "Sheep will never make any insurrections." Virginian Benjamin Harrison proposed a compromise—"two slaves should be counted as one freeman"—that would bear fruit a decade later in the Constitution's notorious Three-Fifths Clause.[32]

Two provisions of the Articles that would arouse heated controversy in later years caused very little at the time: the federal government could not levy taxes, and any future effort to alter the Articles would require the consent of every state. Having just broken away from the British empire, Americans were not about to let their federation evolve into a state. One way to enter into the delegates' mindset would be to consider how modern-day Americans might feel about empowering the majority of the countries belonging to a modern-day federation—the United Nations, for example—to tax U.S. citizens directly.

By August 20, Congress was close to a consensus. Every state, no matter how large or small, would continue to cast a single vote in Congress. In a victory for the freer states, slaves would be included in the apportionment of federal expenses. Only one issue seemed to defy resolution. Six weeks after adopting a Declaration of Independence that mentioned taxation-without-representation once but Native Americans and their land three times, the delegates could not agree on how to handle the region west of the Appalachian Mountains. States with no western claims of their own wanted to assign this land to Congress to be used in discharging its growing war debt. Dickinson and the drafting committee agreed, as did land speculators who did not live in states with sea-to-sea-charters and for that reason expected less favorable consideration from them than from Congress. These hopeful real estate speculators included the Indiana Company and the Grand Ohio Company, both of which were well represented among the delegates. But the sea-to-sea states had no intention of relinquishing their western claims. Unable to find a way out of the impasse, Congress postponed further consideration of the Articles.[33]

CHAPTER 20

You Never Will Have Enough

Summer 1776

Even as Congress debated the future of the west, residents of the region found a variety of ways to express their own views. Shortly before the thirteen colonies formally separated from Britain, most of the Cherokee warriors announced their own independence—not only from the white colonists who desired their land but from the British officials who had bade them postpone their attacks against colonial settlements and even from their more cautious elders.

Sometime in late May or early June 1776, the Cherokees welcomed a fourteen-man delegation representing the Shawnee, Delaware, Mohawk, Nanticoke, and Ottawa nations. Reviving the quest to unite the native nations on either side of the Ohio River in a grand coalition, the envoys had come to invite the Cherokees to attack white settlers. Their mission was clear before they spoke a word, for they were painted black and carried a nine-foot-long belt of red wampum. Dragging Canoe, who was head warrior of a Cherokee town called Malaquo (Great Island), struck the war post with his hatchet, signifying his acceptance of the northerners' proposal.[1]

Most white South Carolinians who fought in the Cherokee War of 1776 considered it a race war, but the incident that triggered it was the Lower Towns' steadfast refusal to give up a white Loyalist who had taken refuge with them. In June 1776, when Whig Maj. Andrew Williamson sent ten soldiers in pursuit of the fugitive, the headmen welcomed them and even treated the leaders to a feast, only to attack the whole party, killing most of them. Then Cherokee war parties started raiding white settlements from Georgia to Virginia, hitting numerous communities simultaneously to prevent them from galloping to each other's defense.[2] White Loyalists often fought alongside the warriors, with some bands containing more whites than Indians.

Maj. Williamson put together a punitive expedition. In late July, shortly after crossing into Cherokee country, he received a visit from Robert Cunningham, a recently released Loyalist. Like most white South Carolinians, Cunningham blamed the imperial government for the Cherokee attacks and was so furious that he now "most heartily desired to take the Oath of fidelity to the United Colonies." Other Loyalists switched sides for the same reason.[3]

By July 31, Williamson's army, having grown to more than one thousand men, captured two white members of a Cherokee war party, who related that British Indian agent Alexander Cameron was only thirty miles away, on Oconore Creek. Convinced that capturing or killing Cameron would stop the Cherokee raids, Williamson sped off at the head of 330 horsemen. Riding with him was Francis Salvador, who had sailed from England to South Carolina less than three years earlier, bought seven thousand acres and a crew of slaves, and established himself as a rice planter. In 1774, when his neighbors sent him to the provincial congress, he became the first practicing Jew to win elective office anywhere in the western world.[4]

The information Williamson had picked up from his two white prisoners turned out to be false. At about 2 a.m. on August 1, as he and his advance party entered the abandoned Cherokee town of Essenecca on the west bank of the Keowee River (opposite today's Clemson University), concealed warriors sprang their trap. Salvador was shot from his horse and then scalped. He lived another forty-five minutes and "retained his senses, to the last," but never realized, according to survivors of the ambush, that he had been scalped.[5]

Reinforced by armies from Virginia and North Carolina, Williamson and his soldiers burned Essenecca and other Cherokee towns, along with thousands of acres of standing corn and the Cherokees' stores of beans, corn, and other food. Whig commanders had vowed that the Cherokee nation would be "extirpated," but every town the soldiers entered had been evacuated. Meanwhile warriors laid additional ambushes that led to brutal fighting, much of it hand-to-hand. In one such clash, a warrior who was grappling with a soldier admitted defeat and appealed for quarter.

"Brother, enough," the Cherokee said.

"You never will have enough, while you are alive," the soldier replied as he killed him.[6]

Williamson disbanded his army on October 7. Cherokee warriors had killed thirty-three of his soldiers and wounded sixty-three. He reckoned native losses at about double these, and in addition, his men had captured an undetermined number of Cherokees to be sold as slaves.[7]

The Cherokee War led southern Indian agent John Stuart to abandon his policy of discouraging British-allied Indians from attacking the United States. In a message that could have come from Pontiac, Red Hawk, or Dragging Canoe, he observed to the Muskogees that "each country singly would become an easy conquest to the rebels; whereas by uniting their strength there is the greatest probability of their being . . . able to repel the enemy." For the duration of the war, Muskogee war parties would occasionally raid Whig settlements. But Stuart's reversal had come too late, for, as he observed, "all the southern tribes are greatly dispirited by the unopposed success of the rebels" against the Cherokees, unaided as they were by the British army.[8]

Even the Cherokees were so desperate to restore peace and trade that in 1777 they signed two treaties ceding more than five million additional acres to Virginia, the Carolinas, and Georgia. South Carolina picked up the entire region east of the Appalachian Mountains, including all of the Lower Towns.[9]

Aghast at the treaties, a group of Cherokees led by Dragging Canoe moved to Chickamauga Creek on the lower Tennessee River and continued their resistance.[10]

Meanwhile Stuart's policy reversal produced tangible benefits for two southern nations that had long been at war with each other, the Muskogees and Choctaws. As outsiders with no obvious biases, European officials in North America had proven effective at negotiating (and sometimes buying) intertribal truces. When asked to play this role for the Muskogees and Choctaws, Stuart had initially put them off in keeping with British colonizers' long-standing policy of protecting themselves by fostering conflict among native nations. But as the Muskogees and Choctaws seemed more and more likely to reconcile on their own, Stuart decided "to make a merit with both nations of being mediator." As he related to Lord Germain, the reconciliation ceremony took place on October 20, 1776, in Pensacola:

> Both parties appointed to meet in the street before my door; each party had a white flag as an emblem of peace and were highly painted. They halted about 300 yards distance from each other, their principal chiefs singing the peace song and waving eagles'

tails and swans' wings over their heads. . . . At a signal given a number of young men sallied out from each party and made a sham fight in the space between them. At last both parties . . . joined hands in my presence.[11]

THE REDCOATS WHO WADED ashore on Staten Island on the evening of July 2, hours after Congress declared independence, were only the first of many. At the end of the month, Gen. Henry Clinton arrived from South Carolina with his 2,500 troops, along with formerly enslaved auxiliaries such as Thomas Peters. They were followed in August by Governor Dunmore's Ethiopian Regiment, which became the nucleus of a New York Black community that would expand over the next seven years, partly through natural increase but mostly through the arrival of additional escapees, to more than three thousand souls.[12]

Howe also received reinforcements from Britain and Germany. The fleet commanded by his brother, Lord Richard Howe, was the largest that had ever crossed the Atlantic. Another squadron, arriving on August 12, brought nearly eleven thousand troops, including eight thousand mercenaries from Hesse and other north German states. (In the coming years, the German contingent would grow to thirty thousand). These soldiers' entrance into New York Harbor marked the beginning of one terrifying ordeal and the end of another; crossing the Atlantic, more than a thousand of their shipmates had died, mostly of malaria. By August 22, Gen. Howe would have 32,000 men at his disposal—not to mention the 10,000 sailors in his brother's fleet. Thus the British force was nearly twice as large as the population of New York City and more than twice as large as the 19,000-man American army that awaited them, which consisted primarily of militia.[13]

The British warships hardly noticed the Americans' laboriously constructed shore defenses. On July 12, the very day Adm. Howe's squadron put into New York Harbor, four Royal Navy vessels sailed up the Hudson past Manhattan, exchanging fire with American cannon onshore as they passed. Several British shells landed in town, and Washington feared the panicked inhabitants would demoralize his men. The four ships blew past Forts Washington and Lee and dropped anchor forty miles up, just to show they could. They came back through the intended American gauntlet a week later, again essentially unscathed.[14]

Along with all these sticks, Admiral Howe had brought carrots. He and his brother proposed to negotiate peace with the rebel colonists. As part of a prospective deal, they were empowered to grant pardons to all but the most senior rebel leaders.

GEN. HOWE DECIDED TO begin his invasion of New York not by landing troops in the obvious place, Manhattan, but by occupying its larger eastern neighbor, Long Island. As long as the rebels controlled the western shores of the island, their cannon crews could harass British vessels in New York Harbor. Moreover, hundred-foot-high Brooklyn Heights, at the western tip of Long Island, was directly across the half-mile-wide East River from New York City, at the southern tip of Manhattan. If the British could install artillery atop Brooklyn Heights, they could force Washington to abandon New York City.[15]

On the morning of August 22, transports carried 15,000 redcoats and Germans from Staten Island eastward through Verrazzano Narrows to Denyse Point and Gravesend on Long Island, where they transferred to flatboats with bow ramps to speed their landing, which was unopposed. Three days later, Gen. Howe sent over two late-arriving German brigades. Within a few months, a never previously seen insect infested crops throughout the mid-Atlantic states; believing the bug had come ashore with the Germans, farmers called it the Hessian fly.[16]

Washington trusted Nathanael Greene implicitly and assigned him the defense of Long Island. Greene's men occupied Brooklyn Heights and protected themselves with a chain of forts running from Wallabout Bay on the East River southwest to Gowanus Bay, emptying into New York Harbor. Meanwhile the general was constantly in the saddle, familiarizing himself with the terrain. But then he contracted a violent fever, forcing Washington to replace him with New Hampshire Gen. John Sullivan, who knew neither the men nor the ground.[17]

On August 23, Sullivan and Washington toured the American redoubts on Brooklyn Heights and made a tactical decision that might have procured an American victory, if only it had been executed properly. They sent about three thousand soldiers forward to a new defensive line along the Heights of Gowan, a ridge running from Gowanus Bay nearly due east for about ten miles. The Heights were only about eighty feet high, but their southern slope, facing the British and Germans, was so steep and thickly wooded that artillery, carts, and men in formation could only reach the ridgeline at four passes. The Continentals' one job was to defend those passes. In America as in Europe, every neophyte officer learned to secure his flanks. Recall that on April 19, 1775, the redcoats' anxiety to avoid being outflanked by the militiamen on Lexington Common had propelled them out onto the common—and into a war. But despite warnings from subordinates, Washington and Sullivan inadequately secured the easternmost opening in the Heights of Gowan: Jamaica Pass, more than five miles inland.[18]

Unaware that Howe had committed 22,000 of his 25,000 soldiers to Long Island, Washington increased his own troop strength there to at most 9,000, less than half the invading force. (The redcoats and Germans also had much more experience, with an average of eight years in uniform as opposed to six months for the Americans.)[19] Still, the Continental detachment at Brooklyn had grown large enough that Washington could justify superseding Sullivan with the higher-ranking Gen. Israel Putnam. But Putnam scarcely surpassed Sullivan, either in knowledge of the terrain or in essential qualities of leadership.[20]

At around 8 p.m. on August 26, Howe mobilized about half of his Long Island force, ten thousand troops. Guided by Loyalists, they easily overwhelmed the five mounted militia officers watching Jamaica Pass. At dawn on August 29, they poured through, then opened fire from *behind* Putnam's left wing. The sound of this fusillade was the signal for British cannon crews on the opposite end of the battlefield, five miles to the west, to begin a massive bombardment of the Continentals guarding the Heights of Gowan. American survivors of the Battle of Long Island would struggle to convey the dread they felt upon suddenly hearing cannon and musket fire emanating from their left and rear. This time, the strategy that had failed Howe at Bunker Hill—of crushing the enemy between a hammer swinging down from their left and a stationary anvil directly in front of them—worked perfectly. As in every successful flanking action, the soldiers at the eastern extreme of the American line were not only disoriented but vastly outnumbered by their assailants. Many did not get off a single shot before fleeing in terror to the redoubts behind them on Brooklyn Heights. Others—including many who might have made it but could not find the path and wrongly concluded that it was blocked—laid down their weapons. Whether a soldier fell into the hands of enemy troops who accepted his pleas for "Quarter! Quarter!" or others who summarily pinned him to a tree with their bayonets was a matter of chance. Several British units rolling east to west through the American line, including the one led by Gen. Charles Cornwallis, made it almost to the East River.[21]

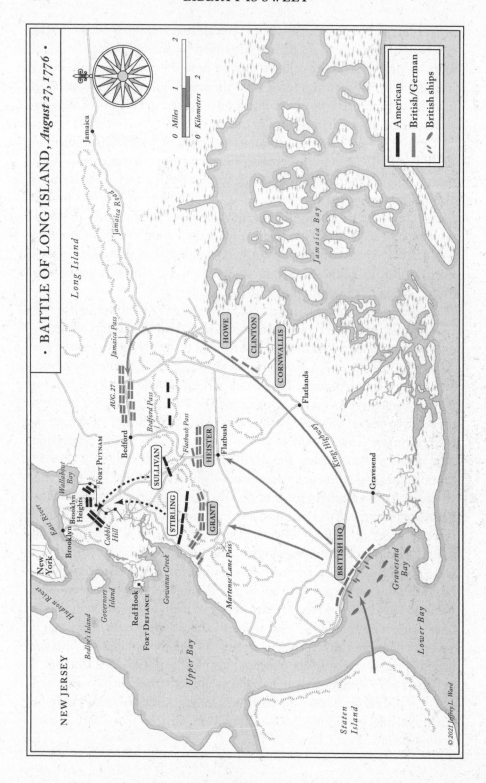

• BATTLE OF LONG ISLAND, *August 27, 1776* •

American
British/German
British ships

Jamaica

Jamaica Road

Long Island

Jamaica Pass

AUG. 27

Bedford Pass

Bedford

Flatbush Pass

HEISTER

Flatbush

HOWE

CLINTON

CORNWALLIS

Flatlands

King's Highway

Gravesend

SULLIVAN

FORT PUTNAM

Wallabout Bay

Brooklyn Heights

Brooklyn

STIRLING

GRANT

Cobble Hill

Gowanus Creek

Martense Lane Pass

BRITISH HQ

Gravesend Bay

East River

New York

Hudson River

Bedloe's Island

Governors Island

Red Hook

FORT DEFIANCE

Upper Bay

Lower Bay

NEW JERSEY

Staten Island

0 Miles 1 2
0 Kilometers 2

Jamaica Bay

© 2021 Jeffrey L. Ward

Before setting out with the flanking column, Howe had given the troops he left behind at the foot of the Heights of Gowan a single task: hold the Americans on the ridgeline in place, preventing them from rushing to the aid of the embattled comrades on their left. But the redcoats and Germans stationed below the Heights nonetheless managed to ascend them, and those on the shore of the East River likewise advanced. The American forces near the river were commanded by Gen. William Alexander. Two decades earlier, he had laid claim to a lapsed Scottish earldom, only to be turned off by the House of Lords. But he continued to call himself Lord Stirling, and so did his friends. As if being outnumbered and outflanked was not enough, Stirling was missing several key subordinate officers, Washington having pulled them over to Manhattan to serve on a court-martial. The commander-in-chief had also reorganized the army at the very last minute, leaving many juniors officers unsure whose orders to follow.[22]

With a British and a Hessian column approaching him head-on and Cornwallis closing in from his left, Stirling sent most of his men scurrying back toward the relative safety of Brooklyn Heights. That meant wading Gowanus Creek, which was eighty yards wide and, in places, over the troops' heads. From the north bank, Pvt. Joseph Plumb Martin witnessed their desperate attempt to pass this gauntlet under heavy enemy fire. "Such as could swim got across," he recalled years later. "Those that could not swim, and could not procure any thing to buoy them up, sunk. . . . Some of us went into the water after the fall of the tide, and took out a number of corpses."[23] Many of the soldiers who made it across Gowanus Creek were shot down as they struggled through the muddy floodplain on its north bank, but officers would later insist that only about a half dozen soldiers were killed at the creek.

To cover his soldiers' escape, Stirling hung back with about 250 Marylanders. To avoid fighting all three enemy columns at once, he marched toward Cornwallis's vastly larger force. "General Lord Stirling fought like a wolf," one eyewitness reported. Not content just to stall the enemy, the Americans attacked, only to be driven back, a sequence that was repeated several more times before Stirling and nearly every man with him was captured.[24]

By noon on August 27, American soldiers on Long Island were either behind the redoubts on Brooklyn Heights, captured, or dead. Roughly two hundred rebels were killed—three times Howe's estimate of sixty-three British and German deaths. The British lost hardly any soldiers to capture but seized something like nine hundred Americans.[25] High-ranking prisoners such as Lord Stirling and John Sullivan could look forward to a comfortable welcome from Howe's generals. But the British saved the expense of building and maintaining prison camps for common soldiers by cramming them into churches (all except Anglican), sugar houses, or the holds of ships.

The Americans had shielded their camp on Brooklyn Heights with a formidable line of forts and redoubts, but it was no Gibraltar, and they were thoroughly demoralized. The British and German soldiers were eager to drive the enemy right into the East River, and most historians agree they could have. Howe acknowledged that "it required repeated orders to prevail on them to desist from this attempt." The general was as determined as his men to capture Brooklyn Heights, but his preferred method was a siege.[26]

By 1776, a besieging army's parallel and ever-closer entrenchments, each communicating with the previous one via a zigzagging access trench, had become so standardized that people called them "regular approaches." Why did Howe choose a siege over a storm? Some historians contend that he feared that annihilating the rebels would interfere with his larger goal of reconciling with them, and that may be, but he was also in the throes of what might be called a Bunker Hill mentality. Behind barriers, he knew, Americans were tenacious fighters, capable of inflicting mass casualties on any army trying to storm their position. Sieges invariably entailed much less loss of life among the assailants (and incidentally among the besieged). "As it was apparent the [Continental] lines must have been ours at a very cheap rate by regular approaches," Howe wrote, "I would not risk the loss that might have been sustained in the assault."[27]

ON AUGUST 28, THE day after the battle, a classic American Nor'easter struck Long Island. Few men in either army had tents, but for the Continentals the storm had a silver lining: the wind blowing in from the north prevented Adm. Howe's fleet from entering the East River to assault rebel boats passing between Long Island and Manhattan. On August 29, Washington, who had joined his troops on Brooklyn Heights, finally decided to escape with them across the river. At about 9 p.m., the Continentals began withdrawing down to the ferry landing (near today's eastern terminus of the Brooklyn Bridge). Joseph Plumb Martin recalled being "strictly enjoined not to speak, or even cough" as he and his comrades were transported over to Manhattan by two ethnically diverse regiments of sailors from Essex County, Massachusetts, north of Boston. A decade earlier, these mariners and fishermen had been among the principal targets of George Grenville's crackdown on North America's trade with the foreign sugar islands.[28]

The honor of covering the retreat—and of being the last ones to leave—went to a Pennsylvania regiment commanded by Thomas Mifflin, whose Quaker meeting back in Philadelphia had expelled him for his military service, initially as one of Washington's aides-de-camp. While holding the line, Mifflin's men made as much noise as they could in order to prevent British and German sentries, some of them only a hundred yards away, from noticing that the army facing them was slipping away.

Then a minor miscommunication threatened disaster. Long before the main body of Continentals had completed their evacuation, Mifflin received an order to withdraw his covering force. He questioned it, but the messenger insisted, so he led his men down toward the ferry. When Washington, who was monitoring the embarkation, spotted Mifflin, he accosted him.

"Good God! Gen'l Mifflin, I am afraid you have ruined us by so unseasonably withdrawing the troops from the lines," Washington shouted.

"I did it by your order," Mifflin replied.

Mifflin's troops hustled back to their posts, and the British never knew they had been gone. By dawn the rest of the soldiers had left, but the rising sun threatened to expose the Pennsylvanians' isolation, very likely prompting Howe to press forward to annihilate them. But then a heavy mist descended, covering their escape. Both fog and the northeasterly winds that had kept the East River clear of British ships are common in the region, but Americans ascribed both to Providence.[29]

Washington blamed the Long Island disaster on his "young Troops," who were not yet capable of "making a brave defence" against a superior force, even when ensconced in "strong posts." But that did not describe what had happened on August 27. True, most of the Continentals had run away, but only because Washington and his generals had left their eastern flank wide open, giving the enemy access to their rear. The men who made it back to the fortifications on Brooklyn Heights provided the same sturdy defense they had on Breed's Hill the previous summer. Granted, rank-and-file troops had less incentive than their officers to expose themselves recklessly in battle. An eighteenth-century gentleman who was killed in war could anticipate glory and might rationally choose that outcome over continued life. By contrast, enlisted men rarely had reason to expect anything more than collective commemoration. Yet they did not believe their reluctance to confront the British out in the open doomed their cause, for on Breed's Hill, they had learned the same lesson as Gen. Howe: that they could win the war from cover.[30]

In mischaracterizing his troops as unwilling even to defend fortifications, Washington appears to have been trying to turn his defeat on Long Island into victory in a different realm. The Continental soldiers had enlisted for at most one year, and their commander did not believe he could win the war until Congress replaced them with a "permanent, standing Army." On September 16, the delegates finally gave in, henceforth requiring new recruits to commit for the rest of the war. In hopes of nonetheless filling eighty-eight battalions, they doubled the enlistment bounty to $20 cash and added the promise of one hundred acres of Indian land.[31]

If the Long Island defeat helped Washington sell Congress on an army of professionals, it also contributed to a crucial change in his own thinking. His description of the Continental soldiers' reluctance to expose themselves in battle was essentially accurate, but in his heart he knew he was wrong to depict them as equally unwilling to defend fortified positions. The obvious message his troops had sent him was that at least for the moment, "on our side the War should be defensive." Indeed, he wrote John Hancock, the enemy was terrified that he might figure that out.[32]

Washington heard something similar from his generals. Congress resolutely opposed abandoning New York City without a fight, and he himself feared it would "dispirit the Troops and enfeeble our Cause." But Charles Lee, who had supervised the construction of breastworks and batteries all around Manhattan's thirty-two-mile perimeter, did not expect them to keep Gen. Howe off the island, just to make him pay dearly for it. He favored evacuation.[33] So did Adjutant General Joseph Reed. "*My* opinion," he had written even before Long Island, "is, we should make it a war of posts, prolong, procrastinate, [and] avoid any general action." The Americans should retain each defensive line only long enough to inflict heavy casualties on the onrushing enemy before retiring to the next one, just as Gen. Howe had feared they would.[34]

Lee, Reed, and other Continental officers promoted a war of attrition not in hopes of exploiting some weakness in the British army but out of admiration for the mother country's economic strength. Having commenced their industrial and financial revolutions well ahead of their European rivals, British merchants and manufacturers could offer both lower prices and more generous credit. They would thus continue to dominate the American market even if Parliament acquiesced in political independence. So ordinary Britons had little practical incentive to keep investing their tax money, much less their husbands and sons, in an endless overseas war. With that in mind, numerous Continental officers urged Washington to stop trying to defeat Howe and instead focus on not losing to him, since in the absence of victories, the British public would grow weary of what would increasingly seem like a quagmire. Fewer than 10 percent of British adults could vote, but as Americans had understood when they boycotted the mother country's merchandise in hopes of provoking riots in its ports and manufacturing towns, public opinion found ways of expressing itself.

Nathanael Greene was the commander-in-chief's most trusted subordinate. Seven months earlier, he had endorsed Washington's bold plan to attack Boston across the frozen Charles River. But in a September 5 letter, he urged him to "take post where the Enemy will be Obligd to fight us and not we them." Three days later—a year to the day after first proposing to storm Fortress Boston—Washington finally embraced the "War of posts." The symbols of his new doctrine would not be the musket and saber but the "Spade & Pickax," the tools his men would use to build defensive works.[35]

Washington's strategic reversal settled the question of whether to try to defend New York City. The longer he stayed, the greater the likelihood that the British would occupy and entrench northern Manhattan. Given that the Royal Navy already controlled the rivers and harbor, the Continentals would then be unable to reach the only two bridges off the island (at its northeastern tip) without throwing themselves against the enemy's fortifications—the precise opposite of the "war of posts" strategy. So on September 12, Washington ordered his troops to leave New York City, moving to the high ground at the northern tip of Manhattan, where they would be much closer to those two bridges.[36]

The Americans' one remaining quandary was whether to burn New York on the way out, preventing the British from using its approximately one thousand buildings as winter quarters. Washington supported the idea, as did nearly all of his generals, but Congress vetoed it.[37]

The British fleet, on the other hand, remained fair game. Back in
1695, the French inventor Denis Papin had designed—but apparently
never built—a one-person, human-powered submarine. Late in the
colonial era, a Yale student named David Bushnell set about realizing
Papin's vision, and in the summer of 1776, while serving in the Connecticut Line—as the captain of Joseph Plumb Martin's company—he
completed work on the *American Turtle*, so named because it resembled two tortoise shells, standing on end and joined together. Constructed of wood secured with iron hoops, Bushnell's submarine also
looked like a bloated barrel, and at six feet high and seven feet long,
including the rudder, it was not much bigger. If the operator ever had
trouble bringing the *Turtle* back to the surface, he could do so quickly
by dropping the two hundred pounds of ballast suspended from the
vessel's hull.[38]

Continental Sgt. Ezra Lee agreed to navigate the *Turtle* to the
underside of Adm. Howe's flagship, the sixty-four-gun *Eagle*, then
drill a hole in its hull and attach a barrel of gunpowder, to be ignited
by a flintlock activated by a timer. On the night of September 6–7, the
Turtle was towed within striking distance of the *Eagle*, and Lee sub-
merged. His first attempt to drill into its hull was stymied by an iron
plate, so he tried to move just a few feet off. Bits of phosphorous on
the tip of Lee's compass needle and at *N* and *E* allowed him to keep his
bearings, but he had no periscope, and as he fought powerful tidal
currents, he lost contact with the *Eagle*. Surfacing in order to find it
again, he noticed dawn approaching and aborted the first submarine
attack in human history. Bushnell would make two more attempts,
equally unsuccessful.[39]

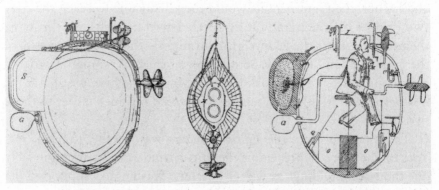

Henry L. Abbott, three views of Bushnell's submarine, *Turtle* (1881)

*   *   *

THE AMERICANS HAD NEARLY completed their evacuation of New York City at 11 a.m. on Sunday, September 15, when five British warships in the East River began bombarding the Manhattan shoreline at Kip's Bay (in the latitude of today's 34th Street and Empire State Building). It was Joseph Plumb Martin's fortune to have been stationed at the very spot Howe had chosen for an amphibious assault. Kip's Bay was one of the weaker stretches of the Continental defenses ringing Manhattan, with nothing more than a trench behind earthworks. That morning, Martin had as usual wandered from his post, and when the first shells hit, he was in an abandoned building nearby. "I made a frog's leap for the ditch," he recalled in his memoirs, "and lay as still as I possibly could, and began to consider which part of my carcass was to go first."[40]

Vastly outnumbered by the four thousand British and German soldiers approaching Kip's Bay in flatboats—and these were merely the first wave—Martin and his comrades fled west. Washington galloped to the scene of action, where he was appalled to find the troops once again running away without a fight. One of his generals later reported that he "threw his hat on the ground, and exclaimed, 'Are these the men with which I am to defend America?'" With their riding crops, Washington and his senior officers slashed not only at common soldiers but at officers, even a brigadier general, in a vain effort to make them turn and fight. Washington was so enraged that he failed to notice that a detachment of Hessian soldiers had approached to within seventy yards. Finally an aide-de-camp grabbed the bridle of his charger and led horse and rider to relative safety.[41]

As Washington tried to rally his men against the British invaders, his chief engineer, Rufus Putnam, dashed south to warn the Continental troops in New York City. The obvious evacuation route was the east bank of the Hudson River (the present-day West Side Highway). But Manhattan is only two miles wide here, and the Continentals feared Gen. Henry Clinton, whom Howe had placed in command of the Kip's Bay landing, would race across to the Hudson River, closing the trap.

But then came a stunning surprise. When Clinton's troops reached the Post Road, which ran the length of Manhattan (roughly along today's Lexington Avenue), they stopped, and most of the Continental soldiers fleeing up the west side of the island got away. Clinton's failure to cut off the rebels' retreat has always seemed as mysterious as Howe's not driving them into the East River three weeks earlier. According to one nineteenth-century writer, in the midst of the battle, local resident Mary Lindley Murray slowed Clinton and his staff by inviting them in for cake and wine. But it seems likelier that Clinton hesitated on September 15 for the same reason Howe had on August 27: he did not wish to subject his soldiers to undue risk.[42]

Indeed, Clinton never intended to attack the Continentals in New York City, just to trap them there. But as his troops marched west across Manhattan, their left flank would be exposed to rebel soldiers exiting the capital. So he refused to budge until joined by his second wave, and the extra hours allowed hundreds of rebels to slip away. When the redcoats and Germans marched unopposed into New York City, they captured nearly all of Washington's supplies, including fifty to sixty cannon, but only three hundred troops. Hardly any Continentals were killed, and no redcoats or Germans were.[43]

On the afternoon of September 15, the Continentals began "fortifying ground naturally strong." Atop a plateau called Harlem Heights, they ran three defensive lines across the island: at modern-day 147th, 153rd, and 159th Streets. If the British and Germans attacked, the rebels would cause them as much "sorrow and loss" as they could from behind the first line before falling back to the next and then the next—a perfect application of the war of posts. On the 16th, Washington sent forward a reconnaissance party: 120 Connecticut rangers led by Capt. Thomas Knowlton, who had first distinguished himself at Breed's Hill. Between the opposing lines, Knowlton's troops collided with a much larger enemy force and withdrew, whereupon British buglers taunted them with a call customarily played after a successful fox hunt. "It seemed to crown our disgrace," Joseph Reed wrote his wife, Esther.[44]

Forgetting what he had said to Congress a week earlier about avoiding conventional warfare in open fields, Washington reinforced Capt. Knowlton and sent him back south toward the British and Germans, this time attempting to outflank them. The flanking maneuver failed, and the captain was killed, but his men drove the enemy troops back, some more than a mile. Soon Howe sent in reinforcements of his own; this was how skirmishes turned into battles. Washington had given his men a look at the enemy's backsides and Whig propagandists a victory to brag about—weak but welcome tonic for the infant nation's depleted morale. It was enough for one day, and he recovered his prudence and his forward troops.[45]

Before the Battle of Harlem Heights, George Washington had established his headquarters at the home of Roger Morris (which still stands at the east end of 161st Street, the oldest surviving house in Manhattan), and a few hours after the battle, a crew that included Joseph Plumb Martin arrived at the Morris estate to bury a fallen comrade. They laid him in the grave and were about to begin shoveling dirt directly onto him when two young women emerged from the Morris mansion. One "took a fine white gauze handkerchief from her neck and desired that it might be spread upon his face," and then she and her companion "retired to the house in the same manner they came."[46]

CHAPTER 21

—•·•—

The Game Is Pretty Nearly Up

Fall 1776

JUST AFTER MIDNIGHT, SEPTEMBER 20–21, SEVERAL FIRES BROKE OUT in British-occupied New York. They may have been accidental; perhaps lightning struck a roof and then the wind carried flaming flakes of its cedar shingles throughout the city. But witnesses claimed to have caught several Whig arsonists in the act. "The first Incendiary who fell into the Hands of the Troops was a *Woman*," a London newspaper reported. "Her Sex availed her little, for without Ceremony, she was tossed into the Flames," along with several male suspects. Citizens and soldiers fought a nine-hour battle against the blaze, and by 10 a.m., when they finally stamped out the last embers, a fourth of the city was gone. British officers never doubted that Continental officers were behind the blaze, and the incident's most careful investigator suspects they were right.[1]

New York City Fire, Sept. 20–21, 1776

The day after the fire, Nathan Hale, a recent Yale graduate and Continental captain who had landed on Long Island in civilian clothes to gather intelligence, was hanged without trial. After mounting the barrel but before he was turned off, he reportedly paraphrased a famous line from Joseph Addison's 1712 play *Cato*, stating something like, "I am so satisfied with the cause in which I have engaged, that my only regret is, that I have not more lives than one to offer in its service."[2]

Gen. Howe had no desire to hurl his men at the Continental fortifications atop Harlem Heights. He also needed to consolidate his supplies, so for nearly a month he did little else. Then on October 12 he struck, not directly at the enemy lines but seven miles to the east at Throgs Neck, which juts from the mainland southward into Long Island Sound. His obvious intention was to trap the Continentals on Manhattan.

Although technically a peninsula, Throgs Neck was actually more of an island, and Pennsylvania riflemen easily sealed off the one bridge and one causeway to the mainland. Howe again hesitated, loath to sacrifice more soldiers in a war that ironically seemed just as hopeless to him as it did to many Whigs.

The British landing on Throgs Neck coincided with the return from the southward of Charles Lee, who had long favored moving the Continental Army off Manhattan. Finally Washington agreed. On October 18, the first wave of U.S. soldiers crossed the Harlem River and headed north toward the village of White Plains. That very day, Howe's troops abandoned Throgs Neck and reembarked in their transports. About four thousand of them landed three miles north at Pell's Point, a half mile west of City Island. They had missed the chance to trap the Americans on Manhattan but might still catch them at their most vulnerable: while on the march to White Plains.[3]

Before leaving Pell's Point, though, the redcoats and Germans would have to contend with Col. John Glover's 750-man Massachusetts brigade, which included many of the same sailors and fishermen who had rescued the Continentals from Long Island seven weeks earlier. In a classic illustration of defense in depth—the war of posts in microcosm—Glover's three regiments crouched behind a succession of stone walls, each firing about ten volleys before pulling back. Although outnumbered five to one, the mariners suffered only about eleven casualties while inflicting hundreds on their assailants—and more importantly, slowing the British advance long enough for their fellow Continentals to complete their trek to White Plains and set up in terrain that a British officer would describe as "inaccessible."[4]

Had Congress and Gen. Washington decided to make the War of Independence a series of Pell's Points—in other words, a series of Bunker Hills—they might have worn out the British much sooner, perhaps even without help from France. But early in the war, the home government's ability and willingness to reinforce its American army seemed limitless. On October 18, the same day Washington left Manhattan and Howe's troops waded ashore at Pell's Point, 120 Royal Navy vessels transported eight thousand reinforcements into New York Harbor.[5]

At White Plains as at Harlem Heights, Washington positioned his troops in a west-to-east defensive line, with most of the army to the east of the southward-flowing Bronx River and a few hundred militiamen atop Chatterton Hill over on the west bank.[6] Howe was growing increasingly reluctant to expend additional British lives on a seemingly hopeless quest, and he did not march his army north to White Plains until October 28. Only that morning did Washington realize that the British could easily seize Chatterton Hill and then use it to fire their cannon over the Bronx River down into his main line. He dispatched a corps of Continentals to the summit just as Howe, who instantly perceived its value, sent British and German infantrymen racing toward the same spot.

The Continentals got there first, and an American officer noted that in the ensuing battle, "The rail and stone fence behind which our troops were posted proved as fatal to the British as the rail fence and grass hung on it did at Charlestown [Breed's Hill] the 17th of June 1775." While the main British and German force assaulted the steep and heavily wooded hill head-on, taking heavy losses, Col. Johann Rall's light infantry and Lt. Col. Samuel Birch's light dragoons swept around the Americans' right flank.[7] The Massachusetts and New York militiamen on the western slope broke and ran, briefly exposing Washington's far right, but Delaware Continentals pivoted to the right to close the breach. Eventually they and the rest of the Americans on Chatterton Hill retreated in good order. On the east bank of the Bronx, the light troops posted in front of the Continental center pulled back as the enemy advanced but fired a volley from behind every stone wall, just as Glover's men had at Pell's Point, and the main line held.[8]

On both sides, casualty estimates for the Battle of White Plains varied widely. Somewhere between 150 and 400 Americans were killed and wounded, and estimates of British and German casualties ranged from the mid-200s to the mid-300s. In the subsequent days, Howe chose not to order a frontal assault against the Continentals, and on October 31, they pulled back seven miles north to a new, more defensible, position: North Castle Heights.[9]

On November 9, Washington began ferrying five thousand American soldiers over the Hudson River into New Jersey. These Continentals are often depicted as fleeing the British, but Howe and his troops had actually disengaged from the rebels four days earlier and returned to Manhattan. The real reason Washington crossed into New Jersey was not to escape the redcoats but to get in front of a large British detachment known to be headed that way. Washington figured it would be easier to prevent the British troops, commanded by Gen. Charles Cornwallis, from establishing themselves in New Jersey than to dislodge them after they dug in.[10]

The reason Howe had brought most of his army back to Manhattan was to capture the Continentals' one remaining toehold there. Fort Washington stood atop a narrow but tall ridge, known then as Mount Washington and today as Washington Heights, that arose just south of the fort and extended two-thirds of a mile northward before sloping sharply downward to Spuyten Duyvil (Dutch for "Spouting Devil")—the boisterous junction of the Harlem and Hudson Rivers. Howe's timing may have been dictated by a lucky break: on November 2, an American ensign in Fort Washington named William Demont turned traitor, slipped out, and delivered Howe a detailed map of its defenses, along with equally useful intelligence of "great dissensions" among its officers. This was more of a temptation than even the increasingly cautious Howe could resist.[11]

Gen. Nathanael Greene, who had jurisdiction over Fort Washington, feared that abandoning it—and with it, Manhattan Island—would spread "Discouragement" among U.S. civilians as well as soldiers. The three thousand men in its garrison could successfully withstand a siege, he believed, and if not, they could always escape across the Hudson to New Jersey, just as their comrades had evacuated Breed's Hill and Brooklyn Heights.[12]

Other Continental commanders feared Greene was deluding himself about the strategic value of Fort Washington (British warships regularly blew past it), the ease with which it could be evacuated, and, most of all, its impregnability. Many surmised that Washington would have intervened if it had not meant undermining Greene, but it was Greene who

warned Washington of another problem: the Fort Washington garrison
was being asked to guard the entire northern tip of Manhattan, which
had a perimeter of about eight miles. That was far more territory than
these three thousand troops could defend, and Greene urged Washington
to shrink the perimeter.

Washington himself believed the only viable alternative to abandoning the fort was to swing to the other extreme, sending the commander
at Fort Washington, Col. Robert Magaw, the seven thousand or more
reinforcements he would need to retain not just the fort but all of Manhattan north of Harlem Heights. As the commander-in-chief wavered
between these two very different objectives, he and Greene inexplicably
permitted Magaw to try to achieve the more ambitious one, retaining his
entire eight-mile perimeter, with the troops already on hand.[13]

The western edge of Fort Washington was protected by a nearly ver-
tical 230-foot drop-off down to the Hudson River, allowing Magaw to
focus on the other three. To guard the northern slope of Washington
Heights, he placed about 250 Virginia and Maryland riflemen in a redoubt named for William Tryon, principal target a half decade earlier for
the Regulator rebellion in North Carolina and now the Loyalist governor of New York. A half mile east of the Heights, two hundred Pennsylvania militiamen awaited the enemy atop Laurel Hill, a parallel but
lower ridge along the west bank of the Harlem River. Redcoats and Germans marching north from New York City would face off against an
eight-hundred-man force commanded by Col. Lambert Cadwalader and
defending the old Continental fortifications on Harlem Heights, a task
previously assigned to the entire U.S. army.[14]

Howe gave the honor of capturing northern Manhattan and Fort
Washington to Wilhelm von Knyphausen, his senior German general,
and thirteen thousand British and German soldiers. On November 15,
when James Patterson, Howe's adjutant general, sent Magaw his (wholly
conventional) threat to massacre the entire garrison if it did not immediately surrender, Magaw gave the customary reply: "I am determined
to defend this post to the last extremity." The next day, Knyphausen
attacked from the north, south, and east. All three of the assaulting corps
suffered terribly; in one regiment that was rowed across the Harlem
River, ninety men never made it to the west bank. But soon most of
the heavily outnumbered units manning Magaw's outer defenses had to
withdraw into the fort—all except the riflemen and artillerymen firing

British troops row down the Harlem River to attack Fort Washington, Nov. 16, 1776

down at the two German units clawing their way up the north side of Washington Heights.[15]

The Continentals defending the north face of Mount Washington included the twenty-five-year-old Margaret Corbin, who assisted her husband, John, a matross (enlisted artilleryman), and this was not her first fight. When she was five, Indians had attacked her family's western Pennsylvania farm, killing her father and capturing and reportedly adopting her mother. John Corbin died defending Washington Heights, and Margaret took his place at the cannon until she herself took enemy grapeshot in the arm (permanently disabling her), chest, and jaw. Three years after the Battle of Fort Washington, Congress, recognizing that Corbin had "heroically filled the post of her husband," awarded her a lifetime pension, and in 1780 she joined the invalid regiment at West Point.[16]

The riflemen defending the northern summit of Washington Heights rebuffed the enemy for two hours, but continuous firing clogged their weapons. In the eighteenth century, muskets carried bayonets, but rifles did not, so the Americans had no choice but to pull back to Fort Washington, which the British and Germans immediately invested. Watching the action from atop the Palisades on the opposite bank of the Hudson, Washington sent Magaw an exhortation to hold on until nightfall, when he and his troops could be evacuated. But the commandant did not feel he could wait that long, for British and German artillerymen were ready to pour "a shower of shells and richochet-balls" into the now overcrowded fort. He surrendered his nearly three thousand troops.[17]

About sixty of Magaw's men and eighty of their assailants (primarily Germans) died on November 16. Nearly four times as many attackers as defenders had been wounded. Elated but also enraged, the victors summarily executed several prisoners. Washington, who would later ascribe the loss to the "warfare in my mind" over whether to order Greene to evacuate, witnessed the slaughter of the American prisoners through his spyglass. According to one of the commander-in-chief's earliest biographers, the men standing nearby—among them, Thomas Paine—then had the dubious privilege of seeing George Washington cry.[18]

BACK IN LATE SEPTEMBER, in the town of Saint-Jean on the Richelieu River, British and German troops had finally managed to float what Gen. Carleton considered a sufficient number of vessels to pursue Benedict Arnold's ragtag Continental squadron. On October 4, Carleton's fleet set sail. Arnold's subordinates advised him to fight the larger British squadron near the middle of Lake Champlain, where he would at least be able to run away. But despite his utter lack of experience in naval warfare, Arnold chose stratagem instead. He anchored his little fleet in the narrow passage between Valcour Island and the western shore of Lake Champlain (just south of modern-day Plattsburgh, New York) with the expectation that Carleton's sailors, sailing fast with a northerly wind at their backs, would pass the island before spotting their opponents. He would then have the crucial advantage of fighting from the windward.[19]

Sure enough, Carleton's fleet did not detect Arnold's until about 10 a.m. on October 11, shortly after passing Valcour Island. As the British ships tacked back upwind toward the rebel fleet, a process that took several hours, they were vulnerable to American broadsides. One of Arnold's ships ran aground and had to be burned, and Carleton landed rangers and Indians on Valcour Island and the mainland to fire into the Americans' flanks. But by the time Carleton's vessels came within striking distance of the rebels, night had fallen, so he postponed his attack to the next day. During the moonless night of October 11–12, Arnold's entire fleet slipped past the British and continued southward up Lake Champlain. In the ensuing chase, Carleton captured an American ship, and most of the rest had to be run ashore and burnt, with their crews escaping toward Fort Ticonderoga on foot. Only three of Arnold's ships made it to the fort, but most of his men did.[20]

Calculating that it was too late in the season to attack Fort Ticonderoga, Carleton ceded the entire lake to the Americans and withdrew to Saint-Jean. Historians err in crediting Arnold's spirited if doomed defense of Lake Champlain with delaying Carleton so long that he had to push his assault on Ticonderoga into the summer of 1777. Actually, the Battle of Valcour Island consumed only two days. On the other hand, Carleton's determination to overpower the rebel fleet had confined him to his makeshift shipyard at Saint-Jean well into October. Arnold had stopped Carleton not so much with his sailors as with his shipwrights.[21]

Still trying to conciliate the enemy, Carleton treated his Continental prisoners well and soon sent them back to Fort Ticonderoga. They had such nice things to say about him that Gen. Horatio Gates, the commandant, hustled them home before the infection spread.[22]

As HOWE PRESSED HIS advantage in New York and Carleton returned to Canada, free male residents of just over half of the newly independent states were writing new constitutions. Connecticut and Rhode Island residents were satisfied with their highly democratic colonial charters, so they kept them, removing only what they had to, such as references to the British monarch. Four states—New Hampshire, South Carolina, Virginia, and New Jersey—had instituted new constitutions before Congress adopted the Declaration of Independence. In most of the remaining seven, voters spent the second half of 1776 battling over just how far to push their governments toward the democratic ideal. Delaware proclaimed its new government on September 21. Then Pennsylvania and Maryland adopted constitutions that stood at polar extremes.

During the colonial era, only about 50 percent of Pennsylvania men possessed at least fifty acres of land, and only they could vote in assembly elections.[23] But in setting the rules for sending delegates to the state constitutional convention, the provincial conference extended the franchise to the 90 percent of adult men who paid taxes. That increased the likelihood that the convention would write a highly democratic document—and so did an eight-month-old organizing effort on the part of rank-and-file militiamen. Throughout Pennsylvania, militia companies had elected committees of privates that in turn sent representatives to city- or county-wide committees. On June 25, 1776, the final day of the provincial conference, Philadelphia's committee of privates warned the state's militiamen against voting for "great and over-grown rich Men" or "Gentlemen of the learned Professions," such as doctors and attorneys. At a time when elite political writers celebrated the enlightened officeholder who stands above party, the privates candidly expressed their desire to be represented by men "of like Passions and Interests" as themselves."[24]

Pennsylvania voters followed the Philadelphians' advice, electing a convention that was all but unique in American history for having so few lawyers (as few as four of the ninety-six) and so many ordinary farmers and artisans. Assembling on July 15, these delegates proceeded to write the most democratic constitution of the founding era. It was apparently the work of Timothy Matlack, a merchant, brewer, and abolitionist—and a Quaker until being disowned ten years previously.[25]

The most democratic feature of the new constitution—its unicameral legislature, all of whose members had to face the voters every year—was actually a carryover from Pennsylvania's colonial government. But because the convention also abolished the position of governor, every measure that made it through that annually elected assembly became law. In addition, the framers retained the liberal voting qualification under which they themselves had been elected, enfranchising all male taxpayers, which expanded the electorate by nearly 50 percent. They also subjected assemblymen to term limits. Moreover, Pennsylvania's was the first constitution in America (and possibly the world) to delay the vote on any legislative proposal until after the next election—a practice that conservative North Carolina congressman William Hooper described as making "the mob . . . a second branch" of the legislature."[26]

Pennsylvania voters would elect justices of the peace, the assembly's sessions would be open to the public, and its votes would be printed. There would be no special property qualification for officeholding. Every seven years, voters would elect a Council of Censors to review the constitution and suggest changes.[27] In a draft version of its declaration of rights, the convention made the extraordinary claim that:

> An enormous Proportion of Property vested in a few Individuals is dangerous to the Rights, and destructive of the Common Happiness, of Mankind; and therefore every free State hath a Right by its Laws to discourage the Possession of such Property.

This defense of wealth redistribution had broad support—for instance, from Benjamin Franklin—but the delegates narrowly defeated it: one of their few concessions to the conservative minority.[28]

One colonial-era policy that the convention did not revisit was the use of Pennsylvania's enormous counties as legislative election districts. Within two years, Pennsylvanians would criticize these countywide election districts as insufficiently democratic. But when the convention presented its handiwork to the public on September 28, all of the rebukes came from elitists. Leading Pennsylvanians derided the new constitution as "sickly," "Damned," "levelling," and "Villanous."[29]

Neighboring Maryland's journey to a new constitution was equally contentious. A June 26 meeting of militiamen in Anne Arundel County sought large strides toward freeholder democracy. Under their proposal, both houses of assembly would be elected every year, the governor would have no power to veto legislation, and lawsuits against debtors would be suspended until after the war. Reviving a technique that had proven effective in the battle for independence, 885 Anne Arundel freemen—40 percent of them—joined in instructing their constitutional convention delegates not only to support the June 26 reforms but also to abolish the state's property qualification for voting. Many of the same Marylanders who had celebrated the "glorious Effects" of county instructions in smoothing the road to independence objected, just a few weeks later, to instructions in favor of democratic reforms. Indeed three of Anne Arundel's four convention delegates resigned in protest.[30]

Thousands of other Marylanders joined Anne Arundel in endorsing the enfranchisement of all taxpaying militiamen, both in choosing constitutional convention delegates and for all subsequent contests. On voting day, freeholders in five counties threw out the election judges and invited all militiamen who paid taxes to vote. The council of safety ordered these counties to hold new elections and they did so, voting the majority of the original delegates right back in.

But in the end the campaign for a more democratic Maryland failed. The document adopted on November 11 reduced but retained the property qualification for voting and imposed lofty minimum-wealth requirements for officeholders. Nine in ten adult freemen would even be shut out of the lower house of assembly, the House of Delegates, owing to its £500 requirement. And the state's sheriffs, senators, congressmen, and council members would all have to possess £1,000, while gubernatorial candidates would need £5,000. The most powerful restraint on the popular will would be Maryland's Senate, whose members were to be selected to five-year terms by a special group of wealthy electors rather than directly by the voters.[31]

On the spectrum between democratic and aristocratic forms of government, the framers of the Pennsylvania and Maryland constitutions had run to opposite extremes, and numerous citizens of both states demanded a new constitutional convention, initially with little success.

The authors of the first state constitution, Virginia's, had prohibited government officials from jailing dissenters, but free Virginians of every religious faith still had to pay taxes to the established Church of England (soon to be rebranded as the Anglican or Protestant Episcopal Church). Conservatives argued that dissenters undermined husbands' authority over their wives and slaveholders' control over their human property—and that disestablishment would threaten Virginia's very existence by encouraging the growth of antiwar and antislavery sects such as the Quakers. For their part, citizens who criticized measures such as church taxes argued that the greatest threat to civil peace was persecution.[32]

By October 1776, Virginia dissenters, especially Baptists, had collected more than ten thousand signatures—an extraordinary number in a state where only about fifty thousand men could vote—on a petition seeking greater religious freedom. This was more grassroots pressure than state legislators could resist. The first statute adopted by the Commonwealth of Virginia revived the tobacco inspection system that underlay Virginia's economy, but the second one, approved on December 9, 1776, exempted dissenters from taxes supporting the Episcopal Church. Not that the strife was over; the act allowed some future assembly to adopt a "general assessment," taxing all freeholders to support the denomination of their choice.[33]

GEN. HOWE ESTABLISHED HEADQUARTERS in New York City, but in the closing weeks of 1776 climate and other considerations compelled him to send detachments into two nearby states. During the night of November 19–20, Charles Cornwallis and four thousand troops crossed the Hudson to begin an extended forage in the fertile fields of eastern New Jersey, where farmers had just harvested their crops. Less than two weeks later, on December 1, Gen. Henry Clinton and six thousand British and German soldiers set sail for Newport, Rhode Island. Fifty miles north of New York City but 150 miles to the east, Newport is close enough to the Gulf Stream that even during that colder era its harbor almost never froze. If both invasions succeeded, Howe could go into winter quarters plausibly claiming to have returned three British colonies to the imperial fold.[34]

Today Lord Cornwallis is best known for surrendering an eight-thousand-man army at Yorktown, Virginia, on October 19, 1781. But Yorktown was actually the only major blemish in an otherwise stellar career that stretched from acclaimed service in 1759 at Minden (the battle that led to the death of Lafayette's father and the court-martial of Lord Germain) to an epic victory over Tipu Sultan, the son and heir of Haidar Ali, in India in 1792 and the successful suppression of the Irish rebellion of 1798. In the House of Lords in March 1766, Cornwallis had been one of the few members of Parliament to oppose both the Stamp Act and the Declaratory Act.[35] This was his first independent command.

Cornwallis and his men rowed undetected across the Hudson, landing at the foot of the five-hundred-foot Palisades. Loyalist guides pointed out a little-used path up the cliff face. It was impassible for oxen or horses, but not for humans, and by midday on November 20, the troops had dragged their cannon to the top without being detected. Then they headed south. Fort Lee, directly across the Hudson from Fort Knyphausen (the former Fort Washington), was only about five or six miles away, and Cornwallis meant to surprise its garrison.[36]

Continental officers learned of Cornwallis's crossing just in time to remove most of Fort Lee's ammunition, field pieces (light cannon), and soldiers. Getting all of that matériel to safety was another matter, as the tangle of wagons, horses, men, and mobile artillery created, not for

British landing below the New Jersey Palisades, Nov. 20, 1776

the last time, some massive traffic problems leaving Fort Lee. Late on November 20, when Cornwallis and his troops occupied the fort without firing a shot, they captured some one hundred stragglers and one thousand barrels of flour, along with tents, blankets, and all the heavy cannon. At Forts Washington and Lee, the British had rolled the enemy on the side. They then proceeded to shadow the Continental Army as it marched south and west across the Jerseys. Howe had ordered Cornwallis's troops not to draw the rebels into a major battle, at least not until he caught up, and they did not so much chase the Continentals across the state from the Hudson to its western boundary, the Delaware River, as shoo them off.[37]

Washington, unaware of Cornwallis's orders, took pains to avoid a battle, for his men were not only outnumbered but "much broken & dispirited." He would have liked to have implemented his new strategy of inflicting heavy casualties on the advancing enemy from behind a succession of fortifications, but he had lost most of his entrenching tools at Fort Lee, and the terrain in New Jersey's midsection was "almost a dead Flat."[38] When the Continentals reached Newark, Cornwallis's seeming sloth permitted them to halt for five days in hopes of being reinforced, either by additional New Jersey militia or by Charles Lee, whom Washington had begged but not ordered to cross the Hudson and join him. Neither came.

After crossing the Raritan River to (New) Brunswick, the Americans were able to rest for another two days, partly on the future site of Rutgers University, because Howe had ordered Cornwallis not to cross the Raritan.[39]

Only once did Washington's and Cornwallis's armies clash. The first British troops reached the north bank of the Raritan at 1:30 p.m. on December 1, and the two sides' artillery came forward to duel across the river. The American cannon were commanded by Alexander Hamilton, a fatherless Caribbean immigrant, originally from the island of Nevis, who had attended King's College (soon to be renamed Columbia University). Hamilton had then read for the law before organizing an artillery company at the age of twenty.[40]

The artillery duel produced few casualties, and late that afternoon the Americans moved out, reaching Trenton and the Delaware River at noon the next day. Although often depicted as a long slog, the Continentals' transit of New Jersey had actually taken only twelve days, six of which they had spent in camp.

Washington halted at Trenton for nearly a week as he contemplated making a stand with his back to the Delaware. But on December 7, he started ferrying his army over to Pennsylvania, careful not to leave his pursuers, if such they can be called, a single boat for thirty-five miles in either direction. Howe had caught up with his army, and his advance troops entered Trenton on the afternoon of December 8, missing the last of the Continentals by just three hundred paces.[41]

On the infamous December 7, 1776, the same day the Continentals began their retreat over the Delaware, the fleet carrying Gen. Henry Clinton's detachment anchored off Newport, Rhode Island, with nary a shot fired in either direction. The troops disembarked the next morning "without the least opposition."[42]

Rhode Island had rebelled against Britain partly in response to the Quartering Acts of 1765 and 1774, neither of which quartered any redcoats in private homes, but during the British soldiers' three-year occupation of Newport, they forced hundreds of residents to board them. Many soldiers were accused of abuse—but none by Sarah Osborn, the impoverished teacher who had once welcomed men as well as women and Blacks as well as whites to her religious meetings. No soldier was quartered in her home, and those she met on the street called her "that *good woman*" and "took care to avoid all profane words when near her," her friend and biographer Samuel Hopkins recalled. Like most Americans, even in occupied cities, Osborn cared more about her private life, especially her religious life, than the American War of Independence. One of her friends reported that during the war and ever afterward, she was often "sick; destitute; and in affliction." And in 1778, two years into the British occupation, she lost her second husband. Still, she enjoyed "almost uninterrupted" assurance of divine favor and thus "serenity of mind." When she died in 1796, her property barely covered her debts and the cost of her funeral, but it was not her only legacy, for Samuel and Elizabeth Hopkins published her memoirs and letters.[43]

IN THE WAKE OF Washington's providential escape from Trenton, nearly everyone in both armies assumed that the British and Germans would follow him across the Delaware as soon as they could construct boats or a pontoon bridge—or when the river froze, as it often did in December. Then, in as little as a day, they would march thirty-five miles downriver to the lightly defended Philadelphia.

Panic-stricken Philadelphians secured their belongings as best they could, and many fled. Up until this time, Congress had prided itself on micromanaging the war, but the delegates delayed their flight south to Maryland long enough to formally entrust Washington with plenary military power for the next six months. They thereby incurred harsh criticism for turning the commander-in-chief into a dictator, but they always denied intending to go that far. Washington made good use of his new power, for instance establishing an artillery division that Congress had never quite gotten around to.[44]

Meanwhile the grim news kept pouring in. On December 2—too late to help Washington fend off Cornwallis—his second-in-command, Charles Lee, finally moved his troops into New Jersey. Lee believed Congress might soon ask him to replace Washington at the head of the army, and he sought to advance that prospect by openly denouncing the chief to his fellow officers. Lee's campaign received unexpected support from Adjutant General Joseph Reed, Washington's supposedly devoted acolyte. Assuring Lee it was "entirely owing to you that this army, and the liberties of America . . . are not entirely cut off," Reed blamed the loss of Fort Washington on his mentor's irresolution. "Oh! General, an indecisive mind is one of the greatest misfortunes that can befall an army; how often have I lamented it this campaign," he wrote. When Lee's reply, which endorsed Reed's aspersions and—still worse for him—recapitulated them, arrived at headquarters, Reed was away. Washington thought the letter might be time-sensitive, so he opened it, suddenly discovering his protégé's "disengenuity." The commander-in-chief's disappointment with Reed suffused their subsequent communications. Before the incident, Washington had adopted the rare practice of closing all twenty-one of his surviving letters to the young attorney with an expression of "affection," always using some form of that word. But his next three letters said nothing about affection, and after that, he expressed it only sporadically.[45]

On December 12, the day Congress gathered for the last time before fleeing Philadelphia, Lee halted his army at Basking Ridge, New Jersey, and then rode three miles farther on to the highly rated White's Tavern near Veal Town. The next morning, shortly after signing a letter describing Washington as "most damnably deficient," Lee, still in his dressing gown, was startled by the sound of musket balls striking the tavern. A Loyalist had disclosed his whereabouts to a company of British dragoons that included the soon-to-be-notorious Banastre Tarleton. The dragoons had Lee surrounded, and he and his guard offered only token resistance before giving themselves up.[46]

For Washington, the removal of the disobedient, even seditious, Lee was in many ways a blessing. Had he known that Lee would soon be advising his captors on how to suppress the rebellion, he would have regretted the loss even less. But the public, including the troops, saw the capture of the army's second-in-command as yet another devastating blow.

On December 13, the same day his troops captured Lee, Howe made a surprise announcement: his army would go into winter quarters without attacking Philadelphia. Still, his troops would guard the New Jersey Loyalists with a T-shaped chain of cantonments extending east to west across the state's waist and then up and down the Delaware River, with the least favored troops, the German mercenaries, garrisoning the posts farthest from New York. Almost immediately, some of the idle soldiers began committing atrocities: beatings, theft, and even rape. A gang of five or six infantrymen attacked a ten-year-old, a pregnant woman was raped over the course of several days by different attackers, and groups of soldiers held women for days at a time, repeatedly assaulting them—all in the town of Pennington, New Jersey. And British and German as well as U.S. sources affirmed that women in other towns endured similar assaults.[47]

During these same weeks, some Loyalists and British officials informally adopted Governor Dunmore's policy of encouraging enslaved people to seize their freedom. Nothing better illustrates the ambiguity of the American Revolution than most white Whigs' belief that John Vandyke, the "Malitious Active Tory" who reportedly "assembled and spirited the Negroes against us," was just as guilty of a war crime as any rapist.[48]

Washington was appalled at the actions of the British occupiers—but even more so at New Jerseyans' seeming unwillingness to rise up against them. "Instead of turning out to defend their Country and affording aid to our Army they are making their Submissions as fast as they can," he wrote. The Howe brothers promised amnesty to anyone who would take an oath of fidelity to the king, and by the end of 1776 at least five thousand New Jerseyans—including Richard Stockton, a signer of the Declaration of Independence—had signed it. Washington warned two of his brothers that unless leading Whigs on the home front—men like Samuel and John Augustine Washington—strained every nerve to replenish the army's ranks, "the game is pretty nearly up."[49]

But Washington's desponding letters did not tell the whole story. The British and German soldiers occupying New Jersey faced constant harassment, not only from Continental patrols but from militia parties and even freelancers. The insurgency drew inspiration from a new publication by Thomas Paine, who had joined the Continental Army's exodus across New Jersey, serving as a volunteer aide-de-camp to Gen. Nathanael Greene. Each night at his campfire, Paine labored over *The American Crisis*, and the first number appeared in Philadelphia on December 19. "These are the times that try men's souls," he wrote. "The summer soldier and the sunshine patriot will, in this crisis, shrink from the service of his country; but he that stands by it *now*, deserves the love and thanks of man and woman."[50]

Many of Washington's advisors implored him to provide more tangible motivation, both for Continental soldiers to fight on and for additional freemen to enlist. Others raised more practical concerns. "Something must be attempted to revive our expiring Credit . . . & prevent a total Depreciation of the Continental Money," Joseph Reed told the chief in a December 22 letter.[51]

If Washington was going to "raise the spirits of the People" and the value of their currency by giving the enemy "a lucky blow," he would have to do so before December 31, when most of his troops' enlistments expired. And maybe he could, for by sticking to his resolution never to engage the British except from cover, he had lulled them into a complacency that he could now exploit. On Christmas night, he marched 2,400 Continental soldiers, nearly half his force, to McConkey's Ferry, where Col. John Glover's Marblehead mariners, assisted by local watermen and dockworkers, shuttled them over to New Jersey. This was the scene immortalized seventy-five years later in Emanuel Leutze's *Washington Crossing the Delaware*, and it played out ten miles upriver from Trenton, New Jersey, winter quarters for about 1,400 Hessian soldiers.[52]

At about 11 p.m., in the midst of the crossing, an arctic storm crashed the mercury and ushered in slashing winds. "It hailed with great violence," artillery commander Henry Knox reported to his wife, Lucy. Observing the operation from the Jersey shore, Washington briefly considered turning the army around but concluded that he could not do so before sunrise, when anyone still waiting his turn to reembark would be spotted and captured. So he "determined to push on at all Events."[53]

Washington had hoped to have all his troops over the Delaware by

Emanuel Leutze, *Washington Crossing the Delaware* (1851)

midnight, but it was 4 a.m. before they were actually ready to head southeast down the river road toward Trenton. The plan had been to arrive just before dawn, but they would not actually make it until "the day was fairly broke."[54]

About halfway to Trenton, Washington divided his army. Gen. John Sullivan's division continued down the river road, while Gen. Nathanael Greene's, accompanied by Washington, doglegged to the left in order to enter Trenton along a roughly parallel road farther east.

Meanwhile two other detachments of Continentals entered New Jersey downriver—or so Washington thought. Knowing that Assunpink Creek hemmed Trenton in on the east and south as it flowed toward its junction with the Delaware, he had directed a five-hundred-man corps under Gen. James Ewing to cross into New Jersey below the town and block the only bridge over the Assunpink. When Sullivan's and Greene's hammers struck from the northwest, Ewing's men would serve as the anvil. An additional force was supposed to cross the Delaware six miles farther down and engage the Hessians at Bordentown, preventing them from sprinting to Trenton to rescue their countrymen. But neither of these downriver detachments made it across the ice-choked Delaware.[55]

POPULAR MYTHOLOGY HAS THE Continental Army catching the Hessians at Trenton off guard on the morning of December 26 because they were hung over from the previous day's revels, but what actually doomed the garrison was a false sense of security. It began, as several survivors conceded, with long-standing contempt for American soldiers, which recent events had only reinforced. Col. Johann Rall, who commanded the three German regiments at Trenton, had seen no reason to put his men to the trouble of fortifying against a possible American attack. "Shit upon shit!" he had reportedly said, "Let them come. . . . We will go at them with the bayonet."[56]

Throughout December, Continental patrollers, New Jersey militiamen, and self-appointed locals had constantly harassed German and British soldiers traveling among imperial cantonments like Trenton and Princeton. And they had occasionally even gnawed at the outer defenses of the garrison towns themselves. Over time, the occupiers had come to accept these raids as an unpleasant fact of life.

What would turn out to be the most significant of these attacks occurred at twilight on Christmas Day, as Washington's expedition mustered in Pennsylvania. Without informing headquarters, fifty Virginians, furious at the Hessians for killing one of their comrades in an earlier skirmish, had struck a German guardhouse on the outskirts of Trenton, only to be repelled without loss on either side. As Washington marched east toward Trenton, he was horrified to meet the Virginians returning from their reprisal raid. When he learned that their commander, Adam Stephen, had given them his blessing, he was livid: "You sir, may have ruined all my plans." Actually, Rall had received reports of a possible U.S. attack, and he apparently believed that by repelling the Virginia raiders, his men had put him in the clear.[57]

All the same, on Christmas afternoon, Rall made his customary tour of the guardhouses. Then the rain changed to sleet and snow. Forgetting that Americans had stormed Quebec on New Year's Eve 1775 in the middle of a blizzard—an easy attack to overlook, since it had so utterly failed—Maj. Friedrich von Dechow canceled the next morning's predawn patrol, and Lt. Andreas von Wiederholdt allowed the pickets guarding the northern approaches to Trenton to do so from indoors.[58] Only a crazy person, they figured, would come out on a night like this.

Both American wings ran into German sentries on the outskirts of Trenton at about 8 a.m. Before withdrawing into town, each sentry fired a single shot to warn their comrades, but not in time for them to muster much of a defense. Crews led by Thomas Forrest and Alexander Ham-

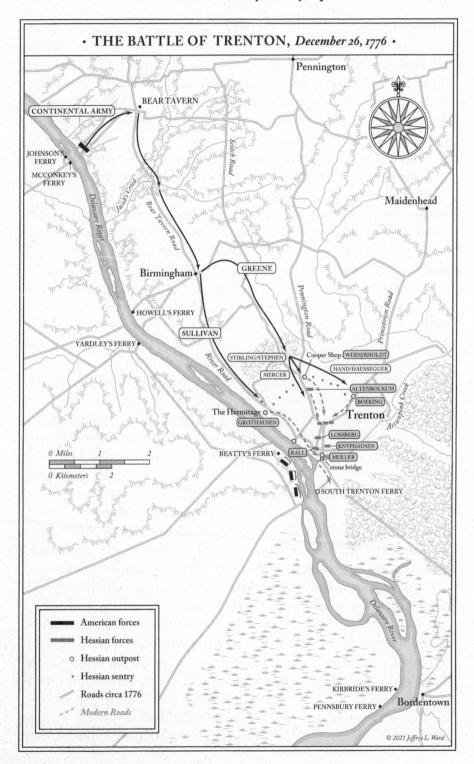

· THE BATTLE OF TRENTON, *December 26, 1776* ·

ilton set up field pieces on a hill north of town and opened up. Meanwhile Sullivan, upon learning that Ewing's corps had failed to cross the Delaware and block the bridge over Assunpink Creek, rushed eastward through the lower part of town in order to do so himself. Twenty British dragoons beat Sullivan to the stone bridge and galloped across, but the several hundred Hessian infantrymen behind them arrived after the Americans had barred the door.

Rall sent two cannon crews north up Trenton's main street, and they got off six shots before the Americans north of town wounded or killed most of them and sent the rest flying. As Continental infantry ran to capture the German cannon, several Americans were shot, among them a Virginian who just a year earlier had been a sophomore at the College of William and Mary. A surgeon's mate clamped his wound, saving his life, and forty years later, James Monroe would be elected president.

Rall led his infantry out of the line of fire, into an orchard east of town. Incredibly, he ordered his men to advance northward toward the Americans, with a view to turning their eastern flank, as Howe had on Long Island. But Greene shifted some of his troops eastward, so Rall redirected his brigade back toward the center of town to try to reclaim its cannon and its honor. The colonel took two musket balls in the side and fell mortally wounded. A short time later, his regiment and one of the others surrendered. The third, under Gen. von Knyphausen, tried to wade across Assunpink Creek. But the soldiers floundered in the marshy creek bottom, easy targets for the Americans, and soon threw down their weapons.

In less than an hour, the rebels had killed more than twenty Hessians and captured about nine hundred. Two American soldiers were killed, five were hurt, and at least four others died of exposure. Only a few civilians had remained in Trenton. At least one died in the crossfire, and a woman reportedly stepped out of her front door and killed a German officer. Washington's fondest hope had been to continue on to Princeton or even to the huge British supply depot at Brunswick. But even after losing the Trenton garrison, the Germans in western New Jersey outnumbered the Continentals. Moreover, the weather was still deteriorating, and many of Washington's troops had gotten drunk on the Hessians' liquor. Finally he bowed to prudence, and the Continentals, accompanied by their prisoners, marched ten miles back to McConkey's Ferry and recrossed the river. Three additional men reportedly froze to death on the return trip, and the rest did not make it back to their tents until dawn on Friday, December 27, having been awake, and mostly on the march, for forty-eight hours.[59]

The Trenton raid was more consistent than it superficially seemed with what "Perseverance," a Massachusetts newspaper writer, called "General Washington's defensive system," since that strategy allowed exceptions whenever the Americans' apparent passivity lulled their pursuers into a false sense of security. But Perseverance and others believed Washington's ultimate weapon remained attrition, since the redcoats would "waste away every campaign by sickness, by skirmishes, through fatigue and hardship, and by the badness and scarcity of provisions," as the government continued to shell out £60,000 per month—equal to the total expenses of the Continental Army—just on cartage.[60]

"In our condition, a defensive war is more prudent than an offensive one," Perseverance insisted, and the initially aggressive Washington had finally grasped this point, with England's *Annual Register* grudgingly honoring him as "the American Fabius." Expertly exploiting North America's "numberless inaccessible posts, and strong natural barriers, formed by the various combinations of woods, mountains, rivers, lakes, and marshes," he and his generals had made the conflict "a war of posts, surprizes, and skirmishes," in which the imperial army could "retain no more territory than what it occupied, which was again lost as soon as it departed to another quarter." Like Gen. Howe, opposition MP Edmund Burke and his fellow *Register* editors gave the mother country's army little chance of winning the war.[61]

CHAPTER 22

The Price of Revolution

Early 1777

S HORTLY AFTER WASHINGTON SETTLED BACK IN AT HEADQUARTERS, he learned to his astonishment that Col. Carl Emil Ulrich von Donop, the Hessian count who commanded the nearest enemy troops, had responded to the devastating news from Trenton not by leading his men toward the scene of action but by abandoning the rest of the Delaware River defensive cordon and retreating all the way to Princeton. John Cadwalader and James Ewing, the Whig commanders who had been unable to get their men across the Delaware on December 26, now managed to do so. At Cadwalader's urging, Washington on December 30 began ferrying his troops back to Trenton.

By sunset on December 31, after Washington's army had returned to New Jersey, the American commander realized he had made a terrible mistake. As he ought to have predicted, senior British and German officers had halted the Hessians' withdrawal, and eight thousand enemy troops were now milling about in Princeton, just twelve miles from Trenton, ready to pounce on the Continentals before they could retreat back across the Delaware.[1] All they were waiting for was their commander.

Two weeks earlier, when Howe sent his army into winter quarters, Cornwallis had sought and received permission to spend the winter break back in England with his invalid wife, Jemima. He had already sent his baggage on board the vessel that was to carry him home when he learned of Washington's master stroke against Trenton—and of Howe's orders indefinitely postponing his leave and sending him to Princeton.[2]

Most of the U.S. soldiers' enlistments were set to expire at the end of 1776. Washington and his officers pleaded with them to stick around, even if only for a few weeks. One soldier recalled years later that on

December 31, the commander-in-chief paraded the men of his regiment and "entreated us to stay. The drums beat for volunteers, but not a man turned out."

Washington tried again: "My brave fellows, you have done all I asked you to do, and more than could be reasonably expected; but your country is at stake, your wives, your houses, and all that you hold dear."

Finally one soldier said to a friend, "I will remain if you will."

Others chimed in — "We cannot go home under such circumstances" — and eventually most of the regiment agreed to stay on.[3]

Washington was also able to offer the men a material incentive. Congress, which had previously granted him nearly total control over military matters, voted on December 27 to give him even more power, and he used it to give soldiers who remained another six weeks a bounty of $10, doubling their salaries. Most of the New Englanders in the Continental Army agreed to that arrangement, but nearly all of the members of a Delaware regiment that had shown amazing valor over the previous months, especially on Long Island, refused to march another step. One of the few who agreed to stay was their colonel, John Haslet.[4]

On January 1, Cadwalader's and Mifflin's armies joined Washington at his direction, giving him a total of about 6,800 troops. Still with fewer men than Lord Cornwallis, Washington considered his options. As ice filled the Delaware, slowing navigation and threatening to forbid it altogether, his most prudent course would be to cross back to Pennsylvania while he still could. But the capture of the Hessian garrison at Trenton had done wonders for American morale — militiamen were "pouring in from all Quarters" — and Washington worried that abandoning New Jersey again would mean "destroying every dawn of hope which had begun to revive in the breasts of the Jersey Militia."[5]

Early on January 2, Cornwallis started his army down the road to Trenton, foreclosing the Continentals' option of recrossing the river, since they could not all make it over before the British arrived. To slow Cornwallis, and thin his ranks, Washington sent a portion of his army forward. All along the Princeton–Trenton road, they repeatedly shot at the redcoats and Germans from cover — ravines, woodlots, houses — before dropping back to the next natural defensive position to begin again. The British did not reach Trenton until 4 p.m. By then Washington had withdrawn his men across the Assunpink and covered the one bridge and every known ford with gun batteries. Cornwallis sent several detachments wading across the creek, but all were badly beaten up and forced to turn back. With dusk approaching, Cornwallis reconciled himself to spending the night in Trenton. Along the road from Princeton and in Trenton, his army had reportedly lost more than three hundred soldiers—more than three times as many as the Americans. But the rebel force was still smaller than his, composed largely of greenhorn militia, and as he understood, shrinking fast. The redcoats and Germans would cross the Assunpink in the morning. With any luck, they would pin the Continental Army against the Delaware River and destroy it.[6]

As Washington agonized over whether to stay and fight or try to escape down the left bank of the Delaware, one of his officers (or possibly the commander-in-chief himself) came up with a third option that would allow the Continentals to escape from Cornwallis and still (as Washington put it) "avoid the appearance of a retreat." They would run away from the British at Trenton—in order to attack them at Princeton. A handful of soldiers kept up a clamor at their campsite south of Assunpink Creek—clanking pots, loudly digging, and keeping the campfires burning brightly—while, starting around midnight, the rest of the army slipped away. Heading north and marching all night, they followed "a roundabout Road" toward Princeton.[7] On January 2, Cornwallis awoke to the sight of an empty American camp across the Assunpink and the distant sound of two of his detached regiments fighting the entire American army on the Trenton–Princeton road.

Shortly after dawn, the American soldiers had reached a crossroads about three miles south of Princeton. Here they divided. Most turned right and headed northeast toward the town's eastern approaches, which were said to be lightly defended. Washington accompanied this wing, which was commanded by Gen. Sullivan. Gen. Greene's somewhat smaller division took the left fork and marched due north up the Stony Creek ravine. These troops' first objective was to secure the bridge, one mile south of Princeton, that carried the road from Trenton over Stony Creek. They would then head north into town. Greene's advance was commanded by Col. Hugh Mercer, a Scottish-born doctor who had served with the rebels at Culloden in 1745, fled to Pennsylvania, received a nearly fatal wound at the Battle of the Monongahela, and subsequently moved to Virginia. Mercer's second-in-command was John Haslet.[8]

If the entire "Grand Army" (as Americans were starting to call it) had attacked Princeton from the east, it probably could have achieved complete surprise and a quick conquest. But the Battle of Princeton was destined for a more ambiguous outcome. Lt. Col. Charles Mawhood, the British commander at Princeton, was leading two of his three regiments to Trenton on the morning of January 3, and he and his men crossed the Stony Creek bridge just as Greene's advance troops came up the ravine. Spotting the Continentals at about the same time they saw him, Mawhood turned his army around to confront them.[9]

Exploiting their initial numerical advantage, the British drove the Americans back, mortally wounding Mercer—who would take nine days to die—and then Haslet as they tried to rally their men. Washington galloped over from the other division, followed by some of Sullivan's infantry. Spurring his white horse, an easy target for British firelocks, to within thirty paces of the enemy, the commander-in-chief succeeded at rallying both the Continentals and—to his great surprise—the Philadelphia Associators (militiamen).[10] He later acknowledged that these city dwellers (or "Citizens," as he called them) had "undergone more fatigue and hardship than I expected Militia (especially Citizens) would have done at this inclement Season." Mawhood's now outnumbered troops broke and ran, with the Continentals in close pursuit and Washington joining in, yelling, "It is a fine fox chase, my boys!"[11]

Greene and Sullivan could now turn their attention to the tiny British garrison in the college town of Princeton, which put up a valiant and well-considered defense, making successive stands at a ravine and then a receding series of redoubts while wagoners hustled the town's stockpile of food and other supplies northeast toward Brunswick. The redcoats took their final refuge in the university's main building, Nassau Hall, where officers soon appeared at the windows to surrender.[12]

Washington's original plan had been to continue on to Brunswick, which was rumored to be as lightly defended as Princeton. But the unexpected clash with Mawhood had delayed the Americans, and now British and German troops were hustling up the road from Trenton. Washington spurred his own exhausted soldiers due north toward the relative safety of Somerset Courthouse (present-day Millstone, New Jersey). Over the next three days, they made their way to Morristown, on a high plateau that Continental officers had previously identified as a relatively safe place to winter, since British attackers sallying out from New York City, thirty miles to the east, would have to traverse narrow and highly defensible passes in the Watchung Mountains.

In the subsequent months, Howe confirmed the Americans' prediction that he would keep his distance from Morristown. Indeed, by winning a major battle at Trenton on December 26 and then not losing there on January 2–3, the Continentals had accomplished a remarkable feat. With just two exceptions—Amboy, on New York Harbor, and Brunswick, just fifteen miles inland—the British had left New Jersey.

LESS THAN A MONTH after reaching Morristown, Washington initiated a maneuver that may have done even more than his Trenton and Princeton victories to advance the Continental cause. Yet hardly anyone outside the army even knew he had done it.

From the start of the war, the redcoats had enjoyed a massive advantage over the rebels in a little-known but crucial metric: many more of them had already survived smallpox, gaining lifetime immunity. Thousands had contracted the virus before leaving the more densely populated mother country. And during the British occupation of Boston, Gen. Howe responded to a smallpox outbreak by inoculating every soldier who had never had it.[13]

Smallpox wrought much suffering and loss of life in the Continental Army. It also tamped down enlistment and encouraged desertion. Generals as well as congressmen blamed it for the Americans' failure to capture Canada. But Washington hesitated to follow Howe's example. Inoculation, unlike the later vaccination with cowpox, immobilized recipients for at least a month, so immunizing the entire army would be tantamount to temporarily disarming it. But if soldiers received the virus in shifts, the first comers might inadvertently transmit it to those waiting their turn, and taking the infection "in the natural way" was ten times more lethal than being inoculated. Little wonder that colonists had periodically rioted against neighbors who assembled to have themselves inoculated. Faced with this conundrum, Washington as well as other Continental officers in independent commands not only decided against inoculating their subordinates but prohibited them from undergoing the operation on their own—though such was the soldiers' and especially the officers' dread of the virus that many violated orders and got inoculated in secret.[14]

William Shippen, an army doctor, tried immunizing new southern and western recruits as they passed through Philadelphia on their way to Morristown. But Washington countermanded his order, not fearing that the inoculated men would spread the virus but that their clothing would—and their old uniforms could not be burned, because most only had one. Then, early in February, Washington brought to the smallpox crisis the same personal quality that had shaped his approach toward African American enlistees more than a year earlier: his ability to change his mind. He ordered doctors at Morristown and other army camps to inoculate the troops. Joseph Plumb Martin underwent the procedure with about four hundred fellow Connecticut infantrymen, and the operation was a complete success, with Martin marveling that "We lost none."[15]

The officers supervising Martin's inoculation so feared spreading the virus to civilians that when a fire broke out in a nearby house, he and his comrades were not allowed to join the bucket brigade, and it burned to the ground. The officers were right to worry, for in other areas the virus did leak out, and hundreds of civilians died. But the leading expert on the wartime smallpox epidemic contends that Washington's belated embrace of inoculation saved his army.[16]

Yet the commander-in-chief's bold approach to the smallpox threat by no means solved his manpower crisis. American freemen eagerly signed up for short stints in the militia to protect their own neighborhoods, but far too few would make multiyear commitments to the Continental Army.[17] The states tried to tempt men to enlist with increasingly generous signing bonuses of cash and land, but often to little avail. And besides, Washington warned, by making a nakedly financial appeal, recruiters ran the risk "of greatly injuring the service by introducing into it Foreigners of no Principle, who seize the first Opportunity of deserting to the Enemy." Washington's prejudice against "Foreigners"—recent immigrants from the German states and northern Ireland—was widely shared. One reason British Gen. Henry Clinton gave Irish-born Loyalists their own separate legion called the Volunteers of Ireland was to avoid "giving umbrage to the natives of America" already fighting for king and country.[18] But the Continental Army had to take recruits where it could get them, and by the "Valley Forge" winter of 1777–1778, nearly half the enlisted men were immigrants and African Americans.[19]

On April 14, 1777, Congress gave up on its all-volunteer army, urging the states to begin drafting soldiers where necessary. Most eventually did. Few of the early statutes required that draftees be selected at random, so in many areas, local officials simply chose men they considered "vagabonds."[20]

Right from the start and all over the country, Americans—even enthusiastic Whigs—resisted the draft. In northeastern North Carolina, this grievance merged with others. Many farmers in the northern reaches of Albemarle Sound feared that the Protestant faith was in danger, both from the secularist gentlemen who had tried to omit any religious test for officeholding from the new state constitution adopted on December 18, 1776, and from the alliance Congress was trying to forge with Catholic France. These men did not want to be drafted at all, but especially not by a country tainted with both papacy and secularism. They formed a sophisticated organization with secret codes, a four-part oath for full membership, and three levels of leadership. Early in the summer of 1776, some of these Associators, as they called themselves, frustrated at their failure to halt conscription or remove secularists or crypto-Catholics from state government, devised a desperate plan: after creating a diversion by encouraging slaves to rebel, they would kill Governor Richard Caswell and other state leaders and turn North Carolina over to the British. The rebellion was quickly suppressed, but draft resistance continued throughout the war, and not just in North Carolina.[21]

As the Continentals constructed their cabins near Morristown, they and the Anglo-German troops in New York settled into a low-intensity battle over the region's human and animal food. In one incident, five hundred of Gen. Adam Stephen's Continentals ran into a British foraging party twice its size at Drake's Farm (modern-day Metuchen, New Jersey). The redcoats killed nine of the rebels and wounded and captured fifteen others, some of whom they summarily executed. Stephen, who had survived the Battle of the Monongahela, told British officers that Braddock's Indian attackers "could not be prevailed on to butcher the wounded, in the manner your Troops have done, untill they were first made drunk." For their part, Continental soldiers, Whig militiamen, and irregulars killed, captured, or seriously wounded something like two thousand British and German soldiers during the spring of 1777—and the "forage war" would continue until the British evacuated New York in 1783.[22]

IN APRIL 1777, HOWE sent a party of about 1,500 light infantry and 500 Loyalists under New York governor William Tryon to destroy the Continental supply depot in Danbury, Connecticut. Sailing through Long Island Sound and landing near Norwalk, Connecticut, on April 25, the corps met little resistance on its twenty-three-mile march to Danbury. But the incursion awakened a sleeping giant: Benedict Arnold.[23]

Arnold had won laurels the previous year for keeping Fort Ticonderoga out of the hands of Guy Carleton, but before that, during the rebel invasion of Canada, he had been accused of plundering Montreal merchants. Although a court-martial cleared him of all charges, he could not shake the scent of corruption. On February 19, 1777, when Congress promoted five brigadier generals to major general, the delegates' lingering doubts about Arnold's integrity, distaste for his imperious manner, desire to exert their authority over George Washington (who had championed Arnold), and determination to distribute preferment equitably among the states caused them to pass him over in favor of less senior men. Arnold repaired to his hometown, New Haven, to stew.[24]

Nor was Arnold alone in his "sense of ravaged honor." John Adams spoke for many contemporaries when he denounced the Continental officers for their constant "Scrambling for Rank and Pay like Apes for Nutts," but the problem was actually institutional.[25] Constantly expanding and continually reorganized, the rebel army offered officers the prospect of rapid advancement. Contrast John Montrésor, who as an ensign took a ball at the Monongahela in 1755 but still had not made captain twenty years later, and Johann Ewald, a Hessian who valiantly commanded troops throughout the American War of Independence without rising above the rank of captain, to Nathanael Greene, who became a militia general and then a Continental general a year before first seeing combat. As a result, American generals often fought British lieutenant colonels, as at Princeton, Stony Point, and Cowpens. And with officers racing to the highest ranks of the Continental Army, the real and apparent snubs piled up.[26]

Still, Arnold set his bitterness aside when he learned of Tryon's incursion. It was too late to save Danbury, but not to make Tryon pay a price for it, and Arnold devised a plan in cooperation with other Connecticut officers, including Gold Selleck Silliman, whose measured response to Mary Fish Noyes's "Portrait of a Good Husband" had recently won him her hand. On April 27, as the British and Loyalist troops marched back toward Long Island Sound, about five hundred Connecticut farmers built a breastwork across their path. Most of the defenders were militia, but they were joined by a handful of Continental soldiers, including Joseph Plumb Martin, who had completed his Continental service on Christmas Day 1776 and headed home before reluctantly agreeing to reenlist for a sizable bounty. Some of Tryon's light infantrymen got around the rebels' line and raked them with enfilade fire, scattering them. Arnold's horse took nine musket balls and collapsed, and he became entangled in the stirrups. A British soldier ordered him to surrender. "Not yet," Arnold exclaimed as he drew his pistol and shot the man dead.[27]

As the redcoats and Loyalists approached their boats, the rebels attacked again, and Tryon fended them off with an artillery barrage and a bayonet charge. Martin recalled years later that the reckless Arnold "had a very close rub, but escaped."[28] Learning of this latest feat, Congress belatedly promoted Arnold but refused to backdate his commission, leaving him junior to the major generals it had created in February. So he tendered his resignation.

ABIGAIL AND JOHN ADAMS spent most of the Revolutionary War agonizingly apart, but the first half of 1777 proved particularly difficult, especially for Abigail, because John had made a brief visit home the previous winter, and they had conceived. For Abigail, enduring pregnancy alone seemed too great a sacrifice. With the baby due in barely a month, she lamented being denied "the privilidge which some of the Brute creation enjoy, that of having their mate sit by them with anxious care during all their Solitary confinement."[29]

On July 12, Adams's fetus, a girl, was delivered dead. At the time the bereaved mother assured John that the loss had been unavoidable, but many years later, she speculated to a male friend that her anxiety during her husband's absence had killed her child. (Three decades earlier, Eliza Lucas Pinckney, best known for introducing indigo to South Carolina, had similarly blamed her own emotional state for the loss of a child. Shock at the news of her father's death in French custody threw her prematurely into labor, and "the dear babe lived but 15 days.")[30]

Even as the war brought tragedy into countless American homes, primarily by accelerating the circulation of contagious disease, it also facilitated, and sometimes compelled, self-assertion on the part of thousands of women—not just Whigs but Loyalists and neutrals. Bostonian Lucy Flucker had defied the wishes of her Loyalist father in marrying Boston bookseller Henry Knox, a Whig. Yet in the early years of their marriage, Henry had routinely referred to her as "his little girl," and she does not appear to have objected. But in the spring of 1776, when Henry traveled to New York as Washington's chief of artillery, Lucy was drawn into his business affairs—just not as deeply as she wished. In a June 1777 letter, Lucy complained about Henry having his brother sell two of his horses. "The horses fetched but seventy five pounds owing to your not entrusting me with the sale of them," she informed him. "You had better make me your future agent. I'll assure you, I am quite a woman of business."[31]

Lucy Knox offered equally bold assessments of Henry's other financial concerns, objecting, for instance, to his investing in a pair of privateers. In an August 23 letter, she confessed a concern that after "being long accustomed to command," he would expect to be "commander in chief" of the Knox household at war's end. In a family, she reminded him, there was "such a thing as equal command."[32] New Hampshire's Mary Bartlett almost imperceptibly reached the same conclusion. In 1776, the year her husband, Josiah, signed the Declaration of Independence, Mary sent him regular reports on what she called "Your farming business." By 1778, she would be briefing him on "our" farm.[33]

No matter what economic role they played, many women felt that the war not only permitted but compelled them to engage in political discourse in a way few previously had. When Gen. Anthony Wayne wrote the poet Hannah Griffitts declaring that "Politics is an unfit subject for a Lady's ear," she conceded that that had been true during peacetime, but not "when all we hold dear is exposed to the rage of War." Indeed, it was women's distinguishing qualities that thrust them into the male sphere. "Can a Heart fraught with sensibility & capable of all those exquisitely fine feelings that Constitute at once our Happiness or Misery be supposed to remain Cold and unmoved[?]," she asked. "No!" Griffitts pronounced herself "so good a whig that of Consequence I must be a little of a Politician." Other women made the same claim, intending the term *politician* not in the careerist twenty-first-century sense but closer to the modern *policy wonk*.[34]

Most women confined themselves to commentary, but circumstances pushed some to act. On July 31, 1777, barely two weeks after losing her child, Abigail Adams told John of an incident that had briefly lightened her mood. Earlier in the year, assemblymen in Massachusetts and the other New England states had agreed to combat inflation by prohibiting the sale of most commodities, including coffee, above a set price. Thomas Boylston, a Boston grocery wholesaler (and "a Batchelor," she archly noted), was accused of withholding coffee from the market in hopes the price controls would soon be repealed. Nearly a hundred women marched to Boylston's warehouse, seized his keys, allegedly spanked him, and then made off with his coffee. The marchers craved more than a caffeine fix, another witness reported; they "kept Little shops to sell Necessarys for Poor People" and needed coffee for their customers.[35]

The Boston coffee riot was part of a wartime wave of crowd action, most often prompted by price spikes. These in turn had several sources. Imports virtually ceased in response to the provincial boycott of the mother country and Britain's aggressive campaign to keep colonists from trading with its European rivals. As their shelves all but emptied, shopkeepers could name their own price. Moreover, with more and more Americans exchanging cornfields for battlefields—as many as 250,000 men and perhaps 100 women fought for the United States at some point during the war, and another 10,000 or more fought as Loyalists—production fell, raising prices. Worst of all, the enormous cost of keeping the army in the field left Congress and the state assemblies with no choice but to plunge deeper and deeper into debt, both to the Continental soldiers and to the merchants and farmers who kept them more or less fed, equipped, and clothed. As promissory notes of various forms inundated the economy, their value inevitably sank.[36]

Historian Barbara Clark Smith has documented more than thirty food riots in 1776 and 1777, nearly a third conducted by women. At this early stage of the war, almost all of the commodities that rioters took or tried to take had been imported from the Caribbean: principally sugar products such as molasses and rum. But the most painful shortage was of salt, which before the war had mostly come from Bermuda. Salt riots had contributed to elite Americans' momentous decision to revive international trade by declaring independence, and the British blockade guaranteed that the salt shortages would continue to fuel civil unrest.[37]

Food rioters often took pains to distinguish themselves from mere thieves. In July 1776, when Longmeadow, Massachusetts, merchant Samuel Colton was accused of holding back his stock of sugar products and salt in anticipation of higher prices, rioters from neighboring towns broke into his store and seized his merchandise but did not make off with it. Instead they turned it over to the town clerk for sale at a price they considered just and then left the proceeds for Colton.[38] For legitimacy, the rioters relied upon a long-standing transatlantic tradition authorizing crowd actions to enforce community norms, a notion that the colonial riots against parliamentary taxation had only strengthened. Longmeadow rioters evoked the spirit of the Boston Tea Party by dressing "like Indians."[39]

Even as ordinary Americans struggled to shield their families from currency depreciation, many of the wealthiest men and women in the country insisted that its worst victims were themselves. Inflation eroded the value of the invisible assets known today as accounts receivable, which sometimes originated as cash loans but more commonly as purchases on credit. Whereas in normal times the creditor often had to chase down his debtor, the rapid depreciation of the state and Continental currencies turned prey into predator: debtors stocked up on cheap paper and then caught their creditors to painlessly liquidate their loans.[40] In a typical case, Thomas Jefferson inherited land from his father-in-law and sold some of it to his fellow Virginians, including his brother-in-law, only to be repaid in paper currency that was "not worth oak leaves."[41]

Everyone agreed on the need to shrink the bloated money supply, but how? Each remedy seemed to victimize a different segment of society. Most of the provincial conventions and state assemblies sought to prop up their paper money by proclaiming it legal tender. But in one state, Maryland, the assembly initially left the status of its currency unclear. Charles Carroll of Annapolis (as people called him to distinguish him from his son, Charles Carroll of Carrollton) was the patriarch of Maryland's wealthiest family, and he had issued £24,000 worth of loans. He believed that legislation permitting his debtors to force him to accept worthless paper would "Surpass in Iniquity all the Acts of the British Parliamt. agt. America."[42]

Both Charles Carrolls implored the state assembly to shore up its currency in a way they considered much more equitable: aggressively taxing it back into the state treasury. But Marylanders, like other Americans, were already staggering under enormous taxes, even as the war dramatically reduced their income, and legislators did not dare add to their burden. In April 1777, they went ahead and made the state currency legal tender, prompting the elder Charles Carroll to insist that his son, a state senator, resign his seat.[43] The assembly had just elected the younger Carroll to Congress, and it retained the power to recall him if he now stood out too much in opposition. So he defied his father's demand. "There is a time when it is wisdom to yield to injustice," he insisted; it was "the price of Revolution."[44]

Since October 1776, Congress had been trying to remove Continental currency from circulation by accepting it in payment for federal loan office certificates, which in many ways resembled modern savings bonds. In September 1777, the delegates found a way to make its bonds more attractive. They would no longer pay bondholders their interest in depreciated paper money but out of the funds they secretly received from Louis XVI. The change dramatically increased the value of loan office certificates; Abigail Adams, who had bought one in June 1777 for $100 in depreciated Massachusetts paper money, would now receive her annual interest using French funds worth 24 Massachusetts dollars—a 25 percent annual return on her investment. Since French aid was coming in covertly, this investment opportunity was available only to Americans with connections to Congress.[45]

While creditors pushed for higher taxes and Congress peddled loan office certificates, many ordinary Americans proposed their own schemes for siphoning off excess government paper. Hermon Husband had made his name in North Carolina in the 1760s and early 1770s as the penman of the Regulator rebellion. When Governor Tryon put a price on his head, the avowedly risk-averse Husband escaped to Bedford County in western Pennsylvania and once again achieved financial competency. But he could not suppress his activist impulse, and in 1775 the Bedford County court indicted him and several neighbors for sedition and riot. In the fall of 1777, Husband was elected to the state assembly, whereupon he devised his own solution to the twin challenges of massive government debt and hyperinflation.[46]

Since currency depreciation was inevitable, Husband wanted Pennsylvania authorities to give up on preventing it and instead focus on distributing its ravages more equitably. He would replace the state's depreciated paper money with new bills, each of which would lose 3 percent of its original value every year until, thirty-three years later, it became worthless.[47]

In the eighteenth century, the standard rate of interest was 6 percent a year, so a government-mandated 3 percent annual erosion in the value of money would, in effect, tax away 50 percent tax of the investor's interest income. In defense of that very high tax rate, Husband noted that for years ordinary American farmers had been paying enormous property taxes. "Money should be taxed, equal with Property," he declared. Husband also proposed other ways to reduce the farmer's fiscal burden, for instance by taxing "Superfluities" (luxuries) and "Office Titles" (documents used in land speculation). He broached his plan at a breakfast meeting with a group of fellow radicals that apparently included Thomas Paine. "We advised him to lay [it] aside for the present," another participant reported.[48] He did, but his career as a political economist was far from over.

*   *   *

BY OCTOBER 1776, WHEN Guy Carleton, the liberator of Quebec, pushed his invasion of the United States into the following spring, his old nemesis, George Germain, had already, unbeknownst to him, taken that operation out of his hand. The news from London did not reach Carleton until May 6, 1777, handed to him by his replacement. Gen. John Burgoyne would conduct not only a larger invasion but a more complex one.[49] As his main army headed south, first up Lake Champlain and then overland to the Hudson River for the final push to Albany, a detachment under Lt. Col. Barrimore St. Leger would approach Albany by a more circuitous route: southwest up the St. Lawrence River to Lake Ontario, then southeast to Albany. A classic eighteenth-century diversion, St. Leger's side expedition would force U.S. commanders to redirect some of their soldiers and other resources away from repelling Burgoyne.

Burgoyne also had instructions to "cooperate" with Gen. Howe, but the familiar textbook map, with arrows labeled *Burgoyne, St. Leger,* and *Howe* all converging on Albany, requires an asterisk. Germain requested but did not require Howe's attendance at the grand rendezvous. A peremptory order would have upset the delicate balance that Britain's civilian leaders and overseas military commanders had worked out over the course of the eighteenth century. To allow for the months-long lag in transatlantic communication, protect overseas commanders' egos, and allow Britain's dominant party to distance itself from disasters, London issued recommendations, not orders. For his part, Howe announced that he had no intention of giving up his own planned invasion of Pennsylvania to meet Burgoyne in Albany.[50]

Burgoyne's proposal also contained other flaws. From Fort Ticonderoga to Albany, about a hundred miles, his soldiers would not have Royal Navy vessels to transport and protect them. The Continentals were certain to try to block the invaders as they had on Breed's Hill, perhaps inflicting comparable casualties. They could then repeat the process farther south. And even a successful march might prove pointless. Burgoyne's whole purpose was to isolate New England, the seat of the rebellion, from the rest of the United States. But he did not have nearly enough troops to establish a chain of forts along this corridor, and even fully staffed forts would not have prevented the passage of American troops and supplies. On the night of April 18–19, 1775, when Paul Revere's co-conspirators rowed him across the Charles River to begin his famous ride, they had escaped detection as they passed within pistol shot of several British men-of-war. The Champlain–Hudson corridor would be infinitely more porous, for it extended 360 miles from Sorel at the mouth of the Richelieu River south to New York City. Burgoyne's whole enterprise assumed the impossible.[51]

Yet the general's delusion was widely shared, by his superiors and even his adversaries. As early as February 1776, George Washington worried that the British would wall off New England, the primary source of Continental recruits, from the rest of the rebel colonies.[52] In subsequent decades, U.S. authorities would discover the difficulty of plugging pathways as diverse as the Underground Railroad and the Ho Chi Minh Trail. But without that history as a guide, the prospect of Britain cutting the rebellion in half seemed as real to Washington as it did to Burgoyne.

As a very limited monarch, George III had played at best a minor role in provoking the American Revolution, but the ensuing war had the ironic effect of temporarily augmenting his clout. George assisted in picking Burgoyne to lead the 1777 invasion from Canada and in drawing up his instructions. Burgoyne wanted the option of proceeding from Quebec to New York entirely by water: down the St. Lawrence River and then the Atlantic coast. But the newly empowered king, enthralled like so many others by the vision of three British armies uniting their strength at the head of the Hudson River, vetoed that idea.

Governor Carleton had kept his shipwrights at Saint-Jean busy all through the winter and spring of 1777, making new ships and refitting old ones, and the fleet shoved off on June 15, three months earlier than in 1776.[53] The transports carried more than eight thousand English rank and file—fewer than half of whom were actually English. More than three thousand were Brunswick and Hesse-Hanau mercenaries who had arrived in Canada in 1776. There were also 250 Canadians and Loyalists— many fewer than war planners back in London had expected—and several hundred Scots and Native Americans.[54]

This time the Americans did not even try to oppose the invaders on Lake Champlain, instead congregating at one of the most active hubs in North America's vast network of inland waterways. When Quebec-based paddlers or sailors ascending Champlain reached Ticonderoga, they could continue southward up either of the lake's principal sources: Lake George or, several miles to the east, South Bay and its tributary, Wood Creek. Fort Ticonderoga stood on an elevated peninsula jutting into Lake Champlain from its west bank. Along with another high peninsula protruding into the water from the east, it created a chokepoint only a quarter of a mile wide that the Americans blocked off with a floating bridge and a lumber-and-chain boom. They named the hill on the east bank Mount Independence and crowned it with an eight-pointed star redoubt.[55]

The commandant of Ticonderoga was Arthur St. Clair, who had first come to America from his native Scotland as a British officer during the Seven Years' War. Burgoyne had no desire to drive St. Clair's three thousand troops out of the fort; he wanted to capture them. So he landed the two wings of his army on the opposite banks of Lake Champlain and marched them south with a view to reuniting them south of the fort, blocking the rebels' escape.[56] On the morning of July 2, the two columns—Brunswickers under Gen. Friedrich Adolf Baron von Riedesel on the east bank and redcoats on the west bank—began seizing Ticonderoga's outbuildings amid scattered fire that produced few casualties.

The highest summit around Fort Ticonderoga was 750-foot Sugar Loaf Hill, southwest of the two American forts and just inside cannon range of both. Months earlier, when the twenty-year-old John Trumbull, the future creator of such iconic scenes as *The Declaration of Independence* and *The Surrender of Cornwallis at Yorktown,* laid out the American defenses, he recommended fortifying Sugar Loaf Hill. Gen. Horatio Gates, who commanded the garrison, dismissed Trumbull's suggestion, saying no artillery crew could ever scale that summit—and that even if one did, it could be driven off by Continental cannon on nearby Mount Hope. Later, after handing command of the fort to St. Clair, Gates had second thoughts and advised him to secure Sugar Loaf. But by then it was too late, for Burgoyne's Indian scouts had already chased the Americans inside their lines. Moreover, St. Clair was so desperately short of soldiers—he had fewer than a third as many as had defended Ticonderoga the previous summer—that he had to abandon Mount Hope.[57]

They should have listened to Trumbull. Burgoyne asked Gen. William Phillips, his artillery commander, if he thought his men could drag cannon to the top of Sugar Loaf Hill. "Where a goat can go, a man can go, and where a man can go, he can drag a gun," Phillips replied. A fatigue party started up the slope, "hoisting cannon from tree, to tree," and the Ticonderoga garrison awoke on July 5 to the sight of British soldiers constructing a gun battery atop the renamed Mount Defiance.[58] St. Clair did not wait for the British artillery crews to open up. During the night of July 5–6, his men slipped out of Ticonderoga and Mount Indepen-

dence. The invalids and heavy equipment traveled due south, up South
Bay, in more than two hundred ships and bateaux; the infantry marched
southeastward toward the town of Hubbardton in the New Hampshire
Grants, the region also known as Vermont.[59]

Just before dawn on July 6, Burgoyne learned that the Ticonderoga
garrison had escaped, and the chase began. British sailors needed only
half an hour to cut through the boom and bridge blocking their path.
By the time the rebel fleet reached Skenesborough (modern-day Whitehall), New York, Burgoyne was at their heels, forcing them to burn most
of the supplies they had salvaged from the fort. They then headed up
Wood Creek. Meanwhile Gen. Simon Fraser's corps was closing in on
the rebels who had fled southeastward by land. At dawn on July 7, he
caught up with their rear guard near Hubbardton. In the ensuing battle, he lost about two hundred men. More than half of the six hundred
Americans were killed, wounded, or captured (mostly captured), but
they had bought their fellow Whigs time to escape.[60]

St. Clair's decision to give up the North American Gibraltar without a
fight disgusted his countrymen. Some claimed Burgoyne had bribed him
by firing silver cannonballs into the fort, and Abigail Adams wondered
whether the evacuation of Ticonderoga proceeded from "Cowardice,
Guilt, [or] Deceit."[61] Congress opened inquiries into both St. Clair and
Philip Schuyler, commander of the northern division of the Continental
Army.[62]

ON JULY 8, THE day after the Battle of Hubbardton, delegates attending
a convention forty miles away in Windsor completed work on Vermont's
first constitution. In addition to defining the government's powers and
the people's rights, the new charter complained, as Jefferson had a year
earlier in the Declaration of Independence, of the enemy having "hired
foreign troops" and "sent the savages on our frontiers, to distress us."
Yet Vermont's accusations were leveled not at Britain but the state of
New York.[63]

For decades, New York had laid claim to this region of rolling hills
and fertile river valleys, but so did New Hampshire. By 1764, when the
British government ruled that New York extended east to the Connecticut River, New Hampshire governor Benning Wentworth had issued
grants for 129 townships west of the river. The New York assembly
refused to recognize the "New Hampshire Grants," setting off a low-
intensity war. For example, New York troops fired on Green Mountain

Boys a month before the Battle of Lexington and Concord, killing one. On January 15, 1777, Vermonters declared independence from New York, initially under the name "New Connecticut." Congress sided with New York, and it was partly in hopes of strengthening their territorial claims that Vermonters drafted a constitution.[64]

Many elements of the new government, including the unicameral legislature whose statutes could not be vetoed, were copied from Pennsylvania's. But Vermont was to be an even more democratic polity. When Pennsylvania abolished its property qualification for voting, it nonetheless confined the franchise to taxpayers, but Vermont allowed all adult men to vote.[65] At a time when many Americans considered the War of Independence a battle for individual property rights, Vermonters adopted an eminent domain clause stating that "private property ought to be subservient to public uses." There could scarcely have been a starker contrast to the conservative constitution New York had adopted the previous April, with its property qualification for voting, powerful governor, and Council of Censors empowered to veto any law passed by the assembly.

The first sentence of the state's new Declaration of Rights—"all men are born equally free and independent"—was cribbed from Pennsylvania's. But the second sentence made history, for it established Vermont, a rogue nation in the eyes not only of Britain but of its powerful western neighbor, as the first in the modern world to abolish slavery.[66]

CHAPTER 23

———— ⋅◆⋅ ————

Above All, Horses

Summer 1777

O N JULY 12, THE TWO DIVISIONS OF CONTINENTALS THAT HAD
fled Ticonderoga a week earlier—one by water, the other overland
across Vermont—rendezvoused at Fort Edward on the Hudson River.[1]
Burgoyne established temporary quarters twenty-five miles to the north
in Skenesborough. By this time, he had been joined by four hundred
Native American warriors, primarily Christians from the St. Lawrence
Valley, and he infuriated the rebels by threatening to "give stretch to
the Indian Forces under my direction."[2] On July 17, two men who had
served as French agents during the Seven Years' War, Charles Langlade
from the region around Fort Michilimackinac and the sixty-five-year-
old Luc de la Corne, led one hundred Great Lakes warriors—including
Matchekewis, the man who had orchestrated the lacrosse game that delivered Michilimackinac into Ojibwa hands in 1763—into Burgoyne's
camp. That was many fewer native fighters than Burgoyne had expected,
but he seized upon their arrival as a potential public relations coup.
Historians doubt that Langlade had actually fought at the Battle of the
Monongahela back in 1755, but he claimed he had, and white Americans
believed him, permitting Burgoyne to boast that his Great Lakes Indians
were led by "the very man who projected and executed with these very
nations the defeat of General Braddock."[3]

Burgoyne's attention to public opinion also influenced his route to
the Hudson River. He had originally planned to head from Ticonderoga
up Lake George and then sixteen miles overland to the Hudson. But his
army had chased part of the Ticonderoga garrison far up Wood Creek,
ten miles to the east, with his most advanced troops coming within
eleven miles of the Hudson. Practical considerations still dictated having most of the army backtrack nearly thirty miles to Ticonderoga for

the much easier route up Lake George. But like many who fought in this war, Burgoyne understood the importance of perception, specifically the "impressions which a retrograde motion is apt to make upon the minds both of enemies and friends." He marched on.[4]

In May and June 1777, William Howe made several efforts to lure the Continental Army down from Morristown and Middlebrook, its strongholds in the hills of central New Jersey. Small parties occasionally raided the plains for food but always returned before the redcoats and Germans could draw them into an open-field fight. Finally Howe tired of playing cat to Washington's mouse and set off for Philadelphia. With a population of about 25,000, Philadelphia rivaled New York as the largest city in the country, and it harbored numerous Loyalists.[5] Howe chose not to take the direct land route southwest across New Jersey (as Interstate 95 does today), because he did not want to expose his right flank to the enemy or force his soldiers to cross the Delaware River under fire. Instead they would travel by water.

The troops sailed out of New York Harbor on July 23 in a fleet of more than 260 vessels. They expected to disembark on the west bank of the Delaware and then march upriver to Philadelphia. But on July 30, Capt. Andrew Snape Hamond, the Royal Navy commander in the area, informed the Howe brothers that the rebels defending the river had assembled a wide array of warships, including fire ships and floating batteries. A British landing might be attended with heavy casualties.[6] So at William Howe's request, his brother's fleet took the soldiers all the way south into Chesapeake Bay, then north toward a landing in Maryland. By forgoing the direct route up the Delaware, Gen. Howe added more than 250 miles to his trip, but they were water miles, and he had greatly increased his chance of landing unopposed.

Burgoyne's expedition was going better than Howe's, in part because his Native American allies not only brought him frequent updates on the Continentals planning to block his path but also stopped deserters from carrying vital information in the opposite direction. During the Revolutionary War, British and German deserters typically ran to the Americans, while most of the men who deserted the rebel ranks simply went home. Yet at least a thousand U.S. soldiers offered their services to the British, with one officer in Brunswick, New Jersey, reporting in May 1777 that deserters from the U.S. army "come in by hundreds."

Soldiers caught trying to switch sides in either direction were hanged, but many were willing to take the risk, since those who got in safely were richly compensated for insight on their former comrades' numbers and disposition. But Burgoyne's secrets were safe. As Benedict Arnold noted, British soldiers were "prevented from deserting [to the Americans] by the Indians between us, so that every source of Information is in a manner cut off." Indians also prevented the Continentals from sending out scouts.[7]

Yet it was also one of Burgoyne's native auxiliaries who inadvertently helped to seal his fate. On its way south, a Wyandot scouting party surprised an American picket, capturing a soldier named Samuel Standish, who later claimed to have been present on July 27, when the warriors entered the recently-evacuated Fort Edward on the Hudson River. There they found Jane McCrea, who had come to meet her fiancé, one of Burgoyne's Loyalist rangers. The ranger had offered a reward to whoever would escort McCrea to him, so two Wyandots seized her. But then, according to Standish, the two quarreled, and one settled the matter by shooting her from her horse. The Wyandots told a different story: that Americans had fired on the natives from a distance, accidentally killing McCrea. Nearly every white soldier in both armies credited Standish's version. Burgoyne assembled his indigenous auxiliaries for an insulting tirade that provoked many to decamp, and McCrea joined men like Joseph Warren and Hugh Mercer on the new nation's roll of martyrs.[8] Horsemen rapidly spread her story, with one newspaper account appearing more than 150 miles away just four days after the attack. Dozens more followed. Yet only *one* Whig newspaper covered the murders of the neutralist Shawnee headman Cornstalk and his son at an American fort on the Ohio River later in 1777.[9] Throughout New York and New England, militiamen who had agonized over whether to join the fight against Burgoyne now rushed to do so.

Even as the enemy's ranks swelled, Burgoyne faced what he had known all along would be his tallest challenge: keeping his troops and livestock fed until they once again reached the head of navigation at Albany. A year earlier, Gen. Howe had worried that the Continental soldiers would discover the wisdom of "retiring a few miles back from the navigable rivers," where "ours cannot follow them from the difficulties I expect to meet with in procuring land carriage."[10] With no help from the Americans, Burgoyne had placed himself in precisely that predicament.

First up: the twenty-five miles from Skenesborough south to Fort

Edward on the Hudson. The army's cannon and other heavy equipment and supplies would begin this leg of the trip on Wood Creek, but when it gave out, everything would have to be transferred to wagons. The rebels strewed countless obstacles in their pursuers' path, tearing up bridges and damming and diverting streams to flood river bottoms, at one point forcing Burgoyne's engineers to build a causeway two miles long. Militiamen chopped down pairs of trees on opposite sides of the path so that they intertwined in impenetrable tangles. Clearing the road consumed two weeks and much of the invaders' food—the real point of all the barricades. But contrary to myth, they completed their march from Skenesborough to Fort Edward in just five days. More effective than any of the rebels' physical obstacles was their successful removal or destruction of most of the region's forage and draft animals, aggravating Burgoyne's already severe transportation crisis.[11]

Shortly before he entered Fort Edward, Burgoyne learned that Barrimore St. Leger's seven hundred British, Loyalist, and German troops had completed their westward journey to Lake Ontario, where they merged with about eight hundred Mississauga and Iroquois warriors led by the Mohawk sachem Joseph Brant (Thayendanegea).[12] Although several Iroquois warriors, including Brant, had fought in the war almost from the start, the nation as a whole stayed out throughout 1775 and 1776, despite tremendous pressure from several British officials to take their side. In 1776, when Indian agent John Butler convened the Iroquois at Fort Niagara and called them "foolish" for giving the Whigs just what they wanted by remaining neutral, the tart reply came from Guyasuta, who had recently received a silver gorget (throat armor) and a colonel's commission from the Continental Congress. Given that the British were trying "to bring us into an unnecessary war," he told Butler, "we must be Fools indeed to imagine that they regard us or our Interest." Other officers, especially Governor Carleton, were initially reluctant to field native warriors. But as soon as Burgoyne returned to Quebec with his plan to invade New York, British and Iroquois leaders agreed that the time had come to activate their alliance.[13]

Once Brant's and St. Leger's forces linked up, they turned east toward Albany. Their first destination was the Great Carrying Place, connecting Wood Creek, which drains into Lake Ontario, to the headwaters of the Mohawk River, which flows east to the Hudson. Reaching the eastern terminus of the portage on August 3, the troops laid siege to Fort Stanwix, which the rebels had renamed Fort Schuyler.[14]

Although most of the Iroquois league allied with the British, two member nations, the Oneidas and Tuscaroras, mostly sided with the rebels. Not only had the Oneidas long been targets of intense missionization by New Light Presbyterians from Connecticut, they believed their only chance of preserving their land lay in supporting the Whigs, who seemed sure to win. Oneidas carried word of the Anglo-Indian siege of Fort Schuyler fifty miles down the Mohawk River to Tryon County militia commander Nicholas Herkimer. He and an eight-hundred-man army that included at least sixty Oneida warriors immediately rode west, preceded only by Joseph Brant's sister Mary, who informed Brant and St. Leger that they were coming. St. Leger directed Brant, British Indian agent and army captain John Butler, two companies of Loyalist rangers, and about four hundred Iroquois to head toward Herkimer and set a trap.[15]

On the night of August 5–6, the Whig militia camped one day short of the besieged Fort Schuyler. Herkimer sent garrison commander Peter Gansevoort a request to have some of his men sally out to attack St. Leger's soldiers the following morning, preventing them from concentrating against the relief force. Gansevoort was to signal receipt of Herkimer's message by firing three cannon at dawn on August 6. When the sun rose on a silent morning, Herkimer hesitated, fearing his messenger had not made it through. But then his officers accused him of cowardice and even treason—he had a brother serving under St. Leger—whereupon he led his soldiers toward the besiegers' camp.

The militiamen's path west ran parallel to the Mohawk River and just south of it. Five miles short of Fort Schuyler, near the Oneida town of Oriske, it crossed, at right angles, a two-hundred-yard-wide ravine cut by a stream flowing north into the Mohawk. The floor of the ravine was a boggy morass, so in traversing it the soldiers had to keep to the narrow corduroy road. As the head of the column emerged from the ravine, the Iroquois, Mississaugas, and Loyalists simultaneously attacked its front and flanks. Butler would later disclaim any role in coordinating the August 6 attack. "We were immediately formed by the Seneka Chiefs, who took the lead in this Action," he wrote.[16]

Herkimer's troops were easy marks for Indians crouching behind trees. Whenever a militiaman got off a shot, he gave away both his position and his need to reload, and an Iroquois warrior would rush him. Seeking to disrupt this strategy, Herkimer instructed the men to pair up, with one reloading while the other leveled his weapon. Others he deployed in circles around trees so that at least their backs would be covered. Blacksnake, a Seneca warrior, recalled years later that the blood shed at the Battle of Oriskany—the first official involvement of the Iroquois confederacy in the American War of Independence—seemed like "a Stream Running Down on the Desending ground."[17] By one estimate, half of the eight hundred Whig militiamen and Oneidas became casualties. Of these, at least two hundred, including Herkimer, suffered mortal wounds, and the survivors fled back down the Mohawk.[18]

In sharp contrast, only about thirty Loyalists and thirty Indians were killed or wounded. But St. Leger understood that the natives' loss was immense according to the more exacting "Indian computation," which reckoned every death a catastrophe.[19] As the historian Barbara Graymont notes, "The Senecas alone had five chiefs killed: Hasquesahah, Gahnahage, Dahwahdeho, Dahgaiownd, and Dahohjoedoh." Equally dispiriting to St. Leger's native allies was that for the first time since the formation of the Iroquois league hundreds of years earlier, one nation, the Oneidas, had gone to war against the rest. In the aftermath of the Oriskany ambush, an Iroquois band destroyed Oriske, and the Oneidas responded in kind. Still, such was both sides' abhorrence of this Iroquois civil war that the Oriskany ambush appears to have been both its first major battle and its last.[20]

The Iroquois and Missisauga warriors were further discouraged when they returned to their camp outside Fort Schuyler to discover that the Americans had scored one success on August 6. With several hundred British troops joining the Iroquois in ambushing Herkimer's militia and as many more improving the supply road from Lake Ontario, St. Leger had left only a handful of men to guard his camp—and none to protect the property of his native allies. At midday, Gansevoort, having finally received Herkimer's plea for a diversion, sent three hundred men into the deserted Iroquois/Mississauga camp, where they seized both military equipment and personal effects, including packs of furs intended for sale and all of the warriors' clothing. (Both nations' warriors typically went into battle nearly naked.) Disconsolate at the loss of their belongings, countrymen, and national unity, St. Leger's native allies began to leave him.[21]

TWO DAYS BEFORE THE Battle of Oriskany, on August 4, Burgoyne made a fateful decision aimed at smoothing St. Leger's path. Until the principal British invasion force drew much closer to Albany, the Continentals were free to concentrate against St. Leger's detachment, possibly annihilating it. But once Burgoyne posed a credible threat to the Continentals, they would have to stay out of St. Leger's way for fear of "putting themselves between two fires."[22]

So Burgoyne's troops needed to speed up—but how? The moment they passed the latitude of Fort George at the southern tip of Lake George, its American garrison ran off, allowing them to transport their food, cannon, and other material southward by water. But all these supplies still had to travel sixteen miles overland from Fort George over to Fort Edward, and it took the soldiers fifteen days to cart over just four days' worth of food. Still more portages lay ahead, around the Hudson River falls, and each would be a bottleneck, with the oxen and horses having to shuttle back and forth between take-out and put-in. The lengthening supply line would also eat away at Burgoyne's army, for he would have to detach troops either to escort every supply convoy or garrison a chain of protective forts.[23]

This was the context in which Burgoyne decided to send part of his army east to Bennington in southwestern Vermont. Farmers throughout "a large tract of country" herded their horses and cattle to Bennington's stockyards, whence they were periodically driven nearly two hundred miles south to the main Continental Army camp in Morristown, New Jersey.[24] Burgoyne believed a side trip to Bennington would actually speed him southward. A thousand additional draft animals and half that many wagons would enable his teamsters to dispense with the shuttle system, complete each portage in a single trip, and quickly amass reserves of food and forage.[25] In a sense, Burgoyne wanted to rustle *camels*. Once self-sufficient in food, his army could cut its tether to Fort George and sweep south, perhaps reaching Albany within a few days. That was why he ordered the Bennington raiders to bring back as much food as they could, but "above all, horses."[26]

Historians criticize Burgoyne for giving command of the livestock raid to Lt. Col. Friedrich Baum, who spoke little English. Actually, then as now, army officers made do with translators, and Baum's lack of English does not appear to have contributed to his fate. The choice of Baum at least fit with another decision Burgoyne made at the same time: the single largest element in the expedition would be 320 Brunswickers, who would be accompanied by another 400 Loyalists, Indians, and Canadians but only a few dozen British riflemen and artillerymen. Acutely conscious that his most precious resource was people, Burgoyne was determined to preserve his dwindling supply of redcoats.[27]

The approximately seven hundred participants in the Bennington raid would be more than Baum had ever commanded. Many of Burgoyne's other officers had more experience, but by the same token they were less expendable.[28]

The expedition got off to a bad start. When Baum's Native American allies brought in several captured horses, he refused to pay for them, and the warriors in their anger cut the horses' hamstrings.[29] On the morning of August 14, still nine miles from the Bennington stockyards, Baum learned that they were defended by two thousand militiamen: triple his own strength. He alerted Burgoyne, but honor prevented him from requesting reinforcements. He did not even seek out a defensible location to await the relief column that he nonetheless expected Burgoyne to send. Convinced that the militia would scatter at the sight of German infantry, he pushed on.[30]

Baum's detachment never made it to Vermont, for a mile and a half west of the state line, it ran into New Hampshire militiamen commanded by Gen. John Stark. The New Hampshiremen were supposed to have left the region more than a week earlier but had been delayed by a point of personal honor. Stark's remarkable courage at the Battle of Bunker Hill had earned him a colonel's commission in the Continental Army, but in February 1777, at the same time Congress refused to advance Benedict Arnold from brigadier to major general, it passed over Stark for promotion to brigadier, and he resigned. When New Hampshire assemblymen sent a militia army to fight Burgoyne, they begged Stark to command it, and he agreed on the condition that he would report only to them, not to Congress or its generals.[31] Once the New Hampshire militiamen reached western Vermont, they were directed to join the Continentals retreating down the Hudson River as Burgoyne advanced. Stark refused and was immediately reported to Congress, which denounced New Hampshire's unusual arrangement with him. But this would not be the delegates' final comment on the matter.[32]

Gen. Benjamin Lincoln asked Stark and his men to join him in striking the British rear, and they agreed. But like Burgoyne, the New Hampshiremen were short on food and wagons, and they did not move out until August 14. And then just as they were setting off, they learned that Baum was headed their way.[33]

Stark's men hurried west to meet the invaders and found them just at sunset, whereupon both armies fell back and camped, ready to do battle the following day. But a hard rain fell throughout August 15, preventing

either side from attacking and giving Baum time to dig in. The delay
should also have allowed Baum's reinforcements—642 Brunswickers
under Lt. Col. Heinrich von Breymann—ample opportunity to reach
him. Burgoyne had given Breymann strict orders: if he and Baum had
to retreat, they must hold on to every wagon and draft animal they had
collected. That way they would "give the enemy no chance to triumph
over us, and no cause for discouragement to the Indians."[34]

Muddy roads, cumbersome artillery, hilly terrain, an inadequate
guide, and perhaps long-standing animosity between Baum and Breymann slowed the relief party to less than half a mile an hour.[35] Meanwhile
Baum made the elemental mistake of dispersing his troops in the face of
superior numbers, posting most in an arrowhead-shaped redoubt atop a
hill but also establishing various satellite positions, including, incredibly,
one on the opposite bank of the Walloomsac River, near the enemy camp.

On August 16, Stark also divided his army and attacked from all directions, picking off Baum's posts two or three at a time. Baum's native
allies left him.[36] The Brunswickers crouched behind the log breastworks
they had constructed the previous day, but in these woods their assailants
could also take cover. Many of Baum's troops ran off, and after he was
mortally wounded, the rest followed. Some of the most vicious fighting
was among Americans. Lt. Col. John Peters of the Queen's Loyal Rangers received a bayonet wound from his old schoolmate Jeremiah Post and
saved himself only by shooting him dead.[37]

Breymann's relief party did not arrive until nearly dusk, and by that
time Stark had also been reinforced. Breymann tried to organize an orderly retreat, but panic turned it into a rout. By day's end, only about
thirty Whig militiamen were dead, with forty injured, but approximately
two hundred of Baum's and Breymann's troops had been killed. Another
seven hundred were captured.[38]

As the survivors of the two expeditions staggered into Burgoyne's
camp, many of his remaining Indian auxiliaries concluded that the whole
enterprise was doomed and struck for home. Others soon followed, for
hunting season was coming on.[39] Members of Congress learned of the
Battle of Bennington (which had actually been fought entirely in New
York, even as defined by Vermonters) three days after criticizing John
Stark's special arrangement with New Hampshire officials. Now they
made him a brigadier general.[40] The American victory also gave the leaders of both armies a newfound respect for militia. A year earlier, Washington had insisted that "to place any dependance upon Militia, is, assuredly,

resting upon a broken staff," but he now echoed Schuyler's praise of Stark and his men for having "pushed the enemy from one work to another, thrown up on advantageous ground, and from different posts, with spirit and fortitude, until they gained a complete victory over them."[41]

Burgoyne's attempt to use Bennington's horses to meet the challenge of overland supply had led instead to his first setback, in turn contributing to his surrender two months later and thus to French entry into the war. Right up until August 16, the general's correspondence exuded confidence that he would succeed without anyone's help. But after Bennington, as his troops spent a month using the inefficient shuttle system to stockpile the additional month's worth of food required for the journey to Albany, he began attributing his troubles to William Howe's troops' failure to draw off his adversaries by ascending the Hudson, as Howe had been asked but not ordered to do.[42]

While Burgoyne tarried on the Upper Hudson, Benedict Arnold, whom Washington had cajoled back into the army, led a second American relief party up the Mohawk Valley toward the besieged Fort Schuyler. On his way west, Arnold sent a white man and at least one Iroquois ahead to spread false and alarming rumors about both the size of his force and its proximity to the British besiegers' camp. St. Leger was already considering abandoning his expedition, and the imminent arrival of the American relief force settled the matter. The British later acknowledged having fallen for Arnold's trick, and historians generally assume that the Iroquois and Missisaugas who fled with them were also taken in. They point out that one of the operatives spreading Arnold's false reports was known to be insane—and that many Eastern Woodlands Indians, including the Iroquois, respected mentally disturbed people as prophets.[43]

St. Leger interpreted Iroquois and Missisauga intentions differently, at least in retrospect. Pointing out that his Indian allies had joined him primarily in the expectation of plunder, only to have their own packs stolen by the American troops who sallied out from Fort Schuyler on August 6, the lieutenant colonel stated that when he refused to make good the Indians' losses, they found a way to reimburse themselves. St. Leger initially planned an orderly withdrawal from his camp outside Fort Schuyler. But then Iroquois headmen "artfully caused messengers to come in one after the other with accounts of the nearer approaches of the rebels." The redcoats felt they had no choice but to drop everything and run—whereupon the Iroquois and Missisaugas finally got their plunder.[44]

Others did, too. After the Battle of Oriskany, Joseph Brant's mother,

Margaret, and sister Molly—now marked women—fled the Mohawk town of Canajoharie, taking refuge in Fort Niagara. The Whigs who joined the Oneidas in pillaging their home were at once angry and gratified to discover fine furniture and clothing, along with jewelry and silverware.[45]

Even though St. Leger had been forced to turn back, Henry Clinton considered his western path to Albany superior to Burgoyne's, and he believed the entire army ought to have used it. It required a much shorter portage, Clinton observed to a fellow British general, and in sharp contrast to the Champlain–Hudson corridor, "the whole country till you come within a few miles of Albany is Indian, and your allies."[46]

BACK IN JULY, GEORGE Washington had spotted opportunity in Burgoyne's penchant for "acting in Detachment." Whig forces might be able to pick off the various portions of his army one at a time and thereby "inspirit the people and do away much of their present Anxiety."[47] U.S. fighters had achieved essentially that result during the third week of August at Bennington and Fort Schuyler. And now they could focus on Gen. Burgoyne.

Burgoyne did not think Washington would be able to spare enough Continental soldiers to give the army resisting the invading Brunswickers and redcoats anything like parity. He was right, but he drastically underestimated the amount of help the Continentals would receive from local militiamen, who swelled their ranks to more than eight thousand, an ever-increasing advantage over the six thousand healthy infantrymen Burgoyne could still muster after garrisoning Fort Ticonderoga and losing troops to disease, desertion, and the New Hampshire militia.[48] The rebels were motivated by rage at the invaders (especially after the murder of Jane McCrea), by the prospect of success (especially after their victories over Baum and St. Leger)—and by a change in their leadership. Philip Schuyler, who owned the entire region where the northern army would fight its climactic battles against Burgoyne, was widely seen as a haughty aristocrat. Congress dismissed him not for that offense but for losing Fort Ticonderoga, and on August 19, he handed the reins to Horatio Gates. By failing to secure Sugar Loaf Hill, Gates had unwittingly helped pave the way for Schuyler's dismissal and his own elevation. And northern rebels finally had a commander they admired.[49]

A WEEK AFTER GATES took command of the northern army, on August 25, more than fifteen thousand British troops disembarked at the mouth of the Elk River, near the northern tip of Chesapeake Bay. For more than two centuries, Howe has been pilloried for sailing his army from Brunswick, about fifty miles northeast of Philadelphia, to the Elk River, about the same distance southwest of the city. Cheek by jowl in the transports, dozens of soldiers and hundreds of horses had sickened and died en route.[50] But Howe had saved his men from having to land on the west bank of the Delaware under fire. His only regret about not marching westward across New Jersey was that it would have lured the Continentals out of their Watchung Mountains lair, opening a corridor by which "the Seneca Indians [could] have joined us."[51]

Soon the British and German soldiers were on the road to Philadelphia. As they passed through the abandoned town of Head of Elk (modern Elkton), Maryland, they lost their way, and a Hessian officer later reported that "men were sent out in all directions until finally a Negro was found, and the army had to march according to his directions." Washington had viewed the British army's extended detour as a grand feint, but once he realized his error, he led his sixteen thousand soldiers down the west bank of the Delaware to meet it. On August 24, the Continentals staged a dramatic march through the politically divided Philadelphia in hopes of exerting "some influence on the minds of the dissaffected there."[52]

Spectator John Adams found much to criticize in the soldiers' form. "They dont step exactly in Time" he complained. "They dont hold up their Heads, quite erect, nor turn out their Toes, so exactly as they ought." Yet their sheer numbers impressed him, as "They marched Twelve deep, and yet took up above two Hours in passing by." Washington's contribution to the performance was to give strict orders regarding the army's female workers, whom he had always considered "a clog upon every movement": "Not a woman belonging to the army is to be seen with the troops on their march thro' the city."[53]

Washington, who rode at the head of the procession alongside his new general and companion, the marquis de Lafayette, found an ideal place to block Howe's path: Brandywine Creek, which flows southward into the Delaware River twenty-five miles southwest of Philadelphia. The swift-moving Brandywine was not really a creek; at Elizabeth Chadds's ferry and ford, where the road from Maryland to Philadelphia crossed it, it was 150 feet wide. Over the centuries it had cut a deep valley, leaving high bluffs on both sides; Howe's soldiers would be vulnerable both as they crossed the river and as they worked their way up its east bank.[54]

Washington established his center at Chadds Ford and covered the downriver crossings one mile to the south, where the bluffs became cliffs and tributaries widened the creek, making a British crossing unlikely. In addition, he sent detachments as far upriver as Buffington's Ford. With no natural anchor for his upriver flank, he placed pickets farther up the Brandywine and sent scouting parties across to the west bank. But for some reason he did not bend the northern segment of his front line back toward the center to face a possible flank attack.[55]

Howe knew frontal assaults rarely succeeded, least of all on North America's forested hills, and he and other British generals had begun adapting as best they could to the terrain. Many lined their men up in "open order," with space between them so they could navigate around trees without breaking ranks. Several had also faced up to the folly of lining up their men in open fields for firefights against Americans crouching behind fences. When attacking, they ordered their men not to pause to fire even a single volley but instead to rush the enemy with their bayonets.[56] Yet the tactic that had defeated the rebels on Long Island in 1776 was an old one, the flank attack, and at Brandywine Creek, Howe once again discovered that his opponent had failed to secure one of his flanks.

Dividing his army into two columns, Howe sent one, under Gen. Wilhelm von Knyphausen, to engage the enemy center at Chadds Ford. At 5 a.m. on September 11, the commander-in-chief set off with the other column, commanded by Lord Cornwallis, on a long march north. By 2 p.m., Cornwallis's troops, with Hessian Capt. Johann Ewald leading the advance guard, had crossed the Brandywine's two forks above the last guarded ford.[57]

Throughout the morning of September 11, Washington received conflicting reports on possible enemy activity to the northward. These ought to have rudely reminded him of how the British had turned his left flank a year earlier at Long Island. And they should have caused him to reinforce his right. Instead the American, still stuck in forward, exulted, for it seemed that his opponent had given him the very gift he had tried to create eighteen months earlier by luring the British up Dorchester Heights: a fatally diminished force at British headquarters. Washington began moving most of his center across the Brandywine. But then Pennsylvania militia Maj. Joseph Spear brought word that the entire British army had actually remained at Chadds Ford. Washington was not going to compel a portion of his troops to face a force that large with a river at their back, so he returned them to the east bank.[58]

At about 2 p.m., Maj. Spear's report was itself contradicted by a Whig

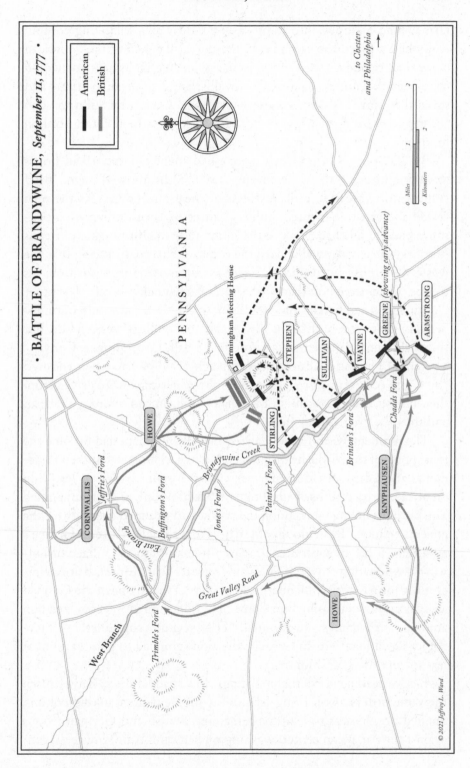

· BATTLE OF BRANDYWINE, *September 11, 1777* **·**

American
British

PENNSYLVANIA

Birmingham Meeting House

to Chester
and Philadelphia

GREENE (showing early advance)

STEPHEN

SULLIVAN

WAYNE

ARMSTRONG

STIRLING

HOWE

Brandywine Creek

Brinton's Ford

Chadds Ford

Painter's Ford

Jones's Ford

KNYPHAUSEN

Buffington's Ford

Jeffrie's Ford

CORNWALLIS

East Branch

Great Valley Road

HOWE

West Branch

Trimble's Ford

0 Miles 1 2

0 Kilometers 2

© 2021 Jeffrey L. Ward

farmer who galloped into camp saying Cornwallis's flanking column really had crossed the creek far to the north. If much of the American center had remained west of the Brandywine, its flanks and rear would have been defenseless against Cornwallis; Spear's mistaken report had saved the army.[59] Washington now instructed Gen. John Sullivan, who commanded his right wing, to head north to face the flanking column head-on.

By 2:30 p.m., Cornwallis's troops had spent ten and a half hours marching fifteen miles in sweltering heat, and he allowed them a brief respite atop Osborne Hill, just east of the Brandywine. As the men rested and ate, one spotted Sullivan's three divisions lining up on another knoll a mile and a half to the south, near the Birmingham Friends Meetinghouse. Cornwallis gave the order to charge. Noticing that the western extremity of Greene's line was still moving into position, his troops concentrated on that weak spot, which quickly broke. The other Continentals had had no time to dig in, so they were not only outnumbered but exposed, both in their front and now on their western side. But they held out for more than an hour and a half; Gen. Thomas Conway, a veteran of countless European campaigns, said he had never endured "So Close & Severe a fire." Five times the Americans were driven from their hilltop, only to regain it. But finally Sullivan had to order a retreat, and the men fired as they fled.[60]

The moment Washington realized that Birmingham had become the focal point of the battle, he dispatched Nathanael Greene with reinforcements and asked an elderly farmer named Joseph Brown to lead him on ahead. Brown refused until one of Washington's aides manhandled him onto his horse, whereupon the two set off at a mad gallop, with the general yelling, "Push along, old man! Push along!"[61] It took Greene's men only forty-five minutes to march five miles to the village of Dilworth, where they covered Sullivan's retreat. Years earlier, before emigrating, John Peter Muhlenberg had briefly served in one of the German army units now pursuing him. Some of his old comrades recognized him among their enemies and shouted, "Hier kommt teufel Piet!"—"Here comes Devil Pete!" Even Greene's division soon had to give way, but at least in an orderly fashion.[62]

Before heading north that morning, Howe had left Gen. Knyphausen the same orders as on Long Island: the moment the flanking column opened fire, he was to lead the remaining British and German troops against the American center. Washington had cannibalized his own center to shore up his threatened flank, and it soon dissolved. The entire Continental army retreated under fire until darkness ended the chase. Later Howe would claim, plausibly, that with "an hour's more daylight," he could have wrought the enemy's "total overthrow."[63]

Washington's error on the left bank of the Brandywine on September 11, 1777, duplicated Col. Rall's on the left bank of the Delaware on Christmas night 1776. Neither could imagine half of the enemy soldiers stationed on the opposite bank of the river marching far to the north, then crossing the river and doubling back south, revealing themselves only with their first volley.[64] Washington cannot be faulted for failing to extend his defensive line farther up the Brandywine, for at nine miles it was already too attenuated, and even if he had run it still farther north, Cornwallis always had the option of crossing at the next ford up. But Washington should have done before the battle what he ended up doing in its midst: pivot his upriver regiments back to face north. That would have given his troops time to throw up breastworks or at least avail themselves of existing features such as stone fences. Howe might still have won the battle, but at least, as at Breed's Hill an exorbitant price. As it was, the Americans suffered at least 1,100 casualties (including young Lafayette, wounded in the leg)—twice as many as the enemy.[65]

CHAPTER 24

Take No Quarter

Fall 1777

IMMEDIATELY UPON TAKING COMMAND OF THE NORTHERN DIVISION of the Continental Army, Horatio Gates set it in motion toward Burgoyne. On September 9, the Continentals reached the crest of Bemis Heights, two hundred feet above the west bank of the Hudson and three miles north of the town of Stillwater. They began building breastworks.[1]

Burgoyne learned of Gates's approach just as his army finally finished laying in a month's supply of food. On September 10, the British and German soldiers began crossing to the west bank of the Hudson at Saratoga (modern-day Schuylerville), New York, for the final push to Albany. A week later, they halted just three miles north of Bemis Heights.[2]

The perennial challenge of feeding the soldiers had given rise both to Baum's ill-fated expedition to Bennington and Burgoyne's month-long layover on the east bank of the Hudson; it now led to the imperial army's first contact with the Continental soldiers blocking its path. On September 18, a group of British women and soldiers ventured five hundred yards south of the fortifications to dig potatoes. A Continental scouting party came upon them and let fly, killing or wounding fourteen and capturing twenty.[3]

The next day, September 19, Burgoyne led his troops forward. A week earlier and 240 miles to the south at Brandywine Creek, William Howe had once again demonstrated his aptitude for turning George Washington's flank. But Burgoyne planned nothing more elaborate than softening up the American lines with a cannonade and then barreling right through.[4]

Gates's initial response to the Anglo-Brunswick army's approach was to stick with the purely defensive strategy that had served the Americans so well.[5] But the instinctively aggressive Benedict Arnold badgered him

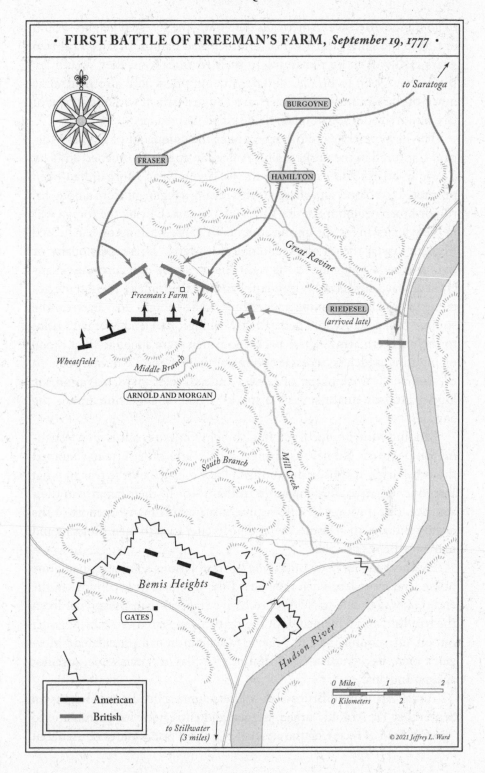

· FIRST BATTLE OF FREEMAN'S FARM, *September 19, 1777* ·

to Saratoga

BURGOYNE

FRASER

HAMILTON

Great Ravine

Freeman's Farm

RIEDESEL
(arrived late)

Wheatfield

Middle Branch

ARNOLD AND MORGAN

South Branch

Mill Creek

Bemis Heights

GATES

Hudson River

American
British

0 Miles   1   2
0 Kilometers   2

to Stillwater
(3 miles)

© 2021 Jeffrey L. Ward

to go on the offensive. Americans defending the forested heights would not have the same clear field of fire they had had on Breed's Hill two years earlier. And by remaining in their fortifications, they would lay themselves open to bombardment. Staying put would also neutralize much of the advantage the Americans had just gained with the arrival of five hundred additional fighters, all skilled woodsmen.

The newcomers were riflemen under the command of Daniel Morgan. Captured in the unsuccessful American attack on Quebec on New Year's Eve 1775 and exchanged the following year, Morgan had been promoted to colonel and charged with raising a regiment from among his rough-hewn neighbors in the Valley of Virginia. During the forage war in New Jersey in the spring and summer of 1777, Washington had helped Morgan master the art of psychological warfare. "Dress a Company or two of true Woods men in the right Indian style," the commander-in-chief advised his fellow Virginian, "and let them make the Attack accompanied with screaming and yelling as the Indians do." Later in the summer Benedict Arnold persuaded Washington to lend Morgan's rifles to the northern army. These backwoodsmen were adept at "that mode of Fighting which is necessary to make them a good Counterpoise to the Indians," Washington observed. Indeed, their mere arrival on the Upper Hudson might suffice to spark "a general Desertion among the Savages."[6]

Sending Morgan north might also help Gates recruit militia, Washington believed. Numerous farmers who might otherwise have joined the rebel army had been discouraged "not a little" by the fear of what Burgoyne's native allies might do to them—or to their families in their absence. But if Morgan's rifle regiment scared off many or most of the enemy Indians, then farmers would be likelier to grab their firelocks and make for Bemis Heights.[7]

By this time most of Burgoyne's First Nations auxiliaries had gone home, and more left when they heard the riflemen were coming. In the end, Gates was able to field more native fighters than Burgoyne. Even the handful who remained with the British "appeared very shy at going out on any scouting parties," just as Washington had anticipated.[8] Morgan's men, by contrast, were destined to play a crucial role, just not against Indians.

As the British and Brunswick soldiers approached Bemis Heights on September 19, Arnold "urged, begged and entreated" for permission to "give instead of receiving the attack." For three hours Gates refused, but finally he partially relented, allowing Morgan's men, working in tandem with Henry Dearborn's light infantry, to move forward. The American column soon collided with a detachment of British irregulars: Loyalists, Canadians, and a few Indians. Almost immediately, the riflemen brought down nearly all of the British officers and many of their men. The survivors ran, followed closely by Morgan's troops, who, showing more zeal than prudence, soon found themselves in enemy territory. They scattered, only to reassemble when Morgan blew his shrill "turkey-call."[9]

Most of this region was heavily wooded, but near the midpoint between the two armies, the British managed to position several cannon at the northern edge of a clearing that extended about 550 yards from north to south and 250 yards from east to west. These guns became the focal point of a three-hour contest. First the Americans would dash across the field, capturing the cannon and driving the enemy into the woods, and then the fugitives would regroup and fight their way back to the clearing. Meanwhile Morgan's riflemen, many perched in trees, picked off the British artillery crews. All but one of the officers and thirty-six of the forty-eight gunners were wounded or killed, and the cannon fell silent.[10]

One regiment in the British center suffered 80 percent casualties. On the American side, at least one woman joined the fight; weeks later, when a British officer came upon her corpse, she was still "grasping cartridges." The rebels were on the cusp of a decisive victory over the outnumbered redcoats when Baron Riedesel, who commanded Burgoyne's left wing down by the Hudson, came huffing up the river bluff with reinforcements and cannon. The German artillery crews began firing grapeshot into the rebels' right flank, forcing them to withdraw as night fell.[11]

Burgoyne had his troops build new fortifications right where they stood: only about a mile ahead of their previous lines. Given the difficulty of obtaining reinforcements, any battle in which the British took so little of the Americans' territory while sustaining comparable casualties must be accounted a defeat, and the hard fact of September 19 was that Burgoyne had lost about six hundred men—killed, wounded, and captured—compared to just over three hundred for the Americans.[12]

Very few Indians served on Burgoyne's side in the First Battle of Freeman's Farm, yet they had still influenced the outcome. Hundreds of militiamen—along with Gates's most valuable fighters, the Virginia rifles—had entered the Upper Hudson Valley for the express purpose of fighting Burgoyne's Indians. And thousands more were coming.

＊　　＊　　＊

Meanwhile in Pennsylvania, Howe's army marched north, roughly parallel to the Delaware, while Washington regrouped east of the Schuylkill River and then headed west, placing him due north of the British, where he posed a threat to their left flank. Howe headed north to confront the Continentals.

On the afternoon of September 16, just as the leading edges of the two armies met near the White Horse Tavern, a classic Nor'easter dumped torrential rain that rendered both sides' firelocks inoperable and turned the soil into an impenetrable muck, forbidding even a bayonet charge. Eighteenth-century soldiers carried their paper cartridges in leather pouches, and during the Battle of the Clouds, many of the Continentals' shoddily made cartridge boxes leaked, spoiling as many as 400,000 cartridges. Washington had no choice but to pull back to Yellow Springs, eleven miles to the north, leaving Howe free to cross the Schuylkill and enter Philadelphia. But he again hung back, apparently out of fear of being attacked from behind during the crossing, and his army camped just west of the river.[13]

The British had unknowingly pitched their tents just five miles southwest of the wartime equivalent of a gold mine. Valley Creek follows a northeasterly course, and near where it empties into the Schuylkill, the rebels had stashed 25 barrels of horseshoes, several thousand tomahawks, 3,800 barrels of flour, and other supplies on the grounds of an iron forge. On September 18, Lt. Col. Alexander Hamilton, Capt. Henry Lee, and a detachment of Continental cavalry galloped out to try to save the Valley Forge larder. As they rolled barrels onto barges, a much larger British cavalry detachment rode up, drove them off, and seized the supplies. The next day, Howe himself visited Valley Forge and the west bank of the Schuylkill. To test American defenses on the opposite bank, he sent an African American man across; he "pass'd over and return'd with only one Shot fired."[14]

On the evening of September 19, the Continentals profited from Howe's halt to ford the Schuylkill thirteen miles above Valley Forge. Only Anthony Wayne and his 1,500 men remained behind, hoping to raid the British baggage. Confident that the enemy knew nothing of him, Wayne camped near the Paoli Tavern, four miles southwest of Howe's camp. But American prisoners, Loyalists, and deserters alerted the British. Eighteenth-century people were surprisingly willing to travel overnight, though their roads and vehicles were unlit, but commanders rarely attacked between dusk and dawn, because it nearly always meant losing control of their troops. But Howe decided to make an exception. At 1 a.m. on September 21, Gen. Charles Grey and five thousand redcoats crept into Wayne's camp. In what survivors called the Paoli Massacre, they killed, wounded, or captured nearly three hundred Continentals. Grey boasted that his soldiers, only two or three of whom were killed, had executed the entire raid with bayonets, not firing a single shot because he had forbade them to carry flints.[15]

At sunrise on the 21st, Howe moved his soldiers to the Schuylkill River near Valley Forge.[16] As many as five thousand Continentals lined the east bank, ready to contest their crossing. As Johann Ewald noted, this stretch of the Schuylkill is "over eight hundred paces wide and about a half-man deep."[17] Wading over to the east bank—sinking into the muck, sliding on stones, and in some cases turning ankles—would slow the troops even more than the consecutive fences on Breed's Hill had two years earlier. It would take a miracle for them to complete the crossing without suffering at least as many casualties as on June 17, 1775.

But that night, Howe got his miracle. He and his soldiers awoke on September 22 to the astonishing discovery that Washington and his soldiers had moved off far to the north, leaving the Schuylkill fords all but undefended. Over the next two days, the entire Anglo-German army waded over without loss, then faced right and commenced a leisurely march south. On the 25th, Howe established his headquarters in Germantown, and the following morning Cornwallis's corps covered the remaining five miles to Philadelphia, occupying the town without firing a shot.

Why had the Americans moved out of Howe's way? Washington would later acknowledge that his adversary had fooled him with "a variety of perplexing Maneuvres." By "marching high up the Schuylkill" along its west bank, Howe had forced the Continentals to shadow him on their side of the river in order to remain between him and the U.S. supply depot in Reading, Pennsylvania, forty miles farther up. Another reason the rebels felt compelled to follow the British upriver was self-preservation. Had Howe crossed the Schuylkill north of them, he could have pivoted south and crashed through their right flank just as he had at Brandywine.[18]

Washington acknowledged learning several days later that the redcoats and Germans had actually marched only a few miles upriver—just enough to catapult the Continentals northward—before cutting back south and slipping across the unguarded Schuylkill at Valley Forge.

There was just one problem with Washington' description of his opponent's northward feint. Howe had not marched any troops up the Schuylkill. Apparently Washington's morbid fear of being outflanked again, just ten days after Brandywine, had caused him to lead his army upriver in imitation of a shadow.

Or did Washington only pretend that the British had duped him? Over the previous two weeks, his soldiers had suffered devastating losses at the Brandywine, White Horse Tavern, and Paoli Tavern. Did he fear that the enemy had annihilated the last vestiges of their self-confidence? If so, then placing them in Howe's path—even in such an advantageous position as the east bank of the Schuylkill—would set them up for another collapse. But Washington could not openly acknowledge having lost faith in the troops, so he devised an alternative excuse for failing to challenge the British: his own phantom fear that they had marched upriver. If accurate, this explanation for Washington's perplexing maneuver indicates that he had become a very different person from the glory hound of the 1750s and land speculator of the 1760s. In order to preserve his army's reputation, he had sacrificed his own.[19]

LESS THAN TWO WEEKS after not contesting Howe's crossing of the Schuylkill, Washington decided to take the offensive.

The British military commanders' belief that the burden of taking territory fell on them allowed the rebels the luxury of playing defense, firing from cover and generally inflicting disproportionate casualties, even when they had to give ground. The one shining exception to the Americans' defensive posture had been their surprise attack on Trenton, and echoes of that triumph rippled through Washington's plan to strike the main enemy camp at Germantown, five miles north of Philadelphia. The harried and defeated Continentals would once again exploit the enemy's assumption that they were too "dispirited" (as one British captain called them) to mount an assault. In October 1777 as in December 1776, the Americans would improve their chances of surprising their enemies by spending the previous day far enough away to lull them into complacency, only to close the distance with a long overnight march. Col. Rall's sense that the Continental Army was on the brink of dissolution had dissuaded him from ringing Trenton with redoubts, and Howe reached a similar conclusion for a different reason. Understanding, as did most commanders on both sides of this conflict, the vital importance of public opinion, Howe feared that constructing fortifications north of Germantown would "induce an opinion of inferiority." So he built none.[20]

Another factor in Washington's favor was that he had just received four thousand reinforcements, giving him eight thousand regular soldiers and three thousand militiamen. Howe, on the other hand, had sent six thousand troops off to occupy Philadelphia, begin clearing the rebel forts blocking the Delaware, and, in the meantime, escort supply trains up the west bank. These detachments left him only about nine thousand soldiers at Germantown—and gave Washington roughly the same numerical advantage Howe had enjoyed at Brandywine Creek. The Virginian also had a more personal reason for proceeding with the attack. Americans were just learning of the battle at Freeman's Farm on September 19, and most considered it a victory for the northern Continental Army. Now it was Washington's turn.[21]

As at Trenton, Washington divided his assault force into columns—this time, no fewer than five. One marched down the west bank of the Schuylkill to fire shot and shell over the river at the redcoats in Philadelphia, ideally tying them down. The other four followed roughly parallel roads south toward Germantown. Though the easternmost and westernmost columns were nearly five miles apart, all four were to attack at the same instant: 5 a.m. on October 4.[22]

The excessive complexity of the plan became clear even before the first British picket came into view. As Gen. John Sullivan reported, "a Thick Fog which being rendered still more So by the Smoke of the Cannon & musketry prevented our Troops from Discovering the motions of the Enemy or Acting in Concert with Each other." A Maryland colonel, perhaps recalling all the talk about the "providential" mist that had helped the Americans escape Long Island a year earlier, stated that the "thick foggy air" seemed to be "designd by Providence to favor the Brittish."[23]

Sullivan's column reached the enemy an hour late—but long before any of the others. Hessian jägers tied up the American militiamen descending the east bank of the Schuylkill. On the opposite or eastern side of the battlefield (the American far left), another militia column, one thousand men under Gen. William Smallwood, had more miles to cover than the others and did not arrive until after the battle. Just to the right of Smallwood, Nathanael Greene's column, comprising two-thirds of the American army, was led astray by its guide and arrived forty-five minutes after the fighting began. Until then, Sullivan commanded the only American column on the battlefield.

Two British light infantry regiments encamped north of Germantown

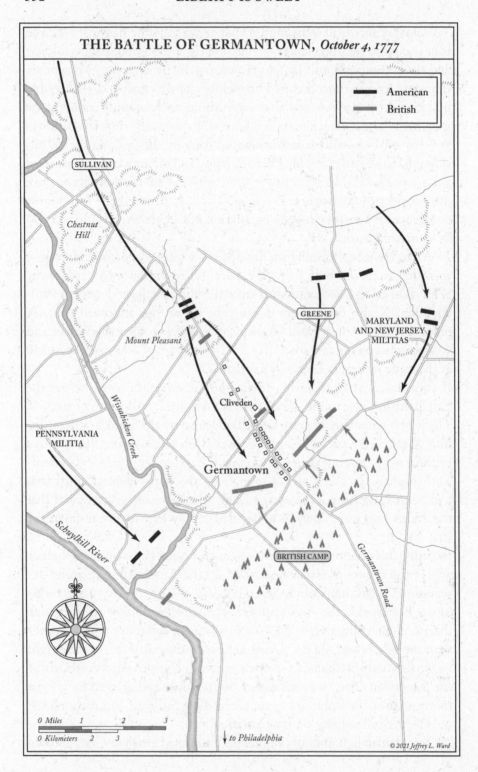

THE BATTLE OF GERMANTOWN, *October 4, 1777*

American
British

SULLIVAN

Chestnut Hill

GREENE

MARYLAND AND NEW JERSEY MILITIAS

Mount Pleasant

Cliveden

Wissahickon Creek

PENNSYLVANIA MILITIA

Germantown

Schuylkill River

Germantown Road

BRITISH CAMP

0 Miles   1   2   3
0 Kilometers   2   3

↓ to Philadelphia

© 2021 Jeffrey L. Ward

had picked up ambiguous intelligence that the Continentals might be coming and were prepared for them. They yielded to superior numbers, but only gradually, grateful for the chance to employ the defense-in-depth strategy that had served the rebels so well since Pell's Point. Making a brief stand "at Every Fence wall & Ditch they passed," they inflicted heavy casualties on their assailants and bought their comrades time to organize.[24] Anthony Wayne's soldiers, bent on avenging the Paoli Massacre, captured several redcoats and refused them quarter. Officers "exerted themselves to save many of the poor wretches," Wayne reported, "but to little purpose."[25]

As the Americans came close to surrounding Britain's 40th Regiment, its colonel, Thomas Musgrave, led about a hundred troops into Cliveden, Benjamin Chew's country home. Like many buildings in the area, Cliveden had stone walls that were "almost impenetrable by Cannon."[26] Minutes later, Washington arrived on the scene and asked an impromptu council of war whether he should detour around the obstruction or take the time to capture it. Henry Knox, who had spent the months leading up to the war poring over military manuals in his Boston bookstore, pressed the ancient doctrine that "it would be unmilitary to leave a castle in our rear," and he eventually prevailed. It was not a stupid mistake, but it was costly. Washington wasted a precious hour and dozens of lives in the ultimately unsuccessful siege of Cliveden. And the Continentals' battle against Musgrave helped turn the tide against them.[27]

Suddenly, Wayne's division, which had proceeded past Cliveden, turned around and retreated. Wayne would later claim that his soldiers had decided, without orders, to assist in capturing Chew's mansion. But in a letter to his wife just two days after the battle, he explained the about-face differently. Wayne's division constituted the left (eastern) flank of Sullivan's column. Detecting troops on his own left (these would later prove to be some of Greene's men) and assuming the British had outflanked him, Wayne had himself ordered the withdrawal.[28] Either way, Wayne's retreat cost the Americans their victory. British and German soldiers detected it and set off in pursuit. So now some Continentals—those who had marched on Wayne's right—really did have enemy troops on their left flank. Some of these men sensed a threat to their right as well, and many had run out of ammunition. For all these reasons, they joined in the retreat.[29]

Just as the redcoats and Germans advanced against Wayne and Sullivan, Greene's division punched through the enemy's line and entered its camp. But with the rest of the Continentals retreating, Howe's troops were able to focus on Greene. Threatening both of his flanks at once, they forced him to withdraw.

Hearing the gunfire five miles away in Philadelphia, Lord Cornwallis made for Germantown at the head of three battalions of grenadiers, who ran the whole way, and a troop of dragoons. They arrived too late for the fighting but took over the pursuit, pushing the rebels no harder than Cornwallis had a year earlier in New Jersey but following them for eight miles before finally breaking off at dusk.[30] At 9 p.m. the first of the Americans made it to the designated rendezvous, Pennybacker's Mill, twenty miles north of Germantown. "I had previously undergone many fatigues," Lt. James McMichael wrote, "but never any that [had] so much overdone me as this." Over the previous twenty-four hours, Washington's men had marched forty-five miles, pausing mid-journey only for a firefight of nearly three hours. Count Casimir Pulaski and Generals Muhlenberg and Conway all reportedly fell asleep in the saddle. A court-martial concluded that Adam Stephen had coped with his stress and exhaustion by getting dead drunk. He was cashiered, and Lafayette took over his division.[31]

In his official report to Congress on the Battle of Germantown, Washington primarily blamed the disaster on the fog. But the previous mornings had also been foggy, and Washington should have known that low visibility would doom a plan that was already far too complicated. Back on December 26, 1776, he had divided his army into only two columns and separated them for only an hour.[32] But on October 4, 1777, no two columns reached Germantown at the same time. Washington's flawed scheme had cost his army about 1,100 casualties—essentially the same as at Brandywine and once again double the enemy's loss.[33] Numerous Americans, especially Continental officers, used the same ancient expression to sum up the day: "We fled from victory." But many insisted that the near success of the rebels' first major offensive against the main British expeditionary force had at least tarnished its aura of invincibility.[34]

EVEN AS HOWE'S SUCCESS at Germantown confirmed his grip on Philadelphia, Burgoyne's situation in the Upper Hudson Valley grew ever more desperate. In the two and a half weeks following the September 19 Battle of Freeman's Farm, as many as six thousand New York and New England militiamen joined Horatio Gates's army at Bemis Heights, giving him nearly twelve thousand effectives to Burgoyne's five thousand.

Indeed, the Americans' only major liability was a dispute within their top brass. Benedict Arnold was furious at Gates for not mentioning him in his official report on the September 19 battle. Gates had not singled out anyone else for praise, either, but his acolyte James Wilkinson spread the false rumor that Gates's internal adversary, Arnold, had not even taken the field. These and other slights led Arnold to confront his commander, who in his fury relieved him of command.[35]

A mile and a half to the north, the barely four thousand British and Brunswick troops still fit for duty built up their fortifications, foraged for increasingly scarce food, and did their best to dodge Gates's snipers and Indians.[36] Often at night they heard packs of wolves roaming the Freeman's Farm battlefield, setting up a howl whenever they sniffed out a shallow grave. "Their noise was hideous till they had scratched it up," one British officer reported.[37] Burgoyne agonized over the ever-expanding human barricade athwart his path. His officers pleaded with him to return to Canada while the path remained relatively clear, but he could not endure the disgrace of abandoning a mission in which he and the nation had invested so much.[38]

Ever since the Bennington disaster, Burgoyne had pinned his hopes on a British fleet sailing up the Hudson River to Albany, forcing Gates to detach part of his army and possibly enabling Burgoyne to defeat the smaller Continental force that remained. Howe had shown no willingness to abandon his own campaign against Philadelphia. But on September 21, Burgoyne learned that Henry Clinton, who commanded the British and German troops remaining in New York City, planned to lead three thousand of them up the Hudson.[39]

On October 6 — much later than Burgoyne had hoped — Clinton captured two U.S. forts about a third of the way to Albany and then continued upriver. But how would he inform Burgoyne that help was on the way? As the lowest-ranking commissioned officers in both armies, captains, ensigns, and especially lieutenants were the redshirts of the American Revolution, inevitably chosen for such missions and often volunteering for them. Clinton sent Lt. Daniel Taylor galloping toward Burgoyne with a simple message: "*Nous y voici* [Here we are], and nothing now between us but Gates." On his way north, Taylor approached some men in red uniforms — which turned out to have been taken from a captured British transport. Discovering his error, he swallowed the tiny silver ball containing Clinton's note, but his American interrogators made him puke it up and then hanged him.[40]

Another messenger made it through to Burgoyne, but only after he had sealed his own fate, personally leading a 1,500-man detachment against the American left on October 7. In his report to Germain, Burgoyne stated that he was covering for a foraging party; many of his horses and cattle were starving. But he also claimed to be probing for a weak spot in the Continental defenses, though he must have known he would not find one, now that he was outnumbered nearly three to one. Apparently he had concluded that his reputation required him to make one last try.[41]

Soon after Burgoyne's detachment moved forward, the Americans launched a furious counterattack that turned into a classic double envelopment and sent the redcoats and Brunswickers scurrying back toward their lines, primarily to a pair of redoubts on their western flank. Benedict Arnold remained without command, but he "volunteered his services" and led three regiments against the larger redoubt. Turned back with heavy losses, he galloped straight "through the fire of the two lines" to the smaller one, atop a high hill, and then cooperated with Daniel Morgan in surrounding and assaulting it. Really just a hundred-yard-long log barricade (as archaeologists have discovered), this redoubt was commanded by Lt. Col. Heinrich von Breymann, who had led the ill-fated rescue mission to Bennington. In fierce fighting, Arnold was shot in the left leg—the same one a British musket ball had shattered outside Montreal two years earlier. Another American's head was blown off, with skull fragments striking his neighbor, knocking him unconscious.[42] Finally the Continentals got around both ends of Breymann's breastwork, and the lieutenant colonel himself took a bullet. One version of the incident had his soldiers fleeing the redoubt, prompting Breymann to kill four of the fugitives before one finally turned around and shot him dead.[43]

By capturing Breymann's redoubt, the Americans turned Burgoyne's right flank as effectively as Howe had turned Washington's at Brandywine less than a month earlier. Like Washington on September 11 and Gates on September 19, Burgoyne was saved only by the arrival of nightfall. His casualties in the Second Battle of Freeman's Farm—at least six hundred killed, wounded, and captured—were four times greater than Gates's.[44] At 11 p.m. on October 8, the Anglo-Brunswick troops broke camp and started north, finally headed back to Canada.

They made it only to Saratoga, seven miles upriver, before the Americans trapped them against the Hudson. On October 13, Burgoyne asked for a parley, and Gates, violating protocol by proffering his terms first, demanded unconditional surrender. Burgoyne's council of war unanimously refused that humiliation, resolving that "it would be better to rush upon the Enemy, determined to take no Quarter."[45] Then as now, a victorious officer who ordered his troops to *take no prisoners* or *give no quarter* was guilty of a war crime. But to *take no quarter* was an action of the vanquished; it meant refusing to be taken alive.

By this time Gates had learned of Clinton's October 6 victories on the Lower Hudson, and he dreaded the arrival of a messenger saying Clinton's troops were closing in on Albany. So on October 15, he agreed to the extraordinary "convention" (not capitulation) that Burgoyne proposed. Under this agreement, signed two days later, the captured British and Brunswick troops would head home to Europe, where their only obligation would be to not return to America for the rest of the war. Counting officers, staff, and the ill, 5,728 men surrendered and set off for Boston.[46] Shipping would not be ready until spring, so they spent the winter of 1777–1778 in the same barracks just outside town where the Continental Army had stayed while besieging Boston two years earlier.

Even if Burgoyne could somehow have driven Gates out of Bemis Heights, he probably never would have made it to Albany. Shortly after the Battle of Bunker Hill in 1775, Burgoyne had foreseen how the rebels were going to win the war. As the British army drove them from each successive hill, always at the expense of numerous casualties, it would find them "continually retrenched upon the next."[47] And there were countless additional hills between Freeman's Farm and Albany. But Burgoyne's mission would have failed even if he had completed his trek, because there were not enough soldiers in the British army to wall New England off from the rest of the rebel colonies. Burgoyne's expedition thus reflected in miniature the absolute futility of the wider British war effort.

Members of Congress were appalled to learn that Gates had authorized the British government to use Burgoyne's troops in the European theater, freeing other redcoats for service in America. They contrived various pretexts for not carrying out his pledge, and ultimately they refused even to exchange them for imprisoned Americans.[48]

Indeed, by the end of 1777, Congress had begun to slow-walk *all* prisoner exchanges—and for good reason.[49] Most redcoats had to spend their entire working lives in the army, so supposedly liberated prisoners actually went straight back to camp. By contrast, Americans served in

the Continental Army for as little as six months or in the militia for just
a few weeks, and their enlistments expired during their confinement.
Others, taken from privateers, had never owed the army anything. A
congressional committee noted that if the Americans in British jails were
exchanged, most would "scatter abroad thro the Country"—in other
words, go home—"and make little or no Addition of Strength to our
Army." In every prisoner exchange, Washington traded soldiers for
civilians.[50]

In a March 8, 1778, letter that demonstrated the continuing influence
of ordinary Americans on red-letter events, Washington told Congress
that "the prevailing Current of Sentiment demands an Exchange" of prisoners. But he and the delegates made the agonizing decision to trade only
enough prisoners to demonstrate goodwill.[51] The human costs of this
policy were enormous. By war's end, disease exacerbated by exposure
and malnutrition would kill something like eighteen thousand Americans in British custody—about three times the estimated four to seven
thousand Continentals and Whig militiamen who died in battle.[52] As
the years passed, the British confined more and more of their American
prisoners in "hulks" (vessels shorn of their masts, rigging, and sails) anchored in the two great rivers bracketing Manhattan. Eventually drawn
together in the East River's Wallabout Bay, the future site of the Brooklyn Navy Yard, Britain's floating prison camps were often compared to
the Black Hole of Calcutta. They also resembled slave ships, with the
captives crammed together in stifling heat and subjected to the stench

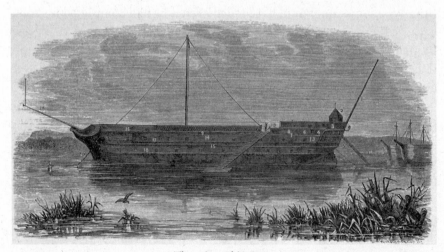

The prison ship *Jersey*

of their own waste and the putrefying bodies of the dying and dead. As on voyages from Africa, there was so little oxygen below decks that guards struggled to keep their lanterns lit as they made their rounds. Perhaps these similarities increased some white prisoners' empathy for the victims of the slave trade, though one jailed officer complained of being "huddled together between decks in a prison-ship, with Indians, Mullattoes, Negroes, &c."[53]

To save money, punish the unruly, and retaliate for Wallabout Bay, the Americans also made use of prison ships. But most of the Saratoga prisoners were sent to western Virginia, then Maryland, then Pennsylvania, and along the way the majority either escaped and made their way back to British headquarters or opted for lives as American citizens. Hundreds died of malnutrition, exposure, and—always foremost—disease.[54] Congress's breach of the Burgoyne-Gates accord elicited much criticism at the time—but then a measure of vindication nearly two centuries later, when historian Jane Clark discovered William Howe's secret letter instructing Burgoyne, once his troops were embarked on British transports, to divert them to British headquarters in New York City.[55]

By October 17, when Burgoyne's troops marched out of their works, Howe had been in Philadelphia for nearly a month, but his triumph remained incomplete, because the rebels had obstructed two Delaware River chokepoints with *chevaux de frise*. For centuries, armies short on cavalry had protected themselves against enemy horsemen with wooden contraptions fitted with spikes. Credited to the people of Friesland on the North Sea (*cheval de frise* is French for "Friesland horse"), these devices had been adapted for use against infantry and even ships. The chevaux de frise anchored in the Delaware were arrays of heavy timbers tipped with iron spikes capable of poking holes in a ship's hull, sending it to the bottom.

Thus all supplies headed to the British troops in Philadelphia and Germantown had to be off-loaded downriver, completing the trip on flatboats hugging the shore on dark nights or overland under heavy guard. Unless the Royal Navy could clear the Delaware and resupply the army by water, Gen. Howe might have to relinquish his hard-won conquest. In combination with Burgoyne's surrender, some Americans dared to believe, a British evacuation of Philadelphia might bring "a speedy and glorious end" to the war.[56]

If permitted to work freely, demolition teams can make short work of chevaux de frise, so the Americans built forts to guard each of their underwater barricades. The British drove the defenders from the lowest fort and destroyed its chevaux de frise, leaving just one range of chevaux de frise and, protecting it, Fort Mercer on the east bank of the Delaware in New Jersey and Fort Mifflin on Fort Island (often conflated with the neighboring Mud Island) near the Pennsylvania side.[57]

During the third week of October, British cannon onshore and on warships anchored just below the chevaux de frise opened fire on Fort Mifflin. Then on October 22, two thousand Hessians under Col. Donop assaulted the four-hundred-man garrison in Fort Mercer, suffering in the space of forty minutes nearly four hundred casualties—ten times as many as the defenders. "I lost five of my oldest friends," one of the attackers, Capt. Johann Ewald, recalled years later. "I have not yet left a battlefield in such deep sorrow." Donop took a musket ball in the groin, was captured by the fort's defenders, and succumbed seven days later, reportedly declaring, "I die the victim of my ambition and of the avarice of my sovereign."[58]

By then Howe had given up on Fort Mercer, at least for the moment, and shifted his focus to Fort Mifflin. During the night of November 14–15, two flat-bottomed boats, mounting a total of thirty guns, crept up a narrow and shallow channel that the rebels had not thought to block and drew within half a mile of the fort. In the ensuing cannonade, Joseph Plumb Martin, a member of the Fort Mifflin garrison, saw several fellow soldiers "split like fish to be broiled."[59]

The fort's largest cannon were 24-pounders, but the defenders had not been able to bring in any ammunition of that weight. No matter; the British fired numerous 24-pound balls into the fort, and American artillery officers offered a gill of rum to any soldier who brought them one. Martin watched "from twenty to fifty men standing on the parade waiting with impatience the coming of the shot, which would often be seized before its motion had fully ceased and conveyed off to our gun to be sent back again to its former owners. When the lucky fellow who had caught it had swallowed his rum, he would return to wait for another."[60]

Yankee thrift only went so far, and by the evening of November 15 the fort had run out of ammunition. At 10 p.m., the garrison rowed across the Delaware River to New Jersey, with only seventy or eighty men lingering to set Fort Mifflin ablaze and demolish its dikes, flooding it. The flames illuminated the fleeing Americans' boats, enabling British gunners to fire at them from seemingly every direction at once.[61] The

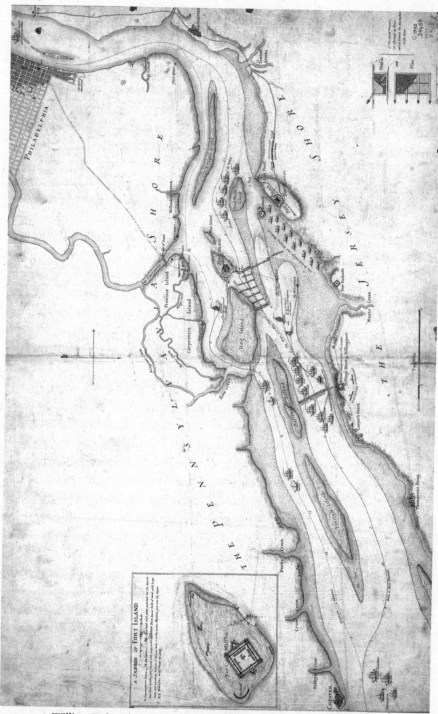

William Faden, drawing of the Delaware River including Fort Mercer,
Fort Mifflin, and the Whigs' chevaux de frise (1777)

very next day, Howe's troops cut through the chevaux de frise, and the first of his ships made it to Philadelphia. Fort Mercer no longer served any purpose, and the Americans abandoned it.

ON NOVEMBER 15, THE very day the British perfected their claim to the Delaware River and Philadelphia, the Continental Congress, meeting a hundred miles to the west in York, Pennsylvania, finally approved the Articles of Confederation. Over the previous year, large-state delegates had repeatedly tried to overturn the one-vote-per-state rule. Under a compromise proposed by Thomas Jefferson, no act of Congress would have taken effect without the consent of the majority of the states *and* of delegates representing the majority of voters. But small-state congressmen successfully clung to the *one state, one vote* principle that had governed Congress since its inception.[62]

Yet the delegates did alter the Articles in other ways, for example confining future Congresses to the powers "expressly delegated" to them and affirming the sovereignty of each state. Ironically, given Virginians' later clashes with the federal government, it was the only state to vote against state sovereignty. On October 14, a month before adopting the Articles, Congress changed the basis for apportioning federal expenses among the states, replacing population with the relative value of the states' land and buildings. Every delegate from south of the Delaware River supported the change, but New Englanders unanimously opposed it, since their real estate was the costliest in the country.[63] The states with clearly defined western boundaries demanded that those with charters running to the Pacific Ocean relinquish their western claims to Congress so it could use Indian land to liquidate its enormous debt. But the sea-to-sea states were able to insert language in the Articles of Confederation guaranteeing that "no State shall be deprived of territory for the benefit of the United States." Another last-minute change benefited slaveholders even as it violated the state sovereignty that most of them had demanded. No state could ever adopt its own version of the *Somerset* verdict, protecting its inhabitants from being dragged away in chains, for the Articles guaranteed slaveholders who visited other states the right to take their human property home with them.[64]

The Articles required the approval of every state. That seemed less than likely, since Congress's acquiescence in some states' vast western claims infuriated the other states—not to mention the land speculators whose imagined paths to western wealth ran straight through Congress.

———•:•———

CHAPTER 25

The Valley

Winter 1777–1778

A<small>T</small> W<small>ASHINGTON'S</small> <small>DIRECTION, HIS ELEVEN THOUSAND SOLDIERS</small> spent the winter of 1777–1778 in an ideal stronghold: eighteen miles northeast of Philadelphia on a 250-foot-high plateau in the peninsula formed by Valley Creek's junction with the Schuylkill River, with both streams serving as moats. The commander-in-chief offered a $12 reward for the first dozen men in each regiment to build their fourteen-by-sixteen-foot log hut. As they chopped down trees, notched logs, raised walls, and mortared them with clay, Thomas Paine said the Continentals looked "like a family of Beavers; every one busy."[1]

Weeks of warfare had drained the region around Valley Forge of most of its food, and Congress inadvertently exacerbated the crisis. Joseph Trumbull, eldest brother of the soon to be famous painter, was an aggressive and highly successful commissary of purchases, but in June 1777 his employers took away his power to hire and fire deputies and stopped paying either him or them commissions. Trumbull quit (as did most of his staff) and Congress replaced him with William Buchanan, who proved incompetent. Three months later, Thomas Mifflin, who as quartermaster general had the crucial responsibility of getting food and other supplies to camp, also resigned. Hoping he would reconsider, Congress refused to appoint a successor, and the post remained vacant for four months.[2]

But the main reason so little food, clothing, and other essentials made it to Valley Forge was financial. In the royal and rebel armies' competition for farm families' crops, livestock, and produce, the British advantage magnified as the Continental currency depreciated, giving birth to the expression "not worth a Continental." In sharp contrast, British commissaries never stopped paying farmers in specie—gold and silver coin—and Col. Walter Stewart fumed that enough flour "to maintain

Eight or Ten Thousand men goes daily to Philadelphia." Farmers caught selling their produce to the enemy were court-martialed, then whipped, jailed, or fined, and Johann Ewald claimed that several "were bound to the tails of horses and lost their lives in this sad way." On March 4, Congress authorized Washington to hire up to four hundred Oneida Indians, to be commanded by Battle of the Monongahela veteran Nathaniel Gist and tasked with interdicting "the pernicious Intercourse which the disaffected Inhabitants of this Country . . . hold with the Enemy."[3]

Among Gist's recruiters was a fellow alumnus of the Battle of the Monongahela, Louis Cook. The son of an Abenaki mother and African American father, Cook had been captured as a child by a pro-French offshoot of the Mohawks known as the Caughnawagas. They adopted him, gave him the name Atiatoharongwen, and eventually made him a sachem. Receiving an officer's commission in the French army, he fought in several battles of the Seven Years' War and then, more than a decade later, opted to oppose the British in the American War of Independence as well. In 1779, Congress would commission him as a lieutenant colonel in the Continental Army, and for the rest of the war he remained the highest-ranking Native American in the Continental officer corps—and its only African American.[4]

John Trumbull, Louis Cook or Atiatoharongwen (c. 1785–86)

Three days into the Valley Forge encampment, Washington warned Congress that the army might soon face a stark choice: "Starve—dissolve—or disperse."[5] And Nathanael Greene feared the shooting war would be eclipsed by the "war of funds," in which the "longest purse will be triumphant"—and everyone knew whose purse that was.[6] This pessimism was widely shared, and it raises a question. Back in 1774, the British secretary of war, Lord Barrington, aghast at the prospect of losing thousands of his soldiers in an unwinnable war, proposed to fight the colonists not by trying to conquer them on land but by completely cutting off their overseas trade. Suppose Parliament had listened to Barrington; might Britain have won the war? With zero export earnings, Congress might have been forced to disband the Continental Army. But that need not have spelled surrender, since the United States was a breadbasket, and its citizens could have kept up their passive resistance forever. Still, without access to foreign markets and supplies, Americans might have been much more open to accommodation—that is, unless London alienated them by shedding their blood, which is almost inevitable when governments rigorously enforce embargoes.[7] Still, a blue-water strategy would have been much easier to sell to Parliament than the fire-and-sword approach that had served Britain so well against Irish, Native American, and Black rebels. And with hindsight it seems that either of these two extremes would have had a better chance of success than the middle course that the North administration imperceptibly fell into.

An astonishing 2,500 soldiers—nearly a fourth of the original contingent—lost their lives during the army's six-month encampment at Valley Forge. But contrary to myth, almost none died of hunger or cold. With rare exceptions, flour continued to flow into the camp, and cornmeal always did, so the men were never without their savory firecake (griddle-cooked batter). Nearly all who died that winter succumbed to disease. Of course pathogens traveled more easily when immune systems were weakened by inadequate clothing and poor nutrition.[8] Moreover, until they got their beds built, the soldiers slept on the cold, wet ground, in most cases without straw, which abounded in the region but could not seem to make its way to Valley Forge. Indeed the army's deficiency in the humble article of straw may have killed more men than its infamous shortages of food and clothing.[9]

In the eighteenth century, alcohol as well as meat were widely considered essential nutrients, but for long periods, neither could be found.[10] Two days after reaching Valley Forge, surgeon Albigence Waldo recorded the daily refrain:

"What have you for your Dinners Boys?"

"Nothing but Fire Cake & Water, Sir."

"What is your Supper Lads?"

"Fire Cake & Water, Sir."

"What have you got for Breakfast, Lads?"

"Fire Cake & Water, Sir."

Waldo hoped "our Commissary of Purchases may live [on] Fire Cake & Water, 'till their glutted Gutts are turned to Pasteboard."[11]

Twice before the end of 1777, Washington contemplated repeating his spectacular triumph at Trenton a year earlier by attacking Philadelphia, thereby shoring up both American morale and the Continental currency. But most of his generals opposed a late November assault against the British defensive line running all the way from the Schuylkill River to the Delaware. One, John Sullivan, reminded Washington that a "Single Redoubt [had] Ruined the British Army at Bunker Hill"—and that behind Gen. Howe's fourteen redoubts lay nasty street combat against an enemy with "Vastly Superiour" artillery. The Americans' much wiser move would be to induce Howe to attack their own fortifications.[12]

At dawn on December 22, Howe, who was suffering from shortages of his own, took the majority of his troops across the Schuylkill to forage, and Washington briefly considered assaulting the diminished Philadelphia garrison on Christmas Day 1777—the anniversary of his crossing of the Delaware.[13] But he had to cancel the attack for lack of food. The enduring image of Valley Forge soldiers leaving bloody footprints in the snow is founded in fact; on December 23, three thousand men were deemed unfit for duty for lack of adequate shoes or clothing. Two years earlier, when an ammunition shortage that Washington could not publicly acknowledge prevented him from attacking Boston, he had endured the humiliation of people mistaking his prudence for timidity, and now the subsistence crisis produced the same effect. "I am obliged to conceal the true state of the Army from public view," he told Henry Laurens, the president of Congress, "and thereby expose myself to detraction & calumny."[14]

Officers suffered less than their men, but like them, they worried about the impact of shortages and hyperinflation on their families. Where officers differed from soldiers was in being free to resign their commissions whenever they wished, and growing numbers did so. On December 27, 1777, alone, fifty officers in a single division, having received "continual letters of complaint from home," returned to their businesses, farms, and families.[15] These departures gave those who remained bargaining power in pursuit of the same perquisite enjoyed by their British counterparts, albeit mostly after serving for a decade or more: lifetime pensions at half pay.[16]

Several high-ranking officers engaged in a still more disturbing form of agitation. Although born in Ireland, Thomas Conway had been raised in France, where he served in the army for twenty-eight years before joining the throngs of French officers sailing to America, where Congress made him a brigadier general.[17] In October 1777, after Washington lost at Germantown and Horatio Gates accepted the British surrender at Saratoga, Conway wrote Gates highlighting the contrast. Several officers who shared Conway's doubts about the commander-in-chief circulated and copied the letter, in some cases magnifying its claims, and an especially inflammatory version reached Washington, convincing him that Conway had drawn numerous officers, including his own former aide-de-camp Thomas Mifflin, into a plot to replace him. The remaining members of the chief's military family were fiercely loyal, and several challenged Gates's partisans to duels. In one encounter, John Cadwalader shot Conway in the jaw, nearly killing him.[18]

The movement to remove Washington did not actually gel into anything so solid as the "Cabal" that he and his supporters imagined. He had made mistakes, but his subordinates admired his legendary grit, displayed most recently in the campaign for their pensions, which he had at first opposed. On April 15, 1778, Washington went so far as to warn a Virginia congressman that disappointing the officers might provoke "a combination in quitting the service"—a mass resignation—and "possibly undo us forever." Three weeks later, Congress finally approved the pensions, though it limited them to seven years.[19]

The one officer who would draw no pension, as he took no pay, was the commander-in-chief. Could this be the same man who had spent much of the 1760s trying to inveigle his Seven Years' War subordinates out of their land bounties? The best explanation for Washington's metamorphosis seems to be that his Revolutionary War service brought him a different kind of compensation. Coming to terms with his apparent infertility, and shortly thereafter taking command of the army, he had learned to define his posterity in a larger, more metaphorical, sense. The transformation was complete by 1778, when an almanac dubbed him the "father of his country."[20] Washington's popularity accrued not only from what he did but from the one thing he could not do: establish a dynasty. Other Founding Fathers also lacked legitimate male heirs: Benjamin Franklin, Thomas Jefferson, and James Madison. Each had plenty of enemies, but none could be said to pose the same sort of generational threat as, say, John Adams, who schooled his sons in politics from an early age and lived to see one enter the White House.

Washington was not alone in his dedication to the troops. With his long nose, selective command of English (confined at first to "goddam"), and inflated rank (he presented himself as a major general, though he had never actually risen above captain), the man originally known as Friedrich Wilhelm Ludolf Gerhard Augustin von Steuben can sometimes seem farcical. But he really had learned the art of war in Frederick the Great's famed Prussian army—just as many of the Hessian officers bivouacked in Philadelphia had. More recently, he had for eleven years served the German principality of Hohenzollern-Hechingen as grand marshal, leaving only after being accused of having "taken familiarity with young boys." He now undertook to turn the amateur fighters encamped at Valley Forge into professional soldiers.[21]

Astonishingly, the Continentals had never learned to march in multiple columns, and by teaching them that one maneuver, Steuben enabled them to move much more quickly into a battle line. American soldiers had often fled at the sight of British and Hessian bayonets, but by constantly drilling them in the use of that weapon, Steuben demystified it. Most Continental officers had deputed sergeants to train their men, but Steuben set them an example, personally drilling a hundred privates from disparate regiments before returning them to their home units to spread the gospel. The troops' growing professionalism further isolated them from civilians but intensified their commitment to seeing the war through.[22]

BY THE SUMMER OF 1777, Philadelphia's population had grown to 35,000 souls, making it second only to London in the English-speaking world. About 12,000 residents—roughly a third—fled the British occupation, so the nearly 24,000 who remained were slightly outnumbered by Howe's 25,000 troops. The absent Benjamin Franklin may have been putting on a brave face when he quipped that "Instead of Howe taking Philadelphia, Philadelphia has taken Howe," but he had a point. Nonimportation and the British blockade had driven fine fabric and other luxuries from the city's display windows, but with the royal army's arrival, businesses scrambled to fill the void. One of the numerous merchants' daughters who entertained officers was the teenaged Rebecca Franks. On February 26, 1778, as Americans shivered and sickened at Valley Forge, she described her "life of continued amusement." Several "Ladies Hair-Dresser[s] from London" followed the redcoats to Philadelphia and set about crowning its upper-class women with "Enormous High head Dresses." Franks's Jewish faith was no bar to fashionable society, and she ended up marrying a British officer.[23]

Back in 1774, the Continental Association had closed the rebel colonies' few playhouses, but the British officers revived Philadelphia's Southwark theater and staged thirteen shows during the winter of 1777–1778. One of the most popular officer-actors was William Cunningham, who as provost marshal supervised American prisoners of war. Cunningham was notorious for underfeeding his inmates—some in their desperation ate clay, wood, and stones, and one man reportedly gnawed on his own fingers—and for such sadistic practices as pouring the prisoners' broth in the dirt just to watch them try to lap it up.[24]

Much of the British merchandise that landed on Philadelphia's wharves made its way across enemy lines into the countryside, where it was exchanged for women's poultry, eggs, dairy products, and vegetables as well as men's grain and livestock. But Whigs such as Anthony Wayne harshly contrasted "those Virtuous Daughters of America who cheerfully gave up ease and Affluence in a city for Liberty and peace of mind in a Cottage" with the women who remained in Philadelphia.[25]

Of course the vast majority of the British occupiers were not officers but common soldiers such as Thomas Peters, the African-born wheelwright who had escaped to Gen. Clinton two years earlier. Ordinary redcoats stayed warmer and ate better than their counterparts at Valley Forge, but an outbreak of scurvy among Hessian occupation forces served as a reminder that their nutrition was also substandard.[26]

Many elite Philadelphians were invited to the officers' "Plays, Balls Concerts [and] Assemblys" but chose not to attend. Most prominent among these were the Quakers whose aversion to luxury combined with their "peace testimony" to bar close association with either army. But Quaker women were by no means inactive. Earlier in the war, several male Friends had been banished to the Virginia backcountry for refusing to swear allegiance to the Whig cause. In the spring of 1778, a delegation of Quaker women obtained both armies' permission to pass through the lines to Lancaster, Pennsylvania, where they appealed to the state assembly and executive council for their husbands' release. Eventually they succeeded.[27]

Late in the spring of 1778, Congress and Washington finally found competent men to run the Continental supply departments. Nathanael Greene initially balked at becoming quartermaster general, since it meant forgoing the prospect of battlefield glory. But Greene was a pragmatist—he once resisted Washington's pressure to attack a larger British force, observing that "The Cause is too important to be trifled with to shew our Courage"—and he eventually agreed to feed the troops he had once commanded. The equally competent Jeremiah Wadsworth became commissary general, and Congress went back to allowing supply officers to earn commissions. The delegates also adopted the same policy by which William Pitt had led Britain to victory in the Seven Years' War, instructing Wadsworth and Greene to pay farmers whatever was required to keep supplies coming in, debt be damned. But the United States in 1778 was not Britain in 1758, and Congress's abandonment of fiscal restraint doomed the already moribund Continental dollar.[28]

ONE OF THE MOST popular assumptions about the American Revolution—that the Saratoga surrender of October 1777 led to the Franco-American alliance of February 1778—omits a crucial intermediate step. When King Louis XVI finally cast his lot with the United States, he was not reacting to Burgoyne's surrender at Saratoga four months earlier but to the British Parliament's response to Saratoga.

Benjamin Franklin's decade in Paris, from December 1776 to July 1785, is often portrayed as one long flirtation with female aristocrats. Actually the widowed septuagenarian endured much frustration during these years. One of his fellow American agents, Arthur Lee of Virginia, accused another, Connecticut's Silas Deane, of dispatching cargoes across the Atlantic and then awaiting their fate before declaring who owned which, labeling captured vessels official U.S. government property and those that successfully ran the British blockade his own. In addition, Lee openly criticized Franklin's diplomacy, which struck him, as it has many historians, as another word for socializing. Franklin was also frustrated that his many sweethearts apparently kept him at arm's length—as did Louis XVI during his first year and a half in France.[29] The king saw no reason to sign a treaty with the Americans, because for him, the informal alliance, centered on trade and secret French gifts and loans, worked just fine. Louis's government was already overstretched, with a debt-to-income ratio of six to one; declaring war against Britain might bankrupt it. Another reason to hesitate was the relative weakness of the French fleet, though a reconstruction program undertaken after the calamitous Seven Years' War was beginning to bear fruit.

But then word of Burgoyne's surrender reached London, and on December 6, 1777, the North ministry informed the American commissioners in Paris that he was prepared to make most any concession to win the colonies back. It was North's gambit, not Burgoyne's surrender, that convinced the comte de Vergennes, the French foreign minister, that France could maintain its relationship with the United States only by putting a ring on it. On February 6, 1778, the American commissioners met him at his office in the Hôtel de Lautrec to sign two treaties, one commercial and one military. In addition to offering the United States protection and trade, Louis XVI renounced any claim to Canada or Louisiana. And both nations pledged not to reconcile with Britain without the other's consent.[30]

France's entry into the war fundamentally transformed it, as Britain's focus shifted to its ancient adversary. Like the Seven Years' War, this one would now be fought not only in America but in Europe, Africa, and Asia.

Even if no French soldier had ever set foot on U.S. soil, as some Americans would have preferred, the transition to global war would have profoundly altered conditions in North America.[31] The North administration has traditionally been portrayed as deciding in 1778 to shift its attention to the southernmost rebel colonies. That characterization is not wrong; indeed, north of the Mason-Dixon line, the British had already launched their last major attack against the Continental Army, at Freeman's Farm in 1777. But the ministry's real focus would shift even farther south than the Carolinas and Georgia. In March 1778, North and his cabinet decided to remove eight thousand redcoats from the North American theater. Some would go to St. Augustine in East Florida—the oldest continuous European settlement in North America—and to Pensacola in West Florida. But most were destined for the Caribbean, home to France's as well as Britain's most valuable overseas possessions. Their first assignment would be to invade the French-controlled island of St. Lucia. Two-thirds of Great Britain's soldiers served in North America in 1778, but over the next two years, as Europeans' focus shifted to the sugar islands and suppression of the rebellion became "a secondary consideration," North America's proportion of the mother country's army fell to one-third.[32]

London was right to worry about the two Floridas, for Whigs had already raided both. At the end of 1777, Congress authorized former Natchez merchant James Willing to assemble a party at Pittsburgh and then float down the Ohio River toward West Florida. Willing's forty-odd freebooters raided Walnut Hills (the future Vicksburg), Natchez, Manchac, and other British plantations and settlements on the east bank of the Lower Mississippi, capturing several British officials, more than one hundred slaves, and a vast quantity of property, including a ship that had been loading for London. In Spanish—and thus officially neutral—New Orleans, Willing's troops sold their booty, including the slaves, some of whom managed to escape back upriver to their families.[33]

More than five hundred miles east of New Orleans, the British garrison in St. Augustine provided crucial support to Loyalists, Indians, and other enemies of the United States and also dispatched its own raiding parties to rustle rebellious South Carolinians' and Georgians' cattle and liberate their slaves. Early in 1777, Whigs invaded East Florida, but did not get far, and by May the expedition's leaders were fighting a duel in which one died. A second attack, early in 1778, was scarcely more successful.

Then in May 1778, about 3,500 Continentals under Gen. Robert Howe (no relation to British Gen. William Howe) joined South Carolina and Georgia militia in a renewed strike at St. Augustine. Late in June, as the invaders approached the St. Mary's River (then as now the border between Georgia and Florida) and Fort Tonyn, on its south bank, the British garrison set it ablaze and withdrew. The redcoats and Loyalists defending East Florida did not manage to recruit many indigenous auxiliaries, but Native Americans helped them indirectly, drawing off numerous Whig fighters who could otherwise have joined in the invasion. Howe's advance force made it only fourteen miles south of the St. Mary's before riding into an ambush and having to turn back.[34]

In a still more lethal encounter, the Americans were "violently attacked by sickness," and more than three hundred died. Also, their rice ran low, and militia commanders refused to take orders from Howe. Sixteen former royal soldiers who had deserted to the Americans tried to desert back to the British; most were recaptured by the expedition's native allies. Howe had occupied the ruins of Fort Tonyn for barely two weeks when he asked his officers to consider whether "the sickness which so fatally prevails in the army, render[s] a retreat immediately requisite?" They "Resolved unanimously in the affirmative."[35]

* * *

THE NORTH MINISTRY'S ORDER transferring nearly half of the North American garrison to the Floridas and the Caribbean was not addressed to William Howe but to Henry Clinton, for the cabinet had finally approved Howe's oft-repeated request to return to England. Lord Germain was excited about the change, since Clinton had a reputation for feistiness, though unfortunately toward his colleagues as well as the enemy. Yet even Clinton could not be expected to hold North America's two largest cities with eight thousand fewer troops than his predecessor, so Germain instructed him to evacuate Philadelphia and consolidate his remaining strength in New York.[36]

At the same time, the North ministry continued its diplomatic overtures to the rebels, even in the face of the Franco-American treaty. Parliament promised never again to levy taxes on them, station troops among them during peacetime, or alter their charters. In April, it sent over a peace commission—known as the Carlisle Commission for the earl who led it—with broad authority to yield to American demands (for instance that Parliament suspend all post-1763 American legislation) and even to permit the popular election of provincial officials such as governors and customs agents, a concession no one in America had sought. The Carlisle commissioners are often described as offering the rebels independence in everything but name, but they held firm on one point: the mother country would not give up its monopoly of American trade.[37]

One of the peace commissioners, Henry Johnstone, asked Elizabeth Graeme Fergusson, a Pennsylvania heiress who had remained in Philadelphia when her Loyalist husband chose exile, to deliver a proposition to Congressman Joseph Reed: if he could effect a reconciliation, the North ministry would give him 10,000 guineas and "the best post in the government." Fergusson indignantly replied that "no pecuniary emoluments" could sway her friend, and when she told him of Johnstone's offer, Reed's response echoed her own. Congress voted unanimously not to speak to the commissioners.[38]

The news from Europe occasioned two very different celebrations in Pennsylvania in May 1778, one in Philadelphia and the other at Valley Forge. Washington set aside May 6 for a day of thanksgiving for the French treaties. Prayers and artillery salutes were followed by troop inspections, rum for all, huzzahs, and a *feu de joie*, with every soldier firing his musket in rapid succession.[39]

The farewell party that General Howe's officers threw him twelve days later was far more glamorous. The officers and their guests paraded down the Delaware River in elaborately decorated boats, serenaded by regimental bands and saluted by the battleships, and then came ashore at the Joseph Wharton estate for a *meschianza*, derived from the Italian words for *mix* and *mingle*. A pageant choreographed by Major John André, Howe's adjutant general, featured a mock joust between the Knights of the Blended Rose and the Knights of the Burning Mountain, each side defending the honor of seven Turkish maidens played by young Philadelphia women. Resplendent in demi-turbans and broad pink sashes, the maidens were attended by slaves "in oriental dresses, with silver collars." Howe's officers split the tab for the extravaganza, which André stated in the African-derived coin of the aristocracy: 3,312 guineas (£3,478).[40] Amid the crusaders, Turkish maidens, African slaves, and Chinese silk and fireworks, the one significant omission was any reference to North America.

Although the meschianza was intended as a celebration of honor and other core British values, it was widely derided as an apt icon of imperial rot—and not just by the rebels. Hannah Griffitts called it "A shameful scene of dissipation, / The Death of sense and Reputation." She and others were especially appalled at the involvement of so many young women from respectable Philadelphia families. "Recollection's pained to know," she wrote, "That *Ladies* joined the frantic show."[41]

By May 25, when Howe sailed for England, Clinton was also preparing to evacuate Philadelphia, along with his army and any Pennsylvania Loyalist who sought the king's protection. Short on transport ships, he decided to embark the baggage, the three thousand Loyalists, and a

John André, a meschianza lady, her escort, and a slave

handful of his men in the few vessels he had and then march across New Jersey with the bulk of his troops. On June 18, the last British soldiers left Philadelphia, accompanied by a contingent of self-emancipated African Americans.[42]

For more than three weeks, the Continentals had known that the British were headed to New York by land, and Clinton feared they would precede him across the Delaware, dig in at some highly defensible location along his path, and then charge him a hefty toll.[43] But Washington hung back, not breaking camp at Valley Forge until the day the British left Philadelphia.

Clinton passed up the most direct path to New York, since it crossed the Raritan River, and he feared having to do so under fire. Instead he took a more easterly road toward Sandy Hook at the mouth of New York Harbor, whence he would ferry his troops into town.[44] On the morning of June 24, Washington convened a council of war at Hopewell, New Jersey, to propose sending several thousand Continentals against Clinton's rear guard. Charles Lee, whom the Americans had just recovered in exchange for a British officer, opposed the attack, primarily out of fear that it would snowball, drawing the entire 12,500-man U.S. army into an open-field battle against Clinton's 10,000, a prospect he viewed as "criminal." Most of the other generals agreed, and they urged the commander-in-chief to do nothing more than send 1,500 light infantry to join the several hundred militiamen and Continentals already harassing Clinton's flanks and rear. But later that day, two of the men who signed this recommendation—Lafayette and Nathanael Greene—privately wrote Washington saying they actually favored a broader assault. "People expects something from us," Greene told his commander, and their morale would suffer if their soldiers marched "with great rapidity until we got near the Enemy and then our courage faild us and we halted without attempting to do the enemy the least injury."

Washington initially accepted the council of war's advice, but the very next day, he changed his mind, endorsing Greene and Lafayette's proposal to send five thousand troops—nearly half his army—to try to beat up Clinton's rear guard without engaging his main army. Per custom, he offered leadership of this detachment to his second-in-command, but Lee declined, allowing Washington to assign the task—and with it, a shot at glory—to Lafayette. But discussions with other officers convinced Lee that he would be "disgrac'd" if he passed up what had become a major assignment, so he asserted his prerogative and displaced Lafayette.[45]

On the morning of June 28, 1778, Lee caught up with the rear of Clinton's army at the town of Monmouth Courthouse (already known to many as Freehold, its current name). The Americans' one chance at victory would be to hit the British rear guard, commanded by Lord Cornwallis and variously estimated at five hundred to two thousand men, after the rest of his army had marched too far east to return in time to save it. But Lee blew that chance, if it ever existed, by splitting his corps into two wings and having one attack straight-on, tying the British down, while he personally led the other half to the northeast before cutting back south to take them in the rear.

Cornwallis saw the Americans coming long before they fired their first shot and induced Clinton, who rode with the rear guard, to call for reinforcements. Soon the two generals had ten thousand troops. By contrast, the main body of the Continental Army was still hours away.[46] Washington had hoped his five-thousand-man detachment would isolate an enemy contingent half its size, but that was precisely the advantage that Clinton and Cornwallis now enjoyed.

Lee would probably have been forced to pull his troops back at some point, but before he could, he suffered the humiliation of seeing them retreat on their own, apparently prompted by a toxic mixture of confusion and intolerable heat. The mercury rose over 100 degrees on June 28, killing about sixty soldiers on each side, which was nearly as many as enemy fire. Artillerymen had the most punishing job of all. Working a cannon— hoisting a shot or shell and a sack of gunpowder into its white-hot barrel, ramming them home, dashing for cover as the gun's discharge rolled it four or five feet backward, then dragging it back into position before swabbing the barrel in preparation for the next shot—was hot work even in winter and actual torture on a day like this. After artillery Capt. Thomas Wells lost two men to enemy fire and many more to heat stroke, his commander, Lt. Col. Eleazar Oswald, had him pull back to an orchard, apparently in hopes the shade would provide some relief. But the sight of the gun crews heading to the rear convinced other American officers and soldiers that a general retreat had begun, and many joined in.[47]

Joseph Plumb Martin and his Connecticut comrades may also have contributed to the stampede. They marched through some woods and then out into an open field that felt, Martin said, like "the mouth of a heated oven." Gasping for air, they broke ranks and returned to the shady area through which they had just passed.[48] Soon Martin saw other Continentals retreating, perhaps mistakenly following Connecticut's lead.

The units that withdrew left their neighbors' flanks exposed, all but forcing them to enlist in the exodus. Lee and his officers quickly gave up on preventing the retreat and bent their efforts toward imposing order on it. They largely succeeded, thanks in part to Baron von Steuben's drills, and as the men reached the crest of a hill west of Monmouth, most, though not all, agreed to turn, stand, and fight.[49]

Just before 1 p.m., the commander-in-chief, riding ahead of his army's main body, reached the outskirts of Monmouth. Wrongly assuming that Lee had either ordered his troops to retreat or lost all control over them, Washington publicly abused him, questioning his commitment to an attack that he had opposed in council and reportedly even calling him a "damned poltroon" (coward). For more than two centuries, historians have echoed this criticism, but the real blunder at Monmouth appears to have been Washington's assumption that his vanguard would be able to hit Clinton's rear guard and get away before British reinforcements arrived.[50]

Soon the rest of the Continentals came up, and Washington instantly and masterfully combined them with Lee's men to form a series of defensive lines. In this crucial phase, the Battle of Monmouth resembled Bunker Hill, with British infantrymen once again taking heavy casualties as they assaulted Americans who in this case covered themselves not with breastworks (no time for those) but trees, a hedgerow, and the crest of a hill.[51] Washington would have earned his reputation for military genius, then and there, if he had deliberately set up the scenario that had accidentally played out: Lee's men picked a fight with a larger body of British troops and then withdrew to a series of defensible positions, whence they and their fellow Continentals thinned the ranks of their pursuers.

Around 1:30 p.m., Clinton decided to pause his infantry attack until his cannon crews could soften up the rebels. American gunners responded, and it was apparently during this artillery duel that Joseph Martin watched the wife of a Pennsylvania gunnery sergeant assist her husband at his trade. "While in the act of reaching [for] a cartridge and having one of her feet as far before the other as she could step," Martin related, "a cannon shot from the enemy passed directly between her legs without doing any other damage than carrying away all the lower part of her petticoat,—looking at it with apparent unconcern, she observed, that it was lucky it did not pass a little higher."[52]

Martin's anecdote may have been fanciful, but Dr. Albigence Waldo, who helped treat the Monmouth wounded, heard that after one infantryman was shot down, his wife took over his musket "and like a Spartan heroine fought with astonishing bravery, discharging the piece with as much regularity as any soldier present." In the nineteenth century, Martin's and Waldo's accounts would coalesce with others into the story of the far less bellicose Molly Pitcher, who brought pitchers of water to cool her husband's cannon and slake its crew's thirst. Molly Pitcher must be understood as a myth, not because no fallen Continental soldier's wife ever took over for him but because so many did.[53]

Finally the Americans managed to place artillery on Combs Hill, on Clinton's left flank, forcing his own cannon crews to withdraw. The two sides suffered roughly the same casualties at the Battle of Monmouth. The Americans had 69 killed and 161 wounded, while 65 British and German soldiers were killed and 170 wounded. And the freakish heat killed more men than either army: about 100 British, German, and American soldiers.[54] The Continentals made no further effort to interfere with the redcoats' and Germans' march to Sandy Hook, and on July 5, the last of them were ferried into New York. By this time, Washington had pointed his army toward White Plains, New York, taking it slow to improve his troops' chances of surviving the continuing heat wave.

The northbound army was the site of a roving court-martial, requested by Charles Lee in hopes of vindication. The commander-in-chief helped draft a three-point indictment alleging that Lee had disobeyed orders to attack, issued his own "unnecessary" order to retreat, and—what Lee could not deny—responded to Washington's battlefield rebuke with a pair of insulting letters. The panel found him guilty on all three charges and suspended him for one year. That drew him into a dispute with Congress, which made the suspension permanent. Here was another sense in which Washington won the Battle of Monmouth: he rid himself of a second-in-command who had become a liability.[55]

Superficially the British and American armies were back where they had been a year earlier, with Clinton's redcoats, Loyalists, and Germans still mostly confined to Manhattan Island and the Americans hovering in northern New Jersey and the Hudson Valley. But there was one crucial difference, for Washington believed that with the aid of French troops and ships, he could finally take the offensive. Over the next three years, he would grow increasingly determined to command a grand amphibious assault against Fortress Manhattan.[56]

Meanwhile, small parties from the two armies patrolled the no-man's-land between them. Although this war nominally pitted British redcoats against rebel colonists, the participants in one of the bloodiest skirmishes of the White Plains encampment were primarily Loyalists, Germans, and Wappinger Indians. A decade after the New York council deprived them of their land on the east bank of the Hudson River, the Wappinger warriors formed a regiment in the Continental Army. On August 31, 1778, the Wappingers, commonly known as the Stockbridge Indian Company, fell into an ambush set for them by Hessian jägers (including Capt. Johann Ewald's company) and Loyalists commanded by Lt. Cols. John Simcoe, Andreas Emmerich, and Banastre Tarleton. About half of the fifty-odd Wappingers, including sachem Daniel Nimham and his son Abraham, were slain, some in the battle and the rest as prisoners.[57]

CHAPTER 26

Southern Strategies

1778–1779

CONGRESS RETURNED TO PHILADELPHIA ON JULY 2, AND ALMOST immediately took up the Articles of Confederation. Back in November 1777, when it had sent the proposed federal government out to the state legislatures, Congress had given them less than four months to vote it up or down. But by the March 10, 1778, target date, only eight states had ratified. The Maryland House of Delegates coupled its rejection with a proposal to give the federal government control over the western domain. If Congress approved Maryland's amendment, then all of the states that had already endorsed the Articles would have to vote again, and those with sea-to-sea charters might well withdraw their support. The proposal failed by a single vote.[1]

But the battle over the Articles was not the only venue in which the states advanced their western land claims. On January 2, 1778, Virginia governor Patrick Henry and his council instructed twenty-six-year-old George Rogers Clark to raise seven companies of volunteers for the defense of the state's Kentucky district, which had been the target of countless Indian raids. Actually, as Clark later noted, Governor Henry had drafted these instructions "designedly for deseption." His real targets were the British forts and nominally British, primarily Francophone, towns in what is now the Midwest. If Virginia could establish a presence in this region, it could prevent Indian attacks by forcing warriors to fall back and protect their own villages. Moreover, as Governor Henry's successor, Thomas Jefferson, noted in a spring 1779 letter to Clark, his expedition would, "if Successful, have an important bearing ultimately in Establishing our North Western boundary" in future negotiations with Congress as well as Britain.[2]

The Upper Mississippi Valley might also serve as a stepping-stone to Britain's Fort Detroit. As he floated down the Ohio River, Clark passed up a fight against an Indian war party on its way to attack settlers on the Greenbrier River in modern-day West Virginia for fear of losing valuable time and men. But Native Americans and their imperial allies were never far from his mind. Although historians have shown that native warriors were no one's puppets, their resistance against U.S. encroachment really did rely upon British guns, ammunition— and leadership. Native war captains were far more willing to accept direction from harmless British Indian agents than from their rivals in other native villages.

Britain's gateway to the Great Lakes and Upper Mississippi Valley Indians was Fort Detroit, and Clark was not the only Whig with designs on that post. On June 11, 1778, Congress, apparently unaware of Clark's plans, approved its own expedition against Detroit, but it had to be canceled barely a month later for lack of funds, food, and fighters. Still, that autumn and again the following spring, when Lachlan McIntosh, the Continental commander at Pittsburgh, led a force of Continentals and Virginia militiamen west into Indian country, he held out the hope, of course unrealized, of marching all the way to Detroit. McIntosh's successor, Daniel Brodhead, ridiculed his schemes but then devised his own strike against Fort Detroit, one that wildly underestimated the distance from Pittsburgh. George Washington, Patrick Henry, and Thomas Jefferson also had their eyes on Detroit. Even David Zeisberger, a minister in the pacifist Moravian sect (the Church of the Brethren) offered that the United States would never know peace with its native enemies "until they are subdued & Detroit is taken." Zeisberger and other Moravian missionaries lived with the Delawares in what is now eastern Ohio and made numerous converts. Like the Presbyterian Oneidas, the Moravian Delawares proved useful to the United States. Late in 1779, in compliance with an order from Washington, Brodhead and Zeisberger sent a party of these native Christians to Detroit with instructions to use their professed pacifism as a cover for spying out its defenses.[3]

By mid-June 1778, Clark had assembled his army on an island in the middle of the Ohio River. Only then did he disclose his "secret Instruction" to attack the British forts and towns west of the river. Most of the troops embraced the change, but some did not, and Clark and his captains were unable to stop "The Greatest part" of one company from slipping back across the Ohio to Kentucky. On June 24, the soldiers headed downriver. They disembarked near the mouth of the Tennessee and struck out overland in hopes of surprising the town of Kaskaskia, nearly a hundred miles to the northwest, on the east bank of the Mississippi, sixty miles below St. Louis.[4]

Reaching the outskirts of Kaskaskia on the evening of July 4, the raiders were alarmed by a commotion in the village but then relieved to learn that it was only "the Negroes at a Dance." Clark would later describe in vivid colors how he surprised and seized Kaskaskia, but the reality was that most of the residents were Francophone *habitants* who leapt at this opportunity to throw off the British yoke. Once Clark informed them that France and the United States had become allies, they agreed "to become Free americans." In the coming weeks, *habitants* would outnumber Clark's original band in the parties that encountered little resistance in obtaining the allegiance of other French-speaking settlements, including Cahokia (across the Mississippi River from St. Louis) and Vincennes (140 miles to the northeast on the Wabash River). At Vincennes, Clark's emissary was the local Jesuit priest. The *habitants* viewed Clark as helping them escape British tyranny, but historians christened him the "Conqueror of the Old Northwest" (the region north and west of the Ohio River). The lieutenant colonel did not neglect civil government, even issuing a proclamation prohibiting freemen from renting or lending buildings to "red or black slaves . . . for the purpose of dancing, feasting, or holding nocturnal assemblies" like the one that had alarmed him on his way into Kaskaskia.[5]

DANIEL BOONE ALSO CROSSED to the west bank of the Ohio in 1778, but not willingly. Modern folklore paints Boone, a veteran of the Battle of the Monongahela, venturing into the American wilderness for long solo hunting trips, but the prey he most cherished was the wilderness itself. In 1773, he had led a group of land hunters west only to turn back after an Indian attack in which his son James was killed. Two years later, when he moved the surviving members of his family from North Carolina to Kentucky, he was in the employ of land speculator Richard Henderson, whose settlements were also the targets of numerous Native American raiders.[6]

Early in 1778, Boone was leading a work party procuring salt for the Kentucky River town of Boonesborough when a group of Shawnees, bent on avenging the murder of Cornstalk and his son the previous autumn, captured him and his men. One Shawnee warrior, Captain Will, had also waylaid Boone eight years before, and the two old adversaries greeted each other with a hearty "Howdydo." Boone was interrogated by the war chief Blackfish, speaking through his African American translator Pompey, whom the Shawnees had seized and adopted years earlier. After transporting Boone and his men across the Ohio River, Blackfish's warriors sent some on to the British at Detroit but adopted others as replacements for deceased kin. Blackfish took Boone. It was an oddly appropriate choice, given that, two years earlier, when Blackfish's son led a war party into Kentucky and captured Boone's daughter and two other young women, Boone had organized the militia band that rescued the three and killed Blackfish's son. But the adoption did not take. On June 16, Boone escaped and returned to Boonesborough, where, three months later, he took the lead in breaking a Shawnee siege.[7]

LATE IN JULY 1778, France and the United States launched their first joint operation. Ten thousand Continentals and New England militiamen under Gen. John Sullivan and a twelve-ship French fleet under the comte d'Estaing, along with transports carrying four thousand French soldiers, all converged on Narragansett Bay in southern Rhode Island in hopes of liberating the island city of Newport, which the British had held for a year and a half.[8]

On August 9, Sullivan's troops landed on the northern tip of Aquidneck Island, ten miles north of Newport. That very day, Adm. Richard Howe's British squadron arrived from New York, and d'Estaing's fleet sailed out to greet it. After two days of maneuvering, both fleets were scattered by a massive storm. Meanwhile the Americans marched to within cannon shot of Newport and began digging siege trenches. D'Estaing finally returned to Rhode Island on August 19, initially elating the Americans, only to announce that he was not going to participate in their attack. The storm had badly damaged two of his ships, and he had heard that a second British fleet was headed to Narragansett Bay, so he was leaving for Boston.[9]

The Americans on Aquidneck Island were furious—and even more so when d'Estaing refused even to set his infantrymen ashore before sailing away. During the night of August 28–29, Sullivan pulled his troops back toward the northern tip of the island, and at dawn the Newport garrison set off to try to run them down.[10] Desperate to avoid a rout, American officers had their men turn and face their pursuers, ensuring an orderly retreat. The "desperate valor" exhibited by the Rhode Island 1st Regiment as it repelled three waves of onrushing Hessians impressed observers in other units — and also surprised them, for two reasons. The first was that most of them had never seen battle before; the second was that they were Black.[11]

Originally organized as a mostly white unit, the 1st Regiment had withered away as soldiers died, deserted, or declined to reenlist. On February 14, 1778, Rhode Island assemblymen voted to replenish the 1st with Native Americans and enslaved as well as free African Americans. Each new recruit received his freedom with his musket, and his owner was paid his market value.[12]

Officially the Continental Army still prohibited African Americans, but they and recruiting officers had routinely ignored the ban, and several whites had advocated enlisting them in larger numbers. In August 1776, when hundreds of New Jersey militiamen marched to New York to fight the British, former New Jersey congressman Jonathan Dickinson Sergeant grew anxious about a possible slave rebellion and proposed to lessen the danger by "employing those Slaves as Soldiers in the publick Service," granting them freedom but using deductions from their monthly pay to compensate their owners. He sent his proposal to John Adams, who replied that "Your Negro Battallion will never do. S. Carolina would run out of their Wits at the least Hint of such a Measure."[13]

The Rhode Island legislators who created the Continental Army's first and only Black regiment were no more motivated by racial inclusiveness than the British commanders who had set them the example. They simply could not interest enough white men in serving. The skittish assembly withdrew its emancipation offer after just three months, but desperate recruiters continued to accept slaves, as many as 250 in all. As was initially the case for African American soldiers in the Civil War, Black Rhode Islanders earned less than their white comrades, being denied the standard subsistence allowance. And yet, unlike the typical white soldier, most agreed to remain for the duration.[14]

The reconstituted Rhode Island 1st Regiment resembled the 186,000 African Americans who fought in the Civil War in another way as well. In both conflicts, many whites feared that Blacks would not fight. Even Jonathan Sergeant shared the common viewpoint that "Slaves generally are Cowards." But no white person who witnessed the August 29, 1778, Battle of Rhode Island would ever again doubt the courage of the recently freed African Americans in the 1st Regiment. Still, whites would have to relearn this lesson over and over again, as evidenced by the doubts that bedeviled the soldiers of the famous Massachusetts 54th Regiment until they kept advancing toward Fort Wagner, near Charleston, South Carolina, on July 18, 1863, even as more than half of their comrades fell (as depicted in the movie *Glory*).[15]

During the night of August 30–31, 1778, Continental mariners rescued the U.S. troops from Aquidneck Island, "mortifying" British officials. By that time, d'Estaing's fleet had sailed into Boston Harbor. Already a drought and the nearly six thousand British and German soldiers captured with Burgoyne and housed in Cambridge had strained the region's grain supply, and the arrival of an additional six thousand French soldiers and sailors aggravated the crisis. When d'Estaing's bakers built field ovens on the waterfront and refused to share the bread with crewmen from an American privateer, the sailors attacked, gravely wounding a French lieutenant, the chevalier de Saint-Sauveur, who in civilian life was first chamberlain to Louis XVI's brother. A week later Saint-Sauveur became the first member of the French expeditionary force to die on U.S. soil.[16]

French and American officers scrambled to prevent the incident from damaging their nations' freshly inked alliance. D'Estaing claimed the melee had been instigated by two groups of Britons: Jack Tars from recently captured merchant ships and Saratoga prisoners who had been permitted to enlist on American privateers. The admiral's U.S. hosts eagerly embraced this fable, and Boston's *Independent Ledger* favorably contrasted the French visitors' restrained response to their friend's death to the redcoats' massacre of five Bostonians on March 5, 1770.[17] The day after Saint-Sauveur died, the Massachusetts assembly voted to raise a memorial in his honor. But after the French fleet sailed out of Boston, the idea languished, not to be revived until the middle of World War I. Dedicated six weeks after the United States entered the war on France's side, the monument still stands in front of the church where Saint-Sauveur is buried.[18]

Memorial to the chevalier de Saint-Sauveur outside King's Chapel in Boston

*   *   *

GEN. SULLIVAN'S FAILURE TO capture Newport in some ways resembled Barrimore St. Leger's unsuccessful siege of Fort Stanwix/Schuyler the previous summer, but St. Leger's expedition had produced results that were not immediately apparent. Determined to revenge their losses at the Battle of Oriskany, numerous young Iroquois eagerly accepted a British invitation to raid Whig settlements in upcountry Pennsylvania and New York. In one of the most notorious of the 1778 attacks, British rangers and Iroquois warriors entered one of the Continental Army's breadbaskets: the Wyoming Valley, on the north branch of the Susquehanna River.[19] Due west of Connecticut, this region was claimed by that state on the basis of its sea-to-sea charter—but also by Pennsylvania. The decade-long feud between Connecticut and Pennsylvania settlers had led to considerable violence, though few fatalities.

The July 1778 assault might also have resulted in little bloodshed, for the settlers spotted the attackers in time to shelter in forts. But the sixty Continental troops and nearly four hundred militiamen in Forty Fort pressured their commander, Col. Zebulon Butler, to confront the Anglo-Iroquois war party, so on July 3 he led them out the gates in an attempt to surprise the besiegers' camp. But instead they walked into an ambush. John Butler (no relation to Zebulon), the onetime Indian agent, had been promoted to major and given command of the British and Iroquois fighters. He reported that in the ensuing violence, which became known as the Wyoming Massacre, the Iroquois took 227 scalps. Still, a short time later, when Forty Fort capitulated, the British and Iroquois complied with their promise not to harm "a single person . . . but such as were in arms."[20]

The term *massacre* is more appropriate for the events of November 11, 1778, in the town of Cherry Valley, New York (fifty miles west of Albany, on a far northeastern tributary of the Susquehanna River). An Anglo-Iroquois party killed sixteen Whig soldiers and thirty-two civilians, mostly women and children. In the four months since the Wyoming Valley raid in July, a combination of factors had eroded British and Indian fighters' compunction about striking civilians. Whigs had attacked several villages in Iroquoia. And the leader of the American militia at Wyoming Valley, who had been released unharmed in return for agreeing to stay out of future fighting, had instead resumed his command, which meant the Iroquois had to "fight the enemy twice." According to British officials, First Nations fighters were also angry at the Whigs for falsely accusing them of killing women and children at Wyoming. Another ingredient in the Cherry Valley massacre was British commander Walter Butler's infuriatingly contemptuous attitude toward his Iroquois allies, especially Joseph Brant (who nonetheless tried to prevent the killing of civilians).[21]

Natives and U.S. citizens continued to raid each other's settlements throughout the war and long afterward, as the revenge cycle rolled on and on.

OFTEN A SOCIETY UNDER external assault at least has the consolation of diminished internal strife. But if Pennsylvania and Virginia, the two most populous states, are any indication, the Indian raids of 1778 did nothing to reduce conflict among whites.

The burning issue in Virginia was military service. When voluntary recruitment failed to fill the state's quota of Continental troops, legislators initiated a draft. At first they permitted local officials to impress the men they deemed most expendable, which often meant free Blacks. But many of the chosen men dropped out of sight, and "friends Secrete[d] them." Others rioted. In an attempt at reform, the assembly decreed on January 9, 1778, that henceforth each county would randomly select its draftees from among its bachelors. But that only provoked still more boisterous draft riots—and also contributed to the defeat of numerous assemblymen. The new legislature that gathered in May 1778 took the extraordinary step of abolishing the year-old draft altogether. After that, Virginia failed to procure even half the soldiers Congress requisitioned.[22]

Neighboring Pennsylvania also tried drafting soldiers only to return to its infinitely more popular and less productive reliance upon volunteers.[23] But Pennsylvanians' most pressing grievance against their ruling party (the defenders of the state's unusually democratic constitution, they would soon be known as the Constitutional Society) was currency inflation. In the October 1778 assembly elections, angry voters elevated numerous members of the rival Republican faction, which opposed the state's 1776 constitution as too democratic. The Constitutionalists' growing isolation helps explain their inflexible attitude toward Pennsylvanians who had collaborated with the British during their occupation of Philadelphia. Juries found John Roberts, who had served the occupiers as a guide, and Abraham Carlisle, who had worked as a gatekeeper, guilty of treason—a hanging offense.[24]

Petitions to spare the two elderly Quakers poured into the state's executive council from all over the state—even from the jurors who had convicted them. But special prosecutor Joseph Reed, an erstwhile moderate who had become a hard-line member of Pennsylvania's Constitutionalist party, warned that pardoning the traitors would itself be "a species of Treason," and Roberts and Carlisle were hanged on November 4.[25] Reed began presenting evidence against twenty additional defendants, and Pennsylvania seemed poised for mass executions. But juries began returning "not guilty" verdicts even in cases where incriminating evidence was overwhelming.[26]

IN NOVEMBER 1778, GEN. Henry Clinton finally carried out Lord Germain's eight-month-old order to send nearly half of his New York troops southward. Five thousand redcoats and Germans wrestled St. Lucia, a sugar island, from France and then remained in the Caribbean to guard this and other British possessions. Hundreds of others went to Bermuda, the Bahamas, and West Florida.[27] And on November 27, a fleet carrying 3,500 English soldiers—the majority of whom were not actually English but Scottish, German, and Loyalist—left New York Harbor and set a course for the Savannah River, the border between South Carolina and Georgia. A Black pilot named Sampson guided the warships and transports up the river to within two miles of Savannah, Georgia's capital and only city of any size. At dawn on December 29, the expedition's commander, Lt. Col. Archibald Campbell, disembarked his troops. Savannah's Whig defenders, 700 Continentals and 150 militia, were outnumbered four to one. But when Lt. Col. Campbell shimmied up a tree to observe them, he discovered that their commander, Gen. Robert Howe, had anchored both of his flanks in swamps and directed his troops to dig a trench all the way from one swamp to the other. A frontal assault would cost Campbell numerous casualties.[28]

Then Quamino Dolly, an elderly slave belonging to Georgia governor James Wright, led Lt. Col. Campbell's light troops down a little known path through the swamp on Howe's right. Their reappearance in the rebels' rear threw them into disorder, whereupon Campbell sent his front line forward. Many American soldiers ran into the swamp and drowned; eighty-three defenders and only three British soldiers were killed. As Campbell's army occupied Savannah without further opposition, he bragged about having "ripped one star and one stripe from the rebel flag of America."[29] Soon the royal governor called the assembly into session—a feat that none of his counterparts had accomplished since July 1776.

The British Regulars and Loyalists in lowcountry Georgia and the

Whigs farther up the Savannah River and on its north bank in South Carolina repeatedly raided each other without either side gaining an advantage. Then on April 20, 1779, Gen. Benjamin Lincoln, the new Continental commander in the south, invaded Georgia, leaving so few troops behind in South Carolina as to practically invite a British incursion. Gen. Augustine Prévost, who had superseded Arthur Campbell in command of the British troops in Georgia, accepted Lincoln's invitation, leading an army of redcoats, Germans, and Muskogees north over the Savannah in hopes of stocking up on food, especially rice and beef, and forcing Lincoln to abandon his own thrust into Georgia. Continental Army Gen. William Moultrie rallied Whig militiamen to block Prévost's path, but his outnumbered army repeatedly fell back and then all but melted away as the men slipped off to defend their own families and farms. According to South Carolina historian David Ramsay, writing in 1785, British depredations "and above all the dread of the royal auxiliaries, the Indian savages, whose constant practice is to murder women and children, diffused a general panick among the inhabitants," leading many to go so far as to seek British protection.[30]

The hundreds of slaves who escaped to Prévost soon discovered that he was no Lord Dunmore. "Great Evel may Result from the Number of Negroes Who hourly Resorts to the army," he declared in a May 5 order. After assigning one hundred African Americans to his headquarters departments and allowing each of his officers several Black servants, the general announced that he would not be "incombered with a multitude of useless people."[31]

Three years earlier, in June 1776, Henry Clinton had failed to capture Sullivan's Island, much less Charles Town. But Prévost, who had not entered the state with any designs on its capital, found himself on the brink of seizing not only Charles Town but Moultrie's army. On May 9, nine hundred British soldiers crossed over to the Charleston Peninsula and started south.[32]

In the midst of this crisis, John Laurens showed up in Charles Town with an extraordinary proposal. The eldest son of Henry Laurens, the onetime slave merchant and president of Congress, and himself a former aide-de-camp to Washington, the twenty-four-year-old Laurens had witnessed the valor of Rhode Island's 1st Regiment on August 29, 1778. He now proposed to liberate up to three thousand enslaved South Carolinians in return for service in the Continental Army. Early in 1779, as the army's manpower crisis worsened, Congress, observing that Carolina authorities had been "unable to make any effectual efforts with militia, by reason of the great proportion of citizens necessary to remain at home to prevent insurrections among the negroes," suggested that white South Carolinians listen to Laurens and enlist those same slaves.[33]

Governor John Rutledge and his Privy Council would do *almost* anything to save Charles Town. They even wrote Prévost offering to pull South Carolina out of the rebel coalition, making it a neutral power: Switzerland with Spanish moss. Yet the rice planters had their limits; they would not free and arm a single slave.[34]

Lincoln finally recrossed the Savannah and made tracks for Charles Town, credibly threatening to trap the British against its walls. Prévost broke off the siege and headed back toward Savannah by way of South Carolina's sea islands, thus leaving a water barrier between himself and Lincoln. Marching south over Johns Island, Prévost left an eight-hundred-man rear guard to fortify a beachhead on the mainland side of Stono Ferry, near the site of the famed September 1739 slave rebellion.[35] On June 20, Gen. Lincoln led 1,200 militiamen and Continentals against the British beachhead. As Whig casualties mounted, the survivors increasingly resisted their commander's repeated orders to renew the charge, and he had to desist. Lincoln thus learned the same lesson the British had imbibed four Junes earlier at Breed's Hill: frontal assaults on entrenched positions seldom succeeded.[36]

Meanwhile Prévost's provisions ran low, and he stopped feeding his Black auxiliaries. And with too few boats to move his entire force to the mainland for the final push to Savannah, he left most of the fugitives behind. Ramsay described their response: "in order to get off with the retreating army, they would sometimes fasten themselves to the sides of the boats. To prevent this dangerous practice the fingers of some of them were chopped off, and soldiers were posted with cutlasses and bayonets to oblige them to keep at proper distances."[37]

A similar attitude toward African Americans opened the proclamation that Henry Clinton published on June 30, 1779, while headquartered at Philipsburg Manor, thirty miles up the Hudson from New York City. The British commander announced that "all Negroes taken in arms" by his army would become its property, not its prisoners. Yet he also offered to free slaves owned by rebels, just as Lord Dunmore had back in November 1775. Since then, numerous imperial officials had quietly enlisted African Americans, but Clinton and his commandant in New York City, David Jones, were the first since Governor Dunmore to put the offer in writing. Dunmore had made freedom contingent on military service, but Clinton promised "every Negro who shall desert the Rebel Standard, full security to follow within these Lines any occupation which he may think proper." Everyone understood the implicit message of the so-called Philipsburg Proclamation: Clinton was headed south.[38]

AT THE END OF 1778, as Archibald Campbell's troops sailed toward Savannah, Henry Hamilton, the lieutenant governor of British Detroit, led a mostly Indian army to Vincennes on the Wabash River and wrested it back from Leonard Helm, one of George Rogers Clark's captains. Hamilton, who was short on food, dismissed his Indian allies for the winter, whereupon Clark and 130 soldiers left the Mississippi for a brutal mid-winter trek, 180 miles east to Vincennes.[39]

Snowmelt had flooded the Little Wabash and Wabash Rivers, merging them into one giant lake, and Clark's troops had no choice but to wade through miles and miles of frigid water. They spent the night of February 21–22, 1779, on a temporary island, and the next morning Clark "took some water in my hand poured on Powder Blacked my face gave the war [w]hoop and marched into the water without saying a word." His men plunged in after him, and on February 23 they emerged from the drowned land, entered Vincennes, and laid siege to its British post, Fort Sackville.[40]

As Clark and Hamilton negotiated surrender terms, a party of native warriors returned from raiding U.S. settlements on the Ohio River. Unaware of Clark's arrival, they walked right up to his men, who killed most of them on the spot. Clark briefly spared the lives of four warriors, only to have them "Tomahawked in the face of the Garrisson" in order to convince the Indians that "Governour Hamilton could not give them that protection that he had made them to believe he could." The one member of the war party Clark spared was its leader, a "White Man" who was the initially unrecognized son of the Virginia soldier Clark had assigned to guard him. Fort Sackville capitulated on February 25. Clark sent Hamilton to Virginia, where he was imprisoned for two years and finally released in return for James Willing, captured at sea shortly after his daring raid down the Mississippi.[41]

As he celebrated his success at Vincennes, Clark proposed another winter trek, 340 miles northeastward to Fort Detroit. But a lack of manpower forced him to hold off until summer.[42]

* * *

THE MISSISSIPPI VALLEY ENGAGED the attention not only of *habitants*, Native Americans, and British and American soldiers but also of the king of Spain. With more extensive American claims than Britain—including New Orleans, everything west of the Mississippi River, much of the Caribbean, and most of Latin America—Carlos III had no desire to see the rebellion spread. For him, the Revolutionary War was an opportunity to extract concessions from Britain—specifically, Gibraltar. But once he determined that Britain was never going to sign away the Rock, he entered into a secret mutual defense pact with France, the Treaty of Aranjuez (April 12, 1779). Within weeks the two Bourbon powers were conducting joint operations, and on June 17, Britain formally declared war against Spain. Americans were disappointed at Carlos's refusal to treat with their representatives, but they knew that his entry into the war would draw off British ships and troops for battles over Gibraltar as well as both Spanish and British possessions in America.

When Bernardo de Gálvez, the twenty-three-year-old governor of Spanish Louisiana, learned that his king had declared war against Britain, he marched 1,300 soldiers north from New Orleans toward British settlements on the Lower Mississippi. Gálvez's army was as diverse as America itself. Its few Spanish soldiers were outnumbered by French-speaking militiamen, including the sons of Acadians (Cajuns) expelled from British Nova Scotia in 1755 as well as free Blacks dressed in "white jackets with gold buttons and round hats topped with crimson cockades." There were also Whig refugees from the loyal British colony of West Florida and warriors from such Indian nations as the Houmas, Alabamas, and Choctaws. By the end of September 1779, Gálvez's troops had captured several British posts, including Natchez and Baton Rouge.[43]

The British could not have won the Seven Years' War without their European allies, but in the American War of Independence they stood alone, even at sea, where the Royal Navy once again fought the fleets of France and Spain, which, between them, possessed 44 percent more ships.[44] Quickly exploiting this advantage, French and Spanish officials made plans to invade southern England in the summer of 1779.

On August 14, the two Bourbon fleets appeared off Plymouth, sowing widespread panic. But four days later, a gale swept most of the ships back out into the Atlantic. As the captains struggled to regain the English Channel, they spotted a Royal Navy fleet and gave chase. The British just barely reached the safety of Spithead, and on September 8, the French and Spanish broke off the attack. The combined fleets had seen little action, capturing only one enemy vessel as disease killed hundreds of crewmen as well as their passengers: the soldiers waiting to hit the beaches.[45]

During these same weeks, though, another, much smaller, anti-British expedition achieved remarkable success, at least in the all-important arena of public opinion. The French government had commissioned John Paul Jones, a thirty-two-year-old former slave ship captain, to sail seven vessels toward Ireland in order to divert Royal Navy resources away from the Franco-Spanish fleet. Jones's flagship was a French veteran of the Canton tea trade that he had rechristened the *Bonhomme Richard* in honor of Benjamin Franklin's *Poor Richard's Almanack*. Accompanied by three smaller French and American vessels, the *Bonhomme Richard* had nearly completed a clockwise circuit of the British Isles when, on September 23, it encountered a British convoy off Flamborough Head on England's northeast coast. Two Royal Navy vessels, the *Serapis* and the *Countess of Scarborough*, screened the merchantmen as they escaped into port unscathed and then turned to engage Jones's fleet.[46]

The forty-gun *Bonhomme Richard* took a thrashing from the agile *Serapis*, which mounted up to fifty cannon. Richard Pearson, the captain of the *Serapis*, called out to ask if Jones had struck his colors (surrendered). Jones yelled something like "I may sink, but I'll be damned if I strike," often rendered as, "I have not yet begun to fight." In desperation, Jones brought his ship alongside the *Serapis*, deliberately intertwining the two vessels' rigging. Riflemen balancing on the *Bonhomme Richard*'s masts and spars picked off crewmen on the deck of the *Serapis* as cannon on each ship fired point-blank into the other. When one of Jones's sailors managed to drop a grenade through *Serapis*'s hatch onto its gun deck, igniting spilled gunpowder, Capt. Pearson surrendered. Two days later, the *Bonhomme Richard* sank, and Jones made the *Serapis* his flagship for the final leg of his journey, to Amsterdam. The government of the Netherlands was officially neutral, but many Dutch citizens were sympathetic to the Americans' cause and willing to suffer or finesse the diplomatic consequences of hosting them.[47]

TRAVELERS SEEKING TO CROSS the Hudson River knew their last chance to do so below the Highlands was the ferry between Stony Point and Verplanck's Point, two rocky promontories protruding toward each other from opposite banks of the river forty miles above New York City. Americans built forts atop the two hills, but on May 31 both fell to the British. Washington resolved to take them back, his primary motive being "to satisfy the expectations of the people and reconcile them . . . to the apparent inactivity, which our situation imposes upon us."[48] He had recently created the perfect brigade for tasks like this one. Commanded by Gen. Anthony Wayne, it consisted entirely of light infantry.

Washington decided to begin with Stony Point, on the west bank of the Hudson, and to schedule the attack for the night of July 15–16. On the 15th, some of Wayne's men were detailed to kill all the dogs in the area so their barking would not alert the British. Since eighteenth-century armies typically attacked enemy posts just before dawn, Washington advised Wayne to preserve the element of surprise by striking several hours earlier.[49] At the head of Wayne's 1,350 troops marched a slave named Pompey with two Continentals disguised as farmers. Having periodically visited the garrison to sell berries and other food, Pompey had been entrusted with its countersign. With it, he and his companions were able to draw near two British sentinels and capture and gag them before they could fire warning shots or cry out.[50]

Only one side of the hill was gradual enough for a road, and Wayne had a column of soldiers march along it, but this was only a feint. The actual attackers, divided into two wings, left the road and waded eastward, just off the promontory's upriver and downriver shores, with a view to scrambling up its northern and southern slopes and meeting in the fort. Per custom, each column was led by an all-volunteer "forlorn hope," commanded by a lieutenant. To retain the element of surprise, Washington and Wayne emulated Charles Grey, whose troops had relied entirely on their bayonets in capturing Wayne's camp at Paoli two years earlier. The advance troops were not even permitted to load their weapons. As for the rest, Wayne warned that "If any Soldier presumes to take his musket from his Shoulder, or attempts to fire, or begins the battle till ordered by his proper officer, he shall be instantly put to death by the officer next him."[51]

The commander of the 650-man garrison in the British fort, Lt. Col. Henry Johnson, was taken in by Wayne's diversionary attack along the road and took nearly half of his troops out to meet it. As the U.S. soldiers ascending the southern slope of Stony Point cut through the first of two lines of abatis, British sentinels spotted them. Hundreds of muskets let fly, and royal artillery fired grapeshot. But in the darkness, the defenders could not get a fix on their targets. Within minutes, the southern column's forlorn hope—animated by pride, patriotism, and

Wayne's promise of cash awards to the first five soldiers entering the fort—had cut through both lines of abatis, clawed their way up the hill, and vaulted the parapet. About sixty British soldiers died in the assault, four times the Continental fatalities.[52]

Washington visited Stony Point the morning after its capture, made the determination that it could not hold out against British warships, and ordered it stripped of its equipment and then abandoned. The British quickly reoccupied Stony Point, this time without firing a shot, only to evacuate it just three months later. But at least the Continental soldiers had successfully rebutted the widespread criticism of their "inactivity."[53]

IN THE CONFLICT BETWEEN the United States and the Six Nations of the Iroquois, 1779 was the most important year of the war. By February 25, when Congress ordered the Continental Army to avenge the previous year's raids on white settlements such as Cherry Valley and the Wyoming Valley, Washington had already developed a plan.[54] The first attack, commanded by Col. Goose Van Schaick, left Fort Stanwix/Schuyler on April 18 and headed west toward the Onondaga towns. The Oneidas were U.S. allies, and their warriors asked to participate, but Van Schaick feared one would warn his intended targets, so instead he sent them on an extended expedition against a remote and unimportant Anglo-Indian post far to the north, on the St. Lawrence River. Van Schaick's men killed twelve Onondagas—including "a Negro who was their Dr."—and took thirty-three prisoners. Most of the captives were women, and several were reportedly raped. On April 24, less than a week after setting out, the Continentals marched back into Fort Schuyler.[55]

For the ensuing summer, Washington planned a far more extensive incursion, involving a fourth of his army. The Continentals were to "rush on with the war [w]hoop," defeat the Six Nations, and then burn their towns, fields, and food and also acquire hostages "of every age and sex" to be traded for Iroquois neutrality.[56] One American army would head north from Pittsburgh, striking the Senecas, who were the westernmost, largest, and most anti-settler of the Six Nations. Farther east, Gens. John Sullivan and James Clinton would join forces at the Susquehanna River town of Tioga, just south of today's New York–Pennsylvania border, and then strike north into the Iroquois heartland. Clinton's soldiers portaged from the Mohawk River to Lake Otsego, the source of the Susquehanna, but faced a difficult passage down the river, which was clogged with downed trees. So they raised the level of the lake two feet by damming its outlet at modern-day Cooperstown, New York. Then they broke the dam, giving the Susquehanna sufficient water to float their boats down to their junction with Sullivan.[57]

The Iroquois counted on help from the Delawares who lived in upstate New York, along with about a hundred rangers and other Loyalists and fourteen British regulars commanded by John Butler. But the four thousand Continentals vastly outnumbered the seven hundred Anglo-Indian fighters. Butler and the sachems resolved to block the invaders near the Delaware village of Newtown (six miles southeast of present-day Elmira, New York) in a narrow defile between the Chemung River and a range of hills. They also made the decision, extremely rare for Indians, to fight from behind a breastwork—a prudent choice, since Sullivan's army, which reached the Anglo-Iroquois defensive line on August 29, had brought cannon.[58]

The Indians' breastwork ran from north to south and presented a concave face to the enemy, enabling the rangers and Indians, as Sullivan noted, "to fire upon our Flank and front at the same time." Mid-battle, a detachment of warriors ascended the hill north of the breastwork with instructions to work their way around the Continentals' right flank. At about the same time, Sullivan launched his own flank attack, also north of the breastwork. When the opposing flankers collided, the outnumbered Iroquois gave way, but the Continentals could not get behind the main body of British and Iroquois troops, who had withdrawn in the face of premature artillery and infantry fire from the U.S. center.[59]

Only about five rangers, five Iroquois, and three Continentals were killed at the Battle of Newtown, though dozens of fighters on both sides were wounded and Sullivan's troops captured two Loyalists, one white and one Black. The Americans scalped their Indian dead, and Maj. Daniel Piatt had a lieutenant skin two slain warriors to make bootlegs for both of them.[60]

After Newtown, the Iroquois retreated in the face of superior numbers. With ample warning of the Continentals' approach, all but a handful escaped. The soldiers killed an elderly Tuscarora who had refused to leave his home but spared a Cayuga woman whose age they estimated at 120 years.[61] The invaders' most significant victory was against the Iroquois's food. Briefly pausing to marvel at the two-foot-long ears of corn that Iroquois women were about to pick from their sixteen-foot-tall stalks, the Continentals burned an estimated 160,000 bushels' worth of corn, along with watermelon, squash, and whole orchards of fruit. When

Sullivan determined that his assault on the Six Nations' food supply would take longer than anticipated, his men magnanimously agreed to stretch their own rations so they could finish the job.[62]

Iroquois scouts shadowed the Continental force—Joseph Brant later boasted to an American officer that "I roasted my venison by the fires that you left"—but made only one more stand against them.[63] Sullivan sent a detachment of Morgan's rifles, commanded by Lt. Thomas Boyd, west through a swamp with instructions to destroy Genesee Castle, a principal Seneca town. Surmising that the rest of the U.S. soldiers intended to follow them, the Iroquois, Delawares, and rangers set up an ambush. Sullivan's main body stayed put, but as Boyd's troops headed back to rejoin their comrades, they stumbled into the trap. At least fourteen were killed on the spot, and Boyd and several others were captured. All were tortured to death, along with an Oneida guide whose captors included his own brother.[64]

By September 30, Sullivan was back in Tioga, bragging about burning forty Indian towns while losing fewer than forty men.[65] Meanwhile, on August 11, the third and last incursion into Iroquoia, commanded by Col. Daniel Brodhead and consisting of six hundred soldiers, left Pittsburgh and followed the Allegheny River northward. The Seneca sachem Guyasuta, who with George Washington had likewise headed north along the Allegheny twenty-six years earlier, sent Mason Bolton, the British commandant at Fort Niagara, an urgent plea for help, but the redcoats could not possibly arrive in time, so all the Senecas could do was stay out of Brodhead's way. He and his troops marched almost to the New York line, skirmished with a small party of Senecas, and burned several Seneca towns before heading back downriver. Although Washington had not accompanied any of the three expeditions into Iroquois country, the Indians knew he had dispatched them, and they revived their old name for him: "Town Destroyer."[66]

The title of the definitive account of the three U.S. incursions neatly sums up their outcome: *A Well-Executed Failure*. Even including Iroquois civilians, roughly equal numbers of attackers and Indians were killed. As one of Sullivan's officers stated, "The nests are destroyed, but the birds are still on the wing."[67]

Sullivan also failed at another of his goals—he did not bring back a single hostage—but he succeeded at provoking a subsistence crisis. "There was not a mouthful of any kind of sustenance left," the Iroquois matron (and former white captive) Mary Jemison recalled in her memoirs. Jemison found a job shucking corn for two African American men who had escaped slavery and established a farm on the Genesee River, fifty miles east of the present-day city of Buffalo. (She was amused that her employers, mistaking her skin tone for her identity, zealously guarded her against the Indians.) But most of the Iroquois had to take refuge with the British at Fort Niagara, essentially becoming their clients. Inadequate and unwholesome army rations increased the refugees' vulnerability to deadly pathogens, and during the extraordinarily cold winter of 1779–1780, when, as Jemison noted, deer froze to death "in vast numbers," scores, perhaps hundreds, of Iroquois succumbed to disease.[68]

—◦•◦—

CHAPTER 27

Dark Days

1779–1780

Like the naval war, the successive British and American seizures of Stony Point, and the U.S. invasion of Iroquoia, another event of the summer of 1779, the "Penobscot Expedition," ended unambiguously.

On June 17, 640 British soldiers under the command of Gen. Francis McLean established a new military post, Fort George, on a peninsula at the mouth of the Penobscot River in what is now Castine, Maine, 250 miles northeast of Boston. It was to be the nucleus of a new British province peopled by Loyalist refugees from the rebel colonies. Bordered by New England to the southwest and Nova Scotia to the northeast, "New Ireland" would give Britain exclusive access to the Penobscot Indians and the mast trees growing alongside the Penobscot River and its tributaries; it would also be a base for Royal Navy vessels protecting Nova Scotia and its shipping from American privateers. Most of all, Fort George would challenge the territorial ambitions of Massachusetts, which insisted that the Penobscot was well inside its District of Maine—in fact a hundred miles west of its border with British Canada. Settlers from Massachusetts had already established the village of Machias, seventy miles east of the Penobscot, and the previous year its residents had successfully resisted a British assault.[1]

As soon as Massachusetts assemblymen learned about New Ireland, they resolved to destroy it. A U.S. Navy captain who had never given orders beyond his own ship, Dudley Saltonstall, was made commodore of a fleet of seventeen warships, including several contributed by New Hampshire and Congress, and twenty-four transports. Massachusetts supplied the bulk of the ground forces: 872 militiamen commanded by Gen. Solomon Lovell.[2]

The U.S. fleet reached Penobscot Bay on July 25, and that very day it skirmished against several British vessels. But Saltonstall held off on a more aggressive attack, against either Fort George or the small British squadron protecting it, saying he did not wish to risk damaging his own vessels. Thirty-two naval officers formally petitioned the commodore to storm Fort George, and the next day, July 28, he set Lovell's troops ashore. They rapidly fought their way to within six hundred yards of the fort but took heavy fire from the British ships, and Lovell declared that he would proceed no farther until Saltonstall engaged the enemy fleet. This Saltonstall would not do until Lovell's men boosted his chances by silencing the Fort George batteries.[3]

Finally the naval and infantry commanders agreed to strike simultaneously on August 13. But that very evening, British reinforcements arrived: a seven-ship squadron commanded by Commodore George Collier. Saltonstall embarked Lovell's troops and retreated up the Penobscot River, with Collier's squadron in close pursuit. As the Americans approached the falls of the Penobscot (at present-day Bangor), they had to beach and burn their ships, leaving the crews, as well as Lovell's infantrymen, to make their own way back to Boston. None of the American officers distinguished himself during the chase, but one, artillery chief Paul Revere, came in for particularly harsh criticism, especially for refusing to help rescue a disabled U.S. vessel drifting toward the enemy. A court-martial later cleared Revere, but Saltonstall was convicted and dismissed. The pointless expedition had cost Massachusetts a million dollars.[4]

The Penobscot disaster would be quickly forgotten if George Washington could accomplish his most ambitious objective for 1779. Late in January, when Congress learned that the British had captured Savannah, its members begged Adm. d'Estaing, then in the Caribbean, to come liberate white Georgians. Soon Conrad-Alexandre Gérard, the French minister (ambassador) to Congress, was reporting that d'Estaing's ships might indeed return to North America—whereupon Gen. Washington essentially tried to hijack the French fleet. He proposed that it sail not to Savannah but to New York, to join the Continental Army in storming Britain's largest North American garrison.[5] The French alliance had rekindled his abiding desire to take the war to the enemy.

D'Estaing ended up remaining in the Caribbean for most of the summer. On July 4, he captured the valuable British island of Grenada, but then in early September, he finally set his course for North America. Washington hoped the French would make directly for New York. But he soon learned that the fleet was headed to Georgia—and that its next stop after that would be France. Still, Washington and his generals persuaded themselves that in conjunction with southern Whigs, d'Estaing's ships and his more than 4,500 troops would capture the Savannah garrison in plenty of time to head north and assist them as well. As he mobilized the resources of the New England and mid-Atlantic states for the climactic Franco-American assault on Fortress New York, Washington ordered Gen. Sullivan and his troops to hustle back from western New York, though it meant abandoning eight hundred head of cattle to the Iroquois families they had spent the summer trying to starve. Horatio Gates neatly summed up the commander-in-chief's goal: "by one Great Stroke to Finish the War."[6]

By September 12, when d'Estaing began disembarking his soldiers about eight miles downriver from Savannah, he was starting to doubt his ability to make quick work of the British garrison. One discouraging sign was that few South Carolina militiamen showed much interest in the effort. "A spirit of money-making has eaten up our patriotism," David Ramsay lamented. "Our morals are more depreciated than our currency." In theory state officials had the option of pressing militiamen into service against Savannah, but Ramsay reported ominously that western settlers, angry at the salt shortage and other privations, "will not submit to a draught." John Laurens, who had secured election to the state House of Representatives during the summer, demanded that the chamber consider enlisting slaves. "Received with horror by the planters," his proposal garnered only twelve votes.[7]

The other side was not so squeamish. A New York newspaper reported that "Betwixt 200 and 300 negroes were ordered in by the Governor and Council, immediately set to work, and 13 good redoubts were soon erected round the town." Prévost also used several hundred African Americans as infantry, and Savannah became a place of refuge for fugitive slaves who feared recapture by the Franco-American army.[8] One of them, David George, had escaped a Virginia tobacco plantation years earlier and fled into the Carolina backcountry, only to be reenslaved by Muskogee-speaking Indians, who eventually sold him to deerskin trader George Galphin. While working for Galphin, who lived on the South Carolina shore of the Savannah River, just down from Augusta, Georgia, he married, fathered two children, and joined with an ex-slave, George Liele, in forming the world's first Black Baptist church, at Silver Bluffs, overlooking the river.

When the British occupied Savannah, Galphin, a Whig, fled, and more than fifty of his slaves, including David George and his family, crossed the Savannah to freedom and British protection. Liele and George continued preaching as well as farming together. When the French troops landed, George and his family joined other African Americans in the provincial capital.[9]

D'Estaing ordered his troops to advance on the town using "regular approaches"—ever-closer trenches. Forced in the meantime to station part of his fleet in the river to shell the town and the rest just off the coast to fend off British warships, d'Estaing worried that the diminished coastal squadron would succumb either to a larger enemy fleet or a hurricane. He soon concluded that creeping forward via regular approaches would take too long. That left him only two options: abandon the attempt or storm the city. "Prudence would have dictated" that d'Estaing simply decamp, as Ramsay noted, but his "sense of honour" compelled him to undertake a frontal assault.[10]

First, though, he would soften up the city with a cannonade. David George reported that after a French cannonball came through the roof of the stable where his family had taken refuge, "we sheltered ourselves under the floor of a house." French artillerymen were not just firing solid shot but also carcasses and exploding shells. Like the Whig garrison in Fort Mifflin two years earlier, some of Savannah's Black children delivered reusable enemy cannonballs to gun crews defending the town, receiving seven pence for each. Some even ran up to exploding shells and kicked sand on them to extinguish the fuse.[11]

D'Estaing decided to begin the final assault before dawn on October 9, with Spring Hill Redoubt on the British right as the main target. Other troops would hit the center and left so Prévost would not know where to send his reserves. Among the units assigned to these feints were the Volunteers of Santo Domingo. Two months earlier, d'Estaing had called at France's largest sugar island, Saint-Domingue, just long enough to put together a militia battalion of 545 free Blacks. One of the youngest Volunteers was a bootblack and mess boy named Henri Christophe. Three decades later, when the world's first successful slave insurrection transformed Saint-Domingue into Haiti, Christophe would become its first king.[12]

Hours before dawn on October 9, fog descended on the lowcountry, helpfully disguising the allies' troop movements. But as the assailants crouched in the darkness, they were unnerved by the wail of bagpipes arising from the Spring Hill redoubt. That sound could mean only one thing: Prévost had stationed his most effective fighters, the 71st Highland Regiment, at Spring Hill. Ominous enough on its own, Prévost's deployment of the 71st indicated that he knew where the allies planned to focus their attack. When James Curry, a sergeant major in the Charles Town Grenadiers, turned up missing, his comrades immediately conjectured that he had defected to Prévost with this crucial intelligence.[13]

Few if any soldiers from the storied 71st were actually among the 110 men guarding the Spring Hill redoubt that day. But fortune smiled on its defenders in other ways. A series of delays postponed the allied assault until after daybreak. A half dozen French and American columns were supposed to strike simultaneously, but as each unit came on line, its commander led it forward without waiting for the others. Inevitably, as Maj. Thomas Pinckney reported, the allied forces were "beaten in detail."[14]

Amazingly, at least one man from each of the six columns managed to scale the British parapet and plant his regimental flag—a proud symbol as well as a rallying point—before being shot down.[15] Back in 1763, when Eastern Woodlands Indians rebelled against the British, they never attacked a settlement or fort unless they had either overwhelming numbers or the element of surprise. William Howe was reminded of the wisdom of this policy at Bunker Hill; the Americans received their reminders at Montreal, Stono Ferry, and Savannah. D'Estaing's haste and fragile sense of honor had added up to a failed frontal assault that cost the French and American armies nearly a thousand casualties. Barely a hundred redcoats died or were wounded.[16]

The news of October 9 had still not reached Washington at West Point on the Hudson by November 5, when he wrote, "We turn an impatient eye to the Sea-board, looking for the arrival of the french fleet." Actually, by that time, d'Estaing and his ships had long since left Georgia, he for the mother country and most of them for the all-consuming Caribbean. Washington had to scrap his grand scheme for capturing New York.[17]

Although African Americans had performed wonders in saving Savannah from Britain's enemies, Prévost immediately set about disarming them, though it meant "shedding much of their blood."[18] David George and his family survived the siege, but amid the massive circulation of people resulting from the Franco-American invasion, he contracted smallpox and nearly died. Well into the spring of 1780, he remained unable to work, and his family scraped by on the pittance Gen. Clinton paid his wife for washing his clothes.[19]

IT MIGHT SEEM RIDICULOUS to compare the travails of David George's family, besieged in Savannah, to those of Benedict Arnold, whom Washington had named as military commissioner of Philadelphia after the June 1778 British evacuation, but Arnold had trouble believing that any American could be as aggrieved as he. Twice, at Quebec on the last day of 1775 and at Freeman's Farm on October 7, 1777, he had been wounded in his left leg, which was now all but useless. And yet the nation had never shown him the least gratitude. Congress had insulted him by passing him over for promotion to major general and since then had fallen far behind in his pay—a grievance he shared with other Continental officers and soldiers—and in reimbursing his public expenditures.

Arnold's worst tormentor was Pennsylvania's executive council, which revived the old charge that he had abused his public office for personal profit, possibly even trading with the enemy. In the spring of 1779, with his grievances as well as his debts mounting, Arnold gave Joseph Stansbury, a Loyalist who had remained in Philadelphia when the British evacuated in June 1778, a message for Henry Clinton: for the right price, he would turn traitor. Although Arnold was prepared to switch sides immediately, Sir Henry informed him, through John André, the British officer who became his handler, that he was actually most useful right where he was—privy to all of the Continental Army's secrets. By the autumn of 1780, Clinton had paid him £500 and promised him much more.[20]

André, who had organized the extravagant meschianza in Philadelphia in May 1778, had not lost his flair for the dramatic, and he devised a variety of ways to communicate with Arnold. For example, he wrote letters to Margaret Chew, his onetime meschianza collaborator, knowing she would write back by way of Arnold and his wife, also named Margaret. Before forwarding Chew's letters to André, Margaret Arnold used invisible ink to interline them with her husband's messages.[21]

ARNOLD WAS BY NO means alone in his mounting sense of grievance against the nation's leaders. Early in the war, American storekeepers had run out of salt as well as sugar products, including rum. But the supply crisis that developed in the spring of 1779 was different, for now Americans were often unable to obtain even domestically produced basic necessities such as grain. Nowhere did rising food prices hit harder than Pennsylvania, which had been colonial North America's granary. Hyperinflation had several sources. Privateering, soldiering, and other wartime employments drew fishermen from their nets and farmers from their fields, decreasing output. In addition, agents for the British, American, and French armies all competed for grain, bidding up the price. And bad weather shortened the 1778 crop.

But the primary culprits were the state and federal governments. Just in 1779, Congress put an additional $125 million into circulation, bringing the total to $226 million. At the start of that year, Continental currency had already lost nearly 90 percent of its value. By the end of December, it would take more than 40 Continental dollars to buy one dollar's worth of gold or silver.[22] Washington complained that "a waggon load of money will scarcely purchase a waggon load of provision."[23] Rising crop prices ought to have motivated farmers to increase production, but the prospect of being paid in depreciated paper money had the opposite effect, and ebbing output pushed prices still higher.

Many Americans, including Washington, attributed hyperinflation to "Monopolizers—forestallers—& Engrossers," who deliberately held goods back from the market in order to drive up the price. And they were not entirely wrong. One of the people accused of jacking up grain prices was Samuel Chase, a Maryland delegate to Congress and future Supreme Court justice. In a brace of *New-York Journal* articles, Alexander Hamilton claimed that Chase was trying to corner the grain market in anticipation of the arrival of the French fleet, whose commissaries would require vast quantities of bread.[24] The Virginia legislature adopted an anti-monopoly law and used it to seize £20,000 worth of woolen clothing and blankets for the army. Throughout 1779, as U.S. and British armies in New York and South Carolina fought to a stalemate, imperial officials believed the rebel colonists would soon come crawling back, defeated not just on the battlefield but by the collapse of their currency.[25]

As Americans struggled to feed their families, other grievances seemed less tolerable than ever. Philadelphia militiamen who had repeatedly been called up became increasingly resentful of well-to-do neighbors who evaded duty by paying fines that common people could not afford. In a May 12 petition, militiamen asked the state's executive coun-

cil to fine every Pennsylvanian who declined to serve "in proportion
to his Estate." Many of Philadelphia's female Loyalists had remained
behind when their husbands joined the British evacuation to New York,
and now their neighbors accused them of transmitting military secrets
to their partners. A May 25 citizens' meeting demanded that Loyalist
women be exiled.[26]

Numerous Pennsylvanians considered their state's 1776 constitution
too democratic, but by 1779, many others viewed state officials as insufficiently responsive to their needs. Taking matters into their own hands,
they declared (in the words of one anonymous broadside), "down with
your prices, or down with yourselves."[27] At a May 25 mass meeting,
Philadelphians established a committee to stabilize and then lower prices,
and other towns followed suit. Thomas Paine and the other members of
Philadelphia's committee labored valiantly to enforce price controls, but
farmers and merchants increasingly diverted their commodities to other
towns, exacerbating shortages and angering one of Paine's core constituencies, artisans.

Paine soon turned against price-fixing, and the members of his committee finally gave up the fight, whereupon frustrated militiamen once
again took to the streets. Suspected forestallers and Loyalist sympathizers, most of whom had broken no law, were nabbed and delivered to the
city jail. On October 4, militiamen seized five residents they believed had
helped the British or violated price controls and paraded them through
town, all the while beating the rogue's march. The crowd then headed
toward the home of James Wilson. The previous autumn, attorney Wilson had defended the men accused of collaborating with the British
during the occupation. He had also opposed the Pennsylvania constitution of 1776 as well as price controls, and on October 4 he harbored
twenty suspected Loyalists and monopolizers.[28]

As the crowd approached Wilson's home at the southwest corner
of Third and Walnut, its leader, Capt. Ephraim Faulkner, tried to slow
the pace in order to avoid or at least postpone a confrontation. But his
followers pushed him forward. As the last militiamen passed Wilson's
house, one of his guests, Capt. Robert Campbell, taunted them from a
second-story window. A shot rang out—each side accused the other of
firing first—and a battle ensued. In short order, one of the "gentlemen"
in the house, five or six of the militiamen in the street, and a Black child
who had been drawing water from a nearby pump all lay dead. More
than a dozen other Philadelphians were injured. There might have been

additional violence if not for the timely arrival of cavalry led by Joseph Reed, who as president of Pennsylvania's executive council sympathized with the rioters' goals but not their methods.[29]

State assemblymen responded to the Fort Wilson riot by pardoning the militiamen, distributing a hundred barrels of flour to the poor (with preference given to those who responded to a militia callout), banning forestalling, and proportioning militia fines to wealth. But they chose not to distribute the burden of military service more equitably.[30]

Within months of the Fort Wilson riot, the misery resulting from inflation and artificial food shortages was exacerbated by a natural cause: the winter of 1779–1780 was the coldest on record. During "the hard winter," as it was called, the Delaware and Schuylkill Rivers froze solid, and New Yorkers marveled at their ability to walk or sleigh over to Long Island or New Jersey or even five miles down the harbor to Staten Island. But the cold—only once in January 1780 did Philadelphia thermometers rise above 32 degrees—also slowed the transport of food and other necessities, and no one suffered worse than the Continental soldiers encamped at Morristown, New Jersey. Much of what American mythology says about the Valley Forge winter of 1777–1778 actually applies to Morristown in early 1780. During one snowstorm, Joseph Plumb Martin "did not put a single morsel of victuals into my mouth for four days and as many nights, except a little black birch bark which I gnawed off a stick of wood."[31]

ICE STILL CLOSED PHILADELPHIA to navigation on March 1, 1780, when the Pennsylvania legislature voted to abolish slavery in the state. Adopted with much fanfare, the law did not actually liberate a single slave. It merely stated that African Americans born after March 1 would be freed after a twenty-eight-year apprenticeship to their mothers' owners. A handful of Black Pennsylvanians born just before the adoption of the law were still enslaved in 1847, when the assembly finally ended Pennsylvania slavery altogether. Pennsylvania was nonetheless the first of the original states to set slavery on the road to extinction. Over the next three decades, four other northern legislatures enacted similar "gradual" emancipation laws.[32]

Unlike in Massachusetts, no Black Pennsylvanians had petitioned the assembly for an abolition law, but many had contributed to its adoption indirectly. As the executive council noted, the dozens of African Americans who had left Philadelphia with the British in June 1778 had undermined the institution of slavery in the state, making it much more vulnerable to a legislative challenge.[33]

By the time Pennsylvania passed its abolition law, Gen. Henry Clinton had begun offering many enslaved South Carolinians a shorter, if less certain, path to freedom. On March 29, he began ferrying ten thousand British soldiers to the east bank of the Ashley River in preparation for a siege of Charles Town. Like the British armies that had failed to capture the city in 1776 and 1778, this one was diverse, with redcoats and German mercenaries but also white and Black Loyalists, including Harry Washington, who had fled Mount Vernon back in 1776. British military planners shifted the war for North America southward for a wide variety of reasons. Like every other region except New England, it was thought to harbor tens of thousands of Loyalists who would unmask themselves the moment redcoats arrived to lead them. The enormous enslaved population of the four southernmost rebel colonies—360,000 souls or about 40 percent of the population—supposedly made it the rebellion's soft underbelly. And even among whites, the opulence of the Few was said to have engendered deep resentment among the Many, making them ripe for revolt against their patriot leaders. Furthermore, if the British could conquer the south, they could divert the revenue generated by its rice and tobacco away from the rebellion and toward its suppression. But Clinton's most pressing concerns as he gathered up more than half of his New York City garrison and headed south on December 26, 1779, were, first, that he could not protect British Savannah against a renewed rebel attack without also taking South Carolina, and, second, that plunging temperatures all but shut down military operations in the north (by eliminating free forage) and finally made them tolerable in the south.[34]

On their way down the coast, Clinton's ships ran into a horrific storm that blew them far out into the Atlantic, prolonging the voyage. Stocks of forage ran out, and wranglers had to cast more than a thousand cavalry and artillery horses into the sea. One troop transport ran aground . . . in England. The remnants of the fleet limped into Savannah for repairs, then headed north, entering the North Edisto River twenty miles southwest of Charles Town on February 11, 1780. The troops began disembarking on Simmons (now Seabrook) Island that very night.[35]

Henry Clinton resembled William Howe in coming into the post of commander-in-chief with a reputation for audacity—but also in quickly learning the value of going slow. Clinton spent seven weeks marching his

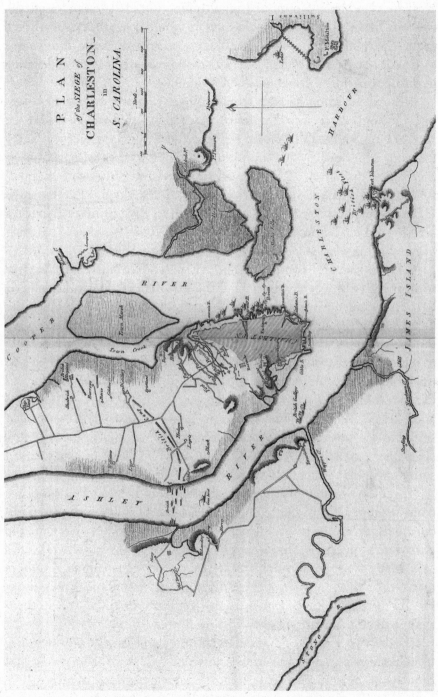

Map of the Siege of Charles Town, South Carolina, from
Chief Justice John Marshall's *Life of George Washington*

army overland from Simmons Island to Drayton Hall, ten miles northwest of Charles Town, where his soldiers would cross the Ashley River
to the Charleston Peninsula. After Augustine Prévost broke off his siege
of Charles Town two years earlier, his troops covered the same distance
in the opposite direction in one-tenth the time.

Meanwhile Adm. Marriot Arbuthnot was deciding that the best way
over the sandbar and into Charleston Harbor was to not tangle with Fort
Moultrie on Sullivan's Island, as Clinton and Commodore Peter Parker
had four years earlier, but simply to blow past it. As the fleet entered
the harbor on March 20, losing no warships and only one transport,
the small Continental squadron withdrew up the Cooper River, east of
Charles Town, leaving the Ashley, to the west, wide open for Clinton's
crossing, which began at dawn on March 29. Two days later the British
began digging siege trenches.[36]

Whig authorities compelled about six hundred enslaved Charlestonians to build a defensive line all the way across the peninsula. The
barriers included a moat and an elaborate redoubt commonly called the
Citadel (later the nucleus of the college of the same name).[37] Before leaving New York City, Gen. Clinton, fearing his men would not be able
to mold South Carolina's sandy soil into effective breastworks, had had
them build hundreds of "mantelets"—freestanding wooden screens, six
to ten feet high and up to sixteen feet long. Sailors from royal warships
and African Americans who had escaped to the British army—or been
seized by it—positioned these prefabricated barriers in front of the redcoats' first parallel. On April 10, having completed that trench, Clinton
summoned Gen. Lincoln to surrender, only to be refused.[38]

Three days later, Governor John Rutledge and three members of his
council slipped out of the capital city in hopes of rallying the militia to
defend its last escape route, the region between the Cooper River and the
coast north of Charles Town. But few militiamen answered Rutledge's
call. Many worried about a recent resurgence of smallpox.[39] Others
feared their slaves would rebel the moment they left home. And militiamen in the upcountry resented eastern authorities' failure to help them
against the Indians or relieve their dire shortage of salt.[40]

As the two sides bombarded each other and British workers dug
trenches ever closer to the American works, Capt. Johann Ewald had
time to look around. The Spanish moss dangling from tree branches "like
horses' tails" gave "a very melancholy appearance to a forest" but also
provided fodder for farm animals. Alligators, snakes, and tropical disease

were all sufficiently alarming, and Ewald "could not put a bite of bread into his mouth which was not covered with sand," but "the intolerable heat, the lack of good water, and the billions of sandflies and mosquitoes made up the worst nuisance."[41]

Within the besieged capital, William Moultrie noted that many soldiers' "faces were so swelled they could scarcely see out of their eyes." He blamed sleep deprivation, though insect bites would have had the same effect. Both armies' artillery captains grew more cunning in their cruelty. British gunners increased the kill radius of exploding shells by filling them with rice and sugar, and American crews replied with canisters of "scrap iron and broken glass." Friendly fire incidents further dismayed both sides.[42]

At an April 20 council of war, the Continental officers concluded that they could not save Charles Town and that their duty now was to escape. But prominent civilians informed Lincoln that they preferred that he surrender rather than abandon the capital, since an attempted military exodus might prompt Clinton to order up a destructive frontal assault. The locals "declared to General Lincoln, that if he attempted to withdraw the troops, and leave the citizens; that they would cut up his boats, and open the gates to the enemy." "This," William Moultrie noted, "put a stop to all thoughts of an evacuation."[43]

PRISON SHIPS ARE GENERALLY thought of as all-male institutions, but the British often allowed women aboard, either to care for kinsmen—as many did, at great risk of infection—or to sell the inmates food and other goods, as New Yorker Elizabeth Burgin did through much of 1779. Months later, British officials learned that Burgin had helped as many as two hundred of her customers escape. With redcoats in close pursuit, she in turn absconded to Philadelphia. Gen. Washington helped her obtain a congressional pension, and in her thank-you letter she could not resist giving him a word of advice. "I Should Be Glad," Burgin wrote, "to See a French Fleett Surrounding New York By Watter & the Brave Americans Storming the Lines By Land & Were I a man I Think I Should not Want Courage to Be one of the Foremost in Mounting one of their Strongest Fortreses."[44]

Washington shared Burgin's desire to storm New York City, and in May 1780 he thought he might finally be able to act on it. For the first time since d'Estaing's unsuccessful attack on Savannah in the fall of 1779, Louis XVI had sent a fleet across the Atlantic. Seven ships of the line and six frigates, commanded by the chevalier Ternay, escorted transports carrying more than five thousand troops under the redoubtable comte de Rochambeau. With Ternay's squadron just over the horizon, Washington came to view the British siege of Charles Town as a blessing for the Continentals, since staffing it had required Clinton to reduce his New York City garrison to just eight thousand troops. The American commander endeavored to prevent the British troops besieging Charles Town from finding out that Ternay and Rochambeau were on their way, lest they raise the siege, take to their ships, and "concenter their force at New York."[45]

But South Carolina Whigs were no longer in a position to tie Clinton down, for on May 12, Lincoln surrendered Charles Town and his army. Given that the two adversaries had exchanged cannon fire for more than a month, casualties had been surprisingly light. Clinton had 76 men killed and 189 wounded. On the American side, about 20 civilians and 89 soldiers died, and an additional 140 militiamen and Continentals were wounded. Clinton's 5,611 prisoners found one of his requirements especially humiliating: marching out of Charles Town to lay down their arms, they had to furl their flags.[46]

Contemporaries had no difficulty explaining why Clinton had succeeded in capturing Charles Town just seven months after d'Estaing, who had also possessed both naval and ground superiority, fell short at Savannah. Whereas the hurried d'Estaing had launched a frontal assault, the patient Clinton had laid a siege.

Only three days after Lincoln surrendered Charles Town, on May 15, the city suffered a blow more fatal than the siege. British soldiers were stacking captured Continental muskets when one went off, igniting a nearby stockpile of gunpowder, and the explosion in turn caused numerous other firelocks to discharge. Nearly all of the fifty men guarding the confiscated weapons and ammunition were killed, along with as many as 250 other soldiers and civilians, Black and white. "One man was dashed with violence against the steeple of the new independant church, which was at a great distance from the explosion, and left the marks of his body there for several days."[47]

Lincoln proposed to trade his army for the roughly equivalent force that had been captured with Burgoyne nearly three years earlier, and the British endorsed the idea. But Congress opposed it, as did the chevalier de La Luzerne, the French representative in Philadelphia. By this time, even George Washington had come around to Congress's conviction that, as he put it in July 1780, "the exchange of the privates, tho strongly urged by humanity, would certainly be against us in a political view." Recognizing that freed redcoats and Germans would return to the fight, while most freed Americans would simply head home, Washington agreed to leave Britain's American prisoners where they were as the only way of subjecting their British counterparts to the same fate.[48]

For the Whigs, the month of May held one more tragedy in store. Abraham Buford had marched his regiment of Virginia Continentals south to help defend Charles Town. Arriving too late, they were ordered back north but soon came to the attention of Charles Cornwallis and Banastre Tarleton.

Cornwallis had returned to England at the end of 1778 to care for his ailing wife. She died on February 16, a month after his arrival, and to "shift the scene," he rejoined the British army in America.[49] Less than a week after Charles Town fell, Gen. Clinton sent Cornwallis to pacify northern South Carolina. In an effort to keep him south of the Santee River, U.S. troops destroyed most of the available boats. They hid the rest in swamps, "but," as an American officer learned, "the negroes discovered them and the army crossed."[50]

Cornwallis ordered Lt. Col. Tarleton and his British Legion, a light infantry and light cavalry force made up of redcoats and New York Loyalists, to rush ahead in hopes of overtaking Buford before he was reinforced. Nearly two-thirds of his 270 troops were cavalry, and to speed the pursuit the infantrymen rode behind the troopers. The horses were ridden so hard that several died, but on May 29 the green-jacketed Legionnaires came within sight of the Virginians.[51]

Buford could have found a defensible position and dug in, but he knew the Legionnaires would soon be reinforced, so he tried to outrun them. Thus he and his men were out in the open, fully exposed, when Tarleton and his men caught up with them in the Waxhaws region, about five miles south of the border between the two Carolinas. Through a messenger, Tarleton promised to parole Buford and all his officers if he surrendered. These were better terms than Lincoln had obtained, but the American force, which now included forty Continental cavalry, was more than 50 percent larger than the army pursuing it, and Buford indignantly refused. As the two negotiated, both violated the rules of war by continuing to march their men northward. Then the British cavalry charged.[52]

Most of the American infantry had never seen battle, while Tarleton's

Legionnaires were veterans. Buford compounded this disadvantage by ordering his soldiers to withhold their fire until the advancing enemy was only ten yards away, but that old axiom did not work against a cavalry charge. Slashing with their sabers, Tarleton's troopers broke through the Continental line, followed in short order by the infantry. Many of the rebels asked for quarter but were refused, giving rise to the term "Tarleton's quarter" for the murder of men trying to surrender. At least 113 of Buford's soldiers died that day. Rejecting any responsibility for the murders, Tarleton (who had only five killed) noted that his horse had taken a round and fallen dead on top of him, not only preventing him from controlling his men but giving many the false impression that he had been killed, which "stimulated the soldiers to a vindictive asperity not easily restrained." Although Tarleton had not ordered the Waxhaws massacre, his actions in the wake of previous engagements had convinced his troops that, despite his public protestations, he welcomed the murder of men who surrendered.[53]

FOR THE WHIGS, THE losses at Charles Town and Waxhaws only added to the gloom caused by persisting aggravations such as the intensifying depreciation of the Continental currency, which impoverished everyone on a fixed income, most glaringly the soldiers, who never got a pay raise during eight years of war. On March 18, 1780, Congress mandated that Continental dollars would be worth only one-fortieth of their face value. So if you owed someone a dollar, you would now need 40 Continentals to settle up. Congress began replacing the old paper money with new interest-bearing Continental bills to be issued by the states in small quantities. But the new currency depreciated as fast as the old.

Continental soldiers also had other grievances, including a food shortage worse than they had known at Valley Forge. On the evening of May 25, after three years of being paid in badly depreciated currency, five months without even that, and ten days without meat, two Connecticut regiments mutinied. When the colonel of another regiment tried to prevent his troops from joining in, one bayoneted him. The colonel lived, and officers appeased their men with promises to find beef. But the mutiny both nourished a British belief that the rebel coalition was cracking up and shook Whig authorities' confidence; Washington confessed that it had given him "infinitely more concern than any thing that has ever happened" since the start of the war.[54]

Even the heavens seemed to reflect the Whigs' depression of spirits.

On the morning of May 19, especially in New England but as far south as New Jersey, the sky grew so dark that roosters crowed and (as Joseph Plumb Martin recalled) "the whip-poor-wills sung their usual serenade."[55] Americans knew from their almanacs that this was no eclipse, and many believed the world was coming to an end. (The most widely accepted modern explanation of the Dark Day is smoke from forest fires.)

In the Americans' despair, Gen. Wilhelm von Knyphausen saw opportunity. As the commander of the British garrison in New York during Clinton's expedition to South Carolina, Knyphausen knew that Washington had had to detach troops to nearly every point of the compass, including south to Charles Town and west to fight Indians. Moreover, the German general had heard about the mutiny in the Connecticut Line—and also that New Jersey militiamen and civilians were just as dissatisfied with the rebel regime, enough, in fact, to fight for their king. Knyphausen believed that if he could strike Morristown quickly enough, possibly with local help, the few Continentals still encamped there would have to run for their lives, abandoning most of their cannon, horses, and other supplies and dealing a perhaps fatal blow to Whig morale.[56]

As the participant-historian Charles Stedman observed, however, the Continentals' and New Jerseyans' resistance against their leaders—like so much of the Whigs' internal insurgency—"arose from distress, and not disaffection." New Jersey militiamen doggedly blocked Knyphausen's path, and then Washington moved much of his army into New Jersey's Short Hills, a highly defensible position that Knyphausen did not dare attack.[57]

Persuaded by Knyphausen's raid that he had spread himself too thin, Washington called numerous troops back to headquarters. Depleting Whig garrisons in northern New York inevitably cleared the path for Iroquois warriors responding in kind to Sullivan's torching of their 1779 corn crop. Meanwhile a delegation of Six Nations sachems, led by Guyasuta and carrying "4 Belts containing 24 thousand wampum" and a call to continue resistance, visited the Detroit Indians, who needed no convincing. Native American warriors were not just defending their land and seeking revenge but obtaining substitutes for deceased kin. At a 1780 conference at Fort Niagara, Guyasuta gave his Iroquois countrymen a settler's scalp "to replace your Chief *Sekanade*, that he may be once more amongst you."[58]

At the same time, a handful of Iroquois warriors continued to provide invaluable assistance to the United States. In June 1780, Washington noted that thirty-one U.S. soldiers stationed at Fort Schuyler, angry at "the want of pay & of necessary cloathing—particularly Shirts," had deserted en masse, fleeing north toward the British Fort Oswegatchie (near modern-day Ogdensburg, New York)—until a party of Oneidas commanded by Lt. Abraham Hardenbergh caught up with them, gunning down thirteen. As the historian Carl Van Doren notes, "This is perhaps the only time in the history of the American Army when an officer used Indians to kill white soldiers." But by this time, many of the Oneidas had rejoined the Iroquois confederation and the British alliance.[59]

A telling symptom of the rebels' despondency was the decision of John Dunlap, editor of the *Pennsylvania Packet*, to step out from behind the conventional editorial "we." "I am," he declared in an unsigned wrap-up of the war news, "like every other loyal and faithful citizen, affected at every disaster which befal us." But he found evidence that Americans were rising to the occasion. One encouraging sign, right there in Philadelphia, was an extraordinary fundraising campaign initiated by a woman named Esther Reed.[60]

Born and raised in England, Reed had immigrated to Pennsylvania in 1770. During the War of Independence, as her husband, Joseph, alternated between Pennsylvania politics and the Continental Army, the couple endured countless separations. Both left Philadelphia during the British occupation, and Esther delivered a son on May 12, 1778. The very next day, her next-youngest child, "a fine little girl near two years old," succumbed to smallpox. Like Abigail Adams the previous year, Reed blamed herself for her child's death; her single-minded focus on her pregnancy had prevented her from exercising "the necessary precaution" against the deadly virus.[61]

In May 1780, the Reeds had another son, naming him for Joseph's onetime mentor, George Washington. The pregnancy and delivery aggravated Esther's chronic ailments, but she was determined to add her mite to a burgeoning civilian campaign to bolster the Continental army. On June 5, Thomas Paine sent Joseph Reed, who was president of Pennsylvania, an extraordinary proposal: wealthy Philadelphians should voluntarily hand over their silverware to be melted down, cast as coins, and paid out to the troops. That was more Paine than the city's merchants could handle, but three days later, they embraced his alternate proposal that they donate to a fund to be used for enlistment bounties.[62]

Esther Reed wished to do something for the troops already serving.

On June 10, she published a broadside entitled *The Sentiments of an American Woman*. Lamenting that Continental soldiers feared "their distresses may be lost, and their services be forgotten," she proposed a house-to-house fund drive on their behalf. It would be conducted entirely by women, since they, no less than their brothers and husbands, were "born for liberty." And they had plenty of role models, since crises throughout history had inspired valiant women to disregard gender norms. As examples, Reed cited biblical figures such as Esther and enlightened queens such as England's Elizabeth and Russia's Catherine the Great, both of whom had "extended the empire of liberty." Now American women felt the same stirrings as the republic's males: "Our ambition is kindled by the [f]ame of those heroines."[63]

Sentiments of an American Woman reminded women of the crucial role they had played in the early years of the imperial struggle. They had given up tea, and their "republican and laborious hands [had] spun the flax" that sustained the boycott of British linen and clothed the soldiers. Now women should abstain from fancy clothing and hairdos and donate the savings. One of the campaign's organizers touted it as also giving female Philadelphians who had consorted with British officers during the 1777–1778 occupations "an opportunity of relinquishing former errors."[64]

Nor were female Philadelphians the only ones to whom the fundraising effort offered the prospect of redemption. Nearly four years earlier, Joseph Reed, then a protégé of George Washington, had insulted him behind his back, gotten caught, and forfeited his trust. In 1778, when a court-martial suspended Gen. Charles Lee for misbehaving at the Battle of Monmouth, he published Reed's insults in a Baltimore newspaper, reopening the wound. Reed's ascension to the presidency of his state that same year only revived the tensions, as the commander-in-chief pressured Pennsylvania and other states to forward more and more supplies to an army that might still be able to capture New York City—if only it was not being undermined by "Mutiny and sedition."[65]

Reed sent what he could but also warned that previous government demands had made Pennsylvania farmers just as mutinous as the troops; more than one state official trying to seize property from delinquent taxpayers had been killed. Washington and President Reed also took opposing positions in Pennsylvania's battle against Benedict Arnold, with Reed at one point warning that unless an upcoming court-martial took Pennsylvania's charges against Arnold seriously, the state would stop supporting the Continental Army in the way it had famously helped Gen. Braddock: with wagons. Meanwhile Reed's political opponents, the Republicans, positioned themselves for the October 1780 legislative elections by sabotaging everything he did. At its best, Esther's fund-raising effort would help repair Joseph's relations with both Washington and the voters.[66]

The women's canvas soon expanded beyond Philadelphia. Reed and fellow organizer Sarah Bache (daughter of Benjamin Franklin) planned to entrust the money to Gen. Washington, with the one condition that he not use it "to procure to the army the objects of subsistence, arms or cloathing, which are due to them by the continent." At a time when the hyperinflation of the Continental currency had wiped out the troops' wages, the women hoped to hand each soldier two dollars' worth of honest-to-God gold and silver coin.[67]

Washington welcomed the ladies' campaign but not their plan to give his soldiers hard money, which he feared might actually generate "much discontent," since the troops were bound to ask how these women could procure coin when their own paymasters could not. He suggested that "the female patriots" instead deposit their money in a bank that Republican merchants had just established to purchase food for the army, thus boosting the bank's cash reserves. In return, they would receive banknotes with which to sew desperately needed shirts for the soldiers.[68]

Reed initially acceded to the commander-in-chief's preference for clothing over cash. (Despite the high cost of importing linen during wartime, neither he nor she considered having the women spin the thread or weave the cloth.) But when she learned that the army would soon receive two large shipments of shirts, she summoned the gumption to tell him that "an Idea prevails among the Ladies, that the Soldiers will not be so much *gratified*, by bestowing an Article to which they are entitled from the Public." Moreover, while Joseph felt compelled to show support for his political opponents' new bank, Esther did not, and she pointed out to Washington that turning her group's money into banknotes would diminish its purchasing power.[69]

Washington backed down from his suggestion about the bank but not from his preference for shirts, and Esther Reed could see that he was "hurt by our . . . not following his directions." Up to this point, her volunteer work had enhanced her husband's standing with his former commander, but with her defiance she risked damaging it. So she and the other women gave in, laid their money out in linen, and sewed more than two thousand shirts, with "no woman of whatever quality neglecting the honour of assisting with her own hands to make them up."[70]

Historians routinely refer to Reed's campaign as "the Ladies' Association," but she and other organizers never actually took that name, or any other, apparently out of fear that founding a formal institution would seem unladylike. (Perhaps we should refer to them the way Washington did, as "female patriots.") They nonetheless spread the movement to other states, generally by writing governors' wives. Like Virginia first lady Martha Jefferson, Esther Reed suffered from chronic health problems that were aggravated by her repeated pregnancies, and she died on September 18 at the age of thirty-three, apparently of dysentery. Very few women's obituaries were published in the eighteenth century, and most of these were so generic as to be interchangeable. Reed's was no exception. Separately, though, the editors of the *Pennsylvania Gazette* described her fundraising effort in loving detail, even speculating that she might have inadvertently taken her own life by "imposing on herself too great a part of the task."[71]

CHAPTER 28

Secret Agency

1780

ON JUNE 3, HENRY CLINTON ISSUED A PROCLAMATION THREAT-ening to hang any free male South Carolinian who refused to join the Loyalist militia. Just five days later, he set sail for New York with about 4,500 of the British and German troops he had brought with him—and also about 500 African Americans who had recently escaped to his lines. More than 5,000 soldiers remained in South Carolina with the earl Cornwallis, who hated his commander-in-chief but zealously implemented his anti-neutrality proclamation. After establishing outposts throughout the state/colony, Cornwallis announced on June 30 that he had "put an end to all resistance in South Carolina."[1]

The earl celebrated too soon, for many Whigs who had accepted British protection responded to his army's with-us-or-against-us approach by resuming their insurgency. Riding south to rendezvous with Georgia rebels, Andrew Pickens, a Whig militia colonel from the Appalachian foothills, stopped to ask directions from a Loyalist woman—who directed him right into the arms of a band of Loyalist fighters. Once again swearing fealty to the king, Pickens stayed out of the fight until learning of British atrocities against Whig prisoners, whereupon he assumed leadership of a band of Whig partisans (guerrillas) in raids against British convoys, patrols, and outposts.[2]

Pickens was an old Indian fighter who now brought frontier tactics to the battle against the British, and farther east, so did Thomas Sumter. A colonel in the Continental Army until September 1778, when he contracted malaria and had to resign, Sumter narrowly escaped Tarleton on May 28, 1780. But when British troopers arrived at the absent Sumter's home and his wife, Mary, refused to disclose his whereabouts, they plundered the plantation, seizing or freeing several slaves and yanking him back into the conflict as the elected leader of a partisan band. Sumter's counterpart in the lowcountry swamps north of Charles Town was Francis Marion, whose multiracial guerrilla unit specialized in raiding British supply convoys. *After* Pickens ("the Wizard Owl"), Sumter ("the Gamecock"), and Marion ("the Swamp Fox") had proven themselves in the field, Whig governor John Rutledge commissioned them as militia generals.[3]

One of the rebels' first targets was Christian Huck, who years earlier had immigrated from Germany to Philadelphia and entered the practice of law. When the city's Whigs confiscated Huck's property, he accepted a captain's commission in Tarleton's British Legion, and in South Carolina his troops became notorious for cruelty to civilians, especially the Presbyterians he blamed for all his losses. On July 11, 1780, while patrolling just south of the border between the two Carolinas, more than one hundred of Huck's British and Loyalist fighters captured five rebels, locked them in a corn crib, and announced plans to execute them the next day. At least three local residents—Mary McClure, sister of one of the captives, an enslaved man named Watt, and the physically handicapped Joseph Kerr—rode to Gen. Sumter's camp with news of Huck's assault, and at dawn on July 12, about 250 Whig militiamen attacked Huck's party, freed the prisoners, and captured or killed all but twenty-four of his troops. Huck himself received a fatal head wound. Years later, a doctor whose family had lost its home to Huck's raiders exhumed his skeleton and displayed it in his office.[4]

On the day of Huck's defeat, the diminutive Jane Thomas, who had traveled to the town of Ninety Six to visit her husband, a captured Whig officer, overheard two female Loyalists discussing their menfolk's plan to surprise a regiment of sixty Whig militiamen encamped fifty miles north at Cedar Springs. She galloped ahead of the raiders and alerted the Whig commander, her son Thomas, allowing him to surprise the Loyalists instead.[5] Astonishingly, less than a month later, on August 8, Mary Dillard made a similar overnight ride—briefer but bareback—to warn a different Whig army, also encamped near Cedar Springs, that the Loyalists were coming. The Whigs' triumph over Huck and the firm stands they twice took at Cedar Springs helped restore spirits crushed by the disasters at Charles Town and the Waxhaws.[6]

And women would continue to carry warnings to men throughout the war. On November 20, Banastre Tarleton resolved to prevent Thomas Sumter and his militia from crossing the Tyger River. Hoping to pin them down at William Blackstock's farm, he gathered his cavalry and a few mounted infantry and rushed ahead of his infantry and artillery. An unknown woman rode ahead to inform Sumter that he and his men would have a vast if temporary numerical advantage over their assailants. The rebels went on the offensive, beating up Tarleton's advance and then escaping across the river before his infantry and cannon arrived.[7]

Why were so many Whig women able to overhear, and then thwart, male Loyalists' plots against their husbands and sons? Elizabeth Ellet, who had lived in Columbia, South Carolina, just before writing her two-volume *Women of the American Revolution* (1848), had a theory about that. Contempt for female influence and intelligence dissolved officers' inhibitions about discussing their plans "in the hearing of weak and despised women." Ellet's correspondence with dozens of women, especially in the South, convinced her that "the tradition of the country teems with accounts" of women's "secret agency," though few were ever "recorded in the military journals."[8]

Sometimes women took up arms. Ellet reported that two sisters-in-law, Grace and Rachel Martin, grabbed pistols and disguised themselves as men to waylay a British courier and his two guards, obtaining valuable intelligence that they passed on to American commanders. The befuddled redcoats then found lodging at a nearby home—the Martin farm—where they failed to recognize their attackers in their hostesses. At about the same time, Deborah Sampson, a Middleborough, Massachusetts, servant, weaver, and teacher, dressed as a man to enlist in the Continental Army. Wounded, she nursed herself back to health to avoid detection and was caught and sent home only after being hospitalized with disease.[9]

Whigs spent much of the summer and fall of 1780 trying to capture the outposts Cornwallis had established throughout the Carolina backcountry. Revolutionary mythology paradoxically paints the Whigs as invincible underdogs, but the reality was that their frontal assaults on fortified positions—for instance at Hanging Rock and Rocky Mount—often failed. They did much better when they employed stratagems. In the wee hours of July 14, Whigs took Gowen's Old Fort by pretending to be Loyalists. On August 19, when the Whigs sent to capture Musgrove's Mill on the Enoree River realized they were outnumbered, they abandoned plans for a frontal assault and instead tricked the garrison into sallying out—and into an ambush. When more than one hundred Loyalists barricaded themselves in Rugeley's Mill, William Washington, second cousin to the commander-in-chief, obtained their surrender on December 4 by menacing them with fake cannon.[10]

Grace and Rachel Martin, disguised in male clothing, waylaying a British
ourier and his guards in modern-day Edgefield County, South Carolina

Neither side could control the backcountry, but that was tantamount to a Whig victory, since the British and the Loyalists bore the burden of proving that they had reintegrated the Carolinas into the empire.[11]

SINCE 1775, AFRICAN AMERICANS had provided crucial assistance to the redcoats, and they had typically received their freedom in return. Once the British captured Charles Town with the help of Black guides, the British hired them for a wide variety of jobs, sometimes paying them twice as much as army privates. But Clinton actively discouraged additional slaves from escaping to his lines. Moreover, when Blacks fell in the redcoats' way as they moved across the countryside, Clinton and his officers usually treated them the same way the Whigs did, as property. When Gen. Lincoln capitulated, many Black Charlestonians were sold, often to the Caribbean, and never saw their families again. Some were distributed to Loyalists in compensation for slaves who had been taken by the Whigs. Still others were set to work growing food for the army on plantations confiscated from enemy combatants; as in the past, those who rebelled were brutally suppressed.[12]

For their part, slaves had numerous reasons of their own for not joining the British—and even, in a few cases, for briefly joining them before returning to their homes. Most prominently, those who escaped to the army, like those who were sold, rarely saw their children and other family members again. One Black South Carolinian, Boston King, undertook the thirty-mile gauntlet to Charles Town only after receiving an additional incentive: having been unavoidably delayed in returning a horse borrowed from a white neighbor, he faced a brutal beating.[13]

Despite all the reasons not to run, as many as one-fifth of enslaved South Carolinians would join the British by the end of the war. But given Britain's inconsistent response to these overtures, the Anglo-Black alliance may have contributed less to the strength of the imperial army than to white Americans' hatred of Britain.[14]

IN JUNE 1780, CONGRESS authorized a new southern army to replace the one Benjamin Lincoln had surrendered the previous month. Since Washington was able to spare only 1,400 Continental troops, this new force would have to consist primarily of militia.[15] Citizen-soldiers had contributed mightily to Horatio Gates's victory at Saratoga, making him their zealous advocate—and the obvious choice to take over the Southern Department. Gates's three thousand fighters, along with "a multitude of women, and not a few children," reached Rugeley's Mill, thirteen miles north of Cornwallis's army at Camden, on August 13. Many modern accounts state that when Gates led his troops out of camp at 10 p.m. on August 15, he rashly intended to strike the British. Actually, he wished only to redeploy seven miles to the south, on the north bank of the all but unfordable Sanders' (or Saunders') Creek, where any attack Cornwallis launched "would have proved disastrous to him."[16]

A mile north of Sanders' Creek, the cavalrymen leading the American column collided with Banastre Tarleton's Loyalist cavalry. "By a singular coincidence," about 2,200 British and Loyalist troops had stepped off at the same time as the rebels, intending to surprise their camp.[17] Tarleton's dragoons charged the Americans "with the yell of an Indian savage" but were driven back, and both commanders tore up their plans. Gates considered retreating. But like Burgoyne in upstate New York three years earlier, he feared that "to have fallen back from thence would have discouraged the good men of the Country, & have given confidence to the opposite party."[18]

Gates had his infantry in line of battle before dawn on August 16. As the enemy approached, one of his officers thought he spotted an opportunity: the redcoats on Cornwallis's right, along the eastern edge of the battlefield, had not finished moving from columns into battle lines. The

American left was composed of Virginia militia. Most had never seen battle before, and many carried rifles, which lacked bayonets—the essential element in any successful charge. Yet Gates spurred them forward in order to take advantage of the apparent disorder on the British right.[19]

Officers on Cornwallis's right quickly perfected their line and also advanced. Just like Gates, Cornwallis thought he spotted a weakness in the enemy line: apparently dissatisfied with the disposition of the troops on his left, Gates was making last-minute corrections.[20] No American source mentions such a maneuver, and it appears that a sanguine Cornwallis magnified a momentary disruption. Thus both commanders sent their eastern flanks forward in order to exploit apparent enemy missteps: one that was quickly redressed and another that never actually existed. But it was too late for either army to turn back.

The Virginians were stunned to find themselves advancing directly into a bayonet charge. Several dropped their weapons and ran, some without firing a shot. Panic flew from one man to the next, and soon the entire brigade was scurrying toward the rear.[21] The troops immedi-

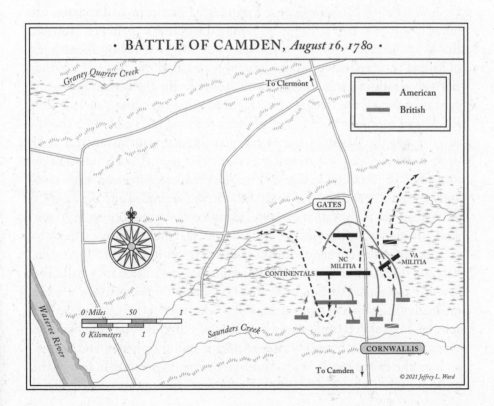

· BATTLE OF CAMDEN, *August 16, 1780* ·

Graney Quarter Creek

To Clermont

American
British

GATES

VA MILITIA

NC MILITIA

CONTINENTALS

0 Miles .50 1
0 Kilometers 1

Saunders Creek

Wateree River

CORNWALLIS

To Camden

© 2021 Jeffrey L. Ward

ately to the right of the Virginians, in the center of the American line, were also militiamen, North Carolinians. When the Virginians' departure exposed their left flank, all but one Carolina regiment also took to their heels, in turn exposing the left flank of the Continental soldiers on Gates's right. By all rights, they ought to have been the next domino. But they continued forward and soon captured fifty British soldiers.[22]

Cornwallis sent in his cavalry. Some pursued the fleeing militiamen, but the Virginians and North Carolinians were too fast for them. Not one Virginian was killed, and few militia from either state were captured. The rest of Tarleton's troopers joined British infantry in a brutal assault on the Continental soldiers' rear and exposed left flank. About 250 Americans died at Camden: nearly all Continentals. An estimated eight hundred men were wounded, many of whom died, with most of the rest falling into British hands. The captives included twelve African Americans, and Cornwallis approved a subordinate's proposal to sell them in order to "convince *Blacke* that he must not fight against us." The British suffered about one-third as many casualties as Gates: just over three hundred killed and wounded.[23]

And what of Horatio Gates? Early in the battle, he had spurred his horse toward the rear in hopes of halting the militia's "pell mell" retreat. But as an American officer recalled, he was "borne away by the torrent of Militia" and ended up riding all the way to Charlotte, North Carolina, sixty-five miles to the north, before stopping for the night. Tarleton's cavalry pursued the fleeing Americans twenty-two miles, to Hanging Rock, and captured twenty ammunition wagons and nearly 150 supply carts. As at the Battle of the Monongahela, many teamsters cut their draft horses loose for a speedier escape. The historian David Ramsay described the road from Camden to Charlotte as "strewed with arms and baggage . . . and covered with the sick, the wounded and the dead."[24]

Success has many fathers; failure, many explanations. For most American officers, including George Washington, Camden once again demonstrated "the fatal consequences of depending on militia." In their own defense, the Virginians and North Carolinians stated that they had been "greatly exhausted by fatigue at that hot season."[25] Gates made an even more inviting target. Thinking his force was twice its actual size, he had sent off several detachments on missions of dubious value. He had also sapped his men's strength with inadequate and unripe fruit and corn—and, on the eve of battle, with stomach-churning molasses in lieu of the customary but unavailable rum.[26] Probably Gates's most consequential error was sending greenhorn militia forward to exploit the apparent disorder on the British right. But that is the nature of sudden opportunities; it can be just as dangerous to let them pass.

Gates predictably blamed his loss on bad luck, and he had a point. As an aide noted, "If the American Army had marched from Rugely's two hours earlier, or Cornwallis had moved from Camden two hours later," the Americans would have been ensconced behind Sanders' Creek by the time he arrived, and "the event of the contest would probably have been very different."[27]

Gates badly damaged his reputation by losing the Battle of Camden—and then destroyed it altogether by running away to Charlotte. Congress asked Washington to name his successor as southern commander, and he did not hesitate a moment in sending Gen. Nathanael Greene. The commander-in-chief also sought to restore Whig morale with a dramatic victory in the north. Rochambeau's troops disembarked at Newport, Rhode Island, on July 10. By this time, Clinton and half the soldiers from his South Carolina expedition had returned to New York, but Washington still thought his own troops could capture the city with the help of their French allies. The joint strike never materialized, but the arrival of the French bolstered Washington's attack plan indirectly. Clinton, hoping to drive Rochambeau and Ternay away from Newport before they could dig in, loaded about eight thousand redcoats and Germans onto transports and sent them eastward through Long Island Sound toward Rhode Island, once again weakening his New York garrison and inviting an American attack.[28]

Washington moved the Continental Army down the Hudson River toward New York City.[29] At the very least, his threatening the British base would force Clinton to cancel his Rhode Island expedition in order to protect the city. The American commander was not happy to be proved right on this last point, since it meant calling off his own assault on Manhattan.

As WASHINGTON POKED AT New York City and Cornwallis contended with Whig guerrillas in South Carolina, Virginia governor Thomas Jefferson faced west. In January 1780, he ordered George Rogers Clark and his troops to bring about either the Ohio Indians' "removal beyond the [Great] lakes or Illinois river" or their "extermination."[30] But U.S. officials such as Clark and Jefferson soon realized that in the Mississippi Valley and Great Lakes regions, they had lost the initiative to the mother country and its First Nations allies. Between February and April, four armies set out from British posts and indigenous villages in what is now the state of Michigan. Picking up reinforcements along the way, they hit Spanish, French, and U.S. settlements in a wide arc from St. Louis through the Illinois and Ohio River watersheds all the way east to Kentucky and Pittsburgh. Back in 1777, John Burgoyne in northern New York and George Washington at Germantown had doomed their armies by dividing them. Detached bands of native warriors ran no such risk, since they traveled light and fast.

The westernmost raiding party, dispatched by Capt. Patrick Sinclair, lieutenant governor at Fort Michilimackinac on the straits between the lower and upper Michigan peninsulas, included at least two veterans of Burgoyne's 1777 invasion of the United States, Matchekewis (Ojibwa) and Charles Langlade. But the force acquired most of its one thousand soldiers on the western shore of Lake Michigan, in modern-day Wisconsin: Lakota Sioux—who were long-standing enemies of the Ojibwas— along with Winnebagos, Menominees, Sauks, Foxes, and other nations that had only recently established ties with Britain. Such was British faith in one Sioux leader, Wabasha, that—like the Seneca sachems at Oriskany three years earlier—he was authorized to command white as well as indigenous troops.[31]

This heterogeneous legion headed down the Mississippi River and on May 26 simultaneously hit the sister towns of Cahokia and St. Louis, on opposite sides of the mile-wide Mississippi. Under Spanish rule, St. Louis had become the gateway to the "rich furr Trade of the Missouri River," which enters the Mississippi just thirteen miles to the north. Although by no means the farthest-west battles fought in North America during the founding era—during these years natives rebelled against Spaniards in what is now the southwestern United States and against Russians in present-day Alaska—the May 26 attacks marked the western boundary of the Revolutionary War.[32]

Scouts had brought Cahokia and St. Louis ample warning, and Cahokia even benefited from the last-minute arrival of George Rogers Clark with a small party of Kentucky militiamen. Despite being vastly outnumbered, both held out. But not everyone made it into the stockades. The Anglo-Indian army captured twenty-four people—eleven whites and thirteen African Americans—and killed more than twenty others.[33]

Meanwhile Arent DePeyster, who had taken charge of Britain's Fort Detroit the previous year, sent war parties against Fort Vincennes and the

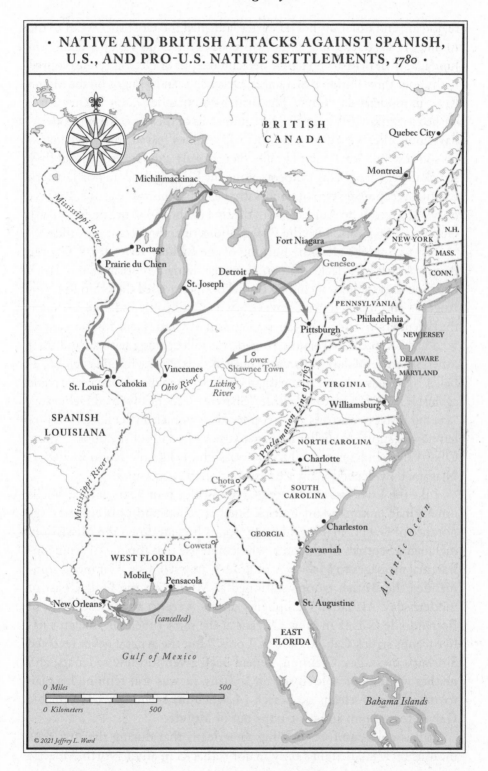

· NATIVE AND BRITISH ATTACKS AGAINST SPANISH,
U.S., AND PRO-U.S. NATIVE SETTLEMENTS, *1780* ·

region around Pittsburgh. DePeyster launched the most successful of the summer 1780 attacks only at the insistence of the Ohio Valley Indians. On June 1, a small British and native detachment out of Detroit rendezvoused with about three hundred Shawnees, Delawares, and Mingos on the Miami River in modern-day Ohio. The British commander, Capt. Henry Bird, wished to strike the Virginians' fort at the falls of the Ohio River (modern-day Louisville, Kentucky). But his native allies feared that traveling so far south would leave their families dangerously exposed, so instead they struck the chain of Whig outposts along the Licking River in northeastern Kentucky, capturing two of them with the help of his two cannon. Bird returned to Detroit on August 4 with the first of about 350 prisoners, mostly German immigrants, with the First Nations retaining countless others.[34]

Just two weeks after the burning of the Licking River forts, George Rogers Clark was back in Kentucky organizing a reprisal raid. Clark's one thousand soldiers, including Daniel Boone, crossed the Ohio River on August 1 and attacked two Shawnee towns, Chillicothe and Piqua. Among the defenders was Joseph Rogers, a cousin of Clark's and former captive who had accepted conversion. Rogers was killed, along with a handful of other Shawnees. Clark's men also burned the two towns and their cornfields. "The loss we have met with of our Friends in the resistance we made against [Clark] is not considerable," Shawnee leaders informed DePeyster, "yet our distress is no less, on account of our women and children who are left now destitute of shelter in the woods or Food to subsist upon." Many Ohio Valley Indians moved to Detroit, where, like the Iroquois at Fort Niagara, they depended on the British for basic necessities.[35]

Like the Loyalists at Moore's Creek Bridge four years earlier, Michilimackinac commandant Patrick Sinclair relied upon his enemies' ignorance of Gaelic, making sure the troops he sent down the Mississippi included a Scottish Highlander who could use that tongue to send confidential messages to a fellow Scot, John Campbell. Gen. Campbell commanded the British troops stationed at Mobile on the Gulf Coast of modern-day Alabama. Campbell's orders were to attack the army of Bernardo de Gálvez in New Orleans at the same time that Sinclair's native troops struck Cahokia and St. Louis.[36] But the general never received Sinclair's messages. Claiming he had been given too few redcoats, and neither willing nor able to recruit Indians, he was still refining his plan to attack New Orleans on March 14, when the seemingly unstoppable Gálvez forced him and his troops out of Mobile.

It was cold comfort to Whig Americans that during the first nine months of 1780, Britain's only major setbacks in all of North America occurred at St. Louis, Cahokia, and Mobile, where there were hardly any Whigs. Britain's only other major loss that summer took place on the other side of the world. In July 1780, Haidar Ali, furious at the East India Company for breaking the promises that had ended the first Anglo-Mysore War in 1769, took his troops through the mountain passes into the British-controlled Carnatic. On September 10, near Conjeveram, Haidar's men wiped out an East India Company army of more than three thousand regulars and sepoys (Indians in British service). "Heyder Ali is the standing toast of my table," Philadelphia physician Benjamin Rush stated.[37]

BENEDICT ARNOLD HAD BEEN sending useful updates to his handler John André since the spring of 1779, but he longed for a larger role, and during the summer of 1780 he landed one. André had become Clinton's adjutant general, and he had an idea. If Arnold could convince George Washington to give him command of West Point, the American citadel on the west bank of the Hudson River, fifty miles north of New York City, he could hand his new masters the supposedly "impregnable" fort, along with its defenders and its vast stores of war matériel. Through André, Clinton had previously assured Arnold that his delivery of "a Corps of 5 or 6000 Men would be rewarded with twice as many thousand Guineas."[38] West Point housed fewer than half that many Continentals, but Clinton saw it as the key to finally realizing Burgoyne's dream of controlling the entire Hudson–Champlain corridor, thereby cutting the American confederacy in two and "finish[ing] the rebellion immediately." He offered Arnold £20,000 for the fort and its garrison.[39]

Arnold set about lobbying Washington for the command of West Point. Despite his leg injuries, Arnold remained one of the Continental Army's best generals, and the commander-in-chief was perplexed at his aiming so low. But finally, on August 3, 1780, Washington informed Arnold the post was his.[40]

Here is how Arnold repaid him. Still fixated upon an Anglo-American assault on Fortress New York, Washington arranged to meet Rochambeau and Ternay in Hartford, Connecticut, in September 1780 to discuss details. On the 16th, he learned that a fleet commanded by Adm. George Rodney had just entered New York Harbor, further strengthening Clinton's defenses, but he did not cancel the Hartford meeting. In fact he convinced himself that Rodney was going to carry much of Clinton's garrison away on an expedition against either Virginia or French-occupied Rhode Island, leaving New York more vulnerable to an allied attack. Washington wrote Arnold informing him he planned to cross the Hudson at King's Ferry on September 17. Before heading downriver to offer a mid-journey greeting to his commander and friend, Arnold sent his British handlers a message: here was their chance to kill or capture George Washington.[41]

The *Vulture*, a British navy sloop, happened to reach King's Ferry on September 17, but Washington had already safely crossed the Hudson by the time its captain received Arnold's tip.

The reason the *Vulture* had sailed upriver was that John André had decided that he needed to meet Arnold face-to-face. Arnold and Joshua H. Smith, a man of flexible loyalties who lived about five miles downriver from West Point, rowed out to the *Vulture* to collect André; Arnold used the threat of prison to compel two of Smith's tenants to handle the oars. Once on shore, André conferred with Arnold about such matters as his compensation—Arnold wanted £10,000 even if his plot was foiled— and possible routes for the British assault.[42]

The riverside discussion ran long; if the two oarsmen rowed André back to the *Vulture*, they could not make it back to shore before sunrise. They refused to go, so André set off for New York on horseback, initially accompanied by Smith and an African American servant. As he approached Tarrytown, New York, he was accosted by three patrollers. Making the fatal assumption that they were Loyalists, he identified himself as a British officer. The patrollers, who were actually Whig militiamen, searched him. In his stockings, they found incriminating evidence, including sketches of West Point. The militiamen sent word of their capture to George Washington and to the highest-ranking American officer in the region: Benedict Arnold.[43]

There now ensued what the historian Carl Van Doren called "a kind of race to decide whether Washington or Arnold would first learn that treason had been discovered." Arnold won, but just barely, receiving the news of André's arrest early on the morning of September 25 at his quarters on the east bank of the Hudson River opposite West Point as he awaited a visit from his commander-in-chief. Washington was on his way back to New York from Hartford (where Rochambeau and Ternay had vetoed his idea of attacking New York City) and had scheduled a tour of the fort's defenses. Arnold knew that from the moment of André's capture, his own hourglass had begun to drain. Telling his aides he had been called over to West Point and would return soon to greet Washington, he instructed his bargemen to row him not across the Hudson to the fort but twenty miles down the river to the *Vulture*, ostensibly for a parley. Once Arnold and his oarsmen had boarded the *Vulture*, he informed them of his true intentions, and they became British prisoners.[44]

Thirty minutes after Arnold's barge pushed off into the Hudson, Washington's entourage reached the Robinson House. The chief was surprised at not finding Arnold either at his headquarters or across the river at West Point, but later in the day the messenger carrying André's papers reached him and cleared up the mystery. Several of the documents, including André's pass, were in Arnold's handwriting. Washington had always worried about Arnold's overpowering resentment at what he considered the nation's ingratitude, but he had never considered his friend a potential traitor. Breaking the news to Lafayette, Washington reportedly asked him, "Whom can we trust now?"[45]

André knew he could not avoid execution, but he held out hope of dying an honorable death before a firing squad instead of being hanged as a common spy. He used his infamous charm to obtain some of his captors' interposition with the commander-in-chief. Washington was unmoved, but his jailers came to see André as the very embodiment of the eighteenth-century ideal of masculine sensibility, and it appears that much of their affection for the foreign agent in their custody derived from the contrast to the traitor who had slipped through their fingers. Washington offered to trade André for Arnold, but Gen. Clinton could not violate the ancient and pragmatic military maxim that soldiers deserting from the enemy are "never given up."[46]

The hanging of John André on October 2 elicited tears from several of the Continental officers in attendance; one said the scene elicited "the compassion of every man of feeling and sentiment."[47] A separate court-martial found insufficient evidence to convict Smith, so he was turned over to civilian authorities, from whom he eventually escaped into New York City. In the aftermath of the affair, George Washington, a militia skeptic who had recently joined in the nationwide condemnation of the citizen-soldiers who had run away at Camden,

John André, self-portrait, sketched on October 1, 1780, the day before his execution

acknowledged that Arnold might have accomplished his purpose but for "the virtuous conduct of [the] three Militia Men" who captured André.[48] He might have added that André would have avoided his perilous over-land journey to New York altogether if the watermen who collected him from the *Vulture* had agreed to row him back.

Washington devised a bold plan to bring Arnold to justice. An American soldier would pretend to desert and then volunteer for the Loyalist legion the turncoat was busy assembling. That would bring him close enough to Arnold to assassinate him—but that was not Washington's intention. Arnold must be taken alive and brought back inside American lines for a public execution. This hazardous assignment went to John Champe, a man "full of bone and muscle" who served as Henry Lee's sergeant major. To maintain secrecy, even Champe's fellow dragoons were not told that his desertion was fake. When he left camp, a party of horse pursued him and nearly managed to bring him down. Reaching New York City, he was accepted into Arnold's legion.[49]

Meanwhile Whig authorities sought to put a positive spin on Arnold's treason, declaring "a day of public Thanksgiving" for the preservation of West Point. And they had a point. The only soldiers Arnold was able to deliver to the British were himself and his bargemen, and the only plunder was their uniforms. The chief beneficiaries of the affair were, ironically enough, the Continental officers Arnold had betrayed. Partly with a view to making treason less appealing, Congress finally yielded to Washington's repeated pleas that it turn the officers' half-pay pensions, which were due to expire seven years after the war, into lifetime sinecures.[50]

The near loss of West Point intensified Washington's long-standing desire to attack the British in New York City, even without French aid. Part of the attraction was that more than two thousand British head-quarters troops had just been transferred to the southern theater. One of the few points that Clinton and his southern commander agreed on was that Cornwallis should move into North Carolina. But as of mid-September, he remained south of the state line, because a combination of heat and disease (a consequence of the heat, he believed) had immobilized much of his force.[51] In hopes of smoothing his passage into North Carolina, Cornwallis asked Clinton to invade the neighboring state of Virginia. The previous year, a British squadron commanded by Commodore George Collier and Gen. Edward Mathew had spent two weeks in the lower Chesapeake, capturing or destroying 137 vessels and £2 million worth of supplies and liberating more than five hundred slaves. Now Cornwallis proposed a permanent base in Virginia to slow the southward flow of Whig soldiers and supplies. On October 16, 2,200 of Clinton's redcoats headed to Virginia.[52]

Then in mid-November, Rodney's fleet sailed out of New York Harbor, headed back to the Caribbean, and Washington convinced himself that Clinton was now vulnerable to assault. In attacking New York, the Americans' principal weapon would be the one that had delivered Trenton into their hands four years earlier: surprise. Keeping the mission secret meant keeping it small, at least in its initial phase: at most seven hundred men would land on Manhattan just below Fort Knyphausen (the former Fort Washington) and then capture that all but inaccessible eminence and at least two well-fortified outposts nearby.[53]

On November 24, ten days after conceiving the idea of assaulting New York, Washington dropped it. When Gouverneur Morris, who had moved to Philadelphia, urged him to storm the citadel, the commander-in-chief was compelled to acknowledge the folly of both Morris's plan and his own. Surely he had been motivated not by rational calculation but by an "earnest desire . . . of closing the Campaign with some degree of eclat." In a letter to Morris, Washington regretted, even more candidly than he had outside Boston four and a half years earlier, that "my wishes had so far got the better of my judgment."[54]

ALL THIS TIME, PARTISAN warfare was intensifying in the southern backcountry. In one incident, a party of British dragoons captured thirteen-year-old Andrew Jackson, who was then ordered to clean the major's boots. He refused, and the officer slashed at him with his saber, leaving a scar that the future president would carry, alongside hatred of Great Britain, the rest of his life. (The fatherless Jackson lost his mother and two brothers to viruses churned up by the war.) The characteristic event of upcountry warfare was not the battle but the raid. A band of Whig or Loyalist militiamen would descend on a small community or isolated farm, liberating or stealing the slaves, grabbing everything valuable and portable, burning everything else, sometimes assaulting women and often whipping, seizing, or even killing white men. "The whole country is in danger of being laid waste by the Whigs and Torrys [Loyalists], who pursue each other with as much relentless fury as beasts of prey," wrote Nathanael Greene. These attacks had both a personal side—a revenge cycle akin to modern-day gang violence—and a practical side: Whigs as well as Loyalists recruited followers in part by threatening atrocities against anyone who resisted the call.[55]

Not that the South lacked for more traditional fighting. On September 14, about five hundred Whigs under the command of Col. Elijah Clarke laid siege to Augusta, Georgia, where the British had stockpiled £4,000 worth of presents headed to the Muskogees and Cherokees. Clarke's men wished both to get their hands on this British merchandise and to keep it away from their indigenous enemies. Soon the rangers, Muskogees, and Cherokees defending the town were reduced to drinking their own urine. But when British reinforcements arrived, Clarke's troops, accompanied—and actually outnumbered—by their wives and children, headed north into the mountains, pursued not only by the British but by their native allies, who killed and scalped many.[56]

Maj. Patrick Ferguson, whose Loyalists had been skirmishing with upcountry insurgents since mid-July, headed toward North Carolina's Great Smoky Mountains to try to cut off Clarke's retreat.[57] He thereby drew the attention of the settlers known to history as the "over-mountain men" and to Ferguson as "the Back Water men," since their rivers flowed west into the Mississippi. The Whigs rendezvoused at Sycamore Shoals on the Watauga River (the site five years earlier of Richard Henderson's outsized and fraudulent land purchase from a group of Cherokees) and rode east through the mountain passes, their force swelling along the way to close to two thousand.[58]

Now the hunted, Ferguson and his 1,125 troops also steered east, toward Cornwallis's army, which had just reached Charlotte, North Carolina. But on October 6, still thirty miles from Charlotte, Ferguson halted and formed a defensive perimeter atop Kings Mountain, an oblong hill rising sixty feet above the rolling fields and forests of the western Piedmont. Most accounts have the over-mountain men gaining on Ferguson, forcing him to make a stand, yet in 1881 the indefatigable researcher Lyman Draper assembled convincing evidence that he could have made it to Charlotte but stopped at Kings Mountain out of an "infatuation for military glory."[59]

An obsession with elevation pervaded the eighteenth-century military class, but its actual benefits were dubious, as soldiers defending heights tended to overshoot. This hill was even less defensible than most, since its sides were forested. "Shelter yourselves, and give them Indian play," the Whig officers told their troops as they started up Kings Moun-

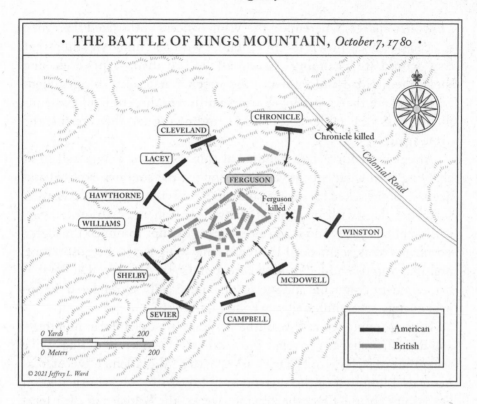

· THE BATTLE OF KINGS MOUNTAIN, *October 7, 1780* ·

CHRONICLE

Chronicle killed

CLEVELAND

LACEY

Colonial Road

FERGUSON

Ferguson
killed

HAWTHORNE

WILLIAMS

WINSTON

SHELBY

MCDOWELL

SEVIER

CAMPBELL

0 Yards   200
0 Meters   200

American

British

© 2021 Jeffrey L. Ward

tain. "Advance from tree to tree." The summit, by contrast, was nearly treeless, giving the attackers a clear field of fire.[60]

Ferguson was well known for inventing a rifle that could be reloaded much faster than existing models, allowing the user to fire up to six rounds a minute.[61] Yet it never caught on. The Whig militiamen who stormed Kings Mountain on October 7 carried traditional rifles, but only a few of Ferguson's defenders had rifles of any kind. Even these few were not used as firearms, Ferguson having fitted them with plug bayonets so all of his infantrymen could join in bayonet charges. At that point the Back Water men would be essentially defenseless, since their rifles did not carry bayonets and took a long minute to reload. Ferguson did not know that the colonels commanding the troops at the foot of Kings Mountain—there was no general present on either side—had decided to add an extraordinary new element to their battle plan: retreat. As each Whig regiment neared the summit, "raising a regular frontier war-whoop, after the Indian style" and firing their rifles with deadly effect, Ferguson blew on his silver whistle to order a bayonet charge, whereupon the Whig officers authorized their men to scamper back down the mountain—with the understanding that they would stop running as soon as the Loyalists stopped chasing them, then reload and return to the attack.[62] As each Whig regiment withdrew, another approached from a different direction, likewise inflicting heavy casualties before also withdrawing and then starting the cycle again.

After about forty-five minutes of this, Ferguson's men balked at charging their assailants, instead huddling at the summit, exposed and helpless. Some asked for quarter, only to have Ferguson slash down their surrender flags with his saber. Finally Ferguson and two other colonels grabbed horses and made a desperate attempt to punch through a seemingly weak segment of the tightening Whig circle. Ferguson took multiple rounds and fell dead, whereupon Capt. Abraham De Peyster, his second-in-command and successor, immediately surrendered the approximately seven hundred surviving Loyalists.[63]

Kings Mountain was the southern Whigs' first victory in months—and their first chance to avenge the Waxhaws massacre. Shouting "Give them Buford's play" and "Tarleton's Quarter," the riflemen executed as many as a hundred of the surrendering Loyalists. Several urinated on Ferguson's corpse. Over the previous weeks, the British and their local supporters had hanged numerous South Carolinians for quitting Loyalist units to fight for the United States. In retaliation, the Kings Mountain victors convened a court-martial, found nine of their captives guilty of "atrocious crimes," and hanged them.[64]

Although much less well known than Burgoyne's surrender at Saratoga three years earlier, Ferguson's loss at Kings Mountain was nearly as crucial a turning point. The British and Loyalists had bested the Whigs in all of the major battles of the summer of 1780: Charles Town, Waxhaws, and Camden. Now their streak had ended, immeasurably boosting Whig morale. Kings Mountain also compelled the formerly indomitable Cornwallis to drop back to Winnsboro, South Carolina (twenty-five miles north of modern-day Columbia), postponing his invasion of North Carolina.

On October 21, Gen. Alexander Leslie landed in Virginia to support Cornwallis's invasion by interdicting the southward flow of supplies to his opponents. Ferguson's defeat two weeks earlier had rendered Leslie's mission at least temporarily obsolete, but he destroyed Whig supplies and freed hundreds of slaves. Leslie's Virginia foray ended not because of Whig resistance but because Cornwallis needed his troops. With too few transports for the trip down the coast to Charles Town, Leslie abandoned the several hundred slaves who had joined him to the mercies of their once and future masters.[65]

THE CAROLINA OFFENSIVE WAS not the only British campaign of 1780 that opened triumphantly only to stall out by autumn. Soon after Spain entered the war, Lord Germain signed off on an invasion of the Spanish Main. An expeditionary force would sail a hundred miles up the San Juan River (today the eastern segment of the border between Nicaragua and Costa Rica) to its source, Lake Nicaragua, with a western shore only eleven miles from Spain's Pacific ports. Plundering the area might force Carlos III to sue for peace; it would certainly enrich the leaders of the expedition.[66]

Well aware of European soldiers' susceptibility to tropical diseases and believing it was not shared by Africans, commander John Polson rounded out his corps with free Blacks from Jamaica. On April 29, 1780, the redcoats captured the Fortress of the Immaculate Conception, sixty-four miles up the San Juan from the Gulf of Mexico. But they never made it to Lake Nicaragua. Yellow fever and other diseases killed about 2,500 of Polson's soldiers—more than in any of the war's battles. One officer who became gravely ill but survived was Horatio Nelson, the future hero of the Battle of Trafalgar. On November 30, the survivors abandoned the fortress and returned to Jamaica.[67]

CLINTON HARRIED CORNWALLIS TO resume his incursion into North Carolina. And still convinced that he needed to stanch the flow of northern supplies to the Southern Department of the Continental Army, Clinton gave Benedict Arnold his first assignment as a British officer: reoccupy Virginia.

As Arnold prepared to embark from New York City, John Champe and another, never-named, American agent were planning to capture him during his nightly stroll through his garden, then bind and gag him and row him across the Hudson River to a waiting U.S. cavalry troop. On December 11, the day before the planned kidnapping, Arnold moved closer to the wharf to focus on final arrangements for Virginia. To discourage the enlisted men from deserting when they discovered their sickly destination, he sent his troops—including Champe—aboard transport ships. These two routine measures saved Arnold's life.[68]

The British fleet passed the Chesapeake capes on December 30—just five weeks after Leslie's departure—and by January 5, 1781, the invaders/liberators had reached Richmond, the new capital. While in Virginia, Arnold "always carried a pair of small pistols in his pocket," not to fend off would-be kidnappers like those he had unwittingly escaped in New York City but, if need be, to cheat the hangman by shooting himself in the head.[69]

Although Alexander Leslie had abandoned the several hundred Black Virginians who joined him the previous fall, such was the slaves' desperation for freedom that nearly three hundred men, women, and children, including several claimed by Thomas Jefferson and George Washington, now joined Arnold. Loyalists asserted ownership of some of these fugitives and enlisted Arnold's aid in recovering them. Governor Jefferson worried that if they succeeded, other white Virginians would declare for the king just to get their slaves back. So he stepped in to stop Arnold from returning the Loyalists' slaves. It was the most tangible step that the nominally antislavery Jefferson ever took toward actually freeing Black Americans. When one Loyalist-leaning white Virginian, Mary Willing Byrd, loaned Arnold a slave guide named Wat, he seized the moment and never returned.[70]

FREE BLACKS IN THE town of Dartmouth on the southeastern coast of Massachusetts also sought to better their condition. The previous February, as numerous Massachusetts towns petitioned the state assembly for relief from oppressive taxation, seven Dartmouth Blacks made the case that no one deserved tax relief more than those whose decades in slavery had prevented them from either inheriting or earning money. They also faced continuing employment discrimination: "we have not an Eaqual chance with white people Neither By Sea nor By Land." And while Massachusetts Blacks had enlisted in the Revolutionary War at a higher rate than whites, Dartmouth and many other towns refused them the vote. The obvious remedy for this taxation without representation would have been the franchise, but instead the petitioners asked legislators to complete their exclusion from white politics by exempting them from taxation. Two of these men, the brothers Paul and John Cuffe, were the sons of a Wampanoag Indian woman and an African-born slave and had recently taken their father Akan's first name as their own surname.[71]

The Dartmouth Blacks' petition failed in the state legislature, so in December 1780 the Cuffe brothers refused to pay their taxes and were briefly imprisoned. Four years earlier, Paul Cuffe, a onetime whaler as well as seaman, had been serving on an American merchant ship when it was captured. He and other crewmen had spent three months as British prisoners in New York, which meant that Cuffe had the dubious distinction of being jailed first by the redcoats and then by the rebels.[72]

CHAPTER 29

———•◦•———

Had I Crossed the River

1781

DURING THE WINTER OF 1780–1781, THE CONTINENTAL ARMY quartered in Morristown, New Jersey, as it had twice before. But this time, Pennsylvania soldiers were quietly plotting a rebellion.

The conspirators were angry at their lack of pay, food, and clothing, but most of all at being tricked into extra service. In sharp contrast to the peacetime British army, where new recruits typically made lifetime commitments, Continental recruiters initially permitted enlistees to commit for as little as ninety days. But in the fall of 1776, Gen. Washington finally persuaded Congress to require soldiers to remain for a minimum of three years and ideally for the duration. The delegates instructed recruiting officers to hand new enlistees different enlistment papers, depending on how long they agreed to serve. But literal-minded recruiters, especially in Pennsylvania, copied Congress's key—and fatefully ambiguous—phrase, signing men up "for three years, or during the war." Hundreds of Pennsylvanians joined in 1777 not expecting to stay in any later than 1780, but as new enlistments dwindled, officers (who themselves always had the option of resigning) and members of Congress increasingly insisted that for privates, "three years, or during the war" meant *whichever comes last.*[1]

Then Washington had an inspiration. On June 9, 1779, he asked Congress to present a $100 *douceur* (sweetener) to every soldier who committed for the duration. When the normally dilatory delegates approved the bonus just thirteen days later, one of their motivations was to mollify the men who had sold their own skins early on for a paltry $20 bounty, only to see Johnny-come-latelies extort princely sums for as little as a few months' service.[2]

The bitter-enders' bonus was also a trap, for officers tendered it not only to soldiers expecting to serve until the end of the war but also to those who had "enlisted upon the alternative of three years or during the war." Many took the money knowing what it meant but figuring they would probably be forced to stick around regardless. Others accepted it without realizing that they had thus committed for the war. But at least Washington had kept his army together.[3]

Or so he thought. On New Year's Day 1781, the soldiers of the Pennsylvania Line agreed, almost to a man, to march on Congress to demand redress. Two captains who tried to stop them were killed. January 1781 being an especially quiet month in the northern theater, this was two more dead Americans than Henry Clinton could claim.[4]

When the rebels reached Princeton, thirty miles to the south, they informed Anthony Wayne, the acting commander of the Pennsylvania Line, that their chief grievance was the "fine deception" Washington had pulled off a year and a half earlier. Wayne tried to quell the mutiny by promising to release any and all who were "justly entitled to their Discharges."[5] Many of these soldiers had entered the army as teenagers, but more than three years later their youthful naïveté was just as spent as their bodies, and they demanded more specific guarantees. And when Wayne suggested that they meet a delegation from the Pennsylvania executive council in Trenton, thirteen miles farther south, they allowed that they would rather stay in Princeton.

Why would the mutineers walk halfway to Philadelphia, posing enough of a threat to that city that Wayne advised Congress to evacuate, and then refuse to take another step, even as the man trying to end their revolt urged them to march on? The answer lies with Gen. Clinton, who ferried an elite corps of redcoats to Staten Island to prepare to land in New Jersey to receive the mutineers. Anticipating Clinton's maneuver, Wayne tried to lure the rebels as far from New York City as possible, while they in turn remained in Princeton in order to better exploit his fears.[6]

Washington was cautiously optimistic that soldiers from other state lines would resist the temptation to rendezvous with the Pennsylvanian rebels, too many of whom were immigrants. "The other troops, who are more generally composed of natives, and may therefore have attachments of a stronger nature, may bear their distresses somewhat longer than the Pennsylvanians," he predicted. (A fifth of the Pennsylvania Line had immigrated from Ireland.) But as a precaution, he informed his officers that the mutiny was not to be "conversed upon, before their

Domestics." When Gen. William Heath, commander of U.S. forces in the Hudson Highlands, sent a camp woman "among the men to hear their conversation," the spy reported that at least some Continentals had declared "they would have no hand" in subduing the mutineers, "as they were contending for a redress of [grievances], under which all are labouring & equally concerned."[7]

But the mutineers were disgruntled Whigs, not Loyalists. The moment two of Clinton's agents appeared in the rebel camp, they were seized and delivered to an astonished Gen. Wayne. Continental officers quickly tried and convicted the two emissaries, then took them to the ferry landing on the Delaware River opposite Trenton, where they made a slave string them up, with their corpses "to be left hanging till they fall from the gallows."[8] For capturing Clinton's agents, the insurgents in Princeton were offered 50 guineas, equal to what a common laborer might earn in two years. But these men who had not enjoyed adequate food, clothing, or shelter for three years declined "any other reward but the love of our country."[9]

For five and a half years, Washington had scrupulously deferred to the nation's civilian leaders. But the Pennsylvania mutiny spooked him into encroaching upon Congress's authority to requisition state funds: he dispatched Henry Knox to beg the New England legislatures to send their lines "at least three Months pay . . . in Money that will be of some value to them." Inaction was not an option, he stressed. "At what point this defection will stop, or how extensive it may prove," he wrote, "God only knows."[10]

Meanwhile the mutineers' representatives met with two members of the Pennsylvania executive council, who agreed to release every soldier who denied having intended to commit for the war. Many of the troops thus discharged just as rapidly reenlisted, finally receiving the same outsized bounty as new recruits.[11]

Appreciating that one of the rebels' principal grievances was the "delay of cloathing," officers and civilian officials made sure that all of them, even those who chose to go home, received shoes, trousers—and a shirt. Philadelphia women had just finished sewing two thousand shirts, and about one-third of these went to their state's mutineers.[12] Esther Reed's widower, Joseph, president of the Pennsylvania council, wanted to further stimulate the rebels' reconciliation by sending much needed clothing—"A new gown, silk handkerchief, and a pair of shoes, etc."—to the wives and children who had marched with them. Anticipating that his fellow councilors might refuse to fund the gift, he counted on finding a hundred Pennsylvania gentlemen to sponsor one camp woman each, so long as the clothing went "only to those soldiers' wives who continue in the service."[13]

The men of the Pennsylvania Line had pulled off the most extensive and effective mutiny of the Revolutionary War—but not the last. On January 20, New Jersey Col. Israel Shreve learned from a woman in his regiment that the men, inspired by the Pennsylvanians' success, were striving to emulate it with their own march to Philadelphia. Washington and other Continental officers blamed this new revolt not on legitimate grievances but on their own lenient response to the Pennsylvania rebels—a mistake they resolved not to repeat. At Washington's direction, New England troops surrounded the mutineers, disarmed them, and arrested their leaders. An impromptu court-martial sentenced two leaders to be shot (a third was reprieved), and other participants in the revolt were forced to serve as their firing squad.[14]

Even as Pennsylvania and New Jersey soldiers tried to fight their way out of the Continental Army, hundreds of other Americans took up arms to avoid being mustered in. Virginia had begun drafting soldiers in 1777, provoking stiff resistance, and then backed down in 1778, precluding the state from meeting even half its congressionally mandated troop quota, whereupon assemblymen gradually resumed the draft.[15] But in 1780, even as British troops roamed the James River watershed, more and more Virginians again resisted induction. So on January 1, 1781, the legislature renewed its effort to avoid conscription, this time by offering anyone who would serve for the rest of the war a seemingly irresistible bonus: $12,000 (albeit in depreciated paper money) up front and the promise of three hundred acres of western land and a slave at war's end.[16]

It was easy enough for legislators to lure new recruits with Indians' land and African Americans' labor, but the cash bounties, payable upon signing, could only be funded through enormous new taxes. In several counties, recruiters managed to fill their quotas of new enlistees but could not pay them their promised bounties, because, as one officer reported, "the Collector of the Tax . . . has been opposed in the Execution of his Duty, and has been obliged to desist."[17] In their desperation to prevent draft riots, state legislators had devised an enlistment bounty so generous and expensive as to provoke a tax revolt.

The Virginians who balked at the new bounty tax even included

George Washington's mother, who had several male friends lobby the Virginia House of Delegates to grant her relief. Aghast at Mary Ball Washington's bid for special favor, her son had it quashed, but even he could not pay his bounty tax without selling several slaves, in some cases permanently dividing their families.[18]

Historian-reformers rightly take inspiration from the Americans of the founding era who tried to turn a mere colonial revolt into an actual revolution. For example, Gary B. Nash's acclaimed *Unknown American Revolution* celebrates agrarian radicals like Hermon Husband and proto-feminists like Abigail Adams. But these were voices crying in the wilderness, for the era's mass movements were mostly defensive. Soldiers would not have mutinied had Congress kept its promises. Draft resisters asked only to be left alone. Even "radicals" primarily resisted their tormentors' new demands rather than making their own (though many sought electoral reforms that shocked contemporaries, and the North Carolina Regulators asked for more than most). Likewise, most Native American rebels fought only for what they already had, even casting their attempts at spiritual transformation as *revivals*—just as evangelicals in the colonies had. Lesser-known revolutionaries thus had something in common with the famous ones, who rebelled against Britain only because it increased its exactions. But the war sparked one mass movement for which the status quo held no attraction: tens of thousands of African Americans struck for freedom.

IF ARNOLD'S OCCUPATION OF Virginia failed to unify free Virginians, it did benefit them in another way, clearing away the last lingering obstructions to the adoption of the Articles of Confederation. As of February 1779, twelve states had signed on, but Maryland legislators refused to ratify until Virginia yielded its western territory to Congress. The Marylanders claimed they wanted to guarantee the federal government the land office revenue it needed to pay off its war debt, but everyone understood their real motive: land speculation firms organized by non-Virginians could expect infinitely better treatment from Congress than from the Virginia assembly. The promoters of some of the more grandiose real estate schemes remained as active as ever. In February 1780, Samuel Wharton and Benjamin Franklin, representing the Indiana Company, which in its previous incarnation as the Grand Ohio Company had come within a hairsbreadth of obtaining a royal charter to the region between the Allegheny Mountains and the Ohio River (modern-day West Virginia and eastern Kentucky), sent Congress a heartfelt appeal. The following December, when Thomas Paine denounced the Virginians' western claims in a pamphlet called *Public Good*, they assumed that the Indiana Company had paid him off (and they were right).[19]

Neither the Virginia land speculators nor their rivals in other states showed any sign of budging. But then on January 2, three days after Benedict Arnold's fleet entered Chesapeake Bay, the Virginia assembly relinquished its claim to the territory west of the Ohio River—on the condition that none of it went to out-of-state speculators such as the Illinois-Wabash Company. Exactly a month later, in the wake of the Pennsylvania and New Jersey mutinies and with the Continental currency continuing its plunge into worthlessness and Arnold's army moving freely through the neighboring state, Maryland ratified the Articles of Confederation, making them the law of the land.[20]

MEANWHILE THE WAR IN the south entered a new and pivotal phase. On December 2, Nathanael Greene reached Charlotte, North Carolina, temporary headquarters for the Southern Department of the Continental Army. The next day, he took over the remnants of Gates's army: only 1,632 healthy soldiers, mostly militiamen, not the Continentals upon whom Greene and other generals preferred to rely. Greene made the extraordinary decision to cut this tiny army in half, marching to the Pee Dee River in northeastern South Carolina at the head of about eight hundred soldiers and assigning the rest to a "flying army" to be stationed on the west bank of the Broad River.

Greene was aware of the ancient warning against dividing one's army in the face of a more numerous adversary, but he had several reasons for disregarding it. With food increasingly scarce, sending the soldiers into two different regions of South Carolina would make it easier to feed both divisions. Moreover, stationing some of his regulars in both the lowcountry and farther west was the only way of "heading and encouraging the Militia" in the two regions.[21]

Greene gave command of his western detachment to the recently promoted Gen. Daniel Morgan. Its numbers grew with the arrival of militiamen from South Carolina and neighboring states. But Morgan was astonished to receive no help at all from Thomas Sumter, who thought he ought to have been offered command.[22] Upon learning of Greene's bifurcation of his army, Cornwallis emulated it, sending Banastre Tarleton with 1,200 troops north up the west bank of the Broad River in pursuit of Morgan and leading his own troops up the east bank of the Broad, several days behind the ever-eager Tarleton.

Morgan enjoyed a favorable defensive position on the north bank of the Pacolet River, and he feared that pulling back would cause his militia to "desert us, & . . . join the Enemy." Yet when he learned of Tarleton's approach, he proposed to dissolve his own army, dispersing its militia units and reincorporating its Continentals into Greene's corps. As he awaited Greene's reaction to that idea, Morgan retreated northward to avoid or delay a confrontation with Tarleton. For most of its passage to the Atlantic Ocean, the Broad River drains toward the south or southeast. But in western North Carolina, just north of the South Carolina line, the Broad flows from west to east for about twenty miles. Morgan knew that if his soldiers could make it to this segment of the river and get across it, they would gain a measure of safety.[23]

At dusk on January 16, Morgan's flying army reached Hannah's Cowpens, five miles south of the Broad. The troops could have kept marching into the evening, but Morgan decided to spend the night at Cowpens and cross the river the following morning. But then, an hour or two before sunrise on January 17, a scout brought shocking news. Late the previous evening, Tarleton had reached Burr's Mill, just twelve miles to the south. Allowing his troops only a few hours' rest, he had roused them at 2 a.m. to resume the pursuit. Tarleton himself apparently got no sleep at all that night, and the entire detachment was exhausted.[24]

Morgan figured he might still be able to get his army across the Broad River, and he had a compelling reason to try: Cowpens was no Kings Mountain. The terrain was nearly flat, and over the years the livestock penned there had consumed the underbrush, creating "an open wood," about five hundred yards square, where Tarleton's three hundred cavalry-men, who outnumbered the American horse three to one, would have free rein. But Morgan dreaded the prospect of the redcoats overtaking his soldiers just as they struggled across the rain-swollen Broad. In addition, he knew his soldiers were tired of retreating. Indeed, fording the river meant crossing into North Carolina, whereupon many South Carolina militiamen, having joined him to fight for their homes and not to tour a neighboring state, would leave him, as their officers bluntly informed him. In the end Morgan decided to stay and fight.[25]

Like Buford at Waxhaws, Morgan had allowed Tarleton's lightning force to overtake him before he could reach favorable terrain. But having entered the war at the head of a rifle company, Morgan did not set his riflemen up for failure, as Gates had at Camden. Instead he arranged his troops in multiple lines. Far to the rear (north), the cavalry would wait in reserve behind two low hills. In front of the horsemen and atop the lower and more southerly of the two hills would be a line of 450 Continental soldiers, Virginia militiamen (most of whom had served stints in the Continental Army), and North Carolina militia, principally armed with bayonets.[26] About 150 yards in front of the musketmen, Morgan positioned four hundred militia, mostly carrying rifles. Another 150 yards ahead were the skirmishers, with the customary orders to fire one or two shots before retiring to the first line.

Military and congressional leaders would express astonishment at Morgan's decision to place his rifle-wielding militiamen at the front of his army, just behind the skirmishers. Five months earlier, Camden seemed to have confirmed the conventional view that militiamen were less likely than regular soldiers to withstand enemy fire. But at Camden, Gen. Gates had sent his militiamen, whose rifles took an eternity to reload and did not carry bayonets, directly into a British bayonet charge. By contrast, the militia colonels who commanded at Kings Mountain on October 7, recognizing that riflemen lacked bayonets, not courage, had allowed them to give way when charged, so long as they returned the moment they could. Similarly, Morgan instructed his riflemen to thin the British ranks with a volley or two and then withdraw to the rear, leaving the hand-to-hand combat to the bayonet wielders 150 yards behind them. In a last-minute refinement, he ordered the rifle companies not to retreat through the Continental ranks, possibly sowing confusion or even panic, but to skirt the American left before heading to the rear to re-form as a *corps de reserve*. Morgan shared his fellow Continental officers' disdain for militiamen. But he recognized that rifles and muskets bestowed different capabilities, and he had found a way to use both.

Tarleton caught up with the rebels at 8 a.m. on January 17 and sent his troops forward before they were even fully aligned. The Loyalists and redcoats "Raised a prodigious yell," whereupon Morgan ordered an American response. "Give them the Indian whoop," he shouted. The American skirmishers performed their part to perfection, as did the militiamen, who shot down numerous redcoats and Loyalists and then exited the battlefield to the left, as ordered. Thinking they had another Camden on their hands, the British infantry "quickened their advance," but they soon discovered the difference.[27] At Camden, where Gates had positioned his militiamen to the left of his Continentals, the militia's departure exposed the regulars' left flank to the advancing redcoats. But at Cowpens, the militia curtain rose to reveal an unbroken line of Continental soldiers. Now ensued the most brutal phase of the battle: a musket duel (supported on the British side by two 3-pound cannon) at almost point-blank range. Neither side yielded.

Tarleton sought to break the impasse by ordering his infantry reserves, the 71st Highlanders, to turn the Americans' right (western) flank. John Eager Howard, who commanded the Continental and Virginia troops, quickly detected the maneuver. He ordered Captain Andrew Wallace's company of Virginia Continentals, on the American right, to form a new line, perpendicular to the main American line and thus facing the British flank attack head-on. Wallace instructed his men to turn around and face the rear, and then, using the man on their far right as an axis, swing 90 degrees, like a minute hand sweeping from 9 p.m. to midnight. Then, with another about-face, they would transform the Highlanders' flanking maneuver into an infinitely more difficult frontal assault.

Wallace's men executed the first about-face, but instead of pivoting until they were perpendicular to the main American line, as ordered, they marched straight ahead—that is, toward the American rear. Witnessing this maneuver, other officers in the American line assumed Howard had ordered a general retreat and instantly joined it.[28]

Although accidental, the American withdrawal proceeded "in perfect order." Still, in the eyes of the oncoming British infantry, the Americans seemed to be fleeing in panic. Eager to complete the rout, individual redcoats and Loyalists disobeyed commands to wait for their comrades and rushed forward "in no Order." Tarleton now paid a price for attempting to Americanize his tactics. European infantry typically marched in an unbroken line, with each man nearly touching his neighbors to the right and left, but Tarleton and other British officers had attempted to adjust to North America's forests by having their men advance in "open order," with gaps of several feet between them. But open order allows individual soldiers unprecedented discretion, and Tarleton's infantrymen now exercised theirs, turning their front line into a footrace.[29]

As the fleetest British runners approached within ten yards of the prize, Morgan and his officers finally got their soldiers to stop retreating and turn to face their pursuers. Suddenly firing a volley, the Americans killed and wounded many and stunned the rest—and then launched a bayonet charge of their own. Every redcoat "took to His heels for security—helter-skelter," Morgan reported, and his own troops had not advanced far when the dazed British officers began waving white handkerchiefs. Only the artillerymen remained at their posts until they were shot down or stabbed. As the Americans raced toward the first field piece, two captains competed for the honor of capturing it. Richard Anderson won the race by using his spontoon (half-pike) to pole-vault the final few yards.[30]

Most of Tarleton's cavalrymen had not yet entered the battle, and he tried to rally them for a desperate effort to "retrieve the day."[31] But, refusing to commit suicide, they joined the exodus, as did Tarleton. Then he and two of his officers caught sight of Morgan's cavalry commander, William Washington. The three British officers faced about. Just as one lunged at Washington with his saber, an American sergeant got between them and parried the thrust. As the officer renewed his attack, an American waiter (servant) shot a pistol at him, wounding him and saving Washington's life. At the time, no one said anything about the waiter's race, but in 1845 the painter William Ranney plausibly depicted him as African American, and the image of a Black man saving the beloved General Washington's cousin became a powerful exhibit against slavery.

Washington's cavalry pursued Tarleton's for another twenty-four miles—about the same distance Tarleton's troopers had chased American

William Tyree Ranney, *The Battle of Cowpens*

militiamen after the Battle of Camden. Most of the British horsemen and a few foot soldiers managed, that day or the next, to reach Cornwallis's army on the east bank of the Broad.[32]

Fewer than 150 Americans were killed or wounded at the Battle of Cowpens. Morgan estimated British casualties at 839, but the true figure may have been closer to a thousand, especially if you count the more than seventy African Americans who had escaped slavery by joining the British only to now be reenslaved. Some who had belonged to Whigs were returned to them; two would remain Daniel Morgan's property for the rest of his life.[33]

Morgan did not exaggerate when he boasted of having given the hated Tarleton "a devil of a whiping," and most historians of the American War of Independence consider Cowpens the turning point of the southern phase of the war, though that distinction must actually be shared with Kings Mountain. Still, Morgan was criticized by many contemporaries, including Tarleton, for allowing his opponent to overtake him in terrain that provided no natural defense. Morgan insisted that he had deliberately chosen to fight Tarleton at Cowpens rather than from the far side of Broad River. Drawing upon most officers' contempt for citizen-soldiers, he explained that he had backed his men up against the Broad in order to force them to fight: "Had I crossed the river, one half of the militia would immediately have abandoned me."[34] Numerous mapmakers have bolstered Morgan's claim by depicting the Broad River just behind the American lines, though it was actually five miles to the north.

THE DAY AFTER THE battle, Morgan's army waded over the Broad and headed north. With the dissolution of Tarleton's Legion, Cornwallis took over the pursuit, now with the primary purpose of recovering Morgan's eight-hundred-odd captives. Ordinarily a commander attempting such a rescue would have sent his light infantry ahead to tie the enemy down until the main army could come up. But Tarleton had lost nearly all of his light troops at Kings Mountain and Cowpens, so he made the fateful decision to turn his regulars into light infantry by destroying most of the army's baggage, including its food, setting the example by publicly burning his own. Perhaps the soldiers took pride in thus unofficially joining the ranks of the elite light infantry, though none could have enjoyed watching the commissary's men stave in the corps' entire supply of rum.[35]

In burning his supplies, Cornwallis emulated the generals of old who

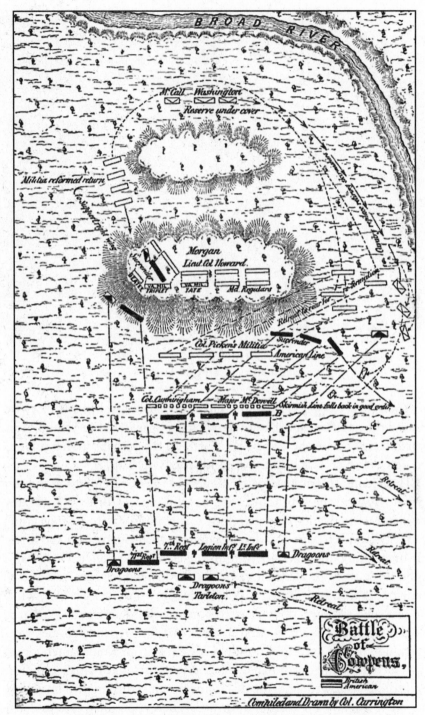

Henry Carrington, *Battle of Cowpens*, incorrectly placing it
directly adjacent to the Broad River

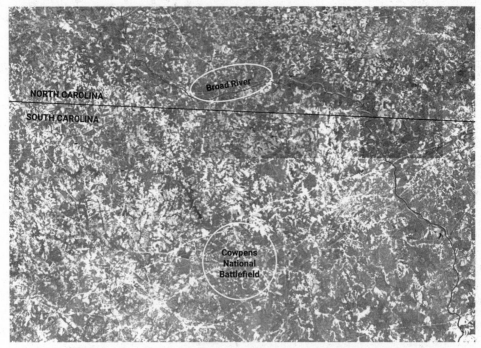

Aerial photograph of the Broad River and the site of the Battle of Cowpens
illustrating the distance between them: five miles

stiffened their troops' resolve by burning their boats, but with a twist.
He had the navy transport ample food and war matériel to Wilmington,
North Carolina, on the Cape Fear River. To reach them, all his soldiers
would have to do was crush the Continentals.

The fleeing Americans crossed numerous rivers, careful never to leave
a single boat on the southern shore. Several times, Cornwallis negated
this natural disadvantage by marching upstream to where his men could
wade. Morgan's troops could still slaughter their pursuers at the fords,
but by sending detachments to multiple crossings at once, Cornwallis
could force them into a shell game. At the Catawba River, he directed
some of his troops to Beatty's Ford, tying down the Americans, while
the rest sped six miles downriver to Cowan's Ford and waded out into
the rain-swollen stream. Several soldiers and two generals' horses were
swept downriver, and eight hundred North Carolina militiamen vigor-
ously defended the north bank. But the Loyalists and British and German soldiers showed amazing discipline in not returning fire until they
had completed the crossing and formed, whereupon their volleys drove
the North Carolinians off. At that point, the Continentals and Whig

militia guarding Beatty's and other fords had to pull back to avoid being pinned against the river.[36]

In North Carolina, Morgan's army linked up with Greene's and continued its celebrated "race to the Dan" River (also called the Roanoke), which flows west to east and, in this stretch, just north of the North Carolina–Virginia line and roughly parallel to it. Severe sciatica and hemorrhoids forced Morgan to head home to northwestern Virginia on February 10. Four days later, Greene's soldiers paddled across the Dan, where they obtained not only supplies and reinforcements from the northward but a measure of safety, since Cornwallis knew better than to contest his reinvigorated opponents' claim to the north bank.[37]

One of Greene's officers aptly described him as "restless in safety."[38] On February 18, just four days after reaching Virginia, his troops began recrossing the Dan into North Carolina. Over the next three weeks, they remained on the move, avoiding a general engagement with Cornwallis but keeping close enough to him to prevent his gathering much food or forage or many Loyalist fighters.

On the other hand, detachments from the two armies clashed frequently. Dr. John Pyle assembled about four hundred fellow backcountry Loyalists as mounted infantry and rode off to join Tarleton. Seeing horsemen approaching and assuming they were Tarleton's, Pyle and his men agreed to let them pass. Only after the two columns had aligned did the newcomers reveal their actual identity—Henry Lee's independent Continental command, known as the American Legion— by opening fire. "The conflict was quickly decided, and bloody on one side only," Lee noted. "Ninety of the royalists were killed, and most of the survivors wounded." After that, few Loyalists joined Tarleton and Cornwallis.[39]

By mid-March, reinforcements had swelled the American army to about 4,400 men. With many veterans about to complete their tours, Greene decided to confront Cornwallis. On March 14, he lined his army up at Guilford Courthouse (in modern-day Greensboro, North Carolina) in order to invite attack from a British army that was now less than half its size. Cornwallis's troops would come from the west, so the Americans faced in that direction. Adopting an even more extreme version of the defense-in-depth strategy that had served Morgan so well at Cowpens, Greene placed two lines of militia in front of his Continentals. Then, as the Germans and redcoats approached on the morning of

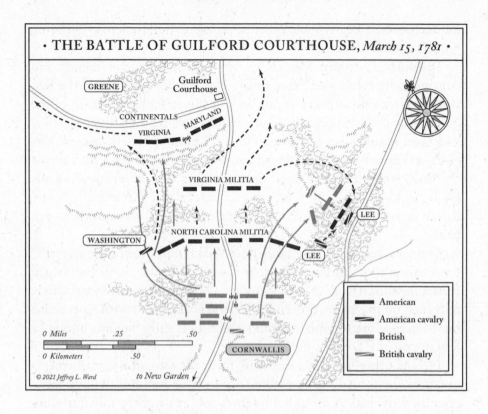

· THE BATTLE OF GUILFORD COURTHOUSE, *March 15, 1781* ·

GREENE
Guilford Courthouse
CONTINENTALS
MARYLAND
VIRGINIA
VIRGINIA MILITIA
LEE
WASHINGTON
NORTH CAROLINA MILITIA
LEE
CORNWALLIS
to New Garden

American
American cavalry
British
British cavalry

0 Miles   .25   .50
0 Kilometers   .50
© 2021 Jeffrey L. Ward

March 15, he sent Henry Lee's Legion and about sixty riflemen forward as a mobile first line of defense that successfully thinned their assailants' ranks.[40]

Cornwallis's troops had to cross an open field to reach Greene's first stationary line: North Carolina militiamen steadying their muskets and (more commonly) rifles atop a rail fence, with a dense forest behind them. Like Morgan at Cowpens, Greene had ordered his front-line fighters to fire two volleys and then retire. He later complained that many of the North Carolinians got off only one shot and indeed that "a considerable part left the ground without firing at all."[41] The coauthors of the most thorough investigation of the battle state that Greene himself had inadvertently contributed to the North Carolinians' flight by leaving four hundred yards of thick woods between them and the line behind them. That was twice the distance Morgan had left at Cowpens, which had much less tree cover, and it deprived the front line of tactical and moral support. Moreover, from his position in the third line, where he could not see his frontline troops, Greene appears to have exaggerated the number of them who fled without firing. Eyewitnesses credited the North Carolinians with significantly degrading Cornwallis's force.[42]

The Virginia militiamen in Greene's second line were covered by dense woods that allowed them to hold out considerably longer. Especially thick cover at the southern end of the battlefield enabled the cavalry, rifle regiment, and musketmen guarding Greene's left flank to offer particularly stout resistance. Eventually they did pull back, but the vegetation was so thick that Henry Lee had to lead his horsemen down a road that veered off to the southeast. The foot soldiers followed, with two enemy regiments, one German and one British, in close pursuit. Soon this battle-within-the-battle had pivoted to a north–south axis and drifted nearly a mile away from the primary engagement.[43] With the rest of the American front giving way more rapidly than its southern fringe, the British center soon reached a point north of the American left, with some redcoats and Germans ending up behind it. When a group of British infantrymen turned to their right to exploit this opportunity, they, too, discovered enemy soldiers on their flanks and in their rear. They were about to surrender when they were saved by the fortuitous arrival of some of Cornwallis's cavalry and the never-explained departure of Lee's.

Back in the main battle, some musketmen in Greene's second line got off as many as fifteen shots—an entire flint's worth.[44] By the time they finally withdrew, they had staggered the redcoats in more than one sense. They had killed many, worn down the rest, and sown disorder. Perhaps most crucially, some of the British and German units had broken through the topographical and human obstacles more quickly than others, and they all emerged at different times into the clearing they would have to cross on their way uphill to the final American line, the Continentals. First the 33rd Regiment emerged from the forest and made a solo assault on the Continental line, only to be turned back. Next came the 2nd Battalion of Britain's Brigade of Guards, also operating independently. They managed to get behind a regiment of Maryland Continentals, who had to execute an about-face to confront them, and soon the antagonists were "so near that the blazes from their guns seemed to meet."[45]

William Washington's cavalry joined in the effort to repel the Guards, and Cornwallis ordered his cannon crews to switch to case shot. Henry Lee later contended that Cornwallis knowingly fired into a mixed scrum that included some of his own soldiers, but he did not actually witness this barrage, and no one who did confirmed his claim.[46]

Eventually the Americans managed to push the Guards all the way back to the edge of the forest. As other British units reached the clearing, their officers halted them long enough to organize a unified assault. But by this time, Greene had decided to retreat. Astride his horse near the northern edge of the battlefield, he had only a murky idea of what was happening to the south. He thought the British had turned his left flank, and he worried that his right flank might soon crumble as well.[47] Had the general known that neither flank was actually in any immediate danger, he undoubtedly would have stayed and fought, and he might have achieved a victory as complete as Morgan's at Cowpens.[48]

Greene posted a rear guard to cover his troops' withdrawal, but the redcoats, Loyalists, and Germans, like the Continentals and Whig militia, had had enough. They pursued the rebels only a short distance.

The American commander believed he had lost the Battle of Guilford Courthouse, and other Continental generals, including Washington, agreed and tried to console him.[49] But historians disagree. Like Howe at Breed's Hill nearly six years earlier, Cornwallis had driven the rebels off, but only at enormous cost. Despite Greene's complaints about the North Carolina militia, his troops had faithfully followed the war-of-posts strategy, each line inflicting heavy casualties on the oncoming British before pulling back. The Americans suffered only 7 percent casualties in the battle: 79 men killed and 184 wounded. As a proportion of his 1,924 men, Cornwallis's loss was four times greater, 28 percent (93 killed, 26 missing, and 413 wounded).[50] After Guilford (indeed, after the war) Greene could still not claim a single victory over the British. And Cornwallis could still say, a little bit longer, that the rebels had never beat him. But this latest British victory was widely described as Pyrrhic, and the same could be said for nearly all of the mother country's triumphs in this distant war, since, win or lose, replacing the dead eroded popular support, the government's financial prospects—and the ministry's majorities in Parliament.[51] The astonishing fact about the Battle of Guilford Courthouse was that so few Whigs commented on how much it had helped their cause. Did they really not see that they were winning a war of attrition? Or did they fear that deliberately creating a quagmire would tarnish their honor?

BY THE TIME OF the Guilford battle, Cornwallis's troops had used up most of their scant food stocks, clothing, and equipment, forcing them to march to the village of Cross Creek, ninety miles up the Cape Fear River from Wilmington, whence the general ordered supplies sent upriver. But the likelihood of a Whig ambush effectively closed the Cape Fear, forcing the troops to march downstream to Wilmington, where they arrived on April 7.

No one but Cornwallis could say where he was headed next, and it was not clear that he himself knew. But for the moment, he had abandoned the backcountry, forcing Greene to choose between following him and returning to South Carolina, where partisans had continued their raids against British posts and convoys. Deciding to head south, Greene once again divided his army, sending the light infantry under Henry Lee southeast toward a junction with Francis Marion in the swamps of northeastern South Carolina while personally leading the main army on a more westerly path toward Camden.[52]

As soon as Lee's and Marion's detachments joined forces, they invested Fort Watson, atop a thirty-foot-high Indian mound on the Santee River.[53] With no cannon, the Americans could not hope to batter down the sturdy stockade, but Maj. Hezekiah Maham suggested an old expedient: a siege tower from which riflemen could shoot down into the fort. The Maham Tower was completed during the night of April 22–23, and the next morning the astonished British commander surrendered the fort and his 114 men.[54]

The nine hundred troops guarding the British fort in Camden presented a more formidable obstacle. On April 19, Greene's army of 1,500 made camp atop Hobkirk's Hill, a mile and a half north of the fort, but prudently balked at a frontal assault. At 10 a.m. on April 25, Lord Rawdon, the British commander at Camden, ordered that it be "manned with Negroes and Tories." Then he marched with his regulars toward Hobkirk's Hill.[55] The British column attacked while it was still evolving into a battle line, presenting a narrow front to Gen. Greene, who sent his own men forward to attempt a double envelopment. But when two Maryland companies fell back sixty yards

Maham Tower used by the Whigs in their siege of Fort Watson

to reorganize, their colonel made the fatal error of ordering the rest of the regiment to join them, and that "broke the line" (as a court-martial would later rule). Up to this point, the Battle of Hobkirk's Hill had borne a striking resemblance to the Battle of Camden, fought just ten miles to the north the previous August. In both, an American army approached British-held Camden from the north, whereupon the Camden garrison sallied northward. Both times, the attackers' transition from column to line looked to the American commander like a vulnerability, and he ordered his men to charge. Then some of the rebels faltered, forcing the rest to pull back as well. But the similarities ended there, for Greene, unlike Horatio Gates eight months earlier, managed to keep his retreat orderly, and even as the British pursued them for about three miles, he and his men ended up inflicting nearly as many casualties (258) as they suffered (270). After the Fort Washington disaster and what he saw as a defeat at Guilford Courthouse, Greene had at least mastered the art of marching backward. "We fight get beat and fight again," he told Washington on May 1.[56]

Even before driving Greene off, Rawdon had received instructions to leave Camden and march his army east to Monck's Corner, just thirty miles north of Charles Town. During the battle, Greene captured several men who had fought on the American side and then deserted to the British. He hanged five of them, and when news of the executions reached the American deserters still with Rawdon, they refused to go out on patrols. The mutinous spirit spread through the Camden garrison, sealing Rawdon's decision to evacuate. Heading east on May 10, the troops were accompanied by numerous Loyalists and as many as five hundred African Americans. Some had escaped from Whigs, while others remained the property of Loyalists—living reminders that Britain's enlistment of rebels' slaves was an alliance of convenience.[57]

The day after Rawdon abandoned Camden, Thomas Sumter captured the eighty-man British garrison at Orangeburg, whereupon other nearby posts "fell in quick succession." Months earlier, British soldiers had driven Rebecca Brewton Motte from her mansion near the confluence of the Congaree and Wateree Rivers, turning it into "the principal depot of the convoys from Charleston to Cambden." Lee and Marion laid siege to "fort Motte" on May 8 and set slaves to work digging approach trenches. On the fourth day of the siege, Motte "presented the besiegers with a quiver of African arrows" that they set ablaze and shot onto her roof, igniting it and forcing the nearly two hundred Loyalists inside to capitulate. (More than two hundred years later, a University of South Carolina archaeologist would dig up one of those arrows.)[58]

By the end of May 1781, the British had lost or left all of their posts in the Carolina backcountry except Ninety Six. London slave trader Richard Oswald was not surprised. When his friend and longtime trading partner Henry Laurens was captured at sea and imprisoned in the Tower of London, Oswald paid him a visit, and the two agreed that "these remote Inland Situations," far beyond the reach of supply ships, placed British regulars and American militia on an "unequal footing." As Laurens explained to Oswald, the militiamen could travel light by subsisting on parched corn boiled into "a Sort of Saloop or Jelly." In other words, an essential ingredient in the Whig victory was that classic First Nations contribution to southern cuisine, grits.[59]

CHAPTER 30

———•◦•———

Nothing but a Treaty

1781

As Britain's South Carolina forts fell, Cornwallis was in Wilmington, North Carolina, refitting his army and undoubtedly cursing the destruction of his detachments at Kings Mountain and Cowpens, which had not only denied him a decisive victory at Guilford Courthouse but also forced him to streamline his regular army by destroying most of its food, in turn dictating the supply run to Wilmington.

Cornwallis's gloom shaped his thinking about where to go next. Heading back to South Carolina would be not only dangerous (since Greene could trap his small corps between any two of the province's great rivers) but, as a retrograde motion, "disgraceful."[1] A return to western North Carolina had even less appeal. The Loyalists upon whom Cornwallis had repeatedly pinned his hopes had just as often disappointed him. As he reported from Wilmington, "Many of the inhabitants rode into camp, shook me by the hand, said they were glad to see us . . . and then rode home again."[2]

Even more discouraging was the matter of supply. Numerous rivers drained the eastern slopes of North Carolina's Great Smoky Mountains into the Atlantic, but none was navigable for large transports. So if Cornwallis headed back inland, he would periodically have to return to Wilmington to resupply.[3]

In sharp contrast, Virginia beckoned. Charles II's "Old Dominion" had become the wealthiest and most populous British colony in North America in part because several of its rivers remained navigable for up to a hundred miles. Indeed, at their mouths, the James, York, Rappahannock, and Potomac were, like the Hudson, so wide that British supply ships could sail right past U.S. shore batteries. The Carolina backcountry was so much less accessible that Cornwallis could only hope to conquer it by cutting off the Whigs' supplies as they passed through Virginia.[4] More than three years earlier, John Burgoyne's struggle to feed his army had prompted him to send part of it on a livestock-rustling expedition to Bennington, Vermont, that doomed his own effort to prevent Whig war materiél from crossing the Hudson. Now Cornwallis's frustration with carting baggage overland similarly directed his course to Virginia, with similarly fateful consequences.

Another reason Cornwallis chose to head north was that his 1,400 troops were "very insufficient for offensive operations," whereas Gen. Clinton had just reinforced the 1,600 British soldiers already in Virginia with 2,000 more under the command of the recently exchanged William Phillips, Burgoyne's onetime second-in-command and Cornwallis's "dear friend."[5] On April 25, 1781, Cornwallis's army left Wilmington, destination Petersburg, Virginia.[6]

IN THE SPRING OF 1781, as the Whigs methodically reconquered South Carolina and Cornwallis slogged toward Virginia, the British army suffered a crucial defeat that was not a U.S. victory. A year earlier, Louisiana governor Bernardo de Gálvez had seized the British fort guarding Mobile Bay on the Gulf of Mexico and immediately targeted the capital of West Florida, Pensacola. A fleet carrying five to six thousand Spanish soldiers sailed out of Havana and dropped anchor just outside Pensacola Bay on March 9. As more and more reinforcements poured in, Gálvez methodically invested the British fort. On May 8, a Spanish shell ignited the British gunpowder magazine, killing seventy-six redcoats. The next day, Gen. John Campbell surrendered the fort—and with it all of West Florida.[7]

France had also sent an expeditionary force to North America: the six thousand troops under the comte de Rochambeau that had landed in Newport, Rhode Island, on July 11, 1780. The French army spent a year consuming supplies without engaging the enemy, but on May 22, 1781, Rochambeau met George Washington in Wethersfield, Connecticut, and agreed to march west to the Hudson River to rendezvous with the Continentals.

Rochambeau wanted the united armies to continue southward, all the way to Virginia, and drive Cornwallis out of that state. Washington was not persuaded. He remembered Lafayette's troops' resistance to marching southward during the hot summer months and feared his own men would raise the same "objections to the climate." Besides,

Washington's army was dangerously understrength, both because of the mutiny and subsequent near dissolution of the Pennsylvania Line and because he had sent a third of his troops to fight the Iroquois in upstate New York and another 1,200 to pursue Arnold in Virginia.[8] He wanted Rochambeau to join him on the Hudson, where they would await an opportunity to execute his long-standing desire to storm New York City. In letters he sent friends and colleagues after the Wethersfield conference, Washington exulted that Rochambeau had agreed to attack the British in New York instead of Virginia. The commander-in-chief of the allied forces had so little cash that he was forced to send many of his letters by regular mail, which British agents easily intercepted. Henry Clinton soon learned of the Continentals' plan to strike him in New York.[9]

Meanwhile Rochambeau wrote the comte de Grasse, admiral of a French fleet sailing toward North America by way of the Caribbean, informing him of Washington's decision—but also of his own preference for invading the Chesapeake.[10]

ON MAY 20, THE remnants of Cornwallis's army—about 1,400 men fit for duty—stumbled into Petersburg, one of several Virginia towns that had recently seen action.[11] At the end of March, the beleaguered general's friend William Phillips had entered the Chesapeake with 2,200 reinforcements, rendezvoused with Arnold (his adversary from the two Battles of Freeman's Farm), taken charge of the combined force, and, on April 25, clashed with one thousand Virginia militiamen commanded by Baron von Steuben in the little town of Blandford, a mile down the Appomattox River from Petersburg. Phillips's soldiers made quick work of Steuben's, then seized more than seven million pounds of tobacco from twelve merchant ships in the Appomattox and James Rivers, burning most of it but sending some to Europe for sale at astronomical wartime prices. They also liberated numerous slaves.[12]

Just two days after the Battle of Blandford, the Whig soldiers in Virginia also acquired a new leader, as Lafayette led his 1,200 Continental reinforcements into Richmond and superseded Steuben. Then on May 15, Phillips died of a fever, and Arnold once again took over the rebel colony's British forces, only to be superseded just five days later with the arrival of the bereaved Cornwallis. More British reinforcements reached Virginia on May 21, bringing the total to seven thousand (at least by Clinton's reckoning). The new arrivals quickly picked up Cornwallis's men's practice of making servants of the African Americans who had escaped to the army. "Every officer had four to six horses and three or four Negroes, as well as one or two Negresses for cook and maid," Johann Ewald reported, and every officer's "woman" had "a Negro and Negress on horseback for her servants." Had these formerly enslaved women and men already mastered horseback riding before the war, or did they learn it on the march?[13]

"I am quite tired of marching about the country in quest of adventures," Cornwallis had written Phillips from Wilmington. But his pursuit of the twenty-three-year-old Lafayette seemed to reinvigorate him.[14] Washington and Nathanael Greene feared the glory-mad Lafayette would provoke a scrape with Cornwallis, whose army surpassed his own in both numbers (by a factor of two) and experience, but the young general tried to reassure his superiors. "I Have Been Guarding Against My Own Warmth," he told Washington. On the other hand, if Lafayette were to "decline fighting" altogether, "the Country would think Herself given up," so he would not pass up opportunities to "Skarmish."[15]

Cornwallis pushed Lafayette's troops northward, over the Rapidan River, sixty miles north of Richmond, before pausing at Hanover Courthouse, twenty miles north of the capital, to send two expeditions west. Lt. Col. Simcoe's troops marched to Point of Fork, where the Rivanna River empties into the James. Swelling his detachment's apparent size by having the teamsters and women mix with the troops in a thick forest, Simcoe scared off Steuben's army and then destroyed Virginia's principal supply cache.[16] Meanwhile Lt. Col. Banastre Tarleton and 250 mounted infantry and British Legion cavalry galloped west on June 3. Days earlier, when the British occupied Richmond, Governor Thomas Jefferson and the Virginia legislature had fled seventy miles west to Charlottesville. Tarleton's orders were to capture both the governor (whose term had actually ended, though the legislature had not yet chosen his successor) and the General Assembly.

Late in the evening of the third, as Tarleton's raiders rested at Louisa Courthouse, they drew the attention of Jack Jouett, a twenty-seven-year-old militia officer. Jouett rode west, took a shortcut, pulled ahead, and reached Jefferson's home, Monticello, just before dawn on June 4. Other riders also warned Jefferson, but like Paul Revere six years earlier, Jouett would become the symbol. Jefferson immediately sent his family off but hung back collecting state papers until a party of Tarleton's raiders reached the foot of his mountain, only minutes away, whereupon he finally mounted his horse and disappeared into the woods.[17]

From Monticello Jouett carried his warning to the assembly in nearby Charlottesville. Several legislators, including Daniel Boone, moved too slowly and were taken and briefly detained. For more than two years, barracks near Charlottesville had housed the British and German soldiers captured with Burgoyne back in 1777. By the time Tarleton's troopers rode up, most of the prisoners had been sent farther west, but about twenty who had found work at local farms and businesses were still in town, and their compatriots had the satisfaction of liberating them.[18]

CORNWALLIS'S SUCCESSES IN VIRGINIA proved costly, for he had not left enough troops behind to hold the Georgia and Carolina backcountry. Fort Cornwallis in Augusta, Georgia, was garrisoned by roughly equal numbers of Loyalists and Muskogee Indians, and the duty of capturing it fell to Lt. Col. Henry Lee. "Lighthorse Harry" was one of more than a hundred Revolutionary War veterans who later published autobiographies, but his was like no other. Released in 1812, shortly after Lee completed a year in debtors' prison, the book was aimed in part at restoring his solvency, and it sometimes veered toward fiction. But Lee also stood out for his willingness to admit mistakes. In May 1781, his troops built a thirty-foot-high Maham Tower outside Fort Cornwallis and even managed to hoist a cannon atop it, but the British almost succeeded in burning it down by setting fire to an adjacent building that Lee had neglected to demolish. "This omission," he admitted in his memoirs, "resulted from that spirit of procrastination common to man, and was certainly highly reprehensible."[19]

In recalling his siege of Fort Cornwallis, Lee praised its commander, Thomas Brown, especially for his handling of a Scottish artillery sergeant who scaled the parapet and made a dash for the American lines. Arriving safely, the sergeant offered to guide the gunners atop Lee's Maham Tower to Fort Cornwallis's powder magazine. They never hit it, though, and Lee would soon find out why. The sergeant had actually been *sent* to the American camp, specifically to burn down the Maham Tower. The idea of misdirecting the cannon crew's fire was apparently his own.[20]

Lee planned his final assault on Fort Cornwallis for June 4. The previous night, he dispatched a squad of riflemen to a house near the fort to assess how many snipers it could accommodate. He then withdrew them, intending to sneak them back in before attacking at dawn. But he never got the chance, because around 3 a.m. on the 4th, an explosion blew the house thirty or forty feet in the air and reduced it to "fragments." Anticipating Lee's use of the building, Brown's sappers had tunneled underneath their stockade and undermined it with explosives. Seeing Lee's riflemen enter the house (but failing to notice their departure), Brown had given the order to blow it up. For all his ingenuity, Brown had failed either to bring down his besiegers' Maham Tower or blow up their riflemen. He had no choice but to accept Lee's surrender terms, managing only to postpone the signing ceremony one day, to June 5, to push it past the king's birthday. By capturing Augusta, the Americans had all but eliminated the possibility of Britain laying claim to Georgia in future peace talks.[21]

Meanwhile Greene's troops had laid siege to Ninety Six, the last major British fort in the Carolina backcountry. Like Fort Cornwallis, this post had no well, and soon "the sufferings of the garrison began to be extreme for want of water." The commandant—Lt. Col. John H. Cruger, the onetime mayor of New York City—would have had to capitulate but for nightly forays to a nearby stream carried out by "naked negroes . . . whose bodies in the darkness were not distinguishable from the trees that surrounded them."[22]

Three thousand British troops under Gen. Rawdon set out from Charles Town to relieve Ninety Six. Realizing they would arrive before he could capture the fort by regular approaches, Greene on June 18 tried to storm it. Unsurprisingly, the assault failed, and rather than risk an engagement with Rawdon, the Americans fled. But like their brethren at Camden two months earlier, the men of the Ninety Six garrison had defended their post only to be ordered to abandon it and head to the coast.[23]

MEANWHILE IN VIRGINIA, CORNWALLIS briefly occupied Elk Hill, a slave labor camp owned by Thomas Jefferson, before heading back east with twenty-three of the Black Virginians who had toiled there.[24] Reaching Williamsburg on June 25, the general received alarming new orders from his commander-in-chief. Having seen Washington's letters rejoicing that Rochambeau's forces would soon unite with his in an all-out assault on British headquarters, Gen. Clinton wanted his subordinate to send him two to three thousand soldiers—nearly half his army. The men were less needed in Virginia, Clinton contended, and anyway it would be unwise to leave them "in that unhealthy climate at this season of the year" (summer).[25]

Cornwallis believed Clinton was operating with faulty intelligence about the belligerents' relative strength in both theaters. Most crucially, Clinton thought Cornwallis's soldiers vastly outnumbered Lafayette's, but in reality the recently reinforced Lafayette could now field 4,000 men against Cornwallis's 4,300 (which Clinton inflated to 7,000).[26]

After sending half of his army to Clinton, Cornwallis was to march the rest to the town of York, eleven miles east of Williamsburg, in order to provide safe haven for British ships anchored in the York River. Cornwallis feared he could not carry out that mission with his diminished force. So on June 30, he informed Clinton that he was going to lead his troops all the way east to the town of Portsmouth, seventeen miles from the mouth of Chesapeake Bay, embark half for New York, and then hunker down with the rest in that disease-ridden but defensible port. It seems clear that Cornwallis was trying to bury Clinton's distant fear of having to repel an American assault on New York City under the more immediate prospect of being blamed for giving up all of Britain's largest North America colony except its "sickly" southeastern tip. That might convince Clinton to reconsider his decision to cannibalize Cornwallis's army.[27]

On his way to Portsmouth, Cornwallis set a trap for Lafayette. Both generals knew the Americans' best chance of defeating the redcoats would be while they crossed the James River. On July 4, the British marched to Green Spring plantation, on the north bank of the James a mile upstream from Jamestown. That evening and the next day, Cornwallis ferried most of his baggage and a portion of his army over the river. On July 6, Lt. Col. Tarleton had "a negroe and a dragoon" fake-desert to the approaching Americans with the "false intelligence" that most of Cornwallis's army had crossed to the south bank, leaving only a small rear guard behind.[28]

Later that day, American scouts riding toward Green Spring learned from "a negroe with a knapsack on his back"—apparently a British soldier—that Cornwallis and most of his army were actually still north of the James. This information was quickly conveyed to headquarters, where it "produced a pause," as Henry Lee reported. But Anthony Wayne, Lafayette's senior general, "disquieted as he always was by losing a chance of battle," yearned to proceed with the assault. Perhaps succumbing to the "ardor natural to the season of youth" (as Lee later suggested), Lafayette gave his consent.[29]

To reach the British soldiers lined up at the edge of a forest, the American troops had to march across an open field. Only with the enemy's first volley did they discover that they should have listened to the "negroe with a knapsack" rather than the Black man and the dragoon. Cornwallis had actually kept most of his troops north of the river. As the British launched their own charge, Lt. Col. Thomas Dundas carefully avoided Tarleton's Cowpens blunder of allowing the troops, scenting victory, to charge ahead pell-mell. As a colleague reported, "this able officer ordered his men to halt [and] formed them in regular order."[30]

Nearly everyone on both sides expected the British onslaught to send Wayne's men scampering. But Wayne knew that armies are never more vulnerable than when they show their backs, so instead he continued to advance. Dundas, having kept his men together, quickly repulsed the Pennsylvanians, though their audacious advance had bought them time to escape.

About 150 Americans were killed or wounded at the Battle of Green Spring: double Cornwallis's casualties.[31] The British also captured Lafayette's only two cannon, one of which, Cornwallis gleefully noted, was inscribed "Taken at Bennington." The Americans' losses would have been even greater if their long march to Green Spring had not delayed their attack until nearly dusk. A wistful Cornwallis observed that "A little more daylight would have given us the whole corps."[32]

As CORNWALLIS'S REDCOATS, BLACK refugees, Loyalists, and Germans completed their crossing of the James and marched east toward Portsmouth, Lafayette explained to Washington why he had followed them across the state and then finally attacked. For several weeks, newspapers had been reporting that Catherine the Great of Russia and Emperor Joseph II of Austria had offered to oversee peace negotiations between Britain and its enemies. For many free Americans, the bright prospect of peace was overshadowed by the specter of France and Spain agreeing to resolve the conflict on the conventional principle of *uti possidetis* ("as you possess"), under which all belligerents retained the territory on which they stood. That would leave most of Georgia and significant swaths of South Carolina, Virginia, and the district of Maine in British hands.[33]

Worse still, France seemed poised to extract consent to *uti possi-*

detis from Congress. In 1780, the delegates had made the notoriously anti-French John Adams their sole peace commissioner and instructed him not to agree to any dismemberment of the Confederation. But in the intervening period, La Luzerne, the French minister in Philadelphia, had found ways to soften the Americans' position. For example, in the fall of 1780, he began dispensing bribes to John Sullivan, the leader of the 1779 expedition into Iroquois country and now a member of Congress.[34]

On June 15, 1781, Congress gave La Luzerne almost everything he wanted. Adams would henceforth share the peace commission with Benjamin Franklin, Henry Laurens, Thomas Jefferson, and John Jay, and they were instructed not to meet George III's representative without the consent of the French and "ultimately to govern yourselves by their advice and opinion." Only after the members of Congress thus made the United States essentially a client state did La Luzerne inform them that France planned to end the war under the principle of *uti possidetis.*[35]

But La Luzerne was not the only French nobleman seeking to influence the peace treaty. As Cornwallis's troops marched eastward across Virginia, Gen. Lafayette labored to give the impression that he was not just following but chasing them. If he could "Give His Lordship the Disgrace of a Retreat," he could possibly influence the "European Negotiations." With the same "political Views" in mind, Lafayette persuaded Virginia to send two thousand militiamen to reinforce Greene in South Carolina. All too aware of the French government's fondness for *uti possidetis,* Lafayette considered it "Important for the treaty that Carolina Be Reconquered."[36]

In the same letter, Lafayette alerted Washington to another diplomatic opportunity. Woefully short of cavalry horses, Lafayette proposed to obtain them, as Cornwallis had, from the Virginians who best knew horseflesh. "Nothing But a treaty of alliance with the Negroes Can find Out dragoon Horses," he wrote.[37]

As Lafayette trailed Cornwallis across southern Virginia, state officials seeking to meet his demand for more militia provoked additional draft resistance. Hampshire County in the northern part of the state emerged as a center of opposition, and in late June, Gen. Daniel Morgan came out of retirement to march four hundred militiamen from neighboring counties into Hampshire. One rebel was killed and several were captured.[38] Farmers in Virginia, and throughout the country, also continued to resist the draft. In May 1782, a western Pennsylvania official sardonically exulted at having successfully enlisted two new Continental soldiers, "only one of which has deserted."[39]

Cornwallis's troops had reached Portsmouth by July 20, and hundreds had already boarded transports for the voyage to New York City when new orders arrived from Gen. Clinton. Furious at Cornwallis's decision "to retire from a district of so much importance" as the peninsula between the York and James Rivers, the commander-in-chief authorized Cornwallis to send him only those soldiers he could safely spare, which for the moment Cornwallis judged to be none.[40]

Lafayette learned of Cornwallis's spat with Clinton from an American spy: a Black Virginian named James who had pretended to join the British and then somehow insinuated himself into Cornwallis's retinue. "A Servant Has opportunities to Hear," Lafayette knew, and sure enough, at the end of July, James informed him that the British were about to leave Portsmouth. They ended up sailing only as far as the York River, where Cornwallis occupied the town of York, along with Gloucester Point on the north bank, in compliance with his earlier instructions to provide safe anchorage for the Royal Navy.[41]

With two sets of fortifications to build, Cornwallis informed Charles O'Hara, whom he had left in command at Portsmouth, of his "great want of negroes to work, as the heat is too great to admit of the soldiers doing it." O'Hara sent over as many able-bodied African Americans as he could find but begged his friend and chief to also make provision at Yorktown for the more than one thousand African Americans who had taken refuge with the British and then contracted smallpox and other diseases. As a British colonial governor on the west coast of Africa, O'Hara had excelled at fomenting wars among local societies in order to draw more Black captives through his port, and in 1775 a group of white, African, and mixed-race colonists had traveled to London to complain of his venality and cruelty. It was apparently the first-ever African delegation to London, and it succeeded in getting him recalled. Yet even O'Hara could not think of "abandoning these unfortunate beings to disease, to famine, & what is worse than either, the resentment of their enraged masters."[42]

Cornwallis would not run the risk of the sick refugees infecting his troops; nor did he wish to waste food on those who survived. When the last of the British troops sailed from Portsmouth to Yorktown, ill African Americans were to be left behind.[43]

As able-bodied Blacks dug trenches and threw up breastworks on both sides of the York River, Cornwallis labored over a different sort of defense. Already glimpsing the coming catastrophe and well aware of Gen. Clinton's determination "to throw all blame on me," Cornwallis began composing a series of documents deflecting the censure right back onto his commander-in-chief.[44]

NATHANAEL GREENE'S CONTINENTALS SPENT the hottest five weeks of the summer in the relatively cool and healthy High Hills of Santee, emerging on August 23 to attack the only British force of any size still operating in the South Carolina backcountry. Lt. Col. Alexander Stewart, who had replaced the ailing Rawdon as Britain's southern commander, awaited Greene at Eutaw Springs on the south bank of the Santee, fifty miles northwest of Charles Town. On September 8, when Greene's army charged through a wooded area toward Stewart's troops, they resisted, counterattacked, and broke the American line. The Continentals rallied and on the second try drove the British all the way back through their camp, but then a regiment of redcoats, taking cover in a brick house, inflicted heavy casualties on the Americans, forcing them once again to withdraw. The Battle of Eutaw Springs brought the opposing armies into closer contact than perhaps any other engagement of the war. Henry Lee recalled years later that "a number of the soldiers fell transfixed by each other's bayonet"; the Americans felled in this way included a Black Marylander. Another anomalous aspect of the battle, unthinkable earlier in the war, was that a large portion of both armies consisted of deserters from the other side.[45]

Eventually the cautious Greene withdrew, leaving the British the official winners of the Battle of Eutaw Springs. But they had suffered heavier casualties: about 40 percent of the Germans, Loyalists, and redcoats engaged as opposed to 25 percent of the Americans. This dubious victory had the same sequel as earlier British successes in South Carolina: Stewart pulled his front line farther back, to Monck's Corner, thirty-five miles up the Cooper River from Charles Town. In all of Georgia and the Carolinas, the British retained only the ports of Wilmington, Charles Town (with its outpost at Monck's Corner), and Savannah.[46]

THE UNITED STATES WAS not faring nearly as well against its native enemies. At the start of 1780, Thomas Jefferson had tried to turn George Rogers Clark away from capturing Detroit and toward the "extermination" of Native Americans in the Ohio Valley. But the Indians' numerous raids against U.S. and Spanish targets that summer, especially their successful attack on the Licking River forts, made a tremendous impression on Governor Jefferson. And 1781 might well be worse, since First Nations leaders in the Ohio Valley appeared to have finally put together the extensive and well-armed anti-settler coalition they had envisioned since before the days of Pontiac. If two thousand Indians attacked western Virginia, Jefferson noted, they would not only spread "destruction and dismay" along "the whole extent of our frontier" but also divert western militia from the showdown with Cornwallis. Embracing Clark's conviction that Detroit was the real engine of native resistance, Jefferson wrote him on Christmas Day 1780 endorsing its capture and noting that it would "add to the Empire of liberty an extensive and fertile Country."[47]

Thousands of orators and authors have picked up on Jefferson's description of the United States as an "Empire of liberty" without taking note of its genocidal origins. The leading prose stylist of the founding era may have come up with that evocative term on his own. But just six months earlier, Martha Washington had sent the governor's wife multiple copies of Esther Reed's *Sentiments of an American Woman*, which celebrated Europe's enlightened queens for extending the "empire of liberty." It seems likely that Martha Jefferson gave her husband a copy of Reed's exhortation—and with it, one of his most memorable phrases.[48]

Jefferson authorized Clark to draft more than two thousand western militiamen for the assault on Detroit, but that proved difficult.[49] With redcoats and Germans marching at will through the southeastern part of the state and native war parties crossing the Ohio River to attack Virginia's western counties, few frontiersmen could be convinced to trek to the far end of Lake Erie.

Finally Clark came up with about three hundred fighters, and Archibald Lochry obtained a hundred more in western Pennsylvania. Knowing that the only way to prevent his men from deserting was to put miles and Indians between them and their homes, Clark sped down the Ohio, and Lochry could not catch up. On August 24, 1781, about ten miles below the mouth of the Great Miami River, his party was attacked by about ninety warriors. Without suffering a single fatal casualty of their own, the natives killed Lochry and about a third of his troops and captured most of the rest.[50]

Alarmed frontier whites learned that Lochry's attackers included at least two Mohawk sachems, one of whom was also a captain in the

British army. Joseph Brant had made it to the age of thirty-eight without succumbing to alcoholism, but on April 6, 1781, he had gotten into a drunken brawl, and his commander, Guy Johnson, sought to defuse tensions by sending him, along with the Seneca leader Guyasuta, on a diplomatic mission to the First Nations villages around Detroit. Many of these Anishinaabegs' forebears had fled Iroquois attacks on their previous homes in what is now Ontario, Canada, but over the intervening decades relations between the Six Nations and the Anishinaabeg—especially the Wyandots (or Hurons), Ojibwas (Chippewas), Ottawas, and Potawatomies—had steadily improved. Brant and Guyasuta were headed west to further strengthen the anti-settler alliance, and they interrupted their journey only long enough to help annihilate Lochry's party.[51]

Early in November 1781, representatives of thirteen indigenous nations converged on Detroit to discuss a possible joint assault against frontier settlements. For decades, native diplomats in what is now the Midwest had occasionally tried to build a pan-Indian coalition to resist encroaching settlers. These efforts had borne fruit in Pontiac's Rebellion in 1763, but the coalition builders achieved their greatest success during the American War of Independence, primarily because they now had help from Britain. Imperial officials could use European manufactured goods, especially arms and ammunition, to reward loyalty to the coalition, and Indian leaders who would not think of deferring to other native nations' sachems readily accepted the leadership of these much less threatening outsiders. By 1781, the British had helped the Indians assemble a confederacy powerful enough to survive even Britain's betrayal the following year.[52]

Joseph Brant made it to Detroit in the fall of 1781—he was a prominent speaker at the pan-Indian conference—but George Rogers Clark did not. The struggle to recruit fighters had fatally delayed his departure, and then the few soldiers he managed to enlist panicked upon learning Lochry's fate. Thus the 1781 expedition against the Indians' principal armory got no further than the dozen or so previous attempts.[53]

Even as some Native Americans worked to build their rebel coalition, others fought to remain neutral (in Michael A. McDonnell's fine formulation), sometimes with tragic results. David Zeisberger, the Moravian missionary, lived among his converts in the town of Gnadenhutten ("House of Grace") on the Tuscarawas River (halfway between Pittsburgh and modern-day Columbus, Ohio). When he learned that non-Christian Indians were planning a surprise attack on the U.S. garrison in Fort Henry (modern-day Wheeling, West Virginia), he warned the soldiers and saved the fort. But when the warriors discovered that Zeisberger had divulged their plans, they seized him, his fellow missionaries, and all of the Moravian Indians, and forcibly removed them 120 miles west to the Sandusky River.[54]

CHAPTER 31

Surrenders

1781–1782

B Y MID-1781, THE WHIGS WERE MAKING STEADY PROGRESS IN
Georgia and South Carolina but flailing nearly everywhere else.
Meeting with Washington in Wethersfield on May 22, the comte de Rochambeau had agreed to march his troops to Peekskill, New York, to
join the Continental Army in storming the British garrison in New York
City. A month later, he had still not arrived, and Washington must have
suspected him of stalling. Constitutionally incapable of continuing to
stand around, Washington cooked up what he called a "Coup de Main."
Benjamin Lincoln would lead eight hundred elite infantrymen onto the
northern tip of Manhattan Island during the night of July 2–3, and then
the next morning, James De Lancey's Loyalists, stationed on the mainland just east of Manhattan (near modern-day Yankee Stadium), would
be attacked by a second division consisting mostly of an independent
legion commanded by the duc de Lauzun. Like the rest of the French
army, Lauzun and his troops were actually still working their way west
through Connecticut, but Washington wrote them into his plan in the
apparent hope of tempting them to hurry up and join him.[1]

When Lincoln reconnoitered the British forts in northern Manhattan
from atop the New Jersey Palisades, he quickly fell back on Washington's much less audacious Plan B, which had him simply taking his men
ashore on the mainland north of Manhattan to support Lauzun against
De Lancey. Lauzun's legionnaires did their best to keep the appointment
Washington had set, marching all day on July 1, then most of that night
and all day on July 2 and all that night. But on the morning of July 3, still
eight miles short of their intended target, Lauzun and his troops learned
that the British had spotted Lincoln and were driving him off. The best
they could do was cover Lincoln's escape.[2]

On July 6, the main French army finally reached the Continental camp at Philipsburg, and Rochambeau ceremonially reviewed the Continental Army. "Three-quarters of the Rhode Island regiment consists of negroes," one of the French commander's aides-de-camp noted, "and that regiment is the most neatly dressed, the best under arms, and the most precise in its maneuvers."[3]

Washington spent the rest of July preparing for a grand assault on the British fortifications on Manhattan and trying to persuade his fellow general officers and himself that they were not, as he had once described them, "impregnable." Rochambeau remained constantly by his side, gently reminding him of the risks involved in an amphibious landing on a heavily fortified island and of the much greater chance of trapping Cornwallis's smaller force in Virginia. Rochambeau's case for Washington's home state was strengthened by the intelligence that Clinton had ordered Cornwallis to send half of his soldiers to New York.[4]

On July 23, the two generals accompanied a team of engineers on a scouting expedition to Throgs Neck, where, five years earlier, William Howe had begun his invasion of the American mainland—or tried to. Throgs Neck had turned out to be a terrible place to establish a beachhead, since high tide transformed it into an island, and the British had been forced to reembark and land farther east. The Neck frustrated Rochambeau and Washington as well. The two paid no attention to the

Jean Baptiste Antoine de Verger, *Soldiers in Uniform* (1781)

desultory fire from the cannon crews on a distant British warship (who would have been astonished to learn the identities of their targets). Indeed, finding themselves with time to kill while the engineers completed their survey, the two old veterans (Washington had first come under fire twenty-seven years earlier, and Rochambeau's first battle was even earlier) lay down together for a nap. They were abruptly awakened by the discovery that the tide had come in, cutting off their escape. Fortunately they were able to flag down a passing boat and return to the mainland.[5]

By the end of July, Washington was almost ready to face facts. The states had managed to recruit only about half the troops he would need to storm Fortress New York. And Adm. de Grasse would no doubt prove just as reluctant as d'Estaing to lead his ships through the narrow channel into New York Harbor under heavy British cannon fire—this assuming that they survived the gauntlet that Adm. George Rodney and his captains were reportedly preparing for them in the Caribbean.

Fortune smiled on de Grasse. On February 3, Rodney captured the Dutch island of St. Eustatius, which had grown rich as a way-station for molasses smugglers, and he was so busy extracting plunder from its merchants, especially the Jewish ones, that he sent a subordinate, Samuel Hood, to deal with de Grasse, giving him only eighteen ships of the line and holding on to the other four to guard his loot. Moreover, Rodney wanted to keep Hood close until he loaded the captured property on freighters bound for Britain, so he forbad him to meet de Grasse out in the open sea. With Hood thus hobbled, de Grasse's supply ships slipped unimpeded into the port of Fort-de-France on Martinique, and three warships from that station joined his fleet.[6]

De Grasse captured the British island of Tobago on June 2, and by July 28, he was anchored off Saint-Domingue, writing the comte de Barras, the admiral of the French fleet off Newport, Rhode Island, to say his twenty-eight ships of the line would soon set sail for North America. The thrilling news reached American headquarters on August 14, but it came with a caveat: de Grasse had decided not to assail Clinton in New York but Cornwallis in Virginia. Washington's initial initial reaction to this announcement was "intemperate passion." Possibly he suspected that de Grasse had chosen a southern state, just as d'Estaing had two years earlier, in hopes of making a quick return to the sugar islands, the real source of France's as well as Britain's colonial riches. But Washington soon gave up "all idea of attacking New York." Accompanied by Rochambeau's 5,500 soldiers and 2,000 (about half) of his own, he headed south toward home.[7]

The American victory in the Revolutionary War is often attributed to the vigor and ingenuity of a young country, but it relied more than anything else on an Old World insight about the advantages that nearly always attend armies defending fortifications. For six years, Washington had yearned to storm the ramparts of Boston and then Philadelphia and then New York. The sheer number of attacks that he called off raises the possibility that he never actually intended to proceed and just went through the motions to avoid accusations of retromingency. But it seems more likely that Washington really had lacked prudence in 1775 and learned it over the course of the war. Vanquishing his own aggressive instincts, he made his single largest contribution to the allied victory by surrendering to de Grasse's fait accompli and heading to Yorktown.

The Americans crossed to the west bank of the Hudson on August 20 and 21, with the French following four days later. One factor that had helped reconcile Washington to marching to Virginia was the intelligence that Cornwallis had been directed to send half his troops to New York, making Virginia an easier target and Clinton's army in New York a harder one. But by the time Washington crossed the Hudson, he knew that this massive transfer of redcoats and Germans from Virginia to New York had been canceled. It was too late to turn back now, and there were a million reasons to press on, but perhaps Washington enjoyed the irony of having agreed to march south partly in response to the troop transfer that the British had arranged after learning of his own, earlier, plan to storm New York City, which had also been aborted after inadvertently influencing the actions of the other side.

Washington's dream of storming New York City actually had one more purpose to serve. Fearing that Clinton might reinforce Cornwallis, the allied commanders concocted an elaborate cover story that their troops were "Marching to Sandy hook to facilitate the entrance of the French fleet" into New York Harbor. Continental soldiers set to work building bread ovens near Sandy Hook, and farmers were directed to send forage there. "Our own army no less than the Enemy are completely deceived," one of Washington's aides noted. The Americans also benefited from earlier misfortune: the British capture of Washington's letters previewing his plan to attack New York City blinded Gen. Clinton to the possibility that they might hit Cornwallis in Virginia instead. By the time Clinton figured out that his garrison was not the French and

American soldiers' actual target, the first of them were already parading through Philadelphia.[8]

Like Joseph Plumb Martin, most of the U.S. soldiers now making their way toward Virginia hailed from north of the Mason-Dixon line. Many, Washington noted, had already "shewn marks of great discontent," especially about not being paid on time or in real money, and for months he had worried that many would balk at having to march 350 miles farther from their homes and closer to the tropical diseases they all dreaded. Indeed, the prospect of mass desertion on the march southward had been one reason he preferred to attack the British in New York rather than Virginia. Four months earlier, the women of Baltimore had helped Lafayette reconcile his troops to their southward journey by sewing shirts for them. Washington cast about for a similar gesture, finally deciding to give the Continentals a "douceur" like the one he had doled out in 1779. "A douceur of a little hard money would put them in proper temper," he reasoned. So as the army headed south, he wrote Robert Morris, Congress's new superintendent of finance, asking that every Continental on the Virginia expedition receive one month's pay in gold and silver coin. A half century later, Martin would still remember that payment—"the first that could be called money, which we had received as wages since the year '76."[9]

On September 6, the first allied troops reached the head of Chesapeake Bay, where William Howe's troops had disembarked at the end of August 1777 to begin their march to Philadelphia. Continental quartermasters were able to procure sufficient shipping for fewer than three thousand advance troops. Martin was one of the fortunate ones and felt even luckier upon discovering that the officers on his vessel had loaded a barrel of rum into their cabin—flush against the bulkhead separating them from "the soldiers in the hold." Once at sea, the enlisted men loosened a board in the partition, pierced the barrel, and got stinking drunk.[10]

The rest of the allied troops headed south on foot, but soon managed to catch a ride on transports provided by the comte de Grasse. He had entered Chesapeake Bay on August 30 with thirty-six ships of the line, along with transports carrying three thousand French soldiers—and 4 million Spanish reales. Although the king of Spain had never formally recognized the United States, de Grasse was able to convince Francisco de Saavedra, the Spanish governor of Havana, to call upon wealthy Cubans to lend these funds, the ultimate source of the Continental soldiers' one month's pay. In addition, Saavedra and his superior, Bernardo de

Gálvez, pledged the Spanish navy for the protection of French as well as Spanish possessions in the Caribbean, allowing de Grasse to continue on to North America with his entire fleet.[11]

ON SEPTEMBER 6, CLINTON assured the increasingly nervous Cornwallis that reinforcements were on the way: he had already loaded four thousand soldiers from his New York garrison onto transport ships that would sail to Yorktown as soon as Adm. Thomas Graves confirmed that the coast was clear. Unbeknownst to Clinton, Graves's fleet had attacked de Grasse's just outside the mouth of the Chesapeake the previous day. Like most of the era's naval encounters, the September 5, 1781, Battle of the Chesapeake Capes ended without a clear victor. About 336 of de Grasse's men were killed or wounded—more than the French would lose in the weeks-long siege of Yorktown. Graves lost only 220 sailors, but two of his nineteen warships were captured and five were damaged, leading him to return to New York City instead of trying to push through to Cornwallis.[12]

Also on September 5, de Grasse landed some two thousand marines on Jamestown Island, fifteen miles west of Yorktown. The French and American armies assembled at Williamsburg and at 8 a.m. on September 28 marched to Yorktown. But they did not storm the parapets, as d'Estaing had at Savannah two years earlier. Instead the allied commanders had chosen to lay a siege, which would cost them (not to mention Cornwallis) many fewer casualties.

With the noose tightening around them, Cornwallis's troops soon ran out of forage. Even as French and American teamsters and cavalrymen scrounged for steeds in the Virginia countryside, their enemies had to kill nearly a thousand horses. Several days after their corpses were cast into the York River, "these poor animals came back in heaps with the tide," German jäger Capt. Johann Ewald reported. "It seemed as if they wanted to cry out against their murder."[13]

On the night of October 5–6, French engineers began laying out the allies' first parallel, seven hundred yards from the British breastworks. As they indicated where they wanted trenches, a crew that included Joseph Plumb Martin, who had recently joined the Sappers and Miners, laid down strips of wood to show fatigue parties where to dig. At one point the engineers wandered off, and a stranger came up and asked which way they had gone. Before setting off after them, he gave the workers a tip: if captured, they should not identify their unit. "We were

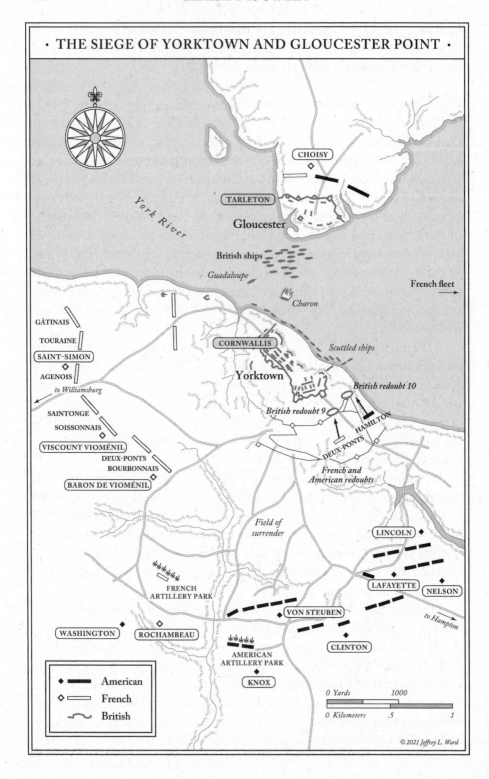

· THE SIEGE OF YORKTOWN AND GLOUCESTER POINT ·

CHOISY

York River

TARLETON

Gloucester

British ships

Guadaloupe

French fleet

Charon

GÂTINAIS

TOURAINE

SAINT-SIMON

CORNWALLIS

Scuttled ships

AGENOIS

Yorktown

British redoubt 10

to Williamsburg

British redoubt 9

SAINTONGE

HAMILTON

SOISSONNAIS

VISCOUNT VIOMÉNIL

DEUX-PONTS

DEUX-PONTS

BOURBONNAIS

French and
American redoubts

BARON DE VIOMÉNIL

LINCOLN

Field of
surrender

LAFAYETTE

FRENCH
ARTILLERY PARK

NELSON

VON STEUBEN

to Hampton

WASHINGTON   ROCHAMBEAU

CLINTON

AMERICAN
ARTILLERY PARK

◆   American
KNOX

◇   French

～   British

0 Yards   1000

0 Kilometers   .5   1

© 2021 Jeffrey L. Ward

obliged to him for his kind advice," Martin recalled, "but we considered ourselves as standing in no great need of it; for we knew as well as he did, that Sappers and Miners were allowed no quarters." When the stranger returned with the engineers, all calling him "Your Excellency," Martin and his coworkers realized they had been speaking with George Washington.[14]

The next night, 1,500 soldiers began digging the trenches, with Washington turning the first shovelful and three thousand additional troops serving as guards. By dawn on October 7, the as yet incomplete ditch provided effective cover. Two days later, when it was finished, "his Excellency General Washington put the match to the first gun," and allied artillery crews delivered a massive barrage.[15] Much of the shot and shell flew slowly enough to be followed by the naked eye, especially at night, when the fuses on exploding shells gave them the appearance of fireworks. When a soldier spotted a ball hurling toward his lines, he would yell "A shot" or "A shell!" Washington had no objection to the troops warning each other about incoming shells, since men could often protect themselves from shrapnel by taking cover. But since each ball only struck a single spot, and no one knew where that would be, he ordered the soldiers not to spread panic by screaming "A shot."[16]

The soldiers were not the only ones following the balls and bombs. Martin noticed a British cannon crew's bulldog chasing its shots and shells across the battlefield.[17]

Nearly all of the soldiers killed at Yorktown were victims of the artillery duel. Martin was standing near a New Yorker when a cannonball passed very close to his head. It left no mark, but the percussion wave killed him. At least two besiegers in a forward trench died when shells fired over their heads exploded prematurely.[18] Among the victims of the shelling were civilians in Yorktown; some had chosen not to evacuate, while others were slaves who had no choice. Many Yorktown residents sought shelter in natural and man-made caves in the bluffs along the York River (as did Cornwallis for part of the siege) but were nonetheless killed by allied artillery.

For all its destructive power, the artillery barrage probably killed fewer people than tropical diseases, which spread rapidly amid this mass of humanity. And yet as the British guns fell silent, the American and French camps began to seem safe enough for civilian visitors. Washington finally ordered the gawkers kept at bay, less for their safety than "to prevent the Provisions & forage being eat up by a Set of idle Spectators, who had before flocked from all parts in thousands to see the Shew," as one such visitor reported.[19]

Cornwallis addressed his own, much more pressing, food shortage by "turning out useless mouths," which primarily meant driving most of the army's African American auxiliaries beyond the breastworks they had helped build. Many of the former slaves were suffering from smallpox, and Continental doctor James Thacher suspected Cornwallis of using them to circulate the virus among the rebels. The expulsions culminated on October 14, when Capt. Ewald, who was stationed in Gloucester, observed in his diary:

> I would just as soon forget to record a cruel happening. . . . We drove back to the enemy all of our black friends, whom we had taken along to despoil the countryside. We had used them to good advantage and set them free, and now, with fear and trembling, they had to face the reward of their cruel masters.

That night, while on patrol outside the British lines, Ewald encountered several of the Black people his commander-in-chief had just set adrift. They were "between two fires"—between the Anglo-German and Franco-American lines—and in Ewald's way, so he drove them farther off.[20]

ON THE NIGHT OF October 11–12, U.S. and French soldiers began their second parallel, just three hundred yards from the enemy's works.[21] Near the York River, four hundred yards in front of the far left of the British line, the troops and their Black auxiliaries had built two redoubts, Number 9 and Number 10, both of which stood in the path of the allies' second parallel and prevented its completion. About four hundred American light infantrymen were ordered to storm Redoubt 10, on the bluff above the river, and an equal number of French chasseurs and grenadiers were assigned to Redoubt 9, nearly a quarter of a mile to the west. Washington initially gave command of the American assault to Lt. Col. Jean Joseph Sourbadère de Gimat, a French officer in the Continental service. But Alexander Hamilton claimed he outranked Gimat, and the commander-in-chief after a quick investigation reassigned the post of honor to him.[22]

This was not the first time during the Yorktown siege that Washington had to settle a command dispute. Since joining the army four years earlier, the marquis de Lafayette had become something like a son to the childless Washington, and he now presumed upon that relationship in asking for command of the American wing, though Benjamin Lincoln outranked him. In the end, an anguished Washington decided not to disrupt the chain of command.[23]

At dusk on October 14, French batteries began bombarding the far western sector of Cornwallis's line—all in order to divert his troops' attention from the allied attack on Redoubts 9 and 10, far to the east. The French assailants set off just after sundown and took few hits as they ran toward the redoubt but a great many, at nearly point-blank range, as they waited for Sappers and Miners to cut through the abatis ringing the redoubt. As the survivors of the artillery and small-arms fire entered the ditch in front of the redoubt, the defenders charged them with their bayonets. Nearly one hundred attackers were killed or wounded, but eventually the 120-man British garrison had no choice but to yield to superior numbers.

Forty-five minutes after the French stepped off, at about 7:30, Hamilton and his officers shouted "up, up," and the American soldiers, including Joseph Plumb Martin and several Black soldiers from Rhode Island, hastened forward. Redoubt 10 proved to have only about forty-eight defenders—fewer than half as many as Redoubt 9. To Martin, the watchword for the operation, Rochambeau, sounded appropriately enough like "rush-on-boys." The infantrymen were supposed to wait while Sappers and Miners cut a hole through the abatis, as the French had, but most just "lifted each other over the Pickets."[24] The Americans did imitate the French in relying entirely upon their bayonets; just to make sure, Hamilton prohibited them from loading their weapons. A flanking party led by John Laurens captured the redoubt's commander, Maj. Patrick Campbell, but most of his men escaped over the low rear wall before making a mad dash for Yorktown. Only eight were killed or wounded.[25]

Once Redoubt 10 changed hands, artillery crews in Fortress Yorktown blasted away at what was now its front wall as the new occupants began rebuilding it, and within forty-five minutes, it could stop cannonballs. The French soldiers in Redoubt 9 performed a similar operation as fatigue parties connected both redoubts to the allies' second parallel. Before dusk on October 15, two howitzers in each of the captured redoubts were dropping exploding shells into Yorktown.[26]

Cornwallis knew his situation was hopeless—but also that honor required one final, desperate effort. On October 16, he made two. At

4 a.m., about 350 redcoats sortied out of the British fortifications and
briefly captured two allied redoubts but were soon driven back with
losses. That evening, the British tested allied defenses over at Gloucester
Point, where the French and Americans had pinned British Col. Banastre Tarleton's forces against the north bank of the York. Cornwallis
thought he might possibly be able to break through the allied lines at
Gloucester and then lead the bulk of his troops on a 350-mile trek to
Clinton's headquarters in New York City.[27] Cornwallis thus spent his
last hours of freedom recapitulating John Burgoyne's final two steps on
the Upper Hudson exactly four years earlier: first a desperate attack on
the far more numerous rebels and then an obviously doomed effort to
break out toward the north. In both cases, the commander's sole motive
was to preserve his army's honor as well as his own.

Cornwallis's escape attempt collapsed even more quickly than Burgoyne's. The first wave of about 1,300 soldiers made it across the York,
but by the time the boats had returned for the next cohort, a squall had
blown in, and heavy winds drove most of the British boats down the
York, many with soldiers still on board. Cornwallis did not record his
feelings about the storm, but he may well have been relieved. In the
first year of the war, when Continental soldiers occupied Dorchester
Heights, overlooking Boston, Gen. William Howe set about driving
them off. But then a storm delayed the British troops' assault, giving the
Americans time to dig in—and Howe a way to save his reputation without sacrificing his army. The October 17, 1781, squall likewise provided
Cornwallis an honorable excuse to abandon his ludicrous Gloucester
breakout. Just after dawn, he informed Washington that he was ready to
negotiate terms. Many on both sides noted the anniversary: Burgoyne
had capitulated to Gates exactly four years earlier.

The British asked for the honors of war, which would mean marching
out of their fortifications with their flags flying, but Washington dictated
the same furled flags that Henry Clinton had imposed upon the Continental garrison in Charles Town a year and a half earlier.[28]

Washington made one other major change to Cornwallis's draft articles of capitulation. "Natives or Inhabitants of different parts of this
Country at present in York or Gloucester," the British commander had
proposed, "are not to be punished on account of having joined the British Army." This provision would have offered at least a thin veneer of
protection not only to the handful of white Virginia Loyalists who had
joined him but also to the Black Virginians who had made it to his lines

and evaded his attempts to banish them. Washington returned the document with a marginal note: "This Article cannot be assented to, being altogether of civil Resort."[29]

The agreement was signed on the morning of October 19, and that afternoon at about 3 p.m., the French and American armies lined up on either side of the road leading out of Yorktown to receive their captives' arms. The British and German troops marching through this mile-long gauntlet were led not by Cornwallis, who claimed illness, but by his second-in-command, Charles O'Hara.[30]

Riding up to the allied commanders, O'Hara, apparently mistaking Rochambeau for Washington, offered him his sword. Rochambeau directed him to the American commander, who in turn passed him off to his own number two, Benjamin Lincoln. A few of the British had evidently fortified themselves for this humiliating scene with strong drink. As they stacked their arms, some wept, one yelled, "May you never get so good a master [as George III] again," and many tried to throw their muskets down hard enough to break them. In all Cornwallis surrendered 7,247 soldiers, 840 sailors, and 244 artillery pieces.[31]

THAT NIGHT WASHINGTON THREW a party for senior officers on both sides; only the accused war criminal Banastre Tarleton "was pointedly not invited to any of the festivities." At this event or shortly afterward, Cornwallis was shocked to spot his former servant James in the American camp. It finally dawned on him that James had not actually been a refugee but an American spy. "Ah you rogue," the general reportedly told him, "then you have been playing me a trick all this time." More than five years after the capitulation, the Virginia legislature, acting on a testimonial from Lafayette, purchased James's freedom. He was thenceforth known as James Lafayette. And he was not alone; more and more Black spies entered both sides' camps in what had increasingly become an involuntary African American civil war.[32]

James Armistead Lafayette

Congress and Gen. Washington could have traded Cornwallis's army, along with the remnants of Burgoyne's, for all of the Americans—at this point mostly privateer crewmen—wasting away in British prison hulks such as the notorious *Jersey*. But civilian and military leaders agreed that the greater good of winning the war required them to starve the enemy of manpower. It was a costly decision; fewer than seven thousand Americans were killed in battle before Yorktown, but more than eight thousand died in prison ships afterward.[33] Washington could have ended all that suffering and dying with the stroke of a pen, but how long might the war have gone on if he had freed Cornwallis's men or helped Burgoyne and his men to their original objective of meeting Clinton in New York?

Nearly all of the giant siege guns that contributed to "Washington's victory" at Yorktown had been French, as were the engineers who positioned them and the month's pay in hard coin that tamped down dissent within Continental ranks. Counting the French sailors who drove off Cornwallis's would-be rescuers and reinforcements, France supplied twice as many fighters as the United States.[34] But saying that the Americans would not have won without French help tells only half the story, because there never would have been a Battle of Yorktown if de Grasse had heeded Washington's plea to sail to New York.

The Yorktown victors viewed themselves the way most people see them today, as the friends of liberty—and that made the battle's sequel all the more incongruous. The British had chased hundreds of African Americans beyond their lines, hundreds more remained in their camp, and their former owners from as far away as South Carolina now converged on Yorktown, offering rewards for their return. On October 22, American Lt. Reuben Sanderson reported "Colecting Nigars till 5 o'clock." Like Johann Ewald, Joseph Plumb Martin was an otherwise decent man who could feel no empathy for African Americans, and he partnered with several messmates in tracking down one of the fugitives. His share of the bounty—$1,200 in depreciated paper money—was just enough for a quart of rum.[35]

Most of the African Americans who had left Thomas Jefferson's plantations and joined Cornwallis had died of disease, especially smallpox, but the former governor was able to recover six of them. As punishment for running, he gave a girl named Isabel to his sister and sold all the rest. These Virginians had sought freedom even at the intolerable cost of never seeing their families again. Now they had lost both.[36]

Even as Continental soldiers tracked down fugitive slaves, a still greater horror was developing in the Atlantic Ocean. Early in 1781, British privateersmen operating off the West African coast had captured the Dutch slave ship *Zorgue*, along with the 244 Africans chained in its hold, and sold it to a Liverpool-based firm whose representatives tweaked its name to *Zong*, purchased additional captives, bringing the total to 442, and set sail for the Caribbean. On November 27 or 28, crewmen spotted their destination, Jamaica, but mistook it for the Spanish province of Santo Domingo and continued westward. By the time they realized their mistake, they were about ninety miles downwind of Jamaica and running low on potable water. Rather than entering an enemy port, which would have meant forfeiting their ship and its human cargo, or reducing everyone's water ration for the long slog back to Jamaica, the sailors threw about 140 of the Africans into the Atlantic.[37]

The *Zong* captives did not die entirely in vain. In the hands of Gustavus Vassa and other abolitionists, the massacre fueled the campaign to convince Britain—at that time the largest carrier of captive Africans to North America—to get out of the slave trade. That effort would require another quarter of a century, but in the months before the *Zong* massacre, enslaved people and their allies won two important victories in Massachusetts. The new state constitution took effect in October 1780, and the following spring four Black Massachusetts residents sued the people who claimed to own them. In the Berkshire County town of Sheffield, an enslaved war widow named Mumbet tried to shield her sister from violence at the hands of Hannah Ashley, their owner's wife, only to be struck in her turn with a red-hot fireplace shovel. Mumbet fled and then sued Hannah's husband, John Ashley, for her

Susan Anne Livingston Ridley Sedgwick, Mumbet or Elizabeth Freeman (1811)

freedom. Two of Ashley's other slaves also filed suits, one echoing Mumbet's claim of physical abuse.[38]

Seventy miles to the east, in the Worcester County town of Barré, a man named Quaco (the Akan day name for Wednesday) or Quock Walker also escaped his owner, Nathaniel Jennison, in the spring of 1781. He took refuge and a job with brothers Seth and John Caldwell, and when Jennison and his friends tracked him down and beat him, he sued for assault. Jennison then filed a suit of his own, not against Walker but against the Caldwells for detaining his property. The two cases came before the state's Supreme Judicial Court in September, and the jury ruled, first, that Walker had in fact been assaulted and, second, that the Caldwells had not harmed Jennison, since Walker was not a slave. The Berkshire County Court of Common Pleas had meanwhile ruled in Mumbet's favor in her freedom suit, and when her former owner saw the higher court's rulings in the Quock Walker cases, he not only declined to file an appeal but also liberated the other two slaves who had sued him. Mumbet took the name Elizabeth Freeman.[39]

Nearly two years later, in April 1783, Walker's criminal complaint against his former owner finally reached the Supreme Judicial Court, giving Chief Justice William Cushing an opportunity to dispel any lingering doubts about the legality of slavery in Massachusetts. Jennison acknowledged beating Walker but stood on his rights as a slave owner. That prompted Justice Cushing to instruct the jurors that the first clause of the state's declaration of rights, which declared that "all men are born free and equal," banned slavery and thus required them to find Jennison guilty. When the jurors complied, they made Massachusetts the first of the original thirteen states to abolish slavery.[40] But the ruling did not automatically free anyone other than Quock Walker. Other slaves had to sue their owners or convincingly threaten to do so. One Black resident of the Bay State who obtained her freedom before the year was out was Phoebe Abdee. As the property of Rev. William Smith of Weymouth, she had helped raise his daughter Abigail. After her mother and father died, Abigail Smith Adams described Abdee as "the only surviving Parent I have."[41]

Massachusetts's 1780 declaration of rights remains in force, and on November 18, 2003, the Supreme Judicial Court cited the same "free and equal" clause that freed Quock Walker in making the Bay State the first in the nation to allow gay couples to marry.[42]

* * *

THE 7,200 SOLDIERS WHO surrendered at Yorktown with Cornwallis constituted only one-fourth of the British army in North America; redcoats and Germans still occupied Quebec and a half dozen coastal enclaves: Penobscot Bay, New York City, Wilmington, Charles Town, and Savannah. But nearly everyone expected Parliament to react to Yorktown by ending the war. The clever gambit by which Cornwallis prevented British headquarters in New York City from purloining half his troops had had the ironic effect of ensuring that his surrender would be significant enough to extinguish Britain's will to fight.

Within a week of the news reaching Philadelphia, Congress had thanked the French and American armies, voted funds for a marble commemorative column—and directed the state assemblies to impose their largest tax increase ever. Previous requisitions had drawn upon the states only for relatively plentiful food and forage or the still more abundant Continental currency. But the $8 million requisition approved on October 30, 1781, had to be paid in either scarce specie (gold and silver coin) or special promissory notes issued by the superintendent of finance.[43]

The author both of these promissory notes and of the October 1781 requisition was Robert Morris. Since taking over Continental finances the previous May, he had kept after the thirteen states to fund the federal debt, both by allowing Congress to tax merchandise entering American ports and by imposing their own heavy taxes and turning the money over to the federal government. Onerous taxes aimed at further enriching elite bondholders invariably provoked rebellions, and state and local officials, unable to cope with insurrection and invasion at the same time, had frequently yielded to grassroots demands for tax relief. But Cornwallis's surrender made British withdrawal all but inevitable, placing Congress in the same advantageous position vis-à-vis Americans that Parliament had enjoyed early in 1763: no longer needing their help to win the war. In 1781 as in 1763, the national legislature could finally summon the courage to tax North Americans with a heavy hand, in the present case by way of their state assemblies. Yorktown also gave Morris another advantage in his battle against taxaphobic state legislators. French subsidies had recently reached unprecedented levels, reducing the pressure on American taxpayers. But shortly after the great allied victory over Cornwallis, the chevalier de La Luzerne, Louis XVI's envoy to the United States, announced that French aid would now cease.[44]

Since the early eighteenth century, Britain's first lord of the treasury

had been considered its prime minister, and the equally influential Superintendent of Finance Morris served in essence as the first prime minister
of the United States. Indeed, Morris had much in common with George
Grenville, Britain's prime minister at the start of the revolutionary era.
Grenville's preference for studying infrastructure legislation over attending
concerts found its reflection in Morris's willingness to guarantee federal
obligations using his own credit (embodied in "Morris's notes") in place
of Congress's, which had long since evaporated. Yet both the Financier (as
Morris was often called) and the Great Financier (as critics dubbed Grenville) made a killing from government service.[45] Grenville and Morris each
took over the treasury of a nation emerging victorious but debt-ridden
from an eight-year global war, and both understood that now was the time
to act, since the government no longer required North Americans' military
service. Neither asked Americans to pay down the war debt, just to take on
a larger tax burden in order to help check its growth. Yet battles over both
financiers' taxes—and over a popular alternative, paper money—helped
spark revolutions, albeit with a twist in Morris's case, for his fiscal policies
would lead, indirectly, to a rebellion against the Articles of Confederation
and the sovereign states, culminating in the U.S. Constitution.[46]

Thomas Paine had once proudly counted himself among Morris's
most vocal critics, but on the crucial issues of taxation and paper money,
he had changed his mind. Moreover, by the time Morris took over the
finance department, Paine, who had donated his *Common Sense* and
American Crisis royalties to the Continental Army, was on the brink of
poverty. In return for a secret government salary, he eagerly accepted
the Financier's invitation to publish essays promoting his onerous new
federal taxes. Pleased to have joined the new nation's fiscal elite, Paine,
the onetime British excise officer, induced Morris and Washington, two
of the most powerful and well-off men in America, to inaugurate the
arrangement at a dinner in his cramped Philadelphia apartment.[47]

TIDINGS OF CORNWALLIS'S SURRENDER reached London on November 25. Lord Germain forwarded the news to George III and observed
that in his reply, the king exhibited his usual sangfroid—except that for
once he neglected to jot down the exact hour and minute. Lord North
was said to have taken the news "like a ball in the breast."[48]

Repeatedly pacing the floor, he exclaimed, "Oh, God! it is all over!"[49]

Since the surrender had occurred on Henry Clinton's watch,
George III felt he had no choice but to accept the resignation Clinton had

repeatedly proffered. Germain wanted to replace Clinton with Charles Cornwallis, but that would have been awkward, since he was officially a prisoner of war, albeit on parole. Next in line was Guy Carleton, who refused to serve under his old adversary, which meant that Germain—the cabinet's last diehard supporter of the American war—had to go. After successfully holding out for a peerage, he resigned on February 9, 1782.

De Grasse and Rochambeau had assured Washington that capturing Cornwallis would be enough to sap Britain's will to fight, and on February 27 the House of Commons proved them right. With the price of a £100 British government bond having fallen from £86 to £54, the MPs voted to halt offensive operations in North America. George III could not bear the idea of becoming known for losing America, and he dropped hints about abdicating. Parliament ignored the threat, showing once again that it had become Britain's premier power. George kept his crown, but on March 27 North had to resign.[50]

The king wished to replace North with one of the few prominent Britons who still opposed recognizing American independence, Lord Shelburne, but the only post he would accept was a new one, Secretary for Home, Irish, and Colonial Affairs. The new prime minister would be the Marquess of Rockingham, who in his previous outing on the front bench had secured the repeal of the Stamp Act.

THE FIRST BRITISH SUBJECTS to reap tangible benefits from Cornwallis's surrender were not the Americans but Ireland's Catholic majority. The war had prompted Parliament to enforce its long-dormant ban on direct trade between North America and the Emerald Isle, devastating the Irish economy. In response, Irish traders had taken a cue from their American brethren, boycotting the mother country's merchandise. Then in 1779, the specter of a Franco-Spanish invasion led several Irish counties to mobilize unsanctioned companies of Volunteers—just as the Americans had five years earlier. In response to the plunge in Irish consumption of British manufactured goods and the ominous if unstated threat posed by the forty thousand Volunteers, Parliament allowed Ireland to trade directly with loyal American colonies.[51]

Yorktown further loosened Ireland's chains. In 1782, Britain granted the Irish parliament full legislative powers—equivalent to what American radicals such as Thomas Jefferson and James Wilson had sought for their provincial assemblies in 1774—whereupon Ireland ended the ban on Roman Catholic clergy and finally permitted Catholics to own land.[52]

Although Rockingham accepted the necessity of acknowledging American independence, he was in no rush to make peace with Britain's other enemies, from the French and Spanish to Haidar Ali. But in 1782, the country's military expenditures exceeded £20 million for the first time ever, and it became clear that the war was going to nearly double the national debt, just as the Seven Years' War had. The East India Company's battle against Haidar Ali's loose confederation of Indian states was going better but remained enormously expensive. By June 20, 1783, when British and French fleets fought the final major battle of the American War of Independence off the southeast Indian port of Cuddalore, Haidar had died of cancer. But his incursions into territory claimed by the East India Company had contributed both to the advent of the American Revolution, by pushing the Company to the brink of bankruptcy and thereby prompting Parliament to adopt the Tea Act of 1773—and to its conclusion, by saddling both the Company and the government with enormous military expenses, all but forcing the ministry to sue for peace.[53]

During his brief initial stint as prime minister sixteen years earlier, Rockingham had persuaded Parliament to insist upon its right to legislate for America "in all cases whatsoever," but he now signaled his willingness to acknowledge the rebels' independence even before peace negotiations began. The ministry's offer was not as generous as it seemed. In February 1778, the United States and France had agreed not to sign treaties with Britain without each other's consent, and Louis XVI had indirectly linked the Americans' fate to Spain's by vowing not to sheathe his sword until his cousin Carlos III recovered Gibraltar. But Rockingham believed that if he agreed to most of Congress's terms, he could inspire ordinary American freemen to pressure their congressmen to make peace at once, without waiting for France and Spain. Could the Americans really be expected to keep fighting and dying to serve the territorial ambitions of a Spanish king who had never even deigned to recognize their independence? They seemed much likelier to agree to Rockingham's separate peace, not only saving their lives and their prostrate economy but also giving them the only major merchant marine plying the Atlantic without fear of enemy seizure. As American vessels' insurance premiums plummeted, they would capture a larger share of the remaining belligerents' freight than they ever had as privateers.[54]

Of course a side deal would also benefit the British, freeing up the troops garrisoning Savannah, Charles Town, and New York for service against France and Spain. Moreover, Lord Shelburne and other members of Rockingham's cabinet had come around to Adam Smith's view that Britain could profit from North America without possessing it—unless American leaders signed an exclusive agreement with France. What better way for Rockingham to head off a Franco-American commercial alliance than to negotiate separately with the Americans, alienating them from their allies?

Breaking up the anti-British coalition would also force Louis XVI to moderate his extravagant war aims. In the negotiations that concluded the Seven Years' War exactly twenty years earlier, France had given up large swaths of its empire, not only in North America and the Caribbean but in Africa and India, and Louis now expected to recover much of what he had lost. Whether he would succeed would depend, as so much of this war had, on events in the Caribbean Sea.

CHAPTER 32

To Amend and Perfect

1782–1783

ONE REASON THE FRANCO-AMERICAN VICTORY AT YORKTOWN did not end the war was that it was quickly followed by French and Spanish disappointments that inspired many British politicians to fight on. Word of the anti-Spanish Yuma Rebellion of July 17, 1781 (in present-day Arizona, southern California, and northern Mexico), did not reach the eastern United States and Europe until the following year, but when it did, many speculated that the so-called Tupac Amaru rebellion (in present-day Perú) had spread to Spain's North American territories.[1]

Louis XVI suffered an even greater loss. Upon learning of Adm. de Grasse's victory in the Battle of the Chesapeake Capes, the French council sent him supplies, modest reinforcements, and a fateful assignment: capture the crown jewel of the British Caribbean, Jamaica. On April 12, 1782, as de Grasse's thirty ships of the line headed to a rendezvous with the Spanish Caribbean squadron, they were overtaken by George Rodney's thirty-six warships. The ensuing duel, known as the Battle of the Saintes for a nearby chain of islets, began in the usual fashion. Each fleet formed a line and sailed toward the other; as they passed, every vessel in both fleets would fire a broadside at each enemy ship. But some disorders in the French fleet, combined with a sudden shift of wind, allowed Rodney and his captains to alter their course, no longer steering parallel to de Grasse's line but toward it. As each of Rodney's warships passed through de Grasse's line, it fired simultaneously at the French vessels on its port and starboard sides, with neither enemy crew able to retaliate, since most eighteenth-century warships mounted no cannon in the bow or stern. Rodney thus broke de Grasse's fleet into three sections, which he then picked off in detail.[2]

More than two hundred of Rodney's men died in the Battle of the

Saintes, but de Grasse's losses were much greater: five thousand sailors and soldiers were captured, and between one and six thousand were killed. The British also seized five French ships of the line, including de Grasse's 110-gun flagship, the *Ville-de-Paris*, along with the admiral, his siege guns, and fifty thousand handcuffs intended for carrying off Jamaica's slaves.[3]

With the exception of the thousands who were killed, wounded, or captured and those Black Jamaicans, no one was more powerfully affected by the Battle of the Saintes than George Rodney. When residents of the mother country learned of his victory, most instantly forgave his rape of St. Eustatius and celebrated him as the captor of de Grasse, savior of Jamaica, and restorer of British naval supremacy in the most valuable corner of America.[4]

The Battle of the Saintes also moderated French diplomatic demands. Wartime expenditures had already set the country on the road to eventual bankruptcy (and, as some anticipated, revolution), and even the most hawkish ministers now pined for peace. Louis XVI had other worries, too. His old enemies, the Russians, had wrested the Crimea from his ally, the Ottoman empire, and showed no sign of stopping there. French officials feared being drawn into that conflict, thus having to fight Britain and Russia at the same time. Moreover, Vergennes did not want to give the impression of lording it over the Americans, so when they requested permission to negotiate separately with Britain, he consented, so long as his allies agreed to await his approval before concluding an agreement.[5]

THE FALL OF THE North ministry and Parliament's decision to halt offensive operations led to an unofficial cease-fire in the northern United States, but not in the lower south or west of the Appalachian Mountains. White westerners had battled Indians long before Lexington and Concord, and Yorktown brought the west no peace. Back in the fall of 1781, when Native Americans fighting the United States had forced the Moravian Indians to move from the Tuscarawas River more than a hundred miles west to the Sandusky, they had not even given them time to harvest their crops. By the start of 1782, the Moravians were close to starvation, and their captors allowed about a third of them to return to their homes to salvage whatever corn had survived the winter.[6]

As they embraced a European religion, the Moravian Indians had also changed their culture, dressing themselves and even their hair as whites did. And in sharp contrast to other native societies, men as well as

women were working in the fields on March 7, when about 160 militiamen from the region around modern-day Wheeling, West Virginia, rode
into Gnadenhutten, the principal Moravian Indian village, gathered the
flock, and then voted to kill every one of them the next morning. Some
of the militiamen wished to burn the Moravians alive, but that would
have prevented them from taking scalps, so they decided to bludgeon
them instead.[7]

The ninety-odd Christian Indians spent the night of March 7–8 praying and singing psalms. Most were still singing the next morning as the
militiamen led them in pairs to two "slaughter-houses"—one for men
and one for women and children. "Many children were killed in their
wretched mothers' arms," an American officer reported to his wife. The
only survivors were three young boys. One hid in the cellar, where he
watched in horror as the blood of his relations dripped down between
the floorboards; another was clubbed and scalped like the rest but somehow clung to life while avoiding detection by lying still among the dead;
the third was adopted by one of the attackers. The militiamen burned all
three towns before returning to Pennsylvania, where, per custom, they
auctioned off their plunder, split the proceeds, displayed the Indians'
scalps, and kept their mouths shut, ensuring that none was ever prosecuted.[8]

Several of the Gnadenhutten killers later traveled to Fort Pitt. U.S. officials had offered asylum to another band of noncombatant Delawares,
and they were living on a nearby island when the militia attacked. The
militiamen killed as many of them as they could, including two Delawares who had been commissioned as captains in the U.S. army. While
on a brief visit back east, Fort Pitt commander William Irvine had left his
post in the hands of Col. John Gibson, whose Shawnee wife had died in
the Yellow Creek Massacre back in 1774. Suspecting Gibson of being "a
friend to Indians," the militiamen contemplated killing him, too. When
Irvine returned to the fort, he allowed that even he did not feel safe. "No
man knows whether I approve or disapprove of killing the Moravians,"
he wrote his wife in Carlisle. Mrs. Irvine must "not express any sentiment for or against these deeds," her husband warned her, "as it may be
alleged, the sentiments you express may come from me or be mine."[9]

In late May, nearly five hundred Virginia and western Pennsylvania
militiamen pushed even farther into Indian country, to the village of
Upper Sandusky, where the original inhabitants, the Wyandots, had long
hosted Delaware warriors who shared their determination to resist U.S.

encroachment. To lead them, the militiamen elected William Crawford, a survivor of Braddock's expedition who was George Washington's long-time friend and land agent. In hopes of surprising Sandusky, everyone on the expedition rode horses. But far from having the drop on the Wyandots and Delawares, the militiamen headed to a town that the rebel Indians had abandoned about a year earlier, moving eight miles to the north. Most of the victims of the Gnadenhutten Massacre had been noncombatants, but Upper Sandusky was a center of determined resistance whose defenders outnumbered their assailants. When they learned of the militia's approach and Crawford realized he had lost the element of surprise, he proposed to turn back, but his subordinates overruled him, and the army rode on.[10]

On June 4—George III's birthday, as one Wyandot leader noted—about a hundred British rangers and several hundred native warriors ambushed and quickly surrounded Crawford's men. Two nights later, the militiamen found a gap in the Anglo-Indian perimeter, slipped through it, and made for home.[11] About fifty militiamen were killed at Upper Sandusky and on the return trek. Others, less fortunate, were taken alive, and these included Col. Crawford. His captors painted him black and then tethered him to a stake. For several hours, natives of both genders and all ages cut off his ears, forced him to walk on hot coals, and poked his body with burning sticks. A warrior then scalped him, being careful not to slice so deep as to kill him, and then used his scalp to slap the face of fellow prisoner John Knight (who later escaped to tell his story). Knight reported that Crawford, "being nearly exhausted . . . lay down upon the burning embers, when the squaws put shovelfuls of coals on his body, which, dying as he was, made him move and creep a little." All of "this the Delawares declare they did in retaliation" for the Gnadenhutten Massacre, according to a British officer. Knight recalled one of Crawford's tormentors telling him that Indians "kill their enemies, but not their friends!"[12]

The last major Iroquois raid of the Revolutionary War was led by Guyasuta, the Seneca sachem who had traveled with George Washington three decades earlier, on the eve of the Seven Years' War. At about 2 p.m. on July 13, he and his troops, including a "great number of whites," struck Hannastown, Pennsylvania, about thirty miles east of Pittsburgh. Most of the inhabitants made it into the fort, but the raiders killed nine, captured twelve, and burned the town. In the wake of the attack, many western settlers, including Hermon Husband and his family, fled east.

Meanwhile Joseph Brant led nearly five hundred warriors to the region around Fort Herkimer (in modern-day German Flatts, New York) on the Mohawk River, inflicting only a handful of casualties before learning that commander-in-chief Carleton had ordered British forces to stand down. Brant's acquiescence to Carleton's order ended Iroquois involvement in the war.[13]

The last major Native American initiative of the Revolutionary War was also one of the most successful. Early in August, an army of about three hundred Indians and fifty British rangers crossed the Ohio into Kentucky and tried but failed to capture the fort at Bryan's Station (near modern-day Lexington) before retreating. The warriors made no effort to hide their escape route. Indeed, several of the approximately 180 mounted Kentucky militiamen who assembled to pursue them, including Daniel Boone, noticed that they had cut blazes into trees along the way, a clear indication that they wanted to be overtaken.[14]

What the warriors did conceal was the size of their force; walking single file, each man stepped in the previous man's tracks. Boone had an inkling that the indigenous army was larger than it seemed. When the cavalry reached the south bank of the Licking River, not far from a salt deposit known as the Lower Blue Licks, and spotted the natives on the opposite shore, the officers held a brief council, and Boone urged against an attack. His prediction of what was about to happen—Native Americans taking cover in a forest ambushing white soldiers, forcing them back into the stream they had just crossed—drew upon his own experience, twenty-seven years earlier, at the Monongahela. Other officers replied that turning back would be cowardly. During a previous Indian encounter, a ranger had "fouled his pantaloons as a consequence of his extreme fear," and he had been known ever since as "dung-breeches." To most of the men attending the council, humiliation seemed worse than death. Even Boone now cried out, "I can go as far in an Indian fight as any other man."[15]

The cavalry crossed the river and had just ascended a hill on the north bank when the Indians sprang the trap. The ensuing melee resulted in the deaths of fewer than twenty Indians and an estimated seventy-seven Kentuckians, making it their "worst defeat of the war." Among the dead was Israel Boone, whose father's push west into Kentucky had now cost him two sons.[16]

In the weeks after the Kentuckians' defeat in the Battle of Blue Licks, William Irvine, the American commander at Fort Pitt, collaborated with

George Rogers Clark in planning a two-pronged incursion into Indian country. As Clark's Kentuckians struck the Shawnees on the Great Miami River (a northern tributary of the Ohio), Irvine's Continentals, supported by militiamen from western Pennsylvania and northwestern Virginia, would hit Sandusky. Irvine was about to set out from Pittsburgh when he received a letter from Secretary of War Benjamin Lincoln calling off the attack. British officers had stopped dispatching native war parties against Whig settlements, and U.S. leaders decided to halt their own western raids lest the British and Indians resume theirs.[17]

Irvine had no choice but to follow Lincoln's orders, but Clark answered only to the governor of Virginia. On November 1, he and more than one thousand militiamen, including Boone, crossed the Ohio River and burned the five largest Shawnee villages on the Great Miami. Resisting the temptation to engage with this outsized U.S. force, Shawnee leaders instead devoted their efforts to getting their wives and children out of its way, and the most significant result of the "last major offensive of the American Revolution" was that the Shawnees rebuilt their towns farther north. Clark's inability to knock the Shawnees out of the war reflected a large American failure. Despite repeated efforts, militiamen and Continental soldiers never captured either Sandusky, which had become the nexus of native resistance, or the Anglo-Indian alliance's most valuable supply depot, Detroit. Native Americans were the primary reason both that U.S. leaders were so determined to capture Fort Detroit and that their armies never got near the place. On the east coast, the Continental Army won the American War of Independence without ever capturing its commander's top objective, New York City. But in the western theater, white Americans' failure to take Detroit denied them a victory. A decade after the United States and Britain made peace, native war parties armed in Detroit would still be hitting white farms and towns in Kentucky, Virginia, Pennsylvania, and Ohio.[18]

After Cornwallis surrendered at Yorktown, Washington took most of his army back north with him but ordered the Pennsylvania, Maryland, and Virginia Lines to reinforce Greene in South Carolina. In the fall of 1781, disease once again intervened in the war, slowing the southward movement of the Virginia Line. When some of the Virginians came down with smallpox, Col. Christian Febiger felt he must inoculate the rest before sending them south. But local citizens, fearing the virus would spill out of Febiger's camp, cut off supplies to his soldiers and even threatened him with violence, forcing him to discontinue the immunizations.[19]

Then the men commanding the planned Carolina expedition vowed to resign unless they received their long overdue pay—and not in depreciated Virginia currency. In a November 26 letter to Febiger, the five officers predicted that the march would entail numerous expenses, especially to combat the diseases they would inevitably contract in "so unhealthy a Climate." Washington suspected that they were actually trying to avoid serving in the sickly lower south altogether—and that many of Febiger's common soldiers were feigning debilitating illness out of the same fear of having to encounter the genuine article in South Carolina.[20]

The General Assembly somewhat satisfied the officers by promising them first crack at the revenue arising from the sale of confiscated Loyalists' estates, but by then enlisted men were in open revolt. In a note signed, "We the honest Politicians," they, too, refused to budge until they were paid, and about a hundred of them tried to free fellow soldiers who had been imprisoned for earlier resistance. On February 14, when Febiger ordered the men to strike their tents and set off for South Carolina, most initially refused, yielding only after he deployed cajolery, threats, and, as he noted, "an excellent Band of Music to play them off."[21]

Smallpox and other illnesses, shortages of food and clothing, and the officers' and enlisted men's rebellions reduced the Virginia reinforcements to about a hundred men and delayed their arrival until late March. The Pennsylvania and Maryland Lines had made it to South Carolina three months earlier, but within days of the Virginians' arrival, Pennsylvania soldiers initiated a revolt of their own. Someone left a placard outside Gen. Arthur St. Clair's quarters asking, "*Can soldiers be expected to do their duty clothed in rags and fed on rice*," and then a Maryland camp woman alerted officers to a larger plot. Several of these men had also participated in the mutiny of the Pennsylvania Line the previous year, but the officers' investigation persuaded them that the new conspiracy was, in Henry Lee's words, "marked by a very different character." Abetted by British emissaries, it allegedly aimed at kidnapping Gen. Nathanael Greene and delivering him to the enemy. Sgt. George Goznall, the reputed ringleader, was executed on April 22.[22]

Greene could at least take comfort in his British counterparts' even more dire labor shortage. Ever since 1775, when African Americans had begun escaping to Governor Dunmore, the imperial army had relied upon their labor. But after Dunmore, British officers had tried, not always successfully, to keep their Black workers—numbering 652 in Charles Town alone as of March 1781—out of combat. But at the end of 1781, after Greene moved his army from the High Hills of Santee to the Round O River, forty miles west of Charles Town, Alexander Leslie, Britain's new southern commander, took the momentous step of creating an African American cavalry company. The Black Dragoons were commanded by a man who had apparently fled Whig politician John Mathews's plantation, where he had been known as March. His new name was Captain Smart, the British army having apparently given him not just an honorific title but an actual captain's commission. His adversaries in the Continental Army and Whig militia found him "extremely active, & very troublesome."[23]

On January 18, 1782, the South Carolina legislature returned to work for the first time in two years. As the delegates gathered in Jacksonborough, on the Edisto River thirty miles west of Charles Town, their greatest challenge was the shortage of Whig fighters. The state could not fight the British with militia, its representatives had explained to Congress three years earlier, "by reason of the great proportion of Citizens Necessary to remain at home to prevent Insurrections among the Negroes, and to prevent the desertion of them to the Enemy." Nor would white South Carolinians submit either to a draft or to the high taxes needed to fund enormous bounties like those Virginia had tried. And northerners'—even Virginians'—"prejudices respecting the climate" of the lower south prompted Continental soldiers to resist being sent there. With Gen. Greene's blessing, Representative John Laurens once again proposed enlisting thousands of African Americans in the Continental Army. Laurens's plan won the votes of only about a dozen of his more than one hundred colleagues, but the legislature found a different way to make enslaved South Carolinians useful to the cause. A year earlier, Virginia had begun offering slaves as bounties to men who enlisted in the Continental Army, and in South Carolina, Thomas Sumter had adopted a similar policy on his own authority. The assembly now massively expanded the slaves-for-service offer, promising new enlistees an enslaved worker at the start of each of the next three years.[24]

The Confiscation Act signed into law on February 26, 1782, by John Mathews, the new governor of South Carolina and the former owner of Capt. Smart, is best known for appropriating nearly four hundred Loyalists' land, but the Whigs' more immediate need was for bounty slaves.[25] The Georgia legislature took the monetization of Loyalists' human property even further, disbursing Black Georgians as salary to the governor and in payment for horses. As historian Jim Piecuch notes, "Slaves became in effect the currency of the financially strapped state government."[26]

Whigs had never previously appropriated enemy planters' human property on this scale, and South Carolina Loyalists cooped up in Charles Town with Gen. Leslie persuaded him to retaliate. Starting in March, British troops descended on Whigs' plantations and seized their Black workforces. Leslie alternately threatened to use these people to reimburse dispossessed Loyalist slaveholders and to arm them against their former owners. One of Leslie's raids turned into a skirmish that cost Capt. Smart his life, but his fellow Black Dragoons kept up the fight—"daily committing the most horrible depredations and murders," an American officer claimed—until they evacuated with the British, headed to a new life in the British West Indies as the royal army's new "Carolina Corps," nearly as free as other redcoats.[27]

If Americans ever choose a day to commemorate the internal struggles that accompanied the battle against Britain, they could hardly do better than the 22nd of April, for on that date in 1782, Capt. Smart died in a clash with Whig cavalry—and Sgt. Goznall faced Gen. Greene's firing squad.

EARLY IN 1782, AS Gen. Greene tightened the noose around Charles Town, Continental Capt. Michael Rudolph devised a plan for eliminating one of the few remaining obstacles: the *Alligator*, a British galley that patrolled the upper reaches of the Ashley River. As in slave societies all around the Atlantic rim, enslaved men transported produce downriver to the capital, where Black women sold it. On the night of March 18, Rudolph embarked a squad of light infantrymen in a vessel commonly used in this farm-to-market trade, concealing some beneath the produce and disguising the rest as Black. Hailed by one of the *Alligator*'s sentinels, one of Rudolph's men "answered in the negro dialect" and was told to come alongside to display his wares. As the two vessels aligned, the light infantrymen vaulted the railing and fought a bloody and successful battle for control of the *Alligator*, which they burned to the water's edge.[28]

Redcoats, Loyalists, and British-allied Native and African Americans also carried out daring raids. One squad ventured all the way from Wilmington on the North Carolina coast 150 miles inland to Hillsborough, where they captured Thomas Burke, the Whig governor, along with several army officers.[29]

Peace seemed equally remote in Georgia. On January 16, Gen. Anthony Wayne ferried about four hundred Continental troops south across the Savannah River into Georgia. Two months later, the British killed one of Wayne's dragoons three miles from Savannah and then allegedly paraded his corpse through town as entertainment for a visiting Native American delegation. According to Gen. Wayne, British officers ordered that the body remain unburied, "but the Ethiopians, more humanized, stole it away & deposited it in the ground."[30]

In June, the noted Muskogee leader Emistisiguo led about three hundred warriors toward Savannah in hopes of breaking Wayne's siege. Led, like so many British and American officers throughout the war, by "negro guides," Emistisiguo surprised Wayne's camp before dawn on June 24. The general and Virginia Lt. Col. Thomas Posey rallied their men for a counterattack. One of Posey's sergeants disobeyed orders by taking off his coat and wearing a handkerchief around his head, and Posey "took him . . . for an Indian, and thrusting his sword through his body, laid him at his feet." The sergeant somehow lived. Later that same morning, Posey's men spied a group whose race they could not initially determine. Finally identifying them as Muskogees, Posey's detachment strode up to them. Since the white men were coming from the direction of Savannah, several Muskogees assumed they were British and approached them. Fourteen were killed and twelve captured. Wayne had the captives executed in what appears to have been the war's last bloodshed in Georgia. But most of Emistisiguo's warriors made it through to Savannah, too late to save the town but in time to join the British in evacuating to East Florida seventeen days later, on July 11.[31]

On August 7, Gen. Alexander Leslie made the long-awaited announcement that his troops would soon evacuate Charles Town as well. In the meantime, he offered to stop sending armed foraging parties into the countryside if Greene would permit British commissaries to continue purchasing food from South Carolina farmers, as they had long done without his consent. Greene was determined to reduce the number of African Americans the British carried off, and he figured, "the more scanty we can render their supplies of provisions," the sooner they would leave, and "the fewer Negroes they will have it in their power to take with them." So he rejected Leslie's proposal, forcing the redcoats to continue foraging in force.[32]

John Laurens had returned to his home state after the capture of

Cornwallis's army, and Gen. Greene had made him his spymaster. Having chaired the legislative committee that wrote the Confiscation Act, Laurens was well poised to obtain exemptions for Loyalist planters willing to spy for Congress. Laurens's informants included Eliza Clitherall, the wife of a Loyalist whose estate had been confiscated. In 1784, the South Carolina assembly reduced the Clitheralls' punishment to amercement: a one-time punitive property tax. Another of Laurens's spies tipped him off not only to British maneuvers but also to a raid by a band of African Americans.[33]

Late in August 1782, Laurens seized what looked to be his last chance to, as a fellow officer put it, "gain a laurel for his brow previous to a cessation of arms." A British foraging party had passed Santa Helena island, fifty miles down the Atlantic coast from Charles Town, and ascended the Combahee River. Laurens left his assigned post without permission and sped off to take command of the soldiers hustling to a narrow stretch of the river to obstruct the foragers' return. He socialized with the women of a nearby plantation until past midnight on August 26 and then, early on the morning of the 27th, led his fifty men toward the river. Prudence dictated that he await reinforcements, hurrying toward him and only two miles back. But he rushed ahead—right into an ambush laid by a British landing party of as many as three hundred men. Their first volley killed Laurens, along with one of his captains; more than twenty others were captured. Just ten days later, the British evacuation fleet reached Charles Town, prompting Gen. Leslie to recall his foraging party.[34]

Gen. Greene's effort to keep the British from carrying off more slaves had led to the "paltry little skirmish" (as he called it) that finally ended John Laurens's campaign to induct Black South Carolinians into the Continental Army. The twenty-seven-year-old lieutenant colonel's death devastated his loved ones—"his father will hardly survive it," Greene predicted—but he had won the fame he craved. Just watch *Hamilton*.[35]

In November 1782, a Black man showed up in the American camp on the outskirts of Charles Town with a tip: soldiers from the British fort on James Island, just south of the capital, had ventured outside its walls to cut firewood, taking along very few guards and thus leaving themselves highly vulnerable to capture. Andrzej Tadeusz Bonawentura Kościuszko, a Polish colonel in the Continental Army, decided to personally lead a mounted Maryland regiment in scooping them up.

Kościuszko's informant was either mistaken or part of a plot, for the wood-cutters were well prepared for his November 14 attack. The colonel narrowly escaped death, but five of his men were killed—the last known Continental fatalities of the war.[36]

By that time, Leslie's forces had already begun evacuating Charles Town, though they would not complete the process until December 14. In a further illustration of the simple truth that Black slaves lost more in the American Revolution than any other group besides Native Americans and at the same time gained more from it than anyone, the African Americans who shipped out of Charles Town and Savannah suffered a wide variety of fates. Leslie and Royal Navy captains moved heaven and earth to enable Loyalists to transfer their slaves to Loyal British colonies, especially Jamaica, the Bahamas, and East Florida. If the British army had captured you from a Whig plantation, you were likely to remain a slave: returned to your owner, used to reimburse some dispossessed Loyalist slaveholder, or snapped up by a British officer with dreams of becoming a sugar baron, making a few quick guineas—or spending the rest of his life with you. An early-nineteenth-century historian attributed much of the enemy's resistance to repatriating Black women to the "thousands of amorous connexions well known to have existed" between Black women and British officers.[37]

If you joined the army on your own initiative in response to one of its offers of freedom, you were likely—but not certain—to obtain it. But it appears that most—though not all—of the "sequestered negroes" who survived the war were reenslaved. One man was crammed into a rice barrel, apparently with his consent, and smuggled onto an outbound ship. He suffocated, but dozens or hundreds of other stowaways must have survived.[38]

The range of fates suffered and seized by Black South Carolinians can be glimpsed in the lives of two women, one white and one Black. In 1771, when Mary Middleton married Pierce Butler, her father made her the sole beneficiary of a "separate estate" containing dozens of slaves, amounting with their children to two hundred souls by 1782. After the British confiscated the Butlers' slaves, Mary asked them to return the people named in her marriage settlement. Leslie did not acknowledge Mary Butler's separate estate but did return some of her and her husband's slaves. Meanwhile Rawlins Lowndes paid homage to a woman named Rynah, who had "raised his children and had the care of their infancy." Escaping him during the war, Rynah and her husband were among the hundreds of African Americans who became servants to British officers. By the time Lowndes, a former Whig president of South Carolina who had later accepted British protection, solicited Gen. Carleton's help in recovering her, she and her husband were already in New York City—together and safe until Lowndes convinced Carleton to send her back to South Carolina.[39]

MEANWHILE, MORE AND MORE free Americans were turning away from the waning conflict against Britain and toward internal battles. While nearly everyone wanted Congress to repay its loans from Dutch bankers and Louis XVI, the federal and state governments' massive debts to their own citizens proved much more controversial. Army officers and civilian officials had issued a variety of IOUs—from Continental currency to loan office certificates to tiny scraps entitling the bearer to payment for a few weeks of militia service or a confiscated cow. All of this paper had depreciated.

Robert Morris, the federal financier, emphasized that the federal government could raise the market value of its securities simply by regularly paying the interest, which explains his support not only for Congress's request for the power to tax imports but also for its October 1781 requisition on the states. He acknowledged that the legislatures could only comply with the requisition by imposing heavy taxes, consuming as much as 40 percent of many people's income. But redistributing wealth from farmers to bondholders would boost the American economy in two distinct ways. "Men are disposed to indolence and profusion," he argued, and heavier taxation would make them work harder and spend less. Free Americans would develop those good habits no matter what the government did with their money, but if it went to bondholders, it would strengthen the economy in another way as well. Once Congress started paying interest on the bonds, "monied men would purchase them up (tho' perhaps at a considerable discount)." Extracting tax money from farmers and disbursing it to bondholders thus meant "distributing property into those hands which could render it most productive." The moneyed class's investments would grow the economy, benefiting even the taxpayers forced to fund them, to include the veterans and other unfortunates who had sold their own bonds to speculators at the bottom of the market.[40]

Nearly two hundred years after Yorktown, Arthur Laffer would take up a paper napkin and draw a backward-bending curve demonstrating that reducing federal taxes could increase the volume of money in the productive economy and thus, paradoxically, boost government revenue.[41] Superficially, Morris's plan stood in stark opposition to Laffer's "trickle-down" economics, since he hoped to save the American economy by granting the federal government the power to tax. But the primary purpose of both proposals was to give wealthy Americans ("job creators" in modern lingo) more money to invest—Laffer by reducing their taxes and Morris by using taxpayers' money to swell the value of their government securities.

As the economy gained strength, Morris predicted, so would Congress. A large federal debt owned by a small number of bondholders would "give stability to Government by combining together the interests of moneyed men for its support."[42]

For the moment, Morris's plan of direct federal taxation proved too radical for the members of Congress, but they continued to press the state assemblies to revive the depreciated war bonds. By the end of the year, every state assembly but Rhode Island's had approved federal customs duties on goods entering the United States, and most had also voted to comply with Congress's 1781 and 1782 requisitions, also aimed primarily at paying interest to federal creditors. And nearly every state levied separate taxes to service its own debt. Clearly the idea of enriching bond speculators at taxpayer expense enjoyed widespread support among the nation's leaders; it did not hurt that many of them possessed securities of their own.

But the immense new fiscal burden provoked "a general outcry against the payment of taxes," and no one objected more strenuously than Hermon Husband, the religious and political radical who had fled North Carolina after the defeat of the Regulators in 1771, resettling in western Pennsylvania. "Raising the Value of Money" after it has been "engrossed from the Publick at low Rates by a few" was "Ratsbane and rank Poison," Husband insisted in a 1782 pamphlet he called *Proposals to Amend and Perfect the Policy of the Government of the United States of America, or, The Fulfilling of the Prophecies in the Latter Days, Commenced by the Independence of America.* It was "as wicked Robbery as House-breaking."[43]

In sharp contrast to Morris, who believed that enriching bond speculators would benefit the whole society, Husband warned that taxing farmers so heavily that they had to forfeit their tools and draft animals would harm both them and the larger economy. To "distress the labouring Part, and take their Implements of Labour, their Horses, Oxen, &c. is to stab ourselves to the very Heart," he declared. Rather than redeem the paper that had funded the war with taxes so high as to impoverish farmers, the legislature should replace it with new currency that lost a fixed portion of its value every year until it became worthless.[44]

Like Robert Morris on the opposite end of the political spectrum, Husband linked economic and political reform. Even though Pennsylvania had the most democratic written constitution on earth, a tiny minority of "Tavern-keepers, Merchants, &c." wielded infinitely more political power than the agrarian majority, Husband believed, and the reason was that the state's legislative districts were too large. Most voters never saw their local representative and could not keep tabs on how he voted, and he in turn was unable to stay abreast of so many constituents' needs. By contrast, elites, especially merchants, ran into each other every day on the streets of Philadelphia, enabling them to unite their strength. Husband urged ordinary farmers to make their own efforts to "associate and join in your Elections," but also proposed to foster unity by reducing the size of election districts—and to submit all major policy questions to a popular vote.[45]

Few Americans ever learned of the link Husband had drawn between the size of the election district and the representative's susceptibility to popular pressure; as he acknowledged, *Proposals* "would not sell." But other writers made the same connection, albeit from a different perspective. A pamphlet published in Connecticut in 1782 celebrated the statewide election of the state's council (upper house) as assuring the members' independence from voters.[46]

But Husband's opposition to taxation for the sake of bondholders was widely shared. The October 1781 requisition had to be paid in gold or silver coin or in Morris's notes, which were nearly as scarce, and observers wondered whether the economy contained that much money, even if tax collectors took every free American's last dollar.[47] Residents of half the counties in Husband's adopted state of Pennsylvania signed antitax petitions, many of which connected the fiscal battle to the ongoing struggle against Native Americans. According to Dorsey Pentecost, the Washington County representative on the state's executive council, western farmers complained "that they are not assisted with either men or money to defend themselves [against] the savages, and yet are obliged to pay a Tax in Specie which they have not towards the general war." Pentecost himself was accused of advocating collective tax resistance.

Other Pennsylvanians took the even more direct approach of robbing tax collectors of their paperwork, but resisters' most common strategy was to threaten violence without actually inflicting it.[48]

Massachusetts attempted to cover its quota of the 1781 requisition with an array of new taxes, including one taking 6 percent of all residents' property—all this just months after levying an even higher tax primarily benefiting the states' bondholders. Soon deputy sheriffs began seizing and selling delinquent taxpayers' belongings. Many farmers found they

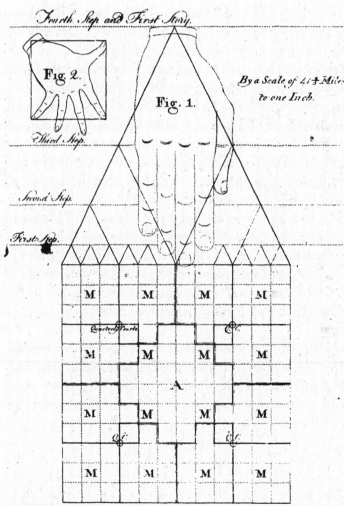

Hermon Husband, diagram showing how county legislatures
will elect state assemblymen

could pay their taxes only by putting off their private creditors, leading to still more property confiscation, some of which ended in violence. On September 24, 1782, a Berkshire County deputy took a yoke of oxen from debtor Enoch Marvin, and the man's neighbors banded together to take them back. When the deputy assembled a posse to confront Marvin and his supporters, they "began a battle with clubs and staves." Other Massachusetts farmers also sought strength in numbers, holding protest conventions and covenanting "to resist all sheriffs and Collectors" who tried to tax them or confiscate their property. In April, Rev. Samuel Ely, an itinerant preacher and veteran of the Battle of Bennington, led a crowd in shutting down the Hampshire County court. Ely was jailed, but about 130 of his supporters broke him out.[49]

Farmers' resistance to debt and tax collection often compelled state and local authorities to back down. Of the $8 million in new revenue that Congress demanded in October 1781, only $1.5 million had been paid two years later.[50] Morris and other leading Americans attributed the taxpayers' delinquency to pure selfishness, but at the end of April 1784, Congress voted to cut every state's quota of the 1781 requisition in half—a tacit admission that the burden had been intolerable. The delegates also had another reason to halve the 1781 requisition: they discovered that Morris, in his zeal to build popular support for tax increases, had deliberately distorted the federal government's balance sheet. Most glaringly, he had omitted a recently received French loan of four million livres.[51] Morris's accounting trick resembled Washington's 1779 attempt to fool Continental soldiers into committing for the war. Both men believed that leaders must sometimes deceive the people for their own good.

In time the war between taxpayers and government bondholders would drive some Americans back to the battlefield, this time to fight their fellow citizens, and others to Philadelphia, where they would launch a campaign to massively strengthen America's federal government.

CHAPTER 33

Like Old Worn Out Horses

1782–1783

ON JULY 1, 1782, DISEASE ONCE AGAIN AFFECTED THE COURSE OF the war, as an influenza epidemic that had killed thousands of ordinary Europeans also carried off the British prime minister, the Marquess of Rockingham. In his place George III got the man he had wanted all along. Lord Shelburne, the new PM, knew he could no longer oppose American independence outright, and in fact he repeated Rockingham's promise to recognize the new nation in advance of peace negotiations, but he kept proposing conditions that were unacceptable to the American peace commissioners—or, more precisely, to one of them.

Only two of Congress's five representatives had made it to Paris by the time Shelburne became prime minister. Frustrated with the slowness of the peace process—and even more so with French officialdom—John Adams had ridden off to Amsterdam, where he inked an alliance with the Netherlands and then stuck around to negotiate loans from the nation's bankers. Thomas Jefferson remained in America dealing with personal crises, culminating in the death of his wife, Martha, in September 1782. And while Henry Laurens had been released from the Tower at the end of 1781, he remained in London, immobilized by illnesses acquired during his long confinement and then by the loss of his son—and also unsure whether he could negotiate with the British while still officially their prisoner, albeit on parole.

That reduced the American peace commission to Benjamin Franklin, who had represented the United States in Paris since 1776, and John Jay, previously the U.S. minister to Spain, who joined him in June 1782. Jay wanted to hold Shelburne to his predecessor's promise to recognize the United States before even sitting down with its commissioners. But the British public recoiled, as Shelburne had, at granting recognition in return for nothing, so he insisted that it be an article of the peace treaty. Franklin, who prided himself on his flexibility, cheerfully acquiesced.[1]

Shelburne's stance received support from an unexpected quarter, America's European allies. France and Spain also opposed allowing citizens of the new republic access to the lush Grand Banks fishing grounds off Newfoundland or the territory out to the Mississippi River. Of special concern to Carlos III, whose troops had just wrested West Florida from Britain, was that province's northern border. He thought it should follow the Ohio River, which would give him the region that is now Tennessee and Kentucky. And he preferred to see the region north of the Ohio go to the weakened British rather than the surging United States. That would place the western boundary of the United States at or near the Appalachian Mountains—the old Proclamation Line that had helped spark the Revolution—and French officials for the most part agreed. The American commissioners insisted that France had ceded the region between the Appalachians and the Ohio to the British, who had in turn lost it to their former colonists. But Joseph-Mathias Gérard de Rayneval, undersecretary to Vergennes, the French foreign minister, knew that the Native Americans who lived and hunted in this region had never given it up. "Neither Spain nor the United States has the least right of sovereignty over the savages," he declared.[2]

Eventually Jay became so frustrated at France and Spain's opposition to his country's demands that he urged Britain to use the twenty thousand redcoats and Germans garrisoning New York City, Charles Town, and Savannah to recapture West Florida from Spain. He also proposed a path through the impasse over whether Britain should recognize American independence before formal peace talks opened: if Shelburne would add the words *United States* to British commissioner Richard Oswald's instructions, that would be sufficient acknowledgment of the new nation's existence, and negotiations could begin. Shelburne agreed, and on October 5, Oswald, Franklin, and Jay settled upon a draft peace treaty. In it, the British government, which had resisted white expansion into Native American territory for two decades, first by forbidding colonial settlement west of the Appalachians and then by arming the Indians, assigned the United States all of the land out to the Mississippi River.[3]

On September 30, Shelburne learned that the British fortress on Gibraltar had withstood a massive Franco-Spanish attack, and the news emboldened him to make additional demands: first, that judges in the thirteen former colonies enable British merchants to collect from their

American debtors and, second, that Congress "earnestly recommend" that the states return Loyalists' property. The U.S. commissioners gave in on both points, though many state courts would actually remain closed to British creditors for another decade and a half and few Loyalists would ever get their property back. John Adams reached Paris on October 26, just in time to take the lead in fending off a British attempt to take away his countrymen's right to fish the Grand Banks.[4]

On November 29, 1782, the last full day of negotiations, one more American commissioner, Henry Laurens, finally appeared in Paris. On the 30th, after the British and American secretaries had copied out the final treaty, Laurens asked for an additional clause prohibiting Royal Navy and army officers overseeing the evacuation of U.S. ports from "carrying away any Negroes, or other Property of the American Inhabitants." In his career as a South Carolina slave importer, Laurens had often sold Africans in partnership with none other than Richard Oswald, who now agreed to his proposal that the British government break its repeated pledges to free Whigs' slaves who left them to fight for king and country. Laurens's amendment was interlined into the engrossed copies of the preliminary treaty, which the commissioners then signed.[5]

In adding a fugitive slave clause to the peace treaty at the eleventh hour, Laurens replicated his fellow South Carolinians' success, back in October 1774, at modifying the completed Continental Association to allow for the continued exportation of rice. The lowcountry planters had obtained crucial last-minute changes both to one of the documents that ignited the American War of Independence and to the treaty that ended it.

Congress had instructed the American peace commissioners to show the preliminary treaty to Vergennes before approving it, and they had promised to do so. Instead they disclosed its contents only after signing. Vergennes protested but soon let the matter drop. The historian Samuel Flagg Bemis speculates that he was actually happy to see the Americans conclude a separate peace, since the loss of this crucial ally gave him an honorable escape from his country's vow to keep up the fight until Spain recovered Gibraltar.[6]

NEWS OF THE PRELIMINARY peace treaty would not reach North America until February 1783, but everyone knew it was coming. Most U.S. citizens were overjoyed at the prospect, but many of the officers and soldiers who had obtained the victory were surprisingly ambivalent. The nation owed them millions of dollars, and they feared that after they dispersed, Congress would forget its promises.[7] Two years earlier, in the wake of Benedict Arnold's treason, the delegates had agreed to match the British officers' retirement benefit of half pay for life. But the pensions had been widely condemned, with numerous critics pointing out that most enemy officers earned their half pay by spending their entire adult lives in the army. Moreover, enlisted men and civilians believed that in the United States as in Britain, an alliance of pensioners and power-hungry officeholders would constantly encroach upon the freedom of their fellow Americans.

With the political tide running against them, the officers began to fear that the federal government or state assemblies might eventually cut off their pensions. So they asked Congress to "commute" each man's half pay into a lump sum equal to five years' salary. Commutation was touted as saving the federal government money, but the reality of eighteenth-century disease was that commutation and half pay amounted to roughly the same sum, since the average middle-aged man could expect to live only ten more years.

Federal financier Robert Morris and like-minded congressmen, including Alexander Hamilton, saw the Continental officers' memorial as an opportunity. Rhode Island had voted down the proposed 5 percent federal tax on imported merchandise, and Virginia withdrew its support just as the officers' memorial reached Philadelphia. With legislators and private citizens asking why Congress should shower yet another windfall on the holders of the loan office certificates, Morris proposed that the bondholders link arms with the more popular, or at least more formidable, Continental officers. As Hamilton later reported to George Washington, "The necessity and discontents of the army presented themselves as a powerful engine" for extracting money from taxpayers. Morris's assistant Gouverneur Morris (no relation) believed the officers would also benefit from their association with the bondholders, who could be counted upon to monitor Congress's and the states' compliance with their commitments. "If you will permit me a metaphor from your own profession," he told Gen. Henry Knox, "after you have carried the post the public creditors will garrison it for you." Robert Morris sealed the alliance with a threat: he would resign his post, deranging federal finances and further infuriating the officers, unless Congress satisfied *all* of its creditors.[8]

Under the Articles of Confederation, financial legislation required the approval of nine state delegations. On March 10, 1783, the officers' bonus came before Congress and only won the support of "Eight states and a half." Oliver Wolcott favored commutation, but the only other Connecticut delegate present, Eliphalet Dyer, opposed it, keeping Connecticut out of the Yes column.[9]

But the fight had barely begun. On the same day that Congress narrowly rejected commutation, a printed address began circulating among the Continental officers encamped at Newburgh, New York, fifty-five miles up the Hudson River from Manhattan. Writing anonymously, Pennsylvania Maj. John Armstrong urged his brother officers to "carry your appeal from the Justice to the fears of government": until Congress met their demands, they should refuse to disband the army. In a second address appearing two days later, Armstrong hinted that the commander-in-chief approved of his scheme.[10]

Actually Washington was aghast, both at the bondholders for using his officers "as mere Puppits" and at the officers themselves for conspiring to subvert civilian rule. Never forget, he told Hamilton, that an army is "a dangerous instrument to play with."[11] Back in the 1760s, Washington had tricked several of the men who had served under him in the Seven Years' War out of their bounty land, and in this new postwar era, he once again found himself battling his subordinates, but this time with a nobler motive. Americans had been referring to their commander-in-chief as the father of his country since 1778, but on March 15, 1783, when Washington assembled his officers, he truly earned the title.

Pleading for patience, Washington read from Congressman Joseph Jones's letter reciting the delegates' enormous fiscal challenges. But Jones's words mattered infinitely less than Washington's performance. He had scarcely started when his voice faltered: the fifty-one-year-old could not decipher Jones's handwriting without spectacles. Taking a pair from his coat, he explained to the officers that "he had grown gray in their service, and now found himself growing blind." Many in the audience cried. Finishing Jones's letter, Washington left the room, whereupon the twenty-odd officers in attendance adopted resolutions condemning the conspiracy and agreeing to await Congress's justice.[12]

Meanwhile in Philadelphia, when Congressman Eliphalet Dyer learned of the Continental officers' threat "to carry their points & do themselves Justice as they call it with their Arms & at the Point of the Bayonet" (as he paraphrased it), he switched his vote on commutation, moving Connecticut into the Yes column and ensuring adoption. Two associates used the same word to explain Dyer's reversal: the officers had "extorted" it from him.[13] But at least Dyer, along with Washington, had ended the Newburgh conspiracy.

Commutation would remain an empty promise until Congress acquired a reliable source of income. Thus on April 18, the delegates asked state assemblymen to ratify a federal import tax, forgo any remaining claims to the western territory (so the federal government could use that land to redeem war bonds), and commit to levying a total of $1.5 million a year in federal taxes. Lest any region suffer disproportionately, none of these provisions would take effect until the states ratified all three.[14]

As the states took up Congress's request, Henry Knox proposed that the Continental officers form an association. At its first meeting on June 19 in a tavern in Fishkill, New York, the group named itself after the victorious Roman general Cincinnatus, who could have parlayed his battlefield laurels into political power but chose instead to return to his plow. The Society of the Cincinnati was (and remains) a commemorative and fraternal organization, but its most pressing objective in 1783 was to keep on Congress and the state assemblies to fund the commutation certificates. The idea of an officers-only political pressure group alarmed enlisted men as well as civilians. Most troublingly, the officers voted to bequeath membership in the Cincinnati to their firstborn sons, *their* firstborn sons, and so on forever, a rule that made them look less like Cincinnatus than Caesar.[15]

George Washington agreed to become the first president of the Society (a decision he would soon regret), and he lent his support to Congress's April 18 revenue package—especially the officers' commutation bonus—in a rare circular letter to the states. Free Americans almost never criticized Washington, but in 1789, just as the electoral college unanimously elevated him to the presidency, Hermon Husband violated the taboo, wishing the former commander-in-chief had "shewn as much care and concern for the people (who were all half ruined in their estates by the war) in his circular letter, as he did for the officers, who made their fortunes by the war."[16]

Husband did not know that behind the scenes, Washington had urged Congress to make good on its promises to the troops. In fact he warned one delegate, Alexander Hamilton, that if nothing was done for them, they would "go home enraged—complaining of injustice—& committing enormities on the innocent Inhabitants in every direction." Eventually Congress granted each private soldier one month's salary ($7) in hard money and an additional three months' pay in Morris's notes, which the man could sell at 50 to 80 percent of their face value.[17]

BACK IN 1780, WHEN both the traitor Benedict Arnold and the slave Boston King escaped to the British, they had embodied the ambiguity of the American Revolution. By March 1783, when Americans learned that U.S. and British diplomats had signed a preliminary peace treaty, King was in New York City, once again well positioned to appreciate the Revolution's multiple meanings. He observed that the treaty "diffused universal joy among all parties, except us, who had escaped from slavery, and taken refuge in the English army." As he recalled years later, "a report prevailed at New-York, that all the slaves, in number 2000, were to be delivered up to their masters." Numerous planters were on their way to Manhattan to take advantage of the fugitive slave clause that Henry Laurens had added to the peace treaty. A still greater number, including Virginia governor Benjamin Harrison and the widowed Mary Willing Byrd, compiled lists of their former slaves and sent agents to recover them.[18]

Carl Leopold Baurmeister, a Hessian major stationed in New York, reported that the three thousand African Americans in the city "refuse[d] to be delivered in so unwarrantable a manner." Their emissaries met with Gen. Carleton, the British commander-in-chief, and "insist[ed] on their rights" under the emancipation proclamations of Dunmore, Clinton, and other British officers. Carleton's response was simple but extraordinary: treaty or no treaty, Great Britain would keep its promise. "Prior Engagements binding the National Honor," he declared, "must be kept with all Colours." The African Americans' former owners were furious. In a May 9 parley with Carleton, Washington insisted on "the Preservation of Property from being carried off, and especially the Negroes."[19]

On May 26, Congress instructed Washington to dismiss all soldiers serving for the duration of the war. Ultimately Continental Army officers would retain fewer than a thousand men to serve alongside state militiamen against the Indians. Years later, Joseph Plumb Martin described the strange mix of emotions he and his messmates had felt in June 1783: pride at defeating the British, sadness at separating from the men with whom they had "lived together as a family of brothers for several years"—and disgust with Congress and the state assemblies for violating their promises. As an example, new Continental recruits who agreed to serve for the duration of the war had been offered land bounties of at least a hundred acres, but Martin reported that "When the country had drained the last drop of service it could screw out of the poor soldiers, they were turned adrift like old worn out horses, and nothing said about land to pasture them upon." Nor had the soldiers received their promised rations, pay, or clothing. "The country was rigorous in exacting my compliance to *my* engagements to a punctilio," he wrote, "but equally careless in performing her contracts with me. . . . She had all the power in her own hands, and I had none."[20]

At Congress's direction, enlisted men as well as officers were sent home not only without pay but without an accounting of what the government owed them. So on June 21, 1783, several hundred Pennsylvania soldiers stationed in their home state decided to emulate their officers in forcing civilian authorities to pay up. They marched to the statehouse, surrounded it, and demanded that the executive council, which met upstairs, give them everything it owed them, especially land bounties and back pay. Ominously, the state's beleaguered militiamen refused to protect the council from their fellow soldiers. The Pennsylvania regulars—like many other Continentals, including Joseph Plumb Martin—also believed Congress and their officers had issued them temporary *furloughs* rather than permanent *discharges* to lull them into the false belief that they would be remembered even after they dispersed.[21]

For once the soldiers' suspicions of their leaders were misplaced; Congress had actually used the term *furlough* to get out of an entirely different jam. Months after receiving word of the preliminary peace treaty, Gen. Carleton was taking his time evacuating his troops from New York City—and scrupulously carrying out his policy of freeing the slaves who had fought for their king. Many southern delegates believed the only way to pressure Carleton to leave his Black allies behind was to keep the Continental Army together. But congressmen from states with few slaves feared such a provocative move would reignite the war. Keeping the soldiers in the field also subjected Congress to the enormous expense of feeding them. Moreover, Washington warned Congress that the Continental Army's ten thousand "Soldiers for the War" interpreted their commitment literally: since the preliminary treaty had ended the fighting, they should be allowed to go home at once. When Congress did not immediately authorize their release, Washington and his officers felt compelled "to increase our gards to prevent rioting."[22] With southern delegates insisting on retaining the troops and nearly everyone else wanting to muster them out, Congress split the difference, sending them home but with furloughs instead of discharges. Designed in part to prevent a mutiny, this compromise provoked one in Pennsylvania.

Congress had responded to the Newburgh conspiracy by adopting commutation and seeking federal taxes to fund it, but when the Pennsylvania privates surrounded their statehouse, the delegates sent in two regiments of Continental soldiers. Unwilling to fight their fellow sufferers, the protesters dispersed. Two of their leaders were captured and condemned to death but pardoned at the gallows.[23]

Although the June 21 march to the Pennsylvania statehouse had targeted the state's executive council, not Congress, it nonetheless spurred the federal government to adjourn to Princeton, New Jersey. In subsequent years, the delegates would move twelve miles southwest to Trenton before also trying Annapolis and New York City. A newspaper writer helpfully suggested that the peripatetic congressmen hold their deliberations "in a little Balloon."[24]

Joseph Plumb Martin was one of the few men in his company who stuck around long enough to collect the "final settlement certificates" Congress owed the soldiers. He reported that most of the men sold their certificates to speculators, for pennies on the dollar, in order "to procure decent clothing and money sufficient to enable them to pass with decency through the country, and to appear something like themselves when they arrived among their friends."[25]

"I was among those," he wrote.[26]

The soldiers with the greatest cause for bitterness were the Native Americans who had taken the American side. They did not share in the bounty land allotted to whites, and most whites' bounties were carved from Indian country.[27]

Enlisted men's sense of betrayal fueled the "great Clamour" against Congress's embrace of commutation. In Connecticut and Massachusetts, dozens of town meetings, several county conventions, and the lower houses of both state legislatures denounced the officers' bonuses, with several towns announcing their "determinations to pay no Taxes for the Commutations." Every year for more than two decades, Connecticut voters had returned Eliphalet Dyer to the council of assistants, but after he cast the deciding vote for commutation, voters turfed him out.[28]

From his home near Paris, Benjamin Franklin kept close tabs on the battle over federal taxation to fund the officers' bonuses and other securities. "I see in some Resolutions of Town-Meetings, a Remonstrance against giving Congress a Power to take as they call it, *the People's Money* out of their Pockets tho' only to pay the Interest and Principal of Debts duly contracted," he told Robert Morris in a Christmas 1783 letter. Franklin conceded the right of individuals to retain whatever property they needed for survival and "the Propagation of the Species" but declared that in a people's republic, "all Property superfluous to such purposes is the Property of the Publick."[29]

Despite entreaties from Franklin and other Founding Fathers, the state assemblies never gave Congress the power to levy taxes on merchandise arriving in American ports.[30] As a result, every year when the interest came due on federal securities, all their owners received was still more paper: interest notes, known as indents, that traded far below their face value, though not as low as the principal bonds. Indents, commutation certificates, the soldiers' final settlement certificates, and other federal and state bonds became the objects of intense speculation, and one of the wiliest and most successful of the speculators was Abigail Adams.[31]

Biographies of the Founders generally depict them as proud and powerful. But the commutation certificates were born of a military coup, only to succumb, at least for the moment, to taxpayer revolts. In this battle as in so many others of the revolutionary era, the Founders served primarily to register the net effect of conflicting external forces.

LIKE CONTINENTAL OFFICERS AND soldiers, most Native Americans were ambivalent about the preliminary peace treaty. No belligerent had suffered more than they, but Indians were shocked that the British had, as Joseph Brant put it, "Sold the Indians to Congress." Alexander McGillivray, the mixed-race Muskogee leader, insisted that Britain had "no right to give up a country she never could call her own." Gen. Allan Maclean, at Fort Niagara, reported that he had distributed rum to the Indians "a little more liberally than usual to keep them in good humour" — but in vain. A group of Iroquois asked Maclean how Britain could consent to a treaty that gave the United States the Indians' land without even mentioning the Indians themselves. They insisted that they "were the faithful allies of the King of England not his subjects; that he had no right whatever to grant away to the States of America their rights or properties." The treaty boundary was null and void.[32]

But what could the Indians do, now that the British had abandoned them? As they had even before Pontiac's Rebellion in 1763, they sought strength in unity. Taking the lead, Joseph Brant and other Iroquois sachems invited other nations to meet at Lower Sandusky town (between modern-day Toledo and Cleveland) in September 1783 to inaugurate a new pan-Indian confederacy. Even as His Majesty's soldiers were evacuating their posts throughout North America, imperial Indian agent John Johnson sent the conferees a supportive speech, two British emissaries, and a schooner called the *Faith* loaded with presents. Coalition leaders played up this British aid on the proven theory that even the illusion of a British alliance could both attract additional warriors and intimidate the United States.[33]

At the Sandusky conference, the Shawnees and Cherokee delegations returned a wampum belt the Iroquois had circulated among them; what made the transaction significant was that they did it together. The Shawnees and Cherokees had spent most of the eighteenth century attacking each other, but in 1770 they had begun peace talks, and during the Revolutionary War they and nearly all of the nations between the Ohio and the Appalachians had united under nominal British leadership. The two delegations now signified that they meant to stay united.[34]

Four months later, Ephraim Douglass, a U.S. official returning from Indian country, quoted the Sandusky attendees as saying the British representatives had asked them not to bury the tomahawk but merely to "lay it down carefully by their side" so they could resume the war at a moment's notice. Douglass may have been lying, for in the British transcripts of the meeting, the only ones who speak of keeping the hatchet close at hand are Joseph Brant and the Wyandots Deyonquat and T'Sindatton. It is also possible that British officials doctored the transcript, but the likeliest explanation for the discrepancy is that the natives exaggerated imperial support for their aggressive stance toward the United States in hopes of further entangling Britain in their alliance.[35]

Over the next decade, the Native Americans resisting the United States would continue to gather for periodic councils and to add new nations to their confederacy.[36]

MEANWHILE THE BRITISH CONTINUED the mass evacuation of New York City that had begun early in the summer. Unlike the African Americans who left Savannah and Charles Town, most of those who sailed out of New York had secured their freedom. With British officers refusing to help visiting slaveholders recover their human property, they and their

agents once again resorted to kidnapping. "We saw our old masters coming from Virginia, North-Carolina, and other parts, and seizing upon
their slaves in the streets of New-York, or even dragging them out of their
beds," Boston King later recalled. Frank Griffin's former owner tracked
him down, tied a rope around his neck, and dragged him onto a sloop.
But then Griffin was liberated by a party of Hessians and a former slave
named Colonel Cuff. "Two weeks later," the historian Cassandra Pybus
notes, Griffin, "his wife, and their baby daughter were evacuated to Nova
Scotia," the destination of most of New York's Black Loyalists.[37]

Carleton expected the British government to reconcile its agents' conflicting promises to the slaves and their former owners by financially
compensating the slaveholders, and to facilitate that process he had his
officers compile capsule biographies of the more than three thousand
African Americans who evacuated, mostly to Nova Scotia. Carleton's
"Book of Negroes," available online, shows that in the spring of 1776,
a slave named Mary escaped her home in Hampton, Virginia, with her
three-year-old daughter, Phillis. They made it to the British lines, spent
the remainder of the war in New York City, took the last name Halstead,
and evacuated in 1783. When James Tucker, formerly of Norfolk, Virginia, evacuated, he was fifty-five years old and "almost worn out"—but
finally free. Another refugee, the thirty-year-old Ralph Henry, formerly
the slave of Patrick Henry, had served in the British army—and joined
other underpaid recruits in attempting to desert to the much more lucrative privateers. Thomas Peters (the African-born wheelwright who
joined Henry Clinton's army on the Cape Fear River in 1776), Harry
Washington, and Boston King and his wife all left for Nova Scotia on the
same vessel, *L'Abondance*. It sailed on July 31. Handfuls of formerly enslaved evacuees chose other Loyal British colonies, and many headed to
the mother country. Samuel Burke, who "could speak the Irish tongue,"
had used his skills to recruit Irish Americans into the army; he and his
wife, of African and Dutch ancestry, resettled in London.[38]

Mary Willing Byrd tried to lure back an especially valuable slave, Wat,
who had taken the last name Harris, by agreeing not to punish him. She
even offered him a "handsome" reward if he could inveigle other slaves
back to Virginia with him. Deploying the planter's ultimate weapon—the
slave family—Byrd informed Wat that "his wife and Children are very
anxious to see him." Wat left for London and, incredibly, later returned
to New York as a free man, but he never saw his family again. Carleton's
criteria for evacuation—he accepted only those African Americans who

reached British lines before the preliminary peace treaty was signed—had the effect of separating families: often the husband or wife qualified but the spouse and children did not and had to remain behind.[39]

Many of Carleton's fellow Britons took pride in the principled stand he took in New York in 1783, and in the ensuing years some followed his lead. Even before the outbreak of the American Revolution, a handful of religious leaders, especially Quakers, had called upon Parliament to shut down the international slave trade. That movement's increased momentum at the end of the American War of Independence was not entirely coincidental, as the Columbia University historian Christopher Brown discovered. Many British subjects worried that the self-styled Sons of Liberty had won not only the war but the moral high ground, and abolitionists soon grasped that this sense of national humiliation could be turned to good use. As one preacher put it, if other Britons followed Carleton's lead, they would show their former colonists in America "that we are no less friendly to liberty than they."[40] Opponents of the slave trade kept pushing this patriotic vision right up until 1807, when Britain—and simultaneously the United States—finally got out of the business of buying human beings on the African coast.

ON SEPTEMBER 3, 1783, as Native Americans made their way to Sandusky to inaugurate a new defensive alliance and African Americans boarded the Royal Navy ships that would transport them from New York Harbor to freedom, British and American representatives met David Hartley, who had replaced Richard Oswald as the British peace commissioner, at the Hôtel d'York in Paris to affix their signatures to the definitive treaty ending the Revolutionary War. Then Hartley rode out to Versailles to sign the Anglo-French treaty.

The final version of the British-American treaty was virtually identical to the preliminary draft agreed to by Franklin, Jay, Adams, Laurens, and Oswald back on November 30, 1782, but the commissioners did make one telling change. The 1782 version had contained no religious language. But just as Congress had added phrases such as "endowed by their Creator," "divine Providence," and "the Supreme Judge of the world" to Thomas Jefferson's rough draft of the Declaration of Independence, the authors of the definitive treaty decided to open it with an invocation—or, more precisely, two: "In the Name of the most Holy and undivided Trinity. It having pleased the divine Providence . . ."[41]

* * *

As THE PEACE COMMISSIONERS signed the treaty, Jefferson was at home in Virginia, completing *Notes on the State of Virginia*. He had it privately printed in Paris in 1785, and the first English edition for mass distribution came out two years later. The book was primarily a work of natural history (which at the time included Native Americans) and geography, and Jefferson's most persistent purpose was to refute French naturalists' claims that the American environment produced animals, including humans, that were smaller and weaker than their European counterparts. *Notes* includes some of Jefferson's most stirring descriptions of the continent's natural wonders, especially Natural Bridge and present-day Harpers Ferry, West Virginia, where the Shenandoah and Potomac Rivers join forces to crash through the Blue Ridge Mountains on their way to the Atlantic.

In addition, Jefferson offered one of history's pithiest defenses of religious liberty: "it does me no injury for my neighbor to say there are twenty gods, or no God. It neither picks my pocket nor breaks my leg." And he warned that the opportunity to establish freedom of religion would soon pass away. "From the conclusion of this war we shall be going down hill. It will not then be necessary to resort every moment to the people for support. They will be forgotten, therefore, and their rights disregarded." Downhill, a wagon easily glides along, and in normal times, so does the governing class. Only when it must "resort every moment to the people for support" will it attend to their demands.[42]

Notes on the State of Virginia also featured Jefferson's most stirring celebration of ordinary white farmers—"the chosen people of God"—and his most sickening references to African Americans. In July 1799, the childless George Washington would write a will liberating all his slaves upon his wife's death. When he died five months later, Martha Washington realized that George's slaves were now only a heartbeat away from freedom—*her* heartbeat—and went ahead and freed them.[43] Jefferson, by contrast, liberated only slaves to whom he was related. In *Notes on the State of Virginia*, he stated that he would like to free all of America's slaves—but then immediately banish them. One of his concerns was that Black anger and white prejudice would fuel racial violence leading to "the extermination of the one or the other race." But he also harbored the contradictory fear that Blacks and whites would get along too well, even intermarrying. That would degrade the white race, for Jefferson considered Blacks "inferior to the whites in the endowments both of body and mind." They sweated more, which gave them "a very strong and disagreeable odour." Lacking the capacity for "forethought," they were more lustful, less imaginative, and less capable of reason. "Never yet could I find that a black had uttered a thought above the level of plain narration," Jefferson wrote. He claimed that even Black men affirmed white superiority by favoring white women as mates, just as, he assured his readers, Africa's male orangutan (never mind that orangutans actually live in southeast Asia) preferred "the black women over those of his own species." Jefferson had had no problem affirming that Africans were "MEN" in his draft of the Declaration of Independence, where doing so had sharpened his barb at George III's connivance in the slave trade. But in *Notes on the State of Virginia* he consigned Blacks to a much lower rung. After insisting upon slaves' "disposition to sleep," he contended that "An animal whose body is at rest, and who does not reflect, must be disposed to sleep."[44]

One Black woman, Phillis Wheatley, especially aroused Jefferson's ire, and he pronounced "the compositions published under her name . . . below the dignity of criticism." In a footnote to the first poem in her 1773 *Poems on Various Subjects*, Wheatley had proudly claimed the enslaved Roman writer Terence, a native of North Africa, as a fellow *"African by birth."* Jefferson owned a copy of Wheatley's book and may have been responding directly to her—and to the threat that she, a classicist as well as a successful poet, posed to the slaveholders' myth of Black inferiority—when he sought to reclaim Terence for "the race of whites."[45]

Reaching for the moral high ground, Jefferson insisted that his plan to banish the African American fifth of the U.S. population would facilitate emancipation by allaying whites' fears of seeing the "dignity and beauty" of their race corrupted. But when he shared a draft of *Notes* with Charles Thomson, the secretary of Congress, his friend suggested that he delete the passages on African Americans, which "might seem to justify slavery." Jefferson refused.[46]

LIKE MOST WARS, THE American Revolution is typically represented as a chess match between commanders-in-chief. In truth, though, the clash of arms between 1775 and 1783 was powerfully influenced by the same little-known conflicts and external forces that had helped to set it off. For example, few modern Americans have heard of Haidar Ali, but his army's incursions into Madras led both to Parliament's Tea Act of 1773 and, a decade later, to the British government's decision to cut its losses by signing a peace treaty with the American rebels. So Haidar had helped both cause and conclude the Revolutionary War.

Charles H. Hubbell, *Battle of Guntur* (1780), depicting Haidar Ali's troops deploying
rockets against the British (which they later copied for use against Napoleon)

The Americans' battle against Britain also felt the influence of other
conflicts that never made it into their textbooks. As Part One showed,
the Native Americans who resisted what historians now call "settler colonialism" helped provoke Britain to adopt a ban on western settlement
and speculation, imperiling the ambitions of American land speculators
like George Washington and Benjamin Franklin, and also the Stamp Act.
Then in the war, Indian country became the one region of North America where Congress and the thirteen states faced constant defeat, for instance never capturing Fort Detroit. The Americans achieved their
greatest western successes not on the battlefield but in negotiations with
British officials, who, in recognizing American independence in 1783
gave up on halting their western advance. According to the "schedule of
property" he compiled on July 9, 1799 — the forty-fourth anniversary of
Braddock's defeat — George Washington alone would acquire more than
forty thousand acres west of the mountains.[47]

In the 1760s and even more intensively in 1774, obscure Americans
like Hannah Griffitts pressured reluctant merchants to stop importing
British manufactured goods, thereby aggravating tensions between Par-

liament and the provincial assemblies. In the ensuing war, Col. James Barrett's subordinates pressured him to lead them into battle against the redcoats at Concord's North Bridge, the civilian leaders of the besieged Charles Town, South Carolina, forced more than five thousand Continental troops to share their fate, ordinary citizens pressured Gen. Washington (albeit with limited success) to trade the British soldiers and sailors he had captured for the militarily less valuable Americans crammed into British prison ships—and so on and on.[48]

In the early 1760s and 1770s, young males dominated the urban crowds that harassed British tax collectors and customs agents. During the war, many of these same men resisted being drafted into the Continental Army, leading three southern states to recruit freedom fighters with the lure of human bounties. In several states, officials tried to preclude the possibility of draft riots by offering everyone who volunteered an enormous bonus, but their efforts to collect sufficient funds to make these payments often led to tax revolts. Continental soldiers also influenced events. For example, Pennsylvanians who thought they had enlisted for three years saw right through Gen. Washington's attempt to trick them into committing for the war, and their mutiny forced him to release them. In October 1775, a Black Virginian, Joseph Harris, provoked the battle that brought the Revolutionary War south of New England, and seven years later, on James Island in South Carolina, another Black man, whose name has not survived, set in motion the last battle in which Continental soldiers died.[49]

Like the political dispute that preceded it, the war was also affected by impersonal forces. North America's distinctive demographics—a sparse but rapidly growing population—helped turn free colonists against the crown both by dooming their attempts at large-scale manufacturing and by making land speculation enormously profitable, that is until Britain shut it down. America's hills and forests—vastly different terrain from the Low Countries where most British army officers had learned the art of war—gave a natural advantage to defenders, which in most cases meant the rebels. North America's geographic diversity influenced the war's direction in a literal sense. William Howe moved his army from Massachusetts, with its short and narrow rivers, to New York early in 1776 largely because his brother's ships could navigate the Hudson for 150 miles. And five years later, Virginia's broad streams similarly enticed Charles Cornwallis and his troops out of the Carolinas. Rivers shaped the war in other ways as well.[50] In August 1777, when Howe landed his troops at the head of Chesapeake Bay, they were no closer to their destination, Philadelphia, than they had been in New Jersey. But they had avoided landing on the west bank of the Delaware River under fire. That same summer, John Burgoyne's frustration with having to shuttle his cannon and other matériel around the rapids of the Upper Hudson River led him to send troops to Bennington, Vermont, to rustle up horses and carts, and the defeat they suffered just short of their objective imperiled his entire expedition.

Of course the war's nominal commanders were sometimes able to execute their commands, but in many cases their subordinates wished they had failed. In October 1777, when Continental troops halted Burgoyne's near Freeman's Farm, and exactly four years later, when the French and Americans besieged Cornwallis at Yorktown, Burgoyne and Cornwallis both felt compelled to launch one last offensive—not with any hope of success but for honor's sake. The honor imperative provoked not only pathetic disputes over rank but several fatal duels, and John Laurens gave his life in a rash and pointless attack late in the war—all for honor.

William Howe is often depicted as lethargic or even cowardly or treasonous for not destroying the Continental Army when he had the chance, at Brooklyn Heights in late August 1776. But the hard-won lesson he had learned at Bunker Hill was not to waste his men on frontal assaults. Many American generals firmly grasped that point, but one who did not was George Washington. From the moment he took command of the Continental Army, Washington resolved to launch a grand assault on an entrenched British army, be it in Boston, Philadelphia, or New York. To be sure, he could find support for such a move in the mother country's military manuals, but his motives seem to have been at least partly personal. As of 1780, he had spent nearly half of his adult life in uniform, but he had led troops to victory only twice: against the Hessian garrison at Trenton on December 26, 1776, and, back in 1754, in a sudden and deliberate attack against a French reconnaissance party that had no reason to think there was a war.[51]

Whatever mixture of rational calculation and thirst for distinction went into Washington's obsession with storming the British trenches, by never acting on it, he made his single greatest contribution to the American victory. The wisdom of the "Fabian" defensive strategy that Washington was pressured into adopting may be summarized in one remarkable fact: the Americans won the war despite failing to capture either New York City or Fort Detroit, their two most enduring targets.

Washington and other commanders also contributed to their soldiers' successes in more positive ways. Officers often concluded that boosting their own side's morale while depressing the enemy's ought to determine how they deployed their troops. More than once, commanders declined to move their men to stronger ground if it required even the slightest movement away from the enemy.[52] Sometimes officers' efforts to project confidence seem foolhardy in retrospect. In late September 1777, when William Howe established his headquarters at Germantown, Pennsylvania, he feared that fortifying his lines would project weakness, so he never gave the order.[53]

Military leaders' determination to discourage enemy troops and inspire their own can help explain many of the war's great mysteries. After the British landed on Manhattan on September 15, 1776, they could have cut off the Continentals' retreat from New York simply by crossing the narrow island. Why did British commander Henry Clinton hold back? Because he believed even the slightest setback would fatally compromise his army's reputation for invincibility. Late in 1778, Gen. Lachlan McIntosh's native allies goaded him into beginning his expedition west from Fort Pitt toward Detroit before he had amassed sufficient supplies, and sure enough, by the time his army reached the Tuscarawas River, its wagons were all but empty. Before heading home, McIntosh built Fort Laurens right there on the Tuscarawas, where he had to know that enemy Indians would pick off any soldier who ventured out for food. Why? Because he feared that turning around would "Confirm the Savages in the Opinion the Enemy inculcates of our weakness" unless he first planted the flag.[54]

McIntosh was not alone in worrying about what the natives thought. Several Continental commanders tried to overawe First Nations leaders, for instance by inviting them to review large troop concentrations in populous eastern cities. In August 1777, Washington sent Daniel Morgan's regiment to fight Gen. John Burgoyne's Indian allies and correctly predicted that just by showing up on the Upper Hudson, the riflemen would persuade many of them to disengage. At the same time, both Britain and the United States tried to use their indigenous allies to intimidate their opponents. With fewer Indians at their disposal, Continental officers sometimes disguised nonnative troops as Indians, for instance by altering their dress and having them give a "war hoop" as they charged.[55]

Commanders understood that battlefield successes and apparent suc-

cesses also crucially affected both sides' civilians. Viewing himself and
other generals almost as stage managers, Nathanael Greene noted that
"It is not the real value of Cities or places that gives the public a good
or bad impression but the imaginary estimation given them." In 1777,
Washington tried to obtain a portable printing press in hopes of relieving the American public "from that despondency, which they are apt
to fall into from the exaggerated pictures our Enemies . . . commonly
draw of any misfortunes we meet with." More than once, Continental
officers designed their tactical maneuvers around shoring up the value
of U.S. currency. Washington at one point believed that even a small
victory would attract enough voluntary recruits to avert a draft, and he
and his generals deployed their troops accordingly. So did the British,
whose success on the battlefield and recruitment of Black as well as white
soldiers each seemed to strengthen the other.[56] Sometimes commanders
designed their strategies around their probable effects on peace negotiations in Europe, as when Lafayette ordered his army to follow Cornwallis's troops as they marched eastward across Virginia in order to give
the appearance of running them off.[57]

In short, thousands of participants in the independence movement
and the Revolutionary War learned—sometimes repeatedly—the same
two lessons that Gen. Braddock had imbibed at such great cost on the
Monongahela. The first was to keep an eye on the invisible enemy; the
second, to realize an invisible ally might just save the day. But focusing
on what Professor Nash calls "the unknown American Revolution" does
not mean ignoring the Founding Fathers. Indeed, research into *the in-
teraction between the known and unknown revolutions* is bound to bear
fruit for years to come.[58]

PART THREE

———◆———

ROADS OPENED,
ROADS CLOSED

INTRODUCTION

I N THE EIGHTEENTH-CENTURY SPIRIT OF MODERATION, THIS BOOK'S comprehensive coverage of the American War of Independence ceases when the belligerents signed peace treaties on September 3, 1783. But a case could be made for ending a decade later, in 1794–1795, when U.S. armies put down rebellions by whiskey distillers in western Pennsylvania and by two coalitions of Native Americans. Enslaved people on the west bank of the lower Mississippi River also rose up in 1795—against Spain, which continued to rule that region, while the east bank was the subject both of a treaty between the United States and Spain and of a massive land fraud that raised fundamental issues that Americans were able to resolve only by amending the Constitution. The United States and Britain nearly went back to war in 1794 but resolved their dispute with a treaty that fell just short of making the United States its former mother country's ally against revolutionary France. These and other events of 1794–1795 are described in chapter 36, but first, chapters 34 and 35 briefly summarize the pivotal decade from 1784 to 1793, with special attention to the adoption of the Constitution. Part Three also describes how the panoply of individuals and groups that shaped the American Revolution in turn felt its influence, and it offers some tentative conclusions about what the conflict meant and means.

CHAPTER 34

A Revolution in Favor of Government

1783–1788

THE AMERICAN REVOLUTION ENDED THE WAY MANY WARS DO, IN a recession. The conflict had not only killed thousands of people and tens of thousands of oxen and horses but also destroyed massive quantities of food, hundreds of ships and farms, and in some regions entire towns. Congress and the thirteen state legislatures had run up towering debts.[1] Free Americans attributed much of the economic distress to deliberate British policy. Lord Shelburne, who became prime minister on July 4, 1782, believed that welcoming the former colonists back to imperial trade networks would be to Britain's benefit. But the House of Commons deemed Shelburne too lenient, and in April 1783 he and his fellow ministers were replaced by an odd coalition of the two factions that had opposed them from more or less opposite directions.[2] On July 2, 1783, the seventh anniversary of American independence, the Privy Council adopted "orders in council" prohibiting U.S. ships from carrying North American fish, grain, livestock, and forest products to Britain's islands in the Caribbean. British sugar planters joined a handful of politicians in pleading for a return to free trade. But they could make no headway against the shipbuilders and British merchants who now enjoyed an official monopoly of the island trade. Retired Continental Army Col. William Stephens Smith believed George III harbored an additional motive for quarantining his people from the new country: "the doctrine of Liberty is sweet and captivating," and he feared they would catch the bug.[3]

The ban on U.S. shipping did much more damage on paper than in practice. As British colonists, North American ship captains had skillfully evaded parliamentary restrictions on trade with the foreign islands in the Caribbean, and they now proved nearly as adept at slipping into

British islands like Barbados and Jamaica. Even during the brief periods when the Royal Navy fully enforced the blockade, Americans simply carried their cargoes to French sugar islands, whence a portion was trans-shipped to British colonies in smaller vessels, many crewed entirely by African Americans.[4]

In the direct trade between North America and Europe, British politicians and merchants would have been happy to pick up where they and the Americans had left off in 1774, but the citizens of the new republic had higher aspirations. As colonists, they had hated Britain's "enumeration" of some of their most valuable crops, including tobacco, which obliged them to send every ounce to the mother country. They rejoiced at their newfound power to sell their produce where they pleased. But Americans proved about as capable of redirecting their Atlantic trade to France and other European countries as Parliament was at keeping them out of the British West Indies. Within weeks of the preliminary peace treaty of November 30, 1782, U.S. and British ships were once again calling at each other's ports. Albion's merchants spoke the former colonists' language both literally and figuratively; as a French historian has noted, even eight years of bitter fighting had not diminished Americans' fondness for "l'English style of life." Furthermore, France had fallen behind Britain both in its industrial revolution—British manufacturers turned out higher-quality merchandise at lower cost—and its financial revolution: British merchants could provide longer credit at lower interest.[5]

By 1799, 40 percent of British woolen exports went to the United States, and half of the ships trading to Georgia, South Carolina, Virginia, and Maryland were British, with only 8 percent flying other European flags; the rest were American. Thus did economic laws guarantee Britain's monopoly of American trade as effectively as its Acts of Trade ever had, and as late as 1820, Henry Clay, the speaker of the U.S. House of Representatives, was still describing the American states as "independent colonies of England."[6] If British leaders could have glimpsed that future in a crystal ball, would they have sacrificed so many lives and so much treasure trying to prevent thirteen colonies from calling themselves states?

In the mid-1780s several state legislatures passed laws favoring French and other continental European vessels over those flying the Union Jack. But most of these initiatives failed, because British captains could always just call at rival ports. For many Americans, the states' need to coordinate their trade war against Britain became a powerful argument for transferring their commercial powers to Congress.

As MUCH AS CITIZENS of the new nation worried about their place in the Atlantic economy, nearly all agreed that the real source of the postwar recession was domestic: misguided legislation emanating from the thirteen state assemblies. But that consensus masked a profound disagreement over what exactly the representatives had done wrong. At various times during the 1780s, most states tried both squeezing debtors and taxpayers and easing up on them, and the central debate of the postwar era was over which of these conflicting policies had wrecked the economy.

One key element in the recession was the $65 million war debt. Americans had rebelled against Parliament partly over taxation without representation, but then their own representatives tried to finance the state and federal debts by, on average, tripling colonial-era taxes. The state assemblies also constricted the money supply, with disastrous results. An anonymous Rhode Island writer declared that paying the enormous new taxes with almost nonexistent gold and silver coin was "harder than being forced to make bricks without straw, it is to make them without clay." "A FRIEND to the PUBLIC" conjured up a farmer who used to pay his taxes every year by selling an ox. Once the shortage of circulating coin cut the price of livestock in half, the ox would only discharge half the farmer's tax bill, prompting the writer to ask, "Pray honest farmer, where is the other half of your ox?"[7] When deputy sheriffs seized and sold delinquent debtors' and taxpayers' livestock—and sometimes threw debtors in jail—their families were not the only ones who suffered, for the nation's output declined. State assemblymen had taxed the economy into recession.

The era's most prominent leaders explained the economic downturn differently. "Our calamities are in a great measure occasioned by the luxury and extravagance of individuals," insisted more than one hundred Hartford, Connecticut, women who gathered on November 6, 1786, to sign an "Oeconomical Association" pledging to "dress their persons in the plainest manner." Patterned on the female frugality pledges that had accompanied the colonists' anti-British boycotts, this one soon spread, for it contributed to a larger campaign to pin the nation's recession on the debtors and taxpayers who persuaded state assemblymen to adopt legislation that gave them temporary relief but wrecked the larger economy.[8]

For many, the most dreaded form of legislative relief was the paper money that seven of the thirteen state legislatures printed in the half decade after the adoption of the peace treaty. Like the British merchants who had obtained the passage of the Currency Act of 1764, leading Americans tarred paper money as a debtors' scheme to cheat their creditors. For their part, the defenders of the treasury bills claimed that thousands of Americans would lose their farms unless assemblymen gave them some medium with which to pay their enormous new taxes. They also noted that paper money often held its value in peacetime—a point that even Hamilton acknowledged—and that the only reason legislators had sparked hyperinflation by firing up the printing presses in the late 1750s and again in the late 1770s was to pay and supply the troops.[9]

Among the most prominent Americans who viewed themselves as victims of state-level debt and tax relief were James Madison and Gouverneur Morris, soon to be the two most frequent speakers at the Constitutional Convention. In the spring of 1786, Madison joined his fellow Virginian James Monroe (who would succeed him in the presidency three decades later) in speculating in Iroquois land in upstate New York. But the two could only afford nine hundred of the thousands of acres they hoped to flip, because they could not obtain loans. Madison asked his friend Thomas Jefferson, then representing the United States in France, to borrow the funds from some of that nation's fabulously wealthy aristocrats, but Jefferson replied that Europeans refused to lend money to Americans for fear of losing it to some politician's debtor protection scheme. Morris's need for cash was even more pressing. Having overextended himself in purchasing his childhood home, Morrisania, he was convinced that the only way to satisfy his creditors was to borrow still more. But like Madison, Morris was unable to raise sufficient funds, and, also like Madison, he blamed his predicament on potential investors' fear of debt relief legislation.[10]

Madison, Morris, and thousands of other would-be borrowers believed that if they could obtain the loans they needed to expand their operations, other Americans would benefit, too. The United States could never attract investment capital, especially from overseas, while the money supply and debtor-creditor relations more broadly were governed by state assemblymen who lived in fear of their indebted constituents. Indeed, many prominent Americans saw the wave of relief legislation emerging from the state legislature in the 1780s as exposing a fundamental flaw in republican government: the rural majority could use their power over state legislators to, in effect, confiscate the wealth of their fellow citizens who had lent money, either privately or to the government. Even the few who conceded that much colonial paper money had held its value went on to contend that fiat currency could never succeed in the U.S. republics, since legislators felt pressure from their indebted constituents but no longer from a pro-creditor Parliament.[11]

Thus the recession of the mid-1780s exposed a deep rift among free Americans. The majority viewed state assemblymen as so beholden to private creditors and the speculators who had bought up the war bonds at a fraction of their face value that they imposed heavy taxes and restrictive monetary policies that not only ruined individual farm families but threw the whole nation into recession. A smaller but more prominent group of Americans offered a diametrically opposed interpretation that blamed the economic crisis on the state legislators who had catered to voters' every whim.

Americans could not even agree on *why* assemblymen sometimes eased up on debtors and taxpayers. No one outdid Alexander Hamilton in promoting the ratification of the U.S. Constitution—or Elbridge Gerry in opposing it. But earlier, at the federal convention, Gerry and then Hamilton had used the same phrase to describe the central defect in the state governments: an "excess of democracy."[12] They and many other elite Americans feared that annually elected state representatives would never muster the courage to deny voters' demands for irresponsible measures such as paper money.

Ordinary farmers scoffed at the notion that they had too much electoral influence over the state representatives who tripled their taxes while sapping the economy of circulating cash. As they saw it, state as well as local officials had granted relief only in response to insurgency. When deputy sheriffs seized farmers' property for nonpayment of debt and taxes and transported it to the county courthouse to be auctioned off, the delinquents and their friends often violently took it back, just as the North Carolina Regulators had. Pennsylvania debtors and taxpayers even blocked roads leading to the county courthouse with ditches and barricades. When a South Carolina deputy tried to deliver a writ to Hezekiah Maham, the inventor of the tower that had facilitated the capture of British forts, he not only refused the writ but made the deputy eat it, helpfully providing a beverage to wash it down.[13]

South Carolina was also the scene of an extraordinary attack on the judicial system. On April 27, 1785, years before the births of his renowned abolitionist daughters Sarah and Angelina, John F. Grimké, judge of the Camden district court, was just sitting down to a long docket of creditors' lawsuits when a thousand people surrounded the courthouse, with many pushing inside. One of the protesters, whom Grimké identified only as Hill, began calling out the names of jurors—in hopes, the judge said, of "intimidating the Jury from appearing." Countering Hill's intimidation in kind, Grimké made sure the whole courtroom could overhear him ordering the sheriff to arrest him. But as the judge later reported, Hill "was so far from being intimidated that he proceeded leisurely in calling over the list of names as before."[14]

Next Grimké translated his threat into body language, rising from the bench in order to "prevent others from supporting [Hill] as they would be more immediately under my own Eye." Also, for the first time, he spoke directly to Hill, "hoping that it would daunt" him. Instead Hill "replied to me tauntingly that it was [']not many words that would fill a bushell'"—in other words, the judge was all talk. So Grimké called upon the grand jury to help him arrest Hill, speaking in "so sudden and decisive a manner" as to have compelled Hill and his supporters "to have abandoned so impudent an attempt." That failed, too. Once again resorting to threatening body language, the judge "suddenly descended from the Bench and invited [the jurors] to assist me." Finally Hill and his friends withdrew, but Grimké learned the next day that his prospective jurors "had quitted the Town with precipitancy and apprehension," preventing him from trying a single case.[15]

Hill and his followers had closed Judge Grimké's court without laying a hand on him, and they were not alone. While farmers throughout the country attacked court officers, many more obtained their ends using threats and warnings—just as Native American diplomats in the 1760s had dictated parliamentary leaders' land policy not with actual violence but with hints about their success at assembling an anti-British coalition.

As more and more free farmers resisted tax debt collection, gentry leaders increasingly feared that enslaved South Carolinians would once again exploit divisions within the free half of the population to liberate themselves. In October 1785, state legislators sought to head off that possibility by printing £100,000 of paper money. Debtors and taxpayers in every state likewise wrung relief from frightened assemblymen and local officials. Each of these victories strengthened leading Americans' conviction that the only way to stop state legislators from granting their constituents' every wish was to transfer some of their most crucial powers to Congress. But farmers and their supporters read the same sequence differently, observing that rebellion and rumors of rebellion could produce relief even when petitioning and voting failed.[16]

IN THE 1783 PEACE treaty, Britain had given the United States all of the territory out to the Mississippi River, doubling its land area. But U.S. citizens hoping to occupy or sell this real estate faced two obstacles. Many U.S. leaders wished to establish a western boundary similar to the old Proclamation Line and barely a hundred miles farther west. For example, George Washington, of all people, warned Congress against allowing "a wide extended Country to be overrun with Land jobbers—Speculators, and Monopolizers or even with scatter'd settlers," provoking attacks by the Indians who denied Britain's right to deed away their land. These were the same concerns that had led the mother country to stand by the Proclamation of 1763 until Americans abrogated it by winning their independence.[17]

Congress held out hope of quieting the Indians' land claims without the expense of a war. Its commissioners could have saved money by assembling representatives from every native nation at once but instead followed Thomas Jefferson's advice to "treat with the several nations at different times and places" in order to "discourage every coalition and consultation which might tend to involve any one nation in the wars of the others." As U.S. representatives invited their native counterparts to a series of meetings, starting with the Iroquois in the fall of 1784 and continuing with various Ohio Valley nations over the next two years, a Shawnee named Piteasewa told them, "We are aware of your design to divide our Councils."[18]

All of these conferences were held in American forts, with soldiers looking on as U.S. commissioners browbeat and deceived a handful of Native Americans into adding their marks to treaties ceding their nations' land. The Oneidas had sided with the United States against Britain, but most of their territory entered the U.S. domain along with the rest. In May 1785, without waiting for the completion of the fort treaties, Congress sent a team of surveyors to the western Ohio Valley to begin dividing it into ranges, townships, and sections that it could auction off to reduce its enormous debt.[19]

But many Indians were as determined as ever to fight for their land, and they courted two European allies: the Spanish, who had regained the Floridas in a 1783 treaty, and the British, who remained in Canada.

Britain also held on to a chain of forts on the U.S. side of the Great Lakes—partly in response to pressure from its native allies and partly to prod the Americans to comply with their treaty obligations. After the fall 1784 Fort Stanwix treaty where U.S. commissioners obtained questionable title to the vast stretch of land west of Iroquoia, two Iroquois attendees, Cornplanter and George Washington's old associate Guyasuta, traveled to Pittsburgh with alarming news: the Mohawk sachem Joseph Brant had sailed to London to seek British arms and ammunition. Brant's winter 1784–1785 visit to Britain was widely reported in American newspapers—even though it was entirely fictitious, apparently a deliberate native effort to inflame U.S. fears of an Anglo-Indian alliance.[20]

Brant really did visit England the following year, and he and other indigenous leaders kept up their negotiations with the British, but they recognized their more reliable allies would always be each other. So, just as they had on the eve of the revolution, they gathered for a series of multination meetings, culminating in a November and December 1786 congress at Brownstown across the Detroit River from the British fort. Today some Americans believe the Iroquois Indians' "Great League of Peace and Power" was the model for the U.S. Constitution, but native spokesmen at Brownstown saw themselves as students rather than teachers. One Iroquois said whites had conquered "that large tract of Country, between our present habitations and the Salt Water" by being "prudent enough to preserve . . . Unanimity," in the face of which "None of the divided Efforts of our Ancestors to oppose them had any Effect." If the Indians wished to keep their remaining land, they must "profit by these things and be unanimous."[21]

As they had in the 1760s, native coalition builders skillfully exploited the European concept of race. For example, the Iroquois delegation at Brownstown told the western nations that the pan-Indian confederacy was of "high importance to all of us of the same Colour." The British had provided abundant encouragement but little ammunition, no troops, and only vague promises of future support, and the native congress pressed them for a "determined answer."[22] And the representatives demanded that the U.S. Congress renounce both its claim to have obtained all of the land out to the Mississippi River from Britain and the "partial" treaties its agents had negotiated with small numbers of Indians within the walls of its western forts. The natives warned that if the United States failed to "meet them upon fair and equal Terms, they are all Unanimously determined to defend their rights and privileges to the last extremity."[23] In

March 1787, federal Indian agent Richard Butler reported that First Nations diplomats had "laboured exceedingly to form a general confederacy among themselves from North to South in order to become formidable." For the United States, that raised the specter of "a general war" against Indian rebels wielding two weapons they had had during the Revolutionary War but not in the 1760s: "*European supplies and friends.*"[24] And that worrisome prospect powerfully influenced U.S. policy.

Congress planned to hold the land west of the Ohio River back from the market until its surveyors completed seven "ranges," whereupon everything would be auctioned off. But in 1785 and again the following fall, Indian threats sent the surveyors scurrying back across the Ohio. Congress had to give up on land auctions for the foreseeable future. "Had it not been for the hostile appearances in the Indians," Massachusetts delegate Nathan Dane declared in November 1786, "7,000,000 acres of the land belonging to the United States would now have been surveyed, and ready for sale." The best the federal government could manage was to sell 1.5 million acres of the best land in the Ohio Valley to a group of Massachusetts investors who had borrowed both the Ohio Company's name and its strategy of distributing shares to members of Congress. The firm paid $1 million—in federal bonds trading at one-eighth of their face value.[25]

Native resistance also forced the United States to drop its claim to have obtained title to all of the land out to the Mississippi River by beating the British. In the Northwest Ordinance of July 13, 1787, Congress acknowledged that it would also have to purchase this territory from its actual owners. In a further concession, the delegates abandoned Jefferson's divide-and-conquer strategy and agreed to treat with all Indian claimants at a single grand conference.[26] Native American rebels had placed Congress in a classic bind: it could not emerge from bankruptcy without selling millions of western acres, but it could not profit from the Indians' land until it drove them off, and that required a much larger army than Congress could afford.

BY 1786, MANY OF the most prominent men in America were growing increasingly alarmed about a host of challenges, from British mercantilism, taxpayer revolts, and the state legislators' willingness to print paper money to border conflicts between neighboring states and the Indians' resolute defense of their land. The only viable response to these threats, more and more U.S. leaders came to believe, was to strengthen the fed-

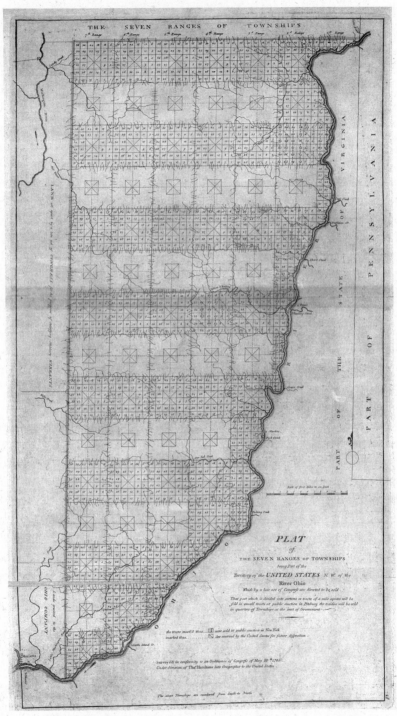

Plat of the Seven Ranges of Townships ordered by Congress in 1785

eral government. When the few delegates who showed up for an unsuccessful multistate convention in Annapolis, Maryland, in September 1786 put out a call for a second attempt in Philadelphia the following May, many Americans remained skeptical. George Washington was an ardent nationalist, but when Virginia placed him at the head of its delegation to Philadelphia, he told friends he planned to decline.

Then a group of Massachusetts farmers, many of them veterans of the Revolutionary War, handed the nationalists what many considered the final argument for a federal convention. Like parliamentary leaders at the close of the Seven Years' War, Massachusetts assemblymen were determined to pay down the war debt, and in March 1786 that led them to impose the heaviest taxes Massachusetts had ever known. The legislators also refused to ease the tax burden with a relief measure such as paper money. Over the next few months, crowds of farmers, many referring to themselves as Regulators, forced several county courts to shut down. The movement had several leaders but ended up being named for a former Continental Army captain, Daniel Shays.

Historians typically depict the farmers who rebelled in Massachusetts and other states during the mid-1780s as desperate debtors. But many of the revolts were actually sparked by massive tax increases like the one that passed the Massachusetts legislature in March 1786, so historians' singular focus on debt is just as inaccurate as the numerous accounts of the origins of the American Revolution that home in on "taxation without representation" at the expense of other battles such as the one pitting British creditors against American debtors.[27]

Over in Paris, Thomas Jefferson reacted to Shays's Rebellion with equanimity. "The tree of liberty," he wrote, "must be refreshed from time to time with the blood of patriots and tyrants"—a statement so timeless and pliable that Timothy McVeigh wore it on his T-shirt on April 19, 1995, when he bombed the Alfred P. Murrah Federal Building in Oklahoma City, killing 168 men, women, and children.[28] But other leading Americans panicked. "The flames of internal insurrection were ready to burst out in every quarter," Pennsylvania's James Wilson recalled less than a year later. "From one end to the other of the continent, we [walk] on ashes, concealing fire beneath our feet." A decade earlier, George Washington had warned that if white Virginians did not immediately crush the royal governor who had offered freedom to their slaves, his army would "Increase as a Snow ball by Rolling." In October 1786, Washington similarly warned that "like snowballs," farmers' rebellions "gather strength as they roll." In a reversal, the former commander-in-chief announced that he would attend the Philadelphia convention after all.[29] Without the popular George Washington, the movement to strengthen the federal government might well have failed, so Shays and his compatriots merit recognition as inadvertent coauthors of the Constitution.

Western Massachusetts newspapers described how the Camden, South Carolina, court riot and other revolts forced Palmetto State assemblymen to issue paper money, and these reports kindled Bay State farmers' hopes of obtaining a relief package of their own. But African Americans had never been numerous in the Bay Colony, and in 1783, the state supreme court had found slavery unconstitutional. Thus Massachusetts authorities felt free to respond to their state's western insurrection not with concessions but with an army.

As Governor James Bowdoin began recruiting troops, he received an extraordinary offer. A decade earlier, Irish Masons serving with the British army in Boston had admitted fifteen African Americans to their order, and after the redcoats left, the city's newest Masons formed an "African Lodge." Seeing Shays's Rebellion as a chance to demonstrate Black Bostonians' loyalty and value, grand master Prince Hall offered the governor up to seven hundred fighters. But Bowdoin spurned the aid, instead finding 4,400 soldiers among the state's poor whites. The governor and Gen. Benjamin Lincoln, his choice to command the expedition against the rebels, funded it by appealing to wealthy merchants and securities speculators to become "loaners of a part of their property if they wished to secure the remainder."[30]

White New Englanders' newfound reluctance to enlist African American soldiers led many Black Bostonians to abandon hope of ever integrating into the dominant society. On January 4, 1787, Prince Hall and seventy-two other free Blacks composed the first of numerous appeals to Bay State whites to aid Blacks in returning to an Africa that most had never seen.[31]

Meanwhile Congress had joined the fight against Shays's Rebellion— or at least tried to. On October 20, 1786, the delegates voted to embody a 1,340-man army, ostensibly to invade Indian country but actually to attack the Massachusetts insurgents. But the states failed to fund Congress's army, and it never took the field. For many Americans, the aborted march sealed the case for radically reforming the federal government.[32]

*   *   *

ASK MODERN AMERICANS WHAT they most appreciate about the Constitution, and you are likely to hear freedom of speech, protection against unlawful search and seizure and cruel and unusual punishment, universal suffrage, gun rights, and freedom of religion. These popular provisions have two things in common. First, almost all focus on protecting civil liberties, especially those of underdogs such as accused criminals and members of minority religions. Second, and more surprisingly, is that none is actually in the Constitution—at least not in the document that the framers presented to the nation on September 17, 1787. They were all added later, in the Bill of Rights and later amendments. And that raises a question: if the framers did not travel to Philadelphia in the summer of 1787 to secure civil liberties, then *why were they there*?

The Constitution strengthened the United States government against its enemies, foreign and domestic, and it tamped down conflicts among states. But it was, above all, an economic document. It created a national market and enabled the federal government to use the threat of commercial retaliation to open British Caribbean ports to U.S. ships. But most popular accounts of the origins of the Constitution do not even mention the economic motivation that was foremost in the minds of the framers themselves. Shortly after the convention adjourned, Madison affirmed that the "mutability" and "injustice" of the laws adopted by the thirteen state assemblies had "contributed more to that uneasiness which produced the Convention, and prepared the public mind for a general reform, than those which accrued to our national character and interest from the inadequacy of the [Articles of] Confederation."[33]

The framers lodged two main grievances against the state legislatures. First, they had caved in to their constituents' demands for tax relief, disabling state and federal officials from paying interest on the war bonds and thus decreasing the likelihood that moneyed men and women would buy future bonds. Second, assemblymen had provided relief to debtors, discouraging wealthy people from making private loans. Madison arrived in Philadelphia with a radical remedy for the state legislators' tendency to cheat creditors (and also persecute religious dissenters, which he had helped outlaw in Virginia): a U.S. Senate veto over state laws. That was too much for Madison's fellow delegates, but they accomplished the same purpose by prohibiting the states from printing paper money or otherwise "impairing the Obligation of Contracts."[34]

The convention also took care of government bondholders. The Articles of Confederation had not allowed the federal government to collect taxes of any kind, but the Constitution gave it several sources of income. For the next century and a half, the most productive of these would be a tariff on merchandise arriving on American wharves. The state assemblies had tried to levy their own taxes on imports, but most of these had failed, because arriving ship captains typically had their choice of where to land, allowing them to incite bidding wars that drastically reduced tariffs. But federal import taxes eliminated this race to the bottom and proved highly lucrative.

Although the Constitution prevented the state legislatures from cheating either private creditors or federal bondholders, the danger remained that the federal government might itself go easy on either taxpayers or debtors. Foreclosing that prospect was the primary reason the framers made the national government much less susceptible to grassroots pressure than any state. First in North Carolina and then in Pennsylvania, Hermon Husband had complained that countywide legislative districts were so large that voters could neither educate their representative about their grievances nor learn what, if anything, he had done about them. But members of Congress would be even more remote, since they would represent up to twenty times more voters. As Madison explained to the federal convention, uniting every American freeholder under a single political roof would, paradoxically, "divide the community into so great a number of interests & parties, that . . . they may not be apt to unite in the pursuit" of any particular goal. And in a private letter to Thomas Jefferson, he made the same point in starker terms, calling the well-known strategy of "divide and conquer" both "the reprobated axiom of tyranny" and "the only policy, by which a republic can be administered on just principles."[35]

During the war, numerous commanders, including Washington at Germantown, had made the mistake of excessively dividing their armies, preventing the constituent parts from "acting in concert." Gouverneur Morris spoke for the worst enemies as well as the best friends of the Constitution when he predicted that shifting certain key powers to the national level would likewise dampen ordinary voters' efforts to "act in concert" to influence legislation.[36] Elites' unity would be less impaired.

Even if a proposal favoring debtors or taxpayers made it out of the House of Representatives, it could still be defeated by the Senate, the president (who would wield more power than George III), or the Supreme Court—none of whom had to face the voters directly (senators were appointed by the state legislatures until 1913) and all of whom served long terms and still do. The federal convention was proposing what one critic called "a revolution in favor of *Government*."[37]

Historians often describe the Constitution as antidemocratic, but a better term might be *paternalist*, since the Founding Fathers believed they had eroded ordinary citizens' political power for their own good—in the same way that loving parents keep the cookie jar on a shelf beyond their child's reach. Since their most pressing motivation for this grand act of political disempowerment was to attract capital to the American economy, the single most apt description of the Constitution may be *capitalist*.

The convention delegates' broad consensus on the need to protect merchant-creditors and securities investors did not prevent them from disagreeing on a host of other issues. The convention nearly broke up over a dispute pitting representatives from the smaller states, who wished to retain the existing apportionment of one vote to each state, against those representing the more populous states, who wanted to make representation proportional to population. The Great Compromise gave every state two senators and doled out seats in the House of Representatives according to population. Another controversy arose when southern delegates insisted on counting slaves in apportioning congressmen among the states. Northern delegates balked at the idea but eventually agreed to a compromise. In distributing congressional seats as well as the federal tax burden among the states, every slave would be considered three-fifths of a person.[38]

The regions also split over overseas trade. Northerners and upper south delegates hoped to empower Congress to abolish the African slave trade. The southernmost delegates opposed that idea but joined the upper south delegations in seeking to require that import tariffs aimed at favoring American manufacturing receive a two-thirds vote in both the House of Representatives and the Senate. In the end, the convention allowed Congress to adopt tariffs by a simple majority—but also prohibited it from interfering in the slave trade for the next twenty years. This "dirty compromise" facilitated a postwar boom in the forced transportation of Africans to the Americas: nearly a million souls between 1783 and 1792. Before the Revolution, only about one-sixth of the Africans arriving in North America had come over in American-owned ships. Afterward, the proportion soared to three-fourths.[39]

Slavery played an equally important, though less heralded, role in the convention's debate over how to pick the president. Many southern delegates believed their region deserved the same outsized influence in presidential elections that it had already obtained in the House of Representatives. But the convention would not be able to give slave-holders extra weight in presidential elections if it left the choice to the voters, so most southern delegates favored selection by Congress. The great exception was Madison, who deeply distrusted legislatures and thus favored a third alternative: allowing the states to choose special electors who would then select the president. By giving each state two electors plus one more for each of its congressmen (elected under the Three-Fifths Clause), the convention could preserve the president's independence of Congress while also weighting presidential elections in favor of the slave states. The convention adopted Madison's proposal, and most historians believe that it was the Three-Fifths Clause and the electoral college that allowed Madison's friend Thomas Jefferson to win the presidency in 1800.[40] The electoral college remains controversial today; two of the twenty-first century's first four presidents entered the White House after winning in the electoral college but losing the popular vote.

To the few schoolchildren who still have to memorize it, the Preamble to the U.S. Constitution sometimes can seem like a string of glittering generalities. Actually, though, at least three of its clauses set forth quite specific goals, all of which came into focus as state conventions debated whether to ratify the Constitution. Nine states would have to do so before it took effect.

One goal announced in the Preamble was to *provide for the common defence*. Now that Congress could finally levy its own direct taxes, it could field a formidable army for the first time since the Revolutionary War. U.S. citizens worried about a wide variety of potential enemies, from the British and Spanish empires, both of which retained footholds in North America, to the Barbary pirates in the Mediterranean. But the new nation also faced immediate adversaries in the Native Americans whose land beckoned not only to individual Americans but to the financially strapped state and federal governments.

When the Constitution reached Georgia, the legislature had already been called into session to prepare for a possible war with the seven to eight thousand fighters of the Muskogee confederacy. That coincidence explains why Georgia became the first state outside the Delaware River watershed to ratify the Constitution. The vote was unanimous, and everyone knew why. "If we are to be much longer unblessed with an efficient national government, destitute of funds and without public credit, either at home or abroad," New Hampshire congressman Nicholas Gilman declared after hearing the Georgia news, "I fear we shall become contemptible even in the eyes of savages themselves." Massachusetts poet and playwright Mercy Otis Warren, who opposed ratification, lamented that Georgia, "apprehensive of a war with the Savages, has acceded in order to insure protection."[41]

In other states, too, settlers' desire for federal protection against the Indians clinched the case for the Constitution. On his second-to-last day presiding over the federal convention, George Washington rejected a lowball offer on one of his western tracts, confident of "obtaining the price I have fixed on the land" if "the Government of this Country gets well toned, and property perfectly secured"—in other words, if his fellow Americans ratified the Constitution.[42] The western Virginians who supplied the votes needed to secure their state's ratification—by just 6 percent—were motivated in part by the expectation that federal judges, unlike their state counterparts, would permit British creditors to collect from their Virginia debtors, as the 1783 treaty required. And only that could persuade London to carry out its own treaty obligation to evacuate Detroit and the other Great Lakes forts that provided crucial supplies and direction to the First Nations violently resisting American encroachment on their land. Britain's western forts had vexed North American settlers since the mid-1760s, when Parliament tried to garrison them at colonial expense.[43]

THE PREAMBLE ALSO PROMISED that the Constitution would *insure domestic Tranquility*. In modern minds, that phrase may conjure up families serenely gathered 'round the fireside, but it actually referred to the need to suppress—or, even better, prevent—rebellions by farmers and slaves.

Reflecting on race relations in *Notes on the State of Virginia*, Jefferson observed that, "considering numbers, nature and natural means only, a revolution of the wheel of fortune, an exchange of situation is among possible events." A decade later, in 1794, President Washington expressed his own expectation that enslaved Americans would become "a very troublesome species of property 'ere many years pass over our heads." Thus did both of the first two southern presidents predict widescale slave rebellions—and in so doing, they helped explain slaveholders' support for a Constitution that massively strengthened their hand. No state would benefit more from a powerful national government than Virginia, Washington wrote during the ratification struggle, since "in point of *strength*, it is, comparitively, weak." Another federal convention delegate, Charles Cotesworth Pinckney of South Carolina, likewise acknowledged "the interest the weak Southn. States had in being united with the strong Eastern [northern] States."[44]

America's first decades under the Constitution transpired very much as Washington, Jefferson, and Pinckney had predicted. States' rights rhetoric notwithstanding, southern governors requested federal troops in response to all of the major slave insurrection scares: Gabriel's Rebellion in central Virginia in 1800; the German Coast, Louisiana, revolt of 1811; the Denmark Vesey conspiracy in Charleston, South Carolina, in 1822; Nat Turner's rebellion in Virginia in 1831; and John Brown's raid on Harpers Ferry, Virginia, in 1859. State militiamen put down most of these uprisings before federal troops could arrive, but U.S. Army dragoons helped suppress the 1811 revolt, and John Brown's band held out until its position was stormed by U.S. Marines. And African Americans who attempted that far more common form of rebellion—escaping to the free states—found the Constitution's fugitive slave clause an effective instrument in the hands of their pursuers.[45]

Not that African Americans posed the only danger. Five days before the federal convention adjourned, the *Pennsylvania Gazette* warned that if Americans rejected the Constitution, the news of June 1789 would read something like this: "We hear from Richmond, that the new statehouse lately erected there was burnt by a mob from Berkeley county, on account of the Assembly refusing to emit paper money." On the other hand, if Americans enabled the federal government to field a powerful army, readers would soon learn that the rebellion of Connecticut squatters in the Wyoming Valley of Pennsylvania had been suppressed—and that the insurgent leaders were "to be tried for their lives."[46]

THE FRAMERS' MOST PRESSING imperative—to *establish justice*—may seem nebulous, but it actually referred to two specific clauses of the Constitution. By empowering the federal government to levy taxes, Article I, Section 8 would enable it to do justice to the people who had invested in its bonds. Section 10 of the same article, which prohibited the states from printing paper money or committing any other injustice against creditors, has become one of the most obscure clauses in the Constitution, but during the ratification battle, it attracted more superlatives than any other. It was "the best in the Constitution," "the soul of the Constitution," and "sufficient to outweigh all Objections to the System." "Nothing, in the whole Federal Constitution, is more necessary than this very section," a New Jerseyan claimed. Two Pennsylvania signers of the Declaration of Independence, attorney James Wilson and physician Benjamin Rush, independently concluded that even if the Constitution had done nothing more than ban paper money, that alone would have been, in Rush's words, "eno' to recommend it to honest men."[47]

DESPITE THE BATTERY OF arguments advanced in favor of the Constitution, historians estimate that about half the voters opposed it. So how did its supporters prevail? Early on, they claimed the name *Federalists*, which implied approval of the existing federation of autonomous states and thus concealed the nationalizing impulse they had avowed behind the closed doors of the Constitutional Convention. The Federalists tarred their opponents as Anti-Federalists, implying that the people defending the Articles were actually trying to tear them up. Like most of the state legislatures, the ratifying conventions were malapportioned, with the more mercantile, more pro-Constitution, coast electing more delegates than its population warranted. In addition, Federalists owned eighty of the nation's ninety-two newspapers, printing many more pro than anti essays. Yet in nearly half the state-ratifying conventions, the Federalists, with all their advantages, got the Constitution through only by vowing to amend it.[48]

On June 21, 1788, New Hampshire became the ninth state to ratify, reducing the holdouts' options to acquiescing to the Constitution or going it alone. About two-thirds of the delegates elected to the New York convention had pledged to vote No, but then New York City threatened to secede from the state and join the new nation on its own, whereupon enough delegates moved over to the pro-ratification camp to give the Constitution a two-vote margin. It would take North Carolina another sixteen months to submit, and Rhode Island did not come in until May 29, 1790.[49]

Federalists in the First Congress kept their promise to amend the Constitution—to a degree. Critics had demanded two root-and-branch changes. Convinced that the Constitution had transferred too much power from the states to the federal government, they wanted to send some back. And they proposed to shift some of the Senate's and president's duties to the House of Representatives, whose members were the only federal officeholders elected directly by the voters for short terms. Congress rejected both of these structural amendments, but James Madison, who had vehemently opposed a bill of rights during the ratification fight, now drafted one. Congress approved it on September 25, 1789, and the states ratified it two years later.[50]

Americans actually owe their celebrated civil liberties, from freedom of speech and religion to gun rights and protection against torture and unlawful search and seizure not to the men who wrote the Constitution but to the people like Mercy Otis Warren of Massachusetts and Patrick Henry of Virginia who hated it. Far from worshipping the Founding Fathers and their works, as today's schoolchildren are often taught to do, they demanded the changes that became the Bill of Rights.[51]

Nor did the transformation of the Constitution end there. Just as abolitionists and women's rights advocates would gradually convert the secession-justifying Declaration of Independence into an egalitarian manifesto, ordinary Americans would, over the decades, turn the Constitutional Convention's antidemocratic, pro-creditor "coup" into an underdogs' constitution. In the 1860s, just as Americans started referring to the first ten amendments as the Bill of Rights, decades of abolitionist agitation, culminating in the Civil War, finally secured the ratification of three additional amendments committing the Constitution to the principle that all men are created equal. Women had to fight another half century for the right to vote, and it was only within my lifetime that pressure from civil rights activists and feminists finally forced Congress, state legislators, and the courts to breathe life into the Fourteenth Amendment's guarantee of "equal protection of the laws."[52]

The path to the Constitution in many ways resembled the one that had led to the Declaration of Independence. Britain in the 1760s and the United States in the 1780s had each just beaten back an existential threat, but only by incurring an enormous government debt that would influence its politics for years to come. Moreover, the Declaration and Constitution both resulted not only from the struggles pitting the thirteen assemblies against the national legislature but also from lesser-known battles among economic interest groups. In both cases, diverse Indian nations came together to resist settler encroachment and hugely influenced relationships among the interlopers. The native resistance of the 1760s prompted Britain to restrict colonial expansion, alienating many North Americans and thereby contributing to the Revolution. Twenty years later, whites' concerns about a similar native coalition helped persuade them to ratify a document giving Congress the revenue it needed to field a western army. Likewise, enslaved and free workers' "domestic insurrections" played complex but crucial roles both in the outbreak of the American Revolution and in the campaign for the Constitution.[53]

Some of the factional conflicts of the 1760s reappeared in the 1780s under slightly different guises. During the late colonial era, British merchants and their American customers tugged from opposite directions at Parliament's monetary policy. After the Revolutionary War, the currency dispute shifted to the state legislatures, with mostly rural taxpayers and debtors campaigning for paper money while coastal merchants and bond speculators dug in against it. The documents adopted at the Pennsylvania statehouse on July 4, 1776, and September 17, 1787, also shared a focus on government finance. During the Seven Years' War, Parliament ran up a huge debt that indirectly fueled conflict between British and American taxpayers. Then during the Revolutionary War, the state and federal governments amassed enormous debts of their own, igniting disputes between their creditors (bondholders) and their debtors (taxpayers). In seeking to tax their neighbors with a heavy hand, investors in government securities received support from policy professionals—men like George Grenville in the 1760s and Alexander Hamilton, Robert Morris, and James Madison in the 1780s—who were motivated less by personal financial interest than by their determination to rein in the national debt.

The Declaration of Independence culminated a decade of tax battles arising out of the Seven Years' War and the Constitution found its genesis in debates about the debts that the state and national governments had amassed during their seven-year War of Independence. Thus both documents reflected, above all, the transforming hand of war.[54]

CHAPTER 35

An Unseen Enemy

1788–1793

JAMES MADISON HAD WRITTEN THE ROUGH DRAFT OF THE CONSTI-
tution, and the final document powerfully influenced Madison in turn.
Hardly anyone in the Piedmont Virginia congressional district that he
wished to represent had any desire to pay new federal taxes for the benefit of bond speculators. Partly by virtue of his about-face on the Bill of
Rights, Madison got elected to the First Congress, but as he prepared to
face the voters again in 1790, his attitude toward government securities
necessarily evolved. He proposed to compel the current owners of the
bonds to share the government's bounty, on a 50/50 basis, with the soldiers and suppliers to whom they had originally been disbursed. Conceived as a matter of simple justice to the people who had wrought the
victory over Britain, Madison's plan would also leave cash in the hands
of ordinary families dispersed across the countryside, fueling economic
development from below.[1]

On February 22, 1790, when the House of Representatives voted on
Madison's proposal, the throngs packing the gallery included the vice
president's wife. It seems clear that Abigail Adams chose this day for
her first and only recorded visit to Congress because her portfolio of
government securities would lose half its value if Madison's amendment
passed. But it failed, 36 to 13. That vote set the stage for the representatives' August 4 decision to fund not only the federal bonds but most of
the war debt still owed by the thirteen states. Altogether, the federal and
state debts added up to an enormous $65 million. But in the end Con-
gress was able to amass most of the necessary revenue by selling Indian
land and taxing merchandise coming in from overseas. With the thirteen
state legislatures no longer having to levy taxes on behalf of Congress,
and with the federal government assuming most of the state debts, the

states were able to reduce their onerous taxes by as much as 90 percent. The one exception to the rosy fiscal picture was that servicing the state debts required Congress to impose a special tax on distilled spirits, including whiskey.[2]

THE BONDHOLDERS' SUCCESS IN the halls of Congress raises the question of just how radical the revolution had turned out to be. Several states reformed inheritance law, abolishing primogeniture (whereby all of the land of decedents who left no wills had gone to their firstborn sons) and entail (which allowed a testator to will his property to his firstborn son, then *his* firstborn son, and so on forever). In a handful of state legislatures, the upper house ceased to be an elite bastion. And several states, including Madison's Virginia, disestablished their official churches.[3]

But other democratic reforms came with asterisks. In 1790, the percentage of freemen who could vote was much higher in North America than in Great Britain—but that had been the case in 1760 as well.[4] After independence as before, ordinary farmers and artisans were severely underrepresented in the assemblies. Most of the states reenacted their colonial legal codes, making only piecemeal amendments. The Revolution wrought even fewer changes at the local level. New England towns retained their highly democratic town meetings, but nearly everywhere else local power remained in the hands of county oligarchs who never had to face the voters.[5] Historians once depicted the departure of seventy thousand Loyalists as removing a significant portion of North America's colonial aristocracy. Something like that happened in New York; although the state's new leaders were nearly as wealthy as their colonial forebears, they forged lasting alliances with farmers and artisans. Overall, though, the Loyalists were so diverse, ethnically as well as economically, that the permanent exile of thousands of them (others left but returned) contributed little if anything to democratization.[6]

During the decade between the adoption of the Declaration of Independence in 1776 and the Constitution in 1787, the thirteen former colonies were significantly more democratic than the colonies they replaced, largely because most power resided in the assemblies, which had to face broad electorates every year.[7] But much of the impact of the American Revolution was blunted when, under the Constitution, a less responsive federal regime took over what were arguably the two most important powers that governments exercise in peacetime: levying taxes to pay off war debt and regulating the money supply.

Several state governments also reversed their earlier strides toward democratization. Eleven days after Congress adopted the Declaration in the assembly room of the Pennsylvania statehouse, delegates from every county in Pennsylvania gathered in the courtroom across the hall to begin drafting what would be hailed throughout the Atlantic world as the most democratic written constitution on earth. On September 28, 1776, when the framers presented their handiwork, some Pennsylvanians, including Hermon Husband, complained that they had not gone far enough.[8] But other Americans denounced Pennsylvania's new constitution, with its single-house legislature and no governor, as well as the similar regime that Georgians adopted the following year, as far too responsive to the whims of ordinary voters. A decade later, when the states ratified an undemocratic federal government, the enemies of the Pennsylvania and Georgia constitutions resolved to effect similar changes at home.

In May 1789, Georgia's antidemocrats secured the adoption of a new constitution requiring laws emerging from the lower house of assembly to run two additional gauntlets: a senate and governor. But when newspapers in Carlisle and Philadelphia printed an essay demanding that Pennsylvania make the same two changes, the octogenarian Benjamin Franklin, who helped draft the 1776 document, wrote a point-by-point reply. Drawing upon his Seven Years' War experience, which had begun with providing carts to Gen. Braddock, Franklin recalled how squabbles between colonial Pennsylvania's assembly and council had impeded "the Defence of the Province during several Years, when distressed by an Indian War." In response to his adversaries' demand for an upper house of the legislature to represent property—under John Adams's Massachusetts constitution, senators had to own at least £300 worth of land or £600 worth of personal property—Franklin pointed out that the government already favored the wealthy by protecting their outsized property holdings. Back in 1783, the well-to-do Franklin had responded to farmers' complaints about excessive taxation with the explosive claim that everything inessential to human survival was actually "the Property of the Publick." He now used the same radical notion—that "private Property . . . is a Creature of Society"—to reject the gentry's demand for its own branch of the legislature.[9]

In the end Franklin decided not to publish his defense of the 1776 constitution. Instead this former slaveholder's last major publication was a forthright denunciation of American slavery, thinly veiled as a salute to the North African pirates who captured and enslaved white Christians. Franklin died on April 17, 1790. Among the numerous innovative provisions in his will was a £2,000 endowment, to be loaned out to artisans, with the interest compounded for a century and then devoted to public works in his two hometowns, Boston and Philadelphia. In 1908, Boston used its endowment to establish an industrial school that still thrives today: the Benjamin Franklin Institute of Technology.[10]

Franklin's 1776 Pennsylvania constitution outlived him by only four months. The 1790 replacement insulated members of the newly created state senate from voters with outsized election districts and staggered four-year terms.[11] In other states, too, many of the American Revolution's most significant reforms—including the all-important annual election of legislators—also proved to be the most fragile.

In several crucial arenas, the Revolution left ordinary Americans with less power than before. Even after approving the Currency Acts of 1751 and 1764, Parliament allowed the thirteen assemblies to print paper money, so long as they gave creditors the option of refusing it. But after 1788 only Congress could issue currency, and it did not do so until the Civil War. Other losses were less obvious. Even colonial conservatives such as Massachusetts governor Thomas Hutchinson had acknowledged that among farmers, tenants, and artisans—in short, everyone but slaves—"Mobs, a sort of them at least, are constitutional." But with the formal advent of republican government, many Americans denied that rebellion could ever be justified. Massachusetts resident William Manning was sympathetic to the aims of Shays's Rebellion but decried "the madness and folly of rising up against a government of our own choice."[12]

Connecticut assemblyman Zephaniah Swift believed the Constitution had disempowered ordinary voters in an especially sinister way: without seeming to. His 1792 pamphlet claimed that large congressional districts were "calculated to induce the freemen to imagine themselves at liberty, while they are thus destined to be allured or driven round as if impounded, being at the same time told that nothing confines them, although they have not the powers of escape."[13] In short, the Constitution was an invisible fence, and even white men made few strides toward democratization before the age of Jackson.

THE CAMPAIGN TO HOLD the infant country to its professed ideals attracted a small but strong band of women, many of whom found or

created surprisingly opportunities to spread the word. In the optimistic aftermath of the Revolutionary War, entrepreneurs in every state
founded newspapers, while a handful of others started magazines, and
nearly all sought to attract female as well as male readers with provocative commentary by authors of both genders. Copy-hungry periodicals
even published a handful of explicitly feminist essays. In October 1784,
Judith Sargent Murray of Gloucester, Massachusetts, took to the pages
of the *Gentleman and Lady's Town and Country Magazine* to warn
that most mothers as well as fathers overdid their efforts to check their
daughters' pride, leaving them with "a low estimation of self." She urged
parents to allow all of their children to develop "a reverence of self."[14]
Six years later, Murray anonymously published a magazine article entitled "On the Equality of the Sexes." Drawing upon her Universalist
faith, which posited a stark separation between body and mind, she insisted that the soul has no gender. Male and female infants possess the
same intelligence, but starting around the age of two, boys' potential
was developed, while girls' was stifled or allowed to languish. In 1792,
an anonymous essayist in the recently launched *Lady's Magazine* lodged
her own bold complaint. "I object to the word 'obey' in the marriage-
service," she wrote.[15]

The postwar era also saw a boom in "female academies." The founders typically sought to inculcate feminine virtues, but the students often
learned much more. In May 1793, Priscilla Mason, one of only four
graduates of the Philadelphia Young Ladies Academy, shocked a commencement audience of men as well as women by defending women's
right to develop their talents—a point she emphasized by using the word
exercise five times in her short speech. Both Mason and Murray bravely
traced patriarchy to its biblical foundations. And like Abigail Adams in
her "Remember the Ladies" letter, both leavened their complaints with
humor, poking fun not only at misogynist male writers (Mason called the
Apostle Paul a "Contemptible little body") but at common stereotypes
about women, including their supposed addiction to gossip and fashion,
with Mason wryly proposing that Congress revive the Roman emperor
Heliogabalus's "senate of women" to regulate dress. Both sarcastically
called men "lords" and complained of their having (in Mason's words)
"denied us the means of knowledge, and then reproached us for the want
of it."[16]

Despite shining exceptions such as Mason, Murray, and Adams, the
Revolution did little for the great mass of American women. Several

states, especially in New England, made it easier for women as well as men to obtain divorces, but only a few wives benefited. Outside New Jersey, no women could vote, and none could serve on juries. And in continuing to follow English common law, including the principle of coverture, all thirteen states denied married women's right to own personal property. Moreover, postwar glimmerings of female activism—and, far less commonly, feminism—provoked a backlash as disproportionate as whites' standard response to rumored slave revolts.[17]

In 1782, Abigail Adams's pessimism about men's capacity for change, coupled with her confidence in herself, drove her to an extraordinary decision: she began defying coverture by setting aside some of the money she had earned for her husband and claiming it as her own. By 1816, when she wrote her will (something married women were not supposed to do), she had amassed $5,000—equivalent to about $100,000 in modern currency. Adams left everything—from furniture and gowns to canal stocks and cash—to her nieces, granddaughters, and female servants. Like her, many of these women were married and thus not permitted to own and control property. And that may actually have been Adams's point: to give her heirs the wherewithal to carry her rebellion against coverture into the next generation.[18]

Recall that John Adams had laughed at his wife's March 31, 1776, "Remember the Ladies" letter. After she died on October 28, 1818, he would have been well within his rights in throwing her will into the fire. Instead he carried it out to the letter, giving it legal sanction—and proving that she had made at least one male convert.[19]

Nothing better embodied the Revolution's ambiguous impact on women than the concept of the "republican woman." On the one hand, the transition to formal republican government accorded public value to mothers and wives as men's preceptors in civic virtue. It also justified giving future mothers a modicum of formal education. On the other hand, republican womanhood paved the way for the nineteenth-century cult of domesticity.[20] But it appears that the Revolutionary War influenced women less as a revolution than as a war. In addition to depriving thousands of their partners, it devastated the economy and spread disease. Bear in mind that bullets and bayonets claimed the lives of about 7,000 Continental soldiers and Whig militiamen—fewer Americans than would perish at Gettysburg. Of the roughly 35,000 Whig soldiers who died during the American War of Independence, approximately 28,000 succumbed to infectious diseases. Even the most heavily fortified army camps had porous boundaries, with male and female farmers (to cite just one example) constantly arriving to sell their produce. Moreover, the vast majority of the roughly 200,000 men who fought in the war returned to their communities after short stints, and even those serving for the duration of the war occasionally obtained furloughs. Total female fatalities resulting from the war have never been compiled but appear to have approached the estimated 35,000 deaths among men. In sum, independence appears to have brought free women more pain than progress.

The impact of the American Revolution on later generations of women was equally ambiguous. The most important benefits were indirect in the extreme. Louis XVI's intervention in the American War of Independence bankrupted him, bringing on the French Revolution and, with it, a radical new form of feminism that eventually blew back to North America, with the single most important vehicle being the English radical Mary Wollstonecraft's *Vindication of the Rights of Woman* (1792). Then in the nineteenth century, the United States acquired considerable territory from France, Spain, and Mexico, where the prevailing civil law allowed married women to own property — as it would continue to, to varying degrees, even after Florida, Louisiana, Texas, New Mexico, and California became American states. This injection of civil law into the American legal system in turn provided inspiration to women fighting coverture in the older states. Still, in 1839, when the common law states began recognizing married women's right to own and control property, their primary purpose was to shield farmers', especially cotton growers', belongings, especially their slaves, from their creditors. The authors of those early statutes were trying to counter the clauses of the Constitution that prevented them from safeguarding debtors' property in more direct ways.[21]

The later marital property laws, which pushed on toward genuine equality between husbands and wives, were the fruits of female activism, and that raises the question of what the American Revolution did for, or to, nineteenth-century women who sought the vote and other rights. Most nineteenth-century freemen were as unlikely to act on the Founders' libertarian ideals as the Founders themselves, but they universally revered revolutionary rhetoric, which thus became immensely useful to women's rights activists. Elizabeth Cady Stanton modeled her 1848 Seneca Falls "Declaration of Sentiments" on the Declaration of Independence, and her revisions — "We hold these truths to be self-evident: that all men and women are created equal" — carried forward Lemuel

Haynes's dream of shifting the focus of the Declaration of Independence from states' rights to human rights.[22]

The Revolutionary War also provided women's rights activists a different kind of inspiration. For seven years, women had taken over their husbands' farms or even accompanied them to war. They had also materially contributed to the victory and occasionally even challenged their subjugation. In 1848, weeks before the Seneca Falls convention, the historian Elizabeth Ellet ticked off one task after another, from foxhunting to rail-splitting, that had become "unfeminine" only after the Revolution. The contrast between the generations threatened nineteenth-century women with a palpable feeling of inferiority. Ellet described how Esther Wake would ride eighty miles across the North Carolina countryside to visit her sister, the wife of Governor Tryon—and then back home the next day. "What would these women have said to the delicacy of modern refinement in the southern country, fatigued with a moderate drive in a close carriage[?]" Ellet asked. The founding mothers had "disdained not labor with their hands," had not seen even "affluent circumstances [as] an excuse for idleness or extravagance." And nineteenth-century women ought to profit from their example.[23]

Most of Ellet's biographers assume she was still living with her husband in Columbia, South Carolina, between 1845 and 1847, when she researched and wrote *Women of the American Revolution*. But the historian Gretchen F. Schoel used the postmarks on her letters, along with other evidence, to show that Ellet spent most of this time on her own in New York City. So as she wrote admiringly of how Mary Slocumb, like countless other founding era women whose husbands went to war, "took the entire charge of the plantation, being obliged to perform many of the duties which usually fall to the lot of the rougher sex," Ellet herself was living independent of her husband, only by choice.[24]

Yet Ellet and others erred in attributing all of the revolutionary era's female activism to the Revolution. The Battle of Lexington and Concord was still two years in the future when Mary Fish boldly set down her "Portrait of a Good Husband." Even before that, the Great Awakening emboldened Phillis Wheatley to become a poet and abolitionist and Sarah Osborn to stand up to the men trying to shut down her ministry. The evangelical insistence that the individual's communion with God be mediated only by the Bible also appears to have outdone the subsequent political revolution in fomenting literacy among both women and men. With their commitment to biblical literacy, the Awakeners also far surpassed the revolutionaries in extending educational opportunities to African Americans like Wheatley and Native Americans like Samson Occom. Modern-day evangelicalism's enmity toward feminism and the stark divide between today's white and nonwhite evangelicals are both products of the nineteenth century, not the first Great Awakening.

IN DECEMBER 1788, SIX months after Virginia ratified the Constitution, George Clendinen, a militia colonel in the Kentucky district, exulted that the long-running stalemate pitting white westerners like himself against their native neighbors would soon be broken. "The next year will put an end to Indian Hostilities, as the General Government will take the business up," he wrote.[25]

Clendinen got everything right but the timing. In 1790, the new federal taxes enabled Congress to send a military expedition to the head of the Maumee River (modern-day Fort Wayne, Indiana), where Miamis, Delawares, and Shawnees had congregated for mutual defense. The 300 regular U.S. army soldiers and 1,100 militiamen were led by Josiah Harmar, a former Quaker who had risen to the rank of lieutenant colonel during the Revolutionary War. On October 17, 1790, the U.S. troops reached the rebel towns and set about burning twenty thousand bushels of corn. But Harmar unwisely divided his army, and native warriors led by Michikinakoua (a Miami leader known to whites as Little Turtle) used a variety of stratagems to defeat two detachments, killing nearly two hundred. As his remaining troops fled back toward the Ohio River, Harmar urged them to take the long view. Whites and Indians had died "man for man," he noted, "and we can afford them two for one."[26]

This was an understatement. As recently as 1700, five out of every six inhabitants of North America had been Indians. But by 1800, the imbalance would be equally lopsided in the other direction: 5.3 million U.S. residents (of all races) would confront slightly more than a million Native Americans, only about 100,000 of whom lived east of the Mississippi.[27]

U.S. officials planned multiple incursions into Indian country for 1791. Armies commanded by Charles Scott and James Wilkinson managed the rare feat of surprising Indian towns, killing fifty warriors and more than 150 women and children. Arthur St. Clair, governor of the Northwestern Territory, led the largest U.S. force, consisting of about two thousand regulars, nearly five hundred militia, and about two hundred women. President Washington assigned St. Clair the same target as Harmar—the cluster of rebel villages at the head of the Maumee River—but gave him the more ambitious assignment of building a U.S. fort in their midst.[28]

Desertion doomed St. Clair's expedition. The general hanged two recaptured deserters as a warning to others, but on October 31 sixty Kentucky militiamen headed home en masse, and the general sent three hundred of his best regulars to track them down and return them. That plus the need to garrison intermediate posts appears to have left him with as few as 1,700 troops—only a handful more than Harmar had led the previous year. On the evening of November 3, the army camped along the Wabash River at present-day Fort Recovery, Ohio. That night, a native force, about the same size as St. Clair's and led by Blue Jacket (Shawnee) and Little Turtle (Miami), quietly approached.[29]

A half hour before sunrise on November 4, the allied Indians struck. During the ensuing three-hour battle, Lt. Col. William Darke, a veteran of Braddock's 1755 campaign and the commander of St. Clair's left wing, repeatedly led his men in bayonet charges, but each time they were driven back by the natives, who "hid in hazle bushes and in the grass."[30] One critic accused St. Clair of repeating Braddock's error of waiting too long to reconcile himself to the "disgrace" of having to "retreat from an *unseen enemy.*" The Americans had cannon, which in the past had proved effective against native attacks, but they were soon silenced by elite warriors commanded by William Wells, a formerly white Miami captive and subsequent adoptee.[31]

Wells's brother Samuel fought on the American side. He survived, but an estimated 660 Americans (including at least thirty women) were killed: more than double the 268 who would die with George Armstrong Custer at the Little Bighorn in 1876. Others, including a woman named Polly Meadows, were captured. By most estimates, fewer than fifty Indians died. Little Turtle's and Blue Jacket's warriors pursued St. Clair's troops about four miles back down the path, then returned to the battlefield to harvest the plunder—and to stuff some of the fallen U.S. soldiers' mouths with the soil for which they had traded their lives. During the next year's Green Corn Ceremony, an Upper Wabash River elder would declare that the First Nations' "late victories over the whites, particularly their signal defeat of St. Clair, were evidences of the returning favor of the Great Spirit."[32]

On the evening of November 4, the first U.S. survivors of "St. Clair's Shame" reached Fort Jefferson, a fallback post thirty miles to the south. An eyewitness claimed that one man staggered in with two tomahawks sticking out of his head. "Braddock's defeat & Harmer's expedition is not to be compared to this," another survivor wrote.[33]

The same December 22 issue of Boston's *Independent Chronicle* that carried multiple accounts of St. Clair's defeat also featured an essay questioning whether the conquest of Indian land was worth the cost. "The blood of our countrymen is too precious, to moisten the soil of the wilderness," the anonymous author declared. Reprinted in newspapers all over the country, this anonymous piece was signed "Braddock." Others made the comparison to the Battle of the Monongahela even more explicit. Meanwhile Hermon Husband, the frontier economist, democrat, and prophet, drew up a plan for restricting the nation's westward expansion in order to keep peace with the Indians. He appears never to have found a publisher.[34]

South of the Ohio River, the battle between Native Americans and the U.S. citizens who coveted their land was complicated by a dispute between the federal government and Georgia over who got to set Indian policy. When Georgia leaders persuaded a small number of Muskogee headmen to add their marks to documents giving the state all of the land east of the Oconee River, the other Muskogees renounced the cession, and so did the Washington administration. On August 7, 1790, Muskogee leaders and Secretary of War Henry Knox signed the Treaty of New York, the first treaty ratified by the U.S. Senate. White Georgians were disappointed at not obtaining "the best winter hunting grounds of the lower Creeks" (Muskogees), but they did get the Oconee River boundary. Knox had procured the consent of the most prominent Muskogee leader, Alexander McGillivray, son of a British army officer and Muskogee matron,

John Trumbull, Muskogee leader Hopothle-Mico (1790)

by adding two secret articles to the treaty. One allowed the Muskogees to import European merchandise by way of the United States duty-free and gave McGillivray a monopoly of this trade. The other made him a brigadier general in the U.S. Army at $1,200 a year.[35]

After signing the public portion of the treaty, the Muskogee delegates, who were staying at an inn called the Indian Queen, "had a great Bond fire dancing round it like so many spirits hooping, singing, yelling, and expressing their pleasure and Satisfaction in the true Savage Stile," as their temporary neighbor Abigail Adams reported.[36]

The Muskogee nation repudiated the Treaty of New York, but its significance lay in Congress's having assumed responsibility for dispossessing the southern Indians. The implications would be massive, not only for whites and Native Americans but for the African Americans who would be forced west from the eastern seaboard. In the nineteenth century, Thomas Dew, a pro-slavery professor at William and Mary, would call Virginia "a *negro* raising state for other states" farther south and west. Most of the more than one million slaves relocated from the upper south to the freshly conquered territories never saw their families again.[37]

THE 1790 TREATY OF New York was thus a significant if overlooked episode in African American history. Two others took place outside the United States. In August 1791, slaves in the French sugar colony of Saint-Domingue launched the insurgency that became known as the Haitian Revolution: the world's first successful slave revolt. North Americans had indirectly and inadvertently contributed to this outcome: the Haitian Revolution was made possible by the disorder of the French Revolution, which was partly the result of the massive debt Louis XVI incurred in the American War of Independence. The Haitian Revolution would in turn massively influence U.S. politics and the lives of African Americans well into the nineteenth century.

More than three thousand African Americans who earned their emancipation by fighting for their king chose to settle after the war in Nova Scotia. But they were not yet fully free. Few obtained the farmland they had been promised. Abuse by white Loyalists who had also settled in Nova Scotia culminated in a 1784 riot, in which whites pulled down the homes of David George and other Black refugees. Loyalists were permitted to bring their slaves with them to Nova Scotia, and several of them falsely claimed ownership of African Americans who had actually freed themselves by escaping Whig owners. For example, Mary (or Molly, as her purported owner, Loyalist Jesse Gray, called her) Postell had fled to Charles Town, South Carolina, where she helped construct the British fortifications. After the war, she moved first to St. Augustine and then, in 1786, to Nova Scotia. When Gray, a fellow South Carolinian and a survivor of the Battle of Kings Mountain, asserted ownership of her, she fled. Gray took her to court and brought in white witnesses to corroborate his claim and ultimately prevailed. In about 1790, a Scottish trader purchased Postell's ten-year-old daughter from Gray and returned her to Carolina to be sold back to the slave labor camps. In an attempt to save her remaining daughter, Postell sued Gray, and a Black man named Scipio Wearing testified on her behalf. As he did, his house was set ablaze, apparently by whites seeking to intimidate him, and he, too, lost a child.[38]

Cheated and abused, the Black Empire Loyalists (as Canadians now call them) appealed to Parliament for permission to resettle elsewhere. In February 1790, a group of British abolitionists, investors, and armchair missionaries decided to establish a new, mostly Black, commercial outpost in Sierra Leone on the West African coast. News of the Sierra Leone venture reached Black Nova Scotians, who sent one of their own, the former millwright and British army sergeant Thomas Peters, to London with their offer to migrate once again. Soon Peters was back home recruiting for an exodus. Having been ruled slaves, Mary Postell and her daughter could not embark. But entire congregations, especially Methodists, decided to emigrate en masse.[39]

On January 15, 1792, fifteen vessels carrying 1,200 Black refugees cleared out of Halifax Harbor and set sail for Sierra Leone. The migrants waded ashore in mid-March, many singing a Methodist hymn:

The day of Jubilee is come!
Return ye, ransomed sinners, home.[40]

A handful of the Sierra Leone settlers found work in West Africa's ubiquitous slave trade. Others were captured by local traders and sold back out into the Atlantic. A few who had been born near Sierra Leone managed to complete the Atlantic circuit, reappearing among their loved ones as if from the dead. But the vast majority knew nothing of the place or people and might just as well have landed in Australia. (Indeed, at about this time, many former American slaves, having joined the London poor and committed petty crimes, were shipped along with whites to what was then called New South Wales.)[41]

As in Nova Scotia, African American refugees had scarcely reached Sierra Leone when white authorities began breaking their promises. Back in Nova Scotia, British officials had assured prospective Sierra Leone settlers they would not have to pay taxes, but they were soon assessed two shillings an acre—a hundred times higher than the land tax they had resisted in Nova Scotia. Starting in 1793, the settlers, most of whom were religious dissenters, were compelled to attend Anglican service twice every day. Three years later, Gov. Zachary Macaulay prohibited dissenting ministers from marrying their parishioners. But the settlers were angriest at once again, as in Nova Scotia, not receiving their promised land. Before leaving Halifax, each couple had received a certificate for thirty acres of farmland (plus five more for each of their children). But the British had bought land for the Sierra Leone colony from the Temne ruler Naimbana, who later acknowledged that he had no right to sell it. After the Nova Scotians (as they often called themselves) arrived, the government reduced the size of the colony by 80 percent, proportionately shrinking each family's farm. And provincial officials were so slow to survey even these tiny plots that settlers missed their first two growing seasons.[42]

The colonists resisted these insults and abuses and demanded representative government. Some simply seceded from Sierra Leone and obtained their own land grants from local rulers. Like their counterparts in North America in the 1760s and 1770s, British colonial officials blamed the rebellion on evangelical Christians—but also, incongruously, on the egalitarian ideas emanating from the French Revolution. Macaulay claimed the Methodist Church in Sierra Leone had become "a kind of Jacobin club."[43]

In June 1794, a visiting slave ship captain taunted two free Black porters, "saying in what manner he would use them if he had them in the West Indies." A riot ensued, and Governor Macaulay arrested eight Black men—including Ralph Henry, who by Virginia law still belonged to the man known for saying, "Give me liberty, or give me death"—and sent them to London for trial.[44] Five years later, in 1799, defiant Black settlers established an extralegal government resembling the conventions and congresses that had briefly ruled Britain's rebel colonies in North America. White officials suppressed this nonviolent revolt with help from a new cohort of African American settlers: five hundred Jamaican Maroons who had made peace with the British only to be driven from the island. Maroons in government service killed two of the Sierra Leone insurgents, and two others were hanged.[45]

On October 10, 1800, three days after authorities back in Virginia executed the slave rebel Gabriel, a court-martial in Sierra Leone banished dozens of participants in the self-government campaign. Among the exiles was a prosperous farmer named Harry Washington. In the fateful year 1776, Washington had absconded from the American commander-in-chief, at some point adopting his last name. Now, a quarter of a century later, the approximately sixty-year-old Washington's fondness for freedom had once again sent him out into the unknown. Sierra Leone officials eventually gave up on taxing the colonists.[46]

ONE OF THE MOST striking features of the post-revolutionary United States was the emergence of a significant free African American population, especially in the north and upper south. Free Blacks experienced continuing oppression, but many proved more than equal to the challenge. Born free in New York and then born again in Charles Town, South Carolina, under the guidance of George Whitefield, John Marrant had been impressed onto a British warship, where he served throughout the Revolutionary War. Afterward the Countess of Huntingdon (who had financed Phillis Wheatley's *Poems on Various Subjects* in 1773) appointed him as one of her ministers, and he later headed back to America to preach, primarily to Blacks but also to whites and Native Americans. In June 1789, shortly after joining Boston's Black Masons, Marrant presented a sermon to the African Lodge. Most whites saw Blacks as "a species below them, and as not made of the same clay with themselves," he noted, but "Ancient history will produce some of the Africans who were truly good, wise, and learned men, and as eloquent as any other nation whatever." Marrant's roster of eminent Africans, which included such church fathers as Cyprian, Tertullian, and Augustine, called to mind Esther Reed's honor roll of queens who had expanded the empire of liberty.[47]

On November 9, 1785, Lemuel Haynes, whose 1776 essay, "Liberty Further Extended," had begun the process of altering the meaning of the Declaration of Independence, became a Congregationalist (Puritan) minister—and the first African American to be ordained by a mainstream Protestant denomination. In 1789, a conservative flock in Rutland, Vermont, chose Haynes as their pastor, and he held the post for the next thirty years. Paul Cuffe, who in 1780 had spent time in prison for refusing to pay taxes to a government in which he was not represented, married a Native American (as his father and sister had) and grew wealthy as a shipbuilder and overseas merchant. Early in the nineteenth century, Cuffe and an all-Black crew would transport thirty-eight free African Americans to Sierra Leone. Had his wife been willing, Cuffe said, he would have emigrated, too.[48]

Free Blacks living south of New England also fought subjugation and the prejudice that justified it. Early in 1791, freeborn Benjamin Banneker, a self-trained mathematician and astronomer from Maryland, traveled to the Potomac River to assist in surveying the new Federal District (Washington, D.C.). Returning home in April, he composed an almanac predicting the following year's celestial events and sent a copy to Thomas Jefferson, Washington's secretary of state and a celebrated man of science. The cover letter gave no indication that Banneker had read what Jefferson had written about Blacks in *Notes on the State of Virginia*, but one indication that he might have was that his only specific request was for Jefferson and other whites to "wean yourselves from these narrow prejudices which you have imbibed" against Blacks. Jefferson replied politely to Banneker but shared with a French friend the suspicion that he had not actually performed the calculations for which he claimed credit.[49] For his part, Banneker kept publishing almanacs.

Richard Allen was a Pennsylvania-born slave who converted to the Methodist faith. After purchasing his freedom, he made his living as a woodcutter, wagoner, shoemaker, and bricklayer but also became an itinerant preacher, exhorting Native Americans and whites as well as Blacks. One day in 1792, Allen and his friend Absalom Jones were worshipping at the mostly white St. George's Methodist Church when Jones was ordered, mid-prayer, to move to the seats designated for Blacks. He finished the prayer and then led Allen and the other Black parishioners in a walkout. Construction of Jones's "African Church of Philadelphia" began the following year, and Allen would later found the African Methodist Episcopal (AME) Church, today one of the largest denominations in the United States. Blacks in other states also formed African churches, at once proclaiming pride in a background that whites had scorned and dissolving the last vestiges of the hostility that had sometimes subsisted between families from different regions of Africa.[50]

In the summer of 1793, a yellow fever epidemic struck Philadelphia, killing more than four thousand. Africans were widely believed to be immune to the disease, and as an estimated twenty thousand whites fled the city, Allen and Jones recruited numerous Blacks to remain behind to serve as nurses and gravediggers. Africans' immunity to yellow fever turned out to have been exaggerated, and they died at nearly the same rate as their patients. But that did not stop newspaper editor Mathew Carey, who had fled the city, from falsely accusing the Black nurses of overcharging and even robbing their patients.[51]

Despite the achievements of African Americans like Haynes, Cuffe, Jones, and Allen, the American Revolution cannot be described as a net contributor to Black freedom. Parliament freed Britain's slaves in a two-step process in 1832 and 1837—three decades before the ratification of the Thirteenth Amendment in December 1865 abolished slavery in the United States.[52]

THE OVERALL IMPACT OF the American Revolution can never be objectively assessed, but the attempt is worth making. Ordinary freemen achieved modest gains, but many of these were erased by the adoption of the Constitution. Free women saw little change. Native Americans had participated actively both in the struggles that led the Whigs to declare independence and in the subsequent war, but they also became the war's worst victims. Thousands of African Americans obtained their freedom, but tens of thousands remained in slavery. And war-churned disease devastated every segment of the population. It seems clear that for the founding generation, the American Revolution produced more misery than freedom.

It nonetheless mattered that most free Americans *thought* the Revolution had sparked a radical transformation and *believed* themselves—and not, say, Eastern Woodlands Indians—the "freest people on the face of the earth."[53] The Great Seal of the United States, which would eventually appear on the dollar bill, proclaimed the new nation a "*Novus ordo seclorum*"—a "new order of the ages." Here was the real American exceptionalism: a vast gap between theory and reality, but one that has almost always seemed bridgeable. Many Americans brandish the Declaration as a trophy, but it owes its continuing relevance to those who take it as a challenge.

CHAPTER 36

Back to Braddock's Field

1794–1795

O NE OF THE REASONS IT IS SO DIFFICULT TO ASSESS THE IMPACT OF the Revolutionary War is that less than a decade after it ended, Americans began to feel the effects of another revolution, in France. Initially most U.S. citizens cheered for the French revolutionaries, who seemed so much like themselves, but by 1793 the French Revolution had divided Americans into parties. Many in the United States were horrified by the Terror, but others supported the French more enthusiastically than ever, because 1793 was also the year France went to war against Britain. Numerous Amercans, especially southerners, believed that the United States had a treaty obligation to help France—and ought to do so anyway, since the infant republic still needed French help to check the British. In the spring of 1794, a decade after the Revolutionary War, many Americans predicted that they would soon be back at war against the former mother country. They cited numerous provocations. For example, in November 1793, as Britain prepared to invade Saint-Domingue, the largest French colony in the Caribbean, the Privy Council adopted a secret order in council requiring Royal Navy captains to seize all vessels trading with the enemy, including dozens flying the American flag. Then Lord Dorchester, the former Guy Carleton, who had once again become governor of Canada, informed a visiting Indian delegation of a possible Anglo-American war, and Dorchester's warning found its way into numerous U.S. newspapers.[1]

President Washington tried to resolve the dispute peacefully, obtaining the Senate's consent to send Chief Justice John Jay to London to see about negotiating a treaty. Jay sailed on May 12.[2]

*   *   *

EVEN AS U.S. CITIZENS faced the prospect of renewed war against Britain, new internal disputes also erupted. At the urging of Washington and Treasury Secretary Hamilton, Congress took over $20 million worth of state obligations lingering from the Revolutionary War. To fund this new debt, the representatives increased the tariff on imported liquor and, for the first time, levied a tax on spirits distilled in the United States. Americans living west of the mountains did not have the option of cheaply transporting their produce to eastern markets by water, so they had to use carts. Since flour could rarely bear this expense, farmers instead distilled their rye into whiskey, which could. Whiskey also served as a medium of exchange in western regions suffering from a chronic shortage of circulating coin; for example, farmers used it to recruit additional hands at harvesttime. Now all of this hard liquor would have to pay a hard-money tax that would consume as much as 25 percent of farmers' profit. For all these reasons, the men sent west to collect the new levy met with stiff resistance. Dressed sometimes as women but more often as Indians, frontiersmen destroyed the collectors' property, cut off their hair, and tarred and feathered them.[3]

Nor was the whiskey excise the frontier rebels' sole grievance. Many were angry at Congress's August 4, 1790, Funding Act, providing enormous windfalls to the securities speculators who had bought up the war bonds at a fraction of their face value—and nothing to the veterans to whom the bonds had initially been disbursed. In addition, white westerners thought state as well as federal officials were overpaid, that courts hit litigants with excessive fees, that Pennsylvania favored absentee real estate speculators over actual settlers, and that the federal government was doing too little to protect whites encroaching on Indian land.[4]

But westerners' paramount grievance was the federal excise, and by early 1794, Washington had decided that the only way to force them to pay it was to make examples. Farmers in four states and the Northwest Territory had resisted the new tax, but the president decided to target western Pennsylvania. One reason was its relative proximity to Philadelphia, which, with more than fifty thousand souls, was the nation's single largest reservoir of potential soldiers. Moreover, by rebelling in the state that hosted Congress, the Pennsylvanians seemed to pose a special threat to its authority. Most of all, they had far exceeded all other opponents of the excise in their level of organization.[5]

Washington appointed John Neville, a veteran of the Battle of the Monongahela and initial critic of the excise, as the top federal tax collector for western Pennsylvania. In July 1794, Neville and federal marshal David Lenox delivered summonses to more than sixty farmers who had refused to register their stills. Then on July 15, thirty to forty locals accosted the pair. One man allegedly fired a round at them, and they barely escaped.[6] By coincidence, local militia officers had mustered their men that very day to choose some to join in the U.S. Army's planned attack against the western Indians. Jettisoning that objective, as many as a hundred militiamen and other tax resisters besieged Neville's mansion, Bower Hill, that night. The next morning, Neville fired out a window, killing one rebel. Then "a horn blowed" inside the house, and, as one insurgent reported, Neville's "negroes fired on our rear [and] wounded several of our people," putting the rebels to flight. Neville had armed slaves for the same reason the British had during the Revolutionary War: sheer desperation. The insurgents returned the next afternoon, July 17, now more than five hundred strong. This time Neville escaped into the woods, federal troops occupying the house killed at least two more insurgents, and only an appeal from the slaves prevented the rebels from burning his house and their cabins.[7]

During the Revolutionary War, when Gen. Washington encountered strategic threats, his first instinct had always been to go on the offensive, for instance by storming British strongholds in Boston, Philadelphia, and New York City. Yet his impetuosity had nearly always given way to prudence. Following that same pattern in his reaction to the Battle of Bower Hill, Washington initially harkened to Hamilton's call to immediately raise an army. But after encountering resistance from an old nemesis, Thomas Mifflin, who had become governor of Pennsylvania, the president took a more measured approach, sending a commission rather than an army to western Pennsylvania. He did not actually expect the conflict to be resolved peacefully, though. As Attorney General William Bradford observed, the commissioners' real purpose was to pave the way for the troops who were sure to follow by swinging "the weight of the public opinion" in their favor.[8]

Meanwhile leaders of the insurrection invited westerners to assemble on August 1, then seize guns and ammunition from Fort Lafayette (which had replaced Fort Pitt), and march into nearby Pittsburgh. Two days before the meeting, the organizers canceled it, claiming to have learned that the weapons in the fort were destined for a purpose no white westerner could oppose: killing Indians. But in defiance of their leaders, the tax resisters went ahead and assembled, five to nine thousand strong, on an open hillside eight miles east of Pittsburgh, the site thirty-nine years earlier of the Battle of the Monongahela. Now known as Braddock's Field, it once again became the locus of western resistance.[9] The next day, August 2, the protesters marched through Pittsburgh, thoroughly intimidating the populace.

By the time President Washington learned of the rebels' march, he had already decided to send an army against them. On August 7, he called up thirteen thousand militia. Many rural draftees refused to serve, but recruiters found all the manpower they needed in Philadelphia and other cities. The army was commanded by Virginia governor Henry Lee, the former Continental Army cavalry officer and future father of Robert E. Lee (who in October 1859 would also head west to put down a rebellion—at Harpers Ferry—only to take command of his own rebels two years later). President Washington accompanied the troops as far west as Cumberland, Maryland, which the Maryland and Virginia divisions used as a staging area, just as Braddock had. Hamilton rode with the troops all the way to Pittsburgh. That made a peculiar kind of sense, since he had taken the lead in convincing Congress first to assume the states' war debts and then to fund assumption with an excise on distilled spirits. Another of Hamilton's creations, the Bank of the United States, had already stirred the suspicions of westerners before lending Washington the money he needed to enlist, pay, and equip the soldiers. The bank's ability to finance an undertaking of this scope stood in sharp contrast to the Confederation Congress's failure to raise sufficient funds to field troops against Shays's Rebellion eight years earlier. Here was the first compelling evidence that the U.S. Constitution was going to succeed at ensuring domestic tranquility.[10]

As the federal government's chief tax collector, Hamilton had a special interest in suppressing its first major tax revolt. So it is fitting that he is credited with coining the term Whiskey Rebellion, which thereby joined Pontiac's Rebellion and Shays's Rebellion in receiving its derisive moniker from the people who put it down.[11]

NORMALLY A MILITIA ARMY of this magnitude would have been led by regular soldiers, but Washington had few at his disposal, because he and Congress had decided to try once again to defeat the rebel Indian confederacy in what is now the Midwest. This time the commander would be Anthony Wayne, the hero of the Battle of Stony Point in 1779 and a principal target of the mutiny of the Pennsylvania Line in 1781. Secretary of War Henry Knox understood, as he and other generals had during the Revolutionary War, that an army's image was everything; he warned that another loss to the natives would be "inexpressibly ruinous to the reputation of the government." As Treasury Secretary Hamilton remade the American financial system in the British image, Congress was able to reduce its reliance on the militiamen who were largely blamed, at least in Philadelphia, for Harmar's and St. Clair's failures. Congress created a brand-new force called the Legion of the United States and staffed it with five thousand regulars—fifteen times the number Harmar had led.[12] Then Wayne took more than two years to recruit troops, train them in forest maneuvers, and build a chain of forts along their route.[13] Thirty years earlier, when Parliament made peace with France but decided to leave an army in Indian country, British colonists were furious, especially after learning that they were expected to foot the bill. But the purpose of Wayne's forts would not be to impede but to facilitate white encroachment.

U.S. officials also laid additional groundwork. They took the extraordinary step of returning some of the land they had taken from the Six Nations of the Iroquois ten years earlier at Fort Stanwix—in return for the Iroquois forfeiting their claim to the Ohio Valley and thus their membership in the rebel coalition.[14] Some U.S. citizens had begun to raise humanitarian objections to the Indian wars, and many more worried about the human and financial cost to their own country. So about the same time the Washington administration made a show of seeking to reach a negotiated resolution with the whiskey rebels, it also sent commissioners to treat with the Indians. With the United States demanding all or most of the land it claimed to have received from Britain and the native confederacy refusing to allow whites west of the Ohio River, these negotiations were doomed. But at least Knox could state that the United States had tried "to obtain peace by milder terms than the sword."[15]

One of Wayne's most potent assets, and at $1,000 a year one of the most expensive, was his chief scout, William Wells. Captured by the Miamis and adopted and trained as a warrior before returning to the United States in 1792, he had maintained good relations with his Miami father-in-law, the noted war chief Little Turtle. At the site of St. Clair's 1791 defeat, Wells helped Wayne's troops find several cannon barrels that the Indians had buried after their victory. Remounted in a new fort called Fort Recovery, the cannon enabled Wayne's advance troops to repel the

Indians' ill-advised frontal assault of June 30, 1794. Like Wells, most of his scouts had learned First Nations languages and tactics as war captives. About a hundred Choctaws and Chickasaws also served with Wayne, and for once a mostly white army had better intelligence than its native adversaries.[16]

Little Turtle, the architect of the indigenous victories over Harmar and St. Clair, had become convinced that continued resistance was futile, and he abdicated leadership of the Indian army to the Shawnee warrior Blue Jacket. As Wayne's troops inched forward, Canada's governor Dorchester built a new fort on the Maumee River, which flows into Lake Erie from the south. Fort Miami, as it was called, not only provided material support to the rebel Indians but gave them "new confidence" in their previously unreliable ally.[17] The war chiefs resolved to give the Americans battle at the falls of the Maumee, five miles upriver from Fort Miami. They also decided to follow British officials' advice that they form a European-style defensive line. As the Legion of the United States approached on August 20, one of Wayne's officers marveled that the native warriors, "whose great power consists in their invisibility . . . now for the first time within the memory of Man, present themselves a fair object, or Station, to the attack of a superior force."[18]

At least the Indians had chosen the perfect place to make their stand: a forest just east of the Maumee where a windstorm had toppled hundreds of trees, obstructing Wayne's infantry and preventing him from deploying cavalry. But once the U.S. soldiers moved forward in open order, slashing with their bayonets, the thin native line melted away. In the Battle of Fallen Timbers, about thirty of Wayne's men were killed, and about one hundred were injured. Wayne claimed that his enemies' casualties were more than double his own, but British observers stated that as few as thirty of Blue Jacket's warriors had died. Wayne's critics played down the U.S. victory, with one of his officers claiming that it did not even "deserve the name of a Battle." But for Native Americans, thirty to sixty deaths was devastating—and so was the battle's aftermath. As the warriors withdrew northward down the west bank of the Maumee River toward Fort Miami, no one from the garrison came out to assist them. Many of the retreating warriors sought refuge in the fort, but the commandant, Maj. William Campbell, barred the gates.[19]

The U.S. army had finally defeated the Indians, but only on the third try and at a tremendous cost. Harmar's and St. Clair's armies had suffered a combined eight hundred fatalities—about sixteen times the number of Indians killed at Fallen Timbers. All three expeditions had been expensive. Between 1790 and 1796, nearly five-sixths of the United States's operating budget went to killing Indians.[20]

KENTUCKY MILITIAMEN WHO HAD fought under Wayne would have to wait for their share of these federal funds; government officials delayed sending their payroll west across Pennsylvania for fear of its being captured by the whiskey rebels.[21] Less than a month after Fallen Timbers, one hundred of these Kentuckians attacked another native nation, this time in conjunction with 450 white residents of what is now Tennessee.

Dragging Canoe had died in about 1792, and during the summer of 1794, the Chickamaugas (better known, after leaving the creek of that name, as the Five Lower Towns) sent several peace overtures to U.S. officials, but small parties continued to attack white settlements along the Cumberland River in the vicinity of Nashville, and the Chickamaugas still harbored numerous white captives and Black fugitives. In defiance of a stand-down order from President Washington, militia Gen. James Robertson ordered an attack on the Chickamauga towns. Joseph Brown, who years earlier had been captured and adopted by the Chickamaugas, and Richard Findleston, a mixed-race man with a wife and son among the Chickamaugas, led about 550 Kentucky and Tennessee militiamen along secret mountain paths to surprise the town of Nickajack, on the Tennessee River near modern-day Chattanooga. They struck on September 13, killing seventy Indians—more than had died at the better-known Battle of Fallen Timbers the previous month. Many were scalped.[22]

By this time, most of the states had ceded their western claims to Congress, but on January 7, 1795, the Georgia legislature sold 35 million acres to four massive land speculation firms. Collectively the deeds became known as the Yazoo sale, since some extended all the way out to the fertile watershed of the Yazoo River, which empties into the Mississippi at modern-day Vicksburg. When President Washington warned that the Yazoo deeds might provoke a war against Georgia's Spanish and native neighbors, and when it came out that all but one of the state assemblymen who supported the land speculation firms had received shares in them, Georgians elected a new legislature that overturned the sales. Eventually white Americans amended the Constitution in hopes of preventing such massive land frauds. But even as real estate developers battled actual settlers, the two groups cooperated in driving the southern Indians from their land.[23]

Other regions' land speculators also asserted themselves in 1795.
For example, the proprietors of vast tracts of Maine wilderness cracked
down on the farm families squatting on their land. Among their targets
was Continental Army veteran Joseph Plumb Martin, who settled on
land patented to Henry Knox. Unable to make his payments, Martin
saw the size of his spread steadily decline, and by 1818 he had no trouble proving his poverty for a small federal pension. Twelve years later,
he published his *Narrative of Some of the Adventures, Dangers, and
Sufferings of a Revolutionary Soldier*, hoping both to memorialize the
enlisted men's sacrifices and support his family, including a mentally disabled son.[24] Early in 1795, the Whiskey Rebellion sputtered to an anti-
climactic conclusion. None of the insurgents resisted the government's
"super abundant force" (as Secretary of War Knox called it). Only two
men, neither of whom had been accused of violence, were killed, one
in a scuffle and the other apparently by accident. After spending the
first three weeks of November in Pittsburgh, the federal troops headed
back to Philadelphia, leaving only a bare-bones garrison under Daniel
Morgan, who knew the region from his service with Braddock four
decades earlier.[25]

The federals had captured dozens of alleged rebels. Mistreating many
but releasing most within days, they sent only about twenty to Philadelphia for trial. Two were convicted, but President Washington pardoned
both. One insurgent who committed no violence but nonetheless caught
the attention of the president as well as other U.S. officials was Hermon Husband, who had served as the pacifist spokesman for the North
Carolina Regulators more than twenty years earlier and as an advocate
for the oppressed ever since. A party of light horse captured Husband
on October 19, and Washington urged that he be sent under guard to
Philadelphia. The seventy-year-old Husband would spend nearly eight
months in a frigid jail in the capital. In the spring of 1795, when he was
finally tried on a misdemeanor and acquitted, he headed home but died
along the way, apparently of pneumonia.[26]

BETWEEN AUGUST 1794 AND October 1795, the United States negotiated four treaties—in Tennessee, England, Spain, and Ohio—that opened
its way to millions of acres of Indian land. Like the American War of Independence, the treaties were powerfully influenced by ordinary Americans of all complexions.

After U.S. troops wiped out Nickajack, even these most resolute of

Cherokee militants concluded that further resistance was futile. On November 7 and 8, 1794, their representatives met U.S. officials at Tellico Blockhouse in present-day East Tennessee to negotiate peace. The treaty marked the end of Cherokee resistance against U.S. encroachment and was thus a crucial step toward the removal of the southern Indians.[27]

Just eleven days after the Tellico treaty, on November 19, John Jay, chief justice of the Supreme Court, signed a treaty aimed at preventing an Anglo-American war. The British signatory to the Jay Treaty was foreign affairs secretary William Grenville, son of George, whose crackdown on the colonies had helped provoke the American Revolution. The agreement would ensure the continued flow of British merchandise into American ports and thus of the customs revenue that sustained Hamilton's financial system, especially his military buildup and his punctual payments to the government's creditors. It also helped delay the next Anglo-American war (for nearly two decades, as it turned out), giving the United States time to grow in wealth and strength. Britain agreed to compensate the U.S. merchants whose ships it had seized for trading with the French. In addition, American vessels gained partial access to British ports in the Caribbean and Far East. Before long, American tea merchants would compete so effectively against the East India Company that British leaders had to abolish the firm's monopoly of their country's tea market. Had they done that in the 1760s, they might have prevented the American Revolution.[28]

In the Jay Treaty, Britain also promised to evacuate its forts on the southern shores of the Great Lakes and compensate free Americans whose slaves had escaped to the British. Yet white southerners believed these concessions had come at an intolerable cost. State courts, especially in Virginia, had used Britain's refusal to pay for the fugitive slaves and its continued military support for Native Americans, both of which violated the 1783 peace treaty, to justify breaking their own promise to allow British merchants to sue their U.S. debtors. Thus the removal of both U.S. grievances opened America's state courts to British creditors. Moreover, many Americans saw the Jay Treaty as making them Britain's unofficial allies against the French. That not only undermined U.S. sovereignty but betrayed France, which had helped secure U.S. independence and was now fighting to preserve its own republic.[29]

On June 24, 1795, the Senate ratified the Jay Treaty without a single vote to spare: 20 votes to 10. The treaty debate defined national politics for the remainder of the 1790s. A northern-based Federalist party would push for good relations with Britain, while a Jeffersonian Republican party, based primarily in the south but with some strength in northern cities, would favor France.

On August 3, 1795, six weeks after Senate ratification of the Jay Treaty, Anthony Wayne and native leaders representing more than a dozen nations signed the Treaty of Greenville. Under its terms, the Indians held on to most of their villages but gave up their hunting grounds—indeed, most of what is now Ohio. Wayne also obtained twenty smaller, noncontiguous parcels on the Indian side of the new boundary. These included the 150,000 acres along the Ohio River that had been granted to George Rogers Clark and his raiders and the sites of the modern-day cities of Chicago, Detroit, and Toledo, where the U.S. government would be permitted to build forts.

Why did inveterate enemies of the United States like Blue Jacket and Little Turtle suddenly reverse course at Greenville and affix their marks to Wayne's treaty? Although the conventional answer is the destruction of their army at Fallen Timbers, that battle was actually more of a draw. The real catastrophe for the native warriors had come later on August 20, 1794. On the eve of the Greenville council, Wayne reported that Indians were telling him they had "lost all confidence in the British since the 20th. of August, Because they remained idle spectators & saw their best & bravest Chiefs & Warriors slaughtered before their faces, & under the Muzzles of their great Guns without attempting to assist them—hence they consider the British not only liars—but also Cowards."[30]

Nor had the Battle of Fallen Timbers been the last instance of British abandonment. In the Jay Treaty, signed just two months later, the imperial government agreed to evacuate all of its posts south of the Great Lakes, including Forts Detroit and Miami. Wayne made a point of obtaining a copy of the Jay Treaty to read to the Indians assembled at Greenville. Relinquishing their last hopes for British backing, indigenous leaders felt they had no choice but to make the best deal they could.[31]

Even as Britain abandoned the native nations north of the Ohio River, Spanish officials, distracted by Spain's war against France, urged the Muskogees and Chickamaugas to "suspend all hostilities" against the United States.[32] And in the October 27, 1795, Treaty of San Lorenzo, also known as Pinckney's Treaty, Carlos III settled his border with the United States at 31 degrees (which remains the northern border of most of the Florida panhandle), giving up several Mississippi and Tombigbee River posts where his countrymen had given and sold arms and ammunition to the Chickasaws and other First Nations. The Spanish king also authorized U.S. citizens to navigate the Mississippi River and to avoid Spanish customs duties on produce stored in New Orleans while awaiting shipment overseas. Thus the treaty facilitated U.S. expansion into the vast Mississippi Valley.

BY 1795, THE TWO thousand white residents of Pointe Coupée on the west bank of the Mississippi River, a hundred miles north of New Orleans and twenty miles upriver from Baton Rouge, included not only Spanish soldiers and officials but expatriates from the former British colonies on the Atlantic coast. The largest number were descendants of the original French settlers or refugees from Saint-Domingue, and they owned some seven thousand slaves. In April, as many as sixty African Americans allegedly plotted a rebellion—reportedly with inspiration from the French and Haitian Revolutions and help from a handful of whites and free Blacks. Like British American slaves in 1775, Black Louisianans spread the rumor that the Spanish government had issued an emancipation decree that local planters and officials had suppressed. Others said France (then at war with Spain) planned to free them. Both rumors were plausible in the context of the successful Haitian Revolution and the French National Convention's February 4, 1794, decree abolishing slavery throughout the empire.[33]

Fearing not only slave unrest but Jacobin infiltration, Spanish authorities reacted to the plot with more than usual savagery. Twenty-six Black Louisianans were executed, and their severed heads were displayed at intervals along the Mississippi. Others were sent to the Spanish fort in Havana to serve long terms at hard labor. And Francisco Luis Hector, Baron de Carondelet, the Spanish governor-general of Louisiana, resorted to the same remedy that British and U.S. officials had often deployed in the face of slave revolts: he instituted a total and complete shutdown of Africans entering Louisiana until he could figure out what the hell was going on. Though he also disarmed Pointe Coupée's slaves, many of whom had been required to hunt much of their own food, Carondelet could not deprive them of their love of liberty. In fact they allegedly plotted another revolt the following year.[34] Historians drawing solely upon the writings of the Founding Fathers may have given the Revolutionary War too much credit for expanding American freedom, but they have not exaggerated the desire of Americans—of every race, rank, and gender—to breathe free.

EPILOGUE

THIS BOOK HAS CONTENDED THAT MUCH CAN BE GAINED FROM bringing all Americans of the founding era into the same timeline. Two examples:

The famous story of Esther Reed's 1780 fundraising effort is all the more interesting in context: Reed's husband was desperate to repair his relationship with Gen. Washington. Knowing that Esther was trying to help Joseph as well as the soldiers makes it all the more remarkable that she initially resisted the general's request that her group give the troops shirts instead of money. As noted above, Reed in turn influenced male politics, helping mollify the 1781 mutineers and perhaps even giving Thomas Jefferson his famous phrase, "Empire of liberty."[1] Similarly, when northern soldiers refused to serve in the disease-ridden south, John Laurens tirelessly lobbied the leaders of his and neighboring states to solve their manpower shortage by enlisting Black men. Instead southern Whigs used slaves as enlistment bounties with which to recruit whites. In 1782, when South Carolina tried to replenish their supply of bounty slaves by sending raiders onto Loyalist plantations, they scuttled the arrangement under which the British purchased food from Whig farmers, leaving them no choice but to forage in force, and one of those raids killed John Laurens.

Historians tend to divide the Revolutionary War into three phases: its origins, battles, and outcome. But numerous concerns loomed large throughout the founding era. Take paper money. The Currency Act of 1764 not only contributed to the American colonists' animus against Parliament but also aggravated many of their internal conflicts, especially the Regulator rebellions in North and South Carolina. After the imperial dispute devolved into a war, commanders on all sides looked for opportunities to shore up the value of their national currencies. For instance, one of George Washington's motives for taking his army across the Delaware River on Christmas Night 1776 was to arrest the depreciation of the Continental dollar. Then in the summer of 1787, when delegates from twelve states gathered in Philadelphia to combat what Madison called the "Injustice of the laws of [the] States," they agreed that the state legislatures' single most egregious crime had been to print paper currency, so they prohibited them from ever doing so again.[2]

MOST NATIONS DEFINE THEMSELVES by their revolutions. The English hark back to 1688, the French to 1789, and so on. In the United States and many other places, the mythologization of the founding rebels has played out as a revolt against complexity. Flattering and flat celebrations of the Founders often proceed from a laudable desire to instill patriotism in the young (they also sell well), but they have always seemed more appropriate to authoritarian regimes, and they have slandered history by making it dull. Thank God for the debunkers, but often their antiheroes have been as crudely carved as the idols of the hero-worshippers. Our real debt is to historians of women, Native Americans, African Americans, and other unknown Americans, for their scholarship on the American Revolution has exposed its most famous participants' multiple dimensions. George Washington was both the "devourer" of Native American villages and the man who, in 1783, ended his brother officers' conspiracy against civilian rule. Thomas Jefferson wrote both *Notes on the State of Virginia*, using fake science to paint a racist caricature of African Americans that justified their enslavement, and the Declaration of Independence. Likewise, in communications with British officers, South Carolina's Mary Butler boldly asserted her right, though married, to a separate estate—which happened to consist of two hundred human beings. In 1780, the British army provided refuge to Boston King, a runaway slave and future evangelist, but also to another American fugitive, Benedict Arnold. The American War of Independence was an involuntary African American civil war but also an essential stepping-stone to the Americas' first successful slave revolt, the Haitian Revolution.[3]

In the mid-1820s, northern newspapers circulated the possibly fictitious story of a Virginia slave named Cunningham, who used the freedom certificate his brother had earned by fighting on the American side in the War of 1812 to escape to Boston. Enemy fire had fractured the brother's arm and leg and cost him a finger, toe, and part of a leg, so before setting out, Cunningham asked a butcher to maim him to fit the physical description set down in the certificate. The horrified butcher at first refused, but Cunningham convinced him with the same phrase Lund Washington, temporary master of Mount Vernon, had used a half century earlier as he warned his cousin the commander-in-chief about the probable impact of Governor Dunmore's emancipation proclamation: "liberty is sweet."[4]

Hermon Husband, the Maryland-born penman of farmers' revolts in colonial North Carolina and independent Pennsylvania, hinted at the Revolution's complexities when he distinguished between the Founding Fathers and their ideals. "Though the men themselves are lost to all truth, reason, and justice," he wrote, "their works will stand the test and trial of fire."[5]

ACKNOWLEDGMENTS

Even more so than my previous books, this one has been a team effort, and I want to thank the many people who carried *Liberty Is Sweet* and me across the finish line. The scarcest ingredient in a massive project like this one is time, and I am grateful that I was able to launch it more than a decade ago with a summer research grant from the University of Richmond and a year-long fellowship from the National Endowment for the Humanities (thank you, fellow taxpayers!). Then Peter and Bonnie McCausland created the professorship that brought me to the research-friendly University of South Carolina and my family to the fun and welcoming city of Columbia. Both at Richmond and Carolina, I benefited from the insights and other assistance of brilliant colleagues. Staff at both institutions, especially Deborah Govoruhk at the University of Richmond and Lori Carey at Carolina, have given me the gift of time, ideas, and friendship.

Fellowships at the Huntington Library in San Marino and the Newberry Library in Chicago enabled me to bring the project close to completion. At both, I ran up intellectual and other debts to staff members and fellow researchers, especially (at the Huntington) Sara K. Austin, María Bárbara Zepeda Cortés, John Demos, Scott Heerman, Steve Hindle, Roy Ritchie, Charles C. Reid, Eileen White Read, Bethel Saler, Olga Tsapina, and Catherine Wehrey-Miller, and (at the Newberry) Christopher Albi, Rowena McClinton, Christopher McKee, and especially D. Bradford Hunt. The UofSC's College of Arts and Sciences provided a Manuscript Completion Grant and other assistance.

As always, Jim Hornfischer early on explained what I was trying to say better than I could, and—not for the first time—Thomas LeBien generously listened. Marjoleine Kars and David Waldstreicher took time away from their own research and writing to edit every chapter. Other friends and colleagues contributed corrections as well as ideas within their areas of specialization. I am especially grateful to works-in-progress seminars at the Newberry, Huntington, Massachusetts Historical Society, and University of Southern California. Not all of the advice came from my fellow academics. I tried out many of my ideas on teachers' continuing-education workshops and got great suggestions, for instance from Texas teacher Richard Kelly, who pointed out that Jefferson encompassed African Americans in "all men are created equal," at least formally, by specifically referring to them, in his rough draft of the Declaration of Independence, as "MEN." The grassroots reviewers on goodreads.com powerfully improved this book by pointing out my tendency to overquote in the last one. I confess to scorning Wikipedia years ago, but I will not make that mistake again, as I found it enormously useful. So I want to thank its millions of volunteer contributors. I also leaned heavily on the often unheralded but always accurate source and context notes produced by the editors of the papers of the American Founders, broadly defined.

While this book is based mostly on printed primary sources, unpublished manuscripts occasionally proved crucial, and I express my thanks to the people who both preserve them and provide access to them, especially the archival staffs at the Huntington, Massachusetts Historical Society, New-York Historical Society, Newberry, and South Carolina Historical Society (housed at the College of Charleston). The staff at New York's Lewey Lake State Park were gracious hosts for three successive summer writing retreats.

The book benefited from the assistance of a host of University of South Carolina librarians, especially Kathy Snediker, Jane Olsgaard, and the staff of the Inter-Library Loan Office. Also at the UofSC, I have been inspired, challenged, and otherwise assisted by amazing graduate students, especially Carter Bruns, Jill Found, Katelynn Hatton, Erin Holmes, Andrew Kettler, James Lockemy, Josh Mayes, M. Patrick O'Brien, Neil Polhemus, Gary Sellick, and Cane West.

It was, however, a University of South Carolina undergraduate who became essentially my coauthor for the final year of the project. Riley Sutherland checked nearly all of the five thousand citations, correcting numerous embarrassing errors. She also contributed ideas of her own as well as better ways of expressing mine. In addition, she chased down both the images and permission to use them and prepared both the bibliography and the population table. I am immensely grateful to her. And Riley in turn reminds me to thank the Mid-Continent Public Library's Woodneath Library Center for aiding her research, especially with books from other libraries all over the country.

Others who provided invaluable assistance include Robert Alexander, Emily E. Ames, Sara Austin, Charles Baxley, Ellen McCallister Clark (Library Director of the Society of the Cincinnati), Marc Egnal, Robert A. Gross, Tim Higgins, T. Cole Jones, Sgt. Stephan Kassza, Andrew B. Lewis, Rowena McClinton, Brendan McConville, Michael A. McDonnell, Christopher McKee, Mary Jo Murphy, David Preston, Ray Raphael, Claudio Saunt, Tim Sumter, Stuart Tolchin, Douglas L. Winiarski, and Rick Wise. I chose the title *Liberty Is Sweet* both because of the context in which the phrase was first used and in homage to my graduate mentor, Peter H. Wood, who gave the name "Liberty Is Sweet" to a pathbreaking article he published in 1993. As he always does, Peter made invaluable contributions both to this book and to its author.

I expect most readers will join me in thanking my editor, Bob Bender, for reining in a manuscript that at one point approached a thousand pages. Bob improved the book in numerous other ways as well, and he also earned my gratitude by holding me to a strict deadline—and then another and another. Also at Simon & Schuster, Johanna Li deftly handled all things visual and Fred Chase not only caught hundreds of errors, subtle and magnificent, but helped Bob smooth out the prose. Thank you, Fred. Also at "Simon," Kirstin Berndt and Leila Siddiqui played at least as large a role as I did in getting this book into your hands, while Charles Newman compiled an index comprehensive enough to reinforce one of its principal themes. I am so glad I decided to commission the best mapmaker in the business, Jeff Ward, and so grateful to him for his patience as well as his gift.

As they have four times before, my parents, Linwood and Jinks Holton, contributed not only encouragement but, even more helpfully, pointed questions about when I planned to finish. My siblings and their families provided homes-away-from-home, abundant insight, and willing ears. Here in South Carolina, Beverly and Henry endured, *usually* with good cheer, my eighteenth-century stories and my aversion to reading and writing in my office while they brought light and life to the kitchen and den. I must also thank them for pointing out that my working title for this book, *The Fire Beneath*, was only going to lead to jokes about Taco Bell. My spouse, Dr. Gretchen Schoel, read . . . not a word of the manuscript, having long ago decided not to be my assistant author at the expense of her own priorities, including managing the kids' school's garden (where I help out only on Family Day) and her thriving editing business (where, since that one time, I *never* help!). She also picked up far more than her share of the parenting, especially the hard stuff, from keeping the pets alive (mostly) to dealing with insurance companies to getting at least some breakfast into the kids. She turned our being uprooted to Chicago and Los Angeles for a year into new friends and amazing adventures for the entire family, peaking, literally, with our ascent of Mount Wilson on our way out of California. For all of these, she has my thanks, and for everything else, my love.

ABBREVIATIONS USED IN
NOTES AND BIBLIOGRAPHY

ANB – *American National Biography*—anb-org
ASPIA – *American State Papers, Indian Affairs*, in *Century of Lawmaking for a New Nation*
BNA – British National Archives
CL – William L. Clements Library
CVSP – *Calendar of Virginia State Papers and Other Manuscripts*
DCB – *Dictionary of Canadian Biography*—biographi.ca/en/
DHRC – Jensen et al., eds., *Documentary History of the Ratification of the Constitution*
DNB – *Oxford Dictionary of National Biography*—oxforddnb.com
DRCHSNY – Brodhead, Fernow, and O'Callaghan, eds., *Documents Relative to the Colonial History of the State of New-York*
HEH – Henry E. Huntington Library
HH – Houghton Library, Harvard University
IHC – *Illinois Historical Collections*
JCC – Ford et al., eds., *Journals of the Continental Congress, 1774–1789*
JHB – Kennedy, ed., *Journals of the House of Burgesses of Virginia*
LC – Library of Congress
LiVi – Library of Virginia
MHC – *Collections and Researches Made by the Michigan Pioneer and Historical Society (Michigan Historical Collections)*
MHS – Massachusetts Historical Society
NAW – James, James, and Boyer, eds., *Notable American Women, 1607–1950*
NCCR – Weeks and Saunders, eds., *North Carolina Colonial Records*
NL – Newberry Library
N-YHS – New-York Historical Society
NYPL – New York Public Library
OED – *Oxford English Dictionary*
OHAR – Gray and Kamensky, eds., *Oxford Handbook of the American Revolution*
RV – Van Schreeven et al., eds., *Revolutionary Virginia: The Road to Independence*
SCHS – South Carolina Historical Society
USNA – United States National Archives
UVA – University of Virginia, Manuscripts Department, Alderman Library
VHS – Virginia Historical Society
W&M – Swem Library, College of William and Mary
WMQ – *William and Mary Quarterly*
YL – Yale University

NOTES

Words and Boundaries

1. Romans, *Concise Natural History of East and West-Florida*, 91.

Prologue: An Invisible Enemy

1. George Washington to John Augustine Washington, July 27, 1775, *Founders Online*.
2. The other future Continental generals were Horatio Gates, Charles Lee, Andrew Lewis, Hugh Mercer, Daniel Morgan, and Adam Stephen. John Weighton, a Sudbury, Massachusetts, minuteman who fought the British on April 19, 1775, had also been at Braddock's defeat. Fischer, *Paul Revere's Ride*, 222–24.
3. Kopperman, *Braddock at the Monongahela*, 30; McDonnell, *Masters of Empire*, 167–68; Preston, *Braddock's Defeat*, 222.
4. Crytzer, *Guyasuta and the Fall of Indian America*, 113.
5. Kopperman, *Braddock at the Monongahela*, 15.
6. The editors of the *Papers of George Washington* state that the young Virginian inherited this name from his great-grandfather John Washington. George Washington, speech sent to Tanaghrisson, n.d., cited in Washington to Robert Dinwiddie, April 25, 1754 (quotation in text is from editors' note), George Washington, "Comments on David Humphreys' Biography of George Washington," [1787–1788] (and editors' note), *Founders Online*; Lengel, *General George Washington*, 33; Calloway, *Indian World of George Washington*, 25, 69–70.
7. Washington, journal, Nov. 30–Dec. 23, 1753, *Founders Online*; Crytzer, *Guyasuta and the Fall of Indian America*, 15–28; Calloway, *Indian World of George Washington*, 73.
8. Anderson, *Crucible of War*, 3–7, 41–65; Lengel, *General George Washington*, 25–48; Calloway, *Indian World of George Washington*, 87–91.
9. Robert Orme to George Washington, March 2, 1755, *Founders Online*.
10. Israel Pemberton to John Fothergill, [May 19, 1755], *Founders Online*; Franklin, autobiography, franklinpapers.org.
11. Preston shows that Franklin got the idea of depicting St. Clair as a Hussar from St. Clair himself, who occasionally wore a Hussar uniform for the same purpose of intimidation. Franklin, advertisement for wagons, April 26, 1755, *Founders Online*; Kopperman, *Braddock at the Monongahela*, 12; Preston, *Braddock's Defeat*, 94–96.

12. Wood, *Americanization of Benjamin Franklin*; Morgan, *Benjamin Franklin*, 220–22.

13. Franklin, autobiography, franklinpapers.org; Preston, *Braddock's Defeat*, 92–96.

14. Shingas, quoted in Bond, "Captivity of Charles Stuart," 63; Tanner and Pinther, eds., *Atlas of Great Lakes Indian History*, 65–66.

15. Shingas and Braddock, quoted in Bond, "Captivity of Charles Stuart," 63.

16. Preston notes that Stuart, a secondhand source, is the only one who has Shawnees attending this meeting with Braddock. Shingas and other Delaware sachems, quoted in Bond, "Captivity of Charles Stuart," 63–64; Preston, *Braddock's Defeat*, 114.

17. Preston, *Braddock's Defeat*, 113–16, 302.

18. Sixteen additional Iroquois would later decide to join Braddock's army, arriving a day *after* the July 9 battle. Calloway, *Scratch of a Pen*, 35; Preston, *Braddock's Defeat*, 112, 115.

19. Braddock, quoted in Franklin, autobiography, franklinpapers.org.

20. Indian trader James Lowry attributed the crucial intelligence about the French reinforcements being stuck on the Buffalo River to William Johnson, a British colonel and Indian agent based on the Mohawk River in present-day upstate New York. But Johnson had last written Braddock on May 17, long before the French reinforcements reached the Buffalo, so the information appears actually to have come from Indians on that river. Another possibility is that George Washington was correct that Braddock only *inferred* that the French *must* have gotten stuck on the Buffalo (as indeed they had, briefly)— and that that inference came from Washington himself. George Washington to John Augustine Washington, June 28–July 2, 1755, *Founders Online*; William Shirley Jr. to Robert Hunter Morris, June 11, 1755, *Pennsylvania Archives*, Ser. 1, 2:357; Lowry, cited in Edward Shippen to [Robert Hunter Morris], June 17, 1755, Pennsylvania Provincial Council, *Minutes of the Provincial Council of Pennsylvania* 6:431; Thomas Butler to William Johnson, May 14, 1755, Johnson to Braddock, May 17, 1755, *Papers of Sir William Johnson* 1:495, 515; Davies, *Virginia's Danger and Remedy*, 5–6; Preston, *Braddock's Defeat*, 131–49, 180–82.

21. Preston, *Braddock's Defeat*, 88, 133, 147; Parrish, *American Curiosity*.

22. Preston, *Braddock's Defeat*, 182, 394n; Dinwiddie to Halifax, July 23, 1755, *Official Records of Robert Dinwiddie* 2:114; Kopperman, *Braddock at the Monongahela*, 9–10, 16–17.

23. Findley, quoted in Faragher, *Daniel Boone*, 36, 69–70.

24. George Washington to John Augustine Washington, June 28–July 2, 1755, *Founders Online*.

25. Harry Gordon, quoted in Preston, *Braddock's Defeat*, 221; [Dr. Alexander Hamilton] to Baillie Hamilton, [Aug. 1755], in Breslaw, "Dismal Tragedy," 136.

26. Adam Stephen, letter, in Kopperman, *Braddock at the Monongahela*, 227, 25; Anderson, *Crucible of War*, 97; Crytzer, *Guyasuta and the Fall of Indian America*, 30–32, 48–53. Contrecoeur's thorough grasp of native culture was by no means unique. Many French Canadian officers were skilled at integrating Indian and French fighters, as they had spent their entire careers navigating the "middle ground" between the two societies. Some, in fact, were products of interracial unions. White, *Middle Ground*.

27. Kopperman, *Braddock at the Monongahela*, 28–30; Anderson, *Crucible of War*, 97.

28. Kopperman, *Braddock at the Monongahela*, 60; Anderson, *Crucible of War*, 99; Jennings, *Empire of Fortune*, 157; Preston, *Braddock's Defeat*, 231–34, 240.

29. Anonymous letter, July 25, 1755, in Pargellis, ed., *Military Affairs in North America*, 117; Kopperman, *Braddock at the Monongahela*, 50; Anderson, *Crucible of War*, 99.

30. Thomas Dunbar to Robert Napier, July 24, 1755, in Pargellis, ed., *Military Affairs in*

North America, 111; Thomas Dunbar and Thomas Gage to William Shirley, [Oct.] 21, 1755, Shirley, *Correspondence of William Shirley* 2:313; Anderson, *Crucible of War*, 100, 102; Taylor, *American Revolutions*, 44.

31. Washington to Mary Ball Washington, [July 18, 1755], *Founders Online*; "British A" (unnamed British officer), quoted in Kopperman, *Braddock at the Monongahela*, 76, 73.

32. Anonymous letter, July 25, 1755, in Pargellis, ed., *Military Affairs in North America*, 117; Jennings, *Empire of Fortune*, 157n.

33. "British A," quoted in Kopperman, *Braddock at the Monongahela*, 83; Washington to Robert Dinwiddie, July 18, 1755, *Founders Online*; Anderson, *Crucible of War*, 102.

34. Adam Stephen, quoted in Ward, *Major General Adam Stephen and the Cause of American Liberty*, 20 ("particular aim"); anonymous letter, July 25, 1755, in Pargellis, ed., *Military Affairs in North America*, 115 ("Whiszing noise"); Wright, "Rifle in the American Revolution," 295; Babits, *Devil of a Whipping*, 12–14. For an opposing analysis, see Preston, *Braddock's Defeat*, 151, 245, 389n, 404n.

35. "British D," in Kopperman, *Braddock at the Monongahela*, 176; Faragher, *Daniel Boone*, 37–38; Preston, *Braddock's Defeat*, 256–59.

36. "British A," in Kopperman, *Braddock at the Monongahela*, 165; anonymous letter, July 25, 1755, in Pargellis, ed., *Military Affairs in North America*, 124; Jennings, *Empire of Fortune*, 158n; Anderson, *Crucible of War*, 105; Preston, *Braddock's Defeat*, 262, 264, 277–78, 347–49, 356.

37. Anderson, *Crucible of War*, 100, 103–4; Richter, "War and Culture"; Calloway, *Indian World of George Washington*, 118–19.

38. "The Journal of Captain Robert Cholmley's Batman," quoted in editors' note to Washington to James Innes, July 17, 1775, Washington to Dinwiddie, July 18, 1755, *Founders Online*; Anderson, *Crucible of War*, 104–5. After a brief pause in eastern Pennsylvania, the army headed on to Albany, New York.

39. Dinwiddie to Halifax, July 23, 1755, in *Official Records of Robert Dinwiddie* 2:114.

40. Dinwiddie to Charles Carter, July 18, 1755, Dinwiddie to Halifax, July 23, 1755, in *Official Records of Robert Dinwiddie* 2:102, 114; "An Act to Incorporate Charlestown," in Edwards, ed., *Ordinances of the City Council of Charleston*, 1; Wood, *Black Majority*, 308–26; Landers, "Gracia Real de Santa Teresa de Mose."

41. Davies, *Virginia's Danger and Remedy*, 10.

42. Morgan, *Benjamin Franklin*, 102, 144.

43. Greene, "Posture of Hostility," 36–58.

44. Calloway, *Indian World of George Washington*, 148–60.

45. *Annual Register . . . for the Year 1763*, 21; Bullion, "Ten Thousand in America"; Brown, *Tacky's Revolt*, 235.

46. Ernst, *Money and Politics in America*, 43–62.

47. Truxes, *Defying Empire*.

48. Thomas Hutchinson to William Bollan, March 6, 1762, Hutchinson, *Correspondence of Thomas Hutchinson* 1:159.

Chapter 1: Awing and Protecting the Indians

1. Jennings, *Empire of Fortune*, 396–409.

2. Nov. 16, 1762, "Journal of James Kenny," 173; Crytzer, *Guyasuta and the Fall of Indian America*, 98; Calloway, *Indian World of George Washington*, 50, 104, 172, 174.

3. Nash, *Unknown American Revolution*, 37.

4. Cogliano, *Revolutionary America*, 32.

5. Holton, "Revolt of the Ruling Class," 45–46; Anderson, *Crucible of War*, 78, 84, 474, 523, 529–31; Ferling, *Ascent of George Washington*, 62; Calloway, *Indian World of George Washington*, 171–72.

6. Hugh Mercer, quoted in Downes, *Council Fires on the Upper Ohio*, 97; Barrow, *Trade and Empire*, 177; Cogliano, *Revolutionary America*, 49; Du Rivage, *Revolution Against Empire*, 77.

7. Guyasuta, speech, Fort Pitt conference, May 10, 1765, in Hildreth, *Pioneer History*, 64.

8. Dowd, *War Under Heaven*, 11, 20–21, 27, 65, 70–78, 88–89, 169, 173; Kane, "Covered with Such a Cappe."

9. Guyasuta, speech, Fort Pitt conference, May [10], 1765, in Hildreth, *Pioneer History*, 63–64; Johnson to Board of Trade, Nov. 13, 1763, *DRCHSNY* 7:575; Downes, *Council Fires on the Upper Ohio*, 109–11; Richter, "Plan of 1764," 180; Peckham, *Pontiac and the Indian Uprising*, 101; Crytzer, *Guyasuta and the Fall of Indian America*, 30–32, 48–53, 84–87. Native American leaders also had other grievances against Amherst. For example, British officers had obtained local Indians' permission to erect forts on their land only after promising to dismantle them at the end of the war. After the French left, the British not only broke this promise but enlarged the forts and encouraged farmers to settle near them to grow food for the soldiers. Calloway, *Scratch of a Pen*, 55.

10. Ayling, *Elder Pitt*, 189, 220; Morgan, *Benjamin Franklin*, 98.

11. Karl Wolfgang Schweizer, "Stuart, John, third earl of Bute (1713–1792)," *DNB*; "Bullion, "Security and Economy," 499–503.

12. Eliphalet Dyer, quoted in Pincus, "Stamp Act Crisis in Global Perspective," 17–18; Greene, "Seven Years' War and the American Revolution," 93–94; Calloway, *Indian World of George Washington*, 179–80.

13. [Thomas Gage], "Report of the Forts in North America . . . ," enclosed in Gage to Barrington, Dec. 18, 1765 (first, second, and fourth quotations), in *Correspondence of General Thomas Gage* 2:319, 321; John Pownall, quoted in Bunker, *Empire on the Edge*, 105 (third quotation); *Annual Register . . . for the Year 1763*, 21; Shy, *Toward Lexington*, 47, 50–68, 79–83, 242, 274; Barrow, ed., "Project for Imperial Reform," 122–26; Bullion, "Ten Thousand in America"; Thomas, *British Politics and the Stamp Act Crisis*, 37–38; Bullion, *Great and Necessary Measure*, 93–94; Anderson, *Crucible of War*, 574; Gould, *Among the Powers of Earth*, 107; Holton, "History of the Stamp Act Shows How Indians Led to the American Revolution."

14. Lawson, *George Grenville*, vi (first quotation), 154; Thomas Pitt, quoted in J. V. Beckett and Peter D. G. Thomas, "Grenville, George (1712–1770)," *DNB* (second quotation); Bullion, *Great and Necessary Measure*, 60.

15. Cogliano, *Revolutionary America*, 49.

16. Moving from north to south, the midpoint of Britain's twenty-six American colonies was not the Mason-Dixon line but modern-day Gainesville, Florida. Smith, "Fourteenth Colony," 66. Historians with different ideas of what constitutes a colony have put the number of British American colonies in 1776 as high as thirty. Bunker, *Empire on the Edge*, 107.

17. Bridges, *Annals of Jamaica* 1:134; McCusker and Menard, *Economy of British America*, 130, 160; McCusker, "Current Value of English Exports," 621, 626 (average for 1771 to 1774); O'Shaughnessy, *Empire Divided*, 60; Mulcahy, *Hurricanes and Society in the British Greater Caribbean*, 163; Marshall, "Britain's American Problem," 20.

18. Johnson, "El Niño, Environmental Crisis, and the Emergence of Alternative Markets in

the Hispanic Caribbean"; Magra, *Fisherman's Cause*, 95; Dunn, *Tale of Two Plantations*, 138, 154–55.

19. Magra, *Fisherman's Cause*, 27, 6–7n; Ragsdale, "George Washington, the British Tobacco Trade, and Economic Opportunity in Prerevolutionary Virginia," 158; Taylor, *American Revolutions*, 19.

20. Defoe, quoted in Sheridan, "Formation of Caribbean Plantation Society," 409; Griffin, *America's Revolution*, 13; Magra, *Fisherman's Cause*, 87.

21. Craig, "Grounds for Debate?"; Peterson, *City-State of Boston*, 19.

22. Cogliano, *Revolutionary America*, 51; O'Shaughnessy, *Empire Divided*, 62–63, 67.

23. O'Shaughnessy, *Empire Divided*, 62.

24. Gipson, *Coming of the Revolution*, 32–33; Stout, *Royal Navy in America*, 14–15; Anderson, *Crucible of War*, 578–79; Truxes, *Defying Empire*, 112; Morgan and Morgan, *Stamp Act Crisis*, 219.

25. Franklin, "Rules by Which a Great Empire May Be Reduced to a Small One," *Public Advertiser*, Sept. 11, 1773 (first quotation), Franklin to Richard Jackson, June 1, 1764, *Founders Online*; John Adams to William Tudor, Aug. 11, 1818 (second quotation), in *Works of John Adams* 10:345; "An Act for the further Improvement of His Majesty's Revenue of Customs . . ." in *Statutes at Large, of England and of Great-Britain* 12:212–18; "Extract of a Letter from One of the Council of Boston, in New-England, to a Merchant in London," *Newport Mercury*, May 21, 1764; "Journal of the Times," July 1, 2, 1769, *Boston Evening-Post*, Aug. 14, 1769; June 1, 1763, in Grant, Munro, and FitzRoy, eds., *Acts of the Privy Council of England* 4:560–62; Ubbelohde, *Vice-Admiralty Courts and the American Revolution*, 38–44; Stout, *Royal Navy in America*, 25–34; Truxes, *Defying Empire*, 173; Morgan, *Benjamin Franklin*, 138–39; Kinkel, "King's Pirates?," 22–24. As its common name suggested, the Hovering Act also extended to America a British law aimed at preventing arriving vessels from loitering offshore awaiting the chance to run cargo ashore without paying applicable port taxes.

26. [John?] Buller, speech in the House of Commons, March 24, 1783, Great Britain, Parliament, *Parliamentary Register*, Ser. 2, 9:514; Shy, *Toward Lexington*, 50–51; Lawson, *George Grenville*, 147–49, 181.

27. Vaughn, "Politics of Empire," 352–67, 522–25. Counting expenses that the colonial assemblies incurred before Pitt made his promise, Parliament reimbursed about two-fifths of what they spent. Anderson, *Crucible of War*, 814n.

28. Grenville, Pitt, quoted in Waterhouse, *Essay on Junius and His Letters*, 191; Ayling, *Elder Pitt*, 312–13; Vaughn, "Politics of Empire," 367–69.

29. Bunker, *Empire on the Edge*, 32–33, 134.

30. Eacott, *Selling Empire*, 163, 189, 196, 204–5.

31. Rhode Island remonstrance against the Molasses Act, Jan. [27], 1764, *Providence Gazette*, Oct. 20, 1764; Andrews, ed., "State of the Trade," 382; Wiener, "Rhode Island Merchants and the Sugar Act," 493; Johnson, "Passage of the Sugar Act," 510; Barrow, *Trade and Empire*, 142; Thomas, *British Politics and the Stamp Act Crisis*, 61.

Chapter 2: The First American Revolution

1. Savannah dateline, *Georgia Gazette*, June 9, 1763; Portsmouth dateline, June 10, 1763, *New-Hampshire Gazette*; Warren, "History of the Ojibways," 201–2; Smith, "Remembering Mary, Shaping Revolt," 532; McConville, *King's Three Faces*, 77–78, 130–31; Bell, *Road to Concord*, 46–50.

2. Peckham, *Pontiac and the Indian Uprising*, 163–64; Van Kirk, *Many Tender Ties*; McDonnell, *Masters of Empire*, 215–21; Widder, *Beyond Pontiac's Shadow*, 141–67.

3. Peckham, *Pontiac and the Indian Uprising*, 164–65; McDonnell, *Masters of Empire*.

4. Gladwin, quoted in Calloway, *Scratch of a Pen*, 70, 56; Jennings, *Invasion of America*, 166; Richter, *Ordeal of the Longhouse*, 37–38.

5. William Johnson, Journal of Indian Affairs, July 11, 1763, quoted in Dowd, *War Under Heaven*, 89.

6. Ohio Company of Virginia, journal, July 4, 1763, George Mercer's Appointment and Instructions as London Agent for the Ohio Company, July 4, 1763, in *George Mercer Papers Relating to the Ohio Company of Virginia*, 182–83; Anderson, *Crucible of War*, 533–34.

7. Anderson, *Crucible of War*, 594; Calloway, *Indian World of George Washington*, 178.

8. Washington to Sarah Cary Fairfax, Sept. 12, 1758, *Founders Online*.

9. Washington to Robert Stewart, April 27, 1763, *Founders Online*.

10. Peter Fontaine to Moses and John Fontaine and Daniel Torin, Aug. 7, 1763, in Maury, ed., *Memoirs of a Huguenot Family*, 372; Benjamin Marshall to James Tapscott, Nov. 12, 1763, "Extracts from the Letter-Book of Benjamin Marshall," 205; "At a Conference with the Six Nations and Delawares at Johnson Hall [between] April 29th and May 22, 1765," *DRCHSNY* 7:726; Peckham, *Pontiac and the Indian Uprising*, 166; White, *Middle Ground*, 269–314; McConnell, *Country Between*, 181–206; Calloway, *Scratch of a Pen*, 76–77.

11. "Narrative of the Captivity of John M'Cullough," 272; Oct. 15, 1762, March 1, 1763, Oct. 18, Nov. 4, 1762, "Journal of James Kenny," 171, 188, 172–73; White, *Middle Ground*, 280–81; Dowd, *Spirited Resistance*, 23, 33–35; Dowd, *War Under Heaven*, 94–105.

12. March 1, 1763, "Journal of James Kenny," 188; Anderson, *Crucible of War*, 535–37; Dowd, *War Under Heaven*, 101–2.

13. Feb. 21, 1763, "Journal of James Kenny," 187; Dowd, "French King Wakes Up in Detroit"; Dowd, *War Under Heaven*, 105–13.

14. Eccles, "New France and the French Impact on North America," 42–43.

15. Johnson, "A Review of the Progressive State of the Trade, Politics and Proceedings of the Indians in the Northern District . . . ," 1767, *DRCHSNY* 7:958; Anderson, *Crucible of War*, 545.

16. Smallpox actually did spread through the Upper Ohio towns in 1763 and 1764, though it cannot be traced with certainty to Ecuyer's blankets. Fenn, "Biological Warfare in Eighteenth-Century North America," 1552–58; Dowd, *War Under Heaven*, 190; Calloway, *Indian World of George Washington*, 176.

17. William Fleming to Francis Fauquier, July 26, 1763, in *Official Papers of Francis Fauquier* 2:998; Peter Fontaine to Moses and John Fontaine and Daniel Torin, Aug. 7, 1763, in Maury, ed., *Memoirs of a Huguenot Family*, 372; David Van der Heyden, quoted in Dowd, *War Under Heaven*, 144.

18. Peckham, *Pontiac and the Indian Uprising*, 239; Anderson, *Crucible of War*, 634, 620; Dunn, *Frontier Profit and Loss*, 3, 182.

19. The Proclamation of 1763 was also expected to confine settlers to the two roles that the mercantilist system assigned them: shipping raw materials to Britain and in return consuming its manufactured goods. George Washington to Lord Dunmore, Sept. 12, 1773, *Founders Online*; avalon.law.yale.edu/18th_century/proc1763.asp; Barrow, ed., "Project for Imperial Reform," 114–16; Greene, "Seven Years' War and the American Revolution," 91; Calloway, *Scratch of a Pen*, 94.

20. Proclamation of 1763, avalon.law.yale.edu/18th_century/proc1763.asp; David Robinson to William Thompson, Feb. 18, 1764, document 2QQ44, Draper Manuscripts; Jonathan Boucher to Rev. James, March 9, 1767, "Letters of Rev. Jonathan Boucher," 344; Fauquier to Board of Trade, Feb. 13, 1764, Board of Trade to Fauquier, July 13, 1764, in *Official Papers of Francis Fauquier* 3:1076–79 (quotation at 1078), 1125; [Young], *Political Essays Concerning the Present State of the British Empire*, 386; Holton, *Forced Founders*, 8–9; Calloway, *Indian World of George Washington*, 179–84.

21. John Penn to William Johnson, Dec. 31, 1763, Thomas McKee to William Johnson, [Feb. 15, 1764], in *Papers of Sir William Johnson* 4:284, 11:55–56; Heckewelder, *Narrative of the Mission of the United Brethren Among the Delaware and Mohegan Indians*, 77–81; Merrell, *Into the American Woods*, 283–88; Dowd, *War Under Heaven*, 192–94; Spero, *Frontier Country*, 63, 153, 160–65.

22. Anderson, *Crucible of War*, 611–12; Morgan and Morgan, *Stamp Act Crisis*, 252–53; Spero, *Frontier Country*, 166.

Chapter 3: Confederacy of Smugglers

1. Bernard, quoted in Morgan and Morgan, *Stamp Act Crisis*, 27; Benjamin Marshall to Hugh Forbes, Nov. 12, 1763, to James Tapscott, June 22, 1764, and to James Brooks, July 28, 1764, in Stewardson, ed., "Extracts from the Letter-Book of Benjamin Marshall," 205, 207; John Temple, notice, *Boston Post-Boy and Advertiser*, Feb. 6, 1764; Schlesinger, *Colonial Merchants and the American Revolution*, 48n; Ubbelohde, *Vice-Admiralty Courts and the American Revolution*, 93.

2. Nicholas Brown, [no first name given] Cooke, quoted in Wiener, "Rhode Island Merchants and the Sugar Act," 472–73.

3. Joseph Green et al. to Gurdon Salstonstal & Nath[anie]l Shaw, Jan. 9, 1764, and introduction, in Andrews, ed., "State of the Trade," 381, 379; Wiener, "Rhode Island Merchants and the Sugar Act," 476, 483, 494; Rhode Island remonstrance against the Molasses Act, Jan. [27], 1764, *Providence Gazette*, Oct. 20, 1764; "Extract of a Letter from a Gentleman in Philadelphia, to his Friend in Providence, dated February 22, 1764," *Boston Post-Boy and Advertiser*, March 26, 1764.

4. American Duties Act, avalon.law.yale.edu/18th_century/sugar_act_1764.asp; Morgan and Morgan, *Stamp Act Crisis*, 24–26; Barrow, *Trade and Empire*, 178–85; Thomas, *British Politics and the Stamp Act Crisis*, 48, 61, 109; Anderson, *Crucible of War*, 574–80; Stout, *Royal Navy in America*, 34–38.

5. Joseph Green et al. to Gurdon Salstonstal & Nath[anie]l Shaw, Jan. 9, 1764, in Andrews, ed., "State of the Trade," 381; Dickinson, *Late Regulations*, 20.

6. Hopkins later freed *some* of his slaves and introduced legislation prohibiting the importation of slaves into Rhode Island. "P.," "The Remainder of the Essay on the Trade of the Northern Colonies," *Providence Gazette*, Jan. 21, 1764 (quotations in text and note); Wiener, "Rhode Island Merchants and the Sugar Act," 482–84.

7. The American Duties Act of 1764 also more than quintupled the tax on the importation of foreign refined sugar into North America (from five shillings per hundred to 27) and, for the first time, completely prohibited the colonists from buying foreign rum. American Duties Act ("Sugar Act"), avalon.law.yale.edu/18th_century/sugar_act_1764.asp; Bullion, *Great and Necessary Measure*, 102–3; Eacott, *Selling Empire*, 182–83.

8. John Watts to John Aberdein, Aug. 11, 1764, May 4, 1765, *Letter Book of John Watts*, 281, 350; Dickinson, "Address Read at a Meeting of Merchants to Consider

Non-Importation," 412–13; Tyler, *Smugglers & Patriots*, 8, 81–83; Hancock, *Oceans of Wine*, 3, 119.

9. Ubbelohde, *Vice-Admiralty Courts and the American Revolution*, 138. Hiller Zobel notes that the Boston merchants' challenge to the writs of assistance followed Prime Minister William Pitt's 1760 effort to crack down on molasses smuggling and posits that it may have come in response to it. Zobel, *Boston Massacre*, 12–14.

10. John Adams to William Tudor, March 29, 1817, in *Works of John Adams* 10:244–49 (quotation at 245); Lynd and Waldstreicher, "Free Trade, Sovereignty, and Slavery," 606.

11. Morgan and Morgan, *Stamp Act Crisis*, 218–20; Ernst, *Money and Politics in America*, 39; Anderson, *Crucible of War*, 669.

12. John Adams to William Tudor, March 29, 1817, in *Works of John Adams* 10:244–49; Adams, Petition of Lechmere (Argument on Writs of Assistance), editorial note, *Founders Online*; Bailyn, *Ordeal of Thomas Hutchinson*, 54–56.

13. Otis, *Rights of the British Colonies Asserted and Proved*, 54, 39–40.

14. Otis, *Rights of the British Colonies Asserted and Proved*, 29–30; Barker-Benfield, *Culture of Sensibility*. Otis had also "asserted the rights of negroes" in his challenge to writs of assistance. John Adams, quoted in Tudor, *Life of James Otis*, 69; Breen, "Subjecthood and Citizenship," 379.

15. Otis, *Rights of the British Colonies Asserted and Proved*, 80.

16. Otis, *Vindication of the British Colonies*, 18–19; anonymous poet, quoted in William Pencak, "Otis, James (2 Feb. 1725–23 May 1783)," *ANB*.

17. Oswald, *Memorandum on the Folly of Invading Virginia*, 45; Rappleye, *Sons of Providence*, 47, 126; Morgan and Morgan, *Stamp Act Crisis*, 44–48; Stout, *Royal Navy in America*, 66–68; Thomas, *British Politics and the Stamp Act Crisis*, 48, 109; Magra, *Poseidon's Curse*, 296–99.

18. Price, *Capital and Credit in British Overseas Trade*, 8; Anderson, *Crucible of War*, 705.

19. Lee, quoted in Holton, *Forced Founders*, 65; "An Act for the More Easy Recovery of Debts in His Majesty's Plantations and Colonies in *America*," *Statutes at Large, of England and of Great-Britain* 9:248–50; [Knox], *Interest of the Merchants and Manufacturers of Great Britain in the Present Contest with the Colonies*, 35–42.

20. Holton, *Unruly Americans and the Origins of the Constitution*, 270.

21. Ernst, *Money and Politics in America*, 37–42.

22. Hopkins, quoted in Job Almy, deposition, n.d., in Lowell and Quincy, eds., "Hopkins vs. Ward," 338.

23. Ernst, *Money and Politics in America*, 41–42.

24. Ernst, *Money and Politics in America*, 47, 51, 56, 59; Greene and Jellison, "Currency Act of 1764 in Imperial-Colonial Relations," 486.

25. Unnamed British merchant, quoted in Charles Carroll of Carrollton to Charles Carroll of Annapolis, Jan. 31, 1763, in Carroll and Carroll, *Dear Papa, Dear Charley* 1:307; Washington to Robert Stewart, May 2, 1763, *Founders Online*; House of Burgesses, address to Fauquier and resolution, May 28, 1763, *RV* 1:2–8.

26. John Watts to [Robert] Monckton, April 14, 1764, *Letter Book of John Watts*, 243; Ernst, *Money and Politics in America*, 82–83; Sosin, "Imperial Regulation of Colonial Paper Money," 179–85.

27. Watts to Monckton, April 14, 1764, *Letter Book of John Watts*, 242; Ernst, *Money and Politics in America*, 89–95, 103–11, 129–35, 227–28.

28. "Essay on the Trade of the Northern Colonies," *Providence Gazette*, Jan. 14, 1764; Rainbolt, *From Prescription to Persuasion*; Norton, *Liberty's Daughters*, 15–16; Hood,

"Material World of Cloth"; Shammas, "How Self-Sufficient Was Early America?"; Ulrich, "Wheels, Looms, and the Gender Division of Labor in Eighteenth-Century New England"; Ulrich, *Age of Homespun*, 95, 156–66, 192, 201.

29. The anonymous author "Linen Draper," who disagreed with this statement, attributed it to "some Persons among us." *Commercial Conduct of the Province of New-York Considered*, 17; Johns, Gilpin, and Goldsborough, "Observations Respecting the Chesapeake and Delaware Canal," [2?]:287; Taylor, *Transportation Revolution*, 32–33; Buchanan, *Road to Charleston*, 59.

30. Morgan, "Puritan Ethic and the American Revolution"; Breen, *Marketplace of Revolution*, 148–92; Bullock and McIntyre, "Handsome Tokens of a Funeral," 320.

31. Newport dateline, *Newport Mercury*, Aug. 20, 1764; "P.P.," "Philo Publicus," *Boston Gazette*, Oct. 1, 1764; *Boston Evening-Post*, Sept. 24, 1764; Morgan and Morgan, *Stamp Act Crisis*, 32–33; Breen, *Marketplace of Revolution*, 213–17; Bullock and McIntyre, "Handsome Tokens of a Funeral," 338–40; Eacott, *Selling Empire*, 186–88.

32. "The Farmer" and "Sophia Thrifty," both quoted in Breen, *Marketplace of Revolution*, 230, 233; "P.P.," "Philo Publicus," *Boston Gazette*, Oct. 1, 1764.

Chapter 4: Hungry Caterpillars

1. Anderson, *Crucible of War*, 618–26.

2. Dowd, *War Under Heaven*, 157, 164; Crytzer, *Guyasuta and the Fall of Indian America*, 135–37.

3. "Narrative of the Captivity of John M'Cullough," 252–60, 276–78, 283–85 (quotations at 260 and 276); Thomas King, quoted in Downes, *Council Fires on the Upper Ohio*, 117; Smith, *Historical Account of the Expedition Against the Ohio Indians*, 26–29; Calloway, *Indian World of George Washington*, 118–19.

4. Croghan to Johnson, July 12, 1765, Croghan to William Murray, July 12, 1765, in *Papers of Sir William Johnson* 11:837–38, 841; Anderson, *Crucible of War*, 628–31.

5. Hopkins, *Memoirs of the Life of Mrs. Sarah Osborn*, 35–49; Brekus *Sarah Osborn's World*, 103–22; Winiarski, *Darkness Falls on the Land of Light*, 141.

6. Brekus, *Sarah Osborn's World*, 16–20, 122, 128, 171–73.

7. Osborn, quoted in Brekus, *Sarah Osborn's World*, 248.

8. Osborn to Fish, Feb. 28–March 7, 1767, introduction, in Norton, "My Resting Reaping Times," 523–24, 519–21; Brekus, *Sarah Osborn's World*, 174, 238–42, 265–75.

9. 1 Corinthians 14:34; Brekus, *Sarah Osborn's World*, 23, 248.

10. Osborn, quoted in Brekus, *Sarah Osborn's World*, 248; Osborn to Fish, Feb. 28–March 7, 1767, in Norton, "My Resting Reaping Times," 526.

11. Osborn to Fish, Feb. 28–March 7, 1767, in Norton, "My Resting Reaping Times," 527.

12. Sellers, "Private Profits and British Colonial Policy," 544, 547–48; Kars, *Breaking Loose Together*, 34–42.

13. Henry Eustace McCulloh, quoted in Kars, *Breaking Loose Together*, 36, 224n.

14. Kars, *Breaking Loose Together*, 27–54.

15. Henry Eustace McCulloh, memorial to the North Carolina Council, April 25, 1765, *NCCR* 7:21, 24.

16. Henry Eustace McCulloh, memorial to the North Carolina Council, April 25, 1765, and Henry Eustace McCulloh to Edmund Fanning, May 9, 1765, *NCCR* 7:24, 32.

17. Henry Eustace McCulloh to Edmund Fanning, May 9, 1765, *NCCR* 7:32; Sims, "Address to the People of Granville County," June 6, 1765, 189–90.

18. Bullion, *Great and Necessary Measure*, 76.

19. Eustace, *Passion Is the Gale*, 406; Siegel, "Mommy Dearest," 209–36.

20. Morgan, "Thomas Hutchinson and the Stamp Act," 490–91.

21. Hutchinson, quoted in Bailyn, *Ordeal of Thomas Hutchinson*, 22, 20, 18.

22. Mihm, "Funding the Revolution," 328.

23. Grenville, quoted in Bullion, *Great and Necessary Measure*, 157, 141–42.

24. Grenville, quoted in Bullion, *Great and Necessary Measure*, 159.

25. Barré, quoted in Jared Ingersoll to Thomas Fitch, Feb. 11, 1765, in Morgan, ed., *Prologue to Revolution*, 32; Anderson, *Crucible of War*, 643; Thomas, *British Politics and the Stamp Act Crisis*, 91–93, 98.

26. Marshall, "Britain's American Problem," 19–20; Lewis, "New Spain During the American Revolution"; Klooster, *Revolutions in the Atlantic World*; Kuethe and Andrien, *Spanish Atlantic World in the Eighteenth Century*, 229–304; Du Rivage, *Revolution Against Empire*, 20; Zepeda Cortés, *Minister, Madman, Mastermind*; Zepeda Cortés, "Empire, Reform, and Corruption"; Adelman, *Sovereignty and Revolution in the Iberian Atlantic*; Navarro García, "Crisis del Reformismo Borbónico bajo Carlos IV."

27. George III to Bute, Feb. 17, 1763, quoted in Bullion, "Ten Thousand in America," 651.

28. Tate, "Coming of the Revolution in Virginia."

29. Mills, *Bishops by Ballot*, 1–154; Isaac, *Transformation of Virginia*, 183–98; Rhoden, *Revolutionary Anglicanism*, 37–63.

30. Breen, *Marketplace of Revolution*, 148; Heimert, *Religion and the American Mind*; Colbourn, *Lamp of Experience*; Bonomi, *Under the Cope of Heaven*, 161–62, 168; Winiarski, *Darkness Falls on the Land of Light*, 373, 506.

31. Gage to Halifax, Jan. 23, 1765, in Alvord and Carter, eds., *Critical Period*, 422–23; Gipson, *Coming of the Revolution*, xi. For a brilliant refutation of Gipson's thesis that the removal of the French threat freed British colonists to begin the push for independence, see Murrin, "French and Indian War."

32. Watts to [Robert] Monckton, May 16, 1764, *Letter Book of John Watts*, 255; Greene, "Seven Years' War and the American Revolution," 94–95.

33. To be sure, in this counterfactual scenario, most of Canada would have remained French!

34. Gage to Halifax, Jan. 23, 1765, in *Correspondence of General Thomas Gage* 1:49; Shy, *Toward Lexington*, 163–81, 187; McCurdy, *Quarters*, 92–94. For earlier provincial resistance to supplying British troops, see Thomas Gage to the earl of Albemarle, Jan. 22, 1756, in Keppel, ed., *Life of Augustus, Viscount Keppel* 1:441.

35. Alden, *General Gage in America*, 109; Shy, *Toward Lexington*, 181–89; Anderson, *Crucible of War*, 647–51; McCurdy, *Quarters*, 94–100.

36. Wood, "Changing Population of the Colonial South," 60.

37. James Maury to the John Camm, Dec. 12, 1763, academic.brooklyn.cuny.edu/history /dfg/amrv/maury.htm. Normally preachers did not receive cash salaries but an annual allotment of sixteen thousand pounds of tobacco. Short crops in 1755 and 1758 had caused the value of tobacco to skyrocket, leading the assembly to adopt legislation depriving ministers of this windfall. Meade, *Patrick Henry* 1:118–34; Kukla, *Patrick Henry*, 39–46.

38. Fauquier to Board of Trade, June 5, 1765, in *Official Papers of Francis Fauquier* 3:1250.

39. Jefferson, quoted in Isaac, "Lighting the Fuse of Revolution in Virginia," 662; Jefferson, quoted in Morgan and Morgan, *Stamp Act Crisis*, 97; [Murray], "Journal of a French Traveller in the Colonies," 745.

40. [Murray], "Journal of a French Traveller in the Colonies," May 30, 1765, 745.

41. A guinea was a gold coin worth 21 shillings. [Murray], "Journal of a French Traveller in

the Colonies," May 30, 1765, 745; Virginia Stamp Act resolutions and Jefferson, quoted in Morgan and Morgan, *Stamp Act Crisis*, 96–97.

42. Bailyn, *Ideological Origins of the American Revolution*, 144–50, 158–59.
43. Whately, quoted in Bullion, *Great and Necessary Measure*, 137, 106, 108.
44. Morgan and Morgan, *Stamp Act Crisis*, 103.
45. Isaac, "Lighting the Fuse of Revolution in Virginia"; Beatty, "'French Traveller,' Patrick Henry, and the Contagion of Liberty."
46. [Murray], "Journal of a French Traveller in the Colonies," June 6, 1765, 747; Henry Conway, speech in House of Commons, Feb. 21, 1766, in Simmons and Thomas, eds., *Proceedings and Debates of the British Parliament Respecting North America* 2:281; Morgan and Morgan, *Stamp Act Crisis*, 211–12; "A Virginia Planter" [George Mason], ". . . Letter to the Committee of Merchants in London . . . ," June 6, 1766, in *Papers of George Mason* 1:67; Rosenblithe, "Where Tyranny Begins"; Siegel, "Mommy Dearest," 214, 217.

Chapter 5: A Hobnail or a Horseshoe

1. George III, quoted in Bullion, *Great and Necessary Measure*, 191. Grenville gave the king a more immediate reason to fire him when he insulted the queen mother by promoting legislation preventing her from becoming regent in the event George III died before his son came of age. Thomas, *British Politics and the Stamp Act Crisis*, 115–19.
2. Grenville, diary, July 10, 1765, in Smith, ed., *Grenville Papers* 3:213.
3. Speck, *Butcher*.
4. Thomas, *British Politics and the Stamp Act Crisis*, 121.
5. As was already the case with processing fees, the recipient of a land grant would incur costs at two separate stages of the process: when the land office granted him or her an order for the land to be surveyed, and again when the surveyors' plat was returned to the land office to be exchanged for a land patent.
6. Cyrus Baldwin to Loammi Baldwin, Aug. 15, 1765, masshist.org/database/601?mode= transcript; Anderson, *Crucible of War*, 646; Ulrich, "Political Protest and the World of Goods," 75.
7. Young, "Ebenezer Mackintosh," 15, 17, 20–23.
8. Mackintosh's participation may have been to some extent coerced, or at least controlled. Just two days before the Stamp Act riot, the sheriff served him and his shoemaking partner with a warrant for unpaid taxes, apparently at the behest of noted Whig Samuel Adams, who had been the local tax collector when this money came due. But the sheriff later returned the warrant unserved, perhaps at Adams's direction. Morgan and Morgan, *Stamp Act Crisis*, 127–35 (quotations at 130); Young, "Ebenezer Mackintosh," 15–16, 23.
9. Morgan and Morgan, *Stamp Act Crisis*, 134–35; Kulikoff, "Progress of Inequality in Revolutionary Boston"; Nash, *Urban Crucible*, 292–98. I am grateful for Peter H. Wood's explication of the crucible comparison.
10. Nash, *Unknown American Revolution*, 56; Morgan and Morgan, *Stamp Act Crisis*, 160.
11. Morgan and Morgan, *Stamp Act Crisis*, 230–68.
12. *Maryland Gazette*, Oct. 17, 1765 (supplement); "An Enemy to Hypocrisy," *Virginia Gazette* (Purdie & Dixon), July 18, 1766; Maier, *Old Revolutionaries*, 177–78; Egnal, *Mighty Empire*, 217–18.
13. White South Carolinians customarily celebrated Christmas Eve by firing their guns,

but that was also how they warned of slave revolts, so the council banned the practice, lest too many false alarms "prevent a True one being attended to." Wood, "'Liberty Is Sweet,'" 157–59.

14. Morgan and Morgan, *Stamp Act Crisis*, 158–60, 163, 172.

15. Ubbelohde, *Vice-Admiralty Courts and the American Revolution*, 82–83.

16. Samuel Rhoads Jr. to Richard Neave & Son, March 1, 1766, in Biddle and Rhoads Jr., "Extracts from the Letter-book of Samuel Rhoads Jr. of Philadelphia," 425.

17. "Declaration of the Congress held at New York Octr. 7. 1765," "Preserving American Freedom: The Evolution of American Liberties in Fifty Documents," digitalhistory. hsp.org/pafrm/doc/declaration-congress-held-new-york-october-7-1765; Morgan and Morgan, *Stamp Act Crisis*, 71, 108–21; Thomas, *British Politics and the Stamp Act Crisis*, 94–95.

18. Anderson, *Crucible of War*, 679; Raphael, *First American Revolution*, 26.

19. Tyler, *Smugglers & Patriots*, 91; Schlesinger, *Colonial Merchants and the American Revolution*, 79.

20. Humphry Ploughjogger [Adams], *Boston Gazette*, Oct. 14, 1765, *Founders Online*; "Y. Z.," *Boston Evening-Post*, reprinted in *Pennsylvania Gazette*, Dec. 26, 1765; Anderson, *Crucible of War*, 653, 682–83.

21. "A Friend to this COLONY," *Newport Mercury*, Nov. 23, 1767; Newport dateline, *Newport Mercury*, March 3–10, 1766; Providence dateline, *Providence Gazette*, March 12, 1766; New London dateline, *Newport Mercury*, May 5–12, 1766; Schlesinger, *Colonial Merchants and the American Revolution*, 76.

22. Breen, *Marketplace of Revolution*, 10–20 (quotation at 11); Benjamin Franklin, marginal note on page 26 of his copy of the anonymous *True Constitutional Means for Putting an End to the Disputes Between Great-Britain and the American Colonies*; Greene, "Seven Years' War and the American Revolution," 95.

23. [Dulany], *Considerations on the Propriety of Imposing Taxes in the British Colonies, for the Purpose of Raising a Revenue*, 4, 7–8; Reid, *Constitutional History of the American Revolution*, 47–48.

24. Burnaby, *Travels Through the Middle Settlements in North-America*, 44.

25. Lee, *Essay in Vindication of the Continental Colonies of America*, 20.

26. Bland, "An Inquiry into the Rights of the British Colonies . . . ," [c. March 14, 1766], *RV* 1:40–41; "Rusticus" [Richard Henry Lee], essay, n.d. [filed at the end of 1769], in Hoffman, *Lee Family Papers*.

27. "R. L—L," *Virginia Gazette* (Rind), Sept. 22, 1768; Benjamin Franklin to William Franklin, March 22, 1775, *Founders Online*; Van Doren, *Benjamin Franklin*, 504; Morgan, *Benjamin Franklin*, 89.

28. George Washington to Robert Cary & Company, Sept. 20, 1765, *Founders Online*; Bland, "An Inquiry into the Rights of the British Colonies . . . ," [c. March 14, 1766], *RV* 1:40–41; "Rusticus" [Richard Henry Lee], essay, n.d. [filed at the end of 1769], in Hoffman, *Lee Family Papers*; Ragsdale, "George Washington," 157.

29. Dickinson, *Late Regulations,* 49; [Dulany], *Considerations on the Propriety of Imposing Taxes in the British Colonies for the Purpose of Raising a Revenue*, 77; "Vindex," *Virginia Gazette, or, Norfolk Intelligencer*, Aug. 11, 1774; Beard and Beard, *Rise of American Civilization* 1:202; Reid, *Constitutional History of the American Revolution*, 38; Crowley, *Privileges of Independence*, 21–23, 174n.

30. Thomas, *British Politics and the Stamp Act Crisis*, 139.

31. New York dateline, *Pennsylvania Gazette*, Feb. 27, 1766; [Robert] Nugent, speech in House of Commons, Jan. 14, 1766, in *Correspondence of William Pitt* 2:364n; Ernst,

Money and Politics in America, 100; Thomas, *British Politics and the Stamp Act Crisis,* 139–41, 149–50.

32. Nelson, "Patriot Royalism," 533–72.

33. Pitt and unnamed MPs, statements in House of Commons, Jan. 14, 1766, quoted in *Correspondence of William Pitt* 2:368n; Pitt, quoted in George Grenville to William Knox, Aug. 15, 1768, in Knox, *Extra-Official State Papers* 2:15 (appendix); Pitt, quoted in Ayling, *Elder Pitt,* 340; Pitt, quoted in George Grenville to William Knox, June 27, 1768, William Knox Papers, CL. Pitt appears to have been responding to James Otis's anonymous essay, published in the *Boston Gazette* and in London as a freestanding pamphlet, lamenting that the Navigation Acts forbad colonists "to push the manufacture of iron much beyond the making a horse-shoe or a hob nail." Otis, *Considerations on Behalf of the Colonists in a Letter to a Noble Lord,* 22. On his "strident commercialism," see Vaughn, "Politics of Empire," 352–67 (quotation at 364n).

34. "EXAMINATION of Doctor BENJAMIN FRANKLIN, before an August Assembly, relating to the Repeal of the STAMP-ACT, &c.," [Feb. 13, 1766], *Papers of Benjamin Franklin.*

35. "EXAMINATION of Doctor BENJAMIN FRANKLIN, before an August Assembly, relating to the Repeal of the STAMP-ACT, &c.," [Feb. 13, 1766], *Papers of Benjamin Franklin.*

36. A year earlier, Franklin had proposed that Parliament print up paper money and offer it to the cash-strapped colonists at 6 percent interest, producing more imperial revenue than the proposed stamp duties. Franklin, Scheme for Supplying the Colonies with a Paper Currency, [Feb. 11–12? 1765], "EXAMINATION of Doctor BENJAMIN FRANKLIN, before an August Assembly, relating to the Repeal of the STAMP-ACT, &c.," [Feb. 13, 1766], *Papers of Benjamin Franklin*; Dickinson, *Late Regulations,* 14; Samuel Rhoads Jr. to Neate, Pigou, & Booth, June 22, 1764, Biddle and Rhoads Jr., "Extracts from the Letter-book of Samuel Rhoads, Jr.," 423.

37. Declaratory Act, March 18, 1766, avalon.law.yale.edu/18th_century/declaratory_act_1766.asp.

38. Thomas, *British Politics and the Stamp Act Crisis,* 271. In yet another effort to placate North Americans trading to the Caribbean, Parliament also established, on the islands of Jamaica and Dominica, five free ports where British subjects could purchase foreign molasses. Thomas, *British Politics and the Stamp Act Crisis,* 254–73.

Chapter 6: Who Should Rule at Home?

1. Vassa [Equiano], *Interesting Narrative,* docsouth.unc.edu/neh/equiano1/equiano1.html. Vincent Carretta, whose excellent biography of Vassa reveals that he was born in South Carolina, not West Africa (as he claimed), calls him Olaudah Equiano, but I have used the name that, as Carretta shows, was most often used by the man himself. Carretta, *Equiano, the African,* xvi; Lovejoy, "Autobiography and Memory," 322; Sidbury, *Becoming African in America,* 220n.

2. Becker, *History of Political Parties in the Province of New York,* 22.

3. Mason indicated on his manuscript copy of this letter that it appeared in the *Ledger,* but if it did, no copy of that issue survives. "A Virginia Planter" [George Mason], ". . . Letter to the Committee of Merchants in London . . . ," June 6, 1766, in *Papers of George Mason* 1:67, 72n; Washington to Capel & Osgood Hanbury, July 25, 1767, *Founders Online*; *Virginia Gazette* (Purdie & Dixon), Nov. 9, 1769 (supplement); Deuteronomy 16:19.

4. Criminal trials, which did not require stamps, continued. Bridenbaugh, "Violence and Virtue in Virginia," 3–4.

5. Jesse Thompson, deposition, *Virginia Gazette* (Purdie & Dixon), Sept. 12, 1766.

6. "Dikephilos," *Virginia Gazette* (Purdie & Dixon), July 18, 1766.

7. "Dikephilos," *Virginia Gazette* (Purdie & Dixon), July 18, 1766.

8. The more common explanation for Robinson's death was kidney stones. Bridenbaugh, "Violence and Virtue in Virginia," 9.

9. Jefferson to Nicholas Lewis, July 29, 1787, *Founders Online*; Price, *Capital and Credit in British Overseas Trade*, 122–23, 15–19, 126.

10. "C. R.," *Virginia Gazette* (Rind), March 3, 1768; Land, "Economic Base and Social Structure," 649–50, 653; Price, *Capital and Credit in British Overseas Trade*, 6; Price, "Rise of Glasgow in the Chesapeake Tobacco Trade."

11. May 20, 1774, *Diary of Colonel Landon Carter of Sabine Hall* 2:813; Watts to Moses Franks, March 30, 1765, *Letter Book of John Watts*, 339; Washington to Robert Cary & Company, Aug. 10, 1760, Jefferson, "Additional questions of M. de Meusnier, and answers," [c. Jan.–Feb. 1786], *Founders Online*; Breen, *Tobacco Culture*.

12. "The Rev. Mr. Davenport's Retractions," July 28, 1744, in Fish, *Church of Christ a Firm and Durable House*, 126n, 132–37, 143; Buel and Buel, *Way of Duty*, 10–17; Winiarski, *Darkness Falls on the Land of Light*, 287–364; Gross, *Minutemen and Their World*, 18–22; Nash, *Unknown American Revolution*, 7.

13. Bushman, *From Puritan to Yankee*, 241, 253–60; Bonomi, *Under the Cope of Heaven*, 166–67.

14. Bushman, *From Puritan to Yankee*, 260–62; Collier, *Roger Sherman's Connecticut*, 36–37, 57, 62.

15. Tryon to Shelburne, July 4, 1767, *NCCR* 7:497; Kars, *Breaking Loose Together*, 150.

16. Husband, "Some Remarks on Religion," 214; Jones, "Herman Husband," 83–86; Kars, *Breaking Loose Together*, 6, 111–16, 121, 133–35, 138–39; Whittenburg, "Planters, Merchants, and Lawyers"; Ekirch, "'New Government of Liberty'"; Stewart, *Redemption from Tyranny*.

17. Husband, *Impartial Relation of the First Rise and Cause*, 10–11; Husband, *Fan for Fanning*, 353; Jones, "Herman Husband," 106–8; Bullock, *Revolutionary Brotherhood*; Kars, *Breaking Loose Together*, 135.

18. Husband, *Impartial Relation of the First Rise and Cause of the Recent Differences*, 18, 12; Kars, *Breaking Loose Together*, 135–36.

19. Humphrey, *Land and Liberty*, 4, 6, 39–41, 63–68, 78–81; Hauptman, "Road to Kingsbridge."

20. Prendergast, quoted in Merrell, "'Exactly as They Appear,'" 203, 214, 228–32. Lord Shelburne, the British cabinet secretary with responsibility for America, instructed the council to try the case again. It did so in March 1767 but reached the same verdict. *Geographic, Historical Summary*, 4–10, 13–56; Mark and Handlin, "Land Cases in Colonial New York," 165–66; Humphrey, *Land and Liberty*, 66–67, 78–80.

21. Henry Moore to Henry Conway, April 30, 1766, *DRCHSNY* 7:825; Nash, *Unknown American Revolution*, 83.

22. Joseph Bates, George Hughson, and Samuel Peters, testimony, in Mark and Handlin, "Land Cases in Colonial New York," 187, 180–81.

23. Simon Calkins, quoted in Samuel Towner, testimony, and Tenbrook, testimony, in Mark and Handlin, "Land Cases in Colonial New York," 189–90.

24. May 1, 1766, *Montresor Journals*, 363; Moss Kent, testimony, in Mark and Handlin, "Land Cases in Colonial New York," 175; Gage to Henry Conway, June 24, 1766, in *Correspondence of General Thomas Gage* 1:95; Humphrey, *Land and Liberty*, 69–70.

25. June 28, July 2, 1766, *Montresor Journals*, 375–76; Humphrey, *Land and Liberty*, 75.

26. Humphrey, *Land and Liberty*, 75 (Prendergast quotation), 77.

27. New Jersey council, quoted in William Franklin to Hillsborough, Nov. 23, 1768, in Ricord and Nelson, eds., *Documents Relating to the Colonial History of the State of New Jersey*, Ser. 1, 10:84; Jensen, *Founding of a Nation*, 212–13; Thomas, *British Politics and the Stamp Act Crisis*, 302; Morgan, *Benjamin Franklin*, 162.

28. Shy, *Toward Lexington*, 43–44; McCurdy, *Quarters*, 19–21.

29. New York City merchants, petition, read on Feb. 16, 1767, *Journals of the House of Commons* 31:158–60; Schlesinger, *Colonial Merchants and the American Revolution*, 87.

Chapter 7: From Bengal to Boston

1. Osborn to Fish, Feb. 28–March 7, 1767, in Norton, "My Resting Reaping Times," 523–24.

2. Osborn to Fish, Feb. 28–March 7, 1767, in Norton, "My Resting Reaping Times," 524–26.

3. Osborn to Fish, Feb. 28–March 7, 1767, in Norton, "My Resting Reaping Times," 526–29; Norton, *Liberty's Daughters*, 129–32.

4. Osborn, quoted in Brekus, *Sarah Osborn's World*, 183; Hopkins, *Memoirs of the Life of Mrs. Sarah Osborn*, 48.

5. Marie Peters, "Pitt, William, first earl of Chatham [*known as* Pitt the elder] (1708–1778)," *DNB*.

6. Chatham to Shelburne, Feb. 3, 1767, in *Correspondence of William Pitt* 3:188–89; Chaffin, "Townshend Acts of 1767," 101–3.

7. Thomas, *Townshend Duties Crisis*, 22; Thomas, *British Politics and the Stamp Act Crisis*, 338–39.

8. Labaree, *Boston Tea Party*, 18; Thomas, *British Politics and the Stamp Act Crisis*, 310, 337–39, 347; Thomas, *Townshend Duties Crisis*, 7.

9. Thomas, *Townshend Duties Crisis*, 7; Bunker, *Empire on the Edge*, 43–45; P. D. G. Thomas, "Townshend, Charles (1725–1767)," *DNB*; Vaughn, "Politics of Empire," 392–93, 557–58; Eacott, *Selling Empire*, 168–69.

10. In the end, P. D. G. Thomas reports, the hole that Parliament had opened in the imperial budget by reducing the landholders' tax was patched up "not by the levy on the East India Company, but by an assiduous scrutiny by Townshend of government departments that uncovered numerous odd sums of money." P. D. G. Thomas, "Townshend, Charles (1725–1767)," *DNB*; Beckford to Chatham, Jan. 27, 1767, in *Correspondence of William Pitt* 3:177; Neal, *Rise of Financial Capitalism*, 241–45; Vaughn, "Politics of Empire," 557; Bunker, *Empire on the Edge*, 45.

11. Townshend, quoted in Thomas, *British Politics and the Stamp Act Crisis*, 350; Labaree, *Boston Tea Party*, 19–20; "Benevolus" [Franklin], On the Propriety of Taxing America, *London Chronicle*, April 9–11, 1767, *Papers of Benjamin Franklin*; Wood, *Americanization of Benjamin Franklin*, 130; Morgan, *Benjamin Franklin*, 164–65.

12. The cost of freeing the highest colonial officials from dependence on the provincial legislatures was not high, since many already had independent sources of income such as dedicated taxes. avalon.law.yale.edu/18th_century/townsend_act_1767.asp; Thomas, *British Politics and the Stamp Act Crisis*, 36, 346–48, 355, 361–62.

13. Since the EIC auctioned off tea for an average of 36 pence per pound, the 25 percent transshipment tax averaged around nine pence per pound—triple the American tea importation duty that replaced it. Labaree, *Boston Tea Party*, 20–21; Thomas, *Townshend Duties Crisis*, 29.

14. Townshend, quoted by George Grenville in Thomas, *Townshend Duties Crisis*, 30;

Townshend, speech in House of Commons, Jan. 26, 1767, in Simmons and Thomas, *Proceedings and Debates of the British Parliament Respecting North America* 2:410; Morgan, *Benjamin Franklin*, 166.

15. Chaffin, "Townshend Acts," 92, 105, 109–11; Thomas, *British Politics and the Stamp Act Crisis*, 359–60; Carp, *Rebels Rising*, 225.

16. Dickerson, "Writs of Assistance as a Cause of the American Revolution," 42, 48–75; Peter D. G. Thomas, "Townshend, Charles (1725–1767)," *DNB*.

17. Pasley, *"Tyranny of Printers"*; Rawson, "Guardians of Their Own Liberty."

18. "A Farmer" [Dickinson], "Letters from a Farmer in Pennsylvania, To the Inhabitants of the British Colonies," *Pennsylvania Chronicle*, Dec. 7, 1767; [Dickinson], *Letters from a Farmer in Pennsylvania*; Elaine K. Ginsberg, "Dickinson, John (8 Nov. 1732–14 Feb. 1808)," *ANB*.

19. "A.F.," *Boston Gazette*, Aug. 31, 1767, Oct. 28, 1767, in *Report of the Record Commissioners of the City of Boston Containing the Boston Town Records, 1758–1769*, 221–25. "If nonimportation was a forceful way to oppose unlawful parliamentary encroachments upon colonial rights, it was also an economic weapon to fight a local depression." Champagne, "Family Politics Versus Constitutional Principles," 64.

20. Oct. 28, 1767, in *Report of the Record Commissioners of the City of Boston Containing the Boston Town Records, 1758 to 1769*, 221–25; Boston dateline, *Boston Gazette*, Jan. 4, 1768; *Providence Gazette*, Nov. 7, 1767; *New-York Gazette*, Nov. 30–Dec. 7, 1767; Ames, *Astronomical Diary, or Almanack, for the Year of Our Lord Christ 1768*; Lepore, *Book of Ages*, 146.

21. Nothing came of the effort. Boston town meeting, Jan. 13, May 4, 1768, in *Report of the Record Commissioners of the City of Boston Containing the Boston Town Records, 1758 to 1769*, 230–32, 249–50; Nellis, "Misreading the Signs"; Ulrich, "Sheep in the Parlor, Wheels on the Common," 182–89.

22. Newport dateline, *Providence Gazette*, Jan. 16, 1768; Schlesinger, *Colonial Merchants and the American Revolution*, 109; Norton, *Liberty's Daughters*, 157–61; Ulrich, "Political Protest and the World of Goods," 64–65, 68–69. The eighteenth-century belief that women drank more tea than men has recently been challenged. Fichter, *Tea's Party*.

23. Providence dateline, *South-Carolina Gazette*, Feb. 22–29, 1768.

24. Jensen, *Founding of a Nation*, 271, 245–46, 265n, 269; "Proceedings of the Merchants of Boston," March 4, 1768, in Elwyn, ed., *Papers Relating to Public Events in Massachusetts Preceding the American Revolution*, 58–59; Bernard to Hillsborough, Aug. 9, 1768, in Bernard, Gage, and Hood, *Letters to the Ministry*, 49; Andrews, "Boston Merchants and the Non-Importation Movement," 201–3; Schlesinger, *Colonial Merchants and the American Revolution*, 115–20; Ubbelohde, *Vice-Admiralty Courts and the American Revolution*, 115.

25. Griffitts, "The Female Patriots" (1768), in Blecki and Wulf, eds, *Milcah Martha Moore's Book*, 172; [Griffitts], "The Female Patriots," *Pennsylvania Chronicle*, Dec. 18–25, 1769; Branson, *These Fiery Frenchified Dames*, 21–22. My thanks to Professor Mary Bilder of Boston College Law School for this point about Griffitts addressing women as possessors of formal political power.

Chapter 8: Red Flag Over Boston

1. Paraphrased in Ann Hulton to [Elizabeth] Lightbody, June 30, 1768, in Hulton, *Letters of a Loyalist Lady*, 11; Bernard to Shelburne, March 19, 1768, in Bernard, Gage, and

Hood, *Letters to the Ministry*, 13; Clark, "American Board of Customs"; Jensen, *Founding of a Nation*, 280.

2. Bernard to Shelburne, March 19, 1768, Bernard to Hillsborough, June 16–18, 1768, in Bernard, Gage, and Hood, *Letters to the Ministry*, 14, 25; Jensen, *Founding of a Nation*, 281–82, 290; Magra, *Poseidon's Curse*, 260. For Bostonians' earlier resistance to Royal Navy impressment, see Brunsman, *Evil Necessity*, 101–5, 222–34, 242. In Restoration England, the term *Whig* had been used for those who sought to exclude the Catholic James, Duke of York, from the line of succession to the throne and more generally to limit the power of the monarchy. Since then, the term *Whigs* had described the champions of parliamentary authority over the crown. Around 1768, it started being applied to Americans who resisted the parliamentary initiatives of the 1760s. The resisters themselves preferred the term *Patriots*, as do most historians, but I have opted for the more neutral *Whigs*. Geiter, "Restoration Crisis and the Launching of Pennsylvania," 301.

3. Middlekauff, *Glorious Cause*, 170, 172.

4. Bernard to Hillsborough, June 11–13, 1768, Richard Acklom Harrison, affidavit, June 11, 1768, Board of Customs Commissioners, minutes, June 13, 1768, in Bernard, Gage, and Hood, *Letters to the Ministry*, 20, 93, 86–88; Jensen, *Founding of a Nation*, 282.

5. Jensen, *Founding of a Nation*, 290. J. L. Bell doubts the flag was entirely red, since that was the warning banner flown outside the homes of people afflicted with smallpox and would hardly seem inviting. But the intended message may have been distress or defiance; the Whigs preparing to defend Fort Ticonderoga from Gen. John Burgoyne flew a red flag. Board of Customs Commissioners, minutes, June 14, 1768, in Bernard, Gage, and Hood, *Letters to the Ministry*, 89; July 3, 1777, in Wasmus, *Eyewitness Account of the American Revolution and New England Life*, 58; Bell, "Newspapers on the Flag at Liberty Tree," April 27, 2007, boston1775.blogspot.com/2007/04/newspapers-on-flag-at-liberty-tree.html.

6. Andrews, "Boston Merchants and the Non-Importation Movement," 204; Jensen, *Founding of a Nation*, 249–50, 253.

7. Champagne, "Family Politics Versus Constitutional Principles," 68–75.

8. Husband, *Continuation of the Impartial Relation*, 16 (first quotation), 22 (third quotation); Husband, *Impartial Relation*, 16 (second quotation); Husband, *Fan for Fanning*, 360; Charles Town dateline, *South-Carolina Gazette*, Sept. 12, 1768; Jones, "Herman Husband," 118; Kars, *Breaking Loose Together*, 138.

9. Kars, *Breaking Loose Together*, 2, 138; Husband, *Fan for Fanning*, 361.

10. Woodmason, *Carolina Backcountry on the Eve of the Revolution*, 214.

11. Since the circuit court bill violated imperial policy by granting judges lifetime tenure, it appeared to be destined for a royal veto, and many westerners considered it a trick. Edgar, *South Carolina*, 212–13; Bartow, "'Several and Very Great Grievances.'"

12. "Plan of Regulation," quoted in Jensen, *Founding of a Nation*, 259; William White, quoted in Klein, *Unification of a Slave State*, 69–71; Edgar, *South Carolina*, 214.

13. Jones, "Herman Husband," 123–24, 128–29; Kars, *Breaking Loose Together*, 139.

14. Husband, *Impartial Relation*, 38, 22–23; Husband, *Continuation of the Impartial Relation*, 15.

15. Husband, *Impartial Relation*, 44–45.

16. Francis Lock, deposition, Oct. 14, 1768, Tryon to Hillsborough, Dec. 24, 1768, in Powell, Huhta, and Farnham, eds., *Regulators in North Carolina*, 191–92, 215.

17. Tryon to Hillsborough, Dec. 24, 1768 (first quotation), Tryon, address to North Carolina legislature, Nov. 15, 1768, Anson County Inhabitants to Tryon, Aug. 1768 (second quotation), Samuel Spencer to William Tryon, April 28, 1768 (third quotation), in Powell, Huhta, and Farnham, eds., *Regulators in North Carolina*, 205–6, 147, 94–96.

18. Kay, "North Carolina Regulation," 90–91.

19. Husband, *Impartial Relation*, 48–50.

20. Fanning resigned his position. Husband, *Impartial Relation*, 54–57; Husband, *Fan for Fanning*, 386; Tryon to Hillsborough, Dec. 24, 1768, *NCCR* 7:884–85.

21. Kars, *Breaking Loose Together*, 171–72.

22. Bernard to Hillsborough, July 9, 11, 1768, in Bernard, Gage, and Hood, *Letters to the Ministry*, 38, 41.

23. Jensen, *Founding of a Nation*, 293–96.

24. Shelburne to William Johnson, Jan. 5, 1768, *DRCHSNY* 8:2; Jensen, *Founding of a Nation*, 229.

25. The Suffering Traders were Pennsylvania merchants whose pack trains had been commandeered during the Seven Years' War by British and provincial officers (including George Washington) or plundered during the native uprising known as Pontiac's Rebellion. "At a Treaty with the 6 Nations, Shawanese Delawares, Senecas of Ohio & Dependants &c. opened at Fort Stanwix on Monday the 24 Oct. 1768," Fort Stanwix deed, Nov. 5, 1768, *DRCHSNY* 8:112–37; Representation of the Board of Trade to the King upon Sir William Johnson's Treaty with the Indians, April 25, 1769, *DRCHSNY* 8:158–63; Calloway, *Indian World of George Washington*, 194.

26. Fort Stanwix deed, Nov. 5, 1768, *DRCHSNY* 8:136.

27. George Washington to Charles Washington, Jan. 31, 1770, William Crawford to George Washington, Nov. 12, 1773, Washington to Presley Nevill, June 16, 1794, *Founders Online*; Calloway, *Indian World of George Washington*, 185–88, 191–95, 199–203.

28. Franklin Minor to Lyman Draper, March 23, 1852, Draper Manuscripts, 13ZZa; Loyal Company and Greenbriar Company surveys in Augusta County, [November 1768–May 1769], Virginia Land Office Records, LiVi; [William Preston], survey for Anne Grayson, March 20, 1769, and William Preston, survey book, [1768–1769], Preston Family Papers, folders 589, 581, VHS; William Preston, receipt to Josiah Ramsay, April 13, 1769, Wyndham Robertson Papers (Manuscripts Department, University of Chicago library; microfilm at LiVi), folder 5; John Norton to Thomas Walker, July 8, 1769, Thomas Walker Papers (part of the Rives-Walker Collection), container 162, LC; Calloway, *Indian World of George Washington*, 109, 191.

29. Jefferson to Robert Smith, July 1, 1805, *Founders Online*; Malone, *Jefferson, the Virginian*, "The Walker Affair, 1768–1809," 447–51.

30. July 18, 1769, New York council minutes 26:153–54, New York State Archives, in Jennings, ed., *Iroquois Indians*; Henry Moore to Hillsborough, Jan. 27, 1769, *DRCHSNY* 8:149; Holton, *Forced Founders*, 11–12.

31. Stuart and the Cherokees later agreed to a compromise boundary between the one they had drawn in October 1768 and the one negotiated at Stanwix a month later. But the new Anglo-Cherokee border only gave Virginia speculators a sliver of Kentucky. In marking it out, Virginia surveyors pushed it farther west, but for the moment the imperial government stuck by its ban on colonial settlement anywhere west of the Appalachian Mountains. Holton, "Revolt of the Ruling Class," 74–79, 93–95.

32. Dec. 16, 1768, April 25, 1769, in McIlwaine, Hillman, and Hall, eds., *Executive Journals of the Council* 6:309, 314–15; House of Burgesses, memorial to Botetourt, Dec. 13, 1769, *JHB . . . 1766–1769*, 334–36; Hillsborough to Johnson, Jan. 4, 1769, Representation of the Board of Trade to the King upon Sir William Johnson's Treaty with the Indians, April 25, 1769, *DRCHSNY* 8:145, 160. With the exception of bounty grants to Seven Years' War veterans, Virginia issued only four more trans-Appalachian patents before independence. Patent Book XLI, 325, 438–40, Virginia Land Office Records, LiVi.

33. George Washington to Charles Washington, Jan. 31, 1770, *Founders Online*; Jefferson, *Notes on the State of Virginia*, ed. Peden, 4.

34. House of Burgesses, memorial to Botetourt, Dec. 13, 1769, *JHB . . . 1766–1769*, 335; Calloway, *Indian World of George Washington*, 11.

35. McKee journal, [summer 1769], enclosed in McKee to William Johnson, Sept. 18, 1769, in *Papers of Sir William Johnson* 7:185.

36. Red Hawk, speech, enclosed in Alexander McKee to Croghan, Feb. 20, 1770, Gage to Hillsborough, Jan. 6, 1770, in *Papers of Sir William Johnson* 7:407, 332; Fur, *Nation of Women*, 160–98.

37. Holton, *Forced Founders*, 14–16.

38. Trowbridge, *Shawnese Traditions*, 13. For additional evidence of female sachems, see Bond Jr., "Captivity of Charles Stuart," 71–72; Dowd, *War Under Heaven*, 89.

39. Gage to Hillsborough, Jan. 6, 1770, in *Papers of Sir William Johnson* 7:332; Wood, "Changing Population of the Colonial South," 60; Holton, *Forced Founders*, 16–17.

40. Johnson to Board of Trade, Nov. 16, 1765, *DRCHSNY* 7:777–78; Alden, *General Gage in America*, 136–37; White, *Roots of Dependency*, 76–78; Braund, *Deerskins and Duffels*, 133–35; Perdue, "Cherokee Relations with the Iroquois in the Eighteenth Century," 137; Richter, *Ordeal of the Longhouse*, 237–38.

41. Fauquier to Johnson, July 22, 1765, in *Official Papers of Francis Fauquier* 3:1, 262; Holton, *Forced Founders*, 17–18.

42. Croghan to Johnson, May 10, 1770, in *Papers of Sir William Johnson* 7:652; Dragging Canoe, quoted in Samuel Wilson, deposition, April 15, 1777, *CVSP* 1:283. Dragging Canoe is commonly quoted as predicting that Kentucky would become a "dark and bloody ground." Osborn, *Dark and Bloody Ground*; Webb, *Dark and Bloody Ground*; Blackmon, *Dark and Bloody Ground*. Actually, that phrase appears only in a marginal note; it was apparently written by the editor of the document in which Dragging Canoe is quoted. The region was *already* bloody, Dragging Canoe insisted, and Europeans who settled there would soon find it dark. Hatley, *Dividing Paths*, 224–25.

43. Stuart to Gage, Dec. 12, 1770, Thomas Gage Papers, CL.

Chapter 9: The Music of the Wheels

1. Boston merchants' committee, nonimportation association, quoted in Andrews, "Boston Merchants and the Non-Importation Movement," 205–6.

2. Washington to Mason, April 5, 1769, *Founders Online*; Jensen, *Founding of a Nation*, 305–6.

3. Feb. 8, 1769, *Journals of the House of Commons* 32:185–86; Jensen, *Founding of a Nation*, 296–97; Thomas, *Townshend Duties Crisis*, 109.

4. George Mason to Washington, April 5, 1769, *Founders Online*; "The following Agreement was entered into by the Merchants of Philadelphia the 10th March 1769," James, Dick, and Stewart, et al. to unnamed Philadelphia merchants, March 1769, in Hamilton, ed. *Letters to Washington and Accompanying Papers* 3:351–54; Virginia nonimportation association, May 18, 1769, *RV* 1:75.

5. Schlesinger, *Colonial Merchants and the American Revolution*, 140–47 (quotation at 142); Charles Town dateline, *Boston News-Letter*, March 9, 1769; Jensen, *Founding of a Nation*, 260; Godbold and Woody, *Christopher Gadsden and the American Revolution*, 81–82.

6. Boston dateline, *Providence Gazette*, Nov. 7, 1767; "Journal of the Times," *Boston Evening-Post*, May 29, 1769.

7. Clarke, quoted in Norton, *Liberty's Daughters*, 169. Elizabeth Foote of Colchester, Connecticut, all but echoed Clarke's language when she observed one day in 1775 that her family's hired spinner had produced less yarn than usual but still "felt Nationaly into the bargain." Foote, quoted in Ulrich, "Wheels, Looms, and the Gender Division of Labor in Eighteenth-Century New England," 20.

8. Ipswich, Rowley, and Wenham datelines, *Boston Evening-Post*, July 3, 1769 (supplement) (first and third quotations); "Journal of the Times," March 30–31, [1769], *Boston Evening-Post*, May 29, 1769 (second and fourth quotations); Norton, *Liberty's Daughters*, 165–69; Dr. Mary Babson Fuhrer, personal communication, Sept. 24, 2019; Fuhrer, "Revolutionary Worlds of Lexington and Concord Compared," 111.

9. Schlesinger, *Colonial Merchants and the American Revolution*, 122–23. For the assumed association between spinning and poor women, see "Squibo," *Massachusetts Gazette*, Dec. 24, 1767; Newport dateline, *New-Hampshire Gazette*, Jan. 22, 1768.

10. Providence dateline, *South-Carolina Gazette*, Feb. 22–29, 1768; Providence dateline, *South-Carolina Gazette*, Sept. 21–28, 1765; "A Friend to this Colony," *Providence Gazette*, Nov. 14, 1767; Rowley dateline, *Boston Evening-Post*, July 3, 1769; Norton, *Liberty's Daughters*, 169.

11. "Journal of the Times," April 1, [1769], *Boston Evening-Post*, May 29, 1769.

12. "Frileuthras," "To the Fair Sex of South-Carolina," *South-Carolina Gazette and Country Journal*, Sept. 12, 1769; "Margery Distaff — Conditionally," *South-Carolina Gazette*, Oct. 5, 1769; "Aspatia, Belinda, [and] Corinna," *Boston Gazette* (supplement), Dec. 28, 1767.

13. Advertisement, *South-Carolina Gazette and Country Journal*, May 6, 1766; Charles Town dateline, *South-Carolina Gazette*, June 15, 1769; P. Giroud, *South-Carolina Gazette*, Aug. 2, 1770; William Sanders, John Sanders, and Josiah Smith Jr., advertisement, *South-Carolina Gazette*, Jan. 30, 1775; Gundersen, *To Be Useful to the World*, 77; Kierner, "Genteel Balls and Republican Parades," 192–93; Kierner, *Beyond the Household*, 76.

14. "C.R.," *Virginia Gazette* (Purdie & Dixon), March 22, 1770; Charles Town dateline, *South-Carolina Gazette*, June 15, 1769; Kierner, "Genteel Balls and Republican Parades," 192–93; Kierner, *Beyond the Household*, 73–81; Holton, *Forced Founders*, 89; Kukla, *Patrick Henry*, 119–20.

15. James Hill to George Washington, Aug. 30, 1772, *Founders Online*.

16. Young, *Liberty Tree*, 349–51.

17. Jensen, *Founding of a Nation*, 340–41; Champagne, *Alexander McDougall and the American Revolution in New York*, 22; Peter D. G. Thomas, "Wilkes, John (1725–1797), politician," *DNB*.

18. Boston dateline, *Boston Gazette*, Nov. 7, 1768; "Journal of the Times," *Boston Evening-Post*, Aug. 14, 1769; Dickerson, comp., *Boston Under Military Rule*, viii; Hinderaker, *Boston's Massacre*, 134–35.

19. Hinderaker, *Boston's Massacre*, 113–14, 121–32.

20. Hutchinson, quoted in Schlesinger, *Colonial Merchants and the American Revolution*, 181, 173; "A List of the Names of Those Who Audaciously Continue . . . Importing British Goods Contrary to the Agreement," *Boston Gazette*, Jan. 22, 1770; Boston dateline, *Boston Evening-Post*, Jan. 29, 1770; Jensen, *Founding of a Nation*, 362–63; Norton, "Cherished Spirit of Independence," 55; Cleary, *Elizabeth Murray*, 133–37; web.csulb .edu/projects/elizabethmurray/EM/pscummings.html.

21. Tyler, *Smugglers and Patriots*, 124–25; Schlesinger, *Colonial Merchants and the American Revolution*, 159–70.

22. Lillie, quoted in Zobel, *Boston Massacre*, 173; Young, *Shoemaker and the Tea Party*, 37; "Christopher Seider: Shooting Victim," boston1775.blogspot.com/2006/05/christopher -seider-shooting-victim.html.

23. Schlesinger, *Colonial Merchants and the American Revolution*, 190, 207, 237–38; Tyler, *Smugglers and Patriots*, 141; Thomas, *Townshend Duties Crisis*, 157.

24. Thomas, *Townshend Duties Crisis*, 137, 264; Thomas, *Lord North*, 32–33.

25. John Adams to Abigail Adams, July 6, 1774, *Founders Online*; Boston dateline, *Boston Gazette*, Jan. 29, 1770; "The following is a Copy of the Agreement of the Ladies in this Town, against drinking TEA, untill the Revenue Acts are repealed," *Boston Gazette*, Feb. 12, 1770; Gross, *Minutemen and Their World*, 58–59; Norton, *Liberty's Daughters*, 160–61; Ulrich, *Midwife's Tale*, 11; Gundersen, *To Be Useful to the World*, 174.

26. Zabin, *Boston Massacre*, 89, 96.

27. Of course there are also differences. Most glaringly, Lincoln always opposed the expansion of slavery and eventually signed the Emancipation Proclamation, while North supported slavery and even the African slave trade. Partly as a consequence, Lincoln proved more adept at suppressing rebellion. The eldest son of the earl of Guilford, Frederick North would not assume that title until his father's death in 1790, but as a courtesy he was known from his youth as Lord North. Thomas, *Lord North*, 1 (Walpole quotation), 7–8, 23–29, 32–35, 43, 55, (melancholy), 147; Bunker, *Empire on the Edge*, 87 (North quotation).

28. Charles Town dateline, *South-Carolina Gazette*, May 17, 1770 (supplement); voyage 91465, *Trans-Atlantic Slave Trade Database*.

29. Charles Town dateline, *South-Carolina Gazette*, May 17, 1770 (supplement).

Chapter 10: Town Born, Turn Out!

1. Green and Walker, quoted in Zobel, *Boston Massacre*, 182.

2. John Hill and Thomas Walker, quoted in Archer, *As If an Enemy's Country*, 183; Zobel, *Boston Massacre*, 182; Shy, *Toward Lexington*, 317.

3. Zobel, *Boston Massacre*, 182; Hinderaker, *Boston's Massacre*, 9–23.

4. Hewes, memoir, in Hawkes, *Retrospect of the Boston Tea-Party*, 28–29; Zobel, *Boston Massacre*, 264; Young, *Shoemaker and the Tea Party*, 33–41.

5. Gerrish, quoted in Goldfinch, testimony, Nov. 30, 1770, Adams' Minutes of Defense Evidence, Continued, *Legal Papers of John Adams*, *Founders Online*; Archer, *As If an Enemy's Country*, 187.

6. John Goldfinch, testimony, Nov. 30, 1770, Adams' Minutes of Defense Evidence, Continued, *Legal Papers of John Adams*, *Founders Online*; Archer, *As If an Enemy's Country*, 187.

7. Gerrish, testimony, Oct. 24, 1770, "Anonymous Summary of Crown Evidence," *Legal Papers of John Adams*, *Founders Online*.

8. *A Short Narrative of the Horrid Massacre in Boston*, 29n.

9. By invoking the color red with a reference to lobster, the crowd enhanced its insult, since lobster was eaten mostly by the poor. [Alexander] Cruikshanks, testimony, Oct. 24, 1770, Anonymous Summary of Crown Evidence, Paine's Minutes of Adams's Argument, Oct. 27, 1770, *Legal Papers of John Adams*, *Founders Online*.

10. White, quoted in Benjamin Lee, testimony, Transcript of Remaining Defense Evidence, Nov. 30–Dec. 1, 1770, unknown crowd member, quoted in Richard Hyrons, testimony, Adams' Minutes of Defense Evidence, Continued, Nov. 30, 1770, *Legal Papers of John Adams*, *Founders Online*.

11. [John] Adams' Argument for the Defense, Dec. 3–4, 1770, *Legal Papers of John Adams*, *Founders Online*.
12. Zobel, *Boston Massacre*, 198, 273, 300.
13. Theodore Bliss, quoted in Archer, *As If an Enemy's Country*, 192.
14. Carr, quoted in Zobel, *Boston Massacre*, 286, 198, 215; Archer, *As If an Enemy's Country*, 193–96.
15. Zobel, *Boston Massacre*, 219–20, 231.
16. By the time of the Boston Massacre, two of the four regiments in Boston had been withdrawn. Hinderaker, *Boston's Massacre*, 147; Zabin, *Boston Massacre*, 141–44.
17. Schlesinger, *Colonial Merchants and the American Revolution*, 212, 220–36; Jensen, *Founding of a Nation*, 365–66.
18. Gage to Barrington, Oct. 6, 1770, *Correspondence of General Thomas Gage* 2:561–62; Zobel, *Boston Massacre*, 237–38; Lambert, *"Pedlar in Divinity,"* 224.
19. Abigail Adams to Isaac Smith Jr., April 20, 1771, *Founders Online*.
20. Wheatley, *Elegiac Poem, on the Death of . . . George Whitefield*; Wheatley, "On the Death of the Rev. Mr. George Whitefield," in *Poems on Various Subjects*, 22–24.
21. [Wheatley], *An Elegiac Poem, on . . . George Whitefield*.
22. [Wheatley], *An Elegiac Poem, on . . . George Whitefield*; Wheatley, *Poems on Various Subjects*; Gates, *Trials of Phillis Wheatley*; Carretta, *Phillis Wheatley*; Waldstreicher, "Women's Politics, Antislavery Politics, and Phillis Wheatley's American Revolution."
23. [John] Adams' Argument for the Defense, Dec. 3-4, 1770, *Legal Papers of John Adams*, *Founders Online*; Zobel, *Boston Massacre*, 244–46, 265.
24. Zobel, *Boston Massacre*, 298; Zobel, "Newer Light on the Boston Massacre," 125–26.
25. Zobel, *Boston Massacre*, 301.
26. Cooper to Franklin, Jan. 1, 1771, *Founders Online*; Ryerson, *Revolution Is Now Begun*, 22; Labaree, *Boston Tea Party*, 80.
27. McCusker, "Current Value of English Exports," 626; Ragsdale, *Planters' Republic*, 132; Holton, "Revolt of the Ruling Class," 195–96, 311–12.
28. Klein, *Unification of a Slave State*, 74–77.
29. Orange County inhabitants, petition to Martin Howard, Maurice Moore, and Richard Henderson, Oct. 19, 1770, in Powell, Huhta, and Farnham, eds., *Regulators in North Carolina*, 271; Jones, "Herman Husband," 164–71; Kars, *Breaking Loose Together*, 183–85.
30. New Bern dateline, Virginia Gazette (Purdie & Dixon), Oct. 25, 1770; Jones, "Herman Husband," 168, 170; Richard Henderson to William Tryon, Sept. 29, 1770, in Powell, Huhta, and Farnham, eds., *Regulators in North Carolina*, 245.
31. Riot Act, quoted in Stewart, *Redemption from Tyranny*, 70; North Carolina assembly, resolution, Dec. 20, 1770, in Powell, Huhta, and Farnham, eds., *Regulators in North Carolina*, 295.
32. Kars, *Breaking Loose Together*, 199–207 (quotation at 201); Stewart, *Redemption from Tyranny*, 81.
33. Jones, "Herman Husband," 193.
34. Holton, *Forced Founders*, 21–24n.
35. The unnamed Shawnee who uttered these words claimed to have previously heard them from William Johnson. Council with Great Lakes nations and John Turnbull, Sept. 25, 1769, enclosed in Turnbull to Gage, Sept. 30, 1769, Thomas Gage Papers, CL.
36. Board of Trade to Shelburne, Dec. 23, 1767, *DRCHSNY* 7:1,004; Red Hawk, speech to George Croghan, McKee journal, Cadwalader Family Collection, Croghan section,

box 6, folder 30, HSP; Croghan to Johnson, [April 28, 1770], in *Papers of Sir William Johnson* 7:609.

37. "A Friend to the True Interest of Britain in America," *Virginia Gazette* (Rind), Jan. 14, 1773; Shy, *Toward Lexington*, 259–66, 274.

38. William Tryon to Dartmouth, Sept. 5, 1775, in Davies, ed., *Documents of the American Revolution* 11:101–2; Holton, *Forced Founders*, 7, 29–31; Banner, *How the Indians Lost Their Land*, 103–4; Calloway, *Indian World of George Washington*, 184, 201; Sadosky, "Rethinking the Gnadenhutten Massacre," 191.

39. Benjamin Franklin to William Franklin, Sept. 12, 1766, *Papers of Benjamin Franklin*; Hillsborough to Johnson, July 1, 1772, *DRCHSNY* 8:302; Thomas, *Townshend Duties Crisis*, 66–72; Taylor, *American Revolutions*, 56; Calloway, *Indian World of George Washington*, 193.

40. Jensen, *Founding of a Nation*, 390, 400.

41. Lord Rochford, quoted in Thomas, *Townshend Duties Crisis*, 73.

42. Sheridan, "British Credit Crisis of 1772 and the American Colonies," 172; Ernst, *Money and Politics in America*, 309; Jacob M. Price, "Fordyce, Alexander (*bap.* 1729, *d.* 1789)," *DNB*; Hancock, *Citizens of the World*, 226–39; Bunker, *Empire on the Edge*, 70–77.

43. "C— R—," *Virginia Gazette* (Rind), April 26, 1770; Ernst, *Money and Politics in America*, 309–11.

Chapter 11: Cry for Liberty

1. Rappleye, *Sons of Providence*, 107–11.

2. Rappleye, *Sons of Providence*, 102–6; Miller, *Origins of the American Revolution*, 326.

3. Bunker, *Empire on the Edge*, 183–84; Messer, "Most Insulting Violation," 591.

4. Unnamed witness, quoted in Darius Sessions to Joseph Wanton, Jan. 18, 1773, Aaron Briggs, deposition, Jan. 14, 1773, in Staples, ed., *Documentary History of the Destruction of the Gaspee*, 41 (first quotation), 32–34; Daniel Horsmanden, quoted in Messer, "Most Insulting Violation," 592, 607–10 (second quotation at 610); Rappleye, *Sons of Providence*, 115–17. Horsmanden had also run the trial that sentenced William Prendergast to death in 1766. Lepore, *New York Burning*; wikipedia.org/wiki/Daniel_Horsmanden.

5. Lepore, *These Truths*, 79; Seymour and Frary, *How the World Votes*, 69.

6. Higginbotham, *In the Matter of Color*, 333–34; Schama, *Rough Crossings*, 44.

7. Carretta, *Phillis Wheatley*, 119–24; Higginbotham, *In the Matter of Color*, 352–53. Dido Elizabeth Belle's story was fictionalized in Amma Asante's 2013 film *Belle*.

8. "A Planter," *Candid Reflections upon the Judgement . . . on What is Commonly Called the Negroe-Cause*; Brown, *Moral Capital*, 96–101; Sword, "Remembering Dinah Nevil," 330; Bradley, "Slavery in Colonial Newspapers." While Bradley and others make it clear that *Somerset* angered slaveholders (especially in the Caribbean), there is much less evidence for the corollary contention that one reason white southerners favored secession from Britain in July 1776 was that they feared Britain's growing anti-slavery movement in Britain would persuade the imperial government to interfere with their control of African Americans. Hannah-Jones, "Introduction" to 1619 Project. This claim vastly exaggerates the size and strength of the British abolition movement in 1772. On the other hand, *African Americans themselves* exerted a decisive impact on Britain's North American policy and thus on their owners' decision to declare independence. See chapters 14 and 16 below.

9. The chief justice of Massachusetts's highest court was already paid out of the royal treasury. Middlekauff, *Glorious Cause*, 223; Jensen, *Founding of a Nation*, 414–17.

10. Thomas, *Townshend Duties Crisis*, 230–31; Messer, "Most Insulting Violation," 583, 618–20. For a contrasting reading of the significance of the committees of correspondence, see Park, "Revising the Gaspee Legacy."

11. Franklin claimed he was just trying to promote mutual understanding, but as the historian John C. Miller writes, "A man who had played with lightning surely ought to have known better." Miller, *Origins of the American Revolution*, 331; Franklin, "Tract Relative to the Affair of Hutchinson's Letters," [1774], *Founders Online*.

12. Hutchinson, quoted in Thomas, *Tea Party to Independence*, 12.

13. Franklin to Jonathan Williams Sr., July 7, 1773, *Papers of Benjamin Franklin*; Wheatley to Countess of Huntingdon, June 27, 1773, in Wheatley, *Complete Writings*, 144; Carretta, *Phillis Wheatley*, 117.

14. Wheatley, *Elegiac Poem, on the Death of . . . George Whitefield*; Wheatley, "On the Death of the Rev. Mr. George Whitefield," in *Poems on Various Subjects*, 22–24; Waldstreicher, "Phillis Wheatley," 105.

15. Recognizing that Woolridge would not be the last white person to doubt her, Wheatley and her friends prefaced *Poems on Various Subjects* with a certificate of authenticity signed by some of the most prominent men in the Massachusetts, including John Hancock, several members of the provincial council, her owner, and seven ministers. Governor Hutchinson also signed the certificate—reason enough for Wheatley to have toned down her pro-American rhetoric. Wheatley, "To the Right Honourable William, Earl of Dartmouth," in *Poems on Various Subjects*, 74; Carretta, *Phillis Wheatley*, 130–33; Waldstreicher, "Women's Politics, Antislavery Politics, and Phillis Wheatley's American Revolution," 148–49.

16. Wheatley, "On Being Brought from Africa to America," in *Poems on Various Subjects*, 18.

17. Wheatley, "On Being Brought from Africa to America," in *Poems on Various Subjects*, 18; Sidbury, *Becoming African in America*, 21.

18. John Andrews to William Barrell, Feb. 24, 1773, masshist.org/database/viewer.php?item _id=789&img_step=1&mode=dual; Sidbury, *Becoming African in America*, 21; Roberts, "'Slavery' and 'To Mrs. Eliot on the Death of Her Child.'" My thanks to Henry Bolin for his help on this point.

19. Carretta, *Phillis Wheatley*, 118, 137.

20. Wheatley to Occom, Feb. 11, 1774, *Massachusetts Gazette*, March 24, 1774; Johnson, *Taxation No Tyranny*, 89.

21. Miller, *Origins of the American Revolution*, 337; Neal, *Rise of Financial Capitalism*, unpaginated index; Bunker, *Empire on the Edge*, 45, 147.

22. Labaree, *Boston Tea Party*, 59; Thomas, *Townshend Duties Crisis*, 252; Carp, *Defiance of the Patriots*, 14; Bunker, *Empire on the Edge*, 149n.

23. Tea Act, [May 10, 1773], ahp.gatech.edu/tea_act_bp_1773.html; Schlesinger, *Colonial Merchants and the American Revolution*, 262–63; Labaree, *Boston Tea Party*, 76–77; Thomas, *Townshend Duties Crisis*, 255; Carp, "Nice Party, but Not So Revolutionary."

24. Philadelphia dateline, *Boston Gazette*, Oct. 11, 1773; Labaree, *Boston Tea Party*, 71, 89–90; Thomas, *Townshend Duties Crisis*, 256; Tyler, *Smugglers and Patriots*, 189; Carp, *Defiance of the Patriots*, 81–82; Eacott, *Selling Empire*, 205–6.

25. About half of all transatlantic trade had been engrossed by storekeepers representing English and (especially) Scottish firms. Schlesinger, *Colonial Merchants and the American Revolution*, 265–66, 268–74; Labaree, *Boston Tea Party*, 91; Price, *Capital and Credit in*

British Overseas Trade, 6; Thomas, *Townshend Duties Crisis*, 256–57; Tyler, *Smugglers and Patriots*, 194–98.

26. Charles Yates to Dixon & Littledale, April 2, 1774, Yates Letterbook, UVA; Holton, *Forced Founders*, 95.

27. Holton, *Forced Founders*, 113–14 (Robison quotation), 94–95; anonymous letter, *Virginia Gazette* (Purdie & Dixon), Nov. 25, 1773.

28. Noyes, "Portrait of a Good Husband," Silliman Family Papers, YL; Buel and Buel, *Way of Duty*, 79–82; Shammas, "Anglo-American Household Government in Comparative Perspective," 104.

29. Noyes, "Portrait of a Good Husband," Silliman Family Papers, YL; Buel and Buel, *Way of Duty*, 76–94.

30. Noyes, "Portrait of a Good Husband," Silliman Family Papers, YL.

31. *Letters of Eliza Wilkinson*, 61; "A New Method for Making Women as Useful and as Capable of Maintaining Themselves, As the Men Are . . ." *Boston Gazette*, March 17–24, 1740; Richardson, *History of Sir Charles Grandison* 6:18, 35 (quoting fictional women); "Sapphira," "To the Author of the Egotist," *Pennsylvania Chronicle*, Oct. 2, 1769 (reprinted from an unnamed English paper); "A Favorite Song, Sung at Vauxhall by Mr. Vernon, Set by Mr. Brewster, *Pennsylvania Chronicle*, Oct. 8, 1770; Cowley, *Bold Stroke for a Husband*, 85; Catharine Louisa Salmon Smith to Abigail Adams, April 27, 1785, *Founders Online*; Breen, *Marketplace of Revolution*, 288–89; Holton, *Unruly Americans and the Origins of the Constitution*, 164.

32. Joseph Fish, quoted in Buel and Buel, *Way of Duty*, 88.

33. Gordon, quoted in Jensen, *Founding of a Nation*, 452.

34. James & Drinker, quoted in Labaree, *Boston Tea Party*, 97–98.

35. "A Ranger," *Boston Evening-Post*, Dec. 6, 1773; "Proceedings of the Town of Bellingham," *Boston Evening-Post*, Oct. 18, 1773; Labaree, *Boston Tea Party*, 126–27.

36. Adams, quoted in Jensen, *Founding of a Nation*, 451; Colson, quoted in Carp, *Defiance of the Patriots*, 123.

37. Carp, *Defiance of the Patriots*, 118.

38. Benjamin Bussey Thatcher, quoted in Young, *Shoemaker and the Tea Party*, 44; Bunker, *Empire on the Edge*, 229. On the earliest known use of "Boston Tea Party," see Glickman, *Buying Power*, 323.

39. Montagu, quoted in Carp, *Defiance of the Patriots*, 125.

40. Bunker, *Empire on the Edge*, 261n.

41. Miller, *Origins of the American Revolution*, 350–51; Hoffman, *Spirit of Dissension*, 133–37; Carp, *Defiance of the Patriots*, 165; Norton, *1774*, 58–59.

42. Rick Santelli, quoted in Meyer, "Tea Party Rally Marks a Moment in Chicago," April 18, 2011, chicagotribune.com.

43. Bailyn, *Ideological Origins of the American Revolution*.

44. Adams, diary, Dec. 17, 1773, *Founders Online*; Chatham, quoted in Middlekauff, *Glorious Cause*, 234; Franklin, quoted in Schlesinger, *Colonial Merchants and the American Revolution*, 299.

45. Jensen, *Founding of a Nation*, 419–22.

Chapter 12: In the Common Cause

1. Franklin to Cushing, March 22, 1774, *Founders Online*; Jensen, *Founding of a Nation*, 454.

2. Van Doren, *Benjamin Franklin*, 461–81; Thomas, *Tea Party to Independence*, 11–12

3. Alexander Wedderburn, Edward Bancroft, and Privy Council, in The Final Hearing before the Privy Council Committee for Plantation Affairs on the Petition from the Massachusetts House of Representatives for the Removal of Hutchinson and Oliver, *Founders Online*. According to the *OED*, a prime conductor is a brass electrical component that is "insulated and fixed to the stand, for collecting the electricity."

4. Franklin to Joseph Galloway, Feb. 18, 1774, *Founders Online*.

5. North, quoted in Jensen, *Founding of a Nation*, 455, and in Labaree, *Boston Tea Party*, 185, 188–89; Van Doren, *Benjamin Franklin*, 486; Jensen, *Founding of a Nation*, 455–56; Norton, *1774*, 68.

6. Hanko, *Life of John Gibson*, 30–31.

7. "Recollections of George Edgington of West Liberty, Pa., related to Dr. Draper in 1845," in Thwaites and Kellogg, eds., *Documentary History of Dunmore's War*, 16–17; Hanko, *John Gibson*, 15–16; Calloway, *Indian World of George Washington*, 207–8.

8. Jefferson, *Notes on the State of Virginia* (1803 ed.), 86–88; Thwaites and Kellogg, eds., *Documentary History of Dunmore's War*, 305n; Faragher, *Daniel Boone*, 103; Calloway, *Indian World of George Washington*, 207.

9. Jefferson, *Notes on the State of Virginia* (1803 ed.), 312–13, 318; Fliegelman, *Declaring Independence*, 98.

10. Jefferson, *Notes on the State of Virginia* (1803 ed.), 86; Edmund Pendleton to Joseph Chew, June 20, 1774, *Letters and Papers of Edmund Pendleton* 1:94.

11. Boston town meeting, May 13, 1774, *Boston Town Records, 1770–1777*, 174; Jensen, *Founding of a Nation*, 465; Norton, *1774*, 78–80.

12. Peter Van Schaack to Peter Silvester, May 21, 1774, in Van Schaack, *Life of Peter Van Schaack*, 16–17; Champagne, "New York and the Intolerable Acts," 198–207.

13. Gouverneur Morris to John Penn, May 20, 1774, press-pubs.uchicago.edu/founders /documents/v1ch15s8.html.

14. Philadelphia meeting and Gage, quoted in Thomas, *Tea Party to Independence*, 125, 123; Miller, *Origins of the American Revolution*, 363–66; Jensen, *Founding of a Nation*, 466, 470–74; New Jersey's initial response to Boston's proposed boycott was also tepid. Gigantino, *William Livingston's American Revolution*, 42.

15. Providence, Rhode Island, town meeting, May 17, 1774, in Force, ed., *American Archives*, Ser. 4, 1:334; Jameson, *American Revolution Considered as a Social Movement*, 11; "A Grate Number of Blackes," petition to Gage, council, and assembly, May 25, 1774, masshist.org/database/549?mode=transcript.

16. Boston committee of correspondence, quoted in Norton, *1774*, 106; Jensen, *Founding of a Nation*, 467.

17. Lind, *Answer to the Declaration of the American Congress*, 88–89; Massachusetts Government Act, May 20, 1774, avalon.law.yale.edu/18th_century/mass_gov_act.asp; Jensen, *Founding of a Nation*, 456–57; Thomas, *Tea Party to Independence*, 24, 62, 79; Miller, *Origins of the American Revolution*, 372–73.

18. Bunker, *Empire on the Edge*, 268.

19. Boston committee of correspondence to Douglas town clerk, June 8, 1774, "Solemn League and Covenant," in Matthews, "Solemn League and Covenant," 106–8 (quotation at 106).

20. Dozens of towns adopted their own nonimportation pledges or endorsed the idea in general terms. Jonathan Williams to John Adams, June 28, 1774, *Founders Online*; Boston town meeting, June 27–28, 1774, *Report of the Record Commissioners of the City of Boston Containing the Boston Town Records, 1770 Through 1777*, 177–78; Worcester com-

mittee of correspondence, circular letter, June 13, 1774, in Matthews, "Solemn League and Covenant," 113–14; Brown, *Revolutionary Politics in Massachusetts*, 198–203.

21. Price, *Capital and Credit in British Overseas Trade*, 122–23.

22. William Lee, quoted in Holton, *Forced Founders*, 115; Westmoreland County resolutions, June 22, 1774, *RV* 1:164.

23. Holton, *Forced Founders*, 115–16.

24. House of Burgesses resolution, [May 24, 1774], *RV* 1:93–95; Holton, *Forced Founders*, 117–19.

25. Holton, *Forced Founders*, 117. Eventually South Carolinians would impose the same rule. Bull to Dartmouth, Jan. 20, 1775, in Davies, ed., *Documents of the American Revolution* 9:30.

26. Miller, *Origins of the American Revolution*, 370; Thomas, *Tea Party to Independence*, 79–80; Bell, *Road to Concord*, 4; Zabin, *Boston Massacre*, 218–21.

27. Washington to George Mason, April 5, 1769, *Founders Online*; [Thomson Mason], "British American," VII, VIII, July 14, 21, 1774, *RV* 1:183, 190; "A Virginia Planter" [George Mason], ". . . Letter to the Committee of Merchants in London . . . ," June 6, 1766, in *Papers of George Mason* 1:69; Friedman, "Shaping of the Radical Consciousness in Provincial New York," 790–91.

28. Young, "On the Present State of the British Colonies," in [Young], *Political Essays Concerning the Present State of the British Empire*, 264, 265n; "An Act to Prevent the Exportation to Foreign Parts of Utensils Made Use of in the Cotton, Linen, Woollen and Silk Manufactures of this Kingdom," in *Statutes at Large, of England and of Great-Britain* 13:712–15; Simmons and Thomas, eds., *Proceedings and Debates of the British Parliaments Respecting North America, 1754–1783* 4:430, 475.

29. New Jersey assembly, petition to the king, Feb. 13, 1775, in Davies, ed., *Documents of the American Revolution* 9:49; Nelson, *General Sir Guy Carleton*, 32; Tanner and Pinther, eds., *Atlas of Great Lakes Indian History*, 66.

30. Wedderburn, quoted in Neatby, *Quebec Act*, 40; Holton, *Forced Founders*, 33.

31. Reed to Dartmouth, Sept. 25, 1774, in Reed, *Life and Correspondence of Joseph Reed* 1:79; William Lee to Richard Henry Lee, Sept. 10, 1774, in *Letters of William Lee, Sheriff and Alderman of London* 1:89; Holton, *Forced Founders*, 35–36.

32. [Young], *Political Essays Concerning the Present State of the British Empire*, 386.

33. Edmund Pendleton to Joseph Chew, June 20, 1774, in *Letters and Papers of Edmund Pendleton* 1:92; Jefferson et al., Resolution on Land Grants, [March 27, 1775], *Founders Online*; Dunmore to Dartmouth, [April 14? (incorrectly dated March 14)], 1775, in Davies, ed., *Documents of the American Revolution* 9:81–83.

34. Ammerman, *In the Common Cause*. Connecticut's and New York City's congressmen were chosen by the committee of correspondence; the rest of New York went unrepresented. Norton, *1774*, 149, 154–56.

35. Jefferson, draft of instructions for Virginia delegates in Congress (published as *A Summary View of the Rights of British America*), [July 1774], *Founders Online* (including editors' notes).

36. Job Alby, deposition, in John and Quincy, eds., "Hopkins vs. Ward," 338; Declaratory Act, March 18, 1776, avalon.law.yale.edu/18th_century/declaratory_act_1766.asp; Wilson and Witherspoon, *Considerations on the Nature and the Extent of the Legislative Authority of the British Parliament*; Reid, *Constitutional History of the American Revolution*, 6; Brooks, "On Creating a Usable Past," 337–41.

37. Jefferson, draft of instructions for Virginia delegates in Congress (published as *A Summary View of the Rights of British America*), [July 1774], *Founders Online*.

38. Jefferson, "original Rough draught" of the Declaration of Independence, [June 11–July 4, 1776], *Founders Online*; Ragsdale, *Planters' Republic*, 111–36; Kukla, *Patrick Henry*, 100, 125–26.

39. Rediker, *Fearless Benjamin Lay*.

40. Byrd to John Perceval, earl of Egmont, July 12, 1736, in Tinling, ed., *Correspondence of the Three William Byrds of Westover, Virginia* 2:488; Berlin, *Many Thousands Gone*, 88–89, 195–96; DuVal, *Independence Lost*, 59; Brown, *Tacky's Revolt*, 224, 228–29.

41. Du Bois, *Suppression of the African Slave-Trade to the United States of America*, 10–11; Wood, *Black Majority*, 325. On some of the ramifications of South Carolina's prohibition, see Polhemus, "Culture of Commodification," 24–76.

42. House of Burgesses, petition against the slave trade, [April 1, 1772], *RV* 1:87; Arthur Lee to Joseph Reed, Feb. 14, 1773, Lee Papers (Fraser Transcripts), UVA; Billings, Selby, and Tate, *Colonial Virginia*, 281; Wood, "Changing Population of the Colonial South," 60.

43. Dunmore, quoted in Ragsdale, *Planters' Republic*, 134; Arthur Lee to Richard Henry Lee, Feb. 14, 1773, Arthur Lee Papers, HH.

44. Carretta, *Phillis Wheatley*, 139; Egerton, *Death or Liberty*, 56–57.

45. Jefferson, draft of instructions for Virginia delegates in Congress (published as *A Summary View of the Rights of British America*), [July 1774], *Founders Online*; Mason, June [17], 1788, in Elliot, ed., *Debates in the Several State Conventions, on the Adoption of the Federal Constitution* 3:452; House of Burgesses, petition against the slave trade, [April 1, 1772], *RV* 1:87; Ragsdale, *Planters' Republic*, 135–36.

46. "Americanus" [Franklin], *Pennsylvania Gazette*, May 9, 1751, *Founders Online*; Holton, "Revolt of the Ruling Class," 223–26; Morgan, *Benjamin Franklin*, 74.

47. Jefferson, draft of instructions for Virginia delegates in Congress (published as *A Summary View of the Rights of British America*), [July 1774], *Founders Online*.

Chapter 13: The Hindmost Horse

1. Wikisource.org/wiki/Boston_Port_Act; Labaree, *Boston Tea Party*, 248.

2. "To the Inhabitants of the Province of South-Carolina, About to Assemble on the 6th of July," in Force, ed., *American Archives*, Ser. 4, 1:510–11; Washington to Mason, April 5, 1769, *Founders Online*.

3. New York committee of correspondence, journal, July 7–27, 1774, in Force, ed., *American Archives*, Ser. 4, 1:310–19; Labaree, *Boston Tea Party*, 240–43.

4. Drayton, *Memoirs of the American Revolution* 1:127–31 (quotation at 131); Jensen, *Founding of a Nation*, 478–79.

5. Editor's note, "Extract of a Letter from a Gentleman in Bristol, To His Friend in Philadelphia, Dated July 20, 1774," "A Brief Examination of American Grievances, Being the Heads of a Speech at the General Meeting at Lewiston on Delaware, July 28, 1774," in Force, ed., *American Archives*, Ser. 4, 1:532n, 614, 661.

6. "To the People of America," September 1774, in Force, ed., *American Archives*, Ser. 4, 1:758.

7. Gross, *Minutemen and Their World*, 52–60; Raphael, *First American Revolution*, 75–80, 122–26; Bell, *Road to Concord*, 4–5; Staiti, "Accounting for Copley," 46, 50n.

8. Raphael, *First American Revolution*, 66–67, 135–36; Bell, *Road to Concord*, 23.

9. Abigail Adams to John Adams, Sept. 14, 1774, *Founders Online*; Raphael, *First American Revolution*, 42–45, 72–75, 110, 154–56; Raphael and Raphael, *Spirit of '74*, 110–11.

10. Gross, *Minutemen and Their World*, 48–53.

11. Jensen, *Founding of a Nation*, 535–36; Raphael, *First American Revolution*, 112–30.

12. William Christian to William Preston, Nov. 8, 1774, in Thwaites and Kellogg, eds., *Documentary History of Dunmore's War*, 303; Downes, *Council Fires on the Upper Ohio*, 170–72, 176–77; Selby, *Revolution in Virginia*, 17.

13. Thomas, *Tea Party to Independence*, 155; Grant, *John Adams*, 136.

14. John Adams, diary, Aug. 22, Oct. 9, 1774, *Founders Online*; Barzilay, "Fifty Gentlemen Total Strangers," 84–85.

15. John Adams to Abigail Adams, Oct. 9, 1774, John Adams, diary, Oct. 23, 1774, *Founders Online*.

16. John Adams to Abigail Adams, Sept. 16, 1774, *Founders Online*; Psalm 35:1; McBride, "Masterly Stroke of Policy," 4–8 (quotation at 5); Jensen, *Founding of a Nation*, 488–89.

17. John Adams, diary, Sept. 6, 1774, *Founders Online*; Jensen, *Founding of a Nation*, 491–92; Barzilay, "Fifty Gentlemen Total Strangers," 293.

18. James Duane's Notes of Debates, [Oct. 15–17? 1774], in Smith et al., eds., *Letters of Delegates to Congress* 1:198; Jones, *Memoir of the Hon. James Duane*, 14.

19. Several Whig assemblies condemned Parliament for (in the words of the Pennsylvania congress) "prohibiting us from slitting iron to build our houses, making hats to cover our heads or clothing to cover the rest of our bodies." Samuel Adams to Arthur Lee, May 18, 1774, Pennsylvania convention, Argumentative Part of the Preceding Instructions, "A Brief Examination of American Grievances, Being the Heads of a Speech at the General Meeting at Lewiston on Delaware, July 28, 1774," in Force, ed., *American Archives*, Ser. 4, 1:332 (first quotation in text), 574 (second quotation in text and quotation in note), 658; Virginia convention, instructions to delegates in Congress, Aug. [1–6], 1774, *Founders Online*; Bunker, *Empire on the Edge*, 335.

20. John Adams, notes on debates in Congress, Sept. 8, 1774, and Adams, diary, Sept. 3, Oct. 13, 1774, *Founders Online*; Jensen, *Founding of a Nation*, 494, 498, 503.

21. Continental Association, Oct. 20, 1774, *Founders Online*.

22. Henry Laurens to Georgia Council of Safety, Dec. 14, 1775, in "Journal of the Second Council of Safety," Dec. 14, 1775, South-Carolina Historical Society *Collections* 3:82; Drayton, *Memoirs of the American Revolution* 1:168–72.

23. Continental Association, Oct. 20, 1774, *Founders Online*.

24. Miller, *Origins of the American Revolution*, 385; Jensen, *Founding of a Nation*, 521–22; Breen, *Will of the People*, 43.

25. Jensen, *Founding of a Nation*, 507.

26. Jensen, *Founding of a Nation*, 522, 551.

27. Oct. 3, 1774, *JCC* 1:54n; Jensen, *Founding of a Nation*, 538; Raphael and Raphael, *Spirit of '74*, 157–59; Rakove, *Revolutionaries*, 60; Bunker, *Empire on the Edge*, 326, 339; Norton, *1774*, 236–39.

28. Raphael, *First American Revolution*, 183–85; Hoffer, *Prelude to Revolution*.

29. New York conservative James Duane warned that the Maryland convention's action could be interpreted as taking the militia into its own hands. Fairfax County independent company, articles of association, [Sept. 21, 1774], in *Papers of George Mason* 1:210–12; Maryland convention, Dec. 8–12, 1774, in Force, ed., *American Archives*, Ser. 4, 1:1032; Norton, *1774*, 253–55, 257.

30. Rakove, *Revolutionaries*, 49–63. For two shining exceptions, see Raphael and Raphael, *Spirit of '74*; and Bunker, *Empire on the Edge*, 326–42.

31. Abigail Adams to John Adams, Sept. 22, 1774, *Founders Online*; Madison to William Bradford, Nov. 26, 1774, *Founders Online*; "Narrative by George Millegen of his Experiences in South Carolina," Sept. 15, 1775, in Davies, ed., *Documents of the American Revolution* 11:110; Wood, "'Liberty Is Sweet,'" 160–61.

32. Wood, "'Liberty Is Sweet,'" 167–68 (Jemmy quotation), 163.

33. [Dawe], *A Society of Patriotic Ladies, at Edenton in North Carolina*; Halsey, *Boston Port Bill as Pictured by a Contemporary London Cartoonist*, 170–76, 275–82, 311–20.

34. Thomas, *Tea Party to Independence*, 145–49; Bunker, *Empire on the Edge*, 319.

35. Thomas, *Tea Party to Independence*, 189–93.

36. Thomas, *Tea Party to Independence*, 193.

37. Burke, speech in House of Commons, March 22, 1775, in *Select Works of Edmund Burke* 1:240, 242, oll-resources.s3.amazonaws.com/titles/796/0005.01_Bk.pdf. Okoye, "Chattel Slavery as the Nightmare of the American Revolutionaries"; Kukla, *Patrick Henry*, 159.

38. Roger Atkinson to Samuel Pleasants, Oct. 1, 1774, "Letters of Roger Atkinson," 356; Mark 3:17; Meade, *Patrick Henry* 1:65, 70–74, 244–50; Isaac, *Transformation of Virginia*, 161–77; Nash, *Unknown American Revolution*, 10; Winiarski, *Darkness Falls on the Land of Light*, 337.

39. Henry, quoted in Wirt, *Sketches of the Life and Character of Patrick Henry*, 123.

40. Brodie erred in stating that Sarah Henry was still alive when Patrick gave his famous speech. Henry, quoted in Wirt, *Sketches of the Life and Character of Patrick Henry*, 121–22; Brodie, *Thomas Jefferson*, 121–22.

41. The Virginians' primary contribution was to give their infantrymen a more Native American or western look: they were to carry tomahawks, wear hunting shirts, and arm themselves, where possible, with rifles instead of muskets. Maryland convention, Dec. 8–12, 1774, in Force, ed., *American Archives*, Ser. 4, 1:1032; Virginia convention, resolutions, March 23, 25, 1775, *RV* 2:366–67, 374–76; Mays, *Edmund Pendleton* 2:353n; McDonnell, *Politics of War*, 43–44.

42. Maryland convention, Dec. 8–12, 1774, in Force, ed., *American Archives*, Ser. 4, 1:1032; Virginia convention, resolutions, March 23, 1775, *RV* 2:366–67; James Parker to Charles Steuart, April 6, 1775, in Steuart, ed., "Letters from Virginia," 158; Wirt, *Sketches of the Life and Character of Patrick Henry*, 116–17, 124–25n; Henry, *Patrick Henry* 1:271; Campbell, *History of the Colony and Ancient Dominion of Virginia*, 601–2; Morgan, "Thomas Hutchinson and the Stamp Act," 491; Mays, *Edmund Pendleton* 2:4–8; McDonnell, *Politics of War*, 43–44; Kukla, *Patrick Henry*, 165–72.

43. Thomas, *Tea Party to Independence*, 198–99.

44. North, quoted in Thomas, *Tea Party to Independence*, 139.

45. Jensen, *Founding of a Nation*, 46; Thomas, *Tea Party to Independence*, 272–76.

46. Dragging Canoe, quoted in Samuel Wilson, deposition, April 15, 1777, *CVSP* 1:283; Saunt, *West of the Revolution*, 17–28.

47. Leslie, quoted in Bunker, *Empire on the Edge*, 297, 75–76; Burke, speech in House of Commons, March 22, 1775, in *Select Works of Edmund Burke* 1:235, oll-resources. s3.amazonaws.com/titles/796/0005.01_Bk.pdf.

48. Emerson, quoted in Gross, *Minutemen and Their World*, 111; Cole, *Mary Moody Emerson and the Origins of Transcendentalism*, 61; Cline, "Men and Women We Must Remember."

49. Otis, *Vindication of the British Colonies*, 18–19; [John] Adams' Argument for the Defense, Dec. 3–4, 1770, *Legal Papers of John Adams*, *Founders Online*; "A Ranger," *Boston Evening-Post*, Dec. 6, 1773.

50. Boston dateline, *Boston Gazette*, Jan. 29, 1770; "The following is a Copy of the Agreement of the Ladies in this Town, against drinking TEA, untill the Revenue Acts are repealed," *Boston Gazette*, Feb. 12, 1770; James Hill to George Washington, Aug. 30, 1772, *Founders Online*.

51. Although Wheatley had never met either of the future missionaries, John Thornton, a

British merchant and her fellow evangelical, suggested that she marry one of them and join them in Africa. She thanked him for his "generous Offer" but politely declined. Wheatley to John Thornton, Oct. 30, 1774, in Wheatley, *Complete Writings*, 159–60; Norton, "My Resting Reaping Times"; Buel and Buel, *Way of Duty*, 79–83; Jones, "Herman Husband," 21–34; Carretta, *Phillis Wheatley*, 25–44; Brekus, *Sarah Osborn's World*, 281–83.

52. John Watts to [Isaac] Barré, Jan. 21, 176[4], Watts, "Letter-Book of John Watts," 218.
53. Jefferson, draft of instructions for Virginia delegates in Congress (published as *A Summary View of the Rights of British America*), [July 1774], *Founders Online*; Francis Fauquier to Board of Trade, Feb. 13, 1764, in *Official Papers of Francis Fauquier* 3:1078.
54. Providence dateline, *South-Carolina Gazette*, Feb. 22–29, 1768; Washington to George Mason, April 5, 1769, *Founders Online*.

Part Two: Push On: Introduction

1. Gottschalk, *Lafayette in America* 1:3–4.
2. July 31, 1777, *JCC* 8:592–93; Benjamin Harrison to George Washington, Aug. 20, 1777, *Founders Online*; Gottschalk, *Lafayette in America* 1:50, 120, 2:22; Lengel, *General George Washington*, 219.
3. In 1778, Congress had sent an expedition commanded by Lafayette to Québec, but the troops had not made it past Albany, New York, when, on Lafayette's recommendation, Washington recalled them. Ferling, *Almost a Miracle*, 292–93.
4. Rochambeau to Washington, Jan. 26, 29, Feb. 3, 8, 12, 1781, Destouches to Washington, Feb. 7, 1781, Washington to John Laurens, April 9, 1781, Washington to Lafayette, Feb. 20, 1781 (both letters), *Founders Online*; Providence dateline, *Providence Gazette*, Jan. 24, 1781.
5. Washington to Benjamin Harrison, March 21, 1781, Washington to John Laurens, April 9, 1781, Washington to Rochambeau, Feb. 7, 15, 19, 1781, *Founders Online*; Philbrick, *In the Hurricane's Eye*, 38.
6. Destouches to Washington, Feb. 20, 1781, Washington to Benjamin Harrison, March 27, 1781, Washington to Lund Washington, March 28, 1781 (my thanks to Katelynn Hatton for this reference), Lafayette to George Washington, April 15, 1781, Washington to Lafayette, April 22, 1781, *Founders Online*; Gottschalk, *Lafayette in America* 3:215–16; United States Congress, Joint Committee on the Library, *Rochambeau*, 371–73. It appears that the first American newspaper to employ the term "Loyalist(s)," on July 1, 1771, was the *Boston Evening-Post*, referring to North Carolinians who had fought on Governor Tryon's side against the Regulators at Alamance Creek the previous May. In 1772, an anonymous critic of Parliament took the pen name "Antiministerial Loyalist," but it was only in 1777 that newspapers began applying the term to pro-British Americans. "To Antiministerial Loyalist," *Massachusetts Gazette*, Aug. 27, 1772; New York dateline, *New-York Gazette*, Sept. 29, 1777.
7. Lafayette's belief that Phillips had commanded the gun battery that killed his father was very likely mistaken. Lafayette to Hamilton, April 10, 1781, *Founders Online*; Lafayette to Greene, April 17, 1781, in *Papers of General Nathanael Greene* 8:110; Gottschalk, *Lafayette in America* 1:11–12, 3:204–19, 216, 218–19.
8. Lafayette to Washington, April 15, 1781, *Founders Online*; Lafayette to La Luzerne, April 22, 10, 14, 1781, "Letters from Lafayette to Luzerne," 598–600 (quotation at 600); Plakas, "Sentiments of an American Woman."
9. Lafayette to Washington, April 18, 1781, Lafayette to Hamilton, April 10, 1781, *Founders Online*.

10. Lafayette to Washington, April 14, 1781, *Founders Online*; *Memoirs, Correspondence, and Manuscripts of General Lafayette* 1:259–60; Lafayette to Greene, April 17, 1781, in *Papers of General Nathanael Greene* 8:108–10; Gottschalk, *Lafayette in America*, 3:213–18.

11. Wood, *Black Majority*, 63–91; Glover, *Eliza Lucas Pinckney*, 145.

Chapter 14: Declare Freedom

1. Gage to Dartmouth, Sept. 2, 1774, in Davies, ed., *Documents of the American Revolution* 8:182; French, *Day of Concord and Lexington*, 14; Gross, *Minutemen and Their World*, 109.

2. John Andrews to William Barrell, March 18, [20], [1775], "Letters of John Andrews," 401; Raphael and Raphael, *Spirit of '74*, 174.

3. Dartmouth to Gage, Jan. 27, 1775, in Davies, ed., *Documents of the American Revolution* 9:8, 37, 39.

4. Gage to Dartmouth, April [22?], 1775, in Davies, ed., *Documents of the American Revolution* 9:102; French, *Day of Concord and Lexington*, 68–70, 73; Jensen, *Founding of a Nation*, 583–84; Bell, *Road to Concord*, 148–54.

5. Jeremy Belknap, quoted in French, *Day of Concord and Lexington*, 74–75; Fischer, *Paul Revere's Ride*, 113; Raphael and Raphael, *Spirit of '74*, 186–88; Bell, *Road to Concord*, 152–53.

6. Fischer, *Paul Revere's Ride*, 109, xv, 138.

7. French, *Day of Concord and Lexington*, 76–79; French, *General Gage's Informers*, 36–38; Fischer, *Paul Revere's Ride*, 139.

8. The patrollers eventually released Revere but not his horse, and he walked back to Lexington. French, *Day of Concord and Lexington*, 91–94.

9. Gross, *Minutemen and Their World*, 117.

10. Sutherland, "Sutherland's Narrative," 16. There is no evidence that the decision to leave the road came from Maj. Pitcairn, but he appears to have approved of it. Fischer (*Paul Revere's Ride*, 127, 189–90) erroneously states that Pitcairn had tasked Lt. Jesse Adair, a fellow marine, to *lead* the column; actually, Adair and at least one other lieutenant, William Sutherland, merely *accompanied* the sergeant's party that led the column. French, *General Gage's Informers*, 48.

11. "An account of the Commencement of Hostilities between GREAT BRITAIN and AMERICA . . . By the Reverend Mr. WILLIAM GORDON," May 17, 1775, in Force, ed., *American Archives*, Ser. 4, 2:629; Fischer, *Paul Revere's Ride*, 190–91; Raphael and Raphael, *Spirit of '74*, 201.

12. Coburn, "Fiction and Truth About the Battle on Lexington Common," 48, 30; Ralph Waldo Emerson, "Concord Hymn," poetryfoundation.org; French, *Day of Concord and Lexington*, 117; Fischer, *Paul Revere's Ride*, 188–200, 400n.

13. Fischer, *Paul Revere's Ride*, 198–200.

14. Fischer, *Paul Revere's Ride*, 206.

15. Fischer, *Paul Revere's Ride*, 205–8; Bell, *Road to Concord*, 160–61.

16. Gross, *Minutemen and Their World*, 65 (Daniel Bliss quotation), 108; Fischer, *Paul Revere's Ride*, 207–9 (Hosmer quotation at 209); French, *Day of Concord and Lexington*, 160n.

17. Fischer, *Paul Revere's Ride*, 212–14.

18. Hugh Percy to Thomas Gage, April 20, 1775, in *Letters of Hugh Earl Percy from Boston and New York*, 51; Francis Smith to Thomas Gage, April 22, 1775, in Davies, ed., *Documents of the American Revolution* 9:104; Ann Hulton to [Elizabeth] Lightbody,

[April 1775?], in Hulton, *Letters of a Loyalist Lady*, 77; James Abercrombie to Lord Loudoun, May 4, 1775, Loudoun Papers, HEH; "An account of the Commencement of Hostilities between GREAT BRITAIN and AMERICA . . . By the Reverend Mr. WIL-LIAM GORDON," May 17, 1775, in Force, ed., *American Archives*, Ser. 4, 2:630; Gage, *Circumstantial Account of an Attack That Happened on the 19th of April 1775*; Stedman, *History of the Origin, Progress, and Termination of the American War* 1:119; Jensen, *Founding of a Nation*, 589–90; Gross, *Minutemen and Their World*, 126–27; Fischer, *Paul Revere's Ride*, 214–19, 406–7n; Bell, *Road to Concord*, 160.

19. James Abercrombie to Loudoun, May 12, 1775, Loudoun Papers, HEH. Correctly conjecturing that the rebels had secured the only bridge over the lower Charles River (near Harvard College), the redcoats spent the night in Charlestown; they were rowed across to Boston the next morning. Percy to Gen. Harvey, April 20, 1775, Percy to Gage, April 20, 1775, in *Letters of Hugh Earl Percy from Boston and New York*, 52, 51n; Fischer, *Paul Revere's Ride*, 321.

20. Percy to Gen. Harvey, April 20, 1775, in *Letters of Hugh Earl Percy from Boston and New York*, 52; Fischer, *Paul Revere's Ride*, 321. For the typical ratio of killed to wounded in eighteenth-century battles, see Anderson, *Crucible of War*, 58–59.

21. Graves to Philip Stephens, April 22, 1775, in Davies, ed., *Documents of the American Revolution* 9:105; Percy to Gen. Harvey, April 20, 1775, in *Letters of Hugh Earl Percy from Boston and New York*, 52–53; "Extracts from Several Intercepted Letters of the Soldiery in Boston," April 28, 1775, in Force, ed., *American Archives*, Ser. 4, 2:439–40; Lord Germain to [Lord Suffolk], June 16 or 17, 1775, in Historical Manuscripts Commission, *Report on the Manuscripts of Mrs. Stopford-Sackville* 2:2; Fischer, *Paul Revere's Ride*, 165, 222–23, 243, 247, 263–64; Spring, *With Zeal and with Bayonets Only*, 60, 106, 120–21, 251–52; Calloway, *Indian World of George Washington*, 215. For their part, Massachusetts residents claimed "that the soldiers are worse than the *Indians*." "An account of the Commencement of Hostilities between GREAT BRITAIN and AMERICA . . . By the Reverend Mr. WILLIAM GORDON . . . ," May 17, 1775, in Force, ed., *American Archives*, Ser. 4, 2:630; Jones, *Captives of Liberty*, 36, 37.

22. Fischer, *Paul Revere's Ride*, 257.

23. Jensen, *Founding of a Nation*, 596–97.

24. Josiah Martin to Dartmouth, May 18, 1775, Hugh Finlay to his brother-in-law Ingram, May 29, 1775, John Wentworth to Dartmouth, June 14, 1775, in Davies, ed., *Documents of the American Revolution* 9:139, 146, 171.

25. Edmund Pendleton to George Washington, April 21, 1775, *Founders Online*; anonymous letter, *Virginia Gazette* (Purdie), June 16, 1775; unnamed merchants, note at the foot of Archibald Cary to James Lyle et al., June 12, 1775, Colonial Office 5/1353, 401, BNA; Hugh Hamilton, deposition, *JHB . . . 1773–1776*, 234; Wood, "Changing Population of the Colonial South," 60–61.

26. Randolph, *History of Virginia*, 219; Dunmore to Dartmouth, May 1, 1775, in Davies, ed., *Documents of the American Revolution* 9:107–9; Sussex County committee, May 8, 1775, and Virginia convention, "A Declaration of the Delegates . . . ," Aug. 26, 1775, *RV* 3:107, 501; Selby, *Revolution in Virginia*, 2, 67; Wood, "Dream Deferred," 174.

27. Dunmore, quoted in "Deposition of Dr. William Pasteur in Regard to the Removal of Powder from the Williamsburg Magazine," 49; Benjamin Waller, deposition, *JHB, 1773–1776*, 232; Mays, *Edmund Pendleton* 2:13–14.

28. Burk, *History of Virginia, from Its First Settlement to Present Day* 3:409–10; queries in Archibald Cary to James Lyle et al., June 12, 1775, C.O.5/1353, 400, BNA; Frederick County committee, June 19, 1775, *RV* 3:208–9.

29. Gloucester County committee, April 26, 1775, New Kent County committee, May 3, 1775, Richmond County committee, May 12, 1775, Mecklenburg County committee, May 13, 1775, *RV* 3:61, 85, 121, 124; "Intelligence Extraordinary," *Virginia Gazette* (Pinkney), May 4, 1775; "Brutus," *Virginia Gazette* (Purdie), Aug. 4, 1775 (supplement); George Dabney to William Wirt, May 14, 1805, Patrick Henry Papers, LC; Benjamin Waller, deposition, *JHB . . . 1773–1776*, 232; Selby, *Revolution in Virginia*, 4.

30. Wood, "'Liberty Is Sweet,'" 164–66 (Simmons quotations at 164).

31. Dealey, quoted in Drayton, *Memoirs of the American Revolution* 1:300.

32. Ketchum, *Saratoga*, 29; Middlekauff, *Glorious Cause*, 281–82.

33. Hugh Finlay to his brother-in-law Ingram, May 29, 1775, in Davies, ed., *Documents of the American Revolution* 9:145.

34. Massachusetts Committee of Safety to New York Committee, April 30, 1775, Massachusetts Committee of Safety, commission to Benedict Arnold, May 3, 1775, in Force, ed., *American Archives*, Ser. 4, 2:450, 485; Martin, *Benedict Arnold*, 64–65.

35. Allen, quoted in Bellesiles, *Revolutionary Outlaws*, 118; *Narrative of Col. Ethan Allen's Captivity*, 19; Ethan Allen to Massachusetts congress, May 11, 1775, Benedict Arnold to [Massachusetts] committee of safety, May 11, 1775, in Force, ed., *American Archives*, Ser. 4, 2:556–57; Jensen, *Founding of a Nation*, 605–6; Martin, *Benedict Arnold*, 65–73.

36. Buel and Buel, *Way of Duty*, 75–83 (Silliman quotation at 82), 94.

37. Quoted in Ketchum, *Saratoga*, 77.

38. Ira D. Gruber, "Howe, William, fifth Viscount Howe (1729–1814)," in *DNB*.

39. William Howe to Richard Howe, June 22, 1775, in Historical Manuscripts Commission, *Report on the Manuscripts of Mrs. Stopford-Sackville* 2:3; Smith, *New Age Now Begins* 1:510.

40. Frothingham, *History of the Siege of Boston*, 122–24; French, *Siege of Boston*, 254–58; Nelson, *With Fire and Sword*, 226–28; Philbrick, *Bunker Hill*, 195–98, 202; Peckham, *Toll of Independence*, 3–128.

Chapter 15: Pyramids of Fire

1. Smith, *New Age Now Begins* 1:513, 536.

2. Nelson, *With Fire and Sword*, 233–34; Philbrick, *Bunker Hill*, 199–200.

3. Ellis, *Revolutionary Summer*, 45.

4. Spring, *With Zeal and with Bayonets Only*, 68.

5. Historians state incorrectly that Howe acknowledged delaying the landing until high tide, when it would be possible to bring the soldiers closer to dry land. Howe actually gave the tide as a reason to *hasten* the movement of the troops; he feared that various delays in getting under way would push the landing into the ebb tide that would begin at 2 p.m. William Howe to Richard Howe, June 22, 1775, in Historical Manuscripts Commission, *Report on the Manuscripts of Mrs. Stopford-Sackville* 2:4; Ward, *War of the Revolution* 1:82–84; Nelson, *With Fire and Sword*, 236–37; Philbrick, *Bunker Hill*, 206, 209.

6. Philbrick, *Bunker Hill*, 204–5, 215–16.

7. Howe, quoted in Philbrick, *Bunker Hill*, 218; Ward, *War of the Revolution* 1:88–89.

8. Burgoyne to Lord Stanley, June 25, 1775, quoted in *Bunker Hill: Its Battle and Monument*, 14.

9. Ward, *War of the Revolution* 1:91; Spring, *With Zeal and with Bayonets Only*, 140; Philbrick, *Bunker Hill*, 221.

10. Smith, *New Age Now Begins* 1:532.

11. Philbrick, *Bunker Hill*, 225; James Grant to [Loudoun], June 24, 1775, Loudoun Papers, HEH.

12. Unnamed British officer(?), quoted in Smith, *New Age Now Begins* 1:524.

13. Smith, *New Age Now Begins* 1:526, 529; Philbrick, *Bunker Hill*, 225–26.

14. Philbrick confuses Peter Salem with another Black man who fought on the American side at Bunker Hill, Salem Poor. He had purchased his freedom six years earlier. J. L. Bell's review of the evidence led him to doubt the Peter Salem story. Smith, Nelson, and others do not mention him at all. Smith, *New Age Now Begins* 1:529–30; Nelson, *With Fire and Sword*; Egerton, *Death or Liberty*, 56; Philbrick, *Bunker Hill*, 228; Quintal, *Patriots of Color*, 170–80, 190–96; Bell, "Peter Salem? Salem Poor? Who Killed Major John Pitcairn?"

15. John Waller, quoted in Philbrick, *Bunker Hill*, 227–29; "Another Account of the Late Action at Bunker's-Hill," *Rivington's New-York Gazetteer*, Aug. 3, 1775.

16. Washington to Richard Henry Lee, Aug. 29, 1775, *Founders Online*; Coffin, comp., *History of the Battle of Breed's Hill*, 37; Freeman, Carroll, and Ashworth, *George Washington* 3:491.

17. Plutarch, *The Life of Pyrrhus*, penelope.uchicago.edu/Thayer/e/roman/texts/plutarch/lives/pyrrhus*.html; James Abercrombie to Lord Loudoun, June 20, 1775, James Johnson to Loudoun, June 23, 1775, John Montrésor to Loudoun, June 23, 1775, Loudoun Papers, HEH; William Tudor to John Adams, June 26, 1775, *Founders Online*; Ward, *War of the Revolution* 1:96; Peckham, *Toll of Independence*, 4; Smith, *New Age Now Begins* 1:532; Philbrick, *Bunker Hill*, 230, 233.

18. Gage to Dartmouth, June 25, 1775, in Davies, ed., *Documents of the American Revolution* 9:199 (first and third quotations); Gage to Barrington, June 26, 1775, in *Correspondence of General Thomas Gage* 2:686 (second quotation); James Abercrombie to Lord Loudoun, May 21, 1775, Loudoun Papers, HEH (fourth quotation); Clinton, *American Rebellion*, 19.

19. Dartmouth to Gage, Jan. 27, Aug. 2, 1775, in Davies, ed., *Documents of the American Revolution* 9:39, 11:62–63; French, *Day of Concord and Lexington*, 60–61; Alden, *General Gage in America*, 280.

20. Howe to [British Adjutant General?], June 22, 24, 1775, in Commager and Morris, eds., *Spirit of 'Seventy-Six*, 1:133; Lee, *Memoirs of the War in the Southern Department of the United States* 1:49–55; Lengel, *General George Washington*, 105.

21. Breen, *Will of the People*, 89, 3; Burgoyne, *Reflections Upon the War in America* [1776?], Burgoyne to Lord Rochfort, [June?] 1775, in Fonblanque, *Political and Military Episodes in the Latter Half of the Eighteenth Century*, 208–9, 148; Bobrick, *Angel in the Whirlwind*, 246; Ellis, *Revolutionary Summer*, 46.

22. Miranda and McCarter, *Hamilton*, 118; Frothingham, *History of the Siege of Boston*, 115, 372–401; Frothingham, *Battle-Field of Bunker Hill*, 18–46; Coffin, comp., *History of the Battle of Breed's Hill*. My thanks to Beverly Ferris Holton for her take on *Hamilton*.

23. Burgoyne, *Reflections upon the War in America* [1776?], quoted in Fonblanque, *Political and Military Episodes in the Latter Half of the Eighteenth Century*, 208–9; Bobrick, *Angel in the Whirlwind*, 246. Thomas Gage agreed with Burgoyne: America's hills and forests made it "naturally strong" against invaders, and the rebels had learned to "assist its natural strength" with their shovels. Gage to Dartmouth, June 25, 1775, in Davies, ed., *Documents of the American Revolution* 9:199.

24. Ellis, *Revolutionary Summer*, 30.

25. Virginia convention, resolutions, March 25, 1775, *RV* 2:376–77; June 15, 1775, *JCC* 2:91; Freeman, Carroll, and Ashworth, *George Washington* 3:426; Chernow, *Washington*, 183, 190.

26. John Adams, diary, [June–July 1775], *Founders Online*; George Washington to the officers of five Virginia independent companies, June 20, 1775, *Founders Online*; Longmore, *Invention of George Washington*, 162–71.

27. "... Extracts from a Sermon Preached by the Late President Davi[e]s ... ," *Pennsylvania Packet*, June 26, 1775; Davies, *Religion and Patriotism the Constituents of a Good Soldier*, 9n; Washington, quoted in Freeman, Carroll, and Ashworth, *George Washington* 3:439–40; Freeman, Carroll, and Ashworth, *George Washington* 3:444.

28. June 14, 22, 1775, *JCC* 2:89–90, 103; Ferguson, *Power of the Purse*, 26.

29. June 1, 27, 1775, *JCC* 2:75, 109–10; Ward, *War of the Revolution* 1:138–40; Cubbison, *Burgoyne and the Saratoga Campaign*, 22.

30. Virginia House of Burgesses, resolutions on Lord North's conciliatory proposal, June 10, 1775, Franklin, Intended Vindication and Offer from Congress to Parliament, [before July 21, 1775], *Founders Online*.

31. "A Declaration by the Representatives of the United Colonies of North-America, Now Met in Congress at Philadelphia, Setting Forth the Causes and Necessity of their Taking up Arms," [July 6, 1775], *Founders Online*.

32. Richard Cranch to John Adams, July 24, 1775, *Founders Online*.

33. H. T. Cramahé to Dartmouth, Sept. 21, 1775, Guy Johnson to Dartmouth, Oct. 12, 1775, in Davies, ed., *Documents of the American Revolution* 11:124, 143; Graymont, *Iroquois in the American Revolution*, 75–79.

34. Guy Johnson to Dartmouth, Oct. 12, 1775 in Davies, ed., *Documents of the American Revolution* 11:143; Graymont, *Iroquois in the American Revolution*, 79; Nash, *Unknown American Revolution*, 175.

35. Nelson, *General Sir Guy Carleton*, 74.

36. George Washington to John Hancock, Sept. 21, 1775, George Washington to John Augustine Washington, Oct. 13, 1775, *Founders Online*; Ward, *War of the Revolution* 1:163–64.

37. "Extract of a letter from Frederick town, August 1," *Virginia Gazette* (Dixon & Hunter), Sept. 9, 1775; Ward, *War of the Revolution* 1:165; Kidd, *Great Awakening*, 288; Goff, "Revivals and Revolution"; McConville, *Brethren*.

38. Ward, *War of the Revolution* 1:170–74.

39. Henry, *Accurate and Interesting Account of the Hardships and Sufferings of That Band of Heroes*, 15, 23–24, 27, 30; Arnold to John Manir, Nov. 1, 1775, in Force, ed., *American Archives*, Ser. 4, 3:1328; Nov. 21, 1775, in William Hendricks, "Journal of the March of a Party of Provincials from Carlisle to Boston and from Thence to Quebec," *Pennsylvania Archives*, Ser. 2, 15:50; Allen, "Account of Arnold's Expedition," 510; Calloway, *Indian World of George Washington*, 228.

40. Allen, "Account of Arnold's Expedition," 507n, 511, 517; Henry, *Accurate and Interesting Account of the Hardships and Sufferings of That Band of Heroes*, 33–34, 74–75.

41. Upon his return to Cambridge, Enos was court-martialed. But after pointing out that he had personally opposed his subordinates' decision to turn back and arguing that it was justified by the expedition's food shortage, he was cleared. Force, ed., *American Archives*, Ser. 4, 3:1709–10; Oct. 24, 1775, Hendricks, "Journal of the March of a Party of Provincials from Carlisle to Boston and from Thence to Quebec," 37–38.

42. Henry, *Accurate and Interesting Account of the Hardships and Sufferings of That Band of Heroes*, 65–66; Nov. 2, 1775, *Interesting Journal of Abner Stocking of Chatham, Con-*

necticut, 19; Berkin, *Revolutionary Mothers*, 59; Sheinkin, *Notorious Benedict Arnold*, 75–76.

43. Henry, *Accurate and Interesting Account of the Hardships and Sufferings of That Band of Heroes*, 71, 74; Downes, *Council Fires on the Upper Ohio*, 223.

44. Washington, general orders, Nov. 5, 1775, *Founders Online*.

45. Washington to John Augustine Washington, Oct. 13, 1775, *Founders Online*; Smith, *Arnold's March from Cambridge to Quebec*, 251–53; Ann Hulton to [Elizabeth] Lightbody, Nov. 25, 1773, in Hulton, *Letters of a Loyalist Lady*, 62.

46. Arnold to Montgomery, Nov. 14, 20, 1775, in Force, ed., *American Archives*, Ser. 4, 3:1684, 1696; Nelson, *General Sir Guy Carleton*, 74.

47. Ward, *War of the Revolution* 1:185–88; Nelson, *General Sir Guy Carleton*, 77; Fenn, *Pox Americana*, 63.

48. Stedman, *History of the Origin, Progress, and Termination of the American War* 1:140.

49. Carleton to William Howe, Jan. 12, 1776, in Davies, ed., *Documents of the American Revolution* 12:41.

Chapter 16: Instigated Insurrections?

1. South Carolina military association, June 4, 1775, quoted in Narrative by George Millegen of his Experiences in South Carolina, Sept. 15, 1775, in Davies, ed., *Documents of the American Revolution* 11:109; Laurens, quoted in Drayton, *Memoirs of the American Revolution* 1:253; Crow, "Slave Rebelliousness and Social Conflict in North Carolina," 84n–85n; John Stuart to Dartmouth, July 21, 1775, Campbell to Dartmouth, Aug. 31, 1775, in Davies, ed., *Documents of the American Revolution* 11:53, 97; *Ramsay's History of South Carolina*, 133; Edgar, *South Carolina*, 222.

2. Parkinson, *Common Cause*, 113; Kidd, *Great Awakening*, 291, Harris, *Hanging of Thomas Jeremiah*, 122; Kars, *Breaking Loose Together*, 214.

3. Wright to Gage, June 27, 1775 (forged version), in Drayton, *Memoirs of the American Revolution* 1:347–48.

4. George, John Simpson, quoted in Wood, " 'Liberty Is Sweet,' " 167, 165; Ryan, *World of Thomas Jeremiah*, 54; Klooster, "Slave Revolts, Royal Justice, and a Ubiquitous Rumor in the Age of Revolutions."

5. Estave's letter is the only surviving account of the incident. *Virginia Gazette* (Pinkney), July 20, 1775.

6. Harris, *Hanging of Thomas Jeremiah*, 2, 133, 145–46.

7. Harris, *Hanging of Thomas Jeremiah*, 146–48, 152; Ryan, *World of Thomas Jeremiah*, 157.

8. Klooster, "Slave Revolts, Royal Justice, and a Ubiquitous Rumor in the Age of Revolutions." For a similar strategic deployment of rumors by African Americans, in this case after emancipation, see Hahn, *Nation Under Our Feet*, 152.

9. Williamsburg dateline, *Virginia Gazette* (Purdie), Sept. 8, 1775; Williamsburg dateline, *Virginia Gazette* (Dixon & Hunter), Sept. 9, 1775; Holton, *Forced Founders*, 133–34; Williams, *Hurricane of Independence*, 32–50.

10. Williamsburg dateline, *Virginia Gazette* (Purdie), Oct. 27, 1775 (supplement); Williamsburg dateline, *Virginia Gazette* (Pinkney), Nov. 2, 1775; Holton, *Forced Founders*, 134.

11. Jan. 2, 1776, Robert Honyman diary, LC; Selby, *Revolution in Virginia*, 64.

12. Debt owed by Edmund Taylor, "British Mercantile Claims," 104–5; Dunmore, proclamation, Nov. 7, 1775 [issued Nov. 5, 1775], *RV* 4:334, 340n; Norton, *Liberty's Daugh-*

ters, 210; "Book of Negroes," 148–49, Nova Scotia Archives, archives.novascotia.ca /africanns/archives/?ID=26.

13. James Parker to Charles Steuart, Jan. 27, 1775, in Steuart, ed., "Letters from Virginia," 157; John Norton Jr., quoted in Berkeley, *Dunmore's Proclamation of Emancipation* (unpaginated); Francis Lightfoot Lee to Landon Carter, Feb. 12, 1776, Benjamin Harrison to Robert Carter Nicholas, Jan. 17, 1776, Thomas Nelson Jr. to Mann Page, Jan. 4, 1776, in Smith et al., eds., *Letters of Delegates to Congress* 3:237, 107, 30. Earlier the House of Burgesses had accused an unnamed British official, perhaps Dunmore, of authoring "a Scheme, the most diabolical," to "offer Freedom to our Slaves, and turn them against their Masters." House of Burgesses, address to Dunmore, June 19, 1775, *JHB . . . 1773–1776*, 256. A rumored British scheme to ally with Native Americans was also described as "Diabolical" and "infernal." George Washington to John Augustine Washington, Oct. 13, 1775, Richard Henry Lee to George Washington, Nov. 13, 1775, *Founders Online*.

14. "Intelligence Extraordinary," *Virginia Gazette* (Pinkney), June 1, 1775; late 1775, *Diary of Colonel Landon Carter of Sabine Hall* 2:960; Tarter, "Some Thoughts Arising from Trying to Find Out Who Was Governor Dunmore's Mistress"; Ward, *Major General Adam Stephen and the Cause of American Liberty*, 167–68; Holton, "Rebel Against Rebel," 177–78.

15. Holton, *Forced Founders*, 159.

16. Richard Henry Lee to [Catherine] Macaulay, Nov. 29, 1775, in *Letters of Richard Henry Lee* 1:162; Archibald Cary, quoted in Holton, *Forced Founders*, 159; Edward Rutledge to Ralph Izard, Dec. 8, 1775, *Correspondence of Mr. Ralph Izard* 1:165; Olwell, "'Domestick Enemies,'" 41. Many Loyalists agreed. In Maryland, William Eddis observed that Dunmore's "measure of emancipating the negroes has excited an universal ferment." Jan. 16, 1776, in Eddis, *Letters from America*, 251.

17. Madison to William Bradford [Jr.], Nov. 26, 1774, *Founders Online.*

18. Wood, *Black Majority*, xiv; Polhemus, "Culture of Commodification," 262–91.

19. Moultrie, *Memoirs of the American Revolution* 1:113; South Carolina Council of Safety, quoted in Olwell, "Domestick Enemies," 43; Scipio Handley, Loyalist petition, Jan. 13, 1784, royalprovincial.com/military/mems/sc/clmhandley.htm; Pybus, *Epic Journeys of Freedom*, 21–23, 37–38.

20. Estimates of the number of Blacks killed on Sullivan's Island on Dec. 19, 1775, ranged from as few as three to as many as fifty. Josiah Smith Jr., quoted in Wood, "Dream Deferred," 178–79; "Journal of the Second Council of Safety," Dec. 16, 20, 1775, South-Carolina Historical Society *Collections* 3:88–89, 102–4; Ryan, *World of Thomas Jeremiah*, 119.

21. Henry Laurens, quoted in council minutes, Dec. 30, 1775, Jan. 30, 1776, in "Journal of the Second Council of Safety," in South Carolina Historical Society *Collections* 3:102, 233; "Extract of a Letter to a Gentleman in Philadelphia, Dated Charlestown, South-Carolina, February 7, 1776," in Force, ed., *American Archives*, Ser. 4, 4:950.

22. Dunmore to Dartmouth, Dec. 6, 1775–Feb. [18], 1776, in Davies, ed., *Documents of the American Revolution* 12:60.

23. Dunmore to Dartmouth, Dec. 6, 1775–Feb. [18], 1776, in Davies, ed., *Documents of the American Revolution* 12:60; Woodford, quoted in *Virginia Gazette* (Purdie), Dec. 15, 1775; Selby, *Revolution in Virginia*, 69–74; J. J., "Battle of the Great Bridge," 1–6; Kukla, *Patrick Henry*, 196.

24. [Paine], *Common Sense*, gutenberg.org/files/147/147-h/147-h.htm.

25. George Gilmer, quoted in Holton, *Forced Founders*, 168.

26. Holton, *Forced Founders*, 166–69, 180.

27. Richard Henry Lee to John Page, March 19, 1776, quoted in Smith et al., eds., *Letters of Delegates to Congress* 3:408n; Holton, *Forced Founders*, 173–74.

28. Lund Washington to George Washington, Dec. 30, 1775, *Founders Online*; Holton, *Forced Founders*, 176–80.

29. A[ndrew] Williamson to Edward Wilkinson, Nov. 6, 1775, South Carolina provincial congress, declaration, Nov. 19, 1775, in Gibbes, ed., *Documentary History of the Revolution* 1:209–14; Ryan, *World of Thomas Jeremiah*, 91.

30. A[ndrew] Williamson to Drayton, Nov. 25, 1775, in Gibbes, ed., *Documentary History of the Revolution* 1:217–19; Greene, "Ninety Six," 4, 66–73; Edgar, *Partisans and Redcoats*, 33; Edgar, *South Carolina*, 226.

31. Fletchall, quoted in Klein, *Unification of a Slave State*, 89 (as related by Oliver Hart); "G.R.," quoted on May 1, 1776, in *Diary of Colonel Landon Carter of Sabine Hall* 2:1030–31.

32. Chernow, *Washington*, 199; Freeman, Carroll, and Ashworth, *George Washington* 3:504–5; McCullough, *1776*, 247 (James Monroe: "dignified"), 43 (Benjamin Rush: "dignity"); Abigail Adams to John Adams, July 16, 1775, *Founders Online* ("dignity").

33. George Washington to Lund Washington, Aug. 20, 1775, George Washington to Richard Henry Lee, Aug. 29, 1775, *Founders Online*; Freeman, Carroll, and Ashworth, *George Washington* 3:529.

34. Artemas Ward to John Adams, Oct. 23, 1775, *Founders Online*; Philbrick, *Bunker Hill*, 261.

35. Council of war, Oct. 8, 1775, Washington, general orders, Dec. 30, 1775, Washington to Hancock, Dec. 31, 1775, *Founders Online*; Freeman, Carroll, and Ashworth, *George Washington* 3:569–74, 586; Royster, *Revolutionary People at War*, 25, 96–97.

36. Jonathan Brewer et al., petition to Massachusetts General Court, Dec. 5, 1775, in Quintal, *Patriots of Color*, 175; Quarles, *Negro in the American Revolution*, 11.

37. Lund Washington to George Washington, Dec. 3, 1775, *Founders Online*; Richard Cary to Esther Reed, May 3, 13, 1775, in Reed, ed., *Life of Esther De Berdt*, 214.

38. Washington to Lee, Dec. 26, 1775, *Founders Online*; Wood, "'Liberty Is Sweet,'" 170.

39. Holton, *Forced Founders*, 136.

40. Phillis Wheatley to George Washington, Oct. 26, 1775, Washington to Joseph Reed, Feb. 10, 1776, Washington to Wheatley, Feb. 28, 1776, *Founders Online*; Wiencek, *Imperfect God*, 205–14; Carretta, *Phillis Wheatley*, 154–57.

41. Lengel, *General George Washington*, 314; Nash, "African Americans' Revolution," 254, 261.

42. Lee to Rush, Nov. 13, Sept. 19, 1775, *Lee Papers* 1:216, 206; Washington, circular to general officers, Sept. 8, 1775, council of war, Sept. 11, 1775, *Founders Online*; Ward, *War of the Revolution* 1:111; Freeman, Carroll, and Ashworth, *George Washington* 3:538–39.

43. Oct. 2, 1775, *JCC* 3:270; council of war, Oct. 18, 1775, Washington to Reed, Dec. 15, 1775, *Founders Online*.

44. Ward, *War of the Revolution* 1:101, 110–12.

45. George III, *By the King, a Proclamation, For Suppressing Rebellion and Sedition*; Samuel Graves to Gage, Sept. 1, 1775, Howe to Dartmouth, Nov. 27, 1775, in Davies, ed., *Documents of the American Revolution* 11:98, 196; Leamon, *Revolution Downeast*, 70–73.

46. Abigail Adams to John Adams, Oct. 25, 1775, "Humanity" to John Adams, Jan. 23, 1776, *Founders Online*.

47. Mackesy, *War for America*, 102; Spring, *With Zeal and with Bayonets Only*, 4; Jones, *Captives of Liberty*, 26.

48. I am grateful for Dr. Roberto Oscar Flores de Apodaca for this point.

49. Germain, quoted in Thomas, *Tea Party to Independence*, 286; Piers Mackesy, "Germain, George Sackville [*formerly* George Sackville], first Viscount Sackville (1716–1785)," *DNB*.

50. Washington, Instructions to Capt. Nicholson Broughton, Sept. 2, 1775, Washington to Joseph Reed, Nov. 20, 1775, *Founders Online*; Fowler, *Rebels Under Sail*, 21–23, 29; Brunsman, *The Evil Necessity*.

51. James Wright to Dartmouth, July 10, 1775, Narrative by George Millegen of his Experiences in South Carolina, Sept. 15, 1775, Richard Maitland et al., deposition, Sept. 21, 1775, in Davies, ed., *Documents of the American Revolution* 11:7–9, 44, 113, 125–28; Bonvouloir to de Guines, Dec. 28, 1775, in Doniol, *Histoire de la Participation de la France à l'établissement des États-Unis d'Amérique* 1:287; Buel, *In Irons*; O'Shaughnessy, *Men Who Lost America*, 13–14; Hulbert, "Vigorous & Bold Operations," 17–20.

52. Observations by Benjamin Thompson (afterwards Count Rumford), Nov. 4, 1775, in Historical Manuscripts Commission, *Report on the Manuscripts of Mrs. Stopford-Sackville* 2:16; Gage to Dartmouth, Sept. 20, 1775, in Davies, ed., *Documents of the American Revolution* 11:124; Buel and Buel, *Way of Duty*, 99–100; Fenn, *Pox Americana*, 263–75; Raphael, *People's History of the American Revolution*, 53–54.

53. Abigail Adams to John Adams, Sept. 8–10, Oct. 1, 9, 21, 1775, *Founders Online*; Bell, "Adams Household 'Dangerously Sick with a Dysentery'"; Cataldo, "Epidemic Behind the American Lines."

Chapter 17: Freedom Hath Been Hunted

1. [Paine], *Common Sense*, gutenberg.org/files/147/147-h/147-h.htm; March 28 and 12, 1776, in *Diary of Colonel Landon Carter of Sabine Hall* 2:1006, 999; William Franklin to Germain, March 28, 1776, in Davies, ed., *Documents of the American Revolution* 12:99; Jan. 19–26, 1776, *Journal of Nicholas Cresswell*, 136; Maier, *American Scripture*, 33; Thomas, *Tea Party to Independence*, 327; Larkin, *Thomas Paine and the Literature of Revolution*.

2. Paine refers to the Bible dozens of times but only once to Rome (in the biblical passage, "Render unto Caesar the things which are Caesar's") and never to Greece. In an appendix to a later edition, Paine finally made a classical allusion, employing the cliché, "The Rubicon is passed." Paine, *Common Sense*, gutenberg.org/files/147/147-h/147-h.htm; Taylor, *American Revolutions*, 156.

3. Paine, *Common Sense*, gutenberg.org/files/147/147-h/147-h.htm. My thanks to Dr. Roberto Oscar Flores de Apodaca for drawing my attention to the globalist dimension of Paine's case for independence.

4. Nelson, *Royalist Revolution*.

5. Paine, *Common Sense*, gutenberg.org/files/147/147-h/147-h.htm; *The People the Best Governors*, 3.

6. Lund Washington to George Washington, Feb. 29, 1776, *Founders Online*.

7. George Washington to Joseph Reed, Feb. 10, 1776, George Washington to Jonathan Trumbull Sr., Feb. 19, 1776, *Founders Online*.

8. Israel Trask, in Dann, ed., *Revolution Remembered*, 409; Bell, "Snowball Fight in Harvard Yard"; Cox, *Boy Soldiers of the American Revolution*, 46, 113.

9. Washington to Joseph Reed, Feb. 1, 1776, *Founders Online*.

10. Nathanael Greene to [Jacob Greene], Feb. 15, 1776, Greene to Samuel Ward, Dec. 18, 1775, in Johnson, *Sketches of the Life and Correspondence of Nathanael Greene* 1:53, 44; Washington to council of war, Feb. 16, 1776, *Founders Online*.

11. Indeed, military leaders of this era believed the odds were so tilted against any army assaulting an entrenched position that they often employed expressions like "disadvantageous circumstances" as synonyms for *on the offensive*. Horatio Gates, "Minutes of a Speech Made at a Council of War held at Boston . . ." (quoted in a footnote to council of war, Feb. 16, 1776), Washington to Landon Carter, March 27, 1776, Greene to Washington, Sept. 5, 1776, Washington to Samuel Washington, Oct. 5, 1776, *Founders Online*; Freeman, Carroll, and Ashworth, *George Washington* 4:21; Lengel, *General George Washington*, 118–20.

12. Washington, council of war, Feb. 16, 1776, *Founders Online*.

13. Washington to Hancock, Feb. 18[–21], 1776, *Founders Online*.

14. Council of war, Feb. 16, 1776, *Founders Online*; Howe to Dartmouth, March 21, 1776, in Davies, ed., *Documents of the American Revolution* 12:81; Philbrick, *Bunker Hill*, 272.

15. Jan. 18, 1776, in *Memoirs of Major-General William Heath*, 30.

16. Council of war, Feb. 16, 1776, Washington to Landon Carter, March 27, 1776, *Founders Online*; Henry Sewall, diary, March 5, 1776, MHS; Gordon, *History of the Rise, Progress, and Establishment of the Independence of the United States of America* 2:24–28; Philbrick, *Bunker Hill*, 273.

17. Feb. 15, 1776, in *Memoirs of Major-General William Heath*, 30–31.

18. March 4, 1776, in Thacher, *Military Journal During the American Revolutionary War*, 46.

19. Unnamed British officer, quoted in Frothingham, *History of the Siege of Boston*, 298; Ward, *War of the Revolution* 1:128. British sentinels noticed activity atop Dorchester Heights on the night of March 4–5 and reported it up the chain of command, but army officers did not believe the Americans could build much of a redoubt by morning— apparently because the ground was frozen. Philbrick, *Bunker Hill*, 280.

20. Washington to Philip Schuyler, Feb. 27, 1776, *Founders Online*.

21. William Howe to Dartmouth, March 21, 1775, in Force, ed., *American Archives*, Ser. 4, 5:458–59; Freeman, Carroll, and Ashworth, *George Washington* 4:64; Smith, *New Age Now Begins* 1:652.

22. Dartmouth to Howe, Sept. 5, 1775, Howe to Dartmouth, Nov. 26, 1775, March 21, 1776, in Davies, ed., *Documents of the American Revolution* 11:99, 191, 12:81; Freeman, Carroll, and Ashworth, *George Washington* 4:42–43.

23. Washington to Landon Carter, March 27, 1776, Washington to Charles Lee, Feb. 26, 1776, *Founders Online*; Philbrick, *Bunker Hill*, 272.

24. Philbrick, *Bunker Hill*, 285.

25. Washington to John Augustine Washington, March 31, 1776, Washington to Joseph Reed, March 19, 1776, *Founders Online*; Henry Sewall diary, March 18, 1776, MHS; March 5, 1776, in Heath, *Memoirs of Major-General William Heath*, 33–34.

26. Nash, *Urban Crucible*, 313, 409; Carp, *Rebels Rising*, 225; Saunt, *West of the Revolution*, 189.

27. Germain to [Lord Suffolk], June 16 or 17, 1775, in Historical Manuscripts Commission, *Report on the Manuscripts of Mrs. Stopford-Sackville* 2:3.

28. Martin, *Narrative of Some of the Adventures, Dangers, and Sufferings of a Revolutionary Soldier*, 13–16.

29. Smith, *New Age Now Begins* 1:715.

30. Dartmouth to Howe, Oct. 22, 1775, Germain to Clinton or southern commander, Dec. 6, 1775, in Davies, ed., *Documents of the American Revolution* 11:158–60, 203–5.

31. Josiah Martin to Dartmouth, March 10, 1775, in Davies, ed., *Documents of the American Revolution* 9:72–73.

32. Kars, *Breaking Loose Together*, 212–14.

33. Stedman, *History of the Origin, Progress, and Termination of the American War* 1:180–81; Wilson, *Southern Strategy*, 22–26.

34. Narrative of proceedings of Loyalists in North Carolina, enclosed in Howe to Germain, April 25, 1776, Josiah Martin to Germain, March 21, 1776, in Davies, ed., *Documents of the American Revolution* 12:116 (quotation), 88–89; Wilson, *Southern Strategy*, 26–35.

35. Davies, ed., *Documents of the American Revolution* 11:13.

36. Davies, ed., *Documents of the American Revolution* 12:14; Edgar, *Partisans and Redcoats*, 35.

37. Clinton, *American Rebellion*, 37.

Chapter 18: The Mouse in the Maze

1. John Adams to Horatio Gates, March 23, 1776, *Founders Online*; "A Dialogue between the Ghost of General Montgomery and a Delegate, in a Wood near Philadelphia," *Pennsylvania Packet*, Feb. 19, 1776; Jensen, *Founding of a Nation*, 664; Maier, *American Scripture*, 34–36.

2. Braxton to Landon Carter, April 14, 1776, in Smith et al., eds., *Letters of Delegates to Congress* 3:522; Washington, quoted in Holton, *Forced Founders*, 193; "Cato," III, *Pennsylvania Packet*, March 25, 1776.

3. "Wrote by the same [Fidelia, Griffitts's pen name] upon reading a Book entituled Common Sense," Jan. 1776, "Fidelia," "Wrote extempore on Tea," Wulf's introduction, "The Ladies Lamentation over an empty Cannister, by the Same [Fidelia]," in Blecki and Wulf, eds, *Milcah Martha Moore's Book*, 255–56, 299, 42, 247–50; Griffitts to Anthony Wayne, July 13, 1777, in Griffitts, "Two Letters of Hannah Griffitts to General Anthony Wayne," 110; "Civis," in Force, ed., *American Archives*, Ser. 4, 5:803.

4. Although Adams was trying to correct the excessively republican government that Paine had proposed in *Common Sense*, even he had felt the adoptive Pennsylvanian's influence, for the constitution Adams sketched out in *Thoughts on Government* was considerably more popular than the one he had described in a Nov. 15, 1775, letter to Richard Henry Lee. Selby, "Richard Henry Lee, John Adams, and the Virginia Constitution of 1776," 392.

5. Braxton wanted to give members of the executive council life terms but allow legislators to remove governors for misbehavior. Spring 1776, Adams diary, *Founders Online*; "A Native" [Braxton], *An Address to the Convention of the Colony and Ancient Dominion of Virginia on the Subject of Government in General, and Recommending a Particular Form to Their Consideration*, RV 6:521–24; "Civis," "To the Inhabitants of Philadelphia," in Force, ed., *American Archives*, Ser. 4, 5:802.

6. James Cleveland, quoted in Lund Washington to George Washington, Feb. 29, 1776, *Founders Online*; Buckingham County, Virginia, freeholders, instruction to convention delegates, [May 1776], in Force, ed., *American Archives*, Ser. 4, 6:460; Ketchum, *Saratoga*, 69; Ellis, *Revolutionary Summer*, 118.

7. Francis Lightfoot Lee to Landon Carter, May 21, 1776, in Smith et al., eds., *Letters of Delegates to Congress* 4:57; "Columbus," "To the Electors of the City and County of New-York," June 12, 1776, in Force, ed., *American Archives*, Ser. 4, 6:825; Ryerson, *Revolution Is Now Begun*, 221, 223 (third quotation).

8. Lee to Carter, April 9, May 21, 1776, Edward Rutledge to Ralph Izard, Dec. 8, 1775, in Smith et al., eds., *Letters of Delegates to Congress* 3:500–501 (including quotation from Carter), 4:57, 2:462–63; Richard Henry Lee to [Patrick Henry], April 20, 1776, Lee to

Robert Carter Nicholas, April 30, 1776, in *Letters of Richard Henry Lee* 1:177, 184; John
Page to Thomas Jefferson, April 26, 1776, *Founders Online*.

9. Charles Carroll of Annapolis to Charles Carroll of Carrollton, Dec. 1–2, 1775, in Carroll
and Carroll, *Dear Papa, Dear Charley* 2:853; "A Native" [Braxton], *An Address to the
Convention of the Colony and Ancient Dominion of Virginia, RV* 6:518; Hoffman, *Spirit
of Dissension*, 150.

10. Quarles, *Negro in the American Revolution*. For a similar argument—that the *Somerset*
decision exerted influence beyond African Americans and the whites who claimed to
own them—see Waldstreicher, *Slavery's Constitution*, 40–41.

11. "The Interest of America," "Spartanus," "The Interest of America," III, in Force, ed.,
American Archives, Ser. 4, 6:842, 994; Adams, "Republicanism in Political Rhetoric Before 1776."

12. "Demophilus," *Pennsylvania Packet*, Feb. 12, 1776; "Salus Populi," "To the People of
North-America on the Different Kinds of Government," in Force, ed., *American Archives*, Ser. 4, 5:183; Rodgers, "Republicanism."

13. James Sullivan to Elbridge Gerry, May 6, 1776, cited in footnote to John Adams to James
Sullivan, May 26, 1776, *Founders Online; People the Best Governors*, 12; "Democrati-
cus," "Loose Thoughts on Government," Charles County, instructions to delegates in
Maryland convention, in Force, ed., *American Archives*, Ser. 4, 6:731, 1018; "The Interest
of America," in Force, ed., *American Archives*, Ser. 4, 6:841; Maier, *American Scripture*,
94–95.

14. "Reasons for a Declaration of the Independence of the American Colonies," *Pennsyl-
vania Evening Post*, April 20, 1776; "Demophilus," *Pennsylvania Packet*, Feb 12, 1776;
"Salus Populi," "To the People of Pennsylvania," in Force, ed., *American Archives*,
Ser. 4, 5:97; "The Interest of America," "Spartanus," "The Interest of America," III, in
Force, ed., *American Archives*, Ser. 4, 6:842, 994.

15. *People the Best Governors*, 7, 10–13.

16. Occoquan Baptist Church, petition, May [19], 1776, in "Virginia Legislative Papers," 39.

17. Aimed at assuaging the fears of Americans who had opposed the Constitution, this
original First Amendment was never ratified. "J.R.," "Considerations on the Mode of
Electing Delegates to the General Congress," in Force, ed., *American Archives*, Ser. 4,
6:800; Labunski, *James Madison and the Struggle for the Bill of Rights*, 256, 278. Other
writers also favored direct election of congressmen. "The Censor," "To the Apologist,"
"Spartanus," "The Interest of America," III, in Force, ed., *American Archives*, Ser. 4,
5:71–72; 6:994.

18. "Spartanus," "The Interest of America," III, in Force, ed., *American Archives*, Ser. 4,
6:995. In 1787 and 1788, many Americans who opposed the Constitution would lean
on Baron Montesquieu's claim that republics cannot function over large areas. In reply,
James Madison and other Federalists would cite David Hume's insistence that larger
republics actually work better. More than a decade earlier, on Feb. 12, 1776, a writer in
the *Pennsylvania Packet* had likewise used Hume to refute the Montesquieuian fear that
his large and growing state would collapse if it became a republic. "Salus Populi," "To
the People of North-America on the Different Kinds of Government," in Force, ed.,
American Archives, Ser. 4, 5:180–81; "Demophilus," *Pennsylvania Packet*, Feb. 12, 1776.

19. Talbot County, instructions to delegates in the Maryland convention, Anne Arundel
County, instructions to delegates in Maryland convention, in Force, ed., *American Archives*, Ser. 4, 6:1021, 1092.

20. Abigail Adams to John Adams, March 31–April 5, 1776, *Founders Online*.

21. Abigail Adams to Mercy Otis Warren, April 27, 1776, *Founders Online* (my thanks

to Zara Anishanslin for drawing my attention to this phrase); Abigail Adams to John Adams, March 31–April 5, 1776, *Founders Online*; Kerber, "Why Diamonds Really Are a Girl's Best Friend," 60.

22. John Adams to Abigail Adams, April 14, 1776, John Adams to James Sullivan, May 26, 1776, *Founders Online*.

23. Richard Henry Lee to Hannah Lee Corbin, March 17, 1778, in *Letters of Richard Henry Lee* 1:392–93; Mary Willing Byrd to [Thomas Nelson?], Aug. 10, 1781, in *Papers of Thomas Jefferson* 5:704; Norton, *Liberty's Daughters*, 226, 360n.

24. Fischer, *Washington's Crossing*, 51–65.

25. John Sullivan to John Adams, May 4, 1776, *Founders Online*; Jefferson's notes on congressional debates on independence, June 8, 1776, *JCC* 6:1091.

26. Inglis, *True Interest of America Impartially Stated*, 51–52; Richard Henry Lee to [Patrick Henry], April 20, 1776, in *Letters of Richard Henry Lee* 1:177–78; Hutson, "Partition Treaty and the Declaration of American Independence."

27. Ellison, "'Reverse of Fortune.'"

28. Carleton to Germain, May 14, 1776, in Davies, ed., *Documents of the American Revolution* 12:137.

29. Ward, *War of the Revolution* 1:198–200; Becker, "Smallpox in Washington's Army," 409–21.

30. Fenn, *Pox Americana*, 74.

31. Mackesy, *War for America*, 94–96; Cubbison, *Burgoyne and the Saratoga Campaign*, 159n.

32. John Stuart to George Germain, Aug. 23, 1776, in Davies, ed., *Documents of the American Revolution* 12:188–89.

33. "Copy of a Letter Addressed to the Frontier Inhabitants, by Mr. [Henry] Stuart . . . ," *Virginia Gazette* (Purdie), June 7, 1776; Hamer, ed., "Correspondence of Henry Stuart and Alexander Cameron with the Wataugans," 451–52; O'Donnell, *Southern Indians in the American Revolution*, 37–39; Dowd, *Groundless*, 171–72.

34. Maier, *American Scripture*, 47–96, 217–23.

35. April 1, 1776, Robert Wormeley Carter diary, W&M; April 1, 4, 1776 in *Diary of Colonel Landon Carter of Sabine Hall* 2:1008–10; Randolph, *History of Virginia*, 234; Holton, *Forced Founders*, 199–204; McDonnell, *Politics of War*, 200–208.

36. Landon Carter to George Washington, May 9, 1776, *Founders Online*; Charles Lee to Patrick Henry, May 7, 1776, in [Charles] *Lee Papers* 2:3; Holton, *Forced Founders*, 201–2.

37. Maier, *American Scripture*, 63.

38. Maier, *American Scripture*, 37–38.

39. Roche, *Joseph Reed*, 82; Ryerson, *Revolution Is Now Begun*, 224.

40. Caroline County committee of observation, June 8, 1776, in Force, ed., *American Archives*, Ser. 4, 6:804; Somerset County committee of observation, quoted in Hoffman, *Spirit of Dissension*, 153.

41. Samuel Chase to John Adams, June 28, 1776, *Founders Online*; Jensen, *Founding of a Nation*, 695–96; Hoffman, *Spirit of Dissension*, 166.

Chapter 19: Liberty Further Extended

1. June 26, July 25, 1776, in *Diary of Colonel Landon Carter of Sabine Hall* 2:1051–52, 1064; Isaac, *Landon Carter's Uneasy Kingdom*, 3–15.

2. Henry Laurens to John Laurens, Aug. 14, 1776, in *Papers of Henry Laurens* 11:223–24n; Morgan, *Slave Counterpoint*, 285. Other Laurens slaves would join the British later in the war. Sandy, "Divided Loyalties in a 'Predatory War,'" 378.

3. Sheridan, "Jamaican Slave Insurrection Scare of 1776 and the American Revolution"; Brown, *Tacky's Revolt*, 219, 237–39.

4. Jefferson, "original Rough draught" of the Declaration of Independence, [June 11–July 4, 1776], *Founders Online*.

5. Jefferson, "original Rough draught" of the Declaration of Independence, [June 11–July 4, 1776], *Founders Online*.

6. In a sense, African Americans not only closed out but headed off Jefferson's list of grievances. His very first complaint was that George III had "refused his assent to laws the most wholesome and necessary for the public good." Jefferson had never criticized the British government for disallowing any colonial legislation other than curbs on the slave trade. Jefferson, "original Rough draught" of the Declaration of Independence, [June 11–July 4, 1776], *Founders Online*; Jefferson, draft of instructions for Virginia delegates in Congress (published as *A Summary View of the Rights of British America*), [July 1774], *Founders Online*. Historians who see Jefferson's slavery paragraph as his capstone grievance include Charles Francis Adams, speech in the House of Representatives, May 31, 1860; Jensen, *Founding of a Nation*, 645; Gittleman, "Jefferson's 'Slave Narrative,'" 251; Maier, *American Scripture*, 121. Among the most recent treatments is Brewer, "Kings as Tyrants and Enslavers."

7. Patrick Henry to Robert Pleasants, Jan. 18, 1773, in Holton, *Black Americans in the Revolutionary Era*, 45.

8. Jefferson, "original Rough draught" of the Declaration of Independence, [June 11–July 4, 1776], *Founders Online*.

9. Jefferson, "original Rough draught" of the Declaration of Independence, [June 11–July 4, 1776], *Founders Online*.

10. Jefferson, "original Rough draught" of the Declaration of Independence, [June 11–July 4, 1776], *Founders Online*; Brodie, *Thomas Jefferson*, 136–41.

11. Jefferson, "original Rough draught" of the Declaration of Independence, [June 11–July 4, 1776], *Founders Online*.

12. Mason, first draft of the Virginia declaration of rights, [c. May 20–26, 1774], Virginia convention, final draft of the declaration of rights, June 12, 1776, in *Papers of George Mason* 1:277, 287; Slauter, "Rights," 454–56.

13. New Jersey constitution, July 2, 1776, avalon.law.yale.edu/18th_century/nj15.asp; Lurie, "Envisioning a Republic," 5–6; Gigantino, *William Livingston's American Revolution*, 66–69, 75, 77–78; Drinker, "Votes for Women in 18th-Century New Jersey"; Klinghoffer and Elkis, "Petticoat Electors."

14. John Adams to Abigail Adams, Aug. 3–4, 1776, Abigail Adams to John Adams, Aug. 14, 1776, *Founders Online*; Kerber, *Women of the Republic*, 228–29.

15. Jensen, *Founding of a Nation*, 699–700. The myth that Congress had decided not to declare independence without the consent of every state may have originated with Peter Stone's play and film *1776*.

16. John Adams to Abigail Adams, July 3, 1776, *Founders Online*.

17. Ketchum, *Saratoga*, 169.

18. A printer used this version of the Declaration of Independence to run off copies for Congress and inadvertently used Jefferson's diacritical marks, which look like random apostrophes and quotation marks. Fliegelman, *Declaring Independence*, 4–15.

19. Boyd, *Declaration of Independence*, 29; Parkinson, *Common Cause*, 252–53, 260. Years

later, Jefferson would state that Congress had to delete his denunciation of the slave trade in order to keep the southernmost states, Georgia and South Carolina (as well as Rhode Island, home to numerous slave traders), in the pro-independence column. But as Denver Brunsman points out (personal communication, Oct. 4, 2016), the debate over whether to denounce the African trade took place *after* Congress's July 2, 1776, vote in favor of independence. The key phrase in the final draft, "excited domestic insurrections," appears to have come from the March 26, 1776, South Carolina constitution, where it also refers to enslaved people. avalon.law.yale.edu/18th_century/sc01.asp.

20. Jefferson, "original Rough draught" of the Declaration of Independence, [June 11–July 4, 1776], *Founders Online*; Declaration of Independence, July 4, 1776, archives.gov /founding-docs/declaration-transcript.

21. Jefferson, "original Rough draught" of the Declaration of Independence, [June 11–July 4, 1776], *Founders Online*; Copy of the Declaration made by Jefferson for Richard Henry Lee (which "approximates" the drafting committee's version), in Boyd, *Declaration of Independence*, 73–77; Declaration of Independence, July 4, 1776, archives.gov /founding-docs/declaration-transcript; Becker, *Declaration of Independence*, 18–20.

22. Boyd, *Declaration of Independence*, 19; Declaration of Independence, July 4, 1776, archives.gov/founding-docs/declaration-transcript; Delaware chief justice Samuel Chew had invoked all three elements of Jefferson's triad in a Nov. 21, 1741, speech justifying defensive war: "Life and Liberty, the immediate Gifts of GOD, were common to all Men; and every Man had a natural . . . Right to preserve and defend them from the Injuries and Attempts of others, as they concern'd his Happiness." Chew's speech was published by Benjamin Franklin. In *Common Sense*, Thomas Paine had made two off-hand references to "all men being originally equals." Chew, *Speech of Samuel Chew, Esq.*, 4–5; Paine, *Common Sense*, gutenberg.org/files/147/147-h/147-h.htm; Eustace, *Passion Is the Gale*, 474.

23. Detweiler, "Changing Reputation of the Declaration of Independence," 558–59. Danielle Allen points out that the opening lines of Jefferson's second paragraph are a syllogism—in the eighteenth-century sense of a series of propositions (men are equal, men have rights, men form governments to protect their rights), leading to a conclusion (the right of revolution). Allen, "Punctuating Happiness," 1–2; Wills, *Inventing America*, 65–66.

24. Danielle Allen makes the intriguing case that Jefferson and Congress did not intend a full stop after the phrase "pursuit of Happiness"—that the period that follows it in most modern editions derives from a printer's error. This seemingly trivial matter of punctuation carries tremendous significance, Allen notes, since in her reading, the authors of the Declaration intended to emphasize that humans could "secure these rights" only by forming governments—and by overturning those that failed to safeguard everyone's rights. Allen may be right about Jefferson and Congress, but abolitionists such as Haynes and Benjamin Banneker pointedly ended their quotations from the Declaration after "Life, Liberty, and the pursuit of Happiness," with the obvious intention of emphasizing that phrase. Starting in the nineteenth century, women's rights advocates would do the same thing. Haynes, in Bogin, ed., "'Liberty Further Extended,'" 93–94; Benjamin Banneker to Jefferson, Aug. 19, 1791, *Founders Online*; Newman, Finkenbine, and Mooney, "Philadelphia Emigrationist Petition," 165; Grimké, *Letters on the Equality of the Sexes*, 16, 98; [Seneca Falls] *Declaration of Sentiments* (1848), nps.gov /wori/learn/historyculture/declaration-of-sentiments.htm; Boyd, *Declaration of Independence*, 19; Maier, *American Scripture*, 160–71; Saillant, *Black Puritan, Black Republican*, 15–16; Armitage, *Declaration of Independence*; Slauter, "Rights," 456–59; Allen, "Punctuating Happiness."

25. The London bell cracked soon after arriving in Philadelphia, so a local foundry recast it. Nash, *Liberty Bell*.
26. Kammen, *Colonial New York*, 371n; McConville, *King's Three Faces*, 308–9; Maier, *American Scripture*, 158; Ruppert, "Statue of George III"; Taylor, *American Revolutions*, 161.
27. Of the approximately five thousand people inoculated in Boston in July 1776, only twenty died. Abigail Adams to John Adams, July 21–22, 1776, *Founders Online*; July 3, 18, 1776, in Thacher, *Military Journal During the American Revolutionary War*, 54–56; Fenn, *Pox Americana*, 36–38; Vine, "For the Peace of the Town," 79, 85–86.
28. Virginia convention, May 15, 1776, *Founders Online*; July 18, 1776, *JCC* 5:575; Armitage, *Declaration of Independence*, 81.
29. Virginia convention, resolutions, May 15, 1776, *Founders Online*.
30. Franklin also offered Native Americans an additional safeguard—"No Colony shall engage in an offensive War with any Nation of Indians without the Consent of the Congress . . . who are first to consider the Justice and Necessity of such War"—that Dickinson watered down. But on another key point, Dickinson took the more progressive approach. By requiring that all future land purchases be made from the Iroquois in present-day New York, Franklin, a beneficiary of the Fort Stanwix land fraud of 1768, would have perpetuated the fiction that the Iroquois owned much of the Ohio Valley land the rebel colonists desired. Dickinson's draft directed Congress to buy land from the Indians who actually owned it. [Franklin], "Articles of Confederation and Perpetual Union . . . ," May 10, 1775, *Papers of Benjamin Franklin*; [Dickinson], "Articles of Confederation and Perpetual Union . . . ," [June 1776], digitalhistory.hsp.org/pafrm/doc/draft-articles-confederation-john-dickinson-june-1776.
31. [Dickinson], "Articles of Confederation and Perpetual Union . . . ," [June 1776], digitalhistory.hsp.org/pafrm/doc/draft-articles-confederation-john-dickinson-june-1776; "The Charter of Privileges Granted by *William Penn*, Esq; to the Inhabitants of *Pensilvania* and Territories," in *Charters of the Province of Pensilvania and City of Philadelphia*, 19; Calvert, "Friendly Jurisprudence and Early Feminism of John Dickinson."
32. Edward Rutledge to John Jay, June 29, 1776, in Smith, ed., *Letters of Delegates to Congress* 4:338; Franklin, July 30, 1776, in John Adams's notes on congressional deliberations, Harrison, n.d., in Thomas Jefferson's notes on congressional deliberations, *JCC* 6:1080, 1100; Blumrosen and Blumrosen, *Slave Nation*, 145–48.
33. Articles of Confederation, Aug. 20, 1776, draft with Charles Thomson's notes, *JCC* 5:678–89; Jensen, *Articles of Confederation*, 138–39, 150–58.

Chapter 20: You Never Will Have Enough

1. John Stuart to Germain, Aug. 23, 1776, in Davies, ed., *Documents of the American Revolution* 12:190; Calloway, "Declaring Independence and Rebuilding a Nation," 185, 189–91.
2. Aaron Smith, deposition, July 1, 1776, David Shettroe, deposition, June 30, 1776, in Force, ed., *American Archives*, Ser. 4, 6:1229.
3. Henry Laurens to John Laurens, Aug. 14, 1776, in *Papers of Henry Laurens*, 11:231; Hamer, ed., "Correspondence of Henry Stuart and Alexander Cameron with the Wataugans"; Ryan, *World of Thomas Jeremiah*, 156.
4. Elzas, *Jews of South Carolina*, 68–77; Rosengarten and Rosengarten, eds., *Portion of the*

People, 79; Pencak, *Jews & Gentiles in Early America*, 124–25; Hagy, *This Happy Land*, 34–36.

5. Drayton, *Memoirs of the American Revolution* 2:347.

6. William Henry Drayton to Francis Salvador, July 24, 1776, in Gibbes, *Documentary History of the Revolution* 2:29; Drayton, *Memoirs of the American Revolution* 2:352.

7. Drayton, *Memoirs of the American Revolution* 2:358–59; Edgar, *South Carolina*, 229.

8. John Stuart to Germain, Oct. 26, 1774, in Davies, ed., *Documents of the American Revolution* 12:240.

9. O'Donnell, *Southern Indians in the American Revolution*, 54–59; Edgar, *Partisans and Redcoats*, 37; Piecuch, *Three Peoples, One King*, 108–10.

10. Piecuch, *Three Peoples, One King*, 110.

11. John Stuart to Germain, Aug. 23, 1776, Stuart to Germain, Oct. 26, 1776, in Davies, ed., *Documents of the American Revolution* 12: 191, 239.

12. Clinton, *American Rebellion*, 37–38; Pybus, *Epic Journeys of Freedom*, 20.

13. Smith, *New Age Now Begins* 1:724, 730; Ward, *War of the Revolution* 1:209; Ellis, *Revolutionary Summer*, 81–82.

14. Ward, *War of the Revolution* 1:210.

15. Howe to Germain, June 7, 1776, in Davies, ed., *Documents of the American Revolution* 12:145.

16. No connection between the Hessians and the Hessian fly was ever proved. Howe to Germain, Aug. 13, 1776, in Historical Manuscripts Commission, *Report on the Manuscripts of Mrs. Stopford-Sackville* 2:39; Ward, *War of the Revolution* 1:211; Pauly, "Fighting the Hessian Fly"; Taylor, *American Revolutions*, 327.

17. Fischer, *Washington's Crossing*, 92.

18. Ward, *War of the Revolution* 1:227; Smith, *New Age Now Begins* 1:739; Schecter, *Battle for New York*, 132–35; Fischer, *Washington's Crossing*, 92–93.

19. Fischer, *Washington's Crossing*, 91; Schecter, *Battle for New York*, 132; Ellis, *Revolutionary Summer*, 84; Spring, *With Zeal and with Bayonets Only*, 106.

20. Johnston, *Campaign of 1776 Around New York and Brooklyn*, 148–50n. Schecter states that Putnam pulled rank on Sullivan, demanding his right to command the enlarged force. Schecter, *Battle for New York*, 131.

21. Clinton, *American Rebellion*, 42; Smith, *New Age Now Begins* 1:741.

22. Ward, *War of the Revolution* 1:222; McConville, *These Daring Disturbers of the Public Peace*, 41–44; Fischer, *Washington's Crossing*, 91–93.

23. Martin, *Narrative of Some of the Adventures, Dangers, and Sufferings of a Revolutionary Soldier*, 21.

24. James Chambers to his wife, Sept. 3, 1776, in Linn and Egle, eds., *Pennsylvania in the War of the Revolution* 1:307; Ward, *War of the Revolution* 1:225–26; Smith, *New Age Now Begins* 1:740–42; Schecter, *Battle for New York*, 150.

25. Ward, *War of the Revolution* 1:226–27, 231; Peckham, *Toll of Independence*, 22; Schecter, *Battle for New York*, 153; Fischer, *Washington's Crossing*, 98.

26. Howe, quoted in Ward, *War of the Revolution* 1:231.

27. Clinton, *American Rebellion*, 43–44; William Howe, quoted in Reed, *Life and Correspondence of Joseph Reed* 1:223–24n; Fischer, *Washington's Crossing*, 99; Spring, *With Zeal and with Bayonets Only*, 31.

28. Martin, *Narrative of Some of the Adventures, Dangers, and Sufferings of a Revolutionary Soldier*, 23; Billias, *General John Glover and His Marblehead Mariners*, 100–104; McCullough, *1776*, 120.

29. "Col. [Edward] Hand's Account of the Retreat," in Onderdonk, *Revolutionary Inci-*

dents of Suffolk and Kings Counties, 164; *Memoir of Col. Benjamin Tallmadge*, 10–11.

30. Washington to Hancock, Sept. 8, 1776, *Founders Online*. On honor as an imperative for elite men of the founding era, see Freeman, *Affairs of Honor*; Wyatt-Brown, *Southern Honor*.

31. Less than two months later, the delegates, fearing too few men would be willing to commit for the duration, gave new recruits the option of signing up for only three years, with the same cash bounty as the others but without the western land. George Washington to Hancock, Sept. 2, 1776, *Founders Online*; Sept. 16, Nov. 12, 1776, *JCC* 5:762–63, 6:944–45.

32. Washington to Hancock, Sept. 8, 1776, *Founders Online*.

33. Washington to Hancock, Sept. 8, 1776, *Founders Online*; Ward, *War of the Revolution* 1:240; Fischer, *Washington's Crossing*, 81–83.

34. Reed to [Pettit], Aug. 4, 1776, in Reed, *Life and Correspondence of Joseph Reed* 1:213; Howe to [British Adjutant General?], June 22, 24, 1775, in Commager and Morris, eds., *Spirit of 'Seventy-Six* 1:133. Even some members of Congress supported this mostly defensive strategy. "Act on the defensive, entrench, fortify and defend Passes," Maryland delegate Samuel Chase advised his colleague John Adams, who chaired Congress's Board of War. "Make it a War of Posts." Chase to Adams, July 5, 1776, *Founders Online*.

35. Greene to Washington, Sept. 5, 1776, Washington to Hancock, Sept. 8, 1776, *Founders Online*.

36. Council of war, Sept. 12, 1776, *Founders Online*.

37. Carp, "Night the Yankees Burned Broadway," 472.

38. Roland, "Bushnell's Submarine."

39. Bushnell, "General Principles and Construction of a Sub-Marine Vessel," 303–12; Ezra Lee to David Humphreys, Feb. 20, 1815, *Submarine Turtle*; Roland, "Bushnell's Submarine."

40. Martin, *Narrative of Some of the Adventures, Dangers, and Sufferings of a Revolutionary Soldier*, 27.

41. Sept. 15, 1776, in *Memoirs of Major-General William Heath*, 52; Ward, *War of the Revolution* 1:242–43.

42. Howe to Germain, Sept. 21, 1776, in Davies, ed., *Documents of the American Revolution* 12:227–28; Clinton, *American Rebellion*, 46–47; Ward, *War of the Revolution* 2:937–39; Willcox, *Portrait of a General*, 111–12; Monaghan, *Murrays of Murray Hill*, 66–69.

43. Clinton, *American Rebellion*, 46–47; Ward, *War of the Revolution* 1:243–44.

44. Joseph Reed to [Esther Reed], [Sept. 22, 1776], in *Life and Correspondence of Joseph Reed* 1:237–38 (first and third quotations); Washington to Jonathan Trumbull, Sept. 23, 1776, *Founders Online* (second quotation); Roche, *Joseph Reed*, 94; Schecter, *Battle for New York*, 197–98.

45. Ward, *War of the Revolution* 1:250–51; Schecter, *Battle for New York*, 198–200.

46. Martin, *Narrative of Some of the Adventures, Dangers, and Sufferings of a Revolutionary Soldier*, 33–34.

Chapter 21: The Game Is Pretty Nearly Up

1. Quoted in Carp, "Night the Yankees Burned Broadway," 482.

2. Hale, quoted in Boston *Independent Chronicle*, May 17, 1781; Donnelly, "Possible Source for Nathan Hale's Dying Words," 394; Anderson, *Martyr and the Traitor*.

3. Robert Hanson Harrison to John Hancock, Oct. 14–17, 1776, council of war, Oct. 16,

1776, George Washington to John Augustine Washington, Nov. 6–19, 1776, *Founders Online*.

4. Simcoe, *Simcoe's Military Journal*, 88; "Extract of a letter from Colonel [John] Glover," Oct. 22, 1776, in Force, ed., *American Archives*, Ser. 5, 2:1188–89; Billias, *General John Glover and His Marblehead Mariners*, 110–23.

5. Ward, *War of the Revolution* 1:261.

6. Ward, *War of the Revolution* 1:260–61.

7. Rufus Putnam, memoir, letter from a British officer, Nov. 2, 1776, in Johnston, *Campaign of 1776 Around New York and Brooklyn*, 139, 135; editors' note to Robert Hanson Harrison to John Hancock, Oct. 29, 1776, *Founders Online*.

8. Robert Hanson Harrison to John Hancock, Oct. 29, 1776 (and editors' note), *Founders Online*; *Memoir of Colonel Benjamin Tallmadge*, 13–14; Buel and Buel, *Way of Duty*, 124; Schecter, *Battle for New York*, 237.

9. John Sullivan to George Washington, Nov. 25, 1777, *Founders Online*; Smith, *New Age Now Begins* 1:788; Ward, *War of the Revolution* 1:266; Peckham, *Toll of Independence*, 25.

10. Washington to Nathanael Greene, Nov. 7, 1776, Washington to Samuel Washington, Dec. 18, 1776, *Founders Online*; Fischer, *Washington's Crossing*, 116–17.

11. Demont, quoted in Fischer, *Washington's Crossing*, 113; Ward, *War of the Revolution* 2:940.

12. Washington to Hancock, Nov. 16, 1776, Greene to Washington, Nov. 9, 1776, *Founders Online*; Fischer, *Washington's Crossing*, 111.

13. Although the shore batteries in Fort Washington and its New Jersey counterpart, Fort Lee, could not prevent British warships from ascending and descending the Hudson, they did successfully protect American boats crossing between the two forts from those same Royal Navy vessels. Greene to Washington, Oct. 29, 31 (including footnote quoting Robert Hanson Harrison to Greene, Nov. 5, 1776), 1776, *Founders Online*.

14. "Extract of a Letter from Fort Lee, Nov. 17, 1776," in Force, *American Archives*, Ser. 5, 3:741; Ward, *War of the Revolution* 1:270–71; Schecter, *Battle for New York*, 246–47.

15. Magaw, quoted in Thayer, *Nathanael Greene*, 119; Ward, *War of the Revolution* 1:271; Middlekauff, *Glorious Cause*, 359; Schecter, *Battle for New York*, 247–49.

16. July 6, 1779, *JCC*, 14:805; Margaret Corbin, in James, James, and Boyer, eds., *Notable American Women* 1:385; Raphael, *Founding Myths*, 54.

17. "Extract of a Letter from Fort Lee, Nov. 17, 1776," in Force, *American Archives*, Ser. 5, 3:741.

18. Washington to Reed, Aug. 22, 1779, *Founders Online*; Irving, *Life of George Washington*, 424; Ward, *War of the Revolution* 1:274; Fischer, *Washington's Crossing*, 113–14; Schecter, *Battle for New York*, 255.

19. Nelson, "Guy Carleton Versus Benedict Arnold," 356; Philbrick, *Valiant Ambition*, 34, 333n.

20. Nelson, *General Sir Guy Carleton, Lord Dorchester*, 100–101. For historic moon calculations, see timeanddate.com.

21. Schnitzer, "Tactics of the Battles of Saratoga," 75n; Nelson, "Guy Carleton Versus Benedict Arnold," 355.

22. Nelson, *General Sir Guy Carleton*, 102.

23. Alternatively, a man could secure the right to vote by owning at least fifty acres of land. Pennsylvania frame of government, Nov. 1, 1686, avalon.law.yale.edu/17th_century/pa06.asp.

24. Philadelphia committee of privates, circular letter, June 25, 1776, quoted in Rosswurm, *Arms, Country, and Class*, 101–2; Pennsylvania constitution, Sept. 28, 1776, avalon.law.yale.edu/18th_century/pa08.asp.

25. *The Proceedings Relative to the Calling the Conventions of 1776 and 1790*, 45; Rosswurm, *Arms, Country, and Class*, 103.

26. Hooper, quoted in Rosswurm, *Arms, Country, and Class*, 105; Pennsylvania constitution, Sept. 28, 1776, avalon.law.yale.edu/18th_century/pa08.asp; Taylor, *American Revolutions*, 359. Pennsylvania's plural executive, known as the Supreme Executive Council, served a purely administrative function and could not veto legislation. None of the other twelve rebelling states imitated Pennsylvania's policy of requiring the intervention of an election between the introduction and adoption of legislation, but the rogue province of Vermont did. Pennsylvania's new constitution also eliminated the disproportionate assembly representation that the eastern portion of the state, around Philadelphia, had enjoyed during the colonial era. Morgan, *Benjamin Franklin*, 240.

27. In addition, the constitution enfranchised the sons of freeholders (even if they themselves owned no property and paid no taxes), banned plural officeholding, and gave more assembly seats to the inadequately represented western counties. Pennsylvania constitution, Sept. 28, 1776, avalon.law.yale.edu/18th_century/pa08.asp; Morgan, *Benjamin Franklin*, 240.

28. Morgan, *Benjamin Franklin*, 307–8. In another victory for elites, the convention adopted a clause apparently aimed at reviving the trans-Appalachian colony of Vandalia. Pennsylvania constitution, Sept. 28, 1776, avalon.law.yale.edu/18th_century/pa08.asp.

29. Quoted in Rosswurm, *Arms, Country, and Class*, 103, 107.

30. At a special election to fill the vacancies, two of the three former delegates were returned, which they interpreted as freeing them from the county's instructions. Samuel Chase to John Adams, June 28, 1776, *Founders Online*; Charles Carroll of Carrollton to Charles Carroll of Annapolis, Aug. 20, 1776, in Carroll and Carroll, *Dear Papa, Dear Charley* 2:941; Hoffman, *Spirit of Dissension*, 169–76, 180.

31. Maryland constitution, Nov. 11, 1776, avalon.law.yale.edu/17th_century/ma02.asp; Hoffman, *Spirit of Dissension*, 179–80.

32. Charles City County citizens, petition, *Virginia Gazette* (Purdie), Dec. 6, 1776; anonymous essay, *Virginia Gazette* (Purdie), Dec. 13, 1776; "A Dissenter from the Church of England," *Virginia Gazette* (Purdie), April 26, 1776; "The sentiments of the several companies of militia and freeholders of *Augusta*, in *Virginia*, communicated by the deputies from the said companies and freeholders to their representatives in the General Assembly of the commonwealth," *Virginia Gazette* (Purdie), Oct. 18, 1776; Ragosta, *Religious Freedom*, 62–63.

33. Dec. 9, 1776, *Journal of the House of Delegates of Virginia, Anno Domini 1776*, 90; "An Act for Exempting the Different Societies of Dissenters from Contributing to the Support and Maintenance of the Church as by Law Established . . . ," in Hening, ed., *Statutes at Large* 9:164–67 (quotation at 165); Isaac, *Transformation of Virginia*, 280–82; Kukla, *Patrick Henry*, 231–32; Ragosta, *Religious Freedom*, 63–67.

34. Fischer, *Washington's Crossing*, 116–17.

35. Fischer, *Washington's Crossing*, 117–21.

36. Ward, *War of the Revolution* 1:276–77.

37. "They make their approaches very cautiously, and seem willing to wait till we evacuate a place rather than to drive us from it." Extract of a Letter from Woodbridge, New-Jersey, Nov. 28, 1776, in Force, ed., *American Archives*, Ser. 5, 3:891; Fischer, *Washington's Crossing*, 121, 128.

38. Washington to Charles Lee, Nov. 21, 1776, *Founders Online*; Ward, *War of the Revolution* 1:280.

39. Howe to Germain, Nov. 30, 1776, in Force, ed., *American Archives*, Ser. 5, 3:925.

40. Fischer, *Washington's Crossing*, 129–31.

41. Washington to Hancock, Dec. 9, 1776, Washington to Samuel Washington, Dec. 18, 1776, *Founders Online*; Dec. 8, 1776, in Ewald, *Diary of the American War*, 27; Fischer, *Washington's Crossing*, 132–35.

42. Clinton, *American Rebellion*, 57; Ward, *War of the Revolution* 1:281.

43. Hopkins, *Memoirs of the Life of Mrs. Sarah Osborn*, 355, 352–53 (first, second, fourth, and fifth quotations); Brekus, *Sarah Osborn's World*, 295–301 (third quotation, from Susanna Anthony, at 297), 334–35, 337–39.

44. Dec. 12, 1776, *JCC* 6:1,027; Washington to Hancock, Dec. 20, 1776, *Founders Online*.

45. In 1777, Washington expressed some form of "affection" in half of his nineteen letters to Reed. Reed to Lee, Nov. 21, 1776, in Reed, *Life and Correspondence of Joseph Reed* 1:255–56; Washington to Reed, Nov. 30, 1776, June 11, 1777, *Founders Online*; Roche, *Joseph Reed*, 98–99; McCullough, *1776*, 57, 254–55; Leibiger, *Founding Friendship*, 2–3, 182.

46. Charles Lee to [Horatio Gates], Dec. 13, 1776, in Wilkinson, *Memoirs of My Own Times* 1:108; Howe to Germain, Dec. 20, 1776, in Davies, ed., *Documents of the American Revolution* 12:267; John Sullivan to George Washington, Dec. 13, 1776, *Founders Online*; Tarleton to his mother, Dec. 18, 1776, in Commager and Morris, eds., *Spirit of 'Seventy Six*, 1:501–2; Ward, *War of the Revolution* 1:289.

47. Ward, *War of the Revolution* 1:288; Dederer, *Making Bricks Without Straw*, 28; Fischer, *Washington's Crossing*, 161, 178–79; Gigantino, *William Livingston's American Revolution*, 105.

48. David Chambers to George Washington, Dec. 16, 1776, *Founders Online*; Fischer, *Washington's Crossing*, 193.

49. George Washington to Samuel Washington, Dec. 18, 1776, *Founders Online*; George Washington to John Augustine Washington, Dec. 18, 1776, in Force, ed., *American Archives*, Ser. 5, 3:1275–76; Taylor, *American Revolutions*, 168.

50. [Paine], *American Crisis*, 1; Fischer, *Washington's Crossing*, 138–42, 179–81, 192–98.

51. Reed to Washington, Dec. 22, 1776, Cadwalader to Washington, Dec. 27, 1776, *Founders Online*; Buel, *In Irons*, 44.

52. Washington to Jonathan Trumbull Sr., Dec. 14, 1776, *Founders Online*; Ward, *War of the Revolution* 1:296.

53. Henry Knox to Lucy Knox, Dec. 28, 1776, Stryker, *Battles of Trenton and Princeton*, 371; Washington to Hancock, Dec. 27, 1776, *Founders Online*; Fischer, *Washington's Crossing*, 212.

54. Washington to Hancock, Dec. 27, 1776, *Founders Online*; Smith, *New Age Now Begins* 1:817.

55. Ward, *War of the Revolution* 1:293.

56. Rall, quoted in Fischer, *Washington's Crossing*, 189, 205, 239–40.

57. Washington, quoted in Memorandum in General Robert Anderson's Letter Book, in Stryker, *Battles of Trenton and Princeton*, 374; Ward, *Major General Adam Stephen and the Cause of American Liberty*, 150–51, 278n; Fischer, *Washington's Crossing*, 517n.

58. Fischer, *Washington's Crossing*, 205.

59. Peckham, *Toll of Independence*, 27; Ward, *War of the Revolution* 1:302; Fischer, *Washington's Crossing*, 249, 254, 405–6, 521.

60. "Perseverance," *Independent Chronicle*, Dec. 13, 1776 (my thanks to Paul Bartow for this reference).

61. "Perseverance," *Independent Chronicle*, Dec. 13, 1776; *Annual Register . . . for the Year 1777*, 20; McGuire, *Philadelphia Campaign* 1:7.

Chapter 22: The Price of Revolution

1. Ward, *War of the Revolution* 1:307–8.
2. Fischer, *Washington's Crossing*, 290.
3. Sergeant R— —, "The Battle of Princeton," (Wellsborough, Pennsylvania) *Phenix*, March 24, 1832, quoted in editors' note to Washington to Commanding Officer at Morristown, Dec. 30, 1776, *Founders Online*.
4. Ward, *War of the Revolution* 1:311.
5. Washington to the commanding officer at Morristown, Dec. 30, 1776, Washington to Hancock, Jan. 5, 1777, *Founders Online*; Ward, *War of the Revolution* 1:463n; Fischer, *Washington's Crossing*, 303.
6. Fischer, *Washington's Crossing*, 290–307, 412–13.
7. Washington to Hancock, Jan. 5, 1777, *Founders Online*; Wilkinson, *Memoirs of My Own Times* 1:140; Fischer, *Washington's Crossing*, 314–15.
8. Wilkinson, *Memoirs of My Own Times* 1:146n–47n; Fischer, *Washington's Crossing*, 324–30.
9. Fischer, *Washington's Crossing*, 325–29.
10. Since the colonial era, when the Quaker-dominated assembly had refused to field a militia, leading to the creation of private associations for self-defense, Pennsylvania militiamen had been known as associators.
11. Fewer than one hundred Americans were killed, wounded, or captured in this battle. More than half of Mawhood's force (about 230 out of 450 men) had been killed or wounded, and many more were missing. Washington to Hancock, Jan. 5, 1777, *Founders Online*; Wilkinson, *Memoirs of My Own Times* 1:145; Ward, *War of the Revolution* 1:314, 316; Fischer, *Washington's Crossing*, 330–36, 413–15.
12. Fischer, *Washington's Crossing*, 338–39.
13. Vine, "For the Peace of the Town," 85–86.
14. Washington to Joseph Reed, Dec. 15, 1775, John Adams to Jonathan Dickinson Sergeant, Aug. 17, 1776, Patrick Henry to George Washington, March 29, 1777, *Founders Online*; Edmund Pendleton to Richard Henry Lee, Feb. 8, 1777, in *Letters and Papers of Edmund Pendleton*, 1:205; Henderson, "Smallpox and Patriotism"; Fenn, *Pox Americana*, 36–39, 62–77, 86–88, 92–93; McDonnell, *Politics of War*, 267; Becker, "Smallpox in Washington's Army," 405–24, 429–30; Wehrman, "Siege of 'Castle Pox.'"
15. Martin, *Narrative of Some of the Adventures, Dangers, and Sufferings of a Revolutionary Soldier*, 48; Washington to Horatio Gates, Jan. 28, 1777, Feb. 5–6, 1777, Washington to William Shippen Jr., Jan. 28, 1777, Feb. 6, 1777, Washington to Hancock, Feb. 5, 1777, *Founders Online*; Fenn, *Pox Americana*, 80–81, 92–95.
16. Martin, *Narrative of Some of the Adventures, Dangers, and Sufferings of a Revolutionary Soldier*, 48; Fenn, *Pox Americana*, 95, 134, 260; Gigantino, *William Livingston's American Revolution*, 104.
17. Edgar, *Partisans and Redcoats*, 42; McDonnell, *Politics of War*, 259–71.
18. Washington to Patrick Henry, May 17, 1777, *Founders Online*; Clinton, *American Rebellion*, 110–11.
19. Neimeyer, *America Goes to War*.
20. Massachusetts (1776) and Connecticut (1777) began drafting soldiers before receiving Congress's recommendation. McDonnell, *Politics of War*, 258, 273–80; April 14, 1777, *JCC* 7:261–63; Samuel Holden Parsons to Washington, April 15, 1777, Thomas Jefferson to John Adams, May 16, 1777 (editors' note), *Founders Online*.

21. McConville, *Brethren*.

22. Stephen, quoted in Ward, *Major General Adam Stephen and the Cause of American Liberty*, 157; Kwasny, *Washington's Partisan War*.

23. Martin, *Benedict Arnold*, 316; Buel, *Dear Liberty*, 112.

24. Feb. 19, 1777, *JCC* 7:133; Martin, *Benedict Arnold*, 305–15.

25. Martin, *Benedict Arnold, Revolutionary Hero*, 310; John Adams to Abigail Adams, May 22, 1777, *Founders Online*.

26. Philbrick, *In the Hurricane's Eye*, 24.

27. Arnold, quoted in Martin, *Benedict Arnold, Revolutionary Hero*, 319; Buel, *Dear Liberty*, 112–13.

28. Martin, *Narrative of Some of the Adventures, Dangers, and Sufferings of a Revolutionary Soldier*, 46; Martin, *Benedict Arnold, Revolutionary Hero*, 319–21.

29. Abigail Adams to John Adams, June 1, 1777, *Founders Online*.

30. Pinckney to Mary Bartlett, Dec. 2, 1747, *Papers of Eliza Lucas Pinckney and Harriott Pinckney Horry*; Holton, *Abigail Adams*, 120–25, 165–66; Glover, *Eliza Lucas Pinckney*, 87–88.

31. Lucy Knox to Henry Knox, April 29 or 30, 1776, June 3–5, 1777, *Revolutionary War Lives and Letters of Lucy and Henry Knox*, 27, 106; Norton, *Liberty's Daughters*, 223.

32. Henry Knox to Lucy Knox, Aug. 12, 1777, Lucy Knox to Henry Knox, Aug. 23, 1777, *Revolutionary War Lives and Letters of Lucy and Henry Knox*, 116, 118–19; Norton, *Liberty's Daughters*, 223–24.

33. Norton, *Liberty's Daughters*, 219. Sara T. Damiano suggests that the wartime letters between women and their absent husbands, which often resembled the correspondence of overseas merchants, may have contributed to the process by which the centuries-old hierarchical relationship between husbands and wives gave way to something more closely resembling partnership. Damiano, "Writing Women's History Through the Revolution," 726–28.

34. Griffitts to Wayne, Oct. 30, 1776 (including her quotation from Wayne), July 13, 1777, "Two Letters of Hannah Griffitts to General Anthony Wayne," 109–10; Norton, *Liberty's Daughters*, 171, 189; Zagarri, *Revolutionary Backlash*, 75–77.

35. Abigail Adams to John Adams, July 30–31, 1777, and editors' footnotes, *Founders Online*.

36. Gross, *Minutemen and Their World*, 142–43; Buel, *In Irons*, 48–52; Spring, *With Zeal and with Bayonets Only*, 28; Kulikoff, "War in the Countryside," 216, 227; Taylor, *American Revolutions*, 224.

37. Bezanson, "Inflation and Controls, Pennsylvania," 8; Hoffman, *Spirit of Dissension*, 187–88; Smith, "Food Rioters and the American Revolution," 4–5, 26–29, 35–38; Jarvis, *In the Eye of All Trade*; Bruns, "'. . . The Whole River Is a Bustle,'" 39–40.

38. Smith, "Food Rioters and the American Revolution," 7, 35.

39. Stephen Williams, quoted in Smith, "Food Rioters and the American Revolution," 6.

40. *A Letter from Charles Carroll, Senior, to the Reader, with His Petition to the General Assembly of Maryland*, in Carroll and Carroll, *Dear Papa, Dear Charley* 3:1,167.

41. Jefferson to Alexander McCaul, April 19, 1786, *Founders Online*.

42. Charles Carroll of Annapolis to Charles Carroll of Carrollton, March 13, 1777, in Carroll and Carroll, *Dear Papa, Dear Charley* 2:974; Hoffman, *Spirit of Dissension*, 211; Land, "Economic Base and Social Structure," 650.

43. Charles Carroll of Annapolis to Charles Carroll of Carrollton, April 1, 1777, Charles Carroll of Carrollton to Charles Carroll of Annapolis, April 4, 1777, in Carroll and Carroll., *Dear Papa, Dear Charley* 2:985, 987; Hoffman, *Spirit of Dissension*, 210–14.

44. Charles Carroll of Carrollton to Charles Carroll of Annapolis, Nov. 13, 1777, in Carroll and Carroll, *Dear Papa, Dear Charley* 2:1082; Charles Carroll of Carrollton, quoted in Hoffman, *Spirit of Dissension*, 210; chapter 9, *Laws of Maryland, Made and Passed . . . in the Year of our Lord One Thousand Seven Hundred and Seventy-Seven*, unpaginated; Hoffman and Mason, *Princes of Ireland, Planters of Maryland*, 317–33.

45. In March 1778, Congress declared that future purchasers of loan office certificates would receive their interest in paper money. But interest on previously issued certificates would continue to be paid out of the French funds, a policy that remained in effect until 1782. Ferguson, *Power of the Purse*, 35–39, 149.

46. Jones, "Herman Husband," 222, 236, 249–53.

47. Husband, *Proposals to Amend and Perfect*, 22, 25.

48. Husband, *Proposals to Amend and Perfect*, 22, 25; March 9, 1778, in *Extracts from the Diary of Christopher Marshall*, 171; Jones, "Herman Husband," 253.

49. Nelson, *General Sir Guy Carleton*, 96–98.

50. Germain to Howe, May 18, 1777, Howe to Carleton, April 5, 1777, in Davies, ed., *Documents of the American Revolution* 14:84, 66; Luzader, *Saratoga*, 353–62. The relationship between civilian leaders and overseas commanders resembled the one the U.S. Congress and president worked out early in the twenty-first century: although the Constitution gave Congress the power to declare war, the representatives in effect ceded that authority to the president, thus shielding themselves from blame for military operations that went awry. And presidents were only too happy to accept Congress's gift. Kaine, "Better Approach to War Powers," 3–7.

51. Ward, *War of the Revolution* 1:400–401; Luzader, "Coming Revolutionary War Battles at Saratoga," 9.

52. Washington to Hancock, Feb. 26, 1776, *Founders Online*.

53. June 15, 1777, in Wasmus, *Eyewitness Account of the American Revolution and New England Life*, 51; Ward, *War of the Revolution* 1:401; Peckham, *War for Independence*, 61; Smith, *New Age Now Begins* 2:896; Ketchum, *Saratoga*, 42, 128.

54. Burgoyne, *State of the Expedition from Canada*, 8; Ward, *War of the Revolution* 1:402–3; Middlekauff, *Glorious Cause*, 377. While Burgoyne stated that he left Canada with 7,006 soldiers, Cubbison uses his returns to show that he actually had 8,118. Cubbison, *Burgoyne and the Saratoga Campaign*, 51.

55. Burgoyne, *State of the Expedition from Canada*, xvi–xvii; Cubbison, *Burgoyne and the Saratoga Campaign*, 54–55.

56. Ward, *War of the Revolution* 1:409; Cubbison, *Burgoyne and the Saratoga Campaign*, 52–53.

57. Ward, *War of the Revolution* 1:407; Ketchum, *Saratoga*, 158, 171n; Cubbison, *Burgoyne and the Saratoga Campaign*, 56–57.

58. Phillips, quoted in O'Shaughnessy, *Men Who Lost America*, 148; July 14, 1777, in Thacher, *Military Journal During the American Revolutionary War*, 102.

59. Bobrick, *Angel in the Whirlwind*, 252; Cubbison, *Burgoyne and the Saratoga Campaign*, 62–63.

60. Burgoyne to Germain, July 11, 1777, in Davies, ed., *Documents of the American Revolution* 14:136; Ward, *War of the Revolution* 1:414; Peckham, *Toll of Independence*, 37; Cubbison, *Burgoyne and the Saratoga Campaign*, 63–72.

61. Abigail Adams to John Adams, July 30–31, 1777, *Founders Online* (my thanks to Anthony Galasso for the Adams reference); July 14, 1777, in Thacher, *Military Journal During the American Revolutionary War*, 103; Ward, *War of the Revolution* 1:420.

62. Aug. 1, 1777, *JCC* 8:596.

63. Vermont Constitution, July 8, 1777, avalon.law.yale.edu/18th_century/vt01.asp.
64. Bellesiles, *Revolutionary Outlaws*, 41–42; Phillips, *1775*, 422.
65. Keyssar, *Right to Vote*, 16–18.
66. The abolition clause only applied to adults. Vermont Constitution, July 8, 1777, avalon. law.yale.edu/18th_century/vt01.asp; Bellesiles, *Revolutionary Outlaws*, 136–41. Harvey Amani Whitfield shows that despite the constitutional prohibition, some Black Vermonters—adults as well as children—would continue to be held as slaves into the early nineteenth century. Whitfield, *Problem of Slavery in Early Vermont*.

Chapter 23: Above All, Horses

1. Ward, *War of the Revolution* 1:411–16; Smith, *New Age Now Begins* 2:904.
2. Burgoyne, proclamation, June 20, 1777, *Hadden's Journal and Orderly Books*, 61; Calloway, *Indian World of George Washington*, 227.
3. Burgoyne to Germain, July 11, 1777, in Davies, ed., *Documents of the American Revolution* 14:141; Gilman, "L'Anneé du Coup," 143; McDonnell, *Masters of Empire*, 282–84.
4. Burgoyne's choice of route also saved him the trouble of laying siege to the American fort at the south end of Lake George. Burgoyne, *State of the Expedition from Canada*, 12; Ward, *War of the Revolution* 1:417.
5. Nash, *Urban Crucible*, 313, 409.
6. McGuire, *Philadelphia Campaign* 1:133.
7. D[avid] Cunninghame to Loudoun, May 2, 1777(first quotation), [Basil Fielding] to earl of Dunbigh, July 7, 1776, Loudoun Papers, HEH; Arnold to Washington, July 27, 1777, *Founders Online* (second quotation); William Burke, memoir, in Hagist, *British Soldiers, American War*, 259.
8. Nearly all historians side with Standish, emphasizing (1) that another Whig fighter claimed to have witnessed what he thought was the murder of McCrea from inside Fort Edward, about a half a mile away, and (2) that Burgoyne would have availed himself of the Wyandots' version if he thought anyone would believe it. But there were holes in Standish's story. For example, he insisted that another Indian captive, a woman named McNeil, also witnessed McCrea's murder, a claim McNeil flatly denied. In addition, McCrea's fiancé denied having sent the Wyandots to collect her. Sparks, *Life and Treason of Benedict Arnold*, 100–107; Stone, *Life of Joseph Brant-Thayendanegea* 1:203–6; Johnson, *History of Washington County*, 51–53; Nash, *Unknown American Revolution*, 379; McDonnell, *Masters of Empire*, 284–85; Starbuck, "American Fortifications," 131. My thanks to Peter H. Wood for alerting me to the possibility that McCrea may have been a victim of friendly fire.
9. Parkinson, *Common Cause*, 339–49, 375–77.
10. Howe to Germain, April 26, 1776, in Historical Manuscripts Commission, *Report on the Manuscripts of Mrs. Stopford-Sackville* 2:30.
11. Francis-Carr Clerke to Lord Polwarth, Sept. 10, 1777, in Kingsley and Clerke, "Letters to Lord Polwarth from Sir Francis-Carr Clerke," 422; July 23, 30, 1777, *Orderly Book of Lieut. Gen. John Burgoyne*, 47–48, 60; Ward, *War of the Revolution* 1:419–20; Cubbison, *Burgoyne and the Saratoga Campaign*, 78–79.
12. Taylor, *Divided Ground*, 92.
13. Crytzer, *Guyasuta and the Fall of Indian America*, 164–68 (Butler and Guyasuta quotations at 165); Jan. 27, 1776, *JCC* 4:95; Graymont, *Iroquois in the American Revolution*, 97–99; Taylor, *Divided Ground*, 83–86, 89–92.

14. The Wood Creek that flows into Lake Ontario via Oneida Lake and the Oneida River must not be confused with the Wood Creek that empties into Lake Champlain a hundred and fifty miles to the east. Cubbison, *Burgoyne and the Saratoga Campaign*, 100–2.

15. Daniel Claus to William Knox, Oct. 16, 1777, in Davies, ed., *Documents of the American Revolution* 14:222; Kelsay, *Joseph Brant*, 203; Ketchum, *Saratoga*, 333; Taylor, *Divided Ground*, 84–85, 92; Miles, "Brief Study of Joseph Brant's Political Career in Relation to Iroquois Political Structure," 18.

16. Butler to Carleton, Aug. 15, 1777 (extract), in Cubbison, *Burgoyne and the Saratoga Campaign*, 285.

17. Blacksnake, quoted in Parkinson, *Common Cause*, 350–51.

18. Taylor, *Divided Ground*, 92; wikipedia.org/wiki/Battle_of_Oriskany.

19. St. Leger to Carleton, Aug. 27, 1777, Claus to Knox, Oct. 16, 1777, in Davies, ed., *Documents of the American Revolution* 14:172, 222; Taylor, *Divided Ground*, 92.

20. The Tuscaroras generally sided with the Americans in the Revolutionary War, but there is no record that any Tuscaroras participated in the Battle of Oriskany on either side. Graymont, *Iroquois in the American Revolution*, 14, 138 (quotation), 142–43; Kelsay, *Joseph Brant*, 207, 226; Miles, "Brief Study of Joseph Brant's Political Career in Relation to Iroquois Political Structure," 17; Richter, *Ordeal of the Longhouse*, 31; Taylor, *Divided Ground*, 96; Kane, "'She Did Not Open Her Mouth Further,'" 84; Calloway, *Indian World of George Washington*, 242.

21. Claus to Knox, Oct. 16, 1777, in Davies, ed., *Documents of the American Revolution* 14:222; Ward, *War of the Revolution* 2:488.

22. Burgoyne to Germain, Aug. 20, 1777, in Davies, ed., *Documents of the American Revolution* 14:163.

23. Burgoyne to Germain, Aug. 20, 1777, in Davies, ed., *Documents of the American Revolution* 14:162–63.

24. The idea of hitting Bennington came from Baron Riedesel, who desperately wanted to capture mounts for his two hundred dragoons, who wore hip-high riding boots and carried heavy broadswords, burdensome encumbrances for cavalrymen having to act as infantry. Aug. 8, 1777, Anburey, *Travels Through the Interior Parts of America* 1:384; Burgoyne to Germain, Aug. 20, 1777, in Davies, ed., *Documents of the American Revolution* 14:163; Francis-Carr Clerke to Lord Polwarth, Sept. 10, 1777, in Kingsley and Clerke, "Letters to Lord Polwarth from Sir Francis-Carr Clerke," 422.

25. Burgoyne to Germain, Aug. 20, 1777, in Davies, ed., *Documents of the American Revolution* 14:163; Notes of General Burgoyne's Speech to the House of Commons, [May 26, 1778], in Historical Manuscripts Commission, *Report on the Manuscripts of Mrs. Stopford-Sackville* 2:113.

26. Account of the Defeat at Bennington, Burgoyne to Skene, Aug. 10, 1777, in Historical Manuscripts Commission, *Report on the Manuscripts of Mrs. Stopford-Sackville* 2:76, 74; Riedesel to Germain, Aug. 28, 1777, Burgoyne to St. Leger, n.d., enclosed in Carleton to [?], Sept. 28, 1777, in Cubbison, *Burgoyne and the Saratoga Campaign*, 302, 292.

27. Ward, *War of the Revolution* 1:421–22; Cubbison, *Burgoyne and the Saratoga Campaign*, 95, 98.

28. Peckham, *Toll of Independence*, 38; Cubbison, *Burgoyne and the Saratoga Campaign*, 94.

29. Baum to Burgoyne, Aug. 13, 1777, in Burgoyne, *State of the Expedition from Canada*, xxxviii; Smith, *New Age Now Begins* 2:916.

30. The widespread modern assumption that Baum requested reinforcements rests upon a

single piece of evidence: Burgoyne's statement, in an Aug. 15, 1777, letter to Breymann, that Baum "expects reenforcements." Yet it appears that Burgoyne was actually referring to Baum's Aug. 14 statement that he expected *the enemy* to be reinforced; there is no evidence that Baum asked for help. Burgoyne, instructions to Baum, Baum to Burgoyne, Aug. 14, 1777, in Burgoyne, *State of the Expedition from Canada*, xxxviii–xxxix; Burgoyne to [Breymann], Aug. [15], 1777, *Memoirs and Letters and Journals of Major General Riedesel* 1:272; Riedesel, Relation of the Expedition to Bennington, in Riedesel to [Germain], Aug. 28, 1777, in Cubbison, *Burgoyne and the Saratoga Campaign*, 310; Aug. 15, 1777, in *Hadden's Journal and Orderly Books*, 118. On troop strengths, see Mackesy, *War for America*, 134; Taylor, *American Revolutions*, 180; Ward, *War of the Revolution* 1:426.

31. Stark's official reason for not wanting to subordinate himself to the Continental generals was his militiamen's alarm at the Continentals' having given up Ticonderoga without a fight. New Hampshire delegates to Meshech Weare, Aug. 22, 1777, in Smith et al., eds., *Letters of Delegates to Congress* 7:528–29; Moore, *Life of General John Stark of New Hampshire*, 278.

32. Moore, *Life of General John Stark of New Hampshire*, 278; Lincoln to Schuyler, Aug. 8, 1777, Schuyler to Lincoln, Aug. 9, 1777, in Lossing, *Life and Times of Philip Schuyler* 2:262–63; Aug. 19, 1777, *JCC* 8:656–57; Ward, *War of the Revolution* 1:423–25; Ketchum, *Saratoga*, 288–91.

33. Schuyler to Stark, Aug. 12, 1777, in Moore, *Life of General John Stark of New Hampshire*, 285.

34. Burgoyne to [Breymann], Aug. [15], 1777, in Riedesel, *Memoirs and Letters and Journals of Major General Riedesel* 1:271–72.

35. Undated entry, *Hadden's Journal and Orderly Books*, 136.

36. Cubbison, *Burgoyne and the Saratoga Campaign*, 96–97.

37. Ketchum, *Saratoga*, 312.

38. Ward, *War of the Revolution* 1:430–31; Peckham, *Toll of Independence*, 38. Burgoyne himself estimated that he lost 1,200 men at Bennington. Burgoyne, *Orderly Book of Lieut. Gen. John Burgoyne*, 153.

39. George Fox, narrative, in Hagist, *British Soldiers, American War*, 207; McDonnell, *Masters of Empire*, 286.

40. New Hampshire delegates to Meshech Ware, Aug. 22, 1777, in Smith et al., eds., *Letters of Delegates to Congress* 7:529; Ward, *War of the Revolution* 1:431.

41. George Washington to John Hancock, Sept. 25, 1776, Washington, general orders, Aug. 22, 1777, Schuyler to Washington, Aug. 19, 1777, *Founders Online*.

42. Aug. 17, 1777, in Hadden, *Hadden's Journal and Orderly Books*, 119; Burgoyne to Germain, Aug. 20, 1777, in Davies, ed., *Documents of the American Revolution* 14:166; Aug. 24, 1777, Anburey, *Travels Through the Interior Parts of America* 1:394–96; Cox, "Continental Army," 165. A better target for this blame shifting might have been Germain, who, on the one hand, gave Burgoyne reason to expect help from Howe, while, on the other hand, failed to give Howe an explicit order to meet him in Albany. Davies, ed., *Documents of the American Revolution* 14:2–7, 14.

43. Ketchum, *Saratoga*, 334; Martin, *Benedict Arnold*, 363–67.

44. St. Leger to Carleton, Aug. 27, 1777, in Davies, ed., *Documents of the American Revolution* 14:173; Sparks, *Life and Treason of Benedict Arnold*, 110–11.

45. Gundersen, *To Be Useful to the World*, 39, 181.

46. Clinton to Gen. Harvey, Sept. 16, 1777, in Albermarle, *Memoirs of the Marquis of Rockingham, and His Contemporaries* 2:344.

47. Washington to Schuyler, July 22, 1777, *Founders Online*; Bobrick, *Angel in the Whirlwind*, 247.

48. Ward, *War of the Revolution* 2:523–24.

49. Ketchum, *Saratoga*, 346; Schnitzer, "Battling for the Saratoga Landscape," 14; Valosin, "Saratoga Battles in Fifty Artifacts," 211.

50. Ward, *War of the Revolution* 1:329, 332.

51. Howe to Germain, April 2, 1777, in Davies, ed., *Documents of the American Revolution* 14:64.

52. Burgoyne and Burgoyne, eds., *Journal of the Hesse-Cassel Jaeger Corps* (2005), quoted in Spring, *With Zeal and with Bayonets Only*, 45–46; George Washington to John Hancock, Aug. 23, 1777, *Founders Online*. Eight months earlier, when Washington ordered Gen. Israel Putnam to pull his army out of Philadelphia, he demurred, fearing that leaving the city unguarded would enable its Loyalists to rebel. Reed, *Life and Correspondence of Joseph Reed* 1:275.

53. John Adams to Abigail Adams, Aug. 24, 1777, *Founders Online*; Washington, general orders, Aug. 4, 23, 1777, *Founders Online*; Treadway, "Anna Maria Lane," 135; Mayer, *Belonging to the Army*, 47.

54. Vowell, *Lafayette in the Somewhat United States*, 1.

55. Washington to Hancock, Sept. 9, 1777, *Founders Online*.

56. *Simcoe's Military Journal*, 98–99; Spring, *With Zeal and with Bayonets Only*, 139–44, 198–201, 216–19.

57. Lengel, *General George Washington*, 235.

58. Lengel, *General George Washington*, 234–35.

59. Fortescue, *History of the British Army* 3:216; Ward, *War of the Revolution* 1:467n.

60. Thomas Conway, quoted in Thayer, *Nathanael Greene*, 194; Ward, *War of the Revolution* 1:342, 348–52. Two and a half centuries later, the Birmingham Friends Meetinghouse continues to host weekly Quaker meetings. fgcquaker.org/cloud/5129/calendar.

61. Washington, quoted in Ward, *War of the Revolution* 1:351.

62. Such at least was the family tradition, reported in 1849 by the general's not always reliable great-nephew. Muhlenberg, *Life of Major-General Peter Muhlenberg of the Revolutionary Army*, 30; Ward, *War of the Revolution* 1:352.

63. Howe to Germain, Oct. 10, 1777, in Davies, ed., *Documents of the American Revolution* 14:204; Ward, *War of the Revolution* 1:353–54.

64. Muhlenberg, *Life of Major-General Peter Muhlenberg of the Revolutionary Army*, 92; Ward, *War of the Revolution* 1:346.

65. Howe to Germain, Oct. 10, 1777, in Davies, ed., *Documents of the American Revolution* 14:204; Ward, *War of the Revolution* 1:353–54; Peckham, *Toll of Independence*, 40.

Chapter 24: Take No Quarter

1. Aug. 4, 1777, *JCC* 8:603–4; Ketchum, *Saratoga*, 347.

2. Sept. 9, 17, 1777, in *Hadden's Journal and Orderly Books*, 142, 160; Ward, *War of the Revolution* 2:505; Ketchum, *Saratoga*, 359; Cubbison, *Burgoyne and the Saratoga Campaign*, 106–8; Schnitzer, "Tactics of the Battles of Saratoga," 41.

3. Bird, *March to Saratoga*, 175.

4. Most historians state that Burgoyne sought to turn the Americans' right flank on September 19, but the general's reports and letters make no such claim; nor do other eyewitness accounts. Burgoyne to Germain, Oct. 20, 1777, in Davies, ed., *Documents of*

the *American Revolution* 14:229–30; Sept. 19, 1777, in Lynn, ed., *Specht Journal*, 78–79; Lamb, *Memoir of His Own Life*, 190; William Digby, journal, Sept. 19, 1777, in Baxter, ed., *British Invasion from the North*, 270–72; Sept. 24, 1777, in Anburey, *Travels Through the Interior Parts of America* 1:410; Sept. 19, 1777, "Lord Francis Napier's Journal of the Burgoyne Campaign," 315–17; Sept. 19, 1777, in *Hadden's Journal and Orderly Books*, 161–63; Martin, *Benedict Arnold, Revolutionary Hero*, 375–77; Cubbison, *Burgoyne and the Saratoga Campaign*, 109.

5. Ward, *War of the Revolution* 2:507; Luzader, *Saratoga*, 231–34.

6. The quoted section of Washington's orders does not appear in the signed version and may have been inadvertently omitted by the copyist. George Washington, orders to Daniel Morgan, June 13, 1777 (quoted in editors' note), Washington to George Clinton, Aug. 16, 1777, *Founders Online*; Higginbotham, *Daniel Morgan*, 58, 61; Philbrick, *Valiant Ambition*, 126.

7. Washington to Hancock, Aug. 17, 1777, *Founders Online*; Ketchum, *Saratoga*, 355; Schnitzer, "Tactics of the Battles of Saratoga," 44.

8. British officer, quoted in Cubbison, *Burgoyne and the Saratoga Campaign*, 119; Notes of General Burgoyne's Speech to the House of Commons [May 26, 1778], in Historical Manuscripts Commission, *Report on the Manuscripts of Mrs. Stopford-Sackville* 2:114; Higginbotham, *Daniel Morgan*, 65; Graymont, *Iroquois in the American Revolution*, 152–55.

9. [Richard] Varick, quoted in Arnold, *Benedict Arnold*, 171; Notes of General Burgoyne's Speech to the House of Commons [May 26, 1778], in Historical Manuscripts Commission, *Report on the Manuscripts of Mrs. Stopford-Sackville* 2:114; Higginbotham, *Daniel Morgan*, 58.

10. Sept. 19, 1777, in *Hadden's Journal and Orderly Books*, 164–66; William Crawford, narrative, in Hagist, *British Soldiers, American War*, 63; Ward, *War of the Revolution* 2:511; Higginbotham, *Daniel Morgan*, 68; Schnitzer, "Battling for the Saratoga Landscape," 14; Cubbison, *Burgoyne and the Saratoga Campaign*, 112; Snow, "British Fortifications," 84.

11. Nov. 10, 1777, in Anburey, *Travels Through the Interior Parts of America* 1:437; Sept. 19, 1777, in Lynn, ed., *Specht Journal*, 80.

12. Ward, *War of the Revolution* 2:512; Peckham, *Toll of Independence*, 41. It would be wrong to say Burgoyne had *no* access to reinforcements. "Hundreds of new recruits" joined him on September 3, 1777. Schnitzer, "Tactics of the Battles of Saratoga," 76n.

13. Sept. 19, 1777, *Montresor Journals*, 455; Ward, *War of the Revolution* 1:357.

14. Sept. 19, 1777, Robertson, *Archibald Robertson*, 148; Trussell, *Birthplace of an Army*, 6; McGuire, *Philadelphia Campaign* 1:296–97.

15. Howe to Germain, Oct. 10, 1777, in Davies, ed., *Documents of the American Revolution* 14:205; Bodle, *Valley Forge Winter*, 40; Ekirch, *At Day's Close*; McGuire, *Philadelphia Campaign* 1:300–318.

16. Howe to Germain, Oct. 10, 1777, in Davies, ed., *Documents of the American Revolution* 14:205–6; McGuire, *Philadelphia Campaign* 1:318.

17. Sept. 23, 1777, in Ewald, *Diary of the American War*, 91.

18. Washington to Hancock, Sept. 23, 1777, Washington to Israel Putnam, Sept. 23, 1777, *Founders Online*.

19. For criticism of Washington, see McGuire, *Philadelphia Campaign* 2:22, 32–33. One indication that Washington's explanations for his northward march may have been contrived is that they evolved over time. On September 21 and 22, while moving his army up the Schuylkill, he claimed to fear that the British might cross the river farther up, then pivot southward and turn his right (northern) flank. But he later attributed his

northward march to concern about the British capturing the Continental supply depot in Reading. Washington to Alexander McDougall, Sept. 22, 1777, to Israel Putnam, Sept. 23, 1777, to John Hancock, Sept. 23, 1777, and to John Augustine Washington, Oct. 18, 1777, council of war, Sept. 23, 1777, *Founders Online.*

20. Richard Fitzpatrick, quoted in McGuire, *Philadelphia Campaign* 2:41; Howe, quoted in Spring, *With Zeal and with Bayonets Only,* 18–19.

21. Washington to Hancock, Oct. 5, 1777, Washington, general orders, Pennybecker's Mills, Sept. 28, 1777, *Founders Online;* Ward, *War of the Revolution* 1:362; McGuire, *Philadelphia Campaign* 2:30, 33–35.

22. McGuire, *Philadelphia Campaign* 2:37.

23. Sullivan, quoted in editors' note to Washington to Hancock, Oct. 5, 1777, *Founders Online; Memoir of Col. Benjamin Tallmadge,* 11; Mordecai Gist, quoted in McGuire, *Philadelphia Campaign* 2:66. Other Americans also noted that the fog prevented them from "acting in concert." Nov. 10, 1777, in Thacher, *Military Journal During the American Revolutionary War,* 141.

24. Sullivan, quoted in editors' note to Washington to Hancock, Oct. 5, 1777, *Founders Online;* John E. Howard to Timothy Pickering, Jan. 29, 1827, in "Col. John Eager Howard's Account of the Battle of Germantown," 320; Oct. 4, 1777, Pickering journal, in Pickering and Upham, eds., *Life of Timothy Pickering* 1:170–71; McGuire, *Philadelphia Campaign* 2:49.

25. Anthony Wayne to [Mary Wayne], Oct. 6, 1777 (extract), in Dawson, *Battles of the United States* 1:328; Lambdin, "Battle of Germantown," 379.

26. Chew, the former chief justice of the Pennsylvania supreme court and a Loyalist, had been exiled to New Jersey. Sullivan, quoted in editors' note to George Washington to John Hancock, Oct. 5, 1777, *Founders Online;* Middlekauff, *Glorious Cause,* 400.

27. Pickering, quoted in editors' note to George Washington to John Hancock, Oct. 5, 1777, *Founders Online;* McGuire, *Philadelphia Campaign* 2:53–61.

28. Wayne to Sullivan, Nov. 21, 1777, in Wilkinson, *Memoirs of My Own Times* 1:360; Wayne to [Mary Wayne], Oct. 6, 1777, in Stillé, *Major-General Anthony Wayne and the Pennsylvania Line in the Continental Army,* 96; Charles Cotesworth Pinckney to Daniel Huger Horry Jr., Nov. 17, 1777, *Papers of the Revolutionary Era Pinckney Statesmen.*

29. Sullivan to Meshech Weare, Oct. 25, 1777, quoted in editors' note to George Washington to John Hancock, Oct. 5, 1777, *Founders Online;* Bobrick, *Angel in the Whirlwind,* 268–69.

30. Howe to Germain, Oct. 10, 1777, in Davies, ed., *Documents of the American Revolution* 14:208; Ward, *War of the Revolution* 1:369–70.

31. Oct. 4, 1777, "Diary of Lieutenant James McMichael," 153. Stephen's biographer points out that on the day of the battle, no one complained about his performance. Also, the accusation against him came from junior officers with whom he had clashed, so it may have been fabricated. Ward, *Major General Adam Stephen and the Cause of American Liberty,* 190–93; Ward, *War of the Revolution* 1:369, 371.

32. James Wilkinson stated that the two columns separated "about twilight" (by which he must have meant *sunrise*), which came at 7:23 a.m.; both attacked Trenton a few minutes after 8 a.m. Wilkinson, *Memoirs of My Own Times* 1:128; Fischer, *Washington's Crossing,* 228–30, 235; timeanddate.com.

33. Ward, *War of the Revolution* 1:371; Peckham, *Toll of Independence,* 42; Mackesy, *War for America,* 129.

34. Henry Miller, quoted in editors' note to Anthony Wayne to George Washington, Oct. 4, 1777, Adam Stephen to George Washington, Oct. 9, 1777, *Founders Online.*

35. Martin, *Benedict Arnold*, 385–92; Luzader, "Coming Revolutionary War Battles at Saratoga," 23.

36. Cubbison, *Burgoyne and the Saratoga Campaign*, 117–124.

37. Oct. 6, 1777, in Anburey, *Travels Through the Interior Parts of America* 1:433; Martin, *Benedict Arnold, Revolutionary Hero*, 392.

38. Ketchum, *Saratoga*, 388.

39. Martin, *Benedict Arnold, Revolutionary Hero*, 385–91; Luzader, "Coming Revolutionary War Battles at Saratoga," 23.

40. Clinton to Burgoyne, Oct. 8, 1777, in Pratt, *Account of the British Expedition Above the Highlands of the Hudson River*, 54–57 (quotation at 55); Oct. 14, 1777, in Thacher, *Military Journal During the American Revolutionary War*, 126–27.

41. Middlekauff, *Glorious Cause*, 389–90. On elite men's conception of honor, see Freeman, *Affairs of Honor*.

42. "Samuel Woodruff's Visit to the Battle Ground in 1827," in Stone, *Visits to the Saratoga Battle-Grounds*, 226; Wilkinson, *Memoirs of My Own Times* 1:273; Arnold, *Life of Benedict Arnold*, 82–83; Philbrick, *Valiant Ambition*, 167; Martin, *Benedict Arnold, Revolutionary Hero*, 399; Cubbison, *Burgoyne and the Saratoga Campaign*, 132–36; Schnitzer, "Tactics of the Battles of Saratoga," 58–59; Snow, "British Fortifications," 91–95. Most historians follow James Wilkinson, who hated Arnold even before his treason, in depicting him as commanding troops in the Second Battle of Freeman's Farm despite having been stripped of all authority by Gen. Gates. But a document that came to light in 2016 indicates that Gates actually consented to Arnold's participation in the battle. Nathaniel Bacheller to [Susanna] Bacheller, Oct. 9, 1777 (transcript), Saratoga National Historical Park (my thanks to National Park Service ranger and historian Eric Schnitzer for producing this transcript and sharing it with me); "Letter of General Ebenezer Mattoon, A Participant in the Battle, with Notes by the Author," in Stone, *Campaign of Lieut. Gen. John Burgoyne*, 374–75; Dearborn, "Narrative of the Saratoga Campaign," 8–9.

43. Doblin and Lynn, ed., "Brunswick Grenadier with Burgoyne," 433n; Martin, *Benedict Arnold Revolutionary Hero*, 399; Schnitzer, "Tactics of the Battle of Saratoga," 78n.

44. Ward, *War of the Revolution* 2:530; Peckham, *Toll of Independence*, 42; Snow, "British Fortifications," 90.

45. Oct. 17, 1777, "Lord Francis Napier's Journal of the Burgoyne Campaign," 328; Gates, proposed surrender terms with Burgoyne's responses, Oct. 14, 1777, *Orderly Book of Lieut. Gen. John Burgoyne*, 135; Cubbison, *Burgoyne and the Saratoga Campaign*, 139–41.

46. On October 16, a detachment of soldiers from Clinton's army attacked Kingston (formerly Esopus), the Whig capital of New York, ninety miles downriver from Albany, burning nearly every building and liberating several slaves, but they returned to New York City soon after learning that Burgoyne had surrendered. John Vaughan to Henry Clinton, Oct. 26, 1777, in Davies, ed., *Documents of the American Revolution* 14:246–47; Pratt, *Account of the British Expedition Above the Highlands of the Hudson River*; Ward, *War of the Revolution* 2:537–39; Cubbison, *Burgoyne and the Saratoga Campaign*, 141–42.

47. Burgoyne to Lord Rochfort, [June?] 1775, in Fonblanque, *Political and Military Episodes in the Latter Half of the Eighteenth Century*, 148.

48. Jones, *Captives of Liberty*, 139–86.

49. Washington to Henry Laurens, Dec. 14[–15], 1777, Henry Laurens to Washington, April 14, 1778, *Founders Online*; Dec. 19, 30, 1777, Feb. 26, March 30, 1778, *JCC*

9:1036–37, 1069, 10:197–98, 294–95; Knight, "Prisoner Exchange and Parole in the American Revolution," 203–6. Elias Boudinot, one of the U.S. commissioners sent to negotiate a prisoner exchange with the British, claimed many years later that a British commissioner, Col. Charles O'Hara, told him that Howe, too, only feigned interest in a formal cartel (whether because he knew that would involve recognizing the independence of the United States or for other reasons), but it appears that Howe and his successors were eager to trade prisoners informally. Boudinot, *Life, Public Services, Addresses and Letters of Elias Boudinot*, 1:80–81; Burrows, *Forgotten Patriots*, 41, 127.

50. Committee at Camp to Washington, March [9?], 1778 (unsent draft), in Smith et al., eds., *Letters of Delegates to Congress* 9:246; Washington to Henry Laurens, March 7–8, 1778, Washington to Samuel Huntington, July 10, 1780, Washington to John Mathews, Oct. 4, 1780, *Founders Online*.

51. Washington to Laurens, March 7–8, 1778, Alexander Hamilton to George Clinton, March 12, 1778, *Founders Online*; Germain to Clinton, Nov. 9, 1780, in Davies, ed., *Documents of the American Revolution* 18:224; Burrows, *Forgotten Patriots*; Watson, *Ghost Ship of Brooklyn*, 141, 195.

52. Hoock, *Scars of Independence*, 193.

53. William Gamble, "A Just Account of the Usage that the American Prisoners Received from Lord Howe" (deposition), *Pennsylvania Evening Post*, April 29, 1777; Watson, *Ghost Ship of Brooklyn*, 78; Jones, *Captives of Liberty*, 108. Continental Gen. William Heath stated that 11,644 Americans died as British prisoners; the specificity of that figure suggests that it was probably compiled by British jailers. An account that circulated widely in Whig newspapers in 1783 (for example, the *Pennsylvania Packet*, April 29, 1783) stated that 11,644 men had died on a single ship, the *Jersey*, which came on line in April 1780. But apparently these reports accidentally or deliberately misapplied Heath's figure for the prison ships *as a whole* to this one ship. Peckham, *Toll of Independence*, 130–32; va.gov/opa/publications/factsheets/fs_americas_wars.pdf; Burrows, *Forgotten Patriots* 197–204, 138; Watson, *Ghost Ship of Brooklyn*, 78 (quotation in text), 79, 83, 124, 211–17; Rediker, *Slave Ship*; Hoock, *Scars of Independence*, 211. "The Americans also employed prison ships in Boston and Providence." Hagist, *British Soldiers, American War*, 158.

54. Jones, *Captives of Liberty*, 140–86.

55. Clark, "Convention Troops and the Perfidy of Sir William Howe"; Ketchum, *Saratoga*, 435; Jones, *Captives of Liberty*, 160–61, 166–67.

56. Reed to [Thomas] Wharton, Oct. 24, 27, 1777, in Reed, *Life and Correspondence of Joseph Reed* 1:329–31; Oct. 20, 1777, in Ewald, *Diary of the American War*, 96–97.

57. The whole region around Mud Island and Fort (also called Port) Island would later become Philadelphia International Airport. Rosswurm, *Arms, Country, and Class*, 144; Martin, *Ordinary Courage*, 56n.

58. Oct. 22, 1777, in Ewald, *Diary of the American War*, 102 (first two quotations), 399; Von Donop, quoted in Lossing, *Pictorial Field-Book of the Revolution* 2:88 (third quotation); Richard Howe to Philip Stephens, Oct. 25, 1777, in Davies, ed., *Documents of the American Revolution* 14:245; Ward, *War of the Revolution* 1:374–76.

59. Martin, *Narrative of a Revolutionary Soldier*, 67; Richard Howe to Philip Stephens, Nov. 23, 1777, William Howe to Germain, Nov. 28, 1777, in Davies, ed., *Documents of the American Revolution* 14:258–59, 263.

60. Martin, *Narrative of a Revolutionary Soldier*, 66.

61. James Potter to Washington, Nov. [16], 1777, *Founders Online*; Martin, *Narrative of a Revolutionary Soldier*, 69; McGuire, *Philadelphia Campaign* 2:212.

62. Jefferson to John Adams, May 16, 1777, *Founders Online*; Jensen, *Articles of Confederation*, 144–45.
63. Articles of Confederation, avalon.law.yale.edu/18th_century/artconf.asp; Articles of Confederation, 1777 printing with handwritten amendments, facsimile at the front of *JCC*, Vol. 9. Shortly after adopting the Articles, Congress sent the states its first requisition for funds. Recognizing that it would take years to assess the value of every acre of the nation's real estate, the delegates provisionally apportioned congressional requisitions according to estimated population but promised to readjust the states' quotas once the real estate assessment was completed.
64. Articles of Confederation, avalon.law.yale.edu/18th_century/artconf.asp; Jensen, *Articles of Confederation*, 159; Blumrosen and Blumrosen, *Slave Nation*, 151–54.

Chapter 25: The Valley

1. Paine to Franklin, May 16, 1778, *Papers of Benjamin Franklin*; Washington, general orders, Dec. 18, 1777, *Founders Online*; Ward, *War of the Revolution* 2:544; Bodle, *Valley Forge Winter*, 105.
2. Washington to Committee at Camp, [Jan. 29, 1778] (including editors' notes), Washington to Patrick Henry, March 28, 1778, *Founders Online*; Risch, *Supplying Washington's Army*, 39–40; Carp, *To Starve the Army at Pleasure*, 38–44, 49.
3. Walter Stewart to George Washington, Jan. 18, 1778, *Founders Online* (first quotation); Feb. 27, 1778, in Ewald, *Diary of the American War* (second quotation); Committee at Camp to Henry Laurens, Feb. [12–25?], 20, 1778, in Smith et al., eds., *Letters of Delegates to Congress* 9:82, 144–46 (third quotation); Oct. 8, 1777, March 4, 1778, *JCC* 9:784, 10:220–21; Bodle, *Valley Forge Winter*, 174; Taylor, *American Revolutions*, 186.
4. Washington to Hancock, Aug. 4–5, 1775 (including footnotes), *Founders Online*; Hough, *History of St. Lawrence and Franklin Counties*, 189; Barbara Graymont, "Atiatoharongwen," *DCB*; wikipedia.org/wiki/Joseph_Louis_Cook; Preston, *Braddock's Defeat*, 324–25; Calloway, *Indian World of George Washington*, 1, 107, 223–24.
5. Washington to Henry Laurens, Dec. 22, 23 (quotation), 1777, *Founders Online*.
6. Greene, quoted in Bodle, *Valley Forge Winter*, 190.
7. Barrington to Dartmouth, Dec. 24, 1774, in Wildman, *Political Life of William Wildman, Viscount Barrington*, 152–53; Conway, "British Army and the War of Independence," 177.
8. Washington to William Buchanan, Feb. 7, 1778 (editors' footnote), Washington, general orders, Feb. 22, 1778, *Founders Online*; Trussell, *Birthplace of an Army*, 23–24; Buel, *In Irons*, 6. Compare Wiencek, *An Imperfect God*, 240. On the relationship between inadequate food and disease, see Kiple and Kiple, "Deficiency Diseases in the Caribbean."
9. Washington to Henry Laurens, Dec. 23, 1777 (including editors' note), *Founders Online*; Committee at Camp to Henry Laurens, Feb. 12, 1778, in Smith et al., eds., *Letters of Delegates to Congress* 9:80; Trussell, *Birthplace of an Army*, 42–43; Huston, *Logistics of Liberty*, 184; Bodle, *Valley Forge Winter*, 123.
10. Nathanael Greene to George Washington, Jan. 1, 1778, *Founders Online*.
11. Shortly after writing these words, a grateful Waldo welcomed the arrival of "a little Mutton." Dec. 21, 22, 1777, in Waldo, "Valley Forge," 309–11.
12. "Genl Cadwalader's Plan for attackg Philadelpa Novr 1777," Greene to Washington, Nov. 24, 1777, John Armstrong, Duportail, James Irvine, William Maxwell, John Pat-

erson, Enoch Poor, William Smallwood, John Sullivan (quotations), Anthony Wayne, William Woodford, Lord Stirling, and Charles Scott to Washington, Nov. 25, 1777 (separate letters), *Founders Online*.

13. Dec. 22, 1777, in Ewald, *Diary of the American War*, 111; John Clark Jr. to Washington, Dec. 22, 1777, "Intended Orders for a move that was intended agt Phila by way of surprize 25th Decr 1777" (Plan to Attack Philadelphia), Arthur St. Clair to Washington, Jan. 5, 1778, *Founders Online*; Bodle, *Valley Forge Winter*, 117–19.

14. Washington to Henry Laurens, Dec. 23, 1777, Washington to John Augustine Washington, March 31, 1776, *Founders Online*; Royster, *Revolutionary People at War*, 192; Lengel, *General George Washington*, 271.

15. Dec. 28, 1777, in Waldo, "Valley Forge," 314; Washington to Henry Laurens, April 30, 1778, *Founders Online*; Bodle, *Valley Forge Winter*, 128–29. In similar fashion, the plaintive correspondence that Confederate fighters received in the later years of the Civil War led numerous officers to resign their commissions and enlisted men to desert. Robinson, *Bitter Fruits of Bondage*; Faust, *Mothers of Invention*. For limited and temporary exceptions to the rule that officers could quit, applying only to the New York militia at a moment of extreme crisis, see "In Convention of the Representatives of the State of New York, at Haerlem," Aug. 17, 1776, *Boston Gazette and Country Journal*, Sept. 2, 1776; Richard Caswell to George Washington, Nov. 25, 1777, *Founders Online*; McConville, *Brethren*.

16. Twentieth-century Americans had to wear the uniform for at least twenty years to receive a half-pay pension for life. Epperson and Young, "Military Personnel Face a Critical Choice for Their Retirement Plan."

17. Trussell, *Birthplace of an Army*, 100–1.

18. Royster, *Revolutionary People at War*, 209.

19. Washington to Patrick Henry, March 28, 1778, Washington to John Banister, April 21, 1778, *Founders Online*; May 15, 1778, *JCC* 11:502–3; Martin and Lender, *Respectable Army*, 107–10; Royster, *Revolutionary People at War*, 201–2; Bodle, *Valley Forge Winter*, 239.

20. Quoted in Chernow, *Washington*, 219; Washington to Committee at Camp, Jan. 29, 1778, *Founders Online*.

21. Trussell, *Birthplace of an Army*, 57–62 (first quotation at 59); Palmer, *General von Steuben*, 92 (second quotation); Royster, *Revolutionary People at War*, 213–35; Godbeer, *Overflowing of Friendship*, 231n.

22. Royster, *Revolutionary People at War*, 192–94, 213–35.

23. Franklin, quoted in Isaacson, *Benjamin Franklin*, 342; Franks, "Letter of Miss Rebecca Franks" (Franks to Anne Harrison Paca, Feb. 26, 1778), 216–17; Fisher, "Social Life in Philadelphia During the British Occupation," 247; Josiah Bartlett, quoted in Shields and Teute, "Meschianza," 204n; Rosswurm, *Arms, Country, and Class*, 149; Irvin, "Streets of Philadelphia," 24n.

24. Fisher, "Social Life in Philadelphia During the British Occupation," 250, 259; Bobrick, *Angel in the Whirlwind*, 290.

25. Wayne to [Richard] Peters, July 12, 1778, in Stillé, *Major-General Anthony Wayne and the Pennsylvania Line in the Continental Army*, 153–54; Shields and Teute, "Meschianza," 200.

26. Trussell, *Birthplace of an Army*, 46.

27. Franks, "Letter of Miss Rebecca Franks," 217; April 9–27, 1778, *Extracts from the Journal of Elizabeth Drinker*, 94–101.

28. Greene to Washington, Nov. 24, 1777, *Founders Online*; Lender and Stone, *Fatal Sun-*

day, 70–71; Scott, "Price Control in New England During the Revolution," 472; Buel, *In Irons*, 125–26.

29. Historians have never reached a definitive verdict on Lee's accusation. Brands, *First American*, 562; Morgan, *Benjamin Franklin*, 242–43.

30. Van Doren, *Benjamin Franklin*, 591–97.

31. Ellis, *Revolutionary Summer*, 118.

32. Admiralty Board, quoted in Bodle, *Valley Forge Winter*, 196. One reason for the mistaken belief that the ministry abandoned Philadelphia in order to focus on Georgia and the Carolinas was that Germain raised the prospect of a southern campaign in a March 8, 1778, letter to Clinton, though this plan was superseded two weeks later. The ministry did in fact order a southward shift of the diminished North American garrison. Germain to Clinton, March 8, 1778, secret instructions for Clinton, March 21, 1778, in Davies, ed., *Documents of the American Revolution* 15:58–61, 74–75; Clinton, *American Rebellion*, 86; Cogliano, *Revolutionary America*, 106.

33. John Stuart to Germain, March 5, 1778, Peter Chester to Germain, March 25, 1778, in Davies, ed., *Documents of the American Revolution* 15:55–56, 77–79.

34. Thomas Pinckney to Harriott Pinckney Horry, July 1, 1778, *Papers of Eliza Lucas Pinckney and Harriott Pinckney Horry*; Bullen, "Fort Tonyn and the Campaign of 1778," 253–60; Wilson, *Southern Strategy*, 65–69; Piecuch, *Three Peoples, One King*, 101–4, 133, 150.

35. Charles Cotesworth Pinckney to William Moultrie, July 10 (first quotation), May 24, 1778, Robert Howe, minutes of a council of war, July 11, 1778 (second and third quotations), *Papers of the Revolutionary Era Pinckney Statesmen*; Thomas Pinckney to Harriott Pinckney Horry, May 23, 1778, July 1, 1778, *Papers of Eliza Lucas Pinckney and Harriott Pinckney Horry*; Thomas Brown to Patrick Tonyn, June 30, 1778, Augustine Prévost to Henry Clinton, July 11, 1778, Historical Manuscripts Commission, *Report on American Manuscripts in the Royal Institution of Great Britain* 1:269, 271–72; Jones, *History of Georgia* 2:297; Wilson, *Southern Strategy*, 66–69; Piecuch, *Three Peoples, One King*, 104–6; Kennedy, *American Revolution*, 135; Smith, "Fourteenth Colony," 183–86; McCandless, *Slavery, Disease, and Suffering in the Southern Lowcountry*, 86–87.

36. Clinton, *American Rebellion*, 105–7; Willcox, "British Strategy in America," 108, 119.

37. Instructions to Commissioners for Quieting Disorders in North America, April 12, 1778, in Davies, ed., *Documents of the American Revolution* 15:81–93.

38. Johnstone and Reed, quoted in Reed, ed., *Life and Correspondence of Joseph Reed* 1:384; Bodle, *Valley Forge Winter*, 241; Lender and Stone, *Fatal Sunday*, 84.

39. May 4, 1778, *JCC*, 11:419–58; Washington, general orders, May 5, 1778, *Founders Online*; Trussell, *Birthplace of an Army*, 109–10.

40. Shields and Teute, "Meschianza."

41. [Griffitts], "Meschianza," in Blecki and Wulf, eds., *Milcah Martha Moore's Book*, 52.

42. Peckham, *War for Independence*, 95; Nash, *Forging Freedom*, 56–60.

43. Gates to Washington, June 25, 1778, *Founders Online*; Clinton, *American Rebellion*, 92.

44. Clinton, *American Rebellion*, 90–91; Gigantino, *William Livingston's American Revolution*, 132.

45. Charles Lee to Washington, June 25, 1778, Washington to Charles Scott, June 24, 1778, Washington to Lafayette, June 25, 1778, *Founders Online*; Lender and Stone, *Fatal Sunday*, 187.

46. Lender and Stone, *Fatal Sunday*, 265, 273.

47. Lender and Stone, *Fatal Sunday*, 262, 266; Ward, *Charles Scott and the "Spirit of '76,"* 49–50.

48. Martin, *Narrative of Some of the Adventures, Dangers, and Sufferings of a Revolutionary Soldier*, 92.

49. Lender and Stone, *Fatal Sunday*, 266, 272, 284–88, 294–95.

50. Lafayette and Scott, quoted in Lender and Stone, *Fatal Sunday*, 290, 254; Ward, *War of the Revolution* 2:575, 581.

51. Lender and Stone, *Fatal Sunday*, 294–97, 314–15.

52. Martin, *Narrative of Some of the Adventures, Dangers, and Sufferings of a Revolutionary Soldier*, 96–97.

53. Waldo, quoted in Lender and Stone, *Fatal Sunday*, 329; Raphael, *Founding Myths*, 49–71.

54. Ward, *War of the Revolution* 2:585.

55. Aug. 12, 1778, *Proceedings of a General Court-Martial Held at Brunswick, in the State of New Jersey*, 238; Lender and Stone, *Fatal Sunday*, 392–401.

56. Washington to d'Estaing, July 22, 1778, Washington to Thomas Nelson, Aug. 20, 1778, *Founders Online*.

57. Charles Scott to George Washington, Aug. 31, 1778, *Founders Online*; *Simcoe's Military Journal*, 83–86; Aug. 31, 1778, in Ewald, *Diary of the American War*, 144–48; Hauptman, "Road to Kingsbridge." On other native allies of the United States, see Calloway, *American Revolution in Indian Country*, 65–107, and Calloway, *Indian World of George Washington*, 218–34.

Chapter 26: Southern Strategies

1. Nov. 17, 1777, June 23, 1778, *JCC* 9:934–35, 11:636–37; Jensen, *Articles of Confederation*, 184, 192, 195.

2. Patrick Henry, instructions to John Todd, Dec. 12, 1778, and Clark, memoir, in *George Rogers Clark Papers*, 85, 217, 220–21 (first quotation at 220); Jefferson to Clark, March or April 1779, *Founders Online* (second quotation); Selby, *Revolution in Virginia*, 189–91.

3. Kellogg, ed., *Frontier Advance on the Upper Ohio*, 132, 17–24, 28–29; Washington to McIntosh, Jan. 31, Feb. 15, 1779, Washington to Brodhead, April 21, 1779, McIntosh to Washington, April 27, 1779, Brodhead to Washington, March 21, May 6, June 25, Dec. 13, 1779, *Founders Online*; June 11, July 25, 1778, *JCC* 11:588–91, 720; Brodhead to [John?] Armstrong, April 16, 1779, Brodhead to [Nathanael?] Greene, May 26, 1779, Brodhead to David Zeisberger, Nov. 26, Dec. 12, 1779, Feb. 10, 1780, "Letters from Col. Daniel Brodhead," in *Pennsylvania Archives*, Ser. 1, 12:109–10, 118, 192, 196, 204; Downes, *Council Fires on the Upper Ohio*, 214–20; Calloway, *Indian World of George Washington*, 268, 271; Dunnigan, "Fortress Detroit."

4. Clark, memoir, in *George Rogers Clark Papers*, 221–23, lxi, 225–26.

5. Clark's proclamation also prohibited the sale of liquor to slaves, imposed a curfew on them, etc. Clark, memoir, and Clark, proclamation, Dec. 24, 1778 (my thanks to M. Scott Heerman for this reference), in *George Rogers Clark Papers*, 227 (first quotation), 231–34 (second quotation at 233), 91–95 (fourth quotation at 92); wikipedia.org/wiki/George_Rogers_Clark (third quotation); Downes, *Council Fires on the Upper Ohio*, 229; Cayton, *Frontier Indiana*, 67–68; Heerman, *Alchemy of Slavery*, 62–63.

6. Faragher, *Daniel Boone*, 92–93.

7. Faragher, *Daniel Boone*, 154–57, 167, 164–66, 173–74, 182–99.

8. Ward, *War of the Revolution* 2:587–88.

9. American officers provided an additional explanation for d'Estaing's abandonment of his

allies. Although he was appointed admiral, his background was in the army, and the navy captains forced to serve under him were "Determined to prevent his Doing any thing that may Redound to his Credit." Sullivan to Washington, Aug. 23, 1778, Laurens to Washington, Aug. 23, 1778, *Founders Online*; Robert Pigot to Clinton, Aug. 31, 1778, in Davies, ed., *Documents of the American Revolution* 15:190; Ward, *War of the Revolution* 1:588–91.

10. Sullivan to Washington, Aug. 31, 1778, *Founders Online*; Ward, *War of the Revolution* 2:591–93; Hatton, "Made to Be Forgotten."

11. Thomas C. Amory, quoted in Ward, *War of the Revolution* 2:592; "Certificate of the Governor of Rhode Island to Colonel William Barton," Feb. 14, 1778, in Bartlett, ed., *Records of the State of Rhode Island and Providence Plantations in New England* 8:358–60; William Greene to [Henry] Marchant and [John] Collins, Sept. 3, 1779, in Staples, *Rhode Island in the Continental Congress*, 249–50; Arnold, *History of the State of Rhode Island & Providence Plantations* 2:427; Greene, "Some Observations on the Black Regiment of Rhode Island in the American Revolution."

12. Greene, "Some Observations on the Black Regiment of Rhode Island in the American Revolution," 149, 152; Van Buskirk, *Standing in Their Own Light*, 95–141; Adams, "Deeds of Desperate Valor."

13. "Speculator" [Sergeant], proposal to create a Black battalion, enclosed in Sergeant to Adams, Aug. 13, 1776, Adams to Sergeant, Aug. 17, 1776, *Founders Online*.

14. Greene, "Some Observations on the Black Regiment of Rhode Island in the American Revolution," 169–70.

15. "Speculator" [Sergeant], proposal to create a Black battalion, enclosed in Sergeant to Adams, Aug. 13, 1776, *Founders Online*; Eustace, *Passion Is the Gale*, 385–88, 577n; McPherson, *Battle Cry of Freedom*, 686–87.

16. Carlisle Commission to Germain, Sept. 21, 1778, in Davies, ed., *Documents of the American Revolution* 15:203; Sullivan to Washington, Aug. 31, 1778, *Founders Online*; Smith, *Memorial to the Chevalier de Saint-Sauveur*, 6; Smith, *French at Boston During the Revolution*, 16.

17. William Heath to d'Estaing, Sept. 9, 1778, d'Estaing to Heath, Sept. 10, 1778, "Heath Papers," 268–71; dateline Boston, *Independent Ledger*, Sept. 14, 1778.

18. Hatton, "Made to Be Forgotten"; Smith, *Memorial to the Chevalier de Saint-Sauveur.*

19. Crytzer, *Guyasuta and the Fall of Indian America*, 199.

20. John Butler to Mason Bolton, July 8, 1778, in Davies, ed., *Documents of the American Revolution* 15:166; Graymont, *Iroquois in the American Revolution*, 167–72.

21. Walter Butler, quoted in Parkinson, *Common Cause*, 422; Graymont, *Iroquois in the American Revolution*, 183–91; Kelsay, *Joseph Brant*, 229–34.

22. Edmund Pendleton to William Woodford, Nov. 29, 1777, *Letters and Papers of Edmund Pendleton*, 1:238; Thomas Nelson Jr. to George Washington, Nov. 21–22, 1777, Washington to James Innes, Jan. 2, 1778 (editors' note), Virginia Council of State, Feb. 27, 1778, George Weedon to George Washington, March 30, 1778, Pendleton to George Washington, Dec. 22, 1778, *Founders Online*; McDonnell, *Politics of War*, 258, 273–80, 284–92, 305–7, 316–21, 327; Tillson, *Accommodating Revolutions*, 207, 209, 211–12.

23. George Washington to George Read, Jan. 19, 1778 (editors' note), Joseph Reed to George Washington, July 15, 1780, *Founders Online*.

24. In addition, both men had allegedly given the redcoats intelligence on the rebels, and Roberts had encouraged others to enlist with the British. Messer, "'Species of Treason & Not the Least Dangerous Kind,'" 303; Larson, "Revolutionary American Jury"; Alexander, "Fort Wilson Incident of 1779," 590–91.

25. Reed, quoted in Messer, "'Species of Treason & Not the Least Dangerous Kind,'" 323.

26. The defendants were also fortunate in having James Wilson as their lead attorney. Pennsylvania courts gave defense attorneys—but not prosecutors—the unilateral right to purge potential jurors, and Wilson used this strategy to good effect. Messer, "'Species of Treason & Not the Least Dangerous Kind,'" 303–32; Tomlins, "Republican Law," 546–47.

27. Clinton's claim that he sent away ten thousand (42 percent) of his 24,000 troops appears to have been an exaggeration, but he did lose more than a third of his troop strength. Clinton, *American Rebellion*, 106–7; Willcox, "British Strategy in America," 119.

28. Clinton, *American Rebellion*, 106; Wilson, *Southern Strategy*, 68–80; Dawson, "Enslaved Ship Pilots in the Age of Revolutions," 87.

29. Campbell, quoted in Taylor, *American Revolutions*, 230; Ramsay, *History of the Revolution of South-Carolina* 2:5.

30. Ramsay, *History of the Revolution of South-Carolina* 2:22–23; Piecuch, *Three Peoples, One King*, 153–54.

31. May 5, 8, 9, 1779, Orderly Book of the 71st Highland Regiment of Foot (Fraser's Highlanders), hdl.huntington.org/digital/collection/p15150coll7/id/8196.

32. May 9, 1779, Orderly Book of the 71st Highland Regiment of Foot (Fraser's Highlanders), hdl.huntington.org/digital/collection/p15150coll7/id/8196.

33. March 29, 1779, *JCC* 13:385–86; Nash, *Unknown American Revolution*, 328.

34. Wilson, *Southern Strategy*, 109–11; Parkinson, *Common Cause*, 461.

35. Wilson, *Southern Strategy*, 111–12, 116–23.

36. Ward, *War of the Revolution* 2:685–86; Wilson, *Southern Strategy*, 123–31; Opal, *Avenging the People*.

37. Ramsay, *History of the Revolution of South-Carolina* 2:32–33.

38. Jones's June 7, 1779, order declared "all Negroes that fly from the Enemy's country are Free." Quoted in Egerton, *Death or Liberty*, 84; Clinton, Philipsburg proclamation, [June 30, 1779], clements.umich.edu/exhibit/proclaiming-emancipation/time line-of-emancipation/.

39. Hamilton to Frederick Haldimand, Dec. 18, 30, 1778, in Davies, ed., *Documents of the American Revolution* 15:289–93; Selby, *Revolution in Virginia*, 194–95.

40. Clark, memoirs, in *George Rogers Clark Papers*, 274.

41. Clark to George Mason, Nov. 19, 1779, Clark, memoir, Hamilton to [Germain], July 6, 1781, all in *George Rogers Clark Papers*, 144–45 (quotations), 288–89, 206.

42. Downes, *Council Fires on the Upper Ohio*, 247.

43. Peckham, *War for Independence*, 115.

44. Taylor, *American Revolutions*, 287.

45. Dull, *French Navy and American Independence*, 156–57.

46. Callo, *John Paul Jones*, 62, 71, 77; Dull, *French Navy and American Independence*, 158n.

47. Schellhammer, "Real Immortal Words of John Paul Jones"; Callo, *John Paul Jones*, 90–91, 96–97.

48. Washington to John Jay, July 21, 1779, *Founders Online*; Clinton to Germain, June 18, 1779, in Davies, ed., *Documents of the American Revolution* 17:145.

49. Washington to Wayne, July 10, 1779, *Founders Online*; Posey, *General Thomas Posey*, 52.

50. Lossing, *Pictorial Field-Book of the Revolution* 1:744n, 746; Kaplan and Kaplan, *Black Presence in the Era of the American Revolution*, 58–59. For a challenge to the Pompey story, see Sheehan, "Mythology of Stony Point."

51. Wayne, Plan of Attack, enclosed in Wayne to Washington, July 15, 1779, Washington to Wayne, July 10, 1779, *Founders Online*; Ward, *War of the Revolution* 2:596–99.

52. Wayne to Washington, July 17, 1779, Washington to Gates, July 25, 1779, *Founders Online*; Ward, *War of the Revolution* 2:602.

53. Washington to John Jay, July 21, 1779, *Founders Online*; Ward, *War of the Revolution* 2:602–3; Posey, *General Thomas Posey*, 60.

54. Feb. 25, 1779, *JCC* 13:252; Ward, *War of the Revolution* 2:638.

55. April 21, 1779, "Journal of Lieut. Erkuries Beatty," in Cook, ed., *Journals of the Military Expedition of Major General John Sullivan Against the Six Nations of Indians in 1779*, 17; Graymont, *Iroquois in the American Revolution*, 196; Calloway, *Indian World of George Washington*, 249.

56. Washington to Sullivan, [May 31, 1779], *Founders Online*; Parkinson, *Common Cause*, 434; Shorto, *Revolution Song*, 353–54.

57. Francis Barber, orders, June 19, 1779, in Murray, ed., *Notes from Craft Collection in Tioga Point Museum on the Sullivan Expedition of 1779*, 17; Cooper, *The Pioneers: Or, the Sources of the Susquehanna* (1823), gutenberg.org/files/2275/2275-h/2275-h.htm; Ward, *War of the Revolution* 2:641.

58. Ward, *War of the Revolution* 2:642; Graymont, *Iroquois in the American Revolution*, 206–8; Kelsay, *Joseph Brant*, 261; Fischer, *Well-Executed Failure*, 86–95.

59. John Sullivan to George Washington, Aug. 30, 1779, *Founders Online*.

60. John Sullivan to George Washington, Aug. 30, 1779, *Founders Online*; Kelsay, *Joseph Brant*, 263; Graymont, *Iroquois in the American Revolution*, 213.

61. Kelsay, *Joseph Brant*, 264, 267; Graymont, *Iroquois in the American Revolution*, 215.

62. John Sullivan to John Jay, Sept. 30, 1779, in *Letters and Papers of Major-General John Sullivan* 3:123–24; Ward, *War of the Revolution* 2:642; Graymont, *Iroquois in the American Revolution*, 213.

63. Brant, quoted in Kelsay, *Joseph Brant*, 267.

64. John Sullivan to John Jay, Sept. 30, 1779, in *Letters and Papers of Major-General John Sullivan* 3:128–31; Seaver, *Narrative of the Life of Mrs. Mary Jemison*, 65–68; Kelsay, *Joseph Brant*, 266–67; Graymont, *Iroquois in the American Revolution*, 216–17.

65. Graymont, *Iroquois in the American Revolution*, 218.

66. Seneca chiefs, quoted in Calloway, *Indian World of George Washington*, 256; Graymont, *Iroquois in the American Revolution*, 204, 214–22.

67. Sept. 30, 1779, "Journal of Major Jeremiah Fogg," in Cook, ed., *Journals of the Military Expedition of Major General John Sullivan Against the Six Nations of Indians in 1779*, 101; Fischer, *Well-Executed Failure*; Calloway, *American Revolution in Indian Country*, 136.

68. Seaver, *Narrative of the Life of Mary Jemison*, 70–71; Graymont, *Iroquois in the American Revolution*, 220–22; Shorto, *Revolution Song*, 365; Taylor, *American Revolutions*, 256.

Chapter 27: Dark Days

1. Norton, "Penobscot Expedition," 1–3, 14.

2. Norton, "Penobscot Expedition," 3–13.

3. Norton, "Penobscot Expedition," 14–19.

4. Apparently most walked fifty miles to the Kennebec River and traveled the rest of the way by water. Clinton, *American Rebellion*, 135; Norton, "Penobscot Expedition," 19–28; Greenburg, *Court-Martial of Paul Revere*, 133, 141.

5. Jan. 22, 1779, *JCC* 13:102; Washington to Gérard, May 1, 1779, Gérard to Washington,

May 5, 1779, Washington to Gouverneur Morris, May 8, 1779, Gérard, "memoire" to Congress, May 9, 1779, quoted in editors' note to John Jay to Washington, May 10, 1779, *Founders Online*; Clinton, *American Rebellion*, 145n, 151.

6. Gates to Washington, Oct. 8 (quotation), Sept. 6, 1779, Washington to Jay, Sept. 12, [19–]20, 1779, Washington to d'Estaing, Sept. 13, Oct. 4, 7, 1779, Washington to Sullivan, Oct. 3, 1779, headnote to "Planning for an Allied Attack on New York, c.3–7 October 1779," *Founders Online*; Arent DePeyster to Alexander McKee, Nov. 5, 1779, *MHC* 10:372; Dull, *French Navy and American Independence*, 160–61; Wilson, *Southern Strategy*, 178–81; Taylor, *American Revolutions*, 287–88.

7. More than three thousand Continentals and Whig militiamen participated in the siege. David Ramsay to William Henry Drayton, Sept. 1, 1779, in Gibbes, ed., *Documentary History of the Revolution* 2:121–22; Ward, *War of the Revolution* 2:690; Quarles, *Negro in the American Revolution*, 63–64; Wilson, *Southern Strategy*, 146–47, 177–81.

8. Dateline Savannah, *Royal Gazette* (Rivington), Dec. 11, 1779; Jones, *Siege of Savannah*, 18n; Wilson, *Southern Strategy*, 149, 187.

9. "Account of the Life of Mr. David George from Sierra Leone," in Holton, *Black Americans in the Revolutionary Era*, 112–15.

10. Ramsay, *History of the Revolution of South-Carolina* 2:39; Charles Cotesworth Pinckney to Eliza Lucas Pinckney, Oct. 15, 1779, *Papers of Eliza Lucas Pinckney and Harriott Pinckney Horry*.

11. "Account of the Life of Mr. David George from Sierra Leone," in Holton, *Black Americans in the Revolutionary Era*, 115; Johnston, *Recollections of a Georgia Loyalist*, 58; Piecuch, *Three Peoples, One King*, 169–70.

12. Quarles, *Negro in the American Revolution*, 82.

13. Lawrence, *Storm over Savannah*, 103.

14. Pinckney, quoted in Wilson, *Southern Strategy*, 172.

15. Lt. Col. John Laurens was not even supposed to attack Spring Hill redoubt, but after seeing the first two assaults fail, he led his troops there nonetheless. In rapid succession three of Laurens's lieutenants and one of his sergeants planted the standard atop the wall, only to be mortally wounded. Wilson, *Southern Strategy*, 166–68.

16. Peckham, *Toll of Independence*, 65.

17. Washington to Henry Laurens, Nov. 5, 1779, Washington to d'Estaing, Oct. 7, 1779, Benjamin Lincoln to Samuel Huntington, Oct. 22, 1779, quoted in editors' note to Huntington to Washington, Nov. 10, 1779, *Founders Online*.

18. Hugh McCall, quoted in Wilson, *Southern Strategy*, 176.

19. "Account of the Life of Mr. David George from Sierra Leone," in Holton, *Black Americans in the Revolutionary Era*, 115.

20. Pennsylvania Supreme Executive Council to Washington, April 24, 1779, *Founders Online*; Arnold to André, May 23, [1779?], June 18, [1779], Jonathan Odell to André, [June 13, 1779], in Van Doren, *Secret History of the American Revolution*, 442, 448–49, 446.

21. André to Stansbury, [May 10, 1779], in Van Doren, *Secret History of the American Revolution*, 440, 200–201.

22. Ferguson, *Power of the Purse*, 30, 32; Buel, *In Irons*, 130.

23. Washington to John Jay, April 23, 1779, *Founders Online*; Taylor, *American Revolutions*, 196.

24. Washington to Joseph Reed, Dec. 12, 1778, *Founders Online*; Foner, *Tom Paine and Revolutionary America*, 166; Van Doren, *Secret History of the American Revolution*, 226.

25. Francis Lightfoot Lee to Samuel Adams, Dec. 22, 1777, James Lovell to Sam Adams,

Dec. 15, 1777, in Smith et al., eds., *Letters of Delegates to Congress* 8:459–60, 418; Alexander MacDougall to Joseph Reed, March 25, 1779, in Reed, *Life and Correspondence of Joseph Reed* 2:58; Clinton, *American Rebellion*, 151, 190.

26. "The Memorial and Petition of the first Company of Philadelphia Militia Artillery," May 12, 1779, *Pennsylvania Archives*, Ser. 1, 7:394; Alexander, "Fort Wilson Incident of 1779," 594, 598, 600.

27. *Come on Coolly!* (broadside), May 23 or 24, 1779, in Rosswurm, ed., "Equality and Justice," 261.

28. Rosswurm, *Arms, Country, and Class*, 211–13.

29. Alexander, "Fort Wilson Incident of 1779," 606.

30. Alexander, "Fort Wilson Incident of 1779," 607–8; Rosswurm, *Arms, Country, and Class*, 220–21, 229–31.

31. Martin, *Narrative of Some of the Adventures, Dangers, and Sufferings of a Revolutionary Soldier*, 123–24; Raphael, "America's Worst Winter Ever"; Philbrick, *Valiant Ambition*, 256.

32. Nash, *Forging Freedom*, 59–63; Philbrick, *Valiant Ambition*, 256.

33. Nash, *Forging Freedom*, 56–60.

34. Pybus, *Epic Journeys of Freedom*, 40; Wood, "Changing Population of the Colonial South," 60–61; Clinton, *American Rebellion*, 158; Edgar, *Partisans and Redcoats*, 49.

35. Edgar, *Partisans and Redcoats*, 49; Wilson, *Southern Strategy*, 199–200.

36. Anthony Allaire, diary, March 29, 31, 1780, in Draper, *King's Mountain and Its Heroes*, 489; Wilson, *Southern Strategy*, 210–12.

37. Clinton to Germain, March 9, 1780, in Davies, ed., *Documents of the American Revolution* 18:54; March 30, 1780, in [De Brahm], "Journal of the Siege of Charleston," in Gibbes, ed., *Documentary History of the Revolution* 2:124.

38. Wilson, *Southern Strategy*, 215.

39. Moultrie, *Memoirs of the American Revolution* 2:44; Wilson, *Southern Strategy*, 203–4.

40. James Williams to Andrew Williamson, Jan. 4, 1780, J[ohn] Rutledge to B.G., Feb. 12, 1780, J[ohn] Rutledge to Col. Garden, March 2, 1780, J[ohn] Rutledge to Col. Goodwyn, April 24, 1780, in Gibbes, ed., *Documentary History of the Revolution* 2:123, 128, 129, 132; Wilson, *Southern Strategy*, 204; Bobrick, *Angel in the Whirlwind*, 398.

41. Feb. 12, April 27, March 13, 1780, in Ewald, *Diary of the American War*, 197, 234, 208.

42. Moultrie, *Memoirs of the American Revolution* 2:83n–84; April 17, 1780, in Ewald, *Diary of the American War*, 231.

43. Moultrie, *Memoirs of the American Revolution* 2:77–78, 80; Borick, *Gallant Defense*, 168–71.

44. Elizabeth Burgin to George Washington, March 16, 1780, Burgin to James Caldwell, Nov. 19, 1779, *Founders Online*; Ellet, *Women of the American Revolution* 1:16, 21, 194, 254, 3:60; Watson, *Ghost Ship of Brooklyn*, 156–58.

45. Philbrick, *In the Hurricane's Eye*, 20–21. On the other hand, Washington recognized that if Clinton was about to capture Charles Town, the news that a French fleet was on its way could be used to convince him to break off his siege. He might simply return to New York City. Or he might try to hasten matters in the same way d'Estaing had at Savannah—by storming the Citadel—most likely with the same disastrous results. Washington to Rutledge, May 16, 1780 (quotation), Washington to Lafayette, May 16, 1780, *Founders Online*.

46. Wilson, *Southern Strategy*, 234, 241.

47. Moultrie, *Memoirs of the American Revolution* 2:109. Mortality estimates ranged from fewer than one hundred to three hundred. W. Croghan to Michael Gratz, May 18, 1780,

in Gibbes, ed., *Documentary History of the Revolution* 2:133; May 18, 1780, in Ewald, *Diary of the American War*, 239.

48. Washington to Samuel Huntington, July 10, 1780, La Luzerne to Washington, Jan. 23, 1780, William Phillips to George Washington, June 19, 1780 (including editors' note quoting Joshua Loring to Abraham Skinner, June 21[*sic*], 1780), Huntington to Washington, June 25, 1780, *Founders Online*; Watson, *Ghost Ship of Brooklyn*, 141.

49. Cornwallis, quoted in Buchanan, *Road to Guilford Courthouse*, 79.

50. Moultrie, *Memoirs of the American Revolution* 2:203.

51. Forty of Tarleton's troopers were from a different unit. Ward, *War of the Revolution* 2:705.

52. Edgar, *Partisans and Redcoats*, 56.

53. Tarleton, *History of the Campaigns of 1780 and 1781*, 32; Ward, *War of the Revolution* 2:706; Wilson, *Southern Strategy*, 259–61; Buchanan, *Road to Guilford Courthouse*, 62–63; Edgar, *Partisans and Redcoats*, 56–57.

54. George Washington to Samuel Huntington, May 27[-28], 1780, *Founders Online*; May 29, 1780, in Thacher, *Military Journal During the American Revolutionary War*, 236; Martin, *Narrative of Some of the Adventures, Dangers, and Sufferings of a Revolutionary Soldier*, 131–35.

55. Martin, *Narrative of Some of the Adventures, Dangers, and Sufferings of a Revolutionary Soldier*, 131.

56. Clinton, *American Rebellion*, 190–92; Kelsay, *Joseph Brant*, 283–84; Graymont, *Iroquois in the American Revolution*, 229–41; Stedman, *History of the Origin, Progress, and Termination of the American War* 2:240–41.

57. Stedman, *History of the Origin, Progress, and Termination of the American War* 2:241; James Robertson to Germain, July 1, 1780, Wilhelm Knyphausen to Germain, July 3, 1780, Clinton to Germain, July 4, 1780, in Davies, ed., *Documents of the American Revolution* 18:107–14.

58. Arent DePeyster to Alexander McKee, June 22, 1780, *MHC* 10:404; Guyasuta, quoted in Graymont, *Iroquois in the American Revolution*, 232; Calloway, *Indian World of George Washington*, 257.

59. Washington to Samuel Huntington, June 20, 1780, *Founders Online*; Van Doren, *Mutiny in January*, 20; Graymont, *Iroquois in the American Revolution*, 229–30, 234–35.

60. Philadelphia dateline, *Pennsylvania Packet*, June 17, 1780; Philadelphia dateline, *Pennsylvania Gazette*, June 21, 1780.

61. Joseph Reed to Dennis De Berdt, May 24, 1778, in Reed, *Life of Esther De Berdt*, 286; Esther Reed to Mrs. Cox, June 1778, in Reed., *Life and Correspondence of Joseph Reed* 2:257.

62. Eventually the donors would be reimbursed. Paine to Blair McClenaghan, May 1780, thomaspaine.org/letters/other/to-blair-mcclenaghan-may-1780.html; Thomas Paine to Joseph Reed, June 4, 1780, in Reed, *Life and Correspondence of Joseph Reed* 2:219; Philip John Schuyler to Washington, June 18, 1780, *Founders Online*; Rappleye, *Robert Morris*, 215.

63. Prior to Reed's broadside, the phrase "empire of liberty" had apparently been used only as a euphemism for Heaven. "An American," "To the Honorable James Otis Esq," *Massachusetts Gazette*, June 27, 1771. Reed's talk of women craving *fame* was so audacious that the man who typeset her broadside (accidentally?) rendered it as *same*. [Reed], *Sentiments of an American Woman*; "Mr. Dunlap," *Pennsylvania Packet*, June 13, 1780; Norton, *Liberty's Daughters*, 177–88.

64. [Reed], *Sentiments of an American Woman*; "A Letter from a Lady in Philadelphia

to her Friend in this Place," in Sklar and Duffy, *How Did the Ladies Association of Philadelphia Shape New Forms of Women's Activism During the American Revolution, 1780–1781?*

65. In his reply to Gen. Lee's *Maryland Journal and Baltimore Advertiser* essay, Reed claimed the only reason he had written the general in November 1776 was to solicit his aid in persuading Washington to save the Fort Washington garrison while there was still time, but Washington knew that was untrue, since the enemy had captured the fort five days before Reed wrote Lee. Washington to Joseph Reed, June 11, 1777, April 28, May 28 (quotation in text), July 4, 1780, Joseph Reed to Washington, June 4, 1777, July 15, 1779, *Founders Online*; [Charles Lee], "Some QUERIES, Political and Military, Humbly Offered to the Consideration of the Public," *Maryland Journal and Baltimore Advertiser*, July 6, 1779; Joseph Reed, letter, *Maryland Journal and Baltimore Advertiser*, Aug. 3, 1779; Roche, *Joseph Reed*, 99–102.

66. Pennsylvania Supreme Executive Council to Washington, April 24, 1779, Joseph Reed to Washington, July 15, 1780, *Founders Online*; Roche, *Joseph Reed*, 174–77.

67. "Ideas, Relative to the Manner of Forwarding to the American Soldiers, the Presents of the American Women," *Pennsylvania Gazette*, June 21, 1780; Joseph Reed to Washington, June 20, 1780, *Founders Online*.

68. Washington to Esther Reed, Aug. 10, July 14, 20, 1780, *Founders Online*; Paine, *Dissertations on Government; the Affairs of the Bank; and Paper Money*, thomaspaine.org/essays/american-politics-&-government/dissertations-on-government.html; Lewis, *History of the Bank of North America*, 17–23; Rappleye, *Robert Morris*, 215–19.

69. Reed to Washington, July 31, 1780, *Founders Online*.

70. Esther Reed to Joseph Reed, Aug. 22, 1780, Joseph Reed to Esther Reed, Aug. 26, 1780, in Reed, *Life and Correspondence of Joseph Reed* 2:267–68 (first quotation), 247; Philadelphia dateline, *Pennsylvania Gazette*, Sept. 27, 1780 (second quotation); Sarah Bache to Benjamin Franklin, Sept. 9, 1780, *Founders Online*.

71. Philadelphia dateline, *Pennsylvania Gazette*, Sept. 27, 1780; Ireland, *Sentiments of a British-American Woman*, 204. Martha Jefferson forwarded a copy of Reed's handbill to her friend Eleanor Madison (mother of the future president). Two years later, Jefferson died, and her widower burned her correspondence. The only surviving letter is the one to Eleanor Madison. Norton, "Philadelphia Ladies Association," 205.

Chapter 28: Secret Agency

1. Cornwallis to Clinton, June 30, 1780, in Tarleton, *History of the Campaigns of 1780 and 1781*, 120; Clinton to Germain, Aug. 25, 1780, in Davies, ed., *Documents of the American Revolution* 18:153; Edgar, *Partisans and Redcoats*, 54–57; Brannon, *From Revolution to Reunion*, 18.

2. Ferguson, "General Andrew Pickens," 101–10.

3. Gregorie, *Thomas Sumter*, 74, 80, 134; Liles, "Thomas Sumter's Law," 80, 84–85; Otho Holland Williams, "A Narrative of the Campaign of 1780," in Johnson, *Sketches of the Life and Correspondence of Nathanael Greene* 1:488.

4. Ellet, *Women of the American Revolution* 3:179–85; Gregorie, *Thomas Sumter*, 84–85; Edgar, *Partisans and Redcoats*, xiv, 73–86.

5. Ellet, *Women of the American Revolution* 1:254–56; Draper, *King's Mountain and Its Heroes*, 73–75; Gordon, *South Carolina and the American Revolution*, 89.

6. Anthony Allaire, diary, July 15, Aug. 8, 1780, in Draper, *King's Mountain and Its Heroes*,

501, 503, 101; Mills, *Statistics of South Carolina*, 738–40; Ellet, *Women of the American Revolution* 1:291–94; Edgar, *Partisans and Redcoats*, 85–86. Draper (*Kings Mountain and Its Heroes*, 73–75) claimed that Dillard's midnight ride of August 7–8, 1780, was a myth; in his reading, she had been wrongly credited with Jane Thomas's deed. But we know that Loyalists attempted to surprise Whigs near Cedar Springs on both July 13 and August 8, and in the absence of other evidence, there is no reason to disbelieve the contemporaries who credited both Whig parties' deliverance to women.

7.   Tarleton, *History of the Campaigns of 1780 and 1781*, 181; Gregorie, *Thomas Sumter*, 120–24.

8.   Ellet, *Women of the American Revolution* 1:284–87 (quotation at 284), 171–77; Schoel, "In Pursuit of Possibility." For a similar discussion of privileged and disparaged historical evidence, see Gordon-Reed, *Thomas Jefferson and Sally Hemings*, xvi.

9.   Ellet, *Women of the American Revolution* 1:274–76; Young, *Masquerade*.

10. Edgar, *Partisans and Redcoats*, 93, 99–106, 114–15; Ward, *War of the Revolution*, 2:745.

11. Spring, *With Zeal and with Bayonets Only*, 4, 9; Dederer, *Making Bricks Without Straw*; Shy, *People Numerous and Armed*, 193–224.

12. May 13, 1780, "Diary of Captain Johann Hinrichs," in Uhlendorf, ed., *Siege of Charleston*, 297; James Simpson to Germain, Dec. 31, 1780, in Davies, ed., *Documents of the American Revolution* 18:264; Frey, *Water from the Rock*, 122–24; Olwell, *Masters, Slaves, and Subjects*, 253; Wilson, *Southern Strategy*, 234.

13. "Memoirs of the Life of Boston King," in Holton, *Black Americans in the Revolutionary Era*, 121; Olwell, *Masters, Slaves, and Subjects*, 251; Brannon, *From Revolution to Reunion*, 5–6.

14. Olwell, *Masters, Slaves, and Subjects*, 254; Parkinson, *Common Cause*.

15. June 17, 1780, *JCC* 17:523.

16. Williams, "Narrative of the Campaign of 1780," in Johnson, *Sketches of the Life and Correspondence of Nathanael Greene* 1:491; Thomas Pinckney to William Johnson, July 27, 1822, John Christian Senf, journal, Aug. 15, 1780, in Piecuch, *Battle of Camden*, 38, 23; Gates to president of Congress, Aug. 20, 1780, in Tarleton, *History of the Campaigns of 1780 and 1781*, 149; Stevens to Thomas Jefferson, Aug. 20, 1780, *Founders Online*; Stevens, ed., "Battle of Camden Described by Major McGill," 278; Buchanan, *Road to Guilford Courthouse*, 161.

17. Guilford Dudley, memoir, Josiah Martin to Germain, Aug. 18, 1780, Cornwallis to Germain, Aug. 21, 1780, in Piecuch, *Battle of Camden*, 73, 69, 53–54; Williams, "Narrative of the Campaign of 1780," in Johnson, *Sketches of the Life and Correspondence of Nathanael Greene* 1:494.

18. Guilford Dudley, memoir, Thomas Pinckney to William Johnson, July 27, 1822, John Senf, journal, Aug.15[–16], in Piecuch, *Battle of Camden*, 74, 39, 41, 23–24; Ward, *War of the Revolution* 2:723.

19. Williams, "Narrative of the Campaign of 1780," in Johnson, *Sketches of the Life and Correspondence of Nathanael Greene* 1:495; Thomas Pinckney to William Johnson, July 27, 1822, in Piecuch, *Battle of Camden*, 41.

20. Tarleton, *History of the Campaigns of 1780 and 1781*, 110, 113, 135 (Cornwallis to Germain, Aug. 21, 1780); Stedman, *History of the Origin, Progress, and Termination of the American War* 2:209; Clinton, *American Rebellion*, 224.

21. Williams, "Narrative of the Campaign of 1780," in Johnson, *Sketches of the Life and Correspondence of Nathanael Greene* 1:495–96.

22. Tarleton, *History of the Campaigns of 1780 and 1781*, 110–11; Ramsay, *History of the Revolution of South-Carolina* 2:149.

23. Nisbet Balfour, quoted in Piecuch, *Three Peoples, One King*, 225–26; Gates to Washington, Aug. 30, 1780, *Founders Online*; Buchanan, *Road to Guilford Courthouse*, 169–70; Ward, *War of the Revolution* 2:732–33.

24. Williams, "Narrative of the Campaign of 1780," in Johnson, *Sketches of the Life and Correspondence of Nathanael Greene* 1:496; Thomas Pinckney to William Johnson, July 27, 1822, in Piecuch, *Battle of Camden*, 41; Ramsay, *History of the Revolution of South-Carolina* 2:152; Tarleton, *History of the Campaigns of 1780 and 1781*, 111–12, 136 (Cornwallis to Germain, Aug. 21, 1780).

25. Washington to Samuel Huntington, Sept. 15, 1780, *Founders Online*; Virginia militiamen, petition to the Virginia General Assembly, Nov. 9, 1780, in Piecuch, *Battle of Camden*, 91; Sellick, "'They Were Marched Almost Day and Night,'" 119–20.

26. Williams, "Narrative of the Campaign of 1780," in Johnson, *Sketches of the Life and Correspondence of Nathanael Greene*, 493–94; Tarleton, *History of the Campaigns of 1780 and 1781*, 112–13; Ward, *War of the Revolution* 2:722–34; Ramsay, *History of the Revolution of South-Carolina* 2:148; Buchanan, *Road to Guilford Courthouse*, 161.

27. Thomas Pinckney to William Johnson, July 27, 1822, in Piecuch, *Battle of Camden*, 40.

28. Washington to Rochambeau, July 31, 1780, *Founders Online*; Philbrick, *In the Hurricane's Eye*, 22.

29. Clinton to Germain, Aug. 25, 1780, in Davies, ed., *Documents of the American Revolution* 18:153.

30. Jefferson to George Rogers Clark, Jan. 1, 17[80], *Founders Online*.

31. Sinclair to Capt. D. Brehm, Feb. 15, 1780, *MHC* 9:542; Gilman, "L'Anneé du Coup," 141–45, 147n.

32. Sinclair to Haldimand, Feb. 17, 1780, *MHC* 9:546. Langlade missed the May 26 attacks. He had stopped by Chicago to recruit additional fighters and was then blocked in his passage down the Illinois River by native nations in alliance with Spain. Gilman, "L'Anneé du Coup," 133, 206–7; Saunt, *West of the Revolution*, 34–71; Taylor, *American Revolutions*, 270.

33. Estimates of the number of defenders killed at St. Louis and Cahokia ranged as high as seventy-two; only a handful of the attackers died. In addition, the Anglo-Indian army captured forty-six French and Spanish settlers as it descended and then ascended the Mississippi. Martin Navarro to Joseph de Gálvez, Aug. 18, 1780, in Houck, ed., *Spanish Regime in Missouri*, 1:168; Sinclair to Haldimand, July 8, 1780, *MHC* 9:559; Gilman, "L'Anneé du Coup," 200–205.

34. DePeyster to [Haldimand], Nov. 20, 1779, June 1, 1780, DePeyster to McKee, June 22, 1780, *MHC* 10:372, 398, 404; DePeyster to Mason Bolton, March 10, May 16, June 8, Aug. 4, 1780, McKee to DePeyster, June 4, July 8, 1780, *MHC* 19:501–2, 519–20, 532, 553, 530–31, 541–43; White, *Middle Ground*, 406–7.

35. "Speech of the Delawares and Shawnese Assembled at the Upper Shawnese Village, to Their Father Major DePeyster Commandant of Detroit," Aug. 22, 1780, William Homan to Henry Bird, Aug. 15, 1780, Haldimand to Germain, Oct. 25, 1780, *MHC* 10:420, 419, 444; James, *Life of George Rogers Clark*, 210–13; White, *Middle Ground*, 391.

36. Germain to Haldimand, June 17, 1779, Germain to John Campbell, June 25, 1779, in Davies, ed., *Documents of the American Revolution* 17:144, 153–54; Sinclair to Haldimand, Feb. 17, 1780, *MHC* 9:546.

37. Rush, quoted in Johnston, *Yorktown Campaign and the Surrender of Cornwallis*, 95; Thomas Munro to his father, Oct. 11, 1780, in Gleig, *Life of Major-General Sir Thomas Munro* 1:23–27; Taylor, *American Revolutions*, 302.

38. André to Arnold, [1779], in Van Doren, *Secret History of the American Revolution*, 448, 207; Smith, *Authentic Narrative of the Causes Which Led to the Death of Major André*, 10.

39. Clinton to his sisters, Oct. 4, 9, 1780, in Van Doren, *Secret History of the American Revolution*, 479.

40. Washington to Arnold, Aug. 3, 1780, *Founders Online*.

41. Washington to Arnold, Sept. 14, 1780, Washington to Greene, Sept. 16, 1780, *Founders Online*; Van Doren, *Secret History of the American Revolution*, 314–15.

42. Sparks, *Life and Treason of Benedict Arnold*, 196–98.

43. Sparks, *Life and Treason of Benedict Arnold*, 232–33.

44. Van Doren, *Secret History of the American Revolution*, 342. British officers soon released Arnold's bargemen on parole. Philbrick, *Valiant Ambition*, 308–10.

45. Washington to Lafayette, quoted in Sparks, *Life and Treason of Benedict Arnold*, 247; Philbrick, *Valiant Ambition*, 311.

46. Clinton, quoted in Philbrick, *Valiant Ambition*, 315; Knott, "Sensibility and the American War for Independence," 24.

47. Richard Meade, quoted in Knott, "Sensibility and the American War for Independence," 22.

48. Washington to John Laurens, Oct. 13, 1780, *Founders Online*; Trees, "Benedict Arnold, John André, and His Three Yeoman Captors."

49. Lee, *Memoirs of the War in the Southern Department of the United States* 2:161–87 (quotation at 162).

50. Nov. 2, 1780, in Thacher, *Military Journal During the American Revolutionary War*, 283; Martin and Lender, *Respectable Army*, 160; Taylor, *American Revolutions*, 208.

51. Cornwallis to Germain, Sept. 19, 1780, Cornwallis to Clinton, Dec. 3, 1780, in Davies, ed., *Documents of the American Revolution* 18:170, 244.

52. Selby, *Revolution in Virginia*, 204–8, 216; Mackesy, *War for America*, 352.

53. Washington to Rochambeau, Nov. 14, 1780, Washington to Knox, November 1780, Plan of Attack on New York, November 1780, *Founders Online*; Freeman, Carroll, and Ashworth, *George Washington* 5:232.

54. Washington to Morris, Dec. 10, 1780, *Founders Online*.

55. Greene to Samuel Huntington, Dec. 28, 1780, in *Papers of General Nathanael Greene* 7:9; Piecuch, *Three Peoples, One King*, 237–42; Kendall, *Life of Andrew Jackson*, 50; Remini, *Andrew Jackson and the Course of American Empire*, 15, 21–24; Opal, *Avenging the People*, 41–44; Taylor, *American Revolutions*, 3.

56. James Wright to Germain, Sept. 18, 1780, Charles Shaw to Germain, Sept. 18, 1780, in Davies, ed., *Documents of the American Revolution* 18:167–68; Cornwallis to Ferguson, Sept. 23, 1780, in Tarleton, *History of the Campaigns of 1780 and 1781*, 197; Lee, *Memoirs of the War in the Southern Department of the United States* 1:204–7; M'Call, *History of Georgia* 2:320–34; Ward, *War of the Revolution* 2:739; Cashin, *King's Ranger*, 113–20.

57. Allaire, diary, Sept. 1, 7, 24, 1780, in Draper, *King's Mountain and Its Heroes*, 505–6, 508–9; Uzal Johnson, diary, July 12, Sept. 28, Oct. 1, 1780, in Johnson, *Captured at Kings Mountain*, 20, 29–30; Lee, *Memoirs of the War in the Southern Department of the United States* 1:203–4, 207; Ward, *War of the Revolution* 2:739–41; Piecuch, *Three Peoples, One King*, 198. The sources conflict on whether Ferguson went after Clarke on his own initiative or on orders from Cornwallis.

58. Draper, *King's Mountain and Its Heroes*, 221, 199, 296, 541.

59. Draper, *King's Mountain and Its Heroes*, 201, 208–9, 212.

60. Isaac Shelby, quoted in Draper, *King's Mountain and Its Heroes*, 196.
61. Ward, *War of the Revolution* 2:740.
62. Draper, *King's Mountain and Its Heroes*, 246, 254, 287; Spring, *With Zeal and with Bayonets Only*, 257–58.
63. Two hundred of Ferguson's men who had been out scouting missed the battle and escaped. Robert Campbell, "Battle of King's Mountain," in Draper, *King's Mountain and Its Heroes*, 479, 539; Edgar, *Partisans and Redcoats*, 119; O'Shaughnessy, *Men Who Lost America*, 265.
64. Campbell, "Battle of King's Mountain," in Draper, *King's Mountain and Its Heroes*, 282, 540; Edgar, *Partisans and Redcoats*, 119.
65. Selby, *Revolution in Virginia*, 216–21.
66. O'Shaughnessy, *Men Who Lost America*, 178–82.
67. O'Shaughnessy, *Men Who Lost America*, 182–85; wikipedia.org/wiki/San_Juan_Expe dition_(1780); Wood, *Black Majority*, 63-91.
68. Lee, *Memoirs of the War in the Southern Department of the United States* 2:184–86.
69. Ewald, *Diary of the American War*, 295.
70. Selby, *Revolution in Virginia*, 268, 221–25; Pybus, *Epic Journeys of Freedom*, 44; Pflugrad-Jackisch, "'What Am I but an American?,'" 180, 183–85.
71. Holton, *Black Americans in the Revolutionary Era*, 75–77; Thomas, *Rise to Be a People*, 9–10. Neither the 1691 charter, under which Massachusetts operated through most of 1780, nor the state's new constitution, which took effect in October 1780, prohibited Blacks from voting, but both documents confined the franchise to landholders.
72. Thomas, *Rise to Be a People*, 10–11.

Chapter 29: Had I Crossed the River

1. Aug. 31, 1778, Sept. 16, Nov. 12, 21, 1776, *JCC* 11:854, 5:762, 6:944–45, 970–71; Peter Scull to Washington, June 3, 1779, *Founders Online*; Hagist, *British Soldiers, American War*, 122.
2. Alexander Hamilton to Nathanael Greene, June 11, 1779, Washington to Board of War, June 9, 1779, *Founders Online*; June 22, 1779, *JCC* 14:758.
3. Hamilton to Joseph Ward, [July 8, 1779], *Founders Online*; Nagy, *Rebellion in the Ranks*, 134. The congressional resolution approving the $100 bounty echoed all of Washington's goals except the essential one: convincing Pennsylvania soldiers who had only committed for three years to stay through the rest of the war. June 22, 1779, *JCC* 14:758.
4. Van Doren, *Mutiny in January*, 13–14, 42–48; Nagy, *Rebellion in the Ranks*, 79–80.
5. Committee of Congress, report, Jan. 24, 1781, *JCC* 19:80; Anthony Wayne, reply to Pennsylvania mutineers, Jan. 4, 1781, enclosed in Wayne, Richard Butler, and Walter Stewart to Washington, Jan. 4, 1781, *Founders Online*; Nagy, *Rebellion in the Ranks*, 134.
6. Clinton to Germain, Jan. 25, 1781, in Davies, ed., *Documents of the American Revolution* 20:43; Van Doren, *Mutiny in January*, 173–76, 245 (Oliver De Lancey's journal); Lengel, *General George Washington*, 327; Nagy, *Rebellion in the Ranks*, 127.
7. Washington to Samuel Huntington, Jan. 6, 1781, *Founders Online*; Washington to Heath, Jan. 14, 1781, *Writings of George Washington from the Original Manuscript Sources* 21:96–97; Heath to Washington, Jan. 13, 1781, Robert Howe to Washington, Jan. 16, 1781 (Howe was skeptical of the "Camp girl's" pessimistic report), *Founders*

Online; Lafayette to La Luzerne, Jan. 4, 1781, "Letters from Lafayette to Luzerne," 579; Stillé, *Major-General Anthony Wayne and the Pennsylvania Line in the Continental Army*, 248; Van Doren, *Mutiny in January*, 137–38, 190–93; Lengel, *General George Washington*, 327; Nagy, *Rebellion in the Ranks*, 82.

8. Letter 148, Jan. 14, 1781, "Extracts from the Letter-Books of Lieutenant Enos Reeves," 78; Van Doren, *Mutiny in January*, 157–58.

9. Board of Sergeants, quoted in "Account of the Late Disturbances in the Pennsylvania Line," *Pennsylvania Gazette*, Jan. 24, 1781. Eventually Pennsylvania president Joseph Reed convinced the mutineers to move to Trenton, eleven miles closer to Philadelphia and farther from New York.

10. Washington, circular to the New England states, Jan. 5, 1781, *Writings of George Washington from the Original Manuscript Sources* 21:61–62; Washington to Samuel Huntington, Jan. 6, 1781, Washington to Hancock, Jan. 5, 1781, Washington to Henry Knox, Jan. 7, 1781, *Founders Online*; Jan. 7, 1781, *Memoirs of Major-General William Heath*, 249.

11. John Sullivan to Washington, Jan. 29, 1781, *Founders Online*; Van Doren, *Mutiny in January*, 200, 203.

12. James Lovell to John Adams, Jan. 2, 1781, Samuel Miles to George Washington, Jan. 3, 1781, *Founders Online*.

13. Van Doren notes that Reed's "petty stratagem was not undertaken." Van Doren, *Mutiny in January*, 194.

14. Israel Shreve to George Washington, Jan. 20, 1781, Frederick Frelinghuysen to George Washington, Jan. 20, 1781, *Founders Online*; Schellhammer, "Mutiny of the New Jersey Line."

15. "An Act for Speedily Recruiting the Virginia Regiments on Continental Establishment," "An Act for Obliging the Several Delinquent Counties and Divisions of Militia in this Commonwealth to Furnish One Twenty Fifth Man," in Hening, ed., *Statutes at Large* 9:588–92, 10:82–83; McDonnell, *Politics of War*, 273–356; Tillson, *Accommodating Revolutions*, 207, 212.

16. On draft resistance, see Samuel McDowell to Thomas Jefferson, May 9, 1781, George Corbin to Thomas Jefferson, May 31, 1781, *Founders Online*. Under the initial legislative proposal, Virginians who owned at least twenty slaves would have been compelled to turn over one in every twenty for use as enlistment bounties. As adopted, the law required all taxpayers to contribute in their usual proportions toward purchasing the human bounties. "An Act for Recruiting this State's Quota of Troops to Serve in the Continental Army," in Hening, ed., *Statutes at Large* 10:326–37; McDonnell, *Politics of War*, 389, 394–95; Philyaw, "Slave for Every Soldier."

17. Garret Van Meter to Thomas Jefferson, April 11 (quotation), 14, 20, 1781, Commissioners for Collecting Taxes in Accomac County to Jefferson, May 15, 1781, *Founders Online*; McDonnell, *Politics of War*, 412, 445–62 (with resistance to taxes, not just the draft, on 455–59).

18. Benjamin Harrison to Washington, Feb. 25, 1781, George Washington to Benjamin Harrison, March 21, 1781, *Founders Online*; Shorto, *Revolution Song*, 379.

19. Franklin and Wharton, memorial to Congress, Feb. 26, 1780, *Founders Online*. Several members of Congress were given shares in the company; Paine received three hundred. Kukla, *Patrick Henry*, 229.

20. Jefferson to Samuel Huntington, Jan. 17, 1781 (including editors' notes), *Founders Online*; Sioussat and Maccubbin, "Chevalier de la Luzerne and the Ratification of the Articles of Confederation by Maryland," 391, 402–3.

21. Greene, quoted in Ferguson, "General Andrew Pickens," 116.

22. Morgan to Greene, Jan. 15, 178[1], in *Papers of General Nathanael Greene* 7:126n, 127, 129n, 145n.

23. Morgan, quoted in Piecuch, *Three Peoples, One King*, 240; *Papers of General Nathanael Greene* 7:157n.

24. Morgan to Greene, Jan. 19, 1781, in *Papers of General Nathanael Greene* 7:153, 157n; Robertson, "Burr's Mill Found?"; Babits, *Devil of a Whipping*, 156; Sellick, "'They Were Marched Almost Day and Night,'" 111–25.

25. Marshall, *Life of George Washington* 1:402; Saye, *Memoirs of Major Joseph McJunkin*, 32–33; Ferguson, "General Andrew Pickens," 127–28.

26. Johnson, *Sketches of the Life and Correspondence of Nathanael Greene* 1:377–78; Greene, *Papers of General Nathanael Greene* 7:157n.

27. Morgan to William Snickers, Jan. 26, 1781, Horatio Gates Papers, N-YHS; Morgan, quoted in Johnson, *Traditions and Reminiscences*, 450; Johnson, *Sketches of the Life and Correspondence of Nathanael Greene* 1:372, 378, 380 (third quotation); Higginbotham, *Daniel Morgan*, 137.

28. Johnson, *Sketches of the Life and Correspondence of Nathanael Greene*, 1:381.

29. John Eager Howard, quoted in *Papers of General Nathanael Greene* 7:159n; Anderson, quoted in Babits, *Devil of a Whipping*, 113; Spring, *With Zeal and with Bayonets Only*, 139–44 (quotation at 139).

30. Daniel Morgan to William Snickers, Jan. 26, 1781, Horatio Gates Papers, N-YHS; Lee, *Campaign of 1781 in the Carolinas*, 97n–98n; Johnson, *Sketches of the Life and Correspondence of Nathanael Greene* 1:380; Higginbotham, *Daniel Morgan*, 140; Babits, *Devil of a Whipping*, 120.

31. Tarleton, *History of the Campaigns of 1780 and 1781*, 224.

32. Morgan to Greene, Jan. 19, 1781, in *Papers of General Nathanael Greene* 7:154; Higginbotham, *Daniel Morgan*, 141.

33. Greene, *Papers of General Nathanael Greene* 7:160–61n; Higginbotham, *Daniel Morgan*, 154. Babits found the names of twenty-four Americans who were killed at Cowpens but emphasizes that there must have been many more, since the data comes from Morgan, who did not count militia in either his troop strength or his casualties. Babits estimates that at least 104 were wounded. Babits, *Devil of a Whipping*, 151–52; Piecuch, *Three Peoples, One King*, 270.

34. Morgan to William Snickers, Jan. 26, 1781, Horatio Gates Papers, N-YHS; Morgan, quoted in Johnson, *Sketches of the Life and Correspondence of Nathanael Greene* 1:376.

35. Cornwallis to Germain, March 17, 1781, in Davies, ed., *Documents of the American Revolution* 20:86.

36. Cornwallis to Rawdon, Feb. 4, 1781, *Correspondence of Charles, First Marquis Cornwallis* 1:83; Cornwallis to Germain, March 17, 1781, in Davies, ed., *Documents of the American Revolution* 20:85–87.

37. Philbrick, *In the Hurricane's Eye*, 87–94.

38. Lee, *Memoirs of the War in the Southern Department of the United States* 1:301.

39. Lee later claimed that he had intended to capture the Loyalists, not kill them, but was forced by circumstances to alter his plan. Lee, *Memoirs of the War in the Southern Department of the United States* 1:308–13 (quotation at 311), 322. Philbrick believes both sides were stunned to discover that they were among enemies—but that Lee's Continentals figured it out first. Philbrick, *In the Hurricane's Eye*, 94–95.

40. Lee, *Memoirs of the War in the Southern Department of the United States* 1:336–39; Buchanan, *Road to Guilford Courthouse*, 372–73; Babits and Howard, *Long, Obstinate, and Bloody*, 51, 77.

41. Greene to Samuel Huntington, March 16, 1781, in *Papers of General Nathanael Greene* 7:434; Babits and Howard, *Long, Obstinate, and Bloody*, 77.

42. Moreover, Greene knew or ought to have known better than to expect riflemen, whose weapons took more than a minute to reload and carried no bayonet, to stick around after two shots or, depending on how quickly the enemy advanced, even one. Weller, "Irregular but Effective," 131; Buchanan, *Road to Guilford Courthouse*, 375; Babits and Howard, *Long, Obstinate, and Bloody*, 110–14; Spring, *With Zeal and with Bayonets Only*, 204.

43. Babits and Howard, *Long, Obstinate, and Bloody*, 129.

44. The Virginians also had several other advantages over the North Carolinians. A higher percentage of them had combat experience; unable to see the entire British army, they were less prone to intimidation; and many had had time to assemble downed logs into makeshift breastworks. Babits and Howard, *Long, Obstinate, and Bloody*, 120; Babits, guide, Battle of Guilford Courthouse Staff Ride for battalion commanders at U.S. Army Training Center, Fort Jackson, March 14, 2018.

45. Babits and Howard, *Long, Obstinate, and Bloody*, 152.

46. Babits and Howard concede that British case shot may have hit some of the Guards but contend that any such friendly fire was accidental. Babits and Howard, *Long, Obstinate, and Bloody*, 161–62. One reason to doubt Lee is that he is known to have enhanced other scenes of the war, claiming, for instance, that John Champe, the principal in the U.S. plot to kidnap Benedict Arnold, believed that by bringing him in he could persuade Washington not to execute John André. Actually, the Americans hanged André eighteen days before Champe fake-deserted to the British in order to get close to Arnold. Lee, *Memoirs of the War in the Southern Department of the United States* 1:347–48, 353n, 2:181; Van Doren, *Secret History of the American Revolution*, 392–94.

47. Greene to Samuel Huntington, March 16, 1781, in *Papers of General Nathanael Greene* 7:435; Babits and Howard, *Long, Obstinate, and Bloody*, 164–65.

48. Henry Lee stated that Greene could have made the Battle of Guilford Courthouse "a drawn day" or even "secured to himself the victory." *Memoirs of the War in the Southern Department of the United States* 1:350–51.

49. Greene, orders, March 16, 1781, in *Papers of Nathanael Greene* 7:431–33; Lafayette to La Luzerne, March 23, 1781, "Letters from Lafayette to Luzerne," 596; Washington to Greene, April 18, 1781, *Founders Online*.

50. Greene reported more than one thousand of his soldiers were missing; I do not treat them as casualties, since most appear to have been militiamen who simply went home. Ward, *War of the Revolution* 2:793; Babits and Howard, *Long, Obstinate, and Bloody*, 173–75.

51. Freeman, Carroll, and Ashworth, *George Washington*, 5:274n; Raphael, *Founders*, 371.

52. Ward, *War of the Revolution* 2:797–99.

53. Ramsay, *History of the Revolution of South-Carolina* 2:229; Lee, *Memoirs of the War in the Southern Department of the United States* 2:51.

54. Buchanan, *Road to Charleston*, 82–83.

55. Samuel Mathis to W[illiam] R. Davie, June 26, 1819, in Lossing, ed., *American Historical Record* 2:106.

56. Buchanan, *Road to Charleston*, 85–103 (quotation at 102); Greene to Washington, May 1, 1781, *Founders Online*; Rawdon to Cornwallis, April 25, 1781, *Correspondence of Charles, First Marquis Cornwallis* 1:97.

57. Lee, *Memoirs of the War in the Southern Department of the United States* 2:73; Ward, *War of the Revolution* 2:800–11; Piecuch, *Three Peoples, One King*, 269; Buchanan, *Road to Charleston*, 108.

58. Lee states that Motte's bow and arrows had been "imported from India." Ramsay, *History of the Revolution of South-Carolina* 2:233–34 (first, third, and fourth quotations); Lee, *Memoirs of the War in the Southern Department of the United States* 2:73–80 (second quotation in text at 73; quotation in note at 77), 86–87; Helsley, "Rebecca Brewton Motte," 109–26; Ward, *War of the Revolution* 2:812; Smith et al., "Obstinate and Strong," 24–26; Keenan, "In Search of Granby," 29–31; Smith et al., "Two Revolutionary War Expedient Fire Arrows from Archeological Contexts in South Carolina."

59. Oswald, *Memorandum on the Folly of Invading Virginia*, 32–33; Romans, *Concise Natural History of East and West-Florida*, 92; thespruce.com/cornmeal-vs-grits-vs-polenta-1328613.

Chapter 30: Nothing but a Treaty

1. Cornwallis to Germain, April 23, 1781, *Correspondence of Charles, First Marquis Cornwallis* 1:94; Ramsay, *History of the Revolution of South-Carolina* 2:224.

2. Cornwallis, quoted in Babits and Howard, *Long, Obstinate, and Bloody*, 180.

3. An eighteenth-century European "army's maximum operational range" was "about fifteen to twenty miles from navigable water." Cornwallis to Clinton, April 10, 1781, Cornwallis to Germain, April 18, 1781, in Davies, ed., *Documents of the American Revolution* 20:108, 113; Cornwallis to Clinton, June 30, 1781, *Correspondence of Charles, First Marquis Cornwallis* 1:102; Spring, *With Zeal and with Bayonets Only*, 35.

4. Cornwallis to Clinton, June 30, Aug. 20, 1781, *Correspondence of Charles, First Marquis Cornwallis* 1:102, 114; Urwin, "When Freedom Wore a Red Coat," 9. In similar fashion, "the want of a water conveyance"—that is, the lack of navigable rivers—in Massachusetts had, back at the start of the war, contributed to William Howe's decision to move to New York. Howe to Dartmouth, Oct. 9, 1775, in Davies, ed., *Documents of the American Revolution* 11:139.

5. Cornwallis to Germain, April 23, 1781, Cornwallis to Phillips, April 10, 1781, *Correspondence of Charles, First Marquis Cornwallis* 1:94, 87. J. R. McNeill (*Mosquito Empires*, 219) and Peter McCandless (*Slavery, Disease, and Suffering in the Southern Lowcountry*, 98–101) powerfully demonstrate the influence of disease on the southern campaigns of the Revolutionary War but err in attributing Cornwallis's move north to his concern about "the fatal Sickness, which so nearly ruined the Army last Autumn." As McNeill acknowledges, Cornwallis stated that escaping disease would have meant moving to "the upper parts of the Country"—the west—rather than Tidewater Virginia. Cornwallis to Clinton, April 10, 1781, in Stevens, *Campaign in Virginia* 1:398.

6. "A View of the Strength of the Two Armies (Regular and Provincial) Acting Under the Commander-in-chief and Lieutenant-General Earl Cornwallis, At Different Periods of the Years 1780 and 1781, and of the Regular Force of the Enemy, French and Americans," in Stevens, *Campaign in Virginia* 2:228.

7. DuVal, *Independence Lost*, 167–71, 188–218.

8. Washington, diary, May 22, 1781, Washington to Benjamin Harrison, March 27, 1781, Washington to Lafayette, May 31, 1781, Washington to Greene, June 1, 1781, *Founders Online*.

9. Washington to John Laurens, April 9, 1781, *Founders Online*; Clinton to Cornwallis, June 8, 1781, in Stevens, *Campaign in Virginia* 2:14–15; Freeman, Carroll, and Ashworth, *George Washington* 5:291; O'Shaughnessy, *Men Who Lost America*, 249.

10. Rochambeau told Washington that he had advised de Grasse to make a brief stopover

in Chesapeake Bay to confront a British navy squadron before moving on to New York; actually Rochambeau had recommended that de Grasse sail to Virginia *instead of* New York. The French ministry shared Rochambeau's skepticism of Washington's plan to attack British headquarters in New York. Rochambeau to de Grasse, May 28, 1781, in Doniol, *Histoire de la Participation de la France à l'établissement des États-Unis d'Amérique* 5:475; John Laurens to Washington, April 11, 1781, Rochambeau to Washington, June 10, 1781, *Founders Online*; Selby, *Revolution in Virginia*, 294.

11. "A View of the Strength of the Two Armies (Regular and Provincial) Acting Under the Commander-in-chief and Lieutenant-General Earl Cornwallis, At Different Periods of the Years 1780 and 1781, and of the Regular Force of the Enemy, French and Americans," in Stevens, *Campaign in Virginia* 2:228.

12. Selby, *Revolution in Virginia*, 269–74.

13. June 21, 1781, in Ewald, *Diary of the American War*, 305.

14. Cornwallis to Phillips, April 10, 1781, *Correspondence of Charles, First Marquis Cornwallis* 1:87. Gottschalk shows that David Ramsay probably invented the disdainful boast that he, Henry Lee, and other authors attributed to Cornwallis: "The boy cannot escape me." Lee, *Memoirs of the War in the Southern Department of the United States* 2:198; Ramsay, *History of the Revolution of South-Carolina* 2:314; Gottschalk, *Lafayette in America* 3:431–32; Lengel, *General George Washington*, 330.

15. Lafayette to Washington, May 24, 1781, *Founders Online*.

16. *Simcoe's Military Journal*, 217–20, 223.

17. Babits and Howard, *Long, Obstinate, and Bloody*, 187; Boles, *Jefferson*, 99–100.

18. Tarleton, *History of the Campaigns of 1780 and 1781*, 305; Lee, *Memoirs of the War in the Southern Department of the United States* 2:210; encyclopediavirginia.org/Jack_Jouett_s_Ride_1781; Taylor, *American Revolutions*, 241.

19. Lee, *Memoirs of the War in the Southern Department of the United States* 2:104n; Cashin, *King's Ranger*, 133–35.

20. Lee, *Memoirs of the War in the Southern Department of the United States* 2:105–7, 117; Cashin, *King's Ranger*, 135–36.

21. Lee, *Memoirs of the War in the Southern Department of the United States* 2:104–10 (quotation at 109); Morris, *Peacemakers*, 188; Buchanan, *Road to Charleston*, 135.

22. Stedman, *History of the Origin, Progress, and Termination of the American War* 2:370; Ward, *War of the Revolution* 2:820.

23. Nisbet Balfour to Germain, June 27, 1781, in Davies, ed., *Documents of the American Revolution* 20:164; Ward, *War of the Revolution* 2:820–23; Greene, *Ninety Six*, 119–73.

24. Pybus, "Jefferson's Faulty Math," 245–46.

25. Clinton to Cornwallis, June 8, 11, 15, 1781, in Stevens, *Campaign in Virginia* 2:15, 19–21, 25 (quotation); H. Brodrick to Thomas Townshend, Sept. 30, 1781, *Correspondence of Charles, First Marquis Cornwallis* 1:122.

26. Clinton to Germain, July 13, 1781, in Davies, ed., *Documents of the American Revolution* 20:186; Greene, *Guns of Independence*, 10.

27. Cornwallis even raised the possibility of returning to Charles Town, South Carolina, abandoning Virginia altogether. Cornwallis to Leslie, June 27, 28, 1781, Cornwallis to Clinton, June 30, 1781, *Correspondence of Charles, First Marquis Cornwallis* 1:101–4 (quotation at 103); Gottschalk, *Lafayette in America* 3:277.

28. Tarleton, *History of the Campaigns of 1780 and 1781*, 363; Wickwire and Wickwire, *Cornwallis*, 343.

29. Lee, *Memoirs of the War in the Southern Department of the United States* 2:223–25; Johnston, *Yorktown Campaign and the Surrender of Cornwallis*, 60–62.

30. George Hanger, quoted in Spring, *With Zeal and with Bayonets Only*, 243.

31. Johnston, *Yorktown Campaign and the Surrender of Cornwallis*, 66–67; Selby, *Revolution in Virginia*, 290–91.

32. Cornwallis to Leslie, July 8, 1781, *Correspondence of Charles, First Marquis Cornwallis* 1:105.

33. Joseph Jones to Washington, May 31, 1781, Washington to Jefferson, June 8, 1781, *Founders Online*.

34. Whittemore, *General of the Revolution*, 165–66; Morris, *Peacemakers*, 210–11.

35. "Instructions to the Honourable John Adams, Benjamin Franklin, John Jay, Henry Laurens and Thomas Jefferson, Ministers Plenipotentiary on Behalf of the United States of America to Negotiate a Treaty of Peace," June 15, 1781, *JCC* 20:651–52; Morris, *Peacemakers*, 214–16.

36. Lafayette to Washington, July 20, 1781, *Founders Online*. As Banastre Tarleton, one of Cornwallis's officers, acknowledged, Lafayette's maneuver also "animated the drooping spirits of the Virginians." Tarleton, *History of the Campaigns of 1780 and 1781*, 308.

37. Lafayette to Washington, July 20, 1781, *Founders Online*; Ellison, "James Armistead Lafayette," 401.

38. Graham, *Life of General Daniel Morgan*, 378–80.

39. Dorsey Pentecost to [William] Moore, May 18, 1782, *Pennsylvania Archives*, Ser. 1, 9:545; Johnson, *Sketches of the Life and Correspondence of Nathanael Greene* 2:393.

40. Clinton to Germain, July 13, 1781, in Davies, ed., *Documents of the American Revolution* 20:186–87; Clinton to Cornwallis, July 11, 1781, in Stevens, *Campaign in Virginia* 2:63–64; Cornwallis to Leslie, July 20, 1781, *Correspondence of Charles, First Marquis Cornwallis* 1:106; *Simcoe's Military Journal*, 239; Wickwire and Wickwire, *Cornwallis*, 349.

41. Lafayette to Washington, July 31, 1781, *Founders Online*; Selby, *Revolution in Virginia*, 291–93. John Salmon points out that while historians often give "Armistead," the name of the family that owned James, as his middle or last name, there is no evidence he ever used that name. Salmon, "'A Mission of the Most Secret and Important Kind,'" 78–85; John Salmon and the Dictionary of Virginia Biography, "Lafayette, James (ca. 1748–1830)," *Encyclopedia Virginia*.

42. Cornwallis to O'Hara, Aug. 4, 1781, *Correspondence of Charles, First Marquis Cornwallis* 1:112; O'Hara to Cornwallis, Aug. 9, 1781, quoted in Sellick, "'Undistinguished Destruction,'" 882; Glickstein, *After Yorktown*, 13–14; Brown, *Moral Capital*, 276, 307; Brown, "Atlantic Slave Trade and the American Revolution."

43. Sellick, "'Undistinguished Destruction,'" 882.

44. One of Cornwallis's letters noted that Clinton's rationale for appropriating nearly half of his troops rapidly evolved: in mid-June he claimed to fear an Anglo-French siege of New York, but within two weeks he acknowledged needing the reinforcements for a (later aborted) move against Philadelphia. Cornwallis to Rawdon, July 23, 1781, *Correspondence of Charles, First Marquis Cornwallis* 1:106; Cornwallis to Clinton, July 27, 1781, Clinton to Cornwallis, Aug. 2, 1781, in Stevens, *Campaign in Virginia* 2:104–19.

45. Lee, *Memoirs of the War in the Southern Department of the United States* 2:283n; Johnson, *Sketches of the Life and Correspondence of Nathanael Greene* 2:242; Ward, *War of the Revolution* 2:826–27; Buchanan, *Road to Charleston*, 215–34.

46. Johnson, *Sketches of the Life and Correspondence of Nathanael Greene* 2:232, 236.

47. Jefferson to Clark, Jan. 1 (first quotation), Dec. 25, 1780 (fourth quotation), Jefferson to Washington, Dec. 13, 1780 (second and third quotations), *Founders Online*.

48. Martha Wayles Skelton Jefferson to Eleanor Conway Madison, Aug. 8, 1780, *Founders Online*.

49. John Smith to Thomas Jefferson, Feb. 9, 1781, Washington, diary, June 9, 1781, *Founders Online*.

50. Haldimand to Germain, Oct. 23, 1781, in Davies, ed., *Documents of the American Revolution* 20:248.

51. Kelsay, *Joseph Brant*, 307–14; Taylor, *Divided Ground*, 94.

52. Irvine to Washington, Feb. 7, 1782, *Founders Online*.

53. Haldimand to Germain, Oct. 23, 1781, in Davies, ed., *Documents of the American Revolution* 20:248.

54. John Gibson to George Washington, Sept. 30, 1781, *Founders Online*; Loskiel, *History of the Mission of the United Brethren Among the Indians in North America* 3:154; McDonnell, "Struggle Within," 116.

Chapter 31: Surrenders

1. Washington to Rochambeau, June 30, 1781, Washington to Samuel Huntington, July 6, 1781, Washington, diary, June 28, 1781, *Founders Online*.

2. Ward, *War of the Revolution* 2:880–81.

3. July 9, 1781, *Revolutionary Journal of Baron Ludwig von Closen*, 91–92.

4. Washington to Henry Laurens, March 7–8, 1778, Washington, diary, Aug. 1, 1781, *Founders Online*.

5. Washington, diary, July 23, 1781, *Founders Online* (editors' note).

6. Baugh, "Sir Samuel Hood," 303–4; Dull, *French Navy and American Independence*, 238; O'Shaughnessy, *Empire Divided*, 213–31; O'Shaughnessy, *Men Who Lost America*, 308–9.

7. Richard Peters, quoted in Simpson, *Lives of Eminent Philadelphians*, 707; Washington, diary, Aug. 14, 1781, *Founders Online*; Dull, *French Navy and American Independence*, 243–45; Buchanan, *Road to Charleston*, 213.

8. Washington, diary, Aug. 30, 19 (Jonathan Trumbull, quoted in footnote), 1781, *Founders Online*; Martin, *Narrative of Some of the Adventures, Dangers, and Sufferings of a Revolutionary Soldier*, 160; Clinton to Cornwallis, Sept. 2, 1781, in Stevens, *Campaign in Virginia* 2:149–50; Ketchum, *Victory at Yorktown*, 163.

9. Washington to Morris, Aug. 27, 17, 1781, Washington to Lafayette, July 30, 1781, *Founders Online*; Martin, *Narrative of Some of the Adventures, Dangers, and Sufferings of a Revolutionary Soldier*, 161. Robert Morris also detected "great symptoms of discontent" in the army. Quoted in Philbrick, *In the Hurricane's Eye*, 308n.

10. Martin, *Narrative of Some of the Adventures, Dangers, and Sufferings of a Revolutionary Soldier*, 162; Ketchum, *Victory at Yorktown*, 178; Philbrick, *In the Hurricane's Eye*, 199.

11. Lewis, "Las Damas de La Havana," 85–86, 93–97.

12. Clinton to Cornwallis, Sept. 6, 1781, in Stevens, *Campaign in Virginia* 2:152–53; Ewald, *Diary of the American War*, 431n.

13. Oct. 14, 1781, in Ewald, *Diary of the American War*, 336.

14. Martin, *Narrative of Some of the Adventures, Dangers, and Sufferings of a Revolution-*

ary Soldier, 166–67; Johnston, *Yorktown Campaign and the Surrender of Cornwallis*, 131.

15. Oct. 8 and 9, 1781, in Thacher, *Military Journal During the American Revolutionary War*, 339; Martin, *Narrative of Some of the Adventures, Dangers, and Sufferings of a Revolutionary Soldier*, 167; Johnston, *Yorktown Campaign and the Surrender of Cornwallis*, 131–32.

16. Ketchum, *Victory at Yorktown*, 228, 236.

17. Martin, *Narrative of Some of the Adventures, Dangers, and Sufferings of a Revolutionary Soldier*, 168.

18. Martin, *Narrative of Some of the Adventures, Dangers, and Sufferings of a Revolutionary Soldier*, 173; Johnston, *Yorktown Campaign and the Surrender of Cornwallis*, 141.

19. Aedanus Burke to Arthur Middleton, Oct. 9, 1781, "Correspondence of Hon. Arthur Middleton" (Oct. 1925), 185.

20. Cornwallis to Clinton, Sept. 16, 1781, *Correspondence of Charles, First Marquis Cornwallis* 1:119; Ewald, *Diary of the American War*, 335–36; Oct. 3–4, 1781, in Thacher, *Military Journal During the American Revolutionary War*, 337; Martin, *Narrative of Some of the Adventures, Dangers, and Sufferings of a Revolutionary Soldier*, 174.

21. Washington, diary, Oct. 12, 1781, *Founders Online*; Martin, *Narrative of Some of the Adventures, Dangers, and Sufferings of a Revolutionary Soldier*, 169; Johnston, *Yorktown Campaign and the Surrender of Cornwallis*, 140–41.

22. Lee, *Memoirs of the War in the Southern Department of the United States* 2:342n; Johnston, *Yorktown Campaign and the Surrender of Cornwallis*, 143–45; Greene, *Guns of Independence*, 238; Burdick, "What They Saw and Did at Yorktown's Redoubts 9 and 10."

23. Philbrick, *In the Hurricane's Eye*, 216.

24. Aedanus Burke to Arthur Middleton, Oct. 16, 1781, Middleton, "Correspondence of Hon. Arthur Middleton" (October 1925), 186; Martin, *Narrative of Some of the Adventures, Dangers, and Sufferings of a Revolutionary Soldier*, 170; Alexander Hamilton to Lafayette, [Oct. 15, 1781], *Founders Online*; Nash, *Unknown American Revolution*, 230.

25. George Washington to Thomas McKean, Oct. 16, 1781, *Founders Online*.

26. Freeman, Carroll, and Ashworth, *George Washington* 5:371–73

27. Cornwallis candidly acknowledged the necessity of "leaving a detachment to capitulate for the town's people, and the sick and wounded." Cornwallis to Clinton, Oct. 20, 1781, in Stevens, *Campaign in Virginia* 2:212; Ketchum, *Victory at Yorktown*, 238.

28. Henry Knox to Lucy Knox, Oct. 19, 1781, *Revolutionary War Lives and Letters of Lucy and Henry Knox*, 160.

29. As Washington knew he would, Cornwallis used the defeated commander's customary prerogative of sending off one ship (or "covered wagon," in the case of inland surrenders) uninspected to protect the white Loyalists who faced the greatest danger of being executed by the rebels. Articles of Capitulation Between Washington and Cornwallis, Oct. 19, 1781, *Founders Online*; Germain to Clinton, Jan. 2, 1782, in Davies, ed., *Documents of the American Revolution* 21:27.

30. Everyone in the allied armies believed Cornwallis, who had never lost a battle since arriving in America five years earlier, was faking indisposition to avoid this mortifying scene. But like many of his troops, he had frequently been sick during his nearly two years in the south, and he may have been legitimately disabled on Oct. 19. According to an 1828 report, the British troops marched out to a tune called "The World Turned Upside Down," but it was not mentioned by anyone in 1781, so historians doubt the

claim. Schrader, "'World Turned Upside Down'"; McNeill, *Mosquito Empires*, 226–27; O'Shaughnessy, *Men Who Lost America*, 281; Glickstein, *After Yorktown*, 20.

31. Ketchum, *Victory at Yorktown*, 252–53.

32. Ketchum, *Victory at Yorktown*, 256; Cornwallis, quoted in John Salmon and the *Dictionary of Virginia Biography*, "Lafayette, James (ca. 1748–1830)," *Encyclopedia Virginia*; Saul, petition to the Virginia State Legislature, with endorsement, Oct. 9, 1792, in Holton, *Black Americans in the Revolutionary Era*, 62–63.

33. Occasional exchanges kept down the number of U.S. *soldiers* in British prisons before 1782; it often approached zero. But there are many fewer estimates of captive American *sailors*. John Beatty to Washington, July 18, 1778, George Washington to Robert Howe, Oct. 14, 1779, Benjamin Lincoln to George Washington, Dec. 23, 1779, [Joshua] Loring to [Abraham] Skinner, June 21[*sic*], 1780, enclosed in William Phillips to Washington, June 19, 1780, *Founders Online*; Davies and Harrison, *Report of Commissioners for Settling a Cartel for the Exchange of Prisoners*, 3–4; Knight, "Prisoner Exchange and Parole in the American Revolution," 220; Burrows, *Forgotten Patriots*, 183–86, 197–203; Watson, *Ghost Ship of Brooklyn*, 141.

34. Gottschalk, *Lafayette in America* 3:324–25; Taylor, *American Revolutions*, 296, 294.

35. Sanderson diary, Oct. 22, 1781, in Johnston, *Yorktown Campaign and the Surrender of Cornwallis*, 172; Martin, *Narrative of Some of the Adventures, Dangers, and Sufferings of a Revolutionary Soldier*, 174–75; Oct. 22, 1781, in Thacher, *Military Journal During the American Revolutionary War*, 349–50; Egerton, *Death or Liberty*, 198; Piecuch, *Three Peoples, One King*, 308–9.

36. Pybus, "Jefferson's Faulty Math," 245–46; Jones, *Born a Child of Freedom, yet a Slave*.

37. Shyllon, *Black Slaves in Britain*, 184–99; Brown, *Moral Capital*, 283–84; Walvin, *Zong*, 68–69, 71, 92, 95. The *Zong* incident was by no means unique. Brekus, *Sarah Osborn's World*, 311.

38. O'Brien, "Did the Jennison Case Outlaw Slavery in Massachusetts?"; Zilversmit, "Quok Walker, Mumbet, and the Abolition of Slavery in Massachusetts"; Massachusetts Constitution and the Abolition of Slavery, mass.gov/guides/massachusetts-constitution-and-the-abolition-of-slavery.

39. O'Brien, "Did the Jennison Case Outlaw Slavery in Massachusetts?"; Zilversmit, "Quok Walker, Mumbet, and the Abolition of Slavery in Massachusetts"; Spector, "Quock Walker Cases"; Higginbotham, *In the Matter of Color*, 91–99.

40. Massachusetts constitution, March 2, 1780, press-pubs.uchicago.edu/founders/print _documents/v1ch1s6.html; Cushing, charge to the jury in the Case of Quok Walker, in Holton, *Black Americans in the Revolutionary Era*, 78–79; Higginbotham, *In the Matter of Color*, 91–98; Blanck, "Seventeen Eighty-Three," 28–29.

41. William Smith, will, Sept. 12, 1783, Abigail Adams to John Adams, Nov. 29, 1798, *Founders Online*; Holton, "Abigail Adams on 'The Only Surviving Parent I Have.'"

42. Wikipedia.org/wiki/Goodridge_v._Department_of_Public_Health.

43. Congress gave Superintendent of Finance Robert Morris discretion to allow states to meet their quotas by supplying the army, and he exercised this authority in the case of South Carolina. Oct. 29, 30, 1781, *JCC* 21:1081, 1087–88; Johnson, *Sketches of the Life and Correspondence of Nathanael Greene* 2:311.

44. *Papers of Robert Morris* 2:340n, 3:90n; Rappleye, *Robert Morris*, 278.

45. Eacott, *Selling Empire*, 187–88; Rappleye, *Robert Morris*, 259.

46. Philadelphia dateline, *Pennsylvania Gazette*, Sept. 5, 1787.

47. Foner, *Tom Paine and Revolutionary America*, 161, 189–91; Rappleye, *Robert Morris*, 293–97.

48. George Germain, quoted in Shorto, *Revolution Song*, 395; "Extract from Wraxall's 'Memoirs' Describing Reception of the News by the Home Cabinet," in Johnston, *Yorktown Campaign and the Surrender of Cornwallis*, 180.

49. Wraxall, *Historical Memoirs of My Own Times*, 398.

50. The bonds referred to here paid 3 percent interest, but others depreciated at about the same rate. Wright, "British Objectives," 11; Ketchum, *Victory at Yorktown*, 275; O'Shaughnessy, *Men Who Lost America*, 77; Thomas, *Lord North*, 100.

51. Thomas, *Lord North*, 117–22; Christie, *Wars and Revolutions*, 131–33; Lockwood, *To Begin the World Over Again*, 84–85, 89–91.

52. Christie, *Wars and Revolutions*, 141–42.

53. British military expenditures increased from £17 million in 1781 to £20 million in 1782. Mitchell, *British Historical Statistics*, 579–80; Sutherland, *East India Company in Eighteenth-Century Politics*, 362–63, 374–75; Marshall, *Making and Unmaking of Empires*, 220, 369; Glickstein, *After Yorktown*, 335–39.

54. Shelburne to Carleton, June 25, 1782 (extract), in John Jay to Robert Livingston, Nov. 17, 1782, in Wharton, ed., *Revolutionary Diplomatic Correspondence of the United States* 6:15–16; Bemis, *Diplomacy of the American Revolution*, 204.

Chapter 32: To Amend and Perfect

1. David, *Dunmore's New World*, 133–36; Taylor, *American Revolutions*, 267–73.

2. Dull, *French Navy and American Independence*, 283–84; O'Shaughnessy, *Men Who Lost America*, 314–17; Glickstein, *After Yorktown*, 238–44.

3. O'Shaughnessy, *Men Who Lost America*, 315.

4. O'Shaughnessy, *Men Who Lost America*, 315–17.

5. Dull, *Diplomatic History of the American Revolution*, 132, 142; Mapp, "Revolutionary War and Europe's Great Powers," 323; O'Shaughnessy, *Men Who Lost America*, 292.

6. Butterfield, ed., *Washington-Irvine Correspondence*, 101n; Loskiel, *History of the Mission of the United Brethren Among the Indians in North America* 3:171, 184.

7. Other militiamen rounded up the people of nearby Salem and brought them to Gnadenhutten; residents of Schoenbrunn, the third Moravian town, received timely warning and escaped into the woods. "Relation of what Frederick Leinbach was told by two of his neighbors . . . who were just returned from the Monongahela," in Butterfield, ed., *Washington-Irvine Correspondence*, 237n; Loskiel, *History of the Mission of the United Brethren Among the Indians in North America*, 3:176–82.

8. Loskiel, *History of the Mission of the United Brethren Among the Indians in North America* 3:179–83 (quotation at 180); Irvine to his wife, April 12, 1782, "Relation of what Frederick Leinbach was told by two of his neighbors . . . who were just returned from the Monongahela," in Butterfield, ed., *Washington-Irvine Correspondence*, 343, 237n–38n; Dorsey Pentecost to [William] Moore, May 8, 9, 1782, *Pennsylvania Archives*, Ser. 1, 9:540–41; Slaughter, *Whiskey Rebellion*, 75–78; White, *Middle Ground*, 389–90.

9. Irvine to Washington, April 20, 1782, *Founders Online*; Irvine to his wife, April 12, 1782, in Butterfield, ed., *Washington-Irvine Correspondence*, 344–45; Dowd, *Spirited Resistance*, 86.

10. Pentecost to Moore, June 17, 1782, in Butterfield, ed., *Washington-Irvine Correspondence*, 292n; Irvine to Washington, May 21, 1782, *Founders Online*; Butterfield, *Historical Account of the Expedition Against Sandusky Under Col. William Crawford in 1782*, 56, 84, 163; Calloway, *Indian World of George Washington*, 185.

11. John Turney to Major A[rent] DePeyster, June 7, 1782, in Butterfield, ed., *Washington-Irvine Correspondence*, 369n.

12. Knight, quoted in William Croghan to William Davies, July 6, 1782, DePeyster to Thomas Brown, July 18, 1782, in Butterfield, ed., *Washington-Irvine Correspondence*, 293n, 372n; unnamed Delaware Indians, quoted in Heckewelder, *Narrative of the Mission of the United Brethren Among the Delaware and Mohegan Indians*, 338, 340 (quotation); White, *Middle Ground*, 394–95.

13. Ephraim Douglass to [?], July 26, 1782, Michael Huffnagle to Irvine, July 14, 1782, in Butterfield, ed., *Washington-Irvine Correspondence*, 251–52n, 381; Jones, "Herman Husband," 279; Crytzer, *Guyasuta and the Fall of Indian America*, 216–8; Graymont, *Iroquois in the American Revolution*, 255; Kelsay, *Joseph Brant*, 327–28.

14. Faragher, *Daniel Boone*, 216–17.

15. John Brady, Daniel Boone, quoted in Faragher, *Daniel Boone*, 215, 218.

16. Harrison, *George Rogers Clark and the War in the West*, 88; Faragher, *Daniel Boone*, 92–93, 216–22.

17. Carleton to Washington, Sept. 12, 1782, Washington to William Moore, Sept. 23, 1782, *Founders Online*; Irvine to George Rogers Clark, Nov. 7, 1782, in Butterfield, ed., *Washington-Irvine Correspondence*, 400.

18. William Irvine to George Washington, Dec. 2, 1781, *Founders Online*; Butterfield, *Historical Account of the Expedition Against Sandusky Under Col. William Crawford in 1782*, 26; Kellogg, ed., *Frontier Advance on the Upper Ohio*, 17–18; wikipedia.org/wiki /Battle_of_Blue_Licks.

19. Posey, *General Thomas Posey*, 83–84; McDonnell, *Politics of War*, 513–14.

20. Thomas Posey and four others, memorial to Christian Febiger, Nov. 17, 1781, enclosed in Arthur St. Clair to Washington, Nov. 26, 1781, Washington to St. Clair, Nov. 30, 1781, Washington to Febiger, Jan. 12, 1782, *Founders Online*; Posey, *General Thomas Posey*, 83–90. For a different reading of the five officers' letter, see Nagy, *Rebellion in the Ranks*, 186.

21. "We the Honest Politicians" to Virginia officers, [January 1782?], enclosed in Benjamin Harrison to Washington, Feb. 8, 1782, Febiger to Washington, March 14, 1782, Feb. 10, 1782, St. Clair to Washington, Nov. 14, 1781, Thomas Posey to George Washington, Feb. 11, 1782, *Founders Online*; "An Act to Adjust and Regulate the Pay and Accounts of the Officers and Soldiers of the Virginia Line . . . ," in Hening, ed., *Statutes at Large* 10:463–64.

22. McCrady, *History of South Carolina in the Revolution*, 620–23 (quotation from mutineers' placard at 621); Lee, *Memoirs of the War in the Southern Department of the United States* 2:417–21 (quotation at 418); Charles Cotesworth Pinckney to Arthur Middleton, April 24, 1782, *Papers of the Revolutionary Era Pinckney Statesmen*; Johnson, *Sketches of the Life and Correspondence of Nathanael Greene* 2:295, 319–20; Nash, *Unknown American Revolution*, 370.

23. Edward Rutledge to Arthur Middleton, April 23–24, 1782, "Correspondence of Hon. Arthur Middleton" (Jan. 1926), 14; Seymour, *Journal of the Southern Expedition*, 35; April 21, 1782, "Extracts from the Journal of Lieutenant John Bell Tilden," 225; April 21, 1782, "Revolutionary War Diaries of Captain Walter Finney," 137; muster roll, carolana.com/SC/Revolution/revolution_tidymans_plantation.html; Quarles, *Negro in the American Revolution*, 149; Piecuch, *Three Peoples, One King*, 268, 316–18; Sellick, "Black Skin, Red Coats," 28–38.

24. South Carolina congressional delegation and Daniel Huger (misidentified as Col. [Isaac] Huger), paraphrased in [Thomas Burke?], draft committee report, [before March 25,

1779], in Smith et al., eds., *Letters of Delegates to Congress* 12:243; Greene to Washington, Jan. 24, 1782, *Founders Online*; Edward Rutledge to Arthur Middleton, Feb. 8, 1782, "Correspondence of Hon. Arthur Middleton" (January 1926), 3, 4; Johnson, *Sketches of the Life and Correspondence of Nathanael Greene* 2:272–75; Haw, *John & Edward Rutledge of South Carolina*, 122; Liles, "Thomas Sumter's Law," 107–46, 234–35.

25. Edward Rutledge, the lead author of the confiscation law, explained the rationale behind it: "We have not the Ability to raise a Tax, our Lads would not be draughted, & we were obliged to turn our thoughts to recruiting—with Negroes." Rutledge to Middleton, Feb. 8, 1782, "Correspondence of Hon. Arthur Middleton" (January 1926), 3; Rutledge to Middleton, Jan. 28, 1782, Middleton, "Correspondence of Hon. Arthur Middleton" (October 1925), 212; Francis Marion to Peter Horry, Feb. 10, 1782, John Mathews to Francis Marion, March 18, 1782, in Gibbes, ed., *Documentary History of the Revolution* 3:249, 275–76; Johnson, *Sketches of the Life and Correspondence of Nathanael Greene* 2:275; Nadelhaft, *Disorders of War*, 77–85; Massey, *John Laurens and the American Revolution*, 207; Brannon, *From Revolution to Reunion*, 48–49.

26. Piecuch, *Three Peoples, One King*, 325.

27. Charles Cotesworth Pinckney to Arthur Middleton, Aug. 13, 1782, *Papers of the Revolutionary Era Pinckney Statesmen*; Leslie to Greene, April 4, 1782, Leslie Papers, NYPL; Sellick, "Black Skin, Red Coats," 33–34, 63–66.

28. Lee, *Memoirs of the War in the Southern Department of the United States* 2:402, 414–16 (quotation at 415); Olwell, "'Loose, Idle, and Disorderly.'"

29. Johnson, *Sketches of the Life and Correspondence of Nathanael Greene* 2:244.

30. Wayne to [John] Martin, March 26, 1782, in Steuart, ed., *Magazine of History, With Notes and Queries* 6:6 (December 1907): 361–62.

31. Lee, *Memoirs of the War in the Southern Department of the United States*, ed. Robert E. Lee (1869 edition) 555–61 (quotations at 556 and 559n); Johnson, *Sketches of the Life and Correspondence of Nathanael Greene* 2:298–300; Posey, *General Thomas Posey*, 94–98; Cashin, *King's Ranger*, 152.

32. Greene to Francis Marion, Aug. 9, 1782, in *Papers of General Nathanael Greene* 11:510; Massey, *John Laurens and the American Revolution*, 222; Piecuch, *Three Peoples, One King*, 287, 323.

33. Massey, *John Laurens and the American Revolution*, 210, 214–23.

34. Bennett, "Delaware Regiment in the Revolution," 461; John Mathews to Middleton, Aug. 25–Sept. 1, 1782, "Correspondence of Hon. Arthur Middleton" (April 1926), 71; Johnson, *Sketches of the Life and Correspondence of Nathanael Greene* 2:339–42; Mordecai Gist to Greene, Aug. 27, 1782, in *Papers of General Nathanael Greene* 11:579–82n; Massey, *John Laurens and the American Revolution*, 225–27.

35. Greene to Otho H. Williams, Sept. 17, 1782, in *Papers of General Nathanael Greene* 11:670; Leslie to Carleton, Sept. 8, 1782, in Historical Manuscripts Commission, *Report on American Manuscripts in the Royal Institution of Great Britain* 3:109–10.

36. A New Jersey militiaman and one from Connecticut, participating in separate December 1782 raids, were apparently the last U.S. soldiers killed in the war. Johnson, *Sketches of the Life and Correspondence of Nathanael Greene* 2:345; McCrady, *History of South Carolina in the Revolution*, 667; Peckham, *Toll of Independence*, 97–98; Piecuch, *Three Peoples, One King*, 319.

37. Johnson, *Sketches of the Life and Correspondence of Nathanael Greene* 2:369, 345; Leslie to Carleton, June 11 (second letter), 27 (2 letters), 28, 1782, in Historical Manuscripts Commission, *Report on American Manuscripts in the Royal Institution of Great Britain*

2:520, 543–44, 546; McCrady, *History of South Carolina in the Revolution*, 662; Frey, *Water from the Rock*, 176, 186; Piecuch, *Three Peoples, One King*, 322–23.

38. Leslie to Carleton, June 27, 1782 (second letter), in Historical Manuscripts Commission, *Report on American Manuscripts in the Royal Institution of Great Britain* 2:544; McCrady, *History of South Carolina in the Revolution*, 662.

39. Rawlins Lowndes to Carleton, Aug. 8, 1782, F[rederick] M[ackenzie] to Lowndes, Sept. 9, 1782, Mary Butler to Carleton, Sept. 16, 1782, in Historical Manuscripts Commission, *Report on American Manuscripts in the Royal Institution of Great Britain* 3:59–60, 111, 118; Quarles, *Negro in the American Revolution*, 164–65; Vipperman, *Rise of Rawlins Lowndes*, 232; Bell, *Major Butler's Legacy*, 17, 40.

40. Morris, report to Congress, July 29, 1782 (received Aug. 5, 1782), *JCC* 22:431, 436; Morris to President of Congress, Feb. 27, 1782, in *Papers of Robert Morris* 4:317–18.

41. wikipedia.org/wiki/Arthur_Laffer.

42. Morris to President of Congress, July 29, 1782 (received Aug. 5, 1782), *JCC* 22:432.

43. Cook to Irvine, May 29, 1782, in Butterfield, ed., *Washington-Irvine Correspondence*, 325; [Husband], *Proposals to Amend and Perfect the Policy of the Government of the United States of America*, 29–30.

44. [Husband], *Proposals to Amend and Perfect the Policy of the Government of the United States of America*, 21, 27–28.

45. [Husband], *Proposals to Amend and Perfect the Policy of the Government of the United States of America*, 4, 33, 3–5, 28.

46. "Lycurgus III" [Hermon Husband?], *XIV Sermons on the Characters of Jacob's Fourteen Sons*, iv; [Gale], *Brief, Decent, but Free Remarks, and Observations*, 32–33; Holton, "'Divide et Impera'"; Holton, *Unruly Americans*, 172.

47. Samuel Livermore to Meshech Weare, Nov. 13, 1781, in Smith et al., eds., *Letters of Delegates to Congress* 18:193. Alexander Hamilton estimated that the country's stock of hard money had fallen 80 percent during the war. Bouton, *Taming Democracy*, 79–80.

48. Dorsey Pentecost to [William] Moore, May 18, 1782, George Wall Jr. to Joseph Hart, April 22, 1782, John Robinson, deposition, June 20, 1782, *Pennsylvania Archives*, Ser. 1, 9:546, 529–30, 572; Bouton, *Taming Democracy*, 80–83.

49. *Salem Gazette*, Oct. 24, 1782 (reprinted from *Massachusetts Gazette*); Brown, *Redeeming the Republic*, 103–4, 247–48; Commonwealth of Massachusetts [General Court], *Act for Apportioning and Assessing a Tax of Two Hundred Thousand Pounds*, 1, 7–8; Jensen, *New Nation*, 309; Taylor, *Liberty Men and Great Proprietors*, 105–9, 112–14, 121, 144, 153–60, 209, 265.

50. George Washington to William Moore, May 4, 1782, *Pennsylvania Archives*, Ser. 1, 9:537; Robert Morris to Daniel of St. Thomas Jenifer, June 23, 1782, Jenifer to Morris, July 5, 1782, in *Papers of Robert Morris* 5:471–72, 537; Minot, *History of the Insurrections, in Massachusetts*, 14–16; Rappleye, *Robert Morris*, 299–300.

51. At about the same time Morris covered up the French loan, he publicly predicted that the Yorktown victory would put a stop to French subsidies, even though he actually expected them to continue into 1782. Robert Morris to Benjamin Franklin, Nov. 27, 1781, *Papers of Benjamin Franklin*; *Papers of Robert Morris* 3:90n; Buel, *In Irons*, 229–30; Rappleye, *Robert Morris*, 278–80.

Chapter 33: Like Old Worn Out Horses

1. Morris, *Peacemakers*, 339; Stockley, *Britain and France at the Birth of America*, 38–39, 140.

2. Jay to Livingston, Nov. 17, 1782, enclosing De Rayneval's Memoir Respecting the Right of the United States to the Navigation of the Mississippi, in Wharton, ed., *Revolutionary Diplomatic Correspondence of the United States* 6:24, 26; Morris, *Peacemakers*, 306–7, 322–23.

3. American Commissioners to Robert R. Livingston, Dec. 14, 1782, *Papers of Benjamin Franklin*; Morris, *Peacemakers*, 335–39, 344–48.

4. Preliminary articles of peace between Britain and the United States, Nov. 30, 1782, avalon.law.yale.edu/18th_century/prel1782.asp; Bemis, *Diplomacy of the American Revolution*, 213; Morris, *Peacemakers*, 341–43.

5. Bemis, *Diplomacy of the American Revolution*, 238.

6. Bemis, *Diplomacy of the American Revolution*, 241.

7. "The Memorial from the Officers of the Army," [December 1782], *JCC* 24:291.

8. Hamilton to Washington, April 8, 1783, *Founders Online*; Gouverneur Morris, quoted in Rappleye, *Robert Morris*, 341, 338, 349–50.

9. Hamilton to Washington, March 17, 1783, *Founders Online*; March 10, 1783, *JCC* 24:178–79.

10. [John Armstrong Jr.], Newburgh addresses, enclosed in Washington to Boudinot, March 12, 1783, *Founders Online*.

11. Decades later, even John Armstrong endorsed Washington's view that he and other officers had been used. Washington to Hamilton, April 4, 1783, *Founders Online*; Kohn, "Inside History of the Newburgh Conspiracy," 187–88.

12. *Journals of Major Samuel Shaw*, 103–4; Freeman, Carroll, and Ashworth, *George Washington* 5:435–36.

13. Dyer to Jonathan Trumbull, Sr., March 18, 1783, in Smith et al., eds., *Letters of Delegates to Congress* 20:43; Madison, notes on debates in Congress, March 20, 1783, *Founders Online*; Benjamin Gale, speech to Killingworth town meeting, Nov. 12, 1787, *DHRC* 3:319, 422, 429n; Kaplan, "Veteran Officers and Politics in Massachusetts," 30; Myers, "Armed with Influence," 28–59.

14. The federal import tax and the supplemental grants totaling $1.5 million per year would all expire after twenty-five years, by which time Congress expected to have paid off its debts. Brown, *Redeeming the Republic*, 23.

15. [Burke], *Considerations on the Society or Order of Cincinnati*, 29; Wood, *Creation of the American Republic*, 400.

16. Washington, circular letter to the states, June 8, 1783, *Founders Online*; "Lycurgus III" [Hermon Husband?], *XIV Sermons on the Characters of Jacob's Fourteen Sons*, 25.

17. Washington to Hamilton, April 22, 1783, Washington to Robert Morris, April 9, 1783, *Founders Online*; Ferguson, *Power of the Purse*, 169–70; Buel, *In Irons*, 239; Rappleye, *Robert Morris*, 336–37.

18. "Memoirs of the Life of Boston King," in Holton, *Black Americans in the Revolutionary Era*, 124; George Washington to Benjamin Harrison, April 30, 1783, *Founders Online*; Pflugrad-Jackisch, "'What Am I but an American?,'" 184–85.

19. Baurmeister, journal, June 17, 1783, in Uhlendorf, trans. and ed., *Revolution in America*, 569; Carleton and Washington, quoted in May 9, 1783, Smith, *Historical Memoirs from 26 August 1778 to 12 November 1783 of William Smith*, 586; Raphael, *Founders*, 408; Schama, *Rough Crossings*, 146.

20. Martin, *Narrative of Some of the Adventures, Dangers, and Sufferings of a Revolutionary Soldier*, 205, 208.

21. Even some officers believed Congress had chosen the word *furlough* for a devious purpose: preventing them and their men from accusing Congress of *discharging* the army without pay. Virginia Delegates to Benjamin Harrison, June 17, 1783, *Founders Online*; Martin, *Narrative of Some of the Adventures, Dangers, and Sufferings of a Revolutionary Soldier*, 202; Rosswurm, *Arms, Country, and Class*, 246–47; Gallagher, "Reinterpreting the 'Very Trifling Mutiny' at Philadelphia in June 1783."

22. Ominously, while every delegate who favored the compromise term *furlough* represented a state with a large slave population, all of those who wanted to fully discharge the army hailed from north of the Mason-Dixon line. April 23, 24, May 23, 26, 1783, *JCC* 24:269–71, 275–76, 361, 363–65; Madison, notes of debates in Congress, April 23, May 8, 20, 23, 26, June 13, 1783, Washington to Elias Boudinot, April 18, 1783, Washington to Hamilton, April 22, 1783 (both quotations in text), Madison to Jefferson, April 22, 1783, Thomas Walke to Virginia Delegates in Congress, May 3, 1783, Madison to Jefferson, May 13, 1783, Washington, general orders, June 2, 1783, William Heath to Washington, June 5, 1783, Washington to Boudinot, June 7, 1783, Washington to Lafayette, June 15, 1783, *Founders Online*; Ralph Izard to Arthur Middleton, May 30, 1783, "Correspondence of Hon. Arthur Middleton" (April 1926), 79.

23. Gallagher, "Reinterpreting the 'Very Trifling Mutiny' at Philadelphia in June 1783," 25–26, 28.

24. "Democritus," Boston *American Herald*, April 5, 1784 (reprinted from *Pennsylvania Journal*); Rakove, *Beginnings of National Politics*, 335.

25. Martin, *Narrative of Some of the Adventures, Dangers, and Sufferings of a Revolutionary Soldier*, 203.

26. Martin, *Narrative of Some of the Adventures, Dangers, and Sufferings of a Revolutionary Soldier*, 203.

27. Hauptman, "Road to Kingsbridge."

28. Tristram Dalton to John Adams, July 16, 1783 (first quotation), Dec. 5, 1783, *Founders Online*; James Warren to John Adams, Feb. 26, 1784 (second quotation), Abigail Adams to John Adams, Dec. 27, 1783, *Founders Online*; March 3, 1782, *Memoirs of Major-General William Heath*, 304; Kaplan, "Veteran Officers and Politics in Massachusetts," 39; Hall, *Politics Without Parties*, 152–58, 183–84; *DHRC* 3:319–22; Grossbart, "Revolutionary Transition," 227, 235; Buel, *Dear Liberty*, 304–13; Willingham, *Connecticut Revolutionary*, 40.

29. Benjamin Franklin to Robert Morris, Dec. 25, 1783, *Founders Online*. My thanks to the Hon. Edith H. Jones for this reference.

30. Historians often blame New York for the failure of the 5 percent federal import tax, since its assembly was the only one that loaded down its ratification resolve with conditions that Congress could not accept. Actually, Connecticut's approval of the tax also contained a poison pill (an anti-commutation stipulation). Moreover, Congress had stated that neither the import duty nor the states' pledge to send Congress an additional $1.5 million per year for the next twenty-five years would take effect until both received unanimous support, and several states withheld their consent from the $1.5 million fund, forestalling the whole package. Only the ratification of the U.S. Constitution in 1788 gave Congress the power to levy taxes.

31. Holton, "Abigail Adams, Bond Speculator," 821–38.

32. McGillivray, quoted in DuVal, *Independence Lost*, 238 (second quotation); Brant, quoted in Allan Maclean to Robert Mathews, May 13, 1783 (first quotation), Maclean

to Haldimand, May 11, 1783 (third quotation), Iroquois delegation, quoted in Maclean to Haldimand, May 18, 1783 (fourth quotation), in Brymner, *Report on Canadian Archives*, B 103, 31–32; Kelsay, *Joseph Brant*, 340; Taylor, *Divided Ground*, 112.

33. "Minutes of Transactions with Indians at Sandusky," *MHC* 20:174–76; Kelsay, *Joseph Brant*, 344–46.

34. "Minutes of Transactions with Indians at Sandusky," *MHC* 20:175.

35. "Ephraim Douglass to Pres. Dickinson, 1784," *Pennsylvania Archives*, Ser. 1, 10:555; "Minutes of Transactions with Indians at Sandusky," *MHC* 20:179, 181; Downes, *Council Fires on the Upper Ohio*, 283–84. On European Americans rewriting the transcripts of Indian congresses to suit their interests, see Jennings, *Empire of Fortune*, 39, 56.

36. Downes, *Council Fires on the Upper Ohio*, 282.

37. "Memoirs of the Life of Boston King," in Holton, *Black Americans in the Revolutionary Era*, 124; Pybus, *Epic Journeys of Freedom*, 63; Schama, *Rough Crossings*, 149.

38. "Book of Negroes," novascotia.ca/archives/Africanns/BN.asp; Holton, *Forced Founders*, 219, 156; Van Buskirk, *Generous Enemies*, 142–43 (third quotation), 151; "DESERTED from the Virginia Company of Blacks . . . ," (New York) *Royal Gazette*, Feb. 6, 1779; May 9, 1783, in Smith, *Historical Memoirs of William Smith*, 586. For a prize-winning fictionalization of the evacuation, see Hill, *Someone Knows My Name*.

39. Byrd, quoted in Morgan, *Slave Counterpoint*, 284–85; Pflugrad-Jackisch, "'What Am I but an American?,'" 184–85; Pybus, *Epic Journeys of Freedom*, 70, 78.

40. Robert Boucher Nickolls, quoted in Brown, "Problems of Slavery," 440; Brown, *Moral Capital*.

41. David Hartley and American commissioners, Definitive Treaty of Peace, Sept. 3, 1783, franklinpapers.org.

42. Jefferson, *Notes on the State of Virginia* (1803 ed.), 216, 220.

43. Jefferson, *Notes on the State of Virginia* (1803 ed.), 224; Wiencek, *Imperfect God*, 353–58.

44. Jefferson, *Notes on the State of Virginia* (1803 ed.), 224, 188–91, 196; Jefferson, "original Rough draught" of the Declaration of Independence, [June 11–July 4, 1776], *Founders Online*; McLaughlin, *Jefferson and Monticello*, 115; Gordon-Reed, *Hemingses of Monticello*; Wiencek, *Master of the Mountain*, 43–61. My thanks to Texas teacher Richard Kelly for the point about Jefferson acknowledging Africans' personhood in the Declaration of Independence.

45. Jefferson, *Notes on the State of Virginia* (1803 ed.), 192, 194; Wheatley, *Poems on Various Subjects*, 11; Waldstreicher, "Women's Politics, Antislavery Politics, and Phillis Wheatley's American Revolution," 160.

46. Jefferson, *Notes on the State of Virginia* (1803 ed.), 197; Thomson, quoted in Wilson, "Evolution of Jefferson's Notes on the State of Virginia," 124–25.

47. Shoemaker et al., "Forum: Settler Colonialism in Early American History"; "Land belonging to the subscriber . . . ," enclosed in Washington to Robert Morris, May 26, 1794, Washington, "schedule of property . . . ," July 9, 1799, *Founders Online*; Calloway, *Indian World of George Washington*, 39–40.

48. Jensen, *Founding of a Nation*, 271; Moultrie, *Memoirs of the American Revolution* 2:77–78, 80; Washington to Henry Laurens, March 7–8, 1778, *Founders Online*.

49. Peckham, *Toll of Independence*, 97; Piecuch, *Three Peoples, One King*, 319, 325; Glickstein, *After Yorktown*, 117–18.

50. Hugh Percy to Gen. Harvey(?), July 28, 1775, Percy, *Letters of Hugh Earl Percy from Boston and New York*, 58.

51. Franklin Roosevelt, address to Congress, Dec. 8, 1941, youtube.com/watch?v=YhtuM rMVJDk.

52. George Washington to Richard Henry Lee, July 10, 1775, *Founders Online*; Burgoyne, *State of the Expedition from Canada*, 12; Williams, "Narrative of the Campaign of 1780," in Johnson, *Sketches of the Life and Correspondence of Nathanael Greene* 1:490–91; John Christian Senf, journal, Aug. 15, 1780, Thomas Pinckney to William Johnson, July 27, 1822, in Piecuch, *Battle of Camden*, 23, 39; Rochambeau to de Grasse, May 28, 31, 1781, in Doniol, *Histoire de la Participation de La France à l'établissement des États-Unis d'Amérique* 5:475–76.

53. Spring, *With Zeal and with Bayonets Only*, 18–19.

54. McIntosh to Washington, April 27, 1779, *Founders Online*.

55. Washington to Sullivan, May 31, 1779, Washington to George Clinton, Aug. 16, 1777, Washington to Continental Congress Committee at Camp, Jan. 29, 1778, *Founders Online*; Committee at Camp to Henry Laurens, Feb. 20, 1778, in Smith et al., eds., *Letters of Delegates to Congress* 9:144–46; Burgoyne, proclamation, June 20, 1777, *Hadden's Journal and Orderly Books*, 61–62; Burgoyne to Germain, July 11, 1777, in Davies, ed., *Documents of the American Revolution* 14:141.

56. Greene to Washington, April 25, 1778, Washington to the Continental Congress Committee to Inquire into the State of the Army, July 19, 1777, Washington to Richard Henry Lee, Dec. 26, 1775, Washington to the commanding officer at Morristown, Dec. 30, 1776, Washington to Patrick Henry, May 17, 1777, *Founders Online*; Ward, *War of the Revolution* 1:463n.

57. Lafayette to Washington, July 20, 1781, *Founders Online*.

58. Nash, *Unknown American Revolution*; Morgan, "Other Founders."

Chapter 34: A Revolution in Favor of Government

1. Nettels, *Emergence of a National Economy*, 45; Kulikoff, "War in the Countryside," 218–27.

2. Christie, *Wars and Revolutions*, 146–48; O'Shaughnessy, *Men Who Lost America*, 42.

3. William Stephens Smith to Thomas Jefferson, Feb. 13, 1786, *Founders Online*. The orders in council also prohibited all vessels, including those flying the Union Jack, from carrying North American products such as salted meat and fish to the British Caribbean. Marks, *Independence on Trial*, 56–66.

4. Royal governors often facilitated this trade, either allowing emergency exceptions to the orders in council or looking the other way when American captains falsely claimed that distress on the high seas had forced them to seek the nearest harbor. Elkins and McKitrick, *Age of Federalism*, 400; Scott, *Common Wind*.

5. Meyer, "Les Difficultés du Commerce Franco-Américain Vues de Nantes," 182; Nettels, *Emergence of a National Economy*, 46–47.

6. Clay, quoted in Gould, "Empire That Britain Kept," 475; Robert Morris to Benjamin Franklin, Sept. 30, 1783, franklinpapers.org; Nettels, *Emergence of a National Economy*, 48; Gould, "Empire That Britain Kept," 469.

7. "A FRIEND to the PUBLIC," *Newport Mercury*, Feb. 13, 1786.

8. Holton, *Unruly Americans and the Origins of the Constitution*, 51.

9. Holton, *Unruly Americans and the Origins of the Constitution*, 113; Bouton, *Taming Democracy*, 62, 75, 110.

10. Madison to Monroe, Feb. 24, May 13, 1786 (including editors' notes), Monroe to Madison, May 18, 1786, Madison to Jefferson, Aug. 12, 1786, *Founders Online*; Holton, *Unruly Americans and the Origins of the Constitution*, 23–26, 230.

11. Bouton, "Foreign Founding Fathers"; Holton, *Unruly Americans and the Origins of the Constitution*, 96–100, 111–13.

12. May 31, June 18, 1787, in Farrand, ed., *Records of the Federal Convention of 1787* 1:48, 301.

13. Nadelhaft, *Disorders of War*, 155; Bouton, "Road Closed," 855–57; Holton, *Unruly Americans and the Origins of the Constitution*, 145.

14. Grimké, "John F. Grimké's Eyewitness Account of the Camden Court Riot," 211–12; anonymous Camden District citizens, resolves, April 23, 1785, Grimké Family Papers, SCHS.

15. Grimké, "John F. Grimké's Eyewitness Account of the Camden Court Riot," 212–13.

16. Holton, *Unruly Americans and the Origins of the Constitution*, 154–55; Charles Pinckney, speech in South Carolina House of Representatives, Jan. 16, 1788, in Elliot, ed., *Debates in the Several State Conventions, on the Adoption of the Federal Constitution* 4:255.

17. Washington to James Duane, Sept. 7, 1783, *Founders Online*; Geib, "Land Ordinance of 1785," 1.

18. March 19, 1784, *JCC* 26:153–54; Piteasewa, council at Wakatomika Council House, Nov. 8, 1785, CO 42/49, f. 21, BNA; Captain Johnny (Shawnee sachem), speech, "At Council held at Wakitomiker, May 18, 1785 By the Chiefs the Shawenese, Mingoes, Dellawares, & Cherokee's," Native American History Collection, CL; Holton, *Unruly Americans and the Origins of the Constitution*, 141.

19. Holton, *Unruly Americans*, 137, 141–42; Taylor, *Divided Ground*, 162–67; Calloway, *Indian World of George Washington*, 303–4.

20. Brant did travel to London the following year, *after* these accounts appeared. Holton, *Unruly Americans and the Origins of the Constitution*, 137–40; Taylor, *Divided Ground*, 113–14.

21. Unnamed Iroquois representative, quoted in Holton, *Unruly Americans and the Origins of the Constitution*, 216. The unnamed speaker had of course overstated white Americans' unity; after all, they had just fought a bitter civil war over whether to leave the British empire.

22. Unnamed Iroquois representative, Brownstown congress, both quoted in Holton, *Unruly Americans and the Origins of the Constitution*, 217; White, *Middle Ground*, 434.

23. *Virginia Gazette and Winchester Advertiser*, July 18, 1787; Daniel Claus to Evan Nepean, May 4, 1787, C.O. 42/19, f. 128, BNA.

24. Butler, quoted in Dowd, *Spirited Resistance*, 99.

25. Dane, speech to Massachusetts legislature, Nov. [9] 1786, paraphrased under Boston dateline, *New-Hampshire Gazette*, Nov. 18, 1786; July 27, 1787, *JCC* 33:427–29. Land sales inside the as yet incomplete seven ranges did not begin until 1787 and then only in New York City. The returns were paltry. And it would be nearly a decade before U.S. officials realized their dream of opening a land office west of the Ohio. Washington to Alexander Spotswood, Nov. 23, 1794, *Founders Online*; Geib, "Land Ordinance of 1785," 9–11.

26. Holton, *Unruly Americans and the Origins of the Constitution*, 143–44.

27. Fiske, *Critical Period of American History*, and Szatmary, *Shays' Rebellion*, emphasize debt; Richards, in *Shays's Rebellion*, and I, in "'From the Labours of Others,'" argue that taxation was paramount.

28. Jefferson to William Stephens Smith, Nov. 13, 1787, *Founders Online*; "McVeigh Blinked First and Americans Won," (Toronto) *Globe and Mail*, Aug. 31, 2002.

29. Wilson, Dec. 11, 1787, in Elliot, ed., *Debates in the Several State Conventions on the*

Adoption of the Federal Constitution 2:521; Washington to Richard Henry Lee, Dec. 26, 1775, Washington to Humphreys, Oct. 22, 1786, *Founders Online*; Maier, *Ratification*, 1–26; Holton, *Unruly Americans and the Origins of the Constitution*, 218–20.

30. January 1777 petition, quoted in Kaplan, "Blacks in Massachusetts and the Shays' Rebellion," 8; Szatmary, *Shays' Rebellion*, 82–89 (Lincoln quotation at 86); Mandell, "Natural & Unalienable Right"; Hinks, "John Marrant and the Meaning of Early Black Freemasonry," 106.

31. Holton, *Black Americans in the Revolutionary Era*, 93–95; Kaplan, "Blacks in Massachusetts and the Shays' Rebellion," 9.

32. Oct. 20, 1786, *JCC* 31:891–93.

33. Madison to Jefferson, Oct. 24, 1787, *Founders Online*; Wood, *Creation of the American Republic*, 467.

34. U.S. Constitution, Sept. 17, 1787, archives.gov/founding-docs/constitution-transcript; Hobson, "Negative on State Laws"; Holton, *Unruly Americans and the Origins of the Constitution*, 182–84.

35. Madison, June 6, 1787, in Farrand, ed., *Records of the Federal Convention of 1787* 1:136; Madison to Jefferson, Oct. 24, 1787, *Founders Online*.

36. Washington (who blamed the fog) to Hancock, Oct. 5, 1777, *Founders Online*. As Morris also noted, acting in concert would be easier for the well-to-do, many of whom were already organized into mercantile, veteran officers', bar, and college alumni associations. Holton, *Unruly Americans and the Origins of the Constitution*, 206–8 (Morris quotation at 207), 234–35, 237–38.

37. Philadelphia dateline, *Pennsylvania Gazette*, Sept. 5, 1787. Unlike British monarchs, the president would have full control of the administrative state. Whereas the president's vetoes could be overturned, the king's were absolute—in theory. But the last British monarch to muster the nerve to veto legislation had been Queen Anne in 1708. "Federal Farmer," Jan. 17, 1788, *Founders' Constitution*; Hill, *Century of Revolution*, 275.

38. Staughton Lynd and Robert Alexander point out that the federal convention approved the Three-Fifths Clause at about the same time the Confederation Congress, meeting in New York City, adopted the Northwest Ordinance, prohibiting slavery in what became the Midwest (but making an exception for slaves already there). Lynd and Alexander believe these two conflicting clauses were the product of a deal between the supporters and opponents of slavery. Lynd, "Compromise of 1787"; Alexander, *Northwest Ordinance*.

39. Brown, "Problems of Slavery," 431.

40. Madison, July 19, 25, 1787, in Farrand, ed., *Records of the Federal Convention of 1787* 2:56–57, 110–11; Lynd, "Abolitionist Critique of the United States Constitution," 178; Finkelman, "Slavery and the Constitutional Convention," 209–10; Richards, *Slave Power*, 42; Wills, *Negro President*; Wegman, *Let the People Pick the President*, 92.

41. Gilman and Warren, quoted in Holton, *Unruly Americans and the Origins of the Constitution*, 246.

42. Washington to John Canon, Sept. 16, 1787, *Founders Online*; Holton, *Unruly Americans and the Origins of the Constitution*, 247; Calloway, *Indian World of George Washington*, 317.

43. Brown, "Role of the Army in Western Settlement," 166; McDonald, *We the People*, 263–64; Shepard, *Reluctant Ratifiers*, 14, 39.

44. Jefferson, *Notes on the State of Virginia* (1803 ed.), 222; Washington to Alexander Spotswood, Nov. 23, 1794, *Founders Online*; Pinckney, Aug. 29, 1787, in Farrand, ed., *Records of the Federal Convention of 1787* 2:449; George Washington to Bush-

rod Washington, Nov. 9, 1787, *Founders Online*; Holton, *Unruly Americans and the Origins of the Constitution*, 220–22; Van Cleve, *Slaveholders' Union*; Waldstreicher, *Slavery's Constitution*, 4–9; Meranze, "Hargrave's Nightmare and Taney's Dream," 220–21, 227–28, 231–35.

45. Rasmussen, *American Uprising*, 142–43.
46. Philadelphia dateline, *Pennsylvania Gazette*, Sept. 12, 1787; Holton, *Unruly Americans and the Origins of the Constitution*, 218–20.
47. U.S. Constitution, Sept. 17, 1787, archives.gov/founding-docs/constitution-transcript; William Davie, speech in the North Carolina ratifying convention, July 29, 1788, in Farrand, ed., *Records of the Federal Convention of 1787* 3:350; Charles Pinckney, speech in South Carolina ratifying convention, May 20, 1788, in Elliot, ed., *Debates in the Several State Conventions on the Adoption of the Federal Constitution* 4:333; Edmund Pendleton to James Madison, Oct. 8, 1787, *Founders Online*; Extract of a letter from Salem County, West Jersey, *Pennsylvania Herald*, Oct. 27, 1787, *DHRC* 3:140–41; Benjamin Rush to Jeremy Belknap, Feb. 28, 1788, in Bailyn, ed., *Debate on the Constitution* 2:256; James Wilson, speech in Pennsylvania ratifying convention, Dec. 4, 1787, *DHRC* 2:500; Fiske, *Critical Period of American History*, 323–26.
48. Taylor, *American Revolutions*, 389.
49. De Pauw, *Eleventh Pillar*; Maier, *Ratification*, 320–459.
50. Labunski, *James Madison and the Struggle for the Bill of Rights*.
51. Bowling, "'Tub to the Whale.'"
52. Klarman, *Framers' Coup*; Taylor, *American Revolutions*, 398–99.
53. Declaration of Independence, July 4, 1776, archives.gov/founding-docs/declaration-transcript; U.S. Constitution, Sept. 17, 1787, archives.gov/founding-docs/constitution-transcript.
54. Jameson, *American Revolution Considered as a Social Movement*, 9.

Chapter 35: An Unseen Enemy

1. Elkins and McKitrick, *Age of Federalism*, 114–23, 136–45; Holton, *Unruly Americans and the Origins of the Constitution*, 167–68, 258, 275–76.
2. Holton, *Abigail Adams*, 226–70; "An Act repealing, after the last day of June next, the duties heretofore laid upon Distilled Spirits imported from abroad, and laying others in their stead; and also upon Spirits distilled within the United States; and for appropriating the same," March 3, 1791, in Peters, ed., *Public Statutes at Large of the United States of America*, 199–214; Edling, *Revolution in Favor of Government*, 191–214; Bouton, *Taming Democracy*, 221.
3. Wood, *Radicalism of the American Revolution*; Brewer, "Entailing Aristocracy in Colonial Virginia"; Wilentz, *Rise of American Democracy*, 5; Wright, *Revolutionary Generation*.
4. Most of the British colonial charters imposed property qualifications similar to Britain's, but North America's lower population density made land there much cheaper, and more than half of adult freemen owned enough to vote (though the percentage varied widely, between colonies and even within them). During the revolutionary era, seven states reduced their property qualifications, but in Massachusetts the threshold was actually slightly *increased*, and "in five states, there was little or no change." Keyssar, *Right to Vote*, 5–20 (quotation at 18).
5. "The American Revolution, in sum, produced modest, but only modest, gains, in the

formal democratization of politics." Keyssar, *Right to Vote*, 24; Main, *Upper House in Revolutionary America*; Wilentz, *Rise of American Democracy*, 17, 33.

6. Keyssar, *Right to Vote*, 20. The minority of Loyalists who fled were generally wealthier than those who stayed (with some very large exceptions such as the Black Empire Loyalists), but even so, the earlier view that the departure of the Loyalists skimmed America's cream cannot be sustained. Van Buskirk, *Generous Enemies*; Jasanoff, *Liberty's Exiles*; Taylor, *American Revolutions*, 214.

7. There were two exceptions to the annual-elections rule: South Carolina representatives served for two years, and their counterparts in Connecticut for just six months. Bailyn, ed., *Debate on the Constitution* 2:1087–92.

8. Etting, *Historical Account of the Old State House of Pennsylvania*, 106.

9. Franklin, "Queries and Remarks on a Paper Entitled 'Hints for the Members of Convention['] No II in the Federal Gazette of Tuesday Nov 3d 1789," franklinpapers.org; Franklin to Robert Morris, Dec. 25, 1783, *Founders Online*; "A Farmer," "Hints for the Members of Convention," II, *Carlisle Gazette*, Oct. 21, 1789 (reprinted in [Philadelphia] *Federal Gazette*, Nov. 3, 1789).

10. "Historicus" [Benjamin Franklin], *Federal Gazette*, March 25, 1790; Waldstreicher, *Runaway America*, 238; Franklin, will, July 17, 1788, franklinpapers.org; Steven Gaetano, personal communication, summer 2012; bfit.edu/about-us/mission-and-values.

11. wikisource.org/wiki/Constitution_of_the_Commonwealth_of_Pennsylvania_1790; Brunhouse, *Counter-Revolution in Pennsylvania*, 222–27.

12. Hutchinson, quoted in Elkins and McKitrick, *Age of Federalism*, 465; "A Laborer" [Manning], "On the Shays Affair in Massachusetts," historymatters.gmu.edu/d/5836/; Slaughter, *Whiskey Rebellion*, 200; Elkins and McKitrick, *Age of Federalism*, 481; Smith, *Freedoms We Lost*.

13. [Swift], *Security of the Rights of Citizens in the State of Connecticut Considered*, 83–85.

14. "Constantia" [Murray], "Desultory Thoughts upon the Utility of Encouraging a Degree of Self-Complacency, especially in Female Bosoms," *Gentleman and Lady's Town & Country Magazine* 1:6 (Oct. 1784), jsmsociety.com/Desultory_Thoughts.html; Norton, *Liberty's Daughters*, 246–47; Branson, *These Fiery Frenchified Dames*, 21–53; Skemp, *First Lady of Letters*, 125–27, 133.

15. "Matrimonial Republican," quoted in Norton, *Liberty's Daughters*, 235; "Constantia" [Murray] "On the Equality of the Sexes," *Massachusetts Magazine* 2:3, 4 (March, April 1790): 132–35, 223–26, jsmsociety.com/On_the_Equality.html. In America, the notion that "There is no Sex in soul" had been articulated as far back as 1750 by the Quaker poet Susanna Wright. "Susanna Wright," in Moore, Brooks, and Wigginton, eds., *Transatlantic Feminisms in the Age of Revolutions*, 130–31; Williams, "Revolutionary Era Women in War," 20, 30–31.

16. Murray's sarcastic appellation for men, the "Lords of the Creation," which appears in three different forms in "On the Equality of the Sexes," was in surprisingly common use in the eighteenth century. It was reportedly derived from Genesis 1:28, though it is not a direct quotation. Mason, "Salutatory Oration," 90–95; "Constantia" [Murray], "On the Equality of the Sexes," *Massachusetts Magazine* 2:3, 4 (March, April 1790): 132–35, 223–26, jsmsociety.com/On_the_Equality.html; Catharine Louisa Salmon Smith to Abigail Adams, April 27, 1785, *Founders Online*; Brewer and Evans, *Brewer's Dictionary of Phrase and Fable*, 659; Knowles, ed., *Oxford Dictionary of Phrase and Fable*, 619. The *Conventus Matronarum* actually long predated Heliogabalus (better known today as Elagabalus). Hay, *Amazing Emperor Heliogabalus*, 121–23.

17. Cott, "Divorce and the Changing Status of Women in Eighteenth-Century Massachu-

setts," 586–614; Branson, *These Fiery Frenchified Dames*, 12; Zagarri, *Revolutionary Backlash*, especially 182.

18. Holton, *Abigail Adams*, ix–xi, 407–12.

19. Abigail Adams to John Adams, March 31–April 5, 1776, John Adams to Abigail Adams, April 14, 1776, *Founders Online*; Holton, *Abigail Adams*, xi.

20. Norton, *Liberty's Daughters*, 242–50, 265–72, 287, 298–99; Kerber, *Women of the Republic*; Lewis, "Republican Wife"; Nash, "Rethinking Republican Motherhood."

21. Olympe de Gouges, *Déclaration des Droits de la Femme et de la Citoyenne*, gallica.bnf.fr /essentiels/anthologie/declaration-droits-femme-citoyenne-0; Wollstonecraft, *Vindication of the Rights of Woman*; Barbara Taylor, "Wollstonecraft [*married name* Godwin], Mary (1759–1797)," *DNB*; Holton, "Equality as Unintended Consequence."

22. In Stanton, Anthony, and Gage, eds., *History of Woman Suffrage* 1:70.

23. Ellet, *Women of the American Revolution* 1:325, 322; Schoel, "In Pursuit of Possibility," v, 78.

24. Ellet, *Women of the American Revolution* 1:325; Schoel, "In Pursuit of Possibility," 45n.

25. [Clendinen] to Beverley Randolph, Dec. 18, 1788, Jan. 1, 1789, *CVSP* 4:534, 543; Downes, *Council Fires on the Upper Ohio*, 312.

26. Harmar, general orders, camp 8 miles from the ruins of the Maumee Towns, Oct. 22, 1790, Return of the killed and wounded upon the expedition against the Miami towns, under the command of Brigadier General Harmar, Nov. 4, 1790, in *ASPIA* 4:106; Downes, *Council Fires on the Upper Ohio*, 315; Tanner and Pinther, eds., *Atlas of Great Lakes Indian History*, 72–73; Sugden, *Blue Jacket*, 99–105; Hogeland, *Autumn of the Black Snake*, 113–15; Calloway, *Victory with No Name*, 64–68. At the time the Maumee River was often referred to as the Miami of the Lakes or the Omie, but for clarity's sake I have adopted the modern term.

27. Henry Knox to Washington, June 15, 1789 and enclosure, *Founders Online*; Wood, "When Will Colonial History Become Truly Continental?," 10–11.

28. St. Clair to Henry Knox, Oct. 6, 1791, Henry Knox, "A summary statement of facts, relatively to the measures taken, in behalf of the United States, to induce the hostile Indians, northwest of the Ohio, to peace, previously to the exercise of coercion against them; and also a statement of the arrangements for the campaign of 1791," Dec. 26, 1791, in *ASPIA* 4:136, 140.

29. *Journal of Capt. Daniel Bradley*, 25–26; St. Clair to Knox, Nov. 1, 1791, Henry Knox, "A summary statement of facts, relatively to the measures taken, in behalf of the United States, to induce the hostile Indians, northwest of the Ohio, to peace, previously to the exercise of coercion against them; and also a statement of the arrangements for the campaign of 1791," Dec. 26, 1791, in *ASPIA* 4:136–37, 140; Downes, *Council Fires on the Upper Ohio*, 318–20; Carter, *Life and Times of Little Turtle*, 105–7; Calloway, *Victory with No Name*, 89–90, 111.

30. "Extract of a Letter from Philadelphia, dated Dec. 9, 1791," *Independent Chronicle*, Dec. 22, 1791; *Journal of Capt. Daniel Bradley*, 31.

31. "Fort Jefferson," (Portland, Maine) *Eastern Herald*, Jan. 2, 1792; Carter, *Life and Times of Little Turtle*, 106–7.

32. Spencer, *Indian Captivity of O. M. Spencer*, 103–4, 96; White, *Middle Ground*, 454; Dowd, *Spirited Resistance*, 107; Sugden, *Blue Jacket*, 127; Taylor, *American Revolutions*, 404; Calloway, *Victory with No Name*, 127.

33. *Journal of Capt. Daniel Bradley*, 34; "Extract of a Letter from Captain John H. Buell, of Hartford, to his friend in this City, dated Fort-Washington, Nov. 8, 1791," *Independent Chronicle*, Dec. 22, 1791; White, *Middle Ground*, 454.

34. "Braddock," *Independent Chronicle*, Dec. 22, 1791; Husband, "'Common Farmer (Number 2)': Hermon Husband's Plan for Peace"; Stillé, *Major-General Anthony Wayne and the Pennsylvania Line in the Continental Army*, 321.

35. Henry Knox to George Washington, Aug. 7, 1790, *Founders Online*; Downes, "Creek-American Relations," 353–54. Fourteen years earlier, the newly independent United States had also signed its first treaty with Native Americans. Calloway, *Indian World of George Washington*, 229, 369–70.

36. Abigail Adams to Mary Smith Cranch, Aug. 8, 1790, *Founders Online*; Wright, "Creek-American Treaty of 1790," 379.

37. Washington to U.S. Senate, Aug. 11, 1790, *Founders Online*; Dew, *Review of the Debate in the Virginia Legislature of 1831 and 1832*, 49; Downes, "Creek-American Relations," 354–56.

38. Troxler, "Re-enslavement of Black Loyalists."

39. In 1787, a group of impoverished Black Londoners had been sent to establish the Province of Freedom in what became Sierra Leone, but most had died of disease. The Sierra Leone Company saw the remnant of the 1787 expedition as troublemakers and tried to keep them away from the settlers arriving from Nova Scotia in 1792. Nash, "Thomas Peters"; Pybus, *Epic Journeys of Freedom*, 108–19, 139–51; Sidbury, "'African' Settlers in the Founding of Freetown," 130.

40. Quoted in Pybus, *Epic Journeys of Freedom*, 151; Schama, *Rough Crossings*, 310–23.

41. Schama, *Rough Crossings*, 207; Pybus, *Epic Journeys of Freedom*, 123–37, 157–68, 203–4; Sidbury, "'African' Settlers in the Founding of Freetown," 129, 136.

42. Pybus, *Epic Journeys of Freedom*, 173, 183–87; Anna Maria Falconbridge to [?], Feb. 10, 1791, Isaac Anderson and Cato Perkins to Henry Thornton, Nov. 20, 1793, in Falconbridge, *Two Voyages to Sierra Leone During the Years 1791-2-3*, 37–38, 266–68.

43. Macaulay, quoted in Pybus, *Epic Journeys of Freedom*, 188.

44. Luke Jordan and Isaac Anderson to [John Clarkson], June 28, 1794, in Fyfe, ed., *"Our Children Free and Happy,"* 43; Pybus, *Epic Journeys of Freedom*, 178–80.

45. Like the 1,200 Black veterans of the American War of Independence who had come to Sierra Leone in 1792, the Maroons had initially been transported to Nova Scotia, where both the climate and the white majority had proved inhospitable. Pybus, *Epic Journeys of Freedom*, 195–202; Chopra, *Almost Home.*

46. Pybus, *Epic Journeys of Freedom*, 199–201, 205, 218.

47. Marrant, *Sermon Preached on the 24th Day of June 1789*, 20; Prince Hall, *A Charge Delivered to the Brethren of the African Lodge on the 25th of June, 1792*, blackpast.org /african-american-history/1792-prince-hall-charge-delivered-brethren-african-lodge; Hinks, "John Marrant and the Meaning of Early Black Freemasonry," 105–16.

48. Thomas, *Rise to Be a People*, 12–16.

49. Banneker to Jefferson, Aug. 19, 1791 (and editors' note), Jefferson to Banneker, Aug. 30, 1791, *Founders Online*; Jordan, *White over Black*, 449–55.

50. Charter of the Free African Society, April 12, 1787, in Holton, *Black Americans in the Revolutionary Era*, 95–96; Nash, *Forging Freedom*, 95–96; Sidbury, *Becoming African in America*, 67–69, 133–42.

51. Nash, *Forging Freedom*, 121–25; Calloway, *Indian World of George Washington*, 2.

52. Historians have questioned the value of comparing U.S. and British emancipation dates by conjecturing that had the southern states of North America remained in the British empire, they would have used their influence to prevent Parliament from abolishing slavery when it did. Of course it is impossible to say.

53. U.S. Congress, quoted in Foner, *Story of American Freedom*, 42–43.

Chapter 36: Back to Braddock's Field

1. Knox to Wayne, June 7, 1794, in Wayne, *Anthony Wayne, a Name in Arms*, 337; Elkins and McKitrick, *Age of Federalism*, 392.
2. Elkins and McKitrick, *Age of Federalism*, 394–95.
3. Hamilton to Washington, Aug. 5, 1794, *Founders Online*; Higginbotham, *Daniel Morgan*, 187–88; Elkins and McKitrick, *Age of Federalism*, 466, 473; Slaughter, *Whiskey Rebellion*, 95–96, 102, 195.
4. Hamilton to Washington, [Aug. 5], 1794, *Founders Online*; Slaughter, *Whiskey Rebellion*, 93–94, 105–8, 163; Elkins and McKitrick, *Age of Federalism*, 473; Jones, "Herman Husband," 352; Bouton, *Taming Democracy*, 220–24, 236–38.
5. Tachau, "Whiskey Rebellion in Kentucky"; Slaughter, *Whiskey Rebellion*, 144, 206–12; Bouton, *Taming Democracy*, 227–28.
6. Hamilton to Washington, Aug. 5, 1794, *Founders Online*; Slaughter, *Whiskey Rebellion*, 177–79; Bouton, *Taming Democracy*, 231.
7. John Holcroft, in Brackenridge and M'Culloch, *Incidents of the Insurrection in the Western Parts of Pennsylvania* [3]:134, [1]:122; Abraham Kirkpatrick to George Washington, July 28, 1794, *Founders Online*; Slaughter, *Whiskey Rebellion*, 178–81; Bouton, *Taming Democracy*, 232–33. Neville denied arming his slaves. John Neville to Tench Coxe, July 18, 1794, cited in Francis Mentges, deposition, [Aug. 1, 1794] (editors' note), *Founders Online*.
8. Kohn, "Washington Administration's Decision to Crush the Whiskey Rebellion," 571–76 (Bradford quotation at 575), 583; Slaughter, *Whiskey Rebellion*, 196–201.
9. Elkins and McKitrick, *Age of Federalism*, 463, 477; Bouton, *Taming Democracy*, 235.
10. Elkins and McKitrick, *Age of Federalism*, 479; Slaughter, *Whiskey Rebellion*, 198, 210–19; Bouton, *Taming Democracy*, 241.
11. Edling, *Hercules in the Cradle*, 122.
12. Knox, quoted in Stillé, *Major-General Anthony Wayne and the Pennsylvania Line in the Continental Army*, 321–22; Downes, *Council Fires on the Upper Ohio*, 317.
13. Stillé, *Major-General Anthony Wayne and the Pennsylvania Line in the Continental Army*, 322–23; Carter, *Life and Times of Little Turtle*, 129.
14. The Treaty of Canandaigua was not actually signed until November 11, 1794, nearly three months after the Americans' August 20, 1794, victory at Fallen Timbers, but the United States had signaled its intentions toward the Iroquois earlier in the year. Taylor, *Divided Ground*, 288–93.
15. Knox to Wayne, Sept. 3, 1793, in Wayne, *Anthony Wayne, a Name in Arms*, 271; Anthony Wayne to Henry Knox, Oct. 3, 1792, Ayer MS 966, NL.
16. Carter, *Life and Times of Little Turtle*, 115, 129–31, 158; Sword, *President Washington's Indian War*, 276–77, 269.
17. Knox to Wayne, June 7, 1794, in Wayne, *Anthony Wayne, a Name in Arms*, 337; Elkins and McKitrick, *Age of Federalism*, 395–96, 438.
18. Aug. 18, 1794, in Smith, *From Greene Ville to Fallen Timbers*, 286. This officer's name was not recorded.
19. Aug. 20, 1794, in Smith, *From Greene Ville to Fallen Timbers*, 295; Ward, *Charles Scott and the "Spirit of '76,"* 143; Sword, *President Washington's Indian War*, 306, 312.
20. To be sure, operating expenditures were eclipsed by the interest paid out to federal bondholders. Miller, *Federalist Era*, 183.
21. Knox to Wayne, Dec. 5, 1794, in Wayne, *Anthony Wayne, a Name in Arms*, 364; Ward, *Charles Scott and the "Spirit of '76,"* 147.

22. Knox to [Blount?], July 26, 1794, James Robertson, order to [James] Ore, Sept. 6, 1794, in *ASPIA* 4:634, 530; Maj. [James] Ore to Blount, Sept. 24, 1794, in Putnam, *History of Middle Tennessee*, 476, 480, 485, 497–98n; Dowd, *Spirited Resistance*, 112; Guy, "Last Battle of the Cherokee."

23. In 1810, the U.S. Supreme Court decreed the February 13, 1796, legislation voiding the Yazoo land deeds an impermissible violation of the Contracts Clause of the Constitution, and Congress compensated the Yazoo claimants. Washington to Congress, Feb. 17, 1795, *Founders Online*; Magrath, *Yazoo*, 4–31, 70; Hobson, *Great Yazoo Lands Sale*.

24. Martin, *Narrative of Some of the Adventures, Dangers, and Sufferings of a Revolutionary Soldier*; Martin, *Ordinary Courage*, xiii–xv; Leamon, *Revolution Downeast*, 192; Taylor, *Liberty Men and Great Proprietors*.

25. Knox, quoted in Elkins and McKitrick, *Age of Federalism*, 479; Slaughter, *Whiskey Rebellion*, 205–6, 220; Higginbotham, *Daniel Morgan*, 193–94.

26. Washington, diary, Oct. 20, 1794, Washington to Hamilton, Oct. 26, 1794, *Founders Online*; Jones, "Herman Husband," 359–63; Slaughter, *Whiskey Rebellion*, 218–20; Bouton, *Taming Democracy*, 242–43; Myrsiades, "Tale of a Whiskey Rebellion Judge," 160; Stewart, *Redemption from Tyranny*, 122–30.

27. "At a conference held on the 7th and 8th of November 1794, at Telico block house . . . ," in *ASPIA* 4:536–38; Dowd, *Spirited Resistance*, 112.

28. Madison, Draft of the Petition to the General Assembly of the Commonwealth of Virginia, c. September 1795, *Founders Online*; Bemis, *Jay's Treaty*, 270; Charles, "Jay Treaty," 594; Estes, *Jay Treaty Debate*.

29. Elkins and McKitrick, *Age of Federalism*, 415–18; Estes, *Jay Treaty Debate*.

30. Wayne was apparently quoting a letter from Maj. Thomas Hunt. Wayne to Pickering, May 15, 1795, in Wayne, *Anthony Wayne, a Name in Arms*, 416–17; Sword, *President Washington's Indian War*, 319; Taylor, *Divided Ground*, 291.

31. Wayne to Pickering, May 15, 1795, Pickering to Wayne, June 30, 1795, in Wayne, *Anthony Wayne, a Name in Arms*, 418–19, 435.

32. Baron de Carondelet, quoted in Dowd, *Spirited Resistance*, 112.

33. Hall, *Africans in Colonial Louisiana*, 343–80; Berlin, *Many Thousands Gone*, 345; Klooster, "Slave Revolts, Royal Justice, and a Ubiquitous Rumor in the Age of Revolutions."

34. Holmes, "Abortive Slave Revolt at Pointe Coupée, Louisiana," 348, 357–58. An 1811 uprising farther down the Mississippi, on the "German Coast," has been described as "the largest slave revolt in United States history." Bell, "Common Wind's Creole Visionary," 16; Rasmussen, *American Uprising*.

Epilogue

1. [Reed], *Sentiments of an American Woman*; Jefferson to George Rogers Clark, Dec. 25, 1780, *Founders Online*.

2. Madison, "Vices of the Political System of the U. States," April 1787, Joseph Reed to Washington, Dec. 22, 1776, Cadwalader to Washington, Dec. 27, 1776, Washington to George Clinton, Oct. 4, 1779, Nathanael Greene to George Washington, April 25, 1778, *Founders Online*; Joseph Reed to Esther Reed, Aug. 9, 1776, Cadwalader to Joseph Reed, Nov. 30, 1777, in Reed, *Life and Correspondence of Joseph Reed* 1:215, 348n; Holton, *Unruly Americans and the Origins of the Constitution*, 9; Lockwood, *To Begin the World Over Again*, 135–36.

3. Washington to Robert Dinwiddie, April 25, 1754 (editors' note), *Founders Online*; Mary Butler to Guy Carleton, Sept. 16, 1782, Historical Manuscripts Commission, *Report on American Manuscripts in the Royal Institution of Great Britain* 3:118.

4. "Seymour Cunningham," (Amherst, NH) *Farmers' Cabinet*, June 2, 1827.

5. I have reversed the order of these two phrases. [Husband], *XIV Sermons on the Character of Jacob's Fourteen Sons*, v.

BIBLIOGRAPHY

Manuscripts

British National Archives, Kew, England (BNA)
    C.O. 5, 42
William L. Clements Library, Ann Arbor, MI (CL)
    Thomas Gage Papers
    William Knox Papers
    Native American History Collection
Henry E. Huntington Library, San Marino, CA (HEH)
    Loudoun Papers
Houghton Library, Harvard University (HH)
    Arthur Lee Papers
Library of Congress (LC)
    Patrick Henry Papers
    Robert Honyman diary
Library of Virginia (LiVi)
Massachusetts Historical Society (MHS)
    Henry Sewall diary
National Archives of the United States, Washington, DC (USNA)
Newberry Library (NL)
New-York Historical Society (N-YHS)
    Horatio Gates Papers
New York Public Library (NYPL)
    Leslie Papers
    Chalmers Papers
South Carolina Historical Society, College of Charleston (SCHS)
    Grimké Family Papers
    Anne Hill Gregorie Papers
Swem Library, College of William and Mary (W&M)
    Robert Wormeley Carter diary
University of Virginia, Manuscripts Department, Alderman Library (UVA)
    Yates Letterbook
    Lee Papers (Fraser Transcripts)

Virginia Historical Society (VHS)
    Preston Family Papers
    Virginia Land Office Records
Yale University Library, Beinecke Rare Book and Manuscript Library (YL)
    Silliman Family Papers

Eighteenth-Century Periodicals

American Herald (Boston)
Annual Register
Boston Evening-Post
Boston Gazette
Boston Gazette and Country Journal
Boston News-Letter
Boston Post-Boy and Advertiser
Federal Gazette (Philadelphia)
Independent Chronicle (Boston)
Independent Ledger (Boston)
London Chronicle
Maryland Gazette
Maryland Journal and Baltimore Advertiser
Massachusetts Gazette
New-Hampshire Gazette
Newport Mercury
New-York Gazette
New-York Journal
New-York Mercury
Pennsylvania Chronicle
Pennsylvania Herald
Pennsylvania Evening Post
Pennsylvania Gazette
Pennsylvania Journal
Pennsylvania Packet
Providence Gazette
Rivington's New-York Gazeteer
Royal Gazette (New York)
South-Carolina Gazette
South-Carolina Gazette and Country Journal
Virginia Gazette (Dixon & Hunter)
Virginia Gazette (Pinkney)
Virginia Gazette (Purdie)
Virginia Gazette (Purdie & Dixon)
Virginia Gazette (Rind)
Virginia Gazette, or, Norfolk Intelligencer
Virginia Gazette and Winchester Advertiser

Websites

Adams Papers Digital Edition, masshist.org/publications/adams-papers/
American National Biography, anb.org
The Annotated Newspapers of Harbottle Dorr, masshist.org/dorr/
The Avalon Project, avalon.law.yale.edu/
boston1775.blogspot.com
Biblegateway.com (King James Version)
A Century of Lawmaking for a New Nation (includes *American State Papers*; Farrand, ed., *Records of the Federal Convention of 1787*; Ford et al., eds., *Journals of the Continental Congress*; Smith et al., eds., *Letters of Delegates to Congress*), memory.loc.gov/ammem/amlaw/
Dictionary of Canadian Biography, biographi.ca/en/
Encyclopedia Virginia, encyclopediavirginia.org
Founders' Constitution, press-pubs.uchicago.edu/founders/index.html
Founders Online, founders.archives.gov/
The Papers of Benjamin Franklin, franklinpapers.org
Gallica.bnf.fr
books.google.com
hathitrust.org
Internet Archive, archive.org
Judith Sargent Murray Society, jsmsociety.com/
Online Library of Liberty, oll.libertyfund.org
Oxford Dictionary of National Biography, oxforddnb.com
Oxford English Dictionary, oed.com
Papers of Eliza Lucas Pinckney and Harriott Pinckney Horry, rotunda.upress.virginia.edu/PinckneyHorry/
Papers of the Revolutionary Era Pinckney Statesmen, rotunda.upress.virginia.edu/founders/PNKY.html
Project Gutenberg, gutenberg.org
poetryfoundation.org
The Submarine Turtle: Naval Documents of the Revolutionary War, history.navy.mil/content/history/nhhc/research/library/online-reading-room/title-list-alphabetically/s/submarine-turtle-naval-documents.html
timeanddate.com
Trans-Atlantic Slave Trade Database, slavevoyages.org
wikimedia.org
wikipedia.org

Microfilm Editions

Draper, Lyman Coleman. *Draper Manuscripts, 1740–1891*. Chicago: University of Chicago Photoduplication Department. 123 reels. 1980.
Hoffman, Paul P. *The Lee Family Papers, 1742–1795*. Charlottesville: University of Virginia Library. 8 reels. 1966.
Jennings, Francis, et al., eds. *Iroquois Indians: A Documentary History of the Diplomacy of the Six Nations and Their League*. 50 reels. Woodbridge, CT: Research Publications, 1984.

Note to Readers

In the endnotes, published works are cited by author's last name and short title. The only complete citations in the endnotes are to entries from biographical dictionaries.

Printed Primary Sources (composed before 1861)

Adams, Charles Francis. Speech in the House of Representatives. *Congressional Globe*, May 31, 1860, p. 2514.

Adams, John. *The Works of John Adams, Second President of the United States: With a Life of the Author, Notes and Illustrations*. Ed. Charles Francis Adams. 10 vols. Boston: Little, Brown and Co., 1850–1856.

Albemarle, George Thomas. *Memoirs of the Marquis of Rockingham and His Contemporaries: With Original Letters and Documents Now First Published*. 2 vols. London: Richard Bentley, 1852.

Allen, Ethan. *A Narrative of Col. Ethan Allen's Captivity, from the Time of His Being Taken by the British, near Montreal, on the 25th Day of September, in the Year 1775, to the Time of His Exchange, on the 6th Day of May, 1778*. Walpole, NH: Published by Thomas & Thomas. From the press of Charter and Hale, 1807.

Alvord, Clarence Walworth, and Clarence Edwin Carter, eds. *The Critical Period, 1763–1765*. Collections of the Illinois State Historical Library, Vol. 10. British series, Vol. 1. Springfield: Trustees of the Illinois State Historical Library, 1915.

American State Papers: Indian Affairs. Vol. 4. Washington: Gales and Seaton, 1832.

Ames, Nathaniel. *An Astronomical Diary, or, Almanack for the Year of Our Lord Christ 1768: Calculated for the Meridian of Boston, New-England, Latt. 42° 25' North*. Boston: n.p., n.d.

Anburey, Thomas. *Travels Through the Interior Parts of America. In a Series of Letters*. 2 vols. London: Printed for William Lane, Leadenhall-Street, 1789.

Andrews, Charles M., ed. "State of the Trade." *Colonial Society of Massachusetts Publications* 19 (1918): 379–90.

Andrews, John. "Letters of John Andrews, Esq., of Boston." Ed. Winthrop Sargent. *Proceedings of the Massachusetts Historical Society* 8 (July 1865): 316–412.

The Annual Register, or, A View of the History, Politicks, and Literature for the Year 1763. London: Printed for R. and J. Dodsley, 1764.

The Annual Register, or, A View of the History, Politics, and Literature for the Year 1777. 3rd ed. London: J. Dodsley, 1785.

At a Town Meeting Called by Order of the Town Council, Thursday, November 26, 1767. Newport, RI: Printed by Samuel Hall, 1767.

Atkinson, Roger. "Letters of Roger Atkinson, 1769–1776." Ed. A. J. Morrison. *Virginia Magazine of History and Biography* 15:4 (April 1908): 345–59.

Bailyn, Bernard, ed. *The Debate on the Constitution: Federalist and Antifederalist Speeches, Articles, and Letters During the Struggle over Ratification*. 2 vols. New York: Library of America, 1993.

Barrow, Thomas C., ed. "A Project for Imperial Reform: 'Hints Respecting the Settlement for Our American Provinces,' 1763." *William and Mary Quarterly*, Third Series, 24:1 (January 1967): 108–26.

Bartlett, John Russell, ed. *Census of the Inhabitants of the Colony of Rhode Island and Prov-*

idence Plantations Taken by Order of the General Assembly, in the Year 1774. Providence: Knowles, Anthony & Co., 1858.

———, ed. *Records of the State of Rhode Island and Providence Plantations in New England.* Vol. 8. Providence: Cooke, Jackson & Co., 1863.

Bauermeister, Carl Leopold. *Revolution in America: Confidential Letters and Journals, 1776–1784, of Adjutant General Major Baurmeister of the Hessian Forces.* Trans. and ed. Bernhard A. Uhlendorf. New Brunswick, NJ: Rutgers University Press, 1957.

Bense, Johann. "A Brunswick Grenadier with Burgoyne: The Journal of Johann Bense, 1776–1783." Ed. Mary C. Lynn. Trans. Helga B. Doblin. *New York History* 66:4 (October 1985): 420–44.

Bernard, Francis, Thomas Gage, and Samuel Hood. *Letters to the Ministry from Governor Bernard, General Gage, and Commodore Hood: And Also Memorials to the Lords of the Treasury, from the Commissioners of the Customs. With Sundry Letters and Papers Annexed to the Said Memorials.* Ed. Samuel Hood. Boston: Edes and Gill, 1769.

Biddle, Henry D., and Samuel Rhoads Jr. "Extracts from the Letter-Book of Samuel Rhoads, Jr., of Philadelphia." *Pennsylvania Magazine of History and Biography* 14:4 (January 1891): 421–26.

Bird, Harrison. *March to Saratoga: General Burgoyne and the American Campaign, 1777.* New York: Oxford University Press, 1963.

Bland, Richard. *An Inquiry into the Rights of the British Colonies, Intended as an Answer to The Regulations Lately Made Concerning the Colonies, and the Taxes Imposed upon Them Considered: In a Letter Addressed to the Author of That Pamphlet.* Williamsburg, VA: Alexander Purdie, & Co., 1766.

Blecki, Catherine La Courreye, and Karin A. Wulf, eds. *Milcah Martha Moore's Book: A Commonplace Book from Revolutionary America.* University Park: Pennsylvania State University Press, 1997.

Bond, Beverly W., Jr. "The Captivity of Charles Stuart, 1755–57." *Mississippi Valley Historical Review* 13:1 (June 1926): 58–81.

Boudinot, Elias. *The Life, Public Services, Addresses and Letters of Elias Boudinot, LL.D: President of the Continental Congress.* Ed. J. J. Boudinot. 2 vols. Boston: Houghton, Mifflin and Co., 1896.

Boyd, William Kenneth. *Some Eighteenth Century Tracts Concerning North Carolina.* Publications of the North Carolina Historical Commission. Raleigh: Edwards & Broughton, 1927.

Brackenridge, Hugh H. *Incidents of the Insurrection in the Western Parts of Pennsylvania, in the Year 1794.* Philadelphia: Printed and sold by John M'Culloch, 1795.

Bradley, Daniel, and Frazer Ells Wilson. *Journal of Capt. Daniel Bradley: An Epic of the Ohio Frontier.* Greenville, OH: Frank H. Jobes & Son, 1935.

Bridges, George Wilson. *The Annals of Jamaica.* Vol. 1. London: John Murray, 1828.

Brodhead, John Romeyn, Berthold Fernow, and E. B. O'Callaghan, eds. *Documents Relative to the Colonial History of the State of New-York: Procured in Holland, England, and France.* 15 vols. Albany, NY: Weed, Parsons and Company, 1853–1887.

"British Mercantile Claims." *Virginia Genealogist* 16 (1972): 104–8.

Brymner, Douglas, ed. *Report on Canadian Archives 1886.* Ottawa: Maclean, Roger & Co., 1887.

Bunker Hill: Its Battle and Monument. Boston: John Sly, 1843.

Burgoyne, John. *Orderly Book of Lieut. Gen. John Burgoyne, from His Entry into the State of New York Until His Surrender at Saratoga, 16th Oct., 1777. From the Original Manuscript Deposited at Washington's Head Quarters, Newburgh, N.Y.* Ed. E. B. O'Callaghan. Munsell's Historical Series, No. 7. Albany, NY: J. Munsell, 1860.

———. *A State of the Expedition from Canada, as Laid Before the House of Commons, by*

Lieutenant-General Burgoyne, and Verified by Evidence... London: Printed for J. Almon, 1780.

Burk, John. *The History of Virginia, from Its First Settlement to Present Day*. 4 vols. Petersburg, VA: Printed for the author, by Dickson & Pescud; M. W. Dunnavant, 1804–1816.

[Burke, Aedanus] "Cassius." *Considerations on the Society or Order of Cincinnati; Lately Instituted by the Major-Generals, Brigadiers, and Other Officers of the American Army. Proving That It Creates, a Race of Hereditary Patricians, or Nobility*... Charleston, SC: Printed for A. Timothy, 1783.

Burke, Edmund. *Select Works of Edmund Burke*. Ed. E.J. Payne and Francis Canavan. A New Imprint of the Payne Edition. Indianapolis: Liberty Fund, 1999. oll.libertyfund.org /titles/burke-select-works-of-edmund-burke-vol-1—5/simple.

Burnaby, Andrew. *Travels Through the Middle Settlements in North-America in the Years 1759 and 1760. With Observations upon the State of the Colonies*. Dublin: Printed for R. Marchbank, 1775.

Bushnell, D. "General Principles and Construction of a Sub-Marine Vessel, Communicated by D. Bushnell of Connecticut, the Inventor, in a Letter of October, 1787, to Thomas Jefferson then Minister Plenipotentiary of the United States at Paris." *Transactions of the American Philosophical Society* 4 (1799): 303–12.

Butterfield, C. W. *An Historical Account of the Expedition Against Sandusky Under Col. William Crawford in 1782*. Cincinnati: Robert Clarke & Co., 1873.

———, ed. *Washington-Irvine Correspondence*. Madison, WI: David Atwood, 1882.

Butterfield, L. H., et al., eds. *Adams Family Correspondence*. 13 vols. to date. Adams Papers. Ser. 2. Cambridge: Belknap Press of Harvard University Press, 1963–.

Campbell, Charles. *History of the Colony and Ancient Dominion of Virginia*. Philadelphia: J. B. Lippincott and Co., 1860.

Carroll, Charles, of Annapolis, and Charles Carroll of Carrollton. *Dear Papa, Dear Charley: The Peregrinations of a Revolutionary Aristocrat, as Told by Charles Carroll of Carrollton and His Father, Charles Carroll of Annapolis, with Sundry Observations on Bastardy, Child-Rearing, Romance, Matrimony, Commerce, Tobacco, Slavery, and the Politics of Revolutionary America*. Ed. Ronald Hoffman, Sally D. Mason, and Eleanor S. Darcy. 3 vols. Chapel Hill: Published for the Omohundro Institute of Early American History and Culture by the University of North Carolina Press, 2001.

Carter, Landon. *The Diary of Colonel Landon Carter of Sabine Hall, 1752–1778*. Ed. Jack P. Greene. 2 vols. Virginia Historical Society Documents. Vols. 4–5. Charlottesville: Published for the Virginia Historical Society by the University Press of Virginia, 1965.

The Charters of the Province of Pensilvania and City of Philadelphia. Philadelphia: Printed and Sold by B. Franklin, 1742.

Chew, Samuel. *The Speech of Samuel Chew, Esq; Chief Justice of the Government of New-Castle, Kent and Sussex upon Delaware: Delivered from the Bench to the Grand-Jury of the County of New-Castle, Nov. 21, 1741; and Now Published at Their Request*. Philadelphia: Printed and sold by B. Franklin, 1741.

Clark, George Rogers. *George Rogers Clark Papers, 1771–1781*. Ed. James Alton James. Collections of the Illinois State Historical Library, Vol. 8; Virginia Series, Vol. 3. Springfield: Trustees of the Illinois State Historical Library, 1912.

Clinton, Henry. *The American Rebellion: Sir Henry Clinton's Narrative of His Campaigns, 1775–1782, with an Appendix of Original Documents*. Ed. William Bradford Willcox. Yale Historical Publications, Vol. 21. New Haven: Yale University Press, 1954.

Clive, Catherine. *The Rehearsal: Or, Bays in Petticoats. A Comedy in Two Acts. As It Is Performed at the Theatre Royal in Drury-Lane*. London: Printed for R. Dodsley, 1753.

Closen, Ludwig von. *The Revolutionary Journal of Baron Ludwig von Closen, 1780–1783*. Ed. Evelyn Martha Acomb. Chapel Hill: Published for the Institute of Early American History and Culture by the University of North Carolina Press, 1958.

Coffin, Charles, comp. *History of the Battle of Breed's Hill*. Saco, ME: Printed by William J. Condon, 1831.

Commager, Henry Steele, and Richard B. Morris, eds. *The Spirit of 'Seventy-Six: The Story of the American Revolution as Told by Participants*. Bicentennial Edition. New York: Harper & Row, 1975.

The Commercial Conduct of the Province of New-York Considered, and the True Interest of That Colony Attempted to Be Shewn, in a Letter to the Society of Arts, Agriculture and Oeconomy. New York: Printed for the benefit of the Society of Arts, Agriculture, and Oeconomy, of New-York, 1767.

Commonwealth of Massachusetts [General Court]. *An Act for Apportioning and Assessing a Tax of Two Hundred Thousand Pounds*. Boston: Benjamin Edes and Sons, 1782.

Cook, Frederick, ed. *Journals of the Military Expedition of Major General John Sullivan Against the Six Nations of Indians in 1779 with Records of Centennial Celebrations*. Auburn, NY: Knapp, Peck & Thomson, Printers, 1887.

Cornwallis, Charles. *Correspondence of Charles, First Marquis Cornwallis*. 2nd ed. Ed. Charles Ross. 3 vols. London: John Murray, 1859.

Cowley, [Hannah]. *A Bold Stroke for a Husband, a Comedy, as Acted at the Theatre Royal, in Covent Garden*. 3rd ed. London: Printed by M. Scott for T. Evans, 1784.

Cresswell, Nicholas. *The Journal of Nicholas Cresswell, 1774–1777*. Ed. Samuel Thornely. New York: Lincoln MacVeagh, The Dial Press, 1924.

Cubbison, Douglas R. *Burgoyne and the Saratoga Campaign: His Papers*. Norman: University of Oklahoma Press, 2012.

Dann, John C., ed. *The Revolution Remembered: Eyewitness Accounts of the War for Independence*. Clements Library Bicentennial Studies. Chicago: University of Chicago Press, 1980.

Davies, K. G., ed. *Documents of the American Revolution, 1770–1783*. 21 vols. Colonial Office Series. Shannon: Irish University Press, 1972–1981.

Davies, Samuel. *Religion and Patriotism the Constituents of a Good Soldier. A Sermon Preached to Captain Overton's Independant Company of Volunteers, Raised in Hanover County, Virginia, August 17, 1755*. Philadelphia: Printed by James Chattin, 1755.

——. *Virginia's Danger and Remedy: Two Discourses Occasioned by the Severe Drought in Sundry Parts of the Country and the Defeat of General Braddock*. 2nd ed. Glasgow: J. Bryce and D. Paterson, 1756.

Davies, William, and Robert Hanson Harrison. *Report of Commissioners for Settling a Cartel for the Exchange of Prisoners*. Philadelphia: Printed by David Claypoole, printer to the Honorable the Congress of the United States of America, 1779.

[Dawe, Philip]. *A Society of Patriotic Ladies, at Edenton in North Carolina*. London: Robert Sayer and John Bennett Firm, 1775.

Dawson, Henry B. *Battles of the United States, by Sea and Land: Embracing Those of the Revolutionary and Indian Wars, the War of 1812, and the Mexican War; with Important Official Documents*. Vol. 1. New York: Johnson, Fry, and Company, 1858.

Dearborn, Henry. "A Narrative of the Saratoga Campaign." *Bulletin of the Fort Ticonderoga Museum* 1:3 (January 1929): 2–12.

Dew, Thomas Roderick. *Review of the Debate [on the Abolition of Slavery] in the Virginia Legislature of 1831 and 1832*. Richmond, VA: Printed by T. W. White, 1832.

Dickerson, Oliver Morton, comp. *Boston Under Military Rule, 1768–1769, as Revealed in a Journal of the Times.* Boston: Chapman & Grimes, 1936.

Dickinson, John. "An Address Read at a Meeting of Merchants to Consider Non-Importation." In Paul Leicester Ford, ed., *The Writings of John Dickinson: Vol. I, Political Writings, 1764–1774,* 14:407–17. Memoirs of the Historical Society of Pennsylvania. Philadelphia: Historical Society of Pennsylvania, 1895.

———. *The Late Regulations, Respecting the British Colonies on the Continent of America Considered: In a Letter from a Gentleman in Philadelphia to His Friend in London.* Philadelphia; London: Re-printed for J. Almon, 1765.

———. *Letters from a Farmer in Pennsylvania, to the Inhabitants of the British Colonies.* London: J. Almon, 1768.

Digby, William. *The British Invasion from the North: The Campaigns of Generals Carleton and Burgoyne from Canada, 1776–1777: With the Journal of Lieut. William Digby, of the 53d, or Shropshire Regiment of Foot.* Ed. James Phinney Baxter. Munsell's Historical Series, No. 16. Albany, NY: Joel Munsell's Sons, 1887.

Dinwiddie, Robert. *The Official Records of Robert Dinwiddie, Lieutenant-Governor of the Colony of Virginia, 1751–1758, Now First Printed from the Manuscript in the Collections of the Virginia Historical Society.* Ed. R. A. Brock. 2 vols. Collections of the Virginia Historical Society. New Series, Vols. 3–4. Richmond, VA: The Society, 1883–1884.

Doniol, Henri. *Histoire de la Participation de La France à l'établissement des États-Unis d'Amérique: Correspondance Diplomatique et Documents.* 5 vols. Paris: Imprimerie Nationale, 1886–1892.

Drayton, John. *Memoirs of the American Revolution, from Its Commencement to the Year 1776, Inclusive; as Relating to the State of South-Carolina: And Occasionally Refering to the States of North-Carolina and Georgia.* 2 vols. Charleston: Printed by A. E. Miller, 1821.

Drinker, Elizabeth Sandwith. *Extracts from the Journal of Elizabeth Drinker, From 1759 to 1807, A.D.* Ed. Henry D. Biddle. Philadelphia: J. B. Lippincott, 1889.

Dulany, Daniel. *Considerations on the Propriety of Imposing Taxes in the British Colonies, for the Purpose of Raising a Revenue, by Act of Parliament.* Annapolis: Jonas Green, 1765. Reprint; London: J. Almon, 1766.

Eddis, William. *Letters from America, Historical and Descriptive; Comprising Occurrences from 1769, to 1777, Inclusive.* London: Printed for the author, and sold by C. Dilly, 1792.

Edwards, Alexander, comp. *Ordinances of the City Council of Charleston, in the State of South-Carolina, Passed Since the Incorporation of the City, Collected and Revised Pursuant to a Resolution of the Council.* Charleston: W. P. Young, 1802.

Ellet, Elizabeth F. *The Women of the American Revolution.* 3 vols. New York: Baker and Scribner, 1848–50.

Elliot, Jonathan, ed. *The Debates in the Several State Conventions, on the Adoption of the Federal Constitution, as Recommended by the General Convention at Philadelphia in 1787.* 2nd ed. 4 vols. Washington: Printed for the editor, 1836.

Elwyn, Alfred Langdon, ed. *Papers Relating to Public Events in Massachusetts Preceding the American Revolution.* Philadelphia: Printed for the Seventy-Six Society by T. K. and P. G. Collins, 1856.

Emerson, William. *Diaries and Letters of William Emerson, 1743–1776: Minister of the Church in Concord, Chaplain in the Revolutionary Army.* Ed. Amelia Forbes Emerson. N.p., 1972.

Etting, Frank Marx. *An Historical Account of the Old State House of Pennsylvania Now Known as the Hall of Independence.* Boston: James R. Osgood and Co., 1876.

Ewald, Johann. *Diary of the American War: A Hessian Journal*. Ed. Joseph P. Tustin. New Haven: Yale University Press, 1979.

Falconbridge, Anna Maria. *Two Voyages to Sierra Leone During the Years 1791-2-3, in a Series of Letters*. 2nd ed. London: Printed for the author, 1794.

Farrand, Max, ed. *The Records of the Federal Convention of 1787*. 3 vols. New Haven: Yale University Press, 1911.

Fauquier, Francis. *The Official Papers of Francis Fauquier, Lieutenant Governor of Virginia, 1758–1768*. Ed. George Reese. Virginia Historical Society Documents, Vols. 14–16. Charlottesville: Published for the Virginia Historical Society by the University Press of Virginia, 1980.

Finney, Walter. "The Revolutionary War Diaries of Captain Walter Finney." Ed. Joseph Lee Boyle. *South Carolina Historical Magazine* 98:2 (April 1997): 126–52.

Fish, Joseph. *The Church of Christ a Firm and Durable House. Shown in a Number of Sermons on Matth. XVI. 18. Upon This Rock I Will Build My Church, and the Gates of Hell Shall Not Prevail Against It, the Substance of Which Was Delivered at Stonington, Anno Domini, 1765*. New London: Timothy Green, 1767.

Force, Peter, ed. *American Archives. Fifth Series. Containing a Documentary History of the United States of America, from the Declaration of Independence, July 4, 1776 to the Definitive Treaty of Peace with Great Britain, September 3, 1783*. 3 vols. Washington, DC: M. St. Clair Clarke and Peter Force, 1848–1853.

——, ed. *American Archives. Fourth Series. Containing a Documentary History of the English Colonies in North America, from the King's Message to Parliament of March 7, 1774, to the Declaration of Independence by the United States*. 6 vols. Washington, DC: M. St. Clair Clarke and Peter Force, 1837–1846.

Ford, Worthington Chauncey, et al., eds. *Journals of the Continental Congress, 1774–1789*. 34 vols. Washington, DC: Government Printing Office, 1904–1937.

Franklin, Benjamin. *Memoirs of the Life and Writings of Benjamin Franklin*. Ed. William Temple Franklin. 3rd ed. Vol. 1. London: Henry Colburn, 1818.

Franks, Rebecca. "Letter of Miss Rebecca Franks." *Pennsylvania Magazine of History and Biography* 16:2 (July 1892): 216–18.

French, Allen. *General Gage's Informers: New Material Upon Lexington & Concord, Benjamin Thompson as Loyalist & the Treachery of Benjamin Church, Jr.* New York: Greenwood, 1968.

Frothingham, Richard, Jr. *History of the Siege of Boston and of the Battles of Lexington, Concord, and Bunker Hill. Also, an Account of the Bunker Hill Monument. With Illustrative Documents*. Boston: Charles C. Little and James Brown, 1849.

Fyfe, Christopher, ed. *"Our Children Free and Happy": Letters from Black Settlers in Africa in the 1790s*. Early Black Writers. Edinburgh: Edinburgh University Press, 1991.

Gage, Thomas. *A Circumstantial Account of an Attack That Happened on the 19th of April 1775 on His Majesty's Troops by a Number of the People of the Province of Massachusetts-Bay*. [Boston: John Howe, 1775].

——. *The Correspondence of General Thomas Gage*. Ed. Clarence Edwin Carter. 2 vols. [Hamden, CT]: Archon Books, 1969.

[Gale, Benjamin]. *Brief, Decent, but Free Remarks, and Observations, on Several Laws Passed by the Honorable Legislature of the State of Connecticut, Since the Year 1775*. Hartford, CT: Hudson & Goodwin, 1782.

A Geographic, Historical Summary; or, Narrative of the Present Controversy, Between the Wappinger Tribe of Indians, and the Claimants, Under the Original Patentee of a Large

Tract of Land in Philipse's Upper Patent, So Called. Hartford, CT: Printed by Green & Watson, 1768.

George III. *By the King, a Proclamation, For Suppressing Rebellion and Sedition.* [Boston: John Howe, 1775].

Gibbes, Robert W., ed. *Documentary History of the American Revolution: Consisting of Letters and Papers Relating to the Contest for Liberty, Chiefly in South Carolina, from Originals in the Possession of the Editor, and Other Sources.* 3 vols. New York; Columbia, SC: D. Appleton & Co.; Banner Steam-Power Press, 1853–1857.

Gleig, G. R. *The Life of Major-General Sir Thomas Munro, Bart. and K.C.B., Late Governor of Madras. With Extracts from His Correspondence and Private Papers.* Vol. 1. London: Henry Colburn and Richard Bentley, 1831.

Gordon, William. *The History of the Rise, Progress, and Establishment of the Independence of the United States of America.* 3rd American ed. Vol. 2. New York: Printed for Samuel Campbell by John Woods, 1801.

Graham, James. *The Life of General Daniel Morgan, of the Virginia Line of the Army of the United States, with Portions of His Correspondence; Compiled from Authentic Sources.* New York: Derby & Jackson, 1856.

Grant, W. L., James Munro, and Almeric W. FitzRoy, eds. *Acts of the Privy Council of England.* Colonial Series. 6 vols. London: His Majesty's Stationery Office, 1908–1912.

Great Britain. *The Examination of Doctor Benjamin Franklin, Before an August Assembly, Relating to the Repeal of the Stamp-Act, &c.* [Boston: Edes and Gill, 1766].

——. *Journals of the House of Commons.* Vol. 31. London: Re-printed by order of the House of Commons by His Majesty's Stationery Office, 1803.

——. *Journals of the House of Commons.* Vol. 32. London: Re-printed by order of the House of Commons by His Majesty's Stationery Office, 1803.

——. *The Statutes at Large, of England and of Great-Britain: From Magna Carta to the Union of the Kingdoms of Great Britain and Ireland.* 20 vols. Ed. John Raithby and Thomas Edlyne Tomlins. London: Printed by George Eyre and Andrew Strahan, 1811.

Great Britain, Parliament. *The Parliamentary Register; or, History of the Proceedings and Debates of the [House of Lords and] House of Commons: Containing an Account of the Most Interesting Speeches and Motions [and] Accurate Copies of the Most Remarkable Letters and Papers . . .* Vol. 9. London: Printed for J. Debrett, 1783.

Greene, Albert G. *Recollections of the Jersey Prison-Ship: From the Original Manuscripts of Captain Thomas Dring, One of the Prisoners.* Ed. Henry B. Dawson. Morrisania, NY: Alvord, 1865.

Greene, Nathanael. *The Papers of General Nathanael Greene.* Ed. Richard Showman et al. 13 vols. Chapel Hill: Published for the Rhode Island Historical Society by the University of North Carolina Press, 1976.

Griffitts, Hannah. "Two Letters of Hannah Griffitts to General Anthony Wayne." *Pennsylvania Magazine of History and Biography* 27:1 (1903): 109–27.

Grimké, John F. "John F. Grimke's Eyewitness Account of the Camden Court Riot, April 27–28, 1785." Ed. Robert A. Becker. *South Carolina Historical Magazine* 83:3 (July 1982): 209–13.

Grimké, Sarah Moore. *Letters on the Equality of the Sexes, and the Condition of Woman: Addressed to Mary S. Parker.* Boston: I. Knapp, 1838.

Hadden, James Murray. *Hadden's Journal and Orderly Books. A Journal Kept in Canada and upon Burgoyne's Campaign in 1776 and 1777, by Lieut. James M. Hadden, Roy. Art.* Ed. Horatio Rogers. Munsell's Historical Series, No. 12. Albany, NY: Joel Munsell's Sons, 1884.

Hagist, Don N. *British Soldiers, American War: Voices of the American Revolution.* Yardley, PA: Westholme, 2012.

Hall, Prince. *A Charge Delivered to the Brethren of the African Lodge on the 25th of June, 1792. At the Hall of Brother William Smith, in Charlestown.* [Boston: Printed and sold by T. & J. Fleet, 1792.]

Hamer, Philip M., ed. "Correspondence of Henry Stuart and Alexander Cameron with the Wataugans." *Mississippi Valley Historical Review* 17:3 (December 1930): 451–59.

Hamilton, Stanislaus Murray, ed. *Letters to Washington and Accompanying Papers.* Vol. 3. Cambridge, MA: Published for the Society of the Colonial Dames of America by the Riverside Press, 1901.

Hawkes, James. *A Retrospect of the Boston Tea-Party, with a Memoir of George R. T. Hewes, a Survivor of the Little Band of Patriots Who Drowned the Tea in Boston Harbour in 1773.* New York: S. S. Bliss, printer, 1834.

Heath, William. "The Heath Papers, Part II." In Massachusetts Historical Society, *Collections.* Ser. 7, Vol. 4 (Boston: Massachusetts Historical Society, 1904), 1–341.

——. *Heath's Memoirs of the American War.* Ed. Rufus Rockwell Wilson. Reprinted from the original edition of 1798. Source Books of American History. New York: A. Wessels Company, 1904.

——. *Memoirs of Major-General William Heath.* Ed. William Abbatt. New ed., with Illustrations and Notes. New York: W. Abbatt, 1901.

Heckewelder, John. *A Narrative of the Mission of the United Brethren Among the Delaware and Mohegan Indians, from Its Commencement, in the Year 1740, to the Close of the Year 1808.* Philadelphia: McCarty & Davis, 1820.

Hening, William Waller, ed. *The Statutes at Large: Being a Collection of All the Laws of Virginia from the First Session of the Legislature, in the Year 1619.* 2nd ed. 13 vols. Richmond: Printed for the editor by R. & W. & G. Bartow, 1819–1823.

Henry, John Joseph. *An Accurate and Interesting Account of the Hardships and Sufferings of That Band of Heroes, Who Traversed the Wilderness in the Campaign Against Quebec in 1775.* Lancaster, PA: Printed by William Greer, 1812.

Hildreth, Samuel P. *Pioneer History: Being an Account of the First Examinations of the Ohio Valley, and the Early Settlement of the Northwest Territory.* Historical and Philosophical Society of Ohio Publications, Vol. 1. Cincinnati: H. W. Derby, 1848.

Hildreth, Samuel P., Edward Deering Mansfield, and Ephraim Culter. *Biographical and Historical Memoirs of the Early Pioneer Settlers of Ohio, with Narratives of Incidents and Occurrences in 1775.* Cincinnati: H. W. Derby, 1852.

Historical Manuscripts Commission. *Report on American Manuscripts in the Royal Institution of Great Britain.* Presented to Parliament by Command of His Majesty. 4 vols. London: Printed for His Majesty's Stationery Office, by Mackie & Co. Ld., 1904–1909.

——. *Report on the Manuscripts of Mrs. Stopford-Sackville, of Drayton House, Northamptonshire.* Presented to Parliament by Command of His Majesty. 2 vols. Great Britain Parliamentary Papers by Command. Cd. 1892, 5038. London; Hereford: Printed for His Majesty's Stationery Office by Mackie & Co. Ld.; the Hereford Times Co., 1904–1910.

Hoadly, Charles J., ed. *The Public Records of the Colony of Connecticut.* Vol. 14. Hartford: Case, Lockwood, and Brainard Company, 1887.

Holton, Woody. *Black Americans in the Revolutionary Era: A Brief History with Documents.* Bedford Series in History and Culture. Boston: Bedford/St. Martin's, 2009.

Hopkins, Samuel. *Memoirs of the Life of Mrs. Sarah Osborn, Who Died at Newport, Rhode Island, on the Second Day of August, 1796. In the Eighty Third Year of Her Age.* Worcester, MA: Leonard Worcester, 1799.

Houck, Louis, ed. *The Spanish Regime in Missouri: A Collection of Papers and Documents Relating to Upper Louisiana Principally Within the Present Limits of Missouri During the Dominion of Spain, from the Archives of the Indies at Seville, etc., Translated from the Original Spanish into English, and Including Also Some Papers Concerning the Supposed Grant to Col. George Morgan at the Mouth of the Ohio, Found in the Congressional Library.* 2 vols. Chicago: R. R. Donnelley & Sons Company, 1909.

Hough, Franklin Benjamin. *A History of St. Lawrence and Franklin Counties, New York, from the Earliest Period to the Present Time.* Albany, NY: Little & Co., 1853.

Howard, John Eager. "Col. John Eager Howard's Account of the Battle of Germantown." *Maryland Historical Magazine* 4:4 (December 1909): 314–20.

Hulton, Ann. *Letters of a Loyalist Lady: Being the Letters of Ann Hulton, Sister of Henry Hulton, Commissioner of Customs at Boston, 1767–1776.* Cambridge: Harvard University Press, 1927.

Husband, Hermon. "'The Common Farmer (Number 2)': Hermon Husband's Plan for Peace Between the United States and the Indians, 1792." Ed. James Whittenburg. *William and Mary Quarterly*, Third Series, 34:4 (1977): 647–50.

———. *A Continuation of the Impartial Relation of the First Rise and Cause of the Recent Differences, in Publick Affairs, in the Province of North Carolina, &c.* [New Bern, NC?]: Printed for the author, 1770.

———. "A Fan for Fanning and Touchstone to Tryon." In Boyd, ed., *Some Eighteenth Century Tracts Concerning North Carolina*, 335–92.

———. *An Impartial Relation of the First Rise and Cause of the Recent Differences, in Publick Affairs, in the Province of North-Carolina; and of the Past Tumults and Riots That Lately Happened in That Province.* [New Bern, NC?]: Printed for the compiler, 1770.

———. *Proposals to Amend and Perfect the Policy of the Government of the United States of America; or: The Fulfilling of the Prophecies in the Latter Days, Commenced by the Independence of America* . . . Philadelphia; Baltimore: Printed for the author, 1782.

———. "Some Remarks on Religion, With the Author's Experience in Pursuit Thereof . . . ," In Boyd, ed., *Some Eighteenth Century Tracts*, 193–246.

[Husband, Hermon?] "Lycurgus." *XIV Sermons on the Characters of Jacob's Fourteen Sons: [Five Lines of Scripture Texts].* Philadelphia: Printed for the author by William Spotswood, 1789.

Hutchinson, Thomas. *The Correspondence of Thomas Hutchinson.* Ed. John W. Tyler and Elizabeth Dubrulle. Publications of the Colonial Society of Massachusetts, Vol. 84. Boston: Colonial Society of Massachusetts, 2014.

[Inglis, Charles] "An American." *The True Interest of America Impartially Stated, in Certain Strictures on a Pamphlet Intitled Common Sense.* 2nd ed. Philadelphia: Printed and sold by James Humphreys, Jr., 1776.

Irving, Washington. *Life of George Washington.* Vol. 2. New York: Putnam, 1856.

Izard, Ralph. *Correspondence of Mr. Ralph Izard, of South Carolina, from the Year 1774 to 1804; with a Short Memoir.* Ed. Anne Izard Deas. New York: Charles S. Francis & Co., 1844.

Jefferson, Thomas. *Notes on the State of Virginia. With an Appendix Relative to the Murder of Logan's Family.* Trenton: Printed by Wilson & Blackwell, for Mathew Carey, 1803.

———. *Notes on the State of Virginia.* Ed. William Harwood Peden. Chapel Hill: Published for the Institute of Early American History and Culture by the University of North Carolina Press, 1955.

———. *The Papers of Thomas Jefferson.* First Series. Ed. Julian P. Boyd et al. 43 vols. to date. Princeton: Princeton University Press, 1950–.

Jensen, Merrell. *The Documentary History of the Ratification of the Constitution*. Ed. Merrell Jensen et al. 32 vols. to date. Madison: Wisconsin Historical Society Press, 1976–.

———. *English Historical Documents: American Colonial Documents to 1776*. Vol. 9. New York: Oxford University Press, 1955.

J. J. "The Battle of the Great Bridge." *Virginia Historical Register and Literary Companion* 6:1 (1853): 1–6.

Johns, Kensey, Joshua Gilpin, and Robert H. Goldsborough. "Observations Respecting the Chesapeake and Delaware Canal." In *American State Papers: Miscellaneous*, 2[?] (1834): 286–91.

Johnson, Joseph. *Traditions and Reminiscences: Chiefly of the American Revolution in the South; Including Biographical Sketches, Incidents, and Anecdotes*. Charleston: Walker & James, 1851.

Johnson, Samuel. *Taxation No Tyranny: An Answer to the Resolutions and Address of the American Congress*. London: Printed for T. Cadell, 1775.

Johnson, Uzal. *Captured at Kings Mountain: The Journal of Uzal Johnson, a Loyalist Surgeon*. Ed. Wade S. Kolb III, Robert M. Weir, and Anne H. Weir. Columbia: University of South Carolina Press, 2011.

Johnson, William. *The Papers of Sir William Johnson*. Ed. James Sullivan et al. 14 vols. Albany: University of the State of New York, 1921–1939.

Johnson, William. *Sketches of the Life and Correspondence of Nathanael Greene, Major General of the Armies of the United States, in the War of the Revolution*. 2 vols. Charleston, SC: Printed for the author, by A. E. Miller, 1822.

Johnston, Elizabeth Lichtenstein. *Recollections of a Georgia Loyalist*. Ed. Arthur Wentworth Eaton. New York: M. F. Mansfield & Company, 1901.

Jones, Samuel W. *Memoir of the Hon. James Duane, Judge of the District Court of the U. States for New York*. Schenectady, NY: Keyser, Printer, 1852.

Journal of the House of Delegates of Virginia. Anno Domini, 1776. Richmond, VA: Printed by Samuel Shepherd & Co., 1828.

Kellogg, Louise Phelps, ed. *Frontier Advance on the Upper Ohio, 1778–1779*. Publications of the State Historical Society of Wisconsin. Collections, Vol. 23, Draper Series, Vol. 4. Madison: The Society, 1916.

Kendall, Amos. *Life of Andrew Jackson: Private, Military, and Civil*. New York: Harper & Brothers, 1843.

Kennedy, John Pendleton, ed. *Journals of the House of Burgesses of Virginia, 1766–1769*. Richmond, VA: The Colonial Press, E. Waddey Co., 1906.

———, ed. *Journals of the House of Burgesses of Virginia, 1773–1776. Including the Records of the Committee of Correspondence*. Richmond, VA: The Colonial Press, E. Waddey Co., 1905.

Kenny, James. "Journal of James Kenny, 1761–1763." Ed. John W. Jordan. *Pennsylvania Magazine of History and Biography* 37:1, 2 (1913): 1–47, 152–201.

Keppel, Thomas Robert, ed. *The Life of Augustus, Viscount Keppel, Admiral of the White, and First Lord of the Admiralty in 1782–3*. 2 vols. London: Henry Colburn, 1842.

Kingsley, Ronald F., and Francis Carr Clerke. "Letters to Lord Polwarth from Sir Francis-Carr Clerke, Aide-de-Camp to General John Burgoyne." *New York History* 79:4 (October 1998): 393–424.

Knox, Henry, and Lucy Flucker Knox. *The Revolutionary War Lives and Letters of Lucy and Henry Knox*. Ed. Phillip Hamilton. Baltimore: Johns Hopkins University Press, 2017.

[Knox, William]. *Extra Official State Papers. Addressed to the Right Hon. Lord Rawdon and the Other Members of the Two Houses of Parliament, Associated for the Preservation of the Constitution and Promoting the Prosperity of the British Empire.* Vol. 2. London: Printed for J. Debrett, 1789.

——. *The Interest of the Merchants and Manufacturers of Great Britain, in the Present Contest with the Colonies, Stated and Considered.* London: Printed for T. Cadell, 1774.

Lafayette, Marquis de. *Memoirs, Correspondence, and Manuscripts of General Lafayette.* 3 vols. London: Published by His Family; Saunders and Otley, 1837.

Lamb, Roger. *Memoir of His Own Life.* Dublin: Printed by J. Jones, 1811.

Laurens, Henry. *The Papers of Henry Laurens.* Ed. Philip M. Hamer et al. Columbia: Published for the South Carolina Historical Society by the University of South Carolina Press, 1968.

Lee, Arthur. *An Essay in Vindication of the Continental Colonies of America, from a Censure of Mr Adam Smith in His Theory of Moral Sentiments. With Some Reflections on Slavery in General.* London: Printed for the author, 1764.

Lee, Charles. *The Lee Papers.* 4 vols. Collections of the New-York Historical Society for the Year 1871[–1874]. Publication Fund Series, Vols. 4–7. New York: Printed for the Society, 1872–1875.

Lee, Henry. *The Campaign of 1781 in the Carolinas; with Remarks, Historical and Critical, on Johnson's Life of Greene. To Which Is Added an Appendix of Original Documents, Relating to the History of the Revolution.* Philadelphia: E. Littell, 1824.

——. *Memoirs of the War in the Southern Department of the United States.* 2 vols. Philadelphia: Bradford and Inskeep, 1812.

——. *Memoirs of the War in the Southern Department of the United States.* Ed. Robert E. Lee. A New Ed., with Revisions, and a Biography of the Author. New York: University Publishing Co., 1869.

Lee, Richard Henry. *The Letters of Richard Henry Lee.* Ed. James Curtis Ballagh. 2 vols. New York: The Macmillan Company, 1911–1914.

Lee, William. *Letters of William Lee, Sheriff and Alderman of London; Commercial Agent of the Continental Congress in France; and Minister to the Courts of Vienna and Berlin. 1766–1783.* Ed. Worthington Chauncey Ford. 3 vols. Brooklyn, NY: Historical Printing Club, 1891.

"Letters from Lafayette to Luzerne, 1780–1782, Part II." *American Historical Review* 20:3 (April 1915): 577–612.

"Letters of Rev. Jonathan Boucher." *Maryland Historical Magazine* 9:4 (December 1912): 337–56.

Lind, John. *An Answer to the Declaration of the American Congress.* London: Printed for T. Cadell, J. Walter and T. Sewell, 1776.

Loskiel, George Henry. *History of the Mission of the United Brethren Among the Indians in North America.* Trans. by Christian Ignatius Latrobe. London: The Brethren's Society for the Furtherance of the Gospel, 1794.

Lossing, Benson J., ed. *American Historical Record, and Repertory of Notes and Queries. Concerning the History and Antiquities of America and Biography of Americans.* 3 vols. Philadelphia: Chase & Town, 1872–1874.

——. *The Life and Times of Philip Schuyler.* Vol. 2. New York: Sheldon and Company, 1873.

——. *The Pictorial Field-Book of the Revolution; or, Illustrations, by Pen and Pencil, of the History, Biography, Scenery, Relics, and Traditions of the War for Independence.* 2 vols. New York: Harper & Brothers, 1860.

Loudon, Archibald. *A Selection of Some of the Most Interesting Narratives, of Outrages, Committed by the Indians, in Their Wars with the White People.* Vol. 1. Carlisle, PA: A. Loudon (Whitehall), 1808.

Lowell, John, and Samuel M. Quincy, eds. "Hopkins vs. Ward, An Ante-Revolutionary Lawsuit." *Monthly Law Reporter* 22 (October 1859): 327–39.

Lynn, Mary C., ed. *The Specht Journal: A Military Journal of the Burgoyne Campaign.* Trans. Helga Doblin. Contributions in Military Studies, No. 158. Westport, CT: Greenwood, 1995.

Mark, Irving, and Oscar Handlin. "Land Cases in Colonial New York 1765–1767: The King v. William Prendergast." *New York University Law Quarterly Review* 19:2 (January 1942): 165–95.

Marrant, John. *A Sermon Preached on the 24th Day of June 1789, Being the Festival of St. John the Baptist, at the Request of the Right Worshipful the Grand Master Prince Hall, and the Rest of the Brethren of the African Lodge of the Honorable Society of Free and Accepted Masons in Boston.* Boston: Printed and sold by Thomas and John Fleet, 1789.

Marshall, Christopher. *Extracts from the Diary of Christopher Marshall, Kept in Philadelphia and Lancaster, During the American Revolution, 1774–1781.* Ed. William Duane. Albany: Joel Munsell, 1877.

Marshall, John. *The Life of George Washington, Commander in Chief of the American Forces During the War Which Established the Independence of His Country, and First President of the United States.* 2nd ed. 2 vols. Philadelphia: James Crissy, 1832.

Martin, Joseph Plumb. *A Narrative of a Revolutionary Soldier.* Ed. Thomas Fleming and William Chad Stanley. New York: Signet, 2001.

——. *A Narrative of Some of the Adventures, Dangers and Sufferings of a Revolutionary Soldier; Interspersed with Anecdotes of Incidents That Occurred Within His Own Observation.* Hallowell, ME: Printed by Glazier, Masters & Co., 1830.

——. *Ordinary Courage: The Revolutionary War Adventures of Joseph Plumb Martin.* Ed. James Kirby Martin. 4th ed. Chichester, West Sussex, UK: Wiley-Blackwell, 2013.

Maryland General Assembly. *Laws of Maryland, Made and Passed at a Session of Assembly . . . Begun . . . On Wednesday the Fifth of February, in the Year of our Lord One Thousand Seven Hundred and Seventy-Seven* (Annapolis: Frederick Green, n.d.).

Mason, George. *The Papers of George Mason, 1725–1792.* Ed. Robert A. Rutland. Vol. 1. Chapel Hill: University of North Carolina Press, 1970.

Mason, Priscilla, "Salutatory Oration," May 15, 1793. In *The Rise and Progress of the Young-Ladies' Academy of Philadelphia: Containing an Account of a Number of Public Examinations & Commencements; the Charter and Bye-Laws; Likewise, a Number of Orations Delivered by the Young Ladies, and Several by the Trustees of Said Institution* (Philadelphia: Stewart & Cochran, 1794), 90–95.

Maury, Ann, ed. *Memoirs of a Huguenot Family: Translated and Compiled from the Original Autobiography of the Rev. James Fontaine.* New York: George P. Putnam & Co., 1853.

Maxwell, William, ed. *The Virginia Historical Register, and Literary Companion.* Vol. 6. Richmond, VA: Printed for the proprietor by Macfarlane & Fergusson, 1853.

M'Call, Hugh. *The History of Georgia, Containing Brief Sketches of the Most Remarkable Events, up to the Present Day.* Vol. 2. Savannah: William T. Williams, 1816.

McClellan, Joseph. *Pennsylvania in the War of the Revolution, Battalions and Line, 1775–1783.* Ed. John Blair Linn and William Henry Egle. Harrisburg, PA: Lane S. Hart, 1880.

McIlwaine, H. R., Benjamin J. Hillman, and Wilmer Lee Hall, eds. *Executive Journals of the Council of Colonial Virginia.* 6 vols. Richmond: Virginia State Library, 1925–1966.

McMichael, James. "Diary of Lieutenant James McMichael, of the Pennsylvania Line, 1776–1778." *Pennsylvania Magazine of History and Biography* 16:2 (July 1892): 129–59.

M'Cullough, John. "A Narrative of the Captivity of John M'Cullough Esq., Written by Himself." In Archibald Loudon, ed., *Selection of Some of the Most Interesting Narratives, or the Outrages Committed by the Indians in Their Wars with the White People* Vol. 1 (Carlisle, PA: A. Loudon, 1808), 252–301.

Mercer, George. *George Mercer Papers Relating to the Ohio Company of Virginia*. Ed. Lois Mulkearn. Pittsburgh: University of Pittsburgh Press, 1954.

Michigan Pioneer and Historical Society and M. Agnes Burton. *Collections and Researches Made by the Michigan Pioneer and Historical Society*. Vols. 9 (with variant title), 10 (with variant title), 19, 20. Lansing: Wynkoop, Hallenbeck, Crawford Company, 1886–92.

Middleton, Arthur. "Correspondence of Hon. Arthur Middleton, Signer of the Declaration of Independence." Ed. Joseph W. Barnwell. *South Carolina Historical and Genealogical Magazine* 26:4 (October 1925): 183–213.

——. "Correspondence of Hon. Arthur Middleton (Continued)." Ed. Joseph W. Barnwell. *South Carolina Historical and Genealogical Magazine* 27:1 (January 1926): 1–29.

——. "Correspondence of Hon. Arthur Middleton (Continued)." Ed. Joseph W. Barnwell. *South Carolina Historical and Genealogical Magazine* 27:2 (April 1926): 51–80.

——. "Correspondence of Hon. Arthur Middleton (Continued)." Ed. Joseph W. Barnwell. *South Carolina Historical and Genealogical Magazine* 27:3 (July 1926): 107–55.

Mills, Robert. *Statistics of South Carolina, Including a View of Its Natural, Civil, and Military History, General and Particular*. Charleston: Hurlbut and Lloyd, 1826.

Minot, George Richards. *The History of the Insurrections, in Massachusetts, in the Year MDCCLXXXVI, and the Rebellion Consequent Thereon*. Worcester, MA: Isaiah Thomas, 1788.

Montrésor, James, and John Montrésor. *The Montresor Journals*. Ed. G. D. Scull. Collections of the New-York Historical Society for the Year 1881. Publication Fund Series, Vol. 14. New York: Printed for the Society, 1882.

Morgan, Edmund S., ed. *Prologue to Revolution: Sources and Documents on the Stamp Act Crisis, 1764–1766*. Documentary Problems in Early American History. Chapel Hill: Published for the Institute of Early American History and Culture by the University of North Carolina Press, 1959.

Morris, Robert. *The Papers of Robert Morris, 1781–1784*. Ed. E. James Ferguson et al. 9 vols. Pittsburgh: University of Pittsburgh Press, 1973–1999.

Moultrie, William. *Memoirs of the American Revolution, so Far as It Related to the States of North and South Carolina, and Georgia*. 2 vols. New York: Printed by David Longworth for the author, 1802.

Muhlenberg, Henry A. *The Life of Major-General Peter Muhlenberg of the Revolutionary Army*. Philadelphia: Carey and Hart, 1849.

[Murray, Charles], "Journal of a French Traveller in the Colonies, 1765, I." *American Historical Review* 26:4 (July 1921): 726–47.

Napier, Francis. "Lord Francis Napier's Journal of the Burgoyne Campaign." Ed. S. Sydney Bradford. *Maryland Historical Magazine* 57:4 (December 1962): 285–333.

Onderdonk, Henry, Jr. *Revolutionary Incidents of Suffolk and Kings Counties, With an Account of the Battle of Long Island and the British Prisons and Prison-Ships at New-York*. New York: Leavitt & Co., 1849.

Orderly Book of the 71st Highland Regiment of Foot (Fraser's Highlanders), 1779. hdl.huntington.org/digital/collection/p15150coll7/id/8196.

Oswald, Richard. *Memorandum on the Folly of Invading Virginia, the Strategic Importance of Portsmouth, and the Need for Civilian Control of the Military; Written in 1781 by the British Negotiator of the First American Treaty of Peace*. Ed. Walter Stitt Robinson Jr. Charlottesville: Published by the University of Virginia Press for the Tracy W. McGregor Library, 1953.

Otis, James. *Considerations on Behalf of the Colonists. In a Letter to a Noble Lord.* 2nd ed. London: Printed for J. Almon, 1765.

———. *The Rights of the British Colonies Asserted and Proved.* Boston: Printed and Sold by Edes and Gill, 1764.

———. *A Vindication of the British Colonies.* Boston: Edes and Gill, 1765.

[Paine, Thomas]. *The American Crisis. Number I. By the Author of Common Sense.* Philadelphia: Printed by Styner and Cist, 1777.

———. *Common Sense: Addressed to the Inhabitants of America . . .* A new edition, with Several additions in the body of the work. To which is added, an Appendix; Together with an address to the people called Quakers. Philadelphia: Printed and sold by W. and T. Bradford, 1776.

———. *Dissertations on Government, the Affairs of the Bank, and Paper Money.* London: W. T. Sherwin, 1817.

Palmer, William Pitt, et al., eds. *Calendar of Virginia State Papers and Other Manuscripts . . . Preserved in the Capitol at Richmond.* 11 vols. Richmond, 1875–1893.

Pargellis, Stanley McCrory, ed. *Military Affairs in North America, 1748–1765: Selected Documents from the Cumberland Papers in Windsor Castle.* New York: D. Appleton-Century Company, Inc., 1936.

Pasteur, William. "Deposition of Dr. William Pasteur in Regard to the Removal of Powder from the Williamsburg Magazine." *Virginia Magazine of History and Biography* 13:1 (1905): 36–50.

Pendleton, Edmund. *The Letters and Papers of Edmund Pendleton, 1734–1803.* Ed. David John Mays. 2 vols. Virginia Historical Society. Documents, Vols. 7–8. Charlottesville: Published for the Virginia Historical Society by University Press of Virginia, 1967.

Pennsylvania Archives. Ser. 1. 12 vols. Philadelphia: Joseph Severns & Co., 1852–1856.

Pennsylvania Archives. Ser. 2. 19 vols. Harrisburg: Lane S. Hart; E. K. Meyers, 1874–1893.

Pennsylvania Provincial Council. *Minutes of the Provincial Council of Pennsylvania, from the Organization to the Termination of the Proprietary Government.* Ed. Samuel Hazard. Vol. 6. Colonial Records of Pennsylvania, Vols. 1–10. Harrisburg: Printed by Theo. Fenn & Co., 1851.

The People the Best Governors: Or a Plan of Government Founded on the Just Principles of Natural Freedom. N.p.: 1776.

Percy, Hugh. *Letters of Hugh Earl Percy from Boston and New York, 1774–1776.* Ed. Charles Knowles Bolton. Boston: Charles E. Goodspeed, 1902.

Peters, Richard, ed. *The Public Statutes at Large of the United States of America.* Vol. 1. Boston: Charles C. Little and James Brown, 1845.

Pickering, Octavius, and Charles Wentworth Upham, eds. *The Life of Timothy Pickering.* Vol. 1. Boston: Little, Brown, and Company, 1867.

Piecuch, Jim. *The Battle of Camden: A Documentary History.* Charleston, SC: History Press, 2006.

Pitt, William. *Correspondence of William Pitt, Earl of Chatham.* Ed. John Henry Pringle and William Stanhope Taylor. 4 vols. London: John Murray, 1838–1840.

A Planter. *Candid Reflections upon the Judgement Lately Awarded by the Court of King's Bench . . . on What Is Commonly Called the Negroe-Cause.* London: Printed for T. Lowndes, 1772.

Powell, William S., James K. Huhta, and Thomas J. Farnham, eds. *The Regulators in North Carolina: A Documentary History, 1759–1776.* Raleigh: State Department of Archives and History, 1971.

Pratt, George W. *An Account of the British Expedition Above the Highlands of the Hudson*

River, and of the Events Connected with the Burning of Kingston in 1777. Albany, NY: Munsell & Rowland, 1861.

Proceedings of a General Court-Martial Held at Brunswick, in the State of New-Jersey, by Order of His Excellency Gen. Washington, Commander-in-Chief of the Army of the United States of America, for the Trial of Major-General Lee, July 4th, 1778. New York: Privately reprinted, 1864.

The Proceedings Relative to Calling the Conventions of 1776 and 1790. Harrisburg, PA: Printed by J. S. Wiestling, 1825.

Putnam, A. W. History of Middle Tennessee; or, Life and Times of Gen. James Robertson. Nashville: Printed for the author, 1859.

Raithby, John, and T. E. Tomlins, eds. The Statutes at Large, of England and of Great Britain: From Magna Carta to the Union of the Kingdoms of Great Britain and Ireland. 20 vols. London: George Eyre and Andrew Strahan, 1811.

Ramsay, David. The History of the Revolution of South-Carolina: From a British Province to an Independent State. 2 vols. Trenton, NJ: Printed by Isaac Collins, 1785.

———. Ramsay's History of South Carolina, from Its First Settlement in 1670 to the Year 1808. Newberry, SC: W. J. Duffie, 1858.

Randolph, Edmund. History of Virginia. Virginia Historical Society Documents, Vol. 9. Charlottesville: Published for the Virginia Historical Society by University Press of Virginia, 1970.

[Reed, Esther]. The Sentiments of an American Woman. Philadelphia: Printed by John Dunlap, 1780.

Reed, Joseph. Life and Correspondence of Joseph Reed, Military Secretary of Washington, at Cambridge; Adjutant-General of the Continental Army; Member of the Congress of the United States; and President of the Executive Council of the State of Pennsylvania. Ed. William B. Reed. 2 vols. Philadelphia: Lindsay and Blakiston, 1847.

Reed, William B. The Life of Esther De Berdt, Afterwards Esther Reed, of Pennsylvania. Philadelphia: C. Sherman, Printer, 1853.

Reeves, John B. "Extracts from the Letter-Books of Lieutenant Enos Reeves, of the Pennsylvania Line." Pennsylvania Magazine of History and Biography 21:1 (1897): 72–85.

A Report of the Record Commissioners of the City of Boston Containing the Boston Town Records, 1758 to 1769. Boston: Rockwell and Churchill, 1886.

A Report of the Record Commissioners of the City of Boston Containing the Boston Town Records, 1770 Through 1777. Boston: Rockwell and Churchill, 1887.

Richardson, Samuel. The History of Sir Charles Grandison. In a Series of Letters. 7th ed., Vol. 6. London: Printed for John Donaldson, 1776.

Ricord, Frederick W., and William Nelson, eds. Documents Relating to the Colonial History of the State of New Jersey. First Ser. Vol 10. Newark: Daily Advertiser Printing House, 1886.

Riedesel, Friedrich Adolf. Memoirs, and Letters and Journals, of Major General Riedesel During His Residence in America. Ed. William L. Stone. Munsell's Series of Local American History, Vols. 8–9. Albany, NY: J. Munsell, 1868.

Robertson, Archibald. Archibald Robertson: His Diaries and Sketches in America, 1762–1780. Reprint ed. New York: New York Public Library and Arno Press, 1971.

Romans, Bernard. A Concise Natural History of East and West-Florida: Containing, an Account of the Natural Produce of All the Southern Part of British America, in the Three Kingdoms of Nature, Particularly the Animal and Vegetable. Printed in New York; sold by R. Aitken, London, 1776.

Rosswurm, Steve, ed. "Equality and Justice: Documents from Philadelphia's Popular Revolution, 1775–1780." Pennsylvania History 52:4 (October 1985): 254–68.

Saye, James Hodge. *Memoirs of Major Joseph McJunkin, Revolutionary Patriot*. Greenwood, SC: Index-Journal, 1925.

Seaver, James E. *A Narrative of the Life of Mrs. Mary Jemison, Who Was Taken by the Indians, in the Year 1755, When Only About Twelve Years of Age, and Has Continued to Reside Amongst Them to the Present Time*. Howden: Printed [by W. Walker, Otley.] for R. Parkin, 1826.

Seymour, William. *A Journal of the Southern Expedition, 1780–1783*. Papers of the Historical Society of Delaware 15. Wilmington: Historical Society of Delaware, 1896.

Shaw, Samuel. *The Journals of Major Samuel Shaw, the First American Consul at Canton. With a Life of the Author*. Ed. Josiah Quincy. Boston: Wm. Crosby and H. P. Nichols, 1847.

Shirley, William. *Correspondence of William Shirley, Governor of Massachusetts and Military Commander in America, 1731–1760*. Ed. Charles Henry Lincoln. Vol. 2. New York: The Macmillan Co., 1912.

A Short Narrative of the Horrid Massacre in Boston, Perpetrated in the Evening of the Fifth Day of March, 1770, by Soldiers of the 29th Regiment, Which with the 14th Regiment Were Then Quartered There; with Some Observations on the State of Things Prior to That Catastrophe. New York: John Doggett, Jr., 1849.

Simcoe, John Graves. *Simcoe's Military Journal. A History of the Operations of a Partisan Corps, Called the Queen's Rangers, Commanded by Lieut. Col. J. G. Simcoe, During the War of the American Revolution . . .* New York: Bartlett & Welford, 1844.

Simmons, R. C., and Peter David Garner Thomas, eds. *Proceedings and Debates of the British Parliaments Respecting North America, 1754–1783*. 6 vols. Millwood, NY: Kraus International Publications, 1982–1987.

Simpson, Henry. *The Lives of Eminent Philadelphians, Now Deceased. Collected from Original and Authentic Sources*. Philadelphia: William Brotherhead, 1859.

Sims, George. "An Address to the People of Granville County," June 6, 1765. In Boyd, ed., *Some Eighteenth Century Tracts*, 182–92.

Smith, Dwight L. *From Greene Ville to Fallen Timbers: A Journal of the Wayne Campaign, July 28–September 14, 1794*. Indiana Historical Society Publications. Vol. 16:3. Indianapolis: Indiana Historical Society, 1952.

Smith, Joshua Hett. *An Authentic Narrative of the Causes Which Led to the Death of Major André, Adjutant-General of His Majesty's Forces in North-America*. New York: Printed for Evert Duyckinck, 1809.

Smith, Paul Hubert et al., eds. *Letters of Delegates to Congress, 1774–1789*. 26 vols. Washington, DC: Library of Congress: for sale by the Superintendent of Documents, Government Printing Office, 1976–2000.

Smith, William. *Historical Memoirs from 26 August 1778 to 12 November 1783 of William Smith, Historian of the Province of New York, Member of the Governor's Council, and Last Chief Justice of That Province Under the Crown; Chief Justice of Quebec*. Ed. William H. W. Sabine. Eyewitness Accounts of the American Revolution. Series III. New York: New York Times, 1971.

Smith, William, and Thomas Hutchins. *An Historical Account of the Expedition Against the Ohio Indians, in the Year 1764: Under the Command of Henry Bouquet, Esq: Colonel of Foot, and Now Brigadier General in America. Including His Transactions with the Indians, Relative to the Delivery of Their Prisoners, and the Preliminaries of Peace . . .* Philadelphia: Printed and sold by W. Bradford, 1765.

Smith, William James, ed. *The Grenville Papers: Being the Correspondence of Richard Grenville, Earl Temple, K.G., and the Right Hon. George Grenville, Their Friends and Contemporaries*. Vol. 3. London: John Murray, 1853.

South-Carolina Historical Society. *Collections of the South-Carolina Historical Society.* Vol. 3. Charleston: South-Carolina Historical Society, 1859.

Sparks, Jared. *The Life and Treason of Benedict Arnold.* Library of American Biography. Boston: Hilliard, Gray, and Co., 1835.

Spencer, Oliver M. *The Indian Captivity of O. M. Spencer.* Ed. Milo Milton Quaife. Lakeside Classics, Vol. 15. Chicago: R. R. Donnelley & Sons, 1917.

Stanton, Elizabeth Cady. *Declaration of Sentiments: Seneca Falls Convention, July 1848.* Tucson, AZ: Kore Press, 2004.

Staples, William R. *The Documentary History of the Destruction of the Gaspee.* Providence, RI: Knowles, Vose, and Anthony, 1845.

———. *Rhode Island in the Continental Congress, with the Journal of the Convention That Adopted the Constitution. 1765–1790.* Ed. Reuben Aldridge Guild. Providence: Providence Press Company, Printers to the State, 1870.

Stedman, C. *The History of the Origin, Progress, and Termination of the American War.* 2 vols. London: Printed for the author and sold by J. Murray, J. Debrett, and J. Kerby, 1794.

Sterne, Laurence. *The Life and Opinions of Tristram Shandy, Gentleman.* 2 vols. York: Printed by Ann Ward, 1760.

Steuart, A. Francis, ed. "Letters from Virginia. 1774–1781." *Magazine of History, With Notes and Queries* 3:3 (March 1906): 151–61.

Stevens, Benjamin Franklin. *The Campaign in Virginia 1781.* 2 vols. London: Printed by Chas. Straker and Sons, 1888.

Stevens, John Austin, ed. "The Battle of Camden Described by Major McGill." *Magazine of American History with Notes and Queries* 5:4 (October 1880): 278–79.

Stewardson, Thomas, ed. "Extracts from the Letter-Book of Benjamin Marshall, 1763–1766." *Pennsylvania Magazine of History and Biography* 20:2 (1896): 204–12.

Stocking, Abner. *An Interesting Journal of Abner Stocking of Chatham, Connecticut: Detailing the Distressing Events of the Expedition Against Quebec, Under the Command of Col. Arnold in the Year 1775.* Catskill, NY: Eagle Office, 1810.

Stone, William L. *Life of Joseph Brant-Thayendanegea: Including the Border Wars of the American Revolution, and Sketches of the Indian Campaigns of Generals Harmar, St. Clair, and Wayne . . .* 2 vols. Buffalo, NY: Phinney & Co., 1851.

Stryker, William S. *The Battles of Trenton and Princeton.* Boston: Houghton, Mifflin, and Company, 1898.

Sullivan, James. *Letters and Papers of Major-General John Sullivan, Continental Army.* Ed. Otis Grant Hammond. 3 vols. New Hampshire Historical Society. Collections, Vols. 13–15. Concord: New Hampshire Historical Society, 1930–1938.

Supplement to the Connecticut Courant: Containing Tales, Travels, History, Biography, Poetry, and a Great Variety of Miscellaneous Articles. Hartford, CT: J. L. Boswell, 1835.

Sutherland, William. "Sutherland's Narrative." In Harold Murdock, ed., *Late News of the Excursion and Ravages of the King's Troops on the Nineteenth of April, 1775* (Cambridge: Printed by the Press at Harvard College for the Club of Odd Volumes, 1927), 11–24.

Swift, Zephaniah. *The Security of the Rights of Citizens in the State of Connecticut Considered.* Hartford: Hudson and Goodwin, 1792.

Tallmadge, Benjamin. *Memoir of Col. Benjamin Tallmadge: Prepared by Himself at the Request of His Children.* New York: Thomas Holman, 1858.

Tarleton, [Banastre]. *A History of the Campaigns of 1780 and 1781, in the Southern Provinces of North America.* Dublin: Printed for Colles, Exshaw, White, H. Whitestone, Burton, Byrne, Moore, Jones, and Dornin, 1787.

Thacher, James. *A Military Journal During the American Revolutionary War, from 1775 to*

1783, Describing Interesting Events and Transactions of This Period, with Numerous Historical Facts and Anecdotes, from the Original Manuscript . . . Boston: Richardson and Lord, 1823.

Thwaites, Reuben Gold, and Louise Phelps Kellogg, eds. *Documentary History of Dunmore's War, 1774.* Draper Series, Vol. 1. Madison: Wisconsin Historical Society, 1905.

Tilden, John Bell. "Extracts from the Journal of Lieutenant John Bell Tilden, Second Pennsylvania Line, 1781–1782 (Continued)." *Pennsylvania Magazine of History and Biography* 19:2 (1895): 208–33.

Tinling, Marion, ed. *The Correspondence of the Three William Byrds of Westover, Virginia, 1684–1776.* 2 vols. Virginia Historical Society Documents, Vols. 12–13. Charlottesville: Published for the Virginia Historical Society by the University Press of Virginia, 1977.

The True Constitutional Means for Putting an End to the Disputes Between Great-Britain and the American Colonies. London: Printed for T. Becket and P. A. De Hondt, 1769.

Tudor, William. *The Life of James Otis, of Massachusetts: Containing Also, Notices of Some Contemporary Characters and Events from the Year 1760 to 1775.* Boston: Wells and Lilly, 1823.

Uhlendorf, Bernhard A., ed. *The Siege of Charleston with an Account of the Province of South Carolina: Diaries and Letters of Hessian Officers from the von Jungkenn Papers in the William L. Clements Library.* University of Michigan Publications. History and Political Science, Vol. 12. Ann Arbor: University of Michigan Press, 1938.

United States Census Bureau. *A Century of Population Growth: From the First Census of the United States to the Twelfth, 1790–1900.* Baltimore: Genealogical Publishing Company, 1969.

Van Schaack, Henry C. *The Life of Peter Van Schaack, LL.D., Embracing Selections from His Correspondence and Other Writings During the American Revolution, and His Exile in England.* New York: D. Appleton & Co., 1842.

Van Schreeven, William James, Robert L. Scribner, and Brent Tarter, eds. *Revolutionary Virginia: The Road to Independence.* 7 vols. Charlottesville: Published for Virginia Independence Bicentennial Commission by University Press of Virginia, 1973–1989.

"Virginia Legislative Papers, From the Originals in the Virginia State Archives (Continued)." *Virginia Magazine of History and Biography* 18:1 (January 1910): 24–44.

Waldo, Albigence. "Valley Forge, 1777–1778. Diary of Surgeon Albigence Waldo, of the Connecticut Line." *Pennsylvania Magazine of History and Biography* 21:3 (1897): 299–323.

Walpole, Horace. *Memoirs of the Reign of King George the Third.* Ed. Sir Denis Le Marchant. Vol. 2. Philadelphia: Lea & Blanchard, 1845.

Washington, George. *The Writings of George Washington from the Original Manuscript Sources, 1745–1799.* Ed. John Clement Fitzpatrick. George Washington bicentennial ed. Vol. 21. Washington, DC: Government Printing Office, 1937.

Wasmus, J. F. *An Eyewitness Account of the American Revolution and New England Life: The Journal of J. F. Wasmus, German Company Surgeon, 1776–1783.* Ed. Mary C. Lynn. Trans. Helga Doblin. Contributions in Military Studies, No. 106. New York: Greenwood, 1990.

Waterhouse, Benjamin. *An Essay on Junius and His Letters; Embracing a Sketch of the Life and Character of William Pitt, Earl of Chatham, and Memoirs of Certain Other Distinguished Individuals* . . . Boston: Gray and Bowen, 1831.

Watts, John. *Letter Book of John Watts Merchant and Councillor of New York, January 1, 1762–December 22, 1765.* Ed. Dorothy C. Barck. Collections of the New-York Historical Society for the Year 1928. The John Watts De Peyster Publication Fund Series 61. New York: Printed for the Society, 1928.

Wayne, Anthony. *Anthony Wayne, a Name in Arms: Soldier, Diplomat, Defender of Expan-*

sion Westward of a Nation. The Wayne-Knox-Pickering-McHenry Correspondence. Ed. Richard C. Knopf. Pittsburgh: University of Pittsburgh Press, 1960.

Weeks, Stephen B., and William Laurence Saunders. *The Colonial Records of North Carolina.* Ed. William L. Saunders. Vol. 7. Raleigh: Josephus Daniels, Printer to the State, 1890.

Wharton, Francis, and John Bassett Moore. *The Revolutionary Diplomatic Correspondence of the United States. Edited Under Direction of Congress.* 6 vols. 50th Cong., 1st Sess. House. Misc. Doc. 603. Washington, DC: Government Printing Office, 1889.

Wheatley, Phillis. *Complete Writings.* Ed. Vincent Carretta. New York: Penguin, 2001.

——. *An Elegiac Poem, on the Death of That Celebrated Divine, and Eminent Servant of Jesus Christ, the Late Reverend and Pious George Whitefield, Chaplain to the Right Honourable the Countess of Huntingdon, &c. &c.* Newport, RI: n.p., 1770.

——. *Poems on Various Subjects, Religious and Moral.* London: Printed for A. Bell, bookseller, Aldgate; and sold by Messrs. Cox and Berry, King-Street, Boston, 1773.

Wildman, William. *The Political Life of William Wildman, Viscount Barrington, Compiled from Original Papers by His Brother, Shute, Bishop of Durham.* Ed. S. Dunelm. London: W. Bulmer and Co., 1815.

Wilkinson, Eliza. *Letters of Eliza Wilkinson, During the Invasion and Possession of Charlestown, S.C. By the British in the Revolutionary War.* New York: Samuel Colman, 1839.

Wilkinson, James. *Memoirs of My Own Times.* 3 vols. Philadelphia: Printed by Abraham Small, 1816.

Willis, William, ed. *Collections of the Maine Historical Society.* Ser. 1. Vol. 1. Reprint. Portland: Bailey and Noyes, 1865.

Wilson, James, *Considerations on the Nature and the Extent of the Legislative Authority of the British Parliament.* Philadelphia: Printed and sold, by William and Thomas Bradford, at the London Coffee-House, 1774.

Wirt, William. *Sketches of the Life and Character of Patrick Henry.* Philadelphia: James Webster, 1817.

Wollstonecraft, Mary. *A Vindication of the Rights of Woman: With Strictures on Political and Moral Subjects.* London: Printed for J. Johnson, 1792.

Woodmason, Charles. *The Carolina Backcountry on the Eve of the Revolution; the Journal and Other Writings of Charles Woodmason, Anglican Itinerant.* Ed. Richard J. Hooker. Chapel Hill: Published for the Institute of Early American History and Culture by the University of North Carolina Press, 1953.

Wraxall, Nathaniel William. *Historical Memoirs of My Own Time.* Ed. Richard Askham. London: Kegan Paul, Trench, Trübner & Co., 1904.

[Young, Arthur]. *Political Essays Concerning the Present State of the British Empire.* London: Printed for W. Strahan and T. Cadell, 1772.

Secondary Books and Articles (composed after 1860)

Adams, Gene. "Dido Elizabeth Belle: A Black Girl at Kenwood." *Camden History Review* 12 (n.d.): unpaginated.

Adams, Gretchen. "Deeds of Desperate Valor: The 1st Rhode Island Regiment." Accessed March 28, 2020. revolution.h-net.msu.edu/essays/adams2.html.

Adams, W. Paul. "Republicanism in Political Rhetoric Before 1776." *Political Science Quarterly* 85:3 (September 1970): 397–421.

Adelman, Jeremy. *Sovereignty and Revolution in the Iberian Atlantic*. Princeton: Princeton University Press, 2006.

Akers, Charles W. *Abigail Adams: An American Woman*. Ed. Oscar Handlin. Library of American Biography. Boston: Little, Brown, 1980.

Alden, John Richard. *General Gage in America: Being Principally a History of His Role in the American Revolution*. Baton Rouge: Louisiana State University Press, 1948.

Alexander, John K. "The Fort Wilson Incident of 1779: A Case Study of the Revolutionary Crowd." *William and Mary Quarterly*, Third Series, 31:4 (October 1974): 589–612.

Alexander, Robert. *The Northwest Ordinance: Constitutional Politics and the Theft of Native Land*. Jefferson, NC: McFarland, 2017.

Allen, Danielle. *Our Declaration: A Reading of the Declaration of Independence in Defense of Equality*. New York: Liveright, 2014.

Allen, William. "Account of Arnold's Expedition." *Collections of the Maine Historical Society* 1 (1865): 499–532.

Ammerman, David. *In the Common Cause: American Response to the Coercive Acts of 1774*. Charlottesville: University Press of Virginia, 1974.

Anderson, Fred. *The Crucible of War: The Seven Years' War and the Fate of Empire in British North America, 1754–1766*. New York: Alfred A. Knopf, 2000.

Anderson, Troyer Steele. *The Command of the Howe Brothers During the American Revolution*. New York: Oxford University Press, 1936.

Anderson, Virginia DeJohn. *The Martyr and the Traitor: Nathan Hale, Moses Dunbar, and the American Revolution*. New York: Oxford University Press, 2017.

Andrews, Charles. "The Boston Merchants and the Non-Importation Movement." *Colonial Society of Massachusetts Publications* 19 (1918): 159–259.

Archer, Richard. *As If an Enemy's Country: The British Occupation of Boston and the Origins of Revolution*. Pivotal Moments in American History. New York: Oxford University Press, 2010.

Armitage, David. *The Declaration of Independence: A Global History*. Cambridge: Harvard University Press, 2007.

Arnold, Isaac N. *The Life of Benedict Arnold; His Patriotism and His Treason*. Chicago: Jansen, McClurg & Co., 1880.

Arnold, Samuel Greene. *History of the State of Rhode Island & Providence Plantations*. 2 vols. 4th ed. Providence, RI: Preston & Rounds, 1894.

Ayling, Stanley. *The Elder Pitt: Earl of Chatham*. New York: David McKay, 1976.

Babits, Lawrence Edward. *A Devil of a Whipping: The Battle of Cowpens*. Chapel Hill: University of North Carolina Press, 1998.

Babits, Lawrence Edward, and Joshua B. Howard. *Long, Obstinate, and Bloody: The Battle of Guilford Courthouse*. Chapel Hill: University of North Carolina Press, 2009.

Bailyn, Bernard. *The Ideological Origins of the American Revolution*. Enlarged ed. Cambridge: Belknap Press of Harvard University Press, 1992.

——. *The Ordeal of Thomas Hutchinson*. Cambridge: Belknap Press of Harvard University Press, 1974.

Ballester, Teresa Gallarza. "An Outline of the Social History of the Creole Language of Antigua (West Indies)." *Lengua y migración* 6:1 (2014): 81–94.

Banner, Stuart. *How the Indians Lost Their Land: Law and Power on the Frontier*. Cambridge: Belknap Press of Harvard University Press, 2005.

Barker-Benfield, G. J. *The Culture of Sensibility: Sex and Society in Eighteenth-Century Britain*. Chicago: University of Chicago Press, 1992.

——. *Phillis Wheatley Chooses Freedom: History, Poetry, and the Ideals of the American Revolution*. New York: New York University Press, 2018.

Barrow, Thomas C. *Trade and Empire: The British Customs Service in Colonial America, 1660–1775*. Cambridge: Harvard University Press, 1967.

Baugh, Daniel A. "Sir Samuel Hood: Superior Subordinate." In Billias, ed., *George Washington's Opponents*, 291–326.

Beard, Charles A., and Mary R. Beard. *The Rise of American Civilization*. 2 vols. New York: Macmillan, 1927.

Becker, Ann M. "Smallpox in Washington's Army: Strategic Implications of the Disease During the American Revolutionary War." *Journal of Military History* 68:2 (April 2004): 381–430.

Becker, Carl L. *The Declaration of Independence: A Study in the History of Political Ideas*. New York: Vintage, 1958.

——. *The History of Political Parties in the Province of New York, 1760–1776*. Bulletin of the University of Wisconsin. No. 286. History Series. 2:1. Madison, 1909.

Bell, Caryn Cossé. "The Common Wind's Creole Visionary: Dr. Louis Charles Roudanez." *South Atlantic Review* 73:2 (Spring 2008): 10–25.

Bell, J. L. "Adams Household 'Dangerously Sick with a Dysentery,'" Oct. 8, 2008. boston1775.blogspot.com/2008/10/adams-household-dangerously-sick-with.html.

——. "Peter Salem? Salem Poor? Who Killed Major John Pitcairn?" *Journal of the American Revolution*, June 18, 2018. allthingsliberty.com/2018/06/peter-salem-salem-poor-who-killed-major-john-pitcairn.

——. *The Road to Concord: How Four Stolen Cannon Ignited the Revolutionary War*. A Journal of the American Revolution Book. Yardley, PA: Westholme, 2016.

——. "Snowball Fight in Harvard Yard," Dec. 2, 2007. boston1775.blogspot.com/2007/12/snowball-fight-in-harvard-yard.html.

Bell, Malcolm. *Major Butler's Legacy: Five Generations of a Slaveholding Family*. Athens: University of Georgia Press, 1987.

Bellesiles, Michael A. *Revolutionary Outlaws: Ethan Allen and the Struggle for Independence on the Early American Frontier*. Charlottesville: University Press of Virginia, 1993.

Bellion, Wendy. *Citizen Spectator: Art, Illusion, and Visual Perception in Early National America*. Chapel Hill: University of North Carolina Press, 2011.

Bemis, Samuel Flagg. *The Diplomacy of the American Revolution*. New York: D. Appleton-Century, 1935.

——. *Jay's Treaty; a Study in Commerce and Diplomacy*. New York: Macmillan, 1923.

Bennett, C. P. "The Delaware Regiment in the Revolution." *Pennsylvania Magazine of History and Biography* 9:4 (January 1886): 451–62.

Berkeley, Francis L. *Dunmore's Proclamation of Emancipation: With an Invitation to the McGregor Library & an Account by Francis Berkeley of the Publication of the Proclamation*. Charlottesville: Tracy W. McGregor Library, University of Virginia, 1941.

Berkin, Carol. *Revolutionary Mothers: Women in the Struggle for America's Independence*. New York: Alfred A. Knopf, 2005.

Berkin, Carol, and Mary Beth Norton. *Women of America: A History*. Boston: Houghton Mifflin, 1979.

Berlin, Ira. *Many Thousands Gone: The First Two Centuries of Slavery in North America*. Cambridge: Belknap Press of Harvard University Press, 1998.

Bezanson, Anne. "Inflation and Controls, Pennsylvania, 1774–1779." *Journal of Economic History* 8, supplement (1948): 1–20.

Billias, George Athan. *General John Glover and His Marblehead Mariners*. New York: Holt, 1960.

——, ed. *George Washington's Opponents: British Generals and Admirals in the American Revolution*. New York: William Morrow, 1969.

Billings, Warren M., John E. Selby, and Thad W. Tate. *Colonial Virginia: A History*. A History of the American Colonies. White Plains, NY: KTO Press, 1986.

Blackmon, Richard. *Dark and Bloody Ground: The American Revolution Along the Southern Frontier*. Yardley, PA: Westholme, 2012.

Blanck, Emily. "Seventeen Eighty-Three: The Turning Point in the Law of Slavery and Freedom in Massachusetts." *New England Quarterly* 75:1 (March 2002): 24–51.

Blumrosen, Alfred W., and Ruth G. Blumrosen. *Slave Nation: How Slavery United the Colonies & Sparked the American Revolution*. Naperville, IL: Sourcebooks, 2005.

Bobrick, Benson. *Angel in the Whirlwind: The Triumph of the American Revolution*. New York: Simon & Schuster, 1997.

Bock, Philip K. "Micmac." In Trigger, ed. *Northeast*, 109–22.

Bodle, Wayne K. *The Valley Forge Winter: Civilians and Soldiers in War*. University Park: Pennsylvania State University Press, 2002.

Bogin, Ruth. "'Liberty Further Extended': A 1776 Antislavery Manuscript by Lemuel Haynes." *William and Mary Quarterly*, Third Series, 40:1 (January 1983): 85–105.

Boles, John B. *Jefferson: Architect of American Liberty*. New York: Basic Books, 2017.

Bolster, W. Jeffrey. *Black Jacks: African American Seamen in the Age of Sail*. Cambridge: Harvard University Press, 1997.

Bonomi, Patricia U. *Under the Cope of Heaven: Religion, Society, and Politics in Colonial America*. Updated ed. New York: Oxford University Press, 2003.

Bonwick, Colin. *The American Revolution*. Charlottesville: University Press of Virginia, 1991.

Borick, Carl P. *A Gallant Defense: The Siege of Charleston, 1780*. Columbia: University of South Carolina Press, 2003.

Bouton, Terry. "A Road Closed: Rural Insurgency in Post-Independence Pennsylvania." *Journal of American History* 87:3 (December 2000): 855–87.

——. "Slave, Free Black, and White Population, 1780–1830." Accessed Dec. 26, 2020. userpages.umbc.edu/~bouton/History407/SlaveStats.htm.

——. *Taming Democracy: "The People," the Founders, and the Troubled Ending of the American Revolution*. New York: Oxford University Press, 2007.

Bowling, Kenneth R. "'A Tub to the Whale': The Founding Fathers and Adoption of the Federal Bill of Rights." *Journal of the Early Republic* 8:3 (Autumn 1988): 223–51.

Boyd, Julian P. *The Declaration of Independence: The Evolution of the Text*. Ed. Gerard W. Gawalt. Rev. ed. Washington, DC: Library of Congress, in association with the Thomas Jefferson Memorial Foundation, 1999.

Bradley, Patricia. "Slavery in Colonial Newspapers: The Somerset Case." *Journalism History* 12:1 (Spring 1985): 2–7.

Brands, H. W. *The First American: The Life and Times of Benjamin Franklin*. New York: Doubleday, 2000.

Brannon, Rebecca. *From Revolution to Reunion: The Reintegration of the South Carolina Loyalists*. Columbia: University of South Carolina Press, 2016.

Branson, Susan. *These Fiery Frenchified Dames: Women and Political Culture in Early National Philadelphia*. Early American Studies. Philadelphia: University of Pennsylvania Press, 2001.

Braund, Kathryn E. Holland. *Deerskins and Duffels: The Creek Indian Trade with Anglo-America, 1685–1815*. Indians of the Southeast. Lincoln: University of Nebraska Press, 1993.

Breen, T. H. *American Insurgents, American Patriots: The Revolution of the People*. New York: Hill & Wang, 2010.

——. *The Marketplace of Revolution: How Consumer Politics Shaped American Independence*. New York: Oxford University Press, 2004.

——. "Subjecthood and Citizenship: The Context of James Otis's Radical Critique of John Locke." *New England Quarterly* 71:3 (September 1998): 378–403.

——. *Tobacco Culture: The Mentality of the Great Tidewater Planters on the Eve of Revolution*. Princeton: Princeton University Press, 1985.

——. *The Will of the People: The Revolutionary Birth of America*. Cambridge: Belknap Press of Harvard University Press, 2019.

Brekus, Catherine A. *Sarah Osborn's World: The Rise of Evangelical Christianity in Early America*. New Directions in Narrative History. New Haven: Yale University Press, 2013.

Breslaw, Elaine. "A Dismal Tragedy: Drs. Alexander and John Hamilton Comment on Braddock's Defeat." *Maryland Historical Magazine* 75:2 (June 1980): 118–44.

Brewer, Ebenezer Cobham, and Ivor H. Evans. *Brewer's Dictionary of Phrase and Fable*. Centenary ed. New York: Harper & Row, 1970.

Brewer, Holly. "Entailing Aristocracy in Colonial Virginia: 'Ancient Feudal Restraints' and Revolutionary Reform." *William and Mary Quarterly*, Third Series, 54:2 (April 1997): 307–46.

Bridenbaugh, Carl. "Violence and Virtue in Virginia, 1766: Or, the Importance of the Trivial." *Proceedings of the Massachusetts Historical Society*, Third Series, 76 (1964): 3–29.

Brodie, Fawn McKay. *Thomas Jefferson: An Intimate History*. New York: W. W. Norton, 1974.

Brooks, Van Wyck. "On Creating a Usable Past." *The Dial* 64:764 (April 1918): 337–41.

Brown, Alan S. "The Role of the Army in Western Settlement: Josiah Harmar's Command, 1785–1790." *Pennsylvania Magazine of History and Biography* 93:2 (April 1969): 161–78.

Brown, Christopher Leslie. *Moral Capital: Foundations of British Abolitionism*. Chapel Hill: Published for the Omohundro Institute of Early American History and Culture by the University of North Carolina Press, 2006.

——. "The Problems of Slavery." In *OHAR*, 427–46.

Brown, Richard D. *Revolutionary Politics in Massachusetts: The Boston Committee of Correspondence and the Towns, 1772–1774*. Cambridge: Harvard University Press, 1970.

Brown, Roger H. *Redeeming the Republic: Federalists, Taxation, and the Origins of the Constitution*. Baltimore: Johns Hopkins University Press, 1993.

Brown, Vincent. *Tacky's Revolt: The Story of an Atlantic Slave War*. Cambridge: Belknap Press, 2020.

Brunhouse, Robert L. *The Counter-Revolution in Pennsylvania, 1776–1790*. Harrisburg: Pennsylvania Historical Commission, 1942.

Brunsman, Denver. *The Evil Necessity: British Naval Impressment in the Eighteenth-Century Atlantic World*. Early American Histories. Charlottesville: University of Virginia Press, 2013.

Buchanan, John. *The Road to Charleston: Nathanael Greene and the American Revolution*. Charlottesville: University of Virginia Press, 2019.

——. *The Road to Guilford Courthouse: The American Revolution in the Carolinas*. New York: John Wiley & Sons, 1997.

Buel, Joy Day, and Richard Buel, Jr. *The Way of Duty: A Woman and Her Family in Revolutionary America*. New York: W. W. Norton, 1984.

Buel, Richard, Jr. *Dear Liberty: Connecticut's Mobilization for the Revolutionary War*. Middletown, CT: Wesleyan University Press, 1980.

——. *In Irons: Britain's Naval Supremacy and the American Revolutionary Economy*. New Haven: Yale University Press, 1998.

Bullen, Ripley P. "Fort Tonyn and the Campaign of 1778." *Florida Historical Quarterly* 29:4 (April 1951): 253–60.

Bullion, John L. *A Great and Necessary Measure: George Grenville and the Genesis of the Stamp Act, 1763–1765*. Columbia: University of Missouri Press, 1982.

——. "Security and Economy: The Bute Administration's Plans for the American Army and Revenue, 1762–1763." *William and Mary Quarterly*, Third Series, 45:3 (July 1988): 499–509.

——. "'The Ten Thousand in America': More Light on the Decision on the American Army, 1762–1763." *William and Mary Quarterly*, Third Series, 43:4 (October 1986): 646–57.

Bullock, Steven C. *Revolutionary Brotherhood: Freemasonry and the Transformation of the American Social Order, 1730–1840*. Chapel Hill: Published for the Omohundro Institute of Early American History and Culture by the University of North Carolina Press, 1996.

Bullock, Steven C., and Sheila McIntyre. "The Handsome Tokens of a Funeral: Glove-Giving and the Large Funeral in Eighteenth-Century New England." *William and Mary Quarterly*, Third Series, 69:2 (April 2012): 305–46.

Bunker, Nick. *An Empire on the Edge: How Britain Came to Fight America*. New York: Alfred A. Knopf, 2014.

Burdick, Kim. "What They Saw and Did at Yorktown's Redoubts 9 and 10." *Journal of the American Revolution*, April 7, 2020. allthingsliberty.com/2020/04/what-they-saw-and -did-at-yorktowns-redoubts-9-and-10.

Burrows, Edwin G. *Forgotten Patriots: The Untold Story of American Prisoners During the Revolutionary War*. New York: Basic Books, 2008.

Bushman, Richard L. *From Puritan to Yankee: Character and the Social Order in Connecticut, 1690–1765*. Cambridge: Harvard University Press, 1967.

Calderhead, William L. "Slavery in Maryland in the Age of Revolution, 1775–1790." *Maryland Historical Magazine* 98:3 (Fall 2003): 303–24.

Callo, Joseph F. *John Paul Jones: America's First Sea Warrior*. Annapolis: Naval Institute Press, 2006.

Calloway, Colin G. *The American Revolution in Indian Country: Crisis and Diversity in Native American Communities*. Cambridge Studies in North American Indian History. Cambridge: Cambridge University Press, 1995.

——. "Declaring Independence and Rebuilding a Nation: Dragging Canoe and the Chickamauga Revolution." In Young, Nash, and Raphael, eds., *Revolutionary Founders*, 185–98.

——. *The Indian World of George Washington: The First President, the First Americans, and the Birth of the Nation*. New York: Oxford University Press, 2018.

——. *The Scratch of a Pen: 1763 and the Transformation of North America*. Pivotal Moments in American History. New York: Oxford University Press, 2006.

——. *The Victory with No Name: The Native American Defeat of the First American Army*. New York: Oxford University Press, 2015.

Calvert, Jane. "The Friendly Jurisprudence and Early Feminism of John Dickinson." In Daniel L. Dreisbach and Mark David Hall, eds., *Great Christian Jurists in American History*. Cambridge: Cambridge University Press, 2019, 72–89.

Carey, Henry Charles and J. Lea. *The Geography, History, and Statistics, of America, and the West Indies*. London: Sherwood, Jones, and Company, 1823.

Carp, Benjamin L. *Defiance of the Patriots: The Boston Tea Party and the Making of America*. New Haven: Yale University Press, 2010.

——. "Nice Party, but Not So Revolutionary," April 19, 2009. washingtonpost.com/wp-dyn/content/article/2009/04/17/AR2009041702664.html.

——. "The Night the Yankees Burned Broadway: The New York City Fire of 1776." *Early American Studies* 4:2 (Fall 2006): 471–511.

——. *Rebels Rising: Cities and the American Revolution*. Oxford: Oxford University Press, 2007.

Carp, E. Wayne. *To Starve the Army at Pleasure: Continental Army Administration and American Political Culture, 1775–1783*. Chapel Hill: University of North Carolina Press, 1984.

Carretta, Vincent. *Equiano, the African: Biography of a Self-Made Man*. Athens: University of Georgia Press, 2005.

——. *Phillis Wheatley: Biography of a Genius in Bondage*. Athens: University of Georgia Press, 2011.

Carrington, Henry B. *Battle Maps and Charts of the American Revolution with Explanatory Notes and School History References*. New York: A. S. Barnes & Company, 1881.

Carter, Harvey Lewis. *The Life and Times of Little Turtle: First Sagamore of the Wabash*. Urbana: University of Illinois Press, 1987.

Cashin, Edward J. *The King's Ranger: Thomas Brown and the American Revolution on the Southern Frontier*. Athens: University of Georgia Press, 1989.

Cataldo, Judith. "Epidemic Behind the American Lines," Aug. 30, 2007. boston1775.blogspot.com/2007/08/epidemic-behind-american-lines.html.

Cayton, Andrew R. L. *Frontier Indiana*. A History of the Trans-Appalachian Frontier. Bloomington: Indiana University Press, 1996.

Chaffin, Robert J. "The Townshend Acts of 1767." *William and Mary Quarterly*, Third Series, 27:1 (January 1970): 90–121.

Champagne, Roger J. *Alexander McDougall and the American Revolution in New York*. Schenectady: New York State American Revolution Bicentennial Commission in conjunction with Union College Press, 1975.

——. "Family Politics Versus Constitutional Principles: The New York Assembly Elections of 1768 and 1769." *William and Mary Quarterly*, Third Series, 20:1 (January 1963): 57–79.

——. "New York and the Intolerable Acts, 1774." *New-York Historical Society Quarterly* 45:2 (April 1961): 195–207.

Charles, Joseph. "The Jay Treaty: The Origins of the American Party System." *William and Mary Quarterly*, Third Series, 12:4 (October 1955): 581–630.

Chernow, Ron. *Washington: A Life*. New York: Penguin, 2010.

Chopra, Ruma. *Almost Home: Maroons Between Slavery and Freedom in Jamaica, Nova Scotia, and Sierra Leone*. New Haven: Yale University Press, 2018.

Christie, Ian R. *Wars and Revolutions: Britain, 1760–1815*. The New History of England. Cambridge: Harvard University Press, 1982.

Clark, Dora Mae. "The American Board of Customs, 1767–1783." *American Historical Review* 45:4 (July 1940): 777–806.

Clark, Jane. "The Convention Troops and the Perfidy of Sir William Howe." *American Historical Review* 37:4 (July 1932): 721–23.

Cleary, Patricia. *Elizabeth Murray: A Woman's Pursuit of Independence in Eighteenth-Century America*. Amherst: University of Massachusetts Press, 2000.

Cline, Andrew. "Men and Women We Must Remember: Paul Revere, Yes. But Many Others Fought America's Battle for Liberty." *Christian Science Monitor*, April 18, 1997.

Coburn, Frank Warren. *The Battle on Lexington Common, April 19, 1775*. Lexington and Concord Anthology. Lexington, MA: The author, 1921.

———. "Fiction and Truth About the Battle on Lexington Common." Lexington, MA: The author, 1918.

Coffin, Charles Carleton. *The Boys of '76: A History of the Battles of the Revolution*. New York: Harper & Brothers, 1876.

Cogliano, Francis D. *Revolutionary America, 1763–1815: A Political History*. 2nd ed. New York: Routledge, 2009.

Cohen, David, and Jack P. Greene, eds. *Neither Slave nor Free; the Freedman of African Descent in the Slave Societies of the New World*. Baltimore: Johns Hopkins University Press, 1973.

Colbourn, H. Trevor. *The Lamp of Experience: Whig History and the Intellectual Origins of the American Revolution*. Chapel Hill: Published for the Institute of Early American History and Culture by the University of North Carolina Press, 1965.

Cole, Phyllis. *Mary Moody Emerson and the Origins of Transcendentalism: A Family History*. New York: Oxford University Press, 1998.

Collier, Christopher. *Roger Sherman's Connecticut: Yankee Politics and the American Revolution*. Middletown, CT: Wesleyan, 1971.

Connecticut Office of the Secretary of State. "Population of Connecticut Towns, 1756–1820." portal.ct.gov/SOTS/Register-Manual/Section-VII/Population-1756-1820.

Conway, Stephen. "The British Army and the War of Independence." In *OHAR*, 177–93.

Cooley, Timothy Mather. *Sketches of the Life and Character of the Rev. Lemuel Haynes, A.M.* New York: Harper & Brothers, 1837.

Cott, Nancy F. "Divorce and the Changing Status of Women in Eighteenth-Century Massachusetts." *William and Mary Quarterly*, Third Series, 33:4 (October 1976): 586–614.

Coulson, David P., and Linda Joyce. *United States State-Level Population Estimates: Colonization to 1999*. RMRS-GTR-111WWW. Fort Collins, CO: U.S. Department of Agriculture, Forest Service, Rocky Mountain Research Station, 2003.

Countryman, Edward. *The American Revolution*. Ed. Eric Foner. American Century Series. New York: Hill & Wang, 1985.

Cox, Caroline. *Boy Soldiers of the American Revolution*. Chapel Hill: University of North Carolina Press, 2016.

———. "The Continental Army." In *OHAR*, 161–76.

Craig, Michelle L. "Grounds for Debate? The Place of the Caribbean Provisions Trade in Philadelphia's Prerevolutionary Economy." *Pennsylvania Magazine of History and Biography* 128:2 (April 2004): 149–77.

Creviston, Vernon P. "'No King Unless It Be a Constitutional King': Rethinking the Place of the Quebec Act in the Coming of the American Revolution." *Historian* 73:3 (Fall 2011): 463–79.

Crow, Jeffrey J. "Slave Rebelliousness and Social Conflict in North Carolina, 1775 to 1802." *William and Mary Quarterly*, Third Series, 37:1 (January 1980): 79–102.

Crowley, John E. *The Privileges of Independence: Neomercantilism and the American Revolution*. Early America. Baltimore: Johns Hopkins University Press, 1993.

Crytzer, Brady. *Guyasuta and the Fall of Indian America*. Yardley, PA: Westholme, 2013.

Damiano, Sara T. "Writing Women's History Through the Revolution: Family Finances, Letter Writing, and Conceptions of Marriage." *William and Mary Quarterly*, Third Series, 74:4 (October 2017): 697–728.

David, James Corbett. *Dunmore's New World: The Extraordinary Life of a Royal Governor in Revolutionary America—with Jacobites, Counterfeiters, Land Schemes, Shipwrecks, Scalping, Indian Politics, Runaway Slaves, and Two Illegal Royal Weddings*. Early American Histories. Charlottesville: University of Virginia Press, 2013.

Dawson, Kevin. "Enslaved Ship Pilots in the Age of Revolutions: Challenging Notions of Race and Slavery Between the Boundaries of Land and Sea." *Journal of Social History* 47:1 (Fall 2013): 71–100.

de Fonblanque, Edward Barrington. *Political and Military Episodes in the Latter Half of the Eighteenth Century. Derived from the Life and Correspondence of the Right Hon. John Burgoyne, General, Statesman, Dramatist.* London: Macmillan and Co., 1876.

De Pauw, Linda Grant. *The Eleventh Pillar: New York State and the Federal Constitution.* Ithaca, NY: Published for the American Historical Association by Cornell University Press, 1966.

Dederer, John Morgan. *Making Bricks Without Straw: Nathanael Greene's Southern Campaign and Mao Tse-Tung's Mobile War.* Manhattan, KS: Sunflower University Press, 1983.

Detweiler, Philip F. "The Changing Reputation of the Declaration of Independence: The First Fifty Years." *William and Mary Quarterly*, Third Series, 19:4 (October 1962): 557–74.

Dickerson, O. M. "Writs of Assistance as a Cause of the Revolution." In Richard B. Morris, ed., *The Era of the American Revolution: Studies Inscribed to Evarts Boutell Greene* (New York: Columbia University Press, 1939), 40–75.

Donnelly, F. K. "A Possible Source for Nathan Hale's Dying Words." *William and Mary Quarterly*, Third Series, 42:3 (July 1985): 394–96.

Dowd, Gregory Evans. "The French King Wakes Up in Detroit: 'Pontiac's War' in Rumor and History." *Ethnohistory* 37:3 (Summer 1990): 254–78.

——. *Groundless: Rumors, Legends, and Hoaxes on the Early American Frontier.* Early America: History, Context, Culture. Baltimore: Johns Hopkins University Press, 2015.

——. *A Spirited Resistance: The North American Indian Struggle for Unity, 1745–1815.* Johns Hopkins University Studies in Historical and Political Science, 109th Series, 4. Baltimore: Johns Hopkins University Press, 1992.

——. *War Under Heaven: Pontiac, the Indian Nations, and the British Empire.* Baltimore: Johns Hopkins University Press, 2002.

Downes, Randolph C. *Council Fires on the Upper Ohio: A Narrative of Indian Affairs in the Upper Ohio Valley Until 1795.* Pittsburgh: University of Pittsburgh Press, 1940.

——. "Creek-American Relations, 1790–1795." *Journal of Southern History* 8:3 (August 1942): 350–73.

Draper, Lyman C. *King's Mountain and Its Heroes: History of the Battle of King's Mountain, October 7th, 1780, and the Events Which Led to It.* Cincinnati: Peter G. Thomson, 1881.

Drinker, Sophie H. "Votes for Women in 18th-Century New Jersey." *Proceedings of the New Jersey Historical Society* 80 (January 1962): 31–45.

Du Bois, W. E. B. *The Suppression of the African Slave-Trade to the United States of America, 1638–1870.* New York: Longmans, Green and Co., 1896.

Duffy, John. *Epidemics in Colonial America.* Baton Rouge: Louisiana State University Press, 1953.

Dull, Jonathan R. *A Diplomatic History of the American Revolution.* New Haven: Yale University Press, 1985.

——. *The French Navy and American Independence: A Study of Arms and Diplomacy, 1774–1787.* Princeton: Princeton University Press, 1975.

Dunn, Richard S. *A Tale of Two Plantations: Slave Life and Labor in Jamaica and Virginia.* Cambridge: Harvard University Press, 2014.

Dunn, Walter S., Jr. *Frontier Profit and Loss: The British Army and the Fur Traders, 1760–1764.* Contributions in American History 180. Westport, CT: Greenwood, 1998.

Dunnigan, Brian Leigh. "Fortress Detroit, 1701–1826." In Skaggs and Nelson, eds., *Sixty Years' War for the Great Lakes*, 167–86.

du Rivage, Justin. *Revolution Against Empire: Taxes, Politics, and the Origins of American Independence*. Lewis Walpole Series in Eighteenth-Century Culture and History. New Haven: Yale University Press, 2017.

DuVal, Kathleen. *Independence Lost: Lives on the Edge of the American Revolution*. New York: Random House, 2015.

Eacott, Jonathan. *Selling Empire: India in the Making of Britain and America, 1600–1830*. Chapel Hill: Published for the Omohundro Institute of Early American History and Culture by the University of North Carolina Press, 2016.

Eccles, W. J. "New France and the French Impact on North America." In W. J. Eccles, ed., *Essays on New France* (Toronto: Oxford University Press, 1987).

Edelson, S. Max. *The New Map of Empire: How Britain Imagined America Before Independence*. Cambridge: Harvard University Press, 2017.

Edgar, Walter. *Partisans and Redcoats: The Southern Conflict That Turned the Tide of the American Revolution*. New York: William Morrow, 2001.

——. *South Carolina: A History*. Columbia: University of South Carolina Press, 1998.

Edling, Max M. *A Hercules in the Cradle: War, Money, and the American State, 1783–1867*. American Beginnings, 1500–1900. Chicago: University of Chicago Press, 2014.

——. *A Revolution in Favor of Government: Origins of the U.S. Constitution and the Making of the American State*. Oxford: Oxford University Press, 2003.

Egerton, Douglas R. *Death or Liberty: African Americans and Revolutionary America*. New York: Oxford University Press, 2009.

Egnal, Marc. *A Mighty Empire: The Origins of the American Revolution*. Ithaca, NY: Cornell University Press, 1988.

Ekrich, A. Roger. *At Day's Close: Night in Times Past*. New York: W. W. Norton, 2005.

——. "'A New Government of Liberty': Hermon Husband's Vision of Backcountry North Carolina, 1755." *William and Mary Quarterly*, Third Series, 34:4 (October 1977): 632–46.

——. *"Poor Carolina": Politics and Society in Colonial North Carolina, 1729–1776*. Chapel Hill: University of North Carolina Press, 1981.

Elkins, Stanley, and Eric McKitrick. *The Age of Federalism*. New York: Oxford University Press, 1993.

Ellis, Joseph J. *Revolutionary Summer: The Birth of American Independence*. New York: Alfred A. Knopf, 2013.

Ellison, Ralph. "James Armistead Lafayette." In Ellison, *The Collected Essays of Ralph Ellison*, ed. John F. Callahan (New York: Modern Library, 1995), 397–403.

Elzas, Barnett A. *The Jews of South Carolina: From the Earliest Times to the Present Day*. Philadelphia: J. B. Lippincott, 1905.

Enthoven, Victor. "'That Abominable Nest of Pirates': St. Eustatius and the North Americans, 1680–1780." *Early American Studies* 10:2 (Spring 2012): 239–301.

Epperson, Sharon, and Katie Young, "Military Personnel Face a Critical Choice for Their Retirement Plan." Jan. 7, 2018, cnbc.com/2018/01/05/us-service-members-face-big-changes-to-retirement-plan.html.

Ernst, Joseph Albert. *Money and Politics in America, 1755–1775: A Study in the Currency Act of 1764 and the Political Economy of Revolution*. Chapel Hill: Published for the Institute of Early American History and Culture by the University of North Carolina Press, 1973.

Estes, Todd. *The Jay Treaty Debate, Public Opinion, and the Evolution of Early American Political Culture*. Amherst: University of Massachusetts Press, 2006.

Etting, Frank Marx. *An Historical Account of the Old State House of Pennsylvania Now Known as The Hall of Independence*. Boston: James R. Osgood and Co., 1876.

Eustace, Nicole. *Passion Is the Gale: Emotion, Power, and the Coming of the American Revolution*. Chapel Hill: Published for the Omohundro Institute of Early American History and Culture by the University of North Carolina Press, 2008.

Faragher, John Mack. *Daniel Boone: The Life and Legend of an American Pioneer*. New York: Holt, 1992.

Faust, Drew Gilpin. *Mothers of Invention: Women of the Slaveholding South in the American Civil War*. Chapel Hill: University of North Carolina Press, 1996.

Fenn, Elizabeth A. "Biological Warfare in Eighteenth-Century North America: Beyond Jeffery Amherst." *Journal of American History* 86:4 (March 2000): 1552–80.

——. *Pox Americana: The Great Smallpox Epidemic of 1775–82*. New York: Hill & Wang, 2001.

Ferguson, E. James. *The Power of the Purse: A History of American Public Finance, 1776–1790*. Chapel Hill: Published for the Institute of Early American History and Culture by the University of North Carolina Press, 1961.

Ferling, John. *Almost a Miracle: The American Victory in the War of Independence*. New York: Oxford University Press, 2007.

——. *The Ascent of George Washington: The Hidden Political Genius of an American Icon*. New York: Bloomsbury Press, 2009.

Fichter, James R. *Tea's Party: The Revolutionary Career of a Consumer Good, 1773–1776*. forthcoming.

Fiering, Norman S. "Irresistible Compassion: An Aspect of Eighteenth-Century Sympathy and Humanitarianism." *Journal of the History of Ideas* 37:2 (June 1976): 195–218.

Finkelman, Paul. "Slavery and the Constitutional Convention: Making a Covenant with Death." In Richard Beeman, Stephen Botein, and Edwin C. Carter II, eds., *Beyond Confederation: Origins of the Constitution and American National Identity* (Chapel Hill: University of North Carolina Press, 1987), 188–225.

Fischer, David Hackett. *Paul Revere's Ride*. New York: Oxford University Press, 1994.

——. *Washington's Crossing*. Pivotal Moments in American History. New York: Oxford University Press, 2004.

Fischer, Joseph R. *A Well-Executed Failure: The Sullivan Campaign Against the Iroquois, July–September 1779*. Columbia: University of South Carolina Press, 1997.

Fisher, Darlene Emmert. "Social Life in Philadelphia During the British Occupation." *Pennsylvania History: A Journal of Mid-Atlantic Studies* 37:3 (July 1970): 237–60.

Fiske, John. *The Critical Period of American History: 1783–1789*. Boston: Houghton, Mifflin and Co., 1888.

Fitch, William Edwards. *Some Neglected History of North Carolina: Being an Account of the Revolution of the Regulators and of the Battle of Alamance, the First Battle of the American Revolution*. New York: The Neale Publishing Company, 1905.

Fitz, Caitlin. *Our Sister Republics: The United States in an Age of American Revolutions*. New York: Liveright, 2016.

Fliegelman, Jay. *Declaring Independence: Jefferson, Natural Language & the Culture of Performance*. Stanford: Stanford University Press, 1993.

Foner, Eric. *The Story of American Freedom*. New York: W. W. Norton, 1998.

——. *Tom Paine and Revolutionary America*. New York: Oxford University Press, 1976.

Fortescue, J. W. *A History of the British Army*. Vol. 3. London: Macmillan and Co., 1902.

Fowler, William M., Jr. *Rebels Under Sail: The American Navy During the Revolution*. New York: Charles Scribner's Sons, 1976.

Freeman, Douglas Southall, John Alexander Carroll, and Mary Wells Ashworth. *George Washington*. 7 vols. New York: Charles Scribner's Sons, 1948–1957.

Freeman, Joanne B. *Affairs of Honor: National Politics in the New Republic*. New Haven: Yale University Press, 2001.

French, Allen. *The Day of Concord and Lexington: The Nineteenth of April, 1775*. Boston: Little, Brown, 1925.

———. *The Siege of Boston*. New York: The Macmillan Company, 1911.

Frey, Sylvia R. *Water from the Rock: Black Resistance in a Revolutionary Age*. Princeton: Princeton University Press, 1991.

Friedman, Bernard. "The Shaping of the Radical Consciousness in Provincial New York." *Journal of American History* 56:4 (March 1970): 781–801.

Frothingham, Richard. *The Battle-Field of Bunker Hill: With a Relation of the Action by William Prescott, and Illustrative Documents*. Boston: Printed for the author, 1876.

Fuhrer, Mary Babson. "The Revolutionary Worlds of Lexington and Concord Compared." *The New England Quarterly* 85:1 (March 2012): 78–118.

Fur, Gunlög Maria. *A Nation of Women: Gender and Colonial Encounters Among the Delaware Indians*. Early American Studies. Philadelphia: University of Pennsylvania Press, 2009.

Gallagher, Mary A. Y. "Reinterpreting the 'Very Trifling Mutiny' at Philadelphia in June 1783." *Pennsylvania Magazine of History and Biography* 119:1/2 (April 1995): 3–35.

Gaspar, David Barry, and Darlene Clark Hine, eds. *More than Chattel: Black Women and Slavery in the Americas*. Blacks in the Diaspora. Bloomington: Indiana University Press, 1996.

Gates, Henry Louis, Jr. *The Trials of Phillis Wheatley: America's First Black Poet and Her Encounters with the Founding Fathers*. New York: Basic Civitas Books, 2003.

Geib, George. "The Land Ordinance of 1785: A Bicentennial Review." *Indiana Magazine of History* 81:1 (March 1985): 1–13.

Geiter, Mary K. "The Restoration Crisis and the Launching of Pennsylvania, 1679–81." *English Historical Review* 112:446 (April 1997): 300–18.

Gelles, Edith B. *Abigail Adams: A Writing Life*. New York: Routledge, 2002.

———. *Portia: The World of Abigail Adams*. Bloomington: Indiana University Press, 1992.

Ghere, David L. "Myths and Methods in Abenaki Demography: Abenaki Population Recovery, 1725–1750." *Ethnohistory* 44:3 (Summer 1997): 511–34.

Gigantino, James J., II. *William Livingston's American Revolution*. Haney Foundation Series. Philadelphia: University of Pennsylvania Press, 2018.

Gilman, Carolyn. "L'Aneé Du Coup: The Battle of St. Louis, 1780." *Missouri Historical Review* 103:3, 5 (April, July 2009): 133–47, 195–211.

Gipson, Lawrence Henry. *The Coming of the Revolution, 1763–1775*. The New American Nation Series. New York: Harper & Row, 1954.

Gittleman, Edwin. "Jefferson's 'Slave Narrative': The Declaration of Independence as a Literary Text." *Early American Literature* 8:3 (Winter 1974): 239–56.

Glickman, Lawrence B. *Buying Power: A History of Consumer Activism in America*. Chicago: University of Chicago Press, 2009.

Glickstein, Don. *After Yorktown: The Final Struggle for American Independence*. Yardley, PA: Westholme, 2015.

Glover, Lorri. *Eliza Lucas Pinckney: An Independent Woman in the Age of Revolution*. New Haven: Yale University Press, 2020.

Godbeer, Richard. *The Overflowing of Friendship: Love Between Men and the Creation of the American Republic*. Baltimore: Johns Hopkins University Press, 2009.

Godbold, E. Stanly, Jr., and Robert H. Woody. *Christopher Gadsden and the American Revolution*. Knoxville: University of Tennessee Press, 1982.

Goff, Philip. "Revivals and Revolution: Historiographic Turns Since Alan Heimert's 'Religion and the American Mind.'" *Church History* 67:4 (December 1998): 695–721.

Gordon, John W. *South Carolina and the American Revolution: A Battlefield History*. Columbia: University of South Carolina Press, 2003.

Gordon-Reed, Annette. *The Hemingses of Monticello: An American Family*. New York: W. W. Norton, 2008.

———. *Thomas Jefferson and Sally Hemings: An American Controversy*. Charlottesville: University Press of Virginia, 1997.

Gottschalk, Louis. *Lafayette in America*. 3 vols. Chicago: University of Chicago Press, 1935–1942.

Gould, Eliga H. *Among the Powers of Earth: The American Revolution and the Making of a New World Empire*. Cambridge: Harvard University Press, 2012.

———. "The Empire That Britain Kept." In *OHAR*, 465–82.

Grant, James. *John Adams: Party of One*. New York: Farrar, Straus & Giroux, 2005.

Gray, Edward G., and Jane Kamensky, eds. *The Oxford Handbook of the American Revolution*. Oxford Handbooks. New York: Oxford University Press, 2013.

Graymont, Barbara. *The Iroquois in the American Revolution*. A New York State Study. Syracuse: Syracuse University Press, 1972.

Greenburg, Michael M. *The Court-Martial of Paul Revere: The Son of Liberty and America's Forgotten Military Disaster*. Lebanon, NH: ForeEdge, 2014.

Greene, Jack P. "'A Posture of Hostility': A Reconsideration of Some Aspects of the Origins of the American Revolution." *Proceedings of the American Antiquarian Society* 87:1 (April 1977): 27–68.

———. "The Seven Years' War and the American Revolution: The Causal Relationship Reconsidered." *Journal of Imperial and Commonwealth History* 8:2 (1980): 85–105.

———. *Understanding the American Revolution: Issues and Actors*. Charlottesville: University Press of Virginia, 1995.

Greene, Jack P., and Richard M. Jellison. "The Currency Act of 1764 in Imperial-Colonial Relations, 1764–1776." *William and Mary Quarterly*, Third Series, 18:4 (October 1961): 485–518.

Greene, Jerome A. *The Guns of Independence: The Siege of Yorktown, 1781*. New York: Savas Beatie, 2005.

———. *Ninety Six: A Historical Narrative*. Historic Resource Study and Historic Structure Report. Denver: Denver Service Center, U.S. Dept. of the Interior, 1978.

Greene, Lorenzo J. "Some Observations on the Black Regiment of Rhode Island in the American Revolution." *Journal of Negro History* 37:2 (April 1952): 142–72.

Gregorie, Anne King. *Thomas Sumter*. Columbia, SC: The R. L. Bryan Company, 1931.

Griffin, Patrick. *America's Revolution*. New York: Oxford University Press, 2012.

Griswold, William A., and Donald W. Linebaugh, eds. *The Saratoga Campaign: Uncovering an Embattled Landscape*. Hanover, NH: University Press of New England, 2016.

Gross, Robert A. *The Minutemen and Their World*. American Century Series. New York: Hill & Wang, 1976.

Gundersen, Joan R. *To Be Useful to the World: Women in Revolutionary America, 1740–1790*. Revised ed. Chapel Hill: University of North Carolina Press, 2006.

Guy, Joe. "Last Battle of the Cherokee," n.d. sites.rootsweb.com/~tnmcmin2/jguylastbattle.htm.

Hagy, James William. *This Happy Land: The Jews of Colonial and Antebellum Charleston*. Judaic Studies Series. Tuscaloosa: University of Alabama Press, 1993.

Hahn, Steven. *A Nation Under Our Feet: Black Political Struggles in the Rural South from*

Slavery to the Great Migration. Cambridge: Belknap Press of Harvard University Press, 2003.

Hall, Gwendolyn Midlo. *Africans in Colonial Louisiana: The Development of Afro-Creole Culture in the Eighteenth Century*. Baton Rouge: Louisiana State University Press, 1992.

Hall, Van Beck. *Politics Without Parties: Massachusetts, 1780–1791*. Pittsburgh: University of Pittsburgh Press, 1972.

Halsey, R. T. H. *The Boston Port Bill as Pictured by a Contemporary London Cartoonist*. New York: The Grolier Club, 1904.

Hancock, David. *Citizens of the World: London Merchants and the Integration of the British Atlantic Community, 1735–1785*. Cambridge: Cambridge University Press, 1995.

——. *Oceans of Wine: Madeira and the Emergence of American Trade and Taste*. Lewis Walpole Series in Eighteenth-Century Culture and History. New Haven: Yale University Press, 2009.

Hanger, Kimberly S. "Household and Community Structure Among the Free Population of Spanish New Orleans, 1778." *Louisiana History* 30:1 (Winter 1989): 63–79.

Hanko, Charles William. *The Life of John Gibson: Soldier, Patriot, Statesman*. Americans of Distinction Series. Daytona Beach, FL: College Pub. Co., 1955.

Harris, J. William. *The Hanging of Thomas Jeremiah: A Free Black Man's Encounter with Liberty*. New Haven: Yale University Press, 2009.

Harrison, Lowell H. *George Rogers Clark and the War in the West*. Kentucky Bicentennial Bookshelf. Lexington: University Press of Kentucky, 1976.

Hatley, Tom. *The Dividing Paths: Cherokees and South Carolinians Through the Era of Revolution*. New York: Oxford University Press, 1993.

Hauptman, Laurence P. "The Road to Kingsbridge: Daniel Nimham and the Stockbridge Indian Company in the American Revolution." *American Indian* 18:3 (Fall 2017).

Haw, James. *John & Edward Rutledge of South Carolina*. Athens: University of Georgia Press, 1997.

Hay, John Stuart. *The Amazing Emperor Heliogabalus.* London: Macmillan and Co., 1911.

Heerman, M. Scott. *The Alchemy of Slavery: Human Bondage and Emancipation in the Illinois Country, 1730–1865*. America in the Nineteenth Century. Philadelphia: University of Pennsylvania Press, 2018.

Heimert, Alan. *Religion and the American Mind: From the Great Awakening to the Revolution*. Cambridge: Harvard University Press, 1966.

Helsley, Alexia Jones. "Rebecca Brewton Motte: Revolutionary South Carolinian." In Spruill, Littlefield, and Johnson, eds., *South Carolina Women* 1:109–26.

Henderson, Patrick. "Smallpox and Patriotism: The Norfolk Riots, 1768–1769." *Virginia Magazine of History and Biography* 73:4 (October 1965): 413–24.

Henry, William Wirt. *Patrick Henry; Life, Correspondence and Speeches*. 3 vols. New York: Charles Scribner's Sons, 1891.

Herbert, Eugenia W. "A Note on Richard Bache (1737–1811)." *Pennsylvania Magazine of History and Biography* 100:1 (January 1976): 97–103.

Higginbotham, A. Leon, Jr. *In the Matter of Color, Race and the American Legal Process: The Colonial Period*. New York: Oxford University Press, 1978.

Higginbotham, Don. *Daniel Morgan: Revolutionary Rifleman*. Chapel Hill: Published for the Institute of Early American History and Culture by the University of North Carolina Press, 1961.

——. *Revolution in America: Considerations & Comparisons*. Charlottesville: University of Virginia Press, 2005.

———. *The War of American Independence: Military Attitudes, Policies, and Practice, 1763–1789*. New York: Macmillan, 1971.

Higonnet, Patrice Louis-René. "The Origins of the Seven Years' War." *Journal of Modern History* 40:1 (March 1968): 57–90.

Hill, Christopher. *The Century of Revolution, 1603–1714*. A History of England, Vol. 5. Edinburgh: Thomas Nelson and Sons Ltd., 1961.

Hill, Lawrence. *Someone Knows My Name*. New York: W. W. Norton, 2007.

Hinderaker, Eric. *Boston's Massacre*. Cambridge: Belknap Press of Harvard University Press, 2017.

Hinks, Peter P. "John Marrant and the Meaning of Early Black Freemasonry." *William and Mary Quarterly*, Third Series, 64:1 (January 2007): 105–16.

———. "Slave Population of Colonial Connecticut, 1690–1774." glc.yale.edu/sites/default/files/files/Citizens%20All%20Doc2.pdf.

Hobson, Charles F. *The Great Yazoo Lands Sale: The Case of Fletcher v. Peck*. Landmark Law Cases & American Society. Lawrence: University Press of Kansas, 2016.

———. "The Negative on State Laws: James Madison, the Constitution, and the Crisis of Republican Government." *William and Mary Quarterly*, Third Series, 36:2 (April 1979): 215–35.

Hoffer, Peter Charles. *Prelude to Revolution: The Salem Gunpowder Raid of 1775*. Baltimore: Johns Hopkins University Press, 2013.

Hoffman, Ronald. *A Spirit of Dissension: Economics, Politics, and the Revolution in Maryland*. Maryland Bicentennial Studies. Baltimore: Johns Hopkins University Press, 1973.

Hoffman, Ronald, and Sally D. Mason. *Princes of Ireland, Planters of Maryland: A Carroll Saga, 1500–1782*. Chapel Hill: University of North Carolina Press, 2000.

Hogeland, William. *Autumn of the Black Snake: The Creation of the U.S. Army and the Invasion That Opened the West*. New York: Farrar, Straus & Giroux, 2017.

Holmes, Jack D. L. "The Abortive Slave Revolt at Pointe Coupée, Louisiana, 1795." *Louisiana History* 11:4 (Autumn 1970): 341–62.

Holton, Woody. *Abigail Adams*. New York: Free Press, 2009.

———. "Abigail Adams, Bond Speculator." *William and Mary Quarterly*, Third Series, 64:4 (October 2007): 821–38.

———. "Abigail Adams on 'The Only Surviving Parent I Have.'" *American History*, March 2010. historynet.com/abigail-adams.

———. "'Divide et Impera': 'Federalist 10' in a Wider Sphere." *William and Mary Quarterly*, Third Series, 62:2 (April 2005): 175–212.

———. "Equality as Unintended Consequence: The Contracts Clause and the Married Women's Property Acts." *Journal of Southern History* 81:2 (May 2015): 313–40.

———. *Forced Founders: Indians, Debtors, Slaves, and the Making of the American Revolution in Virginia*. Chapel Hill: Published for the Omohundro Institute of Early American History and Culture by the University of North Carolina Press, 1999.

———. "'From the Labours of Others': The War Bonds Controversy and the Origins of the Constitution in New England." *William and Mary Quarterly*, Third Series, 61:2 (April 2004): 271–316.

———. "The History of the Stamp Act Shows How Indians Led to the American Revolution." *Humanities* 36:4 (August 2015). neh.gov/humanities/2015/julyaugust/feature/the-history-the-stamp-act-shows-how-indians-led-the-american-revo.

———. "'Rebel Against Rebel': Enslaved Virginians and the Coming of the American Revolution." *Virginia Magazine of History and Biography* 105:2 (Spring 1997): 157–92.

———. *Unruly Americans and the Origins of the Constitution*. New York: Hill & Wang, 2007.

Hoock, Holger. *Scars of Independence: America's Violent Birth*. New York: Crown, 2017.

Hood, Adrienne D. "The Material World of Cloth: Production and Use in Eighteenth-Century Rural Pennsylvania." *William and Mary Quarterly*, Third Series, 53:1 (January 1996): 43–66.

Horne, Gerald. *The Counter-Revolution of 1776: Slave Resistance and the Origins of the United States of America*. New York: New York University Press, 2014.

Hubbard, Vincent K. *A History of St. Kitts: The Sweet Trade*. Oxford: Macmillan, 2002.

Humphrey, Thomas J. *Land and Liberty: Hudson Valley Riots in the Age of Revolution*. DeKalb: Northern Illinois University Press, 2004.

Hunt, Peter H., et al. *1776*. Videorecording. Widescreen ed., Restored director's cut. Culver City, CA: Columbia Pictures Home Video, 2000.

Hurt, R. Douglas. *The Ohio Frontier: Crucible of the Old Northwest, 1720–1830*. A History of the Trans-Appalachian Frontier. Bloomington: Indiana University Press, 1996.

Huston, James A. *Logistics of Liberty: American Services of Supply in the Revolutionary War and After*. Newark: University of Delaware Press, 1991.

Hutson, James H. "The Partition Treaty and the Declaration of American Independence." *Journal of American History* 58:4 (March 1972): 877–96.

Ireland, Owen S. *Sentiments of a British-American Woman: Esther DeBerdt Reed and the American Revolution*. University Park: Pennsylvania State University Press, 2017.

Irvin, Benjamin H. "The Streets of Philadelphia: Crowds, Congress, and the Political Culture of Revolution, 1774–1783." *Pennsylvania Magazine of History and Biography* 129:1 (January 2005): 7–44.

Isaac, Rhys. *Landon Carter's Uneasy Kingdom: Revolution and Rebellion on a Virginia Plantation*. New York: Oxford University Press, 2004.

———. "Lighting the Fuse of Revolution in Virginia, May 1765: Rereading the 'Journal of a French Traveller in the Colonies.'" *William and Mary Quarterly*, Third Series, 68:4 (October 2011): 657–70.

———. *The Transformation of Virginia, 1740–1790*. Chapel Hill: Published for the Institute of Early American History and Culture by the University of North Carolina Press, 1982.

Isaacson, Walter. *Benjamin Franklin: An American Life*. New York: Simon & Schuster, 2003.

Jacobs, Diane. *Dear Abigail: The Intimate Lives and Revolutionary Ideas of Abigail Adams and Her Two Remarkable Sisters*. New York: Ballantine, 2014.

James, Edward T., Janet Wilson James, and Paul S. Boyer, eds. *Notable American Women, 1607–1950: A Biographical Dictionary*. Vol. 1. Cambridge: Belknap Press of Harvard University Press, 1971.

James, James Alton. *The Life of George Rogers Clark*. Chicago: University of Chicago Press, 1928.

Jameson, J. Franklin. *The American Revolution Considered as a Social Movement*. Princeton: Princeton University Press, 1926.

Jarvis, Michael J. *In the Eye of All Trade: Bermuda, Bermudians, and the Maritime Atlantic World, 1680–1783*. Chapel Hill: Published for the Omohundro Institute of Early American History and Culture by the University of North Carolina Press, 2010.

Jasanoff, Maya. *Liberty's Exiles: American Loyalists in the Revolutionary World*. New York: Alfred A. Knopf, 2011.

Jennings, Francis. *Empire of Fortune: Crowns, Colonies, and Tribes in the Seven Years War in America*. New York: W. W. Norton, 1988.

———. *The Invasion of America: Indians, Colonialism, and the Cant of Conquest*. Chapel Hill: Published for the Institute of Early American History and Culture by the University of North Carolina Press, 1975.

Jensen, Merrill. *The Articles of Confederation: An Interpretation of the Social-Constitutional*

History of the American Revolution, 1774–1781. Madison: University of Wisconsin Press, 1940.

——. *The Founding of a Nation: A History of the American Revolution, 1763–1776.* New York: Oxford University Press, 1968.

——. *The New Nation: A History of the United States During the Confederation, 1781–1789.* New York: Alfred A. Knopf, 1950.

Johnson, Allen S. "The Passage of the Sugar Act." *William and Mary Quarterly*, Third Series, 16:4 (October 1959): 507–14.

Johnson, Crisfield. *History of Washington Co., New York. With Illustrations and Biographical Sketches of Some of Its Prominent Men and Pioneers.* Philadelphia: Everts & Ensign, 1878.

Johnson, Sherry. "El Niño, Environmental Crisis, and the Emergence of Alternative Markets in the Hispanic Caribbean, 1760s–70s." *William and Mary Quarterly*, Third Series, 62:3 (July 2005): 365–410.

Johnston, Henry P. *The Campaign of 1776 Around New York and Brooklyn.* Reprint. New York: Da Capo, 1971.

——. *The Yorktown Campaign and the Surrender of Cornwallis, 1781.* New York: Harper & Brothers, 1881.

Jones, Charles C., Jr. *The History of Georgia.* 2 vols. Boston: Houghton, Mifflin and Co., 1883.

——. *The Siege of Savannah in 1779, As Described in Two Contemporaneous Journals of French Officers in the Fleet of Count d'Estaing.* Albany, NY: Joel Munsell, 1874.

Jones, Norrece T., Jr. *Born a Child of Freedom, yet a Slave: Mechanisms of Control and Strategies of Resistance in Antebellum South Carolina.* Hanover, NH: University Press of New England, 1990.

Jones, T. Cole. *Captives of Liberty: Prisoners of War and the Politics of Vengeance in the American Revolution.* Early American Studies. Philadelphia: University of Pennsylvania Press, 2020.

Jordan, Winthrop D. *White over Black: American Attitudes Toward the Negro, 1550–1812.* 2nd ed. Chapel Hill: Published for the Omohundro Institute of Early American History and Culture by the University of North Carolina Press, 2012.

Kaine, Tim. "A Better Approach to War Powers." *PRISM* 5:1 (2014): 2–7.

Kammen, Michael G. *Colonial New York: A History.* A History of the American Colonies. New York: Charles Scribner's Sons, 1975.

Kane, Maeve. "Covered with Such a Cappe: The Archaeology of Seneca Clothing, 1615–1820." *Ethnohistory* 61:1 (Winter 2014): 1–25.

——. " 'She Did Not Open Her Mouth Further': Haudenosaunee Women as Military and Political Targets During and After the American Revolution." In Oberg, ed., *Women in the American Revolution*, 83–102.

Kaplan, Sidney. "Blacks in Massachusetts and the Shays' Rebellion." *Contributions in Black Studies* 8 (1986): 5–14.

——. "Veteran Officers and Politics in Massachusetts, 1783–1787." *William and Mary Quarterly*, Third Series, 9:1 (January 1952): 29–57.

Kaplan, Sidney, and Emma Nogrady Kaplan. *The Black Presence in the Era of the American Revolution.* Rev. ed. Amherst: University of Massachusetts Press, 1989.

Kars, Marjoleine. *Breaking Loose Together: The Regulator Rebellion in Pre-Revolutionary North Carolina.* Chapel Hill: University of North Carolina Press, 2002.

——. "Dodging Rebellion: Politics and Gender in the Berbice Slave Uprising of 1763." *American Historical Review* 121:1 (February 2016): 39–69.

Kay, Jeanne. "The Fur Trade and Native American Population Growth." *Ethnohistory* 31:4 (Autumn 1984): 265–87.

Kay, Marvin L. Michael. "The North Carolina Regulation, 1766–1776: A Class Conflict." In Young, ed., *American Revolution*, 71–123.

Kelsay, Isabel Thompson. *Joseph Brant, 1743–1807: Man of Two Worlds*. An Iroquois Book. Syracuse: Syracuse University Press, 1984.

Kennedy, Frances H., ed. *The American Revolution: A Historical Guidebook*. New York: Oxford University Press, 2014.

Kerber, Linda K. "Why Diamonds Really Are a Girl's Best Friend." *Proceedings of the American Philosophical Society* 153:1 (March 2009): 56–66.

——. *Women of the Republic: Intellect and Ideology in Revolutionary America*. Chapel Hill: Published for the Institute of Early American History and Culture by the University of North Carolina Press, 1980.

Kerr, W. B. "Nova Scotia in the Critical Years, 1775–6." *Dalhousie Review* 12:1 (April 1932): 97–107.

Ketchum, Richard M. "England's Vietnam: The American Revolution." *American Heritage*, June 1971. americanheritage.com/content/england%E2%80%99s-vietnam-american-revolution.

——. *Saratoga: Turning Point of America's Revolutionary War*. New York: Henry Holt, 1997.

——. *Victory at Yorktown: The Campaign That Won the Revolution*. New York: Henry Holt, 2004.

Keyssar, Alexander. *The Right to Vote: The Contested History of Democracy in the United States*. New York: Basic Books, 2000.

Kidd, Thomas S. *The Great Awakening: The Roots of Evangelical Christianity in Colonial America*. New Haven: Yale University Press, 2007.

Kierner, Cynthia A. *Beyond the Household: Women's Place in the Early South, 1700–1835*. Ithaca, NY: Cornell University Press, 1998.

——. "Genteel Balls and Republican Parades: Gender and Early Southern Civic Rituals, 1677–1826." *Virginia Magazine of History and Biography* 104:2 (Spring 1996): 185–210.

Kinkel, Sarah. "The King's Pirates? Naval Enforcement of Imperial Authority, 1740–76." *William and Mary Quarterly*, Third Series, 71:1 (January 2014): 3–34.

Kiple, Kenneth F., and Virginia H. Kiple. "Deficiency Diseases in the Caribbean." *Journal of Interdisciplinary History* 11:2 (Autumn 1980): 197–215.

Klarman, Michael J. *The Framers' Coup: The Making of the United States Constitution*. New York: Oxford University Press, 2016.

Klein, Rachel N. *Unification of a Slave State: The Rise of the Planter Class in the South Carolina Backcountry, 1760–1808*. Chapel Hill: Published for the Institute of Early American History and Culture by the University of North Carolina Press, 1990.

Klinghoffer, Judith Apter, and Lois Elkis. " 'The Petticoat Electors': Women's Suffrage in New Jersey, 1776–1807." *Journal of the Early Republic* 12:2 (Summer 1992): 159–93.

Klooster, Wim. *Revolutions in the Atlantic World: A Comparative History*. New York: New York University Press, 2009.

——. "Slave Revolts, Royal Justice, and a Ubiquitous Rumor in the Age of Revolutions." *William and Mary Quarterly*, Third Series, 71:3 (July 2014): 401–24.

Knight, Betsy. "Prisoner Exchange and Parole in the American Revolution." *William and Mary Quarterly*, Third Series, 48:2 (April 1991): 201–22.

Knott, Sarah. "Female Liberty? Sentimental Gallantry, Republican Womanhood, and Rights

Feminism in the Age of Revolutions." *William and Mary Quarterly*, Third Series, 71:3 (July 2014): 425–56.

——. "Sensibility and the American War for Independence." *American Historical Review* 109:1 (February 2004): 19–40.

Knowles, Elizabeth, ed. *The Oxford Dictionary of Phrase and Fable*. 2nd ed. New York: Oxford University Press, 2005.

Kohn, Richard H. "The Inside History of the Newburgh Conspiracy: America and the Coup d'Etat." *William and Mary Quarterly*, Third Series, 27:2 (April 1970): 188–220.

——. "The Washington Administration's Decision to Crush the Whiskey Rebellion." *Journal of American History* 59:3 (December 1972): 567–84.

Kopperman, Paul E. *Braddock at the Monongahela*. Pittsburgh: University of Pittsburgh Press, 1977.

Kuethe, Allan J., and Kenneth J. Andrien. *The Spanish Atlantic World in the Eighteenth Century: War and the Bourbon Reforms, 1713–1796*. New Approaches to the Americas. New York: Cambridge University Press, 2014.

Kukla, Jon. *Patrick Henry: Champion of Liberty*. New York: Simon & Schuster, 2017.

Kulikoff, Allan. "The Progress of Inequality in Revolutionary Boston." *William and Mary Quarterly*, Third Series, 28:3 (July 1971): 375–412.

——. "The War in the Countryside." In *OHAR*, 216–33.

Kwasny, Mark V. *Washington's Partisan War, 1775–1783*. Kent, OH: Kent State University Press, 1996.

Labaree, Benjamin Woods. *The Boston Tea Party*. New York: Oxford University Press, 1964.

Labunski, Richard. *James Madison and the Struggle for the Bill of Rights*. Pivotal Moments in American History. New York: Oxford University Press, 2006.

Lachane, Paul. "New Orleans in the Era of Revolution: A Demographic Profile." Paper presented at the "Revolution et Contre-Revolution a la Nouvelle-Orleans et dans le Monde Creole" symposium, American Society for Eighteenth-Century Studies Twentieth Annual Meeting, New Orleans, LA, April 1, 1989.

Lambdin, Alfred C. "Battle of Germantown." *Pennsylvania Magazine of History and Biography* 1:4 (1877): 368–403.

Lambert, Frank. *"Pedlar in Divinity": George Whitefield and the Transatlantic Revivals, 1737–1770*. Princeton: Princeton University Press, 1994.

Land, Aubrey C. "Economic Base and Social Structure: The Northern Chesapeake in the Eighteenth Century." *Journal of Economic History* 25:4 (December 1965): 639–54.

Landers, Jane. "Gracia Real de Santa Teresa de Mose: A Free Black Town in Spanish Colonial Florida." *American Historical Review* 95:1 (February 1990): 9–30.

Larkin, Edward. *Thomas Paine and the Literature of Revolution*. New York: Cambridge University Press, 2005.

Larson, Carlton F. W. "The Revolutionary American Jury: A Case Study of the 1778–1779 Philadelphia Treason Trials." *SMU Law Review* 61:4 (October 2008): 1441–1524.

Lassiter, Francis Rives. "Arnold's Invasion of Virginia." *The Sewanee Review* 9:2 (April 1901): 185–203.

Lawrence, Alexander A. *Storm over Savannah: The Story of Count d'Estaing and the Siege of the Town in 1779*. Athens: University of Georgia Press, 1951.

Lawson, Philip. *George Grenville: A Political Life*. New York: Oxford University Press, 1984.

Leamon, James S. *Revolution Downeast: The War for American Independence in Maine*. Amherst: University of Massachusetts Press; Published in cooperation with the Maine Historical Society, 1993.

Leibiger, Stuart Eric. *Founding Friendship: George Washington, James Madison, and the Creation of the American Republic*. Charlottesville: University Press of Virginia, 1999.

Lender, Mark Edward, and Garry Wheeler Stone. *Fatal Sunday: George Washington, the Monmouth Campaign, and the Politics of Battle*. Campaigns and Commanders; Vol. 54. Norman: University of Oklahoma Press, 2016.

Lengel, Edward G. *General George Washington: A Military Life*. New York: Random House, 2005.

Lepore, Jill. *Book of Ages: The Life and Opinions of Jane Franklin*. New York: Vintage, 2014.

———. *New York Burning: Liberty, Slavery and Conspiracy in Eighteenth-Century Manhattan*. New York: Alfred A. Knopf, 2005.

———. *These Truths: A History of the United States*. New York: W. W. Norton, 2018.

Levin, Phyllis Lee. *Abigail Adams: A Biography*. New York: St. Martin's Press, 1987.

Lewis, James A. "Las Damas de La Havana, El Precursor, and Francisco de Saavedra: A Note on Spanish Participation in the Battle of Yorktown." *The Americas* 37:1 (July 1980): 83–99.

Lewis, Jan. "The Republican Wife: Virtue and Seduction in the Early Republic." *William and Mary Quarterly*, Third Series, 44:4 (October 1987): 689–721.

Lewis, Lawrence, Jr. *A History of the Bank of North America, The First Bank Chartered in the United States, Prepared at the Request of the President and Directors*. Philadelphia: J. B. Lippincott & Co, 1882.

Little, Ann M. *The Many Captivities of Esther Wheelwright*. Lewis Walpole Series in Eighteenth-Century Culture and History. New Haven: Yale University Press, 2017.

Lockwood, Matthew. *To Begin the World Over Again: How the American Revolution Devastated the Globe*. New Haven: Yale University Press, 2019.

Logan, Rayford W. Review of *Historia de la Esclavitud Negra en Puerto Rica (1493–1890)*, by Luis M. Díaz Soler. *Hispanic American Historical Review* 34:3 (August 1954): 332–34.

Longmore, Paul K. *The Invention of George Washington*. Berkeley: University of California Press, 1988.

Lovejoy, Paul E. "Autobiography and Memory: Gustavus Vassa, Alias Olaudah Equiano, the African." *Slavery & Abolition* 27:3 (December 2006): 317–47.

Lurie, Maxine. "Envisioning a Republic: New Jersey's 1776 Constitution and Oath of Office." *New Jersey History* 119 (Fall–Winter 2001): 3–21.

Luzader, John. "The Coming Revolutionary War Battles at Saratoga." In Griswold and Linebaugh, eds., *Saratoga Campaign*, 1–38.

———. *Saratoga: A Military History of the Decisive Campaign of the American Revolution*. New York: Casemate Publishers, 2008.

Lynd, Staughton. "The Abolitionist Critique of the United States Constitution." In Lynd, *Class Conflict, Slavery, and the United States Constitution: Ten Essays* (Indianapolis: Bobbs-Merrill, 1967), 153–84.

———. "The Compromise of 1787." *Political Science Quarterly* 81:2 (June 1966): 225–50.

Lynd, Staughton, and David Waldstreicher. "Free Trade, Sovereignty, and Slavery: Toward an Economic Interpretation of American Independence." *William and Mary Quarterly*, Third Series, 68:4 (October 2011): 597–630.

MacGregor, Roy. "McVeigh Blinked First and Americans Won." *Globe & Mail* (Toronto), August 31, 2002.

Mackesy, Piers. *The War for America, 1775–1783*. Cambridge: Harvard University Press, 1964.

Magra, Christopher P. *The Fisherman's Cause: Atlantic Commerce and Maritime Dimensions of the American Revolution*. Cambridge: Cambridge University Press, 2009.

———. *Poseidon's Curse: British Naval Impressment and Atlantic Origins of the American Revolution*. Cambridge: Cambridge University Press, 2016.

Magrath, C. Peter. *Yazoo: Law and Politics in the New Republic, The Case of* Fletcher v. Peck. Providence, RI: Brown University Press, 1966.

Maier, Pauline. *American Scripture: Making the Declaration of Independence.* New York: Alfred A. Knopf, 1997.

——. *The Old Revolutionaries: Political Lives in the Age of Samuel Adams.* New York: Alfred A. Knopf, 1980.

——. *Ratification: The People Debate the Constitution, 1787–1788.* New York: Simon & Schuster, 2010.

Main, Jackson Turner. *The Upper House in Revolutionary America, 1763–1788.* Madison: University of Wisconsin Press, 1967.

Malcolm, Joyce Lee. *The Tragedy of Benedict Arnold: An American Life.* New York: Pegasus Books, 2018.

Malone, Dumas. *Jefferson, the Virginian.* Vol. 1. Jefferson and His Time. Boston: Little, Brown, 1948.

Mandell, David R. "A Natural & Unalienable Right: New England Revolutionary Petitions and African American Identity." In Michael McDonnell, Clare Corbould, Frances M. Clarke, and W. Fitzhugh Brundage, eds., *Remembering the Revolution: Memory, History, and Nation-Making from Independence to the Civil War* (Amherst: University of Massachusetts Press, 2013), 41–57.

Mapp, Paul W. "The Revolutionary War and Europe's Great Powers." In *OHAR*, 311–26.

Marks, Frederick W., III. *Independence on Trial: Foreign Affairs and the Making of the Constitution.* Baton Rouge: Louisiana State University Press, 1973.

Marshall, P. J. "Britain's American Problem: The International Perspective." In *OHAR*, 15–29.

——. *The Making and Unmaking of Empires: Britain, India, and America c. 1750–1783.* New York: Oxford University Press, 2005.

Martin, James Kirby. *Benedict Arnold, Revolutionary Hero: An American Warrior Reconsidered.* New York: New York University Press, 1997.

Martin, James Kirby, and Mark Edward Lender. *A Respectable Army: The Military Origins of the Republic, 1763–1789.* Arlington Heights, IL: Harlan Davidson, 1982.

Massey, Gregory D. *John Laurens and the American Revolution.* Columbia: University of South Carolina Press, 2000.

Matthews, Albert. "The Solemn League and Covenant, 1774." *Publications of the Colonial Society of Massachusetts* 19 (1917): 103–22.

Mayer, Holly A. *Belonging to the Army: Camp Followers and Community During the American Revolution.* Columbia: University of South Carolina Press, 1996.

Mays, David John. *Edmund Pendleton, 1721–1803: A Biography.* 2 vols. Cambridge: Harvard University Press, 1952.

Mazyck, Walter H. *George Washington and the Negro.* Washington, DC: Associated Publishers, 1932.

McBride, Spencer. "A 'Masterly Stroke of Policy': The American Revolution and the Politics of Congressional Prayer," *Journal of Religion, Identity, and Politics* (April 2013).

McCandless, Peter. "Revolutionary Fever: Disease and War in the Lower South, 1776–1783." *Transactions of the American Clinical and Climatological Association* 118 (2007): 225–49.

——. *Slavery, Disease, and Suffering in the Southern Lowcountry.* Cambridge Studies on the American South. New York: Cambridge University Press, 2011.

McClellan, Joseph. *Pennsylvania in the War of the Revolution, Battalions and Line, 1775–1783.* Ed. John Blair Linn and William Henry Egle. 2 vols. Harrisburg, PA: Lane S. Hart, 1880.

McCleskey, Turk. *The Road to Black Ned's Forge: A Story of Race, Sex, and Trade on the*

Colonial American Frontier. Early American Histories. Charlottesville: University of Virginia Press, 2014.

McConnell, Michael N. *A Country Between: The Upper Ohio Valley and Its Peoples, 1724–1774*. Lincoln: University of Nebraska Press, 1992.

McConville, Brendan. *The Brethren: A Story of Faith and Conspiracy in Revolutionary America*. Cambridge: Harvard University Press, forthcoming.

——. *The King's Three Faces: The Rise & Fall of Royal America, 1688–1776*. Chapel Hill: Published for the Omohundro Institute of Early American History and Culture by the University of North Carolina Press, 2006.

——. *These Daring Disturbers of the Public Peace: The Struggle for Property and Power in Early New Jersey*. Ithaca, NY: Cornell University Press, 1999.

McCrady, Edward. *The History of South Carolina in the Revolution, 1780–1783*. New York: The Macmillan Company, 1902.

McCullough, David. *1776*. New York: Simon & Schuster, 2005.

McCurdy, John Gilbert. *Quarters: The Accommodation of the British Army and the Coming of the American Revolution*. Ithaca, NY: Cornell University Press, 2019.

McCusker, John J. "The Current Value of English Exports, 1697 to 1800." *William and Mary Quarterly*, Third Series, 28:4 (October 1971): 607–28.

McCusker, John J., and Russell R. Menard. *The Economy of British America, 1607–1789*. Needs and Opportunities for Study Series. Chapel Hill: Published for the Institute of Early American History and Culture by the University of North Carolina Press, 1985.

McDonald, Forrest. *We the People: The Economic Origins of the Constitution*. A Publication of the American History Research Center. Chicago: University of Chicago Press, 1958.

McDonnell, Michael A. "Class War? Class Struggles During the American Revolution in Virginia." *William and Mary Quarterly*, Third Series, 63:2 (April 2006): 305–44.

——. *Masters of Empire: Great Lakes Indians and the Making of America*. New York: Hill & Wang, 2015.

——. *The Politics of War: Race, Class, and Conflict in Revolutionary Virginia*. Chapel Hill: Published for the Omohundro Institute of Early American History and Culture by the University of North Carolina Press, 2007.

——. "The Struggle Within: Colonial Politics on the Eve of Independence." In *OHAR*, 103–20.

McGuire, Thomas J. *The Philadelphia Campaign*. 2 vols. Mechanicsburg, PA: Stackpole Books, 2006.

McLaughlin, Jack. *Jefferson and Monticello: The Biography of a Builder*. New York: Henry Holt, 1988.

McNeill, J. R. *Mosquito Empires: Ecology and War in the Greater Caribbean, 1620–1914*. New Approaches to the Americas. New York: Cambridge University Press, 2010.

McPherson, James M. *Battle Cry of Freedom: The Civil War Era*. New York: Oxford University Press, 1988.

Meade, Robert Douthat. *Patrick Henry*. 2 vols. Philadelphia: J. B. Lippincott, 1957–1969.

Meranze, Michael. "Hargrave's Nightmare and Taney's Dream." *UC Irvine Law Review* 4:1 (March 2014): 219.

Merrell, James H. " 'Exactly as They Appear': Another Look at the Notes of a 1766 Treason Trial in Poughkeepsie, New York, with Some Musings on the Documentary Foundations of Early American History." *Early American Studies* 12:1 (Winter 2014): 202–37.

——. *Into the American Woods: Negotiators on the Pennsylvania Frontier*. New York: W. W. Norton, 1999.

Messer, Peter C. "A Most Insulting Violation: The Burning of the HMS 'Gaspee' and the Delaying of the American Revolution." *New England Quarterly* 88:4 (December 2015): 582–622.

———. " 'A Species of Treason & Not the Least Dangerous Kind': The Treason Trials of Abraham Carlisle and John Roberts." *Pennsylvania Magazine of History and Biography* 123:4 (October 1999): 303–32.

Meyer, Erin. "Tea Party Rally Marks a Moment in Chicago." *Chicagotribune.Com*, April 18, 2011. chicagotribune.com/news/ct-xpm-2011-04-18-ct-talk-talk-tea-party-0418-2011 0417-story.html.

Meyer, Jean. "Les Difficultés du Commerce Franco-Américain Vues de Nantes (1776–1790)." *French Historical Studies* 11:2 (Autumn 1979): 159–83.

Middlekauff, Robert. *The Glorious Cause: The American Revolution, 1763–1789*. Rev. and expanded ed. Oxford History of the United States, Vol. 1. New York: Oxford University Press, 2005.

Mihm, Stephen. "Funding the Revolution: Monetary and Fiscal Policy in Eighteenth-Century America." In *OHAR*, 327–54.

Miles, George. "A Brief Study of Joseph Brant's Political Career in Relation to Iroquois Political Structure." *American Indian Journal* 2:12 (1976): 12–20.

Miller, John Chester. *The Federalist Era, 1789–1801*. New American Nation Series. New York: Harper & Brothers, 1960.

———. *Origins of the American Revolution*. Rev. ed. Stanford: Stanford University Press, 1959.

Mills, Frederick V., Sr. *Bishops by Ballot: An Eighteenth-Century Ecclesiastical Revolution*. New York: Oxford University Press, 1978.

Miranda, Lin-Manuel, and Jeremy McCarter. *Hamilton: The Revolution, Being the Complete Libretto of the Broadway Musical, with a True Account of Its Creation, and Concise Remarks on Hip-Hop, the Power of Stories, and the New America*. New York: Grand Central Publishing, 2016.

Miranda, Lin-Manuel, and Alex Lacamoire. *Hamilton: An American Musical*. Vocal selections. Los Angeles: Warner/Chappel, 2015.

Mitchell, B. R. *British Historical Statistics*. New York: Cambridge University Press, 1988.

Monaghan, Charles. *The Murrays of Murray Hill*. Brooklyn, NY: Urban History Press, 1998.

Moore, Howard Parker. *A Life of General John Stark of New Hampshire*. New York: Howard Parker Moore, 1949.

Moore, Lisa L., Joanna Brooks, and Caroline Wigginton, eds. *Transatlantic Feminisms in the Age of Revolutions*. New York: Oxford University Press, 2012.

Morgan, Edmund S. *Benjamin Franklin*. Yale Note Bene. New Haven: Yale University Press, 2003.

———. "The Other Founders," *New York Review of Books*, Sept. 22, 2005, nybooks.com.

———. "The Puritan Ethic and the American Revolution." *William and Mary Quarterly*, Third Series, 24:1 (January 1967): 4–43.

———. "Thomas Hutchinson and the Stamp Act." *New England Quarterly* 21:4 (December 1948): 459–92.

Morgan, Edmund S., and Helen M. Morgan. *The Stamp Act Crisis: Prologue to Revolution*. 1995 ed. Chapel Hill: Published for the Institute of Early American History and Culture by the University of North Carolina Press, 1995.

Morgan, Philip D. *Slave Counterpoint: Black Culture in the Eighteenth-Century Chesapeake and Lowcountry*. Chapel Hill: Published for the Omohundro Institute of Early American History and Culture by the University of North Carolina Press, 1998.

Morris, Richard B. *The Peacemakers: The Great Powers and American Independence*. New York: Harper & Row, 1965.

Moss, Bobby Gilmer. *The Patriots at the Cowpens*. Blacksburg, SC: B. G. Moss, 1985.

Mulcahy, Matthew. *Hubs of Empire: The Southeastern Lowcountry and British Caribbean*. Regional Perspectives on Early America. Baltimore: Johns Hopkins University Press, 2014.

——. *Hurricanes and Society in the British Greater Caribbean, 1624–1783*. Early America. Baltimore: Johns Hopkins University Press, 2006.

Murphy, Tessa. "A Reassertion of Rights: Fedon's Rebellion, Grenada, 1795–96." *La Révolution française: Cahiers de l'Institut d'histoire de la Révolution française* [online] 14 (June 18, 2016): 1–26.

Murray, Louise Welles, ed. *Notes from Craft Collection in Tioga Point Museum on the Sullivan Expedition of 1779 and Its Centennial Celebration of 1879, Including Order Book of General Sullivan, Never Before Published, Original Manuscript in the New Jersey Historical Society*. Athens, PA: Tioga Point Museum, 1929.

Murrin, John M. "The French and Indian War, the American Revolution, and the Counterfactual Hypothesis: Reflections on Lawrence Henry Gipson and John Shy." *Reviews in American History* 1:3 (September 1973): 307–18.

Myrsiades, Linda. "A Tale of a Whiskey Rebellion Judge: William Paterson, Grand Jury Charges, and the Trials of the Whiskey Rebels." *Pennsylvania Magazine of History and Biography* 140:2 (April 2016): 129–65.

Nadelhaft, Jerome J. *The Disorders of War: The Revolution in South Carolina*. Orono: University of Maine at Orono Press, 1981.

Nagy, John A. *Rebellion in the Ranks: Mutinies of the American Revolution*. Yardley, PA: Westholme, 2008.

Nash, Gary B. "The African Americans' Revolution." In *OHAR*, 250–72.

——. *Forging Freedom: The Formation of Philadelphia's Black Community, 1720–1840*. Cambridge: Harvard University Press, 1988.

——. *The Liberty Bell*. Icons of America. New Haven: Yale University Press, 2010.

——. "Slaves and Slaveowners in Colonial Philadelphia." *William and Mary Quarterly*, Third Series, 30:2 (April 1973): 223–56.

——. "Thomas Peters: Millwright and Deliverer." In David G. Sweet and Gary B. Nash, eds., *Struggle and Survival in Colonial America* (Berkeley: University of California Press, 1981), 69–85.

——. *The Unknown American Revolution: The Unruly Birth of Democracy and the Struggle to Create America*. New York: Viking, 2005.

——. *The Urban Crucible: Social Change, Political Consciousness, and the Origins of the American Revolution*. Cambridge: Harvard University Press, 1979.

Nash, Margaret A. "Rethinking Republican Motherhood: Benjamin Rush and the Young Ladies' Academy of Philadelphia." *Journal of the Early Republic* 17:2 (Summer 1997): 171–91.

Navarro García, Luis. "La Crisis del Reformismo Borbónico bajo Carlos IV." *Temas Americanistas*: 13 (1997): 1–22.

Neal, Larry. *The Rise of Financial Capitalism: International Capital Markets in the Age of Reason*. Studies in Monetary and Financial History. Cambridge: Cambridge University Press, 1990.

Neatby, Hilda. *The Quebec Act: Protest and Policy*. Canadian Historical Controversies. Scarborough, ON: Prentice-Hall of Canada, 1972.

Neimeyer, Charles Patrick. *America Goes to War: A Social History of the Continental Army*. The American Social Experience Series 32. New York: New York University Press, 1996.

Nellis, Eric G. "Misreading the Signs: Industrial Imitation, Poverty, and the Social Order in Colonial Boston." *New England Quarterly* 59:4 (December 1986): 486–507.

Nelson, Eric. "Patriot Royalism: The Stuart Monarchy in American Political Thought, 1769–75." *William and Mary Quarterly*, Third Series, 68:4 (October 2011): 533–96.

———. *The Royalist Revolution: Monarchy and the American Founding*. Cambridge: Belknap Press of Harvard University Press, 2014.

Nelson, James L. *With Fire and Sword: The Battle of Bunker Hill and the Beginning of the American Revolution*. New York: Thomas Dunne Books/St. Martin's Press, 2011.

Nelson, Paul David. *General Sir Guy Carleton, Lord Dorchester: Soldier-Statesman of Early British Canada*. Cranbury, NJ: Associated University Presses, 2000.

———. "Guy Carleton Versus Benedict Arnold: The Campaign of 1776 in Canada and on Lake Champlain." *New York History* 57:3 (July 1976): 339–66.

Nettels, Curtis P. *The Emergence of a National Economy, 1775–1815*. Economic History of the United States, Vol. 2. New York: Holt, Rinehart & Winston, 1962.

Newman, Richard S., Roy E. Finkenbine, and Douglass Mooney. "Philadelphia Emigrationist Petition, Circa 1792: An Introduction." *William and Mary Quarterly* 64:1 (January 2007): 161–66.

Newman, Simon P. "Reading the Bodies of Early American Seafarers." *William and Mary Quarterly*, Third Series, 55:1 (January 1998): 59–82.

Noll, Mark A. *In the Beginning Was the Word: The Bible in American Public Life, 1492–1783*. New York: Oxford University Press, 2016.

Norton, Louis Arthur. "The Penobscot Expedition: A Tale of Two Indicted Patriots." *The Northern Mariner / Le Marin Du Nord* 16:4 (October 2006): 1–28.

Norton, Mary Beth. *1774: The Long Year of Revolution*. New York: Alfred A. Knopf, 2020.

———. "A Cherished Spirit of Independence: The Life of an Eighteenth-Century Boston Businesswoman." In Berkin and Norton, eds., *Women of America*, 48–67.

———. *Liberty's Daughters: The Revolutionary Experience of American Women, 1750–1800*. Boston: Little, Brown, 1980.

———. "'My Resting Reaping Times': Sarah Osborn's Defense of Her 'Unfeminine' Activities, 1767." *Signs* 2:2 (Winter 1976): 515–29.

———. "The Philadelphia Ladies Association." *American Heritage* 31:3 (April–May 1980): 102–7.

Oberg, Barbara B., ed. *Women in the American Revolution: Gender, Politics, and the Domestic World*. Charlottesville: University of Virginia Press, 2019.

O'Brien, William. "Did the Jennison Case Outlaw Slavery in Massachusetts?" *William and Mary Quarterly* 17:2 (April 1960): 219–41.

O'Donnell, James H., III. *Southern Indians in the American Revolution*. Knoxville: University of Tennessee Press, 1973.

Okoye, F. Nwabueze. "Chattel Slavery as the Nightmare of the American Revolutionaries." *William and Mary Quarterly*, Third Series, 37:1 (January 1980): 3–28.

Olwell, Robert A. "'Domestick Enemies': Slavery and Political Independence in South Carolina, May 1775–March 1776." *Journal of Southern History* 55:1 (February 1989): 21–48.

———. "'Loose, Idle and Disorderly': Slave Women in the Eighteenth-Century Charleston Marketplace." In Gaspar and Hine, eds., *More than Chattel*, 97–110.

———. *Masters, Slaves, and Subjects: The Culture of Power in the South Carolina Low Country, 1740–1790*. Ithaca, NY: Cornell University Press, 1998.

O'Neall, John Belton, and John A. Chapman. *The Annals of Newberry: In Two Parts*. Newberry, SC: Aull & Houseal, 1892.

Opal, J. M. *Avenging the People: Andrew Jackson, the Rule of Law, and the American Nation*. New York: Oxford University Press, 2017.

Osborn, Samuel D. *The Dark and Bloody Ground: A History of Kentucky*. Bristol, TN-VA: King Printing Co., 1907.

O'Shaughnessy, Andrew Jackson. *An Empire Divided: The American Revolution and the British Caribbean*. Early American Studies. Philadelphia: University of Pennsylvania Press, 2000.

———. *The Men Who Lost America: British Leadership, the American Revolution, and the Fate of the Empire*. Lewis Walpole Series in Eighteenth-Century Culture and History. New Haven: Yale University Press, 2013.

Paley, Ruth. "Imperial Politics and English Law: The Many Contexts of 'Somerset.'" *Law and History Review* 24:3 (2006): 659–64.

Palmer, John McAuley. *General von Steuben*. New Haven: Yale University Press, 1937.

Park, Steven. "Revising the Gaspee Legacy." *Journal of the American Revolution*, July 28, 2015. allthingsliberty.com/2015/07/revising-the-gaspee-legacy/.

Parkinson, Robert G. *The Common Cause: Creating Race and Nation in the American Revolution*. Chapel Hill: Published for the Omohundro Institute of Early American History and Culture by the University of North Carolina Press, 2016.

Parrish, Susan Scott. *American Curiosity: Cultures of Natural History in the Colonial British Atlantic World*. Chapel Hill: Published for the Omohundro Institute of Early American History and Culture by the University of North Carolina Press, 2006.

Pasley, Jeffrey L. *"The Tyranny of Printers": Newspaper Politics in the Early American Republic*. Jeffersonian America. Charlottesville: University Press of Virginia, 2001.

Pauly, Philip J. "Fighting the Hessian Fly: American and British Responses to Insect Invasion, 1776–1789." *Environmental History* 7:3 (July 2002): 485–507.

Peckham, Howard H. *Pontiac and the Indian Uprising*. Princeton: Princeton University Press, 1947.

———. *The Toll of Independence: Engagements & Battle Casualties of the American Revolution*. Clements Library Bicentennial Studies. Chicago: University of Chicago Press, 1974.

———. *The War for Independence: A Military History*. The Chicago History of American Civilization. Chicago: University of Chicago Press, 1958.

Pencak, William. *Jews & Gentiles in Early America, 1654–1800*. Ann Arbor: University of Michigan Press, 2005.

Perdue, Theda. "Cherokee Relations with the Iroquois in the Eighteenth Century." In Daniel K. Richter and James H. Merrell, eds., *Beyond the Covenant Chain: The Iroquois and Their Neighbors in Indian North America, 1600–1800* (Syracuse: Syracuse University Press, 1987), 135–50.

Peterson, Mark. *The City-State of Boston: The Rise and Fall of an Atlantic Power, 1630–1865*. Princeton: Princeton University Press, 2019.

Pflugrad-Jackisch, Ami. "'What Am I but an American?' Mary Willing Byrd and Westover Plantation During the American Revolution." In Oberg, ed., *Women in the American Revolution*, 171–91.

Philbrick, Nathaniel. *Bunker Hill: A City, a Siege, a Revolution*. New York: Viking, 2013.

———. *In the Hurricane's Eye: The Genius of George Washington and the Victory at Yorktown*. New York: Viking, 2018.

———. *Valiant Ambition: George Washington, Benedict Arnold, and the Fate of the American Revolution*. New York: Viking, 2016.

Phillips, Kevin. *1775: A Good Year for Revolution*. New York: Penguin, 2012.

Philyaw, L. Scott. "A Slave for Every Soldier: The Strange History of Virginia's Forgotten

Recruitment Act of 1 January 1781." *Virginia Magazine of History and Biography* 109:4 (2001): 367–86.

Piecuch, Jim. "Francis Marion Meets His Match: Benjamin Thompson Defeats the 'Swamp Fox.'" *Journal of the American Revolution*, April 29, 2014. allthingsliberty.com/2014/04 /francis-marion-meets-his-match-benjamin-thompson-defeats-the-swamp-fox/.

———. *Three Peoples, One King: Loyalists, Indians, and Slaves in the Revolutionary South, 1775–1782.* Columbia: University of South Carolina Press, 2008.

Plakas, Rosemary. "Sentiments of an American Woman," n.d. guides.loc.gov/american-women -essays/sentiments-american-woman.

Posey, John Thornton. *General Thomas Posey: Son of the American Revolution.* East Lansing: Michigan State University Press, 1992.

Preston, David L. *Braddock's Defeat: The Battle of the Monongahela and the Road to Revolution.* Pivotal Moments in American History. Oxford: Oxford University Press, 2015.

Price, Jacob M. *Capital and Credit in British Overseas Trade: The View from the Chesapeake, 1700–1776.* Cambridge: Harvard University Press, 1980.

———. "The Rise of Glasgow in the Chesapeake Tobacco Trade, 1707–1775." *William and Mary Quarterly*, Third Series, 11:2 (April 1954): 179–99.

Pybus, Cassandra. *Epic Journeys of Freedom: Runaway Slaves of the American Revolution and Their Global Quest for Liberty.* Boston: Beacon Press, 2006.

———. "Jefferson's Faulty Math: The Question of Slave Defections in the American Revolution." *William and Mary Quarterly*, Third Series, 62:2 (April 2005): 243–64.

Quarles, Benjamin. *The Negro in the American Revolution.* Chapel Hill: Published for the Institute of Early American History and Culture by the University of North Carolina Press, 1961.

Quintal, George, Jr. *Patriots of Color: "A Peculiar Beauty and Merit": African Americans and Native Americans at Battle Road & Bunker Hill.* Boston: Division of Cultural Resources, Boston National Historical Park, 2004.

Ragosta, John A. *Religious Freedom: Jefferson's Legacy, America's Creed.* Jeffersonian America. Charlottesville: University of Virginia Press, 2013.

———. *Wellspring of Liberty: How Virginia's Religious Dissenters Helped Win the American Revolution and Secured Religious Liberty.* New York: Oxford University Press, 2010.

Ragsdale, Bruce A. "George Washington, the British Tobacco Trade, and Economic Opportunity in Prerevolutionary Virginia." *Virginia Magazine of History and Biography* 97:2 (April 1989): 132–62.

———. *A Planters' Republic: The Search for Economic Independence in Revolutionary Virginia.* Madison, WI: Madison House, 1996.

Rainbolt, John C. *From Prescription to Persuasion: Manipulation of Eighteenth Century Virginia Economy.* Kennikat Press National University Publications. Series in American Studies. Port Washington, NY: Kennikat Press, 1974.

Rakove, Jack N. *The Beginnings of National Politics: An Interpretive History of the Continental Congress.* New York: Alfred A. Knopf, 1979.

———. *Revolutionaries: A New History of the Invention of America.* Boston: Houghton Mifflin Harcourt, 2010.

Rana, Aziz. *The Two Faces of American Freedom.* Cambridge: Harvard University Press, 2010.

Ranlet, Philip. "The British, Slaves, and Smallpox in Revolutionary Virginia." *Journal of Negro History* 84:3 (Summer 1999): 217–26.

Raphael, Ray. "America's Worst Winter Ever: And Why Mythmakers Chose to Forget It." *American History* 45:1 (April 2010): 52.

——. *The First American Revolution: Before Lexington and Concord*. New York: New Press, 2002.

——. *Founders: The People Who Brought You a Nation*. New York: New Press, 2009.

——. *Founding Myths: Stories That Hide Our Patriotic Past*. Revised ed. New York: New Press, 2014.

——. *A People's History of the American Revolution: How Common People Shaped the Fight for Independence*. New Press People's History. New York: New Press, 2001.

Raphael, Ray, and Marie Raphael. *The Spirit of '74: How the American Revolution Began*. New York: New Press, 2015.

Rappleye, Charles. *Robert Morris: Financier of the American Revolution*. New York: Simon & Schuster, 2010.

——. *Sons of Providence: The Brown Brothers, the Slave Trade, and the American Revolution*. New York: Simon & Schuster, 2006.

Rasmussen, Daniel. *American Uprising: The Untold Story of America's Largest Slave Revolt*. New York: Harper, 2011.

Rediker, Marcus. *The Fearless Benjamin Lay: The Quaker Dwarf Who Became the First Revolutionary Abolitionist*. Boston: Beacon Press, 2017.

——. *The Slave Ship: A Human History*. New York: Viking, 2007.

Reid, John Phillip. *Constitutional History of the American Revolution*. Abridged ed. Madison: University of Wisconsin Press, 1995.

Remini, Robert V. *Andrew Jackson and the Course of American Empire, 1767–1821*. New York: Harper & Row, 1977.

Rhoden, Nancy L. *Revolutionary Anglicanism: The Colonial Church of England Clergy During the American Revolution*. Houndsmill, Basingstoke, Hampshire, England: Macmillan, 1999.

Richards, Leonard L. *Shays's Rebellion: The American Revolution's Final Battle*. Philadelphia: University of Pennsylvania Press, 2002.

——. *The Slave Power: The Free North and Southern Domination, 1780–1860*. Baton Rouge: Louisiana State University Press, 2000.

Richter, Daniel K. *The Ordeal of the Longhouse: The Peoples of the Iroquois League in the Era of European Colonization*. Chapel Hill: Published for the Institute of Early American History and Culture by the University of North Carolina Press, 1992.

——. "The Plan of 1764: Native Americans and a British Empire That Never Was." In Daniel K. Richter, ed., *Trade, Land, Power: The Struggle for Eastern North America* (Philadelphia: University of Pennsylvania Press, 2013), 177–201.

——. "War and Culture: The Iroquois Experience." *William and Mary Quarterly*, Third Series, 40:4 (October 1983): 528–59.

Risch, Erna. *Supplying Washington's Army*. Special Studies. Washington, DC: Center of Military History, United States Army: for sale by the Supt. of Docs., Government Printing Office, 1981.

Roberts, Cokie. *Founding Mothers: The Women Who Raised Our Nation*. New York: William Morrow, 2004.

Roberts, Wendy Raphael. " 'Slavery' and 'To Mrs. Eliot on the Death of Her Child': Two New Manuscript Poems Connected to Phillis Wheatley by the Bostonian Poet Ruth Barrell Andrews." *Early American Literature* 51:3 (2016): 665–81.

Robertson, John A. "Burr's Mill Found?" *Southern Campaigns of the American Revolution* 2:12 (December 2005): 8–11.

Robinson, Armstead L. *Bitter Fruits of Bondage: The Demise of Slavery and the Collapse of the Confederacy, 1861–1865*. Carter G. Woodson Institute Series. Charlottesville: University of Virginia Press, 2005.

Robinson, Donald L. *Slavery in the Structure of American Politics, 1765–1820*. Founding of the American Republic. New York: Harcourt Brace Jovanovich, 1971.

Roche, John F. *Joseph Reed: A Moderate in the American Revolution*. Columbia Studies in the Social Sciences, no. 595. New York: Columbia University Press, 1957.

Rodgers, Daniel T. "Republicanism: The Career of a Concept." *Journal of American History* 79:1 (June 1992): 11–38.

Roland, Alex. "Bushnell's Submarine: American Original or European Import?" *Technology and Culture* 18:2 (April 1977): 157–74.

Rosengarten, Theodore, and Dale Rosengarten, eds. *A Portion of the People: Three Hundred Years of Southern Jewish Life*. Columbia: University of South Carolina Press in association with McKissick Museum, 2002.

Rosswurm, Steve. *Arms, Country, and Class: The Philadelphia Militia and "Lower Sort" During the American Revolution, 1775–1783*. Class and Culture. New Brunswick: Rutgers University Press, 1987.

Royster, Charles. *A Revolutionary People at War: The Continental Army and American Character, 1775–1783*. Chapel Hill: Published for the Institute of Early American History and Culture by the University of North Carolina Press, 1979.

Ruppert, Bob. "The Statue of George III." *Journal of the American Revolution*, Sept. 8, 2004. allthingsliberty.com/2014/09/the-statue-of-george-iii/.

Rusert, Britt. *Fugitive Science: Empiricism and Freedom in Early African American Culture*. America and the Long 19th Century. New York: New York University Press, 2017.

Ryan, William R. *The World of Thomas Jeremiah: Charles Town on the Eve of the American Revolution*. New York: Oxford University Press, 2010.

Ryerson, Richard Alan. *The Revolution Is Now Begun: The Radical Committees of Philadelphia, 1765–1776*. [Philadelphia]: University of Pennsylvania Press, 1978.

Sadosky, Leonard. "Rethinking the Gnadenhutten Massacre: The Contest for Power in the Public World of the Revolutionary Pennsylvania Frontier." In Skaggs and Nelson, eds., *Sixty Years' War for the Great Lakes*, 187–214.

Saillant, John. *Black Puritan, Black Republican: The Life and Thought of Lemuel Haynes, 1753–1833*. Religion in America Series. New York: Oxford University Press, 2003.

Salmon, John. "'A Mission of the Most Secret and Important Kind': James Lafayette and American Espionage in 1781." *Virginia Cavalcade* 31:2 (Autumn 1981): 78–85.

Sandy, Laura. "Divided Loyalties in a 'Predatory War': Plantation Overseers and Slavery During the American Revolution." *Journal of American Studies* 48:2 (May 2014): 357–92.

Saunt, Claudio. *West of the Revolution: An Uncommon History of 1776*. New York: W. W. Norton, 2014.

Schama, Simon. *Rough Crossings: Britain, the Slaves and the American Revolution*. London: BBC, 2005.

Schecter, Barnet. *The Battle for New York: The City at the Heart of the American Revolution*. New York: Walker, 2002.

Schellhammer, Michael. "Mutiny of the New Jersey Line." *Journal of the American Revolution*, March 19, 2014. allthingsliberty.com/2014/03/mutiny-of-the-new-jersey-line/.

———. "The Real Immortal Words of John Paul Jones." *Journal of the American Revolution*, Jan. 19, 2015. allthingsliberty.com/2015/01/the-real-immortal-words-of-john-paul-jones/.

Schlesinger, Arthur M. *The Colonial Merchants and the American Revolution, 1763–1776*. Studies in History, Economics and Public Law, Ed. by the Faculty of Political Science of Columbia University, Vol. 78; whole no. 182. New York: Columbia University, 1918.

Schnitzer, Eric H. "The Tactics of the Battles of Saratoga." In Griswold and Linebaugh, eds., *Saratoga Campaign*, 39–80.

Schrader, Arthur. " 'The World Turned Upside Down': A Yorktown March, or Music to Surrender By." *American Music* 16:2 (Summer 1998): 180–216.

Scott, Julius S. *The Common Wind: Afro-American Currents in the Age of the Haitian Revolution*. Brooklyn, NY: Verso, 2018.

Scott, Kenneth. "Price Control in New England During the Revolution." *New England Quarterly* 19:4 (December 1946): 453–73.

Selby, John E. *The Revolution in Virginia, 1775–1783*. Williamsburg: Colonial Williamsburg Foundation, 1988.

——. "Richard Henry Lee, John Adams, and the Virginia Constitution of 1776." *Virginia Magazine of History and Biography* 84:4 (October 1976): 387–400.

Sellers, Charles G., Jr. "Private Profits and British Colonial Policy: The Speculations of Henry McCulloh." *William and Mary Quarterly*, Third Series, 8:4 (October 1951): 535–51.

Sellick, Gary. "Black Skin, Red Coats: The Carolina Corps and Nationalism in the Revolutionary British Caribbean." *Slavery & Abolition* 39:3 (July 2018): 459–78.

——. " 'They Were Marched Almost Day and Night': The Effects of Sleep Deprivation on the Southern Campaign of the American Revolution." *European Journal of American Culture* 35:2 (June 2016): 111–25.

——. " 'Undistinguished Destruction': The Effects of Smallpox on British Emancipation Policy in the Revolutionary War." *Journal of American Studies* 51:3 (August 2017): 865–85.

Sen, Amartya. "Imperial Illusions." *The New Republic*, Dec. 30, 2007. newrepublic.com /article/61784/imperial-illusions.

Seymour, Charles, and Donald Paige Frary. *How the World Votes: The Story of Democratic Development in Elections*. Vol. 1. Springfield, MA: C. A. Nichols, 1918.

Shammas, Carole. "Anglo-American Household Government in Comparative Perspective." *William and Mary Quarterly*, Third Series, 52:1 (January 1995): 104–44.

——. "How Self-Sufficient Was Early America?" *Journal of Interdisciplinary History* 13:2 (Autumn 1982): 247–72.

Shannon, Timothy J. *Indians and Colonists at the Crossroads of Empire: The Albany Congress of 1754*. Ithaca, NY: Cornell University Press, 2000.

Sheehan, Michael J. F. "The Mythology of Stony Point." *Journal of the American Revolution*, November 3, 2016. allthingsliberty.com/2016/11/mythology-stony-point/.

Sheinkin, Steve. *The Notorious Benedict Arnold: A True Story of Adventure, Heroism, & Treachery*. New York: Roaring Brook Press, 2010.

Sheldon, Richard N. "Editing a Historical Manuscript: Jared Sparks, Douglas Southall Freeman, and the Battle of Brandywine." *William and Mary Quarterly*, Third Series, 36:2 (April 1979): 255–63.

Shepard, E. Lee. *Reluctant Ratifiers: Virginia Considers the Federal Constitution*. Richmond: Virginia Historical Society, 1988.

Sheridan, Richard B. "The British Credit Crisis of 1772 and the American Colonies." *Journal of Economic History* 20:2 (June 1960): 161–86.

——. "The Formation of Caribbean Plantation Society, 1689–1748." In P. J. Marshall, ed., *The Oxford History of the British Empire: Vol. II: The Eighteenth Century* (New York: Oxford University Press, 1998), 394–414.

——. "The Jamaican Slave Insurrection Scare of 1776 and the American Revolution." *Journal of Negro History* 61:3 (July 1976): 290–308.

——. "The Rise of a Colonial Gentry: A Case Study of Antigua, 1730–1775." *Economic History* 13:3 (1961): 342–57.

Shields, David S., and Fredrika J. Teute. "The Meschianza: Sum of All Fêtes." *Journal of the Early Republic* 35:2 (Summer 2015): 185–214.

Shoemaker, Nancy, et al. "Forum: Settler Colonialism in Early American History." *William and Mary Quarterly*, Third Series, 76:3 (July 2019): 361–450.

Shorto, Russell. *Revolution Song: A Story of American Freedom.* New York: W. W. Norton, 2018.

Shy, John W. *A People Numerous and Armed: Reflections on the Military Struggle for American Independence.* New York: Oxford University Press, 1976.

——. *Toward Lexington: The Role of the British Army in the Coming of the American Revolution.* Princeton: Princeton University Press, 1965.

Shyllon, F. O. *Black Slaves in Britain.* London: Published for the Institute of Race Relations by Oxford University Press, 1974.

Sidbury, James. "'African' Settlers in the Founding of Freetown." In Paul E. Lovejoy and Suzanne Schwarz, eds., *Slavery, Abolition and the Transition to Colonialism in Sierra Leone.* Harriet Tubman Series on the African Diaspora. (Trenton, NJ: Africa World Press, 2015), 127–41.

——. *Becoming African in America: Race and Nation in the Early Black Atlantic.* New York: Oxford University Press, 2007.

Siegel, Nancy. "Mommy Dearest: Britannia, America, and Mother-Daughter Conflicts in Eighteenth-Century Prints and Medals." In George W. Boudreau and Margaretta M. Lovell, eds., *A Material World: Culture, Society, and the Life of Things in Early Anglo-America* (University Park: Pennsylvania State University Press, 2019), 209–36.

Sioussat, George L., and J. Maccubbin. "The Chevalier de La Luzerne and the Ratification of the Articles of Confederation by Maryland, 1780–1781: With Accompanying Documents." *Pennsylvania Magazine of History and Biography* 60:4 (October 1936): 391–418.

Skaggs, David Curtis, and Larry L. Nelson, eds. *The Sixty Years' War for the Great Lakes, 1754–1814.* East Lansing: Michigan State University Press, 2001.

Skemp, Sheila L. *First Lady of Letters: Judith Sargent Murray and the Struggle for Female Independence.* Early American Studies. Philadelphia: University of Pennsylvania Press, 2009.

Sklar, Kathryn Kish, and Gregory Duffy. *How Did the Ladies Association of Philadelphia Shape New Forms of Women's Activism During the American Revolution, 1780–1781?* Women and Social Movements in the United States, 1600–2000. Binghamton: State University of New York, 2001.

Slaughter, Thomas P. *The Whiskey Rebellion: Frontier Epilogue to the American Revolution.* New York: Oxford University Press, 1986.

Slauter, Eric. "Rights." In *OHAR*, 447–64.

Smith, Barbara Clark. "Food Rioters and the American Revolution." *William and Mary Quarterly*, Third Series, 51:1 (January 1994): 3–38.

——. *The Freedoms We Lost: Consent and Resistance in Revolutionary America.* New York: New Press, 2010.

Smith, Fitz-Henry, Jr. *The French at Boston During the Revolution: With Particular Reference to the French Fleets and the Fortifications in the Harbor.* Boston: T. R. Marvin & Son, 1913.

——. *The Memorial to the Chevalier de Saint-Sauveur; the History of the Monument and of the Votes to Erect It, and an Account of the Ceremonies at the Dedication, May 24, 1917.* Boston: T. R. Marvin & Son, 1918.

Smith, Justin Harvey. *Arnold's March from Cambridge to Quebec: A Critical Study, Together with a Reprint from Arnold's Journal.* New York: G. P. Putnam's Sons, 1903.

Smith, Mark M. "Remembering Mary, Shaping Revolt: Reconsidering the Stono Rebellion." *Journal of Southern History* 67:3 (August 2001): 513–34.

Smith, Page. *A New Age Now Begins: A People's History of the American Revolution.* 2 vols. New York: McGraw-Hill, 1976.

Smith, Steven D., James B. Legg, Tamara S. Wilson, and Jonathan Leader. "'Obstinate and Strong': The History and Archaeology of the Siege of Fort Motte, South Carolina." *Journal of Middle Atlantic Archaeology* 26 (2010): 31–42.

Smith, Steven D., Brian Mabelitini, James B. Legg, and Ellan Hambright. "Two Revolutionary War Expedient Fire Arrows from Archeological Contexts in South Carolina." *Military Collector and Historian* 71:3 (Fall 2019): 243–46.

Snow, Dean R. "The British Fortifications." In Griswold and Linebaugh, eds., *Saratoga Campaign*, 81–104.

Sosin, Jack M. "Imperial Regulation of Colonial Paper Money, 1764–1773." *Pennsylvania Magazine of History and Biography* 88:2 (April 1964): 174–98.

Speck, W. A. *The Butcher: The Duke of Cumberland and the Suppression of the 45.* Oxford: B. Blackwell, 1981.

Spector, Robert M. "The Quock Walker Cases (1781–83)—Slavery, Its Abolition, and Negro Citizenship in Early Massachusetts." *Journal of Negro History* 53:1 (January 1968): 12–32.

Spero, Patrick. *Frontier Country: The Politics of War in Early Pennsylvania.* Early American Studies. Philadelphia: University of Pennsylvania Press, 2016.

——. *Frontier Rebels: The Fight for Independence in the American West, 1765–1776.* New York: W. W. Norton, 2018.

Spero, Patrick, and Michael Zuckerman, eds. *The American Revolution Reborn.* Philadelphia: University of Pennsylvania Press, 2016.

Spring, Matthew H. *With Zeal and with Bayonets Only: The British Army on Campaign in North America, 1775–1783.* Campaigns and Commanders, Vol. 19. Norman: University of Oklahoma Press, 2008.

Spruill, Marjorie Julian, Valinda W. Littlefield, and Joan Marie Johnson, eds. *South Carolina Women: Their Lives and Times.* Vol. 1. Athens: University of Georgia Press, 2009.

Staiti, Paul. "Accounting for Copley." In Carrie Rebora Barratt et al., eds., *John Singleton Copley in America* (New York: Metropolitan Museum of Art, 1995), 25–52.

Stanton, Elizabeth Cady, Susan B. Anthony, and Matilda Joslyn Gage, eds. *History of Woman Suffrage.* Vol. 1. New York: Fowler & Wells, 1881.

Stanton, Lucia C. *"Those Who Labor for My Happiness": Slavery at Thomas Jefferson's Monticello.* Jeffersonian America. Charlottesville: University of Virginia Press, 2012.

Starbuck, David R. "American Fortifications." In Griswold and Linebaugh, eds., *Saratoga Campaign*, 127–44.

Stempel, Jim. *American Hannibal: The Extraordinary Account of Revolutionary War Hero Daniel Morgan at the Battle of Cowpens.* Tucson, AZ: Penmore Press, 2017.

Stewart, Bruce E. *Redemption from Tyranny: Herman Husband's American Revolution.* Early American Histories. Charlottesville: University of Virginia Press, 2020.

Stillé, Charles J. *Major-General Anthony Wayne and the Pennsylvania Line in the Continental Army.* Philadelphia: J. B. Lippincott Company, 1893.

Stockley, Andrew. *Britain and France at the Birth of America: The European Powers and the Peace Negotiations of 1782–1783.* Exeter: University of Exeter Press, 2001.

Stone, Peter, and Sherman Edwards. *1776: A Musical Play (Based on a Conception of Sherman Edwards).* Book club ed. New York: Viking, 1970.

Stone, William L. *The Campaign of Lieut. Gen. John Burgoyne, and the Expedition of Lieut. Col. Barry St. Leger.* Albany, NY: Joel Munsell, 1877.

——. *Visits to the Saratoga Battle-Grounds, 1780–1880. With an Introduction and Notes.* Munsell's Historical Series, no. 23. Albany, NY: Joel Munsell's Sons, 1895.

Stout, Neil R. *The Royal Navy in America, 1760–1775: A Study of Enforcement of British Colonial Policy in the Era of the American Revolution.* Annapolis: Naval Institute Press, 1973.

Sugden, John. *Blue Jacket: Warrior of the Shawnees.* American Indian Lives. Lincoln: University of Nebraska Press, 2000.

Sutherland, Lucy S. *The East India Company in Eighteenth-Century Politics.* Oxford: Clarendon Press, 1952.

Sword, Kirsten. "Remembering Dinah Nevil: Strategic Deceptions in Eighteenth-Century Antislavery." *Journal of American History* 97:2 (September 2010): 315–43.

Sword, Wiley. *President Washington's Indian War: The Struggle for the Old Northwest, 1790–1795.* Norman: University of Oklahoma Press, 1985.

Szatmary, David P. *Shays' Rebellion: The Making of an Agrarian Insurrection.* Amherst: University of Massachusetts Press, 1980.

Tachau, Mary K. Bonsteel. "The Whiskey Rebellion in Kentucky: A Forgotten Episode of Civil Disobedience." *Journal of the Early Republic* 2:3 (Autumn 1982): 239–59.

Tanner, Helen Hornbeck, and Miklos Pinther, eds. *Atlas of Great Lakes Indian History.* Civilization of the American Indian Series, Vol. 174. Norman: Published for the Newberry Library by the University of Oklahoma Press, 1987.

Tate, Thad W. "The Coming of the Revolution in Virginia: Britain's Challenge to Virginia's Ruling Class, 1763–1776." *William and Mary Quarterly,* Third Series, 19:3 (July 1962): 324–43.

Taylor, Alan. *American Revolutions: A Continental History, 1750–1804.* New York: W. W. Norton, 2016.

——. *The Divided Ground: Indians, Settlers and the Northern Borderland of the American Revolution.* New York: Alfred A. Knopf, 2006.

——. *The Internal Enemy: Slavery and War in Virginia, 1772–1832.* New York: W. W. Norton, 2013.

——. *Liberty Men and Great Proprietors: The Revolutionary Settlement on the Maine Frontier, 1760–1820.* Chapel Hill: Published for the Institute of Early American History and Culture by University of North Carolina Press, 1990.

Taylor, George Rogers. *The Transportation Revolution, 1815–1860.* Economic History of the United States, Vol. 4. New York: Rinehart, 1951.

Thayer, Theodore. *Nathanael Greene: Strategist of the American Revolution.* New York: Twayne, 1960.

Thomas, Lamont D. *Rise to Be a People: A Biography of Paul Cuffe.* Blacks in the New World. Urbana: University of Illinois Press, 1986.

Thomas, P. D. G. *British Politics and the Stamp Act Crisis: The First Phase of the American Revolution, 1763–1767.* Oxford: Clarendon Press, 1975.

——. *Lord North.* British Political Biography. London: Allen Lane, 1976.

——. *Tea Party to Independence: The Third Phase of the American Revolution, 1773–1776.* Oxford: Clarendon Press, 1991.

——. *The Townshend Duties Crisis: The Second Phase of the American Revolution, 1767–1773.* Oxford: Clarendon Press, 1987.

Tillson, Albert H., Jr. *Accommodating Revolutions: Virginia's Northern Neck in an Era of Transformations, 1760–1810.* Charlottesville: University of Virginia Press, 2010.

Tomlins, Christopher. "Republican Law." In *OHAR,* 540–59.

Treadway, Sandra Gioia. "Anna Maria Lane: An Uncommon Soldier of the American Revolution." *Virginia Cavalcade* 37:3 (1988): 134–43.

Trigger, Bruce, ed. *Northeast*. Vol 15. of William C. Sturtevant, ed., *Handbook of North American Indians*. Washington: Smithsonian Institution, 1978.

Trees, Andy. "Benedict Arnold, John André, and His Three Yeoman Captors: A Sentimental Journey or American Virtue Defined." *Early American Literature* 35:3 (2000): 246–78.

Trowbridge, C. C. *Shawnese Traditions: C. C. Trowbridge's Account*. Ed. W. Vernon Kinietz and Erminie Wheeler-Voegelin. Museum of Anthropology, University of Michigan. Occasional Contributions: 9. Ann Arbor: University of Michigan Press, 1939.

Troxler, Carole Watterson. "Re-enslavement of Black Loyalists: Mary Postell in South Carolina, East Florida, and Nova Scotia." *Acadiensis* 37:2 (Summer/Autumn 2008): 70–85.

Trussell, John B. B., Jr. *Birthplace of an Army: A Study of the Valley Forge Encampment*. Harrisburg: Commonwealth of Pennsylvania, Pennsylvania Historical and Museum Commission, 1976.

Truxes, Thomas M. *Defying Empire: Trading with the Enemy in Colonial New York*. New Haven: Yale University Press, 2008.

Tyler, John W. *Smugglers & Patriots: Boston Merchants and the Advent of the American Revolution*. Boston: Northeastern University Press, 1986.

Ubbelohde, Carl. *The Vice-Admiralty Courts and the American Revolution*. Chapel Hill: Published for the Institute of Early American History and Culture by the University of North Carolina Press, 1960.

Ulrich, Laurel Thatcher. *The Age of Homespun: Objects and Stories in the Creation of an American Myth*. New York: Alfred A. Knopf, 2001.

——. "Political Protest and the World of Goods." In *OHAR*, 64–84.

——. "Sheep in the Parlor, Wheels on the Common: Pastoralism and Poverty in Eighteenth-Century Boston." In Carla Gardina Pestana and Sharon V. Salinger, eds., *Inequality in Early America*. Reencounters with Colonialism: New Perspectives on the Americas. (Hanover, NH: University Press of New England, 1999), 182–200.

——. "Wheels, Looms, and the Gender Division of Labor in Eighteenth-Century New England." *William and Mary Quarterly*, Third Series, 55:1 (January 1998): 3–38.

United States Census Bureau. *Historical Statistics of the United States, Colonial Times to 1970*. Bicentennial ed. 2 vols. Washington, DC: U.S. Census Bureau, 1975.

United States Census Bureau and W. S. Rossiter. *A Century of Population Growth, from the First Census of the United States to the Twelfth, 1790–1900*. Baltimore: Genealogical Publishing Company, 1967.

United States Congress, Joint Committee on the Library. *Rochambeau: A Commemoration by the Congress of the United States of America of the Services of the French Auxiliary Forces in the War of Independence*. Washington, DC: Government Printing Office, 1907.

Urwin, Gregory J. W. "When Freedom Wore a Red Coat: How Cornwallis' 1781 Campaign Threatened the Revolution in Virginia." *Army History* 68 (Summer 2008): 6–23.

Valosin, Christine. "The Saratoga Battles in Fifty Artifacts." In Griswold and Linebaugh, eds., *Saratoga Campaign*, 195–228.

Van Buskirk, Judith L. *Generous Enemies: Patriots and Loyalists in Revolutionary New York*. Early American Studies. Philadelphia: University of Pennsylvania Press, 2002.

——. *Standing in Their Own Light: African American Patriots in the American Revolution*. Campaigns and Commanders Series, Vol. 59. Norman: University of Oklahoma Press, 2017.

Van Cleve, George. "Mansfield's Decision: Toward Human Freedom." *Law and History Review* 24:3 (2006): 665–71.

——. *A Slaveholders' Union: Slavery, Politics, and the Constitution in the Early American Republic*. Chicago: University of Chicago Press, 2010.

——. "'Somerset's Case' and Its Antecedents in Imperial Perspective." *Law and History Review* 24:3 (2006): 601–45.

Van Doren, Carl. *Benjamin Franklin*. The American Past. New York: Book-of-the-Month Club, 1980.

——. *Mutiny in January: The Story of a Crisis in the Continental Army Now for the First Time Fully Told from Many Hitherto Unknown or Neglected Sources Both American and British*. New York: Viking, 1943.

——. *Secret History of the American Revolution: An Account of the Conspiracies of Benedict Arnold and Numerous Others Drawn from the Secret Service Papers of the British Headquarters in North America Now for the First Time Examined and Made Public*. New York: Viking, 1941.

Van Kirk, Sylvia. *Many Tender Ties: Women in Fur-Trade Society in Western Canada, 1670–1870*. Norman: University of Oklahoma Press, 1980.

Vipperman, Carl J. *The Rise of Rawlins Lowndes, 1721–1800*. Tricentennial Studies: 12. Columbia: Published for the South Carolina Tricentennial Commission by the University of South Carolina Press, 1978.

Vowell, Sarah. *Lafayette in the Somewhat United States*. New York: Riverhead Books, 2015.

Waldstreicher, David. "Ancients, Moderns, and Africans: Phillis Wheatley and the Politics of Empire and Slavery in the American Revolution." *Journal of the Early Republic* 37:4 (Winter 2017): 701–33.

——. "Phillis Wheatley: The Poet Who Challenged the American Revolutionaries." In Young, Nash, and Raphael, eds., *Revolutionary Founders*, 97–113.

——. *Runaway America: Benjamin Franklin, Slavery, and the American Revolution*. New York: Hill & Wang, 2004.

——. *Slavery's Constitution: From Revolution to Ratification*. New York: Hill & Wang, 2009.

——. "Women's Politics, Antislavery Politics, and Phillis Wheatley's American Revolution." In Oberg, ed., *Women in the American Revolution*, 147–68.

Walker, Peter W. "The Bishop Controversy, the Imperial Crisis, and Religious Radicalism in New England, 1763–74." *New England Quarterly* 90:3 (September 2017): 306–43.

Walvin, James. *The Zong: A Massacre, the Law and the End of Slavery*. New Haven: Yale University Press, 2011.

Ward, Christopher. *The War of the Revolution*. Ed. John Richard Alden. 2 vols. New York: Macmillan, 1952.

Ward, Harry M. *Charles Scott and the "Spirit of '76."* Charlottesville: University Press of Virginia, 1988.

——. *Major General Adam Stephen and the Cause of American Liberty*. Charlottesville: University Press of Virginia, 1989.

Warren, William W. "History of the Ojibways, Based Upon Traditions and Oral Statements." In *History of the Ojibway Nation*, Collections of the Minnesota Historical Society, Vol. 5, 1885, 21–394.

Watson, Robert P. *The Ghost Ship of Brooklyn: An Untold Story of the American Revolution*. New York: Da Capo, 2017.

Webb, Roberta. *The Dark and Bloody Ground*. La Vergne, TN: Turnkey Press, 2005.

Webb, Stephen Saunders. *1676: The End of American Independence*. New York: Alfred A. Knopf, 1984.

Wegman, Jesse. *Let the People Pick the President: The Case for Abolishing the Electoral College*. New York: St. Martin's Press, 2020.

Wehrman, Andrew M. "The Siege of 'Castle Pox': A Medical Revolution in Marblehead, Massachusetts, 1764–1777." *New England Quarterly* 82:3 (September 2009): 385–429.

Weller, Jac. "Irregular but Effective: Partizan Weapons Tactics in the American Revolution, Southern Theatre." *Military Affairs* 21:3 (Autumn 1957): 118–31.

Wells, Robert V. *Population of the British Colonies in America Before 1776: A Survey of Census Data.* Princeton: Princeton University Press, 1975.

White, Richard. *The Middle Ground: Indians, Empires, and Republics in the Great Lakes Region, 1650–1815.* Cambridge Studies in North American Indian History. New York: Cambridge University Press, 1991.

———. *The Roots of Dependency: Subsistence, Environment, and Social Change Among the Choctaws, Pawnees, and Navajos.* Lincoln: University of Nebraska Press, 1983.

Whitfield, Harvey Amani. *The Problem of Slavery in Early Vermont, 1777–1810: Essay and Primary Sources.* Barre: Vermont Historical Society, 2014.

Whittemore, Charles Park. *A General of the Revolution: John Sullivan of New Hampshire.* New York: Columbia University Press, 1961.

Whittenburg, James P. "Planters, Merchants, and Lawyers: Social Change and the Origins of the North Carolina Regulation." *William and Mary Quarterly*, Third Series, 34:2 (April 1977): 215–38.

Wickwire, Franklin, and Mary Wickwire. *Cornwallis: The American Adventure.* Boston: Houghton Mifflin, 1970.

Widder, Keith R. *Beyond Pontiac's Shadow: Michilimackinac and the Anglo-Indian War of 1763.* East Lansing; Mackinac Island: Michigan State University Press; Mackinac State Historic Parks, 2013.

Wiegand, Steve. *American Revolution for Dummies.* Hoboken, NJ: John Wiley & Sons, 2020.

Wiencek, Henry. *An Imperfect God: George Washington, His Slaves, and the Creation of America.* New York: Farrar, Straus & Giroux, 2003.

———. *Master of the Mountain: Thomas Jefferson and His Slaves.* New York: Farrar, Straus & Giroux, 2012.

Wiener, Frederick Bernays. "The Rhode Island Merchants and the Sugar Act." *New England Quarterly* 3:3 (July 1930): 464–500.

Wilentz, Sean. *The Rise of American Democracy: Jefferson to Lincoln.* New York: W. W. Norton, 2005.

Willcox, William B. "British Strategy in America, 1778." *Journal of Modern History* 19:2 (June 1947): 97–121.

———. *Portrait of a General: Sir Henry Clinton in the War of Independence.* New York: Alfred A. Knopf, 1964.

Williams, Eric. *From Columbus to Castro: The History of the Caribbean, 1492–1969.* Illustrated ed. New York: Vintage, 1984.

Williams, Tony. *Hurricane of Independence: The Untold Story of the Deadly Storm at the Deciding Moment of the American Revolution.* Naperville, IL: Sourcebooks, 2008.

Willingham, William F. *Connecticut Revolutionary: Eliphalet Dyer.* Connecticut Bicentennial Series 19. Hartford: American Revolution Bicentennial Commission of Connecticut, 1976.

Wills, Garry. *Inventing America: Jefferson's Declaration of Independence.* Garden City, NY: Doubleday, 1978.

———. *Negro President: Jefferson and the Slave Power.* Boston: Houghton Mifflin, 2003.

Wilson, David K. *The Southern Strategy: Britain's Conquest of South Carolina and Georgia, 1775–1780.* Columbia: University of South Carolina Press, 2005.

Wilson, Douglas L. "The Evolution of Jefferson's Notes on the State of Virginia." *Virginia Magazine of History and Biography* 112:2 (2004): 98–133.

Winiarski, Douglas L. *Darkness Falls on the Land of Light: Experiencing Religious Awakenings in Eighteenth-Century New England*. Chapel Hill: Published for the Omohundro Institute of Early American History and Culture by the University of North Carolina Press, 2017.

Wood, Gordon S. *The American Revolution: A History*. Modern Library Chronicles 9. New York: Modern Library, 2002.

——. *The Americanization of Benjamin Franklin*. New York: Penguin, 2004.

——. *The Creation of the American Republic, 1776–1787*. Chapel Hill: Published for the Institute of Early American History and Culture by the University of North Carolina Press, 1969.

——. *The Radicalism of the American Revolution*. New York: Vintage, 1993.

Wood, Peter H. *Black Majority: Negroes in Colonial South Carolina from 1670 Through the Stono Rebellion*. New York: Alfred A. Knopf, 1974.

——. "The Changing Population of the Colonial South: An Overview by Race and Region, 1685–1790." In Gregory A. Waselkov, Peter H. Wood, and M. Thomas Hatley, eds., *Powhatan's Mantle: Indians in the Colonial Southeast*, rev. and expanded ed. (Lincoln: University of Nebraska Press, 2006), 57–132.

——. "'The Dream Deferred': Black Freedom Struggles on the Eve of White Independence." In Gary Y. Okihiro, ed., *In Resistance: Studies in African, Caribbean, and Afro-American History* (Amherst: University of Massachusetts Press, 1986), 166–87.

——. "'Liberty Is Sweet': African-American Freedom Struggles in the Years Before White Independence." In Young, ed., *Beyond the American Revolution*, 149–84.

Wright, Conrad Edick. *Revolutionary Generation: Harvard Men and the Consequences of Independence*. Amherst: University of Massachusetts Press, 2005.

Wright, Esmond. "The British Objectives, 1780–1783: 'If Not Dominion then Trade.'" In Ronald Hoffman and Peter J. Albert, eds., *Peace and the Peacemakers: The Treaty of 1783*. Perspectives on the American Revolution (Charlottesville: Published for the United States Capitol Historical Society by the University Press of Virginia, 1986), 3–29.

Wright, J. Leitch, Jr. "Creek-American Treaty of 1790: Alexander McGillivray and the Diplomacy of the Old Southwest." *Georgia Historical Quarterly* 51:4 (December 1967): 379–400.

Wright, John W. "The Rifle in the American Revolution." *American Historical Review* 29:2 (1924): 293–99.

Wyatt-Brown, Bertram. *Southern Honor: Ethics and Behavior in the Old South*. New York: Oxford University Press, 1982.

York, Neil Longley. *The American Revolution, 1760–1790: New Nation as New Empire*. New York: Routledge, 2016.

Young, Alfred F., ed. *The American Revolution: Explorations in the History of American Radicalism*. DeKalb: Northern Illinois University Press, 1976.

——, ed. *Beyond the American Revolution: Explorations in the History of American Radicalism*. DeKalb: Northern Illinois University Press, 1993.

——. "Ebenezer Mackintosh: Boston's Captain General of the Liberty Tree." In Young, Nash, and Raphael, eds., *Revolutionary Founders*, 15–33.

——. *Liberty Tree: Ordinary People and the American Revolution*. New York: New York University Press, 2006.

——. *Masquerade: The Life and Times of Deborah Sampson, Continental Soldier*. New York: Alfred A. Knopf, 2004.

——. *The Shoemaker and the Tea Party: Memory and the American Revolution*. Boston: Beacon Press, 1999.

Young, Alfred F., Gary B. Nash, and Ray Raphael, eds. *Revolutionary Founders: Rebels, Radicals, and Reformers in the Making of the Nation*. New York: Vintage, 2012.

Zabin, Serena. *The Boston Massacre: A Family History*. Boston: Houghton Mifflin Harcourt, 2020.

Zagarri, Rosemarie. *Revolutionary Backlash: Women and Politics in the Early American Republic*. Early American Studies. Philadelphia: University of Pennsylvania Press, 2007.

——. *A Woman's Dilemma: Mercy Otis Warren and the American Revolution*. 2nd ed. Hoboken, NJ: Wiley-Blackwell, 2015.

Zepeda Cortés, María Bárbara. *Minister, Madman, Mastermind: José de Gálvez and the Transformation of the Spanish Empire* (New Haven: Yale University Press, forthcoming).

Zilversmit, Arthur. "Quok Walker, Mumbet, and the Abolition of Slavery in Massachusetts." *William and Mary Quarterly*, Third Series, 25:4 (October 1968): 614–24.

Zobel, Hiller B. *The Boston Massacre*. New York: W. W. Norton, 1970.

——. "Newer Light on the Boston Massacre." *Proceedings of the American Antiquarian Society* 78:1 (April 1968): 119–28.

Theses, Dissertations, Conference Papers, and Other Unpublished Scholarship

Allen, Danielle. "Punctuating Happiness." N.d.

Bartow, Paul. "'Several and Very Great Grievances': Petitioning for County Courts in Colonial South Carolina, 1740–1767." Paper presented at the Consortium of the Revolutionary Era, 1750–1850, Philadelphia, PA, 2018.

Barzilay, Karen. "Fifty Gentlemen Total Strangers: A Portrait of the First Continental Congress." PhD diss., College of William and Mary, 2009.

Beatty, Joshua. "The 'French Traveller,' Patrick Henry, and the Contagion of Liberty." Paper presented to the Virginia Forum, March 26, 2011.

Bouton, Terry. "Foreign Founding Fathers: Rethinking American State-Creation as a Story About a Developing Nation and International Capital." Paper Presented at the Seminar on the Political Economy of Modern Capitalism, Harvard, Cambridge, MA, Nov. 5, 2007.

Brewer, Holly. "Kings as Tyrants and Enslavers: Reconsidering the Declaration of Independence Through the Lens of the Original Draft." Speech presented at the Punctuating Happiness symposium, USNA, June 23, 2013.

Brown, Christopher. "The Atlantic Slave Trade and the American Revolution." Talk at the Henry E. Huntington Library, San Marino, CA, Jan. 13, 2017. huntington.org/videos-recorded-programs/atlantic-slave-trade-and-american-revolution.

Bruns, Carter. "'. . . The Whole River Is a Bustle Some About Their Children, Brothers and Husbands and the Rest of Us About Our Salt': The Antebellum Industrialization of the Kanawha Valley in the Virginia Backcountry." MA thesis, Western Carolina University, 2013.

Ellison, Amy Noel. "'A Reverse of Fortune': The Invasion of Canada and the Coming of American Independence, 1775–6." Paper presented at the "So Sudden an Alteration" conference, Massachusetts Historical Society, Boston, MA, April 11, 2015.

Ferguson, Clyde Randolph. "General Andrew Pickens." PhD diss., Duke University, 1960.

Grossbart, Stephen Reed. "The Revolutionary Transition: Politics, Religion, and Economy in Eastern Connecticut, 1765–1800." PhD diss., University of Michigan, 1989.

Hatton, Katelynn. "Made to Be Forgotten: The Chevalier de Saint-Sauveur & the Franco-American Alliance." MA thesis, University of South Carolina, 2019.

Holton, Woody. "The Revolt of the Ruling Class: The Influence of Indians, Merchants, and Laborers on the Virginia Gentry's Break with England." PhD diss., Duke University, 1990.

Hulbert, Kylie Alder. "Vigorous & Bold Operations: The Times and Lives of Privateers in the Atlantic World During the American Revolution." PhD diss., University of Georgia, 2015.

Jones, Mark H. "Herman Husband: Millenarian, Carolina Regulator, and Whiskey Rebel." PhD diss., Northern Illinois University, 1982.

Keenan, Kathryn F. "In Search of Granby: A Colonial Village of South Carolina." MA thesis, University of South Carolina, 2016.

Lewis, James A. "New Spain During the American Revolution, 1779–1783: A Viceroyalty at War . . ." PhD diss., Duke University, 1975.

Liles, Justin S. "Thomas Sumter's Law: Slavery in the Southern Backcountry During the American Revolution." PhD diss., University of South Carolina, 2011.

Muller, John. "Historic Southeastern Native American Population" (Excel spreadsheet in author's possession).

Myers, Sara Beth. "Armed with Influence: The Political Origins of the Society of the Cincinnati." Honors thesis, Duke University, 2003.

Pincus, Steven. "The Stamp Act Crisis in Global Perspective." Paper discussed at the Atlantic History Workshop at New York University. New York, NY, Oct. 24, 2014.

Polhemus, Neal D. "A Culture of Commodification: Hemispheric and Intercolonial Migrations in the Trans-Atlantic Slave Trade, 1660–1807." PhD diss., University of South Carolina, 2016.

Rawson, David Andrew. "'Guardians of Their Own Liberty': A Contextual History of Print Culture in Virginia Society, 1750 to 1820." PhD diss., College of William and Mary, 1998.

Rosenblithe, Bryan. "Where Tyranny Begins: British Imperial Expansion and the Origins of the American Revolution, 1758–1766." Paper presented at the American Revolution Reborn conference, Philadelphia, PA, June 1, 2013.

Schnitzer, Eric. "Battling for the Saratoga Landscape." N.d.

Schoel, Gretchen Ferris. "In Pursuit of Possibility: Elizabeth Ellet and the Women of the American Revolution." MA thesis, College of William and Mary, 1992.

Sellick, Gary. "Black Men, Red Coats: The Carolina Corps, Race, and Society in the Revolutionary British Atlantic." PhD diss., University of South Carolina, 2018.

Smith, Roger C. "The Fourteenth Colony: Florida and the American Revolution in the South." PhD diss., University of Florida, 2011.

Spinelli, Joseph. "Land Use and Population in St. Vincent, 1763–1960: A Contribution to the Study of the Patterns of Economic and Demographic Change in a Small West Indian Island." PhD diss., University of Florida, 1973.

Tarter, Brent. "Some Thoughts Arising from Trying to Figure Out Who Was Governor Dunmore's Mistress." N.d.

Vaughn, James M. "The Politics of Empire: Metropolitan Socio-Political Development and the Imperial Transformation of the British East India Company, 1675–1775." PhD diss., University of Chicago, 2009.

Vine, Benjamin David. "For the Peace of the Town: Boston's Politics in the American Revolution, 1776–1787." PhD diss., University of Sydney, 2018.

Williams, Claire. "Revolutionary Era Women in War: A Move for Societal Reform." BA thesis, James Madison University, 2016.

Wood, Peter H. "When Will Colonial History Become Truly Continental? A Pacific Perspective on North America's Intercultural Frontiers in the Eighteenth Century." N.d.

Zepeda Cortés, María Bárbara. "Empire, Reform, and Corruption: José de Gálvez and Political Culture in the Spanish World, 1765–1787." PhD diss., University of California, San Diego, 2013.

MAP AND ILLUSTRATION CREDITS

174 From The New York Public Library, https://digitalcollections.nypl.org/items/510d47 d9-7eaf-a3d9-e040-e00a18064a99

180 From Frothingham, *Battle-Field of Bunker Hill*, 4–5

183 Jeffrey L. Ward, "Battle of Bunker Hill"

189 *George Washington as Colonel of the Virginia Regiment* (1772) by Charles Willson Peale, U1897.1.1. Courtesy of the Museums at Washington and Lee University

197 Yale University Art Gallery

236 Drawings by Thomas Whyte, from Gerald F. Schroedl et al., eds., *Overhill Cherokee Archaeology at Chota-Tanasee* (University of Tennessee Department of Anthropology and Tennessee Valley Authority, 1986). Courtesy Frank H. McClung Museum, University of Tennessee, Knoxville

246 Library of Congress, Manuscript Division (detail)

248 From Cooley, *Sketches of the Life and Character of the Rev. Lemuel Haynes*, unpaginated

258 Jeffrey L. Ward, "Battle of Long Island"

264 Library of Congress, Prints and Photographs Division

268 Franz Xaver Habermann, *Représentation du feu terrible à Nouvelle Yorck*, Library of Congress, Prints and Photographs Division

273 Thomas Davies, *A View of the Attack Against Fort Washington and Rebel Redoubts Near New York on the 16th of November 1776 by the British and Hessian Brigades*, New York Public Library, https://digitalcollections.nypl.org/items/510d47 d9-7aee-a3d9-e040-e00a18064a99

279 Thomas Davies, *The Landing of the British Forces in the Jerseys on the 20th of November 1776 under the command of the Rt. Hon. Lieut. Genl. Earl Cornwallis*, New York Public Library, https://digitalcollections.nypl.org/items/510d47d9-7aef-a3d9-e040 -e00a18064a99

285 The Metropolitan Museum of Art, New York, NY

287 Jeffrey L. Ward, "Battle of Trenton"

321 Jeffrey L. Ward, "Battle of Brandywine"

325 Jeffrey L. Ward, "First Battle of Freeman's Farm"

332 Jeffrey L. Ward, "Battle of Germantown"

338 From Greene, *Recollections of the Jersey Prison-Ship*, 17

341 Library of Congress, Geography and Map Division

344 Yale University Art Gallery

354 Courtesy of Cliveden, a Historic Site of the National Trust for Historic Preservation

365 From Smith, *Memorial to the Chevalier de Saint-Sauveur*, unpaginated

389 Marshall, *Life of George Washington*

403 Darley, *Elizabeth, Grace and Rachel Martin* (Paris: Goupil & Co, n.d.), The Society of the Cincinnati, Washington, D.C.

405 Jeffrey L. Ward, "Battle of Camden"

409 Jeffrey L. Ward, "Native and British Attacks Against Spanish, U.S., and Pro-U.S. Native Settlements"

413 Yale University Art Gallery

417 Jeffrey L. Ward, "Battle of Kings Mountain"

431 From the Collection of the State of South Carolina, Columbia

433 From Carrington, *Battle Maps and Charts of the American Revolution*, 71.

434 Topographical map from United States Geological Survey (detail)

436 Jeffrey L. Ward, "Battle of Guilford Courthouse"

439 From Coffin, *The Boys of '76*, 363

457 Jean Baptiste Antoine de Verger, "Soldiers in Uniform," Anne S.K. Brown Military
Collection, John Hay Library, Brown University
462 Jeffrey L. Ward, "Siege of Yorktown and Gloucester Point"
467 Smithsonian American Art Museum
469 Collection of the Massachusetts Historical Society
491 From [Husband], *Dialogue Between an Assembly Man and a Convention Man*, unpaginated
508 Division of Political and Military History, National Museum of American History,
Smithsonian Institution
526 From the Collection of Cincinnati & Hamilton County Public Library
548 Yale University Art Gallery

INDEX

Page numbers in *italics* refer to illustrations, maps, and tables. Page numbers beginning with 577 refer to notes.

ABOUT THE AUTHOR

Woody Holton is the Peter and Bonnie McCausland Professor of History at the University of South Carolina in Columbia. His 2009 book, *Abigail Adams*, which he wrote on a Guggenheim fellowship, won the Bancroft Prize. Holton is also the author of *Unruly Americans and the Origins of the Constitution* (2007), which was a finalist for the National Book Award. His first book, *Forced Founders: Indians, Debtors, Slaves and the Making of the American Revolution in Virginia* (1999), won the Fraunces Tavern Museum Book Award (presented by the New York Sons of the Revolution) and the Organization of American Historians' Merle Curti Social History Award. His books are required reading on more than two hundred college campuses, and his work has been widely anthologized and also translated into German, Arabic, and Chinese. In 2016–17, while writing *Liberty is Sweet*, he was the *Los Angeles Times* Distinguished Professor at the Henry E. Huntington Library in San Marino, California.

Between 1990 and 1996, Holton served as founding director of Clean Up Congress, which helped elect pro-environment candidates to Congress.

Holton and his partner Gretchen Schoel, a freelance editor, live near Columbia, South Carolina, with their son Henry, a video game designer and temporary black belt in tae kwondo, and daughter Beverly, a runner, lacrosse player, and future fifth woman president of the United States.

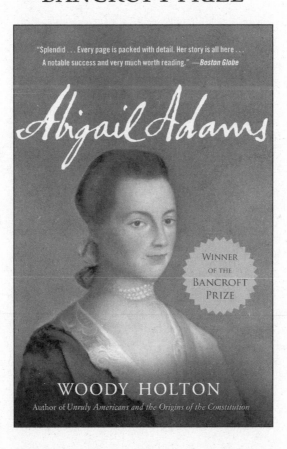